Peter Kuo

SAMS
PUBLISHING

201 West 103rd Street
Indianapolis, Indiana 46290

This book is dedicated to all those that have worked on "The Book from Hades" project, in particular to Rudy Koehle; and to all the (present and future) NetWare 4 administrators.

"Yea, though I walk through the valley of the shadow of death, I will fear no evil 'cause I have the NetWare 4.1 Survival Guide."

PUBLISHER AND PRESIDENT	Richard K. Swadley
ACQUISITIONS MANAGER	Greg Wiegand
DEVELOPMENT MANAGER	Dean Miller
MANAGING EDITOR	Cindy Morrow
MARKETING MANAGER	Gregg Bushyeager

ACQUISITIONS EDITOR
Rosemarie Graham

DEVELOPMENT EDITOR
Angelique Brittingham

PRODUCTION EDITOR
Jill D. Bond

TECHNICAL REVIEWERS
Bob Bailey
Frank Nicholas

EDITORIAL COORDINATOR
Bill Whitmer

TECHNICAL EDIT COORDINATOR
Lynette Quinn

FORMATTER
Frank Sinclair

EDITORIAL ASSISTANT
Sharon Cox

COVER DESIGNER
Tim Amrhein

BOOK DESIGNER
Alyssa Yesh

PRODUCTION TEAM SUPERVISOR
Brad Chinn

PRODUCTION
Mary Ann Abramson, Carol Bowers, Georgiana Briggs, Michael Brumitt, Charlotte Clapp, Michael Dietsch, Louisa Klucznik, Ayanna Lacey, Kevin Laseau, Paula Lowell, Donna Martin, Steph Mineart, Brian-Kent Proffitt, SA Springer, Mark Walchle

INDEXERS
Jeanne Clark, Cheryl Dietsch

Overview

Introduction   xxxvi

PART I   INTRODUCTION TO NETWARE 4
  1   Networking Technology   3
  2   How NetWare Fits In   15
  3   Features of NetWare 4   35
  4   Related Products   71

PART II   PLANNING A NETWARE NETWORK
  5   Networking Standards   89
  6   Selecting and Configuring Server Hardware   111
  7   Workstation Hardware   151
  8   Working Within Your Budget   165
  9   Media Types   181
 10   Determining Personnel Roles   239

PART III   UNDERSTANDING NETWARE DIRECTORY SERVICES
 11   Defining Network Resources   255
 12   Establishing Naming Conventions   271
 13   Designing the NetWare Directory Services Tree   279
 14   Partitioning and Time Synchronization   291

PART IV   PREPARING FOR THE INSTALLATION AND UPGRADE
 15   Developing an Install Plan   303
 16   Protecting the Data and Hardware   321
 17   Configuring Server Hardware   347
 18   Workstation Configuration   369
 19   Installing Media and Connectors   405

PART V   IMPLEMENTING THE NETWORK
 20   Installing and Using DynaText   431
 21   Installing NetWare 4.1 on New Servers   441
 22   Upgrading an Existing Server   467
 23   Installing New Workstation Software   503
 24   Upgrading Existing PC Workstations   523

PART VI   OPERATION

25	Configuring User Accounts	533
26	Menuing	567
27	MHS Services	591
28	Implementing Security	607
29	Auditing	643
30	Documenting Your Network	671
31	Working with Users	695
32	Network Printing	715
33	Selecting Network Applications	753
34	Remote Access	795

PART VII   MAINTENANCE AND TROUBLESHOOTING

35	Network Management	825
36	Archiving and Backup	863
37	Accounting	883
38	Tuning for Performance	901
39	Troubleshooting NetWare 4.*x*	929

PART VIII   INTERNETWORKING AND EXPANSION

40	Internetworking	961
41	Expand Your NetWare Installation	985

PART IX   COMMAND REFERENCE

42	Server Console Commands	1013
43	User Command Line Utilities	1131
44	NWADMIN and NETADMIN Utilities	1159
45	NWUSER and NETUSER Utilities	1199

PART X   APPENDIXES

A	Glossary of Networking Terms	1227
B	Where to Go for More Information	1235
C	Network Management Forms and Lists	1253
D	Cabling Rules	1257
	Index	1267

Contents

Introduction   **xxxvi**

PART I   INTRODUCTION TO NETWARE 4

1   Networking Technology   **3**

Components of a Distributed Processing Network 4
   File Server 4
   Client Workstations 5
   Network Interface Cards (NIC) 5
   Cabling 5
   Other Shared Devices 5
   Software 6
Network Types 6
Network Topologies 7
   Mesh Networks 8
   Star 8
   Bus 9
   Ring 9
   Hybrid 9
Capabilities of a Network or Internetwork 10
   Shared Files 10
   Shared Resources 10
   Shared Applications 11
   E-Mail and Other Utilities 11
   Security 11
A Historical Perspective 11
   Early Network Types 12
   Hardware and Media Advances 12
   Internetworking 12
   Future Developments 13
Features of Network Operating Systems 13
   File and Directory Services 13
   Global View of Network 14
   System Fault Tolerance 14
   Print Services 14
Summary 14

2   How NetWare Fits In   **15**

Specialization 16
   An Event-Driven System 16
   Traditional Design Components 16

A Rich Service Environment 17
Platform for Server-Based Applications 18
The Role of the Network Operating System 19
The Foundation of the Enterprise Network 19
Scalable from Workgroup to Enterprise 20
Expandability 21
Dynamic Discovery 21
Loadable Device-Driver Interface 21
Dynamic Volume Size Increases 22
Fault Tolerance 22
System Fault Tolerance Level I (SFT I) 22
System Fault Tolerance Level II (SFT II) 24
System Fault Tolerance Level III (SFT III) 26
Capacity 28
Memory Capacity 28
File System Capacity 28
Client Support 29
Open Data Link Interface 29
Name Space Architecture 30
Protocol Support 31
Server-Based Applications 32
NetWare Loadable Modules 32
Optional Memory Protection 33
Summary 33

3   Features of NetWare 4   35

NetWare Directory Services (NDS) 36
A Single Logical Entity 37
Easier Management 37
NDS Applications 38
Architecture of NDS 38
Organization of NDS 39
NDS is Backward Compatible 41
Merging and Renaming Trees 42
New Workstation Software 42
More NDS Information 42
High-Performance Scheduler 42
Memory Management 43
Returning Freed Memory 43
Faster Memory Allocation 44
Data Migration 44
Block Suballocation 45
Background File Compression 46

Auditing 47

RSA Security 49

Optional Memory Protection 50

    Preventing Illegal Memory Operations 50

    Performance Hit 52

    Part of an Overall Strategy 52

WAN Enhancements 53

    Packet Burst and Large Internet Packet Protocols 53

    New Routing Protocol Support 55

    Replaceable Router 56

Internationalization 56

Print Services 57

    Print Queues 58

    Print Servers 59

    Associating Printers, Print Servers, and Print Queues ... 59

    Additional Print-Service Protocols 60

    NetWare 4 Print Services 60

Storage Management Services (SMS) 61

    What Is SMS? 61

    SMS Implementations 62

    NetWare 4's SMS Implementation 63

    Archival of NDS 63

    Third-Party Support 63

Electronic Mail 64

Flexible Licensing 64

NetWare 4.1 for OS/2 65

Image-Enabled NetWare 66

Enhanced User Utilities 66

Online Documentation 67

Improved NLM Development Tools 68

Summary 68

4   Related Products   71

NetWare for SAA 73

NetWare HostPrint and NetWare HostPrint/400 75

NetWare Access for DEC 77

NetWare NFS Services—NetWare 4 Edition 78

NetWare Multi-Protocol Router 80

    IPX Support 81

    TCP/IP Support 81

    AppleTalk Support 82

    Source Route Bridging Support 82

NetWare Connect 83

    Remote Control 83

Remote Node 83
Dial-Out Communications 85
Summary 85

PART II   PLANNING A NETWARE NETWORK

5   **Networking Standards**   **89**
How Standards are Set 90
Proprietary Standards 90
De Jure Standards 91
De Facto Standards 91
New Technologies 92
Networking Standards 92
Communications Protocols (Physical and Data Link Layers) 94
Network Interface Methods (Network Layer) 101
Application Services (Application Layer) 104
Network Management 106
Simple Network Management Protocol 106
Other Management Protocols 108
Summary 108

6   **Selecting and Configuring Server Hardware**   **111**
File Server Definitions 112
Traditional File Servers 113
Application Servers 113
Selecting the Correct Equipment 114
Vendor Certification 115
Service Contracts 115
A Balanced Approach 117
System Memory 117
Selecting the Correct Processor 119
Bus Architectures 123
Fixed Disk Drives 130
NetWare's Read/Write Request Handling 131
ESDI 133
IDE 134
SCSI 135
Redundant Array of Inexpensive Disks (RAID) 136
RAID Implementations 137
Understanding the Different RAID Levels 137
Network Design 148
Expendability and Upgradability 148
Drive Bays 148
RAM Expansion 148
Summary 149

7   Workstation Hardware   **151**

   Determining User Profile 152

      Case and Power Supply 152

      Motherboards..154

      Bus Types...157

      Disk Drives 160

      Video 161

      Accessories 161

      Uninterruptable Power Supply (UPS) 162

      Of Clones and Dealers 162

      System Requirements and Recommendations 163

   Summary 164

8   Working Within Your Budget   **165**

   Start with Your Shopping List 166

   Novell-Approved Hardware 167

   Hiring Consultants 168

      Certified NetWare Engineer (CNE)..168

      Network Professional Association (NPA) 169

   Hiring Technicians 170

   Training Your Staff 171

   Putting Together the Budget 172

      Constructing a Budget 172

      Researching Prices 173

      Research Site Licensing and Corporate Rates 177

   Justifying Costs 178

   Summary 179

9   Media Types   **181**

   Topologies..183

      The Bus Topology 183

      The Mesh Topology..184

      The Ring Topology 184

      The Star Topology 185

      The Hybrid Topology 186

   Network Cabling 187

      External Influences 187

      Attenuation 188

      Coax Cable 189

      Twisted Pair Cable 191

      Fiber-Optic Cable 195

   Local Area Network Architectures 196

      ARCnet: The Persistent Architecture.......................................196

      ARCnet Plus: The New and Improved ARCnet 201

Ethernet: How It All Began 203
Running Ethernet At 100 Mbps.. 210
Fiber Distributed Data Interface (FDDI) 214
Token Ring.. 216
Communicating Without The Wires 221
Connecting the Networks Together 224
Repeaters 224
Bridges 225
Routers 226
Wide Area Networks (WANs).. 228
ATM 228
Frame Relay 232
Integrated Services Digital Network (ISDN) 235
T Carrier Lines 236
Summary 237

10 Determining Personnel Roles   239

NetWare Administration Staff... 240
Administrators 241
Group Administrators 242
Area Administrators.. 242
Printing Operators 243
Applying the Concept 244
How to Organize Network Administration 246
Centralized Network Administration 246
Distributed Network Administration 247
Hierarchical Network Administration 248
Departmental Liaisons 248
Network Implementation and Migration Team 250
Summary... 251

PART III   UNDERSTANDING NetWare DIRECTORY SERVICES

11 Defining Network Resources   255

Global View of the Network 256
Tree Analogy 257
What are Objects?.. 259
Container Objects 260
Leaf Objects 267
Summary... 270

12 Establishing Naming Conventions   271

Why Use Naming Conventions?... 272
Naming Conventions 272

Suggestions for Naming Conventions 273
   General Suggestions 273
   Suggestions for Container Objects... 273
   Suggestions for Leaf Objects 275
   Suggestions for File Server Names 277
  Summary 277

13 Designing the NetWare Directory Services Tree   279

What Does the Directory Services Tree Consist of? 280
   The Root 280
   Container objects 280
Number of Trees per Organization 281
Designing the NetWare Directory Services Tree 281
   Coordination of Planning 281
Coordination Checklist 283
   Major Design Elements of the NDS Tree 284
   Partition Replication Blueprint 288
   IPX Network Map 289
   Responsibilities of Central IS 289
   Coordination of an NDS Tree Through
     Central IS 290
Utilities Associated with the NDS Structure 290
Summary 290

14 Partitioning and Time Synchronization   291

Architecture of NDS 292
   Organization of NDS 292
   NDS is Backwards Compatible 293
   The Bindery 293
NDS Partition Management 295
   Partition Replication 295
   Partition Summary..297
NDS Time Synchronization 298
   Types of Time Servers 298
   Advantages of Multiple Primary or Reference Time Servers 300
   Time Zones 300
   Time Synchronization Summary 300
Summary 300

Part IV Preparing for the Installation and Upgrade

15 Developing an Install Plan   303

Constructing Your Schedule 304
   Using Project-Management Software... 304
   Scheduling Technicians and Consultants 305

Scheduling Training 306
Scheduling Installation 307
Importance of a Test Network 308
Phases of Implementation 309
Planning and Testing 310
Purchase and Installation 312
Installation and Training 313
Production 315
Unanswered Questions 315
Consultants 315
Maintenance Contracts 316
Network Support Encyclopedia 316
Per-Incident Support from Novell 316
NetWire 317
The Internet 319
Summary 319

16   Protecting the Data and Hardware   321

Hardware 322
Electricity 323
Redundancy 327
Environmental 330
Software 331
Network Backup 332
Tape Device Management 334
Tape Rotation 334
Directory and File Management 337
SBACKUP.NLM 339
NetWare Directory Services 340
Hardware Issues 340
Media Defects 341
Testing and Maintaining the Backup System 342
Offsite Storage 342
Hierarchical Storage Management 343
Viruses 343
Bugs, Patches, and Fixes 344
Summary 345

17   Configuring Server Hardware   347

The Problems 348
Memory Conflicts 348
Interrupt Request Line (IRQ) Conflicts 348
Port Address Conflicts 348
Memory Conflicts 349

HDDirect Memory Access (DMA) Conflicts 349
Assembly and Initial Hardware Testing: Two Strategies 349
  The Normal Way 349
  The Careful and Methodical Way 350
Burn In 351
Setting Up Hardware: Possible Sources of Conflict 351
  Overview: Focusing on NICs 351
  Base Port Addresses 358
Hard Disk Setup Issues 360
  Setting Up for Multiple Drives 360
  Setting Up BIOS Types 362
Installing CD-ROMs 364
  SCSI CD-ROMs 364
  Proprietary CD-ROMs 364
Make a DOS Partition 364
  Create the Partition 365
  Install DOS 365
  Install Utilities and DOS Drivers 365
Burning In 365
  Thermal Cycling 366
  Simple Burn In 366
  Exercise the Disk 366
  Complete Testing 366
Final Touches 367
  Document It 367
  Have Spares 367
Power Conditioning 368
Summary 368

18 **Workstation Configuration**   **369**

Communication Basics 370
  Configuration 371
Initial Hardware Setup 371
  Configuring BIOS Options 372
  POST Test 372
  Changing Initial CMOS Settings 374
  Standard CMOS Settings 374
Workstation Memory Configurations 379
Floppy Drive Configuration 382
Installing a Network Card 384
Hardware Settings 386
  Avoiding Interrupt Conflicts 387
  Avoiding Address Conflicts 389
  Avoiding DMA (Direct Memory Access) Conflicts 391

Workstation Software 392
    Selecting a Client Installation Method 393
    Creating Client Diskettes 394
Client Driver Options 396
    The NetWare DOS Requester Layers and Modules 397
    NET.CFG File 400
    Creating a NET.CFG File 400
    Optimizing VLMs for Performance 401
Summary 403

19   Installing Media and Connectors   405

Local Area Network (LAN) Cabling 406
    Coax 406
    Twisted Pair (Phone Cabling) 412
MSAUs and Concentrators 418
    Fiber-Optic Cable 419
    Cabling Testing Equipment 420
Bridges and Routers 424
    Bridges 424
    Routers 425
Mainframe and Mini-Computer Connections 426
    NetWare for SAA 426
    Matching the Host Packet Format 426
    Cabling Contractors 427
Summary 428

Part V   Implementing the Network

20   Installing and Using DynaText   431

What is DynaText? 432
Installing DynaText 433
    Installing DT on Your Workstation 433
    Installing DT on Your File Server 435
Using DynaText 435
Using DT Before and During Your Installation 439
Summary 440

21   Installing NetWare 4.1 on New Servers   441

Installing and Configuring
NetWare 4.1 442
    Installation Overview 442
    Installing a DOS Partition 443
    CD-ROM Setup 444
    Begin Installation 445
    Assign Server Name and Internal IPX Network Number 446

Copy Boot Files to DOS Partition 447
Configure Country Code, Code Page, and Keyboard Mapping 448
Select Filename Format for File System 450
Specify *SET* commands for STARTUP.NCF 450
Modify AUTOEXEC.BAT 451
Load and Configure Disk and LAN Driver(s) 452
Set Up NetWare Partition and Volumes 454
Install License Disk 456
Copy NetWare Files to *SYS:* Volume 457
Install NDS Tree 459
Set Time Zone Information 460
Create STARTUP.NCF 462
Create AUTOEXEC.NCF 463
Install Optional Programs and Files 463
Possible Problems and Solutions 464
Disk Driver Problem 465
Hard Disk Problem 465
LAN Driver Problem 465
Ethernet Frame Format Problem 465
Insufficient RAM 465
Incompatible NLMs 465
Summary 465

22 Upgrading an Existing Server   467

Methods of Upgrade 468
Across-the-Wire 469
Same-Server 476
In-Place 485
What to Do After the Migration 500
Upgrading NetWare 4.*x* 501
Summary 501

23 Installing New Workstation Software   503

Open Data-Link Interface (ODI) 504
NETX Versus VLM 505
Workstation Client Files 507
DOS/Windows Client Diskettes from CD 508
OS/2 Client Diskettes from CD 509
DOS Client Diskettes from Server 510
OS/2 Client Diskettes from Server 510
Installing DOS/Windows Clients 510
Windows-Related Changes 515
NET.CFG File for DOS 515
Installing OS/2 Requester 516

NET.CFG File for OS/2 521

Summary 522

24 Upgrading Existing PC Workstations   523

Workstation LAN Driver 524

Installing NetWare DOS Requester 524

AUTOEXEC.BAT 525

CONFIG.SYS 525

SYSTEM.INI 525

WIN.INI 526

PROGMAN.INI 526

Windows Files 526

Updating NET.CFG 527

Upgrading OS/2 Requester 528

Updating NET.CFG 528

Summary 529

PART VI OPERATION

25 Configuring User Accounts   533

Creating Users 534

Creating a User with NETADMIN 534

Creating a User Using the NetWare Administrator 535

Creating Groups 536

Creating a Group with NETADMIN 536

Creating a Group Using the NetWare Administrator 537

Login Scripts 537

Types of Login Scripts 537

Login Script Essentials 538

Creating, Copying, and Modifying Your Login Scripts 539

Creating or Modifying a Login Script Using NETADMIN 540

Associating a Profile Script to a User Using NETADMIN 541

Copying a Login Script Using NETADMIN 542

Creating or Modifying a Login Script Using
    NetWare Administrator 543

Associating a Profile Script to a User Using
    NetWare Administrator 544

Copying a Login Script Using NetWare Administrator 545

Login Script Commands and Variables 545

Login Script Commands 546

.... 546

ATTACH 546

BREAK 547

CLS 547

COMSPEC 547
CONTEXT 548
DISPLAY 548
DOS BREAK 549
DOS SET 549
DOS VERIFY 550
DRIVE 550
EXIT 550
FDISPLAY 551
FIRE PHASERS 551
GOTO 551
IF...THEN 552
END 553
INCLUDE 553
LASTLOGINTIME 554
MACHINE 554
MAP 554
NO_DEFAULT 557
NOSWAP 557
PAUSE 557
PCCOMPATIBLE 558
REMARK 558
SET 558
SET_TIME 559
SHIFT 559
SWAP 560
TEMP SET 560
WRITE 561
Login Script Identifier Variables 561
    Date Identifier Variables 561
    Time Identifier Variables 562
    User Identifier Variables 562
    Network Identifier Variables 563
    Workstation Identifier Variables 563
    DOS Environment Identifier Variables 564
    Miscellaneous Identifier Variables 564
    Object Properties Identifier Variables 564
Login Script Example 565
Summary 566

26 Menuing   567
Previous NetWare Menu System 568
NetWare Current Menu System 568

Designing a Menu 570
Security Issues 570
Designing, Creating, Compiling, and Executing a Menu 572
  Designing a Menu 572
  Creating a Menu Source File 573
  Compiling the Source Script File 573
  Executing the Menu 575
  Breaking Down the Script File 575
  Placement of Menus Onscreen 577
  Menu Color and Sizes 577
  EXEC Options 578
  ITEM Options 579
  Submenus 581
  Advanced Menu Options 583
Building a Turnkey System 587
Converting the Old 588
Summary 589

27 MHS Services   591

MHS Services and NDS 592
Installing MHS Services 593
Configuring MHS Services 595
  MHS Console 595
  Mailboxes 599
  Message Routing Groups 600
  Distribution Lists 601
Using FirstMail 602
  FirstMail for Windows 603
  FirstMail for DOS 604
Summary 605

28 Implementing Security   607

Components of NetWare Security 608
Login/Password Security 609
  RSA Public-Key Cryptosystem 609
  NCP Packet Signatures 611
  Optional Login Security Features 612
NetWare Directory Services Security 618
  Object and Property Rights 618
File System Security 624
  Directory and File Rights 625
  Trustee Assignments 626
  File System Rights Inheritance 627
  Attribute Security 628

Administering Rights Using NWAdmin 630
  NDS Rights 630
  File System Rights 631
Administering Rights Using NETADMIN.................................... 632
  NDS Rights 632
  File System Rights 633
Administering File System Rights Using FILER...................... 634
Administering File System Rights Using
  the *RIGHTS* Command 635
Administering File and Directory Attributes 636
  Administering Attributes Through NWAdmin 637
  Administering Attributes through FILER 637
  Administering Attributes Using the *FLAG* Command 638
File Server Console Security 639
Summary 641

29   Auditing   643

The Need for Auditing 644
Auditing Principles and Practices.. 646
Audit Preparation 650
  Volume Audit Preparation 651
  Enabling Auditing for a Directory Services Container 652
Using AUDITCON 653
Audit Files Maintenance 656
Auditor Configuration 657
  Audit by DS Events 657
  Audit by User.. 658
  Audit Options Configuration 659
  Change Audit Password 662
  Disable Container Auditing 662
  Display Audit Status 662
  Auditing Reports 663
Understanding the Audit Files 666
  The Audit History File 666
  Resetting the Audit Data File 666
  Display Audit Status 667
  Change Session Context.. 668
  Change Current Server 668
Summary 668

30   Documenting Your Network   671

The Ups and Downs 672
  The Upside to Configuration Management 673
  The Downside to Configuration Management 676

The Basics 678
    Topography 678
    Topology 679
    Information and Data.. 680
    Business Processes 681
Doing the Work 681
    Establish Goals 682
    Use the Right Tools 682
    Examine and Document the Network 690
Summary 692

31   Working with Users   695
User Training.. 696
    Networking Terminology 696
    Loading the NetWare Client 696
    Logging In 697
    NetWare Directory Services and Contexts................. 698
    Using CX and NLIST 699
    Login Scripts 700
    Using the File System 701
    Using NetWare Print Services 703
    Using E-Mail for Communicating
        with your Users 704
    Reporting Problems 705
Workgroup Administrator Training 706
    Defining Networking Terminology 707
    Establishing Standards 707
    Hardware Acquisitions.. 708
    Software Acquisitions.. 708
    Adding New Users 708
    Security 709
    Troubleshooting Procedures.................................... 710
    Virus Identification and Elimination 711
Ongoing User Support 712
    DynaText 712
    Phone Support 713
    Remote Control Software 713
    Help Desk 714
Summary 714

32   Network Printing   715
Overview 716
NetWare Print Services 717
    Create Print Queues... 717
    Create Print Server 719

Create and Configure Network Printers 720

Starting the Print Server 724

Test Printing... 727

Workstation Setup 729

Managing Print Jobs 731

Print Jobs... 732

Status 735

Attached Servers 735

Information 736

Users 737

Operators 737

Print Servers.. 737

Managing Print Servers 737

Setting Up and Customizing Printing 742

Redirecting Printer Output.. 742

The *CAPTURE* Command 743

To Stop Redirecting Print Jobs 746

The *NPRINT* Command 746

Using *PRINTCON* 747

Setting up Print Devices using *PRINTDEF*............................ 747

Creating Forms using *PRINTDEF* 750

Summary 751

33   Selecting Network Applications   **753**

The Value of Network Applications 755

The Ideal Application 756

Database 757

Rightsizing, Downsizing, and Upsizing 761

Workflow 762

Messaging 766

Imaging 768

Multimedia 770

General Data Communications 772

Basic Features of a Network Application 775

Network Integration: The OSI Model 775

Determining Network Awareness 778

Support for Network Application Program Interfaces (APIs) 780

Taking the Plunge: From Sale to Service 782

Before You Buy 782

After You Buy and Before You Install 785

After You Install and Before You Go Crazy 788

Summary 792

34   Remote Access   **795**

When Wiring Doesn't "Reach" Far Enough 797
  Dial-In Access 797
  Remote Node Versus Remote Control 798
  Remote-Access Protocols 804
  Dial-Up Routers 805
  Novell-Supplied Communications Products 806
Selecting a Modem 811
  V.DOT International Modem Standards 812
  Speed Versus Standards 812
  V.32 813
  V.32*bis* 813
  Error-Correction and Data Compression 813
  MNP 813
  V.42 814
  V.42*bis* 814
  High-Speed UARTS 815
  Alternative High-Speed Communications Links 816
Selecting a Communications Server 818
  Multiprotocol Support 819
  Standards-Based Management Capabilities 819
  Security Capabilities 820
  Easy Migration Path 820
Summary 821

PART VII   MAINTENANCE & TROUBLESHOOTING

35   Network Management   **825**

Taking a Proactive Approach 826
  Deciding on a Strategy 826
  Areas of Management 827
  Enterprise Managing Platforms 828
Tools for Management Your Network 829
  Products Available with NetWare 829
  Products from Other Sources 832
  Support for Enterprise Management Systems 834
NDS Partition Management 835
  Creating Partitions 837
  Merging Partitions 837
  Moving Containers/Partitions 837
  Aborting Partition Operations 838
  Creating Replicas 841
  Deleting Replicas 842
  Changing Replica Type 842

Rebuilding Replicas 843
Viewing Replicas on a Server 844
Using NetSync 844
Installing and Configuring NetSync 845
Cautions about NetSync 845
NetWare's Remote Management Facility 846
Remote Management Facility (RMF) 846
Setting Up Remote Management Facility 847
Security Precautions 848
Running a Remote Console Session 850
Specific Administrative Tasks 853
Enterprise Management Systems: Novell's NMS 855
Architecture 855
Database 857
Management Protocol 857
Management Agents 857
Console Interface 860
Third-Party Add-ons 861
Summary 862

36   Archiving and Backup   863

Importance of Archiving Network Data 864
Data Archiving Requirements for NetWare 4.x 865
The NetWare File System 865
NetWare-Specific File Attributes 866
Support for Name Spaces 866
Awareness of File Congruency Issues 867
Background File Compression 868
Awareness of the NetWare 4.x Data Migration System 869
NetWare Certification 870
Archiving Methods 870
Image 871
File-by-File Backup and Restore 871
Rotating Media 873
Journalized Archive 874
Perpetual Archive 874
Archiving Hardware and Software 874
Archiving Hardware 875
Archiving Software 876
Storage Management Services (SMS) 877
Archiving Server Data 878
Archiving Workstation Local Data 879
Disaster Recovery 881
Summary 881

37   Accounting   **883**

Purpose of Accounting 884
What Accounting Is 884
What Accounting Is Not 885
Practical Uses 887
Installation 888
Configuration 890
Resource Types 890
Determining Charge Rates 890
Adding and Deleting Charge Rates 891
Managing User Account Balances 893
Maintenance 894
Removal 895
NETADMIN Differences 895
Utilities 896
Novell's ATOTAL Utility 896
Third-Party Tools 897
Other Sources of Accounting Information 898
Novell Sources 898
Other Books 899
CompuServe 899
Summary 900

38   Tuning for Performance   **901**

Dynamic Configuration 902
Directory Cache Buffers 904
File Cache Buffers 905
Disk Elevator Seeking 906
Setting the Number of Packet Receive Buffers 908
Number of Minimum Packet Receive Buffers 912
File Locks 912
Prioritizing Server Processes 913
Memory for NLMs 914
Determining Block Size 915
Large Internet Packet (LIP) 915
Assessing Server RAM 916
Understanding and Tuning Packet Burst 917
Understanding Protocols 919
Understanding Frame Types 920
Finding the Bottlenecks 925
Trend Analyzers 926
Summary 927

39   Troubleshooting NetWare 4.x   **929**

Change Management 930
   Identifying Change Events 932
   Network Inventory Packages 933
Developing a Troubleshooting Methodology 933
Preproduction Testing 934
What Are Server Abends? 934
The NetWare Debugger 936
   Entering the Debugger 936
   Retrieving the Status of Active Threads 936
   Viewing Console Screens 937
   Viewing Loaded Modules 937
   Other Debugger Options 938
LAN Problems 938
   Incorrectly Loading LAN Drivers 940
   Incorrect Protocol Binding 941
   Using Protocol Analyzers 943
   Alleviating Errors 943
Disk Problems 949
   Automatic Volume Dismounts 950
   Errors Updating the FAT table 951
   Failure to Mount a Volume 951
   Read-After-Write Verification Errors 951
   Drive Mirroring and Duplexing 952
NDS Problems 952
   Breakdown of Time Synchronization 953
   Network and Routing Problems 953
   Time Synchronization Problems 954
   Partitions Stored on Downed Servers 954
Technical Support Sources 955
   NetWire 955
   ElectroText and DynaText 956
   Network Support Encyclopedia (NSEPRO) 956
   Novell Resellers, Service Centers, and User Groups 956
   Novell 957
Summary 958

PART VIII   INTERNETWORKING AND EXPANSION

40   Internetworking   **961**

Examples of Internetworking 962
Multi-Protocol Internetworks 964
   What is a Protocol? 965

The OSI Reference Model 965
How NetWare 4.1 provides
  Multi-Protocol Support 967
    How ODI Works 967
    Frame Types 972
  Routing NetWare's Native Protocols 974
    Internetwork Packet Exchange (IPX) 975
    Sequenced Packet Exchange (SPX) 975
    NetWare Core Protocols (NCP) 976
    Routing Information Protocol (RIP) 976
    Service Advertising Protocol (SAP) 977
    NetWare Link Services Protocol (NLSP) 977
  INETCFG 980
    Configuring IPX to use RIP/SAP or NLSP 982
  Host Connectivity 984
  NetWare/IP 984
  Summary 984

41 Expand Your NetWare Installation   985

  Expanding Existing Servers 986
    NetWare Loadable Modules (NLMs) 986
  Adding Additional Hard Drives to Your Server 988
  Adding Memory to Your File Server 991
  Adding a Network Card to Your Server 992
    Specifying a Frame Type 992
    Network Address Considerations 993
    Adding a Network Card Using INSTALL.NLM 997
    Adding a Network Card Using INETCFG.NLM 998
  Adding Name Space Support 1000
    Calculating Memory Requirements 1001
    Removing Name Space from a Volume 1002
  Adding Additional File Servers 1003
  Adding a Server to the NDS Tree 1005
    Default Partitions for Newly Installed Servers 1008
  Summary 1009

PART IX COMMAND REFERENCE

42 Server Console Commands   1013

  Syntax 1014
  Server Console Commands Summary 1015
  New Server Console Commands 1018
    ABORT REMIRROR 1018
    ADD NAME SPACE 1019

BIND 1020
BROADCAST 1022
CLEAR STATION 1024
CLS 1025
CONFIG 1026
DISABLE LOGIN 1027
DISABLE TTS 1028
DISMOUNT 1029
DISPLAY NETWORKS 1030
DISPLAY SERVERS 1031
DOWN 1032
ENABLE LOGIN 1033
ENABLE TTS 1034
EXIT 1035
HELP 1036
LANGUAGE 1037
LIST DEVICES 1038
LOAD 1039
MAGAZINE 1041
MEDIA 1042
MEMORY 1043
MIRROR STATUS 1043
MODULES 1044
MOUNT 1045
NAME 1047
OFF 1047
PROTOCOL 1048
REGISTER MEMORY 1049
REMIRROR PARTITION 1051
REMOVE DOS 1052
RESET ROUTER 1053
SCAN FOR NEW DEVICES 1054
SEARCH 1055
SECURE CONSOLE 1056
SEND 1058
SET 1060
SET TIME 1098
SET TIME ZONE 1100
SPEED 1101
TIME 1102
TRACK OFF 1103
TRACK ON 1103

UNBIND 1105
UNLOAD 1107
UPS STATUS 1108
UPS TIME 1110
VERSION 1111
VOLUMES 1112
NetWare Loadable Modules 1113
NetWare NLM Summary 1113
CDROM 1115
DOMAIN 1118
DSREPAIR 1119
KEYB 1122
RPL 1123
RTDM 1123
SBACKUP 1124
SERVMAN 1126
TIMESYNC 1128
Summary 1130

43 User Command Line Utilities   1131

ATOTAL 1132
Purpose 1132
Syntax 1132
AUDITCON 1132
Purpose 1132
Syntax 1133
CAPTURE 1133
Purpose 1133
Syntax 1135
Example 1135
COLORPAL 1135
Purpose 1135
Syntax 1136
CX 1136
Purpose 1136
Syntax 1137
Example 1137
DOSGEN 1137
Purpose 1137
Syntax 1137
FILER 1137
Purpose 1137
Syntax 1138

FLAG 1138
   Purpose 1138
   Syntax 1139
LOGIN 1140
   Purpose 1140
   Syntax 1140
LOGOUT 1140
   Purpose 1140
   Syntax 1141
MAP 1141
   Purpose 1141
   Syntax 1141
NCOPY 1142
   Purpose 1142
   Syntax 1142
NDIR 1143
   Purpose 1143
   Syntax 1144
NETADMIN 1144
   Purpose 1144
   Syntax 1144
NETUSER 1145
   Purpose 1145
   Syntax 1145
NLIST 1145
   Purpose 1145
   Syntax 1146
NMENU 1146
   Purpose 1146
   Syntax 1146
NPRINT 1146
   Purpose 1146
   Syntax 1147
NVER 1148
   Purpose 1148
   Syntax 1148
NWXTRACT 1148
   Purpose 1148
   Syntax 1148
PARTMGR 1148
   Purpose 1148
   Syntax 1148

PCONSOLE 1149
  Purpose 1149
  Syntax 1149
PRINTCON 1150
  Purpose 1150
  Syntax 1150
PRINTDEF 1150
  Purpose 1150
  Syntax 1150
PSC 1151
  Syntax 1152
PURGE 1152
  Purpose 1152
  Syntax 1152
RCONSOLE 1153
  Purpose 1153
  Syntax 1153
RENDIR 1153
  Purpose 1153
  Syntax 1153
RIGHTS 1153
  Purpose 1153
  Syntax 1154
SEND 1154
  Purpose 1154
  Syntax 1155
SETPASS 1155
  Purpose 1155
  Syntax 1155
SETTTS 1155
  Purpose 1155
  Syntax 1155
SYSTIME 1156
  Purpose 1156
  Syntax 1156
UIMPORT 1156
  Purpose 1156
  Syntax 1156
WHOAMI 1156
  Purpose 1156
  Syntax 1156
WSUPDATE 1157
  Purpose 1157

Syntax 1157
WSUPGRD 1158
Purpose 1158
Syntax 1158
Summary 1158

44   NWADMIN and NETADMIN Utilities   1159

NWADMIN 1160
Using NWADMIN 1162
NWADMIN's Object Menu 1163
NWADMIN's Create Menu Option 1164
Object Details Menu Option 1167
Trustees of this Object Menu Option 1170
The Rights to Other Objects Menu Option 1174
The Move and Copy Menu Options 1176
The Rename Menu Option 1176
The Delete Menu Option 1176
The User Template Menu Option 1176
The Print Option 1177
The Search and Exit Menu Options 1177
The View Menu 1178
The Set Context Option 1178
The Include Option 1178
The Sort by Object Class Option 1178
The Expand/Collapse Option 1178
The Options Menu 1179
The Tools Menu 1179
Partition Manager 1179
The Browser Menu Option 1181
The Salvage Menu Option 1181
The Remote Console Menu Option 1183
The Window Menu 1183
The Help Menu 1184
NETADMIN 1184
The Manage Objects Menu Option 1186
View or Edit Properties of This Object 1188
Manage According to Search Pattern 1194
Summary 1197

45   NWUSER and NETUSER Utilities   1199

Starting NWUSER 1200
Mapping Drives 1203
Capturing Printer Ports 1206
Capture Settings 1208

Attaching to Servers 1210
    Getting NetWare Connection Information 1212
Sending Messages 1214
NetWare Settings 1215
User-Definable Buttons 1216
NETUSER 1218
Printing 1219
Capture Printers 1220
Messages 1220
Drives 1221
Attachments 1222
Changing Context 1223
Summary 1224

PART X   APPENDIXES

A   Glossary of Networking Terms   1227

B   Where to Go for More Information   1235

Novell Authorized Education 1236
    Novell Authorized Education Centers (NAECs) 1238
    Certified Novell Instructors (CNIs) 1239
Computer Based Training (CBTs) 1240
Novell CBTs 1242
Books 1243
Magazines 1243
Trade Shows 1244
User Groups 1244
Professional Associations 1245
Bulletin Board Systems 1246
    A Quick NetWire Tour 1246
    Communications Software 1246
    Benefits of NetWire 1247
    Posting Messages on NetWire 1247

C   Network Management Forms and Lists   1253

Documents and Records 1254
    The LAN 1254
    History of the LAN 1255

D   Cabling Rules   1257

    LAN Resources 1256
ARCnet 1258
Ethernet 1259

The 5-4-3 Rule 1260
10Base2 1260
10Base5 1261
10BaseT 1262
Token Ring 1262

Index   **1267**

Acknowledgments

The *NetWare 4.1 Survival Guide* has been the collective effort of many NetWare experts who unselfishly shared their real-world experiences. In particular, I would like to extend my sincere thanks to my friend, Rudy Koehle, who was instrumental in designing the book outline and set the direction for the book; Rudy initially brought me into the project as the technical editor, and later I took over as the Chief Author. The efforts and the expertise of Doug Archell and Jim Henderson are very much appreciated.

Bob Bailey and Frank Nicholas provided an excellent level of assistance to this project as technical editor. His suggestions and comments about various topics are invaluable to the accuracy of the material presented in this book.

Angelique Brittingham and Jill Bond, my editors at Sams, did an outstanding job in providing the much needed prodding and shaping of the book. I am very much in debt to their tenacity in catching and correcting the silly errors I made. This book would never have made it out of the writing and development stages to print if not for the persistence of my Acquisitions Editor, Rosemarie Graham. For that, I am eternally grateful.

I also want to thank the following people for their contributions in the writing of this book: Blaine Homer, Doug Archell, Todd Brown, Mark Campbell, Jim Carr, Lisa Donald, Thomas Foley, Jim Henderson, Pam Koehle, George Kulman, Ranji Latchmansingh, Ed Serreze, Tom Stearns, Sandy Stevens, Richard Verlaque, and Robert Zych. A special thanks to Brad Drew for his additional contributions

I extend my appreciation and thanks to all of the Novell's NetWire volunteer SysOps and volunteer assistants for putting up with the time I hid from the 'Wire to finish this project. In particular, I thank Sandra Harrell, Chris Patron, and Martin Kirchhoefer for keeping the NOVMAN and NCONNECT forums in one piece while I was away.

Last, but not least, my sincere gratitude to my friend, MT, who helped to keep my sanity and kept me focused on the project.

About the Author

Peter Kuo, Ph.D., is the president of DreamLAN Network Consulting Ltd., a Toronto-based firm specializing in connectivity and network management. Peter is the first Canadian Enterprise Certified NetWare Engineer (and Master CNE) and is a Certified Novell Instructor (CNI) and a Certified Network Expert (CNX). His areas of expertise include advanced NetWare topics such as network management, NetWare 4, NetWare Directory Services, and IBM and UNIX connectivity issues. Peter is a SysOp on NetWire (CompuServe), supporting many advanced sections for Novell, such as connectivity, network management, NetWare 4, and client software. He also is a member of Novell's Professional Developer's Program. Peter has written many computer books, such as *NDS Troubleshooting* and *NetWare Unleashed*. You can reach Peter at 71333,1700@compuserve.com.

Introduction

INTRODUCING NOVELL NETWARE 4.1

NetWare 4.1 is Novell's latest networking offering, the flagship product of a company that dominates computer networking. NetWare 4.1 shares many characteristics with previous versions of NetWare and introduces some dramatically new features that have a large impact on the way network administrators and managers work with their LANs.

NetWare has been around for over ten years and is the most popular local area network operating system in the world.

THE LESSONS OF HISTORY

The history of LAN technology in general and NetWare in particular clearly indicates that your NetWare installation will have three distinct phases during its useful life. These phases are

- ◆ Implementation
- ◆ Operation
- ◆ Expansion

IMPLEMENTATION PHASE

The implementation phase occurs when you install a NetWare LAN. This could mean you are installing a NetWare LAN for the first time, that you are upgrading your NetWare LAN, or that you are moving applications to a new NetWare LAN from another platform.

Activities you must accomplish during the implementation phase include selecting hardware and software components, developing an implementation plan, installing networking hardware, and installing server and workstation software.

OPERATION PHASE

The operation phase begins after you successfully implement your NetWare LAN and continues for the duration of NetWare's operation at your site. In other words, the operation phase is an ongoing process and is the most important phase of your installation's life.

Activities you must accomplish during the operation phase include working with users, documenting your network, configuring user accounts, implementing network security, implementing network printing, implementing network applications, enabling remote access to the network, performing network management, tuning the network for performance, and performing troubleshooting.

Expansion Phase

The expansion phase occurs when you add new capacity, new services, new versions of NetWare, or new NetWare servers to your installation. During the life cycle of a NetWare LAN, you will pass through the operation and expansion phases many times. The most important component of a successful expansion is that you perform this phase without disrupting the normal operation of your NetWare installation.

Activities you may need to perform during expansion include upgrading to a new version of NetWare, moving your network, adding a new service to your network, and implementing new transport protocols on your network.

The Life Cycle of a NetWare LAN

This book is organized around these three phases of NetWare's life cycle. You will find sections on implementation, operation, and expansion of your NetWare LAN.

Each activity associated with the specific phases of your NetWare LAN's life cycle is covered in detail. The *NetWare 4.1 Survival Guide* is designed to serve you well during all phases of your NetWare LAN's life cycle. You can use this book as a tutorial, reference guide, and network manager's handbook.

- Networking Technology

- How NetWare Fits In

- Features of NetWare 4

- Related Products

P A R T I

Introduction to NetWare 4

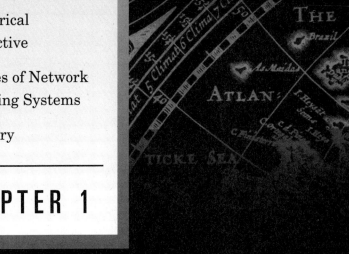

- Components of a Distributed Processing Network

- Network Types

- Network Topologies

- Capabilities of a Network or Internetwork

- A Historical Perspective

- Features of Network Operating Systems

- Summary

CHAPTER 1

Networking Technology

A computer network may be defined as two or more computers connected in such a way that they are able to share files, printers, and other resources. These networks can be very simple or very complex, but they all start with certain basic components. This chapter begins by defining the building blocks of a network, and then looks at what a network will do for you. Finally, this chapter describes the overall features of a network operating system. If you are already familiar with these fundamentals, move on to Chapter 2.

COMPONENTS OF A DISTRIBUTED PROCESSING NETWORK

Whereas a mainframe system does all of the "brain work" for the dumb terminals connected to it, a distributed processing network shares the work among the connected computers. Each node is responsible for its own processing rather than one central unit doing all the work. Novell NetWare is based on this distributed processing model. All distributed processing networks have some common elements (see Figure 1.1).

Figure 1.1.
Components of a
network.

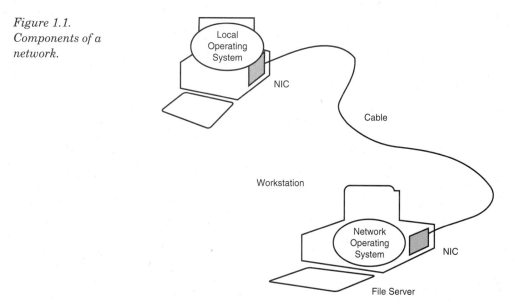

FILE SERVER

The *file server* is a fast computer that runs the network operating system software. It has a large capacity hard drive that is used to store personal and shared files, including network-specific user and management utilities. File servers can store multi-user applications, provide electronic mail service, store shared databases and other common data files as well as personal files and single-user applications, and provide printing services. (Chapter 6 covers choosing appropriate server hardware for your needs.)

CLIENT WORKSTATIONS

Users work on *client workstations*. These can be IBM compatible PCs (using either DOS or Windows), UNIX systems, Apple Macintoshes, or OS/2 machines. Application programs often are run from these workstations and files can be stored on a local drive. The most significant aspect of client workstations is that all of their processing is done at the workstation rather than by the server. Some workstations may be "diskless" devices possessing no local storage capacity. (For information about choosing client workstation hardware, see Chapter 7.)

NETWORK INTERFACE CARDS (NIC)

Network interface cards (NIC) allow the computer to communicate on a network. The NIC, or network adapter, is responsible for converting digital messages to a pattern of electrical voltages on the network medium, or cable. Only a few years ago, ARCnet and Ethernet cards used coaxial cable while token ring used twisted pair. Now you can use a number of different cable types with certain NICs. The most common NIC types are Ethernet, ARCnet, and token ring. (Chapter 5 explains the various network protocol standards.)

CABLING

Cable refers to the wires connecting the workstation to the server and other network resources. The combination of all servers, workstations, and resources at all sites make up the network. Twisted pair, coaxial, and fiber optic are the most common types of cable available. It is common to find multiple types of cabling used in large networks. Systems are available that use radio waves, infrared light, or other wireless transmission methods instead of physical wiring. (Cable choice is covered in Chapter 9.)

OTHER SHARED DEVICES

A wide variety of other devices can be connected to a network. The most common of these is a printer. Other devices include plotters, modems, gateways to mini- or mainframe computers, optical disk readers, and others.

SOFTWARE

The *network operating system* (NOS) of the file server and client workstation software are the final components of the network. These software programs provide file access, system security, printing services, and user-management facilities, as well as many other management and troubleshooting services.

NETWORK TYPES

The components discussed previously can be used in either of two types of network operating systems: peer-to-peer or dedicated-server systems. The file server is the only exception: it is not used in a peer-to-peer setup.

With *peer-to-peer networks*, the processing and storage is shared among the users on the network so that all of the computers are used for word processing, database work, and so on. Because there is no shared hard disk, users store information at their local drives. They can, however, make a portion of their hard disk available to be shared with other users (see Figure 1.2). This is how information is passed from one user to another on a peer-to-peer system.

Peer-to-peer networks are most appropriate for small workgroup situations or where power requirements or budget constraints prohibit a company from investing in a so-called non-productive computer. Microsoft's Windows for Workgroups, Apple's System 7 File Sharing, Artisoft's LANtastic, and Novell's Personal NetWare are examples of peer-to-peer networks.

Figure 1.2.
A peer-to-peer network.

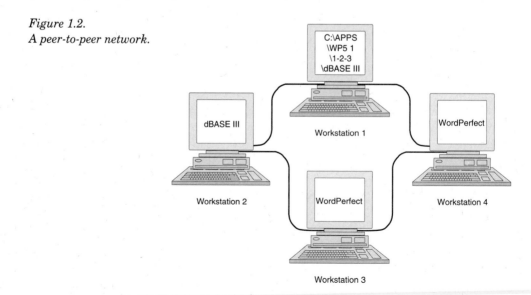

Dedicated-server networks, also called *client/server networks*, have a shared file server as the main component (see Figure 1.3). The server machine is set aside to function only as a shared resource and it is not available for use as an individual's workstation, for word-processing purposes, for example. Users can work with files from the server, but they cannot access each other's computers directly. NetWare 4 is a dedicated-server network system.

Figure 1.3.
A dedicated-server network.

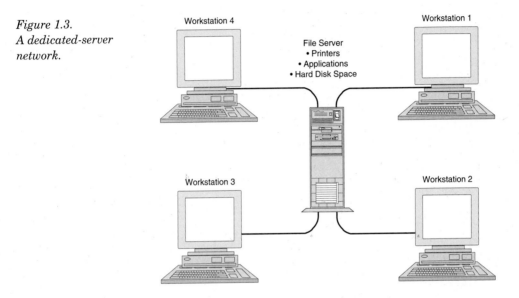

Typically, the server component of a client/server network is designed to work with hundreds, or even thousands of client components. Client/server computing has garnered praise from corporate computing managers because it allows very large and complex data processing applications to run on inexpensive networks.

Unlike the peer-to-peer network on which users share files by making a portion of their hard disk available assessable by others, the NOS in the file server of a client/server network makes its hard drive available to all users, subject to security assignment. This makes the server look like a network from a user's perspective.

NETWORK TOPOLOGIES

Topology refers to the way in which the network components, the computers, the nodes, and connecting cables, are arranged. There are several standard methods for connecting networked computers, as in the following:

◆ Mesh

◆ Star

- ◆ Bus
- ◆ Ring
- ◆ Hybrid network topologies

MESH NETWORKS

In a pure *mesh* topology, each node is connected to every other node, a rather expensive and impractical method of connecting many computers (see Figure 1.4). Today, some of the nodes of a network may be directly connected to each other, particularly in a mainframe computer environment, but seldom will all the devices in a network be connected directly to one another. Although many of the early networks used this method, it is not particularly common at present.

Figure 1.4.
Mesh networks.

Mesh

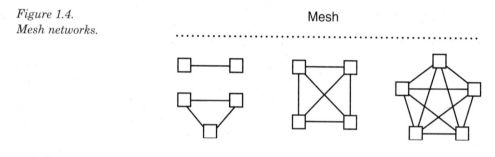

STAR

In a *star* network, a group of nodes are connected to a single computer (see Figure 1.5). This hub (also called a *multiport repeater* or *concentrator*) provides a hierarchical link to the rest of the network. While these topologies are relatively easy to troubleshoot, failure of a hub can disable a large portion of the network. ARCnet and Farallon are examples of star topologies. The Farallon Star Controller is a common hub for Macintosh networks.

Figure 1.5.
Star network.

Star

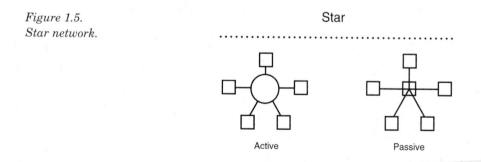

Active   Passive

BUS

The *bus* network topology has a linear arrangement of the computers and other resources on the network and terminators at each end of the cabling medium (see Figure 1.6). This method uses a minimum of cable, but because there is no central connection point, it can be difficult to troubleshoot. Ethernet uses a bus arrangement.

Figure 1.6.
Bus network.

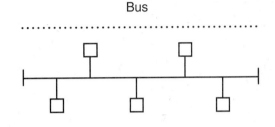

Bus

RING

The *ring* network is a closed loop with each device acting as a signal Repeater (see Figure 1.7). A ring network can be subject to failures. A problem with any component "breaks" the ring. For this reason IBM's token ring specifications include extensive component self-diagnostics. Token ring is the most common ring topology.

Figure 1.7.
Ring Network.

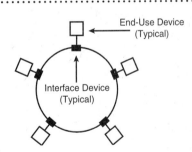

Ring

End-Use Device
(Typical)

Interface Device
(Typical)

HYBRID

Whenever you mix more than one of the preceding topologies, you have a *hybrid* network (see Figure 1.8). In large companies, it is very common to have a Macintosh section in a star network connecting to an OS/2 token ring network attached to a UNIX Ethernet bus network.

Figure 1.8.
Hybrid network.

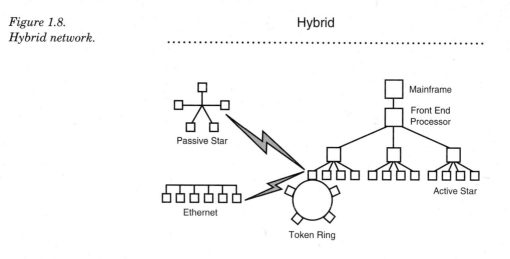

Each type of topology has its own advantages and relative disadvantages, and each is appropriate in particular environments. Most larger networks use a mix of these arrangements to communicate effectively.

Capabilities of a Network or Internetwork

When more than one computer is connected together they make a network. When more than one network is connected, either similar or dissimilar, they form an *internetwork*. Networks provide basic capabilities, as discussed in the following sections.

Shared Files

Any network, whether it is peer-to-peer or dedicated server, will allow you to share files with other users on the network. This is particularly helpful in situations in which a number of people need access to a single file or set of files. Databases, financial data, clip-art libraries, and template files are all examples of files commonly shared over a network.

Shared Resources

A *network resource* could be a printer, plotter, modem, or any device connected to the network that is shared between users. Companies can save a great deal of money by adding these devices to a network because this allows multiple users to access each resource.

SHARED APPLICATIONS

Many common applications are available in network or multi-user versions. Database applications, such as dBASE and Oracle, are among the most often used multi-user environments. Many common applications, such as WordPerfect, are available in multi-user network versions. Instead of having the program reside on each user's local hard drive, one copy can be installed and shared from the server. Again, this results in a tremendous cost saving for large companies, as well as making end-user support easier.

Database management systems optimize the use of both file server and client workstation because they are split into two parts: a data engine, which runs on a network server, and a client data entry program, which runs on a workstation.

E-MAIL AND OTHER UTILITIES

E-mail (electronic mail) has changed the face of interoffice communications. Other users can leave you messages, send you files, even send you pictures via e-mail. Other utilities may include schedulers that remind you of meetings and due dates, backup utilities that are run from the server, and dozens of other third-party utility programs.

SECURITY

Having the access to files controlled and monitored is a great stress reducer to many network users. As you work on sensitive projects, personnel data, marketing information, new products, and so on, you don't want to worry about someone picking up the diskettes on your desk and getting to the confidential data. In a dedicated server environment, you can determine which user or group of users have access to a directory or even an individual file.

A HISTORICAL PERSPECTIVE

The sophisticated networks on the market today didn't just appear. They have been advancing for the past ten years or so and have responded to user interest and market pressure in certain areas.

The original "networked" computer was the mainframe with a central processor and storage facility. The terminals were considered "dumb" in that they were only a window into the main computer rather than stand-alone systems. With the invention of the personal computer, desktop computing was born. For a while, each computer had a printer and files were shared by "sneaker net," that is, walking a disk to whoever needed the files. Soon it became apparent that a better method of sharing printers, modems, hard disks, and files was needed and PC networking was begun.

EARLY NETWORK TYPES

In the early days of desktop computers, hard disk space storage was very expensive. It was not unusual to spend several thousand dollars on a 10MB drive—at that time considered a huge capacity. In order to better utilize the drives, disk serving systems were developed to section the disk, allowing it to be shared by multiple computers. Each user could store data on their own section of the disk, but they couldn't access anyone else's data on the same physical drive. Because of the inflexible nature of these systems, the limitations of the disk serving model quickly became apparent.

The next major step in the industry was the introduction of true file serving network operating systems. A file serving operating system provides network workstations with a remote file system rather than merely a remote disk media partition. These systems provided users with shared storage, as the earlier disk serving systems had, but files on the server could now be accessed by more than one connected user. In addition, the file servers provided access to shared printers, databases, and electronic mail. While these early networks could often connect with the other systems from the same manufacturer, systems from any other manufacturer could not communicate. Customers were unable to tie together their dissimilar systems.

HARDWARE AND MEDIA ADVANCES

As early as 1960, the General Accounting Office found that they were over-utilizing portions of their resources and under-utilizing others. They needed a system to transfer data between sites without regard to format. A system was developed, the ARPANET (Advanced Research Projects Agency NETwork), which linked a number of government agencies regardless of installed computer base. The market continued to standardize on certain formats and protocols, such as TCP/IP, Ethernet, and IBM's SNA (Systems Network Architecture). TCP/IP (Transmission Control Protocol/Internet Protocol) is a group of network protocols that allow dissimilar network resources to communicate with each other. Ethernet, Token-Ring, and ARCnet networks are supported by NetWare TCP/IP. SNA was developed by IBM to interconnect relatively similar components of an IBM network.

INTERNETWORKING

Customers can now create large, networked systems containing many servers, many network segments, and hundreds or even thousands of network workstations around the world. These global networks can connect manufacturers, suppliers, management, and so on, to exchange databases and other files.

FUTURE DEVELOPMENTS

Network operating systems of the future will do much more than integrate computing resources. Current areas of development include true distributed processing, which requires the capability of one computer to address another's memory and send instructions to its processor. Network operating systems also are branching out into non-traditional areas, such as telephony and sound, and video processing.

Some vendors are starting to use the NetWare operating system in embedded systems, or specialized controllers such as the computers that manage your car's engine and suspension system. These developments will make networking technology prominent, not only in the business data processing world, but also in homes and home appliances, cars, ships, airplanes, trains, and more.

The next two chapters explore where Novell NetWare fits into today's market and describe the new features of NetWare 4.

FEATURES OF NETWORK OPERATING SYSTEMS

The network operating system is the power behind any network. It must bind the disparate computing resources of a business into a logical framework that is both user friendly and easily administered by the network manager. A network operating system also must work with many different types of hardware, client networking platforms, protocols, and applications.

FILE AND DIRECTORY SERVICES

File and *directory services* control how files are accessed, where they are stored, who has access to them, and when they are deleted. Network operating systems must have concurrency control so that the network operating system can resolve conflicts that arise when multiple workstations request access to the same file at the same time.

The logical framework that NetWare 4 uses is called *NetWare Directory Services* (NDS). NDS is a global, distributed database containing information about all the computers and users, printers, file servers, or other resources in an organization. You read more about NDS in Part III, "Understanding NetWare Directory Services." A number of chapters are devoted to this particular topic.

GLOBAL VIEW OF NETWORK

NetWare 4 with NDS enables a company's entire network to be viewed as a single logical structure. The administrator can set up the network in whatever way makes sense for that company. Some organizations set up the network based on the structure of the company. Others prefer a geographical approach to designing their network. Part III, "Understanding Network Directory Services" provides a number of chapters with complete descriptions of the logical internetwork.

SYSTEM FAULT TOLERANCE

Fault tolerance defines a system's capability to survive failures of one sort or another. This can be as simple as ensuring that any data written to a disk can be retrieved through a "read-after-write" verification process to guaranteeing non-stop processing, even in the event of catastrophic failure of an entire file server hardware system. As companies place more of their "mission critical" applications on PC networks, the capability to provide increasingly sophisticated levels of fault tolerance becomes essential to the survival of the company. NetWare 4's fault tolerance features are discussed in more detail in Chapter 2.

PRINT SERVICES

Sharing high-cost laser printers or plotters is a major feature of any network operating system. The file server acts as a print server, managing which print jobs go to which print queues, and thus to which printers. Large print jobs can be deferred. Important jobs can be submitted with a high priority. For a complete description of printing with NetWare, see Chapter 31.

SUMMARY

Networks of all sizes are designed as a way to share information and resources between users. Peer-to-peer networks do not feature a central file server and, therefore, no shared hard disk, so they most often are found in smaller environments. Distributed processing is how NetWare 4 operates; each user has a local computer with a processor where most of the programs are run and files stored. Finally, NetWare allows diverse network topologies to connect so that large internetworks are formed.

The next few chapters examine how NetWare fits in the network market and look at the features of NetWare 4 and its related products.

- Specialization

- The Foundation of the
  Enterprise Network

- Expandability

- Fault Tolerance

- Capacity

- Client Support

- Protocol Support

- Server-Based
  Applications

- Summary

CHAPTER 2

How NetWare Fits In

This chapter describes the characteristics of NetWare 4, including its design goals, overall architecture, and behavioral aspects. Although this chapter doesn't discuss specific features of NetWare, it provides important conceptual information that can help you install, administer, and expand your NetWare installation.

SPECIALIZATION

NetWare's origins are different than those of other popular operating systems, such as UNIX, VMS, OS/2, and so on. NetWare began life as a disk-serving operating system and quickly expanded to provide full file service over a network.

NetWare is the only operating system on the market today that began as a strictly back-end, network-based product. *Back-end* services are network-based operating system components, such as file systems. This focus on network-based, back-end services is the motivation for NetWare to provide maximum throughput and reliability, which explains some of its unique characteristics and differences when compared to other network operating systems.

AN EVENT-DRIVEN SYSTEM

Because NetWare's role is to provide back-end services over a network, it is an *event-driven* system. When a network workstation (front end) requests to read a file residing on the server, for example, it sends a request packet to the server. The request packet triggers activity on the NetWare server: the server checks for concurrency conflicts, security violations, reads the file data, and sends the data back to the workstation over the network.

All this activity on the NetWare server is driven by an event: the reception of a request packet from the front-end workstation. This means that NetWare's capability to perform is dictated by its capability to receive and process packets that come to it over the network. NetWare, therefore, is designed to handle thousands of hardware interrupts and hundreds of network request packets per second. This high-throughput design requires an efficient overall operating system architecture and a particularly robust device driver interface.

TRADITIONAL DESIGN COMPONENTS

Some traditional operating system design components, such as virtual memory, memory protection, and preemptive multitasking, pose significant performance problems to device drivers. NetWare device drivers make heavy use of shared memory and Direct Memory Access (DMA). All three of these traditional design components negate or negatively impact the capability of device drivers to use shared memory and DMA. Because of this, NetWare's designers decided to forgo virtual memory, memory protection, and preemptive multitasking. This was not an oversight or mistake, but a decision consistent with NetWare's focus on providing back-end services over a network.

Note

Preemptive multitasking, virtual memory, and memory protection all contribute to an operating system's capability to run multiple front-end (interactive) applications concurrently. These design features were specifically introduced into general-purpose operating systems to allow users on terminals to run front-end applications. NetWare specializes in back-end services, which in traditional operating systems typically run at the *kernel* level anyway (without memory protection) and must deal with the negative consequences of virtual memory and preemption.

NetWare makes use of the fact that it is generally much faster—about 100 times—to access information from RAM than it is from hard disk; it tries to keep as much information in RAM as possible. File Allocation Tables (FATs), most recently used Directory Entry Tables (DETs), and most recently accessed files are all cached in RAM for fast access.

NetWare obtains excellent performance from commodity PC hardware because of the reasons mentioned previously. In order to take full advantage of NetWare's initial concept, you must install and configure NetWare in a manner consistent with its design characteristics.

A Rich Service Environment

NetWare's event-driven design and the consequential requirements for high throughput demand a minimalist philosophy on the part of NetWare's designers. Each component of NetWare is designed with this philosophy in mind. NetWare's kernel is exceedingly simple and elegant.

NetWare, despite its simplicity, presents a rich environment to developers and systems designers. This is possible because of the fortunate rule that complex systems can be constructed by integrated simple components in a modular fashion. Each basic component of NetWare is sparsely coded and simple in design; however, because of the modular integration of the many basic components of NetWare, the NetWare environment is rich and complex.

This enables NetWare to present a complete back-end service platform to server-based applications developers and still maintain its high throughput. NetWare can service network request packets very quickly because it is "flat" (it has few OSI layers; see Chapter 5 for more information on OSI). Being flat means that it is only concerned with the lowest layers of the OSI model: physical, data link, network, and transport. Another reason NetWare can handle request packets quickly is because its modular design leverages the basic kernel to its maximum potential.

Examples of services offered by NetWare 4 include the following:

- ◆ Kernel-level scheduling and memory management
- ◆ Interprocess communication
- ◆ LAN communications
- ◆ Hardware device driver support
- ◆ File system
- ◆ Print services
- ◆ Messaging and e-mail
- ◆ Internetwork routing
- ◆ Programming interfaces and development environment
- ◆ Network management
- ◆ Network hub support
- ◆ Built-in support for multiprotocol operation
- ◆ Support for multiple-file formats
- ◆ Built-in support for database management systems

PLATFORM FOR SERVER-BASED APPLICATIONS

As a result of its focus, design, and characteristics, NetWare 4 is an ideal platform for server-based applications. (Server-based applications provide the "server" component of client/server computing.)

Server-based applications running on NetWare can gain increased performance over other platforms because of NetWare's high-throughput, event-driven design. Specifically, server-based applications running on NetWare automatically enjoy the following benefits:

- ◆ Multi-threaded (or multi-process) execution
- ◆ Full 32-bit protected mode
- ◆ Flat memory model with up to 4GB of addressable memory
- ◆ Full access to NetWare OS services

Developers, such as Oracle, Sybase, and Informix, that have ported their multi-platform database management systems to run as NetWare server-based applications, have expressed that NetWare provides the highest possible performance, given the hardware on which it is running. This means that a NetWare server can run such applications just as fast or faster than platforms that cost many times more than a NetWare system.

These developers note that NetWare has a different design than other platforms they support. These design differences must be accounted for in the development process, such as changing the application to work well in a non-preemptive multitasking system. The benefits of non-preemption, however, include increased performance and better overall efficiency.

THE ROLE OF THE NETWORK OPERATING SYSTEM

As you read in Chapter 1, the history of network operating systems indicates that their role expanded over time. NetWare went from disk-serving to file-serving, to internetworking and multiprotocol service. Today, network operating systems are expected to perform all of these functions and more.

NetWare 3.1x has proven the utility of a network operating system that supported multiple network protocols and client file systems. In addition, NetWare 3.1x has proven the effectiveness of NetWare as a platform for server-based applications, based on the excellent performance and reliability of NLM-based applications, such as Oracle, Informix, Sybase, and Gupta.

NetWare 4 is designed to extend the role of the network even further, to the point that NetWare might become the foundation of an enterprise network.

THE FOUNDATION OF THE ENTERPRISE NETWORK

NetWare 4 is designed to provide the foundation of the enterprise network. *Enterprise networks* tie together the disparate computing resources of the organization, enabling unlike systems to act together as a cohesive whole.

NetWare 4 binds an organization's computing resources in two ways. First, the versatile protocol and file services of NetWare enable communication among disparate computing systems. Second, NetWare Directory Services (NDS) provides a systematic and intuitive method of managing, administering, and using all the computing resources of an organization.

Interestingly, NDS calls on all the lower-level services provided by NetWare:

◆ Communications protocols are necessary to query and respond to queries from other systems on the internetwork.

◆ File services are necessary to store the NDS Directory Information Base (DIB).

◆ Security services are necessary to ensure that the distributed NDS system allows only authorized information to be obtained across the internetwork.

◆ Transaction and concurrency control is necessary for the smooth operation of the distributed NDS DIB, such as tracking file updates on remote computers.

NetWare 4's role as the "glue" that binds an enterprise together is its most ambitious goal to date, one which draws on the heritage of NetWare's past and requires all the lower-level services that have evolved over the years to work correctly and reliably.

NDS has started to shape the future of using the network. The built-in services provided by NDS, combined with the NDS programming interface, create the potential for a new generation of distributed "glue" applications—modules that bind different types of computers across geographical and organizational boundaries.

Glue applications provide a logical framework that destroys such boundaries and makes resources available universally. While NDS is itself such a glue application, it also creates the potential for any number of higher-level modules that enable computing activities not foreseen by the designers of NDS.

SCALABLE FROM WORKGROUP TO ENTERPRISE

NetWare 4 is designed to be *scalable* from the work group to the enterprise because the concept of the network is logical rather than physical. You can add to your NetWare installation one server at a time and even one user at a time. This scalability primarily is achieved through the distributed design of NDS. NDS enables you to create a multileveled global directory tree one server at a time, with no restrictions on the timing or number of servers you add to the tree.

UNLIMITED NDS

The NDS was designed to have unlimited size, which is to say, an unlimited number of levels. This design allows a single NDS database to contain not only information about very large organizations, but also to allow the linking of multiple organizations through the merging of trees. The algorithms built into NDS for replicating the database and checking distributed links in the tree are highly scalable—they perform very well even when the database becomes extremely large.

Expandability

Many computer programmers believe that the role of a computer operating system is to provide a programming interface to the underlying computer hardware, and to provide a systematic way of obtaining hardware resources.

With this view in mind, NetWare's expandability becomes particularly important. NetWare enables you to add hardware resources to the server machine easily without having to reconfigure the NetWare operating system.

Dynamic Discovery

NetWare provides expandability through its dynamic discovery of underlying hardware resources installed on the server machine. Because NetWare discovers all server memory during the NetWare boot routines, it can make use of additional server memory automatically.

Loadable Device-Driver Interface

NetWare's loadable device-driver interface means that you can add storage devices, LAN cards, and other hardware devices to the server machine without reconfiguring the NetWare operating system. To activate such devices, you only need to load the device's driver from the NetWare server console prompt. (Conversely, you can deactivate hardware devices simply by unloading their drivers from the console prompt.)

Note

> As an analogy, you can consider the NetWare operating system as a "Lego set"—you add and remove pieces from it as you see fit (see Figure 2.1).

NetWare's loadable device-driver interface especially is attractive when you consider that UNIX (and other similar operating systems) require you to relink the entire operating system simply to add a driver. DOS requires a complete reboot in order to add device drivers.

You can change certain server resources, such as LAN receive buffers, directory cache buffers, and others, simply by entering commands at the server console prompt while the server is running.

Figure 2.1.
Device drivers can
easily "snap" into the
operating system.

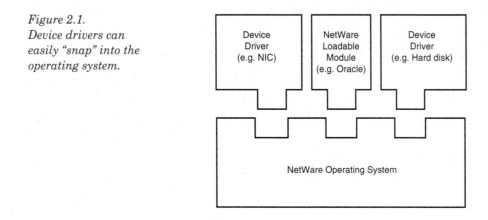

DYNAMIC VOLUME SIZE INCREASES

The most spectacular aspect of NetWare's expandability is the capability to increase the size of a NetWare volume while the server is running.

To do this, simply add a prepared storage partition to a volume: NetWare increases the size of that volume dynamically.

FAULT TOLERANCE

Fault tolerance is a design philosophy that has been part of NetWare from the beginning. Fault tolerance means that NetWare can continue operating in the face of hardware errors.

NetWare contains different levels of *system fault tolerance* (SFT). The need for fault tolerance became evident early in the life of NetWare because NetWare, as a server operating system, was responsible for concurrently providing resources to many workstation computers. This amounted to a single point of failure—the machine on which NetWare was running. This had the potential to bring down many other machines—the workstation machines requesting services from NetWare.

SYSTEM FAULT TOLERANCE LEVEL I (SFT I)

Level I fault tolerance is built into the core routines of all versions of the NetWare file system. It provides for automatic, on-the-fly remapping of bad hard drive media sectors. Novell calls this feature *Hot Fix*, referring to the automatic and transparent remapping of bad media sectors. If a sector on a hard drive goes bad, NetWare automatically maps that sector to a good one from a pool of reserved sectors (see Figure 2.2).

Figure 2.2.
Dynamic bad block
remapping (Hot Fix).

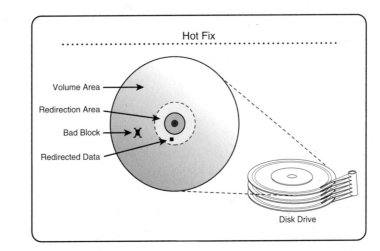

To detect bad media sectors, NetWare uses read-after-write verification. This verification involves reading data into a special buffer after NetWare has written that same data to disk. NetWare compares the data it just read to the data it just wrote and, if the two are not the same, infers that the media has suffered an error. This triggers the Hot Fix feature you just read about (see Figure 2.3).

Figure 2.3.
Read-After-Write
verification process.

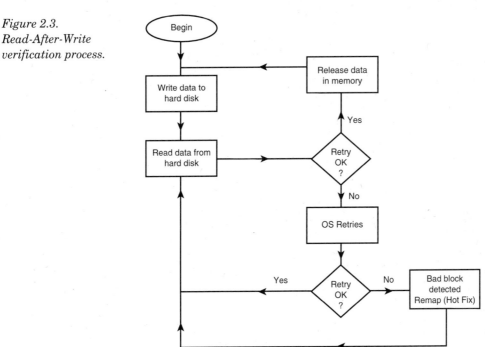

REDUNDANT VOLUME DATA STRUCTURES

Another aspect of SFT I is *redundant volume data structures*. Volume data structures contain essential information regarding the NetWare file system, files, directories, and free space on the media. Without these data structures, the NetWare file system cannot function.

NetWare maintains redundant copies of all volume data structures and performs routine comparisons of the primary and redundant data structures. If either a primary or redundant data structure becomes corrupted, NetWare repairs it using the other copy as a reference.

CONSISTENCY CHECK ON VOLUME MOUNTS

Each time a volume mounts, NetWare checks each set of directory tables and FATs for internal consistency and then compares it with the other copy to ensure that both copies are valid. If a discrepancy is found, the volume will not be mounted and a warning message displayed on the server console.

Note

> If any of your volumes failed to mount, you need to run VREPAIR to correct any inconsistencies before trying to mount them again.

SYSTEM FAULT TOLERANCE LEVEL II (SFT II)

Level II fault tolerance consists of *disk mirroring* and *duplexing*. Both mirroring and duplexing enable you to configure redundant storage devices for use with NetWare.

DISK MIRRORING

A mirrored drive consists of two physical drives connected to the same hard drive controller (see Figure 2.4). NetWare duplicates all write operations to both drives of a mirrored set.

If one of the drives fails, NetWare continues to run, using the remaining drive for all read and write operations. All data on the remaining drive is up-to-date, meaning that no data loss occurred when the failed drive went down. When you replace the failed drive, NetWare automatically restores the mirror using a special background process that allows the server to remain up and running throughout the entire process.

Figure 2.4.
Disk mirroring.

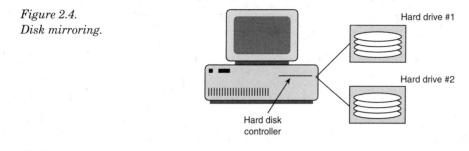

Note

Depending on the amount of disk space that needs remirroring, the process can take up to several hours.

Warning

It is always important to keep track of which disk is being mirrored onto which other disk. Choosing the wrong disk as the primary could destroy valuable data!

DUPLEXING

The difference between mirroring and duplexing is simple. Mirroring occurs when two or more drives (the mirrored set) are attached to the same drive controller. *Duplexing* occurs when each drive in the mirrored set is attached to a different controller (see Figure 2.5).

Figure 2.5.
Disk duplexing.

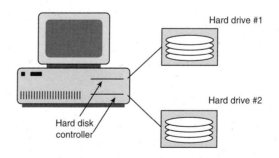

Duplexing is more robust than mirroring because it protects against drive and controller failure, while mirroring only protects against drive failure.

Most people don't realize that you can mirror or duplex a drive to several or more redundant drives—you can construct a mirrored set of many drives, rather than just two. This isn't always practical because of the cost of hard drives. You can, however, construct multi-drive mirrored sets if you want.

Mirroring and duplexing were built into the NetWare operating system at a time when drive failure was more frequent than it is today (around the mid-1980s). Despite the gains in reliability of magnetic media that have occurred in the last several years, disk drives are still among the least reliable components of a computer system. Therefore, disk mirroring and duplexing are extremely important features of NetWare's fault-tolerance system.

TRANSACTION CONTROL

Finally, SFT II also includes *transaction control,* or, as Novell refers to it, the *Transaction Tracking System* (TTS).

TTS enables programs to associate groups of write operations into logical transactions. Each transaction is guaranteed to succeed (meaning that all the individual write operations are successful) or, if it doesn't succeed, NetWare restores all affected files to their pre-write state—a roll-back. NetWare then can retry the transaction, knowing that it is starting from the same point.

TTS is of interest primarily to database-management programs, which frequently make groups of updates to database files. If one update in a group fails, the database becomes corrupted. NetWare uses TTS to ensure the integrity of the NDS database files. TTS is fully integrated with the NetWare file system. Most database-management systems that are written for use with NetWare use TTS.

SYSTEM FAULT TOLERANCE LEVEL III (SFT III)

Level III fault tolerance consists of server mirroring, or redundant servers. Level III fault tolerance is provided in the NetWare 4.1 operating system, called System Fault Tolerance (SFT) III.

SFT III provides non-stop operation through the use of an entirely redundant server machine, including CPU, power supply, drives, network interface cards, and everything else. You have two completely separate server machines (see Figure 2.6).

Two server machines are connected via a high-speed Mirrored Server Link (MSL). The job of the MSL is to maintain synchronization between the two machines. The entire memory image of the NetWare Server is duplicated on both machines. If one machine goes down, the other machine remains running. NetWare clients experience no loss of state or interruption in service. Server-based applications, such as Oracle, run mirrored automatically.

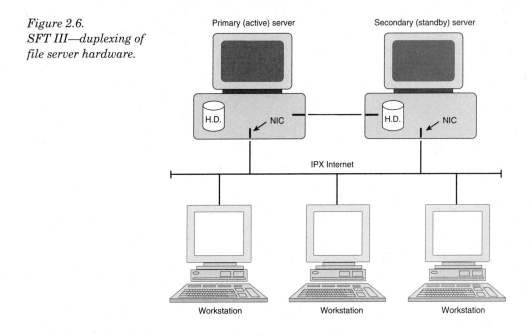

Figure 2.6.
SFT III—duplexing of
file server hardware.

Software-Based Non-stop Computing

SFT III NetWare is the first and only software-based solution to provide non-stop computing. Other vendors, such as Tandem and Stratus, provide non-stop operation using specially constructed redundant machines that cost hundreds of thousands of dollars. SFT III uses a patented architecture invented by Novell. Novell intentionally designed SFT III to run on high-quality, inexpensive PC hardware.

Administrators may purposefully bring one SFT III system machine down for repair or maintenance, and the other machine will continue to service NetWare clients. This allows maintenance to occur at the time of the administrator's choosing, such as in the middle of the day, rather than over a weekend or in the middle of the night.

Non-Identical Configuration

Both machines of the SFT III mirrored pair need not be identically configured. Each may have different network interface cards and storage devices, and even may be of different brands. This is possible because SFT III NetWare isolates all hardware device drivers from the server operating system in order to provide synchronization between the two machines.

Current MSL hardware allows the two mirrored machines to be up to two kilometers apart from each other. Future MSL hardware may work using satellite links, providing the potential for disaster-proof NetWare systems. Each server of the mirrored pair may reside hundreds or even thousands of miles apart.

CAPACITY

NetWare 4 features prodigious capacity, both in the amount of RAM the server can address and in the amount of data the server's file system can store and use. The following two subsections cover the memory capacity and file system capacity of NetWare 4.

MEMORY CAPACITY

NetWare 4 can address all physical RAM installed in the server machine, up to 4GB. Servers containing 128MB of RAM or more are common as hardware prices decline.

Why would you want so much memory in your server? Servers with multi-gigabyte file systems require more memory than you would expect. This additional memory is needed by NetWare to cache important volume structures. The greater the size and number of volumes on a server, the more memory required to cache important volume data structures.

NetWare uses all its free memory to provide a file-system cache. The file-system cache speeds up server performance by holding the data of active files in fast server RAM. This reduces the need for NetWare to read data from physical media devices, which increases performance. The greater the size of the file-system cache, the greater the increase in performance. That's why many administrators install over 100MB of RAM in their NetWare servers.

NetWare 4 was designed to work well with large amounts of memory installed on the server machine. Its internal memory management algorithms do not slow down or become complex when they must deal with large amounts of memory. Adding RAM to your server machine is one of the most effective things you can do to improve server performance.

FILE SYSTEM CAPACITY

Presently, the capacity of the NetWare file system is as follows:

- ◆ Up to 4 terabytes (TB) of online storage
- ◆ A single file may be up to 4GB in size
- ◆ A single server may have up to 64 Volumes
- ◆ A volume may consist of up to 32 physical media devices
- ◆ Up to 100,000 concurrently open files
- ◆ Up to 100,000 concurrent record or file locks
- ◆ Up to 100,000 concurrently active transactions
- ◆ Each physical media device may be mirrored to up to 15 redundant devices

In addition to the capacity of the NetWare file system, NetWare 4 includes a feature called *data migration*. Data migration enables developers to write NLMs that migrate files from the NetWare file system to offline or near-line storage devices.

When a file is migrated, its data no longer resides on a NetWare volume, yet it still has an entry in the NetWare volume directory table. This enables users to retrieve the file by opening it, just as they would a normal file. When a user opens a migrated file, the data migration module retrieves the file from the offline or near-line storage device and restores the file data to the NetWare volume.

Data migration is intended to provide a hierarchical storage system. The NetWare volume remains the primary storage system for file data. Files that have not been recently accessed, however, can be migrated to slower near-line media such as magneto-optical or read-write optical.

Files that have not been accessed for a long time can be further migrated from the near-line storage media to offline storage media, such as tape. All such files still have an entry in the volume directory table, so users can gain access to them in the standard way, even though the file's data does not reside on the NetWare volume.

CLIENT SUPPORT

As in Chapter 1, file serving operating systems really took off as mainstream business products when they began to support multiple-client operating systems. This occurred for NetWare in 1988 with NetWare 2.15's support of Macintosh clients.

Today, NetWare 4 provides the greatest support for multiple-client operating systems on the market: DOS/Windows, OS/2, UNIX, Macintosh, OSI, and Microsoft's Windows NT. Each of these client operating systems requires a different file format, and the UNIX, Macintosh, and OSI clients each require a different non-IPX/SPX protocol stack and file-service protocol.

NetWare 4 provides a wide range of client operating system support through two mechanisms: the Open Data Link Interface (ODI) protocol architecture and the file-system name space architecture.

OPEN DATA LINK INTERFACE

ODI (Open Data Link Interface) is a protocol architecture jointly developed by Novell and Apple Computer. The purpose of ODI is to allow for multiple network protocol stacks to be serviced concurrently by an operating system, using any combination of network interface cards.

A single Ethernet card, for example, may service IPX/SPX and AppleTalk concurrently. Or, a single token-ring card may service TCP/IP and OSI TP0-TP4 concurrently. Under ODI, a single network interface card may service multiple protocol stacks (see Figure 2.7), a single protocol stack may be serviced by multiple network interface cards, or any variation thereof.

Figure 2.7.
ODI allows multiple
protocols sharing the
same network interface
card.

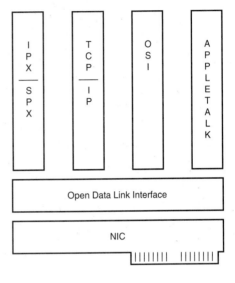

NAME SPACE ARCHITECTURE

The *name space architecture* is an open-ended mechanism whereby the NetWare file system can concurrently maintain files in several different formats.

Name space support allows NetWare to present a single file to different clients, with each client viewing that file in its (the client's) native format (see Figure 2.8). A Macintosh client and UNIX client, for example, may both have the same server-based file open: to the Macintosh client the file appears as a standard Macintosh file; to the UNIX client the same file appears as a standard UNIX file.

Both ODI and the name space architecture are open-ended—Novell can extend NetWare to support any number of client operating systems with relatively little effort and no redesign of the core operating system. This allows for support of future client operating systems.

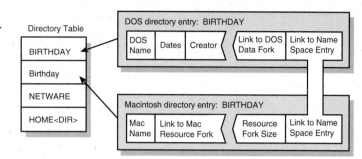

Figure 2.8.
Name space support for
non-DOS clients.

PROTOCOL SUPPORT

You just read about ODI and how it enables multiple-protocol support for NetWare 4. Without additional software, NetWare 4 supports IPX/SPX, AppleTalk, and TCP/IP. One thing you may not have known is that NetWare can *route* each of these protocol stacks. Protocol stacks written for NetWare have historically provided full-fledged internetwork routing.

NetWare 4 extends routing support in a couple of ways. First, the built-in NetWare IPX router has been optimized for use in a wide area network (WAN) environment. Second, and most importantly, the core routing services in the NetWare operating system are now open for developers. This is called the "replaceable router" API (Application Programming Interface) for NetWare 4. What it means is that developers can create specialized multiprotocol router modules and load them on a NetWare server, thus replacing NetWare's built-in routing features. This opens the door for better and more specialized routing support under NetWare 4.

NetWare's native protocol suite, IPX/SPX, has been optimized in several key ways under NetWare 4. A fully new version of SPX is present in NetWare 4 called SPX II, and some of the critical paths in NetWare's IPX protocol have been optimized for performance.

For developers, there are several different programming interfaces that provide access to active network protocol stacks. These APIs include the standard IPX/SPX, TCP/IP, and AppleTalk interfaces, plus standard portable interfaces including Berkeley sockets and the AT&T Transport Layer Interface (TLI).

Developers are free to create additional protocol stacks for NetWare 4. The areas that show the greatest potential right now are for specialized WAN protocol stacks, such as Point-To-Point Protocols (PPP), and versions of existing protocol stacks optimized for satellite or wireless operation. NDS, in fact, creates a real need for specialized protocol stacks because it practically demands that large NetWare sites have efficient WAN links.

SERVER-BASED APPLICATIONS

Server-based applications are the back-end components of client/server computing. A database server such as Oracle runs on NetWare, for example, while client workstations run a data-entry or reporting program that communicates with the Oracle database server.

This is only one example of a server-based application running on NetWare. As client/server computing becomes ever more popular, NetWare will be called on to run ever more sophisticated and numerous server-based applications.

NETWARE LOADABLE MODULES

Server-based applications running on NetWare are called *NetWare Loadable Modules* (NLMs). NLMs, when loaded on the NetWare server, are actually linked into the core operating system (just like device drivers discussed earlier; refer to Figure 2.1). This allows developers to extend the NetWare operating system by creating NLMs. All NetWare device drivers and protocol stacks, in fact, are NLMs, as are server-based applications such as Oracle.

NLMs gain the following benefits directly from the NetWare operating system design:

◆ Full access to operating system services and data structures

◆ 32-bit protected mode execution

◆ Flat memory addressing model

◆ Multi-threaded execution and inter-process communication

◆ Fault tolerance

The NetWare 4 environment makes it especially appropriate for running server-based applications. Every type of service required in order to have an effective "back-end" application, in fact, is provided by the NetWare operating system, including the following:

◆ Rich network communications, including multiple concurrent protocol suites

◆ Memory allocation

◆ Scheduling

◆ A fast and robust file system designed specifically for server-based applications

◆ A fully implemented network security and naming service

◆ Programming API designed specifically for distribution of the application across the internetwork

Oracle reports that its NetWare-based product is experiencing faster growth than any other version of Oracle. The success of vendors such as Oracle, Sybase, Informix, Gupta, and others, demonstrates the effectiveness of NetWare as a platform for server-based applications.

OPTIONAL MEMORY PROTECTION

Some trade journalists and industry analysts have criticized NetWare for its lack of memory protection. Memory protection refers to the capability of the operating system to prevent use of illegal memory references made by applications. As you read earlier, NetWare's designers did not include memory protection in NetWare for performance reasons.

NetWare 4, however, features optional memory protection. With memory protection activated, you can load NLM applications in protected memory, or memory that is monitored by the operating system. If such an NLM attempts an illegal memory access, the operating system disallows the memory access and unloads the offending NLM. Without memory protection, such illegal memory accesses go unchecked and have the potential to crash the NetWare server.

Memory protection on NetWare 4 decreases NLM performance by between 3 percent and 10 percent, depending on the specific NLM and how it was designed. (This is not out of line with the performance penalty paid by other operating systems with memory protection.) Novell recommends that all NLM developers use memory protection to trap programming errors during development.

Novell suggests that server administrators run third-party NLMs in protected memory space for about a month. During that time, if the NLM did not attempt any illegal memory references, the administrator may move the NLM to unprotected memory in order to gain a slight increase in NLM performance. Or, the administrator may choose to leave the NLM loaded in protected memory.

Optional memory protection allows those who are concerned about illegal memory accesses by NLMs to protect the NetWare operating system. At the same time, however, those who run trusted applications are free to do so in unprotected memory without the slight performance penalty associated with memory protection.

SUMMARY

This chapter discussed the characteristics of NetWare 4, including its design goals and overall architecture. It also discussed the various levels of system fault tolerance available for NetWare. The next chapter examines, in some detail, the various features of NetWare 4.

- NetWare Directory Services (NDS)

- Memory Management

- Background File Compression

- RSA Security

- Storage Management Services (SMS)

- Electronic Mail

- Image-Enabled NetWare

- Online Documentation

- Improved NLM Development Tools

- Summary

CHAPTER 3

Features of NetWare 4

This chapter describes features of NetWare that are new or significantly improved in version 4, especially ones available in NetWare 4.1. NetWare 4 is not a total rewrite of the popular NetWare 3.*x* operating system, but it is radically different. The most publicized new feature of NetWare 4 is *NetWare Directory Services* (NDS). All portions of the NetWare 4 operating system, however, have new or improved features.

Note

Unlike the change from NetWare 2.*x* to NetWare 3.*x*, which is a total rewrite and design of the operating system, the difference between NetWare 3.*x* and 4.*x* is small in certain areas, but drastically different in others.

Warning

You should not consider the upgrade from 3.*x* to 4.*x* is as simple as it was moving from 2.*x* to 3.*x*. NetWare 4.*x* is not "NetWare 3.*x* on steroids," as some people (wrongly) think.

You should carefully consider and understand the changes and implications due to the additional and new features offered by NetWare 4 before committing to using it.

After reading this chapter, you will have a good understanding of what is new and improved in NetWare 4, and specifically NetWare 4.1. You won't read specific technical or hands-on information; that comes later in this book. If you already have a good understanding of NetWare 4, you probably can skip this chapter.

NetWare Directory Services (NDS)

One of the major changes in this version of NetWare as compared to previous ones is the replacement of the bindery by *NetWare Directory Services* (NDS). The bindery is what is called a *server-centric entity*—the users are defined on a per server basis, for example. Conversely, NDS maintains a global, distributed, replicated database of information about all network resources. These resources include, but are not limited to, users, servers, volumes, and printers. That means, you need to only define the user once for the network, and the user may have access to the various network resources, regardless of location.

Note

For those of you that have used Novell's NetWare Naming Services (NNS), you can consider NDS as a superset of NNS. It does everything NNS promised to do, and more.

A Single Logical Entity

With NDS, you no longer log into a specific NetWare server, but you log into the *network*. All servers and resources are presented to you as a single, logical entity, and you gain access to the entire logical entity with a single login. Servers, users, resources, and so on, are globally defined. You, as a user, are defined once within NDS, and your user object definition is available across the entire network.

NDS makes resource access (such as gaining access to printers and servers) transparent. To gain access to files located on two different servers under NetWare 3.11, for example, you must log in to one server, attach to the other server, and map drives to both servers. Under NetWare 4 with NDS, you only need to log into the network once, and you can map drives to the appropriate volumes on the two servers.

Easier Management

NDS not only makes it easier for you to use a multi-server NetWare installation, it also makes it easier for you to *manage* a multi-server installation. You only need to create user definitions, including security privileges, once. These user definitions then are globally defined throughout the internetwork.

Note

User attributes, such as login scripts, user names, and so on, are also defined globally. You need to maintain file system securities separately, however, just like in previous versions of NetWare.

The global scope of NDS is its primary advantage over the bindery. NDS also stores much more information than the bindery, and presents that information in a more user-friendly fashion. For example, NDS can store each user's name, mail stop, phone number, fax number, home address, and more, within the global definition of that user.

New types of resources, including server machines, workstations, fax machines, printers, organizational units, meeting rooms, and so on, can be globally defined within NDS. This presents some interesting possibilities for third-party applications based on NDS, including network inventory programs, group scheduling software, telephony applications, and more.

Users and administrators can perform global searches on NDS objects. For example, you can print a list of all employees with a last name beginning with the letter *S*, or a list of all server machines in your company manufactured by Compaq. All this information can be stored in NDS and is globally available across the network.

NDS APPLICATIONS

Novell is primarily touting NDS as a tool that makes it easy to use and administer a large, multi-server NetWare network. Although this is appropriate, NDS has the potential to be much more than an ease-of-use aid. As third-party developers become familiar with NDS and what it offers, innovative applications based on NDS will come to market. These applications will extend the usefulness of NDS in ways unforeseen by Novell and will lead to new areas of use for NetWare.

ARCHITECTURE OF NDS

All information stored by NDS resides in a distributed and replicated database called the *Directory Information Base* (DIB). The DIB is *distributed*, which means that portions of it (known as partitions; this is discussed in details in Chapter 14) reside on different NetWare servers. It is also *replicated*, which means that specific portions of the DIB are duplicated on other NetWare servers.

Distribution and replication serve several purposes. Distribution of the DIB eliminates any size limits on the DIB. (If the DIB were stored entirely on one server, the size limit would be the storage capacity of that server.)

Replication provides performance benefits and fault tolerance. When different portions of the DIB are replicated on one or more secondary servers, NDS can service requests for data from the DIB using the replicated portion of the DIB that is closest to the source of the request. Also, when one server holding a replicated portion of the DIB is unavailable, NDS can obtain the requested information from another server that holds a replica of the information contained on the downed server.

ORGANIZATION OF NDS

Logically, NDS is organized as a tree—an inverted tree. Each portion, or branch, of the tree is called a *container*. Each container contains either more containers or *leaves* (end points), or a combination of both. Figure 3.1 illustrates the logical structure of NDS.

Figure 3.1.
Logical structure
of NDS.

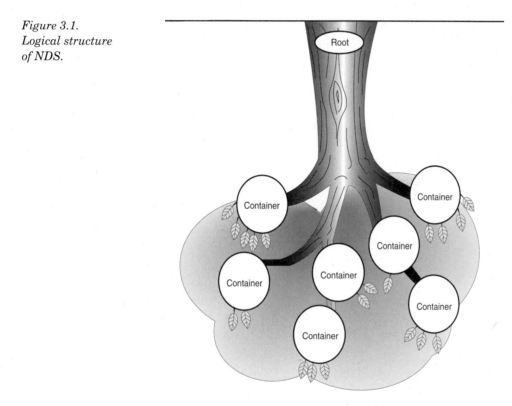

A NDS tree is made up of *objects*. There are different types of objects. At the very top is the *Root* object, denoted as [Root]. Below the [Root] are *container* objects. Each container object can either contain more container objects, or simply leaf objects. The following sections examine the different types of container and leaf objects. A more "standard" format of representing NDS tree is shown in Figure 3.2.

Figure 3.2.
A more conventional
way of representing
NDS tree structure.

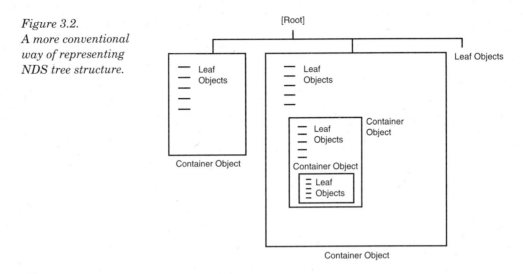

> ## Note
>
> As a rough analogy, you can compare NDS to the file system directory structure you have on your workstation hard disk. The [Root] object is your root directory (\); container objects are your directories and subdirectories; leaf objects are your files.

A more detailed discussion of the various types of objects is given in Chapter 11.

OBJECT NAMES PROVIDE THEIR LOCATIONS

A key design feature of NDS is that the name of an object also defines its location in the DIB tree. For example, a user named Joe Schmoe in the Accounting department of the Utopia Services Company has the following NDS name:

```
CN=Joe Schmoe.OU=Accounting.O=Utopia Services
```

where CN stands for common name, OU stands for organizational unit, and O stands for organization. Note that a period is used as delimiter between "fields."

Joe Schmoe's object is located in the DIB as shown in Figure 3.3.

Joe Schmoe's object name therefore provides a global location with which other NDS objects may locate and query Joe Schmoe's object, regardless of the location of the querying object.

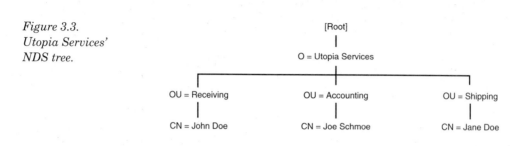

Figure 3.3.
Utopia Services'
NDS tree.

REPLICATED PARTITIONS

As you read earlier, partitions (different portions of the DIB) can be replicated. When replication occurs, the original partition is designated as the primary partition, while the other replicas are designated as replicated partitions.

Each replicated partition is defined either as *read-write* or *read-only*. Administrators can make changes to the DIB, such as defining objects, adding of new objects, or deleting of objects, using either the primary or any of the read-write replicated partitions. Read-only replicated partitions can only be used to look up object data; they cannot be used to change any information in the DIB.

When NDS is executing a search for information about an object, it may retrieve that information from a replica of the primary partition, which contains the object being searched for. This can significantly speed NDS performance.

Replication, however, requires that changes made to one DIB partition also be made to replicas of that partition. NDS uses a background process to synchronize DIB partitions.

Updates occurs continually in the background over the internetwork. You cannot easily control the frequency—it is done on an as needed basis in NetWare 4.*x*. However, starting with NetWare 4.1, at certain update times you can have control over using some console SET parameters.

NDS IS BACKWARD COMPATIBLE

NetWare 3.1*x* and earlier versions use a server-based directory called the *bindery*. The bindery serves many of the same functions as NDS, except that the bindery has a scope limited to the server it is running on. If you are at all familiar with NetWare, you know about the bindery, so this book will not discuss it in detail.

All NetWare 4 servers are backward compatible with bindery-based servers (version 3.12 and earlier). NDS has a *bindery emulator*, which is active by default, that allows NetWare 4 servers to coexist with 3.12 and earlier servers.

NetWare 3.1*x* utilities also work with NetWare 4's bindery emulator, as do third-party products that use the NetWare bindery. To such utilities and products, a NetWare 4 server appears as a NetWare 3.1*x* server. This provides NetWare 4 with full backward compatibility with the huge installed base of NetWare 3.1*x* and earlier.

A set of tools called *NetSync* are shipped with NetWare 4.1, which allows you to administrator user information, such as passwords, using NetWare 4's administration tools.

MERGING AND RENAMING TREES

Prior to NetWare 4.1, it was not possible to change the name of your NDS tree once you have installed it. In order to change the tree name, you had to deinstall the entire NDS and reinstall. NetWare 4.1 is shipped with an NLM called *DSMERGE*. It allows you to easily rename a tree.

The other function of DSMERGE is its capability of merging two different trees into one. This is helpful for sites that have multiple trees (perhaps due to lack of coordination by a central department or due to wanting a separate testing environment) and administrators that want to consolidate them into one, without having to reinstall.

NEW WORKSTATION SOFTWARE

NetWare 4 comes with NDS-aware workstation software, called *Virtual Loadable Modules* (VLMs), and utilities. In order to take advantage of NDS, you must run the new workstation software and use the new utilities for full access to NDS.

MORE NDS INFORMATION

This concludes the summary discussion of NDS. Chapters in Parts III, V, and VI of this book contain in-depth discussion and information on designing, installing, and configuring NDS for your network.

HIGH-PERFORMANCE SCHEDULER

NetWare has always had a high-performance, non-preemptive scheduler. The scheduler controls when a given process is executed. A process (also known as a *thread*) typically is a running NLM or program on the server. *Non-preemption* means that every process running on the operating system remains in control until it relinquishes access to the server's CPU. Sometimes a non-preemptive scheduler is referred to as a *run-to-completion* scheduler. In other words, each task (or process) runs until it has completed the processing it needs to accomplish at a given time.

Note

> Non-preemption is the most efficient type of scheduling algorithm used today. However, non-preemption allows poorly programmed software to monopolize CPU cycles, which prevents operating system tasks from being accomplished in a timely manner. This is cited by some as a weakness of NetWare. However, problems are rare and, when they arise, are easier for developers to fix.

NetWare 4 features a rewrite of the NetWare scheduler. The scheduler is now more robust and can deal with ill-behaved software that in previous versions could monopolize CPU cycles. In addition, some of the scheduler's algorithms have been changed to make them more efficient. The NetWare 4 operating system now is able to schedule critical processes more quickly than in previous versions of NetWare, and the overall execution time consumed by the scheduler is greatly reduced over previous versions of NetWare.

The NetWare 4 scheduler optimizations improve all areas of operating system performance. These performance improvements are more likely to become noticeable under high load conditions, such as when hundreds of users are logged into the server. In addition, software developers now have a more flexible scheme for writing multithreaded applications for NetWare.

MEMORY MANAGEMENT

The NetWare 4 memory management routines are new and provide two types of performance improvements over NetWare 3.1x. The following two subsections give an overview of how memory is managed in NetWare 4.

RETURNING FREED MEMORY

The first type of performance improvement provided by the new NetWare 4 memory allocator is that all freed memory can be returned to the NetWare file system cache buffers.

In NetWare 3.x, when you unload a NetWare Loadable Module (NLM) the memory freed is not necessarily all returned to the cache buffer pool, some may be placed in an allocation pool for use by other NLMs. This means that you could deplete the amount of memory used by the file cache system when you load and unload NLMs.

In NetWare 4, however, unloading an NLM returns all the memory used by that NLM to the file cache buffer pool. This allows the operating system to dedicate as much memory as possible to the file cache buffer pool at all times. And the more memory that is dedicated to the file cache buffer pool, the better the NetWare operating system performs.

FASTER MEMORY ALLOCATION

The second type of performance improvement provided by the new NetWare 4's memory allocator is that the memory allocation routines execute faster.

This improvement is of interest primarily to software developers. Under certain conditions, such as when a NetWare server has been running nonstop for several months, users have noticed a slowdown in 3.1*x* memory allocation. The cause for this slowdown in NetWare 3.1*x* is both rare and obscure (it involves the fragmentation of freed memory in the operating system). Fragmentation of memory in NetWare 4 has virtually been eliminated by the new memory allocator.

DATA MIGRATION

NetWare 4 features a developer's interface for *data migration*, or the movement of infrequently used data to online or offline secondary-storage media.

Note

> You can use the NetWare FLAG utility to prevent a file from being migrated by marking it as Don't Migrate (DM).

For example, a third-party storage management NLM based on data migration could scan a server and migrate all files that have not been accessed in the past month to a relatively inexpensive, high-capacity, magneto-optical storage device. The migrated files still appear in the server's directory tables, but the actual file data resides on the magneto-optical storage device (not on the server's NetWare volumes). This technology is referred to as the *High Capacity Storage System* (HCSS).

Note

> The migrated file will have a file attribute of M (Migrated) associated with it.

This provides more free space on the NetWare server's primary storage media (fast, but expensive, hard drives). If a user attempts to access a migrated file, the NLM retrieves the file from the magneto-optical device, restores the file's data to the server's primary media, and then opens the file for the user.

Note

> Under data migration, the user will never know the file was not located on the server's hard drive, except for a slower response time on the initial access.

Data migration has the capability to support all types of storage devices, including tape drives, jukeboxes, hard drives, WORM opticals, and magneto-opticals. The primary purpose of data migration is to allow for transparent off-loading of infrequently accessed data to secondary and tertiary storage media, thus freeing up space on NetWare volumes.

There are many potential applications for the data migration interface, however, including perpetual backup systems and virtual file systems.

Note

> Note that data migration isn't actually a feature or product, but is a programming interface. It remains for third-party developers to build actual products based on the data migration interface.

It is interesting to note that one such product has already received a lot of attention in the press: image-enabled NetWare, which was co-developed by Novell and Kodak, is based on the data migration interface. See the section on "Image-Enabled NetWare," later in this chapter.

BLOCK SUBALLOCATION

Block suballocation is a new feature of the NetWare file system that makes it more efficient when storing files. In NetWare 3.12 and earlier versions, the smallest storage unit available for storing files was a 4K block. A file of one byte always consumed 4K of volume storage space.

In NetWare 4, the file system can suballocate storage in 512-byte groups, so a single 4K block may hold data from up to eight different files. Now a 1-byte file will only consume 512 bytes of storage space, rather than 4K, which, in this particular example, shows an eight-fold increase in the efficiency of the file system's storage algorithm.

The degree of efficiency that you gain in your NetWare 4 server depends on several factors, including the average size of files stored on the server and the number of files stored. However, block suballocation provides some gains in efficiency for every NetWare 4 server and, in some cases, frees many megabytes of volume disk space.

The feature is called block suballocation because the file system still allocates storage in block increments (blocks are at least 4K in size), but is able to *suballocate* 512-byte portions of each block for storing portions of different files.

BACKGROUND FILE COMPRESSION

Perhaps the greatest increase in NetWare 4 file system storage efficiency is provided by background compression. A special low priority thread runs during predefined time periods (unless you deactivate background compression) and compresses files according to criteria you set at the server console.

Note

The default time period in which file compression thread runs is between midnight and 6:00 am. You can adjust this depending on your working environment to decrease the impact of the file compression thread on your server performance.

Warning

File compression requires CPU cycles as well as RAM in your server. Make sure you have sufficient free RAM or you will receive a `Cannot allocate RAM for file compression` error message on your server console.

When the file compression thread is running, your server CPU utilization may shoot up to about 80 percent or higher for an extended period of time.

For example, you can set the file compression process to compress all files that haven't been accessed in the past thirty days or more. The compression process runs in the background and compresses all such files that it discovers in the file system.

The compression algorithm used by NetWare reduces the size of each compressed file by 30 to 60 percent, depending on the content of the file. It is not unlikely that total volume space available for new files will double compared to a 3.1*x* server. (It may be possible to store 100MB of data in compressed format on 50MB of NetWare volume space.)

Note

For an executable program, the typically compression rate is about 45 percent. For a text file or graphics image file, the compression rate could be as high as 60 percent or more.

When a user requests access to a compressed file, NetWare 4 automatically decompresses that file before providing the user access. This means that file compression and decompression occurs transparently to users. The time required to provide access to a compressed file is greater than that required for a non-compressed file because NetWare has to decompress the file. Therefore, you should configure background compression to ignore files that frequently are read and written by users.

Because the background compression process is a low-priority thread, NetWare ensures that compression doesn't run unless the operating system is otherwise idle. This means that important processing tasks, such as sending and receiving network packets, or reading from and writing to disks, always run when they need to run. Background compression therefore does not have a negative impact on server performance.

Note

You can use the NetWare FLAG utility to mark a file for Immediate Compress (IC) if you want to compress during the next compression thread execution. Or mark it Don't Compress (DC) to never compress this file.

Warning

It has been reported that certain applications will not execute properly if any of their files are compressed. For example, a custom application (BWEVAL) used by Novell Education for performing course evaluations will fail to execute if its executable and overlay files are compressed.

AUDITING

NetWare 4 features a much more comprehensive auditing capability than in any previous versions of NetWare. This implementation is a very secure auditing system. NetWare can audit all file accesses, plus all accesses to NDS objects (including emulated bindery objects). Auditing information, including access dates, times, filenames, NDS object names, and names of users or objects requesting access, is stored in a secure audit log. Previous versions of NetWare only allowed tracking of user logins and logouts. Auditing of file system changes and access require third-party add-ons.

Auditing is activated (on a per-volume basis for file system auditing, and at the container level for NDS events) and maintained by a user designated as the *auditor*. In order to provide the highest level of security, this person should be someone other than the administrator of the network. No one may gain access to the auditing system unless that person knows the auditing password, which should be different from the supervisor password.

Users have no way of knowing whether auditing is active on a NetWare 4 server. The auditor alone may define which files and NDS objects are subject to auditing.

In addition, the auditor can define which operations are subject to auditing. For example, the auditor may activate auditing only for a select group of files and NDS objects, and then only when those objects are written to or altered. The auditor also may determine that every file and NDS object should be subject to auditing, and for every type of access or operation.

Note

Auditors should not have access to network files other than the audit-related files, unless they are granted rights by the administrator.

The auditor can know just about everything that occurs on a NetWare server or NDS container, and he or she alone can view the auditing reports. This provides for an extremely secure environment. The auditing system may also cause apprehension for users, because it can track all their activity on the entire internetwork.

Note

The auditing only tracks which files are accessed and in what manner. Contents of the files are not recorded.

The auditor can configure the auditing system, view audit logs, and perform other auditing-related tasks using the AUDITCON utility provided by Novell. In addition, the auditing system has a programming interface that third-party developers can use to extend the range of auditing so that it includes their applications.

The auditing system has potential, not only as a security tool, but also as a performance monitoring tool for users performing data entry operations or similar functions. So auditing, if activated on a server, should be managed in a low-key fashion and should not be used to intrude on users' privacy or to unnecessarily intimidate users. Nevertheless, significant needs are served by the auditing system. Every business has data that is private, such as the salaries of workers and their personnel files. Auditing is an excellent feature for increasing the security of these types of data.

Note

By knowing how often a given file is used and how it is accessed, the network administrator may be able to justify a faster storage device, or the programmer may be able to fine-tune the application and/or database.

RSA SECURITY

The Rivest-Adleman-Shamir (RSA) public-key crypto-system is one of the most robust computer security models invented to date. Novell has licensed the RSA code and incorporated it into the security system of NetWare 4.

Note

Due to export license restrictions, the full-key is not used in NetWare 4's implementation.

The RSA public-key crypto-system is used by NetWare whenever an NDS client logs into the network. The client and NDS generate an authenticated image, or *mint*, which verifies the identity of the client. The mint is used by NDS as proof of the client's identity, and NDS bases its granting (or not granting) of access to NDS objects on the existence of the mint.

The algorithm used by NetWare to obtain the mint is highly complex and involves the exchange of public keys between NDS and the client, and the derivation of an encrypted footprint that, when combined with random information, becomes the mint. The mint precedes the client throughout NDS and the authentication procedure occurs transparently to the client whenever the client requests access to NDS objects throughout the NetWare internetwork.

The RSA crypto-system used by NetWare 4 provides the highest level of authentication possible today. Note that the RSA crypto-system simply ensures that an NDS client is precisely who it/he/she claims to be. The establishment of other aspects of security—such as assigning privilege levels to specific clients for files and NDS objects—remains the responsibility of the network administrator.

For example, once the RSA crypto-system within NDS has established that user JOE is actually JOE, that doesn't really help you unless you have ensured—through privilege settings—that JOE cannot view private files.

Note

NetWare 4 is designed to be compliant with U.S. Government C2 and European E2 security criteria. At the time of this writing, proceedings have begun for these classifications.

OPTIONAL MEMORY PROTECTION

Previous versions of NetWare (including 3.12) did not provide memory protection. That is, server-based applications were not restricted by the operating system from writing to critical areas of server memory, including memory in which the operating system itself resides. This allowed programming errors in server-based applications to trash the operating system, which could bring down the NetWare server.

Many operating systems establish *memory protection*, which prevents applications from corrupting operating system memory. However, because memory protection decreases overall system performance (the checking of memory addresses and disallowing of errant writes to memory requires additional processing overhead), NetWare's designers decided to forgo memory protection in the interest of providing the highest possible level of system performance.

In previous versions of NetWare, including 3.12 and earlier, the lack of memory protection made it more difficult for programmers to detect bugs in their applications, and in some cases caused production servers to go down when running server-based applications with bugs in them.

PREVENTING ILLEGAL MEMORY OPERATIONS

The answer to the problem of errant NLMs accessing wrong memory locations is NetWare 4's optional memory protection. Intel defined a memory protection model that divides the memory into concentric rings (see Figure 3.4): Ring 0 through Ring 3. Ring 0 maintains the highest privilege level and cannot be preempted by processes in other rings. Ring 3 has the lowest privilege, and does not have direct access to the kernel. The rings also prevent processes from inadvertently accessing each other's codes and data that concurrently reside in memory ("access violation").

Note

Under the Intel memory protection model, a process cannot gain access to memory at a greater privilege level (lower numerical level) unless explicitly allowed, or indirectly allowed via some "gateway" mechanism. This protection is achieved by using the built-in Intel 386/486 segmentation features, which are the following:

♦ Segment size limits

♦ Privilege levels

♦ Segment attributes (read only, read/write, and so on)

The hardware (386/486 CPU chip) generates an error condition when an NLM tries to execute instructions or access memory beyond the limit of the memory segment. This error then can be trapped and handled by the operating system.

NetWare 4 implements the Intel ring protection model slightly differently. It divides the memory into two rings: Ring 0 (where the operating system runs) and "the rest." It considers rings 1 through 3 to be the same—their ring number or privilege level is irrelevant. Instead, NetWare 4 "reserves" an area of RAM to run NLMs in a protected manner (see Figure 3.4). The legal addressing space for a process within a given "ring" is known as the *domain*.

Figure 3.4.
In NetWare 4, there are only two domains: the OS Domain at Ring 0 and the "protected" domain.

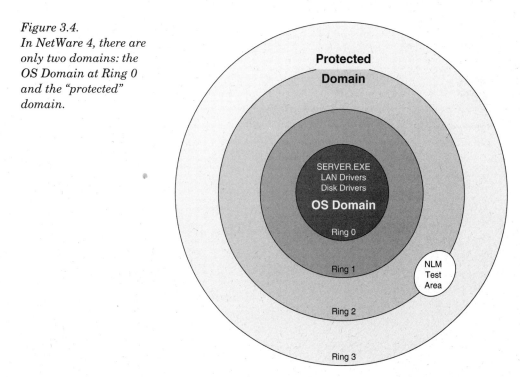

3

You can activate NetWare 4's memory protection scheme by loading on the NetWare server a special program called *DOMAIN.NLM*. Then, by loading NLM applications within the protected memory space, the operating system can detect and prevent illegal memory operations. When an NLM attempts an illegal memory operation, the operating system disallows the memory operation and unloads the offending NLM, thereby preventing memory corruption and ensuring that the server remains up and running.

You can configure NetWare's memory protection system to notify you in several ways—including console messages—that a particular NLM has attempted an illegal memory operation. So you can know the specific NLM that has the programming error in it. If this ever occurs with an NLM you purchased from a software vendor, you should contact that vendor and report the bug.

PERFORMANCE HIT

When memory protection is active, NLMs running in the protected memory space experience about a 10 percent decrease in performance. That's why memory protection is optional.

Novell recommends that you run NLMs in protected memory space for a test period of several weeks. After that time, if the NLM has not attempted any illegal memory operations, you can be confident that the NLM is free from memory addressing bugs. You then can load the NLM in nonprotected memory space, thereby gaining increased performance for that NLM.

PART OF AN OVERALL STRATEGY

NetWare 4's optional memory protection is part of an overall strategy announced by Novell to provide greater memory addressing options, including cross-machine multiprocessing.

The memory protection mechanism itself is based on *Remote Procedure Call* (RPC) technology. This technology will be extended in the future so that applications running on one NetWare server or workstation can use memory residing on a different machine connected to the network.

Note

This RPC technology has been used by the UNIX operating systems for the past number of years. However, its use in the LAN arena is just starting to develop.

WAN ENHANCEMENTS

NetWare, historically, has not performed as well in wide-area network (WAN) environments as have other network operating systems, such as Banyan VINES.

This weakness primarily is due to NCP protocol that NetWare nodes (servers and workstations alike) use to communicate with each other. That is not to say that NetWare is ineffective in WAN environments. It is effective. Rather, the efficiency of NetWare's network communications is lower in a WAN environment.

PACKET BURST AND LARGE INTERNET PACKET PROTOCOLS

Beginning with NetWare 3.11, Novell improved NetWare's performance in WAN environments. Two important WAN features introduced for NetWare 3.11 and later versions were the *Packet Burst* and *Large Internet Packet* (LIP) protocols.

Note

Packet Burst protocol is sometimes referred to as *PBurst* or *Burst Mode protocol*.

The PBurst protocol is a new NCP technology that sharply reduces the number of packets a server must exchange with a NetWare client in order to fulfill file service requests. Although packet burst can improve local performance, its primary benefit is improved client/server performance over WAN links.

Note

.It is a common misconception that the request/response nature in NetWare is due to IPX. It is not. It is due to NCP at the upper layers of the protocol stack.

The original NetWare NCP was designed and optimized for high speed links (2.5 Mbps and higher). It used a one-request-one-respond ("ping-pong") means of communicating between the client workstation and server. It was not a big problem for local area communication. However, over (slow) WAN links, this becomes noticeable.

The first implementation of PBurst was to modify the number of packets sent in response to a request. This gives a many-to-one ratio rather than the one-to-one ratio (see Figure 3.5). This is very similar to the traditional windowing protocols.

Figure 3.5.
Packet Burst protocol
allows a group of
packets to be sent for a
single request packet.

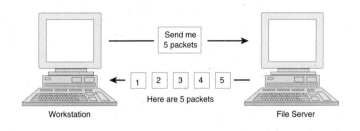

Warning

The original PBurst was implemented using BNETX. However, due to a (rare) potential data corruption problem, Novell no longer recommends or supports the use of BNETX.

In order to use PBurst, Virtual Loadable Modules (VLM) drivers, the new generation of workstation drivers, are to be used.

Note

OS/2 Requester for NetWare v2.01 and higher has built-in PBurst support. Previous versions of OS/2 Requesters do not support PBurst.

Current implementation of PBurst also allows for better dynamic configuration (such as change of window size) and self-adjustment to network conditions (such as congestion). This was not possible with the original implementation.

Note

You can find an in-depth discussion of the current implementation of PBurst in the November 1993 issue of *NetWare Applications Notes*, published by Novell.

Large Internet Packet (LIP) support allows NetWare servers and workstations to negotiate a very large maximum packet size for file service requests. Previously, the largest packet allowed for a file service request across a router was 512 bytes. This limit was to ensure that file service request and reply packets could safely traverse an internetwork via (IPX) routers in case there is an ARCnet segment somewhere along the path (see Figure 3.6). However, this is not very efficient if all the intermediate networks are of the same topology or can pass large packets.

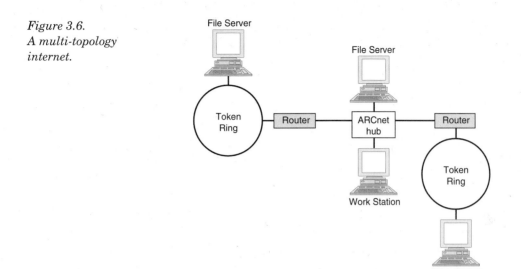

Figure 3.6.
A multi-topology
internet.

LIP queries bridges and routers on the network to determine the maximum packet size that can be safely transmitted across a specific internetwork route. This becomes the actual maximum packet size that workstations can use to request file service from the NetWare server.

Note

> Large Internet Packet protocol has been built into NetWare 4.*x* and 3.12. In order to allow LIP on NetWare 3.11, you need to load PBURST.NLM on the servers.

Depending upon the network media configuration of your NetWare site, LIP can allow maximum packet sizes of up to 64K, which can provide dramatic performance improvements in a bridged- and routed-environment.

Warning

> Before you enable LIP support, ensure all your intermediate networks, routers, and bridges can support the larger packet size being used. Otherwise, it will result in workstation hangs or loss of connections.

NEW ROUTING PROTOCOL SUPPORT

NetWare 4.1 is shipped with new routing protocol support for both IPX and TCP/IP. On the IPX side, *NetWare Link State Protocol* (NLSP) can be used either in conjunction or replace the traditional RIP/SAP (Routing Information Protocol/ Service Advertising Protocol) protocols that have been a common cause of broadcast traffic on WAN links.

On the TCP/IP side, NetWare 4.1 provides support for the new enhanced *RIP II* protocol as well as *Open Fastest Path First* (OSPF).

REPLACEABLE ROUTER

NetWare 4.1 has a *replaceable router* application programming interface (API). This enables developers to create routers optimized for a WAN environment and to load those routers on a NetWare 4.1 server. When a router is loaded on a NetWare 4.1 server, NetWare's built-in router is deactivated, and the loaded router takes its place.

Novell offers a WAN-optimized multi-protocol router that you can load on NetWare 4.1 servers when appropriate. The product is called the *Multi Protocol Router*. Other vendors are developing WAN-optimized routers for use on NetWare 4.

INTERNATIONALIZATION

NetWare 4 is the first fully *internationalized* operating system offered by Novell. Internationalize means that the operating system can be configured dynamically to support multinational internetworks. For example, your company may have divisions in more than one country, and employees at different divisions may speak different languages.

Each site of a multinational company can be configured to work using a different language. Actually, each workstation on the same network can be configured to use a different language! This enables employees at different sites to use their native languages when working with NetWare, yet at the same time be able to fully participate with other sites using NDS.

Internationalization is not automatic. The activation of a language on a server and workstation requires a language-specific message file. The message file contains a specific translation of all messages, prompts, window titles, and so on, that are used by the operating system or NDS utilities. The default language module is English.

Note

Keep in mind that even with multilingual support, not all information will be automatically translated. For example, utility program messages, such as error messages and prompts, will be displayed in the

> appropriate language. But if you use the SEND utility to send an English message to a workstation using German language module, the message will still come out in English.

Novell is providing message files for the major international languages including, but not limited to, English, German, French, Spanish, and Japanese. However, because these are just a few of the many languages spoken on the planet, Novell has a program that allows third-party translation houses to develop language-specific message files for NetWare 4. This means that over time, NetWare 4 can support hundreds of different languages and dialects.

Novell also has provided third-party developers with internationalization tools. Developers can use these tools to make their software products for NetWare multilingual, just as NetWare 4 itself is multilingual. This also requires the translation of software messages and the creation of language-specific message files. Of course, third-party developers are not bound to make their software multilingual. But it is hoped that market forces will encourage them to do so before long.

PRINT SERVICES

Many NetWare users first installed NetWare in order to share expensive laser printers. NetWare's printing services have long been a key selling point, from the very early days until today.

However, as LANs have evolved to the point where they are poised to become the central computing platform of worldwide enterprises, the printing needs of users have also evolved.

NetWare 4's printing services are designed to allow the following configurations:

- ◆ Easy sharing of printers across the enterprise
- ◆ Total freedom regarding the physical location of printers
- ◆ Support for all printer types and page description languages and control protocols
- ◆ Security and configuration management of printers
- ◆ Cross-platform printing (additional software required)
- ◆ Customization of printer configuration on a per-user basis

In earlier versions of NetWare (pre-2.2), printing services were built into the NetWare operating system and printing hardware was attached directly to the NetWare server. This was referred to as "core printing."

Note

Remote printing capability for NetWare was available starting with NetWare 2.15. Prior to this, third-party software solutions, such as LANSpool, were often used.

Today, however, core printing has been replaced with a more modular and flexible printing-service architecture that is consistent with the overall design of NetWare. Printing services under NetWare (all versions since v2.0a) consist of the following modules:

◆ Print queues

◆ A print server

◆ A printing device

◆ Configuration, administration, and management software

PRINT QUEUES

Print queues are special directories that hold printer jobs and dole them out to printers a little at a time. When a NetWare user prints a job, the workstation software writes that job to a print queue, along with management and configuration information, such as the identity of the user who submitted the print job, and formatting information for the print job (see Figure 3.7). As soon as the print job is written to the print queue, the user who submitted it is free to continue performing other work.

Figure 3.7.
Printing path in
NetWare.

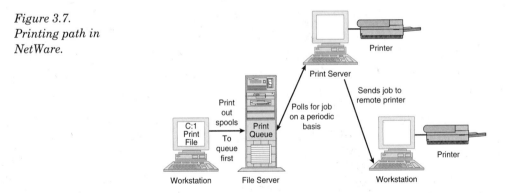

Print queues can hold many specific print jobs at any one time. The print server "spools" each job to an available printer based on that job's order in the queue, the priority of the queue, and other information.

NetWare allows specific print jobs to be preceded by control codes for a specific printer type, thus allowing reinitialization or reconfiguration of the actual printer producing the hard copy output. In addition, NetWare allows post-printing initialization and configuration.

Each print job in a NetWare print queue contains information that allows the Print Server to notify the user when the print job is complete, notify an administrator or other person when the printer is suffering an error, or notify a user when the printer needs more paper, toner, and so on.

Print queues, and consequently the actual printers associated with the print queues, are subject to NetWare security. This means there can be limits on the users who can submit jobs to a given print queue, thus using a given printer. Limits also can be placed on users allowed to configure and manage printers, queues, and print servers.

Print Servers

The function of a *print server* is to periodically check (poll) the print queues for jobs, and transfer those jobs to the corresponding printers.

Print servers under NetWare are software modules that advertise their presence over the network, thus providing a way for remote printers to identify them and getting services from them. Each print server is associated with one or more actual printers and one or more print queues.

Note

Pre-NetWare 4 print server software from Novell, including NetWare v3.12, only supports 16 printers. The new print server NLM for NetWare 4 can service up to 256 printers. PSERVER.EXE is no long included in NetWare 4.

Associating Printers, Print Servers, and Print Queues

With the exception of print queues, which always reside on a NetWare server, the administrator is free to locate any component of NetWare's print services anywhere on the network. Print servers can be running on dedicated workstations attached to the network (pre-NetWare 4 implementation), NetWare servers, or can be embedded as firmware into "black boxes" (such as Intel NetPort) or into actual printers (such as HP LaserJet 4).

3

FEATURES OF NETWARE 4

Actual printers can be attached directly to the network, to a network workstation, or to a NetWare server. A single print server can manage multiple printers. A single print server can service multiple print queues on multiple servers.

In the past, one cannot reference a printer directly—one needs to reference by the print queue name associated with the printer. With NetWare 4 and NDS, you now can directly reference a printer by name.

ADDITIONAL PRINT-SERVICE PROTOCOLS

NetWare supports the inclusion, in a modular fashion, of alternative print-service protocols. Presently, support for Macintosh print-service protocols can be added by purchasing the NetWare for Macintosh product. Support for UNIX print-service protocols on NetWare 4.1 can be added by purchasing NetWare NFS Services v2.1—NetWare 4 Edition or NetWare UNIX Print Services v2.1—NetWare 4 Edition.

Note

A 5-user NetWare for Macintosh is shipped with NetWare 4.1.

When support for alternative print-service protocols, such as Macintosh and UNIX, is added, NetWare integrates those protocols into its overall print-service architecture. This allows for cross-platform printing.

For example, Macintosh users might submit print jobs to a "NetWare" print server, and DOS or Windows users may submit print jobs to a Macintosh print server. UNIX clients may submit print jobs to a "NetWare" print server, and so on. Users of NetWare print services, therefore, don't even need to be aware of NetWare's existence.

NETWARE 4 PRINT SERVICES

While the basic print-service architecture remains the same under NetWare 4, the presentation of print services to the user and administrator is dramatically different.

By taking advantage of NDS, the information available to users regarding printers, print servers, and printer queues is much more useful and relevant. It is easier under NetWare 4 to configure and manage components of NetWare's print services, and the configuration and management options available are more extensive. Printing is discussed in more detail in Chapter 32.

Storage Management Services (SMS)

Storage Management Services, or SMS, is a collection of services and specifications designed to make cross-platform network backup easier and more effective, both now and in the future.

Novell hopes SMS will become an industry-wide standard for network backup, encompassing not only NetWare systems, but also systems from other network vendors.

What Is SMS?

Novell's goals in designing the SMS specification were to make it easier to back up NetWare data and to make it easier for third-party developers to support new versions of NetWare. Both the Storage Independent Data Format (SIDF) and the Storage Device Interface (SDI) were specified to make new product development easier. Also, Novell wanted to make archival and retrieval of data completely media- and platform-independent.

The primary components of SMS include the *Storage Independent Data Format* (SIDF), a high-level device interface, and a group of services designed to enable different types of archiving and restoring of data.

SIDF is designed to be a general-purpose data format suitable for archival of data from any operating system, including future operating systems. SIDF is important now because of the explosion of multi-platform, multi-vendor networks. However, Novell feels SIDF will be even more important in the future when new types of data, such as audio and visual data, emerge.

The *Storage Device Interface* (SDI) is a high-level interface that enables SMS to store and retrieve data from archive hardware without having explicit knowledge of the hardware's configuration. SDI is designed to make it easier to develop SMS archiving software and device drivers by modularizing hardware drivers and archive logic, and making them independent of each other.

A long-range goal of SDI is to allow users to restore very old data using very new hardware. For example, a user should be able to archive his or her data today, and then restore that same data ten years from now, using hardware that didn't exist when the data was originally archived.

SMS provides a core group of services to applications wishing to archive and restore data. These services include different types of scopes of archival and restore operations. As SMS matures, so will the services it provides.

3

FEATURES OF NETWARE 4

Note

In order to backup compressed files (compressed by NetWare 4) without first decompressing them, your tape backup software must support SMS as special APIs are required.

Otherwise, the files will be decompressed first before copying onto the tape.

SMS IMPLEMENTATIONS

An implementation of SMS consists of a service provider and one or more service responders, called *Target Service Agents*, or TSAs. The service provider is the actual archive unit, consisting of hardware and software. You can think of the service provider as an "archive server." The TSA is any network resource that has data to be archived. You can think of the TSA as an "archive client."

When archiving data, the TSA provides a stream of SIDF data to the service provider. The service provider archives the SIDF data. When restoring data, the process works in reverse.

Note

SMS does not require service providers to be NLMs. Rather, they can be DOS .EXEs, Macintosh programs, UNIX processes, or any other executable program running on any operating system. The only requirement is that a service provider must be able to communicate with TSAs. However, current service providers are all implemented as NLMs.

By the same token, TSAs may be implemented in any executable format, provided they can communicate with the service provider. Hence, SMS allows archival of client workstation local data, provided the client workstation is running a TSA.

The first implementation of SMS was released in April 1991, and consisted of SBACKUP.NLM (an archive server) and a TSA for archival of NetWare 3.11 servers. As such, this first release of SMS was rather incomplete, and raised some concerns in the marketplace that Novell would only support server-based archive systems in the future. Some of these concerns have disappeared, however, as third-party SMS-compliant products from vendors such as Legato and Cheyenne have appeared on the market.

NetWare 4's SMS Implementation

The NetWare 4 implementation of SMS, on the other hand, goes much further than the 3.11 implementation: it supports archival and restoration of 4.x servers, 3.1x servers, plus DOS and OS/2 workstation data. The capability to archive and restore Macintosh, UNIX workstation, and new file systems (such as Windows/NT) is built into the SMS specification, and Novell has plans to introduce those capabilities in the future.

In addition, Novell expects third-party vendors to introduce SMS-compliant products that add value to Novell's implementation. Specifically, some vendors are developing TSAs that support specialized network servers, such as database servers, electronic-mail servers, and so on.

Novell also says that it has been working with third-party vendors to assist their SMS development by providing engineering support and even source code when appropriate. This support is especially critical because of recent changes to the SMS specification that may cause problems for existing SMS-compliant products.

Archival of NDS

NDS is based on a distributed database of network resources. Novell provides a special TSA that allows the archival and restoration of a distributed and replicated NDS DIB. Archival of the NDS DIB would have been extremely difficult without the NetWare 4 implementation of SMS.

Third-Party Support

Virtually all backup vendors in the NetWare market have announced their support for SMS. These vendors include Mountain, Emerald, Palindrome, Archive, Cheyenne, Legato, Hewlett-Packard, and others. Each of these vendors is currently doing development work on SMS-compliant products.

Note

Not all third-party tape backup software will backup NDS. Check with your vendor.

ELECTRONIC MAIL

The NetWare 4.1 NOS comes with integrated messaging capabilities. NetWare *Message Handling Service* (MHS) is a store-and-forward message transfer service that provides a back-end solution to more than 250 third-party applications and services. This messaging service can be configured to run on any NetWare 4.1 server and is the basis for building a fully interconnected message-distribution system. Because NetWare MHS for NetWare 4 is integrated with Novell's NDS, you can administer your messaging environment with the same utilities used to manage the rest of your network.

Note

Similar to the Basic MHS e-mail package shipped with NetWare 3.12, the NetWare MHS for NetWare 4 will only route mail within the same NDS tree. In order to exchange mail with users on a different NDS tree or a different email package, Novell's Global MHS or a similar product is required.

NetWare MHS for NetWare 4 also provides a server-based utility (MHSCON) that supports event monitoring, operational statistics and message flow control.

Note

MHS Services is not available for NetWare 4 versions prior to NetWare 4.1.

To get you up and running quickly on e-mail, NetWare 4.1 also comes with the FirstMail client application for DOS, Windows, and Macintosh workstations. Installation and configuration of MHS Services will be discussed in Chapter 27.

FLEXIBLE LICENSING

The NetWare 4.1 NOS provides increased flexibility for customers who want to have more control over the number of user connections supported by the network. You can increase the number of simultaneous user connections in five-user increments.

Suppose that you have installed a 100-user NetWare 4.1 server. Six months down the road you need to allow for 20 more connections. Under the previous NetWare 4 version, you need to upgrade to a 250-user license. However, with NetWare 4.1, the "additive licensing" allows you to install a 20-user license *in addition* to your already installed 100-user license, giving you a total of 120 connections. There is no limit on how many licenses you can install on the same server, as long as your server hardware can support the load. There are cases where 2000-user and 5000-user (e-mail) servers have been installed this way.

NETWARE 4.1 FOR OS/2

Included with your NetWare 4.1 is the option to install the NOS to run under OS/2. This is an extension of the NetWare 4.1 network operating system that provides NetWare services in a nondedicated environment. It enables one computer to function simultaneously as a NetWare server, an OS/2 application server, and a NetWare client.

Note

Prior to NetWare 4.1, NetWare for OS/2 support was a separately purchased item from Novell.

With NetWare 4.1 for OS/2, you can work in an OS/2, DOS, or Microsoft Windows session on the OS/2 side of your computer while the NetWare server side supports you and other users on your network. NetWare 4.1 for OS/2 uses the same source code and provides the same features as the NetWare 4.1 NOS.

NetWare 4.1 for OS/2 is for those who need to run strategic applications in both the NetWare and OS/2 environments. For example, it can greatly benefit companies that require remote mainframe access, local network support, and support for OS/2 application servers. With NetWare 4.1 for OS/2, a single computer can perform all three functions, thereby saving significant hardware expense.

NetWare 4.1 for OS/2 provides all the standard features found in NetWare 4.1 plus some enhancements. For example, it includes a driver, DSKSHARE.DSK, that enables you to run both the NetWare 4.1 NOS and OS/2 from a shared hard disk. DSKSHARE.DSK acts as the interface between the NetWare NOS and an OS/2 disk device driver, enabling the NetWare NOS to use disks controlled by OS/2. The NetWare partition of the shared disk is formatted and managed solely by the NetWare network operating system.

To preserve security, the DSKSHARE.DSK driver does not enable transparent access between the NetWare partition and the OS/2 partitions. OS/2 applications cannot use the space allotted to the NetWare file system and vice versa.

Hard-disk sharing is an option, not a requirement. You also can install NetWare NOS-dedicated disks (not recognized by OS/2) and OS/2-dedicated disks.

NetWare 4.1 for OS/2 can share a network adapter with NetWare clients running on the OS/2 portion of a computer. This is accomplished through the use of two drivers: LANSHARE.SYS and LANSHARE.LAN. LANSHARE.SYS is installed as the driver for the NetWare Client for OS/2, and LANSHARE.LAN is installed as the driver for NetWare 4.1 for OS/2.

NetWare 4.1 for OS/2 also can share a network adapter with other protocols, such as NDIS in a token-ring environment. This enables you to run the NetWare server on the same computer as IBM Extended Services and still use only one network adapter.

IMAGE-ENABLED NETWARE

Image-enabled NetWare is the result of a collaboration between Novell and Kodak. Image-enabled NetWare is a group of services and an environment based on NetWare, and designed specifically for the storage, manipulation, retrieval, and maintenance of computerized images.

Image-enabled NetWare consists of the following components:

◆ A special high-capacity file system based on the Data Migration interface

◆ A programming interface for manipulating images, including support for all the popular graphics formats in use today. This interface includes scanner support, image compression, rotation, bit-map manipulation, scaling, and more.

◆ A programming interface for document management, retrieval, indexing, and searching

Novell and Kodak are encouraging developers of imaging software to standardize on the environment provided by image-enabled NetWare. When this happens, it will create a standard environment and programming interface for imaging software and, hopefully, make imaging applications more practical and more affordable than they are right now.

ENHANCED USER UTILITIES

NetWare 4 includes a new set of user and administration utilities. These utilities are all designed to support NDS. The design of NDS allowed Novell to integrate many of the functions of the 3.1x utilities into several NetWare 4 utilities, reducing the number of programs that users and administrators must learn in order to take advantage of NetWare.

Note

As a result of the restructuring of utilities, some of your more "favorite" utilities are no longer available in NetWare 4: SYSCON, FCONSOLE, SALVAGE, and NDIR, just to name a few.

However, you can copy some of these file-system-related utilities onto your 4.*x* servers.

Most NetWare 4 utilities come in two versions: a graphical version based on Microsoft Windows, and a text-mode version for DOS. Users and administrators will notice that many routine operations with NetWare now are much easier, including mapping network drives, searching for files, sending jobs to network printers, creating users and groups, defining security privileges, and so on.

NDS enables the administration and user utilities to work on the entire network without requiring you to attach to multiple servers. This alone makes the NetWare 4 utilities much more friendly and powerful than the 3.1*x* utilities.

Because of the bindery emulation provided by the 4.*x* servers, most of the "older" (3.12 and earlier) utilities still work with NetWare 4. However, the old utilities are ignorant of NDS, so they don't gain the benefits offered by NDS. NetWare 4 servers appear to these utilities as 3.1*x* bindery-based servers.

ONLINE DOCUMENTATION

All the NetWare 4 documentation is available online. Novell includes software that enables users to graphically view the documentation, search for commands or text, print the documentation, and so on. The software that controls the online documentation behaves like some of the really good context-sensitive help available in the latest Windows and Macintosh applications.

Note

Unlike the online help shipped with NetWare 2.*x* and 3.*x*, which is based on Folio VIEWS, ElectroText is a customized version of DynaText v1.5 from EBT Inc.

The online help for NetWare 4.0*x* was in ElectroText (or ET) format. Starting with NetWare 4, however, Novell converted from ElectroText to DynaText v2.1.1, which supports Windows, Mac, DOS, and major UNIX implementations, such as Sun, DEC, and IBM.

Currently, the online documentation is available only to Windows and OS/2 clients. Macintosh users, however, will be able to view the online documentation in the near future.

IMPROVED NLM DEVELOPMENT TOOLS

NetWare *Loadable Modules* (NLMs) are server-based applications for NetWare. Novell has gone to great lengths to improve the NLM development environment for NetWare 4. These improvements include a more powerful and open programming interface to NetWare, better documentation, and better support through the Novell Professional Developers Program (PDP).

Novell also has made agreements to license several important third-party tools and object frameworks and make those products available to NLM developers. In the near future, NLM developers will have object-oriented frameworks available to them that will make development of sophisticated client/server applications easier. Right now, the NLM programming environment is based on the popular C programming language. However, Novell has announced that the NLM environment will support other programming languages, including FORTRAN.

SUMMARY

NetWare 4 is an ambitious operating system from Novell. NetWare Directory Services, the most widely touted feature offered by NetWare 4, is extremely important and will have a powerful effect on the way you use NetWare in your business. However, NetWare 4 has several additional new features that, all by themselves, are important as well.

The new features discussed are the following:

- ◆ NetWare Directory Services (NDS)
- ◆ New NDS tools for managing trees and bindery-based servers
- ◆ A new high performance scheduler
- ◆ Better memory management and protection
- ◆ Data migration
- ◆ Enhanced file system (block suballocation and file compression)
- ◆ Better security
- ◆ Enhancements for wide area networks
- ◆ Multilingual support
- ◆ Enhanced print services

♦ Enhanced storage management services

♦ Built-in electronic mail support

♦ Additive license feature

♦ Bundled support for NetWare for OS/2

♦ Better user utilities and online documentation

♦ Improved NLM development tools

Chapter 4 discusses some of the NetWare add-on products that will help with your connectivity and remote access issues.

- NetWare for SAA

- NetWare HostPrint and NetWare HostPrint/400

- NetWare Access for DEC

- NetWare NFS Services—NetWare 4 Edition

- NetWare Multi-Protocol Router

- NetWare Connect

- Summary

CHAPTER 4

Related Products

While LANs exist in most corporations today, they are frequently not the only computing platforms used by these organizations. There exists a need in many firms to provide connectivity services to corporate IBM and DEC mainframes and midrange computers, such as the IBM AS/400, DEC VAX, HP9000, and assorted UNIX systems. Over the past several years, many solutions for such connectivity needs have existed.

Looking back to the early 1980s, the solution was quite simple. People who needed LAN access were given PCs with network cards, people who needed host access were given terminals. Those individuals needing both LAN and host access were given credenzas on which to place both pieces of equipment.

As technology advanced, PCs were given host connectivity access by installing terminal emulation hardware and software, such as IRMA boards. Terminal emulation enables a PC computer to behave as if it were a host terminal. This includes among other things, mapping PC keyboard function keys that are used by host terminals and do not exist on standard computer keyboards, but still has its drawbacks, namely the following:

◆ Emulation boards had to be purchased for every LAN station needing host access. This created very high implementation costs.

◆ Terminal emulation boards had to be installed in every LAN station needing host access. This labor added to high implementation costs.

◆ Terminal emulators and LAN connections both require their own cabling. By running two separate cables to the workstations, you once again are faced with high implementation costs.

◆ Terminal emulators are usually physically cabled to some communication device, such as a cluster controller in the IBM installations. In addition to the costs involved at the workstation, additional sums of money to install and maintain the adequate number of cluster controllers to support these users also are an issue.

With the proliferation of laptop and notebook computers, demands for mobile computing needs are rising every day. Also, as you expand to extend your network to remote sites, communications between various locations becomes a concern as well.

This chapter identifies several Novell products that can enhance the connectivity functionality of your NetWare 4.1 network. While there literally are thousands of packages that easily could have been included in this chapter, the following are indicative of various product categories. The goal of this chapter is to provide enough detail on each product and category to help you identify how the product may be used, rather than a totally comprehensive review.

The following Novell products are discussed in this chapter:

- NetWare for SAA
- NetWare HostPrint and HostPrint/400
- NetWare Access for DEC
- NetWare NFS Services—NetWare 4 Edition
- NetWare Multi-Protocol Router
- NetWare Connect

NetWare for SAA

Many of the large enterprise networks that exist today have been built around IBM's System Network Architecture (SNA). With the evolution of the NetWare operating system, corporations have been driven to provide their network users with the resources that both SNA and LANs have to offer by integrating NetWare servers into legacy SNA networks. An SNA *gateway* provides the means of interconnecting between LANs and IBM hosts.

NetWare for SAA has been available for a number of years. In 1995 Novell released NetWare for SAA 2.0 that provides support for NetWare 4.1 systems and is compatible with NDS.

For those not familiar with IBM host environments, a very simplified picture of the architecture is given in Figure 4.1. Terminals and printers are the devices that you are most familiar with and can easily imagine needing connectivity to the host computer. These devices are often wired to a device called a *cluster controller*, which is in turn connected to a device called a *communications controller* (or *front-end processor*). The FEP is in turn connected to the host computer. Cluster controllers are commonly connected to FEPs over token ring links or over WAN links using synchronous modems and the SDLC (Synchronous Data Link Control) protocol.

Where does NetWare for SAA fit into this? You still have terminals. However, the terminals are now PCs running terminal emulation software, and you still have your printers. Rather than the cluster controller, a NetWare server running NetWare for SAA is used. Instead of being wired to the cluster controller, the terminals and printers are LAN connected to the NetWare for SAA server using the standard IPX/SPX protocol. The NetWare for SAA server acts as a gateway to convert this IPX/SPX data into IBM SNA data recognizable by IBM hosts and intermediary devices, such as the FEPs. To the SNA network, the NetWare for SAA server looks and acts as though it were an IBM cluster controller.

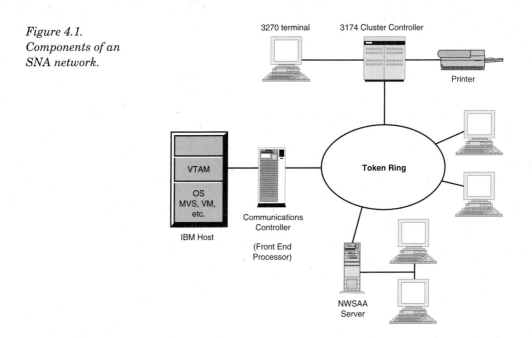

Figure 4.1.
Components of an
SNA network.

If you are using IBM AS/400, then chances are you are familiar with the IBM PC Support/400 software package. This software allows PCs to emulate IBM 5250 terminals, and provides file and print access. You can use NetWare for SAA in this environment by replacing the "PC Support Router" software with the version shipped with NetWare for SAA. This enables you to reduce the memory requirement by PC Support/400 by as much as 60K.

NetWare for SAA is implemented as a set of NLMs. You can load them on your production server or on a dedicated "application server" using a copy of Runtime NetWare supplied with NetWare for SAA. Connections to the host computer may be made either using token ring, Ethernet, SDLC, X.25/QLLC, or "channel-attached" devices. LAN workstations may utilize any topology supported by Novell's ODI drivers.

The following is a list of some of the new features that are incorporated into NetWare for SAA v2.0:

◆ Multiple PU emulation with the capability to support up to 2000 sessions

◆ Support for SNA *Low Entry Networking* (LEN) nodes with dependent and independent LUs

◆ Expanded support for AS/400 connections

◆ Load Balancing

◆ Hot Standby

◆ TN3270 (TCP/IP support)

◆ Enhanced network management capabilities (via NetView)

◆ New Windows-based configuration utility

◆ LUx/LUA support

◆ New support for CPI-C transaction program

◆ Compatible with NetWare 4.1

◆ Compatible with NDS

Note

For more information about NetWare for SAA 2.0, consult the *NetWare for SAA 2.0 Info Guide*, available from Novell.

NETWARE HOSTPRINT AND NETWARE HOSTPRINT/400

As discussed previously, LAN workstations can be configured to support terminal and printer sessions through the NetWare for SAA servers. Running printer sessions in this fashion, however, puts the processing and memory overhead at each workstation. *NetWare HostPrint* is designed to reduce and move this overhead to the NetWare for SAA server. HostPrint operations are simpler, faster, and more efficient than workstation-based print emulation sessions.

NetWare HostPrint 1.11, a NetWare Loadable Module (NLM) that runs on a NetWare for SAA server enables users to send host print jobs to networked printers through server-based IBM 3278 LU1 and LU3 printer emulation sessions (see Figure 4.2). The NetWare HostPrint NLM routes host print jobs directly from the host to NetWare print queues, reducing network traffic and providing centralized administration and control. In contrast to traditional workstation-based host printer emulation, NetWare HostPrint 1.11 does not require a workstation to run the host printer emulation. NetWare HostPrint 1.11 provides a reliable, high-performance alternative to workstations dedicated to 3270 emulation.

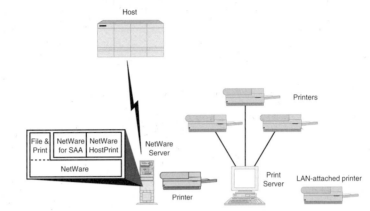

Figure 4.2.
Using NetWare
HostPrint with
NetWare for SAA to
send host print jobs
directly to LAN-based
printers.

Because NetWare HostPrint v1.11 interfaces directly with NetWare print queues, it reduces traffic on the network. Print jobs go directly to the print queue on the server instead of being sent to the client and redirected to the print queue. NetWare HostPrint also provides automatic queue reconnection, a critical feature for printing to remote printers over WAN connections. The reconnection feature will automatically reestablish a connection with an out-of-service server and its associated print queues once the server comes back online.

Note

NetWare HostPrint v1.11 can be purchased for either 16 sessions or 256 sessions.

Similar to NetWare HostPrint for IBM mainframes, a version of HostPrint is available for printing from AS/400 machines. *NetWare HostPrint/400* v1.0, a NetWare Loadable Module (NLM) that runs on a NetWare for SAA server, enables users to send host print jobs to networked printers through server-based, IBM AS/400 host-compatible printer emulation sessions. HostPrint/400 routes host print jobs directly from the host to NetWare print queues, reducing network traffic and providing centralized administration and control.

In contrast to 5250 emulators, NetWare HostPrint/400 provides efficient, centrally administered, server-based printing. NetWare HostPrint/400 also provides printing features, such as multiple fonts and more than 132 characters per line for AS/400 environments. Unlike emulators using the AS/400 3270 Remote Attach feature that requires a link reserved for itself, NetWare HostPrint/400 can share the same link to the AS/400 for both display and printer emulation.

NetWare HostPrint/400 can emulate as many as 253 host printer sessions—many more than a workstation solution. All 253 host printer sessions can be located on a single AS/400 host system or spread out over as many as 32 AS/400 host systems. The print output from these sessions can be redirected to any NetWare print queue on the network.

Note

For more information about HostPrint and other add-on products for NetWare for SAA, consult *NetWare for SAA Solutions Guide*, available from Novell.

NETWARE ACCESS FOR DEC

Similar in function to NetWare for SAA described previously, *NetWare for DEC Access* is a NetWare connectivity gateway product that provides transparent access to DEC (Digital Equipment Corporation) systems over the LAT (Local Area Transport) protocol (see Figure 4.3). The product integrates NetWare and DEC environments to preserve investments in DEC hardware, applications, and data. Built as a set of NetWare Loadable Modules (NLMs), NetWare for DEC Access takes advantage of the high-performance, reliability, manageability, and security features of the NetWare operating system.

Figure 4.3.
Using NetWare for
DEC Access to connect
a NetWare LAN to the
DEC/LAT network.

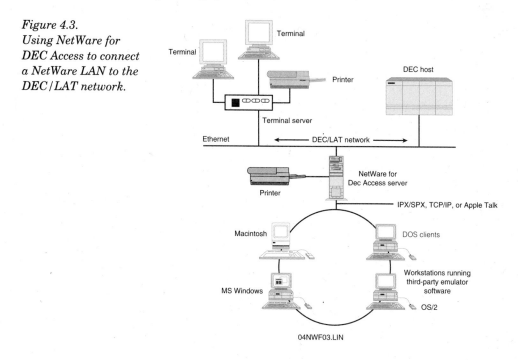

Because LAT is not a routable protocol, the use of NetWare for DEC Access reduces the complexity of wide-area-connectivity to DEC systems by providing remote access to central DEC systems using TCP/IP, IPX/SPX, or AppleTalk WANs; you no longer need to set up separate LAT bridging networks or DECnet routers. In addition, NetWare for DEC Access simplifies the administration of DEC connectivity, enabling administrators to configure, secure, and monitor DEC system access using familiar-looking NetWare utilities.

Note

> Formally NetWare Access for DEC was known as NetWare for LAT. Because of the addition of new client workstation protocol (such as TCP/IP) support in the newer version, the product was renamed.

Each NetWare for DEC Access server enables as many as 128 concurrent users to transparently access DEC applications over any topology supported by the NetWare NOS.

If you want to make your DEC machines reachable by certain TCP/IP clients over the Internet, you can configure the DEC Access server to permit connections from only pre-authorized TCP/IP telnet clients, thereby providing a security firewall from the TCP/IP network to the DEC network. This can be especially useful in preventing unauthorized access from TCP/IP users. Also, each DEC Access server can be configured to force authorized telnet clients to a particular DEC system.

Note

> For in-depth information about NetWare for DEC Access client emulators, print services, and file transfer software, refer to the *NetWare for DEC Access Info Guide*.

NETWARE NFS SERVICES—NETWARE 4 EDITION

Do you have the need to share file and print resources between your NetWare 4.1 network and UNIX machines? If your answer is yes, NetWare NFS Services— NetWare 4 Edition could be your solution.

Note

> TCP/IP and NFS services are not limited to only UNIX hosts. They are available for many platforms, such as DOS, DEC VMS, and Apple Macintosh. In this section, UNIX and TCP/IP hosts are used interchangeably.

NetWare NFS Services—NetWare 4 Edition is a set of NLMs designed for NetWare 4.1 with built-in NDS support. The product transparently integrates UNIX systems with NetWare 4 file and print services to give UNIX users access to the NetWare environment, yet at the same time it also enables DOS and Microsoft Windows users to access files and printers on local and remote NFS servers. It enables you to use familiar NetWare commands to access files or submit print jobs to printers that reside on NFS (UNIX) servers. With NetWare NFS Services—NetWare 4 Edition, UNIX users can share files and other network resources with NetWare 4 clients, such as DOS, Macintosh, and OS/2 computers, in a fully integrated, seamless manner.

Note

> For those of you familiar with the NetWare NFS and NetWare NFS Gateway products, the NetWare NFS Services product is simply a combination of them, with NetWare 4.1 support included.

The following are some of the product highlights:

- Transparent file access to NetWare volumes by NFS users
- Transparent file access to NFS file systems by NetWare users
- Allows NetWare users to spool print jobs to UNIX TCP/IP servers using familiar NetWare utilities, such as CAPTURE and NPRINT
- Enables UNIX TCP/IP host to submit print jobs to standard NetWare print queues via the lpr protocol
- Turn your NetWare 4.1 server into an FTP server using the included File Transfer Protocol daemon (FTPSERV), a standard TCP/IP file transfer service
- Enables any FTP client with valid NetWare access to connect to any NetWare server not running FTPSERV and initiate file transfers to and from any NetWare volume or directory
- Support for Domain Name services
- Supports remote administration from any client that supports VT100, VT220, or the X Window System

Note

> If you do not require the file sharing facilities in this product, but need the FTP and bi-directional printing, you can use *NetWare UNIX Print Services—NetWare 4 Edition* instead; this is much like the NetWare FLeX/IP product.

NETWARE MULTI-PROTOCOL ROUTER

Over the past decade, companies have begun to realize the need and value of intercommunications between various locations. Most major companies that have multiple sites now rely heavily on their communication infrastructure to carry voice, data, and sometimes video between these locations. The need for reliable, efficient, and cost-effective communication is increasing at a fast pace. And to make life more interesting for the network administrators, multiple protocols need to be supported over such connections. You can create your wide area network (WAN) using either software-based or hardware-based routers, depending on the functionality and throughput you need from the routers.

Novell's *NetWare Multi-Protocol Router* (MPR) 3.0, implemented as a set of NLMs, provides extensive internetwork routing and source route bridging services, which enable systems on separate LAN segments to communicate, even when the LAN types are different. It routes the most popular network protocols (IPX, AppleTalk, and IP) using the most popular data-link protocols (Ethernet, Fast Ethernet, token ring, ARCnet, LocalTalk, and FDDI). MPR also supports source route bridging for remote token ring networks.

NetWare Multi-Protocol Router 3.0 also enables systems on geographically distant LANs to communicate through multiple network protocols across the same (or multiple) synchronous or asynchronous WAN link using NetWare Link/PPP.

You can use MPR 3.0 as a dedicated (NetWare 4.1) router, which provides multi-protocol routing and source route bridging services to an internetwork, or as a (NetWare 4.1) server based router, which combines internetworking services and NetWare file and print services on the same system.

Note

> MPR 3.0 also can be installed on NetWare 3.12 servers.

MPR 3.0 provides the same set of enhanced protocol support that is included with the basic NetWare 4.1 server software, *except* for the WAN and Source Route Bridge support. These enhancements are discussed in the following sections.

IPX SUPPORT

IPX is the traditional network-layer protocol used by NetWare systems. IPX bases its routing decisions on the address fields in its header and on the information it receives from its routing protocols.

MPR's IPX implementation provides the following features:

- ◆ **Link state routing**: In addition to providing full Routing Information Protocol/Service Advertising Protocol (RIP/SAP) functionality, Novell's new IPX protocol stack provides NetWare Link Services Protocol (NLSP), Novell's link state routing protocol for IPX networks. NLSP offers faster convergence and better reliability and scalability than the RIP/SAP routing traditionally employed by NetWare servers.

- ◆ **Filtering**: The Filter Configuration utility (FILTCFG) enables the router to filter services, incoming and outgoing routes, IPX packets, and NetBIOS packets at all or selected router interfaces.

- ◆ **IP tunneling**: This encapsulation method provides a way for two or more IPX networks to exchange IPX packets over an IP network. For this purpose, IPX uses IPRELAY, a WAN driver that models the IP internetwork as a collection of point-to-point PVCs (permanent virtual circuits).

- ◆ **Point-to-point (PPP) WAN connections**: You can set up either permanent or on-demand PPP connections over synchronous, asynchronous, X.25, and Frame Relay links.

Note

In MPR 3.0, Novell implemented the IETF Point-to-Point Protocol (PPP), which enables point-to-point high-speed transmission of data over synchronous dedicated communications media (leased lines) or asynchronous/synchronous switched transmission facilities at up to T1/E1 speeds. (In Europe, the equivalent to T1 (1.544 Mbps) is E1, which operates at 2.048 Mbps.) PPP is recognized throughout the industry as a multi-vendor means of establishing WAN connectivity between two LANs requiring high bandwidth and low delay.

TCP/IP SUPPORT

TCP/IP is a suite of networking protocols that is widely used to enable dissimilar nodes in a heterogeneous environment to communicate. The suite of protocols defines formats and rules for the transmission and receipt of information independent of any given network organization or computer hardware.

4

RELATED PRODUCTS

Novell's implementation of TCP/IP provides the following features:

◆ **Multiple routing protocols**: IP traffic can be routed between networks using the RIP, EGP (Exterior Gateway Protocol), or OSPF (Open Shortest Path First) protocol.

◆ **Filtering**: FILTCFG enables the router to filter incoming and outgoing RIP and EGP routes, OSPF external routes, and many different TCP/IP and UDP/IP services, such as finger, telnet, and who.

◆ **WAN support**: Numbered and unnumbered point-to-point (PPP) connections over synchronous, asynchronous, X.25, and Frame Relay links. Permanent or on-demand links are supported.

APPLETALK SUPPORT

AppleTalk provides complete native mode AppleTalk connectivity with other AppleTalk nodes in the internetwork. With packet forwarding enabled, the router routes AppleTalk packets to and from any AppleTalk node, such as a Macintosh, LaserWriter or ImageWriter, or a server that supports AppleTalk.

Novell's implementation of AppleTalk provides the following features:

◆ **Routing Table Maintenance Protocol (RTMP)**: This protocol transmits routing information every 10 seconds to neighboring AppleTalk routers.

◆ **AppleTalk Update-based Routing Protocol (AURP)**: This protocol provides a means of connecting isolated AppleTalk networks through an IP internetwork (IP tunneling).

◆ **Filtering**: FILTCFG enables the router to filter services and routes.

◆ **Point-to-Point WAN Connections**: Permanent unnumbered and numbered point-to-point links over synchronous, asynchronous, X.25, and Frame Relay networks. On-demand connections over the same links are supported.

SOURCE ROUTE BRIDGING SUPPORT

Source Route Bridge enables you to link token ring networks. The bridge allows segmentation of network traffic to reduce the load on any one segment and provides parallel bridging, a fault-tolerant technique of determining alternate routes for data when a bridge fails.

Novell's Source Route Bridge software in MPR 3.0 provides the following features:

◆ **Multiple protocol support**: Source Route Bridge bridges any protocol that supports source route bridging on token ring networks, including, but not limited to, IPX, IP, SNA, AppleTalk, and NetBIOS.

- ◆ **Filtering**: FILTCFG enables the source route bridge to filter packets by protocol ID or ring number.
- ◆ **Internal virtual ring**: Source Route Bridge supports the use of multiple interfaces for creating backup bridging paths.
- ◆ **WAN support**: Source Route Bridge provides extensive WAN support, using leased-line synchronous links over PPP, or over X.25 and Frame Relay networks.

NetWare Connect

A well designed and implemented LAN often leads to the need for employees and customers to gain remote access to critical data and resources. LAN users also will find the need to access data external to the LAN, perhaps on bulletin boards (BBS) or other hosts (such as CompuServe). NetWare Connect is Novell's solution to both dial-in, remote users, and dial-out services.

There has long been two distinct schools of thought concerning dial-in access to a LAN. The first camp supports a methodology known as remote control, the second an approach called remote node.

Remote Control

Remote control dial-in access calls for the dial-in user to physically capture control of the host it is calling. Keystrokes typed by the remote user are transmitted across the telephone lines and are "fed" to the host computer. All program execution takes place on the host computer, and screen updates are "echoed" back to the dial-in user.

This solution often is used for remote program execution because it minimizes the amount of data actually transmitted across telecommunication links—only keystrokes and screen updates are sent. The downside to this approach is the dedication of home office PCs which wait for dial-in users to call in.

Some popular remote control software packages are PC Anywhere, CarbonCopy, and ReachOut.

Remote Node

Remote node allows a dial-in user to be connected to LAN resources as if he or she were a local station on the LAN. Upon successful remote connection, remote node stations can access the LAN under the same distributed processing environment as local users. Remote node is useful for copying files, but often suffers from poor performance when executing programs from across the LAN.

It is worthwhile to briefly review how LAN applications execute user remote node. For this purpose the process of loading WordPerfect from the server, retrieving and editing a document, and saving the changes will be examined in the following steps:

1. Remote node user types WP. The user's workstation sends a request to the file server to open and read the WP program.

2. Remote node user waits, and waits, and waits.... This is often a good time for the remote user to grab a fresh cup of coffee. Today's applications are more powerful than ever and require larger program executable files to provide this functionality. Under remote node configuration, the entire executable program, along with any necessary overlay files, must be transmitted over the phone link. With programs requiring several hundred kilobytes of executables, and telecommunication links typically in the 9600 bps to 28.8 kbps range, this could easily exceed five minutes of load time.

3. Remote node user retrieves his or her document. Again the user will wait as his or her document is sent across the phone lines. The wait time usually will be much shorter than for application loading because most documents are smaller in size.

4. User makes edits. This step executes at normal speed because the program and document have been transferred and are now executing at the remote site—local to the user. Telecommunication charges (if any) are still racking up as the user is still online with the remote LAN.

5. The user saves the document. The revised document is transmitted across the link as in step 3.

Because of this service performance issue when loading remote software, it is often that remote node users launch applications from their local hard drive and save and retrieve data files from the remote LAN. This dramatically reduces waiting, but file retrieves and saves are still more time consuming than remote control, where data never crosses the phone lines.

Note

Administrators should be aware of application software licensing issues when configuring remote users. Many accounting packages, such as Real Time, license their software on a per site basis. Remote users with copies of the accounting software local to each office and centralized data are subject to additional application software charges of $5,000 per site. Remote control is the solution of choice for these instances because all the software resides at one location.

Remote node access is best used for connecting to a LAN, transferring files to the remote site, disconnecting, and using the file locally.

The nice thing about NetWare Connect is that it supports both modes of operation. NetWare Connect provides software that functions as a "modem LAN driver." The use of the NASI (Novell Asynchronous System Interface) driver provides support for configuring third-party remote control software, such as PC Anywhere. When you choose the NASI connection type within the modem software (as opposed to COM1 or COM2), you instruct the software that the modem will not be on the local machine, but on another machine acting as a communication server.

When utilizing remote control, administrators have a tremendous level of flexibility in hardware configuration. For example, if five simultaneous dial-in sessions are needed, you can configure five LAN workstations as dedicated to this purpose. If you don't want to use that many PCs, you have the option of purchasing specialty hardware such as Cubix boards.

DIAL-OUT COMMUNICATIONS

NetWare Connect provides an excellent modem pooling mechanism for LAN users to dial out of the network to remote resources such as CompuServe, without having to install individual modems and phone lines at each user's workstation. You can use any terminal emulation software that supports either NASI or INT14 interface. For example, Procomm Plus network version supports NASI. For those of you using CompuServe's WinCIM program, it supports the INT14 interface.

SUMMARY

This chapter covered several Novell products that you can utilize to enhance the connectivity functionality of your NetWare 4.1 network. The following Novell products were discussed in this chapter:

- ◆ NetWare for SAA
- ◆ NetWare HostPrint and HostPrint/400
- ◆ NetWare Access for DEC
- ◆ NetWare NFS Services—NetWare 4 Edition
- ◆ NetWare Multi-Protocol Router
- ◆ NetWare Connect

- Networking Standards

- Selecting and Configuring Server Hardware

- Workstation Hardware

- Working Within Your Budget

- Media Types

- Determining Personnel Roles

PART II

Planning a NetWare Network

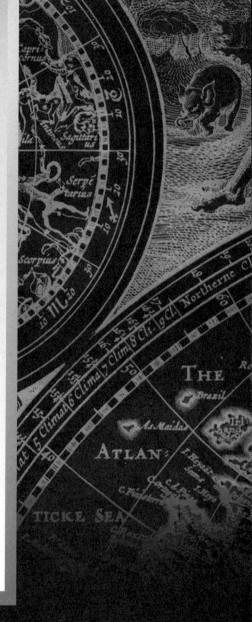

- How Standards are Set

- New Technologies

- Networking Standards

- Network Management

- Summary

CHAPTER 5

Networking Standards

Networking standards refer to publicly accepted rules for various types of communication among operating systems, computers, networks, and so on. In the early days of networking PCs, there were no standards between manufacturers, so a client was locked into a particular brand once they had made the initial choice. Because of the networking standards, communication protocols have been proposed and accepted so that, to some extent, components can be mixed-and-matched, as long as they adhere to the standards.

Selecting networking software that supports established industry standards protects the client's investment. This chapter introduces the importance and scope of networking standards as they relate to purchasing decisions.

HOW STANDARDS ARE SET

There are several types of recognized standards within the networking industry. This chapter discusses proprietary standards, de jure (dee zhur-ay) standards, and de facto (dee FAC-to) standards. While these standards are established in different ways, the effect is the same: the user can count on various pieces of the network being able to work together.

PROPRIETARY STANDARDS

Proprietary standards are developed and controlled by a single corporate entity. The specifications for proprietary standards are usually not available to the public or available only in a limited fashion. Proprietary standards are therefore usually vendor specific. IBM's System Network Architecture, SNA, is an example of a proprietary standard. It was designed to work exclusively with IBM hardware and facilitate communication among IBM systems.

Today proprietary standards generally are maintained only in highly specialized areas. Most companies have opened the books, so to speak, on much of their technology, but some have chosen to keep a particular jewel to themselves. IBM's Advanced Peer-to-Peer Networking PU (Physical Unit) Type 2.1 is an example of such a protected technology. While it has remained a proprietary standard, recently IBM has begun licensing other companies to use it.

The biggest advantage of proprietary standards is that new technology can be brought to market faster because the standards don't have to be accepted by a committee. The owner of the technology standard is free to alter, extend, or replace its specifications without having to gain the approval or cooperation of its competitors. Thus many new emerging technologies may first appear as vendor-specific solutions. High-speed Ethernet is an example of such a technology that several companies have been promoting in recent months. However, it is to a company's advantage to keep their products compatible with others, so they often will seek to have their proprietary standards accepted as de jure standards, which is discussed in the following section. As a network manager, you will find most components on the market today will work fine together. Some additional examples of proprietary standards are Novell's NetWare Core Protocol (NCP), Compaq Computer's multi-processor hardware specification, and IBM's MicroChannel bus architecture.

DE JURE STANDARDS

De jure standards are set forth by a board of representatives from the major players in a particular technological area who agree to conform to a specified standard in the interest of keeping the technology moving forward. These boards are comprised of government, industry, educational, and company representatives. To be accepted as a standards-setting body, an organization must be founded by an unbiased group of participants, such as a government or public sector organization, or by a representative group of private concerns, such as companies who lead a particular industry. Additionally, a standards-setting body must offer membership to all interested parties. Such parties should be able to qualify for membership without facing any impractical or unfair restrictions.

De jure standards are adopted after a thorough process of proposal, study and testing, committee review, improvement or alteration, and finally membership acceptance by balloting. Only then is the standard accepted as "official." Changes made to industry standards occur rarely and only after a long and careful review process so that they do not favor any specific company or vendor. Although de jure standards are very reliable as far as interoperability is concerned, some argue that the process is too slow for the industry since technological advances tend to outpace committees.

DE FACTO STANDARDS

De facto standards are "unofficial" industry standards that generally are determined through market share. If a particular company is making an item with a specialized protocol and there are more of this company's product in the client's hands than anyone else's, then that protocol becomes the de facto standard. The IBM PC is a good example of de facto standards. IBM didn't design the PC with the intention of becoming a new standard in the computer world, but that's what happened. Because the technology was made available to other vendors, another characteristic of de facto standards, other vendors were able to create their own compatible versions of the PC. Novell's NetWare enjoys a majority share of the Local Area Networking industry, and thus constitutes a de facto standard for LANs. As a result, any vendor seeking to market hardware or software will ensure that it is compatible with NetWare.

While there is not single company or governing body determining de facto standards, they generally are sound because of the influence of the customers on the manufacturer to maintain a compatible product. For example, when a group of PC manufacturers jointly specified a high-performance PC architecture, they ensured that it was backwards-compatible with the de facto ISA design on which the original IBM PC AT was based. When IBM improved the performance of a token ring by boosting its speed from 4 to 16 Mbps, they ensured that the new faster token ring could still work with rings of the original specifications.

NEW TECHNOLOGIES

Standards are in place so that when you purchase new equipment, you have a base of comparison. As long as the technology you buy is compatible with established standards, you can feel comfortable with your choice. It's a good idea to let a new technology "settle" before implementing it in a large networking situation. When purchasing a technology for use with NetWare, look for products that are NetWare Certified. This means that they have been tested and judged to be compatible with NetWare.

Some system administrators like to experiment with new technologies by purchasing a sample so that they can test to see if it works with their existing system. If you are the leading edge daredevil type, go for it! Buy the latest of everything. But be forewarned that you may find yourself down a blind alley if the latest thing is not fully compatible with the rest of the market, or if the rest of the market moves on but the specialized technology you chose does not.

Warning

Intel introduced a new bus architecture in 1994 called *PCI*. However, due to its initial lack of good standardization and certification process, and the other vendors' interpretation of the PCI specification, often PCI devices from different vendors did not interoperate successfully. This often leads to NetWare server crashes. Early in 1995, Intel revoked all its previous certifications and started on the PCI II specification, working in conjunction with a number of other vendors, towards a better "standard."

NETWORKING STANDARDS

Today there is great market pressure for the use and adoption of "open" systems; that is, systems and components that will communicate with products from a wide variety of vendors and can be integrated into whatever systems a customer may already have in place. The Open Systems Interconnections (OSI) model is the standard for network compatibility developed by the International Standards Organization (ISO). The model is sometimes called ISO/OSI model.

The model was developed to facilitate the understanding of protocols and to help in the design and development of various industry standards. Rather than define each specification, the OSI model specifies which layers should be present and which tasks each layer should perform. The model sets out the functions that should be performed at each layer without mandating how the tasks are to be accomplished. The "how" is left to the vendor to decide as their implementation of the particular layer is developed. Each layer connects only to the ones directly above and below it.

The OSI model is important in the creation and adoption of standards. The U.S. Federal Government has specified that all products it purchases must meet GOSIP requirements. *GOSIP* is the Government OSI Profile, which specifies a minimum degree of open functionality. Other nations have drafted similar requirements based upon the OSI model.

Figure 5.1.
The ISO/OSI model.

Headers and the OSI Model

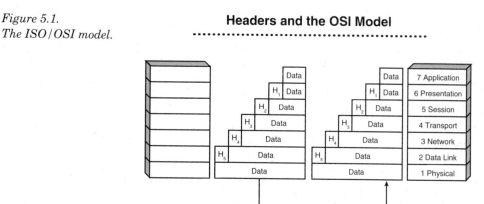

Actual OSI protocols are infrequently used in their pure form due to their current comparative limitations, including limited network management or security, difficulty in implementation, and poor performance. However, the creation of the OSI standard has led to many advances in networking, and has provided rich ground for further research. Some parts of the OSI specification have been adopted by vendors and integrated with existing technologies. One example of this is the NetWare 4.1 Directory Service, which is generally compliant with the OSI specification for global naming known as X.500.

The OSI model specifies seven layers of network services. Layers one through five are concerned with network media and network protocol stacks. The top two layers are concerned with application services, including global naming. NetWare supports layers one through four at the device and protocol level, and the top two layers using NDS.

TABLE 5.1. THE OSI MODEL.

LAYER	FUNCTION
7 Application	Responsible for the interface with the user
6 Presentation	Transforms data into a format that can be understood by the Application layer
5 Session	Establishes, maintains, synchronizes, and manages the dialog between communicating applications
4 Transport	Ensures reliable delivery of data over the network
3 Network	Moves data over a network comprised of more than one segment
2 Data Link	Builds frames of bits with logical meaning. Controls information from the Data Link layer, including source and destination hardware addresses
	The Data Link layer is separated into a Logical Link Control (LLC) sublayer and a Media Access Control (MAC) sublayer
1 Physical	Defines the specifications of the network medium (usually the cable), and the interface hardware (the NIC)

COMMUNICATIONS PROTOCOLS (PHYSICAL AND DATA LINK LAYERS)

The *Physical layer* establishes a physical connection between a computer and a network. It controls how the information is transmitted. The *Data Link layer* packages data for transmission over the Physical layer and unpacks the data when it gets there. The Data Link layer places a header and trailer field on the data it receives from the Network layer above it. The *header* includes destination and source address fields. The *trailer* includes a *Cyclical Redundancy Check* field (CRC) which helps detect transmission errors. A unit of data surrounded by such a header and trailer is called a *frame*. Data is transmitted over the wires (the media) in information units called *packets*. Some media can support more than one *frame type*, as you will read in this section.

5

The Data Link layer is actually subdivided into two components. The *Logical Link Control layer* (LLC) lies above the *Media Access Control layer* (MAC). The IEEE (Institute of Electrical and Electronics Engineers) has separate standards for each of these. The 802.2 specification addresses the LLC layer and is common to all the network types considered in the following pages. The MAC layer resides directly above the Physical Layer and is specific to the underlying medium. The 802.3 standard defines the Physical and MAC layers for IEEE Ethernet-like networks. The 802.5 standard defines the same layers for the IEEE token ring networks.

While there are many types of cabling available, the most common is discussed here: Ethernet, token ring, Fiber Distributed Data Interface (FDDI), ARCnet, and IEEE 802 Series.

Note

A number of IEEE committees were put together to establish standards for LAN interface and protocol specifications. Their Project 802 standards correspond with the Physical and Data Link layers of the OSI model.

ETHERNET NETWORKS

Ethernet means many things. It was made a de facto standard by Digital Equipment Company, Intel, and Xerox in 1980 (*Ethernet Blue Book*). Today the IEEE standard for Ethernet-type networks is 802.3. This specifies the Physical and Data Link layer functions.

Any networking protocol must regulate media access by specifying the "rules of the road" for using the cable. Ethernet networks use *CSMA/CD*, Carrier Sense Multiple Access/Collision Detection. Every network node monitors the cable at all times "listening" for any traffic, "carrier sense," and may use the cable whenever it is idle, "multiple access." Thus, all nodes attached to the cable may freely attempt to use it whenever it is available. However, the cable can carry only one message at a time. If two nodes transmit at the same time, their packets will "collide" on the wire. Each node is responsible for continuing to "listen," even as it transmits in order to detect any collision. Because collisions inhibit communication, nodes detecting collisions when transmitting must re-transmit their data.

Ethernet networks can be installed over a variety of cable types including 50-ohm coaxial "thick net" cable (10BASE-5), 50-ohm "thin net" or "cheaper net" coax (10BASE-2), 10BROAD-36 which also uses coax cable over broadband (multiple frequencies) rather than baseband (single frequency) technology, and twisted-pair cable (10BASE-T). The specific rules for the use of each of these cable types are provided in Appendix D.

Ethernet networks can use a number of different frame types. NetWare 4 uses the IEEE 802.2 standard by default, although, this can be reset using a frame statement to either the LOAD command (servers and routers) or the NET.CFG file (workstations). There is more about setting this up and configuring the hardware in Chapters 17 and 18.

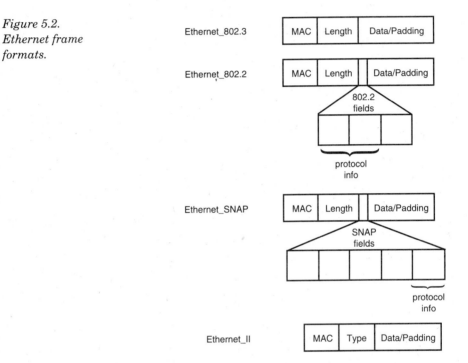

Figure 5.2.
Ethernet frame
formats.

Ethernet_802.3 is the standard frame type for pre-NetWare 4 (and pre-NetWare 3.12) and also is referred to as the *raw* frame. It is raw because it lacks the 802.2 header that usually follows the MAC header. This type of frame is only appropriate for IPX communications (Internetwork Packet eXchange, a Novell communication protocol). The Ethernet_II frame type (Ethernet version 2) is used for communications with DEC minicomputers or UNIX computers using TCP/IP or AppleTalk Phase I. The Ethernet_II frame differs from the IEEE 802.3/802.2 frame in only minor details; nonetheless, they are incompatible. The 802.3/802.2 frame contains a 2-byte field, which indicates the higher level protocol data contained in the frame, TCP/IP or IPX, for example. The older Ethernet_II frame indicates the length of the frame in the corresponding 2-byte field.

AppleTalk Phase II uses Ethernet_SNAP, a frame type that adds the SNAP (Sub-Network Access Protocol) header to the basic IEEE 802.2. This frame type is an interim solution in that it provides the upper protocol type field previously included in the Ethernet II frame, but does so within a fully compliant 802.3/802.2 frame.

NetWare 3.*x* and 4.*x* servers can use more than one frame type at the same time, and IPX can be used with any or all of the frame types described. Clients using different Ethernet types can coexist on a network, although they must have help communicating with each other. An internal IPX router in the server can provide frame-type conversions, for example. It is Novell's Open Data-Link Interface (ODI) that makes it possible for stations with different frame types to coexist on the same network.

While most Ethernet networks run on a bus topology (Ethernet backbone), many vendors have developed sophisticated hub-and-star media for Ethernet, building in various diagnostic and management features. More vendors offer Ethernet products than any other type of media, and Ethernet is among the most inexpensive types of media you can use.

Today Ethernet runs at 10 Mbps (megabits per second), which provides performance sufficient for most networking purposes. Some vendors, such as Intel, are offering new Fast Ethernet media, which works the same as regular Ethernet, but runs at 100 Mbps—ten times as fast as standard Ethernet. Most Fast Ethernet implementations are compatible with standard Ethernet, which means you don't need to change your cabling plant to use Fast Ethernet. Fast Ethernet is one of those rapidly emerging new technologies for which IEEE or other de jure standards do not yet exist.

TOKEN RING NETWORKS

Token ring was developed by IBM but is now fully standardized (IEEE 802.5) and available from many other vendors. It takes its name from the theory by which it operates: stations are arranged in a ring with a special electronic signal, called a token, cycling the ring at a predetermined rate.

For a station to transmit data, it captures the token and attaches data to it. The token then continues around the ring and the station to which the data is addressed then captures the token and reads the data attached by the transmitting station. The receiving station then sets a bit in the circulating frame indicating that the data was received and the token continues around the ring until returning to the sender. The sender confirms that the destination received the data, removes the data it had attached to the token, and releases a "free token." The token is now available for further attachment of data, and it proceeds to cycle around the ring once more.

Token ring is sometimes called a "deterministic" protocol because stations can only transmit and receive data at predetermined intervals. The length of this interval is determined by the speed at which the token circles the ring. This speed is in turn determined by the electronic characteristics of the media. It is available at either 4 Mbps or 16 Mbps. The 16 Mbps offers performance that rivals standard Ethernet. Token ring networks are particularly effective where the timing of network data transmissions must be known, as in real-time and factory-automation systems.

Figure 5.3.
Token ring networks pass a token around a ring.

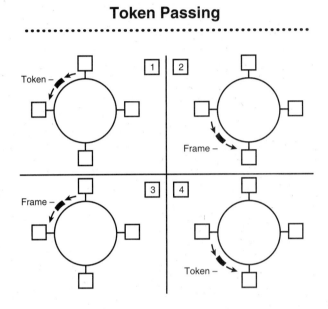

Token Passing

Warning

Although many token ring NICs are capable of operating in either 4 Mbps or 16 Mbps environments, it is critical that all the stations on a particular ring are configured to operate at the same speed. Token ring NICs may have their operating speed set using jumper switches or through configuration software.

On a token ring network, each node acts as a repeater, receiving the frame from its "upstream neighbor" and sending it on to its "downstream neighbor." Adding nodes to a token ring network may require bringing down the entire network segment and running two cables, one to each "neighbor" on the ring. This occurs whenever it is necessary to add a new *Multi-Station Access Unit* (MSAU) to the cabling plan. Each MSAU will allow up to eight workstations to attach to the ring.

Note

A token ring network behaves like a logical ring, but it is cabled as a physical star.

Token ring usually is more expensive than Ethernet, both to purchase and to maintain. Network interface cards and cabling are typically priced higher than comparable Ethernet elements. However, collisions are impossible on a token ring network because stations must capture the token before transmitting data. There can be only one token circulating the ring at a time.

Token ring provides some important safety mechanisms to ensure consistent data transmission. Token ring networks go through a self-diagnostic procedure to discover a station that has had a hardware error. If the token "disappears" because of a hardware fault, a protocol exists for introducing a new token into the ring. If a station on a token ring network suffers a hardware failure, for example, the token ring media on the faulty station trips a relay to physically remove itself from the ring. These two mechanisms allow a token ring network to heal itself when it suffers a fault, something which is impossible for Ethernet to accomplish.

NetWare supports two frame types for token ring networks. Most protocols will use the standard token ring frame. However, TCP/IP and AppleTalk must use token ring SNAP. The SubNet Access Protocol for token ring serves the same purpose as the Ethernet SNAP frame. It provides a method to identify higher level protocols in use.

FIBER DISTRIBUTED DATA INTERFACE (FDDI)

FDDI, Fiber Distributed Data Interface, is a high-speed network media system based on fiber-optic technology. The fibers are thin, clear filaments of glass or plastic through which light is beamed. This medium can carry high quantities of data with protection against eavesdropping and other interference.

While FDDI is essentially a souped-up version of token ring, there are necessary differences in the area of fault recovery. FDDI includes an optional dual-ring configuration, wherein each station is attached to a primary and redundant fiber-optic ring. If a cable break occurs, the entire ring may reconfigure itself, mending the break. Because of the use of fiber-optic media, FDDI does not need to protect against the electronic characteristics of faulty media or devices.

FDDI runs at 100 Mbps, which is 10 times faster than standard Ethernet. It is the most expensive of the network types because of the cable and NIC cost.

Note

It also is possible to run FDDI over copper cables. This implementation is known as CDDI and also runs at 100 Mbps.

ARCNET

ARCnet was developed prior to Ethernet and token ring by DataPoint. They developed ARCnet to allow their minicomputers to communicate over a network in a peer-to-peer fashion. DataPoint did not make the specification of ARCnet public and the media remained obscure until 1982 when DataPoint began to license the design of ARCnet to chip manufacturers. ARCnet media became available for use with non-DataPoint systems and it quickly became popular with PC LANs, especially due to its reliability, simplicity, and low cost. In fact, most early NetWare LANs ran on ARCnet.

Note

If you examine an ARCnet card, you will generally find a black plastic coated chipset. That is the proprietary ARCnet chipset.

Figure 5.4.
ARCnet operates on a token bus.

An ARCNET Network Configuration

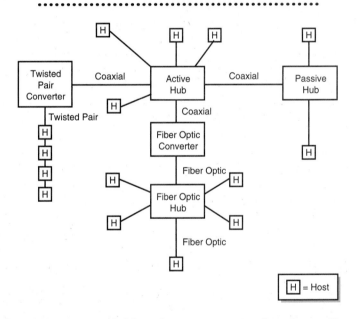

ARCnet operates on a token bus. It is much like token ring, except that the media is arranged in a bus, or linear fashion, rather than in a ring. In addition, the electronic characteristics of ARCnet are much simpler than token ring, which makes ARCnet more tolerant to hardware faults. ARCnet, therefore, does not require the extensive fault-recovery mechanisms provided by token ring.

The original 2.5 Mbps ARCnet specification recently became accepted as an industry standard. However, a group of ARCnet vendors has promoted a new specification for ARCnet, called ARCnet II (or ARCnet Plus), which runs at 20 Mbps. ARCnet II is not yet an official industry standard. In addition, Thomas-Conrad, a networking media vendor that sells many ARCnet media products, has developed a proprietary version of ARCnet, called TCNS, that runs at 100 Mbps.

ARCnet remains popular today, if not as popular as Ethernet or token ring. The benefits of ARCnet—reliability, simplicity, and low cost—ensure that it will remain a popular and viable networking media in the future. Many users of ARCnet have had it installed for years, and swear by the reliable media.

NETWORK INTERFACE METHODS (NETWORK LAYER)

Network protocols are one layer up the OSI model from the Physical and Data Link layers. After an interface card receives a network packet, it strips the media-specific information from the packet and hands it off, now formatted with an LLC header, to a network-protocol stack. The network-protocol stack then decides what to do with the packet, such as forwarding it to another station such as a router, or copying the data to an application or the operating system.

Popular network-protocol stacks include IPX/SPX, TCP/IP, AppleTalk, DECNet, SNA, and others. The network-protocol stack is entirely a software construction: it is concerned with the logical characteristics of data transmitted and received over a network, rather than the physical characteristics. The job of the network protocol stack is to route data through the segments of a network (internetwork) making sure that the packets arrive in the same order they were transmitted.

IPX/SPX

IPX/SPX (Internetwork Packet eXchange/Sequenced Packet eXchange) is a Novell communication protocol that can send and receive data packets over physically different networks. The specification of the IPX/SPX protocol stack are available to the public to be used as a standard.

IPX/SPX is based on a network protocol, called the *Xerox Network System* (XNS), developed by Xerox in the late seventies. Xerox actually proposed XNS as an industry-standard protocol, but XNS was rejected in favor of TCP/IP. Novell, recognizing some of the benefits of XNS, developed a slightly different implementation, which later became IPX/SPX.

Many third-party products feature implementations of IPX/SPX. Because of the huge installed base of NetWare products, vendors support IPX/SPX as a means of ensuring their product's viability in the marketplace.

Among the benefits of IPX/SPX are the following:

◆ Network nodes may discover their IPX addresses, rather than reading their addresses from a static database. This makes IPX addressing more dynamic and flexible than other protocol stacks.

◆ IPX is a routable protocol. A station may perform internetwork routing since routing is built into the IPX/SPX specification.

Novell decided early on to include a full-blown router in the NetWare operating system. This made constructing complex internetworks with NetWare relatively easy. The NetWare IPX router makes good use of the routable design of IPX/SPX. Customers don't have to purchase specialized, stand-alone router machines when using NetWare, as they do with other protocol stacks such as TCP/IP.

Novell recently has made some minor changes in the IPX/SPX specification that improve its performance in wide area network environments. With NetWare 4.*x*, IPX/SPX performs just as well in a WAN environment as any other protocol. These improvements include implementation of Packet Burst and LIP (Large Internet Protocol) as discussed in Chapter 3.

TCP/IP

TCP/IP (Transmission Control Protocol/Internet Protocol) is a suite (group) of protocols accepted as a standard by the Internet Advisory Board (IAB) and the U.S. Department of Defense (DoD) over XNS (Xerox Network System). The Internet is an international research network sponsored by academic institutions and the DoD, interconnecting virtually all TCP/IP stations in the world. As a result of this standardization, TCP/IP has traditionally been built into the UNIX operating system as a basic feature. Most of the networking research performed in the United States and around the world has been based upon the TCP/IP networking protocol.

Because of its standardization and roots in the research community, TCP/IP is the best network-protocol stack for interoperability among dissimilar computer hardware and operating systems. Many large organizations, both in the public and private sectors, have standardized on TCP/IP.

TCP/IP was designed to work well in a WAN environment. and is implemented on virtually every type of computer system. NetWare TCP/IP supports Ethernet, token ring, and ARCnet networks by using the Open Data-Link Interface (ODI). However, it was specified nearly twenty years ago, and has since remained virtually the same. The TCP/IP addressing system will need a major overhaul to accommodate the projected increase in stations in the near future.

APPLETALK

AppleTalk is a network protocol suite developed by Apple Computer for its Macintosh systems. Apple freely licenses the source code for the AppleTalk protocol stack to developers and as a result, AppleTalk has obtained the status of a de facto standard and has expanded its base to include many non-Macintosh computer systems.

AppleTalk Phase II supports huge internetworks, full routing, and dynamic station addressing. All Macintosh computers have AppleTalk built into their operating systems, although they can support other protocols as well. In addition to the LocalTalk Link Access Protocol (LLAP), the AppleTalk protocol suite includes Ethernet LAP (ELAP) and Token-Ring LAP (TLAP). The AppleTalk Address Resolution Protocol (AARP) is used to translate AppleTalk addresses into addresses that can be read by other token ring or Ethernet devices.

Figure 5.5.
The AppleTalk Protocol suite.

ISO-OSI Model	AppleTalk Protocol Suite
7-Application Layer	Application-specific protocols
6-Presentation Layer	AFP (Filing Protocol), PostScript
5-Session Layer	ASP (Session Protocol), ADSP (Data Stream Protocol), PAP (Printer Access Protocol)
4-Transport Layer	ATP (Transport Protocol), NBP (Name Binding Protocol), ZIP (Zone Information Protocol) Echo
3-Network Layer	DDP (Datagram Delivery Protocol)
2-Data Link Layer	LLAP (LocalTalk Link Access Protocol), ELAP (Ethernet LAP), TLAP (Token-Ring LAP)
1-Physical Layer	Twisted Pair, Coax, Fiber Optic, PBX

NETBIOS

NetBIOS is an application programming interface developed by IBM in the early eighties. It was originally encoded directly onto networking adapter cards manufactured by IBM, but was later transferred to software and implemented by Microsoft as part of their PC LAN program.

NetBIOS was not designed for internetworking, WAN use, or interoperability with unlike systems. It was not even designed to be a networking protocol in the first place. Nevertheless, it has become a standard, largely through the influence of Microsoft and IBM rather than based upon its technical merits.

Network operating systems based on NetBIOS, including Microsoft's LAN Manager, are incapable of performing internetwork routing. This makes multi-server sites impossible to construct without the purchase of specialized routing systems produced by third-party vendors. NetBIOS is also exceedingly inefficient when multisegment networks are constructed.

Many networking applications written during the early days of PC networking, such as electronic mail and database systems, were written to use NetBIOS. For this reason, NetWare 4.1 supports NetBIOS through a NetBIOS emulator.

Note

Novell's NetBIOS encapsulates NetBIOS function calls within IPX/SPX packets. It is not compatible with IBM NetBIOS. Both stations must be using the same NetBIOS interface.

In general, NetBIOS is not routable. It must be bridged. However, because Novell's NetBIOS is encapsulated within IPX/SPX packets, which is a routable protocol, it can be routed.

APPLICATION SERVICES (APPLICATION LAYER)

The *Application layer* is the top level of the OSI networking standard. It has become common practice in the networking business to refer to any protocol layer above the networking protocols you just read about as application services.

The Application layer standards are not themselves applications; rather, they are well-defined networking services made available to applications. Examples of applications that make use of these services are file systems, electronic mail, database systems, and so on.

NETWARE CORE PROTOCOL (NCP)

NetWare Core Protocol (NCP) is NetWare's built-in Application layer protocol. Stations on the network use NCP to request login to a server, to access a server-based file, to submit a print job to a print server, to navigate NetWare Directory Services (NDS), and more.

NCP is the rules the server must follow when handling workstation requests for service. The request for service for a NetWare server is begun in the RAM on the client workstation using a utility called the *DOS Requester* (or *Requester for OS/2*). The Requester sends the request to the communication protocol, which passes the request on after adding a header with source and destination information. The server removes the header and reads the request. NCP is now compatible with TCP/IP as well as IPX/SPX. Formerly NCP required IPX/SPX transport services.

Figure 5.6.
How NCP forms a
NetWare server request.

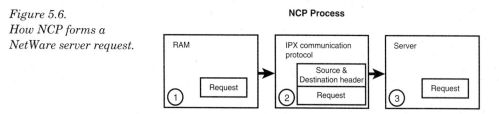

NCP is a proprietary standard used exclusively by NetWare. Novell licenses NCP specifications to software developers but reserves the exclusive right of specifying NCP services. Changes made to the NetWare operating system, such as the NetWare Directory Service (introduced with NetWare 4.0), require commensurate changes in the NCP specification.

NETWORK FILE SYSTEM (NFS)

The Network File System, or NFS, is an application layer protocol for remote file service. NFS was developed by Sun Microsystems to allow UNIX stations access to files located on other computers and has become an industry standard protocol. NFS is a complete file-service protocol, and it represents a subset of the functionality offered by NCP.

You can load NFS on a NetWare 3 or 4 server in order to provide UNIX stations with access to files located on the NetWare server. Presently, NFS works only in conjunction with the TCP/IP network-protocol stack. Sun liberally licenses NFS source code for a trivial license fee and as a result, most brands of UNIX on the market today include NFS.

APPLETALK FILING PROTOCOL (AFP)

The AppleTalk Filing Protocol (AFP) was developed by Apple Computer as a file-service protocol for working with the AppleTalk protocol stack. AFP is similar to NFS in that it is a file-service protocol.

AFP is a de facto standard file-service protocol for the Macintosh arena. Although Apple grants source code licenses for AFP, the specification is controlled tightly by Apple, and has not been accepted as an official industry standard. Nevertheless, AFP is an important file-service protocol because it is the only one that truly addresses the unique file format of Macintosh files. Hence, it is very important for any networking product that will support Macintosh computers to be in compliance with AFP.

AFP is supported by the NetWare 2, 3, and 4 operating systems. AFP was the first non-NCP file-service protocol to be supported by NetWare.

NETWORK MANAGEMENT

The main objective of network management is to allow network managers to mange devices (such as servers), monitor critical network events (such as errors), and gather long term usage statistics for network growth planning, all from a central management station.

Because internetworking allows different types of devices to participate on the internetwork, these components (such as routers and hubs) will usually be multi-vendor and heterogeneous in nature. It is clear that a particular vendor's network management technology is unusable in such environments. A non-vendor specific solution is needed.

The first widely accepted nonproprietary network management protocols were developed by the Internet community for the TCP/IP network—the *Simple Network Management Protocol* (SNMP)—in the late 1980s.

SIMPLE NETWORK MANAGEMENT PROTOCOL

Simple Network Management Protocol (SNMP) is a set of specifications that provides a means for collecting network management-related data from different devices on the network. Reporting capability is also provided to the "managed" devices to report errors to the management station.

The SNMP protocol suite consists of the following:

◆ Structure and Identification of Management Information (SMI)

◆ Management Information Base (MIB)

◆ Simple Network Management Protocol (SNMP)

SMI defines the structure of the SNMP database agent. This defines the number of fields and the type of data that will go in each field. This is very much similar to any database you work with.

MIB describes the objects, or entries, that are to be included in the database. For example, device up time and network address are objects in a MIB. Each object has a predefined name so developers of the management station software will know what objects are available, their names, and the type of values (characters for names, integer for counters, and so on). Currently, there are five types of MIB specifications, as follows:

◆ Standard—version I

◆ Standard—version II

◆ Standard—RMON (Remote MONitoring)

◆ Experimental

◆ Private (Enterprise)

Three standard MIBs are in use today. The first standard MIB was known as MIB I and contains about 114 objects. It soon was updated and replaced with MIB II, which contains about 172 objects. The newest standard MIB ratified by the Internet community is the RMON MIB. It is different from MIB II in that it contains objects for monitoring networks.

The Experimental MIB includes specific information about other aspects of network and device management that is not yet part of the standard MIBs. Once an Experimental MIB has been "approved" then it moves from this category to the standard specification.

Private or Enterprise MIBs are vendor-specific. They provide information about their own network devices that is not available in the standard MIBs.

Finally, the SNMP protocol itself is a client/server protocol with four basic operations, as follows:

◆ GET: Used to obtain a single object from the MIB

◆ GET-NEXT: Used to obtain the next entry in a table

◆ SET: Used to change information

◆ TRAP: Used to report error conditions

A new version of SNMP, SNMP II, is currently under ratification by the Internet standards body. It adds enhanced security among other features.

Note

Although the majority of SNMP implementation is over TCP/IP, SNMP is specifically designed to be transport-protocol independent. For example, Novell has implemented SNMP over IPX with its NetWare Management System (NMS).

OTHER MANAGEMENT PROTOCOLS

Even though SNMP is the most widely implemented network management protocol in the industry, two other standards are available.

Common Management Information Protocol (CMIP) was developed by the ISO committee. It is a far more comprehensive and complex protocol than SNMP. Due to its complexity, however, it is not expected to be widely available for some time yet.

Keeping in mind that CMIP may become the standard one day, the Internet community ensured that the SMI specification is consistent with the OSI ASN.1 (Abstract Syntax Notation) format for a network management database. This provides an easy migration path for CMIP-based products when they become available.

Because the Internet uses TCP/IP as the transport protocol, the implementation of CMIP over TCP/IP is known as *CMOT*.

Another popular management protocol among the IBM mainframe installations is *NetView*. It is a proprietary protocol and uses the virtual terminal telecommunications access method (VTAM) to communicate with the network management console. NetView agents on SNA devices are known as "entry points" (as compared to MIBs in SNMP).

SUMMARY

This chapter outlined some of the more important standards supported by NetWare, which include the following:

- ◆ IEEE 802 series specifications
- ◆ Ethernet II frame encapsulation
- ◆ SNAP frame encapsulation
- ◆ IPX/SPX
- ◆ AppleTalk
- ◆ TCP/IP
- ◆ NetBIOS
- ◆ OSI layers 1-4
- ◆ NCP
- ◆ NFS
- ◆ AFP
- ◆ SNMP

Standards are a very important part of the networking industry and there are many different types of standards. While it is safest to rely on tried-and-true vendors and products, sometimes a beneficial technology is too new to have any standards set.

It is best to take a balanced approach when considering nonstandard technology: weigh the benefits of such technology against the risks. Purchase all your technology from established vendors with good support records. Purchase your technology from vendors with a history of support for NetWare. Then you can benefit from standard technology and, if necessary, nonstandard technology as well.

- File Server Definitions

- Selecting the Correct Equipment

- A Balanced Approach

- Fixed Disk Drives

- Redundant Array of Inexpensive Disks (RAID)

- Expendability and Upgradability

- Summary

CHAPTER 6

Selecting and Configuring Server Hardware

In the last couple of years, the term "file server" has evolved into having several different meanings. It used to be that a file server was a file server, and when you went shopping for a server you simply wanted the biggest, the best, the fastest hardware available. This type of selection process was also easy to justify—all the network client stations could take advantage of the faster and usually more expensive machine. But, because of the advent of new and more powerful hardware, as well as the advances in application and operating system software, this simple assumption, unfortunately, is only partially true. Today, with all the available options, finding the perfect server hardware is a much more difficult task.

In fact, the task or process of determining which server or server components would best fit your needs should actually begin before you have chosen an operating system. This journey should begin as you strategize how the purchasing of an extra machine will provide you with additional benefits. In other words, you should decide exactly what you want to get from the machine, then decide what specific types of tasks the server will perform. Only after you have the tasks in mind, should you start shopping for hardware. Remember, that it is the server's tasks that will determine the type of server hardware you need, as well as the how the hardware should be configured.

This chapter defines the different types of servers. It also discusses the following:

◆ Server performance considerations

◆ Network communication subsystems

◆ Fixed disk options

◆ Memory configuration options

◆ Advantages of certain bus types

◆ System processor options

After reading this chapter, you will have gained direction in selecting suitable hardware for a network file server.

FILE SERVER DEFINITIONS

Before selecting server hardware, it is first necessary to determine which type of file server you are shopping for, such as the following:

◆ File server

◆ Database server

◆ Application server

◆ Communications server

◆ A fax server, and so on

The key distinction among the different types of servers is simply the duties you expect the server to perform. Often, the hardware is similar; the difference is how the hardware is configured. To optimize performance in a traditional file server, for example, you would optimize the file server's memory for file transfers, which for the traditional file server environment, is more important than processing speed. This is true because the processing is generally done by the workstations.

In the traditional file server setting, the file server simply retrieves and then sends files to the workstations at the workstation's request. In a database server environment, however, you not only need to be concerned about file transfers, but also about the processor's capabilities (speed).

TRADITIONAL FILE SERVERS

Traditionally, a file server used to be a computer that distributed files to workstations on a network. Often, although not always, the file server would have significantly more data storage capacity, memory, and power than other computers on the network. With the reduced cost of high-powered PC hardware, however, it is no longer this simple.

The concept of a file server, in the traditional sense, has not changed. It is still one of the most popular types of file servers and basically is a PC-based computer that houses the network operating system software and provides connectivity, file sharing, printer sharing, as well as access to other network resources. The perspective that has changed is the hardware used to build the traditional file server.

No longer is the file server just a personal computer on steroids (although there are still a lot of these machines being used as servers). Today's server manufactures are trying to differentiate file servers from PCs by designing a PC-file-server architecture that will take advantage of today's networking features.

APPLICATION SERVERS

An *application server* is a server that is dedicated to running a single application. Application servers are very commonly used when a proprietary application has been downsized from a mainframe environment and placed on a LAN.

An application server's hardware configuration will depend on the type of application the server is currently running. Because each and every application server has the potential to be slightly different, it is very difficult to recommend any specific set of hardware configurations. However, understanding the different types of application servers will help you in determining the appropriate hardware.

There also are several other types of servers that are not running proprietary applications but are still classified as an application server. The following provides a simple definition of several of these types of application servers:

Database server: A database server is a form of application server because it usually will be dedicated to running one of several client server database platforms, Oracle, Sybase, SQL server, and so on. These servers usually are very processor intensive; performing searches, queries, and other database functions requires the server to do the processing. Therefore, database servers require more processing power, more memory, and more hard disk space than traditional file server.

Communication server: Communication servers can be of several types, but they have one thing in common—they are dedicated to communications. Communication servers can be set up to receive multiple incoming or outgoing calls (often creating modem pools). Communication servers generally house multiple communication devices (modems, fax modems, and so on). Because these devices are usually the bottleneck, a fast processor is not particularly important.

Fax server: Fax servers sometimes are classified as a communications server but really are dedicated to a more specific purpose—faxing. Fax servers consist of one or more fax boards, and some type of network fax software. This software-hardware combination enables users on the network to send or receive faxes from their PC. The amount of processor speed and power that you need generally will be determined by the fax software. If the software has the workstation do the graphics rendering and conversion, then the speed of the file server is not that critical (this type of fax software usually is placed on a file server that is also responsible for the more traditional duties of sharing files and printing documents). If the network fax software, on the other hand, requires the server to do the routing, rendering, and conversion of fax image files, then processor speed, memory, and bus type indeed will affect the server's performance.

One thing that all application servers have in common, regardless of type, is that they leave the file and print duties to the more traditional file server.

SELECTING THE CORRECT EQUIPMENT

Determining down time costs will provide you with the best guidance on selecting the appropriate hardware for your server. Because, regardless of the type of server you have, or are looking for, if the file server is down, certain network functions also will be down. Thus, in an attempt to maximize server up-time, you will want to weigh the "cost" of having your server go down.

The importance of selecting quality hardware for your network server will increase as the cost of down time increases. Thus, hardware should be viewed from a cost-performance-quality perspective. So, considering budget constraints and the cost of downtime in your particular environment, decide on the necessary quality.

Tip

Too often people make the mistake of using poor quality hardware in a mission-critical environment. When selecting server hardware, follow one simple rule: the network will only be as good as the server. If the server goes down the network goes down.

A server can only be as good as any one of its internal components: if the hard drive fails, the server fails; if the power supply dies, the server dies. So, during your server purchasing decision, you should not overlook the hard drive, memory, processor, power supply, and so on.

Unfortunately, this does not explain how to determine the quality of the hardware. The next section helps in this difficult endeavor, by listing and explaining several elements of quality hardware.

VENDOR CERTIFICATION

Vendor certification programs are one source for determining the quality of hardware. If a vendor has submitted its products to Novell or any other manufacturer for certification, it usually means the vendor has spent the necessary time, effort, and sometimes money, to ensure a certain level of quality, as well as compatibility. The process of certification usually involves in-house testing by the operating system manufacture.

Note

Hardware that has been certified by Novell will bare a "Novell Labs Tested and Approved" logo. Software that has been certified by Novell will bare a "YES, It runs with NetWare" logo.

Certification programs do not completely ensure quality or compatibility. The certification is done using a very specific hardware and software combination. Using different "certified" components in the same server does not necessarily guarantee that they will work together perfectly. They do, however, provide some assurance that the hardware manufacture will work with the software vendor if problems do arise.

SERVICE CONTRACTS

Service contracts are another indication of quality—if the company selling the machine is willing to send a representative out to fix a problem, the company usually will be careful with the quality of the hardware they are sending out its doors. Do not rely on service contracts alone, however. Finding quality hardware that is the perfect fit for your needs involves looking at several other aspects. One factor that helps determine the quality of the hardware is the special features that are integrated into the hardware, for example, fault tolerance.

FAULT TOLERANT HARDWARE

Network manufactures are beginning to implement *fault tolerant* features into their hardware, which have been utilized in main frame and minicomputer environments for some time. These fault tolerant features are of two main types: Operating system fault tolerance and hardware fault tolerance.

Operating system based fault tolerant features are part of the operating system. In NetWare, for example, these are SFT-III, Read-After-Write verification, Hot-Fix, and so on (some third party software fault tolerance components are also available).

The second category of fault tolerant devices are hardware based. This category would include things such as error correcting hardware, automatic revision tracking, server critical error log, error correcting code memory (ECC), automatic restart, and so on.

Sometimes hardware dependent fault tolerant features are referred to as error-checking or error-correcting hardware. The following items covers some of the error-correcting hardware that are available in today's PC servers.

Automatic revision tracking (ART) tracks hardware upgrades. When hardware that is ART-compliant is changed, the configuration change is recorded in an independent log file. This creates an audit trail that can help associate problems with specific board upgrades or revisions.

Server critical error logs are becoming more popular in the high end hardware market. This feature allows the machine to keep track of errors every time they occur, independent of the operating system. Without a server error log, if the server is down and the operating system will not load, getting to the internal operating system's error logs is pretty close to impossible. If there is an independent error log and the server fails, looking at the last error recorded in the server's error log is simple, and it may make discovering the cause of the server's failure a much quicker process.

Error Correcting Code memory (ECC) is usually found in high-end servers. ECC memory is built around fault correction circuitry, which assures that the information the system reads from memory is the same information that was written into memory. This allows the server to detect and actually correct single bit (most common) memory errors.

Automatic restart is a function, as its name implies, that automatically brings the server back up if it goes down. Although this feature may seem trivial, it can be a big time-saver. For example, if the server goes down when the server administrator is not available, automatic restart would be there to bring the server back up.

Not all vendors are implementing these types of fault tolerant feature into server hardware, but in the process of choosing your server hardware you should decide if you need these types of features — they separate the PCs on steroids from the PCs designed and built specifically for the use as a file server.

A BALANCED APPROACH

Quality and fault tolerance are important, but are certainly not the only categories that need to be evaluated when looking for a server. You also want to consider price and performance. It is easy to compare machines according to price, but the saying "You get what you pay for" is especially relevant when talking about server hardware. Performance, on the other hand, is not as easy to explain.

Determining the performance of a server is complicated, because a server is not made up of a single device, but rather a collection of hardware components. However, there is one key concept that is often overlooked, which can be used as a guideline when evaluating server performance—make sure that all the components are "balanced."

Balancing a server is vital to performance because a server can only be as fast as its slowest part. In other words, if you have a server that is using a Pentium processor, has plenty of RAM, yet has a slow hard drive, then the server will obviously have to wait for the hard drive to store and retrieve data, slowing down the entire server in the process. To completely balance a server, look at the following server components:

- System memory
- System Processor
- Bus architecture
- Primary disk storage
- Network channel and design

The performance of each of these components affects the performance of all the other components in the server. The following section describes and discusses the more popular options for each of these components and relates each to performance.

SYSTEM MEMORY

The amount of memory and the speed of the system memory are two considerations when purchasing a server. Since the speed of the memory is easier to explain than the amount, it is addressed first.

Memory is designated in nanoseconds. The lower the number, the faster the memory (60ns is faster than 70ns, for example). The best way to determine the speed of the memory that you need is to follow the recommendations of the system board manufacture.

Determining the amount of memory you need is more difficult. In fact, there is a good chance that after you purchase a file server, regardless of the amount of memory that you get, you will want to add more. For this reason, be doubly sure that the server you purchase takes a standard type memory module and it can be upgraded.

It is also just as important to appropriately allocate the system's memory to the different NetWare resources. NetWare does dynamically allocate system memory to resources that require system memory, such as sending and receiving network packets, reading and writing information to disk, and so on, but more memory doesn't just mystically appear in the server. If the amount of memory is increased in one memory pool, then another memory pool is being decreased.

NetWare divides the system into the following three main memory pools:

◆ Cache Buffers

◆ Permanent memory

◆ Alloc memory

NetWare uses all memory, beyond the system memory required by the Operating System, and then allocates the remaining memory to the Cache Buffers memory pool. Then when the Permanent memory pool or the Alloc memory pools needs more memory, memory is taken from the Cache Buffers memory pool and added to the memory pool that needs it. This important to understand, because the Cache Buffers memory pool is responsible for disk caching, and disk caching is one of the more noticeable network performance parameters—the more memory available for disk caching, the faster the overall network performance. To help you optimize memory utilization, NetWare 4 includes a memory optimization screen, as seen in Figure 6.1.

Figure 6.1.
NetWare 4.1's memory
utilization screen.

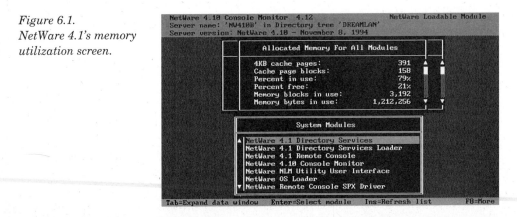

Of course, there is a point where you reach saturation and disk cache memory is wasted. This point of saturation depends on several variables; the type of data that is being retrieve, the number of users, and so on.

Note

> In NetWare 3, if an application uses memory from one of the allocated memory pools, the memory is not always returned, which means that it is possible that a large portion of your memory eventually will not be used at all.
>
> In NetWare 4, this situation does not occur. Improved memory management returns allocated memory back to the main memory pool so that it can be efficiently reused.

Because this chapter is concerned with helping you purchase the correct hardware, it will not go into depth on optimizing performance. For this type of information, see Chapter 38. The main thing to understand here is that memory is a very important component of a NetWare server. So important that having the appropriate amount of memory and having the memory correctly configured can often make more difference than moving to the next faster processor, hard disk, LAN card, and so on.

Selecting the Correct Processor

This section briefly discusses available Intel processors, beginning with the 386. It will provide you with enough information so you can inquire of the vendor as to the implementation and use of the processor. But before discussing 32-bit processors you must first understand some terms: truly preemptive multitasking, multi-threaded, and virtual memory management.

The processor is the center of your server and determines the speed at which computations are performed. So if the task that you expect from your server is running a processor intensive application, such as a database server, you will want to make sure that you get a fast processor. In a traditional file server setting, however, NetWare is very seldom, if ever, processor bound. If you currently have a server and are looking to upgrade, look at the server utilization value on the MONITOR.NLM's main screen as seen in Figure 6.2.

The CPU utilization percentage will dynamically change indicating the amount of compute cycles the current tasks are taking. If this number is low (below 25 percent), your server is not currently performing processor intensive tasks (this value should be evaluated over time). If the average server utilization is high (above 70 percent), you may need to get machine with a faster processor, or you may simple need to eliminate a bottle neck (perhaps adding a new LAN card to create a new segment can make the server utilization value drop).

Figure 6.2.
NetWare 4.1's Main
MONITOR.NLM
screen.

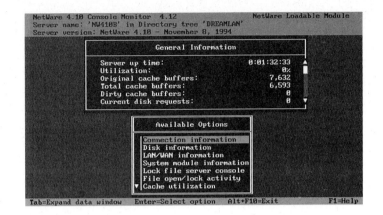

Truly preemptive multitasking simply implies that more than one application can operate at the same time, which means that the processor will allow an application, such as NetWare, to take control of the processor so that it can control time-critical tasks when it needs to.

Multithreading enables an application to use several threads to simultaneously run sub-programs. Or in other words, the application can performing more than on simultaneous function.

Virtual memory management enables the processor to access memory beyond the previous 16MB limit.

The following are short descriptions of available Intel server class processors. These descriptions provide a technical explanation of why the processors differ, and in which situations they should or should not be used.

386 SX

The 386 SX is Intel's low end 32-bit processor and is the minimal requirement for most network operating systems. The 386 SX has limited capabilities; specifically, the limitation of only being able to transfer memory in a 16-bit fashion. Furthermore, it can only address a total of 16MB of memory. There is not much room for the 386 SX as a server processor.

386 DX

The 386 DX processor is a true 32-bit processor capable of handling a 32-bit data path, 4GB of physical memory, and 64TB of virtual memory. This true 32-bit processor makes *concurrent network processing* possible. Concurrent network processing consists of several connections (workstations) that can simultaneously utilize different portions of the server's processor. The 386 DX line of Intel processors is indeed useful in the network server market; filling the low-end traditional file server role.

486

The 486 is offered in several models: the SX line, the DX 25, DX33, the DX 50, the DX2, and the DX4. The DX indicates that it is a "true" 486 and not a 486 SX. The number behind the DX (25, 33, 50, and so on) represents the speed at which the processor can operate (the higher the number the faster the processor). The 486 SX line of processors, like the 386 SX counterpart, are the "low-end" of Intel's 486 chip family. The 486 SX processor has the same optimized instruction set and internal cache as the DX line but does not offer a floating point unit (FPU). Because of this, as a server processor, it will not provide a significant amount of advantage over the 386 DX processors. Furthermore, the cost difference between a 486 SX and a 486 DX is minimal. So, if at all possible, you should purchase a 486 DX server; it is definitely faster. The server will be faster because, sophisticated network operating systems, such as NetWare, can sense that a 486 CPU is on-board, and automatically takes advantage of the special instruction set that the 486 offers.

The 486's memory interface benefits from a cache controller and 8KB of *internal cache*. The internal cache is located inside of the 486's architecture, where it increases the speed at which it processes commands, especially 32-bit commands (network type instructions). A 486's cache uses what is called *four-way set association*. This is basically a data transfer burst mode that allows the processor to send four 32-bit instructions in five clock cycles (in a best case scenario the 386 would take eight clock cycles). Thus, the cache controller, internal cache, burst transfers, built-in math co-processor, and 1.2 million transistors resoundingly make the 486 chip preferred over the 386 processor for a network server.

DX (Overdrive) Processors

There are two versions of the speed doubling processors: the DX2 and the DX4. The DX2 series of processors will internally double the speed at which the 486 DX 33 MHz (also a 25 MHz version) processor can compute, becoming a 486 DX2 66 MHz (meaning it takes half the time to perform the same calculations as its DX counterpart). The DX4 processor triples the speed at which the processor can normally compute, becoming a 486 99 MHz. Both of these processors are based on the 486 processor and will increase the internal speed of the processor.

The only doubling or tripling that actually takes place in either of the CPUs is the core logic processing and internal operations; all other operations remain in sync with the system's clock. So, in a server, the speed of the traffic moving across the network segment and from the disk channel is not going to double; once the traffic is in the processor, calculation will be faster. The only portion of the server that will be directly affected is the CPU processes, this means that database servers, or servers running CPU intensive applications benefit the most from a speed doubling processor.

Note

> Doubling or tripling the speed of the processor only changes the server's utilization by cutting the "CPU busy time" in half (the processors are completing the calculations in a shorter time). Thus, cutting *average CPU utilization* in half.

The performance of an application server, or other uses of the server's processor, will improve with a speed DX2 or DX4 processor. With a "speed enhanced" processor, functions such as a database sort will be improved. Even a traditional file server will see increased performance by using a "boosted" CPU, but in all cases, only those functions that directly use the server's processor will show increased performance.

PENTIUM

The Pentium is Intel's newest processor. This is the only Intel processor that is officially rated in millions of instructions per second (Mips) rather than MHz. Even though the Pentium is hard to compare with the 486, it boasts five times as much speed as the fastest 486 processors. The speed of the Pentium processor makes it Intel's most aggressive attempt at entering the market for non-Intel networking systems.

The Pentium includes a 64-bit data bus (twice as wide as a 486) and supports the new generation of 10-nanosecond error checking, data integrity, dynamic RAM. The Pentium operates at 66 MHz, 90 MHz, 99 MHz, and 128 MHz. It has 16K internal cache (twice as much as the 486), has a 32-bit instruction set, and uses a 64-bit data path. Intel Pentiums also use a *superscalar architecture*, which has two integer units that can process instructions in parallel, thus giving the Pentium the capability to process two instructions per clock cycle (in a best case scenario the 386 consumes eight clock cycles for four 32-bit instructions, while the bursting capabilities of the 486 accomplishes the same task in five clock cycles).

Note

> Just purchasing a motherboard with a Pentium processor will not automatically give you better, or the best performance. Some motherboard designs are not capable of handling the data path demands of the Pentium processors. To take advantage of the Pentium, motherboard manufactures need to design the motherboard around the advantages of the Pentium.

This section contains a large amount of information, but the important point is that the processor affects server performance and is a vital component of the motherboard. Do not purchase the server strictly on the processor's performance, however; the processor is only one component of a server that affects the file server's speed (the amount of memory your server has is usually more of a determining factor of a traditional file server's speed). Another factor, and usually the most limiting factor of a file server's speed is the bus. The following section discusses the available bus architectures and briefly hits each architecture's highlights.

Bus Architectures

When the desktop computer was first introduced, vendors used proprietary bus designs. But it did not take long for vendors and users alike to realize that if a standard were created, third party vendor products would work in any bus. Understanding the different bus standards is an important consideration to understand when selecting a server.

The computer's bus is one of the most often overlooked, and yet important components of a file server's speed; it is important because all the data coming and going from the file server has to be passed across the bus from the server's memory, to the processor, and then back across the bus to the appropriate channel (disk controller or LAN adapter).

The speed of the bus is determined by three variables: the bus transfer rate, the amount of parallel data bits that it can transfer, and the amount of cycles consumed to complete the transfer. This means that if the bus cannot "keep up" with the processor, the processor will simply have to wait.

ISA

The *Industry Standard Architecture* (ISA) bus was first introduced as an 8-bit bus released in the IBM PC. The standard ISA bus transfers data in 8-bit chunks at 4.77 MHz. The fist ISA buses had transferred data at the same speed as the processor.

IBM then introduced the AT computer, with a bus and processor speed of about 6 MHz. Shortly after the 6 MHz version, IBM introduced an AT computer that had an 8 MHz processor and the AT bus speed was also increased to 8 MHz. Thus, when clone manufactures began to introduce AT machines, they rightly assumed that an AT with a 12 MHz processor should have a 12 MHz bus speed. This soon led to incompatibilities with earlier expansion boards designed for the slower bus speeds. The solution was to set a standard, thus the ISA bus was destined to run at 8 MHz.

Note

Every card in the ISA bus needs to use a different interrupt line to signal the PC's Processor that it needs to access or use the bus. So when putting cards in the bus be sure that you are not duplicating interrupts on any of the expansion cards.

One of the biggest disadvantages of the ISA bus, besides bandwidth, is the lack of capability to arbitrate control, or to have multiple expansion cards have direct memory or CPU access. This disadvantage is expounded with the advent of Intel's 386 processor capable of preemptive multitasking, multithreading, and virtual memory management. To take advantage of the 386 capability to perform these higher functions, some manufactures began to build and sell proprietary 32-bit memory boards (so they could at least get around the ISA buses memory access limitations). After seeing the extraordinary throughput of the 32-bit bus, it did not take long for developers to realize its efficiency and potential.

Note

The first ISA busses boasted an 8-bit data path. Not far behind the 8-bit path was development of the 16-bit path. Since the birth of the 16-bit ISA bus, it has not changed and is currently used in original form today. The speed of the 16-bit ISA bus is a little over 8 MHz and it takes two cycles to transfer 16 bits. This means that 2 bytes are transferred per cycle. Therefore, the theoretical maximum transfer is a little over 8 MB/sec.

Regardless of bus design, memory access usually takes up about one-third of the theoretical maximum transfer rate. So after memory access overhead, an ISA bus computer's *theoretical sustained transfers* reaches its limit at about 5 MB/sec.

A theoretical sustained transfer is the most data that could possibly be transferred, after accounting for memory overhead. In other words, if there were no other limiting factors, and a card was as fast as it possibly could be, it could still only transfer 5 MB/sec. But there are other limiting factors, besides memory overhead. Other cards in the bus have to also have a turn to transfer data. After taking this into consideration, the maximum sustained transfer rate of today's ISA bus is about 1 to 2 MB/sec. This is why there is not much argument against the fact that if the wrong bus is used in a server, it is the most limiting factor of the server.

Motherboard manufactures began looking for a technology to enable the bus to better take advantage of the processor's increased power. One example that was introduced is the bus-mastering technology. Bus-mastering is not a bus redesign, but rather, a technique available for all current 16-bit and 32-bit buses. It enables an expansion device (such as a disk controller or network interface card), to move control of the bus from the processor to the expansion device itself. This technique temporarily releases the processor of its data flow obligations, freeing it up to process something else. However, this didn't completely solve the problem because the ISA bus design—it does nothing to solve the ISA buses bus management or bus arbitration deficiencies, which *are* methods of negotiating which bus-mastering device has control of the bus. Thus, problems can occur when more than one bus-mastering device is installed in the same machine.

For this reason advanced bus technologies where designed. Some of the new designs include following:

◆ Micro Channel architecture (MCA)

◆ EISA

◆ VLB

◆ PCI

◆ Proprietary bus designs

MCA

IBM led the way into the 32-bit bus world by introducing the Micro Channel architecture. This bus design makes bus-mastering devices arbitrate for control by forcing them to send signals that indicate a priority rating. This full arbitration adeptness is fully manageable with priorities assigned during system setup, along with interrupts, I/O addresses, and other configuration parameters.

In the Micro Channel architecture, arbitration can be set up in one of two methods: *linear*, which returns control to the master with the highest priority until the transfer is completed; and *fairness*, which in a sense, divides the pie into equal slices. No device, regardless of priority, can regain control of the bus until each device that is contending for the bus has equal opportunity to use it.

Typically, control or the right to generate a transfer across the bus must be arbitrated for every 32-bits. This overhead can be somewhat eliminated by implementing "burst mode" (not to be confused with a processors burst mode). Bursting allows a device to resume control of the bus for approximately 15 milliseconds. During this period of time, a device can carry out multiple transfers, but once time is up, the device has to relinquish control and once again contend for the right to make a data transfer.

Micro Channel theoretically reaches a maximum speed of 40MB/sec. Additional mechanisms, called streaming and multiplexing, push the MCA's bus to its limits. For example, when a device gets control of the bus, every transfer has to be accompanied by a beginning address; likewise, an ending address must also be sent. Generally, every chunk of data (roughly a word) has to communicate a beginning and ending address. Streaming on the other hand, allows a beginning address to be delivered at the beginning and end of a "paragraph" rather than a word. Multiplexing simultaneously transfers streamed bytes across the address lines as data is being transferred across the standard data path. In effect, this creates a 64-bit bus. The disadvantage of MCA is its lack of backward compatibility with the ISA bus.

EISA

A group of reputable clone manufactures decided to develop a 32-bit bus of their own, the *Extended Industry Standard Architecture* (EISA). The most notable advantage of the EISA design is that it remained backward compatible with the ISA bus. This enabled users to utilize existing ISA cards. And EISA, unlike the ISA bus, has an arbitration mechanism that enables it to take advantage of bus-mastering techniques mentioned earlier.

Note

Originally, the industry called the ISA bus computers AT class machines. It wasn't until after the EISA (Extended Industry Standard Architecture) bus was released that somebody thought that if the industry was going to have an Extended Industry Standard Architecture that there should be an Industry Standard Architecture, and so the AT machines were referred to as Industry Standard Architecture (ISA).

EISA mediates control of the bus in cycles and *epicycles* (cycles within cycles). Each of the three system functions is assigned a cycle: memory refresh, direct memory access (DMA), and the necessity to relinquishing control of the bus to a bus-mastering device. In similitude of the MCA design, each bus-mastering device (or master) in an EISA machine must also be assigned a priority level.

During a single cycle, each epicycle has to be completed. In other words, all three of the previously mentioned functions are completed at least once during a given cycle. For each cycle, according to the devices priority, a different bus-mastering device is given the opportunity to gain control of the bus and initiate its transfer.

During burst mode transfers, the theoretical maximum speed of the EISA bus approaches 33MB/sec. After system functions (memory access) gobble up approximately a third of the theoretical maximum, the maximum sustainable rate drops to approximately 22.33MB/sec (MCA is no different). At first, when you look at sustained transfer rates of a fast disk controller at about 10MB/sec, it seems significantly fast. However, if you place two controllers in the bus you quickly reach 20MB/sec. It won't take long for the EISA bus to be inadequate. This issue will be addressed later, for now, let's concentrate on the EISA advantage.

Tests performed on Ethernet cards show the efficiency of the EISA (or MCA) style bus versus the ISA. If the same data intensive test is executed on ISA and EISA cards, for example, average aggregate throughput could very possibly be the same. In fact, it is possible that some ISA cards could outperform an EISA adapter. However, if average CPU utilization (the amount of time the processor is free to do other tasks) is tracked, you will find that the EISA cards will generally use less than a third as much CPU processes as its ISA counterpart. Thus, if your plans are to use multiple LAN segments (more than one NIC), EISA or MCA would be the bus of choice.

With a single bus-mastering device installed, EISA and MCA machines are fairly equivalent. But, MCA has enhancements that allow for greater system configuration and subsequently greater optimization and performance. When multiple bus-mastering devices are present, for example, streaming and multiplexing can provide an advantage.

The biggest downfall of IBM's MCA technology is that it has not been as widely accepted as the EISA bus. But, IBM might be able to stretch the life of the MCA bus by implementing Intel's Pentium processor, which will utilize MCA's 64-bit capabilities. Conversely, EISA's life may be limited. Unlike MCA, EISA does not have the backing of IBM, nor does it allow for 64-bit transfers. EISA's only hope for prolonged life is for a new EISA standard to be developed that supports faster 64-bit transfers. If such a standard is ever agreed on, people might not be as quick to dump a machine with an EISA bus, especially if the new standard is backward compatible. A standard, called FAST EISA is, in fact, on the drawing table. It is touting a 64-bit 130MB/sec I/O bus.

VESA (Local Bus)

There is not much doubt that today's bus technologies are a major contributing factor to the performance limits of the PC. For this reason, a consortium of more than 120 companies allied as VESA (Video Equipment Standards Association) came together and developed a standard called VL-Bus or VESA (VLB). This bus implementation enables the video cards, as well other cards, to directly access the processor, meaning that they can transfer data at the speed of the processor (up to 33 MHz).

The advantages of the Local Bus solution are actually very plentiful: it will coexist with all former bus designs. It offers backward compatibility with the 8-bit and

16-bit ISA standards, and it offers improved performance; theoretically, it can transfer data at rates as high as 132MB/sec.

The disadvantages, however, limit the usefulness of the VESA standard in network implementations. Its biggest disadvantage is that it was implemented with Video in mind, and while it produces some phenomenal benefits for Video it limits its usefulness in the networking community. It biggest limitation is that the current VESA committee only recommends three VL-Bus slots per machine. This means that this solution will only be suitable for small networks.

Note

With only three slots available, the VLB bus design has limited functionality for a Network server: one slot will be used by the disk controller, one by the Ethernet card. This means that you have one left. You can use it to duplex drives or to put in another NIC. However, you often need to do both.

The VESA committee claims that provisions are being made so that the standard will accommodate as many as 10 VL-Bus slots per motherboard, and these provisions also include support for a "mezzanine" bus (64-bit). The mezzanine bus will take advantage of the Pentium processor. Until that time, however, the VESA local bus will have a hard time capturing any significant interest in the networking arena (at least as a serious server).

PCI

In 1994, Intel also entered its Peripheral Component Interconnect (PCI) into the bus race. Intel's solution is more complex and farsighted than VESA's proposed solution. Besides the obvious (tighter integration with the CPU and support for future processors), Intel's solution has the following benefits:

◆ It brags of supporting concurrent bus-mastering

◆ It suggests a pipelining queue that will ultimately minimize the number of wait-states

◆ It offers a full burst mode, sports reflective wave signaling that reduces noise problems

◆ It boasts of implementing multiplexing

OTHER BUS TYPES

The concept of bus technologies and their bottlenecks gets even more confusing, not to mention heated, when you start discussing the bus technologies around "high-end server" manufactures. Each has its own ideas as to the appropriate way a bus should be designed. This section quickly introduces some of the more popular, yet proprietary "high-end" network server bus designs.

TriFlex

TriFlex architecture is a proprietary, yet backwards compatible bus, designed by Compaq for its System Pro-XL line of servers. The TriFlex Architecture splits the standard bus implementation into three individual subsystem components I/O bus, memory access, and processor.

The purpose driving the TriFlex architecture is performance without sacrificing upgradability or backward compatibility. It features a 64-bit processor bus that is capable of transferring data from the processor to RAM at a rate of 256MB/sec. It uses a 128-bit memory bus to transfer data from the memory to the processor at 267 Mb/sec. It also uses a 32-bit EISA bus for the I/O path. In the center of the busses, Compaq uses a bi-directional, multi-stage, buffering system called a data-flow manager. It can buffer or cache up to 16 EISA transfers, as well as four processor transfers, at the same time. This allows EISA devices to simultaneously access memory more than 70 percent of the time.

The reason that Compaq elected to use the EISA bus for the I/O pathway is that it ensures backward compatibility with EISA cards. The overall design provides backward compatibility and future upgradability. For example, straight off the "press" can house a 386 32-bit processor, a 486 32-bit processor, a Pentium 64-bit processor, or all three.

Powerbus

The *Powerbus* is Tricord's answer to high-end bus design and is found in its Powerframe machines. These servers are designed around intelligent subsystems and targeted at the enterprise networking market. These servers offer symmetrical processing, a 32-bit 132MB/sec powerbus, which boasts individual proprietary disk channels capable of transferring 30MB/sec. These disk channels house intelligent I/O processor disk controllers that can effectively manage four disks. It has an EISA I/O bus for backward EISA NIC compatibility with the EISA bus being independent of the disk channel bus.

Hierarchical Bus

The *Hierarchical Bus* is yet another proprietary bus architecture designed by NetFRAME. The NetFRAME family of servers designed around a *Multi-Processor Server Architecture* (MPSA). The MPSA architecture uses multiple independent buses for I/O, with each independent bus being capable of transferring 12.5MB/sec.

The I/O bus is designed to support multiple processors. All the data passing through the bus is independent of the other buses that might be in use.

The data is then aggregated into a wider bus (100MB/sec). This hierarchical approach is accompanied by a 200MB/sec memory channel. In a sense, this design starts with small independent pipes, with each pipe running into a bigger pipe. A server with this kind of speed is designed and priced for the medium to large network.

These are not the only "other bus" designs available. Several other vendors have designed and manufactured computers directly aimed at the network server environment.

FIXED DISK DRIVES

Because fixed disk reads and writes comprise a major part of the daily network operations, the *fixed disk drive* subsystem is another important performance factor of a NetWare server. In fact, the majority of the server activity is fixed disk drive access and data retrieval, so it is very important.

This section provides information on how NetWare handles read and write requests, and how this affects overall network performance. It also covers some of the more popular drive implementations as well as explains the Redundant Array of Inexpensive disk (RAID) technologies.

To understand how the disk channel can be such a major contributor to the performance of your NetWare server, it is necessary to understand how NetWare's disk caching handles disk requests. Understanding NetWare's disk caching also will help you determine whether your particular environment would benefit from having a caching hard drive or controller. With this understanding, you will be able to configure your server to help alleviate fixed disk drive subsystem bottlenecks.

Note

The most common bottleneck in a NetWare environment usually is the disk or NIC channel. These bottlenecks can result from inefficient use of NetWare's cache, the disk driver, the disk itself, the amount of memory in the server, and so on.

NETWARE'S READ/WRITE REQUEST HANDLING

NetWare's disk caching, under normal circumstances, satisfies most disk I/O requests.

As the system processes read\write requests, these requests are posted or written into the cache area. To provide faster access, when a user station requests the data, the data is actually obtained from the cache memory and not from the fixed disk. Because almost all requests go through the cache, caching makes disk reads far more efficient.

When a write request enters the cache, NetWare reports to the application that the write operation has been completed successfully, multiple write requests will then accumulate. Netware can then pass these request to the elevator, and when the cache is full, or when the DIRTY DISK CACHE DELAY TIME is reached, these write requests can then be written. To determine how effective your cache configuration is, look at the cache hit ratios found in the Cache Utilization screen of the MONITOR.NLM utility. As seen in Figure 6.3, the short term utilization is better, the closer it is to 100 percent.

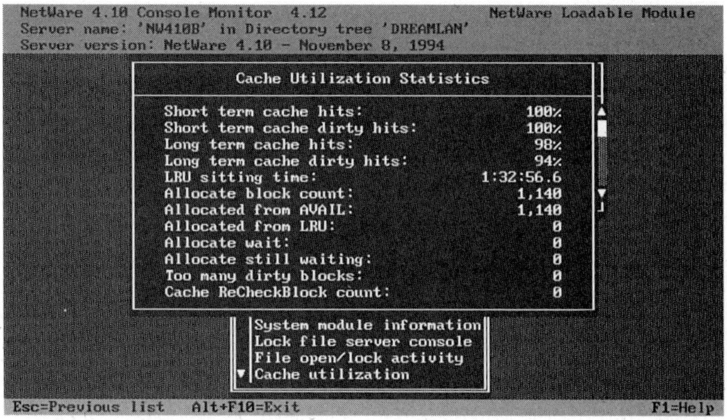

Figure 6.3.
NetWare 4's Cache
Utilization screen.

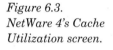

By delaying writes NetWare can provide a more effective method of processing requests. For example, if a user requests to write 512 bytes of data to the server, (since the 512 bytes of data is only equal to one sector) NetWare's cache stores that data and combines it with another write request. NetWare, will thus, have better response times. Because read requests "data that needs to be retrieved from the file server" will be serviced first.

Note

When configuring your server's subsystems there are two console settings that you can use to alter NetWare's settings: SET MAXIMUM CONCURRENT DISK CACHE WRITES, and SET DIRTY CACHE DELAY TIME. Both of these setting can be changed using the new NetWare 4 utility called SERVMAN.NLM.

The first setting can be used to tell NetWare to hold more write requests in the queue, before writing them to disk. Users usually are unaware that writes are being delayed. By delaying writes you enable NetWare to service more reads (which improves performance). However, delaying writes also introduces some risk. If you have transaction tracking enabled and you also have UPS, however, you probably will never have a problem.

The second setting, SET DIRTY CACHE DELAY TIME enables you to control the amount of time the cache will hold a request that does not fill the buffer. By forcing the cache to hold write requests longer, you make more efficient use of the cache area.

Because all requests pass through the fixed disk device driver, the device driver plays an very important role in the network server's overall performance. In other operating systems, such as DOS, the BIOS of the computer handles the disk I/O. In NetWare, however, the BIOS is not used; rather, a device driver handles all disk I/O requests.

When shopping around for a disk drive, most people tend to get stuck in the search for the physical device, the drive. However, the drive doesn't have as much to do with the speed of a disk subsystem as the devices driver does. In fact, some manufactures can claim as much as 25 percent increase in speed, just by updating a device driver. So, the importance of understanding that the disk driver is largely responsible for the disk's speed can not be stressed enough.

With this in mind look for a disk subsystem that offers "NetWare aware" features. For instance, Data unmingling, Data fusion, Tagged command queuing, and so on.

If you find yourself responsible for the task of finding the perfect server, remember that technology is changing quickly, especially the technology used in the drive subsystems. The trick is to find a drive that will support the high-performance systems of today, and yet not be obsolete tomorrow. When looking for a disk subsystem, be sure to balance the drive system with the overall capabilities of the server. This includes looking at the bus, the controller, and even the disk driver. Also, when considering storage technology, try to determine capacity needs. Only after defining these needs can a storage device be chosen.

Note

NetWare mingles, or mixes, read and write requests together on its elevator queues. By mixing read and write requests, NetWare assumes that both are equally important. In some situations, however, you want the users to have immediate access to data, meaning that in your environment, reads are more important. Some disk drivers will allow you to "unmingle" read and write requests. The result is improvement in the apparent response time perceived by the users on the network.

Data fusion is a technique that combines requests so that one large access from the drive can be performed, rather than multiple small requests. This type of feature will improve performance by enabling NetWare to retrieve data in a more sequential fashion.

Tagged command queuing is used by several of the faster SCSI disk subsystems. This feature enables several requests for a single drive to be grouped together and delivered at a single time. Drives that support tagged command queuing are able to queue up to as many as 256 requests. Just because a drive has the capability to queue up commands, however, it does not mean that the driver is taking advantage of this feature. Besides increasing performance, tagged command queuing can increase drive efficiency by reducing mechanical movements of the drive.

For background information, the following section discusses various physical disk storage technologies and implementations. It is important to understand the advantages and disadvantages of each of these technologies, but the difference in a high performance system and a mediocre system is more often the device driver and memory configuration.

ESDI

ESDI (pronounced Ess-dee) stands for *Enhanced Small-Device Interface*, which was a technology one step up from the old ST-506 drives. At the time, these drives offered better throughput than the ST-506 drives. They also enabled the user to store greater capacities on a single drive. ESDI also offered greater intelligence, by reducing the amount of communication needed between the drive and the controller, which in turn, increases efficiency. ESDI, however, was simply a stepping stone that was passed up by IDE and SCSI.

With the ESDI technology, the CPU of the file server is forced to manage the ESDI drives, which limits its usefulness or suitability for the networking environment. In addition, ESDI drives have a serial interface, which sends format and sector information as well as data. So, the transfer rate of ESDI drives are not that impressive, especially in a multitasking environment, such as NetWare.

IDE

As its name implies, *IDE* (Integrated Drive Electronics) combines both the disk and the controller on the same unit, the drive. IDE uses a 16-bit parallel interface that is responsible for transferring data (no format of sector information). Because of this, IDE drives offer better transfer rates, higher throughput, and even faster access than ESDI drives. IDE drives are very reasonably priced, which makes them an attractive alternative for the "small" (those that do not need large data storage capacities) price-sensitive customer.

IDE, however, has some disadvantages, specifically storage capacity and data throughput. IDE drives generally are thought of as having medium-capacity storage capabilities, which range from 40MB to 1.2 gigabytes. Also, IDE drives are not a physically formatted device, which makes it difficult for them to be efficiently accessed by a network operating system. Each time the operating system tries to transfer data to the drive, for example, the drive must read the data, translate the appropriate place to put the data, and then write the data. Furthermore, normal IDE implementations only support two devices on the same controller: the first is the master, and the second the slave. The IDE drive slave-master routine is not optimized for multiple drive circumstances that abound in network implementations.

Tip

You cannot perform low-level format on most IDE drives without special utilities because it is not a device-level interface. IDE has the capability to give your BIOS the logical appearance of a known drive type, while physically it may be different. This is the reason you will not see bad tracks on your disk—IDE hides them from you. With translation mode, IDE drives are capable of automatically matching their logical drive appearance with the drive type your computer expects to see.

The overhead that IDE drives impose, the limited storage capacities, and the slave-master routine restricts IDE drives to small networks that are not particularly concerned with expansion, storage capacity, or speed.

SCSI

The technology pronounced "Scuzzy" is today's resounding choice for network drive implementations. There are a couple of reasons for this almost unanimous vote. First, SCSI stands for Small Computer Systems Interface technology. The word "small," however, is often misunderstood.

SCSI technology offers the largest capacity devices and the most flexible implementations in the "small" (network server rather than mainframe) LAN environments. Second, the SCSI technology and its implementation in the LAN environment is supported by a large number of vendors. This means that drives, controllers, subsystems, and so on, do not have to be purchased from the same vendor. Another compelling reason that SCSI has been so widely accepted is its capability to hook attach unlike devices to the same channel. For example, you can have your SCSI controller run you hard disk, your tape backup, and your CD-ROM devices.

All SCSI drives are not created equal, however. Simply purchasing a SCSI drive will not solve all of your problems; it merely narrows the available selections. Also, the SCSI technology has undergone several revisions in its life, and it is necessary that these SCSI revisions be carefully implemented to correctly balance the capabilities of your server and operating system.

Note

SCSI controllers can currently sustain the highest data throughput; however, there is a significant difference between the capabilities of an ISA SCSI controller and a EISA controller.

So, when looking for a SCSI device, remember that what you are trying to do is balance all the server's systems—match the bus and processor, purchase a disk controller that is equally suited for the bus, and select a hard drive that can function at the same operating speed as the controller. For example, it makes no sense to purchase the power of an EISA server without using EISA NIC's or EISA SCSI disk controllers, other than for possible upgrades options. By balancing the system, you can get the most out of each component; you do not want to purchase an expensive machine and then handicap it with an inappropriate drive system.

As mentioned previously, SCSI has undergone several revisions, or enhancements. Fast SCSI-2, for example, has a transfer rate that peaks at 12MB/sec and can sustain an equally impressive 9MB/sec. Other SCSI implementations directed at boosting speeds are Fast SCSI, Wide SCSI, and Fast Wide SCSI. Fast SCSI doubles the clock speed, while Wide SCSI increases the bus width, and Fast Wide SCSI combines the options. Each of these options then have the capability to add additional performance-boosting features, including controller-based RAM caching and tag-command queuing. By queuing commands from the CPU, the processor is immediately free to process other requests while the drive finishes its task. The SCSI technology can prioritize commands in the queue to maximize efficiency.

SCSI hard disks tout the fastest transfer rates of the discussed technologies, boasting the capability to transfer data at rates of up to 40MB per second. Two Fast SCSI-2 controllers in a duplexed mode could come close to completely utilizing an EISA server's power. Duplexing controllers creates two independent disk channels, especially when used in a redundant fashion. This dual channel configuration allows disk transfer rates to peak at an incredible 24MB/sec and sustain an even more incredible 20MB/sec.

Plans for SCSI 3 include enhancements of current features and the capability to handle more than eight daisy-chained devices. So, for high performance, high capacity, and high flexibility in a high-traffic LAN environment, SCSI "fits the bill."

All these improvements are building on the reason that SCSI is the resounding choice for a network server drive technology. Although the SCSI drive technology has passed the bottleneck blame to other portions of the server, however, it, by itself, does not accommodate for the massive amounts of storage space that is needed and supported by today's network Operating Systems. For this reason, a new market has emerged—the disk subsystem market. Vendors participating in this market usually include several disks that operate on the same SCSI controller(s).

REDUNDANT ARRAY OF INEXPENSIVE DISKS (RAID)

NetWare's capability to access massive amounts of disk storage has prompted the development of disk storage systems. One of the most popular being *RAID* (Redundant Array of Inexpensive Disks).

RAID is basically a method of spreading your data over multiple drives and then introducing redundancy into a disk subsystem to improve reliability. This redundancy allows the network to continue at almost normal capacities (parity information cause some overhead), it even allows you to recover or reconstruct the lost data onto a new disk drive.

RAID originally was developed to increase drive capacity and performance. Because of its natural drive redundancy, however, it is now being marketed as a fault-tolerant storage solution. The redundancy factor is simply a way of mitigating the negative effects of daisy-chaining drives. Without redundancy, chaining or spanning drives increases the chance of drive failure. If a single drive had a Mean Time

Between Failure (MTBF) of 50,000 hours and two spanned drives create a single volume, for example, the MTBF is cut in half, meaning that the volume is twice as likely to go down.

Numerous manufacturers are now implementing RAID using the SCSI technology. These implementations improve drive performance, storage capacity, and overall disk subsystem reliability. The following section ("RAID Implementations") takes and in-depth look at this technology.

Note

The name RAID stands for Redundant Array of Inexpensive Disks, but is often said to refer to Redundant Array of Independent Disks.

RAID IMPLEMENTATIONS

There are two types of RAID technology: software and hardware. A software RAID solution checks and stores parity information, reconstructs drives, and provides warnings by software. Software RAID implementations use the server's CPU and RAM. But, these are insignificant tradeoffs when considering the cost a complete hardware RAID solution.

Hardware solutions do not burden the server, but rather use proprietary components to check parity, track data, and rebuild the drive. Being proprietary, these hardware components often are expensive. Hardware RAID devices do not necessarily increase fault tolerance or performance.

UNDERSTANDING THE DIFFERENT RAID LEVELS

Because the RAID implementations are designated as levels 0 through 5, a hierarchical misconception of 5 being better than one has emerged. This fallacy draws support from RAID 5 being the newer technology. The truth is that a RAID 5 subsystem is not inherently better than a RAID 1 subsystem. RAID is simply a different designation of how the data is to be stored on the disk subsystem; each has a different purpose. To understand which RAID level is best for your specific needs, you must first understand the different levels. However, this is not a simple task.

Understanding RAID is confusing because each vendor has its own idea of what RAID means. To add disarray to confusion, each vendor uses a proprietary method to implement the different levels of the RAID technology. Each RAID level is at best a conceptual standard; how the concept is implemented is not; therefore, it is impossible to describe every possible RAID implementation.

RAID 0

RAID 0 is actually disk stripping, which allows information to be written across multiple disks rather than onto a single disk. This allows the network operating system to view multiple small drives as a single large component, even though they are physically distinct, as seen in Figure 6.4.

Figure 6.4.
An example of disk
spanning.

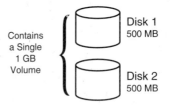

Although RAID 0 is not a true RAID solution, an understanding of RAID 0 remains important because it used in conjunction with other RAID levels. In fact, RAID 0 is very similar to disk spanning, but unlike disk spanning, RAID 0 or stripping balances the load across all the disks in the array, as seen in Figure 6.5.

Figure 6.5.
An example of a disk
stripping.

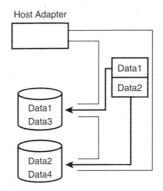

When drives are spanned, data is written sequentially by segment across the array. (A segment is a definable number of blocks—if you are using a 512-byte block size and define the segment to be eight blocks, your segment size would be 4K.) RAID 0 is not a true RAID level because it does not introduce any redundancy. Disk stripping simply allows data to be written across multiple drives, which in turn allows network operating systems to view multiple drives as a single component; even though they are physically separate.

Disk stripping will copy or save a file to the disk in the following manner: the first segment will be written to Drive 0, the second segment to Drive 1, the third segment to Drive 2, and so on, as seen in Figure 6.6. When it reaches the end of the drive array, it returns to Drive 0 and the process starts again.

Figure 6.6.
An example of how
data is stored on a
spanned stripped disk.

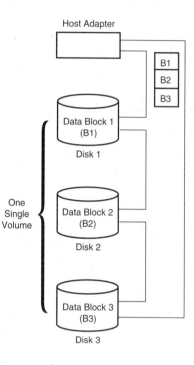

If the software is written correctly, RAID 0 will provide a certain amount of increased performance. In order for RAID 0 to demonstrate an increase in speed, the software has to allow the disks in the array to write data across the spanned devices concurrently.

Warning

Disk stripping and spanning allows several multiple small drives to function as a single large unit and, therefore, is very useful. However, it does nothing to increase overall reliability. What happens to one drive happens to all. For example, if a single drive in the array fails, so does the entire array. Because the chances of an array failing increase as you increase the number of spanned drives, the chance of the entire subsystem failing increases.

If networking is going to be the downsizing answer that people believe it to be, fault tolerant spanning of data is mandatory. The drawbacks of RAID 0 have made it obvious that other fault tolerant schemes must be implemented; by itself, simple spanning is not the solution. Consequently, other levels of RAID address the issue of spanning drives and also implementing a level of fault tolerance.

RAID 1

RAID 1 often is referred to in simple terms, such as drive mirroring or drive shadowing; this section refers to it as drive mirroring. *Drive mirroring* provides subsystem fault tolerance and can boast 100 percent data redundancy, because as its name implies, drive mirroring completely duplicates any information that is written to the first drive onto the second drive.

Drive mirroring was one of the first fault tolerant technologies available to network subsystems. In fact, most of the network operating systems built mirroring capabilities into the actual operating system. It is the primary method of adding fault tolerance to networks because it is the best understood and easiest to implement.

There are several ways of implementing drive mirroring. The first and most common is simply known as *standard mirroring*. In a standard mirror implementation, a single host adapter (controller) runs both drives. When data is manipulated on one of the drives, an exact mirror is reflected on the other drive. The drawback of standard mirroring is the single host adapter (controller), it is a single point of failure, as well as a potential bottleneck.

The second implementation of mirroring, *duplex mirroring*, alleviates the bottleneck and can eliminate the single point of failure (if used redundantly). Figure 6.7 shows the difference between a standard mirroring and duplexed mirroring.

Figure 6.7.
Standard mirroring
versus duplexing.

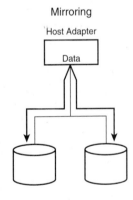

Mirroring

Host Adapter

Data

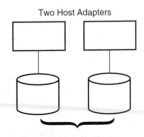

Duplexing

Two Host Adapters

Duplexing uses two host adapters and allows the drives to be accessed simultaneously, or in a parallel fashion. The capability for an operating system to split disk reads between the two disk channels is one of RAID 1's advantages; however, this advantage is almost nullified, because data must be written on both drives. This duplication of writes means a 100 percent increase in disk space. The disadvantage, or cost of 100 percent more drive space has to be weighed against the advantage of having an exact duplication or mirror image of your data.

RAID 2

RAID 2 is an attempt to reduce the requirement of 50 percent more disk space, and at the same time still provide a complete duplication of data. Unlike mirroring, RAID 2 takes advantage of the Hamming codes. *Hamming codes* are an error detecting correction solution that was originally written for communications systems. This mathematical solution for storing data lent itself well for disk drives.

RAID 2 accomplishes redundancy by distributing data over multiple drives and bit-interleaving check information with each disk write. The first data-bit is written to the first drive, the second to the second, and so on. In other words, the data spans all the drives in your array. If one drive should fail, RAID 2 uses the data on the remaining drives to rebuild the data on the "crashed" drive.

For a number of reasons, however, RAID 2 is not commonly used in a networking environment. First, the performance is not conducive; in order for a read to take place, all the disks must spin to the correct location on the disk before it can actually pull data off the drive. After the disks retrieve the data, each drive must again find the correct location before writing the data. Second, the Hamming error correction code achieves integrity, but the process requires multiple drives just for error checking. If a system had eight data drives, for example, it would require three drives to store the error correction code information, as seen in Figure 6.8.

Figure 6.8.
An example of RAID 2's
storage technique.

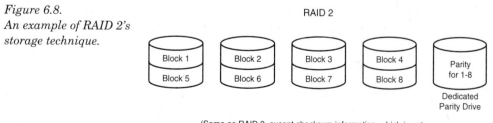

Usable disk space, therefore, ranges from 50 percent in a four-drive system to 73 percent in an 11-drive system. The Hamming error correction code (RAID 2) is, however, useful in the mini- and mainframe-computing environments. Mainframe and mini computers do not use checksumming to track the data bit that contains the error, which is mandatory to rebuild the information from the remaining data; RAID 2 supplies this information for them. PC hardware already provides data bit error information through hardware checksumming; so tracking and storing the data bit that contains the error is expensive and needlessly redundant.

RAID 3

Because drives (such as in the micro computer hardware) can detect and report errors, *RAID 3* is an option. Unlike RAID 2, RAID 3 focuses on maintaining the redundant data necessary to correct any errors rather than store the data bit that contained the error.

RAID 3 stores parity information on a dedicated parity drive as shown in Figure 6.9.

Figure 6.9.
An example of RAID 3's storage technique.

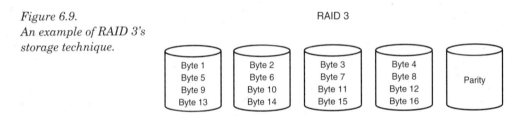

If your system requires four data drives, a fifth drive will be needed to hold the parity information. When a RAID 3 drive fails, the parity on the remaining drives are examined and the information then goes through a bit-by-bit reconstruction; thus, information is accurately restored on the new drive.

Like RAID 2, RAID 3 must access every drive in the array for every single disk request. This allows RAID 3 to process only one disk request at a given time, making it inefficient when operating in transaction mode. For this reason, RAID 3 has not overpopulated the network file server arena. Vendors in the server market, however, have not given up on implementing RAID 3. They still are working on an implementation that would allow RAID 3 to access the data in such a way as to provide concurrent access, or at least a way to increase the throughput of a RAID 3 implementation.

RAID 4

In RAID 3, a block of data is divided and striped across the drives in the array. In *RAID 4*, the entire first block gets written on Drive 1, the second block on Drive 2, and so on. For an example of how data and parity are stored in a RAID 4 system, see Figure 6.10. Because most read transactions involve a single drive, this method of stripping data dramatically increases disk read performance because disk transaction can be independent, allowing the drives in the array to service concurrent read requests.

Figure 6.10.
An example of how
data and parity are
stored in a RAID 4
system.

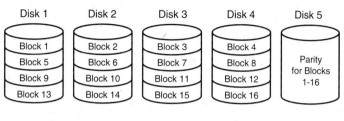

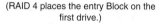

(RAID 4 places the entry Block on the
first drive.)

Note

The question is, "Can data be effectively segmented to individual drives?" Additionally, does the operating system support independent read transaction to each disk? If so, in theory, RAID 4 can effectively lower the mean access time of reads; for example, six drives with an 18ms access time will access information across the array at close to 3ms. But, in practice it is almost impossible to accomplish (as soon as this is said, somebody will accomplish it).

In RAID 4, writing is done to the disk in a fashion similar to the dedicated parity drive of RAID 3, meaning that every write transaction requires a write to the parity drive (not to every drive, just the parity drive).

This limits performance to a single-write transaction at a time. RAID 4 improves throughput over RAID 3, however, because it can use the array's entire bandwidth. So, if your network read-to-write workload ratio is heavy on reads and those reads can be effectively segmented, RAID 4 might be a possible solution. If the write workload ratio is even close to 50 percent, however, then in its current state, RAID 4 would not be the best choice for a RAID implementation.

RAID 5

A *RAID 5* implementation strays from the practice of using a dedicated drive to store parity information. Instead, parity information is spread over all the drives in the array as shown in Figure 6.11.

Combining the parity data and the actual data onto each drive alleviates the single file write restriction present in other levels of RAID. In turn, RAID 5 is capable of multiple concurrent writes, because the transactions are independent. If a drive fails in a RAID 5 system, the controller rebuilds the data from the data and parity on the remaining good drives: if a drive fails, for example, the controller looks at the parity and data on the remaining drives—from this, it could rebuild the data on the lost drive.

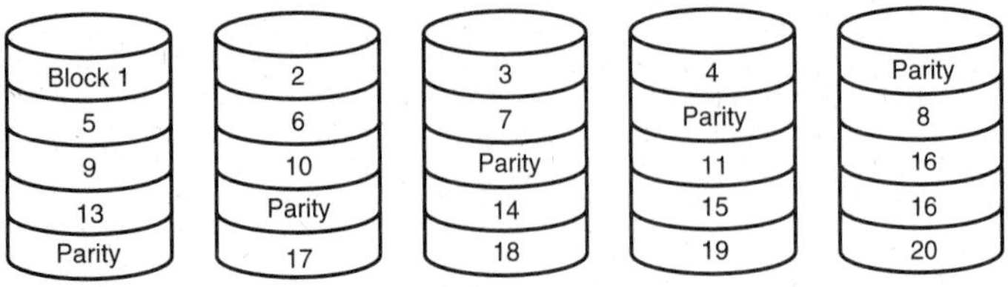

Figure 6.11.
An example of how
RAID 5 combines data
and parity on the same
drive.

Block 1	2	3	4	Parity
5	6	7	Parity	8
9	10	Parity	11	16
13	Parity	14	15	16
Parity	17	18	19	20

This level of RAID is well-suited for file server applications in which there is a high small-block I/O transaction rate. It does well because it is able to do multiple, simultaneous reads and writes. In fact, as you search for a disk subsystem, do not be surprised if the only RAID implementation that you are confronted with is the RAID 5 solution.

THE TRUTH ABOUT RAID SUBSYSTEMS

RAID technology was developed for the mainframe environment with three purposes in mind. In no specific order, these purposes are as follows:

◆ To reduce the costs of disk storage

◆ To increase performance

◆ To increase fault tolerance

Alone, any of these benefits would be marvelous, but together, RAID would provide Local Area Networks with a technology that was extremely valuable. Because of this value, drive manufactures began to "downsize" RAID technology to the LAN, and today, there are several versions, sizes, and shapes of RAID technology available for the LAN environment. Before you run out and purchase a RAID system for your network, however, you should consider the following.

First, are you expecting RAID to be a cheaper option? The LAN market has flourished and been successful, in large part, because it is an inexpensive, flexible, computing solution. This success has attracted more players, which, in turn, has driven the cost of PC components down at a staggering pace. Disk drives are a good example of this competitive market. Not more than a year ago, disk space sold for about three dollars a megabyte; now you can buy physically smaller drives that have the same large capacity, for less than one dollar per megabyte. Remember that one of the reasons RAID was introduced into PC environment was to save money on disk storage costs; but in today's competitive market, does RAID actually equate to a savings? No.

Note

One of the main marketing pitches that you will hear is that RAID solutions save you money because you do not "waste" 50 percent of your disk drive space. But if you look at it from a cost perspective, who cares if you "waste" disk space if that solution is cheaper? In other words, it is less expensive to purchase six 1GB drives and completely mirror the drives, than it is to purchase a four-drive RAID solution—both options provide you with a 3GB storage capacity.

Second, are you hoping that RAID will improve disk performance? There are some situations in which RAID does indeed increases performance, but these situations are the exception and not the rule. Even RAID proponents agree that one of the fastest configurations is RAID 1 (drive spanning) with duplexed controllers. This configuration allows simultaneous reads and writes on separate SCSI channels. And, unlike other version of RAID, this configuration is not slowed down by having to create and store parity information on other drives in the drive span. Furthermore, mirroring and other fault tolerant features comes as a feature of most network operating systems. The bottom line is that all the network environments indicate that RAID will not generally increases performance.

Third, does RAID provide increased fault tolerance? To say, "RAID provides fault tolerance" is a correct statement. But one must hesitate before they say, "RAID provides increased fault tolerance." Certainly there are some nice options in today's RAID devices: hot swappable redundant power supplies, hot pluggable drives, floating spares, increased cache buffers, and so on. But to say, "These features increase fault tolerance" is incorrect; because simple statistics shows that the more components introduced into a system, the greater the chance is for a component failure. So, a more correct statement would be, "RAID devices provide us with more fault recovery options, if a failure does occur."

Another correct statement would be to say, "When a drive fails, RAID allows continued operation." However, it is not correct to say, "Operations continue normally." In order to retrieve data from a failed RAID 3 or RAID 5 drive, parity information must be gathered and used to reconstruct the lost data. This takes time, and all other network operations will be slowed. In a mirrored environment, the drive simply fails and data can be retrieved from the second copy of the drive, without having to reconstruct the data (if your drives are duplexed, performance will also go down).

6

SELECTING AND CONFIGURING HARDWARE

Furthermore, it is incorrect to say, "RAID solutions allow drives and other components be exchanged without taking the network down." This statement is absolutely incorrect because these are not functions of RAID. They are welcomed, value-added features that specific vendors have chosen to include in their subsystems.

Another feature being pushed by RAID vendors is the concept of continued operation. This means that if you have a drive failure, drives can be replaced, data can be restored, and operations never have to stop. But again, these are options of the subsystem and not the functions of RAID.

The original reasons for buying a RAID box are becoming weaker and weaker as single drives become cheaper and faster. But there are still some reasons that can be found for purchasing a RAID system. Not all Network operating systems, for example, provide spanning and mirroring capabilities, more manageable features, remote administration, and so on.

THE FUTURE OF RAID

Competition from "single large drives" and from "just a bunch of drives" will force the price of these systems down, or will cause RAID solutions to offer more valuable options, such as management, remote control, hot swap features, and so on. Network Operating Systems also will begin to include more native RAID options (RAID 5). These forces will cause RAID vendors will to market their RAID boxes for what they really are—a disk subsystem that offers increased disk management, improved awareness of fault tolerance, enhanced alarming features, and finally, RAID support.

DON'T FORGET TO CONSIDER CASE DESIGN

The design of the subsystem case may seem simple and unimportant, but it can play a big part in the amount of flexibility the subsystem has to offer. A small unobtrusive design will fit on a desk, or under a table, or it could even be rack mounted.

A question to ask is, "Are the drives hot swappable, and if so, how easy is it?" Some RAID subsystems come with each of the drives individually housed. The housings have handles and can be easily pulled out. Also look for redundancy in the power supplies. Most subsystems have two power supplies, but not all of these systems allow the power supplies to be changed while the system is running. Also watch out for RAID systems that go completely overboard on redundancy; some systems include a motherboard, a couple of controllers, several power supplies, two or three backup drives, and so on. With all this duplication, the key words "inexpensive array," are thrown out the window.

Because the only standard in RAID implementations is in the way the data is to be stored, the real advantages of RAID will show up in the design and functionality of the overall system. Some vendors will implement software features that provide the subsystem with superior flexibility. The next section discusses some features that you might look for.

RAID SOFTWARE FEATURES

A valid reason for purchasing a RAID solution would be to get the software enhancements that it offers. For example, because most network traffic consists of reads, network disk systems often will allow the reads to be serviced before writes, which helps the performance of the majority of networks. If your network is not conventional, however, it can suffer.

A *mingle* option will allow the network administrator to define whether or not the reads and writes should be serviced equally. A single large request is processed faster and with less overhead than several small requests, so some vendors are increasing performance by implementing an option that allows multiple smaller sequential reads and writes to be *fused* together into a large single request.

The disk driver will directly affect server utilization, and server utilization will affect all other portions of your network. A good disk driver will establish an efficient communications channel across the bus with the processor and host adapter; this passes the processing duties to the host adapter. All the data will then be passed over this channel, and thus, off-load the work from the server. Some vendors will establish this connection for every transfer; others will predict the size of the transfer and establish this connection only if overall performance will be increased.

The software also is responsible for the reconstruction of a downed RAID systems, and, therefore, is different on just about every RAID implementation (it ships with the RAID system). In fact, the software, in a large part, will determine the difference between a good RAID system and a poor one. Be sure that the system can reconstruct "on-the-fly," or rebuild the data without interrupting the network. It also is important to verify that the reconstruction can be assigned to run by the system clock. If and when the drive needs to be reconstructed, you will want to be able to have it start in the middle of the night (perhaps after the backup). This may seem obvious, but many systems don't allow unattended reconstruction.

Furthermore, as data reconstruction can take a significant amount of time, be sure the software offers the capability to designate the reconstruct block size and the time interval. (The larger the block size and the smaller the time interval, the faster the drive will be reconstructed; however, network usage is inversely related.) Another tip is to verify that the reconstruct parameters are changeable, even after the rebuild process has already begun. Finally, look for RAID software that offers a familiar interface, sends good prompt warnings, offers management, and has good technical support.

NETWORK DESIGN

When shopping for a "file server," spend time to design your network. This means planning the physical implementation, wiring, routers, hubs, and so on, all the while looking ahead and planning for expansion.

Part of this planning is a component directly associated with the file server's performance. The NIC channel (network interface card) is associated with the network topology; however, planning the NIC channel design consists of more than just deciding on a topology. It is planning and distributing the network loads across the different LAN segments. This means you need to be aware of the NIC's capabilities and balance those capabilities with the file server, as well as with the entire physical design of the network. If you plan to purchase two Ethernet cards, for example, you will want to purchase hubs that are also segmentable. This will allow your network, as well as your file server, to take full advantage both interface cards (theoretically doubling overall network performance).

EXPENDABILITY AND UPGRADABILITY

When you go through the trouble of selecting a server, one item that you do not want to overlook is the capability of that server to grow with your organization. When looking for expansion capabilities, consider the following, which are discussed in the following sections:

- ◆ Drive bays
- ◆ RAM expandability
- ◆ Expansion slots
- ◆ Power supply
- ◆ Bus scalability

DRIVE BAYS

It used to be that *drive bays* were a critical part of a server's expandability, and to an extent, they still are; however, external storage devices offer significant expansion. If you plan to use internal drives, be sure to leave enough room to *at least double* the amount of your current disk space.

RAM EXPANSION

RAM expandability is also an issue (RAM requirements are discussed earlier in this chapter); for example, for every 300MB of disk storage, your NetWare server needs at least 8 additional MB of RAM. Besides supporting additional disk capacities, memory is also used for other important sever operations; in fact, it is the one component that you will never be able to get enough of. Thus, when purchasing a server, be sure that it is capable of handling sufficient amounts of RAM. If you neglect this issue, it will not take long for your server to become obsolete.

Expansion Slots

When a network begins to grow (has more users), certain elements of the server may begin to experience saturation, such as the LAN channel. If the LAN segment is saturated (too much traffic), adding a second Ethernet card is the best resolution. In effect, it cuts the work of a single network card in half. If the bottleneck is the disk channel, adding a second controller and drive will alleviate the bottleneck. This duplexes the drives, which usually doubles the amount of data that can be transferred. Each of these resolutions requires a free expansion slot in the server. So, as you evaluate candidate machines look ahead and consider the number of expansion slots the server has (eight expansion slots is standard).

Summary

A server is the focal point of the network. If it has troubles the network has troubles; thus you have troubles. To avoid trouble, look for a server that is more than just a PC on steroids; select one that is high quality, offers increased network aware hardware, and one that offers the type of performance that your users will expect.

There are several methods available to help in your search for quality hardware. Look for hardware that offers "special" LAN correcting-hardware. Such features will save a considerable amount of time and effort, specifically time spent on troubleshooting. Also look for hardware that comes form a hardware manufacture that offers the type of support that you would expect. At times, this will be as important as actually having quality hardware—you can sometimes tell what a manufacture thinks of its computer by the warranty and server specific features it has implemented into it.

There are several options to consider when selecting the exact hardware for your network server, such as the processor, the bus, the drives, expandability, and so on. Each of these components play a vital role in the server's capability to perform.

The processor is the heart of the server. The 386 DX 33 MHz processor is a good entry level processor for small to medium sized networks. However, the prices of the 486 chip have almost made selecting a processor a mute point: at least get a 486 server. The integer instruction set, cache, and FPU make it worth while. The Pentium chip is currently the ultimate processor, but if you are considering the Pentium, be sure that the manufacturer is actually taking advantage of the Pentium's capabilities. The choice of which processor to get will actually be one of the easiest.

The bus type is also an easy selection, although with all the new arrivals, the choice is not as clear as it used to be. EISA is currently the bus of choice for the masses. It has a theoretical maximum transfer rate of 33MB/sec. This means that the sustained rate is somewhere around 20MB/sec. The fastest I/O cards are SCSI disk controllers and they can only sustain about 10MB/sec. This is further reduced by the need to relinquish the bus to other devices; therefore, the rates are more realistically around 4–5MB/sec. Moreover, fast Ethernet controllers can only realistically transfer 1MB/sec. With eight bus slots in an EISA machine, it is doubtful that a current real-world situation could ever completely saturate the bus. This doesn't eliminate the fact that the bus is a considerable factor of performance, it just proves that the bus should be balanced for optimal performance.

SCSI's capability to offload the work from the server's processor to the host adapter has made it the paramount choice for today's network storage solutions. Developers have spent continued efforts to improve the implementation of the SCSI technology. These efforts have introduced several levels of RAID technology, which take the storage challenge seriously. They offer fault-tolerance features, management, higher storage capacities, and overall, a flexible-modular storage solution.

Server performance is a vital portion of network longevity and productivity. To be efficient, all the server's components must be well balanced, such as having a fast processor, but a slow I/O bus creates a bottleneck and thus cripples the server's performance. The conclusion, therefore, is an obvious one—a high performance server has to have more than just a fast processor, the server has to have a fast bus. In fact, the server must be completely balanced. To balance a server, you must give thought to the motherboard design, the bus, the disk channel, the network adapter, and so on. If any one system is lackluster in performance, a bottleneck is created and the server's overall performance sacrificed. If all the components of server are quick but the drive system is slow, for example, the server will be slow—a server can only be as fast as its slowest part. The next chapter provides more insight on selecting a primary and secondary storage system.

- Determining User
  Profile

- Summary

CHAPTER 7

Workstation Hardware

In Chapter 6, an in-depth discussion on how to select your server hardware was presented. In this chapter, the selection process for workstation hardware is presented. Although both are "computers," the needs are different; therefore, different selection rules need to be established and applied.

DETERMINING USER PROFILE

The first step in deciding which hardware to buy for your workstations is asking yourself the following questions:

◆ **What uses (applications) will you need to provide for?** A workstation that will be mostly word processing will need less resources than one that will be creating graphic presentations.

◆ **If you will be running database applications, will they be client/ server or workstation based?** A client/server application will require less workstation resources because a large amount of the processing takes place on the server.

◆ **If you will be doing a lot of spreadsheet work, will the application support a numeric co-processor?** If so, get a CPU that has one built-in (486DX or Pentium) or plan on adding one.

◆ **Do you need to store a large amount of data on your local hard disk (for either security or speed of access)?** You'll want a larger-than-standard disk, and if speed is the concern, you'll want a faster disk subsystem (perhaps a caching controller with a fast, SCSI-2 hard disk).

◆ **Will you be doing a lot of high resolution graphics?** Get a high speed, co-processed video system connected to a high performance bus such as VESA Local Bus or PCI.

These and many other questions need to be examined before you can determine the proper selection of workstation attributes. The basic workstation choices are discussed in the next section. Following that section will be considerations on the various operating system environments and how they affect your choices. The focus will be the Intel PC-based platforms (DOS, Windows, OS/2). Macintosh and UNIX clients will also be addressed.

CASE AND POWER SUPPLY

Starting at the basics, you should consider various case type and power supply requirements. Most vendors offer their machines with varying types of cases and making a good choice will make life easier down the road.

THE DESKTOPS

These are cases meant to be laid horizontally and put on the desktop, although some will be put sideways on the ground. The usual choices are *full-sized* (room for three or more 5.25-inch devices, such as floppies, CD-ROMs, or tape backups—some also have room in the case for at least one full-height 5.25-inch hard drive) and *slim profile* (usually two 5.25-inch bays and one internal 5.25-inch or 3.5-inch hard drive bay).

The slim line cases are appealing because they often are only a couple of inches high and are easy to place in a work area. The two things to consider before selecting slim line cases are the number and size of accessory bays (for hard disks, floppies, and so on) and the layout and limitations of card slots (where, for example, NICs will go). Usually, if you are considering a slim line case, you will not be putting many drives in the workstation. Perhaps a floppy and a 3.5-inch hard disk so you will have plenty of room, but think ahead—will you be considering putting a CD-ROM in later? Make sure that your plans will not make the case obsolete. Many slim line cases have limitations on the number and size of accessory cards you can install. They often will allow only three to four cards and sometimes will not accommodate full length or full height cards, so check in advance.

The reigning standard is the desktop case. It normally accommodates three 5.25-inch accessories and often two 3.5-inch ones as well. They also will normally have internal space for 5.25-inch and 3.5-inch hard drives. They will not have a problem with full-height cards, and at least some of the slots will accommodate full-length cards.

As a general rule, the full sized desktop is the best choice. It offers more flexibility of accessories and, usually, lower cost than the slim line cases. If you need the slim line's low profile, make sure that you will be able to install all the accessories you will need.

TOWERS

Growing more popular are the *tower cases*. These are aligned vertically and are intended to be set on the floor. This configuration allows for easier access to floppy drives than a desktop that has been flipped and laid on its side. Lately, the mini-tower case has gained support. It is still aligned vertically but is shorter, allowing it to be set on a desktop and take up less desk space.

The full-sized tower usually offers a great deal more space for drives. They often have four or five accessible 5.25-inch bays and three or four internal bays for hard disks. They are at the top of the heap for this kind of storage. Also, many offer auxiliary fans to keep your components cool. The mini-tower usually has less space, two to three accessible bays, and a 3.5-inch internal bay for hard disks.

Note

Accessory card slots are not usually an issue on tower cases: full-length and full-height cards are no problem.

OTHER CASE ISSUES

The power switch should be on the front of the case. Older cases used a switch on the side in the back, which is very inconvenient. The reset switch should be specially marked, or better yet recessed to avoid accidentally hitting it.

Turbo switches are a throwback to the early PC days. People would hot-rod their machines with a faster crystal (making it run faster), but some functions, such as the DOS FORMAT command, would not operate properly. The turbo switch allowed users to restore the normal speed to run these commands. Modern operating system software does not cause these problems and the trouble now is that accidentally hitting this switch and putting it in a slower mode will cause a real speed degradation. If your case has a turbo switch, disable it. Use a jumper on the motherboard to ensure that it will stay in its high-speed mode.

Most cases will have a lock on the front panel. These usually just prevent the keyboard from being used, but some will actually lock the case so that it cannot be opened with the lock closed. Both types of locks have advantages, but proper security on your network limits the usefulness of the keyboard lock and locking the case may prevent the curious from tinkering inside their workstation.

POWER SUPPLIES

Often, you are not given a choice of *power supplies*, the case just comes with one. It is sufficient that you make sure that the supplied unit will handle your needs. A 200-watt power supply will power a normal workstation. If your machine will have fax/modems installed internally or a sound card, you should get a 250–300 watt supply. You also should make sure that, when installing the machine, the fan on the power supply is running. There is nothing more destructive to the components in your workstation than overheating. Also be sure that the fan is relatively quiet in its operation. A noisy fan is sure to cause user complaints.

MOTHERBOARDS

The *motherboard*, with its CPU, RAM and bus connections, is the centerpiece of your workstation. Taking the time to select the right one for your uses will be time well spent.

CPUs

The CPU (Central Processing Unit) is the chip that does most of the work. It is the one referred to when asked, "What kind of machine do you have?" Sometimes people will refer, in error, to the whole case as the CPU; the CPU is the chip in the box.

In 1995, the two major contenders are Intel's i486 and the Pentium. If you have 80386 workstations, these will run fine, assuming that you have enough RAM for them and you put them in places where processing power is not at a premium. No new 386s should be bought. Application-software vendors are now assuming that the standard is at least a 486 and will be basing their performance expectation on this.

Note

The power of processors is constantly changing. By the time you read this, it will have changed again. I have always used the following rule of thumb for workstation:

Unless the application requires processing power, get a machine on the second tier of pricing.

There is big price difference between a "first tier" machine and a "second tier" system. At the time of this writing, first tier systems are the Pentium 90 and faster machines, while second tier systems are the 486DX4–100, Pentium 60, and Pentium 66 machines. Using the rule of thumb, you can get the best price for performance when purchasing workstations.

486DX processors are currently available in speeds of 33 and 50 MHz. These are not the doubled or tripled processors. The DX50 has been reputed to cause some bus problems, but there have not been any NetWare-related problems experienced that can be directly attributed to the speed. These days, the DX2 and DX4 chips (doubled and tripled) are usually the cheaper for a given speed, so these chips will probably be dropped from the market soon.

The 486DX2 and 486DX4 processors employ "clock multiplication" to get extra speed out of the processor so that a 486DX2-66 actually runs from a 33 MHz external clock, but internally runs at 66 MHz. The 486DX4 processors work the same way, but the clock is tripled so that an external 33 MHz clock yields an internal 99 MHz (rounded up to 100 MHz).

Note

Some magazine reviews have indicated that a doubled or tripled chip is not as fast as a native chip of the same speed. For example, a 486DX-50 is faster than a 486DX2-50, which runs an external clock speed of 25 MHz. The reviews base this finding on the fact that the only thing doubled, or tripled, is the CPU. Memory and bus speed stay at the unmultiplied rate. This is not a problem, however, because even the unmultiplied rate is faster than any other device on the bus, so the processor waits anyway.

The 486DX processors make a good entry-level machine. For machines that are not going to do a heavy processing load, 486DX processors will work well. For heavier use, a 486DX2–66 or 486DX4–100 will work well. For the heaviest use, you should go to the Intel Pentiums.

In early 1994, the Intel Pentium hit the market after much anticipation. The Pentium (not called the 586) offers dual pipelines and other architectural features that make it a major improvement over the previous x86 CPUs and gives a glimpse of things to come. As of this writing, the most commonly shipped Pentiums are the 90 MHz and 100 MHz models. 120 MHz have been announced for some time and are just now becoming readily available.

The announcement and anticipation of these faster Pentiums has driven down the prices of the 60 MHz and 66 MHz processors. These currently are the leaders of the "bang-for-the-buck" class. By the time you read this, they may even be cheaper, and higher speed models may be available (rumors are of a 120 MHz machine). In addition, the as-yet unannounced (and unnamed) "P6" processor, which is to be the successor of the Pentium, is being shown around and stories are that Intel will bring this new processor rapidly to market.

Tip

One of the difficulties of writing about this type of information is that the market is so dynamic. With that in mind, remember to apply the underlying structure rather than the actual advice. From a software perspective remember this: most software written today, and for the next year or so, will be based around the 486. This means that most software will run on a 486 (there will not be much Pentium-specific software) and that it will perform adequately (from the vendor's perspective) on a 486.

Pentiums will run faster, and you should get one if speed is what you need. Pentium machines also will be more likely to offer the latest hardware advances, such as the PCI bus and 4-byte (72 pin) memory modules (SIMMs). For some time to come, however, a 486 will be an adequate machine.

Late in 1994, Intel announced a flaw in all the Pentium processors that were shipped up to that point in time. The flaw has to do with a floating point (basically big numbers and or numbers with a decimal point) calculations. Intel has said that all Pentiums will be replaced, on request, with fixed processors. Depending on the type of applications you use, you should check that you have one of the newer chips. If you are unsure, there are a number of free software applications available from various sources, such as CompuServe, that can test your Pentium to see if it contains the flaw.

Tip

How do different processors stack up? As a rule of thumb, each new family (386, 486, and so on) will perform at about twice the rate of its predecessor, clock for clock. A 486DX–33, for example, is almost twice as fast as a 386DX–33.

BUS TYPES

On your motherboard is a *bus*. A bus is the slot in which you insert an accessory card. Currently, there are five major bus types in common use, as shown in the following list:

- ◆ **Industry Standard Architecture (ISA)**: This is the original bus introduced by IBM on the PC AT. It was an extension of the PC bus. It contained two slots in tandem, the second, smaller slot being the addition. It had eight more IRQ lines and four more address bits, taking the amount of accessible memory up to 16MB. This bus lives on even though it is the oldest and has the lowest performance. If you have a PCI or VESA Local Bus machine, you also will have some ISA capable slots. The ISA bus is the reigning bus champion because its performance for most purposes is good enough.

- ◆ **Micro Channel Architecture (MCA)**: Introduced by IBM with the PS/2 line, MCA has not really taken hold. It is a very capable bus with some advanced features but suffers from having no backward compatibility with the ISA bus (which the other three contenders do).

7

WORKSTATION HARDWARE

◆ **Extended Industry Standard Architecture (EISA)**: Created by a consortium of hardware manufacturers, EISA was the first successful attempt to bring the bus up to 32-bit performance. It was created to compete with IBM's MCA and is still seen, but with decreasing frequency. As with ISA, EISA has two tandem connectors. These are compatible with ISA cards so that a slot can be used for either ISA or EISA. EISA cards need to be configured using software supplied with the computer and drivers supplied by the card manufacturer. Setup information is stored in non-volatile RAM. EISA offers a full 32-bit connection to the memory bus and 4-byte access. It has mainly been used for disk controllers.

◆ **VESA Local Bus (VLB)**: VESA is an acronym for the *Video Electronics Standard Association*. This association felt that even EISA was not fast enough for their needs. As the name implies, the VLB initially was used for connecting fast video cards. The Local Bus part means that the card was connected directly to the CPU's bus. For video, the VLB was faster than EISA, and EISA video cards never caught on. Soon after, another VLB card popped up; the disk controller. VLB is limited to two to three slots because it is connected directly to the CPU bus. Many early adopters of this bus had trouble getting two cards to work in one machine. Like EISA, VLB is an extension of the ISA bus, and this time has three connectors in tandem. The third connector (the one closest to the front of the machine) is the VLB and the slot can be used for ISA cards as well.

Tip

The VLB connector can be much harder to seat than a normal, ISA, card. Be sure that you seat it fully.

◆ **Peripheral Connect Interface (PCI)**: Intel, working separately from the VESA group, developed another local bus design. PCI has theoretical advantages over all the other bus designs but is slow in getting adopted. The setup, while not difficult, can be tricky, and the PCI bus is not compatible with ISA; that is, a PCI slot cannot be used for a ISA card. PCI is made to work with ISA so that the two can coexist, but each slot is either one or the other. Hard disk controllers and NICs are the main PCI cards now and video controllers are being introduced. These three types probably will be the mainstay of PCI so, except for servers, three PCI slots should be enough, although the PCI standard uses buffered access to the CPU bus, so there is not the limitation that VLB has.

◆ **Combination bus designs**: There are combinations of EISA and VLB, EISA, and PCI, and even all three together. Combinations enable you to use existing EISA cards in newer designs but have little advantage other than that. All cards available in EISA configurations will be, or are already, available in VLB or PCI designs and usually are less expensive than EISA.

Which bus should you choose? VLB and PCI are the only real players for new hardware (with their attendant ISA slots). EISA is a good but rapidly diminishing standard. For workstations, VLB has a slight edge because it is usually easier to install VLB cards and the performance advantages of PCI are not usually realized in a workstation. Either bus type should serve you well.

RAM (Random Access Memory)

This section discusses how much RAM you need when dealing with Operating Systems. First, you need to understand the different types of RAM packaging. In the early days, RAM came in chips called *DIP* (Dual Inline Package, and leading to the obvious jokes about "DIP chips")—these are the chips that look like caterpillars. Around the time the 80386 came out, a new type of packaging was introduced called the *SIMM* (Single Inline Memory Module). The SIMM had memory chips on a small circuit board. A variant of the SIMM was the *SIPP* (Single Inline Pin Package). A SIPP is a SIMM with legs soldered on.

The reason for the popularity of these packages has to do with the CPU's memory access. The original IBM PC had an Intel 8088 processor. It accessed memory eight bits (one byte) at a time. This meant that in adding RAM, you had to add nine chips at a time (eight data bits and one parity bit).

The AT introduced 16-bit memory access. This meant that you added memory 18 bits (16 data bits, 2 parity bits) at a time. At that time, this was not a problem because many machines had only a 1MB of RAM, which was accomplished with 4 rows (2 banks) of 256 Kilobit RAM chips.

The 80386 came out with 32-bit (4 bytes) memory access. Now memory had to be added 36 bits at a time or 4 rows of 9 chips. Because you usually had at least 2 banks (72 sockets), this took up too much motherboard real estate. Not only did this take up space, but each of those chips had to be inserted and seated properly. This left a small margin for error.

The first SIMMs replaced a row (9 DIP chips) so that you had 4 SIMMS taking the place of 36 DIPs on a 386 machine. Recently, the original SIMM package has been eclipsed by the "72-pin" SIMM that has 32 data bits so it replaces 4 original SIMMS or 36 DIPs. With these newest SIMMs, you can add one at a time to increase your memory on a 486 (or 2 at a time for the Pentium).

72-pin SIMMs are the way of the future (at least for a while). If you are buying new hardware, try to get a motherboard that uses them.

7

Workstation Hardware

DISK DRIVES

Most workstations will have at least one floppy drive and a hard disk. The following subsections cover the choices of floppy and hard drives.

FLOPPIES

Your workstation normally will have a floppy disk. Most software is available in the 3.5-inch format, which probably is the best choice. Because data security and viruses present possible problems, you may want to consider disabling the floppy drive on users workstations after you install your software.

Tip

> You should have an automated procedure that will scan new data for viruses before you release the data on your network.

HARD DISKS

You have a choice between two hard drive types: IDE and SCSI. IDE (Integrated Drive Electronics) have staked out the small-drive market (less than 500MB). An IDE drive has most of its electronics on the drive itself. The IDE design is a big improvement over the older MFM, RLL, and ESDI standards. In larger drives, SCSIs (Small Computer System Interface) are more popular. In fact, until mid-1995, IDE drives were "limited" to just over 500MB, so SCSI was the only real choice.

One of the limitations of IDE is that it is limited to two drives. Non-hard-drive IDE devices, such as CD-ROMs and tape backups were not readily available until early 1995. On the other hand, SCSIs can have up to seven devices (actually eight but the controller is considered one). SCSI CD-ROMs, tape backups, scanners, and so on, are readily available. Therefore, when making your hard disk decision, take into account the availability of any add-on devices you may need, and the number of devices.

Note

> Most new drives are 3.5-inch low profile (1-inch high), so space normally is not a problem. Prices for high capacity have plummeted, so if there is any chance that you will need a larger drive, now is the time to get it. In 1995, 1 Gigabyte (1000MB) drives sell for roughly $500.

VIDEO

Your video subsystem consists of two parts: a monitor and a video controller. If you have PCI or VLB workstations and are going to run any graphical Operating Systems, such as IBM's OS/2 or Microsoft's Windows, you should get a video controller that will take advantage of your bus. You can consult the manufacturer of the controller for software drivers for the operating system or operating environment you use.

The other part of the video subsystem is the monitor. This is the main way for the computer to communicate with you. Because your users will be looking at it for long periods of time, be sure to get a good quality monitor. While you are selecting monitors, ask for a demonstration that uses the video controller you plan to purchase. Examine it under bright lights for glare and florescent light for flicker. Florescent lights flicker at 60 Hz (cycles per second)—you normally don't notice it, but if the monitor redraws its screen at about the same rate as the florescent lights, you will see it flickering noticeably under this lighting. View the monitor at its (or the video controller's) maximum resolution—is the image clean and square?

ACCESSORIES

There are still many things you need to consider while contemplating the purchase of computers for a network. This section discusses some of the purchasing decisions you will have to make, such as which keyboards to use and which mouse will work best for your users. Because many peripherals are a matter of choice and preference, there are no absolutes.

KEYBOARDS

Along with the video subsystem, the keyboard is the way you interact with your computer. Because a good keyboard increases the productivity of your users, this is not a place to scrimp.

There are two basic feels to keyboards: the "clacky" IBM-type and the "squishy" IBM-type keyboards that have a long key travel and give good feedback when you press a key. They are also somewhat noisy when in use. The squishy type generally has a shorter key travel, is quiet, and feels like pushing a spring, offering little tactile feedback that a key has been struck. Users usually prefer one type or the other, so you may want to have both types available.

Standard keyboard layout is important. As with so many other things, IBM has led the way. Their PS/2 keyboard is the industry standard, with the exceptions of the size of the Enter key and the size and position of the Backspace key and Backslash key. Some manufacturers offer different layouts for function and cursor (arrow) keys. Unless you have only one style of keyboard at your location the non-PS/2 style keyboard will be a poor choice. Switching from a keyboard you are familiar with is hard enough without having to learn new key layouts as well.

THE MOUSE

As with the monitor and keyboard, the mouse is something you use frequently, so be sure to purchase one of good quality. Some models offer three buttons, but two buttons are standard and all you really need. Some keyboards incorporate a mouse-like pointing device, such as a trackball. Keyboard/trackball combinations have the advantage of always being at hand, and never buried under a stack of papers.

UNINTERRUPTABLE POWER SUPPLY (UPS)

Some consumers will only consider a UPS (Uninterruptable Power Supplies) for their server, but this is folly. If you have a brief power drop, it does your data no good if the server is left up but all the workstations crash; the workstations have data, too.

Fortunately, good UPSs that have the capacity to handle crash situations are available for around $100. These units supply five or more minutes of reserve power. You should make it a rule that if the power is off for more than 60 seconds, you need to start closing applications and powering down the computers. Doing these things ensure that all data is saved before the UPS quits. Don't forget to plug your monitor into the UPS; you'll need it to properly shut down your applications.

OF CLONES AND DEALERS

You have seen the ads—tantalizingly low prices on systems with "the works." Should you indulge or should you stay with name brands? To answer the last question first, it depends. What you need to consider is the effect of a down machine on your operation. You need to know how quickly you can expect repair of machines. Generally this means buying from a local dealer who stocks repair pieces or can give you a loaner. If you go mail order, get references and ask about repair policies; specifically, will they cross-ship?

It is better to know and trust your dealer than to blindly buy a brand name. Most dealers who have been in business very long have learned that poor quality comes back to hurt them.

As for the low-priced systems, steer clear. Many of these are made tantalizing by "specification selling," hyping a specification rather overall quality. Often you will find a cheap monitor that claims to work at 1024x768 resolutions, but it is no good at even normal VGA resolution.

SYSTEM REQUIREMENTS AND RECOMMENDATIONS

So now you have a lot of information; what else would you need to know? You need to know about the Operating System for your workstations.

MS-DOS

MS-DOS is the least taxing environment in terms of RAM and disk space requirement. Nonetheless, it is generally recommended that you plan on at least a Windows capability, for many of the applications today require the Windows environment.

MICROSOFT WINDOWS 3.1 OR WINDOWS FOR WORKGROUPS

If you plan to use the Windows environment, you should consider a 486DX-33 machine as a bare minimum. If your budget allows it, consider a 486DX2-66 or 486DX4-100, or even a Pentium. Get 4MB RAM minimum for Windows, but realistically get 8MB, and 16MB will not be too much. Get a big disk because some Windows applications can use over 100MB. As for monitors, get a minimum of a 14- or 15-inch monitor, which gives you a resolution of 800x600. 17-inch monitors can exploit the higher 1024x768 resolution, and 20-inch monitors can go up to 1280x1024. If you need to go above 800x600 resolution, consider getting an accelerated video card to speed up your video.

IBM OS/2 WARP

To run OS/2, a minimum hardware requirement is a 486DX-33 machine, but consider going to a Pentium. With the NetWare Client for OS/2 installed, you'll need at least 8MB RAM. If you can jump to 16MB, the extra RAM gives a big boost in performance. This is the same as in Windows—a big disk is the best choice. Warp itself is about 100MB if you install all the options. The same video choices apply as with Windows.

UNIX

Hardware requirements for UNIX workstations vary from vendor to vendor. It is best to check with them to ensure you purchase a system with sufficient horsepower and resources to run that version of UNIX. The general rule of thumb for UNIX workstations is to get a fast processor, 486DX2-66 or better. Also stock up on RAM, 16MB or more. You also will need a lot of disk space. 300MB of disk space is not an uncommon requirement for UNIX workstations.

MACINTOSH

As a general rule, to run the System 7 Operating System on your Mac, you'll need a Mac with at least 8MB of RAM. As with previous comments, the more RAM, the better is the performance.

WINDOWS NT AND WINDOWS 95

The hardware and resource requirements for Windows NT and Windows 95 workstations are pretty similar to those for OS/2 Warp. You should consider getting a 486/66 machine with 16MB or more RAM and a lot of disk space.

SUMMARY

A lot of ground was covered here, and most of it only briefly. Two rules stand out as the essence of workstation choice:

◆ Buy more than you think you'll need. Computer technology moves along quickly. Yesterday's high performance machine is today's door stop. Get more RAM, more disk capacity, and more processing power than you "need" now; if you don't, you'll be replacing sooner than you think.

◆ Buy from someone you trust. When problems crop up—and they will—the vendor will not be remembering the price you paid for the machine. If you haven't used a supplier before, try asking around and make sure they understand that after-sale service is the key to your continued business.

The next chapter in this book gives you guidelines for how to tailor your hardware and software needs to fit your budget.

- Start with Your Shopping List

- Novell-Approved Hardware

- Hiring Consultants

- Hiring Technicians

- Training Your Staff

- Putting Together the Budget

- Justifying Costs

- Summary

CHAPTER 8

Working Within Your Budget

When planning the implementation of a network, you must plan your budget carefully. This chapter provides tips developed through hard-earned experience on getting the best prices and working with management to implement the network you want. These tips enable you to develop a flexible but precise plan for implementing NetWare.

In Chapters 6 and 7, you learned how to determine what type of machine you need. Coming up with the "wish list" is the first step in formulating your budget. Next, you will need to factor in personnel costs for hiring any consultants or technicians needed to set up your network. Finally, your staff, both network administration and end-users, must be trained to operate and manage the system. To ensure approval of your plan by management, you must plan the justification for each item on your list.

START WITH YOUR SHOPPING LIST

The starting point for your budget is the shopping list you created according to the process detailed in Chapters 6 and 7. Here is a sample shopping list:

SHOPPING LIST: CLEARWATER RESOURCES

Number of Servers: 5
Number of Users: 300

High-end server machines	3 @ $12,000	=	$36,000
Medium server machines	2 @ $5,000	=	$10,000
High-end workstations	35 @ $3,000	=	$105,000
Medium workstations	250 @ $2,500	=	$625,000
Macintosh stations	10 @ $6,000	=	$60,000
UNIX stations (includes OS)	5 @ $8,000	=	$40,000
Hubs, MSAUs	25 @ $1,000	=	$25,000
Cabling plant Ethernet	1 @ $1,150	=	$1,150
Cabling plant token ring	1 @ $4,500	=	$4,500
FAX servers	15 @ $2,000	=	$30,000
Modem servers	10 @ $3,000	=	$30,000
Laser printers	6 @ $3,000	=	$18,000
Line printers	2 @ $800	=	$1,600
Backup systems	5 @ $1,500	=	$7,500

Cable testers	3 @ $250	=	$750
Network analyzer	1 @ $ 3,000	=	$3,000
NetWare operating system	5 @ $6,000	=	$30,000
Server management tools	15 @ $300	=	$4,500
Word processing	300 @ $250	=	$75,000
Spreadsheet	150 @ $250	=	$37,500
Graphics tools	25 @ $2,500	=	$62,500
Engineering tools	30 @ $3,000	=	$90,000
Scheduling	15 @ $150	=	$2,250
E-mail	300 @ $150	=	$45,000

Preliminary Total Budget $1,344,250

(Does not include consulting fees, installation labor, training fees.)

The sample shopping list just shown is for demonstration purposes only. This sample list assumes you are starting from scratch—no computers, no cabling plant, no software, no management tools, and so on. Prices on the sample shopping list are rough estimates, working numbers for purposes of seeing the big picture.

NOVELL-APPROVED HARDWARE

When planning your budget and selecting your hardware, you will want to ensure that the computers you select are fully compatible with NetWare. Fortunately, Novell has extensive testing facilities so that you can purchase equipment that you know will work reliably. Look for products that indicate they are "NetWare Labs Tested and Approved" under the Novell "YES" ("Yes, it runs with NetWare") program. You can confirm approval by contacting the manufacturer or Novell.

Failure to choose approved products could prove quite expensive. Should you have problems later and contact Novell for support, you might be told that your server platform is not approved, and hence, you are "on your own." Although an approved server hardware platform may be more expensive than a "no-name" box with the same speed CPU and hard drive capacity lacking certification, purchasing the "bargain" computer is likely to result in BIOS problems, driver incompatibilities, memory errors resulting in server ABENDS, or countless other potential problems.

Novell tests and approves server platforms, workstation computers, network interface cards, hard drives and controllers, and many other components. However, as mentioned in Chapter 6, the certification does not guarantee that different vendors components will function within the same machine. The certification *does* mean that the certified components will most likely work together without giving you too much grief. A good consultant or systems integrator can help you greatly. The following section provides some information on how to locate qualified assistance.

Note

> If you absolutely must cut hardware costs, make sure that the file server computer is approved by Novell as this is the most critical element of your network. In addition, you should purchase at least a few approved workstations so that you can ensure that any problems you might encounter in the future are not the result of hardware incompatibilities. All network interface cards should be approved without exception.

HIRING CONSULTANTS

Even if your full-time staff is knowledgeable about administering a NetWare network, you may want to hire a consultant to help you plan the network and oversee the installation. Once the basic network is in place, the consultant can be a continuing source for advice about expansion, troubleshooting, and so on.

Whenever a company hires a consultant, they want to make sure that the person they hire knows what he or she is doing. Novell has several levels of professional certification for those who have successfully completed a series of training sessions and passed the related examinations. By hiring consultants with these certifications, you can be assured that the level of technical expertise is in line with Novell's expectations.

CERTIFIED NETWARE ENGINEER (CNE)

Other than hardware certification, Novell also sponsors a number of certification programs for engineers and technicians who work with NetWare. Most consultants and technicians who work with NetWare are *Certified NetWare Engineers*, or CNEs, which means they have successfully completed a specific course of study in Novell products and networking technologies. They have demonstrated mastery of various subjects by passing certification exams that test their knowledge in detail. Novell provides extensive training opportunities through associated training companies (NAECs, or Novell Authorized Education Centers) and selected colleges and universities (NEAPs, or Novell Education Alliance Partners) located around the world. These NAECs and NEAPs deliver Novell-developed courseware that helps network professionals learn about NetWare and associated products, and prepare for the certification tests. To maintain certification, a CNE may be required to take courses and pass recertification tests every year in order to remain up-to-date with new technology provided by Novell.

There are four different CNE "tracks" one can pursue—CNE-NetWare 3, CNE-NetWare 4, CNE-UnixWare, and CNE-GroupWare. This provides the candidates a more focused direction, in much the same way a university student chooses a major.

The *Enterprise Certified Network Engineer*, ECNE, recognizes those individuals who have exceeded the requirements for CNE by passing additional certification tests. All ECNEs must demonstrate familiarity with NetWare 4.*x* as well as NetWare 3.1*x* by passing tests specific to those products. Not all CNEs may yet be "up to speed" with the latest version of Novell's NetWare product, however. Make sure that consultants you hire have experience with NetWare 4.*x*.

In mid-1995, Novell introduced the *Master CNE* program, not as a replacement to the ECNE program, but as a parallel certification. In the MCNE program, the candidates are required to specialized in one of the following three areas:

◆ Network Management
◆ Infrastructure and Advanced Access
◆ GroupWare Integration

Similar to ECNEs, an MCNE is required to have NDS knowledge.

All consultants and technicians that you hire to work with NetWare should be CNEs in the respective area with practical hands-on experience. It is also a good idea for your own networking staff to participate in the training and to gain the CNE certification.

To entice NetWare administrators to gain more NetWare knowledge, Novell has a Certified NetWare Administrator (CNA) program. It is designed for people that work with NetWare but have no immediate need to pursue the CNE designation.

NETWORK PROFESSIONAL ASSOCIATION (NPA)

The *Network Professional Association* (NPA), formally known as the Certified NetWare Engineers Professional Association (NEPA), is an independent professional society for CNEs. While Novell recognizes NPA and provides its members with information and access to Novell technology and personnel, the society is not affiliated with Novell.

NPA provides a newsletter, training, conferences, and other resources to its members. It also provides an ethical code for CNEs. Members of NPA frequently refer consulting business to each other and share information about their professional experiences. Not all CNEs are members of NPA; however, most major consulting organizations provide memberships to NPA for staff who work with NetWare.

When drawing up a contract to hire consultants, make sure that the contract specifically addresses the tasks for which you are hiring the consultants. Enumerate in your contract the tools and equipment you will provide and the tools and equipment you expect the consultants to provide. By dealing with these issues up front, you can avoid misunderstandings later.

The following list provides criteria for hiring consultants to assist in designing, installing, and troubleshooting a NetWare 4.x installation.

◆ Insist on CNE/ECNE certification for your staff and consultants you hire.

◆ Prefer consultants who are members of NPA.

◆ Obtain from each consultant a list of previous clients and call to check the references.

◆ Prefer consultants who have had experience with sites similar to yours.

◆ Include incentives in the contract for meeting your schedule.

HIRING TECHNICIANS

Faulty cabling is one of the most common sources of problems in networks, and cabling-related problems can be one of the most difficult and expensive to resolve. Do not skimp on this item when planning or installing your network. For all but the smallest organizations, it is a good idea to hire professional technicians to install and test your cabling plant. If your building already has a cabling plant that is compatible with NetWare and the physical network media you will be using, have the existing cable tested by a professional. A technician doesn't require any NetWare-specific knowledge to install a good cabling plant for your NetWare system. It is important, however, to hire a technician who has experience installing cabling for use by data-processing equipment.

The technician you hire can ensure that your cabling plant meets local building-code requirements. For example, cabling installed near heat ducts may need to have a special heat-resistant Teflon jacket. Also, local fire codes may have changed since the cable was first installed.

One of the most reliable and least expensive ways of installing cabling (that is, if you are planning to use twisted-pair cabling) is to have your cabling plant installed at the same time your phone system is installed. In this case, the phone company technicians can simply install extra cable for your network at a small incremental cost. This also allows you to locate twisted-pair hubs and repeaters in phone closets, which is a logical place for them to be. The phone company can also come back after the phone system is installed and put in the cabling, but that is generally more costly. When using twisted-pair cabling, be certain that the proper grade cable is used. Not all twisted-pair cable used for telephone systems is suitable for LANs.

Electrical contractors who work on commercial buildings can install a cabling plant for your NetWare network. Remember that your cabling plant must meet electrical standards specific to data-processing equipment and must be tested prior to use. Not all electrical contractors can provide this level of service. Make sure that any contractor you employ has experience installing digital computer cabling. The coaxial cable used for cable television looks very much like the coax used for Ethernet or ARCnet networks *but it is not the same*! As with twisted-pair cabling, insist that the proper approved medium is used. It will be a little more expensive, but failure to use it will undoubtedly cause communication problems in the future.

Finally, many consulting organizations either have technicians on staff who are qualified to install a cabling plant, or work with other organizations that have qualified technicians. This is something to ask about when you hire a consulting organization.

Note

Do not try to cut corners when installing your cabling plant. Insist on the use of high quality materials approved for use in a digital computer network environment.

Hire a qualified professional to install and/or test your cabling. Insist on a guarantee. This may require that cabling be tested or re-tested after new walls or ceilings are built or other renovations to your building are completed.

TRAINING YOUR STAFF

While you may have staff already employed by your organization who can install everything from the network design to the follow-up training, you may find yourself in need of some expert help. Consultants and technicians are available to assist with every step of the implementation process, but you need to be careful in choosing your consultants for quality, availability, and compatibility.

Because you will need full-time staff to maintain, configure, and administer your NetWare system over time, make sure that they are trained by a Novell-certified institution. If you plan on training more than a few of your staff, it may be the most cost-efficient to have the training at your site. Many Novell-authorized institutions offer training at your site provided you meet a minimum class size.

As mentioned earlier, Novell ensures the quality of NetWare training by certifying educational institutions to deliver Novell-developed course materials. These institutions must meet strict requirements regarding their facilities. When an institution is approved by Novell, they are awarded the status of *Novell Authorized Educational Center* (NAEC), or in the case of colleges or universities, *Novell Education Alliance Partner* (NEAP). In addition to certifying the NAEC facility, the trainers presenting the courses must all go through a stringent program of testing and evaluation to become Certified Novell Instructors (CNIs). Worldwide Novell Authorized Educational Centers and Novell Education Alliance Partners offer a wide range of courses, from basic networking technology to advanced NetWare 4.*x* systems administration. Only CNIs working for NAECs or NEAPs are authorized to offer the courses written and developed directly by Novell.

PUTTING TOGETHER THE BUDGET

Although NetWare could be considered the most cost-effective computing platform for businesses today, that doesn't mean it's cheap—it's not. NetWare is, however, many times cheaper than other computer systems, including mainframes and minicomputers. It also is less expensive than a pool of PCs that are not networked. If you don't have enough money allocated to install NetWare correctly, your project will be a failure.

Your budget must allow for the purchase of high-quality server hardware, appropriate workstation hardware, and effective cabling. If you do not choose quality over bottom-line price, your network will not be reliable. You must also consider costs associated with staffing and training when constructing your budget.

CONSTRUCTING A BUDGET

Your budget will be based on the "shopping lists" you draw up for server and workstation hardware (refer to Chapters 6 and 7). The budget should be a formalized working document, rather than a set of "commandments." As you negotiate purchases, and throughout the implementation phase, you should work with your budget. You can use your budget to track your financial outlays against the plan and to catch problems early. Your budget may need to be reformulated midstream if you have not done sufficient research early on. The following list is a checklist you can use during your budget-making process:

◆ Start with your shopping list.

◆ Research manufacturers suggested retail prices (MSRPs).

◆ Research site licensing and corporate rates.

- ◆ Update your shopping list with new pricing information.
- ◆ Investigate staffing costs for consultants and technicians.
- ◆ Research pricing for training, both at a training center and at your site.
- ◆ Make the first draft of your budget.
- ◆ Track cost variance during purchase of items, hiring of consultants and technicians, and arranging for training.

RESEARCHING PRICES

The more you know about hardware and software, the more success you will have with your budget. Researching prices is time consuming, but not at all difficult.

The first step is to gather manufacturers' suggested retail price (MSRP) data for the products on your shopping list. After obtaining the MSRP for the products on your shopping list, negotiate with resellers to establish a budget price.

COMPUTER BUYER'S GUIDE

If you were to call each vendor of each product on your shopping list and ask for the MSRP of a specific product, it would take far too long. A better approach is to use available collections of pricing information, such as the *Computer Buyer's Guide*.

The *Computer Buyer's Guide* is a database sponsored by Ziff-Davis (publisher of several computer magazines) and is available via CompuServe, an online information service. To use the *Computer Buyer's Guide*, you must have a CompuServe account, a modem, and telecommunications software (see Appendix B for more information about CompuServe).

You can search the *Computer Buyer's Guide* for product data using product categories (such as 486 PCs, laser printers, VGA monitors), keywords (such as EISA, local bus, PostScript, NetWare-certified), and manufacturers. The more keywords on which you base your search, the more narrowly focused your search will be. Data produced by the *Computer Buyer's Guide* includes MSRP, add-on options and their prices, available configurations, manufacturer's address and phone number, warranty information, and more.

Although a fee is charged for each session of the *Computer Buyer's Guide* ($10 to $30 per session is not uncommon), it represents a way to save a whole lot of time and can easily pay for itself many times over by increasing the accuracy of your finished budget. You can probably obtain MSRP information for every product category on your shopping list for less than $100 in session fees.

COMPUTER DATABASE PLUS

Ziff-Davis sponsors a sister database to the *Computer Buyer's Guide*, called the *Computer DataBase Plus*, also available via CompuServe. The *Computer DataBase Plus* contains product reviews from trade publications. Using the *Computer DataBase Plus,* you can search for and retrieve reviews and test results about specific products or product categories. This information is especially useful for evaluating new equipment with which you may not be familiar.

Ziff-Davis sells a subscription service containing both the *Computer Buyer's Guide* and the *Computer DataBase Plus* on CD-ROM. Subscribers receive updated CDs regularly. By subscribing to these databases, you don't need to pay access fees for each session. If you use these databases regularly, you may be able to save a substantial amount of money by subscribing to the CD-ROM service, rather than gaining access to the databases via CompuServe.

SAMPLE COMPUTER BUYER'S GUIDE SESSION

Included in this section are some examples of a sample session with the *Computer Buyer's Guide* so you can see how beneficial this service can be.

In this sample session, we searched for information on 486DX 50 MHz EISA computers. We retrieved the data on one of these product listings to demonstrate the depth of information provided by the *Computer Buyer's Guide*. The connect-time charge for our database query was only $1.00, but would have been higher had we extracted information on more than one product.

```
Computer Buyers' Guide                                        Main Menu

                            Welcome to...
                        Computer Buyers' Guide
              Copyright 1990, 1995 Ziff-Davis Publishing Company

   1 Search Computer Buyers' Guide
       For information on computer products and manufacturers
       (69,881 products; last updated May 24, 1995)

   2 Exit
   Enter choice (? for help) ! 1

Computer Buyers' Guide                                Search Methods Menu

How would you like to begin your search for products?

   1  Product Name
   2  Manufacturer Name

   3  Product Category

   4  Not sure — Try All Three
```

```
Enter choice (? for help) ! 3
Enter word(s) in Product Category
(? for help): 486dx

Searching..

Computer Buyers' Guide                                    Browse Menu
Categories that contain "486dx"                              Products
    1  486DX [actual term: Desktop Computers]                   2448
    2  486DX [actual term: Notebook Computers]                   820
Enter choice (? for help) ! 1
...
Computer Buyers' Guide                             Restrict Your Search
Product Category:      Desktop Computers
Processor Chip
    1  Pentium class                                             909
    2  486DX4 class                                              204
    3  486DX2 class                                              604
    4  486DX class                                               185
    5  486SX2 class                                               31
    6  486SX class                                               110
    7  486SL class                                                37
    8  ALPHA                                                      37
    9  PowerPC class                                              51
   10  MIPS series                                                60
   11  SPARC series                                               72
   12  PA-RISC                                                    61
   13  i860                                                       18
Enter as many as 13 choices (<CR> for more, ? for help) ! 4
...
Product reports:      12 from 7 manufacturers

Product Category:      Desktop Computers
Processor Chip         486DX class
Clock Rate             50 MHz
Bus Type               EISA
...
Computer Buyers' Guide                                   Product Report

Product Name:     BCG 486-50 EISA
Manufacturer:     Blue Circle Group, Inc.
                  9967 Valley View Rd.
                  Eden Prairie, MN 55344

Phone:            612-829-7710
800 Number:       800-701-4747
FAX:              612-829-7748
Tech support:     Use main no.

Data Sources Report COPYRIGHT 1995 Information Access Company

--------------------------------------------------------------------

Mfr. base system price: $3,199. Standard warranty included: 5 yr.. Date
announced: 1992
```

8

```
Specifications...
  Category: Desktop Computers
  Software included: DOS 6.21; Windows 3.11
  Processor chip: i486DX
  Clock rate: 50 MHz
  Bus type: EISA
  RAM included in base system: 4MB
  System memory expandable to: 128MB
  Cache RAM: 256KB
  BIOS: AMI
  Ports: 2 serial; 1 parallel; 1 game
  Floppy drive(s): 1.44MB 3.5"; 1.2MB 5.25"
  Hard drive: 340MB
  Access time: 15 ms
  Hard drive type: SCSI
  Controller: SCSI caching
  Power supply: 230 watts
  Keyboard: 101-key enhanced
  Display: 14" Color .28mm 1024x768 NI SVGA
  Graphics adapter: 1024x768 SVGA adapter

Reference #:   T14226

Blue Circle Group, Inc.
9967 Valley View Rd.  Eden Prairie, MN 55344


Computer Buyers' Guide                              Charge Summary

  2  Minutes Connect Time
  1  Product Report Display/Download         @ $ 1.00  = $   1.00
  0  Manufacturer Profile Displays/Downloads @ $ 1.00  = $   0.00
                                                       --------
                                            Total  = $   1.00


Note: These charges do not reflect
rebates or other special offers.


Thanks for using Computer Buyers' Guide
```

LAN TIMES BUYER'S GUIDE

A second source of MSRP information is the *LAN Times Buyer's Guide* published by McGraw-Hill. You can purchase an electronic version of the *LAN Times Buyer's Guide*, which makes finding specific data much easier. (See Appendix A for information on purchasing this publication.)

The advantage of the *LAN Times Buyer's Guide* is that it focuses only on networking products, while the *Computer Buyer's Guide* contains information on all categories of PC and PC-related products. The *LAN Times Buyer's Guide* is published once a year, however, so some of the information it contains will be outdated by the end of the publication year. If you need up to the minute pricing, the online databases, such as *Computer Buyer's Guide* on CompuServe, are continually updated with new product and pricing information.

USE BOTH SERVICES

The best approach for obtaining MSRP information is to use both the *Computer Buyer's Guide* and the *LAN Times Buyer's Guide*. The more information you have, the better your budget will be. Both databases are available in electronic format, which means you can extract only the information relevant to you.

RESEARCH SITE LICENSING AND CORPORATE RATES

It's a well-known fact that "street" prices paid for computer hardware and software are less than MSRPs. However, if your organization is purchasing more than a few of any item—hardware or software—you can do much better than even street prices.

Software vendors usually offer special licensing agreements to customers purchasing large quantities of software. Site licenses generally provide you with one copy of the software, a certain number of user manuals, and the manufacturer's permission to duplicate the software at will, up to a certain number depending on the agreement, for that site. Each additional site would be required to purchase another site license. Some software vendors offer extra technical support to site licensees, as well as special deals on software upgrades.

Most software vendors negotiate site-licensing agreements directly with customers rather than through a local computer store. The easiest approach is to call the software vendor's main switchboard and ask for a sales representative. If you use the *Computer Buyer's Guide* to get product MSRP information, you will already have found the vendor's main switchboard number. Whenever possible, deal with a sales representative who handles large accounts because they will be particularly in tune with the needs of a large corporation.

Hardware manufacturers as well usually offer "corporate rates" to customers purchasing in bulk. Each vendor offers a slightly different type of license package or corporate rate. Some vendors discount more deeply than others, so research in this area can pay big dividends. In addition, hardware vendors offering corporate rates frequently extend the warrantee of hardware purchased in large quantities, and usually offer attractive service contracts as part of the deal.

The fictitious organization mentioned previously, ClearWater Resources, on which the sample shopping list is based, would be able to negotiate some very lucrative licensing agreements and corporate rates because of the size of its purchase.

Although specific site licensing agreements and corporate rates differ from vendor to vendor, you should be able to trim 10 percent to 15 percent off the "street price" of the goods you are considering for purchase by working with a knowledgeable sales representative.

Training companies also offer special pricing for "bulk" training. Request bids from a number of firms in your area and choose the best based on quality, price, and added-value services (such as phone support).

Justifying Costs

Justifying costs is critical to gaining management support for your NetWare installation. It is far easier today to justify the costs associated with a NetWare installation than even a couple of years ago because NetWare is viewed as an effective and less-costly alternative to large host systems.

Justifying costs in a smaller organization is a different matter. Rather than justifying NetWare by showing it is less costly than a large host computer, you must justify it by showing it is less costly than no network at all. Most small organizations already have PCs that are not networked. Therefore, you must show how purchasing more hardware and software to create a network can save a small organization money.

When constructing a cost-justification report, concentrate on the organization's needs that are to be filled by the new computer system: interdepartmental electronic mail, a corporate-accounting system, or an inventory system, for example. Then, tally up the costs of different possible solutions: a new minicomputer, a peer-to-peer network, and so on.

Next, list the advantages and disadvantages of each system. These advantages and disadvantages may not represent costs associated with implementation of the system, but they should provide an indication of the long-term costs associated with each alternative solution. Examples of advantages and disadvantages include system reliability, projected downtime, compatibility with standards, compatibility with existing systems, security, lack of features, lack of capacity, and so on.

Next, list the costs to expand each proposed system. Make several columns of expansion costs: one showing the cost to expand the system by 2 to 5 percent, another showing the cost to expand the system by 50 percent, and so on.

You then want to list the day-to-day maintenance costs associated with each proposed system. If any maintenance contracts are involved with specific systems, list those. List the warranty or service contract expenses. List the salaries of persons required to administer the systems.

Finally, establish your conclusion. Back up your conclusion using data listed in the body of your cost justification. If you recommend NetWare, your conclusion should be based on sound analysis of the data in your report.

After considering your cost-justification report, management may request that you do more research. Perhaps they will request that you investigate further alternatives such as time-sharing or postponing the purchase. In any case, you should work with management until they have "signed off" on your proposal. A lack of management support may cause you irritations when you go into the implementation phase.

SUMMARY

Implementing a reliable NetWare network depends on reliable equipment. Remember, do not try to save money by using substandard cabling, network interface cards, or server hardware. While high-quality equipment can be expensive, you can greatly reduce the cost by shopping around for the best values. If you do your homework, justifying the costs should be a snap.

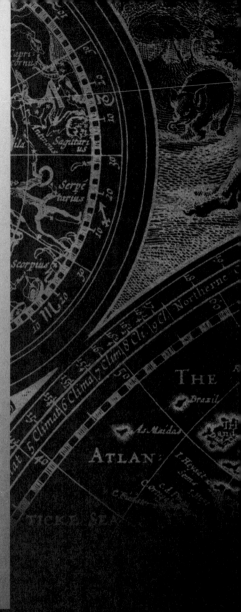

- Topologies

- Network Cabling

- Local Area Network
  Architectures

- Connecting the Net-
  works Together

- Wide Area Networks
  (WANs)

- Summary

CHAPTER 9

Media Types

In this chapter, you are introduced to the different types of transmission media and technologies used in local area networks.

Have you ever wondered what makes your network tick? Or maybe you're looking to install a LAN in your company, yet all of the different pieces of hardware used to connect everything together is confusing you. Alternately, maybe you called in a consultant to make some recommendations and they told you the following:

> Using a router attached to the second ring, you can then link the segment in Toronto with Montreal's through the ATM packet switching network. Once this is done, you should really change that Type 3 UTP to Level 5. By upgrading, you would be better prepared for future upgrades to FDDI or 100VG-AnyLAN.

ATM? Type 3 UTP? Level 5? FDDI? *What are they talking about?*

If you're confused, don't worry, you're not alone. The one aspect of networking that confuses a lot of people is the hardware involved. Just for the cabling alone, there are so many different types that you could give yourself a headache just trying to keep them all straight!

While other areas of this book show you about the types of servers and disk drives available to you, the purpose of this chapter is to discuss what your options are regarding your network's media and how it can be configured. Rather than taking a traditional approach by only showing you the most basic and common options, this chapter provides detailed information on the following:

◆ The different topologies

◆ Cabling varieties and their specifications

◆ Older Network Architectures such as the following:

   ◆ Token ring

   ◆ Ethernet

   ◆ ARCnet

◆ The latest architectures available, such as the following:

   ◆ Frame Relay

   ◆ Asynchronous Transfer Mode (ATM)

   ◆ 100 Mbps Ethernet

   ◆ ARCnet Plus

While it is not possible to discuss everything there is to know about these products, this chapter provides you with a sound knowledge on what's available to you.

TOPOLOGIES

For some people, the word *topology* brings back memories of sitting in a geography class trying to remember the capitals of each state or province. In geography, the word topology is used to describe the physical layout of an area. In networking, the term topology defines, on a basic level, how the nodes of a LAN or WAN are connected together.

At this point, you may be thinking that your network is based on a token ring topology. While many people feel the same way, it is not entirely accurate. There is a clear distinction between what a topology is and what an architecture is. The network architecture provides detailed information as to how the network nodes communicate back and forth. Specifications such as maximum cable distances and the maximum number of nodes are noted within the architecture's standards. A network architecture is based on the topology. For example, the token ring architecture is physically based on the star topology.

Now that you can distinguish between the two, look at each of the topologies available. While there are only five different topologies, there are many different types of architectures, such as ARCnet, FDDI, Ethernet, and token ring. Depending on the architecture, there may be several alternatives available to you as a topology. For example, while token ring will only operate when physically wired as a star, Ethernet comes in several different "flavors." Some versions use a bus topology, while another operates as a star. Network architectures will be covered later within this chapter.

THE BUS TOPOLOGY

A *bus topology* is created when each node is connected onto a common cabling system. The ends of the cabling do not connect together and, in most cases, have some type of terminator attached. The bus is fairly straightforward as you can see from Figure 9.1.

Figure 9.1.
The bus topology.

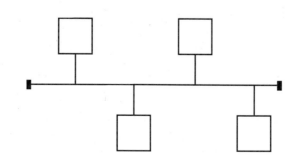

While the bus is a basic topology, it can be one of the most difficult to troubleshoot when a problem arises. Because all nodes are connected onto the same length of cable, a break in this cable will make the entire segment unusable.

THE MESH TOPOLOGY

When someone thinks about what a mesh is, they usually envision some type of material where threads spread out in various directions. For networks, a mesh topology is quite similar. In a mesh, each node is connected to every other node within the LAN or WAN (see Figure 9.2).

Figure 9.2.
The mesh topology.

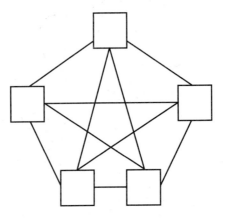

In theory, this approach provides a high level of fault tolerance by establishing various routes that a packet can travel to reach the ultimate destination. In practice, the mesh is usually only seen in large scale packet-switching networks, such as Frame Relay. The problem with this topology is that it is extremely expensive and difficult to implement.

THE RING TOPOLOGY

The *ring topology* bears many similarities to a bus. When configured as a ring, the nodes of the network connect to a common cabling system. Where the ring differs from the bus is at the ends of the common cabling. While the bus terminates the ends of the cable, the ring topology requires the two ends to connect to each other, thus forming a complete ring (see Figure 9.3).

One problem with the standard ring topology is that a single break in the cabling will make the network unusable. Certain architectures, such as FDDI, are based on the ring topology, but offer a degree of fault tolerance to protect the network against failures. FDDI and other architectures are covered later in this chapter.

Figure 9.3.
The ring topology.

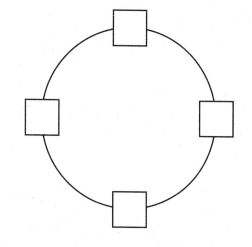

THE STAR TOPOLOGY

The most flexible and probably the most popular topology is the *star*. In a star topology, each node on the network is wired into a central point that can be a hub, concentrator, or MSAU (see Figure 9.4). Unlike the ring or bus topologies, the cabling layout of a star is far more resilient to problems. In most cases, a break in the cabling between the central point and node will not cause the entire network to collapse.

Figure 9.4.
The star topology.

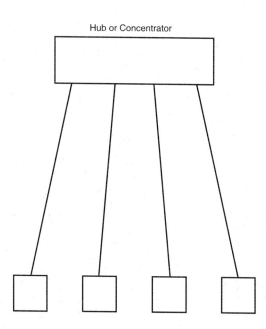

Hub or Concentrator

The star has enjoyed great success in the networking world and is supported by almost all of the architectures available. The only drawback to the star is that the central point acts as a single point of failure. Because all nodes are wired into this point, a failure will most probably result in a complete network shutdown.

THE HYBRID TOPOLOGY

Anyone that is involved in horticulture knows that a plant that is a hybrid has been created from two different plants. Some horticulturists do this to try and develop plants that are stronger and bring the "best of both worlds" into one form. Well, replace the plants with topologies and you have a *hybrid topology*.

Out of the five topologies, the hybrid is the most complex. Other topologies have a single definition as to how they are laid out. In a hybrid, there are several possibilities. Why? Because the hybrid is a topology that is based on a mixture of at least two other topologies, as shown in Figure 9.5. With companies expanding their networking systems and connecting existing LANs into one large WAN, hybrids are being created.

Figure 9.5.
The hybrid topology.

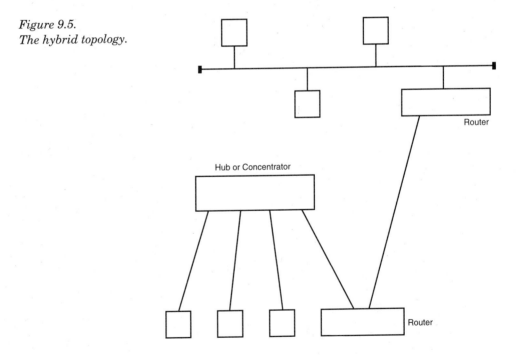

NETWORK CABLING

Building any network from the ground up takes time and resources. When looking at the different types of Network Operating Systems (NOS) and file server hardware, there are many different alternatives available to you. Because you are reading this book, chances are that you picked NetWare as your NOS of choice—wise move. Now, ask yourself two questions: first, how long did you spend researching NetWare, and second, how long did you spend researching your cabling? Having a great NOS is one thing, but install a NetWare server on a network with a substandard cabling plant and you're just asking for trouble.

Some companies spend tens of thousands of dollars buying high performance file server hardware, yet when it comes to cabling, little or no time is spent researching the alternatives. Even though there are only three main types of cable—coax, twisted pair, and fiber—there are several classes of each. A perfect example would be twisted pair (TP) cable. Currently there are three main organizations that certify TP into almost twenty different classifications! Sure, token ring uses twisted pair cable, but which type?

At home, you may be an excellent handyman, or handywoman for that matter. Changing some of the wiring in your house so that you have cable TV in your bedroom is one thing. But what is the worst case scenario if you make a mistake? Probably it would force you to call the cable company to do it right. Now, what could the same mistake cost your organization? Do you think that Fred from the Accounts Receivable Department would be happy if his server went down due to cabling problems? Probably not.

The worst mistake that any network administrator can make is to assume that he or she can just walk down to the local electronics store and purchase a bundle of any old type of cable and then install a 100-node network. Knowing the type of cabling to use, the classification to use, and how to install it properly is essential for any network. While detailed instructions on how to install the cable is beyond the scope of this book, knowing some of the related terminology and your alternatives is not.

Are you intimidated or discouraged yet? Hope not. Cabling may be complex, but what better time to learn than now! Maybe you won't be able to install the WAN all by yourself, but knowing the basics will give you the opportunity to communicate more effectively with your local cabling expert.

EXTERNAL INFLUENCES

Most network cabling consists of some type of copper wire surrounded by one or more sheaths. While the bare wires may be covered, they are still susceptible to interference from outside the cable. So what makes transmissions over a cable difficult?

To answer that question, look around your office for all of the things that make your life simple.

Fluorescent lights provide comfortable levels of illumination in your offices; radios play music in the background and generally provide a happier environment. As you sit back in your chair listening to "Old Blue Eyes," the network cable that passes within a few inches of a radio is being bombarded by interference, thus scrambling the data on the wire.

In any office, or especially in a factory, it is very important to survey where you plan on installing cable *before* you install it. Radios, fluorescent lighting, elevators, and some types of heavy machinery can generate different forms of interference that will create problems when trying to transmit data over your network cabling. When discussing the types of interference, you should concern yourself with the following two items:

◆ **Electromagnetic Interference (EMI)**: EMI can be caused by certain types of office and lighting equipment. The most common cause is fluorescent lights.

◆ **Radio Frequency Interference (RFI)**: RFI is generated by various forms of radio transmitters.

When surveying your environment, take note of where the fluorescent light fixtures, PA systems, microwaves, or any other electrical equipment is installed. During the planning stage, you should try to avoid laying the cabling too close to any of these items. Unfortunately, in some cases, you will not have the luxury of running cabling wherever you want. In times like this, knowing your cabling types and specifications will be important. Different types of cabling have different levels of tolerance towards EMI and RFI interference. Depending on the severity of the situation, you may even decide to use fiber-optic cable, which is completely immune to EMI and RFI.

ATTENUATION

Imagine that you are standing at the corner of your street speaking to a friend. Unfortunately, your friend really isn't that interested so he starts walking away. While he can still hear you speaking when he has gotten ten feet away, by the time he is 50 feet away, he can no longer hear what you are saying. Too bad, too, after all, you did offer to take him to that football game!

Why couldn't your friend hear you when he was further away? While the signal (your voice) continued with the same amplitude (strength), as the signal traveled further away from the source (your mouth), the amplitude decreased to the point that it could no longer be heard.

This same theory applies to data communications. As a signal is traveling down a segment of cable, the amplitude slowly decreases. If the distance between two nodes is too great, the amplitude eventually will decrease so much that the data contained within will not be recognizable. This process is commonly referred to as *attenuation*.

Later in this chapter, detailed specifications are given on the maximum distances for each of the network architectures. One of the purposes for imposing these limitations is to ensure that the packets traveling through the network will reach their destination before the signal attenuates too much. Problems with attenuation are most commonly seen when a segment of cabling is greater than the maximum specifications. When this occurs, intermittent problems or complete network failures are possible.

COAX CABLE

Of the three different types of cabling that are discussed in this section, *coax* is the simplest. At the center of the coax cable is a single copper conductor used to transmit and receive data (see Figure 9.6). While the conductor is fairly stiff, there are several layers of shielding to protect the copper from the possibility of breaking and from external interference. The first shield is a thick layer of plastic that gives the cabling a little more rigidity and acts as an insulator.

Surrounding the first layer, a layer of wire mesh is added. Since coax cabling is susceptible to electromagnetic interference, this wire mesh acts as another insulator. Finally, to hold everything together and protect the cable from cuts, a thick plastic sheath encloses the wire mesh.

Figure 9.6.
Inside the coax cable.

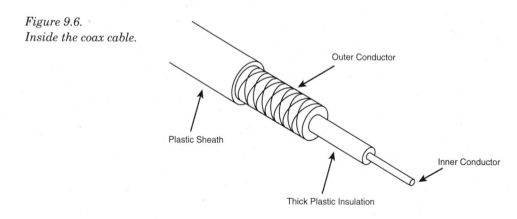

Outer Conductor

Plastic Sheath

Inner Conductor

Thick Plastic Insulation

Compared to twisted pair cabling, coax is not cheap. Depending on the vendor that you are dealing with, and the quantity that you will be buying, coax can cost you roughly twice as much as TP. This may be acceptable for a small 10-node bus topology, but when you're installing large networks, coax could add a significant expense to your company. Although coax costs a little more, it is still widely used in the networking industry and is supported by ARCnet and Ethernet architectures.

INSTALLING COAX CABLE

Coax cable can be easy to install, yet at the same time, can also provide some difficulties for you to overcome. The difficult part is related to the cable's shear bulk. Because it is heavier than twisted pair cabling, moving a large bundle of cabling around the floor and pulling the wires through conduits will be a little more difficult than moving twisted pair cabling around.

Where your life really gets easier is when it comes time to attaching the connectors to the ends of the cable. There are two main types of connectors, known as *British Naval Connectors* (BNC), that you can use, twist on or crimp on. Before attaching the connectors, you must strip the layers of shielding away to expose the inner conductor. Once exposed, you screw on or crimp the connector into place.

TYPES OF COAX CABLING

Unlike twisted pair cabling, which has many different classifications, coax cabling can be summed up into only five different types. This is actually a blessing in disguise. Of the five cables, three look almost identical in shape and size (RG58A/U, RG59/U and RG62). While they may look and feel similar, their electrical characteristics are completely different. Install the wrong cable, and your network will either suffer from intermittent errors, or it just won't work. In Table 9.1, the five key varieties of coax cabling are shown with their corresponding architectures. Remember, making a mistake by choosing the wrong type could be a very costly experience!

TABLE 9.1. COAX CABLING SPECIFICATIONS.

Cable Type	Terminating Resistance	Architecture
RG-8	50 Ohms	10Base5
RG-11	50 Ohms	10Base5
RG-58A/U	50 Ohms	10Base2
RG-59/U	75 Ohms	ARCnet
RG-62/U	93 Ohms	ARCnet

TWISTED PAIR CABLE

Unlike coax cabling which has a single inner conductor, twisted pair cables have a minimum of two copper wires enclosed in a sheath. Wires are paired together within the sheath and twisted a certain number of times per foot: the number of twists per foot varies, depending on the cable.

There are two general classifications for twisted pair cable: Unshielded Twisted Pair (UTP) and Shielded Twisted Pair (STP). While both types of TP contain two or more wires twisted together, both are bundled differently.

The cheapest type of twisted pair cabling is UTP (unshielded twisted pair) (see Figure 9.7). Pairs of wires are enclosed in a single sheath of plastic. While UTP may be cheaper, it is far more susceptible to the effects of EMI and RFI interference. STP (shield twisted pair) cabling may be more expensive, but the wiring is surrounded by a protective layer of shielding which drastically minimizes the effects of EMI or RFI (see Figure 9.8).

Figure 9.7.
Inside an unshielded
twisted pair cable.

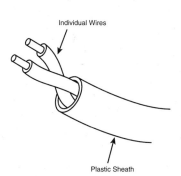

Figure 9.8.
Inside the shield
twisted pair cable.

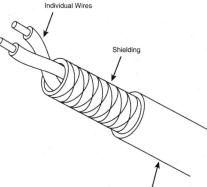

When discussing coax cabling, a point was made to survey your install site *before* you actually do the installation. The same procedure applies to twisted pair cabling, or any cabling for that matter. If you feel that the installation area is not suitable for UTP wiring, you may want to consider using STP. You would be far better off to spend a little bit extra at the beginning rather than having to redo your entire cabling plant from scratch.

TWISTED PAIR LEVELS, GRADES, AND STANDARDS

Now that you know there are two main categories of twisted pair cabling (UTP and STP), how do you know whether your cabling is meant for a network and not your phones? You may be telling yourself that cable is cable, right? Wrong. While the cabling that you use for your phone may *look* like the same type of cabling, it's not. Like many of the wonderful little "gotcha's" in the world of computers, choose the wrong product and you could be spending some long sleepless nights at the office.

So how do you know what the differences are between phone cabling and network cabling? Well, you have two alternatives. First, you could determine the gauge, capacitance, resistance, and number of pairs required to support your architecture, or you could find out what level, category or type of TP that you need. As you might have guessed, the latter is by far an easier solution.

There are several organizations that have developed a series of standards that classify cabling with specific characteristics into certain "grades" or "levels." Therefore, instead of having to memorize the specific electrical characteristics for your cabling, all you need to know is the classification. Now it's time to take a look at some of these organizations and what they have done for you.

IBM TWISTED PAIR TYPES

International Business Machines' (IBM) position within the computer world is formidable. While many competing organizations are out there, IBM is viewed as a reputable organization with decades of expertise. Their work in the networking arena has brought architectures, such as token ring, to the market. As such, it only seems natural that they provide a set of standards regarding the types of cabling that should be used. What separates IBM's cabling standards from the others is that their's are geared specifically towards the token ring architecture (see Table 9.2). These standards cover unshielded and shielded twisted pair cabling with an impedance of 100 and 150 Ohms, respectively.

TABLE 9.2. IBM CABLE SPECIFICATIONS.

Type	Description
Type 1	Type 1 cable contains two pairs of 22 AWG shielded wire. It will support token ring networks up to 16 Mbps with a maximum of 260 nodes.
Type 2	Intended for use in token ring networks up to 16 Mbps, Type 2 cable contains two shielded pairs of 22 AWG plus four pairs of 26 AWG cable between the insulating sheath and shield.
Type 3	Generally intended as a voice grade cable, Type 3 can be used for transmissions up to 4 Mbps with a maximum of 72 nodes when a media filter. Type 3 unshielded cable contains four pairs of 24 AWG wire.
Type 5	Type 5 cabling is a 100/140 micron fiber-optic cable.
Type 6	Type 6 cabling is comprised of two shielded pairs of 26 AWG wire. The purpose of this cable is to be used as patch cables to connect ports on the MSAU.
Type 8	Type 8 is a flat cable (no twists) intended for use under carpeting with two pairs of 23 AWG wire.
Type 9	Type 9 shielded cabling is intended for use in plenum installations. It contains two shielded pairs of 26 AWG wire.

UNDERWRITERS LABORATORIES

In the past, you may have heard of an organization called the *Underwriters Laboratories* (UL). This organization is responsible for the standardization and certification of various products. Their work is highly reputable and they have developed a certification for twisted pair cabling called the *Data Transmission Performance Level Marking* (DTPLM) program. Based on the results of these tests, TP cable is classified within one of five levels that cover both data grade and voice grade cabling, as shown in Table 9.3.

TABLE 9.3. UNDERWRITERS LABORATORIES CABLE SPECIFICATIONS.

Level	Description
Level 1	Level 1 cabling has no preset performance specifications. It is a voice grade cable that is not suitable for data transmissions.
Level 2	Level 2 cable is also intended for voice grade transmissions, or data transmissions up to 1 Mbps. Due to the low data transmission rate, Level 2 cable should not be used for anything other than voice.

continues

Table 9.3. continued

Level	Description
Level 3	Tested up to 16 MHz, Level 3 cable can be used for voice or data transmissions up to 10 Mbps. The most common implementation of Level 3 cable is for use within a 10BaseT environment.
Level 4	Comparable to the EIA/TIA Category 4 cable, Level 4 cabling is tested up to 20 MHz. Typical implementations of Level 4 cable are for large 10BaseT networks or 16 Mbps token ring.
Level 5	Tested up to 100 MHz, Level 5 cable is intended for use in high speed networks operating up to 100 Mbps such as CDDI, TCNS, or other 100 Mbps architectures over copper.

The UL and Safety

Certifying cabling with their DTPLM tests is not the only task of the Underwriters Laboratories. Another key responsibility of the UL is to certify cabling for fire and safety regulations.

While a well-known fact to professional cable installers, the novice may not realize that there are strict codes that stipulate which types of wiring can be used within a building. Should you choose the wrong cable, you are risking the possibility of a fine from your local fire inspector. Don't worry, the fine is the least of your worries. The inspector will most likely force you to remove all of the offending cable and replace it with the appropriately certified version. After spending weeks or even months wiring a building, this will not be an easy, or inexpensive task. Think that's bad? How about risking the life of your co-workers and your own?

Many of the networks in today's companies span an entire floor or through a building. In cases like this, cabling is run from one floor to another through a Riser Room: a.k.a., the wiring closet. Any wiring that connects two or more floors together must be certified by the UL for this purpose. Testing by the UL ensures that if a fire were to start on one floor, the cabling would not carry the fire to other areas of the building.

When nodes are wired together on the same floor, cabling usually passes through the building's plenum: for those of us who are not up on building terminology, this is the area between the ceiling and the floor above. Whenever cabling is run through the plenum, it must pass a test by the Underwriters Laboratories called the Modified Steiner Tunnel Test. This test ensures that the cabling is fire-resistant and will not produce an excessive amount of smoke.

EIA/TIA

In 1991, the Electrical Industries Association published a report categorizing several types of unshielded twisted pair cabling. This report, referred to as the EIA/TIA-568, is comprised of five categories, covering both voice and data communications grade cable (see Table 9.4). Each category in the report is backwards-compatible. For example, an installation requiring Category 3 wiring could also use Category 4 or 5 cable.

TABLE 9.4. EIA/TIA CABLE SPECIFICATIONS.

Category	Description
Category 1	Category 1 cable has no performance specifications for its usage. As such, it is not suitable for data communications.
Category 2	Category 2 cable is a low speed data medium that can be used with some types of alarm wiring. It is not a data grade cable.
Category 3	Tested up to 16 MHz, Category 3 cable can be used for voice or data communications. Typical implementations are for 10BaseT or 4 Mbps token ring.
Category 4	Category 4 cable is intended for voice grade communications or 16 Mbps Token ring. It is tested up to 20 MHz.
Category 5	Tested up to 100 MHz, Category 5 cabling is for use in 16 Mbps token ring, FDDI over UTP, or voice grade communications.

FIBER-OPTIC CABLE

When considering the type of cabling to use on your network, you are not restricted to the copper mediums discussed previously. For a couple of years now, fiber-optic cabling has been making a lot of headway in the world of networking.

Made of a plastic or glass core, fiber-optic cable uses pulses of light, not electricity, to transmit data down the line. Surrounding the core, a thick layer of "cladding" is used for protection and to "bounce" the pulse of light down the stretch of cable. Finally, surrounding the cladding there is an additional layer of plastic whose purpose it is to protect the cable from typical wear and tear (see Figure 9.9).

Fiber-optic cable provides a medium that has a very high potential bandwidth, yet it is not susceptible to EMI interference. Previously, it was noted that EMI (Electromagnetic Interference) is a form of electrical interference that can be created by various pieces of equipment in your office. Well, because fiber-optic cable uses light to transmit data, EMI cannot have any adverse affects on its transmission capabilities.

Figure 9.9.
Fiber-optic cable.

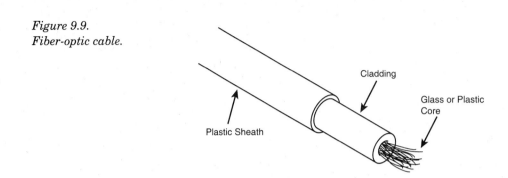

Sound too good to be true? It is. While fiber is probably *the* best medium for your network, it is extremely expensive to implement. At more than 10 times the cost of UTP or coax cabling, using fiber throughout your entire network can be a very costly experience. An additional cost associated with fiber-optic cabling is the tools required to install it. These precision tools are unlike the standard crimpers used for coax cable and they are very expensive.

LOCAL AREA NETWORK ARCHITECTURES

When the use of LANs first started to take off, your choice for the network architecture was limited. At that time, you could choose between ARCnet, 10Base2, or 4 Mbps token ring. Since that time, many advancements have been made in the LAN marketplace. While it would be impossible to discuss every option in complete detail within a single chapter, you will find some valuable information within the pages coming up.

ARCNET: THE PERSISTENT ARCHITECTURE

With so many vendors competing for your business, some products will realize a great deal of success while others never get off the ground. Although a product is in high demand today, who knows where it will be next year or even next month? In the computer field, products come and go.

Introduced in 1977 by DataPoint Corporation, ARCnet is neither a raging success nor a failure. Although many of the industry "experts" have predicted the demise of ARCnet, it is still with us today. You may be asking yourself how a network that only operates at 2.5 Mbps could survive this long; well, the answer can be summed up in the following two points:

◆ **Cost**: While prices for Ethernet and token ring architectures are reasonably affordable today, this was not always the case. In the past, when
competing technologies demanded a higher price tag, ARCnet was the

cost- effective solution. Today, depending on the manufacturer, ARCnet cards can be purchased for roughly $100.

◆ **Vendor Backing**: DataPoint may have brought ARCnet to the marketplace, but in 1981 other companies, such as Standard Microsystems Corporation (SMC), began marketing their own versions of the ARCnet NIC, and two years later, other companies joined in. When Novell first introduced their NetWare NOS, ARCnet was one of the first architectures supported. Novell felt that ARCnet would be a great success due to its low cost and ease of installation. Their confidence was so high that Novell introduced their own board called the RX-NET interface card. Unfortunately, even with its proven stability, ARCnet has not enjoyed the success that some people feel it deserves.

CONNECTING ARCNET NODES

ARCnet is an extremely flexible and resilient architecture. To examine how the ARCnet network is set up, you should first take a look at the possible topologies and wiring configurations.

For your topology, there are two choices available to you: the star or the bus. When wired as a star, each node is physically wired directly to a hub (see Figure 9.10). Depending on the proposed size of your network, and the monetary resources available, there are two types of hubs that you can use: passive or active. *Passive hubs* are generally better suited towards the smaller-sized LANs where money is a concern. While passive hubs will operate perfectly well within the network, you must be careful when working with them. Any ports which are not being used on the passive hub must be terminated with a 93 Ohm Terminator (when using coax cable). Problems arise when nodes are moved or removed from the network, and the port is no longer in use. It is very easy to forget to attach a terminator to the port.

Figure 9.10.
ARCnet LAN based on
a star topology.

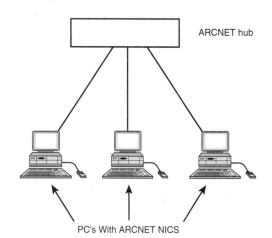

ARCNET hub

PC's With ARCNET NICS

Active hubs will cost you a few hundred dollars more, but they make your life as the network administrator much easier. First off, ports on an active hub do not have to be terminated manually, they are self-terminating. This feature may only save a couple of dollars from purchasing external terminators, but at least you don't have to worry about remembering to terminate the hubs ports when you're in the middle of a big move.

The next point to consider when choosing your hubs is the overall size of your network. Passive hubs only allow you to place a node no more than 100 feet away. Remember, this is the *cable distance*, not walking distance. A node that is 80 feet away for you to walk may actually require 110 feet of cabling to connect to the hub after it travels through conduits and plenums. Active hubs increase this distance by twenty times (see Table 9.5).

TABLE 9.5. ARCNET WIRING CONSIDERATIONS WHEN USED IN A STAR TOPOLOGY.

Maximum distance between passive hub and active hub	100 feet
Maximum distance between two active hubs	2,000 feet
Maximum distance between two passive hubs	N/A
Maximum distance between the two farthest nodes	20,000 feet
Maximum distance between node and passive hub	100 feet
Maximum distance between node and active hub	2,000 feet

Another size related problem with passive hubs is that they cannot be connected together. If you have a passive hub with eight ports and all of them are currently in use, you *cannot* use another passive hub for the same network. Alternately, you can use active hubs to connect to other active or passive hubs.

ARCnet requires a 31 microsecond propagation delay to communicate properly. So what does this mean? It means when a node sends a frame onto the cabling, it expects to see a response within 31 microseconds. If your cabling is too long, the node will not receive a response in the required amount of time and will then assume that an error has occurred. The result will either be a very poorly performing network, intermittent network errors, or possibly a complete network failure. Therefore, you must be careful to observe the restrictions imposed by the ARCnet architecture, or any other architecture for that matter: they also have similar restrictions.

Cabling your ARCnet network is fairly straightforward, but choosing the type of cabling isn't. The recommended standard cable for ARCnet is RG62 coax, which terminates at 93 ohms. Remember, earlier it was stated that ARCnet was flexible *and* resilient? Well, ARCnet can also run on UTP cabling terminated at 100 Ohms

9

or even fiber. Other architectures can also use different types of cabling, but ARCnet will usually work on almost any type of cabling. While you should always use the cabling that is recommended, some ARCnet proponents have used several types of coax and even modified speaker wire to connect nodes to the hub, although this is *not* recommended!

ARCnet Network Interface Cards

ARCnet may be fairly straightforward to install, but there are a few manual steps that are required where you must be extra careful. Architectures such as Ethernet and token ring use NCIs where the physical addresses have be burned in. The possibility of having two Ethernet NICs with the same burned-in ID is highly unlikely. In ARCnet, you must manually set the station ID to a number between 1 and 255 using a set of dip switches on the back of the card. If you are not careful, this can create the following two problems:

- ◆ You cannot have two nodes with the same physical station ID. For example, if a station is currently logged into the network with an ID of 187 and another node with the same ID attempts to attach, the second station will be denied access and the network will continue to operate. Where you will have a serious problem is during the recon (reconfiguration) process. During the ARCnet reconfiguration, two nodes with the same physical ID will cause the recon to fail.

- ◆ Because the dip switches to set the ID are on the back of the card, there is a possibility that the station's ID can be changed by accident when a user is moving his or her PC around or if someone is working in the computer.

Establishing Order Within the ARCnet Network

Nodes can be connected to any port on the hub, regardless of their physical ID, but it is to your advantage to consider the ID before making any connections. ARCnet frames are passed between stations based on the node's physical ID, also referred to as the node's *Source ID* or *SID*. The SID is used in a process called the ARCnet reconfiguration that determines the exact order that a node will receive information from the network. The recon process is initiated whenever a station enters the network or during certain errors.

When a node first joins, it issues a recon request onto the network, which disrupts the logical flow of the token. The node that has the highest SID value, such as 255 if it exists, releases a new token. The node with the lowest value then captures the token and attempts to find out what the next available station ID is. If the first SID is 1, this node will send out a frame looking for SID 2. Should node 2 be connected to the network, the first node then creates a local table that contains its SID ID (1), the ID of the next station (NID), which in this case would be 2, and then passes the token to this station. The entire process continues until all nodes on the network have been given a chance to hold the token.

When a node sends a frame, it will check its local tables to determine what the NID station is. The frame will then be passed to this station and the process will continue until the ultimate destination is reached.

Now that you know how data is passed throughout the network, imagine the kind of chaos that could be created if you do not plan out where nodes will be attached. Figure 9.11 shows a network that has been put together haphazardly during the reconfiguration process. Figure 9.12 is a network that has been properly planned out undergoing the ARCnet recon. As you can see, planning can improve network performance by minimizing the workload that is being created. Another benefit to proper planning pertains to network troubleshooting, especially on large installations. A well organized network will make your life much easier when trying to determine the causes of problems during failures or intermittent problems.

Figure 9.11.
The ARCnet recon on a
poorly organized
network.

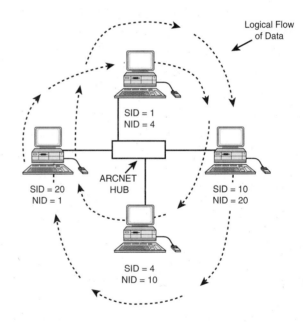

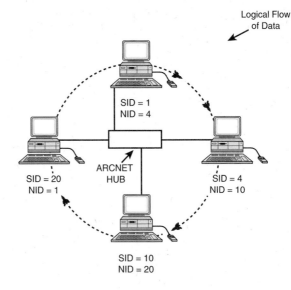

Figure 9.12.
The ARCnet recon on a
well-organized network.

ARCNET PLUS: THE NEW AND IMPROVED ARCNET

ARCnet was, and still is, an affordable networking architecture. Although it had the backing of some very powerful computer companies, the marketplace was never waiting for it with open arms. One reason why many feel that it never really took off was due to its operating speed. With end users looking for higher bandwidth solutions, ARCnet's 2.5 Mbps architecture is just not suitable for the large scale network. To try and satisfy these increased requirements, in 1992 DataPoint introduced ARCnet Plus. This latest architecture allows data to be transferred at 20 Mbps, a significant improvement over previous ARCnet implementations.

When DataPoint developed ARCnet Plus, they addressed the following three factors:

♦ Speed
♦ Cost
♦ Compatibility

ARCnet Plus's 20 Mbps bandwidth is sufficient to handle almost all of the current requirements from the end users community. While there are many up and coming architectures that will offer 100 Mbps bandwidths or more, ARCnet Plus offers more than double the effective throughput of current Ethernet implementations and almost one and a half times that of 16 Mbps token ring at a lower cost!

SAVING MONEY WITH ARCNET PLUS

If you have ever had the "pleasure" of undergoing a large scale network upgrade, you are probably aware of the associated costs and "gotcha's." Depending on what you are upgrading to, in some cases you will have to change all of your wiring and upgrade all stations at once. This is not the case with ARCnet Plus.

Should you decide to upgrade from ARCnet to ARCnet Plus, you will be pleasantly surprised to know that cabling changes are not mandatory; ARCnet Plus will operate on your existing cabling plant. Depending on the size of your network, this could save you thousands or even tens of thousands of dollars. The only hardware costs that you will incur will be for new ARCnet Plus hubs and NICs.

COMPATIBILITY WITH ARCNET

Another important feature of ARCnet Plus is compatibility with existing ARCnet networks. Upgrades can be completed all at once or gradually; the two architectures can be easily combined onto the same network. While upgrades are fairly seamless, you must observe the following three rules:

◆ ARCnet nodes can connect to ARCnet Plus or ARCnet hubs.

◆ ARCnet Plus nodes can *only* connect to ARCnet Plus hubs.

◆ ARCnet Plus Hubs can be attached to ARCnet Plus or ARCnet hubs.

IMPLEMENTING ARCNET PLUS

Figure 9.13 shows how ARCnet Plus can be implemented into a current ARCnet network. Using the intelligence that is built into the ARCnet Plus hubs, an ARCnet node can communicate seamlessly through the ARCnet Plus hub at 2.5 Mbps and when an ARCnet Plus node connects, the hub will automatically grant speeds up to 20 Mbps.

Figure 9.13.
ARCnet and ARCnet
Plus on the same
network.

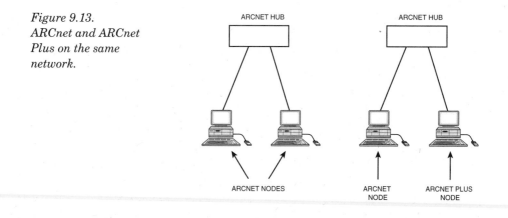

Note

If you are not planning on upgrading the entire network at once, first identify the nodes with higher bandwidth requirements. The NICs contained within these nodes will have to be upgraded to the ARCnet Plus NICs. Finally, to ensure the best possible performance in this mixed environment, upgrade the current ARCnet card in your file server to ARCnet Plus. While your network's effective bandwidth will not be 20 Mbps when mixing the two architectures, it will be still be a considerable improvement over the 2.5 Mbps that you are currently getting.

ETHERNET: HOW IT ALL BEGAN

The invention of Ethernet came about in 1973 through the work of Xerox at their Palo Alto research facilities. It wasn't until years later that three companies, Digital Equipment Corporation, Intel, and Xerox (collectively known as *DIX*) came together to try and really make something of this invention. While initially targeted at connecting high speed printers in a mainframe environment, in 1980 DIX had completed the first revision of their work. Today, DIX's earlier work is commonly referred to as *Ethernet, Version 1*. After a few more years of development, DIX introduced a revised version now called *Ethernet II*.

About the time when Ethernet II came out, the IEEE 802 workgroup was attempting to establish a standard for connectivity within a networked environment. Realizing the potential that official standardization from the IEEE had, DIX submitted Ethernet II as the proposed standard. After a few modifications to the submission, the IEEE announced its 802.3 standard as one method to connect nodes of a network. Except for a few differences within the frames, Ethernet II and the IEEE 802.3 are almost identical.

THE ETHERNET ADVANTAGE

There are many benefits to using Ethernet as your network architecture. One of the most important is Ethernet's widespread use. To date, Ethernet is the most widely used network architecture. Additional benefits can be summed up in the following four points:

◆ Installation of an Ethernet LAN is fairly easy and straightforward. Depending on your requirements, you can choose between different cable types and topologies.

◆ While Ethernet is not the cheapest architecture on the market, it offers a cost-effective solution to your networking needs. Compared to 4 Mbps token ring, Ethernet can be installed for less than half the cost.

◆ DIX may have first introduced Ethernet, but today there are many other organizations developing Ethernet products. NCIs, hubs, and various troubleshooting tools are readily available from almost any computer vendor.

◆ Ethernet offers high performance in the small- to medium-sized network with speeds up to 10 Mbps.

WHAT'S WRONG WITH ETHERNET?

Ethernet may be affordable, widely used, and easy to install, but it is not ideal for all implementations. Like anything, before choosing a product, you must try to determine how it will be used within your environment. If you are planning a network that will be using robust database packages, multimedia, or many users, Ethernet may not be the architecture for you. Even with its advantages, Ethernet has the following two disadvantages:

◆ Ethernet may be rated at 10 Mbps, but this is the effective throughput. In ideal situations or on the small- to medium-network, 10 Mbps may actually be possible. Unfortunately, CSMA/CD, the protocol used for Ethernet, does not perform well under heavy loads. When there are large database applications or an excessive number of users on any one Ethernet LAN, packet collisions can increase dramatically on your network. Whenever a collision occurs, data must be retransmitted, thus reducing the overall performance. Depending on various criteria, your *effective* bandwidth could drop to 6 Mbps or even lower.

◆ There are probably more troubleshooting tools available for Ethernet than any other architecture. There's a reason for that. When wired as a bus, a break or faulty node anywhere along the length of a segment's cabling can bring the entire segment down. Even when you have physically wired your network as a star, electrically it is still operating as a bus. Some of the hubs available on the market will isolate faulty branches of the star, but problems can still arise on a single segment.

10BASE5

When Ethernet was first introduced, it was known as *10Base5* by the IEEE 802.3 workgroup. Operating as a bus topology, 10Base5 networks used drop cables called *Attachment Unit Interface* (AUI) cables or transceiver cables, to connect each node onto a common cabling system. To attach the AUI cables to the common cabling, a small wire tap called a *Medium Attachment Unit* (MAU) or transceiver is used. When all the nodes have been connected to the cabling, the network will look similar to Figure 9.14.

Figure 9.14.
Physical layout of a
10Base5 network.

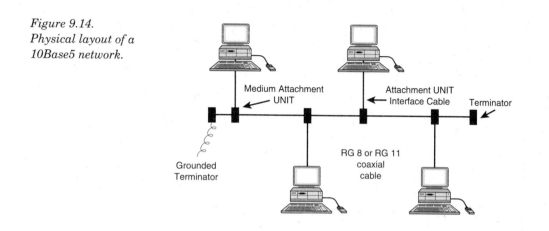

While 10Base5 networks satisfied the user's need for speed, there were a few problems inherent to its use. The first problem is related to its cost. While as a whole Ethernet may be cheaper than token ring, the coax cabling and transceivers required to run 10Base5 were expensive. The thick coax cabling used for 10Base5 is roughly twice the price of thinner varieties of coax. As for the transceivers, at several hundred dollars each, they added a significant expense to the medium or large scale network.

The second problem with 10Base5 relates to its installation. The coax cabling used in 10Base5 is a thick and hard-to-manage cable. It doesn't bend easily and is quite heavy compared to thinner versions. When you're wiring a network, carting heavy cabling around with you is not something that will make the installation a pleasant experience!

Finally, 10Base5 introduced several failure points within the network. For a node to operate, it requires an internal interface card, a transceiver, and transceiver cable. Therefore, for each node installed on your network, there are three possible points of failure. Because 10Base5 operates as a bus topology, a problem with any one of these components could result in a complete network failure. Just imagine if you have a network with 100 nodes and you must worry about a minimum of 300 points of failure. This could really be a nerve-racking experience for the network administrator!

When wiring your 10Base5 network, there are several restrictions that you must be aware of that are noted in Table 9.6. Aside from these restrictions, each end of the thick coax segment must be terminated with a 50 Ohm terminator. To protect the network from certain electrical problems, one end of the segment must also be connected to a suitable ground.

TABLE 9.6. 10BASE5 WIRING RESTRICTIONS.

Minimum length between transceivers	2.5 Meters
Maximum transceiver cable length	50 Meters
Maximum segment length	500 Meters
Maximum network length	2500 Meters
Maximum node separation	5 segments/4 repeaters
Maximum taps per segment	100
Maximum populated segments	3
Cabling used	RG8 or RG11 Coax

10BASE2

While the first implementation of Ethernet (10Base5) provided a high speed network (for the times) to the PC community, expensive components and complicated installations were preventing it from gripping a real hold on the networking world. In 1985, a second "flavor" of Ethernet called *10Base2* was introduced.

Like its predecessor, 10Base2 operates as a 10 Mbps bus topology network. Each end of the coax cabling segment must be terminated with a 50 Ohm terminator, and one end must be connected to a suitable ground. Another similarity between 10Base2 and 10Base5 is what is known as the *5-4-3 rule*.

Note

> The 5-4-3 rule states that in the network you may have 5 segments that are separated with 4 repeaters, but only 3 of these segments can actually be populated with nodes. While two segments cannot have any nodes attached to them, their purpose is to allow you to extend the length of your network. Figure 9.15 depicts the 10Base2 network under the 5-4-3 rule.

10Base2 was seen as an improvement over 10Base5 because it addressed the two key drawbacks that were stifling Ethernet's popularity: cost and installation.

Cabling the 10Base2 network is much easier than 10Base5. Each node uses a network interface card that has a built-in transceiver. From the NIC, a T-connector is used to connect the node directly to the common cabling. By doing so, you eliminate two failure points for every node on your network and your overall cost is drastically reduced. Technically, the T-connector still could be viewed as one failure point, but the chances of a T-connector failing are far less than a transceiver failure.

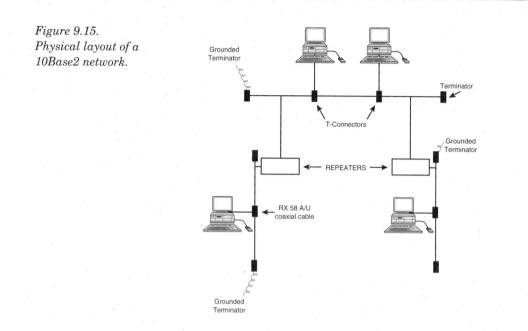

Figure 9.15.
Physical layout of a
10Base2 network.

You may have heard someone referring to 10Base2 as "thinnet." The reason for this is due to the cabling being used. While 10Base2 still uses coax cabling, it makes use of a thinner and lower cost coax. The reduced cable size will make your life much easier. The recommended RG58A/U coax cable bends easier than the thicker coax and is much lighter.

So, 10Base2 is less expensive than 10Base5 and easier to install; therefore, no one would use 10Base5 anymore right? Wrong. 10Base2 may improve on certain aspects of Ethernet networking, but it creates another potential problem that can affect your decision-making process. Depending on the size of your current or proposed network, 10Base2 may not be your ideal choice. The problem here is that the overall size of your network is affected with 10Base2. As shown in Table 9.7, segment lengths and the number of nodes per segment is roughly 1/3 that of 10Base5.

TABLE 9.7. 10BASE2 WIRING LIMITATIONS.

Minimum distance between stations	.5 meters
Maximum segment length	185 meters
Maximum network length	925 meters
Maximum node separation	5 segments/4 repeaters
Maximum taps per segment	30
Maximum populated segments	3
Cabling used	RG58A/U Coax

10BASET

Introduced in the early 90s, *10BaseT* breaks away from the traditional bus topology Ethernet implementation towards an easier-to-manage star topology. While electrically 10BaseT is still a bus, nodes are connected directly to a port on the central hub (see Figure 9.16).

Figure 9.16.
Physical layout of a
10BaseT network.

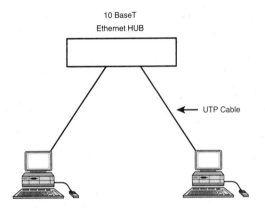

10Base2's popularity may have had some people thinking that there was little that could be improved for Ethernet. With 10BaseT, those opinions were changed.

Unlike previous versions of Ethernet, 10BaseT does not use coax cabling; instead, it uses unshielded twisted pair (UTP). With this switch, manageability is improved while cost is reduced. Not only do you save on the actual cable cost, but there is an additional benefit to using UTP cable for your network. When using coax cable, you must pull one set of wires for your network and another for your phone system. Depending on the type of UTP that you choose, it is possible to only pull one cable to each workstation. Within this cable certain pairs can be used for the network while others can be used for the phones.

So how much will you save? For installation alone, you can possibly reduce your bill in half. Assume that your cable installer charges you $50 per port (which is cheap); if you have a 100-node network, pulling a single UTP cable to each desktop will cost $5,000 for installation. Alternately, when using coax, pulling two different cables to each desktop could easily cost you $10,000!

10BaseT networks further simplify installation by directly wiring each node to the hub. If you currently have a 10Base2 or 10Base5 network, you know that you must bring the network down whenever you want to add a station. With these bus topologies, the segment will not function once the cable length has been broken. In a 10BaseT network, nodes can be wired to the hub without disruption of service.

Another enhancement brought about with 10BaseT is the use of intelligent hubs. Many of the hubs currently on the market have built-in intelligence which, through the use of a corresponding software package, you can use to manage your network as a whole. Statistics on network traffic, bandwidth utilization, collisions, and many other items can be easily collected.

In Table 9.8, some of the limitations of 10BaseT are noted. From this table, you will find that 10BaseT further improves on previous Ethernet implementations by increasing the overall size of your network. Not only can your network be physically larger, but you can have five times the number of nodes that are possible in a 10Base5 environment.

TABLE 9.8. 10BaseT WIRING LIMITATIONS.

Maximum node to concentrator distance	100 meters
Maximum nodes per segment	512
Maximum concentrators in sequence	4
Maximum node separation	5 segments / 4 repeaters
Cable type	UTP

CSMA/CD

No discussion about Ethernet would be complete without mentioning the CSMA/CD protocol. *CSMA/CD* stands for *Carrier Sense Multiple Access with Collision detection* and is the basis of the IEEE 802.3 standards. What is CSMA/CD and how does it work?

Basic contention systems allow each node of a network to transmit whenever they are ready to do so. While CSMA/CD is a contention-based protocol, it does instill a certain degree of order onto the network. The CSMA/CD protocol can really be broken up into two parts: CSMA and CD. The first half (Carrier Sense Multiple Access), checks the wire to see if it is currently in use. When the cable is free, the node can transmit any data that it must send. On its own, CSMA reduces the amount of collisions on the network by listening to the cable before it transmits.

Problems can arise when two nodes check the cable at the same time, detect nothing, and then transmit. When this happens, you have what is known as a *collision*. The CSMA protocol on its own requires a lot of overhead to resend packets when this occurs. This is where the CD part of CSMA/CD steps in. Operating at a lower layer in the OSI model, CD is capable of detecting collisions on the cable and retransmitting the packet after a random period of time. Overall, CD reduces the amount of time to retransmit and decreases the number of secondary collisions.

One well-known problem with CSMA/CD is its performance when subjected to heavy loads. When used in a small- to medium-sized network, CSMA/CD operates quite well. Unfortunately, under heavy loads, the number of packet collisions can increase dramatically. When this occurs, your effective bandwidth level can drop significantly from the 10 Mbps rating.

RUNNING ETHERNET AT 100 MBPS

If you have been using PCs since the days of the IBM XT, think back to what computer technology had to offer. That external 10MB hard drive seemed huge. The 512K of memory on your PC, well, you would never need more memory than that, right? While the PC market has grown exponentially through the years, there have also been some changes in the networking arena. The 2.5 Mbps ARCnet architecture and 4 Mbps token ring were both revamped with "new and improved models." Yet, since Ethernet was first introduced, there has not been any improvement on its throughput; that is, until now.

The improvements to ARCnet and token ring increased the overall network speed to 20 Mbps and 16 Mbps, respectively. This may seem to be a pretty respectable increase, but the new improved Ethernet is jumping up to a whopping 100 Mbps!

Depending on your experience and exposure to different architectures, you may be thinking to yourself that 100 Mbps networks are nothing new. FDDI has been available for a few years now, and it also offers 100 Mbps transmissions. So what sets 100 Mbps Ethernet and FDDI apart?

For starters, one important difference between the two is cost. FDDI connections are not cheap. Depending on the size of your network, implementing FDDI can (and most probably will) put a sizable dent in your organization's pocketbook. When developers were working on 100 Mbps Ethernet, one of the primary goals was to make it cost-effective. If greater throughput is your desire, 100 Mbps Ethernet may be the answer to your problems, but first, you must decide on which version you want.

Currently, there are two proposals for a 100 Mbps Ethernet. The first is called *100VG-AnyLAN* and was proposed to the IEEE as the 100 Mbps standard by Hewlett Packard and IBM. To research this proposal, the IEEE established the 802.12 committee. The second proposal was submitted by Grand Junction Networks and is known as 100BaseX or Fast Ethernet. This proposal has been assigned to the 802.3 committee for closer examination. Read on to look at these two architectures in further detail.

100VG-ANYLAN: ETHERNET WITHOUT CSMA/CD

100VG-AnyLAN is a 100 Mbps architecture that was developed by Hewlett Packard and IBM. One of the biggest differences between 100VG-AnyLAN and Ethernet is the protocol it uses. While the standard Ethernet implementation is known for its CSMA/CD protocol, 100VG-AnyLAN does away with CSMA/CD in favor of a new protocol called *Demand Priority*.

Earlier, the need for a cost-effective networking solution was mentioned. If a company is expected to upgrade their architecture, they want to realize the biggest "bang-for-their-buck." 100VG-AnyLAN is a perfect example of an architecture that brings greater performance to the desktop without breaking your pocketbook. At approximately two or three times the cost of 10BaseT, 100VG-AnyLAN can deliver more than 10 times the bandwidth.

No, your math is not wrong; 100 Mbps is only 10 times 10 Mbps. So how can 100VG-AnyLAN deliver more than 10 times the bandwidth? The answer lies in the new protocol. Earlier discussions on CSMA/CD pointed out that a 10 Mbps network using CSMA/CD with a medium-to-heavy load would actually have a lower overall effective throughput. The CSMA/CD network depends on each node to transmit data when it is ready. As the number of workstations increases, the number of packet collisions increases. Eventually, that 10 Mbps 10BaseT network is only moving data at 9, 8, or maybe even 7 Mbps.

A network that uses the Demand Priority protocol does not suffer from increased packet collisions because they don't even exist. When a node wishes to transmit, it must first send a request to the hub. If the network is idle, the request will be acknowledged and the node will then begin to transmit. As the hub receives the packets, it decodes them to reveal the destination address contained within. Packets are then automatically sent to the appropriate outbound port to reach this destination. Because packets are not passed through each node on the network, an improved level of Link Privacy is afforded to the network. Should the network be busy when a request to send is submitted to the hub, the Demand Priority protocol implements a round-robin arbitration scheme to ensure that each request is serviced in order until all requests have been completed. Figure 9.17 provides a visual comparison of how 100VG-AnyLAN transmits data compared to a 10BaseT network.

While on the topic of Demand Priority, another important issue to look at is the implementation of a prioritization scheme within the network. With 100VG-AnyLAN, it will be possible to have time-sensitive applications, such as multimedia and teleconferencing, to transmit packets that are flagged as being at a higher priority level than the standard network traffic. When the hub receives these packets, it knows that it must transmit these requests before any normal priority packets. By doing so, the higher priority applications will be granted a continuous amount of guaranteed bandwidth, a must for any teleconferencing application!

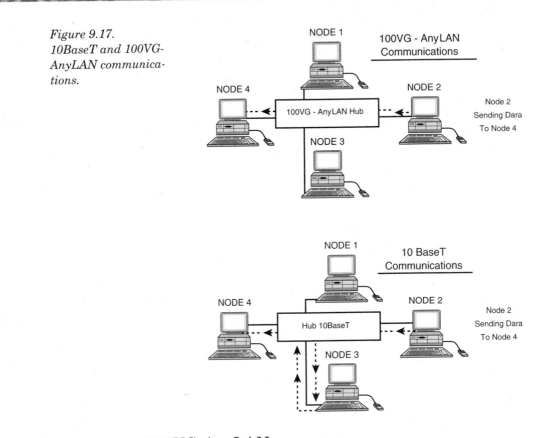

Figure 9.17.
10BaseT and 100VG-
AnyLAN communica-
tions.

IMPLEMENTING 100VG-ANYLAN

An important consideration before any upgrade is compatibility with existing hardware and software. Unless your company has money to burn, you will want to try and use as much of your current equipment as you can. Depending on your current cabling plant, implementing 100VG-AnyLAN may save you thousands, possibly tens of thousands of dollars. While many of the more recent network installations have been done with Category 5 UTP cable, a fair number of Category 3 installs are still out there. The developers of 100VG-AnyLAN realized this and have built a greater degree of cable support into their architecture. With 100VG-AnyLAN, you have the option of using f, shielded twisted pair, or Category 3, 4, or 5 unshielded twisted pair cable.

Standard Ethernet transmissions are sent over two pairs of a four-pair wire. The first pair is used to listen for a carrier while the second is used to transmit. To transmit over UTP cabling, 100VG-AnyLAN uses a new signaling method called *Quartet Signaling*. With Quartet Signaling, data is transmitted down all four pairs of the wire at the same time. Coupled with a more efficient encoding scheme (5B/6B NRZ), data is transmitted on each pair at 2 bits per cycle. By changing the encoding scheme and implementing a new signaling method, 100VG-AnyLAN is able to transmit 100 Mbps over UTP cable.

Up until this point, 100VG-AnyLAN has been compared to Ethernet. For those of you that use token ring, you will be happy to know that 100VG-AnyLAN will also support token ring packets. Because the Demand Priority protocol operates at a lower level, 100VG-AnyLAN can handle token ring packets as easily as it does Ethernet. By supporting both architectures, 100VG-AnyLAN is positioning itself to be one of the most successful 100 Mbps networks around.

FAST ETHERNET/100BASEX

In September of 1992, Grand Junction Networks announced that it was beginning to work on an improved version of Ethernet known as *Fast Ethernet* or *100BaseX*. With this introduction, and up to the last quarter of 1993, there was a lot of hype surrounding this new technology and how it should be addressed within the IEEE. Initially, certain officials within the IEEE tried to block this project from entering into the 802.3 workgroup because there were modifications as to how the CSMA/CD protocol would access the medium compared to a traditional 802.3 network. After many months (and political arguments), Grand Junction Network's proposal was accepted by the IEEE and is under investigation by the 802.3 workgroup.

What separates Grand Junction's Proposal from HP's is that Fast Ethernet retains the CSMA/CD protocol. To achieve the faster throughput, Grand Junction implements an additional layer between the protocol and the physical medium.

By itself, the Ethernet protocol can be broken down into two parts, the CSMA/CD MAC layer and a physical layer used to communicate between the medium and the MAC. Since the MAC layer parameters are specified as bits versus time, the transfer rate can be altered without affecting any of the other parameters within the MAC. To achieve this increased transfer rate, Grand Junction has implemented an additional physical layer known as the ANSI X3T9.5 PMD.

Because the CSMA/CD MAC remains unchanged, Fast Ethernet can be easily integrated into your current Ethernet network. Dual speed NICs that will operate at 10 Mbps or 100 Mbps (similar to 4/16 Mbps token ring NICs) can be used to upgrade portions of the network as the demand or resources allow. Like the ARCnet Plus hubs, which offer speed-matching capabilities, Fast Ethernet can be merged with current 10 Mbps networks through the use of a speed-matching bridge, which operates similarly to any standard Ethernet-Ethernet bridge.

Aside from the PMD layer implementation, Fast Ethernet is very similar to 10BaseT. Operating in a star-wired configuration with a central hub, Fast Ethernet can use fiber, Type 1 shielded twisted pair or Category 5 unshielded twisted pair cabling.

FIBER DISTRIBUTED DATA INTERFACE (FDDI)

For several years now, the need for faster and more efficient network architectures has created a stir in the networking community. While there are several products that are expected to be available in the next year or two, Fiber Distributed Data Interface (FDDI) was one of the first architectures available to the masses. Operating at 100 Mbps, FDDI traditionally uses fiber-optic cabling to connect the nodes of a network. Through the work of the American National Standards Institute, (ANSI) a standard called X3T9.5 has been developed for this architecture.

While FDDI has similarities to the IEEE 802.5 token-passing ring network, there are several improvements such as the following:

◆ Dual attachment

◆ Different encoding scheme

◆ Improved fault tolerance

◆ Physical Medium Dependent (PMD) sublayer

The 802.5 standard states that nodes are wired to a concentrator with a single connection. Within the concentrator an electrical ring is formed. The fundamental problem with this configuration is that a break in the cabling will make the entire ring unusable. FDDI improves upon this token passing topology by implementing a second ring. The first ring is called the *primary ring*. Under normal operation, data transmissions are restricted to this ring. When a node fails or if there is a break on the cabling, data can be rerouted to the secondary ring to bypass the fault point.

To understand how the dual ring can improve the network's fault tolerance, look at Figure 9.18. This figure depicts a network with five nodes with a break in the cabling. Because this network uses the dual-ring topology, packets are rerouted onto the secondary ring to avoid the fault.

Figure 9.18.
FDDI dual-ring
recovery.

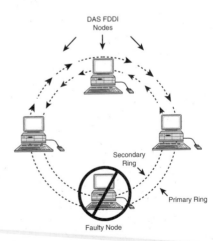

THE DAS AND SAS

Under FDDI, stations are classified as being one of two types. The first type is called a *Dual Attachment Station*, or DAS for short. DASs are stations that connect to both rings at the same time. When a higher degree of fault tolerance is required, DASs are the way to go. For those stations that do not require the same level of fault tolerance, a single connection to the network may be all that is required. These stations are known as *Single Attachment Stations* (SAS). Unlike the DASs that are wired together in a point to point configuration, an SAS is wired directly to an FDDI concentrator which is then connected into the dual-rings or into another concentrator.

FDDI offers greater flexibility for the topology of your network. Some architectures may allow you to choose between different topologies, but it is not always that easy, or even possible, to mix them together within the same network. Following are some of your options:

- ◆ Dual Ring with Dual Attachment Stations
- ◆ Dual Ring with Dual *and* Single Attachment Stations
- ◆ Single Ring

FDDI may normally be classified as a dual-ring topology, but it is possible to only use a single-ring for the entire network. Why? The answer is *size*. When configured as a dual-ring, the maximum length of the network cannot exceed 100 Km with 500 stations. If for some reason this is insufficient, the FDDI network be extended to 200 Km and 1000 stations over a single ring.

The other two configurations (dual-ring with DAS and dual-ring with DAS and SAS) are shown in Figures 9.19 and 9.20 respectively.

Figure 9.19.
FDDI network with
Dual Attachment
Stations.

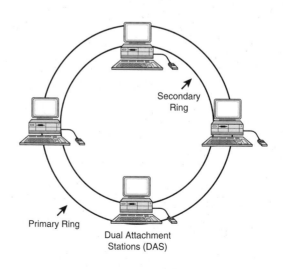

Secondary Ring

Primary Ring

Dual Attachment
Stations (DAS)

Figure 9.20.
FDDI network with
Dual and Single
Attachment Stations.

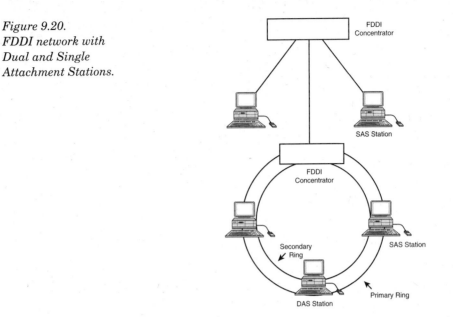

So, FDDI is flexible, fast, and, due to the fiber-optic cable, immune to EMI. Yet, why hasn't it enjoyed greater success than it has? The only real drawback to using FDDI is its price. Fiber-optic cable has dropped in price over the years, but it is still a lot more expensive than copper. Then there's the FDDI adapter cards and concentrators. By some estimates, the per port cost of FDDI could be as high as two or even three thousand dollars. Unless costs drop dramatically, FDDI will probably never be run to the desktop. Instead, most implementations of FDDI will be to connect separate networks or LANs over long distances.

TOKEN RING

Developed by IBM, *token ring* is one of the most complicated network architectures currently on the market. One of the first things that confuses some people about token ring is actually the name itself. While the name implies that it operates on a ring topology, this is not the case. Token ring, electrically, is a ring, yet physically it is wired as a star. At the center of the network is a series of hubs or Multi Station Access Units (MSAUs). To understand how token ring operates electrically as a ring, you must look inside the MSAU or hub.

Note

For the longest time, MSAUs were known as *MAUs*. However, when IEEE published the 802.3 specification that contains a MAU—Media Attachment Unit, IBM changed the name from MAU to MSAU to avoid confusion.

THE MULTI-STATION ACCESS UNIT (MSAU)

In the token ring network, nodes are wired directly to the MSAU or hub. Within the MSAU, each port is wired together to form the actual ring. Confused? If so, take a look at Figure 9.21. In this figure, a cut-away view of an MSAU is shown. The MSAU has eight ports to be used by network nodes and two special ports called the *Ring-In* and *Ring-Out* ports, which are only used when two or more MSAUs are required. For this example, just ignore these two ports and focus your attention on the other eight. When nodes are wired directly to each of the eight ports, wiring within the MSAU forms the ring. As you can see in this figure, port one is wired to port two, which is then wired to port three, and so on until the last port connects back to the first one.

Figure 9.21.
The Multi-Station
Access Unit.

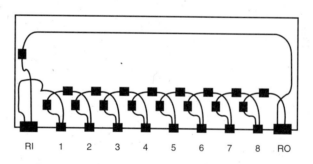

If your network has more than 8 workstations, multiple MSAU's will be required. You already know that the formation of the ring lies within the MSAU, but does this mean that you must have a separate ring for every 8 users? Of course not; this is where those two special ports come in. For this example, assume that there are 11 workstations that must be connected into one ring (see Figure 9.22). The first 8 stations are connected to MSAU #1, and the last three are connected to MSAU#2. At this point, the network is comprised of two separate rings, but as pointed out here, only one ring is desired. To complete the wiring job, the two MSAUs must be connected together in some fashion. To do this, two IBM patch cables will be required to connect the MSAUs as follows:

- ◆ Ring-In (MSAU #1) to Ring-Out (MSAU #2)
- ◆ Ring-Out (MSAU #1) to Ring-In (MSAU #2)

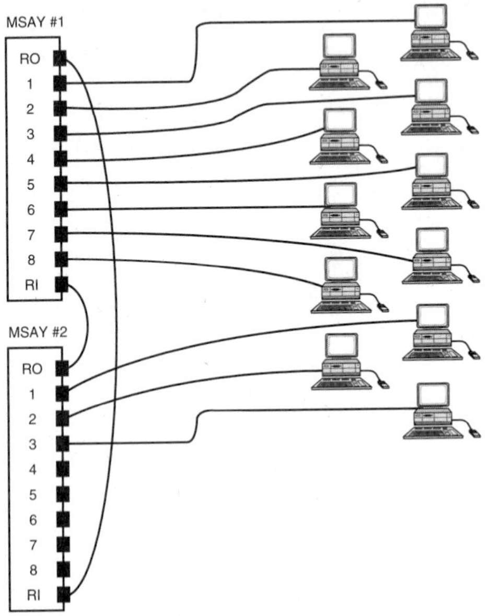

Figure 9.22.
Using two MSAUs for a
token ring network.

Once the Ring-In and Ring-Out ports have been connected, presto, you now have one large ring. Whether the network uses two MSAUs or five MSAUs, the principal is still the same. As a final example, take Figure 9.23. Five MSAUs have been connected together to form one large ring that will let you have 40 workstations. Whenever several MSAUs are being used for the same ring, just remember that the first and last MSAU must be connected together. In this example, the MSAUs are wired as follows:

◆ Ring-In (MSAU #1) Ring-Out (MSAU #2)

◆ Ring-In (MSAU #2) Ring-Out (MSAU #3)

◆ Ring-In (MSAU #3) Ring-Out (MSAU #4)

◆ Ring-In (MSAU #4) Ring-Out (MSAU #5)

◆ Ring-In (MSAU #5) Ring-Out (MSAU #1)

CONNECTING TOKEN RING NODES

Now that you understand how a token ring is actually a ring (even though it is wired as a star), take a look at what it takes to get those nodes up and running.

Your first decision will be to determine whether you are going to follow IBM's Small Movable token ring System or the Large Non-Movable Architecture. If your company is like many other companies, you will probably choose the Small Movable token ring system. For the Small Movable System, Table 9.9 lists some of the important restrictions that must be observed during installation. Detailed information on the Large Non-Movable Architecture is out of the scope of this book, but for further information you can consult one of the following IBM manuals:

♦ *IBM Cabling System Planning and Installation Guide*
♦ *IBM Token Ring Network Introduction and Planning Guide*
♦ *IBM Token Ring Network Installation Guide*
♦ *IBM Building Planning Guide for Communication Wiring*

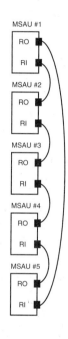

Figure 9.23.
Using multiple
MSAUs.

TABLE 9.9. THE SMALL MOVABLE TOKEN RING NETWORK RESTRICTIONS.

Maximum patch cable distance between two MSAUs	150 feet
Maximum patch cable distance connecting all MSAUs	400 feet
Maximum distance between an MSAU and a node	150 feet
Maximum number of MSAUs	12
Maximum number of nodes	96

The next task is to determine whether you are going to use shielded twisted pair or unshielded twisted pair cabling. Previously, it was noted that choosing between STP and UTP cabling will be affected by the amount of interference that could be generated within your office. While this consideration still holds true for token ring, another issue that you must consider is the size and proposed speed of your network. STP Cabling may be more expensive, but it will support a greater number of users over a larger area. Another benefit to using STP cable is that it will support 4 Mbps or 16 Mbps transmissions; UTP cable is usually used for 4 Mbps transmissions. While it is possible to use UTP cabling for a 16 Mbps token ring network, media filters are required and the overall size of your network is reduced.

If you choose UTP cabling, you will probably be familiar with the connector, which is an RJ45, but if you end up using STP cabling, a new cable connector is used. With an STP adapter cable, usually an eight-foot cable made from IBM Type 6 cable, one end has a DB9 connector while the other uses IBM's own data connector (see Figure 9.24). These connectors are fairly easy to attach, but make sure that you use the little locking clip that is included; without it, the cable can come loose fairly easily.

Figure 9.24.
IBM data connector.

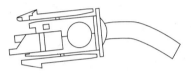

MOVING DATA AROUND THE RING

Compared to Ethernet, token ring instills a greater degree of order onto the network by restricting when a node can transmit a frame. A small 24-bit frame called a *token* is passed around the ring to each station. When in possession of the token, the station can transmit any data that it might have queued to send. While still in possession of the token, the station will transmit a frame that will travel all the way around the ring until it is returned to the sending station. Once the frame has returned, the station will then pass the token off to the next station and must then wait until the token makes its way through the network before it can transmit again. This process is demonstrated in Figure 9.25.

Figure 9.25.
Sending frames
throughout the ring.

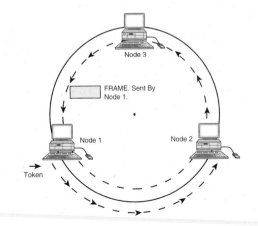

BUILT-IN DIAGNOSTICS

Token ring may be confusing to some, but that is in large part due to the "features" that it has. Of all the network architectures, token ring is the only one that has diagnostic facilities built right into it. Described within the 802.5 specification, these diagnostic facilities are usually controlled by a node on the network, which operates as a monitor. Every node on the network acts as one type of monitor or as a background process. While detailed information on each monitor type is out of the scope of this book, read on to look at two of them: the active monitor and the standby monitor.

THE ACTIVE MONITOR

In the world of token ring, the *active monitor* can be classified as the boss. One of its primary responsibilities is to ensure that the token is flowing properly throughout the network. Should something happen to the token, whether it is damaged or lost, the active monitor will issue a new token onto the ring. Because stations cannot transmit any data unless they are in possession of the token, this obviously is a very critical task.

Another responsibility of the active monitor is to insert a latency buffer onto the ring when required. Remember from previous discussions how frames and tokens are sent around the ring and eventually are returned to the initial station? Well, if the token ring network is too small, it is possible that parts of the frame or token will be returned to the sending station before this station has had the opportunity to transmit the entire token or frame. The latency buffer inserted by the active monitor is a small delay which ensures that this type of wrap-around transmission does not occur.

THE STANDBY MONITOR

On any given network, there will only be one active monitor; alternately, there will be many standby monitors. The *standby monitor* is essentially every node on the network that is *not* the active monitor. If the active monitor can be compared to a b, then the standby monitors acts like a board of directors. Each standby monitor watches to see how the active monitor is performing. Should the active monitor encounter a failure, or just plain disappear, one of the standby monitors will take its place.

COMMUNICATING WITHOUT THE WIRES

So you're sitting at home watching a little TV, relaxing from a long hard day at the office. Sure, management thinks it's easy to install those 50 new PCs—guess they have never pulled wiring throughout the floor's conduits! As the first commercial comes on, you reach down and pick up that little black box with the small buttons. Pointing the box at the TV, you press the button with the up-arrow, continually scanning through the channels until all those dreaded commercials are over.

Just as your show comes back on, the phone rings. Reaching in between the cushions of the sofa, you find the phone and then it hits you like a brick wall: *no wires makes your life easy!* Why get up to change the TV station when you can "point and click." Imagine how much easier your life will be in the office if you could just get rid of those dreaded wires!

While wireless networking does hold a certain degree of appeal, it tends to be drastically overrated. Take a look at some of the pros and cons about wireless networking. Because it is such a "bleeding edge" technology, it will be hard to discuss too many specifics as many of the vendors have come out with their own standards and methods of connectivity. For more detailed information on wireless products, you consult with some of the vendors, such as Motorola or Xircom, that are offering these products.

STANDARDIZING WIRELESS COMMUNICATIONS

Although many of the organizations developing wireless communications products are coming out with their own distinct systems, there currently are moderate levels of standardization.

The IEEE has recognized the importance of wireless communications (yes, even those high-tech professionals watch TV) and has thus assigned two workgroups to examine this technology in more depth. The first committee, the *IEEE 802.10*, is looking at the various security issues involved with network communications over a wireless medium. The second committee, the *IEEE 802.11*, is examining all other aspects of wireless communications such as low level protocols and other connectivity issues.

THE PROBLEMS ASSOCIATED WITH WIRELESS COMMUNICATIONS

Like any emerging technology, several problems with the implementation of any wireless network are involved. These problems can be summed up into the following three key points:

◆ **Cost**: The wireless components currently available are by no means cheap or even economical for that matter. Depending on the product and vendor that you have chosen, your per node connection cost could run you anywhere between a few hundred dollars to more than one thousand dollars. Remember, you get what you pay for.

- **Speed**: The transfer rates offered by most wireless architectures are far below what the industry has been asking for, which was 100 Mbps. 100 Mbps may not be needed at the desktop right now, but the 19.2 Kbps to 5.7 Mbps transfer rates of wireless communications is far off. Another problem regarding speed is that the distance between a transmitter and receiver can drastically affect the overall throughput of the connection. Some wireless products may operate at 5 Mbps, but this may only be when the transmitter and receiver are within 50 feet of each other. Outside of the specified range, the communications speed may drop drastically or it may not work at all.

- **Availability**: With all the attention that wireless products are getting from the media, they sure aren't widely available. Depending on your location, you will most probably be pretty hard-pressed to find a vendor that supplies wireless products.

SECURITY

Whenever people ask about wireless networking, at one point or another, the topic of security is bound to come up. While at first glance it may seem that security would be a weak link in the wireless networking game, it's not as bad as some may think. Depending on the product and your specific application, wireless networking may be almost as secure as your local wire-based communications.

Currently, there are three main types of wireless communications that are being used, as follows:

- **Infrared**: You probably are the most familiar with the infrared technology; if not, just take a look at your TV's remote control—if it's wireless, it's probably infrared. Because it uses beams of light to transmit data, it is not susceptible to EMI or RFI. While data usually is not encrypted with this technology, a direct line of sight between the sending and receiving stations is required. As such, it provides a certain degree of security for your network communications. The only way to "tap into" an infrared network is to change the positioning of all the sending and receiving stations so the "tap" will also be in the line of sight.

- **Spread spectrum**: There are two types of Spread Spectrum wireless LANs: frequency hopping and direct sequence. The *frequency hopping* method sends frames over multiple frequencies. Under this format, the receiving station must know the correct frequencies to switch between to receive the entire frame. The second method, *direct sequence*, spreads a single transmission over several frequencies at once. Finally, *spread spectrum* uses data encryption and low power levels to ensure that transmissions cannot be captured from outside of the office.

◆ **18 GHz Radio**: This technology uses one of 1,024 possible encryption keys to transmit data between User Modules (UM) and Control Modules (CM). In addition to encryption, 18 GHz requires that each node address must be preconfigured for access from the Control Modules. While this may create a minimal amount of extra work, it ensures that un-authorized nodes cannot tap into your network.

CONNECTING THE NETWORKS TOGETHER

As a network administrator, you may be faced with one of the following two problems:

◆ You have one large LAN that you would like to split into smaller, more manageable segments.

◆ You have several LANs that you would like to connect somehow to create an "internetwork."

In either case, there are several options available to you. Knowing your goals is one thing, but how are you going to do it?

Luckily, there are several pieces of hardware that can be used for either of these tasks. In this section, some of the options that are available are presented.

REPEATERS

Of all the devices to be discussed in this section, the repeater is the most basic. Operating within the bottom layer (layer 1) of the OSI Reference Model, it is not aware of the nodes that are actually attached to the network. When a signal is received by the repeater, its electrical composition is regenerated and passed on to the other side of the connection.

The primary role of the repeater is to extend the length of a network segment. Because it is a physical layer device that cannot determine the addresses associated with a packet, it is not suitable for use when load-balancing or splitting up your network. In Figure 9.26, an Ethernet network is depicted using a repeater to extend one of the segments.

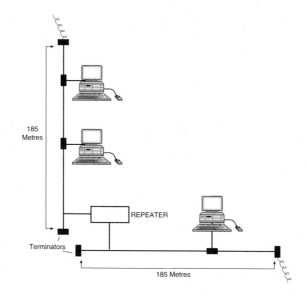

Figure 9.26.
Using repeaters in an
Ethernet environment.

9

MEDIA TYPES

BRIDGES

More advanced than the repeater, a bridge is capable of determining the physical layer addresses contained within a packet. As a device which operates in the Data Link layer (layer 2) of the OSI Reference Model, the bridge is commonly used to split a network into smaller, more manageable sections and for load-balancing. Like the router, the bridge is not restricted to splitting a network, it can also be used to join two networks together. The difference here is that the bridge is generally used to connect like systems: Ethernet to Ethernet, token ring to token ring.

Note

It is possible to get a bridge to connect a token ring to Ethernet. IBM's 8208 Bridge is such an example. This is known as a translational bridge. Such bridges are generally used in environments where mainframe (SNA) protocol is involved and the data needs to transit between Ethernet and token ring.

Because the bridge is capable of reading the physical address contained within a packet, it can either grant or deny passage between the networks that it is connected to. As an example, Figure 9.27 depicts three Ethernet networks connected together using bridges. Connected to each network are two workstations. As you can see from this figure, if the packet is destined for a node attached to the same network as the sending station, the bridge will not pass the packet onto the other side. When the bridge receives a packet *not* destined for the same network as the sending station, the bridge will then pass the packet onto the other side.

Figure 9.27.
Ethernet networks
connected with bridges.

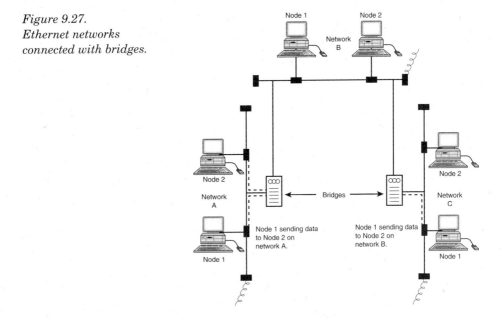

ROUTERS

Unlike the bridge that is usually used to connect like architectures, the router is usually used to connect dissimilar systems (such as Ethernet to token ring, or token ring to ARCnet) with the same network layer protocol such as IPX/SPX.

Operating within the Network Layer (layer 3) of the OSI Reference Model, the router is capable of examining the network address contained within a frame. Based on the network address, the router can determine the most efficient path for a frame to reach its destination.

Since the router is capable of reading the addresses contained within a frame, it can grant or deny access to networks attached to it. As such, it can be used effectively to split your networks into smaller, more manageable sections, or to link networks together to form an internetwork.

9

Routers are generally known as being more "intelligent" than a bridge. To determine the most efficient path of a frame, the router builds internal tables that tell it about the networks currently available. Using this table, the router "measures" the distance between itself and another network in "*hops.*" A hop signifies the number of routers that must be traversed before the ultimate destination is reached. For example, in Figure 9.28, four networks are connected into one large internetwork using routers. Each router within the internetwork builds an internal table, which tells it about the other networks currently online. In this figure, router A's internal table tells it that network D is 3 "hops" away.

Figure 9.28.
Using routers to
connect your networks
together.

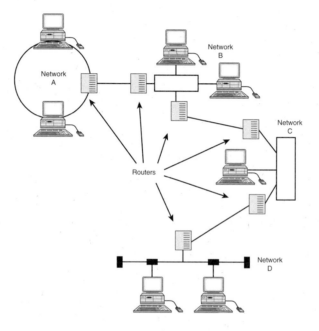

NetWare's Internal Routing

Previously thought of as internal bridging, NetWare has a feature known as internal routing. Compared to using dedicated bridges or routers, NetWare's internal routing offers a cost-effective solution to splitting a large LAN into smaller, easier-to-manage segments or rings. While internal routing does place an additional load on the file server, it is not usually substantial enough to make any significant impact on your server.

Unlike external bridges or routers, internal routing in your file server is fairly easy to implement. While you should check your NetWare manuals for the exact instructions for installation, the only hardware usually required to use your NetWare server as a router is an additional network interface card (NIC) for each network that the file server will service. Once the additional cards have been installed in the file server, you must then make a few changes to your server's AUTOEXEC.NCF file and some rewiring will be required to the MSAU or hub. Upon completion, your network will look similar to the one shown in Figure 9.29. In this figure, a NetWare server has been equipped with three NICs, one Ethernet, and two token rings. While each network appears to be separate, the internal routing in the file server makes it possible for nodes on each network to make use of a resource on another network. Therefore, the printer that is installed on the Ethernet segment of this figure can also be used by nodes that are attached to the token ring segments.

Figure 9.29.
Using NetWare's
internal routing.

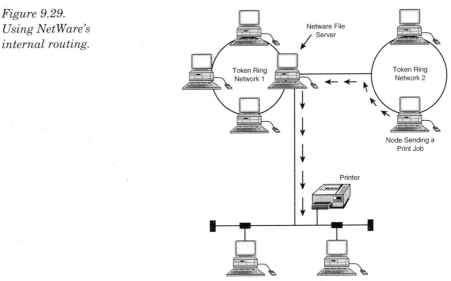

WIDE AREA NETWORKS (WANS)

As organizations continue to implement LANs, the desire to link these LANs together in some fashion will grow. By linking these separate networks together into a *wide area network* (WAN), the administration of the network is simplified and users are given access to a greater number of resources.

There are many different options that are available when considering how you are going to connect these networks together. Each option ranges in price and performance from the cheap and mediocre to the fast and expensive solution. This section looks at a few of these options and how they operate.

ATM

If you're asking yourself why a book on NetWare would talk about banking machines, don't worry; it is not what you think! In this case ATM is not your local

Automatic Teller Machine but rather *Asynchronous Transfer Mode*, the high speed networking architecture of the future. ATM was the brainchild of the Consultative Committee for International Telegraph and Telephone. Since its initial designs, a group of vendors have joined together as the ATM Forum to continue the work of the CCITT.

ATM is a flexible network architecture that can be configured in a variety of ways. Before discussing the different topological options, take a closer look at how ATM actually operates. During the past year or so, many comparisons have been made between ATM and Frame Relay. These comparisons may have confused some people into thinking that ATM is only a wide area networking solution. As you will soon see, this is not the case.

While compared to other packet-switching architectures, ATM is generally referred to as a cell-relay network. Aside from speed, the first thing to differentiate between ATM and Frame Relay is that ATM uses a fixed cell length of 53 bytes; packet sizes in other architectures can vary.

The ATM protocol is a low level protocol that operates within the first two layers of the OSI Reference model. Because the upper layers remain untouched, network layer protocols such as IPX/SPX will be able to operate throughout your ATM network.

So what is all the hype about ATM? For starters, ATM is a high speed networking solution that does one better than the 100 Mbps architectures. Rather than operating at a 100 Mbps, which is a pretty respectable speed, ATM blows the doors wide open with proposed transfer rates up to 622 Mbps. Think that's impressive? Some vendors are claiming that several years down the road, there will be a 10 Gbps ATM network available!

What is important to understand is that the proposed ATM bandwidths are "guaranteed." Architectures such as Ethernet, token ring and ARCnet are noted as being 10 Mbps, 4/16 Mbps or 2.5 Mbps solutions, respectively. These numbers are based on the throughput of the entire network, whether there are two workstations or one hundred workstations. Each of these architectures handles stress differently, but none guarantee this amount of bandwidth for every station. With the intelligence of the ATM hubs and switches, nodes are given a guaranteed amount of bandwidth, no matter how many stations there are or how busy the network is.

Another area that may be confusing pertains to the proposed ATM bandwidths. Some publications may say that ATM is a 45 Mbps solution, others may call it a 622 Mbps solution. The important thing to know is what medium will be used to carry the ATM protocols. Some proposals call from SONET connections such as OC-3 or OC-12, which will operate at 155 Mbps or 622 Mbps, respectively. Alternately, it will also be possible to use ATM on T-carrier lines such as the 45 Mbps T-3.

ATM TOPOLOGIES

Earlier, it was noted that ATM is a flexible architecture with several options available to you during configuration. While other architectures may permit two or three different topologies, ATM is the only architecture to date that can service almost all of your networking needs. Competing technologies may be used for your wide area connections, but they stop at your doorstep. As you will now see, ATM can be used for WANs, LANs, or even your entire network!

The first option to be considered is using ATM as your LAN architecture. Many organizations out there are feeling the crunch of bandwidth restrictions as they attempt to expand their networks. Adding those high-powered applications, such as multimedia or CAD systems, can significantly impact the performance of the network overall. When the power and high performance of ATM is required at the desktop, ATM switches can be used to replace your current hubs or concentrators and after the workstation hardware has been upgraded with ATM interfaces, each station will have guaranteed bandwidth over a high speed connection (see Figure 9.30).

Figure 9.30.
Local area network
using ATM to the
desktop.

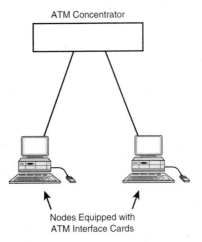

ATM Concentrator

Nodes Equipped with
ATM Interface Cards

If you are in a position of supporting several networks that are in different geographic locations, the thought of connecting them together in some fashion has probably crossed your mind. By joining the two together, administration is simplified and users will be able to communicate with each other far more effectively. The question may not be "should you do it" but "how should you do it." Because ATM is a LAN or WAN solution, there are a few alternatives available to you.

To start with, assume that you have two LANs that are each running ATM to the desktop. A cost-effective solution to connect these two LANs would be to make use of a public switched ATM network (see Figure 9.31). By going with this route, the high costs of leased lines can be avoided while still providing a high bandwidth level. For this scenario, a connection between each ATM switch and the public network would satisfy the user connectivity requirements while satisfying your manager's needs to keep costs down.

Figure 9.31.
Connecting two ATM
LANs through the use
of an ATM public
switched network.

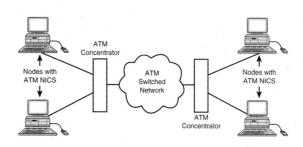

This may be well and good for the company that can afford to bring ATM to the desktop, but what about the rest of us with Ethernet or token ring networks that must satisfy your WAN connectivity needs? Well, if you have had the opportunity to look into other public switched networks such as Frame Relay, you will remember that all that is required is a router at each location. This same principal also applies to ATM WAN implementations. As shown in Figure 9.32, the three Ethernet LANs that you have spread out across the country can be connected into an ATM public switched network by placing an ATM router at each location. While this setup would not improve the local performance of each network, communications with remote sites will be over a high speed connection that is far more efficient than competing technologies.

Figure 9.32.
Using ATM routers to
connect geographically
different LAN architec-
tures.

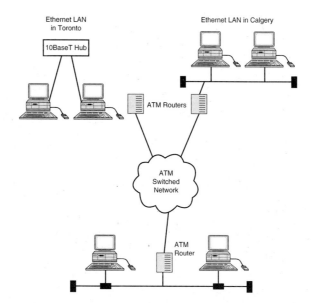

For some organizations, the use of a public switched network may not be an option. Certain government agencies or financial institutions cannot afford the *potential* security risks involved in a public network. While the use of encryption and other security features can make the public network almost infallible, the key word is almost. There is that old adage which says that "where there's a will, there's a way." A system may be impenetrable today, but some devious mind will find a way to beat the system eventually. For these cases, ATM can be used over dedicated or leased lines such as T-1, T-2, T-3, or SONET to achieve the required high bandwidth requirements (see Figure 9.33).

Figure 9.33.
Using dedicated lines
to connect remote
networks with ATM.

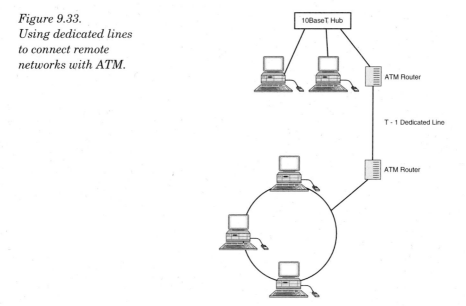

FRAME RELAY

When LANs first started to make it big in the computing world, they generally were used for small workgroups or to fill departmental needs. As the years have gone by, the size and number of LANs has continued to grow to the point where many organizations rely on them for their day-to-day operations.

As LAN usage increases, there is also an increasing need to connect LANs in different geographic locations. One alternative is to use a dedicated or leased line service, such as T-carrier lines. Unfortunately, depending on the amount of usage, these services can be fairly expensive and are generally only used by the larger companies. Another alternative is *Frame Relay*.

Frame Relay first hit the market back in 1991. Vendors and the media alike placed a lot of stress on this technology as the "solution to your wide area networking needs." Yet, like anything which receives too much press, manufacturers, vendors, and the networking community itself were disappointed when Frame Relay didn't take off as quickly as they might have hoped. After a couple of years, Frame Relay is back in the headlines of many of the industry magazines. So what is Frame Relay, and what can it do for you?

Frame Relay is similar to older packet-switching architectures, such as X.25. While many of the X.25 networks out there are privately owned by individual organizations, Frame Relay is a public service available through many of the phone companies and several other service providers.

While X.25 and Frame Relay networks are both packet-switching architectures, Frame Relay improves on the X.25 technology in many ways. Operating within the bottom two layers of the OSI model, Frame Relay is independent of the network layer protocol, such as TCP/IP, being used. Therefore, most networks can be connected through a frame relay service with a minimal amount of overhead that could be created from protocol conversions; something that X.25 networks must do since they operate within the bottom three layers of the OSI model.

Network performance has been improved in several other ways besides the elimination of protocol conversions. First off, X.25 uses a form of error checking that is time-consuming and can impose a severe impact on network performance. Frame relay does away with this method in favor of CRC checks that are performed within the network layer device such as the router. Second, Frame Relay networks offer speeds up to 2 Mbps, X.25 is a 56k solution; a fraction of Frame Relay's capabilities.

Another important benefit to Frame Relay is what is known as "one-stop shopping." In this day and age, consumers are always looking for ways to save time. Vendors know that if they are going to compete, they must offer a wide range of services; specialty shops rarely excel. With Frame Relay, service providers can handle almost every aspect of your connectivity requirements. Most vendors have Frame Relay "packages" that will include all the hardware necessary to turn those remote LANs into one seamless WAN, and they will handle all of the necessary connections and diagnostic requirements. Unlike many of the private X.25 networks available, in-house expertise is not a requirement for Frame Relay consumers.

Overall, Frame Relay offers an economical and simplified solution for connecting remote LANs. Onsite hardware requirements for each network consist of a Frame Relay router bundled with DTE/DCE equipment to connect with the nearest access point. Once your local network is connected to the Frame Relay service, data transmissions are sent through the mesh or "cloud" until they reach their ultimate destination (see Figure 9.34).

Figure 9.34.
Novell NetWare LANs
linked together through
a Frame Relay service.

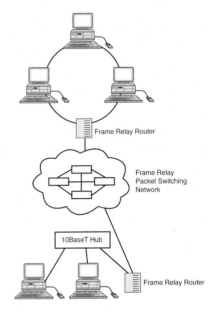

PROBLEMS WITH FRAME RELAY

Like all things that sound too good to be true, there are a few problems with current Frame Relay implementations. While not necessarily an issue for everyone, knowing what the potential problems are could assist you in determining whether Frame Relay is right for you. Following are some of these areas of concern:

◆ **Accessibility:** Frame Relay may be receiving a lot of media attention as a wide area networking solution, but it is not available in a wide number of areas. Currently, coverage across North America is fairly poor. Depending on the locations of your networks across the continent, it may not be possible to have them all linked together with Frame Relay.

◆ **Standardization:** Frame Relay is an improvement on previous X.25 implementations but, unlike X.25, it is not fully standardized. Many of the Frame Relay service providers use hardware that may not be compatible with equipment from other vendors. This could pose a problem if you are looking to different sites where you cannot use the same vendor.

◆ **Fault Tolerance Flaws:** Because Frame Relay operates as a mesh topology, it generally is seen as a reasonably fault-tolerant network. When one of the connections within the mesh fails, data can be rerouted through another path. To some, this offers a false sense of security. Unlike some architectures, which will only slow down when the network is overloaded, Frame Relay drops any excessive packets. It then is up to the network level device to determine that packets have been dropped and to then resend them. This is not always acceptable for mission-critical or time-sensitive applications such as voice and video.

♦ **Moderate Transfer Rates:** No one doubts that Frame Relay's performance is far greater than previous architectures, yet is 2 Mbps really acceptable? Well, that all depends on your application. With talk of technologies such as ATM that will run at hundreds of Mbps or even Gbps, a 2 Mbps solution may not be the best choice for running multimedia or even standard windows applications over the WAN.

INTEGRATED SERVICES DIGITAL NETWORK (ISDN)

Like Frame Relay, *Integrated Services Digital Network* (ISDN) has received a lot of attention from the media. Also like Frame Relay, its success so far has been far less than anticipated.

One of the biggest setbacks for ISDN so far has been the availability from the service providers. By some estimates, ISDN connections are only available from 50 percent of the phone companies. This is by no means an impressive level of support. The next problem that ISDN has had to face pertains to interoperability. Like the Frame Relay service providers, ISDN vendors have not standardized the hardware and communications equipment. Therefore, as you might imagine, ISDN may be accessible in the same locations as all of your offices, but the services may not be compatible with each other.

Currently, communications usually are achieved through the use of some type of analog carrier, such as your phone line. While analog lines can be used to transfer digital data, this was not their initial purpose. If you have ever used a modem on your home PC to dial into a service such as Prodigy or CompuServe, you are probably well aware of the effects that some types of interference, even bad weather, can have on your connection. These problems are minute compared to the slow transfer rates of the analog line. Sure, 9600 bps may be "okay" for transferring small files or e-mail, but it's not exactly ideal for business applications.

If you are fortunate enough to live in an area where ISDN connections are available, you may want to take a look at some of the options available to you. Currently, there are two "flavors" of ISDN available known as *BRI-2B+D* and *PRI-23B+D*. Don't worry, these cryptic names actually do mean something. First look at the following different ISDN channels:

♦ **Bearer Channel:** The Bearer Channel (noted as a B) is used to carry actual data between the sending and receiving nodes.

♦ **Delta Channel:** The Delta Channel (noted as a D) is used to initiate and terminate connections between two nodes. Depending on the configuration, this channel can also be used to transmit low speed packet traffic.

Now, call upon some basic math skills and you will easily be able to decipher the following ISDN coding:

◆ **BRI-2B+D:** The Basic Rate Interface (BRI) service offers two bearer channels (2B) operating at 64 Kbps and one Delta channel combined onto a single line of twisted pair phone wire.

◆ **PRI-23B+D:** The Primary Rate Interface (PRI) service contains 23 bearer channels (23B), each operating at 64KB plus a Delta channel operating at 16 Kbps or 64 Kbps.

Having a 64 Kbps channel for your data communications needs is by far better than those analog lines pushing 9600 bps, but there's more (does this sound like a game show yet?). If you are familiar with the term *multiplexing*, you will know that some architectures can use multiplexing to take one large channel and break it into several smaller channels that can be used for a variety of purposes. Well, ISDN has the capability to offer "inverse multiplexing." Yes, you guessed it, ISDN can take several channels and bring them together as one logical channel. Therefore, the BRI service with two 64 Kbps channels could actually offer a single 128 Kbps channel while the PRI service could merge the 23 bearer (B) channels to offer a single 1,536 Kbps channel!

T CARRIER LINES

Connecting LANs or other networks that are in geographically different locations is not a recent requirement. Since the early 60s, companies have been making these connections with what is known as a "T" carrier line. While the operation of the local architecture of each network remains unchanged, routers can be added to each network to allow connectivity to remote sites or resources.

The term *T-carrier* can be broken down into three distinct services: the T-1, T-2, and T-3.

T-1

The *T-1* line was the first service offered to organizations to provide a high speed connectivity solution for their wide area requirements. Operating at 1.544 Mbps, the T-1 is a synchronous communications link comprised of 24 separate channels capable of transmitting at speeds up to 64 Kbps. With the T-1, two options are available to the consumer, as follows:

◆ Use all 24 channels combined as a single pipe.

◆ Use only a few of these channels individually.

When all 24 channels are combined into a single pipe, this is what is known as multiplexing. Multiplexing takes several normally separate channels and combines them into one usable pipe.

T-2

Not nearly as well known as the T-1 line, the *T-2* is capable of transmission speeds up to 6.312 Mbps. Even though the T-2 is roughly four times as fast as the T-1, it never really had a chance in the limelight due the introduction of an even faster T-carrier service, the T-3.

T-3

The T-3 may not be as fast as some of the other wide area networking architectures that are coming to market, but at 45 Mbps, it is an incredible improvement over the initial T-1. Like the T-1, the T-3 is made up of several channels that can be used individually or on their own. Yet, instead of 24 channels operating at 64 Kbps, the T-3 is comprised of 28 T-1 lines. Unfortunately, due to the problem which plagued the T-1 in the earlier days, extremely high cost, the T-3 is not a cheap solution to your wide area networking requirements. But, with its high throughput, the T-3 can be more economically utilized by combining your voice and data communications together.

SUMMARY

Well, you finally made it! There was a lot of material covered within this chapter. That just goes to show you how expansive networking can really be.

If, after reading this chapter, you don't have everything memorized and down pat, don't worry; no one can be expected to absorb all of this information in one reading. Besides, as a LAN Administrator, you probably won't need to know everything that was covered here. But, like everything in life, a little knowledge can make your life a lot easier.

Throughout this chapter, the different types of cabling and several of the architectures that are available were discussed. While you may never get to use them all, just knowing what's available will be a great help whenever you are looking to install or upgrade one of your networks.

- NetWare Administration Staff

- How to Organize Network Administration

- Departmental Liaisons

- Network Implementation and Migration Team

- Summary

CHAPTER 10

Determining Personnel Roles

In this chapter a discussion on how the network administration tasks can be structured and distributed as far as the personnel is concerned will be presented. To start off, the different types of administrative personnel roles will be defined, followed by a description of what their respective responsibilities will be.

NETWARE ADMINISTRATION STAFF

NetWare 2.x and 3.x environments have the following six types of administrative users:

- ◆ Supervisor
- ◆ Supervisor Equivalent
- ◆ Print Queue Operator
- ◆ Print Server Operator
- ◆ Workgroup Manager
- ◆ User Account Manager

Under NetWare 4.x, there are only the following four administrative user types:

1. Admin
2. Admin Equivalent
3. Print Queue Operator
4. Print Server Operator

There are no more Workgroup Manger and User Account Manger user types. You will not find a utility with an option to assign such users as you could before using SYSCON in NetWare 2.x and 3.x. However, you can set up users with similar capabilities through the use of NDS security.

In every NDS installation, there will be at least one administrator. Depending on the size of your organization and geographical layout, you may have multiple (central) administrators, group administrators, and (remote) area administrators (see Figure 10.1).

In the following sections, the responsibilities of the different administrator types are identified.

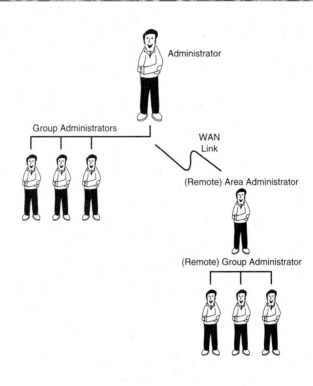

Figure 10.1.
The hierarchy of
administrator types.

ADMINISTRATORS

As the administrator of your network, you may be responsible for the following, other than the day-to-day routine, such as installing and updating application software and assisting users:

◆ Designing and implementing the NDS tree

◆ Specifying and implementing NDS security

◆ Specifying and implementing file system security

◆ Maintaining file systems, including security

◆ Maintaining NDS objects

◆ Specifying and implementing time synchronization

◆ Managing NDS partitions

◆ Maintaining the smooth running of your network, including file servers and workstations

◆ Planning for future expansion of your network

Parts III, VI, VII, and VIII of this book have a number of chapters specifically designed to address the preceding needs. Chapter 13, for example, presents information to aid you to properly design a NDS tree that is effective, secure, and easy to use.

There are times and situations that more than one administrator is responsible for your network. Sometimes these other administrators will not be responsible at the same level as you will be. For example, others may only be responsible for a portion of your network. These administrators are sometimes known as *group administrators*. Their role is very similar to that of Workgroup and User Account Managers in that they are only responsible for a group of users or a combination of users and devices (NDS objects).

GROUP ADMINISTRATORS

In general, group administrators are only responsible for a portion of the network (or a "branch" of the NDS tree in NetWare 4's terminology). Their responsibilities usually are not as extensive as that of the administrators described in the preceding section. Most of the time, their job consists of the following:

◆ Maintaining file systems (backup and restore files, installing and updating applications, for example)

◆ Maintaining file system security

◆ Maintaining NDS objects within the NDS tree branch

◆ Ensuring the smooth running of network, including file servers and workstations

It is more likely that group administrators are the first line of support for end users. They usually are part of the Help Desk. This leaves the administrator to manage the "bigger picture" of the network issues and problems.

In large organizations, it is often that each department has their own file server and someone from within that department is the administrator. This picture does not change with the introduction of NDS in NetWare 4. The only difference is that these administrators will not have NDS rights to other departments (containers), therefore, they are effectively group administrators.

If your network includes wide area connections to remote sites, then the group administrators in those (remote) locations may be considered area administrators.

AREA ADMINISTRATORS

Depending on the size of your remote sites, you may have a complete administrator-group administrator structure implemented in those places. But in most cases, there will be a single group administrator located in the remote sites. The group administrator's role is to provide local support so that users do not have to call the head office.

In some organizations, the users will call a central Help Desk, and the Help Desk will relate the information to the area administrators. If the problem is related to WAN connections, then the local (to Head Office) administrators or group administrators will be involved.

The terminology of administrator, group administrator, and area administrator only differs in the scope of their responsibilities and their location with respect to the head office.

Note

> If the size of your organization warrants it, it is recommended that you establish some structure based on the previously mentioned types of administrators. This will help you and your team to be more productive because responsibilities will distributed and better defined.

No matter how you organize your management team, make sure that each everyone understands which areas they are responsible for and what their responsibilities are. It is also important to have an escalation procedures (chains of command) from one level to the next. If there is a WAN connectivity problem, for example, the area administrator should contact the (Head Office) group administrator responsible for the routers.

PRINTING OPERATORS

Lastly, there are Print Queue and Print Server operator assignments that you need to consider. In most installations, the Print Server operator is the network administrator. In the case of NetWare 4.*x*, this can still be the case. However, if you have group administrators, make them Print Server operators for the print servers located in their own NDS branch. The same goes for Print Queue operators.

You may want to assign certain users as Print Queue operators. These users can be members of your Help Desk, for example.

Note

> You cannot be everywhere at the same time. It is important to delegate some of these "less important" functions, such as clearing a print job from the print queue, to chosen users so you can spend your time in dealing with more important issues, such as monitoring and solving network problems.

APPLYING THE CONCEPT

NetWare Directory Service (NDS) allows for the establishment of different network administrators for different container objects throughout the NDS tree. In a large organization, it would be a good idea to assign specific people the responsibility of administering NDS on a per-container basis. That means that each container object (Organization, Country, or Organization Unit) will have an individual assigned as that container's network administrator. These are your group administrators.

Note

You were briefly introduced to some NDS terms in Chapter 3, such as container and leaf objects. Container objects can be, roughly, compared to the group concept you may be familiar with from NetWare 2 and 3 environments. A container can hold other (sub)containers and leaf objects. More in-depth information on the subject of NDS is forthcoming in the next few chapters.

Depending on the size and structure of your NDS tree, you may assign one individual the responsibility of administering multiple containers (the part of the tree that is remote, for example), as long as each container has a network administrator assigned to it.

Figure 10.2 shows an NDS tree for ClearWater Resources, having six container objects, and being administered by three individuals.

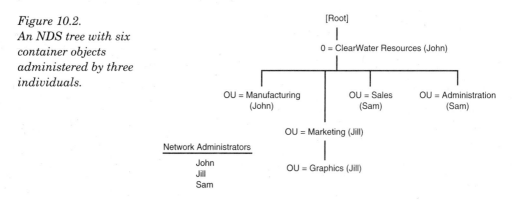

Figure 10.2.
An NDS tree with six
container objects
administered by three
individuals.

In Figure 10.2, ClearWater Resources has a network administration staff of three people: John, Jill, and Sam. Each person on the network administration staff is responsible for administering two container objects, as follows:

◆ **John**: O = ClearWater Resources

◆ **John**: OU = Manufacturing

- ◆ **Jill**: OU = Marketing
- ◆ **Jill**: OU = Graphics
- ◆ **Sam**: OU = Sales
- ◆ **Sam**: OU = Administration

Under this arrangement, you have the option of isolating the different container objects (using NDS security) from one another, in effect forcing them to be administered independently. For example, this would mean that Jill is unable to perform administration tasks on the ClearWater Resources, Manufacturing, Sales, and Administration containers. Likewise, neither Sam nor John are able to perform administration tasks on the Marketing or Graphics containers.

If Marketing and Graphics are located in a separate building than the rest of the departments, then Jill may be considered an area administrator according to the definition presented in the previous section.

Partitioning the administration of different containers requires that you make use of *Object Rights* and the *Inherited Rights Filter* (IRF), which are discussed in Chapter 27. Without the use IRF, John will, by default, have full rights to all the other containers located below O=ClearWater Resources because NDS rights flow downwards through the tree structure. The related security issues are discussed in Chapter 28.

Smaller organizations may want to ensure that network administrators have the capability to administer all container objects within the organization. However, larger organizations frequently prefer to limit access to their container objects to persons actually working within specific organizational units.

Note

It is a good idea to have a "global administrator" who has access to the entire tree. This will come in handy if a group administrator manages to lock themselves out of their portion of the tree.

There is no "right" way or "wrong" way to set up your network management. It varies from company to company. You should adhere to the company structure and policy, if and whenever you can.

HOW TO ORGANIZE NETWORK ADMINISTRATION

When planning how network administration should be done, you need to consider the following factors:

◆ Is there more than one physical location for this (inter)network?

◆ Does the company have a Information Services (IS) department?

◆ At the remote sites, are there experienced users or administrators?

◆ Do the various departments have their own administrators already?

Depending on your answers to the preceding questions, there are three possible ways of organizing your network administration—a centralized approach, a distributed approach, or a combination of both.

CENTRALIZED NETWORK ADMINISTRATION

A centralized organization for administration can be used by large organizations in which there is an Information Services (IS) department. In this case, everything is controlled centrally. Usually a Help Desk is available where all users will call in with problems. Support technicians will then be dispatched (from Head Office or locally) to solve any problems, if they cannot be solved over the phone (see Figure 10.3).

Figure 10.3.
Centralized network
management.

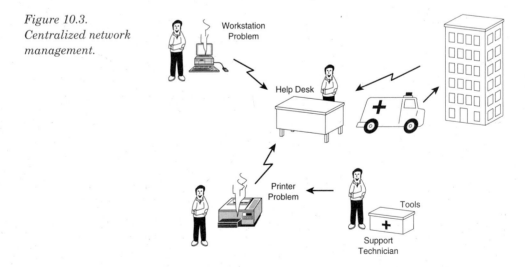

Some of the advantages of this approach are centralized resources (you can afford to purchase better and more troubleshooting equipment), a central tracking system for problem reports, and solution databases (such as "trouble ticket" systems used by many service organizations). The Head Office (usually where IS is located) would be able to dictate the network administration needs, thus uniformity on network devices, applications, and so on, making support easier.

The main disadvantage of this type of scheme is the possible slow response time should you have remote sites. It may be hours or days before a technician can be on-site to start the troubleshooting process. There is also a high communication cost involved (long distance phone calls, for example), which can be resolved by having technicians on site at your remote locations; however, this is not always possible.

In addition, with large networks, it is difficult for a centralized management group to have a proper understanding of the needs of the individual local networks, which leads to the distributed network administration strategy.

Note

For small and some medium size companies, due to the limited resources (people of equipment), centralized management is the preferred (logical) network administration scheme.

DISTRIBUTED NETWORK ADMINISTRATION

A *distributed* management scheme divides the responsibility of various network administration tasks among the various locations or departments. Each department is responsible for supporting their own group of users and associated network equipment. This can be compared with the group administrators concept presented earlier.

The advantage of the distributed scheme is that local administration groups are in touch with the needs and requirements of the workgroups within their portion of the network. Each "center" may have their own Help Desk so that users can obtain help locally, without having to wait for someone from the Head Office (see Figure 10.4).

The down side of this scheme is that each location or group is autonomous—no central network management group oversees the entire network to make global decisions. Another problem is the budget—expensive diagnostic equipment would be duplicated, or is not affordable.

Note

Some of the largest draw backs of autonomous network administration groups include non-sharing of information and tools among groups (due to competition), and competing for resources (such as equipment and budgets).

Figure 10.4.
Distributed network
management.

Head Office - Sales Department

Remote Office

Head Office - Manufacturing

HIERARCHICAL NETWORK ADMINISTRATION

You can get the best of both worlds by combining centralized and distributed network management schemes into a hierarchical network administration system. Each major department and remote site would have their own network support centers. A central management group (most likely headed by the IS department at the Head Office) oversees the entire internetwork (see Figure 10.5).

In a hierarchical setup, individual local administration groups will act on local problems that do not affect the entire internetwork without having to involve central management team. Each distributed support center can serve as a backup for other centers, depending on their geographic locations.

To minimize equipment duplication and to maximize resource usage, remote offices may be equipped with some tools, such as diagnostic software and low end cable scanners, that are essential for dealing with day-to-day troubleshooting. The central support team will maintain the more costly tools, such as a protocol analyzer.

DEPARTMENTAL LIAISONS

In large organizations, the Information Services (IS) department should designate individuals to serve as *departmental liaisons*. Such individuals are responsible for ensuring effective communication between central IS and departmental computer managers. Liaisons typically are members of the central IS group; however, this does not have to be the case. In certain instances, department computer managers may serve as liaisons with central IS, such as when the central IS staff is too small to provide departmental liaisons.

Figure 10.5.
Hierarchical network
management.

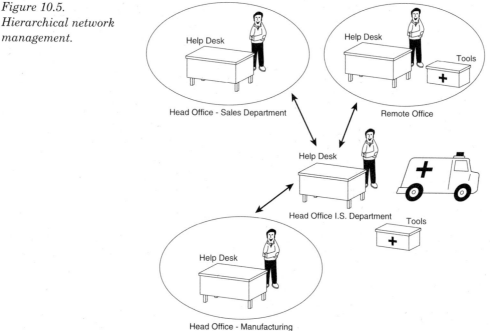

The responsibilities of departmental liaisons are as follows:

◆ Oversee all NetWare 4.*x* upgrade activities for the site or department specified

◆ Distribute NetWare licenses and new IPX addresses for all upgrades

◆ Ensure the completion of the NetWare 3.11 to 4.*x* upgrade checklist by server administrators prior to inserting servers into the NDS Tree

◆ Encourage adherence to corporate directory standards

◆ Provide first line 4.*x* support for all servers at his or her site

◆ Provide users with a phone number they can call for support during the first 30 days of NetWare 4.*x* operation

Note

You will find that no matter what (new) operating system is being installed, users will need about 10 working days to become accustomed to it.

NETWORK IMPLEMENTATION AND MIGRATION TEAM

For any significant network implementation or migration project, you should put together a support team. If you are implementing NetWare 4.*x* for the first time, your team members should have experience in NetWare 4.*x*.

Note

If there is a need, hire a consultant to help you initially get through the learning curves. A good NetWare 4.*x* consultant can save you many hours of frustration dealing in this new environment. The consultant can also help you design your NDS to make your first implementation relatively easy and smooth.

If you are migrating to NetWare 4.*x*, rather than having NetWare 4.x experts on your team, you should also have experts on the platform from which you are migrating. For example, if you are migrating from IBM LAN Server environment to NetWare 4.*x*, you need both 4.*x* and LAN server experts on your team.

Also as part of the team, the following two positions should be specified by central IS and incorporated into the organization's NDS blueprint:

◆ Departmental computer managers who will be installing NetWare 4.*x*

◆ Liaisons between departments and central IS

You may want to have departments nominate individuals to serve in the preceding capacities. Central IS may want to assign individuals to serve as departmental liaisons.

Prior to planning major design elements of the NDS tree, central IS should hold a meeting of all departmental computer managers and departmental liaisons to go through the items discussed in Chapters 12, 13, 14, and 32. It also may be appropriate at this meeting to develop a schedule or project plan for the conversion to or installation of NetWare 4.*x* and NDS.

Note

It is not uncommon that part of the responsibilities of the liaison team is to set up a test bed to test the design ideas.

It also is important that some team members be assigned to test currently used applications to ensure that they will work in the new environment. Sometimes software upgrades from vendors are necessary.

SUMMARY

In this chapter, various roles of network administrators were discussed. Depending on the size of your company, you may have simply the administrator or will have additional assistance from group administrators and area administrators. Also discussed were the three methods of implementing network administration. For small and medium size companies, the centralized administration is the logical option, while large organizations usually implement the hierarchical scheme. Lastly, some of the roles and responsibilities of the network installation and migration team were presented.

In the next section of the book, insights on NetWare Directory Services are given.

- Defining Network Resources

- Establishing Naming Conventions

- Designing the NetWare Directory Services Tree

- Partitioning and Time Synchronization

PART III

Understanding NetWare Directory Services

- Global View of the
  Network

- Tree Analogy

- What are Objects?

- Summary

CHAPTER 11

Defining Network Resources

Understanding how NetWare thinks of your network resources is the first step to designing the structure of your network. For those of you who have used previous versions of NetWare, you will find things have changed quite a bit.

NetWare 4.*x* now thinks of the entire network as one logical entity. Each computer, user, printer, group, and so on, has an identity on the network. These items are logically organized into a hierarchical structure called the *Directory tree*.

GLOBAL VIEW OF THE NETWORK

NetWare Directory Services (NDS) allows the entire network to be viewed as a single logical entity. With NDS, network administrators can perform their jobs from a single point on the network, even administering nodes around the world. NDS information is stored in a global, distributed, loosely synchronized database, the *Data Information Base* (DIB). This single global database defines *objects*, or named items, to the entire network. Formerly, object definitions were stored in server-specific bindery files.

The DIB, like the bindery, stores information in terms of "objects," "properties," and "values." Anything with a unique name is an object, including users, file servers, print servers, and more. Objects have associated properties, or characteristics. Different types of objects will have different properties. For example, *User objects* will have a property that identifies the groups to which the user belongs, while the *Group objects* will have a property that identifies users who are members of the group.

The actual contents of the properties are their "values." For example, a User object may have a *password property* associated with it. If the user account BILL has a password of GREENSFEE, then that is the value of the password property for the User object BILL. Some properties may be multi-valued. For example, a user may have only one password, but can belong to several groups. The name of each group is a value of the groups member of property.

Under NetWare 3.1*x*, a network administrator was needed to establish a separate account on each server for each user who required access. For example, if user JOHN needed access to files located on three different servers, the network administrator would have to establish and maintain three distinct accounts for user JOHN; that is, one account on each of those servers. As a user, JOHN could be required to remember multiple passwords, one for each server.

With NetWare 4.*x*, users and resources are defined globally throughout the entire system, so a network administrator only needs to establish a user's account one time in order for that user to be eligible to have access to all resources on the network. JOHN is defined as a user on the network, and he can be granted privileges to use any network resources he may require. It is easier than ever before for administrators to manage large NetWare internetworks.

The users benefit from NDS also. User JOHN can now log into the "network" rather than logging in specifically to one or more servers. Users can search globally—throughout the network—for available resources, such as printers and modems. To search for a printer compatible with his software, JOHN can use the workstation software and find any such printer located on the entire internetwork. User JOHN doesn't need to worry about attaching to servers before searching for resources attached to that server. Instead, the search is performed transparently in the background by NDS.

If user JOHN decides he wants information about specific network resources, NDS can provide him with that information. In fact, NDS maintains more information about network resources than was available under previous versions of NetWare. Information is stored about printers, servers, users, and other resources located on servers throughout the entire network.

The logical view of the network provided by NDS is intuitive to both administrators and users because NDS is designed to resemble the structure of your organization. Much like a common hierarchical organization chart, the resources on your network are organized in a tree-like structure.

Tree Analogy

The entire NDS logical framework is based on the tree analogy—an upside-down tree, that is. Imagine a tree turned upside-down, with its tap-root at the top. Below the root is the main trunk. Branches extend directly off the main trunk and grow downward; branches may split once or several times. Finally, at the bottom of the upside-down tree, leaves sprout. Leaves are the terminal objects of the tree (see Figure 11.1).

Most organizations are structured in a similar manner. At the top is the CEO, Board of Directors, owner, or other similar organizational leader. Extending downward, the organization chart branches out—divisions, subsidiaries, departments, or similar large suborganizations. Continuing downward, there are further subdivisions. At some point, the organization chart terminates at individual employees or members. Figure 11.2 shows a typical organization chart.

Figure 11.1.
NDS is structured like
an upside-down tree.

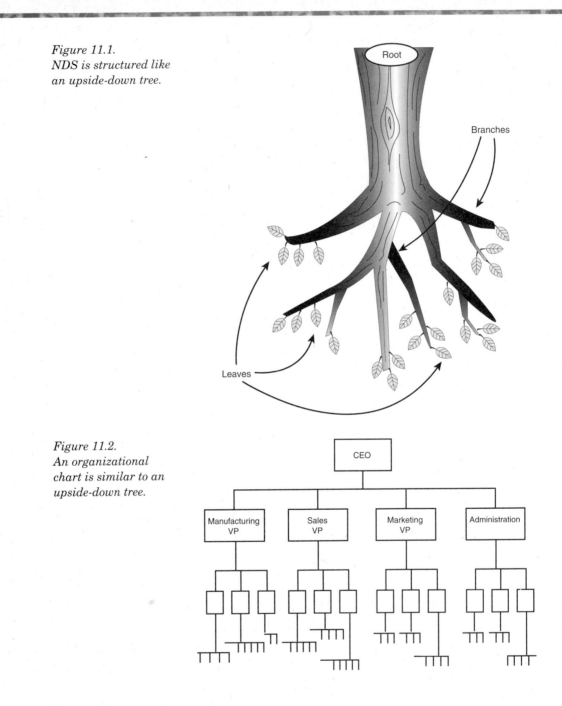

Figure 11.2.
An organizational
chart is similar to an
upside-down tree.

Note

Communication between NDS trees is limited. There should be only one NDS tree for any group that wants to take full benefit of the advantages of NDS. Some companies or university campuses have been tempted to create multiple trees on a single physical network in an attempt to maintain autonomy of different departments. However, a user may only be logged in to a single NDS tree at a time. The user can only access resources in other trees through *Bindery Emulation mode* after logging in to the "foreign" servers independently, and he or she will be limited to using the objects in "foreign" servers Bindery Emulation context.

WHAT ARE OBJECTS?

The items that make up a network are represented as objects in the Directory tree. Objects are the building blocks of the tree. An *object* is a structure where information about a particular network resource is stored; it is not the actual resource itself. An object holds types of information, called *properties*, about itself and its relationship to other objects. At the top of the Directory tree is the [Root] and under it will be container objects and leaf objects arranged in a hierarchical manner (see Figure 11.3).

Figure 11.3.
Possible configurations of the Directory tree objects.

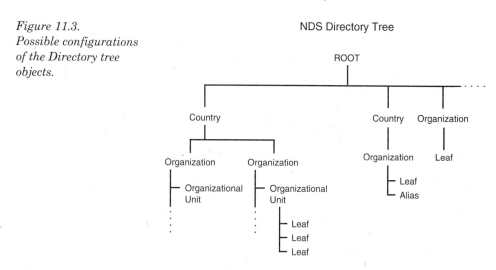

The structure of the tree, as well as the naming conventions and abbreviations used, are derived from the X.500 standard for global naming which is currently under study by the group within the International Standards Organization (ISO). It is Novell's announced intention to fully support this and other standards. Thus NDS will cooperate with other X.500 compliant applications, which may be developed to provide e-mail or other services. These naming conventions include "root," "container" objects or branches (which may in turn contain or hold other objects), and "leaf" or terminal objects which are end points on a tree and represent actual network resources. A leaf object cannot contain other objects.

[Root] is a special object created by NDS. [Root] is always the first object created for any NDS tree. [Root], sometimes referred to as TOP, only does one thing: it contains all other objects on the NDS tree, either directly or indirectly. In Figure 11.4, [Root] contains directly only one other object (the Organizational Unit object ClearWater Resources). Just like the roots of a real tree are hidden underneath the ground, the [Root] object remains hidden most of the time from users and network administrators. Each NDS tree has one and only one [Root], and unlike other objects we will consider, [Root] can never be moved, deleted, or renamed.

Figure 11.4.
ClearWater Resources
Directory tree.

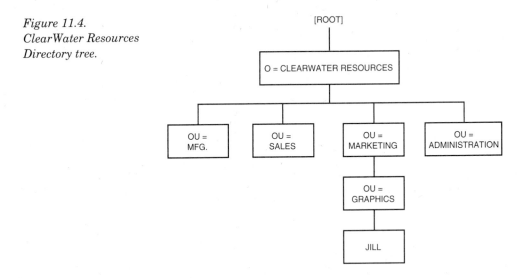

CONTAINER OBJECTS

Container objects contain other objects and are used to logically organize the objects in a Directory tree. Container objects that have other container objects or leaf objects in them are called *parent container objects*. Table 11.1 lists the three possible container objects.

TABLE 11.1. CONTAINER OBJECTS.

Name	Abbreviation	Mandatory
Country	C	No
Organization	O	Yes
Organizational Unit	OU	No

Country objects are optional. The Country object may be used to designate the different countries where your network resides. If used, they must be created immediately beneath [Root]. Country objects may directly contain only Organization container objects or Alias objects, which refer to Organization objects. Before creating any Alias objects, be sure to read the following note.

Note

With the announcement between AT&T and Novell in late 1994 to provide a global IPX "Internet"—the AT&T NetWare Connect Service (ANCS), the use of Country object may become a necessity in the near future.

Country objects must have a name that is exactly two alpha characters. The Country object is provided because it is defined in the emerging X.500 specification. The International Standards Organization maintains a list of two character abbreviations for country names. The list of supported country abbreviations is shown in Table 11.2.

TABLE 11.2. INTERNATIONAL STANDARDS ORGANIZATION TABLE OF COUNTRY ABBREVIATIONS.

ISO 3166 Alphabetic Country Codes (1992)			
AD	Andorra	AE	United Arab Emirates
AF	Afghanistan	AG	Antigua and Barbuda
AI	Anguilla	AL	Albania
AN	Netherland Antilles	AO	Angola
AQ	Antarctica	AR	Argentina
AS	American Samoa	AT	Austria
AU	Australia	AW	Aruba
BB	Barbados	BD	Bangladesh
BE	Belgium	BF	Burkina Faso

continues

11

DEFINING NETWORK RESOURCES

TABLE 11.2. CONTINUED

ISO 3166 Alphabetic Country Codes (1992)

BG	Bulgaria	BH	Bahrain
BI	Burundi	BJ	Benin
BM	Bermuda	BN	Brunei Darussalam
BO	Bolivia	BR	Brazil
BS	Bahamas	BT	Bhutan
BU	Burma	BV	Bouvet Island
BW	Botswana	BY	Byelorussian SSR
BZ	Belize	CA	Canada
CC	Cocos (keeling) Islands	CF	Central Africa Republic
CG	Congo	CH	Switzerland
CI	Cote d'Ivoire	CK	Cook Islands
CL	Chile	CM	Cameroon
CN	China	CO	Colombia
CR	Costa Rica	CS	Czechoslovakia
CU	Cuba	CV	Cape Verde
CX	Christmas Island	CY	Cyprus
DD	German Democratic Republic	DE	Federal Republic of Germany
DJ	Djibouti	DK	Denmark
DM	Dominica	DO	Dominican Republic
DZ	Algeria	EC	Ecuador
EG	Egypt	EH	Western Sahara
ES	Spain	ET	Ethiopia
FI	Finland	FJ	Fiji
FK	Falkland Islands	FM	Micronesia
FO	Faroe Islands	FR	France
GA	Gabon	GB	United Kingdom
GD	Grenada	GF	French Guiana
GH	Ghana	GI	Gibraltar
GL	Greenland	GM	Gambia
GN	Guinea	GP	Guadeloupe
GQ	Equatorial	GN	Guinea
GR	Greece	GT	Guatemala

ISO 3166 Alphabetic Country Codes (1992)

GU	Guam	GW	Guinea-Bissau
GY	Guyana	HK	Hong Kong
HM	Heard & McDonald Islands	HN	Honduras
HT	Haiti	HU	Hungary
ID	Indonesia	IE	Ireland
IL	Israel	IN	India
IO	British Indian Ocean Territory	IQ	Iraq
IR	Islamic Republic of Iran	IS	Iceland
IT	Italy	JM	Jamaica
JO	Jordon	JP	Japan
KE	Kenya	KH	Democratic Kampuchea
KI	Kiribati	KM	Comoros
KN	Saint Kitts and Nevis	KP	Democratic Republic of Korea
KR	Republic of Korea	KW	Kuwait
KY	Cayman Islands	LA	Lao People's Democratic Republic
LB	Lebanon	LC	Saint Lucia
LI	Liechtenstein	LK	Sri Lanka
LR	Liberia	LS	Lesotho
LU	Luxembourg	LY	Libyan Arab Jamahiriya
MA	Morocco	MC	Monaco
MG	Madagascar	MH	Marshall Islands
ML	Mali	MN	Mongolia
MO	Macau	MP	Northern Mariana Islands
MQ	Martinique	MR	Mauritania
MS	Montserrat	MT	Malta
MU	Mauritius	MV	Maldives
MW	Malawi	MX	Mexico
MY	Malaysia	MZ	Mozambique
NA	Namibia	NC	New Caledonia
NE	Niger	NF	Norfolk Island
NG	Nigeria	NI	Nicaragua

11

DEFINING NETWORK RESOURCES

continues

TABLE 11.2. CONTINUED

ISO 3166 Alphabetic Country Codes (1992)

NL	Netherlands	NO	Norway
NP	Nepal	NR	Nauru
NT	Neutral Zone	NU	Niue
NZ	New Zealand	OM	Oman
PA	Panama	PE	Peru
PF	French Polynesia	PG	Papua New Guinea
PH	Philippines	PK	Pakistan
PL	Poland	PM	St. Pierre and Miquelon
PN	Pitcarin	PR	Puerto Rico
PT	Portugal	PW	Palau
PY	Paraguay	QA	Qatar
RE	Reunion	RO	Romania
RW	Rwanda	SA	Saudi Arabia
SB	Solomon Islands	SC	Seychelles
SD	Sudan	SE	Sweden
SG	Singapore	SL	St. Helena
SM	Svalbard & Jan Mayen Islands	SN	Sierra Leone
SO	Somalia	SR	Suriname
ST	Sao Tome and Principe	SU	USSR
SV	El Salvador	SY	Ayrian Arab Republic
SZ	Swaziland	TC	Turks and Caicos Islands
TD	Chad	TF	French Southern Territories
TG	Togo	TH	Thailand
TK	Tokelau	TN	Tunisia
TO	Tonga	TP	East Timor
TR	Turkey	TT	Trinidad and Tobago
TV	Tuvalu	TW	Province of China Taiwan
TZ	United Republic of Tanzania	UA	Ukrainian SSR
UG	Uganda	UM	US Minor Outlying Islands
US	United States	UY	Uruguay

ISO 3166 Alphabetic Country Codes (1992)

VA	Vatican City State	VC	St. Vincent & the Grenadines
VE	Venezuela	VG	British Virgin Islands
VI	US Virgin Islands	VN	Vietnam
VU	Vanuatu	WF	Wallis and Futuna Islands
WS	Samoa	YD	Democratic Yemen
YE	Yemen	YU	Yugoslavia
ZA	South Africa	ZM	Zambia
ZR	Zaire		

The *Organization* object is next in the hierarchy and is a required object. You must have at least one Organization object in your tree. You will probably want more. Organization objects must be created directly under [Root] or directly under a Country object, if you choose to use Country objects. Organization objects may contain Organizational Unit objects, or any type of leaf object. Note that this is the first level of the tree which will permit the creation of leaf objects. Leaf objects cannot be placed directly under [Root] or Country objects.

The Organization, O, container object can be used to represent an entire company, or any logical organization on the network. It could be a branch office, a particular division of a company, engineering or sales perhaps, or it might represent a particular department within a university, such as Physics or Mathematics.

Note

Rather than using the optional Country objects discussed previously, consider using Organization container objects to represent foreign offices, as illustrated in Figure 11.5. If you do plan to connect to the ANCS, however, consider using Country objects in your planning and design.

The *Organizational Unit*, OU, object is the level below Organization. In the previous examples, the OUs would be the divisions or committees. Organization objects are optional but very useful. You will want to make use of them unless your network is very small and simple.

Organizational Unit objects may contain other Organizational Unit objects or any of the types of leaf objects, such as Users or Printers. You could use OU units to distinguish OU=Domestic-Sales from OU=Foreign-Sales within the larger common container OU=Sales, which might fall under the Organization object O=Marketing (see Figure 11.6). You may "nest" Organizational Units as deep as you choose; however, making the tree structures too deep will complicate user access.

Figure 11.5.
Sample #2 (top) (using only Organization objects) and Sample #1 (bottom) (with Country objects).

Figure 11.6.
Organizational Units in use.

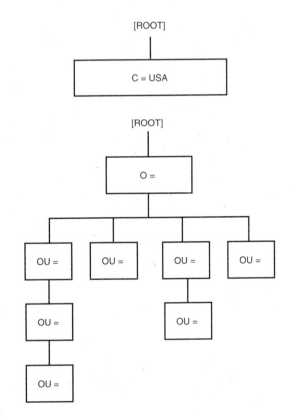

Both the Organization object and the Organizational Unit object may contain leaf objects. If you wanted to, for example, you could create a User object which was contained directly by an Organization object. Case in point: at installation the Admin user object is placed in the Organization container object. This is analogous to a tree with a leaf sprouting directly from the trunk.

Organizational Unit objects may contain further OU objects, leaf objects, or both. OU objects often contain further OU objects and leaf objects. Figure 11.7, for example, shows an OU object representing a company division. In the illustration, the OU object Manufacturing contains a further OU object called Plant, plus User objects for the Manufacturing Vice President and his staff, and a Printer object for the VP's private printer.

Figure 11.7.
Organizational Unit
objects may contain
further OU objects plus
leaf objects such as
Users and Printers.

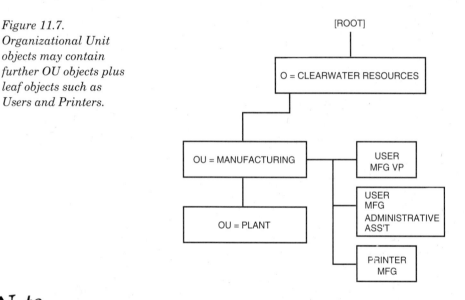

Note

Some corporations have chosen to use only a single Organization container object when defining their tree. After all, they reason, the entire network is part of the XYZ Corporation, so the only Organization object they need is O=XYZ-Corp. They then proceed to build their NDS tree by defining the various field offices of the company as Organizational Unit objects.

It would simplify the network to define those field offices as Organization container objects. This sacrifices nothing in terms of clarity.

LEAF OBJECTS

In the Directory tree, a *leaf* is at the end of the branch. The abbreviation for referencing all leaf objects is *CN*, for *Common Name*. The population of the NDS tree by leaf objects, combined with the containment of those leaf objects, forms the entire logical framework of NDS. Leaf objects are considered *terminal objects* and as such, cannot contain other objects. Rather, they represent the actual network resources, such as users, printers, computers, and so on. As referenced earlier, leaf objects must be contained by an Organization or Organizational Unit object.

Leaf objects represent the real "stuff" of your NetWare 4.*x* network. Every user, user group, printer, phone number, FAX machine, NetWare server, NetWare volume, and so on, on your network will be represented in the NDS tree as a leaf object. NDS provides many other types of leaf objects that you can define and place in the NDS tree according to your organization's requirements. You can even create new types of objects.

Note

In addition to information useful to humans, such as phone numbers and addresses, NDS leaf objects contain information required by the NetWare operating system such as network addresses, node addresses, security information, and more.

Properties, or categories of information, about various leaf objects depend on the type of leaf object. For example, a User object may have a PASSWORD property but a File Server object will not. As a different class of object, it will have its own unique characteristics. The User object known as JILL, for example, holds data that describes the user JILL. This information, called *values*, is stored in properties such as login name, password restrictions, Login script, and so on. In the user JILL, for example, the user name property value is Jill Johnson. Containment is a property of all objects except the [Root] object. It describes the relationship of a specific object to other objects in the same tree.

Note

NDS tracks objects using unique hexadecimal object ids rather than names. This is what permits renaming objects.

The following list gives descriptions of the common leaf objects you will have in your NDS:

AFP server   AppleTalk Filing Protocol-based server connected
                                   to the network. It is probably acting as a router for
                                   the Macintoshes connected to it.

Alias	Points to the original object to make it possible to access an object from two or more places in the tree. You must set an option in NETADMIN (see Chapter 25) to see the alias as a reference to another object or you won't be able to work with the properties or access rights of the object the alias points to.
Bindery object	Object created by an upgrade or migration utility and is something Directory Services can't identify.
Bindery queue	Queue created by an upgrade or migration utility and is something Directory Services can't identify.
Computer	A computer on the network. The properties include the serial number and the person to which the computer is assigned.
Directory map	Used by login scripts to map frequently used applications. If the application is moved, only the map must be changed; login scripts do not change.
Group	A list of users used to assign access rights to multiple users.
NetWare server	Server running any version of NetWare. Server's location is recorded in the Network Address property.
Organizational role	Used to create a user without a specific name, such as a Task Leader or Chairman.
Print queue	A print queue.
Print server	A print server.
Printer	A printer.
Profile	A login script for users who need to share commands from the login script even though they are not located under the same container object.
User	People who use the network. Properties include user name, address, telephone number, password restrictions, print job configuration, and so on.
Unknown	Object that has become corrupted and cannot be identified by NetWare Directory Services.
Volume	Physical volume on the network. Properties include which server the volume is located on, name, owner, space restrictions, and so on.

11

SUMMARY

NetWare Directory Services provides a logical structure for the entire internetwork. It uses various types of objects to organize the structure of the network, usually matching the structure of your organization. There is no limit to the number of containers or leaves you can have in a tree. Use as many as necessary to accurately and logically represent your actual network.

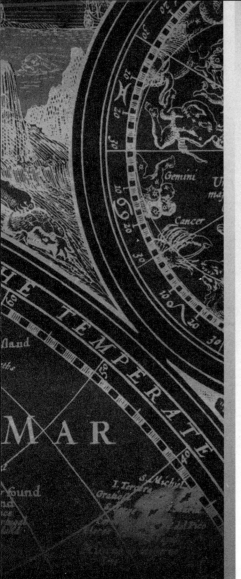

- Why Use Naming Conventions?

- Naming Conventions

- Suggestions for Naming Conventions

- Suggestions for Leaf Objects

- Suggestions for File Server Names

- Summary

CHAPTER 12

Establishing Naming Conventions

Each organization should have a set of naming conventions defined before the network is ever installed. This chapter looks at what naming conventions are, how they are established, and provides several examples of how naming conventions might be set up.

WHY USE NAMING CONVENTIONS?

Naming conventions are a set of rules that govern how objects will be defined on the network. NetWare 4 allows you to have full object names (including container information) that are up to 255 characters long with almost all alphanumeric and punctuation characters. Because of practical considerations, it is important to set up some form of guidelines on how network objects are to be named. For example, a file server with the name SUPERCALIFRAGILISTICEXPEALIDOCIOUS is a valid name, but it has two major drawbacks. The first drawback is the length of the name. The second drawback is that it is not very descriptive of the group the server services. By establishing naming conventions, you can ensure that across the network there will be consistency, usability, and ease of use in the names assigned.

Note

Naming conventions are not restricted to only NDS object naming. You should have a naming standard for your IPX network addresses as well. This will help you and your Help Desk staff to quickly locate the segment on your internet.

NAMING CONVENTIONS

Naming conventions should be established by the central IS (Information Services) department. The naming conventions should then be documented for each type of directory object that will be used. Common types of objects included in the naming conventions document user names, server names, and printers. It also might be helpful to define guidelines for the properties of each object. The key to establishing effective naming conventions is consistency in the implementation. To ensure consistency, a naming conventions document should be created and distributed to each network manager who will create or edit objects on the NDS structure. Network managers should also be highly encouraged to *follow* these guidelines.

It obviously is easier to plan this in the beginning stages rather than retrofit your network later on. Thus, naming conventions should be established *before* the network is ever installed. It will be next to impossible to affect the changes after the fact.

Factors that determine naming conventions include things such as corporate culture, personal preference, and ease of use. In a small network environment, it might be easier to be more flexible and informal with naming conventions than in a larger environment. In a larger network, it might be more appropriate to have a more formal, well-defined set of naming conventions.

Suggestions for Naming Conventions

The following guidelines are examples of how naming conventions might be set up. Keep in mind that there is not one correct way of setting this up, and what might be appropriate for one organization might not be appropriate for another organization.

General Suggestions

◆ Keep names short and descriptive. This makes it easier to remember and less typing for the user.

◆ Be consistent with naming throughout the network.

◆ Use alphabetic and numeric characters where possible; they are easier for people to remember and type.

Tip

> Avoid using spaces because they require you to use " " (quotation marks) when specifying names. The use of underscore (_) or dash (-) can usually serve the same purpose. For example, `"acct printer"` would be `acct printer`. A better way of specifying (and avoiding quotes) would be to specify `acct_printer`.

Suggestions for Container Objects

Container objects are the objects that hold or contain other objects. In NetWare 4 these are `[Root]`, Country, Organization, and Organizational Unit. These objects are used to logically organize all other objects in the NDS tree and special care should be give when determining their naming conventions.

[Root]

`[Root]` is predefined in NetWare 4. You can only have one root *per* NDS tree and you cannot change the name.

COUNTRY

The Country container object is the only container object that only allows a two character name. The Country code is determined from the country code table (refer to Table 11.2 in the previous chapter), so the naming convention is already defined.

Tip

The Country object is optional and is not normally used unless you require x.500 compliance. If you do not require x.500 compliance, it is recommended that you leave this option off because it can cause confusion in specifying current context. Or, as mentioned in Chapter 11, if you do not plan on connecting to the AT&T NetWare Connect Service, you can omit the use of Country object.

ORGANIZATION

Organization names should be the name of the organization. For example, ABC Corporation should be ABC or ABC_CORP. Remember to stay away from using spaces as this will require you to put the name in quotes, as in "ABC CORP," when specifying context. It also is a good idea to avoid using two character names because they might be interpreted as a country code.

ORGANIZATIONAL UNIT

The Organizational Unit should be the name of the organization's departments. You can have more than one level of Organizational Unit (OU), but you do not want to have more than three to five levels total (including the Organization level). If you have a department that is located in more than one OU, you will want to make the name the same. For example, your organization is spread out over a large geographical area and the accounting department is located in Los Angeles, Tokyo, and Paris. In this case, you may have OUs named after the geographical area as shown in the following code:

```
.OU=LA
    .OU=TOKYO
    .OU=PARIS
```

Under each OU, you would specify the department. It is important to make the names uniform. You do not want LA to specify ACCT and TOKYO to specify ACCOUNTING. An example of uniform names for specifying the Accounting department for each of your Los Angeles, Tokyo, and Paris locations is shown below.

```
.OU=ACCT.OU=LA
    .OU=ACCT.OU=TOYKO
    .OU=ACCT.OU=PARIS
```

SUGGESTIONS FOR LEAF OBJECTS

This section examines naming conventions for the more common leaf objects, such as users, printers, print queues, print servers, and file servers. It also looks at establishing naming conventions for properties of an object, such as the user properties.

SUGGESTIONS FOR USER OBJECTS

In NetWare 4, the *login name* is defined by the user object name. Therefore, you should give careful consideration when assigning user object names.

The first tip is planning a naming convention. You can do this in many ways. One example is to use the user's first name. This is somewhat informal and causes confusion when you have two users named John in the same context, especially since you can't have two objects with the same name in the same context. A more common way of specifying naming conventions is to use the user's first initial and up to seven characters of their last name. For example, John Donaldson would use JDONALDS. If a user had a last name of less than six characters, his or her entire last name would be specified;, for example, John Smith would be JSMITH. This is more likely to be unique and descriptive of the user's name. You might be tempted to use the user's entire last name in the naming convention, but stay away from this. Almost all directory structures provide users with a home or personal directory. By default, the home directory uses the user's login name. In a DOS environment, the directory length is limited to eight characters (assuming no extension will be used).

Another possible naming convention is to use the user's last name first. The advantage to this naming convention is that NetWare utilities list object names alphabetically, and it is more logical to see your names listed by last name rather than first name. Think of it like a telephone book—do you expect to see names alphabetized by first or last name?

Warning

> Stay away from special characters, such as /, \, :, ., *, ?, +, =, and spaces. Some of these characters are incompatible with older versions of NetWare that use bindery based services and other characters that require control characters when used. They also are more difficult for the users to remember and type.

SUGGESTIONS FOR USER PROPERTY VALUES

After you assign the user object, you can define additional property values to the user. This is optional, but highly recommended. Standards can also be defined for property values, which will assist in NDS searches. Following are some of the user properties you might define:

Other Name	Usually use user's first name here because login ID is first initial plus first seven characters of last name
Title	Use organization's formal title
Location	Especially important when organization has several sites
Department	Specify organization's formal department name
Telephone	Make sure you are consistent (area code) 555-1234
Fax	Same convention as phone number
E-mail Adresses	E-mail address

By requiring and using consistent property values within each user object, you will make NDS searches much easier to use. If you want to find out John Smith's fax number, for example, rather than phoning him and asking for it, you can do a search starting from the [Root] for User object with the last name equal to SMITH. When the search locates John Smith, you then can look at properties of the user and find his fax number. NDS searches can be performed using any of the defined property values, but this only works if property values have been assigned.

SUGGESTIONS FOR PRINTING LEAF OBJECTS

Printing leaf objects are made up of printers, print queues, and print servers. It is a good idea to pay special attention when setting up naming conventions for these objects because printing has traditionally been an area of confusion for most network users.

A good suggestion for naming printers is to be descriptive! For example, you might want to precede all the HP LaserJet printers with HPL_. After the prefix, you could use the suffix to describe where the printer is kept; for example, an HP LaserJet in the Sales department would be HPL_SALES. This also makes it easier to find resources using directory searches if you know that all HP LaserJets always have the same prefix. Following is one possible way of setting up printer naming conventions:

APL_	Apple LaserWriter Printer
HPL_	HP LaserJet Printer
HPD_	HP DeskJet printer
PLOT	Plotter
OKI_	Okidata Printer
PAN_	Panasonic Printer

The printing naming conventions should be easy for the users to use. Luckily, NetWare 4 allows print jobs to be sent to either queues or printers (in contrast to earlier versions of NetWare that required jobs to be sent to only queues). One way of differentiating queues from printers is the icon used within the graphical interface, the NetWare Administrator.

Another way is by defining naming conventions. One suggestion is to always precede queue names with a Q_. For example, the queue that services the dot matrix printer would be Q_DOT_MAX, while the printer would simply be DOT_MAX. This also ensures uniqueness because no two objects in the same context can have the same name. This naming convention is good because it is descriptive (avoiding problems of Q_1 through Q_20) and users can easily identify queue names versus printer names. Print servers should be preceded by a PS_. The Sales print server, for example, would be PS_SALES.

Note

> When a user sends a print job to a printer, the job is actually being sent to a queue. The user sees his or her job being serviced by the queue name rather than the printer name. This can lead to confusion when printer names and queue names are significantly different, such as when a user sends a job to the HPL_ACCT printer and sees it being serviced by Q_1. It is more intuitive to see the job being serviced by Q_HPL_ACCT.

SUGGESTIONS FOR FILE SERVER NAMES

You might want to specify server names using workgroup or location names. In a small organization, workgroup names alone would probably be sufficient, such as FS_SALES, FS_ACCT, and FS_HR. In a larger, more geographically distributed network, a geographical designation would be more descriptive, such as LA_ACCT or TOKYO_ACCT. Naming conventions that are not descriptive will not be user-friendly. In one network environment, the supervisor named the file servers FS1-FS20. The names are consistent, but it's hard to remember which group is FS17 services or where it is located.

SUMMARY

Naming conventions will make your network more user-friendly and easier to manage if you establish naming conventions before you start creating container and leaf objects. The naming convention you use depends on the environment in which you will be working; there is not a "right" way of establishing naming conventions. The key to successful implementation is to document the conventions that are established, distribute them to anyone who will manage the network, and make sure the rules are followed.

- What Does the Directory Services Tree Consist of ?

- Number of Trees per Organization

- Designing the NetWare Directory Services Tree

- Utilities Associated with the NDS Structure

- Summary

CHAPTER 13

Designing the NetWare Directory Services Tree

The *network directory services tree* is the network "blueprint." It provides access to all the network's resources. It is essential to plan the tree so that it is easy for the users to access the resources they need. Proper planning at this stage will save many headaches later on. This section provides tips and suggestions on how you might want to plan your tree.

WHAT DOES THE DIRECTORY SERVICES TREE CONSIST OF?

The NetWare Directory Services (NDS) tree is made up of the root, container objects, and leaf objects. The NDS is called a tree because the way that it is logically defined is similar to the definition of a tree, or more accurately an upside-down tree. When you install the first NetWare 4.*x* server, you will name the tree and define the context (or location within the tree) the server object will reside in. Before you ever get to that step, you will need to plan the NDS structure. In a way, NDS planning is similar to building a house. You logically define which functions you want the house to incorporate, and then build the house to those specifications. You would not just pick up a hammer and start building without a blueprint. In a NetWare 4 NDS tree, you do not, and should not, start installing without planning. This section focuses on the branches or container objects of the tree.

THE ROOT

The first level of the NDS structure is called the *root*. The root is created upon installation of the first NetWare 4.*x* server, and there is only one root per NDS tree. The root cannot be renamed or deleted and is always enclosed in brackets when referenced—[Root].

CONTAINER OBJECTS

Container objects hold or contain other container objects. These are the branches of the NDS. The three types of container objects are Country (C=), Organization (O=), and Organizational Unit (OU=).

COUNTRY

The Country container is an optional container object. It is a two-letter designation that specifies a country code. It is used in international NDS structures that are organized geographically. In the cases of non-international networks, it is probably easier to omit this level. If, however, there is the possibility of your network connecting to the AT&T NetWare Connect Services (ANCS) in the future, you should consider using Country as part of your design. Should you have to need to, you can create multiple Country objects under [Root].

ORGANIZATION

The Organization container object (usually) holds the name of the organization. It is a required component of the NDS tree. Organizational objects can contain organizational units and leaf objects. You can, however, use O= to denote geographical locations since you can have multiple Organization objects under [Root] or C=.

ORGANIZATIONAL UNITS

Organizational Units hold subunit groups of an organization. It is an optional, but commonly used container object. OUs be must located under another OU or O.

NUMBER OF TREES PER ORGANIZATION

Although it is possible to have more than one NDS tree, it is *not* recommended. If you do have more than one tree, their databases will be separate and independent from each other. A user can only log in to one tree at a time and access resources from one tree at a time. So, unless there are special circumstances, there should only be one tree per organization.

DESIGNING THE NETWARE DIRECTORY SERVICES TREE

Planning is essential for the NDS tree. This section looks at coordinating the NDS structure within different-sized organizations, why coordination is important, and provides a checklist for designing the NDS structure.

COORDINATION OF PLANNING

Because of its enterprise-focus, NetWare 4.*x* is the first operating system released by Novell, which requires extensive pre-installation planning and coordination. Almost all the pre-installation planning and coordination you must perform prior to installing a NetWare 4.*x* network is related directly to NetWare Directory Services (NDS).

NDS is designed to integrate the disparate computing resources of an entire organization and to create a single logical viewpoint of those computing resources. By its nature, NDS requires cooperation among different parts of an organization when planning and installing a NetWare 4.*x* network.

Coordination of planning for NDS, then, is the process of establishing an organization-wide plan for implementing NDS, while allowing specific groups within your organization to fit their NetWare 4.x servers into the organization-wide plan. (The days when a single department could install and manage an isolated NetWare server by itself are gone.)

Most organizations have a central Information Services (IS) department that is responsible for the strategic planning, implementation, and management of the organization's computing resources. However, departments or groups within the organization typically perform most of the day-to-day management of their specific computer systems. Hence, strategic management of computing resources usually is done by the centralized IS department, while day-to-day management is performed on a per-department basis.

The coordination that must occur for a successful implementation of NetWare 4.x, then, is between central IS and the various individuals performing day-to-day management of computers on a departmental level.

NDS requires both types of management: strategic and routine. It is convenient to have the central IS group chart a blueprint of an organization's NDS tree, including facilities for expansion of the tree, while making the departmental computer managers responsible for installing individual NetWare 4.x servers and placing those servers into the organization's NDS tree.

COORDINATION IN SMALLER ORGANIZATIONS

Smaller organizations without a central IS department obviously do not need to perform coordination among central IS and departmental computer managers. However, even in smaller organizations, the need for strategic planning and management of NDS and NetWare 4.x persists. (The NDS tree still needs to be designed, and steps for adding new NetWare 4.x servers still need to be established.) If your organization is a smaller one without a central IS department, the coordination guidelines presented in this chapter still apply to you. However, you should pay more attention to the information that needs to be coordinated, rather than the department doing the coordinating.

IMPORTANCE OF COORDINATION

Central IS, in order to maintain a functional NDS tree and the resulting complex NetWare internetwork, must be apprised of new NetWare 4.x servers prior to their installation. If not, your organization will experience major headaches that could cost it dearly in both money and time.

The necessity of coordination among departments when planning and installing a NetWare 4.*x* is somewhat ironic, given the history of NetWare. Earlier versions of NetWare tended to come into an organization through the "back door," so to speak, when departments installed and maintained NetWare servers on their own, without cooperation from central IS. Central IS departments in most large organizations were slow to recognize the usefulness of NetWare as the organization's primary computing platform and began to integrate the network into the overall computing architecture of the organization only when NetWare achieved a critical mass within the organization as a whole.

Today, however, NetWare 4.*x* requires that central IS perform a key role in the integration of new NetWare servers. There can be no more "back door" NetWare servers.

COORDINATION CHECKLIST

On a macro level, the items that must be coordinated by the central IS department are as follows:

1. **Major Design Elements of the NDS Tree**
   (a) NDS template
   (b) Template for NDS container objects
   (c) Leaf objects and the NDS blueprint
   (d) How servers fit into the NDS blueprint
   (e) How deep should the NDS tree be?
2. **Partition Replication Blueprint**
3. **IPX Network Map**
4. **Responsibilities of central IS**
5. **Coordination Through Central IS**
   (a) Central IS plans and distributes NDS template
   (b) No renegade structures allowed on the network

Each of the items on the preceding checklist should be planned by central IS and communicated to the departmental computer managers who will be installing and managing specific NetWare 4.*x* servers. The remainder of this chapter discusses each item on the preceding checklist.

MAJOR DESIGN ELEMENTS OF THE NDS TREE

Central IS is responsible for constructing a "blueprint" of the organization's NDS tree. This blueprint should be complete with container objects down to the Organizational Unit (OU) container object, and should be three levels deep for large organizations. Smaller organizations may elect to construct an NDS blueprint that is only two levels deep.

The NDS blueprint should reflect the structure of your organization. For example, in the previous chapter you read about an organization called ClearWater Resources having the structure shown in Figure 13.1

Figure 13.1.
A three-level organizational chart for ClearWater Resources.

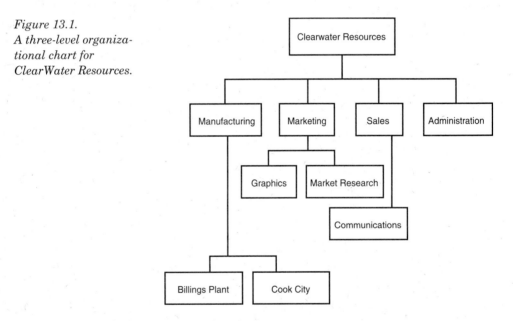

The organizational chart for ClearWater Resources shows the major divisions in the company, and the major groups under each division. The Divisions—Manufacturing, Marketing, Sales, and Administration—are at the second level of the organizational chart. The groups within divisions—Graphics, Communications, Market Research, and so on—are at the third level of the organizational chart.

NDS TEMPLATE

The organizational chart for ClearWater Resources serves as a template for that company's NDS blueprint. Organizations larger than ClearWater Resources may need to use a four-level template, while organizations smaller than ClearWater Resources may only need a two-level template.

TEMPLATE TO NDS CONTAINER OBJECTS

The next step is to convert the organizational chart into an NDS blueprint that shows the major NDS container objects. For ClearWater Resources, this is a simple step that results in the NDS blueprint shown in Figure 13.2.

Figure 13.2.
A three-level NDS blueprint for ClearWater Resources, showing only NDS container objects.

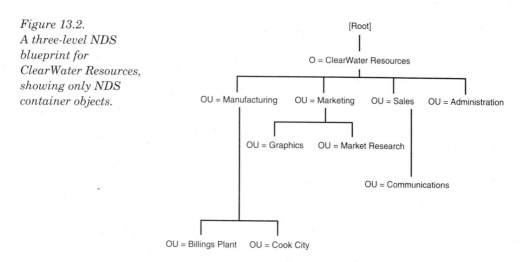

As you read in the previous chapter, NDS container objects are allowed to be superior in the NDS tree to other container objects and to NDS leaf objects. Container objects should represent divisions and groups within your organization. Leaf objects, which are not allowed to be superior to any objects within the NDS tree, represent the actual resources located within your organization: people, computers, printers, and so on.

The NDS blueprint for ClearWater Resources, presented in Figure 13.2, shows only container objects. Leaf objects are, at this point, not filled in to the blueprint.

Note the NDS context of various container objects. The Manufacturing division is `OU=Manufacturing.O=ClearWater Resources`. The Billings manufacturing plant is `OU=Billings Plant.OU=Manufacturing.O=ClearWater Resources`. The Cook City manufacturing plant is `OU=Cook City.OU=Manufacturing.O=ClearWater Resources`. In other words, the three-level NDS blueprint for ClearWater Resources is an exact mirror of that company's organizational chart.

LEAF OBJECTS AND THE NDS BLUEPRINT

When is the best time to sketch leaf objects into your organization's NDS blueprint? Generally, it is the job of departmental computer managers to sketch leaf objects into the NDS blueprint created by central IS. However, the procedures for doing so should be specified by central IS and followed closely by the departmental managers. The departmental computer managers know best which users exist within that department, which servers will be installed or upgraded to NetWare 4.*x*, which printers, and so on. In turn, the departmental computer managers should work with the management personnel in each group (OU) to ensure that the NDS leaf objects contained by that OU are sufficient and appropriate, given the actual human and computing resources within that group.

HOW SERVERS NEED TO BE SPECIFIED ON THE NDS BLUEPRINT

The NDS database is stored on NetWare 4.*x* file servers within partitions. When you install a NetWare 4.*x* file server, you create a new partition when you place the file server object within a new organizational container. If the file server is placed within an existing organizational container, a new partition is not created. So, in order to have an NDS database, you must have a least one NetWare 4.*x* file server.

The rules for storing the NDS database are as follows:

◆ The NDS database is stored on a NetWare 4.*x* server or servers.

◆ A file server created under a new organizational unit implicitly creates a new NDS partition.

◆ A NetWare 4.*x* server may store more than one container object and corresponding NDS partitions.

◆ A NetWare 4.*x* server can be added to an existing container object. If so, the new server does not create a new NDS partition.

As a result of these rules, some servers (those storing NDS container objects and their corresponding NDS partitions) must be specified on the NDS blueprint created by central IS. A portion of the NDS blueprint for ClearWater Resources, with some NetWare 4.*x* servers specified, is shown in Figure 13.3.

In Figure 13.3, ClearWater Resource's central IS department has specified the NetWare 4.*x* servers that will store the NDS container objects for a portion of that company's NDS tree. The [Root] and O=ClearWater Resources container objects are stored on server CLEARWATER. The OU=Manufacturing container object is stored on server CLEARWATER_MFG. The OU=Billings Plant container object is stored on server CLEARWATER_BILLINGS.

Figure 13.3.
Servers storing NDS
container objects
should be specified on
the NDS blueprint.

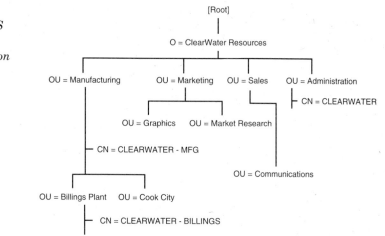

Note the following aspects of ClearWater Resource's NDS blueprint as it is up to this point:

◆ NDS Container objects are named to reflect corresponding divisions or groups on the company's organizational chart.

◆ Where appropriate, NDS container objects contain geographical information.

◆ NetWare 4.*x* servers that store NDS container objects are named to reflect the container object(s) they store.

Note that central IS does not need to specify all servers on the NDS blueprint; only those servers that hold NDS container objects. It is likely that department computer managers at the Billings Manufacturing plant, for example, plan on adding several servers under the `OU=Billings Plant` container object. However, because these additional servers will not store any NDS container objects, ClearWater Resource's central IS department does not need to specify them at this juncture. In fact, the number of such servers does not need to be known at this point.

One final note on partitions—because users access network resources via the NDS partitions, it is critical that they are replicated for fault tolerance and speedy access. This is such an important topic that the Chapter 14 is dedicated to partitioning.

How Deep Should the NDS Tree Be?

NDS allows your tree to be arbitrarily deep. Because of the internal architecture of NDS, there is no performance penalty associated with an NDS tree more than three levels deep. (Partition replication can have a large effect on the performance of NDS, but this is not directly related to the depth of the NDS tree.)

Some marketing information released by Novell when NetWare 4.0 shipped recommended a maximum tree depth of three levels. However, this recommendation was based on shortcomings in administration software and NDS synchronization, which have since been resolved.

Note

> The only drawback to a four-or-greater level NDS tree is that distinguished (fully specified) NDS names can become too long for ease of reference. However, by using the NDS context (tree path) within user login scripts, you can allow users to work with short NDS names (names that omit the full NDS context).

The guideline you should follow when determining the initial depth of your NDS blueprint should be that the NDS blueprint will reflect that actual structure of your organization. In other words, don't restructure your organization so you can limit the depth of your NDS tree to three levels.

Smaller organizations should be content to have a two-level (or perhaps even a one-level) NDS tree. In general, your NDS tree should be as simple as it can be while still reflecting the structure of your organization.

Partition Replication Blueprint

The second item on the preceding checklist is the partition replication blueprint. Partition replication may seem like a less important checklist item than the major design elements of your NDS tree. However, partition replication affects both the fault tolerance and the efficiency of your NetWare 4.x network.

Partitioning and partition replication are related directly to the number of NDS container objects in your tree, and the location within the tree of those container objects.

In this discussion of NDS partitions, it is assumed a one-to-one correspondence between partitions and NDS container objects. Partitions are referred to by the name of the container object they store, such as the O=ClearWater Resources partition, the OU=Manufacturing partition, and so on.

You will read in Chapter 14 about three different types of partitions: Master replica, Read/Write replica, and Read-Only replica. The Master replica is created automatically by NDS when you install the first server object into the NDS tree. A Read/Write replica is a copy of the Master replica stored on a different NetWare 4.x server. Users may read and update information stored on a read/write replica. Users may read but not update a Read-Only replica.

Updates to a Master replica are automatically made to Read/Write and Read-Only copies of the Master replica. Updates made to a Read/Write replica are automatically made to the Master replica. No direct updates are allowed to a Read-Only replica.

IPX Network Map

All NetWare 4.*x* servers have an internal IPX address. The internal IPX network is a "virtual network," not connected to any physical network media. The internal IPX network serves as a stable destination for all IPX packets sent to the server.

Furthermore, NetWare 4.*x* servers have external IPX networks. These are real, physical networks to which the server is attached. NetWare 4.*x* servers will typically attach to several external IPX networks.

IPX network addresses are 4-byte hexadecimal numbers. The rules for assigning IPX network addresses are as follows:

◆ Internal IPX addresses must be unique for the entire internetwork.

◆ External IPX addresses must be consistent (all servers attached to an external IPX network must assign the same address to that network).

If your organization breaks the rules for assigning IPX addresses, you will experience routing problems. It is essential, therefore, that central IS manage the assignment of IPX addresses, both internal and external, throughout the entire organization.

As part of the organization's overall NDS blueprint, central IS should construct an IPX network map, showing the addresses of all IPX external networks. Optionally, central IS may elect to assign all IPX internal networks as well.

Responsibilities of Central IS

Because of the relationship between container objects, which are defined by central IS, and partition replication, it is the responsibility of central IS to create the partition replication blueprint. Central IS needs to ensure the following conditions are met:

◆ Each NDS partition is replicated to a server different from the one storing it.

◆ NDS partitions accessed via WAN links are replicated to the far end of the WAN link.

◆ All servers storing NDS partitions are production servers (not test or development servers).

COORDINATION OF AN NDS TREE THROUGH CENTRAL IS

Before new container objects can be added to the NDS tree, there should be a mechanism in place with central IS to ensure that the new branch follows the guidelines set forth for the NDS tree and the naming conventions mentioned in Chapter 12. Renegade branches can cause confusion and problems and should not be allowed to be a part of the production network. Central IS must be given the authority to manage and regulate the network as it grows. Another critical area of planning should be expansion for future growth or mergers.

UTILITIES ASSOCIATED WITH THE NDS STRUCTURE

The following utilities are used when accessing and defining the NDS database. This is only meant as an overview as these utilities are covered in more detail within other chapters.

- ◆ The NetWare Administrator (NW Admin) is a GUI that allows management of the NDS database. It only manages NDS and not the file system.
- ◆ NETADMIN is the DOS text menu utility, which is the functional equivalent of the NetWare administrator.
- ◆ NLIST is a command line utility used to display information regarding the NDS structure.
- ◆ CX is the command line utility used to display the NDS structure or change context within the NDS structure.

SUMMARY

In this chapter, the basics of NDS are presented and an overall picture necessary in designing an NDS tree is given. In the next chapter, details of NDS partitioning, replication, and time synchronization are discussed.

- Architecture of NDS

- NDS Partition
  Management

- NDS Time
  Synchronization

- Summary

CHAPTER 14

Partitioning and Time Synchronization

The Directory Services tree information is stored in the NetWare Directory Information Base (DIB). It does not need to be contained in a single location but can be replicated throughout the network. You also can partition (break it apart) into smaller pieces before replicating them. The first topic of this chapter examines (in some detail) NDS partitioning and replication.

The second main topic of this chapter is time synchronization. Time synchronization is used with NDS to ensure that all servers attached to the network keep accurate, synchronized time. Keeping accurate time in any directory service environment is critical. The NDS tree is updated and replicated; the newest information should be used and not accidentally replaced or updated with older information with a newer time due to an incorrect server clock.

ARCHITECTURE OF NDS

All information stored by NDS resides in a distributed and replicated database called the *Directory Information Base* (DIB). The DIB is distributed, which means that portions of it reside on different NetWare 4 servers. It also is replicated, which means that specific portions of the DIB are duplicated on other NetWare 4 servers.

Note

> NDS information cannot be stored on servers running NetWare 3.*x* or older versions.

Distribution and replication serve several purposes. Distribution of the DIB eliminates any size limits on the DIB. (If the DIB was stored entirely on one server, the size limit would be the storage capacity of that server.) Replication provides performance benefits and also fault tolerance. When the different portions of the DIB are replicated on one or more secondary servers, NDS can service requests for data from the DIB using the replicated portion of the DIB, which is closest to the source of the request. Also, when one server holding a replicated portion of the DIB is unavailable, NDS can obtain the requested information from another server holding a replica of the information contained on the downed server.

ORGANIZATION OF NDS

Each portion of the DIB is called a partition. The top of the tree is the *root partition*, and each further partition is said to be *contained by the root*. Each further partition can itself contain other partitions. Partitions that contain other partitions are called *branches extending from the root*.

Typically, each partition of the DIB will reside on its own NetWare 4 server. However, there is no technical reason why a single NetWare server may not contain several partitions.

PARTITIONS CONTAIN OBJECTS

Each partition in the DIB contains *objects*. These objects will be users, printers, servers, groups, and so on. The relationship between partitions and objects contained by partitions is what makes possible the global definition of each object within the DIB. To find information about a specific user within your organization, for example, NDS first finds the partition that contains the user object (which entails locating the server on which that partition resides). Once NDS has found the partition containing the user object, it can retrieve the data stored in that user object.

The DIB should reflect the structure of your organization. In a medium-sized company, each partition typically will correspond to a group within the organization. A user object is contained by the partition corresponding to the group in which that user works. Hence, the logical structure of NDS corresponds to an organizational chart of your company. This has been discussed previously in Chapter 13.

NDS IS BACKWARDS COMPATIBLE

NetWare version 3.12 and earlier use a server-based directory called the *bindery*. The bindery serves many of the same functions as NDS, except that the bindery has a scope limited to the server it is running on. (See the following section for more information on the bindery.)

All NetWare 4.*x* servers are backwards compatible with bindery-based servers (3.12 and earlier). NDS has a *bindery emulator*, which is active by default. This allows 4.*x* servers to coexist with 3.12 and earlier servers. NetWare 3.12 utilities work with NetWare 4.*x*'s bindery emulator, as do third-party products that use the NetWare bindery.

THE BINDERY

Until NetWare 4.*x*, naming services for NetWare have been supplied by a flat-file database, called the *bindery*. The bindery is a per-server, unique-key, variable-length database that contains information about all resources associated with a specific server. It also contains information about network-based resources known to that server.

In the bindery, all objects have a unique key that also is the offset within the bindery file of that object's record. Each object has a variable number of properties. Properties are contained in 128-byte segments of raw information associated with their object.

For example, registered users of a NetWare server each have a corresponding bindery object and ID number. The ID number of a user also is the user object's unique bindery key, which also is the offset of the user object's record within the bindery database. Each user object in the bindery has a password property, a security property, and other properties that combine to form a user identity. Print servers, groups, server-based applications, and other network resources may also have objects (and hence properties) in a NetWare server's bindery.

ADVANTAGES OF THE BINDERY

The bindery has served NetWare well over the years for the following reasons:

◆ The bindery is simple and very robust.

◆ The bindery offers excellent performance.

◆ Dynamic objects are easy to add and delete from the bindery.

◆ The bindery is easy to customize, but only by adding objects of a simple data type.

DISADVANTAGES OF THE BINDERY

When NetWare servers were used primarily in workgroup settings, the bindery provided a robust and efficient naming service that was appropriate for the tasks required of it. However, as NetWare became more popular in large multi-server installations, its shortcomings became evident. These shortcomings include the following:

◆ The bindery is local (server) in scope.

◆ Information stored in the bindery must be interpreted by its creator; it is not in human-readable format.

◆ Most object properties consume far less than 128 bytes; therefore space is wasted because the smallest segment of the bindery is 128 bytes.

◆ The bindery is inappropriate for the storage of complex data types.

The most telling disadvantage of the bindery is its local scope; that is, every server on an internetwork contains its own bindery, and there is no coordination of objects among binderies. Administrators must add users to each server, one user at a time. Because each bindery stores information about network-based resources (such as print servers), this information is duplicated throughout a multi-server network. (The information is stored once on every server, although only one instance of the information would suffice.)

The other disadvantages of the bindery are a result of the algorithms used to store and retrieve bindery information. Information stored in the bindery was designed primarily for use by the NetWare operating system, and not for consumption by users. Therefore, the meaning of the bindery-based information is not obvious to users. Clever programmers have devised methods for "hiding" the format of bindery-based data and presenting this data in a more "human-friendly" format. These methods, however, only serve to mask some of the binderies shortcomings, not fix them.

NDS PARTITION MANAGEMENT

As you just read, NDS data is stored in a distributed and replicated database. Distribution allows the amount of data stored by NDS to become arbitrarily large because you can divide the task of managing that data among many different physical server machines. Distribution of NDS data, however, also allows you to place the data in the physical location where it is referenced most frequently. If you are careful with your planning, you can distribute NDS data over different physical servers in such a way that overall NDS performance is enhanced dramatically.

The process of distributing NDS data over two or more physical servers is called *partitioning*. An NDS partition is a discrete portion of the NDS database residing on a separate physical server machine from other portions of the NDS database.

PARTITION REPLICATION

By default, NDS partitions are automatically *replicated*; that is, when you create an additional NDS partition, NDS automatically creates a copy of that partition on a different physical server. The replicated (duplicate) partition increases fault tolerance by providing a secondary source for the data stored on the original partition. Replication of partitions can also serve to increase NDS performance in certain situations. If you have two sites separated by a 56 KB leased line, and users from one site constantly look up NDS information that resides on the remote server, it will serve you well if you replicate the remote partition onto your local server so that all the look-ups can be done locally, rather than having to cross the (slower) WAN link. Otherwise, if look-ups are infrequent, you do not necessary need a replica locally.

DEFAULT PARTITIONING

Prior to NetWare 4.1, the most frequent method of partitioning the NDS tree occurs when you add a new NetWare 4.*x* server to the network. Each new server will, by default, contain a new NDS partition if the server is placed in a new Organization or Organizational Unit. Placing file servers in existing containers will not cause a new partition to be created. Starting with NetWare 4.1, however, you need to create the partitions manually, using either the DOS PARTMGR.EXE or Partition Manager from within NW Admin's Windows interface.

When you install the first NetWare 4.*x* server, INSTALL.NLM creates the [Root] container object and allows you to create one or more additional container objects. Because there is (at this point) only one NetWare 4.*x* server in the new NDS tree, all containers are part of a single partition.

Note

The first NetWare 4.*x* server you create is called the *Root Server* because it contains the partition holding the special [Root] object.

Prior to NetWare 4.02, when you installed the second and all further NetWare 4.*x* servers, INSTALL.NLM placed a copy of the partition you installed the server into on the new NetWare 4.*x* server. You need to tell INSTALL.NLM which existing container object will contain the new container object(s) on the server you are bringing up. With NetWare 4.02 and higher, only the first three servers will receive a copy of the partition. For additional copies, you must create them manually using PARTMGR or Partition Manager.

Note

The default partitioning performed by INSTALL.NLM ensures that at least three copies of the partition exist to offer fault tolerance. Should you need more copies, for performance reasons, for example, you should manually replicate the partition using software provided by Novell.

TYPES OF REPLICATES

NDS supports different types of partitions. The original partition is always the Master partition. Replicates of the Master may be either Read/Write partitions, or Read-Only partitions. Read/Write replicates allow you to add, delete, or edit NDS objects using the replica, just like working with the Master. Read-Only replicas enable you to read NDS objects, but not create new objects or alter existing objects.

LARGE NDS TREES AND DEFAULT PARTITIONING

On large NDS trees, the default partition and replication rules do not offer good performance. You should carefully examine your network configuration and NDS information flow, and create more partitions and replicas as necessary.

SPLITTING PARTITIONS

If a single partition becomes too large, you can split that partition using either the PARTMGR or NWADMIN software provided by Novell. When you split a partition, replicates of the original partition remain on the same server. A replicate of the new partition is created and placed on the server holding the original (unsplit) partition. You also may decide to split a partition in order to increase NDS performance.

SKULKING

NDS maintains and synchronizes replicate partitions using a special background process called the *Skulker*. Whenever you alter an existing partition (or replicate of that partition) by adding, deleting, or editing an NDS object, the Skulker duplicates that alteration to all replicates of the affected partition.

If you add a new User object VERONICA to the Marketing container object, for example, the Skulker will ensure that the new object VERONICA is present in all replicate partitions of the partition containing the Marketing object.

You cannot easily control the timeliness of the Skulker and its associated process. During the beta phase of NetWare 4.0, it was found that many administrators do not fully understand the implications of changing the various NDS update timers, and as a result, on large NDS trees, frequent running of the Skulker clogged the internetwork and slowed the performance of NetWare 4.*x* servers. In some cases, by causing the Skulker to run less frequently, this performance degradation issue was eliminated. However, changes made to NDS partitions took several minutes (up to half an hour in extreme cases) to appear on replicates of the affected partition, and that sometimes resulted in security issues. A user object was deleted from the NDS, for example, but because it took a long time to propagate that information to the other replicas, there was a chance that the user could still access the network by using a remote copy of the replica. Therefore, Novell Engineering took the timer options out of NetWare 4.*x*; some, however, were introduced back into NetWare 4.1.

PARTITION SUMMARY

Partitioning is the process of distributing NDS data across different physical servers. The main points you need to remember about NDS Partitioning are as follows:

14

PARTITIONING AND TIME SYNCHRONIZATION

◆ Partitioning allows the NDS database to become arbitrarily large.

◆ Partitioning can increase NDS performance by causing NDS data to be stored in close physical proximity to the workstations which most often refer to that data.

◆ Partitions are replicated to provide NDS with fault tolerance.

◆ The default partitioning and replicating rules may cause the performance of large NDS trees to suffer.

◆ You can change NDS Partitioning and partition replication manually, using either the PARTMGR or NWADMIN software provided by Novell.

NDS TIME SYNCHRONIZATION

In order to allow for replicated operation of the NDS DIB, each creation, deletion, or modification of an NDS object must be accompanied by an accurate *time stamp*. The distributed nature of NDS, however, leaves the possibility that different servers' internal clocks will not be synchronized. This can lead to problems in the skulking process because the Skulker relies on time stamps to know the exact order of events that occurred on different NDS partitions and replicas.

As a result, NDS requires full synchronization of server internal clocks across the NetWare 4.*x* network. Time synchronization is a feature of NetWare 4.*x* that can ensure that all server clocks are synchronized.

Note

As a side benefit of time synchronization, NetWare 4 servers understand time zones and daylight savings time information. Therefore, you no longer have to reset the server clocks twice a year, if your server is located in a time zone that uses daylight savings time.

TYPES OF TIME SERVERS

NetWare 4.*x* enables you to create different types of time servers, as follows:

◆ Primary time server

◆ Reference time server

◆ Single Reference time server

◆ Secondary time server

PRIMARY TIME SERVER

A *Primary time server* works together with other Primary time servers on the network to establish the correct network-wide time. Typically, a NetWare 4.*x* network will have at least two Primary time servers, that, together, negotiate the correct network time. It is important to have at least two Primary time servers, because with only one Primary time server, NetWare 4.*x* will consider the time unsynchronized. When using Primary time servers, central IS must ensure that each remote site has reliable access to a Primary time server. Preferably, a Primary time server should reside at each remote site on the network.

REFERENCE TIME SERVER

A *Reference time server* receives the correct time from a remote time source, such as a radio signal from an atomic cesium clock. Most networks that use Reference time servers will have several Reference time servers all synchronized to the same outside time source. Reference time servers do not negotiate with each other to establish the correct network time—they rely on the external time source completely. Therefore, Reference time servers should be synchronized to the same external time source.

Reference time servers can reside on the same network with Primary time servers. In this case, the Primary time servers change their internal clock to synchronize it with the time as reported by the Reference time servers. Reference time servers never change their clock, except as the result of the external time source.

Installing a Reference time server means that you must disable the server's internal clock during the installation procedure. INSTALL.NLM allows you to do this.

SECONDARY TIME SERVER

A *Secondary time server* synchronizes its internal clock to the nearest Primary or Reference time server. Secondary time servers do not negotiate the correct network time with Primary or Reference time servers. They simply accept the time given to them by a Primary or Reference time server.

SINGLE REFERENCE TIME SERVER

A *Single Reference time server* should only be used on very small networks, preferably only on single-server networks. The Single Reference time server is the sole source of time for the entire network. It cannot coexist with Primary time servers or other Reference time servers.

ADVANTAGES OF MULTIPLE PRIMARY OR REFERENCE TIME SERVERS

NetWare 4.x clients and Secondary time servers can only obtain the correct network time by querying Primary or (Single) Reference time servers. If your network has only one Primary or Reference time server, network clients and Secondary time servers will not be able to determine the correct network time if the Single Primary or Reference time server is down or otherwise inaccessible.

Therefore, it is to your advantage to establish multiple Primary or Reference servers. Moreover, you should ensure that all sites—especially sites linked over a WAN—have a local Primary or Reference time server.

TIME ZONES

NDS time synchronization calculates the correct time for each time zone in the world, and takes into account geographical factors, such as daylight savings time. When you install a NetWare 4.x server, you must provide the correct time zone information of the geographical area in which that server resides. Failure to do so may render time synchronization inaccurate.

TIME SYNCHRONIZATION SUMMARY

NetWare 4.x requires time synchronization to ensure that all NDS modifications, additions, and deletions take place in an orderly fashion, without corrupting the NDS due to inaccurate server time. The four types of time servers are Primary time server, Reference time server, Single Reference time server, and Secondary time server. Depending on the size of your network, a time synchronization scheme should be chosen with care.

SUMMARY

In this chapter, an overview of NDS partitioning considerations was covered. Also presented was an overview of time server types available in NetWare 4 environments.

The four chapters on NetWare Directory Services presented in this section of the book do not do real justice to NDS.

- Developing an Install Plan

- Protecting the Data and Hardware

- Configuring Server Hardware

- Workstation Configuration

- Installing Media and Connectors

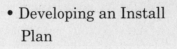

PART IV

Preparing for the Installation and Upgrade

- Constructing Your Schedule

- Importance of a Test Network

- Phases of Implementation

- Unanswered Questions

- Summary

CHAPTER 15

Developing an Install Plan

Just as you constructed a detailed plan for spending money (your budget), you need to make an equally detailed plan for spending time. You need to provide upper management with the date that the new NetWare system will be online and functioning. This "time budget" is your schedule, and it is very critical to the success of your project.

Note

To get a proper feel of the time frame needed for the implementation and find out about some of the pitfalls to avoid, it is to your benefit to talk to network administrators at a number of other sites that are similar to the size of your site.

If you are not sure to whom you should talk, your reseller or your local Novell Sales office would be able to give you referrals.

CONSTRUCTING YOUR SCHEDULE

The most important factor in constructing your schedule is to research the time necessary to perform specific tasks. For a new administrator, this can be an extremely difficult task, because there will be a large number of unknowns. Implementing a test network will help you determine the time it will take to complete most tasks; this data can be used to finalize the schedule.

Once you have completed the tasks discussed in the "Planning and Testing" section, you can put together a first draft of your budget. Many people find it helpful to put together a spreadsheet that shows different vendor's price quotes. This type of spreadsheet enables you to compare the different products and services available, and also enables you to include or exclude certain services or products.

USING PROJECT-MANAGEMENT SOFTWARE

Project-management software automatically creates schedules for projects and enables you to track and alter project schedules while they are active. The software can also track labor and material costs, and can alert you when schedule conflicts occur. You provide data—such as tasks to be completed, due dates, human resources assigned to tasks, dependencies among tasks, and man-hours required to accomplish specific tasks—and the software displays a graphical representation of your schedule.

The schedule includes "critical-path analysis," or analysis of dependencies among individual tasks. The *critical-path analysis* identifies tasks that have the potential to throw off the entire project schedule. For example, if the computers cannot be delivered until March 1, you cannot schedule the installation of the software before that date. Information provided by the critical-path analysis can be used to re-allocate resources to the most critical tasks, as necessary.

The primary advantage of project-management software is that it never forgets even the smallest details and the effects those details have on the project at large. If you enter data into the software, that data is always factored into the schedule. Humans are not always as attentive about details!

If there is a weakness in project-management software, it is that the software depends on the entry of accurate data. If you are providing faulty information to the software, it will provide you with a faulty schedule ("garbage in, garbage out"). Of course, that's a problem with any scheduling system, whether it is manual or automatic.

It is highly recommended that you purchase and use a project-management package to manage your NetWare implementation. All major software vendors sell project-management software, including Microsoft, Symantec, Claris, and others. Some project-management packages are designed for multi-user operation over a network.

If your NetWare implementation project is large, you should consider one of these high-end project-management packages. A good, high-end project-management package enables you to subdivide a large project into many smaller projects. Each smaller project has its own schedule, resources, and critical path. However, you can combine many smaller projects into a large "super project" that tracks everything.

If you need information on purchasing a project-management package, a suggestion is to use the Ziff-Davis *Computer Directory* and *Computer DataBase Plus* that is available on the CompuServe Information Service.

Scheduling Technicians and Consultants

When contracting with technicians to install your cabling, the technicians will tell you how long the installation will take. If you are hiring consultants to help you bring the system online, the consultants will be able to tell you how long it will take to complete their tasks. Although you, as the hiring agent, have the ability to dictate schedules to those with whom you contract, you need to respect the experience of consultants and technicians when it comes to making scheduling decisions.

If you are under a time crunch, consultants and technicians can frequently perform tasks more quickly by putting more people and resources on the job. While this will cost you more, sometimes you need to make that judgment call based on your organization's needs. You also need to take this into account in your budget planning.

Tip

As in any major project planning, you should include a line item for "miscellaneous" or "contingency" in your budgeting so that you will be prepared for unexpected expenses.

When looking for consultants, make sure the consultants have implemented NetWare 4 networks of similar size to the one you are installing. That way, they will be able to provide advice and timing information based on their experience. If you are installing a 100-node NetWare 4.1 network with 2 servers, for example, there is no point in hiring a consulting firm that has only worked with 20-node installations or a consultant that only works with sites with more than 500 nodes. They will not be able to give you a proper perspective as the scale and types of problems are not linearly scaled with the size of the network.

SCHEDULING TRAINING

It will take about two weeks to initially train those who will be administering the NetWare 4 network. Depending on the complexity of your network, for example, if there are routers and gateways involved, it may take longer to fully train your staff.

If you send your staff to a Novell-Authorized Education Center for training, the schedule of the training will more or less be dictated to you by the availability in your area of the appropriate classes. If you contract for training at your site, that training can usually be made to fit in your schedule. You should schedule administration training to occur as close as possible to the installation of your test network. Remember, however, the training of your administration team is an ongoing process.

If your staff plans to get their hands "dirty" during the implementation phase, make sure they attend the *NetWare 4 Installation and Configuration Workshop* course. You also should plan to send at least two of the senior staff to the *NetWare 4 Directory Services Design* course so that someone within your organization can work on and understand the NDS tree design. For more information about training centers and options, see Appendix B.

Depending on each user's usage of the network and level of computer knowledge, each user should receive anywhere from a few hours (if you already had a network) to a few days of training. This training can occur in-house, given by either one of your staff or an outside training specialist. Making training videos available can be helpful to your users as a resource for review. Users can reinforce their initial training on a flexible basis. Training videos are available for NetWare and many major software packages (see Appendix B for more information).

If you have a test network in-house, your staff and users can practice what they have learned, and when the production network is in place, the transition will come much smoother and take much less time.

Scheduling Installation

It will take a couple of hours to install the NetWare 4.1 operating system on each server. The bulk of the time is spent on transferring files from the CD to the server's hard disk. Therefore, the faster the hardware, the quicker the transfer process will be. If you run into problems with device drivers or peripherals, it may take much longer.

Note

If your installation includes wide area network links, the placement of your Master replica becomes important. When a new server is installed, the NDS information is retrieved from the Master replica. Therefore, if the server hosting your Master replica is across a (slow link) WAN, the latter part of the installation of your new server may take longer than if the Master replica is local.

Client workstation software takes anywhere from 5 to 15 minutes to install, depending on whether you are installing from diskettes, or a faster medium, such as the server. Again, this may take longer if you experience problems with device drivers or peripherals.

Installation time for non-NetWare workstation software, such as workstation operating systems, word-processing applications, and so on, varies according to individual products. To get a handle on the time required to install such software, install the software on a node of your test network. When installing the workstation software, determine the time based on an average installation with no problems. Don't rush yourself through the installation, as an inaccurate configuration at this point will result in a prolonged installation schedule.

The transition from installation and training to production may take from a couple of days to a week. You should *always* build some flexibility into your schedule with regard to this transition, as you and your staff will be especially busy bringing users online and training them, as well as troubleshooting any problems your users may have. It is helpful to bring users online, one department or group at a time, so that users can be trained in workgroups and the network administrators can keep track of which network segments are operational.

IMPORTANCE OF A TEST NETWORK

Earlier in this chapter, it was recommended to have a test network. One reason given was that this gives you a feel for the amount of time required to implement the real network. However, there are many more reasons for having a test network.

Many system administrators, both new and experienced, ask why this is a necessary step to the successful implementation of a NetWare (or any kind of) network. After all, don't hardware and software vendors test their products to make sure they work before releasing them?

The answer to this question is a qualified "Yes." Nearly all products designed to be used in a NetWare environment are put through an extensive testing process. During this extensive testing (commonly called a *beta*), many problems are found and are corrected before the product reaches the market.

Additionally, many products are tested and certified by Novell Labs for compatibility with Novell products. The tests that products are put through by Novell Labs are complex; however, even after those tests, Novell Labs only certifies products for the server configuration in which they are tested. The reason for this is because the diverse nature of PC hardware and the increasing complexity of modern networks makes it impossible to test for every possible failure or unusual software interaction in every possible hardware configuration.

As discussed previously in this chapter, the implementation of a test network is critical for two important reasons. First, a test network gives you a chance to practice installing and configuring a new NetWare network before you have to do it "for real" with your production network. Your network administrators can, and should, assist in the construction and maintenance of the test network. During the implementation of the test network, they will gain valuable experience with the product that will be very useful when you switch to the production environment. A test network serves as a test-bed for new procedures and applications—an error that could be potentially disastrous in a production environment is not as critical if it happens in a test environment.

Second, it gives you a chance to evaluate on a smaller scale the products you may purchase to ensure their compatibility with each other and your hardware. In effect, a test network gives you a chance to detect any "surprises" or unwanted side effects generated by product combinations. You do not want to find out about problems while or after you put these products into production.

Following are some guidelines for implementing your test network:

◆ The test network should have at least two servers, if possible. Much of the success of NetWare 4 depends on how servers interact, and a single server may not be sufficient for a thorough test of a new piece of software.

- The test network should have at least one segment of every type of physical network media you are planning to use in your production network.
- The test network should have at least one of every type of workstation you are planning to use on your production network (such as DOS, Windows, OS/2, Macintosh, UNIX, and so on).
- Workstation applications should be installed on the test network before purchasing multiple copies of that particular software.
- The test network should be kept up and running throughout the implementation phase for use as a troubleshooting platform whenever you have problems. If you can duplicate a problem that exists in a production environment in a test environment, the problem will be much easier to resolve.
- The test network should be isolated from the other computers and networks running at your site.
- The test network should be used to ensure the integrity of your archival and retrieval hardware and software.

If your budget allows, it is a good idea to keep the test network up and running after you have completed the implementation of your NetWare system and throughout the production phase. This enables you to keep a good training and troubleshooting platform available that does not affect the operation of your production network.

PHASES OF IMPLEMENTATION

Your schedule for implementing NetWare 4 should reflect the following stages of implementation:

- Planning and testing
- Purchasing and installation
- Installation and training
- Production

Each of these four phases represents a different group of activities for which you must develop a schedule.

In scheduling the different phases of implementation, it is important to realize that there is significant overlap between them. This overlap demonstrates that it is difficult to divide the total implementation of a NetWare 4 network into neat and clean components. Implementing NetWare 4 is more of a process than a procedure. This section looks in detail at each phase and discusses specific tasks you will need to perform.

PLANNING AND TESTING

Planning your NetWare 4 network consists of the following:

◆ Determining the needs of your users

◆ Researching products that meet those needs and the people who will support those products

◆ Designing your NetWare Directory Services tree and the physical layout of your network

◆ Putting together a first draft of your budget

Determining the needs of your users can be done in several ways. You may elect to sit down with them in small groups to discuss how they use computers in their day-to-day work and find features that they would like to have included, or you may choose to have them fill out a short questionnaire. Encourage your users to use their imaginations to find ways they could become more efficient in their jobs by using networked resources. If, for example, a user spends a lot of time running down to the fax machine to pick up incoming faxes, that user might benefit from a network fax solution. If a significant number of users share a similar need, add the item to your shopping list.

Once you have your shopping list, start shopping around for various products that fulfill your users' needs. Read magazine reviews of different products and see how they compare. Also, look at how the various products can be expanded. For example, in the hypothetical network fax solution presented previously, it may be desirable to integrate a fax solution with an electronic mail solution. Which products will support that type of solution? Will the products that support it do so easily, or is there additional setup or software involved? Which products can do the job effectively without requiring additional computer systems dedicated to single tasks?

Tip

If you find a software product that is close to what you are looking for, but is missing a few important features, ask the publisher if there is planned support for the features you want, and if there will be an upgrade path available from the current version of the software. Most software companies will provide a free or low-cost upgrade to users who purchased their software within a certain time period prior to a new release. If you wait until you are within that time period, you potentially could save the cost of the upgrade.

Carefully weigh the different product features and prices. If a product requires a dedicated workstation to function, include the cost of an additional workstation as part of your estimate, even if you already own the necessary equipment. In addition, you will want to find out ahead of time what problems or potential problems each product you are evaluating has, and if there are work-arounds or fixes. An excellent place to conduct this type of research is on CompuServe, as many vendors—including Novell—maintain forums to answer questions and provide support for their products.

In addition to evaluating products, you also will want to evaluate vendors. Work with a few vendors and determine not only which products you need to fill your needs, but also which services the vendors can provide. Consider not only the prices given, but also the vendor's level of expertise, how prompt the representative is in returning phone calls, whether the vendor can fill all your current and future networking needs, and the general level of enthusiasm the vendor has for your project. Be sure to have the vendor include the cost of any support contracts, maintenance agreements, and the cost to have them send a consultant out to your site to assist with a problem.

Also have the vendor give you several references, and follow up on the references you are given. Ask the references how well the vendor has supported their installation, how knowledgeable the vendor is, and where the vendor could improve. Another important question to ask the references is if the vendor has ever had problems providing support in a timely manner.

While you are putting together the products that will fulfill the needs of your users, you will also want to start planning a structure for your NetWare Directory Services (NDS) tree. There are several things to consider in designing the tree; if the NDS tree design is properly done, your network will be much easier to administer. However, if the NDS tree is not set up properly, it will become increasingly more difficult to administer as the NDS tree becomes more complex.

A common suggestion for designing an NDS tree is to follow an organizational chart of the company. For some sites, this seemed to be a logical method to use for NDS design—several sites installed trees in this manner and were happy with this design. Some organizations, however, had problems with this design because the organizational chart did not accurately represent the way people in the organization worked together. The best recommendation is to evaluate how your organization's users interact, and design a tree based on functional working groups. For more information about NDS design, refer to *NDS Troubleshooting*, from New Riders.

If you are installing at a site where a network has not yet been installed, you also will want to contract to have the building cabled. As with determining the needs of your network with your network vendors, you will want to refer to the information presented in Chapter 5 and discuss the cabling needs for your network with a cabling vendor. Whatever type of cabling you have installed, make sure that you have it tested and certified.

Tip

Although having the cable tested and certified is not a necessary step in network installation, a significant percentage of networking problems can be traced down to faulty cabling. Testing and certifying the cable can save you time and money when troubleshooting.

The most important part of the planning phase is setting up a test network. The test network is important for two primary reasons. First, it allows the administration team to learn how to administer the network. Second, it enables you to test the interaction of the various components of your network. The functions and importance of having a test network are discussed in more detail, later in this chapter.

When installing your test network, try to match hardware configurations as closely as you can. It should not be a problem if the production does not yet have all the disk space or memory; however, do make sure that the memory in your test server does fulfill the memory requirements of the hardware and software in the test server. The idea behind the test server is to enable you and your administrators to start learning and experimenting to find out what's going to work for your installation, and also to give you a platform on which to evaluate third-party software.

PURCHASE AND INSTALLATION

Be sure to maintain your budget spreadsheet during the negotiation of your purchase deals. By now, you should have a good feel for the vendor from whom you want to purchase your network.

Warning

If you can, avoid building your network with pieces from multiple vendors or suppliers. If you have problems down the road with part of the network, you may find the vendors and suppliers unwilling to take ownership of the problem, each claiming that the problem belongs to another vendor. The money you save by avoiding this type of "finger-pointing" scenario will outweigh any savings you may get by purchasing pieces from different vendors and suppliers.

Negotiate with your selected vendor on components when the prices seem a bit high. Let the vendor know that the price for certain components is too high, and find out why. In many cases, vendors will be willing to modify those prices unless they provide something with the product that other vendors do not—for example, they may have a more direct means of support.

Find out the product availability from each of your vendor candidates. Keep in mind that most vendors will provide you with a "best case" availability schedule, and ask if they have a contingency should something not be delivered to them by their suppliers on time. If the vendors maintain their own warehouse and have the components in-stock, that will be a definite bonus. At this point, you can select your vendor and agree on a delivery date.

Once you decide on a product, use your test network (if you have one) to perform some testing to ensure that the product works properly in the NetWare 4 environment. Do not wait until production time to find out that you need certain upgrades or an entirely different product.

If you are installing a network in a site in which a network has not been installed before, and will be installing new cabling, make sure that the cable is installed before or during the time you are performing evaluations, using your test network, and training the administrators.

INSTALLATION AND TRAINING

Now that the test network is set up, you will want to evaluate the various products you intend to use with your network. If, while assessing needs, you determine that there are many different things your users will want to be doing with the network, restrict yourself to the most important items. The key to making it past this point of your installation is to avoid trying to do too much. If you try to evaluate too many packages at once, you will lose sight of your initial goal, which is to have a functional network. First evaluate the products that will give you the most value, and work your way through the list. If necessary, change the components that don't work as expected.

Tip

During the evaluation phase, try to anticipate questions your users might have about each product and tasks they might try to perform that the software may not be designed to do. While the components will have been tested by the manufacturer or publisher, it is very useful to know how hardware and software react to being asked to do things they weren't designed to do. If your users have problems, they will thank you if you already have seen the problem and immediately know the answer.

Administrator training can be done a number of ways—you can allow the administrators to learn on the test network, giving them practical hands-on experience with the different products. You may decide to have some, or all, the administrators attend classes in administering a NetWare 4 network. Novell provides a training curriculum consisting of three classes—*NetWare 4 Administration*, *NetWare 4 Advanced Administration*, and *NetWare Directory Services Design*. For more information on these classes, contact your local NetWare Authorized Education Center, or contact the nearest Novell office.

During this part of this phase, you should start receiving your hardware and software for your production installation. Once the administrators are comfortable with their tasks and the initial group of products has been evaluated, you are ready to perform the installation.

You should carefully plan the installation process. Install your server hardware and software and bring each server online. Allow yourself plenty of time to install the hardware and software for each server. Most experienced administrators can install the software in a couple of hours per server; however, they usually allow themselves a weekend in which to do the job, just in case problems arise.

Once the servers are up and running, you can begin to install the client software on the workstations. This can be accomplished a few different ways, but however you choose to do the installations, keep in mind that the users will need to be trained. It might make more sense to install the workstation software on small groups of workstations, and train groups of users as you go along.

Each workstation installation should take 5 to 20 minutes to install, depending on the workstation's configuration, whether the networking hardware is already installed in the machine, and whether the workstation requires support for Microsoft Windows.

Tip

Rather than install each workstation from a set of client installation diskettes, copy the minimum amount of necessary files from one installed workstation to a diskette to get a new workstation connected to the network. Use that diskette to connect the new workstation to the network. You then can install the rest of the workstation files (such as Windows support files) using the INSTALL program located in `SYS:PUBLIC\CLIENT\DOSWIN`. This enables you to avoid swapping diskettes at each workstation.

You may elect to train your users before installing the workstation client software; however, most administrators find that users retain what they learn if they can leave the training session and immediately begin to use what they've learned. A combination of training methods may be the most beneficial—provide a brief introduction to logging in and basic network functions, and schedule a class for the users to attend so that they can learn some of the finer points of using a network.

PRODUCTION

The production phase consists of ongoing tasks that you will have when using and maintaining your network. Continue to install workstation software and train users as necessary. You may want to have periodic meetings with your users to find out what concerns they have about using the network or problems they may have encountered. An important key in maintaining a successful network is communication with the users. Be open to suggestions from them, as they are the ones who are using the resources you provide.

Periodically, step back and evaluate the network. Determine whether you have outgrown the installation and make changes to the configuration, as needed. Before performing any sort of major change capable of crippling your production network, test it out on your test network, when possible. As the network grows and users become comfortable with using it, new needs may arise that were not anticipated at the outset. If the network needs to grow to accommodate more users or services, determine whether the growth is feasible, and then expand as necessary.

UNANSWERED QUESTIONS

During the course of planning and testing your implementation, you will have many unanswered questions. For example, how many network administrators do I need? Should I hire or otherwise allocate full-time network administrators? This section provides sources from which you can get some of your questions answered, quickly and efficiently.

CONSULTANTS

Retaining a NetWare 4-qualified consultant can answer questions that come up during the planning, testing, and implementation phases, based upon their experience with similar projects. Additionally, because most consultants work on multiple projects at the same time, they are more in tune to problems related to NetWare, and the solutions to those problems.

15

DEVELOPING AN INSTALL PLAN

MAINTENANCE CONTRACTS

If your network is considered a "mission critical" network by any of your groups, you will want to have the hardware placed under a maintenance contract. Depending on how severe it would be for a server to go down, your vendor should be able to provide you with information about onsite service agreements and other special programs designed to ensure that if a server goes down because of a hardware failure, your network can be brought back up as soon as possible.

Most vendors provide telephone support as a part of a maintenance contract. Telephone support can range from 9 a.m. to 5 p.m. support from Monday through Friday to a 24-hour support provided 7 days a week.

NETWORK SUPPORT ENCYCLOPEDIA

Novell provides an annual subscription service called the *Network Support Encyclopedia—Professional Edition*, or *NSEPro*. Novell's NSEPro is distributed on CD-ROM, and is updated on a regular basis.

The NSEPro comes with technical bulletins and support documents for Novell products, and includes all of the current patches, fixes, and updates for Novell products.

For administrators in a complex network environment, the NSEPro subscription service is an invaluable tool for tracking down solutions to known problems. In many cases, when a vendor provides support, the NSEPro is one of the resources the vendor's support staff uses to solve problems and answer questions.

For more information on the Network Support Encyclopedia, contact either your vendor or Novell.

PER-INCIDENT SUPPORT FROM NOVELL

Novell also provides a pay-per-incident support channel through their own technical support group. This support is available around the clock; however, it is a bit more expensive than a maintenance contract. Many administrators believe that when they have a problem, it is best to eliminate any people between them and the company that wrote the software.

Members of the Novell support staff undergo a fairly constant education on Novell products. They are very dedicated people who will do everything they can to get a problem resolved. For example, Novell will attempt to duplicate the problem when necessary. In some cases, Novell will ask the administrator to send in a memory dump from their server and examine the dump to determine what was happening at the time of a server problem.

NetWire

NetWire, a Novell-sponsored service on CompuServe, is another place to go for answers to your questions. NetWire consists of many forums, including those for NetWare administrators, programmers, and users. If you have a question regarding your NetWare implementation, you can post a message on one of the forums, generally addressed to SysOp (System Operators) or All. You will most likely receive several answers to your question within a day, although many people receive responses within as little as a few hours. If you don't know which forum is most appropriate for your question, you can post a message to the SysOp and he or she will direct you to the correct NetWire forum.

Note

None of the SysOps are Novell employees. They are all computer professionals who volunteer their time to help answer your questions and resolve any problems that you may have.

If you are looking for an official Novell answer, you need to contact Novell directly.

The NetWire system operators (SysOps) suggest the following guidelines that will help to speed up the process of getting your questions answered:

- ◆ Check the current messages that are in the forum and section that relate to your question to see if your question has already been answered. Oftentimes, you will find a solution to your problem or answer to your question without even having to ask!

- ◆ If you are not sure where to post a question, post a brief description of the problem in the forum or section you think is appropriate.

- ◆ Post questions to which you need answers (as opposed to messages where you want a general opinion from the forum membership) directly to SysOp. This will help ensure a quicker response.

- ◆ Post as much information as possible about your configuration, but do not overdo it. For example, if your server abends, post the contents of the abend message, the brand and hardware configuration of the server, the NetWare Loadable Modules and drivers loaded on the server, and the total amount of server memory and disk space. Make sure that you mention the version of NetWare, as well as any patches and updates that may have been applied. This will help speed the process of getting an answer to you, because if the information is complete, the SysOps will have to ask fewer questions about the configuration.

Tip

You should always check the library sections for updates and patches that may address your problem before posting a question. It is likely that your issue is a known problem and a fix is readily available.

◆ If you do not see any responses to a question you asked within a couple of days, post a second message to the SysOp referencing the original message number. If you cannot see your original message, check your forum settings to ensure that you are able to read messages you have posted. If you post the same message multiple times, you may only receive responses indicating "duplicate message" or something similar.

◆ Post your messages to a single forum and section only. If a SysOp feels that the question will get a better or more complete response in a different forum, he or she will redirect you to the appropriate place.

◆ Do not send private e-mail directly to a SysOp, unless you have been directed to do so. Posting your questions publicly will not only allow other SysOps the chance to help you, but also will allow users who may have had the same problem the opportunity to jump in and provide you with a solution.

◆ If a response from a SysOp isn't clear, feel free to ask for a further explanation. The SysOps are there to help you with your problems.

◆ When working with a SysOp on a problem, reply to any messages left to you instead of composing a new message. This helps the SysOp keep track of individual problems more easily, as CompuServe will chain responses to the original message.

◆ If you were working on a problem with a SysOp and they seem to have forgotten about you, post a follow-up reminder to the SysOp in the original message thread.

◆ Novell maintains a downloadable list of all the NetWire forums and libraries. To access this list, go to the NOVLIB forum and download the file FRMORG.EXE from Library 2.

◆ Read the forum announcements. They include information for upcoming events, including online conferences with Novell employees, where to find information, and other special projects related to the NetWire forums.

A list of NetWire forums that would be of interest to you as a NetWare 4 administrator is given in Appendix B of this book.

NetWire is a good place to report problems you have with the NetWare operating system, device drivers, or peripherals. If there is a solution to your problem, chances are you will find it on NetWire first. Novell uses NetWire to provide fixes to bugs discovered by users via the NOVLIB forum. In addition, many vendors of NetWare-compatible products make fixes to bugs available on NetWire as well.

Several vendors also provide support for their NetWare-related products on CompuServe outside of the NetWire forums.

THE INTERNET

If you are familiar with the Internet, there are a few additional resources available to you. There is an unmoderated Usenet newsgroup called `comp.sys.novell` that discusses Novell-related products and issues. While it is not necessarily monitored by Novell, the users of that newsgroup have a considerable amount of networking experience, and they may be able to provide answers to questions you may have.

There also is an anonymous FTP mirror of the NetWire libraries maintained at the site `ftp.novell.com`. To use this FTP server, connect to it using your FTP package, and sign in as user `anonymous`. When prompted for your password, enter an e-mail address where you can be reached. The files are organized into directories that correlate the NetWire libraries on CompuServe, so it is useful to know which library the file you need is located in, as well as the filename. For those who have both CompuServe access and Internet access, you can use CompuServe to locate the files you need, and then download them from the Internet. For many people, this is more cost-effective than downloading the files from CompuServe.

SUMMARY

The planning and installation of a NetWare 4 network can be a very complex task. The easiest way to approach the process is to break it down into four phases—planning and testing, purchasing and installation, installation and training, and production. While these four phases overlap, there are specific tasks you perform during each phase. The use of project management software can help you plan the steps to successfully install and implement a usable network.

Throughout the entire planning and implementation phases and into the production phase, a test network is an essential component of a successful installation, as it will enable you to determine how much time will be needed to perform specific tasks, and also enable you to safely evaluate software outside of your production network. If you encounter problems at any time, there are a number of support avenues available to you to provide answers and fixes quickly and efficiently.

- Hardware

- Software

- Summary

CHAPTER 16

Protecting the Data and Hardware

When discussing the topic of protecting your hardware and data, it is important to note that they are very different issues. Although one will tend to mimic the other, they are quite different in design, technique, and technology. For example, disk duplexing redundantly creates both hard drive space and the controller channel; if a failure occurs in either the primary hard drive or its controller channel, the secondary equipment seamlessly takes over. This is designed to protect the hardware, but to the new administrator, it may seem to protect the data. To truly protect your data, it must be removed from the system to some sort of tape or optical media and be stored in a safe location so that it can be restored to the system (or some other system), thus protecting it and also isolating the data from the hardware.

The primary technique for protecting your data is very straightforward. *Back it up*. Use a certified tape backup system and be faithful about scheduling the backup and testing restore procedures, making sure that the NetWare Directory Services (NDS) information is able to be backed up and restored as well as the file and directory structure. These issues are discussed in the second section of this chapter. The primary technique in protecting your hardware against failure is redundancy. The redundant issue raises questions about performance and cost. These issues are discussed in the opening section of this chapter. The other issue to keep in mind as you read this chapter is that of awareness. It is important for you to understand that awareness on the part of the administrator is a primary tool in the fight against data loss and hardware failure, and awareness on the part of the user is paramount in protecting the local workstation profile and user data.

This chapter has isolated what the authors believe are the primary areas that pose threats to the integrity of your data: hardware and software. Each area is discussed in detail and identifies the actual threats, offers some preventative measures, and discusses how NetWare built-in features and third-party utilities can provide a fault tolerant system.

Tip

The amount of fault tolerance you build into your system should be a compromise between how mission critical your data is and your budget—the more protection the greater the cost, as a general rule of thumb.

HARDWARE

When dealing with hardware protection, there are three main areas on which to focus. The area of major concern is electricity, where there are power outages and fluctuations. Other areas of hardware protection and concerns are redundancy and environmental issues. All these topics are discussed in this chapter.

ELECTRICITY

Electricity is the biggest threat to your system. We could not run the equipment without it; however, it also is the single biggest culprit behind both the blatant failures and a huge amount of the mystery problems that occur in the computing environment in corporate America. Perhaps the most common, and easiest failure to prevent, is the sudden and complete cutoff of power. This can happen by fate, equipment failure, and lack of proper training.

POWER OUTAGES

Fate, sometimes referred to as "acts of God," would be the blackouts, winter snow, ice storms, lightning, earthquakes, and other natural events that are virtually impossible to prevent. The idea then would be to provide electrical backup via an *uninterruptable power supply* (UPS) and provide data redundancy across wide-area links. Equipment failure will be covered in detail later in this section under "Redundancy."

The reference to "lack of training" would be to anyone who has ever turned off the file server without first typing in the DOWN command at the server console prompt. The DOWN command warns you about any active files, updates server cache buffers to hard drives, synchronizes the servers' duplicate file allocation and directory entry tables (FATs and DETs), and other internal preparation for shutdown. I receive many calls from former students that involve the scenario of someone (not them of course, they already had the training!) prematurely shutting off the file server without first DOWNing it. The error message they see is as follows:

```
:The mirror copies of the FAT don't match volume SYS was NOT mounted
```

Sometimes I've also seen the following:

```
: A Files FAT chain contains entries out of order.
```

These students want to know if there is anything they can do to remedy the problem. NetWare comes bundled with a utility called VREPAIR that is designed to make a best effort at repairing and resynchronizing these tables. It is not uncommon to have the volume unmountable for several reasons, this is just the most common in my experience. Following are the manual recovery steps:

1. From the server prompt type

   ```
   :LOAD VREPAIR
   ```

A menu driven VREPAIR screen will appear with three choices, one to repair a volume, the second to go into VREPAIR options, and the third to exit the utility (see Figure 16.1). The options are set by default to the following:

a. Quit if a required name space support NLM is not loaded

b. Write only changed directory and FAT entries out to disk

c. Write changes to disk immediately

d. Retain deleted files (see Figure 16.2)

These default settings are correct for what you need to do.

Figure 16.1.
VREPAIR main menu.

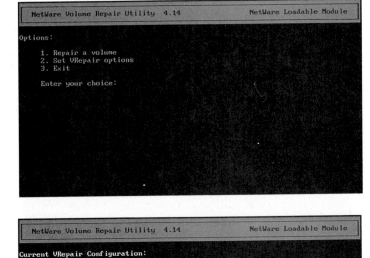

Figure 16.2.
Default VREPAIR options.

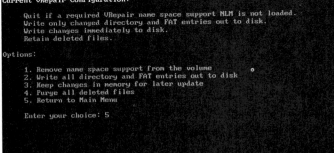

2. From the opening menu, choose Repair a volume (item 1).

VREPAIR will only work on a dismounted volume; if there are no dismounted volumes, VREPAIR will inform you of this. If more than one volume is dismounted, VREPAIR will ask you to choose the volume you want to repair (see Figure 16.3). If there is only one volume, VREPAIR will start its process.

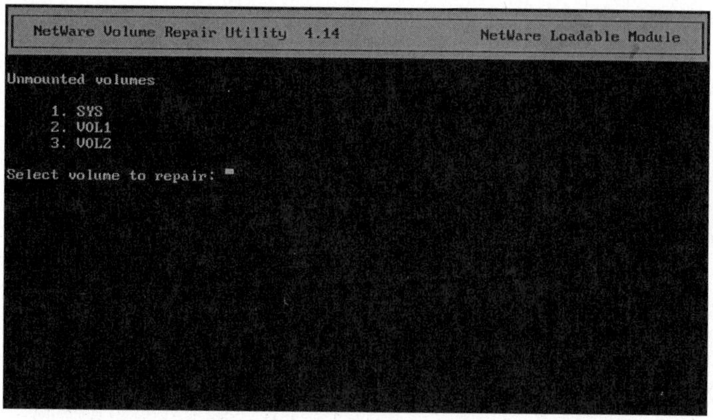

Figure 16.3.
Select a volume
to repair.

```
NetWare Volume Repair Utility  4.14              NetWare Loadable Module

Unmounted volumes

        1. SYS
        2. VOL1
        3. VOL2

Select volume to repair: ▪
```

3. When VREPAIR starts finding errors in the tables, it will pause after each error (it is conceivable that you may have hundreds of errors in these tables). To bypass the pause after each error, press F1 during repair and choose "Do not pause after errors" from the options list and continue the repair.

4. When VREPAIR is done, it will automatically write changes to disk.

   Now it is time to exit VREPAIR and try to mount the volume SYS:.

Note

It is not uncommon to have to run VREPAIR several times in order to get a complete repair. It is important that you repeatedly run VREPAIR until *zero* error is reported.

It is a feature of NetWare 4.*x* that if the SYS: volume cannot mount, then VREPAIR will kick in and try to fix the mismatched FATs and DETs (or whatever problem prevented SYS: from mounting). Most administrators would never even notice if the VREPAIR went through its steps flawlessly as the volume would mount and continue the normal startup procedures. However, a certain percentage of the time VREPAIR may need several passes to completely recover from the problem, or may have difficulty loading at all. In this case, you must manually perform the VREPAIR procedure.

16

PROTECTING THE DATA AND HARDWARE

Note

Because of the auto-VREPAIR feature in NetWare 4, it cannot be emphasized enough how important it is to periodically check the file server error log for instances in which the volumes could not mount unless VREPAIRed. Without knowing the failure occurred, it is impossible to take preventive steps against future failure.

Another product that helps recover servers after quick and total power loss is *Ontrack Data Recovery for NetWare* by Ontrack Data Recovery. While VREPAIR does a great job at synchronizing FATs and DETs, it does not permanently delete corrupted files and table entries; however, Ontrack will. Ontrack Data Recovery for NetWare also provides routines that will enable you to rebuild file structures within a damaged volume, examine and modify any sector on a server device, as well as perform a nondestructive media analysis.

POWER FLUCTUATIONS

Besides the quick and total loss of power, there is the problem of power fluctuations, be they brownouts, spikes, or surges, or the "choppy" power that often is associated with backup generators or sky-rise buildings. Even if you are told you have a dedicated electrical line with filtering on it, you should test the power on a regular basis, as components wear and standards vary between electrical vendors. Intermittent failures, corrupted files, servers restarting themselves for no apparent reason, lost data, and system lock-up are all symptoms of "flaky" power. Physical damage to the system, as well as data loss, can be prevented by using an UPS.

UPS

UPS—what is it? A *UPS* is a battery backup unit that sits between your vital components and the source of power. The UPS should be matched to the load that it would actually have to carry if the power was indeed cut off. If you only have one server and a handful of services to provide, your protection needs would not be as great as someone with multiple servers, gateways, and concentrators. The UPS should have some sort of cable running from it to your primary server that is used to alert the server if it is on standby power. There should also be some kind of notification and shutdown procedure. This can be done with Novell's UPS NLM that ships with NetWare 4.*x* or with the application software that you can get from the manufacturer.

In my office, for example, I use an American Power Conversions (APC) BK900 attached via an RS-232 port, which is my primary server. I also run PowerChute

Plus, which is a nice program that not only provides shutdown procedures but also comes with power diagnostics and power management tools.

A battery backup is fine for the scenario in which the power goes off quickly and completely, but it does not address the issue of fluctuating or choppy power. In high-end UPS's, *line conditioning* is another feature that can be added to provide protection from other electrical threats. A line conditioning UPS does everything the basic model does and also provides the capability to monitor and correct fluctuating power. A line conditioning UPS can be worth its weight in gold (and they are not light!).

STATIC ELECTRICITY

Static electricity is another potential area of electrical damage. Have you ever felt a shock when you walked across a carpeted floor and touched a doorknob? It would take an electrical charge of over 3,000 volts to feel that type of momentary shock. A silicon chip, however, can suffer severe damage with just 30 to 50 volts, one one-hundredth of what we notice. I wonder how many people have carpeted rooms where their servers are kept, or where their wiring closets are. Anti-static mats should be on the floors and anti-static wrist straps should be used whenever repair work is being done. A slight amount of chip damage can change flow of electrical current, thus producing faulty logic and intermittent errors.

Proper grounding is another electrical issue that is essential for the protection of your hardware. Many electrical contractors ground according to building code specifications that may not be tough enough to adequately protect delicate electronic equipment. Buildings age, and over time can settle, electrical demands can triple or quadruple over short periods of time, and physical changes can all alter the original grounding.

REDUNDANCY

The second major topic of protecting your hardware is the issue of *redundancy*. The basic idea here is that system components do fail. They are, after all, just mechanical devices. So, it would make sense to build into the systems the capability for components to fail without bringing down the entire system. The problem is, of course, which components will fail? Hard drives, controllers, and NICs are very common areas in which failure occurs. Any place where there is a single point of failure, a malfunction could bring the entire network down.

MIRRORING AND DUPLEXING

NetWare's built-in *system fault tolerance* (SFT) features include support for two hardware redundancy schemes. The first is *disk mirroring* and the other is *disk duplexing*. In actuality, duplexing is just a sophisticated form of mirroring and is set up and monitored exactly like mirroring using the INSTALL and MONITOR NLMs.

Note

A SCSI controller/drive combination is a great choice in duplexing as it provides two truly independent channels and good throughput. Other technologies will not perform as well, especially under a heavy load.

Disk mirroring is a basic duplication scheme that keeps two hard drives synchronized. If the primary hard drive fails, then the secondary can take over invisibly. This prevents a single hard drive failure from taking down the whole system. Of course, the system needs to eventually have its primary drive replaced and the drives resynchronized. You are without proper protection until you do.

Warning

An IDE drive in a slave relationship to another IDE drive uses the controller mounted on the actual master's hard drive. If the master drive fails, then the slave drive fails as well, making IDE a poor choice in a mirroring environment.

The next most likely area of failure is in the *controller channel*. From past experience, one would say that 15 to 30 percent of hard drive crashes are not due to the hard drives themselves but are failures in the controller channels. Disk duplexing redundantly creates both of these components, thus, a failure in either the primary hard drive or controller cannot bring down the entire network.

Tip

If you have decided to mirror your hard drives, why not go a little further for just a few more dollars and go with duplexing instead? Most controllers cost only a fraction of the drive space they manage, and for the extra hardware protection and increased throughput, it's a great buy.

RAM

The next place to look for potential disaster would be in the server *RAM*. Most of today's high-end concentrators and routers also have RAM built into them. RAM errors are very common, and the following are a few tips to help prevent them.

- Always use the same speed RAM when installing memory and if possible the same manufacturer.

- The chips on a SIMM module and the small board that they are mounted on should be from the same manufacturer, if possible.

- Some IBM compatible SIMMs have nine chips on them; some have three: Try not to mix these in the same system.

- If possible, use error correcting code (ECC) chips in servers. This type of memory is not immune to failure, but does try to isolate memory errors and correct them.

SFT III

The area to look at next, assuming that you are using a UPS, could be anything from processor malfunction, to the motherboard, to the battery powering CMOS. It is difficult to pinpoint where exactly the next most likely failure may occur. You can always have spare inventory around—a spare NIC, an extra CMOS battery, extra SIMMs—but this implies that the server must be powered down, diagnosed, and repaired, thus incurring downtime. To prevent this from happening, you may decide to use Novell's SFT III.

SFT III keeps two identical servers synchronized so that if any critical error takes down the primary server, the secondary can take over without any users even being aware that this is happening. As an added benefit, the primary can be taken offline and worked on right away so that your backup server will only be left unprotected for a minimal period of time. SFT III can also improve performance by splitting the burden of routing requests and disk reads between the two servers.

Some administrators find the cost of SFT III (both the software and the duplicate server) prohibitive; it certainly isn't for everyone, but you must decide what level of redundancy is needed and how much downtime you are willing to accept. As I always remind my students: it's not a case of *if* your server crashes, it's a case of *when* it crashes, and how prepared are you to recover and get back online. The more fault tolerance you build into a system, the more expensive it will be and the less likely it is to crash.

Note

The SFT III feature is built-in to NetWare 4.1. You need a SFT III license to activate its features.

COMPONENTS

Other issues relative to this topic include components (concentrators, routers, bridges, etherswitching engines, intelligent hubs, and so on) and the actual cabling structure itself. Most of today's high-end wiring boxes have built-in fault tolerance features and other options you can buy. For example, I use a great deal of SynOptics (now Bay Networks) equipment; besides the built-in diagnostics and problem isolation features, I have added a redundant power supply and keep on hand a hot swappable fan unit. As far as a redundant cabling layout, most people find this very difficult to justify. Most that I have seen are from a cabling upgrade where the original was left in place for just this purpose. With a big trend towards the star-wired topologies, getting away from the linear bus, most wiring structures cannot be brought down with a single cable break. So, an effective means of protection now can be as simple as a spare spool of cable, a good crimper, and a box of connectors.

PERFORMANCE

The issues of hardware redundancy also bring up the issue of *performance*. To have two hard drives on the same controller would imply twice the number of writes and, therefore, a hit in performance. By stepping up the level of protection to duplexing, the second controller can actually give performance back to the system through *split seeking*. A split seek is when the primary drive is busy and the secondary drive executes a read request. As mentioned with SFT III, the second server can actually give performance back to the overall network throughput. Most well designed networks will experience little or no degradation by implementing SFT features, and some will actually increase throughput by wisely using the extra hardware.

The life expectancy of hardware is measured by the manufacturer as *mean time between failures (MTBF)*. Some software techniques, such as caching and hashing, can actually reduce the amount of times that information is read off the hard drives, thus increasing the MTBF. Other techniques may extend the life span of your equipment, sometimes significantly, but when it's all said and done, your server is just a mechanical device. Many companies take their file servers every two years or so and rotate them into the workhorse or use them as fax servers, or maybe as a dial-in dial-out hub where they are still useful but not in the front lines. This also allows for newer, faster technologies to be brought in for the new server and tested while the server being phased out can still jump in if problems arise.

ENVIRONMENTAL

The third area of concern is what I call the *environmental* issues. Heat, cold, dust, moisture, electro-magnetic interference (EMI), and radio frequency interference (RFI) are all high contributors to hardware failure.

Noise

Both EMI and RFI are considered *noise*. The electrical definition of noise is a low-voltage, low-current, high-frequency signal that creates disturbance in a re-occurring pattern. In contrast to this is the *transient*. A transient is a high-voltage, high-current burst of energy that usually is an isolated event (such as lightning or a generator startup). Typical creators of EMI are fluorescent lights, communication electronics, power tools, and motors. The culprits behind RFI are cordless communication devices, microwaves, or even your desktop PC itself! Proper grounding, careful cable runs (away from devices and lights), and shielding materials are the best way to combat noise.

Heat, Cold, Dust, and Moisture

Besides out-and-out failure, heat and cold combined can create a unique problem to your systems known as *creep*. Creep is when chips or boards rise out of their mounting and become loose. Besides becoming nonfunctional, they can short out other components, compounding the problem. Creep can be fought with good preventative maintenance by periodically opening systems and reseating boards and checking chips. The issue of dust can be addressed in the same way, with a solid quarterly, biannually, and yearly maintenance plan that opens up the systems and blows out the dust-bunnies while checking and running diagnostics on the hardware. Moisture, in combination with other elements, can create condensation and corrosion. A good visual inspection can go a long way during preventative maintenance to locate potential areas of failure.

Clean Room

Another technique to fight all the issues mentioned previously is a clean room. Sometimes called a *safe room*, a clean room is designed to be a temperature-controlled, dust-free, well-ventilated, and high-secure area. It should be a highly-visible, well-protected area with its own electrical feeds (preferably from a reliable generator) and filters. It should be static- and EMI-free, as well provide protection from RFI. Due to the nature of the clean room, high security should be enforced to help prevent unauthorized access. Many businesses prefer a glass room centrally located for this very reason.

Software

Given the amount of data stored on a file server, and its importance to your business as a whole and your day-to-day operations, it is important that you back up your hard drives. In this section, an in-depth look into choosing backup software for your network is presented.

NETWORK BACKUP

Today's business information is no longer the domain of a single company, department, or user. The business community needs timely access to critical information distributed throughout the world. Global decisions are made using this information, which needs to be both accurate and current. A business's competitive advantage comes from its capability to act upon and distribute this information in real time.

This information network is largely distributed across a variety of NetWare file servers, application servers, and workstations. Disk hardware failure, fire, or a natural disaster could severely compromise a company's capability to conduct business and could require a substantial monetary expenditure for its recovery. The disruption of services and the inconvenience to customers add to its costs. Also, in addition to safeguarding this information, an organized manner of data archiving is necessary. Records and files must be stored for future use without consuming valuable hard disk space. With this in mind, the important aspects of a backup strategy must be understood and implemented.

STORAGE MANAGEMENT SERVICES

With the variety of workstations running distinct operating systems that connect and exchange information with different versions of NetWare file servers, the task of backing up this data presents a formidable challenge to the network administrator. With Novell's NetWare, a new methodology was devised to standardize network-based data backup and restores, provide flexibility in selecting backup media, and insulate third-party backup and storage applications from changes in the NetWare operating system. This new architecture is known as *Storage Management Services* (SMS).

SMS is a set of application programming interface services (APIs) that allows the backup program access to a variety of network objects. These objects represent network resources and include NetWare file servers, the NetWare Directory Service database, the Bindery, and a workstation's local hard drive. SMS is implemented as a series of server-based network loadable modules (NLMs) and workstation executable files and consists of the following three components:

- ◆ Storage Management Engine (SME)
- ◆ Target Service Agents (TSAs)
- ◆ System Independent Data Format (SIDF)

The Storage Management Engine is the backup engine that can either be a third-party backup application or SBACKUP (shipped with NetWare), the SME included in NetWare. The SME is separate from the target file system and relies on the Storage Management Data Requester (SMDR) and the Target Service Agents to get the required data. Because of SMS's modularity, third-party vendors can add value to their backup products in the form of replacement backup engines, which add additional bells and whistles. This flexibility provides administrators choices in backup software selection.

Executing the appropriate Target Service Agent (TSA) on a network device requiring backup provides controlled access to the network resource. The TSA is a software module that translates the data from the target and prepares the data for backup.

Information recorded to tape is placed in a System Independent Data Format (SIDF). This allows network administrators to exchange information among disparate operating systems and third-party backup products. To ensure both acceptance and compatibility with tape backup products, Novell co-developed SMS with backup vendors. SMS is becoming a de facto standard as support is growing. The new architecture will provide a migration path toward future versions of NetWare. The SMS standard will be an important piece when developing a backup strategy and deciding on a particular backup software product.

BACKUP SOFTWARE

There are numerous software products available for backup. Some of these are very similar, while others incorporate special features that cater to particular needs. The software features of a particular backup product will determine the hardware's functionality. When evaluating backup software, some important considerations should include ease of use, reliability, device management, tape rotation, directory and file management, virus protection, and workstation support.

EASE OF USE

The user interface to your backup program should be clear and helpful when navigating through a daily backup. The program should be intuitive and not require hours of training or a manual at your side. Good error messages for mistakes should be displayed. Standardizing on a single interface, such as Microsoft Windows, will help ease the learning curve when training new operators.

RELIABILITY

Check to see whether the software program provides a tape-to-disk verification. This method ensures accurate data recovery, although it is very time consuming. Novell's Product Information Group tests third-party products for SMS compliance. Most leading third-party backup products are undergoing certification procedures or currently are Novell-certified. Watch for reviews in trade magazines for specific software features or problems. NetWire on CompuServe is a helpful resource for up-to-date software revisions, reviews, and Q&A.

TAPE DEVICE MANAGEMENT

Look for programs that will enable you to display tape device information. This would include tape configuration information, such as installed tape devices and adapter card, real-time statistics about which tape(s) are in use, and the current status of the tape.

You should be able to format and erase tapes. Re-tensioning a tape is important if you are using quarter-inch cartridges (QIC): this will ensure the tape is evenly wound and properly tensioned. Some tape drives support hardware data compression; check to see if your software supports this feature and whether you can enable/disable this feature. If you have multiple tape drives, the software may support tape-to-tape copying and tape-to-tape comparing. This enables you to make backup tapes and to verify that the data on both tapes is the same.

An important performance feature is *parallel streaming*. This enables you to perform simultaneous processing of backup and restore operations to separate tape devices attached to the same server.

How often to perform backups, what data should be backed up, and how to rotate tapes are issues that can be quite confusing to the network operator. There are backup software programs available that will aid in the management of backups and automate the archival strategy. More and more, the effectiveness of backup software is being determined by how well it performs tape management. The industry is headed toward completely automated storage management software. It will be the software that reacts to both network and human errors and provide continuous management and protection of information across the enterprise. Thus, it will be ease of use, flexibility, and the necessary features to meet your defined backup requirements that will be the major points of a purchasing decision.

TAPE ROTATION

Your backup system strategy should be based on a tape rotation scheme that guarantees complete recovery in case of disaster. The purpose of a rotation scheme is to distribute both old and new information across several tape cartridges or cassettes to reduce the risk of data being lost due to media set corruption. The backup and storage media rotation method you use are determined by the following:

- **File restoration decision**: How many tapes will you need to restore information in the event of complete hard drive failure?
- **Storage facilities**: How many tapes are you physically capable of storing?
- **Aging process**: How long must you keep files archived?

GRANDFATHER-FATHER-SON METHOD

To implement the *Grandfather rotation scheme* (shown in Table 16.1) would involve using 21 tape sets. Four daily tape sets should be labeled Monday, Tuesday, Wednesday, and Thursday. Another four weekly sets should be labeled Friday1, Friday2, Friday3, and Friday4. For months that have five Fridays, you may want to add another set of weekly tapes. Also mark twelve monthly sets labeled January, February, March, and so on. This rotation scheme rewrites daily backups the following week, weekly backups after the five weeks, and monthly backups the following year.

TABLE 16.1. GRANDFATHER-FATHER-SON TAPE ROTATION SCHEME.

	Week1	Week2	Week3	Week4
Daily	Monday	Monday	Monday	Monday
Daily	Tuesday	Tuesday	Tuesday	Tuesday
Daily	Wednesday	Wednesday	Wednesday	Wednesday
Daily	Thursday	Thursday	Thursday	Thursday
Weekly	Friday1	Friday2	Friday3	Friday4
Monthly				**January**

	Week5	Week6	Week7	Week8
Daily	Monday	Monday	Monday	Monday
Daily	Tuesday	Tuesday	Tuesday	Tuesday
Daily	Wednesday	Wednesday	Wednesday	Wednesday
Daily	Thursday	Thursday	Thursday	Thursday
Weekly	Friday1	Friday2	Friday3	Friday4
Monthly				**February**

TEN-TAPE FULL ROTATION TECHNIQUE

As the name implies, the ten-tape rotation method requires ten tapes. Each tape should be labeled with a number from one to ten. Unlike the grandfather method where daily tapes are used more often than monthly tapes, the ten-tape rotation method is meant to ensure that each tape is used an equal number of times.

A forty-week rotation period is used where there are a series of ten four-week cycles within this period. For the first four weeks, use the same tapes for Monday (1),

Tuesday (2), Wednesday (3), and Thursday (4) backups. For the first four Fridays, change the sequence number by one (5 through 8). For the second four week cycle, you must increment the daily tape numbers by one, Monday (2), Tuesday (3), Wednesday (4), Thursday (5), and also increment Friday tapes by one (6 through 9). The ten-tape rotation method is illustrated in Table 16.2.

TABLE 16.2. TEN-TAPE ROTATION SCHEME.

Week1	Week2	Week3	Week4
M,T,W,TH,F	M,T,W,TH,F	M,T,W,TH,F	M,T,W,TH,F
1,2,3,4,5	1,2,3,4,6	1,2,3,4,7	1,2,3,4,8
2,3,4,5,6	2,3,4,5,7	2,3,4,5,8	2,3,4,5,9
3,4,5,6,7	3,4,5,6,8	3,4,5,6,9	3,4,5,6,10
4,5,6,7,8	4,5,6,7,9	4,5,6,7,10	4,5,6,7,1
5,6,7,8,9	5,6,7,8,10	5,6,7,8,1	5,6,7,8,2
6,7,8,9,10	6,7,8,9,1	6,7,8,9,2	6,7,8,9,3
7,8,9,10,1	7,8,9,10,2	7,8,9,10,3	7,8,9,10,4
8,9,10,1,2	8,9,10,1,3	8,9,10,1,4	8,9,10,1,5
9,10,1,2,3	9,10,1,2,4	9,10,1,2,5	9,10,1,2,6
10,1,2,3,4	10,1,2,3,5	10,1,2,3,6	10,1,2,3,7

After the end of the first four-week tape cycle, tape 1 is not used for another twelve weeks. The "Monday" tape set of each subsequent four-week cycle is treated the same way. If you plan to implement this rotation scheme, backup to tape 10 as well as tape 1 on Monday of week 1. This will ensure you have a four-week-old copy of your data at the end of the first four-week cycle.

TOWER OF HANOI

This backup scheme is named after the mathematical game, *Tower of Hanoi*, which sometimes is referred to as the *ABACABA* method. Five or more tapes are needed. For this discussion, we will use five tapes. Label the tapes A, B, C, D, and E. Each tape is used at different rotation intervals. Tape A is used every day, Tape B every fourth day, Tape C every eighth day, Tape D every sixteenth day, and so on. The resulting pattern is shown in Table 16.3. The larger letters represent the first use of the tape.

TABLE 16.3. TOWER OF HANOI ROTATION SCHEME.

Week1	Week2	Week3	Week4
M,T,W,TH,F	M,T,W,TH,F	M,T,W,TH,F	M,T,W,TH,F
A,B,a,C,a	b,a,D,a,b	a,c,a,b,a	E,a,b,a,c

Week5	Week6	Week7	Week8
M,T,W,TH,F	M,T,W,TH,F	M,T,W,TH,F	M,T,W,TH,F
a,b,a,d,a	b,a,c,a,b	a,e,a,b,a	c,a,b,a,d

Week9	Week10	Week11	Week12
M,T,W,TH,F	M,T,W,TH,F	M,T,W,TH,F	M,T,W,TH,F
a,b,a,c,a	b,a,d,a,b	a,c,a,b,a	e,a,b,a,c

The following mini-table shows the age of the oldest copy of data for different numbers of tapes used.

Number of Tapes	Oldest Copy
5	16 days
6	32 days
7	64 days
8	128 days

DIRECTORY AND FILE MANAGEMENT

A well-designed file directory structure should be a fundamental design concern of a well-conceived and implemented backup strategy. Separation of static files from those that change frequently simplifies the backup and restore process. Directory/file searching and selective backup capabilities is made easier because of this distinction. Isolating user data files from executable files enables the administrator to effectively monitor and groom files and directories and to plan future disk space requirements. Because of a multi-client environment, special consideration should be taken to ensure backup and restore capability of the name space support of the file server. Open files require special attention. Some products can back up open files while others skip over them and attempt to back them up once the backup is complete.

Certain files will remain open permanently. In this case, the backup software must report those files that were not backed up so that proper administrative action can be taken. One overlooked aspect of backup is the need to close down applications that hold open configuration or database files prior to performing the backup. The backup software attempts to back up these open files, but the tape copies of these files are often unusable. If you can shut down applications that normally are left running or have files open, this would avoid this situation. A utility such as *NetWare Console Commander* by Frye Computer Systems will schedule the unloading of NLMs and automatically reload the NLM after the backup is complete.

The timeliness of your backup should also be of concern. As the "backup window" diminishes due to the fact that disk drive sizes and the number of new and updated files are growing rapidly, an efficient, workable backup schedule must be employed. A backup time must be chosen that will render the least amount of inconvenience to both users and administrators.

The frequency of a system backup depends on the applications being executed and the value of the information being stored. As a minimum, the daily changes should be backed up. Others will find it necessary to provide continuous, online backup because the cost of recreating the information, such as in an order entry system, is warranted. Planning which data will be backed up each day will lead to a backup schedule. Remembering that backups are performed so as to quickly recover from a system failure or if file errors or corruption occur, restoring files can be difficult if backups are performed without proper planning and concern.

The person responsible for the backup strategy—and there must be one—must visualize what constitutes a viable, daily procedure to perform a system backup. This involves estimating the total costs of backup. This is more than the initial price of the hardware and software, but it includes the labor involved in performing the backup and most importantly, and I can't emphasize this enough, the time it takes to fully restore the information after a major catastrophe.

The backup strategy you choose actually may be a composite of many smaller systems. For example, you may choose to perform an image backup of the file server, as well as doing file-by-file backups of particular data volumes to have more flexibility in selecting which files to restore.

With this in mind, the backup/restore software should act as an extension of your directory and file management goals. Being able to filter or include specific directories or files should be performed easily. Selected options within a particular vendor's menu or window should easily match your desired backup needs. Some form of scripting or programming capability should be permitted to accommodate repetitive type backups. Monitoring services and report generation to verify its success should also be provided.

VIRUS PROTECTION

Some software can work in conjunction with a server-based virus protection program that offers virus detection capabilities. You can elect to scan for viruses before or during execution to ensure a "clean" tape.

WORKSTATION SUPPORT

Inadvertent erasure of workstation files is one of the most common causes of data loss on the network and presents a particular problem for the network administrator who is responsible for its protection. Software that will allow backup and restore facilities of the client as well as the file server is a plus. The capability to not only backup DOS workstations but Macintosh, UNIX, and OS/2 clients makes implementing a total backup strategy more manageable.

As with any software program you buy, you should check the vendor's support policy of the program. This can range from three months to three years. Phone and technical support after the purchase is important for both installation and technical questions concerning use of the backup product.

SBACKUP.NLM

SBACKUP is Novell's implementation of the SMS architecture and marks a step forward when compared with the version shipped with NetWare 3.*x*. This is a server backup and restore solution. You can run SBACKUP only from the system console or from a workstation using the remote access facility running RCONSOLE. NetWare 4.1 ships with TSAs that support NetWare 3.1*x* file servers and binderies, NetWare 4.*x* servers, 4.*x* NDS databases, and DOS and OS/2 workstations. TSAs for server file systems provide full name space support for DOS, OS/2, Macintosh, Network File System (NFS), and FTAM (OSI protocol).

SBACKUP is interactive (see Figure 16.4). It requires the network administrator to back up only one target per session. The program offers no scripting or job control administration features and is adequate for a single server or small network environment that operates under very tight budgetary constraints.

Third-party vendors' products, such as Cheyenne Software's ARCserve, Palindrome's Network Archivist, and Legato Systems' NetWorker, provide many of the features lacking in Novell's SBACKUP program. They continue to define "state-of-the-art" in NLM-based network backup.

16

PROTECTING THE DATA AND HARDWARE

Figure 16.4.
SBACKUP's Main
Menu.

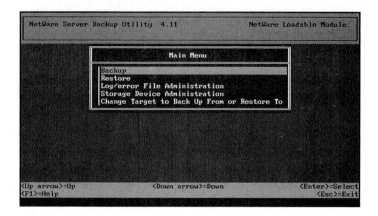

NetWare Directory Services

The *NetWare Directory Services* (NDS) database is a distributed database that contains information about resources and users. It is functionally equivalent to the bindery in previous versions of NetWare. But unlike the bindery, NDS is partitioned and copies of these partitions (replicas) are placed on selected servers. Replicas provide fault tolerance by ensuring that more than one copy of the partition information is available. If the replica becomes corrupted, you can use the master replica to recreate it. Partitions and replicas of the NDS database are created and managed using the PARTMGR text utility or the NetWare Administrator (NWAdmin) graphical utility. Novell's SBACKUP program and leading third-party tape vendors provide a TSA to backup NDS, although replication of the database is the preferred method of ensuring fault tolerance.

Hardware Issues

The hardware you select for your backup system is an important consideration. Tape is the storage medium of choice. Many factors need to be considered before choosing a particular tape drive system. Cost, capacity, and speed are the essential items to look for when making a selection.

Cost

This is one of the most important issues people consider when choosing a tape drive system. Although no one has money to burn, cost must be balanced with other factors. Your tape rotation strategy will dictate how many tapes to buy. Hidden costs, such as operator time, onsite and offsite storage fees, tape replacement, and tape drive repair and maintenance must be included. In the end, you are looking for value in your purchase.

CAPACITY

If at all possible, the capacity of your tape drive should be greater than the disk system on your file server and workstations. It is helpful if a complete backup of your file server can be achieved on a single tape. As your network grows, it may outgrow the capacity of a single tape and require additional tapes to complete a full backup. Support of tape spanning will be necessary and involves both hardware and software. The hardware will know when the end of the tape has been reached and alert the software to prompt the operator to insert the next tape. The software will have the capability to know what has been successfully written to tape and begin writing where it has left off.

Note

> Backups running unattended that perform tape spanning require operator intervention to insert the next tape, unless you have a tape-changer unit.

SPEED

Speed becomes a key issue if users are not permitted to log in to the system while the backup is being performed. Backups must be performed as quickly as possible so as not to impinge on the upcoming workday.

File compression on NetWare 4 servers occurs by default from 12 a.m. to 6 a.m. The backup time slot is now shortened and must be matched with tape speed.

Restoration of files *must* be a speedy process. Downtime increases the cost of doing business. Studies have shown that most companies that experience a data disaster that lasts ten days or more either are acquired by another company or file bankruptcy within a year. It means your job!

MEDIA DEFECTS

As with disk drives, tape drives also can have defects. Almost every tape cartridge has some imperfections. Software must be able to detect these defects and prevent information from being written to the defective areas. These are known as *hard errors*. A report generated by the software listing files skipped due to read errors or why the backup was prematurely aborted is a must.

SOFT ERRORS

Unlike hard drives, tape cartridges are not sealed and are subject to smoke and dust. Over time, the tape read/write heads accumulate dirt and need to be properly maintained to prevent errors from occurring. If not, the software supplied with the hardware will be unable to read past the damaged area, thus making the tape unusable.

Mechanical Breakdown

Tape drives are mechanical devices and if not maintained break down. The internal mechanical components do wear down over time and can change the alignment of the read/write heads. Replacing a tape drive with a new one does not ensure that the old tapes will work. Proper maintenance is required.

Testing and Maintaining the Backup System

Once you have made your hardware/software selection, it is important to test and maintain the hardware and software on a regular basis. Testing ensures what you back up today can be restored tomorrow. Maintenance increases the life span of the equipment you purchased.

After installation of the hardware and software, test drive your backup system. Test anything that might prevent you from getting a good backup. This includes hardware, software, and any scripted or automated procedures you might have created. You should test the hardware/software as a complete system and individually. Diagnostic software is usually provided by the vendor.

From time to time, you will need to continue to test how the software and hardware are functioning. Everyone has a tape backup story of how they performed a backup of the system every day only to find out to their horror that they could not restore the files from tape. The moral of the story is "You can test your system or fall victim to your hardware/software."

Maintenance is another issue that many put off until it is too late. Every tape drive on the market today requires cleaning and physical head inspection. Every tape drive manufacturer includes cleaning instructions in their manuals. Like the auto mechanic who is selling FRAM oil filters says: "You can pay me now or pay me later." Your move.

Offsite Storage

Unfortunately, creating a backup and properly maintaining your hardware does not prevent against fire, earthquakes, theft, disgruntled employees, and other catastrophes. The need to place your information in more than one location helps reduce the chance of tape destruction due to disaster. A consistent schedule of moving tapes to another location, returning them for upgrades, and rotating them back offsite will ensure the tape security. Many companies specialize in providing offsite storage services. This is an additional cost and must be figured in as part of the total backup strategy. This is *not* an option and should be thought of as a mandatory part of the backup process. Besides the cost factor, you should examine the types of services offered by the company. Many offer 24 hours service at a premium, while others have daytime only services. Remember, bad things happen at night and on weekends. Don't shortchange your backup program.

Note

Tapes melt in fireproof vaults. Only your papers will be safe.

HIERARCHICAL STORAGE MANAGEMENT

Spurred by this explosion of data on PC networks and the demand for automated storage management, several vendors are bringing to market their *Hierarchical Storage Management* (HSM) products. Originating from the mainframe and UNIX worlds, HSM is the process of automatically migrating data off the server's hard drive onto a hierarchy of less expensive media, based on the frequency of data access. This migration of data is transparent to the user, and its retrieval is automatic.

By migrating infrequently accessed data to less expensive storage options, such as optical jukeboxes and tape libraries, companies are keeping their most active files "online," using quick access disk drives and still having access to less active files "near-line." HSM is supposed to save money. Costs incurred administering traditional storage systems would pay for HSM. Alphatronix's Inspire Migrator, Palindrome's HSM, and Novell's High Capacity Storage System (HCSS) are such examples.

VIRUSES

Viruses are programs written by angry people who have no respect for others. What you have read or heard about viruses may or may not be true. What you must separate is fact from fiction, although fiction may be more interesting.

Every network administrator fears the devastating effect of a network virus. Viruses should be an important concern but not something to panic about. Viruses are not magic, but programs like any other DOS program. What makes a virus different from a DOS program is that the virus is intended to spread undetected and to be disruptive, possibly destructive.

Note

No viruses capable of infecting NLMs have been found.

To protect your network, NetWare enables you to set a number of file rights and attributes. These security features determine whether particular operations can be performed on a file. Some methods can be used to combat viruses. Where you can, you should deny the W(rite) privilege from directories holding executable files. If executables and data must be stored in the same directory, the agent-orange attribute, Execute-only, can be useful to slow down the spread of file viruses. Viruses don't affect data files.

Note

The execute-only attribute can only be removed by deleting the file. Make sure you have a copy of the file before you set this attribute.

Also, not all executables will run correctly if you use this attribute. Test it before you put it into production. If you cannot use this attribute, flag your executable files Read-Only and deny the Modify right in the directory in question.

Because Admin or Admin equivalent has the write privilege to all directories, when you log in as a super user, be sure you have no viruses resident in memory. When in doubt, log-in as a user who lacks write privileges in directories where executables are stored.

For total network protection, it is advisable to use some form of virus protection software. This software can reside on the file server or a local workstation. The file server solution offers a centralized solution, whereas the workstation version saves file server memory and doesn't degrade network performance by using valuable CPU clock cycles.

The result in using any virus protection software is that you are less likely to become infected. You will be able to detect and remove the virus before it becomes a problem.

BUGS, PATCHES, AND FIXES

Software also is a villain when it comes to data loss. Programmers call these software failures *bugs*; network administrators have other ways to label them. Whatever name they go by, it always means trouble. With NetWare 4.*x*, Novell has included a means to protect against problematic NLMs through memory protection. Memory resources are structured so that processes are unable to corrupt each other's memory space or that of the network operating system. A legal addressing space for the process or domain is provided to test third-party NLMs.

NLMs loaded in this protected domain are unable to corrupt the network operating system. This memory-protected area is enabled by loading the DOMAIN.NLM. This NLM must be defined as the first line of your STARTUP.NCF file before any other

NLMs. With DOMAIN, you can specify which area the NLM will run. Two areas are defined by Novell: OS and OS_PROTECTED. NLMs wishing to run in the OS_PROTECTED domain must be written to function properly within memory protection.

SUMMARY

This chapter has focused on those issues that will help increase the fault tolerance of your hardware system and ensure the integrity of your data. These issues were broken down into both hardware and software considerations. Working to bring about a cohesive plan that will weave together both hardware and software will be your next step. This plan will evolve over time to match both the changes in your business and in the technology. Use this chapter as a template when planning, selecting, and maintaining hardware and software to protect your NetWare 4.x information network.

- The Problems

- Assembly and Initial Hardware Testing: Two Strategies

- Burn In

- Setting Up Hardware: Possible Sources of Conflict

- Hard Disk Setup Issues

- Installing CD-ROMs

- Make a DOS Partition

- Burning In

- Final Touches

- Power Conditioning

- Summary

CHAPTER 17

Configuring Server Hardware

Getting the server up and running under DOS is the first challenge you face when installing a NetWare server. If the machine does not operate properly under DOS, you will not get it to run NetWare correctly. In this chapter, common problems, issues, and possible resolutions are outlined and discussed.

THE PROBLEMS

Setting up your server hardware can be, and often is, easy. There may be problems though, and this chapter will help you to develop a plan to configure your hardware that will enable you to locate and resolve those problems quickly. The following sections briefly indicate some potential problem areas.

MEMORY CONFLICTS

Many interface cards use a portion of RAM addressed near the top of the first megabyte of RAM. These include, but are not limited to, video interface cards, network interface cards (NICs), and hard disk controllers. Having more than one card addressed in the same memory range can lead to intermittent lockups or perhaps even the refusal to boot at all.

Memory address conflicts are the most common cause of lockups due to hardware conflict; if you are experiencing unexplained lockups, especially on a new machine or one that has just had a card added, this is a good first place to look.

INTERRUPT REQUEST LINE (IRQ) CONFLICTS

Many interface cards, such as serial and parallel ports, hard disk adapters, and NICs, use an IRQ. IRQs are also used by motherboard and CPU functions. Addressing an IRQ where one already exists may not cause a problem; some published uses (such as LPT1's use of IRQ 7) are commonly ignored. And some devices, under a single-tasking operating system such as DOS, can share interrupts. Again, however, they can cause subtle problems or even prevent the machine from booting if not properly configured.

PORT ADDRESS CONFLICTS

Least likely to cause subtle problems are port address conflicts. Many cards and devices use port addresses, but presenting a conflict will normally cause one or either of the devices to fail to work. Most common uses are serial ports and the computer's speaker. Some NICs also use a port address, but because there are many of these addresses, most cards will default to an unused address (at least unused by other types of devices).

MEMORY CONFLICTS

When IBM introduced the PC-AT so many years ago, it was powered by an Intel 80286. Along with it came a new bus (the "16-bit" or AT bus, now referred to as ISA for Industry Standard Architecture) that could address up to 16MB of RAM (from the 1MB in the 8088 and 8086 of the original PCs). As you will see, this "unused" space proved too great a temptation for some.

HDDIRECT MEMORY ACCESS (DMA) CONFLICTS

As its name implies, DMA is a method that allows devices to directly access memory rather than accessing it through the CPU. This can provide a performance boost, as when a hard disk adapter is writing a block of data from a disk into RAM, but it is also a possible area of conflict.

ASSEMBLY AND INITIAL HARDWARE TESTING: TWO STRATEGIES

So all you have are hardware in boxes around you. You need to decide how to best go about putting it together with the least trouble. There are two basic strategies that you employ:

a. The careful, methodical approach

b. The normal approach

Reality shows that the normal approach is the one ordinarily applied by the majority of the installers, and with good reason—if all goes well, it is the fastest and least trouble.

The "If all goes well" scenario is not the reason that you normally dive into the books. Therefore, the normal approach will only be discussed briefly. Note that the normal approach also applies to hardware purchased, fully or near-fully assembled (lacking only NICs for example).

THE NORMAL WAY

Don't read the manual(s). Open the case and install all cards and connect cables, as necessary. This approach usually assumes that you have some experience so that you can perform these tasks without instructions.

This approach works remarkably well assuming, as previously mentioned, that you have the experience to perform the basic chores. It works so well because many, if not most, hardware suppliers do not want you to have trouble, so they have tried to make good assumptions about the kinds of conflicts, such as interrupt conflicts, and work around them.

Warning

Frankly, the "normal way" usually works and most people get away with it. Because a server is a critical part of your network, however, be sure to allow time for plenty of burn in (described later) and testing before releasing the server for general use.

Still, however, there can be problems with some of the hardware and all the assumptions hardware vendors make are not benign. Many NICs, for example, come with a default IRQ of 3, the same IRQ as the serial port COM2 (and COM4). You probably won't be using a serial port on your server, but you might, and here is a problem laying in wait for you. All this leads to the second strategy.

Tip

If you start to assemble your server the normal way and run into trouble with the installation, back off and go to the careful, methodical way. Chances are that you'll need to be careful and methodical, so save time and go right back to square one. Even the simplest server is a complex interaction of parts, and isolating one problem (and there may be more than one) is best done carefully and methodically by reducing, as much as possible, the number of variables you are working with at one time.

THE CAREFUL AND METHODICAL WAY

This approach does not take a lot longer, but is often eschewed until problems crop up. Basically, the approach has three parts, as follows:

◆ **Get the most basic machine running:** In case you bought a nearly complete machine (lacking the NICs, for example), this is the starting point. If it doesn't work, refer to your vendor for service. If you are building the machine, try to get the machine with just the video, hard drive and floppy drives, and keyboard, installed and running. The idea is to have a known starting point, so no NICs, CD-ROMs, excess RAM (more than 16MB). Preferably, there will be no printer or serial ports, but they often come on the motherboard or hard disk adapter, so don't overdo it.

- ◆ **Add a single device**, such as a NIC or CD-ROM and test that it, and the machine in general, are working properly. Set the device so that it will not conflict with other devices you have already installed (or may install).
- ◆ **Repeat the preceding step** as necessary, until all additional devices are installed.

Warning

The key to this approach, or troubleshooting if you started out using the other approach, is to do only one thing at a time. This way, if you run into trouble, you will know which device is causing the conflict.

Burn In

Generally, the last step of server hardware configuration and testing is a *burn in*. This phase will be discussed in detail later in the section entitled "Burning In," but it also is discussed now, to emphasize that a thorough burn in process should always be done prior to bringing a server online.

Warning

Be sure to do a burn in on all server hardware before bringing it online. Also, if you have the time, burn in any hardware that is critical to your network, such as hubs and gateway machines.

Setting Up Hardware: Possible Sources of Conflict

This section goes into detail about the kinds of settings you may need to make, uses of these settings by other hardware, and where to be especially careful.

Overview: Focusing on NICs

The main accessory you will be installing in your server is a NIC (or several NICs). These are how your server will communicate with users and other servers on the network. All the NICs we are aware of require at least two of the following:

- ◆ Base memory address
- ◆ Interrupt Request Line (IRQ)

◆ Base port address
◆ Direct Memory Address (DMA) channel

Each one is examined in turn.

Note

Communications is the key for the peripherals you will be installing, especially NICs. Broadly speaking, a device (such as a NIC) can communicate with another device (such as the CPU) using either a base port address (serial and parallel ports) or a memory address (video drivers often do this). NICs can use either or both methods.

Just having a path to communicate is not enough, however; there must be a way of knowing that communication needs to take place. There are two general ways to do this:

◆ An IRQ can be raised, the equivalent of saying "excuse me." The software device driver is then invoked to handle whatever is needed.

◆ On many DOS systems, the software driver for the device will "poll" the port or address every so often to see if anything is there. This is actually a variation of the first method because it uses the "clock-tick" IRQ to determine when to poll.

In a single-tasking environment, such as DOS, polling is a workable technique because the computer is not really doing anything else. In many DOS programs, the keyboard, mouse, and serial ports are polled. Even though an IRQ is established for each of them, it is not used because polling gives peppier performance. This explains why several devices may claim an IRQ—in DOS—without causing problems; the software driving the device may not actually use it.

In multitasking operating systems, such as IBM's OS/2 and Novell NetWare, polling will not work well because the CPU may be off doing something else when the data arrives and before it gets around to polling the device another piece of data may have come in and displaced it. This is why some DOS communication programs lose data when running under Microsoft's Windows or OS/2. Multitasking operating systems require IRQs, and most current motherboards and peripherals will not allow sharing an IRQ.

Base Memory Addresses

Base memory address conflicts are the leading cause of hardware conflicts. Every device that uses a base memory address must have its own address range. Sometimes your machine will be able to boot DOS, but as soon as any of the devices trying to use the address are accessed, you will probably get a crash; it certainly will not work as expected.

Tip

Your NIC may not use a base memory address, refer to your manual. It may not identify it using the same terms used here. If you are unsure, call the manufacturer's support line for help.

Any time you see a 4- or 5-digit number that contains one or more letters (for example, C800, D0000, or CC00), you will know that this is a base memory address. The numbers are given in hexadecimal (base 16) notation and the letters A–F are used to represent the values 10 through 15. The numbers may be followed by an *h* (C800h), but this is not always so. Just learn to look for the pattern.

Base memory addresses are memory locations in the region above the 640 Kilobytes that DOS uses and below 1 megabyte. Refer to Table 17.1 for a list of the commonly used addresses of many devices. Use the column under *Your Server* to record settings for your server.

TABLE 17.1. BASE MEMORY ADDRESSES AND COMMON USAGE.

Address	Common Usage	Your Server
A000–A3FF	VGA Graphics	
A400–A7FF	VGA Graphics	
A800–ABFF	VGA Graphics	
AC00–AFFF	VGA Graphics	
B000–B3FF	Video (usually available)	
B400–B7FF	Video (usually available)	
B800–BBFF	Text Mode Video	
BC00–BFFF	Text Mode Video	

continues

TABLE 17.1. CONTINUED

Address	Common Usage	Your Server
C000–C3FF	Video BIOS	
C400–C7FF	Video BIOS	
C800–CBFF	Some Hard Disk Adapters	
CC00–CFFF	Some SCSI Adapters	
D000–D3FF	(usually available)	
D400–D7FF	(usually available)	
D800–DBFF	Some SCSI Adapters	
DC00–DFFF	Some SCSI Adapters	
E000–E3FF	Reserved for BIOS (may be available)	
E400–E7FF	Reserved for BIOS (may be available)	
E800–EBFF	Reserved for BIOS (may be available)	
EC00–EFFF	Reserved for BIOS (may be available)	
F000–FFFF	ROM BIOS	

Note

The original IBM PC used an Intel 8088 CPU. This is a 16-bit processor with an 8-bit data bus (eight bits of data, one byte, could be read at a time). A 16-bit processor would normally have 16 bit memory addressing. This would only allow for 64 kilobytes (2^{16} or 65,536 bytes).

Because Intel had a 64K CPU in their 8080, they decided to enlarge the memory address range to an unheard of 1MB (2^{20} or 1,048,576 bytes). They did this by *segmenting* the memory addresses into two 16-bit values. The arithmetic is not discussed here, but suffice it to say that the two 16-bit addresses were combined to form one 20-bit address.

When IBM designed the PC, they decided to reserve the top 384K for system devices. This allowed the user to roam free in 640K, an huge amount then—the original PC came with 16K of memory standard.

The offshoot of this segmented architecture is that all peripherals that use a memory address are mapped to fall on a segment boundary, usually 32K apart, although both 16 and 64K are not uncommon, and some will use 128K.

If you are assembling the whole machine (that is, installing the drives and so on), it is probably best to make a copy of Table 17.1 and fill it is as you install devices. As you install a device, mark the range it uses out. Make sure that you mark off the whole range the device uses (this is usually available in the manual, but you may need to call the manufacturer's support line). The table is incremented every 16K (except for F000–FFFF, which generally is unavailable because that's where the ROM BIOS is located), and even if your device uses less than this, mark off the whole portion as used.

If you have an already assembled machine to which you are adding peripherals, such as NICs, you have the following two choices:

◆ Go through the documentation and determine the addresses of your installed devices and then proceed.

◆ Use a program such as Quarterdeck's QEMM to map out RAM addresses that are in use. This approach is often better, as long as you use it with care. You will need a DOS partition on the machine and you must be sure to follow the instructions which come with QEMM carefully.

Briefly, what you must do is load QEMM and all the drivers for your software (if you already have NICs installed, then you will need to load the DOS drivers for them). Run all the normal tasks you might have, load a word processing document, get into a spreadsheet, or look up data in a database program. After you have done this, you can run QEMM's Analyze function to see which memory regions were accessed (see Figure 17.1). You then can use this to fill in Table 17.1.

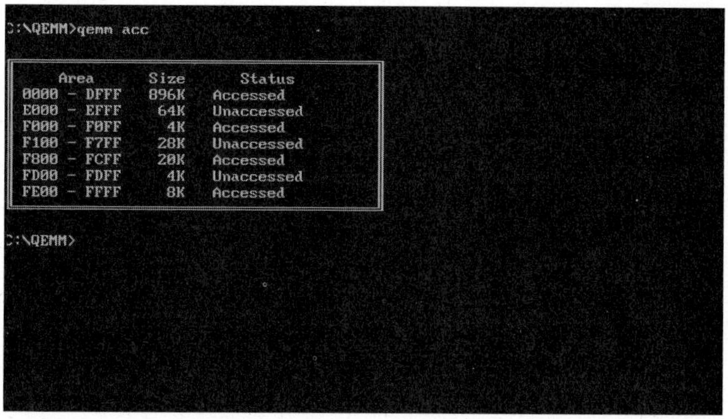

Figure 17.1.
QEMM analysis screen
output.

```
C:\QEMM>qemm acc

     Area     Size        Status
  0000 - DFFF  896K     Accessed
  E000 - EFFF   64K     Unaccessed
  F000 - F0FF    4K     Accessed
  F100 - F7FF   28K     Unaccessed
  F800 - FCFF   20K     Accessed
  FD00 - FDFF    4K     Unaccessed
  FE00 - FFFF    8K     Accessed

C:\QEMM>
```

Warning

You *must* follow the instructions carefully to have QEMM find all memory in use. Failing to do this may result in a region being marked as unused when it is in use.

Probably the best approach, if you are dealing with an already assembled machine, is to do both; research as best as possible and then let QEMM verify your findings.

INTERRUPT REQUEST LINES (IRQS)

Hardwired right to your motherboard, IRQs, also called hardware interrupts, are a way for devices to signal that they need, or have something. Most of the time, this communication is from a device to the CPU, or vice versa, although there is no reason that other devices cannot signal each other. For example, every time you press a key on your keyboard, an interrupt (IRQ 1) is *raised* (*raised* refers to the fact that a voltage is put on the hardwired line). The BIOS (Basic Input Output System) and the operating system check to see whether it is a key they need to notice (Ctrl+Alt+Del, for example, indicating a reboot), and if not, pass it along to the running program.

Multiple software routines can look at an interrupt. The BIOS gets it first, and if it is not needed by the BIOS, it passes the interrupt along to the operating system, and so on. This is called *chaining*, and your computer couldn't work without it. This trick, for example, enables you to have a clock display on your screen while you are working on something else. The clock program chains the System Timer interrupt (IRQ 0) and updates the clock display every time a second passes.

If it is so that different routines can deal with an interrupt, why can't more than one device use that interrupt to get attention with control passing down until the proper routine is found? For example, you could have two doors, front and back, connected to one door bell. You would, upon hearing the door bell, first check the front door and, if someone is there, deal with them. If no one is at the front door, you then could check the back door.

This scenario, two devices (front and back door) connected to one interrupt (door bell) can work in computers, too. In fact, in DOS, it is somewhat common. The problem is that in a high-performance multitasking operating system, such as Novell's NetWare, you can get a second interrupt before the first one gets serviced. To follow the previous example: your door bell rings. As you are getting up to answer it, it rings again. Did the second ring come from the same door as the first, or the other door? Which door do you answer first?

Some newer bus designs (such as IBM's Micro Channel) do allow devices to share interrupts, but you should still avoid it at all costs. On your server, you will probably have plenty of free interrupts (most servers, for example, will not need two printers and two serial ports which use up four interrupts). The reason is that interrupt conflicts can be very difficult to identify and track down. Your server may run fine for months and then start crashing irregularly or corrupting data.

Tip

> Avoid trouble, if at all possible. Even if your server will allow it, do not have devices share interrupts.

The Table 17.2 shows the available interrupts (from an ISA bus machine) and their commonly assigned uses. IRQs 9–15 are not available in 8-bit slots. IRQ 2 is shown as the Cascade interrupt, and its usual function is to activate the IRQs (9–15) available in the 16-bit bus. On most machines, IRQ 2 is also wired as IRQ 9, so use only one or the other.

TABLE 17.2. COMMON DEVICES AND THEIR CONFIGURATIONS.

Device	IRQ	I/O Port
Timer	0	N/A
Keyboard	1	N/A
[Cascade	2]	
COM2	3	2F8—2FF
COM1	4	3F8—3FF
LPT2	5	278—27F
Floppy controller	6	1F0—1F8
		3F0—3F7
LPT1	7	378—37F
Clock	8	N/A
EGA	2/9	3C0—3CF
AT hard disk controller	14	1F0—1F8
		170—177

Tip

> Even if a device is not in use, it may still be present and must be disabled if you want to use that interrupt. For example, so called "multi-IO" cards are popular and come in many machines. They have an IDE hard disk controller, floppy disk controller, serial ports, and a printer port (and maybe even a game port) all on one card. If you want to use IRQ 5, for example (normally the second printer port), you will

need to make sure that the multi-IO card does not have its printer port addressed there. Most cards like this will allow you to disable the various ports with jumpers. Also look out for ports built in to the motherboard. It is not usually enough that the port is unused; it must be disabled.

Most NICs will use an IRQ, so take Table 17.2 and cross off the ones in use in your machine (remember 2 and 9 are usually the same) and use that as a guide as you set your cards.

If you are unsure of what IRQs are in use, you can use a diagnostic program such as Touchstone Software Corporation's CheckIt. See Figure 17.2 for the Interrupt Usage function. CheckIt has been found to be pretty good at finding IRQs in use, although not fool-proof, so the best approach is to find out for sure.

Figure 17.2.
CheckIt's IRQ usage
report screen.

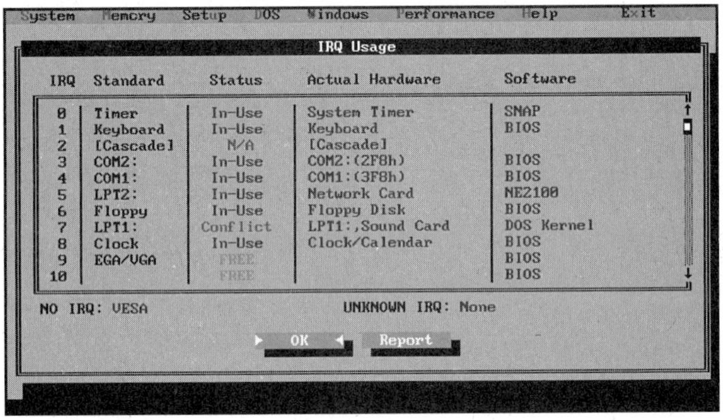

BASE PORT ADDRESSES

The Base Port Address is another way for devices to communicate. This is how the serial port and the PC speaker works. If your card uses this type of I/O, you will see addresses that are three characters long (they could also be one or two characters, but I've never seen I/O cards that use these low addresses). As with memory addresses, base port addresses are given in hexadecimal format (numbers 0–9 and letters A–F) and may or may not include a trailing h, as in 300h.

Base port addresses are blocked in groups of 16 so that the address may be given as a range (300–30F). As a general rule, the addresses in the 300–3AF range are available for use, except for 378–37F, which is used for the first parallel port (LPT1).

DMA CHANNELS

DMA channels enable a device to write directly to memory rather than moving data through the CPU. This can free your CPU to perform other tasks. Devices that use DMA are usually called "bus mastering" devices because, along with the CPU, they can control the memory bus.

Floppy drive controllers and most SCSI controllers are the most common bus mastering devices. There are normally 8 DMA channels available and, in a normal situation, only the floppy controller has one by default so there is a lot of room to experiment.

Tip

If you are installing bus mastering devices (either NICs or hard disk controllers), be sure that you read the next section about 16MB or more of RAM).

16 OR MORE MEGABYTES OF RAM

When the Intel 80386 was introduced, it had unbelievable capabilities. Its predecessor, the 80286, could address up to 16MB of RAM. The 80386 could address 4 gigabytes (4,096MB) of RAM. When the first 80386 machines came out they ignored this because nobody was running more than 4MB to 8MB of RAM anyway. This allowed them to keep the AT's (ISA) bus design with its 16MB limit.

As you have seen so many times in the computer industry yesterday's wonder is today's commonplace. Soon we wanted more than 16MB, and machines were introduced that would take 32MB or even 64MB. But if they ran the ISA bus, and many did, and you wanted to use a SCSI controller (or other bus mastering controller) you had a problem. The controller was connected to the ISA bus with its 16MB limit; it could not directly access the memory above 16MB.

Today's file servers should not be running on an ISA bus, but because of this used-to-be limit in the older architecture, many cards will still have instructions for machines with greater than 16MB installed. Be sure you read these and follow the instructions.

You also should be aware that some manufacturers used the memory addresses right at the top of the 16MB region in order to improve performance, assuming that nothing else would be there. Most of these were video cards, so beware if you are using a hand-me-down video card in your server.

BIOS Settings

Modern BIOSs use the memory management capabilities of the 386 and later processors to move slower ROM BIOS code into faster RAM. This gives a performance boost in DOS, but for protected mode operating systems like NetWare, it is of no use and may introduce trouble. Check your BIOS setup screen(s) for these options. They usually will be labeled as "shadowing" and there may be one setting (such as BIOS Shadowing) or many (such as Video Shadowing, BIOS Shadowing, and so on). Just turn them all off.

Another thing to watch for in the BIOS setup is a *RAM cache setting*. A RAM cache works just like a disk cache; recently-used memory is stored in an area that offers quicker retrieval on the theory that you may need it again soon. This will speed up the operation of your system, perhaps considerably. Check to make sure that the setting is for `All RAM available`. Some BIOS default to caching only the first 16MB and because most servers will have more RAM, you will need to cache it, too.

Hard Disk Setup Issues

This section discusses a couple of issues: cabling for multiple drives, and BIOS setup for the popular IDE and SCSI drives. If your system uses another format or RAID (Redundant Array of Inexpensive Drives), be sure to follow the manufacturers instructions.

Setting Up for Multiple Drives

If you have only one physical drive in the machine, set up is quite straightforward, as follows:

1. Connect the cable between the hard drive and controller card.
2. Connect the power cable from the PC's power supply to the hard drive.
3. If you are using a SCSI hard drive, set the SCSI drive address to `0`. All SCSI devices need a unique address `0–7`, where the controller usually uses `7`. The best practice is to assign SCSI devices numbers starting from 0 and going up.

   If you are using an IDE drive, make sure the jumper is set for Master, and not Slave.

If you have two or more drives to set up, the following sections tell you about a couple of tricks.

Multiple IDE Drives

Current standards allow for two IDE drives. The second drive must be installed as the *slave* (see your drive's documentation). The slave usually is set by a jumper on the drive itself. The first drive should be set up as *master*, but because this is the default of most drives, you will probably not need to change it.

Tip

If you are to use two IDE drives, try to use the same vendors, and if possible, the same model.

MULTIPLE SCSI DRIVES

Make sure that all the drives to be attached to the controller are of the proper type. SCSI-2 (the second generation of the Small Computer System Interface standard) allows for Fast, Wide, and Fast-Wide drive types. Most drives today are Fast SCSI. Just make sure that the drives and controller match.

As mentioned previously, you need to set the address (sometimes called the *Target Address*) for each device to a different value; remember that the controller also is a device. The common address for controllers is 7. It is suggested that you number your drives, starting at 0 and going up.

Tip

It is not uncommon to see the SCSI controllers boot-up screen showing seven drives found (all the same). This is caused by addressing the drive the same as the controller. Most SCSI drives will come with a default address of 7, which usually is the controller's address. While this sometimes will work, it is a time bomb. The boot screen for the controller should show each SCSI device and only show it once.

The order the drives are connected to the physical cable does not need to match the drives address, but the last drive on the physical cable needs a terminator. Many drives have built-in terminating resistors. These need to be removed from every other drive, except the last one.

Note

Each end of the SCSI bus (its cable or cables) needs a termination and there should be no other terminators on the line. The SCSI controller normally is terminated on the assumption that you will have either internal or external devices, but not both. If you do have both external and internal devices, remove the controller's terminator (refer to your manual) and terminate the far end of both the internal and external cables.

SETTING UP BIOS TYPES

You will need to configure the BIOS for your drive types. As you will see, both IDE and SCSI setup usually is easy, but the steps are different for each.

IDE DRIVES

With IDE drives, you will need to have the drive's parameters set in the BIOS table. Many newer BIOS will be able to read your drive's information and select the proper values for you. Do not despair if your BIOS will not do this. Unlike the older days, the IDE drive will mask the real information so that all you really need to set is the proper size. In the old days, you needed to have the drive's number of heads, cylinders, and sectors per track. These figures are collectively referred to as the drive's *geometry*.

When the consortium that created IDE got going, it was apparent that troubles were ahead. For example, the maximum number for cylinders (or tracks, the number of concentric circles the drive could store information on) in the BIOS area is 1024, but many drives now have 2000–4000 or more cylinders, and this is necessary to get the high capacities we now take for granted.

Note

The PC can ask for a specific sector of disk information in two ways (this is at the hardware level). It can ask for a specific combination of head number, cylinder number, and sector number. Or, it can ask for an absolute sector. The absolute sector addressing starts at the first head, first cylinder, and first sector, and starts counting until it reaches the sector requested (actually, it does not count anew each time but knows how to get there).

The controller takes any request made by the head/cylinder/sector method and converts it into an absolute sector before passing it on to the drive. This means that you do not have to put the real values in the BIOS (and you may not be able to if you drive has more than 1024 cylinders); all you need to do is put in values such that `heads * cylinders * sectors/track` equal the total number of sectors on the disk. If you do not know the number of sectors, refer to your documentation or see the following tip.

Tip

To get the total number of sectors on your disk, take the total number of bytes it holds (not the megabyte, such as 170MB, but the real size, which might be something like 178,257,920 bytes) and divide by 512 (the number of bytes per sector).

If you cannot get the actual number of bytes, use the megabyte rating (170,000,000). Be aware, however, that some of the disk will not be used.

Most BIOS drive tables have a couple of user settable drive types (typically the last two on the list). To arrive at a proper figure for your particular IDE drive, follow these steps:

1. Divide the real number of cylinders by a factor to get it under 1024. For example, if the real number of cylinders is 2700, divide it by 3 to get a number that is less than 1024. It is not important to have the number come out with no remainder, but it is desirable.

2. Put this number (from the preceding example, 900) in the cylinders field.

3. Multiply the number of heads by the same number you just divided the number of cylinders by (3 in this example).

4. As long as the number of heads does not go over 64, you are all set. In this case, just put in the real number of sectors per track for your hard drive into the table.

If the heads go over 64, split the factor between the two settings. For example if you had divided by 4 you could multiply heads by 2 and sectors per track by 2, you will need an even factor (2,4,6) to use this technique.

To make life simple for yourself, shop around for a hard drive whose geometry is easy to set up.

Tip

Remember, `heads * cylinders * sectors/track` must not be greater than the number of real sectors on the disk. It is okay if they are a little less, but you should go for as good a match as possible. Many disks will offer alternative settings in their documentation using the method just shown. If yours does show these, use them: it is much easier.

SCSI Drives

Unlike most other drive types, you usually tell the BIOS that there are no drives if you are using SCSI disks. This is because the SCSI controller will interrogate the drive at boot-up and will set the drive tables correctly. This is certainly the easier way to go.

Tip

With most SCSI controllers, you tell your machine's BIOS that there are no hard drives attached. The controller will properly set up the machine each time it is booted.

INSTALLING CD-ROMs

NetWare 4.1 is distributed on a CD-ROM and the documentation is on another. Installing a CD-ROM drive on your server is a good idea for this reason alone, but you probably will find plenty of uses for a networked CD-ROM. Check your documentation for a list of supported drives and use one listed. While it is sometimes possible to make a non-supported drive work, it is unlikely to be worth the trouble.

SCSI CD-ROMs

Probably best choice for CD-ROMs is the one that comes with a SCSI-2 interface. Many brands that fit this bill are available. SCSI CD-ROMs also allow for expansion; one SCSI controller can drive up to seven devices (such as CD-ROMs or hard drives).

PROPRIETARY CD-ROMs

Many popular CD-ROM drives come with a controller that is not SCSI, but rather, a *proprietary driver card*. Some, or many, of these are not supported. Be certain that you check for NetWare support before selecting one of these drives.

MAKE A DOS PARTITION

In order to install NetWare 4.1, you will need to have a small DOS partition on the first disk in your server. Novell recommends a partition size of 15MB or one megabyte for every megabyte of RAM installed. This later recommendation is so that if you need to create a memory image (core dump), you will have sufficient space on your DOS partition.

Tip

Because disk space has become so inexpensive and enlarging this partition at a later date is not easy, you may want to add a little to this figure of 15MB.

CREATE THE PARTITION

Using DOS's FDISK command, create a partition of the proper size and make it active (*active status* means that this partition will be booted). Many disks that come with a machine will already have a DOS partition that uses the whole disk. If this is the case, you need to delete the existing DOS partition(s) and create a smaller one.

INSTALL DOS

Once you have properly partitioned the disk, let the DOS setup program do the install by booting from the first DOS floppy. Or if you want, you can shortcut the process by manually install DOS—you do not need all the DOS programs, just enough to boot the hard drive with DOS and allows you to edit and copy files.

INSTALL UTILITIES AND DOS DRIVERS

You should install any testing utilities such as CheckIt and QEMM. You also should install and test your DOS CD-ROM drivers.

It is also a good idea to install the DOS workstation drivers for NetWare. This way, you can, if needed, run the server as a workstation. This will be handy for some types of testing, such as to ensure that your NIC is properly installed and configured.

BURNING IN

Burning in your system, especially a network server, is critical. Electronics suffer from a tendency called *infant mortality* and should be run for several days to get past the point when most would fail.

INFANT MORTALITY

Modern electronic components, such as those in your computer, are very rugged. Once they get past the first several hours of operation, they will likely run for a very long time. The tendency to fail in the first several hours is referred to as infant mortality. While a failure in this period is still not very common, it pays to get past it before putting your server online. The technique for getting past this period is referred to as *burn in* and it can be done very simply.

The following sections detail the four different ways to perform a burn in, and range from the simple to the complete. Any of these will work for the burn in purpose, but a complete burn in is recommended for its additional diagnostic capabilities.

THERMAL CYCLING

All three methods described in this chapter share a common point: *thermal cycling*. Thermal shock—going from cold to hot or vice versa—is the most common cause of electronic failure. During your burn in, you should turn off the machine after running it for six to eight hours and let it cool down completely (one to two hours) and then restart it. This process should be done at least three to four times over a period of a couple of days.

SIMPLE BURN IN

For a simple burn in, just turn on the machine and let it "sit idle." This process is simple, but usually good enough strictly for burn in purposes, especially if you perform several thermal cycles during this process.

EXERCISE THE DISK

In the process of exercising the disk, you call a simple DOS batch file to run the disk. This process adds some heat stress to the machine while being simple and inexpensive. Again, be sure to thermal cycle the machine during the burn in phase. Create a file called BURNIN.BAT on your C: drive with the following statements:

```
REM a batch file to do a burn in on a computer
REM this file should be called BURNIN.BAT

REM first make a temporary directory
MD C:\TEMP

REM copy the contents of the DOS directory to it
COPY C:\DOS\*.* C:\TEMP /V

REM now the batch file calls itself, this makes it run continuously
BURNIN
```

To run this batch file you just created, go to the directory where you created BURNIN.BAT and type **burnin** at the DOS prompt. Because the files being copied are just test files, you can simply turn off the machine when you need to do a thermal cycle or when you complete the testing.

COMPLETE TESTING

To perform a complete burn in, you can use a utility such as Touchstone Software's CheckIt. The SYSTEST program has a burn in function that is available from the File menu. This will thoroughly test your machine, including the motherboard functions, memory, and hard disk. It stores the results in a file that you can view later.

17

This approach is probably the best because most every aspect of your server is tested, as well as burnt in. Simply select the continuous test function (on older versions of CheckIt, you do this by telling to run 999 iterations).

Again, be sure to thermal cycle the machine several times during the burn in process.

FINAL TOUCHES

The last couple of steps are important. Although you may not need them now, a little thought and work will leave you well prepared for future problems or upgrades.

DOCUMENT IT

Use a stick-on label to document all parameters. Following are some items you will want to document:

- ◆ Disk parameters, model, manufacturer. If it is an IDE, include the BIOS parameters you used (heads, cylinders, sectors/track)
- ◆ Amount of RAM
- ◆ Network Interface Card specifications. If you have more that one NIC, use a magic marker to write the number (1,2,3,...) on the board and then use this number on your label. Be sure to write all parameters you use (IRQ, memory address, port address, DMA channel).
- ◆ Date of purchase and supplier
- ◆ SCSI addresses in use by devices

Warning

Documenting your system is important. You may think you can remember it or figure it out later, but do not succumb to this temptation. Some day, this information will save you a great deal of trouble.

It is also a good idea to write all this information in the owners manual for your computer. Do not rely on this alone, however, because you may not be able to find that manual when you need it.

HAVE SPARES

Because your server is a critical link in your network and its failure will have a big effect on your operation, you should have spare parts for your server. It's not always necessary to have a complete spare machine, although sometimes that is the best choice. You should have spare video cards, NICs (at least one of each type you use in your server), drive controllers, and hard drives.

Consider the availability of the spare parts: do you have local outlets for parts or do you need to order them from out of state? If you cannot get replacements on the same day that you need them, you probably will want a spare server. It should be an exact copy of your work unit so that you can replace just a failed part or the whole machine.

If you can get replacement parts locally, you may be tempted to skimp on spares. This is not a good choice. A carefully chosen set of spares usually will cost a lot less than an entire machine, and it may save the day.

POWER CONDITIONING

Be sure that your server(s) is plugged into a good quality power conditioning device, such as an Uninterruptable Power Supply. It also is important that all external accessories (monitor, CD-ROM drives, RAID devices) be plugged into one, too.

SUMMARY

A lot of territory has been covered in this chapter, and the broad set of possibilities leaves you with many choices. The following is a short list of the important points you learned in this chapter:

- ◆ Install accessories (such as NICs or disk drives) one at a time, and test the system after each device is installed
- ◆ Perform a through burn in
- ◆ Make a DOS partition and install DOS
- ◆ Document the system completely

- Communication
  Basics

- Initial Hardware
  Setup

- Workstation Memory
  Configurations

- Floppy Drive
  Configuration

- Installing a Network
  Card

- Hardware Settings

- Workstation Software

- Client Driver Options

- Summary

CHAPTER 18

Workstation Configuration

In Chapter 7, you learned about the available types of network workstation hardware. This chapter helps you understand the basics of network communications and how the configuration of a workstation can affect those communications.

This chapter is designed to teach you the basic operations of a workstation, as well as to help you understand how to initially configure the workstation for use on a network. It also will provide information for troubleshooting existing workstations, as well as how to maintain a network from a workstation point-of-view.

COMMUNICATION BASICS

To understand the basic principles of which role a workstation plays in the overall network environment, you first must have a basic understanding of how communication takes place between a file server and workstation.

Note

A LAN consists of four basic communication components:

Server: This is the device that transmits the data. In a NetWare environment, it may be a file server or workstation. The sender also creates the data for transmission. In a NetWare network, the sender can be the file server or workstation.

Message: This is the digital data that is transmitted. The message is sent over a physical medium that connects the sending and receiving stations.

Medium: The medium is the communications path between the source and the destination devices. It is the physical devices that enable the sender and the receiver to communicate. The medium can be bounded or unbounded. Bounded media consists of wire types that include coaxial cable, fiber-optic cable, twisted pair, and so on. Un-bounded media carries signals using electromagnetic waves and include communication methods, such as microwave, radio, or infrared light. Regardless of the type of medium, its purpose remains the same, to transport the message from one location to another.

Client: The receiver is the device that has requested, or will be accepting the message. In a NetWare environment the receiver can be a file server or workstation.

Each time a network workstation (client) requires a network-provided service, it sends a request to the file server. The file server will then provide a valid response to the client's request. This communication mechanism is referred to as the *client-server computing model*. In this model, a server is usually associated with a network resource as well as with the responsibility of distributing and controlling the access and use of resources to the client that is requesting a service.

A workstation is a personal computer that is attached to a network. However, because you communicate on a Local Area Network (LAN), your PC is no longer just a personal computer; it is an extension of the network. The connection between the PC and the network file server is what enables you to access the services and equipment provided by the network.

All the appropriate hardware and software must be present to establish communications between the PC and the file server. Thus, understanding how to properly configure your personal computer, as well as configuring it properly as a network workstation, is vital to a successful operation of the overall network.

CONFIGURATION

This section on configuration explores the configuration of a workstation from the initial setup. It then will be followed by a section discussing the optimization of workstation software. Both these sections assume that you are somewhat familiar with hardware discussed in Chapter 7 of this book.

This chapter also covers the different methods used for installing workstation software, but the actual installation of the workstation software is covered in Chapter 23.

INITIAL HARDWARE SETUP

Before an IBM-type personal computer can be used, it must first be "set up." This setup procedure consists of defining the system's parameters. The system parameters (such as amount of memory, disk drives, video displays, and numeric coprocessors) are stored in the CMOS RAM. When the computer is turned off, a battery located on the motherboard retains the system parameters. Every time the system is powered on, it is configured with these values.

Note

It is not uncommon for a workstation to lose power to the CMOS, and thus lose the initial setup values. Each time the values are lost, the CMOS must be restored to the correct settings. So, make it common practice to store a hard copy of the CMOS values.

To set the initial system configuration parameters, a BIOS (Basic Input Output System) program is stored in computer's ROM (Read Only Memory). This program is designed to work with your motherboard's particular type and version of BIOS.

Note

Most BIOS setup programs are usually accessible while the computer is in the initial boot-up stage. During the boot sequence, a message will appear informing you how to launch a setup program.

On most late-model computers, depending on the BIOS used, the message usually will be as follows:

```
Hit <Del> if you want to run SETUP.
```

On older model computers (286 and above), you often had to press a combination of keys to access the setup program. For example, the following combinations where popular:

```
F1
<Shift> and <Esc>
<Alt> and <Esc>
<Shift> and <F1>
```

Some 286 machines (IBM AT) required that you load the BIOS setup program from diskette.

XT machines do not have a setup routine and must be configured using software drivers.

EISA machines use a configuration program, known as "EISA Config," which is run after booting to DOS.

CONFIGURING BIOS OPTIONS

As mentioned earlier, most computers will display a message on screen each time the computer boots, which reads something similar to Hit Del, if you want to run SETUP. There is much more to know, however, about setting up a computer than just seeing the message and starting the CMOS configuration routine.

This section covers some of the features found in the BIOS setup program. This section cannot, however, cover every feature for every BIOS. It is even impossible to cover all of the available options for a single version of an AMI (American Megatrends, Inc.) BIOS. This section *does* cover the basics, and should prepare you for the majority of the types of values you will have to enter to initially configure a network workstation.

POST TEST

Each time a computer is powered up, it performs a diagnostics Power-On Self Test, which often is referred to as the *POST* test. This power-up routine consists of two basic phases. The first phase is a System Test and Initialization, and the second is a System Configuration Verification. These two phases usually are separated by the initialization of the display device. In other words, if an error occurs before the display device (video card) is initialized, the error occurred during the first phase, which means it occurred during the System Test or Initialization Test. If an error occurs after the display device is initialized, the error is said to occur in the second phase of the POST diagnostics test, which is the System Configuration Verification phase.

If errors occur in the first phase of the POST test, the machine usually will emit a series of beeps, indicating that a fatal error has occurred; however, it will not display any error messages. Therefore, it is very useful to know what the beeps mean. The following mini-table shows the number of beeps and their common respective meanings:

# of Beeps	Error
1	Refresh Failure
2	Parity Error
3	Memory Failure
4	Timer Not Operational
5	Processor Failure
6	8042/GATE A20 Failure
7	Processor Exception Interrupt Error
8	Display Memory Read/Write Error
9	ROM Checksum Error
10	CMOS Read/Write Error

If an error occurs during the second phase of the POST test diagnostic routine, beeps will not be sounded. Rather, a message indicating the error will appear. You then can check your motherboard's documentation to determine the appropriate meaning of the error message.

Tip

If you need to call the technical support line for your motherboard, the technical support person will want to know which version of BIOS your machine is running. The best way to identify the BIOS version is to use the identification string, which is located on the bottom left corner of your screen during the initial boot process.

If you do not have much RAM (which lengthens the time it takes for you machine to boot) or if your machine is fast, it is almost impossible to write down this long number before the POST test moves to the next phase. Pressing down a key during the memory test will cause the POST test to return a keyboard error, halting the POST test process so that you will be able to write down the BIOS's identification string.

Changing Initial CMOS Settings

In order to change the standard CMOS settings, you will need to load the setup program. This usually is done by pressing the Delete key before the memory count is completed

Tip

You may need to press the Delete key three or four times.

You will know that you succeeded when the BIOS setup utilities main menu appears. The following is a list of the options that are available on the AMI BIOS's main menu:

- ◆ Standard CMOS Setup
- ◆ Advanced CMOS Setup
- ◆ Advanced Chipset Setup
- ◆ Power management setup
- ◆ Auto configuration with BIOS defaults
- ◆ Auto Configuration with Power-On settings
- ◆ Change Password
- ◆ Auto Detect Hard Disk
- ◆ Hard Disk Utilities
- ◆ Write to CMOS and Exit
- ◆ Do not Write to CMOS and Exit

To select one of these options, use the arrow keys to move the cursor to the desired option and press Enter.

Standard CMOS Settings

The Standard CMOS setting option will enable you to specify your machine's exact configuration. Any time you change the configuration of the machine (adding a hard drive, floppy drive, memory, and so on), you will need to designate the change in the

Standard CMOS setting area. The following section describes the options found in the main setting that will appear if you select the Standard CMOS settings option.

BASE AND EXTENDED MEMORY SIZES

Most AMI BIOS versions will automatically update and register the base memory and extended memory sizes. However, if you add memory (or remove memory) in your machine, you will need to enter the Standard CMOS setting screen (the change in memory will be displayed) so that the change can recorded. After entering this screen, you simply need to press Esc and save the changes to the CMOS.

Note

If your machine used to count a higher amount of memory, or if your machine periodically counts different amounts of memory, it probably means it has some bad memory.

Date and Time: As the name implies, this option sets your computers internal clock. To alter the settings, highlight the field that you want to change and use the PgUp and PgDn keys to select the appropriate time and date.

Note

Some BIOS CMOS Setup programs use the + and - keys to change the date and time values.

HARD DISK TYPE

If you have a hard disk installed, you will need to inform the computer of the disk's physical parameters (Heads, Cylinders, Sectors, Landing Zone, and Read-Write precomp). There are a couple of ways to determine the correct values for your particular hard drive. The first way is to contact the drive manufacturer to obtain the appropriate drive specifications (some drives have the specification printed on the drive's label). The second and simplest way is to let the AMI BIOS determine the correct drive type for you (if your BIOS is new enough to have the automatic drive detection feature).

After obtaining the correct drive setting you need to find a drive type (1-46) that matches your drive's parameters. If you do not find an exact match you can usually use drive type 47, which is a user definable drive type.

Warning

Selecting the wrong drive type or drive parameters may result in data loss. This becomes especially important if you have a drive installed in the computer and the CMOS information is lost. In this situation, resetting the drive with the wrong parameters eventually will cause problems.

This actually is a common problem with intelligent drives (IDE), because an intelligent drive can actually be formatted using any drive type, as long as the specified capacity does not exceed the drive's actual capabilities.

It is good practice to label the drive's parameters on the drive, as well as on the exterior computer case. This way, if the drive settings are lost, you can simply re-enter the correct parameters, without worrying about the loss of data.

The following information will have to be entered to correctly configure you hard drive's parameters:

◆ **Type**: The number for a drive with certain identification parameters

Tip

Most new drives will need to use drive type 47, which is a user definable drive. This means that no predefined information has been programmed in for that particular drive type.

SCSI drives almost always rely on the controller for enhanced translation, and should use drive type 0.

ESDI drives also will rely on the controller for translation, but generally use drive type 1.

◆ **Cylinders**: The number of cylinders in the disk drive
◆ **Heads**: The number of heads in the drive
◆ **Write Precomp**: The size of a sector becomes progressively smaller as the track diameter diminishes, yet each sector must still hold 512 bytes. Write precompensation circuitry on the hard disk compensates for the physical difference in sector size by boosting the current sectors on the inner tracks of a drive's surface. This parameter is the track number where write precompensation begins. (Most new drives (IDE) do not require a precompenstation track.)
◆ **Landing Zone**: This number is the cylinder location where the heads normally park when the system is shut down. It usually is set to the last cylinder of the drive (same number as the cylinder).

◆ **Capacity**: This is the total physical format table space of the drive. This number is not user-definable; it is filled according to the number of heads and cylinders entered.

AUTO DETECT HARD DISK

Some of the newer AMI BIOSes have an Auto Detect Hard Disk option. This option, as its name implies, will automatically detect and find all of an IDE's drive parameters. These auto-detected parameters are then presented to you for your acceptance. If you accept them, they will be placed in the user-definable drive type option, which for most BIOSes will be option 47.

FLOPPY DRIVE TYPES

If you select a floppy drive, the POST test will do a "floppy seek," unless the floppy seek is disabled in the Advanced BIOS settings. Most BIOSes support 360K to 2.88MB floppy drives.

Note

If you have an older BIOS and want to add a disk drive that your BIOS does not support, you can call the BIOS manufacture and get an updated BIOS. Sometimes, however, (depending on your board) it is better, and almost cheaper, to upgrade your motherboard.

PRIMARY DISPLAY

Selecting the primary display is very simple, especially since most of the newer BIOSes will automatically detect the type of monitor that is installed. If, however, the display type is incorrect, you can use the arrow keys to move to the display selection and then press the PgUp and PgDn keys to change the setting.

Note

It is very common for a motherboard to have a jumper that must be set according to the type of monitor you are using (monochrome or color). If this jumper is improperly set, the computer will display an error message during the boot sequence similar to the following:

`display type mismatch`

This motherboard jumper is not overridden by the setting in the CMOS and must be changed physically.

18

KEYBOARD

The keyboard option is a toggle, which can indicate that a keyboard is installed or not installed, and usually is automatic.

POWER MANAGEMENT

All the new BIOSes are now supporting power-management features. These features are known as "green features" and follow the Energy Star-compliant specifications. In order to take full advantage of all the power management functions, you must have a complete Energy Star-compliant machine, which includes a power supply, monitor, and motherboard.

An Energy Star-compliant system will enable users to configure the power management options through the CMOS setup. These options provide the user with the capability to configure how much power continues to be consumed when the machine senses inactivity. For example, you can have the machine automatically "spin down" the hard drive, or power down the monitor or the entire machine. These options often are time selectable (after a certain amount of time of inactivity turn off the monitor). The machine then will be powered back up (to the same state as when powered down) when the computer once again becomes active (a key is pressed, or the mouse is moved).

Some of the BIOSes are also now offering more intelligent wake-up features, such as the capability to power up when an interrupt is used. These intelligent wake-up features are very useful in certain situations, such as when your computer is being used as an answering machine or a fax machine. This is useful because you can have the computer activate when the modem requests the use of the computer. Thus, the machine is only consuming power when it is being used.

Also, an energy-compliant motherboard will allow your system the expandability that is needed for interfacing with future Green-PC peripheral devices.

CACHE MEMORY

Most motherboards also now boast cache memory, which is a technique that places a block of high-speed memory between the computer's processor and memory. This high-speed memory is then used to cache, or store, the most recently read data in memory, which allows for faster retrieval by the microprocessor. This type of cache (located between the CPU and main memory) can be of two types. The first type is known as *internal cache*. This internal cache, sometimes referred to as *primary cache*, is imbedded in the CPU and should always be enabled in the BIOS settings. The second kind of cache is called *external cache*, which is also sometimes referred to as the *secondary cache*. Both types of cache, internal and external, can be configured to run in one of two schemes: Write-Through or Write-Back.

Note

If you have a machine that is performing slower than it should, or perhaps slower than it used to, you may want to verify that the internal cache is enabled.

In a write-through caching scheme, information is written to the cache and main memory simultaneously. By writing to memory and the CPU at the same time, information is said to be *guaranteed*, meaning that the information in the CPU is exactly the same as the information written to memory. However, this sacrifices performance because the cache, and therefore the machine, can only be as fast as the memory. If internal cache is set up in the write-through scheme, it can take advantage of the 80486's built-in post-write buffer, which can temporarily store information, allowing the processor to perform other tasks before the data is actually written to the computer's main memory. External caches cannot take advantage of the 80486's built-in buffer.

Write-back cache is another method of configuring cache memory, which increases performance. This cache configuration, however, does not "guarantee" that the information in the processor is the same information that is placed in memory. With a write-back cache, only write commands will be sent to the cache. The write-back cache controller will then determine when the contents of the cache need to be flushed to the computer's main memory.

Some motherboards will not allow you to configure the caching scheme. In this case, they are usually set in what the manufacturer believes to be the most optimal configuration.

WORKSTATION MEMORY CONFIGURATIONS

In a DOS environment most workstations will have four basic types of memory or memory combinations available:

- Conventional
- Upper
- Extended
- Expanded

Conventional memory often is referred to as the base memory. It is the first 640K of memory that is made available to your computer. It is within these 640K confines that DOS will load and run your software programs. Besides the applications that your computer is running, the 640K of conventional memory must also be used by a portion of DOS itself. This means that the entire 640K is not available for your application.

Upper memory is the 384K of RAM located between 640K and 1MB (1024K). This area was reserved for future expansion and for use by the ROM. The first 128K of the upper memory is reserved for video memory, the next 128K of upper memory is reserved for devices that have installable ROMs, such as video ROM and the hard disk controller ROM. The last 128K of upper memory is reserved for ROM BIOS. However, not all of these sections are fully utilized and thus, a user with little knowledge of DOS can take advantage of this memory area.

Note

Because these upper memory segments have been reserved for a specific purpose, using them can sometimes be tricky. For example, it is possible that some of the ROM's functions will not load until they are used, or perhaps when the devices need for increases. Because the area is "reserved" for a specific device, the device may assume that it can use the memory segment, even if something else is loaded in the same memory segment. The result often is that the workstation will hang, or that a function such as a network connection or video display will be lost.

If you are going to use this area of memory, it is best if you use a memory manager that will compensate for the expansion and use of memory. Some motherboard chipsets, such as the Chips and Technologies chipsets (NEAT and SCAT versions), can use the upper memory area fairly efficiently. Thus, it is a good idea to consult your motherboard's documentation to determine whether it specifies any stipulations for using these memory areas.

Your success of using the upper memory blocks will depend on the specific hardware that is being used, the chipset of the motherboard, the EMS and XMS expanded memory configuration and memory driver, as well as the amount of permanent upper RAM.

Tip

Most motherboard chipsets will not allow you to use the upper segments if you do not have the Shadow RAM function in the BIOS set to Enabled.

Expanded memory takes advantage of an unused area of upper memory, yet still works within the 640K DOS confines, reserving one 64K block of memory called the page frame. The EMM device driver makes expanded memory available to application software as four 16K pages mapped into the page frame. This memory is bank-switched by the hardware and software, meaning that the 1K pages can be swapped in and out of the page frame as needed. As soon as it is in the page frame, a page can be accessed by the microprocessor because it falls within the 1MB confines of the DOS operating system.

Extended memory is a contiguous block of memory, which means there can be no breaks or missing sections. A computer using an 8086 processor is limited to the use of 1MB of RAM. Processors above a 286, such as a 386 or 486, are not limited to 1MB and can address extended memory. Extended memory starts above the 1MB memory address and continues until all available RAM is consumed.

Note

Some of the older machines (for example, a Novell 386 AE) actually reserved memory just above the 1MB memory locations, so its extended memory actually began at 1408.

Extended memory also includes the high-memory section, which is the first 64K of extended memory. The high-memory segment usually begins at the memory address of FFFF. This area of memory can usually only be used to store one program at a time. For this reason, it has become a very popular place for the section of the DOS kernel that can be loaded high.

Tip

When you include the following line in your CONFIG.SYS file, the DOS kernel will be loaded into high memory.

```
DOS=HIGH,UMB
```

However, to use this high memory, you must have a machine with a processor that is at least a 286 and that has more than 1MB of memory and has a memory manager loaded.

Today, most of the extra memory in your workstation should be set up as extended memory.

Expanded memory is a means of working with reserved memory which usually lies above the 640K limit, but below 1MB. One 64K block of this unused upper memory is set aside as a page frame. A group of vendors, specifically Microsoft, Intel, and Lotus, collaborated to set a LIM EMS (Expanded Memory Specification) standard.

This enabled applications to access memory through an EMM device driver. This driver makes expanded memory available to application software as four 16K pages mapped into the reserved 64K page frame. Applications using expanded memory are swapped in and out of the 64K page frame as the application needs more memory.

Expanded memory, is not as popular or as flexible as extended memory and, therefore, is not used as often. In fact, if you do not have an application that specifically requires the use of Expanded memory, you should include the following section to your EMM386 line in your CONFIG.SYS file:

```
DEVICE=c:\DOS\EMM386.EXE NOEMS
```

Doing so will allow your computer to use the 64K section of memory for other purposes.

Each memory type serves a purpose in the DOS environment, and some applications and utilities take advantage of one memory type but not the other. PCs running DOS require a good understanding of how memory works. DOS vendors seem to realize the need for this knowledge, however, and have thus started shipping memory managers with the latest versions DOS. For example, Microsoft's DOS 6.*x* has a program called MEMMAKER. Running MEMMAKER usually will take advantage of most of your computer's memory capacities.

FLOPPY DRIVE CONFIGURATION

Floppy drives started out at 90K, but quickly moved to a 180K. IBM then introduced the revolutionary double-sided 360K drive. Shortly thereafter, the 1.2MB and 1.44MB floppy drives emerged and quickly dropped to a very reasonable price. Developers assumed that the 2.88MB floppy drive was the next logical step; however, this particular drive has not been very well accepted. One reason for its lack of acceptance is that software vendors began to ship applications on CD-ROM drives, which hold up to 600MB, rather than floppies, which hold only 2MB each at most.

Regardless of the size of floppy drives, they remain a very slow, dreaded form of storing data. However, the flexibility and usefulness of floppy drives remain.

If you are currently considering purchasing a machine, or upgrading your old machine, the 1.44MB 3.5-inch floppy drive is the best choice. Almost all vendors are now shipping applications on 3.5-inch media. Oddly enough, these drives are actually the cheapest and can be purchased for about $35.

Installing a Floppy Drive

Installing a floppy drive in an existing machine is a very simple task. Simply open the machine and mount the drive.

Mounting the drive usually consists of using two screws on each side of the drive. If you have a drive bay made to take the large 1.2MB drives, you will need to purchase a conversion kit. These kits are fairly inexpensive, costing approximately $5. If the kit is needed, mount the drive to the kit and then mount the kit in the drive bay. After the drive is mounted, find an unused power lead of which there are two types; a large one and a small one. Most 1.44MB drives use the smaller of the two connectors, while 1.2MB drives use the large connector.

If you had to purchase a conversion kit, there is a good chance that your computer also will need a power lead converter (to convert from the large power connector to the small power connector). This connector should be included in the drive rail kit. The small connectors are flat on the bottom, while the large connector is rounded on the corners, so regardless of the connector type, it is virtually impossible to plug it in wrong. After plugging in the power cord, the last step is to plug in the data cable.

The smaller 1.44MB drives take a different connector than do the larger 1.2MB drives. The 1.2 MB drive connector is similar to a "slot," while the 1.44MB connectors are "holes." In either case, it is important to get the number one cable to the drive's number one pin. The floppy cable usually has the first cable marked with a differentiating color. For example, it will be blue, red, or red-white striped. This designates the first pin of the cable, which needs to line up with the first pin of the drive. The drive will designate the number one pin location with a number "1" printed on the bottom of the drive. If your cable does not have the connectors for both types of drives, a floppy cable can be purchased from any computer store for around $10.

The 1.2MB floppy connectors are usually notched, making it impossible to put them on backwards. Some 1.44MB cable connectors also have a notch, but the notch is along the top. Another hint for matching the 1.44MB drive to the number one pin is to place the red cable closest to the power plug; however, this only works about 90 percent of the time.

If you power-up the machine and the floppy cable is plugged in backwards, the light on the floppy drive will never shut off.

Floppy drives rarely go bad, and if they do, it is cheaper to replace them rather than repair them.

If a floppy drive is having problems, however, it is very possible that the read-write heads are simply dirty. Floppy drive heads should be cleaned about every 100 hours of computer operation time.

Cleaning a floppy drive is similar to cleaning a VCR or cassette deck head. You purchase a cleaning diskette and a cleaning solution (rubbing alcohol). You apply the cleaning solution to the cleaning diskette and place it in the drive and follow the instructions that came with the cleaning diskette.

Note

There are two adjustments on most floppy drives: the azimuth and the read-write head alignment. A computer repair technician can actually re-align the drives using these adjustments, but this process is time consuming and usually fairly expensive (at $50 an hour, it is cheaper to replace the drive).

All computers also have a BIOS (Basic Input Output System). The BIOS is ROM that holds the information about your computer's configuration, including the type of floppy drives that you have installed. If this information is lost (which happens fairly frequently), and a different drive type than what is actually installed is specified, the computer usually will return a floppy error.

It is no longer necessary for a computer to have a floppy. In the past, floppy drives were checked at boot-up; however, most current BIOSes now allow you to disable the floppy seek at boot-time. This was done for several reasons. The first two most prominent reasons are that it drastically reduces the time it takes for a machine to boot, and second, it provides heightened security. In fact, because the disk drives are not very expensive, about the only reason for not having a floppy drive is for security reasons. By not putting a floppy drive in a PC, your IS department has control over which files can get on and off the network, which drastically reduces the risk of virus infestation as well as workstation network driver versions.

INSTALLING A NETWORK CARD

Before a workstation can communicate with a file server, it must have a network card. A network interface card (NIC) creates a physical connection to the file server through the medium (the wire). Network cards are available from a vast number of vendors; however, most are very similar.

NETWORK CARDS

The vast number of available network cards makes selecting the best card for your network implementation seem very daunting. When it comes down to it, however, there is very little difference in how NICs perform fundamental communication tasks. There is extremely little difference in how these different cards perform in a workstation (cards do perform and handle loading differences when placed in the server).

The one criterion that you do want to evaluate is the stability and longevity of the company that produces the candidate cards. This criteria is critical because network drivers change quite frequently, which makes it very difficult for card manufactures to keep up with the driver changes. If the company leaves the business of making network cards it will be impossible to keep your network updated with the latest drivers, meaning that if you select a card, and the vendor decides to leave the network card market, to stay current you will have to replace all your network cards.

The only other difference you need to be aware of is the type of topology support that the card has to offer. For example, does it support 10BaseT, does it support thin Ethernet, and so on. Most cards are now supporting multiple topologies, which makes the topology issue much less of a concern. However, you still need to make sure that the selected cards meet the correct topology criteria.

Another nice feature of modern day NICs you may want to evaluate is the card's capability to be configured via software. Software configuration reduces the possibility of losing the jumper settings and not being able to change the IRQ setting and I/O address (however, you have to keep the software). It also eliminates the need to take the computer apart to change your network card's configuration.

Some of the newer NICs are taking the onboard ROM one step further and including Flash ROM, which stores the network drivers. This means that from one location on the network, the network administrator can update all workstation client drivers.

You also may want to check the card's options for boot PROM (Programmable Read Only Memory) support. Checking these options is more than just finding out whether the card will support a boot PROM; it also includes checking on the setting option that are supported when the boot PROM is installed. Some cards, for example, will not support your computer's upper interrupts (8–15) while the boot PROM is installed.

Note

Boot PROMs used to be a popular way of eliminating the expense of having to have a floppy drive in every machine. Floppy drives are now almost the same price as boot PROMs. Boot PROMs, however, still offer enhanced security.

The procedure of setting up a boot PROM will differ with each NIC manufacture, so for instructions on setting up the boot PROM, consult the documentation that came with the Ethernet card or boot PROM.

After selecting a network card, you will have to install it in the workstation. This task is generally very simple and straightforward—shut the machine off, unplug the cable, open the case, put the card in, configure the card using the card's software or configuration settings, and then plug in the network cable. If you do not have success, however, determining the cause of the failure can be time consuming.

If you do not succeed in making a connection to the file server, you will want to start the troubleshooting process by verifying that you do not have any internal conflicts. Do so by checking the IRQ, I/O, DMA, and memory settings of the card, verifying that none of these are set to the same location as another device.

HARDWARE SETTINGS

The computer is almost always performing more than one task at a time. For example, while printing, the computer will be accepting commands from the network, refreshing information on the screen, and interpreting mouse movements. Each of these tasks requires use of the computer's processor. With DOS, it is not possible for each of these tasks to completely control the use of the processor; therefore, they must somehow get equal opportunity to gain access to the valuable computing time.

There are two methods that DOS and other operating systems commonly use to allow the computer to share CPU time. The first is called *polling*. Polling is a process where all those resources that require time register themselves with the operating system. Once registered, the operating system knows that the device may need some of the computer's CPU time. Thus, every so often, the computer will check with each of the registered devices to see if it needs serviced. Polling, however, requires the computer to spend most of its time determining what work needs done, rather than actually doing any work.

The second method of determining which devices need to be serviced is through the use of *interrupts*. Interrupts, as the name implies is a method that the device can use to "tap the computer on the shoulder" to inform the computer it needs to use the processor. The processor will then stop what it is doing and allow the device at the assigned interrupt to perform its computing task.

Almost all the common devices found in a PC will use the interrupt method of gaining access to the processor. These devices include such things as a mouse, a floppy drive controller, a hard drive controller, a printer port, and even a network card. The computer becomes confused when more than one of these devices, such as a mouse and network card, are assigned to the same interrupt. This confusion often is called an *I/O conflict*. To make matters worse, interrupts are fairly scarce. So, when adding a new device to a PC, be sure that you are not putting in a device that will conflict with an existing device. The following section will help avoid interrupt and other I/O conflicts.

AVOIDING INTERRUPT CONFLICTS

Unfortunately, confusion explodes when more than one device is using the same interrupt (IRQ). Even more unfortunate is the difficulty of determining which devices are using which interrupts. The scarcity of interrupts and the confusion caused by not understanding which devices commonly use which interrupts makes interrupt conflicts one of the most common network workstation problems. An example of this is if a network workstation is properly functioning and a sound card or modem is added to the machine, and the workstation starts to have problems, it is likely that you have placed a new device at the same interrupt as an existing device.

Each card in the computer's bus must use a different IRQ setting, including the Ethernet, token ring, or ARCnet card that hooks your computer to the network cable.

Note

An IRQ is an Interrupt Request Line that enables the computer to interrupt whatever the processor is doing so that some other "important" job can be completed, such as receiving a packet coming across the Ethernet card.

If two cards are using the same IRQ setting, a conflict occurs and the machine usually will hang or one of the cards will be completely ignored. The best way to determine the current setting is to use a software diagnostic utility or consult your PC documentation. You also can consult generic charts, such as the ones shown in Tables 18.1 and 18.2. These charts are based on the IBM AT architecture, on which ISA, EISA, and MCA bus technologies are based.

IBM's AT standard allows for sixteen interrupts, many of which are designated for a particular function. For example, interrupts 0 and 1 are used by the system and not available for any other device. Interrupts 6, 8, and 14, respectively, are used by your machines floppy controller, real-time clock, and hard disk controller. Other interrupts, such as interrupts 3, 4, 5, 7, respectively, are used by the serial and parallel ports. If you disable the COM or LPT port that is using that interrupt, however, you can use the interrupt for another device.

Note

XT machines are based on an 8-bit bus and only have 8 available interrupts (0–7). Likewise, 8-bit cards can only use interrupt 0–7.

For general guidance use the Tables 18.1 and 18.2 to help you avoid interrupt conflicts.

TABLE 18.1. XT, OR 8-BIT MACHINES.

IRQ	Used by
0	Timer Output 0
1	Keyboard Output
2	EGA/VGA
3	COM2
4	COM1
5	Hard Disk
6	Floppy Controller
7	LPT1

TABLE 18.2. AT, 286, 386, 486, AND PENTIUM MACHINES.

IRQ	Used By:
0	Timer Output 0
1	Keyboard Output
2	Cascade for Interrupt 9-15 (EGA/VGA)
3	COM 2
4	COM 1
5	LPT 2
6	Floppy Controller

IRQ	Used By:
7	LPT 1
8	Real Time Clock
9	EGA/VGA (optional)
10	(Available)
11	(Available)
12	PS/2 Mouse Port
13	Math Coprocessor
14	Hard Disk Controller
15	(Available)

18

As you can see from the preceding tables, it can be very difficult to find an "open" interrupt.

Note

It is important to note that even some 16-bit cards do not support the use of the "higher" interrupts. In either case, the only option you have is to disable one of the existing functions, which will disable any peripheral that is connected.

It is possible for an Ethernet card or other network board to use an interrupt currently being used by another function. For example, many programs do not address the LPT ports at the interrupt level. If you load a new application (or driver such as a mouse driver), however, or even use a new feature of the application (printing direct to port), errors (disconnect from the network) may occur. Hence, even if the machine has been functioning properly, it does not mean that there are no interrupt conflicts.

AVOIDING ADDRESS CONFLICTS

Now that you understand that each card must have a unique interrupt, it will be easier to explain that your computer hardware also must have a section of memory that it can call its own. This section of memory often is referred to as a *I/O address*. So, besides having to have a unique IRQ, each NIC as well as other expansion cards (scanner cards, BUS mouse cards, sound cards, and so on) must also have a unique I/O address.

I/O addresses, or port addresses, usually will use the range of memory between 100 hexadecimal to 3FF hexadecimal. The amount of memory that the program, driver, or device uses will vary, but generally range between 8 to 32 bytes. As with interrupts, if two devices try to use the same memory address the computer will not function properly.

You can use Table 18.3 can be used for a general reference to avoid I/O address conflicts. I/O addresses are not stringently adhered to by PC vendors, however.

TABLE 18.3. I/O ADDRESS CONFLICTS.

I/O Address range	Used by
000—01F	8237-1 DMA Controller
020—03F	8259-1 Interrupt Controller
040—05F	Timer
060—06F	8042 Keyboard Controller, PS/2 Mouse
070—07F	146818 RTC-NMI Mask
080	Status Register (POST CARD out port)
081—09F	74LS612 DMA Page Register
0A0—0BF	8259-2 Interrupt Controller
0C0—0DF	8237-2 DMA Controller
0F0—0FF	FPU Reserved
1F0—1F8	Fixed Disk
200—207	Game Controller I/O
278—27F	LPT 2
2E0—2EF	COM 4
2F8—2FF	COM 2
378—37F	LPT 1
380—38F	SDLC BISYNC 2
3A0—3AF	SDLC BISYNC 1
3B0—3BF	Monochrome Display, Printer Adapter
3C0—3CF	EGA Display
3D0—3DF	CGA Display
3E0—3EF	COM 3
3F0—3F7	Disk Controller
3F8—3FF	COM 1

From Table 18.3, you can tell that getting your Ethernet card to fit into an IRQ and I/O setting that does not conflict is not an easy task, but it can be done.

Table 18.4 lists some of the most common I/O options that are given by an Ethernet card's driver as well as some common conflicts. It is not as specific as the chart above, but can be used to find an open I/O area.

TABLE 18.4. COMMON I/O OPTIONS.

I/O Port	Used by
220	(Available)
240	(Available)
260	LPT2 (278–27F)
280	LCD Display on Wyse 2108 PC
2A0	(Available)
2E0	COM4 (2E1)
300	COM2 (300–31F)
320	XT Hard Disk Controller (320–32F)
340	(Available)
360	LPT1 (378–37F)

The comprehensive list (refer Table 18.3) should be used if you are having problems; however, the "generic" list (Table 18.4) can be used to provide guidelines. For the best results, check your computer's documentation or use a software diagnostic program to verify settings.

AVOIDING DMA (DIRECT MEMORY ACCESS) CONFLICTS

After correctly setting the IRQ and I/O addresses, the only other potential conflict would be the DMA channel that the device uses. A *DMA address* is a channel directly connected to the computer's memory, which allows a device to by-pass the use of the CPU and read or write directly the computer's memory.

As with IRQ settings and I/O addresses, no two devices should be set to use the same DMA channel.

Note

> DMA addresses are ranked by priority, with lower numbers having priority over higher numbered addresses. This means that a device setting a DMA 1 will have access to the memory more often than a device setting a DMA 7.

The list in Table 18.5 should help you avoid any DMA conflicts.

TABLE 18.5. DMA CONFLICTS.

DMA number	Used by
DMA0	Available (8-bit)
DMA1	SDLC (8-bit)
DMA2	Floppy Controller (8-bit)
DMA3	Available (8-bit)
DMA4	Cascade for DMA 5, 6, 7
DMA5	Available (16-bit)
DMA6	Available (16-bit)
DMA7	Available (16-bit)

Again, the list in Table 18.5 is very general and you should consult your computer's documentation, as well as each device's documentation to properly configure any settings.

Note

> If you are trying to put two Ethernet cards into the same machine and they are both using the reserved area, you will experience problems. You can disable the cards' use of memory, if it is allowed, or find a different memory segment for one of the cards. One suggestion would be to use the segment 0E0000–0EFFFFh, which is reserved for Ethernet boot ROM, unless of course, both cards are using a boot ROM.

Troubleshooting the workstation is in large part as simple as verifying each of the workstation's IRQs, I/O addresses, and DMA channels.

WORKSTATION SOFTWARE

This section of the chapter focuses on the configuration of client software. A step-by-step installation process is covered in Chapter 23. This chapter discusses the available installation methods as well as provides technical detail on configuring the NetWare client software.

SELECTING A CLIENT INSTALLATION METHOD

The process of installing workstation software will be different, depending on the type of network card you are using, as well as the version of NetWare drivers you are attempting to load. This chapter makes the assumption that you will be using an Ethernet card and that you are using the drivers that come with NetWare (opposed to the ones that ship with your network card).

Tip

> Because it is possible that both the network cards, as well as NetWare itself, could have been sitting on a vendor's shelf, you will want to verify that you are installing the latest drivers—never assume that the drivers that come with the card or the drivers that come with NetWare are the latest.

Note

> Each time a new application is loaded on the workstation, there is the risk of introducing faults. So, before loading any application, even if it is an upgrade, you should test the procedure in a controlled environment. If you do not have this luxury, be sure that it is possible to get back to the original position. This means having a workstation-based backup, or having an emergency disk from which you can boot.

The client software can be installed from the server operating system CD with one of the following different methods:

- ◆ Directly from the NetWare CD-ROM to each individual client
- ◆ From the NetWare CD-ROM to the server, which then will require you to access the server and install the client software to each client
- ◆ Create client diskettes from the NetWare CD-ROM and then use the newly created diskettes to install the client software

Note

> Installing the client software directly from the NetWare Operating System CD-ROM is a simple and quick process. However, it will require that you have a CD-ROM drive in every workstation.

18

WORKSTATION CONFIGURATION

When you install the NetWare server, you have the option to create and install the client software. Installing the client software to the server is always recommended, even if it is not your preferred choice of client installation. It is recommended because having the software on the server will enable you to update any client software from the server, if the clients are currently connected. This method of installing client software assumes that you already have a client-to-file server connection, and is best in a situation where you are upgrading.

Creating a set of client diskettes will be absolutely necessary if all your workstations do not have CD-ROMs or if you do not currently have a client to server connection (and is recommended even if the one of both of the preceding conditions is met). Creating a set of client diskettes will require you to have several pre-formatted diskettes ready before you begin the duplication process.

CREATING CLIENT DISKETTES

To start the duplication process, place the Operating System CD-ROM in a machine with a CD-ROM (this could be the file server at the DOS prompt) and from the root directory, type **install**. The screen shown in figure 18.1 will appear.

Figure 18.1.
NetWare 4.1's Main
installation screen.

After you select the Create Diskettes option, you will be presented with a screen asking which type of diskette set you want to create. You will see the screen shown in Figure 18.2.

After selecting the disk set that you want to create, a DOS prompt screen will appear indicating the number of required blank formatted diskettes. This screen also will prompt you to indicate the target disk drive. Depending on which diskette set you chose to create, the screen will be similar to Figure 18.3.

Figure 18.2.
Diskette Set creation
screen.

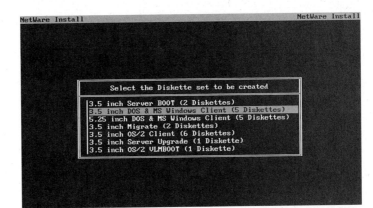

Figure 18.3.
Select target disk drive.

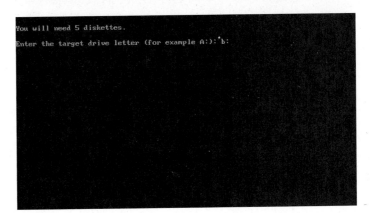

Enter the target drive by typing the drive designation letter followed by a colon, such as B:. After entering the drive letter, you are prompted to place the blank target diskette in the drive.

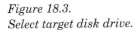

The disk creation procedure will simply copy the client files from the CD-ROM to diskette. Thus, it is important that the diskettes be blank. If the diskettes are not blank, the copy procedure will return an error indicating that the diskette does not have enough room. If this situation occurs, you will have to start the entire copy procedure over again, regardless of the progress already made. In other words, if the last diskette that you attempt to make is not blank, you will have to re-create the first four.

Once the copy procedure is started, a message will indicate the copy is in progress. After the first diskette is completed, the copy routine will inform you to label the diskette and to put in the next diskette. After all the diskettes in the set are created, you will not be returned to the installation menu; instead, you will be returned to a DOS prompt.

The next section covers the basic tasks that must be performed, regardless of the client installation method used.

CLIENT DRIVER OPTIONS

There are currently two types of "drivers" that can be used to make a client communicate with the server. The first is the *shell* (NETX.COM and NETX.EXE) and the second is a *Requester*, or better known as *VLMs*.

A shell is an interpreter that intercepts network requests before they reach the computer's operating system (DOS). In essence, a shell is positioned between the workstation operating system and the network operating system (NetWare). Any commands heading for the workstation operating system will be intercepted, interpreted, and then passed to the appropriate location—DOS or NetWare. This means the shell has to run "in front" of DOS. So, if the request is not for the network, then the shell will pass the instructions onto DOS. If the request is for the network, the instructions are passed to NetWare.

Note

NetWare 4 clients can access the server using either type of client software. However, if the client is running a shell client (NETX) rather than a requester, the client will not be able to take full advantage of NetWare 4's features, such as accessing the NDS information.

In the past, Novell has used the shell; however, there are several technical reasons they are moving to a requester-style client.

The NetWare DOS Requester consists of a series of files that provide NetWare workstation connectivity for DOS and Windows. These files consists of what is called *Virtual Loadable Modules* or *VLMs*, one of which is a single executable file called VLM.EXE. The files that compose the VLM technology, as seen in Figure 18.4, can be grouped into the three following layers:

◆ **DOS Redirection Layer**: Provides all the DOS file services through the DOS redirecter (REDIR.VLM).

- **Service Protocol Layer**: Contains several parallel services, such as NWP.VLM, RSA.VLM, FIO.VLM, and PRINT.VLM. Each of these parallel services contains several other "child" VLMs.

- **Transport Protocol Layer**: The mechanism responsible for maintaining the connections, providing packet transmissions between connections, and performing other transport-specific functions.

*Figure 18.4.
DOS Requester
modules.*

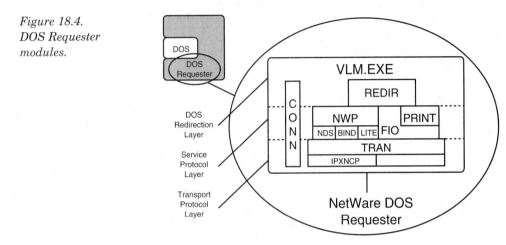

18

THE NETWARE DOS REQUESTER LAYERS AND MODULES

The requester performs the same functions as a shell—it passes information from the client to the network operating system—but in a different fashion. The NetWare shell had to retain its own set of internal resource tables for network file and print services. In contrast, the more tightly integrated DOS Requester can actually share resource tables with DOS. This eliminates the need to maintain redundant tables, decreasing memory requirements for the DOS Requester.

On a more technical note, the DOS Requester uses Interrupt (INT 2Fh Function 11) to pass information to NetWare. This enables DOS to recognize foreign file systems, such as networks, CD-ROMs, and so on, and in theory, will allow DOS to access these file systems through any number of redirects.

If DOS receives a request it cannot service, it will use the interrupt to call a redirected service (REDIR.VLM). For example, when an application makes a request to DOS, DOS first attempts to qualify the request in order to determine ownership of the requested resource, such as a drive letter, a file handle, or a print device. If DOS determines it does not own the resource, DOS polls the redirecters to allow them to determine ownership. If a redirector claims ownership, then DOS makes the appropriate calls to that redirector so it can complete the request.

For example, if the workstation is running the DOS Requester and an application makes a DOS INT 21–3fh "Open File" request, DOS attempts to qualify the request. If DOS can't, it issues an INT 2F–1123h call to the REDIR.VLM in order to qualify the file name. When DOS receives a successful return code from REDIR, DOS issues an INT 2F–1116h call to open the file. The REDIR.VLM then requests other services within the DOS Requester that forwards the call to the file server. The file server returns the resulting information and status to the DOS Requester, which then returns the information to the REDIR.VlM module, then to DOS, and then to the application.

As part of the Requester technology, Novell has made it possible for workstations running applications that use the old DOS shell calls to be compatible with the new Requester technology. If, for example, a workstation loads the Shell emulator, NETX.VLM, the emulator will act like the NetWare shell and intercept INT 21h requests.

Note

The INT 21h requests are the requests that are within the range of the old NetWare APIs B0h through E3h. If one of these calls is made, it will be automatically routed immediately to the network and will bypass DOS entirely. Thus, backward compatibility is established, yet functionality is not lost.

Warning

Because of the different methods the two requesters use to manage resources, the NetWare shell (NETX.EXE) and the DOS Requester (VLM.EXE) cannot coexist, meaning that they cannot be loaded together. In fact, once you install the VLM client kit for Windows, the VLMs need to be used.

The architecture of the Requester technology is much more modular than its shell counterpart. This modularity allows the VLMs to be set up in a variety of memory configurations: they can be loaded into extended memory, expanded memory, or conventional memory. It is even possible to make the VLMs use the upper memory blocks, if any exist. When VLM.EXE is loaded, it relocates its startup code at the top of conventional memory. This small footprint enables the VLM to load and unload modules as needed, which means that memory is not unnecessarily wasted. In a sense, the VLM.EXE file is its own memory manager. Because, the VLM.EXE is loaded, it temporarily loads each of the VLM modules specified to load in the NET.CFG file. When each module is loaded, it reports its ID, memory requirements, and global transient information.

Note

> This temporary loading procedure causes a series of dots to appear onscreen. During this initialization stage, each VLM module executes its initialization code, which includes initializing internal variables, hooking interrupts, notifying other VLMs of it presence, and detecting the presence of other dependent VLMs.

Because VLM.EXE now knows the amount of memory each module will use, it can calculate the total memory requirement for the overall configuration. It then will set aside enough memory for both the transient portions, as well as the global portions for each requester module. The global portion will contain the global segments of each VLMs code. After initialization the global segment will be stored in conventional memory, or in the upper memory blocks if they are available. This code often has to remain in conventional memory for compatibility or backward compatibility issues.

Note

> VLM.EXE will automatically detect and select the type of memory that is available. Once it has determined which memory is available, it will allocate its use. It will attempt to use the best possible configuration by using extended memory first, expanded memory second, and conventional memory last. If you do not have a memory manager loaded, VLM.EXE will have to reserve space in conventional memory for both the global and transient portions of VLM module code. This can quickly "eat-up" memory.
>
> To determine where the VLM's transient portions are loaded, use the following command-line commands (extended, expanded, and conventional, respectively):
>
> ```
> /mx
> ```
>
> ```
> /me
> ```
>
> ```
> /mc
> ```

18

WORKSTATION CONFIGURATION

The transient portion often is called the *swap block*. It is the section of requester code that does not always have to be loaded into memory, and thus, is swapped in and out of memory. At initialization, the transient swap block is roughly the size of the largest VLM module. After initialization, it will be reduced to match the largest transient segment of the largest VLM module.

NET.CFG FILE

Because the VLM-Requester technology is so modular, it often is misunderstood as being big, bulky, and slow. These observations are only partially true—on the surface. Because the Requester is such a modular technology, you can configure and optimize the Requester configuration to meet your exact needs. The following section provides you with some examples of different configurations optimized for different situations.

Note

Before you get into the technical specifics, you must understand that all configurations are done via the NET.CFG file. The NET.CFG file should be located in the same directory as the rest of the VLM files.

CREATING A NET.CFG FILE

The NET.CFG file is a configuration file that contains all the non-default settings for your environment. There are several different types of configuration options that are set in the NET.CFG file, such as network interface card settings, protocol settings, and so on. The NET.CFG file is created when you install the client software, and can be edited with any text editor.

Note

The NET.CFG file can be created any time you want to change your configuration's default settings. There is nothing special about a NET.CFG file; it is simply a text file that is read at initialization to determine which hardware settings should be used and which VLM modules should be loaded.

It is similar to the old SHELL.CFG file, as well as the NET.CFG file used with the ODI drivers.

Although there is nothing special about the file, it does require that you know and follow some specific conventions:

◆ Each Option section must be started at the very left of the file (flush left)

◆ Only one option can be listed per line

Note

An option section is a line that performs some function, such as the following:

```
LINK DRIVER NE2000
```

Each option section can have several parameters, such as the following:

```
INT 4
PORT 340
Frame Ethernet_802.2
```

Each parameter line is indented, located beneath its respective options section, with only one parameter per line. Each line must have a hard return at the end of each parameter setting (including the last line of the file.) A text or comment line can be remarked out by placing REM or a (;) in front of the line.

Note

The NET.CFG file is not sensitive to capitalization.

OPTIMIZING VLMS FOR PERFORMANCE

Because the VLM is so configurable, you may want to read this next section—it covers how you would configure your VLM drivers for performance, memory optimization, and a configuration that combines performance and memory optimization.

It would be nice to tell you that the best configuration of the VLMs would optimize your environment for performance and memory; however, this is not the case and probably never will be. This performance versus memory dilemma is an issue that you have probably gotten used to, and have learned to deal with.

When optimizing the VLMs to conserve memory, be sure you are not loading any VLMs that you do not need. The following is a list of the optional VLMs:

◆ AUTO.VLM

◆ PRINT.VLM

◆ SECURITY.VLM

◆ NDS.VLM

◆ BIND.VLM

◆ PNW.VLM

◆ NETX.VLM

◆ RSA.VLM

◆ WSSNMP.VLM

◆ WSREG.VLM

◆ WSTRAP.VLM

◆ MIB2IF.VLM

◆ MIN2PROT.VLM

◆ NMR.VLM

Warning

Disabling VLMs means that you will be disabling their respective functions. For example, disabling the last seven in the list will effect SNMP services, disabling PRINT.VLM will mean that you cannot print. Disabling NDS.VLM will mean that you cannot access NetWare 4 Directory Services. Disabling BIND.VLM will mean that you cannot connect to a NetWare 3.*x* server, and so on.

Following are the three different ways to disable, or not load specific VLMs:

◆ Delete the VLM

◆ Rename the VLM file to a different name, using an extension other than VLM

◆ Include the line Exclude VLM = <VLM name> under the NetWare DOS requester section of the NET.CFG file.

The VLM comes with default configuration that is optimizing for both memory and performance. The default NET.CFG values are as follows:

```
AUTO LARGE TABLE = OFF
AUTO RECONNECT = ON
AVERAGE NAME LENGTH = 48
CACHE BUFFERS = 5
CACHE BUFFER SIZE = MAX MEDIA SIZE
CACHE WRITES = ON
CHECKSUM = 1
CONNECTIONS = 8
LARGE INTERNET PACKET = ON
LOAD LOW CONN = ON
```

```
LOAD LOW IPXNCP = ON
MINIMUM TIME TO NET = 0
NETWARE PROTOCOL = NDS BIND PNW
NETWARE PRINTERS = 3
PB BUFFERS = 3
PRINT BUFFER SIZE = 64
PRINT HEADER = 64
PRINT TAIL = 16
SIGNATURE LEVEL = 1
TRUE COMMIT = OFF
```

SUMMARY

From this chapter, you should have learned that a workstation is nothing more than a PC connected to a network. Thus, the first part of configuring a workstation is to properly perform the initial setup on the PC. Once the values have been saved in the CMOS, the computer is ready to be hooked to the network with a network card. You should also understand that one of the most difficult parts of hooking a workstation to a network is resolving IRQ, I/O, and DMA conflicts. And finally, you should understand some of the basic procedures of configuring NetWare 4's VLM architecture.

- Local Area Network
  (LAN) Cabling

- MSAUs and
  Concentrators

- Bridges and Routers

- Mainframe and
  Mini-Computer
  Connections

- Summary

CHAPTER 19

Installing Media and Connectors

The purpose of this chapter is to allow you, the NetWare 4 administrator, to better understand, if not install, the physical pieces necessary to communicate between network components. All the pieces must be connected with a type of media or connector—whether from the server to a local workstation or from a remote user to a network printer. Even if you are not the individual who installs this equipment, you, as the administrator, will need to be familiar with its operation in order to be able to better troubleshoot your entire network later. Many of the network problems that you encounter after the initial install will involve some form of cabling or communications issue.

There are numerous types of connections made throughout a network. This chapter discusses those connections being made from the perspective of you, the network administrator, in either a local area network (LAN) or a wide area network (WAN). A LAN is the connection of network nodes within a single building to allow sharing of data and peripherals. A WAN is much the same as a LAN, but consists of network nodes and peripherals spanning more than one building. Each of these broad types of networks has its own unique set of hardware and problems to solve.

LOCAL AREA NETWORK (LAN) CABLING

It is necessary to plan in advance the individual needs of your particular project when cabling a LAN for NetWare 4.*x*. Each different type of cable has a different behavior and maintenance need. You need to be aware that simple issues, such as "What type of ceiling do you have in your area?" will affect the type of cabling you need as much as complex issues such as "How much interference will your office atmosphere create on the physical line?". You also need to keep in mind that your cable choice needs to be something you can live with in the future. Cable standards change, just as processors do. This chapter discusses the three most popular types of cabling and provides information to help you decide which cabling system best meets your needs.

COAX

You may have already used coaxial cable without realizing it. One form of thin coax you may be familiar with is the cable that your television signal comes through when delivered by the cable company, or possibly the cable that carries the sound from your stereo to the speakers in your car. *Coaxial cable* has been around for a very long time and it is a widely used and well-known form of cabling.

Coaxial cable is a very versatile form of cabling because it can carry more than one form of transmission at one time. It can be used for networks that carry both broadband and baseband forms of transmission. It is also very useful for sites that have a need to transmit video, audio, and network traffic within one cabling scheme.

For these reasons, even though coaxial cable may be the more expensive installation at the time, the prospect of cabling once for all your transmission needs may prove to be less expensive in the long run.

There are two basic types of coaxial cable: thick and thin. Both have a center core wire (strands or solid), insulation, and an outer second wire (woven or pressed) covered with a protective outer coating (see Figure 19.1).

Figure 19.1.
Physical cutaway of
coax wire.

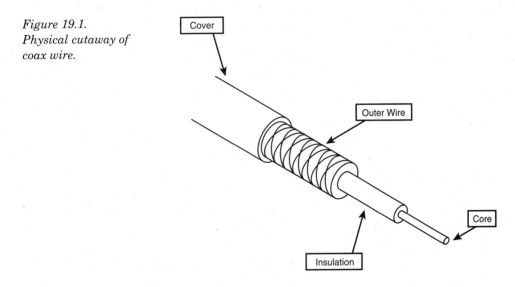

COAX Cable

THIN

Thin coax cable is most often used today for smaller networks between network nodes or as a connector between concentrators. It is the same in appearance (possibly even specification) to your cable television wiring. One major difference in these two types of coax is the connector used to connect them to their respective attachments. Thin coax network connections are made using *Bayonet Nut Connectors* (BNCs). See Figure 19.2.

Thin coax is found in both ARCnet and Ethernet topologies, although the same coax is not used in both. The different forms of thin coax are discussed, as well as some of the possible configurations you may want to implement.

Figure 19.2.
BNC connections.

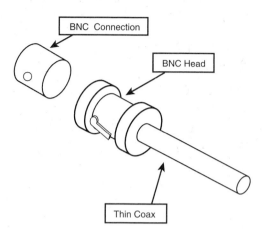

ETHERNET USING THIN COAX (10BASE2)

Ethernet networks are a linear bus topology, meaning that each segment of the LAN is a contiguous line, even though it may not appear so on the surface. RG58U thin coaxial cable is used in the 10Base2 environment. Each connection of the chain is made by a "T" connector connected to a BNC connection on the network interface card in the PC. At the end of each segment, a 50 Ohm terminating resistor (terminator) is needed to terminate the line (see Figure 19.3).

Figure 19.3.
Thin Ethernet network.

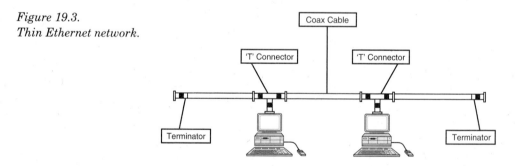

The weakness of such an installation is that should the physical chain be broken at any time, the entire network segment will fail. If the segment fails, all the nodes on that segment will lose connection until the break is repaired. This is exactly why this type of install is not often used in large installations. Imagine trying to physically inspect each component on the network, attempting to find the break that caused the failure—hoping that you do not cause another failure during the inspection. It can be at the least very time consuming, or worse, nearly impossible to inspect depending on the accessibility to the cabling.

The following list shows limitations of thin coax Ethernet cabling.

- ◆ Maximum single segment length is 607 feet
- ◆ Maximum total trunk length (including repeaters) is 3,000 feet
- ◆ Maximum segments connected by repeating devices is 5
- ◆ Minimum distance between devices is 1.5 feet
- ◆ Maximum nodes on one segment is 30

ARCNET USING THIN COAX

ARCnet is used for small networks, as well as networks that involve odd placement of network nodes. Because of the freedom of movement it gave in the placement of hubs, it provided for a very portable network scheme in a time when such schemes were hard to configure. Because of the faster speed of Ethernet and the advent of 10BaseT wiring schemes (discussed later), ARCnet has become less popular over the past few years, but you still might encounter some of these network segments.

In an ARCnet network, the cable is distributed to the network nodes from hubs. Hubs, also known as concentrators, can then be connected together and this provides the freedom for movement discussed earlier.

There are two kinds of hubs in an ARCnet configuration: passive and active. An *active hub* is a hub that provides AC power and is capable of servicing a connection to passive hubs or to network nodes. *Passive hubs* are unpowered hubs that depend on active hubs for signal and may only service network nodes. No passive hub may connect to another passive hub; only to active hubs. Each open connection on a passive hub must be terminated, but an open connection on an active hub does not require termination. A typical ARCnet configuration is shown in Figure 19.4.

THICK

Thick coax is used for longer connections and network backbones in your Ethernet network scheme. It is approximately three times as thick as standard coax television cable (approximately the thickness of a man's thumb) and often is orange or yellow in color.

In your network topology, you may need to make a connection between several smaller networks or across a plant floor that requires a cable be strung over a long distance. In this case, it would make sense to run one super cable across the entire installation and tap into it at given points along the line. This type of installation is known as a *backbone* (see Figure 19.5). Thick coax makes a good choice for this installation because it is capable of spanning a much greater length than thin coax or twisted pair, without losing signal strength. The total maximum distance for a single segment of thick coax is 1,600 feet.

19

INSTALLING MEDIA AND CONNECTORS

Figure 19.4.
ARCnet network.

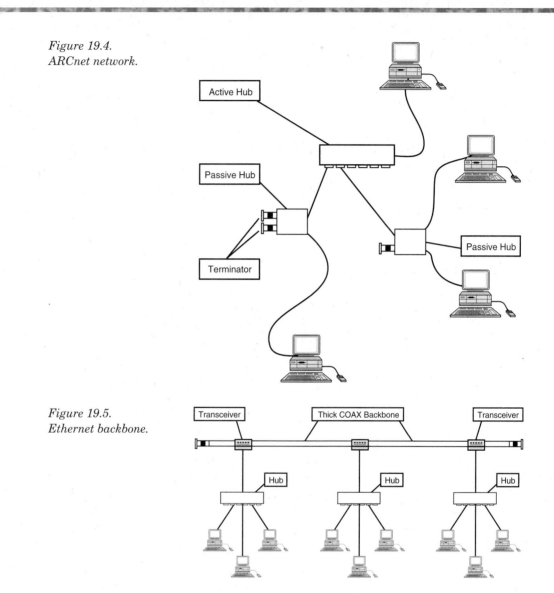

Figure 19.5.
Ethernet backbone.

This application for thick coax wire is most often found in Ethernet networks between twisted pair concentrators (hubs) in a 10BaseT implementation. Thick coax allows the freedom of placing the hubs at any point along the line, then you can branch out to the network nodes from the hub. This allows the physical network to span out much farther than the limitation of twisted pair.

Following are the pieces involved in connecting to thick coax:

♦ **Terminators** (one for each end of the total segment)

On each end of a thick coax line, you will need to place a terminator to maintain the continuation of signal through the line. Failure to terminate the line will stop signals from passing back and forth through the cable.

♦ **Transceivers**

In order to patch into the thick coax line, you must convert the cable type into a usable form for the segment that follows. A transceiver will attach to the outside of the coax cable. It has leads that burrow to the inside of the coax and an external connection to whatever type of cable you have chosen to convert to at that point in the network. An example would be a thick coax to AUI (DIX) connection (see Figure 19.6).

Figure 19.6.
AUI (DIX) Connector.

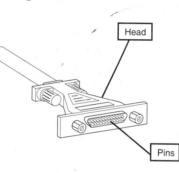

♦ **Coring Tool**

For a transceiver to cleanly burrow into the side of the COAX cable, you first must drill or core out a small hole for the center pin of the transceiver to fit into. A coring tool often comes with most transceivers to facilitate this drilling (see Figure 19.7).

The following list shows the limitations of thick coax Ethernet cabling:

♦ Maximum single segment length is 1,600 feet

♦ Maximum total trunk length (including repeaters) is 8,000 feet

♦ Thick coax must connect through a transceiver

♦ Maximum distance between the transceiver and device is 165 feet

♦ Maximum segments connected by repeating devices is 5

♦ Minimum distance between transceiver taps is 8 feet

♦ Maximum nodes on one trunk is 100

Figure 19.7.
Transceiver attachment
to thick coax.

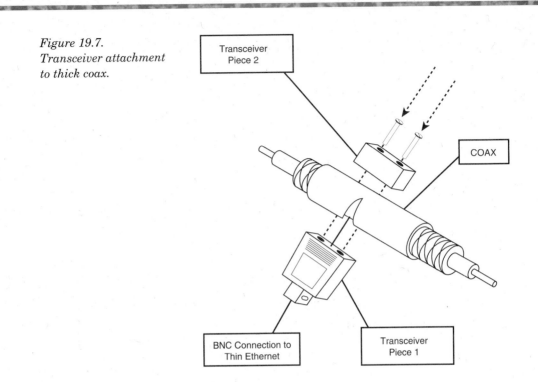

TWISTED PAIR (PHONE CABLING)

Twisted pair cabling is used to connect network nodes to many computer network topologies. It is the most popular cabling system in buildings today because it also is used for phone wiring. It is common today to find a building being built with an extra run of twisted pair wire for each wall plate. This is done in consideration of the fact that a computer network may be installed in the future.

The twisted pair wiring schemes that we will discuss for the purposes of this book are Ethernet and token ring. In both applications, twisted pair cable is used to connect the network node to a central device in a "home run" fashion. A "home run" configuration is a configuration that specifies all the cabling for each network node to come back to a central (home) location. This central device can be an Ethernet Concentrator or a token ring Multi-Station Access Unit (MSAU), but for purposes of simplicity, we will call them a hub.

There are many choices to be made when installing twisted pair cable. First, you must decide where you want to place the hub. With the forms of cabling we have discussed to this point, most of the cable will be inside the walls, but with hubs involved, there is more external exposure and chances for complication. It is necessary to pick a central place, but also a location that is not subject to a large amount of traffic. This location will be the heart of your network communications and you do not want people to disturb the exposed wiring (accidentally or otherwise).

For this reason, a phone closet usually makes a good choice. Phone closets also are good locations simply because most of your wiring will already be centered in this location.

Once you decide on a location for your hub placement, you must decide how the cabling will be physically distributed to the hub. There are several ways to accomplish this, but for now, the following two methods will be considered:

♦ **Direct connection:** Direct connection involves taking the cable ends as they come to the hub and simply attaching the proper head to plug into the hub directly (see Figure 19.8).

Figure 19.8.
Hub to workstation
connection.

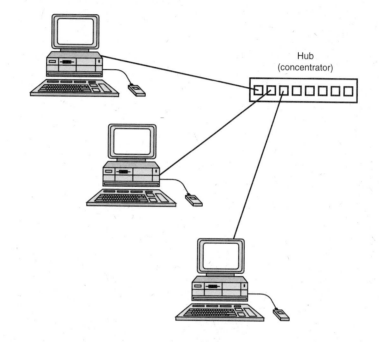

♦ **Punch-down block connection:** The primary difference between a punch-down block install and a direct connection is the punch-down block. A punch-block is a device used to give twisted pair a manageable area for doing cross-connections. When the cable arrives at the hub location, it is first attached (punched down) to the punch-down block. Then separate cables are attached on the opposite side of the block running to the hub. This convention has been used for many years for phone systems and allows for easy identification and change in cabling schemes. If your building was preconfigured with extra twisted pair cable, you may find that these extra wires already come to a punch-down block. You then simply need to make the connection between the proper wires on the block and your hub (see Figure 19.9).

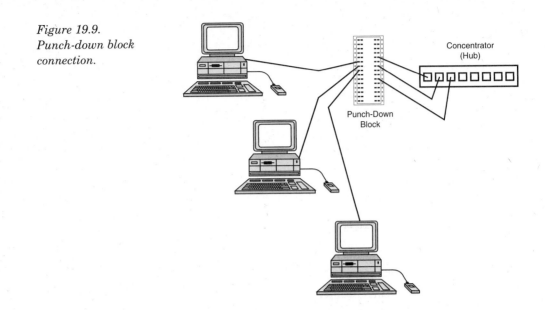

Figure 19.9.
Punch-down block
connection.

There are many different ways to configure this type of connection. We have only discussed the most simplistic form of punch-down installation, and your wiring professional should be relied on heavily in these installs. Unless you have considerable experience in phone wiring schemes, it would be best to hire a professional installer.

ETHERNET USING TWISTED PAIR (10BASET)

In a 10BaseT install, the hub will be an Ethernet concentrator. This device is deceptive because it makes the Ethernet install look as if it were no longer a linear bus or chain, but a star with all nodes coming back to a central location. Actually, the chaining still occurs inside the concentrator. A concentrator allows the chain to be concentrated into a smaller, more manageable format. By containing the chain, the concentrator can allow those nodes connected to continue to be connected even when a particular node is physically disconnected. Even if the cable to one node is cut, the rest of the nodes will maintain connection. This is possible because the concentrator continually monitors each connection for continuity (physical connection).

To continue the bus beyond the capacity of the concentrator, you simply connect one concentrator to another. This is most often done by using a BNC (thin coax) connection or AUI (thick coax) connection on the surface of the concentrator. Some concentrators will even have a particular 10BaseT port that can be set for a chained connection from one concentrator to the other. A typical 10BaseT hub is shown in Figure 19.10.

Figure 19.10.
Ethernet Concentrator
(hub) for 10BaseT.

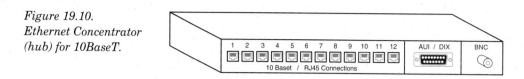

10BaseT installs use either AT&T Type 3 or Type 5 unshielded twisted pair wire (see Figure 19.11). Four conductors (two pairs) of this wire are used by attaching one end to an RJ45 wall plate at the node end and the remaining end to the hub (as discussed previously). The wires are attached to pin positions in the RJ45 head of the cable or on the inside of the RJ45 outlet wall plate. Pins 1, 2, 3, and 6 are the pins that need to be connected for Ethernet. Usually the 1 and 2 pins are attached from one conductor pair and the 3 and 6 pins are attached to the other pair. It is critical that the same conductors are used on each end (Pin 1 at the wall plate to Pin 1 at the wiring closet, Pin 2 to Pin 2, and so on). Twisted pair in these cable types actually contains eight wires (four pairs), but Ethernet will only use four wires (two pairs).

Figure 19.11.
Unshielded twisted
pair.

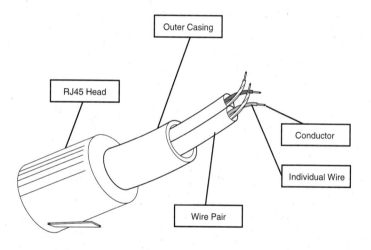

19

Note

The RJ45 connector used in 10BaseT cabling is very much like the modular head of your phone wire. It is wider, thicker, and is sometimes keyed so those business phones that use the same head will not be accidentally plugged in to the same wall plate. It contains eight conductor positions instead of four or six, as many RJ11 heads used for phone systems (see Figure 19.12).

Figure 19.12.
RJ45 wall plate.

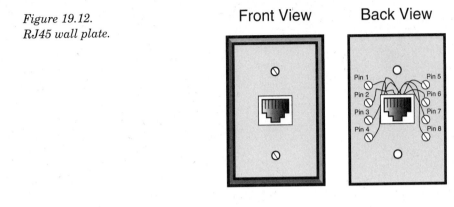

Wall Plate

Note

Type 5 cable is not necessary today, but new technologies are waiting on the horizon that will require Type 5 twisted pair to function. These technologies will use all eight conductors and will carry data at a much faster rate. By choosing the right cabling system today, you can be prepared to take advantage of future technologies as they are introduced in the market without increasing additional wiring cost.

Once the wiring is in the wall and attached to the hub, it needs to be attached to the nodes. The attachment to the node is done by using a patch cable. Patch cables are cables plugged into the wall plate and then plugged into the network interface card (NIC). These short cables are able to be purchased pre-made or custom-made, but in either case they need to be configured in the same way that the cabling system has to this point. Pins 1, 2, 3, and 6 need to be attached to the RJ45 head on each end using the same conductors on each end. Keep in mind that your patch cable is part of the total length and could push you over the 300 foot limit.

The following list shows the limitations of 10BaseT Ethernet cabling.

◆ Maximum single segment length is 300 feet.

◆ Twisted pair must connect through a concentrator (hub)

◆ Maximum distance between the hub and the network node is 300 feet

◆ Maximum recommended number of *active* nodes per (hub) is 30

◆ Twisted pair type is AT&T Type 3 or AT&T Type 5

TOKEN RING USING TWISTED PAIR

Token ring cabling uses a hub referred to as a Multi-Station Access Unit (MSAU). This device is also deceptive because it makes a ring network look like a star with all nodes coming back to a central location. The token "ring" is inside the MSAU and is referred to as a *star ring topology*. An MSAU creates the ring in a smaller, more manageable form. If a node is disconnected from the MSAU, the MSAU trips a solenoid that will remove that connection from the ring.

To continue the ring beyond the capacity of the MSAU (usually eight ports, depending on the vendor and model), you need to connect to another MSAU (see Figure 19.13). To connect to another MSAU, you need to connect the ring-in port of the MSAU to the ring-out port of the other MSAU and vice versa.

Figure 19.13.
Token ring MSAU.

Token Ring MSAU

Token ring installations use either unshielded twisted pair cabling (Type 3 or Type 5) or they use IBM certified Type 1 shielded twisted pair (STP). The difference in these types of cables primarily is the the shielding. The shielded IBM cables are capable of running IBM configurations at 16 Mbps speeds. If you do not use IBM Type 1 cabling, you still may be able to achieve 16 Mbps line speeds, but IBM will not support the install. AT&T Type 5 or Type 3 cabling requires that you use a media filter to connect to the MSAU or the NIC, unless your MSAU or NIC has the RJ45 jack.

The cable is used by attaching one end to a token ring wall plate (IBM Token Ring port or RJ45) at the node end and the remaining end to the MSAU. Token ring is different from 10BaseT in that it often comes back to a modular connection block, then connected to the MSAU (see Figure 19.14). It is also different in that it uses conductors 3, 4, 5, and 6 (4/5 as one pair and 3/6 as another). This connection is like the punch-down block scenario because it allows for better management and selective connection of nodes to the MSAU.

Figure 19.14.
IBM token ring cable
connector.

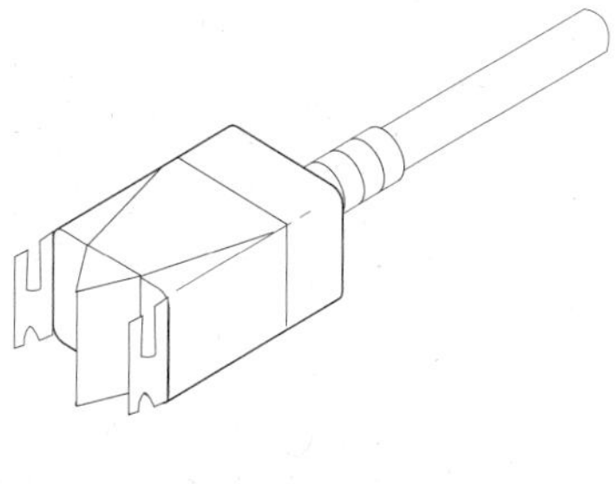

Once the wiring is in the wall and attached to the MSAU, it needs to be attached to the nodes. The attachment to the node is done by the using a *patch cable*. Patch cables are cables plugged into the wall plate and then plugged into the network interface card (NIC). These short cables are able to be purchased pre-made or custom-made, but in either case, they need to be configured in the same way that the cabling system has to this point. Wire needs to be attached to the head on each end using the same conductors on each end. Keep in mind that your patch cable is part of the total length of your run of twisted pair and could push you over the length limit.

The following list shows the limitations of token ring cabling.

◆ Maximum length connecting all MSAUs is 400 feet

◆ Token ring must connect through an MSAU

◆ Maximum distance between the MSAU and the network node is 150 feet

◆ Maximum number of nodes per segment is 96

◆ Maximum number of MSAUs per segment is 12

◆ Twisted pair type is AT&T Type 3, Type 5, or IBM Type 1

MSAUs AND CONCENTRATORS

When purchasing the MSAUs or concentrators for your network, you may want to consider intelligent devices. These devices are able to report back information about the condition of the network to a software agent on a workstation or server. The information that is collected will make it possible for you to manage the network from one location and eliminate the need to physically inspect cable throughout the entire network in the event of a failure or problem.

Devices with this type of intelligence use a reporting protocol called *Simple Network Management Protocol* (SNMP). The SNMP agents on the management machine collect and report the information being brought in from intelligent devices. They report this information to an application, such as Hewlett-Packards' OpenView product or Novell's NetWare Management System (NMS), and it allows the network administrator to see network errors as they occur and possibly even before the users are affected.

Such software and hardware have limited use in a small network environment, because the capability to visually inspect and troubleshoot issues locally is often far less costly and easier. In a larger environment or WAN, the capability to monitor a problematic hub or MSAU from miles away can be an incredible cost savings.

FIBER-OPTIC CABLE

Fiber-optic cable is literally glass fibers with one outer optic layer and an inner optic core running through an insulating cover and uses light pulses to communicate (see Figure 19.15). Because light does not have the physical limitations that an analog or digital signal does, fiber-optic cable is able to deliver its signal across much greater distances (up to 2 kilometers). Because fiber-optic cable is glass, it is fragile and does not bend at sharp angles, making it hard to install in workstation sites. For these reasons, fiber is normally used for backbone applications and long runs to work stations in remote sites.

Figure 19.15.
Fiber-optic cable.

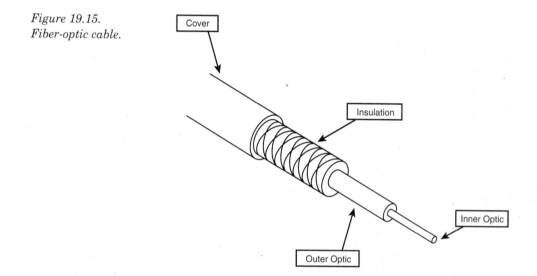

Fiber is not affected by ambient noise or electrical interference. Fiber also does not emit an electrical or magnetic current, so it will not interfere with sensitive equipment around it. Because of these strengths, it is a great choice for noisy plant floors, airports, radio transmitters, and any area where the noise or interference levels are too much for coaxial cable or twisted pair.

Most of the topologies that use fiber exclusively are very fast (100 Mbps or better) but are proprietary and very expensive, meaning that the complete set of hardware involved is manufactured and supported by one vendor. The fact that the administrator is locked into one vendor and because fiber is so expensive, most of these schemes are not used for communications directly to each node. For the most part, the fiber-optic topology is exclusively the realm of high-powered workstations and backbone communications.

Fiber can be used in Ethernet and token ring topologies as a backbone or to connect routers or bridges (discussed later). The length of a single run of fiber dwarfs the possibility of even thick coax. So, if your need is to attach a group of users 3,000 feet away across a campus site, fiber-optic cabling makes this possible while maintaining the speed and convenience of a local connection.

FIBER-OPTIC CABLE IN AN ETHERNET ENVIRONMENT

In order to use fiber-optic cable in an Ethernet installation, you must use a transceiver. This device will connect at one end to your fiber optic cable and on the other end to an AUI connection. AUI connections can then be attached to the concentrator or directly to the network node. In this scenario, the fiber installation is not providing any more speed than a backbone of thick coax or a connection of twisted pair, but instead is providing a more reliable and longer connection capability.

FIBER-OPTIC CABLE IN A TOKEN RING ENVIRONMENT

Fiber-optic cable in a token ring configuration is being used to provide a more reliable or longer connection. Standard token ring cable is used to connect from the MSAU or node to a fiber repeater that will carry the signal down the line to the next repeater and up to the next MSAU or node through another token ring cable. In a token ring installation, a repeater must be used in order to allow communication.

CABLING TESTING EQUIPMENT

For the most part, the average network administrator will not be doing network cable troubleshooting on a segment after the first month of the segment being installed. Cable, if installed well, is a constant. It is installed inside walls, and if the proper topology is chosen for that segment, your user should have little reason to bother that cable. Occasionally, cable problems do happen. The next few sections look into some of the possible avenues you might take to find and solve those cabling problems.

There are many different ways to troubleshoot cable. One very simple way is to call on your cabling contractor to determine why you are having the problem. In many cases, you will find that the cable was not the problem and incur a bill for nothing. It would be nice to have a piece of equipment that you could attach to the line and check it before calling the contractor. The types of devices you will find break down into two basic categories, simple continuity and resistance checking devices, and more complex devices that check line load and utility.

SIMPLE: CONTINUITY AND RESISTANCE

In this section, you will read about a number of simple test tools that you can obtain quite inexpensively from your local electronic stores. These tools test for continuity in the wiring and report the resistance of the wiring. The first wiring testing device to be discussed is a multi-meter.

Most electrical shops or computer shops have, on hand, a simple multi-meter. This device is used to check continuity, AC and DC current, and Ohm resistance. You can use these devices to check your network cabling as well. If you do not have a multi-meter, they are easily purchased at any local electronics outlet or hardware store. Do not spend the extra money on the fanciest one in the shop. Get a compact multi-meter that will be easy to carry around.

When using a multi-meter to check coax cable you can check for two basic items: resistance and continuity. The first test you perform should address the question: "Does it return the proper Ohm resistance when you attach probe 1 to the center conductor and probe 2 to the outer ring of the BNC head?" An example would be if you find that your coax segment is down. Start at the furthest machine from a terminator. Remove the cable from the connector. Set the multi-meter to Ohm and apply the two probes to the separate conductors in the coax (center core and outer ring of the BNC head). The Ohm reading on the multi-meter should read close to the same Ohm resistance as your terminator, depending on how long your segment is. What you essentially have done is attach the multi-meter to the terminator. If you get a reading of 0 (zero), the next step would be to continue to the next connector and continue. Repeat this step until you get a proper reading or reach the terminator. Then test the terminator. If you receive a much greater reading than your terminator's Ohm resistance, immediately move to the terminator and check it. It is possible you were given the wrong terminator or that it has been switched.

Secondly, you should determine whether you have continuity through the cable. In other words, is it physically making the connection or is the cable still in one piece? This test is rather simple. With a terminator connected to the opposite end of the cable, set your multi-meter to continuity checking and attach the probes to the inner core and outer ring of the BNC head. The multi-meter should sound an alert if the connection is complete. If no sound is made, there is a break somewhere in the segment of cable being tested.

When testing twisted-pair cabling with a multi-meter, you must either remove the head of the cable or have probes that are able to reach the conductors in the head of the cable without removing it. Removing the connector may cause additional problems; therefore, it is not recommended.

You can really only run one test on twisted pair cabling with a multi-meter, and this is the continuity test. This test can only be done on patch cables. Simply attach one probe to a conductor and the other to the corresponding conductor on the other end of the twisted pair. This can be a bit tricky. It works best if you have a device to hold both cable ends close together and still. Once the probes are attached, you should hear the multi-meter sound an alert that physical connection has been made. The results of this type of testing are questionable at best, however, because the conductors are so close together, and you may be receiving crossover signals from an adjoining conductor. Only use this type of testing if you have no other option and do not depend on the results for mission critical installs. Testing new patch cables with this method, however, can be an added comfort.

Other than a multi-meter, there also are preconfigured devices that you can find for simple cable testing. These devices are usually continuity checking devices. These devices consist of two pieces; one for each end of the connection. One piece will produce a signal that will be interpreted by the other. The advantage to these devices is that they are able to be used to test larger segments of cable, because each piece can be placed at any point in the cable. A disadvantage to these devices is that they are usually very specific in their application, limiting your return on your investment.

In a coaxial cable testing device, one end will attach to the BNC connection of your cable and the other will attach to the opposite end (see Figure 19.16). When this connection is made, an alert will be sounded or a light will be produced to indicate that either connection has been made or a "short" has been found. A "shorted" condition indicates that both conductors in the cable have somehow made connection with each other and the cable needs to be repaired. No alert indicates that no connection can be made between the two pieces of the test device and the cable needs to be repaired. Obviously, if all alerts are correct, then your cabling segment is fine. Better devices will indicate the condition of each conductor separately so that you can better service the situation.

Figure 19.16.
Coaxial cable testing
device.

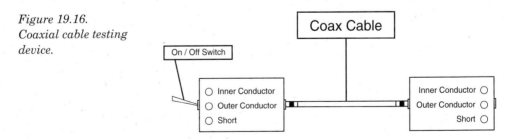

In a twisted-pair cable testing device, one end will attach to the RJ45 or token ring connection of your cable, and the other will attach to the opposite end (see Figure 19.17). When this connection is made, an alert will be sounded or lights will be

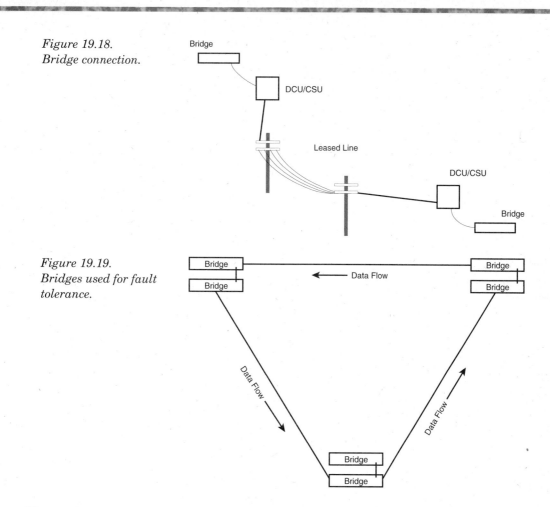

Figure 19.18.
Bridge connection.

Figure 19.19.
Bridges used for fault
tolerance.

ROUTERS

Routers behave in much the same way as do bridges, with one added advantage. Routers are used to connect nodes across segments with unlike frame types and unlike topologies, such as Ethernet to token ring. You could think of a router as an interpreter that allows diverse segments to share data even if their topology needs are different. For example, you may have one group of users operating on a token ring topology that needs to communicate with a group using Ethernet. Although both groups are using IPX packets to communicate over the network, they are unable to communicate without the intervention of a router.

MAINFRAME AND MINI-COMPUTER CONNECTIONS

Now that you have spent all of this time and money on cabling your building to communicate with your Novell 4.*x* server, it would be advantageous if you could use those same connections to communicate with your host systems (mainframe or mini-computer). This can be achieved and often far easier than you might imagine.

In order to achieve this connection, you must find a way to route the signal from your host systems. This can be done in one of two ways. One way would be to use a product like NetWare for SAA to imbed the host packets inside the packets currently being used to communicate across the network. You also could simply use the same type of packet to communicate on your network that your host system is using.

NETWARE FOR SAA

If you are using an IBM host system (3090 series, AS/400, or other), then NetWare for SAA is an option that you may want to look at. NetWare for SAA is discussed in more detail in Chapter 4, but simply put, IBM host systems use a set of communications rules called SAA. These systems follow a uniform communication plan and NetWare for SAA makes a NetWare server appear as a controller for a PU (physical unit) that controls several (between 16 and 2,000) LUs (logical units or terminals and printers). Once the server has established this link, it then administrates the use of the LUs it has been put in charge of.

A node attached to this server can make use of these LUs by running a terminal emulation package to appear to the host as a terminal or printer. Several different packages exist for this application—among them is Attachmate's 3270 Workstation package. The primary requirement is that they be compatible with the NetWare for SAA/host packets.

MATCHING THE HOST PACKET FORMAT

Host systems that use packet forms that are compatible with NetWare make it possible to share a single wiring scheme with the rest of your network. An example of this would be Digital VAX line of mini- and mainframe computers. These systems can use TCP/IP to communicate across Ethernet cables. If this is the case, then you may want to consider using TCP/IP as the protocol for your network. This would allow users to have access to both the network and the host.

CABLING CONTRACTORS

It is important to be very careful when choosing a cabling contractor because you will need to live with the decision daily if you are not. Cabling contractors come in many different flavors.

There are thousands of individuals who have found that they are able to connect network wiring. Many of these people are only part time cable installers and because of this, they are unable to help you in your time of need because of prior engagements. Depending on the work load, however, you may feel that the relationship is more personable and easier to communicate through.

Independents are less likely to have a large staff of assistants—so the work could take longer. Independents are also often less knowledgeable about building codes and could cause you a problem if you need to pass a building inspection. These individuals are awfully tempting because the pricing they offer can be as much as half the cost of the larger firms. Simply put, it is not wrong to use an independent cable installer, but you should be very careful when evaluating your needs versus their ability to deliver.

Large firms offer the comfort factor of having a larger target to aim at in the event of a problem, but you may also find that you disappear in a sea of customers when the going gets tough.

These groups are usually very good about keeping the proper number of staff on hand to meet your needs, and you most often will find that your cabling job is going to be done by a team of qualified installers. Teams of installers allow for a quicker installation and often are able to spend the time to better check their work. Because they are a bigger "target," they also must be more conscious of building and cabling code. Although the cost is considerably higher, it may be in your best interest to go with a larger firm.

In conclusion, just because a contractor is small does not mean that they will be unresponsive or do bad work. The fact that they are big does not mean you will be ignored. You simply need to be careful to select the contractor that will meet your needs. Spend the time to interview the companies. Make sure that they can meet your time schedule. Discuss your particular installation and make sure that they understand what you have in mind. Do not spend your time explaining to a contractor which conductors you want connected. If the contractor is not familiar with network cabling schemes, you should be looking elsewhere.

Note

Be sure that you or your cabling contractor is aware of the need for plenum (fire resistant) cable coatings on the cable in your ceilings. Plenum cabling will stop the fire from following the cable throughout the building. It often can be required in some areas by building code and could be a fire code violation if your friendly neighborhood fire marshal should come to visit. It is often quite expensive by comparison, but it could save a life.

SUMMARY

In this chapter, you learned about the different types of cabling options available to you when installing your network. Also discussed were some ways of troubleshooting cabling issues.

This concludes Part IV of this book, which focused on topics that helped you to prepare your network installation or upgrade. The next section deals with the actual installation of NetWare on your servers and workstations.

- Installing and Using
  DynaText

- Installing NetWare
  4.1 on New Servers

- Upgrading an
  Existing Server

- Installing New
  Workstation Software

- Upgrading Existing
  PC Workstations

P A R T V

Implementing the Network

- What is DynaText?

- Installing DynaText

- Using DynaText

- Using DT Before
  and During Your
  Installation

- Summary

CHAPTER 20

Installing and Using DynaText

NetWare 4.1 is shipped with a new online help package called *DynaText*, or *DT* for short. This replaces the Folio Views and ElectroText packages that were shipped with previous versions of NetWare. DynaText viewer is available as a Windows-based application as well as for Macintosh and UnixWare.

In this chapter, the installation, configuration, and use of DynaText will be discussed. You will find that DT is a very valuable resource that can help you to understand and troubleshoot your new NetWare 4.1 server.

Note

It is not necessary for you to install NetWare 4.1 server before you can make use of DynaText. As a matter of fact, many people will install and use DT first, to gather information, before installing their first NetWare 4.1 server.

WHAT IS DYNATEXT?

DynaText (DT) is Novell's new direction on providing online documentation. If you have used its predecessor, ElectroText, you will find DynaText much easier to use and much faster. The opening screen shows the document sets available from the "collection." Shown in Figure 20.1 are the various book "titles" that are available on your NetWare 4.1 Documentation CD.

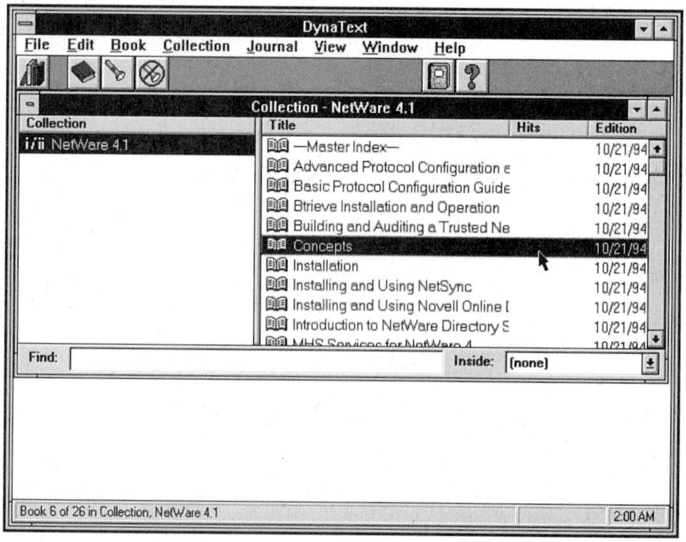

Figure 20.1.
DynaText NetWare 4.1 book "collection."

A total of 26 books are available in the NetWare 4.1 collection. By default, NetWare 4 is not shipped with any printed manual set (except for a couple of "Getting Started" type books). If you were to print out the whole manual set from DynaText, the printout could be well over 3,000 pages. If you want to have a set of printed manuals, you can order it using the Order Form included in your NetWare 4.1 kit. DynaText, however, eliminates your need for printed manuals. You may want to print out selected chapters for reference during your initial installation and later for any troubleshooting needs.

You can install and use DT in a number of ways. Given that the English version of the NetWare 4.1 DT manual set is well over 60MB in size, you may not want to install it onto your server or a workstation. You can access it right from the CD-ROM, if you want. Described in the following section are some ways of installing and running DT from different sources.

INSTALLING DYNATEXT

Many people will use DynaText to look up the installation procedures for NetWare 4.1 before they actually perform the task. In this case, it is easiest if you connect your CD-ROM reader to your workstation and access it from there. There are four ways in which you can access DT, depending on your available resources:

- ◆ DOS CD-ROM drive connected to your workstation
- ◆ Install DT onto the hard drive of your workstation
- ◆ CD-ROM drive connected to your file server
- ◆ Install DT onto a volume of your file server

Tip

It is always better to be well prepared before you start the install.

A CD-ROM reader is not (yet) a common resource for many people, so perhaps installing DT onto the hard disk of your workstation may be the best first step.

INSTALLING DT ON YOUR WORKSTATION

Following are the steps to install DT onto your local DOS hard drive. The following example assumes that the English version will be installed:

Note

DT is currently available in five different languages: Dutch, English, Spanish, French, and Italian. By default, the English version is shipped.

1. You need to first install the CD-ROM reader (and controller card if applicable) on your workstation. The exact procedure for doing this varies depending on the model and make of your CD-ROM reader.

2. Make sure you have at least 70MB of free space available for DT files. You need to have Windows installed as well.

3. Create a PRVNOTES directory off the root on your hard disk.

4. Use the XCOPY command to transfer the entire directory contents from the CD-ROM (assuming that it's drive D:) to your hard drive (assuming that it's drive C:):

   ```
   XCOPY D:\*.* C:\ /S /E /V
   ```

5. Copy DYNATEXT.INI from the \DOCVIEW\DTAPPWIN directory to your Windows directory.

6. Edit DYNATEXT.INI to reflect the correct drive and language directory (see Figure 20.2).

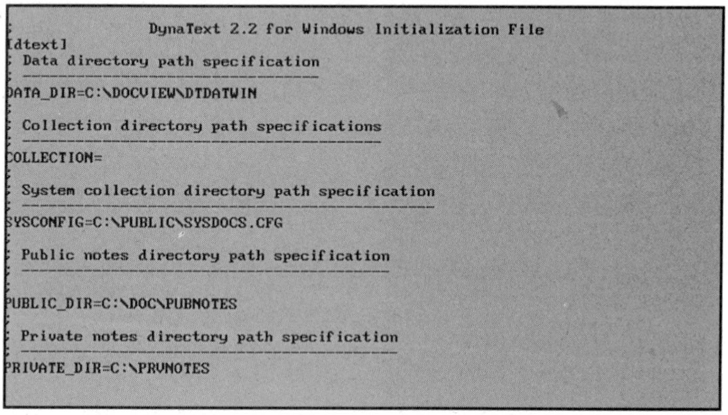

Figure 20.2.
Sample
DYNATEXT.INI for
workstation-based
access.

```
                    DynaText 2.2 for Windows Initialization File
[dtext]
; Data directory path specification
--------------------------------------
DATA_DIR=C:\DOCVIEW\DTDATWIN

; Collection directory path specifications
--------------------------------------
COLLECTION=

; System collection directory path specification
--------------------------------------
SYSCONFIG=C:\PUBLIC\SYSDOCS.CFG

; Public notes directory path specification
--------------------------------------
PUBLIC_DIR=C:\DOC\PUBNOTES

; Private notes directory path specification
--------------------------------------
PRIVATE_DIR=C:\PRVNOTES
```

7. Add the DT icon to your Windows Desktop. Edit the icon's Properties to be sure the command is referencing the correct drive (see Figure 20.3).

Figure 20.4 shows what the DynaText icon looks like.

Figure 20.3.
Icon Properties settings.

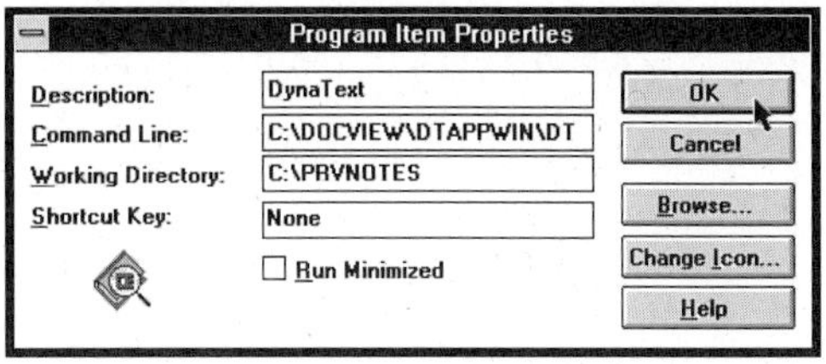

Figure 20.4.
Icon Properties settings.

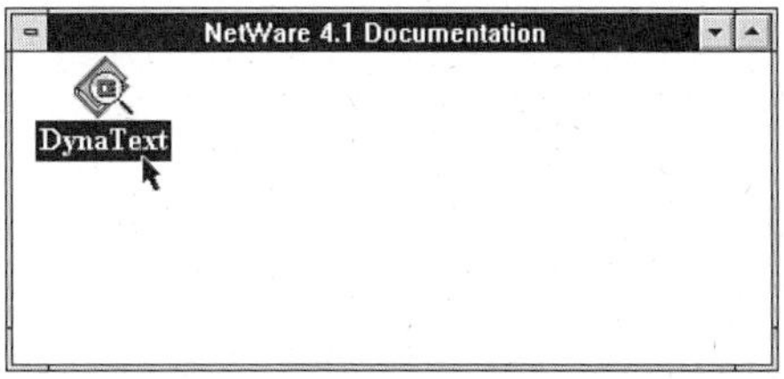

INSTALLING DT ON YOUR FILE SERVER

You can use a procedure similar to the one just described to install DT onto your existing file server, be that a NetWare 2.*x*, 3.*x*, or 4.*x* server. You just need to substitute the destination drive (C: in the preceding example) for the proper MAP'ed drive letter.

Note

If you want users other than those with supervisor rights to also use DT, be sure you give them the proper security rights to \DOC, \DOCVIEW, and \PUBLIC. Users should have their own PRVNOTES (private notes) directory. See Chapter 28 for more information about file system security.

You will have a chance to install DT onto your new NetWare 4.1 during the installation procedure. This is discussed in Chapter 21.

USING DYNATEXT

In DT terminology, the documentation set is made up as follows:

- ◆ Individual manuals called "titles"
- ◆ A set of titles makes up a "collection"
- ◆ You can have one or more collections—for example, to include DynaText for NetWare 4.1 and 3.12 manuals.

Upon opening the collection, you will see a list corresponding to each book (or manual) within the set (refer to Figure 20.1). For NetWare 4.1, the following 26 books are in the set:

◆ A Master Index

◆ Advanced Protocol Configuration and Management Guide

◆ Basic Protocol Configuration Guide

◆ Btrieve Installation and Operation

◆ Building and Auditing a Trusted Network Environment

◆ Concepts

◆ Installation

◆ Installing and Using NetSync

◆ Installing and Using Novell Online Documentation

◆ Introduction to NetWare Directory Services

◆ MHS Services for NetWare 4

◆ Migrating an IPX Network to NLSP

◆ NetWare AppleTalk Reference

◆ NetWare Client for DOS and MS Windows Technical Reference

◆ NetWare Client for DOS and MS Windows User Guide

◆ NetWare Client for OS/2 User Guide

◆ NetWare for Macintosh File and Print Services

◆ NetWare IPX Router Reference

◆ NetWare TCP/IP Reference

◆ New Features

◆ Print Services

◆ Supervising the Network

◆ System Messages

◆ Upgrade

◆ Using MacNDS Client for NetWare 4

◆ Utilities Reference

On each screen, you have the option of searching for keywords. Depending on the screen you are at, you either search the whole collection or a single title. Figure 20.5 shows the results of searching through the collection—each title that contained the keyword is identified by a number that represents the number of "hits" within.

Figure 20.5.
Search results for the
whole collection.

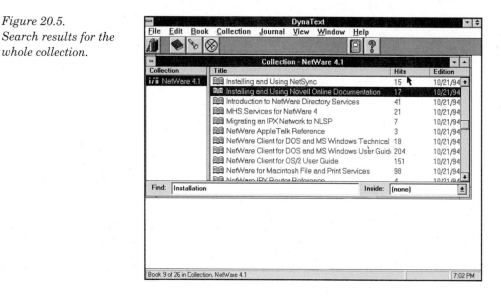

When you open a particular title, you will see a screen similar to Figure 20.6. This figure shows the TCP/IP Reference book. By default, you see the outline shown on the left side and the text on the right. You can change the outline placement via the File/Preferences pull-down menu (see Figure 20.7).

Figure 20.6.
Opening screen for a
book.

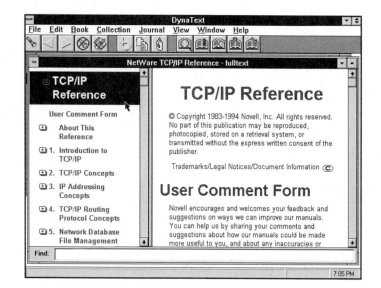

Figure 20.7.
Preferences setting for
Table of Contents
outline.

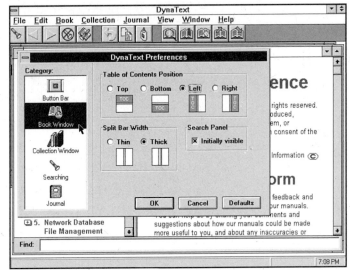

By clicking on the text portion of the outline, DT takes you directly to the starting page of that particular section (see Figure 20.8); you do not have to scroll the window. If a plus sign (+) is shown on the left side of a topic, clicking it will display the subsections within (see Figure 20.9).

Figure 20.8.
Going directly to the
starting page of the
section.

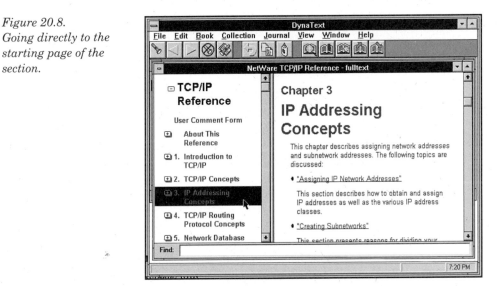

Figure 20.9.
Expanding the outline
to show subsections.

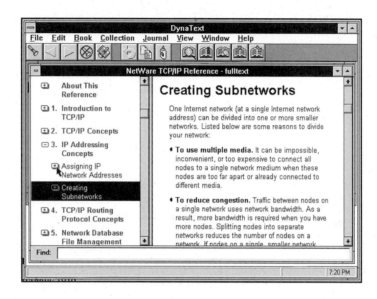

USING DT BEFORE AND DURING YOUR INSTALLATION

If this is your first NetWare install, it is strongly advised that you read the "Custom NetWare 4.1 Installation" chapter in the Installation (DT) book (see Figure 20.10). Even if you are an experienced NetWare 3.1x installer, it does not hurt to quickly check through the information. Although most the installation steps in 4.x are the same as 3.1x, there are additional steps that are unique to NetWare 4.x that you need to be aware of.

You may even want to print out the chapter so that you can check items off during your install as they are performed. This serves as a great record for your reference and subsequent installs.

You should have DynaText available online during your installation, just in case you need to look up the meaning of one of the question prompts or error codes.

20

Figure 20.10.
NetWare 4.1 custom
installation chapter.

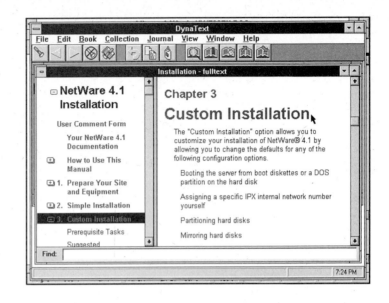

SUMMARY

Given that DynaText is a graphical user interface-based search engine, it is a much simpler and easier tool to use than the previous Folio Views-based product. Many of you will find it more readily accessible than the printed manual, since DT can be installed on your file server and workstation. If you have a portable CD-ROM reader, you can carry the CD anywhere you go. You cannot easily do that with printed books, especially with the amount of information that accompanied NetWare 4!

Should you find the need to have printed manuals, you can either print out the relevant DT chapters or order the printed books through Novell's fulfillment company. An order form is enclosed with each copy of NetWare 4.1 you purchased.

- Installing and Configuring NetWare 4.1

- Possible Problems and Solutions

- Summary

CHAPTER 21

Installing NetWare 4.1 on New Servers

This chapter presents step-by-step procedures necessary for a successful NetWare 4.1 server installation. The end of the chapter lists some possible problems and solutions you may encounter during your server installation. The installation of workstation software will be discussed later in Chapter 23.

INSTALLING AND CONFIGURING NETWARE 4.1

If you have installed earlier versions of NetWare before, such as NetWare 2.15, you know from experience that there are many tedious steps involved, especially the infamous COMPSURF procedure. NetWare 4.1's installation steps have automated much of the steps, and menu selections are used whenever possible.

This chapter assumes that you have fully and correctly installed all necessary hardware, and resolved any potential hardware conflict.

Tip

As discussed in Chapter 20, it would be handy and useful to have the DynaText online documentation installed and available on a workstation where you can have easy access during your installation.

INSTALLATION OVERVIEW

There are two components in installing a NetWare 4.1 server: the DOS component, and NetWare itself. Starting with NetWare 3.0, DOS is used to "bootstrap" NetWare. Previous NetWare uses its own boot code.

By default, your copy of NetWare 4.1 will be shipped on two CDs rather than diskettes. Therefore, you need to have a CD-ROM reader that has a DOS device driver to be used for installation.

Note

You can order diskettes from a third-party Novell fulfillment house by filling out the order form that came with your NetWare. In general, you would not want to install from diskettes as it is very time consuming.

NetWare 4.1 consists of more than 300MB of files, which translates easily into over 100 diskettes, assuming that the files are compressed with a 50 percent efficiency.

Following are the 20 steps necessary for a NetWare 4.1 server installation:

1. Install a DOS partition on your server hard drive.
2. Install and setup CD-ROM reader to be accessed under DOS.
3. Execute the INSTALL.BAT file from the CD to start the menu driven installation process.
4. Assign a server name and a unique internal IPX network number.
5. Copy server boot files from the CD to the DOS partition.
6. Configure country code, code page, and keyboard mapping for your server.
7. Select filename format for the file system.
8. Specify any special SET commands for STARTUP.NCF file.
9. Allow AUTOEXEC.BAT to autoload SERVER.EXE.
10. Load and configure the correct disk driver(s).
11. Load and configure the correct network card driver(s).
12. Set up and configure NetWare partition and volumes.
13. Install the license disk.
14. Copy selected NetWare files to SYS: volume.
15. Install an NDS Tree if the server is the first server.
16. Select and specify time zone information.
17. Enter NDS information if the tree is new.
18. Create STARTUP.NCF.
19. Create AUTOEXEC.NCF.
20. Install optional programs and files.

These steps are discussed in detail in the following sections.

Note

All examples shown in this chapter are based on the English-language support module. Dutch, Spanish, French, and Italian language modules also are available for installation. They are shipped as part of standard NetWare 4.1. You do not need to order them separately.

INSTALLING A DOS PARTITION

Because of the number of files, and their sizes, required by SERVER.EXE during boot, it is best to have a bootable DOS partition on your server. Novell recommends a minimum of 5MB DOS partition. However, it is best to have a bigger one (10MB to 15MB) so that you have some working room.

Note

You can use any version of DOS; however, most installations today are using DOS 5.0 or higher. If you encounter any problems, try MS-DOS 5.0.

CD-ROM SETUP

You need to set up your CD-ROM drive and controller so that the drive can be addressed as a DOS device. A sample AUTOEXEC.BAT and CONFIG.SYS for Adaptec 1542B SCSI controller is shown in Figures 21.1 and 21.2, respectively. In this example, the CD-ROM drive is set up as drive D:.

Figure 21.1.
Sample
AUTOEXEC.BAT
for Adaptec 1542B
controller.

```
@echo off
C:\SCSI\MSCDEX.EXE /D:ASPICD0 /M:12
C:\WINDOWS\SMARTDRV.EXE
cls
SET  path=C:\NMS\bin;C:\WINDOWS;C:\DOS
SET  TEMP=C:\WINDOWS\TEMP
prompt $p$g
SET HELPFILES=C:\NMS\help\*.HLP
```

Figure 21.2.
Sample CONFIG.SYS
for Adaptec 1542B
controller.

```
DEVICE=C:\SCSI\ASPI4DOS.SYS /D
FILES= 60
BUFFERS=40
DEVICE=C:\WINDOWS\HIMEM.SYS
STACKS=9,256
LASTDRIVE=Z
DEVICE=C:\SCSI\ASPICD.SYS /D:ASPICD0
```

You can use almost any CD-ROM drive/controller combination for the installation, as long as you have a DOS driver for it. However, if you want to later make this CD-ROM drive a sharable volume on the server, it must be a SCSI device.

Tip

It is to your advantage to use the fastest CD-ROM drive possible for the installation. The faster the drive, the shorter your installation time.

Novell has not published a list of certified CD-ROM drives; however, the author's experience suggests that the best SCSI controller and CD-ROM drive combination is the Adaptec controller and NEC CD-ROM.

If you are using a SCSI CD-ROM for the installation, it is important to ensure that it is not on the same controller as your SYS: volume. Otherwise, when you get to steps 10 through 13 as listed previously, you can potentially hang the server due to conflict between the DOS CD-ROM driver and the NetWare disk driver. Although the installation process in NetWare 4.1 has been modified to take this into account, it is still a noteworthy caution.

Note

This conflict problem only exists during the installation phase. Afterwards, you can have both the CD-ROM drive and SYS: on the same SCSI controller.

The easiest way to circumvent this issue is to temporarily install a second SCSI controller for the CD-ROM drive during the installation phase.

BEGIN INSTALLATION

The installation batch file, INSTALL.BAT, can be found off the root directory on the CD. Select the first option, NetWare Server Installation, to start the installation process (see Figure 21.3).

Figure 21.3.
Select NetWare Server Installation to start the installation process.

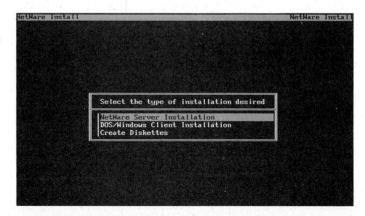

Note

Pay attention to the bottom of the menu as you proceed with the installation steps. The program alternates between ENTER and F10 for selection. Pressing ALT+F10 any time will exit the menu.

Should you have doubts about the prompts on the menu, press F1 to bring up a help screen, or consult DynaText.

If you have purchased an SFT III license, you can select the SFT III installation option instead. In this chapter, the "standard" NetWare 4.1 installation is shown. Select NetWare 4.1 to start the install process.

The next screen you will see offers the following three options:

◆ Simple installation of NetWare 4.1

◆ Custom installation of NetWare 4.1

◆ Upgrade NetWare 3.1*x* or 4.*x*

Simple installation assumes a number of defaults, such as code page and network number. If you want to have full control, select the Custom option. The following sections show the Custom installation steps.

ASSIGN SERVER NAME AND INTERNAL IPX NETWORK NUMBER

Each server must be assigned a unique server name (see Figure 21.4) and internal IPX network number (see Figure 21.5). A default internal IPX number is provided should you want to use it; however, it is best to assign your own numbering system, if you have one.

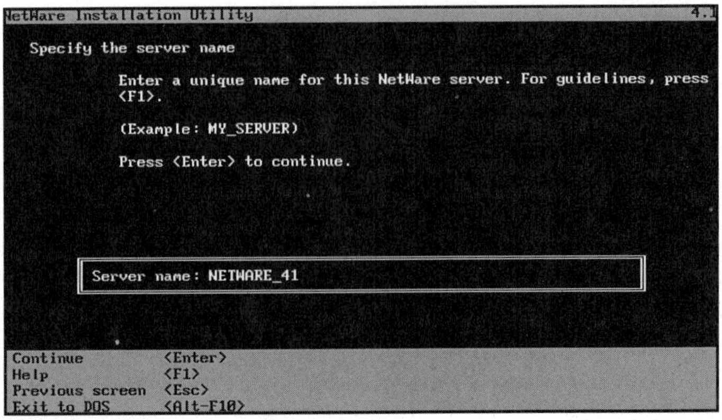

Figure 21.4.
Enter a unique server
name.

Figure 21.5.
Enter a unique internal
IPX network number.

```
NetWare Installation Utility                                        4.1
Assign an internal IPX number to the server

        A unique IPX internal network number is required. You may accept
        this default or modify it to create a number for your server. For
        guidelines, press <F1>.

        (Example: AEFD2498)

        Press <Enter> to continue.


             ┌──────────────────────────────────────────┐
             │     Internal network number:  F410        │
             └──────────────────────────────────────────┘




Continue              <Enter>
Help                  <F1>
Previous screen       <Esc>
Exit to DOS           <Alt-F10>
```

Tip

It is best to develop some naming and numbering conventions for your servers and IPX network addresses. For example, use a location code as part of your server name. This will help you to quickly locate a given server on your network.

COPY BOOT FILES TO DOS PARTITION

Next, you need to decide where on your DOS partition you want to have the server boot files be copied to. The default location is C:\NWSERVER (see Figure 21.6). You can change the destination directory by pressing F4. Once you have decided the destination path, server boot files are transferred from the CD to the DOS partition (see Figure 21.7).

Figure 21.6.
Select destination DOS
directory path for the
server boot files.

```
NetWare Installation Utility                                        4.1
Copy server boot files to the DOS partition

        The server boot files will be copied from the source directory to
        the destination directory.

        Press <Enter> to continue.




     ┌─────────────────────────────────────────────────────────────────┐
     │  Source path:   D:\NW410\INSTALL\ENGLISH                          │
     └─────────────────────────────────────────────────────────────────┘

     ┌─────────────────────────────────────────────────────────────────┐
     │  Destination path:  C:\NWSERVER                                   │
     └─────────────────────────────────────────────────────────────────┘
Continue                             <Enter>
Change current source path           <F2>
Change current destination path      <F4>
Help                                 <F1>
Previous screen                      <Esc>
Exit to DOS                          <Alt-F10>
```

Figure 21.7.
Server boot files copy
progress bar graph.

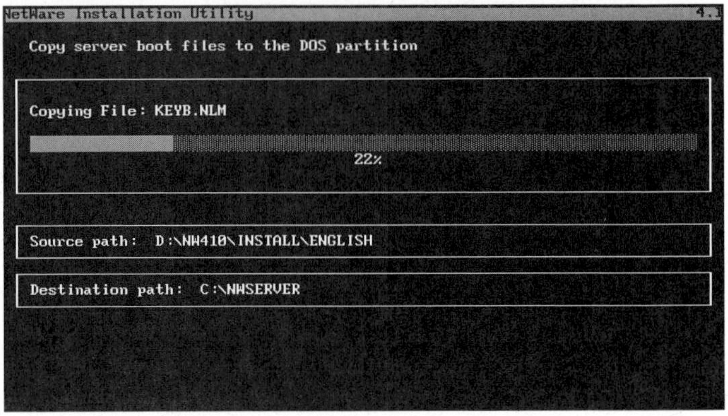

```
NetWare Installation Utility                                              4.1
Copy server boot files to the DOS partition

┌────────────────────────────────────────────────────────────────────────┐
│ Copying File: KEYB.NLM                                                   │
│ ████████████                                                             │
│                              22%                                         │
│                                                                          │
│ ┌──────────────────────────────────────────────────────────────────┐   │
│ │ Source path:   D:\NW410\INSTALL\ENGLISH                            │   │
│ └──────────────────────────────────────────────────────────────────┘   │
│ ┌──────────────────────────────────────────────────────────────────┐   │
│ │ Destination path:  C:\NWSERVER                                     │   │
│ └──────────────────────────────────────────────────────────────────┘   │
└────────────────────────────────────────────────────────────────────────┘
```

Shown in Figure 21.8 is a list of server boot files that were copied. They take up about 2MB of disk space.

Figure 21.8.
Server boot files.

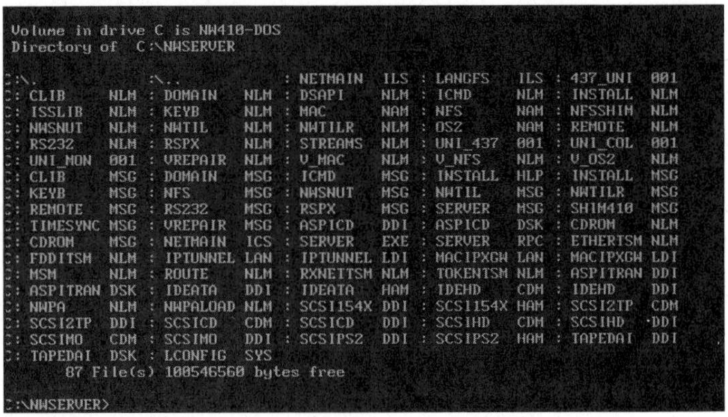

```
Volume in drive C is NW410-DOS
Directory of  C:\NWSERVER

C:\            C:\..           : NETMAIN  ILS : LANGFS   ILS : 437_UNI  001
C: CLIB    NLM : DOMAIN   NLM : DSAPI    NLM : ICMD     NLM : INSTALL  NLM
C: ISSLIB  NLM : KEYB     NLM : MAC      NAM : NFS      NAM : NFSSHIM  NLM
C: NWSNUT  NLM : NWTIL    NLM : NWTILR   NLM : OS2      NAM : REMOTE   NLM
C: RS232   NLM : RSPX     NLM : STREAMS  NLM : UNI_437  001 : UNI_COL  001
C: UNI_MON 001 : VREPAIR  NLM : V_MAC    NLM : V_NFS    NLM : V_OS2    NLM
C: CLIB    MSG : DOMAIN   MSG : ICMD     MSG : INSTALL  HLP : INSTALL  MSG
C: KEYB    MSG : NFS      MSG : NWSNUT   MSG : NWTIL    MSG : NWTILR   MSG
C: REMOTE  MSG : RS232    MSG : RSPX     MSG : SERVER   MSG : SHIM410  MSG
C: TIMESYNC MSG : VREPAIR MSG : ASPICD   DDI : ASPICD   DSK : CDROM    NLM
C: CDROM   MSG : NETMAIN  ICS : SERVER   EXE : SERVER   RPC : ETHERTSM NLM
C: FDDITSM NLM : IPTUNNEL LAN : IPTUNNEL LDI : MACIPXGW LAN : MACIPXGW LDI
C: MSM     NLM : ROUTE    NLM : RXNETTSM NLM : TOKENTSM NLM : ASPITRAN DDI
C: ASPITRAN DSK : IDEATA  DDI : IDEATA   HAM : IDEHD    CDM : IDEHD    DDI
C: NWPA    NLM : NWPALOAD NLM : SCSI154X DDI : SCSI154X HAM : SCSI2TP  CDM
C: SCSI2TP DDI : SCSICD   CDM : SCSICD   DDI : SCSIHD   CDM : SCSIHD   DDI
C: SCSIMO  CDM : SCSIMO   DDI : SCSIPS2  DDI : SCSIPS2  HAM : TAPEDAI  DDI
C: TAPEDAI DSK : LCONFIG  SYS
        87 File(s) 100546560 bytes free

C:\NWSERVER>
```

Configure Country Code, Code Page, and Keyboard Mapping

Depending on whether you want foreign language and keyboard mapping support, you can specify the country code, code page, and keyboard mapping to be used for your server. Figures 21.9, 21.10, and 21.11 show these steps.

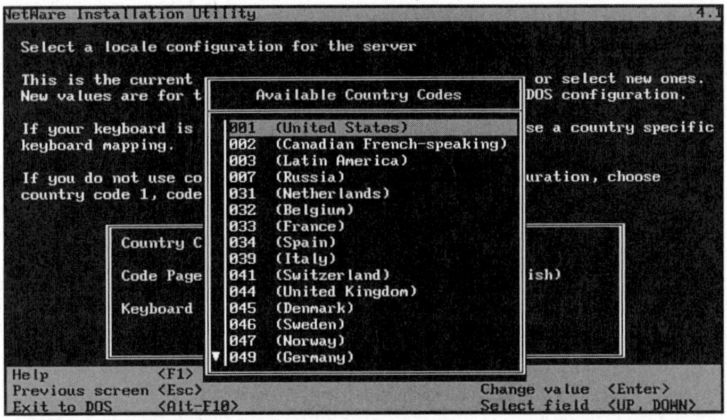

Figure 21.9.
Country code selection.

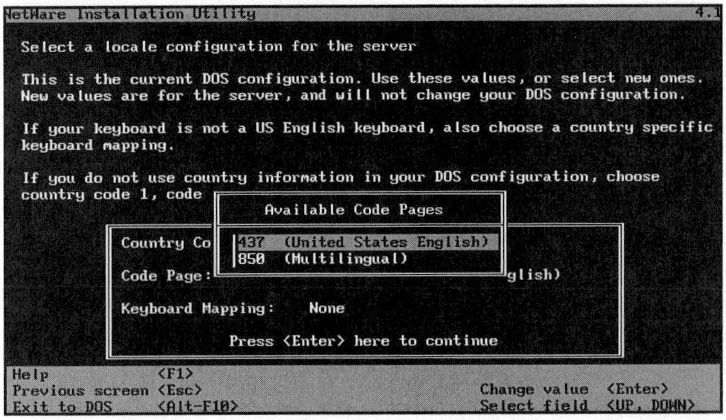

Figure 21.10.
Code page selection.

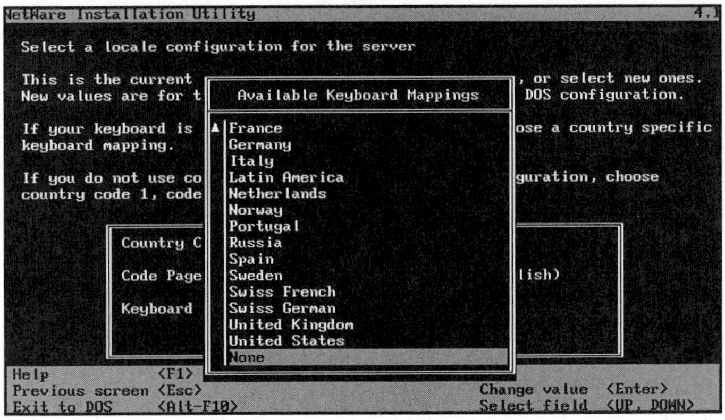

Figure 21.11.
Keyboard mapping selection.

SELECT FILENAME FORMAT FOR FILE SYSTEM

You need to tell NetWare which filename format to use when storing files on the NetWare volumes (see Figure 21.12). Choose DOS Filename Format.

Figure 21.12.
Filename format
selection.

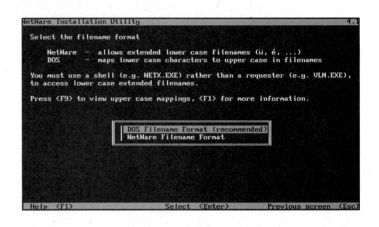

Note

Use the DOS Filename Format unless you have a compelling reason not to. This allows compatibility with DOS and future versions of NetWare.

SPECIFY *SET* COMMANDS FOR **STARTUP.NCF**

If you have an EISA or MCA type machine and have more than 16MB of RAM installed, and you have network card or disk drivers that cannot address more than 16MB of RAM, this is the time to inform the operating system you want "special handling" (see Figure 21.13). Include in your STARTUP.NCF file the following command:

```
SET AUTO REGISTER MEMORY ABOVE 16 MEGABYTES=OFF
```

and you manually register the extra memory using your AUTOEXEC.NCF file later.

Warning

If you fail to perform the preceding step of non-registering the memory, and if you have drivers incapable of addressing memory above 16MB, you can crash the server.

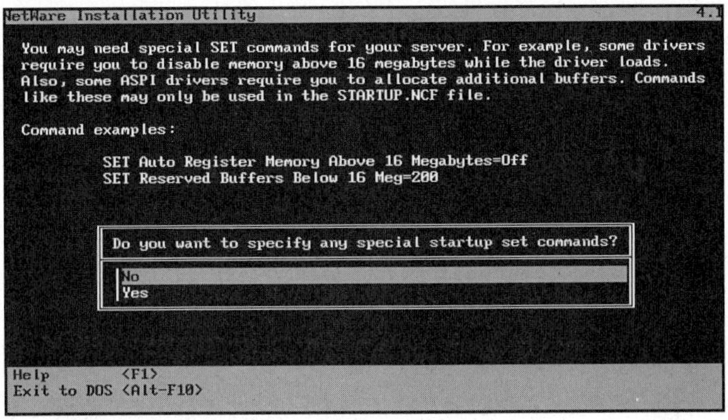

Figure 21.13.
Specify SET commands
in STARTUP.NCF.

```
NetWare Installation Utility                                              4.1
  You may need special SET commands for your server. For example, some drivers
  require you to disable memory above 16 megabytes while the driver loads.
  Also, some ASPI drivers require you to allocate additional buffers. Commands
  like these may only be used in the STARTUP.NCF file.

  Command examples:

        SET Auto Register Memory Above 16 Megabytes=Off
        SET Reserved Buffers Below 16 Meg=200


      ┌──────────────────────────────────────────────────────────────┐
      │ Do you want to specify any special startup set commands?       │
      │┌─────────────────────────────────────────────────────────────┐│
      ││No                                                             ││
      ││Yes                                                            ││
      │└─────────────────────────────────────────────────────────────┘│


  Help         <F1>
  Exit to DOS  <Alt-F10>
```

MODIFY AUTOEXEC.BAT

You should then allow your AUTOEXEC.BAT file to be modified so SERVER.EXE
will be started every time you boot up the machine (see Figure 21.14).

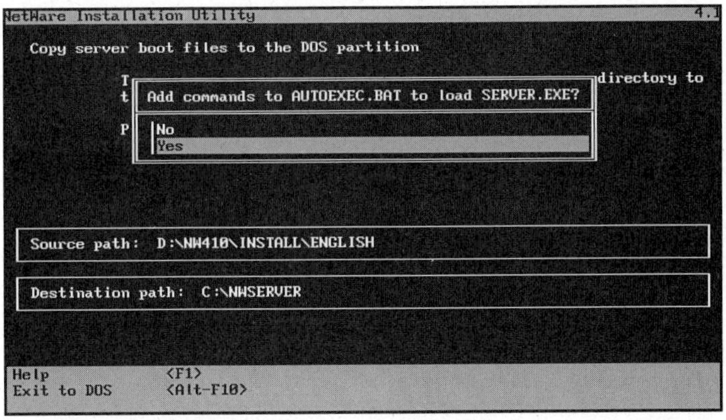

Figure 21.14.
Modify
AUTOEXEC.BAT file.

```
NetWare Installation Utility                                              4.1
    Copy server boot files to the DOS partition
        ┌─────────────────────────────────────────────┐ directory to
    t   │ Add commands to AUTOEXEC.BAT to load SERVER.EXE? │
        │┌──────────────────────────────────────────────┐│
    P   ││No                                             ││
        ││Yes                                            ││
        │└──────────────────────────────────────────────┘│



      ┌────────────────────────────────────────────────────────────┐
      │ Source path:  D:\NW410\INSTALL\ENGLISH                      │
      └────────────────────────────────────────────────────────────┘

      ┌────────────────────────────────────────────────────────────┐
      │ Destination path:  C:\NWSERVER                              │
      └────────────────────────────────────────────────────────────┘

  Help         <F1>
  Exit to DOS  <Alt-F10>
```

Figure 21.15 shows a sample AUTOEXEC.BAT after modification.

Figure 21.15.
Sample server
AUTOEXEC.BAT file.

```
C:\>type autoexec.bat
@ECHO Off
PROMPT $P$G

:BEGIN_SERVER
C:
cd C:\NWSERVER
SERVER
:END_SERVER

C:\>
```

SERVER.EXE is then executed so you can proceed to the next phase of the installation.

LOAD AND CONFIGURE DISK AND LAN DRIVER(S)

A `please wait` message is displayed while disk drivers are being searched for. From the displayed list of drivers, select the most appropriate driver for your hard disk controller (see Figure 21.16). You then need to specify the hardware settings used by the controller (see Figure 21.17).

Figure 21.16.
Available disk drivers.

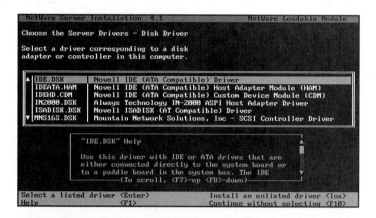

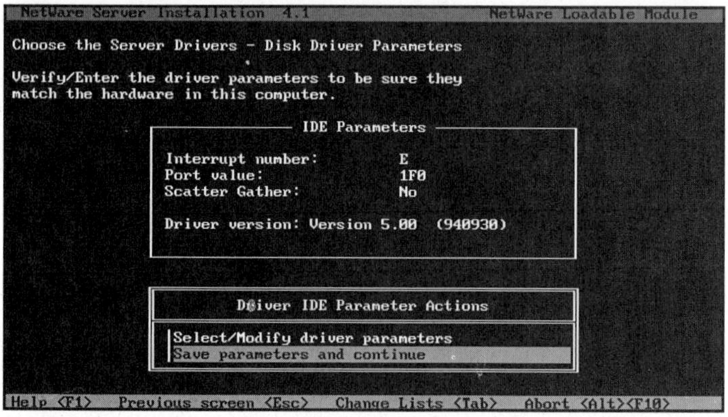

Figure 21.17.
Configure the disk driver.

Tip

If you are using IDE drives, select the IDE.DSK driver. There are some rare instances that the ISADISK.DSK works better than the IDE.DSK driver. Try it only if you experience problems with IDE.DSK.

If you have multiple IDE controllers, you can load the IDE.DSK driver re-entrantly. If you have a different controller, you can load a different disk driver (see Figure 21.18).

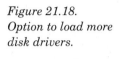

Figure 21.18.
Option to load more
disk drivers.

```
NetWare Server Installation  4.1                    NetWare Loadable Module

Choose the Server Drivers - Disk Driver

Select a driver corresponding to a disk
adapter or controller in this computer.

  ▲ IDE.DSK        Novell IDE (ATA Compatible) Driver
    IDEATA.HAM     Novell IDE (ATA Compatible) Host Adapter Module (HAM)
    IDEHD.CDM                                                    (CDM)
    IN2000.DSK   Do you want to select an additional Disk driver?  er
    ISADISK.DS
  ▼ MNS16S.DSK    No                                              r Driver
                  Yes

                 "IDE.DSK" Help                                   ▲
                 Use this driver with IDE or ATA drives that are
                 either connected directly to the system board or
                 to a paddle board in the system bus. The IDE    ▼
                           (To scroll, <F7>-up <F8>-down)

Select a listed driver <Enter>              Install an unlisted driver <Ins>
Help                    <F1>                 Continue without selecting <F10>
```

When you are done with selecting the disk drivers, you are presented with a summary screen. At this point, you can go back and select more disks (or LAN driver) or continue with the installation. Select and configure the LAN driver using the similar steps as outlined for the disk drivers, discussed previously.

Warning

It is important to note the frame type(s) you have chosen. When you configure the workstation software, you need to specify the same frame type else it will not communicate with the server.

For each frame type, the INSTALL program will check the segment to see whether an IPX network address is already out there. If it finds one, it will automatically be bound to the frame type. Otherwise, a random network address will be generated. As discussed earlier with the internal IPX network number, you should use your own numbering system for good documentation and easy troubleshooting.

Note

At this point, if you have a SCSI CD-ROM, you can allow the install to mount the CD-ROM as a NetWare volume, which can speed up the install. If it turns out there is a driver conflict, however, you will lock up the server.

SET UP NETWARE PARTITION AND VOLUMES

There are two ways in which you can create the NetWare partition: automatically or manually (see Figure 21.19). If you choose Automatically, the NetWare partition will use all available free disk space, and all free space is assigned to SYS: volume. (see Figure 21.20). If you have more than one hard drive, each drive will have its own volume.

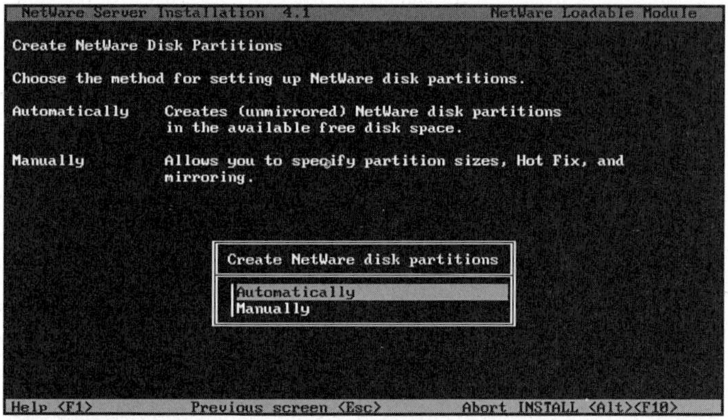

Figure 21.19.
Options to create
NetWare partition.

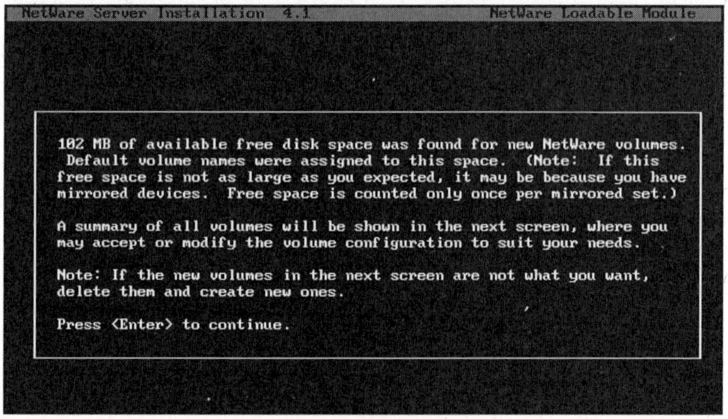

Figure 21.20.
Select automatic disk
partitioning.

If you choose Manually, you can modify your partition table (see Figure 21.21). When you choose Create NetWare disk partition, you can specify the size of the partition and size of redirection area (Hot Fix) (see Figure 21.22). If you previously installed NetWare 3.*x*, you will find this familiar.

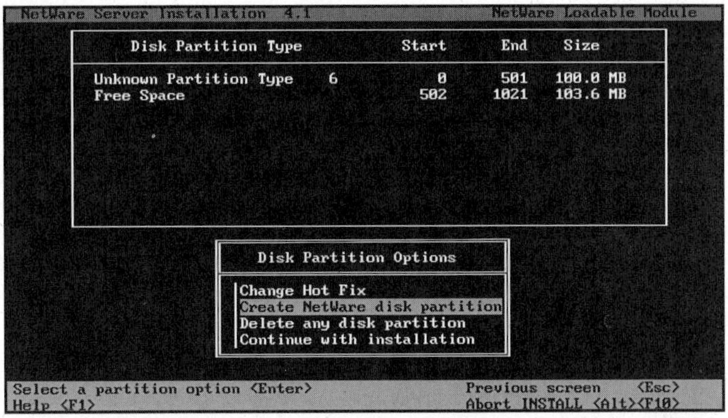

Figure 21.21.
Select manual disk
partitioning.

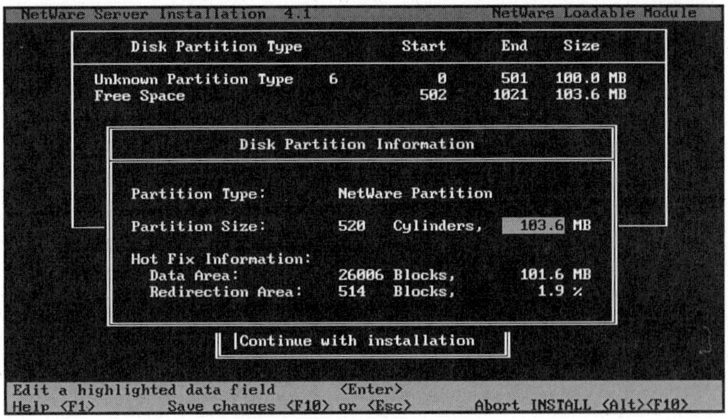

Figure 21.22.
Options for creating
NetWare partition.

The way the installation goes, all free space on the first hard drive is assigned to volume SYS:. Each hard drive will have its own volume. Should you want to have multiple volumes on the drives, delete the volume, re-create it with a smaller size, and then add the new volumes (see Figures 21.23 and 21.24).

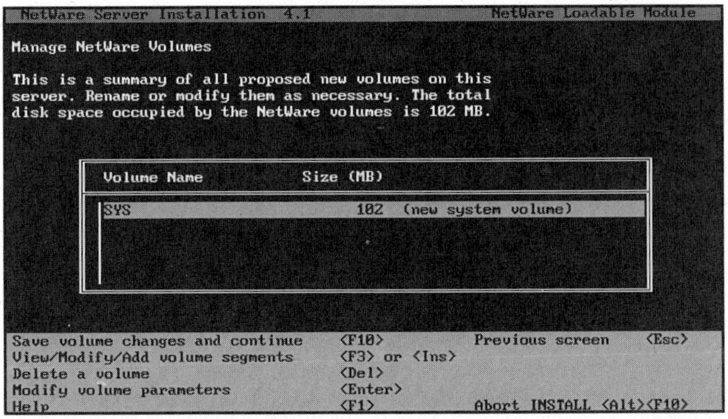

Figure 21.23.
Menu to manage
NetWare volumes.

Figure 21.24.
SYS: and DATA:
volumes defined.

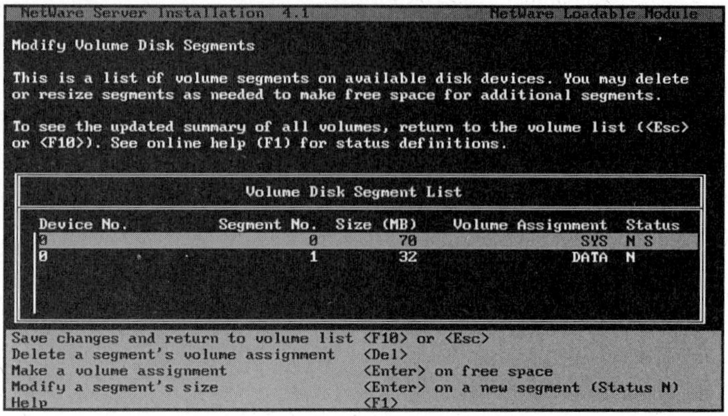

```
NetWare Server Installation  4.1                NetWare Loadable Module
Modify Volume Disk Segments

This is a list of volume segments on available disk devices. You may delete
or resize segments as needed to make free space for additional segments.

To see the updated summary of all volumes, return to the volume list (<Esc>
or <F10>). See online help (F1) for status definitions.

        ┌──────────────────────────────────────────────────────────────┐
        │              Volume Disk Segment List                        │
        │                                                              │
        │ Device No.        Segment No.  Size (MB)  Volume Assignment  Status│
        │ 0                     0           70            SYS  N S     │
        │ 0                     1           32            DATA N       │
        │                                                              │
        │                                                              │
        └──────────────────────────────────────────────────────────────┘
Save changes and return to volume list <F10> or <Esc>
Delete a segment's volume assignment   <Del>
Make a volume assignment               <Enter> on free space
Modify a segment's size                <Enter> on a new segment (Status N)
Help                                   <F1>
```

Before the volumes are actually created, you can highlight and select each volume
to change the settings for volume block size, file compression flag, block suballocation
flag, and data migration flag (see Figure 21.25).

Figure 21.25.
Volume options.

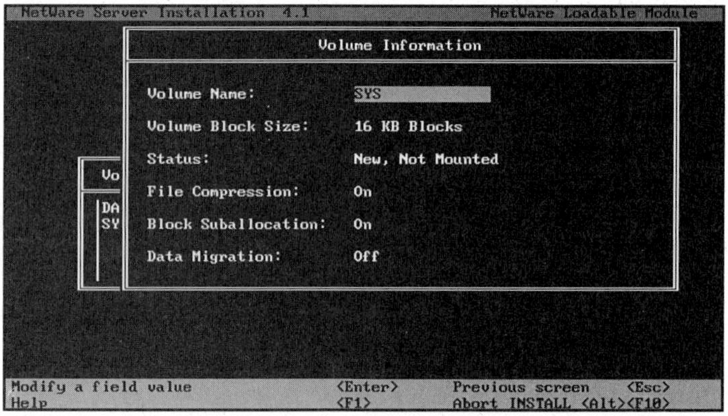

```
NetWare Server Installation  4.1                NetWare Loadable Module
              ┌──────────────────────────────────────────────┐
              │              Volume Information               │
              │                                               │
              │   Volume Name:          SYS                   │
              │                                               │
              │   Volume Block Size:    16 KB Blocks          │
      ┌──┐    │                                               │
      │Vo│    │   Status:               New, Not Mounted      │
      │  │    │                                               │
      │DA│    │   File Compression:     On                    │
      │SY│    │                                               │
      │  │    │   Block Suballocation:  On                    │
      │  │    │                                               │
      │  │    │   Data Migration:       Off                   │
              │                                               │
              └──────────────────────────────────────────────┘
Modify a field value            <Enter>      Previous screen       <Esc>
Help                            <F1>         Abort INSTALL <Alt><F10>
```

Warning

Note that once volume size, file compression flag, and block
suballocation flag are set, they cannot be changed unless you re-
create the volume.

Data migration flag may be toggled at any time.

INSTALL LICENSE DISK

After setting up NetWare volumes, you are asked to insert the license disk (see
Figure 21.26).

Figure 21.26.
Install license diskette.

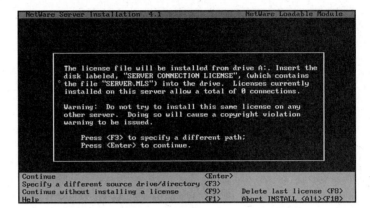

Unlike NetWare 2.*x* and 3.*x*, licensing information for NetWare 4.1 comes on a "license diskette." This diskette contains information about the serial number as well as number-of-connections.

Warning

Make sure you keep track of which license diskette was installed on which server. Mixing licenses on the same internet may cause your server licenses to be deactivated, reverting your servers (ones with duplicated licenses) back to Runtime.

If you provide an invalid license diskette, you will receive a Not Valid message, and the server will become a Runtime (one-user).

Tip

NetWare 4.1 has what is called the "additive" licensing feature. You can install as many licenses as you want onto a single server, and their license counts will be added, one on top of another. For example, if you have installed a 50-user license, you can later install a 100-user one and have a total of 150 user connections.

Following the successful installation of the license diskette, you are now ready to copy NetWare files to the SYS: volume.

COPY NETWARE FILES TO *SYS:* VOLUME

You need to copy certain operating system related files to the SYSTEM, PUBLIC, LOGIN, and ETC directories on the SYS: volume. You can specify the source of these files if they are not on the default path (see Figure 21.27). You also can select which file groups (or sets of files) to copy to conserve disk space (see Figure 21.28).

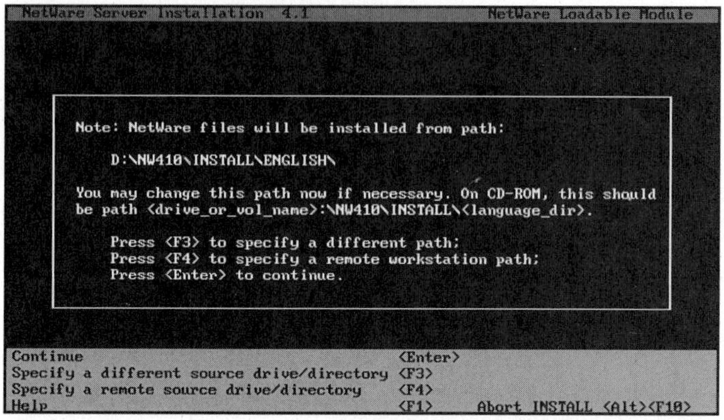

Figure 21.27.
Confirm source path
and directory for files.

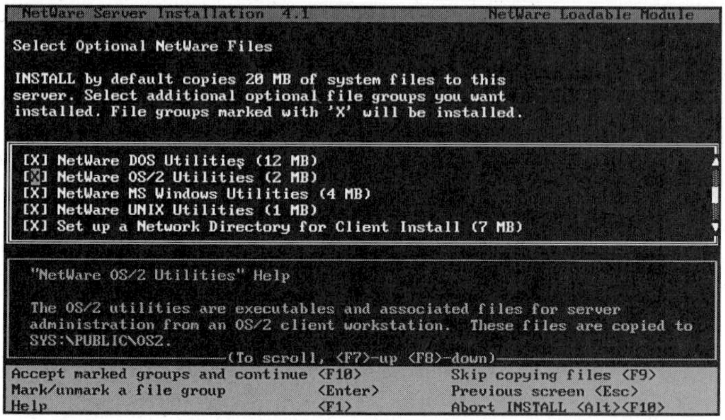

Figure 21.28.
Select file groups to be
copied.

To select or deselect a file group for copying, simply highlight the entry and press Enter. When you are done, press F10 to start copying. A File Copy Status bar graph will appear onscreen (see Figure 21.29).

The copying is done in two steps. The first step copies only selected files, and the bulk of the copying is done after the AUTOEXEC.NCF file is created. Depending on the number of file groups, speed of your CD-ROM, speed of your hard drive, and amount of RAM for file caching, the file copying process will take from about 30 minutes to about an hour or more.

Figure 21.29.
File Copy Status bar
graph.

```
NetWare Server Installation 4.1                 NetWare Loadable Module

                    File Copy Status (Preliminary Copy)

    ┌──────────────┐
    │              │
    └──────────────┘
                              20%

    File group: Pre-Install Files
    Source path: D:\NW410\SYSTEM\PREINST
    Destination path: SYS:\SYSTEM

    ┌────────────────────────────────────────────────────────┐
    │ ->Copying file "CLIB.NLM".                               │
    │ ->Copying file "CONVINET.NLM".                           │
    │ ->Copying file "CSLCNVRT.NLM".                           │
    │ ->Copying file "CSLSTUB.NLM".                            │
    │ ->Copying file "DS.NLM".                                 │
    │ ->Copying file "DSAPI.NLM".                              │
    │ ->Copying file "DSI.NLM".                                │
    └────────────────────────────────────────────────────────┘
```

INSTALL NDS TREE

INSTALL will automatically search for any NDS trees that may exist on your network. If no tree is readily found, you have the option to search again or create a new tree (see Figures 21.30 and 21.31).

Figure 21.30.
Option to attach to
existing Tree or create a
new tree.

```
NetWare Server Installation 4.1                 NetWare Loadable Module

Install NetWare Directory Services (NDS)

No other NetWare 4 servers are accessible on any networks visible to this
server. Either this is the first NetWare 4 server, or there is a network
problem that prevents this server from seeing other NetWare 4 servers.

            ┌──────────────────────────────────────────────┐
            │      Is this the first NetWare 4 server?       │
            ├──────────────────────────────────────────────┤
            │ Yes, this is the first NetWare 4 server         │
            │ No, connect to existing NetWare 4 network       │
            └──────────────────────────────────────────────┘

Help <F1>          Previous screen <Esc>      Abort INSTALL <Alt><F10>
```

Figure 21.31.
Option to search for
Tree again.

```
NetWare Server Installation 4.1                 NetWare Loadable Module

Connect to NetWare 4 Network

Recheck    - After verifying that:
                - An existing NetWare 4 server is up and physically
                  connected to this server.
                - Both are bound to IPX with the proper LAN driver,
                  frame type, network number (<F1> for Help).
             Note: You may need to wait 2 minutes before rechecking.

Specify    - If your network has SAP filtering and you know the IPX
Name and     internal network number of an existing NetWare 4 server.
Number       Note: This may not work if your network has RIP filtering.

            ┌──────────────────────────────────────────────┐
            │           Select NetWare 4 Network             │
            ├──────────────────────────────────────────────┤
            │ Recheck for NetWare 4 network                   │
            │ Specify NetWare 4 server network name and number│
            └──────────────────────────────────────────────┘

Help <F1>          Previous screen <Esc>
```

Warning

While it is possible to have multiple trees on the same physical network, it is not possible for the trees to communicate with each other. Therefore, objects (users, for example) in one tree will not see objects (a server, for example) in another tree.

By selecting Yes to the This the first NetWare 4 server? prompt, you create a new NDS tree. You will need to provide a tree name (see Figure 21.32).

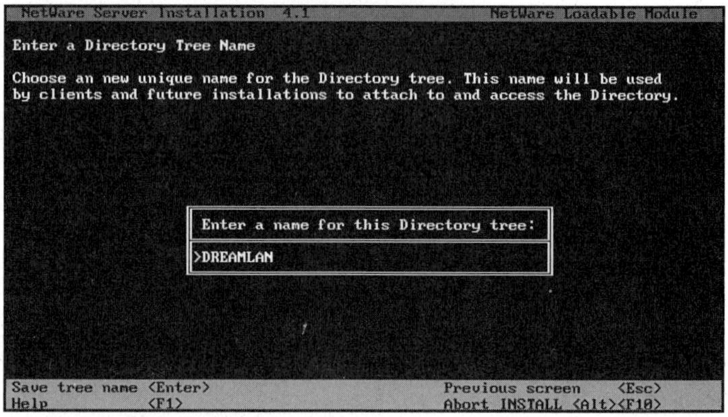

Figure 21.32.
Enter a new NDS tree name.

```
NetWare Server Installation  4.1                    NetWare Loadable Module
Enter a Directory Tree Name

Choose an new unique name for the Directory tree. This name will be used
by clients and future installations to attach to and access the Directory.




                         ┌─────────────────────────────────────┐
                         │ Enter a name for this Directory tree: │
                         │ >DREAMLAN                             │
                         └─────────────────────────────────────┘




Save tree name <Enter>                        Previous screen    <Esc>
Help          <F1>                            Abort INSTALL <Alt><F10>
```

If this is not the first server within your NDS tree, but you want to add this server to an existing tree, select the listed tree name. Make sure you select the correct tree name. Other than this one step, the rest of the installation steps are identical as described in this chapter.

SET TIME ZONE INFORMATION

You need to correctly identify the time zone in which this particular server resides in (Figure 21.33) and any daylight savings time deviations (Figure 21.34). The network time is computed based on these entries.

The daylight savings time information will also save you the trouble of having to reset the server clocks twice a year.

It is important the time server type is set correctly. See Chapter 14 for more details. The default time server for the first server in the tree is Single Reference; subsequent time servers default to Secondary.

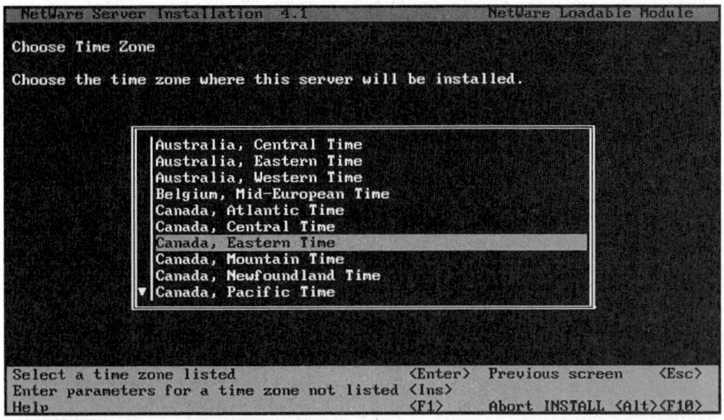

Figure 21.33.
Enter time zone
information.

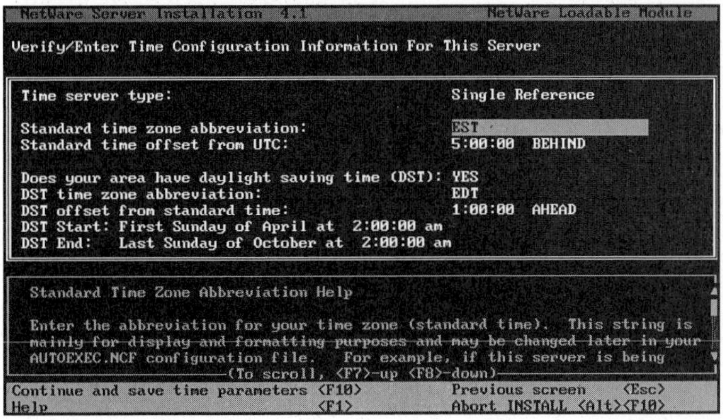

Figure 21.34.
Specify time server type
and daylight savings
information.

You then need to specify the context into which this server is to be located within the
NDS tree (see Figure 21.35). It is here that you specify the password for the Admin
user.

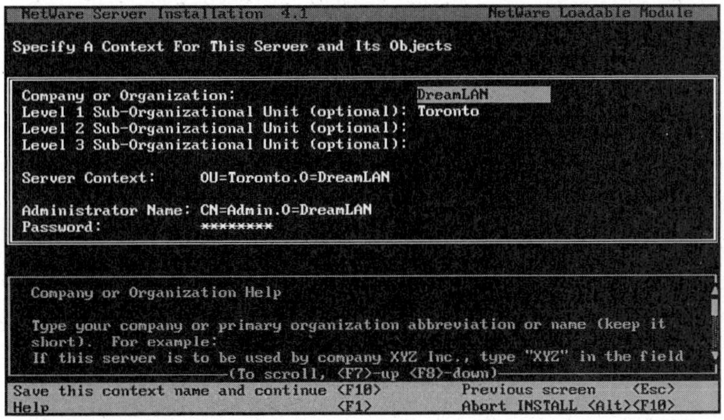

Figure 21.35.
Specify the NDS context
for the server.

Warning

When entering the Admin password, make sure no special characters, such as ! or :, are used. You may experience problems when logging in as Admin using this password.

NDS is then installed and you are informed of the results (see Figure 21.36).

Figure 21.36.
Summary of NDS
installation.

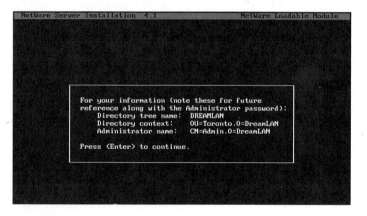

CREATE STARTUP.NCF

After the NDS is installed, you need to create the STARTUP.NCF file. The disk driver information is filled in automatically (see Figure 21.37). Any additional SET and LOAD commands must be entered manually.

Figure 21.37.
Create STARTUP.NCF
file.

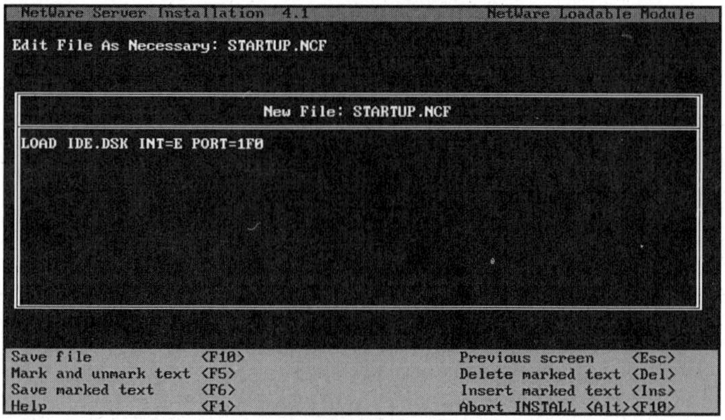

CREATE AUTOEXEC.NCF

The AUTOEXEC.NCF file will be created next (see Figure 21.38). The necessary time zone and LAN driver information are included automatically. Any additional LOAD and SET commands, such as LOAD MONITOR, must be entered manually.

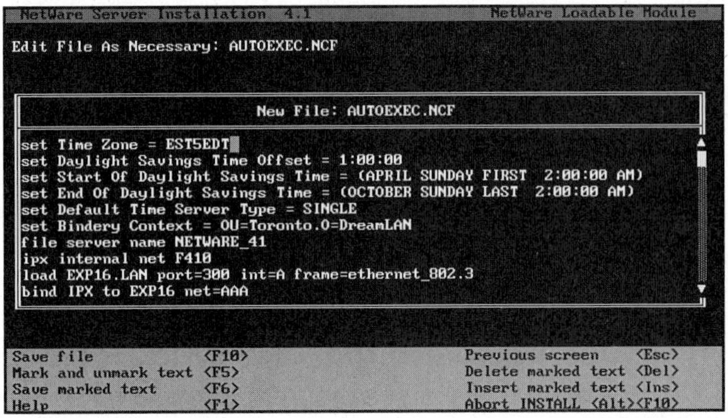

Figure 21.38.
Create
AUTOEXEC.NCF file.

After this point, the rest of the system files are copied (see Figure 21.39).

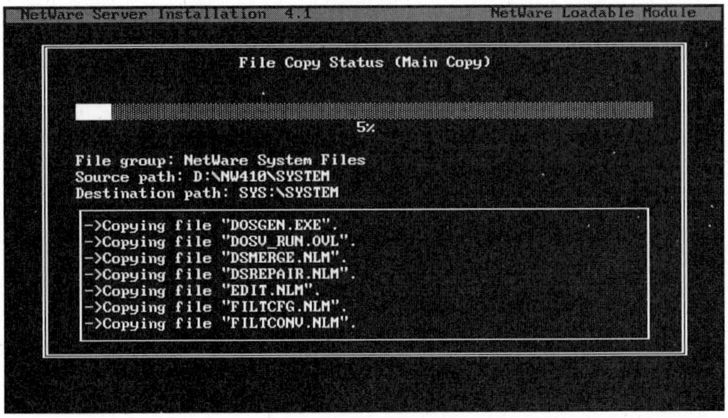

Figure 21.39.
Copy the remaining
system files.

INSTALL OPTIONAL PROGRAMS AND FILES

The next installation screen, shown in Figure 21.40, allows you to perform a number of functions, such as the following:

◆ Create registration diskette

◆ Create client software installation disks

◆ Install MHS Services

Figure 21.40.
Other installation
options.

The NetWare 4.1 package provides a preformatted Registration diskette. Register your software so that you will be mailed any free updates you are entitled to, as well as be put on a mailing list for new updates and information.

The final screen in the installation process (as shown in Figure 21.41) confirms the completion of your installation. You should reboot the server to make sure all the settings made to STARTUP.NCF and AUTOEXEC.NCF are correct.

Figure 21.41.
Installation complete.

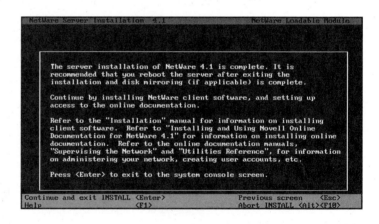

POSSIBLE PROBLEMS AND SOLUTIONS

Listed in this section are some common problems that you may come across during your server software installation. Some solutions and work-arounds are presented. The list is by no means exhaustive. It is assumed here that you have resolved any possible hardware conflicts.

DISK DRIVER PROBLEM

There are some instances that the ISADISK.DSK driver needs to be used instead of IDE.DSK for "IDE" drives.

HARD DISK PROBLEM

Because different manufacturers have different ways of accessing drives, especially large capacity drives, it is best not to mix hard drives from different manufacturers on the same controller.

LAN DRIVER PROBLEM

Very often, LAN drivers for v3.11 servers do not work well in the NetWare 4.1 environment. Check with your vendor for the latest NetWare 4.*x* compatible driver. Under rare conditions, however, a v3.*x* .LAN driver works better than does a v4.*x* version.

ETHERNET FRAME FORMAT PROBLEM

Due to the change in the default frame format of LAN Ethernet drivers, your v4.1 server may not "see" other v3.*x* and v2.*x* servers. Make sure that you are using the same frame format among all the servers using the CONFIG console command.

INSUFFICIENT RAM

Novell recommends 8MB of RAM for a NetWare 4.1 server. However, it is found that a *minimum* of 12MB is required, and if you are going to load CDROM.NLM, for example, 16MB is a good *starting* point. There are known instances where a server abends due to insufficient RAM.

INCOMPATIBLE NLMS

Not all v3.*x* NLMs will run (correctly) on a v4.1 server. Check with your vendor to see whether a v4.*x* version is available. Unfortunately, at the time of this writing, there was no Novell-published document on certified NLMs for v4.*x* platform. At best, the NLM will not load. At worst, it will abend your server.

SUMMARY

A step-by-step installation procedure for a NetWare 4.1 server was presented in this chapter. Also presented were some troubleshooting hints for possible server-related installation problems.

- Methods of Upgrade

- Upgrading NetWare
  4.*x*

- Summary

CHAPTER 22

Upgrading an Existing Server

This chapter discusses the various methods in which you can upgrade a server from an earlier version of NetWare to NetWare 4.*x*. Also discussed are the merits of the different methods, as well as the detailed steps involved.

The upgrade utility from Novell can perform the following types of upgrade:

◆ NetWare 2.*x* to NetWare 4.*x*

◆ NetWare 2.*x* to NetWare 3.12

◆ NetWare 3.1*x* to NetWare 3.1*x*

◆ NetWare 3.1*x* to NetWare 4.*x*

◆ Another network operating system to NetWare 4.*x*

Note

The version of the migration utility (MIGRATE v4.00b) shipped with NetWare 4.01 supports other network operating systems, such as IBM LAN Server v1.0-v1.3 and IBM PCLP v1.3 Extended Services. The latest version of MIGRATE available from Novell also supports Microsoft LAN Manager v2.0. You can download this copy (v4.01e) from the NetWire forum on CompuServe. MIGRATE v4.12, which also supports MS LAN Manager v2.0, is shipped with NetWare 4.1.

This chapter concentrates on the NetWare upgrade paths from NetWare 2.*x* and 3.1*x* to NetWare 4.*x*. However, there is no reason why you cannot use the MIGRATE program for other versions of NetWare upgrade (such as NetWare 2.*x* to NetWare 3.12, or NetWare 3.*x* to NetWare 3.1*x*). You can use the steps outlined in this chapter to upgrade to any version of NetWare 4; therefore, the generic reference of NetWare 4.*x* is used.

METHODS OF UPGRADE

Following are the three ways to perform the upgrade:

◆ **Across-the-wire**: Use MIGRATE to move data from the old server to a new server. Can be used to perform NetWare 2.*x* and 3.1*x* to 4.*x* migration.

◆ **Same-server**: Use MIGRATE to move data offline, upgrade the server operating system/hardware, and then use MIGRATE to move the data back to the same server. Can be used to perform NetWare 2.*x* and 3.1*x* to 4.*x* migration.

◆ **In-place**: Without moving the data, 2XUPGRDE.NLM and INSTALL.NLM are used to perform the operating system upgrade on the same server. Can be used to perform NetWare 2.*x* to 3.12, then 3.1*x* to 4.*x* migration.

The migration program makes use of bindery emulation on a NetWare 4 server. This means that all bindery information transferred is located in the container to which the destination NetWare 4 server's bindery emulation context points. You can manually move the user objects to their final destination at a later time.

Tip

> If you use the across-the-wire and same-server migration methods, you have the option of creating the volumes with a large volume block size because you will be creating the volumes. At the same time, you can enable suballocation. This, however, is not possible if you use the in-place migration method.

On the NetWare 4.1 CD, you will find the necessary files needed for running MIGRATE in the MIGRATE directory off the root; on the NetWare 4.0x CDs, MIGRATE can be found under the \CLIENT_____\MIGRATE directory. You also can obtain the latest version from CompuServe, NSEPro, or Internet FTP sites.

Note

> The necessary files (including a NetWare 3.12 Runtime license) for performing the in-place migration comes on the NetWare 4.1 CD. The files, however, are stored in an image file format. You need to create an update diskette using the INSTALL.BAT file. From the opening menu, select Create Diskettes, and then select 3.5 inch Server Upgrade (1 Diskette).

The following sections discuss the pros and cons of the three upgrade methods. Detailed steps for each migration method are given.

Note

> The migration steps given are based on MIGRATE v4.01e, which functions in the same manner as v4.12 shipped with NetWare 4.1.

Across-the-Wire

In an *across-the-wire* migration, data files are directly moved across the network from the original server to a new server (see Figure 22.1). The bindery information is first moved to the working directory on the workstation that is running the MIGRATE utility, translated to the NetWare 4 format, and then migrated to the destination server. The users created in this manner are NDS objects.

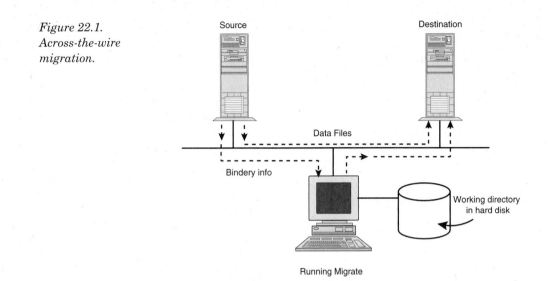

Figure 22.1.
Across-the-wire
migration.

The across-the-wire migration method enables you to preserve the original server environment (both users' information, such as trustee rights, and server configuration). This means there is no risk of data loss should something happen (such as a power outage) during the migration process. You also can choose to migrate multiple source servers to the same destination server. This is useful if you are combining a number of smaller servers into a larger, more powerful server.

The disadvantage of using the across-the-wire migration method is that you need to already have a NetWare 4.*x* server installed. This also means double hardware— your original server plus the new destination server.

This across-the-wire method, however, is the preferred method of upgrade because of the insurance it provides. Also, this is the only option available if you need to upgrade from a different operating system other than NetWare.

Following are a number of prerequisite tasks you need to perform before starting the across-the-wire migration:

◆ On the NetWare 4.*x* server, you need to have created the volumes you want to migrate data to. You cannot create volumes using the migration utility.

◆ Back up the source server. Although this is not necessary, it nevertheless is a good precaution.

◆ Make sure that all users are logged out of both the source and destination servers. Ensure all data files are closed.

◆ If you are logged in to a NetWare 4.*x* server in the NDS mode, log out and re-login using bindery mode. You cannot use the migration utility to log in to a NetWare 4.*x* server.

Note

Make sure you are logged into the NetWare 4.*x* server under bindery emulation before running MIGRATE.

◆ Remove any files that you do not want to migrate, such as .BAK files. This will help to reduce the amount of time required for the migration.

◆ If you are upgrading from NetWare 2.*x* to NetWare 4, make sure you have replacement NLMs for any of the VAPs (Value Added Processes) you are using.

◆ Rename DOS files and directories that have long names. NetWare 2.15 or earlier allows you to create files and directories with 14-character names. This is incompatible with NetWare 4.

◆ Files other than PRINTCON.DAT, LOGIN (DOS user login script) , and LOGIN.OS2 (OS/2 user login script) are not migrated from the SYS:MAIL directories. If you have other files in the SYS:MAIL directories, you need to move them manually. DOS and OS/2 user login scripts are combined in NetWare 4.

◆ Make sure you have sufficient volume space on the destination server. This especially is true if you plan to migrate multiple servers to a single NetWare 4.*x* server.

◆ Run BINDFIX on the source server. This helps to ensure the integrity of the bindery files, as well as to delete mail directories and trustee rights of all users who no longer exist on the source server.

◆ Ensure that the workstation to be used to run MIGRATE has at least 5MB of free disk space to hold the bindery information temporarily.

◆ Ensure the same workstation can login to both the source and destination servers.

◆ Make sure that you do not have objects that have the same name but are of different object types; for example, a user object and a print server object with the same name. Otherwise, you will have objects with names such as *name*+bindery type=1.

Tip

To aid sites in preparing upgrades from NetWare 2.*x* and 3.1*x* to NetWare 4.*x*, Novell's Systems Research Department released a set of unsupported utilities called PRINTUSR (gives listing of users in bindery), PRINTGRP (gives listing of groups in bindery), and DUPBIND (lists objects with the same name but of different object types). For more information about these utilities, consult the April 1993 issue of *NetWare Application Note*. These files can be found on CompuServe's NetWire area—NOVLIB forum—in a file called AN304X.ZIP. This file is also available on the NSEPro and on Novell's Internet FTP sites.

To start, copy the migration utility files from the CD to the workstation that you will be using. Execute MIGRATE.EXE. From the main menu, select Across-The-Wire migration (see Figure 22.2). Then select the source LAN type (see Figure 22.3).

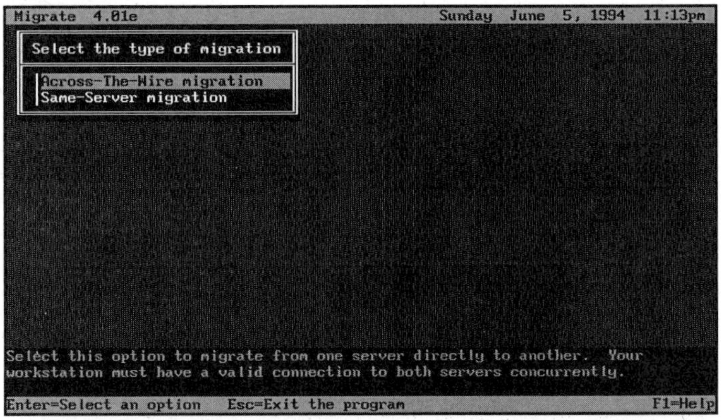

Figure 22.2.
Select the Across-The-Wire migration option from the main menu of MIGRATE.EXE.

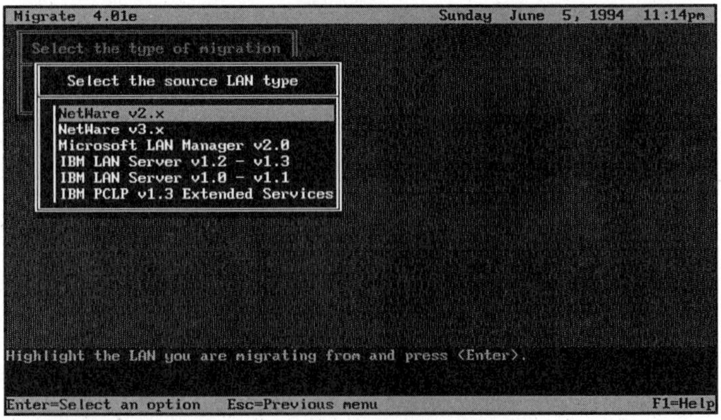

Figure 22.3.
Menu to select the source LAN type.

Tip

Any time you are unsure of a selection, press the F1 key to display context-sensitive help.

Quick Help is available at the bottom of the screen for each selection. It changes when you move the highlight bar using the arrow keys.

After selecting the source LAN type, you are prompted to select the destination LAN type. Select NetWare 4.*x*, and you are presented with the menu to configure your migration options (see Figure 22.4).

Figure 22.4.
Migration option menu.

From this menu, you need to specify the following:

◆ Working directory. This is where the bindery information and migration reports are stored. Data files are not stored here. You need 5MB of free disk space in this directory. The default is the current working directory.

◆ Action when errors and warnings are encountered. The default is Pause after errors and warnings. Press Enter for choices.

◆ Select the name of the source server. You will be presented with a server list that shows the NetWare 4 server, plus any other servers to which you are attached. If the source server you want is not listed, press Insert to display a list of available servers. Highlight the server you want and log in. Then select the server as the source server.

◆ Select the type of information you want to migrate (see Figure 22.5). The default is All Information. Press F5 to select multiple types to migrate.

◆ Select only the volume(s) containing the information you are migrating. Press F5 to select.

◆ Select the destination NetWare 4.*x* server. If you chose a server that is not running NetWare 4, MIGRATE will display an error message (see Figure 22.6).

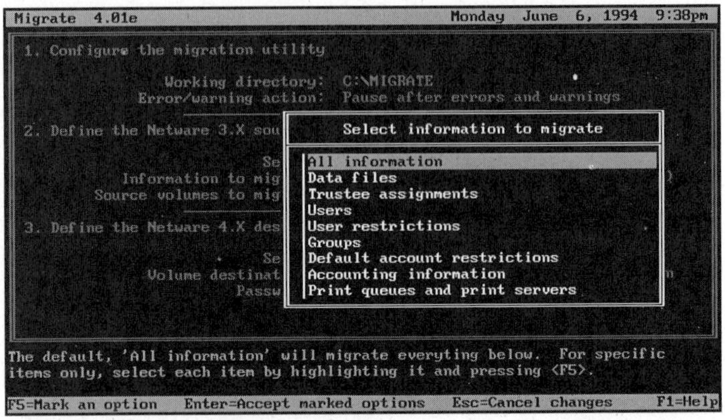

Figure 22.5.
Select which type of
information to migrate.

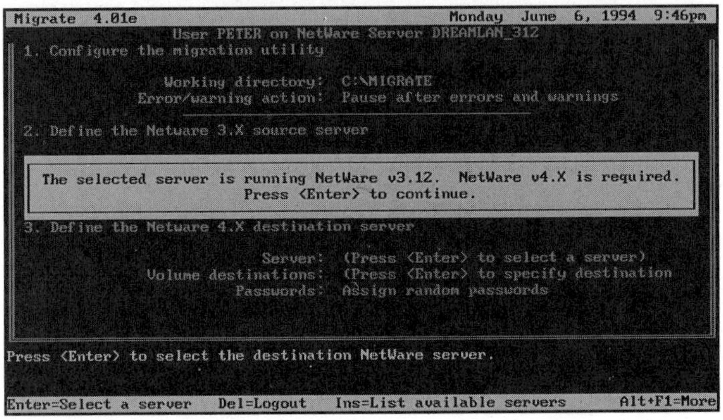

Figure 22.6.
Error in selecting
server.

◆ Select destination volumes if migrating information related to volumes. By
default, the volume migration is one-to-one (for example, SYS: to SYS:);
however, if you want, you can modify the destination path by highlighting
it and pressing Enter.

◆ Lastly, if you are migrating users, you need to select the way new passwords are assigned. You can either assign random initial passwords or no
initial passwords for the users on the NetWare 4 server (see Figure 22.7).
The reason for not carrying over the old passwords is security. The default
is to assign random passwords.

Note

When you choose the Assign Random Password option, the generated passwords are stored in SYS:SYSTEM\NEW.PWD on the destination NetWare 4.*x* server.

New passwords are only assigned to users and print servers that had a password on the source server.

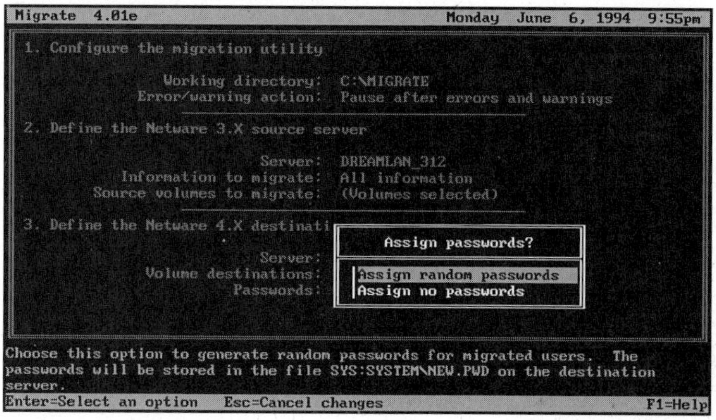

Figure 22.7.
Password assignment
options.

22

To proceed with the migration, press F10 to display the Select a Migration Action menu.

A running summary of the migration process appears on-screen. The same information also is logged into a report file with a name starting MIG000.RPT (see Figure 22.8). The filename is incremented automatically each time a migration is performed. You can view this file from the MIGRATE utility (one of the options on the Select a Migration Action) or any text editor.

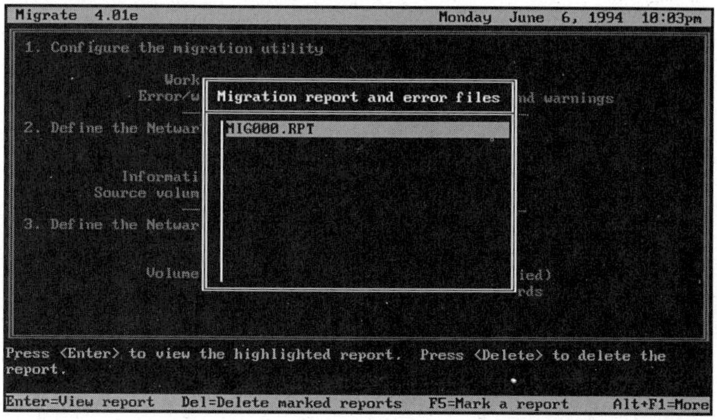

Figure 22.8.
Migration report file.

When the migration is complete, the following message appears:

```
Migration from the source server to the destination server is complete.
Press <Enter> to continue.
```

At this point, the across-the-wire migration is complete. The full migration to NetWare 4, however, is not yet finished. See the later section entitled "What to Do After the Migration" for more information.

SAME-SERVER

The *same-server* migration method is used to upgrade a server that will be installed on the same hardware as the old source server, enabling you to change your NetWare 2.*x* or 3.1*x* server into a NetWare 4.*x* server.

Note

Same-server migration assumes that your existing server is capable of being a NetWare 4.*x* server; that is, a 386-type processor or better and sufficient RAM. Keep in mind that NetWare 4 requires more space on the SYS: volume than NetWare 3.1*x* and 2.*x*.

This method enables you to use only one server, but there are some risks involved with the data during the conversion process. Also, you may not be able to migrate file attributes and trustee rights. If, for any reason, there is a failure in the migration process, you may not have a server to fall back to, and will have to reinstall the original operating system and restore from tape.

Note

You need to use a third-party backup program when performing the same-server migration. NetWare backup tools are not supported by the migration utility.

Because few DOS-based backup software support NetWare 4.*x* fully, you may not be able to restore NetWare file attributes and trustee information.

The same-server migration method is a three-step process. First, you back up the data files onto a tape drive and migrate the bindery information to the working directory on a workstation (see Figure 22.9). Then you install NetWare 4.*x* on your (original) server. Lastly, you restore the data from tape, and translate and migrate the bindery information from the workstation back to the new NetWare 4.*x* server (see Figure 22.10).

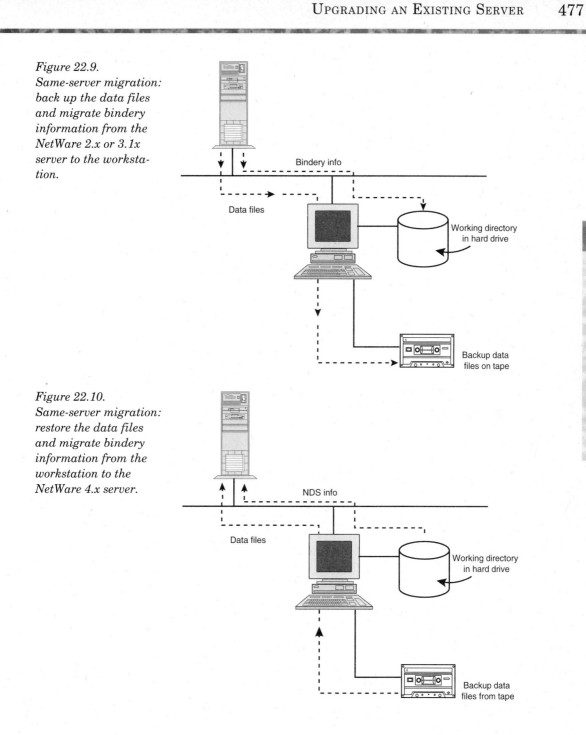

Figure 22.9.
Same-server migration:
back up the data files
and migrate bindery
information from the
NetWare 2.x or 3.1x
server to the worksta-
tion.

Bindery info

Data files

Working directory
in hard drive

Backup data
files on tape

Figure 22.10.
Same-server migration:
restore the data files
and migrate bindery
information from the
workstation to the
NetWare 4.x server.

NDS info

Data files

Working directory
in hard drive

Backup data
files from tape

22

Following are a number of prerequisite tasks you need to perform before starting the same-server migration:

◆ On the new NetWare 4.*x* server, you need to create the volumes you want to migrate data to. You cannot create volumes using the migration utility.

◆ Back up the source server twice. It is absolutely critical that you have *good* backup since the original data will be destroyed.

Tip

The general recommendation is to perform the tape backup twice. It is unlikely that two tapes will fail at the same place or on the same file.

◆ Make sure that all users are logged out of the server and all data files are closed.

◆ If you are logged in to the NetWare 4.*x* server in the NDS mode during the second half of the migration process, log out and re-login using bindery mode. You cannot use the migration utility to login to a NetWare 4.*x* server.

Note

Make sure you are logged in to the NetWare 4 server under bindery emulation before running MIGRATE.

◆ Remove any files that you do not want to migrate, such as .BAK files. This will help to reduce the amount of time required for the migration.

◆ If you are upgrading from NetWare 2.*x* to NetWare 4, make sure you have replacement NLMs for any of the VAPs (Value Added Process) you are using.

◆ Rename DOS files and directories that have long names. NetWare 2.15 or earlier allows you to create files and directories with 14-character names. This is incompatible with NetWare 4.

◆ Files other than PRINTCON.DAT, LOGIN (DOS user login script), and LOGIN.OS2 (OS/2 user login script) are not migrated from the SYS:MAIL directories. If you have other files in the SYS:MAIL directories, you need to move them manually. DOS and OS/2 user login scripts are combined in NetWare 4.

◆ If the source file server has a deep directory structure (more than 25 levels), you need to increase the directory depth on the destination server with the SET MAXIMUM SUBDIRECTORY TREE DEPTH command in STARTUP.NCF.

- Make sure you have sufficient volume space on the destination server. This is especially true if you plan to migrate multiple servers to a single NetWare 4.*x* server.

- Run BINDFIX on the source server. This will help to ensure the integrity of the bindery files, as well as to delete mail directories and trustee rights of all users who no longer exist on the source server.

- Ensure the workstation to be used to run MIGRATE has at least 5MB of free disk space to hold the bindery information temporarily.

- Although the minimum RAM requirement for NetWare 4*x* is 8MB, it is recommended that you have at least 16MB of RAM.

- Make sure that you do not have objects that have the same name but of different object types, such as a user object and a print server object with the same name. Otherwise, you will have objects with names such as `name`+bindery type=1.

Tip

To aid sites in preparing upgrades from NetWare 2.*x* and 3.1*x* to NetWare 4.*x*, Novell's Systems Research Department released a set of unsupported utilities called PRINTUSR (gives listing of users in bindery), PRINTGRP (gives listing of groups in bindery), and DUPBIND (lists objects with the same name but of different object types). For more information about these utilities, consult the April 1993 issue of *NetWare Application Note*. These files can be found on CompuServe's NetWire area—NOVLIB forum—in a file called AN304X.ZIP. The file can also be found on the NSEPro and Novell Internet FTP sites.

To start the first phase of the same-server migration process, copy the migration utility files from the CD to the workstation that you will be using. Execute MIGRATE.EXE. From the main menu, select Same-Server migration (see Figure 22.11). Then select the source LAN type.

Tip

Any time you are unsure of a selection, press F1 to display the context-sensitive help.

Quick Help is available at the bottom of the screen for each selection. It changes when you move the highlight bar using the arrow keys.

Figure 22.11.
Select the Same-Server
migration option from
the main menu of
MIGRATE.EXE.

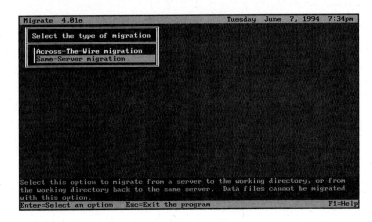

After selecting the source LAN type, you are prompted to select the destination LAN type. Select NetWare v4.*x*, and you are presented with the menu to configure your migration options (see Figure 22.12).

Figure 22.12.
Migration option menu.

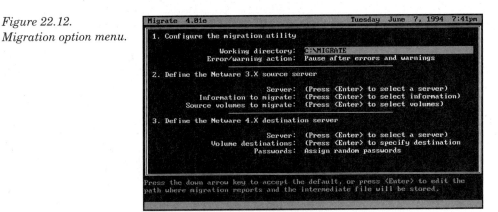

From this menu, you need to specify the following:

◆ Working directory. This is where the bindery information and migration reports are stored. Data files are not stored here. You need 5MB of free disk space in this directory. The default is the current working directory.

◆ Action when errors and warnings are encountered. The default is Pause after errors and warnings. Press Enter for choices.

◆ Select the name of the source server. You will be presented with a server list showing any servers you are attached to. If the source server you want is not listed, press Insert to display a list of available servers. Highlight the server you want and login. Then select the server as the source server.

◆ Select the type of information you want to migrate (see Figure 22.13). The default is All Information. Press F5 to select multiple types to migrate.

◆ Select only the volume(s) containing the information you are migrating. Press F5 to select.

At this point, because you do not yet have a NetWare 4.*x* sever up and running, you cannot select the destination. But instead, press F10 to display the Select a Migration Action menu (see Figure 22.14).

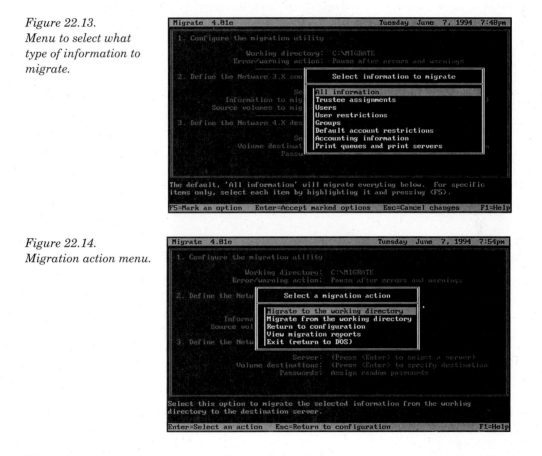

Figure 22.13.
Menu to select what type of information to migrate.

Figure 22.14.
Migration action menu.

The selection here is slightly different from the one from the Across-The-Wire migration option. You have the option to Migrate to the working directory and Migrate from the working directory. For Phase 1, choose Migrate to the working directory.

A running summary of the migration process appears on-screen (see Figure 22.15). The same information is also logged into a report file with a name starting

MIG000.RPT (see Figure 22.16). The filename is incremented automatically each time a migration is done. You can view this file from the MIGRATE utility (one of the options on the Select a Migration action) or any text editor.

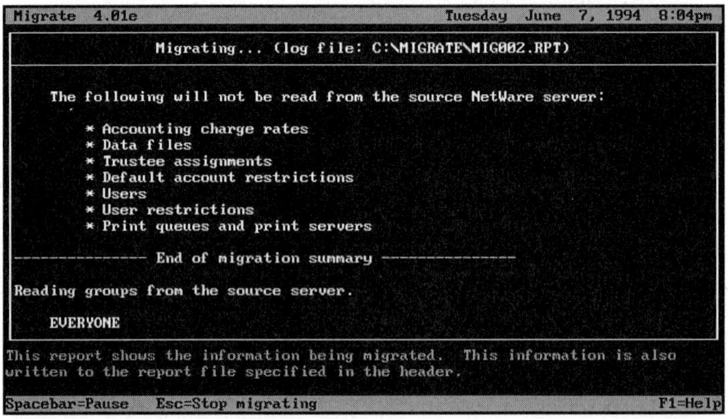

Figure 22.15.
Onscreen migration
summary.

Figure 22.16.
Migration report files.

When the import is complete, the following message is displayed:

```
Migration from the source server to the working directory is complete.
Press <Enter> to continue.
```

Exit back to DOS using the Exit (return to DOS) option.

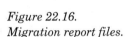

Warning

It is *very* important that you use the Exit (return to DOS) option to exit to DOS, rather than pressing ESC to back out to the main menu like many NetWare utilities. If you fail to do so, a MIGRATE.CFG file will not be created and you will not be able to proceed with Phase 3 of the Same-Server migration.

If you have not already done so, this is a good place to back up your NetWare 2.x or 3.1x server before upgrading it to NetWare 4.

In Phase 2 of the same-server migration process, you need to install NetWare 4 on your old server. Detailed steps for a new NetWare 4.x server is given in Chapter 21.

Next, restore the data files from your backup device to the NetWare 4.x server.

Warning

It is important that you only restore the data files and not any trustee or bindery information.

To complete the third and final phase of the same-server migration process, log in using bindery emulation mode into your new NetWare 4.x server, and restart MIGRATE. Follow the same steps as in Phase 1 to get to the Migration Options menu. Fill in the following information for step 3 *only*:

◆ Select the destination NetWare 4.x server. If you picked a server that is not running NetWare 4, MIGRATE will display an error message.

◆ Select destination volumes if appropriate. By default, the volume migration is one-to-one (such as SYS: to SYS:); however, you can modify the destination path by highlighting it and pressing Enter.

◆ Lastly, if you are migrating users, you need to select the way new passwords are assigned. You can either assign random initial passwords or no initial passwords for the users on the NetWare 4.x server (see Figure 22.17). The reason for not carrying over the old passwords is security. The default is to assign random passwords.

Note

When the Assign Random Password option is chosen, the generated passwords are stored in SYS:SYSTEM\NEW.PWD on the destination NetWare 4 server.

New passwords are only assigned to users and print servers that had a password on the source server.

To proceed with the migration, press F10 to display the Select a Migration Action menu. From this menu, select Migrate from the working directory (see Figure 22.18).

Figure 22.17.
Password assignment
options.

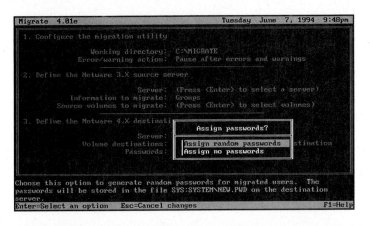

Figure 22.18.
Select Migration from
the working directory.

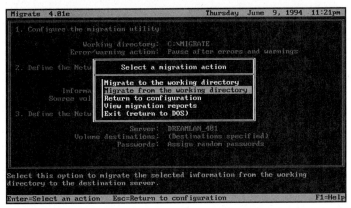

A running summary of the migration process appears on-screen. The same information is also logged into a report file with a name starting MIG000.RPT. The filename is incremented automatically each time a migration is done. You can view this file from the MIGRATE utility (one of the options on the Select a Migration Action menu) or any text editor.

When the migration is complete, the following message is displayed:

```
Migration from the source server to the
destination server is complete. Press
<Enter> to continue.
```

At this point, the across-the-wire migration is complete. However, the full migration to NetWare 4 is not yet finished. Refer to the later section entitled "What to do After the Migration" for more information.

IN-PLACE

The *in-place* upgrade is similar to the same-server migration, except everything is done on the server machine. In this case, however, no intermediate workstation is involved. There are more disadvantages for using this method than there are advantages.

Following are the disadvantages:

◆ Cannot upgrade from NetWare 2.0a. You must upgrade it to at least NetWare 2.10 first

◆ The original server must be a 386 or better machine

◆ If upgrade fails during any of the phases, you may have to restore everything from backup

◆ Requires a two-part upgrade process, if going from NetWare 2.x to NetWare 4.x—upgrade NetWare 2.x to NetWare 3.12, then from NetWare 3.12 to NetWare 4.x

There are three (small) advantages in using the in-place upgrade:

◆ Only one server machine is required, provided it is at least a 386-class machine

◆ When moving from NetWare 3.1x to NetWare 4.x, user passwords are retained

◆ If both DOS and OS/2 user login script exists, the following combined script is created:

```
IF OS="OS2" THEN
    ... OS/2 login script commands
ELSE
    ... DOS login script commands
END
```

Unless you have no other choices, the use of the in-place upgrade is not recommended.

In-place upgrade involves a number of steps. If you are upgrading from NetWare 2.x, you must first perform a NetWare 2.x-to-NetWare 3.12 in-place upgrade using the 2XUPGRDE.NLM. Then use INSTALL from NetWare 4.x to perform an in-place upgrade from NetWare 3.12 to NetWare 4.x.

Following are a number of prerequisite tasks you need to perform before starting the in-place migration:

1. Back up the source server twice. It is absolutely critical that you have *good* backup since the original data will be destroyed.

Tip

> The general recommendation is to perform the tape backup twice. It is unlikely that two tapes will fail at the same place or on the same file.

2. Make sure that all users are logged out of the server and all data files are closed.

3. Remove any files that you do not want to migrate, such as .BAK files. This will help to reduce the amount of time required for the migration.

4. If you are upgrading from NetWare 2.x to NetWare 4, make sure you have replacement NLMs for any of the VAPs (Value Added Process) you are using.

5. Rename DOS files and directories that have long names. NetWare 2.15 or earlier allows you to create files and directories with 14-character names. This is incompatible with NetWare 4.

6. If the original file server has a deep directory structure (more than 25 levels), you need to increase the directory depth on the "final" server with the SET MAXIMUM SUBDIRECTORY TREE DEPTH command in STARTUP.NCF.

7. Make sure you have sufficient disk space on the server to accommodate the new system files.

8. If you are going to create a DOS partition, make sure you have enough free space on all volumes. For example, if you have two volumes and want to create a 15MB DOS partition, 5MB will be taken from each volume for the DOS partition. Therefore, make sure your volumes are not filled to capacity.

9. Make sure that no disk has more than eight volumes on it.

10. Attach the server machine to a UPS unit. If you suffer a power failure during the upgrade process, you need to restore the 2.x system and start all over again.

11. Run BINDFIX on the original server. This will help to ensure the integrity of the bindery files, as well as to delete mail directories and trustee rights of all users who no longer exist on the server.

12. Although the minimum RAM requirement for NetWare 4.x is 8MB, it is recommended that you have at least 16MB of RAM.

13. Make sure that you do not have objects that have the same name but are different object types, such as a user object and a print server object with the same name. Otherwise, you will have objects with names such as *name*+bindery type=1.

Tip

To aid sites in preparing upgrades from NetWare 2.*x* and 3.1*x* to NetWare 4.*x*, Novell's Systems Research Department released a set of unsupported utilities called PRINTUSR (gives listing of users in bindery), PRINTGRP (gives listing of groups in bindery), and DUPBIND (lists objects with the same name but of different object types). For more information about these utilities, consult the April 1993 issue of *NetWare Application Note*. These files can be found on CompuServe's NetWire area—NOVLIB forum—in a file called AN304X.ZIP.

14. The necessary files (including a NetWare 3.12 Runtime license) for performing the in-place migration comes on the NetWare 4.1 CD. However, the files are stored in an image file format. You need to create an update diskette using the INSTALL.BAT file. From the opening menu, select Create Diskettes, and then select 3.5 inch Server Upgrade (1 Diskette).

15. Obtain from your vendors the necessary disk and LAN drivers for NetWare 3.12 and 4.*x*.

Discussed first are the steps for (in-place) upgrading NetWare 2.*x* to NetWare 3.12. After that, instructions for (in-place) NetWare 3.12 to 4.*x* upgrade are provided.

NETWARE 2.*x* TO 3.12 IN-PLACE UPGRADE

The NetWare 2.*x*-to-3.12 in-place upgrade changes the file system from NetWare 2.*x* format to NetWare 3.12 format. All files are left intact. The bindery files are upgraded and new passwords can be assigned.

Note

Core printing services from NetWare 2.*x* are not upgraded. You need to delete any printing services and re-create them after the upgrade.

User volume and disk restrictions are not upgraded because of differences between NetWare 2.*x* and 3.12 file systems. In NetWare 2.*x* the restrictions are server-wide, whereas in 3.12 the restrictions are only per volume.

Before you start the upgrade, obtain the following information from your 2.*x* server:

◆ Server name
◆ Network addresses

◆ LAN hardware configuration information, such as interrupt and I/O address

◆ Disk channel configuration

You can obtain this information by entering the CONFIG command at the server console (see Figure 22.19).

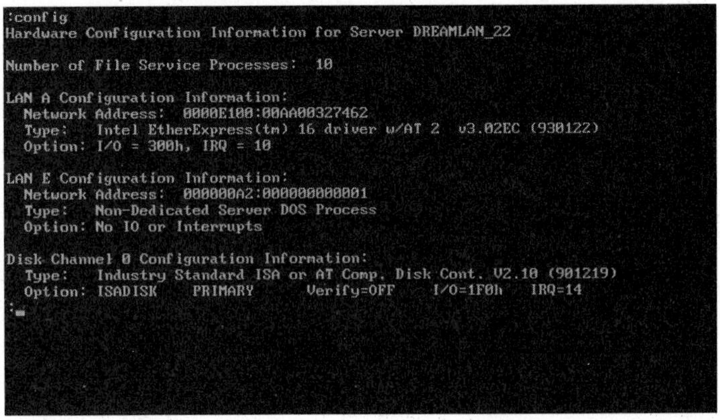

Figure 22.19.
Use CONFIG *to obtain*
server configuration
information.

```
:config
Hardware Configuration Information for Server DREAMLAN_22

Number of File Service Processes:  10

LAN A Configuration Information:
  Network Address:  0000E100:00AA00327462
  Type:   Intel EtherExpress(tm) 16 driver w/AT 2  v3.02EC (930122)
  Option: I/O = 300h, IRQ = 10

LAN E Configuration Information:
  Network Address:  000000A2:000000000001
  Type:   Non-Dedicated Server DOS Process
  Option: No IO or Interrupts

Disk Channel 0 Configuration Information:
  Type:   Industry Standard ISA or AT Comp. Disk Cont. V2.10 (901219)
  Option: ISADISK    PRIMARY     Verify=OFF    I/O=1F0h   IRQ=14
:
```

Boot up the server using the bootable upgrade diskette (refer to step 14 in the preceding section). Execute the SERVER.EXE for NetWare 3.12. Enter the old NetWare 2.*x* server name when prompted with File server name:. Assign an arbitrary IPX number (in hexadecimal) to the IPX internal network number when prompted. The v3.12 console prompt (:) appears after these two steps:

1. At the console prompt, load the disk driver (refer to step 15 in the preceding section) for your hard drive by entering:

   LOAD A:\disk_driver_name

2. Answer the disk driver configuration information prompts by entering the information you obtained using the CONFIG command earlier.

Note

The interrupt number used in NetWare 2.*x* is decimal, whereas in NetWare 3.1*x*/4.*x* it is hexadecimal.

Next, load the in-place upgrade utility:

LOAD A:\2XUPGRDE

You will be presented with a warning screen prompting you to ensure that you have a recent backup of your server.

After confirming with a Y answer, you are presented with a brief description of the four phases of operation of 2XUPGRDE.NLM (see Figure 22.20).

Figure 22.20.
Phase descriptions.

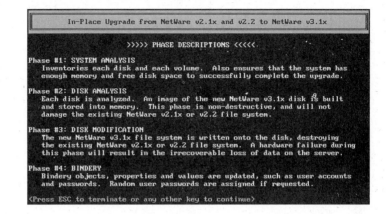

You will have the option to create a DOS partition for boot files (see Figure 22.21). It is strongly recommended that you do so; otherwise, the booting time will be dramatically increased. NetWare 4.*x* requires a minimum of 5MB; however, 15MB is recommended.

Keep in mind, however, that the space for the DOS partition comes off the volume(s) residing on the first (bootable) hard drive of your server. Make sure you do have the free volume space on the disk before you choose this option.

If there is insufficient space on the disk to create the DOS partition, the upgrade stops and displays the following message:

```
This NetWare server has insufficient free hard disk space
to complete the upgrade. The In-Place Upgrade process is now
being aborted.
```

To rectify this problem, delete unnecessary files to free more space on the disk, and restart the upgrade process.

At this point, the disk scanning phase starts (Phase 1; see Figure 22.21). This phase ensures that there is sufficient RAM in the server to build and translate the volume information. Phase 2 of the operation is to build the image of the new NetWare 3.12 disk image in RAM (see Figure 22.22). This is a non-destructive process and will not damage the existing NetWare 2.*x* file system.

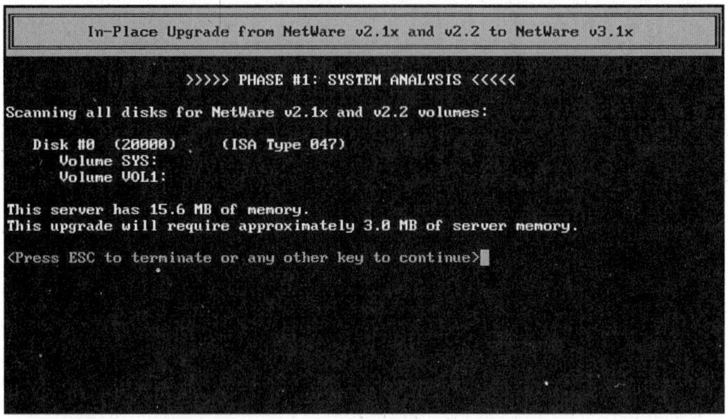

Figure 22.21.
Phase 1: System
analysis screen.

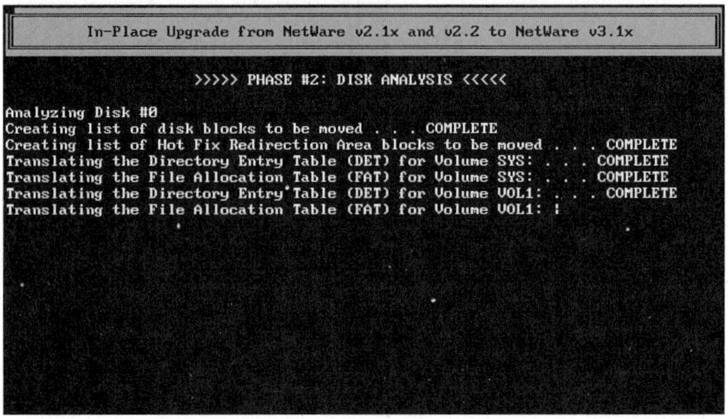

```
┌──────────────────────────────────────────────────────────────────┐
│       In-Place Upgrade from NetWare v2.1x and v2.2 to NetWare v3.1x │
├──────────────────────────────────────────────────────────────────┤

              >>>>> PHASE #1: SYSTEM ANALYSIS <<<<<

Scanning all disks for NetWare v2.1x and v2.2 volumes:

    Disk #0  (20000)     (ISA Type 047)
        Volume SYS:
        Volume VOL1:

This server has 15.6 MB of memory.
This upgrade will require approximately 3.0 MB of server memory.

<Press ESC to terminate or any other key to continue>█
```

Figure 22.22.
Phase 2: Disk
analysis screen.

```
┌──────────────────────────────────────────────────────────────────┐
│       In-Place Upgrade from NetWare v2.1x and v2.2 to NetWare v3.1x │
├──────────────────────────────────────────────────────────────────┤

              >>>>> PHASE #2: DISK ANALYSIS <<<<<

Analyzing Disk #0
Creating list of disk blocks to be moved . . . COMPLETE
Creating list of Hot Fix Redirection Area blocks to be moved . . . COMPLETE
Translating the Directory Entry Table (DET) for Volume SYS: . . . COMPLETE
Translating the File Allocation Table (FAT) for Volume SYS: . . . COMPLETE
Translating the Directory Entry Table (DET) for Volume VOL1: . . . COMPLETE
Translating the File Allocation Table (FAT) for Volume VOL1: ▌
```

Phase 3 of the operation (disk modification) actually overwrites the 2.*x* file system with the 3.12 image from RAM. This is a non-recoverable step. If there is a failure, you need to restore the 2.*x* file system and restart the upgrade. You still have a chance to back out at this point if you need to (see Figures 22.23 and 22.24).

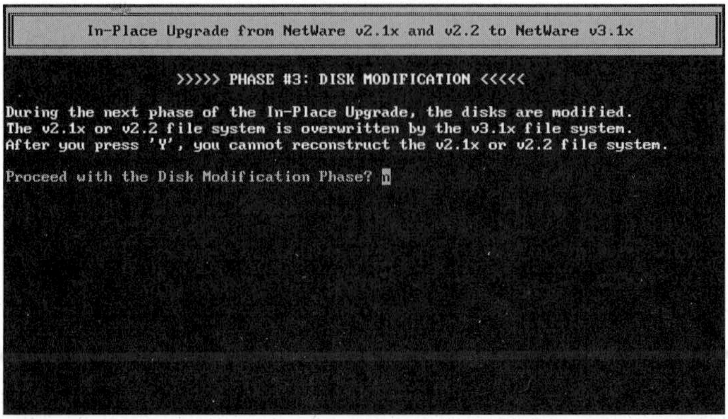

Figure 22.23.
Phase 3: Disk modifica-
tion screen with option
to back out.

```
┌──────────────────────────────────────────────────────────────────┐
│       In-Place Upgrade from NetWare v2.1x and v2.2 to NetWare v3.1x │
├──────────────────────────────────────────────────────────────────┤

              >>>>> PHASE #3: DISK MODIFICATION <<<<<

During the next phase of the In-Place Upgrade, the disks are modified.
The v2.1x or v2.2 file system is overwritten by the v3.1x file system.
After you press 'Y', you cannot reconstruct the v2.1x or v2.2 file system.

Proceed with the Disk Modification Phase? █
```

Figure 22.24.
Phase 3: Disk modifica-
tion process in progress
(a non-reversible
process).

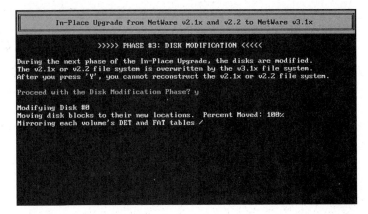

The last phase is to upgrade the bindery file (see Figure 22.25). Because the upgrade process cannot transfer user passwords, you are given the choice of assigning no passwords or assigning random passwords.

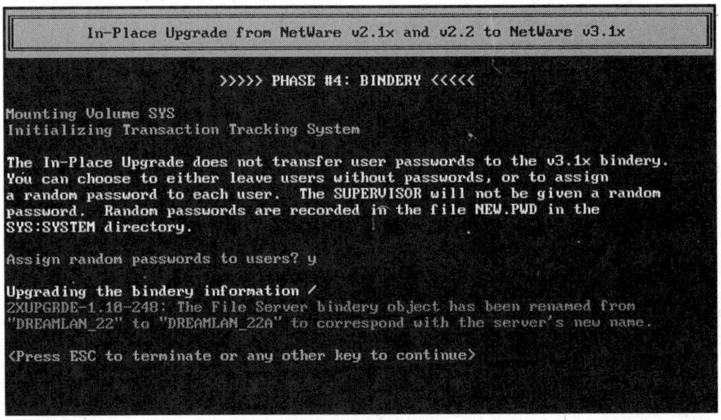

Figure 22.25.
Phase 4: Bindery
upgrade.

If you choose to use random passwords, the list of assigned passwords is recorded in SYS:SYSTEM\NEW.PWD file.

Note

SUPERVISOR is *not* given a password. Therefore, you should promptly set a password to prevent unauthorized access.

If you changed the name of the server between NetWare 2.*x* and 3.12, you will be notified.

The final status screen displays how your disks and volumes were affected by the upgrade (see Figure 22.26).

22

Figure 22.26.
Final status screen.

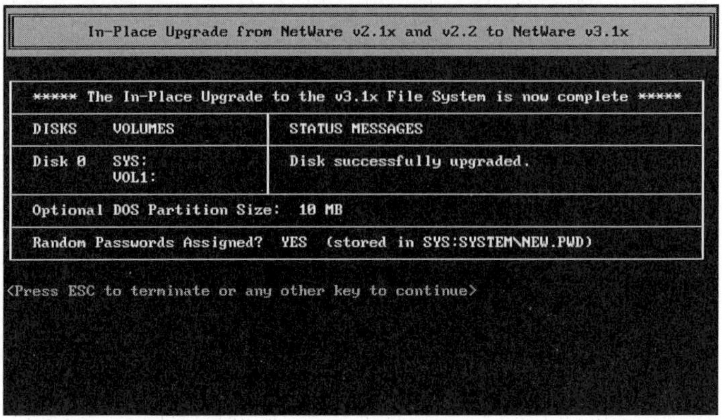

```
┌──────────────────────────────────────────────────────────────────────┐
│         In-Place Upgrade from NetWare v2.1x and v2.2 to NetWare v3.1x  │
├──────────────────────────────────────────────────────────────────────┤
│                                                                        │
│  ***** The In-Place Upgrade to the v3.1x File System is now complete ***** │
│  DISKS    VOLUMES           STATUS MESSAGES                            │
│                                                                        │
│  Disk 0   SYS:              Disk successfully upgraded.                │
│           VOL1:                                                        │
│  Optional DOS Partition Size:   10 MB                                  │
│  Random Passwords Assigned?  YES  (stored in SYS:SYSTEM\NEW.PWD)       │
└──────────────────────────────────────────────────────────────────────┘

<Press ESC to terminate or any other key to continue>
```

You may find that during the upgrade process a number of beeps were sounded. If
that is the case, when you exit back to the console prompt, you may see a number
of messages as shown in Figure 22.27. This is normal during the upgrade process.
However, if you experience this message during normal operation of your server, you
should check your hardware for possible conflicts or faults.

Figure 22.27.
Console messages
during upgrade.

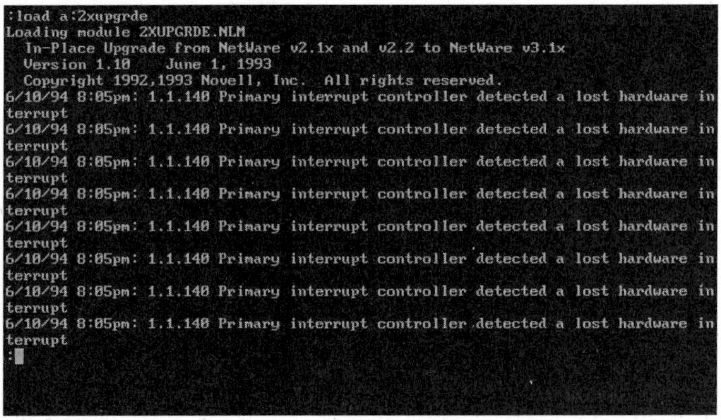

```
:load a:2xupgrde
Loading module 2XUPGRDE.NLM
  In-Place Upgrade from NetWare v2.1x and v2.2 to NetWare v3.1x
   Version 1.10   June 1, 1993
   Copyright 1992,1993 Novell, Inc. All rights reserved.
6/10/94 8:05pm: 1.1.140 Primary interrupt controller detected a lost hardware in
terrupt
6/10/94 8:05pm: 1.1.140 Primary interrupt controller detected a lost hardware in
terrupt
6/10/94 8:05pm: 1.1.140 Primary interrupt controller detected a lost hardware in
terrupt
6/10/94 8:05pm: 1.1.140 Primary interrupt controller detected a lost hardware in
terrupt
6/10/94 8:05pm: 1.1.140 Primary interrupt controller detected a lost hardware in
terrupt
6/10/94 8:05pm: 1.1.140 Primary interrupt controller detected a lost hardware in
terrupt
6/10/94 8:05pm: 1.1.140 Primary interrupt controller detected a lost hardware in
terrupt
6/10/94 8:05pm: 1.1.140 Primary interrupt controller detected a lost hardware in
terrupt
:
```

Verify that all the modified volumes can mount under NetWare 3.12 by entering:

MOUNT ALL

If any volume fails to mount, you'll need to restore the original NetWare 2.*x* file
system and restart the upgrade. Or, simply re-create the volume under NetWare
3.12 and restore the data from backup.

If you have opted to create a DOS partition, then you need to use the DOS FDISK
and FORMAT utilities. The upgrade utility simply "made room" on the hard drive
so you can create the DOS partition. You will find FDISK and FORMAT on your

"upgrade" diskette, but they are for DR DOS 6.0. If you booted the server with a different version of DOS, make sure you use the correct copy.

The following discussion is based on MS-DOS 5.0. Upon running the FDISK utility, you are presented with four options. Choose option 1, then 1 again, to create a primary DOS partition. Use the maximum available size for your DOS partition. Then the system will reboot for the change to take effect. Make sure you have the bootable diskette in drive A:.

After the machine reboots, format the C: drive and make it bootable. If you forget to format drive C: you will get an invalid media type when you try to access it (see Figure 22.28).

Figure 22.28.
Invalid media error if
drive C: was not
formatted.

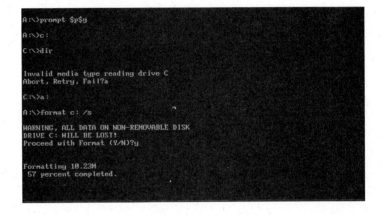

You now have completed the NetWare 2.*x*-to-3.12 in-place upgrade. Proceed to the next section for NetWare 3.1*x*-to-4.*x* in-place upgrade.

NetWare 3.1*x* to 4.*x* In-Place Upgrade

If you are upgrading the 3.1*x* server into an existing NDS environment, make sure you have the following information before starting the upgrade:

◆ Name of NDS tree

◆ Context into which this server will be installed

◆ User id that has Supervisor object rights to the context you are installing the server into (could be Admin)

◆ Password for the preceding user id

If user objects already exist in the context you are adding the server into, you want to make sure that the names of users in the bindery of your 3.1*x* server are different from the existing objects. If there are duplications found during the upgrade, you have the option to rename the conflicting bindery object names. Otherwise, the different user restrictions and information will be merged.

The easiest way to perform the NetWare 3.1x to 4.x in-place upgrade is to use the CD-ROM. Set up your CD-ROM drive and controller so that the drive can be addressed as a DOS device. A sample AUTOEXEC.BAT and CONFIG.SYS for Adaptec 1542B SCSI controller is shown in Figures 22.29 and 22.30, respectively. In this example, the CD-ROM drive is set up as drive D:.

Figure 22.29.
Sample
AUTOEXEC.BAT for
Adaptec 1542B
controller.

```
@echo off
C:\SCSI\MSCDEX.EXE /D:ASPICD0 /M:12
C:\WINDOWS\SMARTDRV.EXE
cls
SET path=C:\NMS\bin;C:\WINDOWS;C:\DOS
SET TEMP=C:\WINDOWS\TEMP
prompt $p$g
SET HELPFILES=C:\NMS\help\*.HLP
```

Figure 22.30.
Sample CONFIG.SYS
for Adaptec 1542B
controller.

```
DEVICE=C:\SCSI\ASPI4DOS.SYS /D
FILES= 60
BUFFERS=40
DEVICE=C:\WINDOWS\HIMEM.SYS
STACKS=9,256
LASTDRIVE=Z
DEVICE=C:\SCSI\ASPICD.SYS /D:ASPICD0
```

You can use almost any CD-ROM drive/controller combination for the installation, as long as you have a DOS driver for it. However, if you want to later make this CD-ROM drive a sharable volume on the server, it must be a SCSI device.

Tip

It is to your advantage to use the fastest CD-ROM drive possible for the installation. The faster the drive, the shorter your installation time.

Novell has not published a list of certified CD-ROM drives. However, the author's experience suggests that the best SCSI controller and CD-ROM drive combination is the Adaptec controller and NEC CD-ROM.

If you are using a SCSI CD-ROM for the installation, it is important to ensure that it is not on the same controller as your SYS: volume. Otherwise, when you go to copy files from the CD to SYS: volume, you can potentially hang the server due to conflict between the DOS CD-ROM driver and the NetWare disk driver.

Note

> The conflict just mentioned only exists during the installation phase. Afterwards, you can have both the CD-ROM drive and SYS: on the same SCSI controller.

The easiest way to circumvent this conflict is to temporarily install a second SCSI controller for the CD-ROM drive during the installation phase.

Make drive D: (CD-ROM) your default directory, and execute the INSTALL.BAT file that is located in the root directory. From the main menu, select NetWare Server Installation, and then from the second menu, select NetWare 4.1. From the next screen, select Upgrade NetWare 3.1*x* or v4.*x*. From this point on, the screens and steps are very similar to a new server installation. Therefore, the screen shots are not shown here, but refer to Chapter 21 should you need more information.

Note

> Pay attention to the bottom of the menu as you proceed with the installation steps. The program alternates between ENTER and F10 for selection. Pressing Alt+F10 at any time will exit the menu.
>
> Should you have doubts about the prompts on the menu, press F1 to display a help screen, or consult DynaText.

Server boot files (such as NetWare 4's SERVER.EXE) are copied from the CD to your DOS partition. You need to specify the destination path. If the directory does not exist, the INSTALL program will create it for you.

Next, depending on whether you want foreign language and keyboard mapping support, you can specify the country code, code page, and keyboard mapping to be used for your server.

You need to tell NetWare which filename format to use when storing files on the NetWare volumes. Choose DOS Filename Format.

Note

Use the DOS Filename Format unless you have a compelling reason not to. This allows compatibility with DOS and future versions of NetWare.

By default, your old STARTUP.NCF will be copied from the previous SERVER.EXE directory to the new area. You then are asked whether the next phase of the install procedure should use the settings you had in the previous STARTUP.NCF. You typically should answer Yes.

If the disk driver specified in your STARTUP.NCF file is loaded successfully, all volumes will be mounted. Otherwise, if the driver does not exist in the DOS partition or did not load due to incompatibility, you will be prompted to enter the server name and IPX internal address. Verify that all disk drivers have loaded correctly. If they have, press F10 to continue. Otherwise, select the driver from the list presented, configure it, and then continue with installation.

Tip

If you are using IDE drives, select the IDE.DSK driver. There are some rare instances that the ISADISK.DSK works better than the IDE.DSK driver. Try it only if you experience problems with IDE.DSK.

If you have multiple controllers, you can load the same DSK driver re-entrantly. If you have a different controller, you can load a different disk driver.

Next, you are prompted for a license diskette. Insert the diskette that came with your copy of NetWare.

Unlike NetWare 2.x and 3.1x, licensing information for NetWare 4.01 comes on a "license diskette." This diskette contains information about the serial number as well as number of connections.

Warning

Make sure you keep track of which license diskette was installed on which server. Mixing licenses on the same network may cause your server licenses to be deactivated, reverting your servers (ones with duplicated licenses) back to Runtime.

If you provide an invalid license diskette, you will receive a Not Valid message, and the server will become a Runtime (one-user) server.

Following the successful installation of the license diskette, you are now ready to copy NetWare files to the SYS: volume.

The next step in the upgrade is to copy all NetWare 4.*x* system files and utilities to the SYS: volume. In addition, you can copy file groups such as DOS and OS/2 utilities to the SYSTEM, PUBLIC, and LOGIN directories. The default is to copy all file groups.

To select or deselect a file group for copying, simply highlight the entry and press Enter. When you are done, press F10 to start copying. A File Copy Status bar graph will be displayed.

Depending on the number of file groups, speed of your CD-ROM, speed of your hard drive, and amount of RAM for file caching, the file copying process will take from about 30 minutes to an hour or more.

The original AUTOEXEC.NCF file (you will not have this if upgrading from NetWare 2.*x*) is first scanned for LAN drivers that have no frame type specified and is then executed. You are warned that the Ethernet default frame type has been changed from Ethernet_802.3 to Ethernet_802.2.

INSTALL will automatically search for any NDS trees that may exist on your network. If no tree is found, you have the option to search again or create a new tree.

Warning

While it is possible to have multiple trees on the same physical network, it is not possible for the trees to communicate with each other. Therefore, objects (users, for example) in one tree will not see objects (a server, for example) in another tree.

By selecting Yes to the `Is this the first v4.x server?` prompt, you create a new NDS tree. You will need to provide a tree name.

If this is not the first server within your NDS tree, but you want to add this server to an existing tree, select the listed tree name. Make sure you select the correct tree name. Other than this one step, the rest of the installation steps are identical as described earlier in this section.

Note

If you are installing the server into an existing NDS tree, you can use either the Admin userid and password or a userid/password that has the Supervisor object rights to the context into which you are installing the server.

You need to correctly identify the time zone and any daylight savings time deviations in which this particular server resides. The network time is computed based on these entries.

The daylight savings time information also will save you the trouble of having to reset the server clocks twice a year.

It is important that the time server type is set correctly. See Chapter 14 for more details. The default time server for the first server in the tree is Single Reference; subsequent time servers default to Secondary.

You then need to specify the context into which this server is to be located within the NDS tree. It is here that you specify the password for the Admin user.

Warning

> When entering the Admin password, make sure no special characters, such as ! or : are used. You may experience problems when logging in as Admin using this password.

NDS is then installed. The bindery is upgraded next into the NDS, followed by the file ownership id being changed from the old (bindery) ids to the new (NDS) ones (see Figures 22.31 and 22.32). The file ownership change is performed for all volumes.

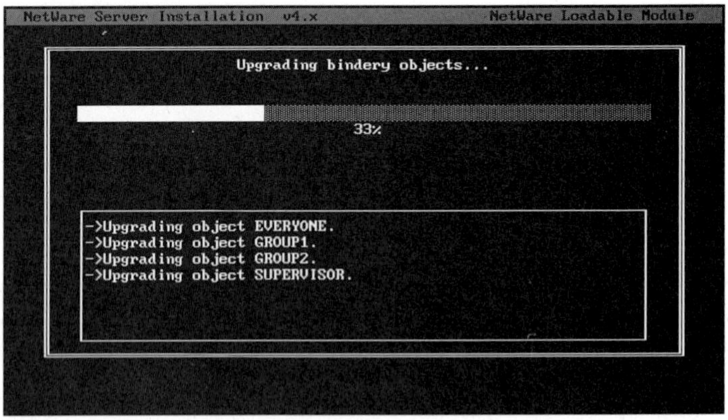

Figure 22.31.
Upgrading bindery
information into NDS.

Bindery object properties such as passwords and group memberships are upgraded into NDS object properties. This is the *only* upgrade that does not require you to change user passwords.

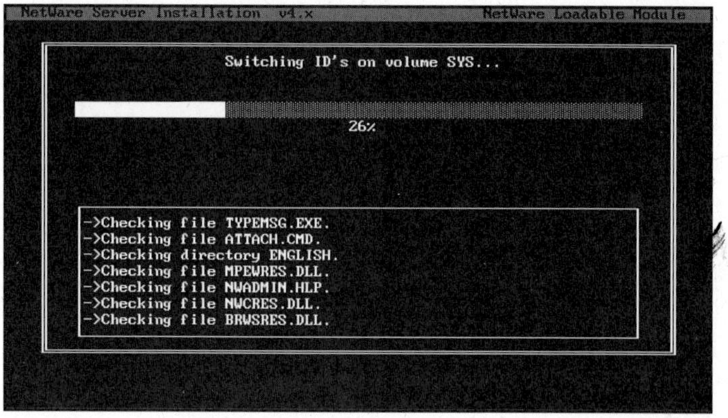

Figure 22.32.
Switching IDs for file
ownership.

```
NetWare Server Installation v4.x                    NetWare Loadable Module

                        Switching ID's on volume SYS...

    ┌──────────────────────────────────────────────────────────────────────┐
    │███████████████                                                         │
    └──────────────────────────────────────────────────────────────────────┘
                                     26%


    ┌──────────────────────────────────────────────────────────────────────┐
    │->Checking file TYPEMSG.EXE.                                            │
    │->Checking file ATTACH.CMD.                                             │
    │->Checking directory ENGLISH.                                           │
    │->Checking file MPEWRES.DLL.                                            │
    │->Checking file NWADMIN.HLP.                                            │
    │->Checking file NWCRES.DLL.                                             │
    │->Checking file BRWSRES.DLL.                                            │
    └──────────────────────────────────────────────────────────────────────┘
```

If there are any name conflicts during the upgrade process, you have the option to either rename the bindery object, or to merge the conflicting objects. Press F1 for more information on these options. At the end of the upgrade process, the number of volumes upgraded is displayed. A summary screen also is shown to remind you of the NDS information.

Once again, the AUTOEXEC.NCF is scanned to ensure it contains time and NDS information. You will have the option to compare the old and new AUTOEXEC.NCF and edit the new one before saving it.

The last installation option screen allows you to perform a number of functions, such as the following:

◆ Create registration diskette

◆ Copy DynaText (online documentation) from CD-ROM to server

Your NetWare 4 package contains a preformatted Registration Diskette. Register your software so that you will be mailed any free updates to which you are entitled, as well as be put on a mailing list for new updates and information.

The final screen in the installation process confirms the completion of your installation. You should reboot the server to make sure all the settings made to STARTUP.NCF and AUTOEXEC.NCF are correct.

You now have completed a new NetWare 3.1*x* to NetWare 4.*x* in-place upgrade. Proceed to the following section, "What to Do after the Migration," for the "clean up" phase of the upgrade.

WHAT TO DO AFTER THE MIGRATION

After the migration is complete, you need to complete the following steps on the NetWare 4 server:

> **Tip**
>
> Make sure you always use the latest UIMPORT.EXE from Novell.

◆ If you migrated user login scripts, you need to run the UIMPORT program (part of NetWare 4) to "import" the contents of the login script files into NDS, by completing the following steps:

  1. Log into the new NetWare 4 server as Admin under NDS mode.

  2. Make SYS:SYSTEM your current working directory.

  3. Execute the UIMPORT program using the following syntax:

```
UIMPORT UIMPORT.CTL UIMPORT.DAT
```

◆ Although user login scripts are migrated, you need to update the scripts to reflect the correct server name as well as any directory path changes.

◆ If you had both DOS and OS/2 user login scripts on the old server, check that they are combined correctly after an In-Place upgrade. If you performed Across-the-wire or Same-server migration, you have to manually combine the scripts; otherwise, only the DOS script will be upgraded.

◆ You may need to reinstall some third-party applications due to a change of directory structure.

◆ If you have chosen Assign Random Passwords during migration, check SYS:SYSTEM\NEW.PWD. Make sure the users have the new passwords. The users should change their passwords immediately upon login.

  If users were migrated from multiple servers, the current password is the last one listed in the report.

◆ You may need to upgrade migrated print queues and print servers using PUPGRADE.NLM (see Figure 22.33). This usually is the case for same-server or in-place migration methods.

◆ If you were using Novell's menu system in NetWare 2.x or 3.1x, you need to convert them into NetWare 4's menu system using the MENUCNVT utility.

◆ Verify that user restrictions, if any, are migrated correctly.

Figure 22.33.
PUPGRADE.NLM
main menu.

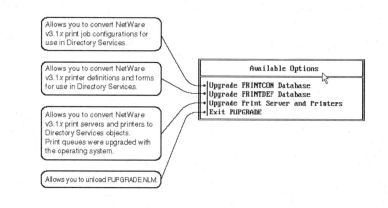

> ## Tip
>
> There is never enough testing before you allow a new server to go into production. Ask some of your more experienced users to test all the (mission-critical) applications for you.

UPGRADING NETWARE 4.*x*

It is important that you keep your NetWare 4 server up-to-date with the patches and updates, especially those specific to NDS. Often, when fixes are first available, they are released to the NetWire forum by Novell. You also can obtain these files from the Internet (`ftp.novell.com`) or your local Novell Authorized Service Centers (NASCs).

SUMMARY

In this chapter, you learned about the different methods available to upgrade from a server running a previous version of NetWare to NetWare 4.*x*. The pros and cons of the different methods were discussed. Detailed procedures for each of the upgrade methods also were presented.

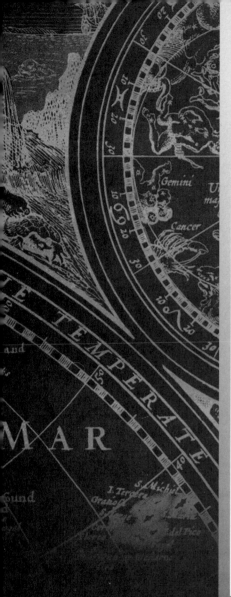

- Open Data-Link Interface (ODI)

- NETX Versus VLM

- Workstation Client Files

- Installing DOS/ Windows Clients

- Installing OS/2 Requester

- Summary

CHAPTER 23

Installing New Workstation Software

This chapter presents step-by-step instructions that will enable you to perform a successful workstation client installation (it is assumed that this is a new station install). Steps to upgrade a workstation that was running the (older) NetWare Shell (NETX) are discussed in the next chapter.

A brief discussion of Open Data-Link Interface (ODI) and the difference between the old NetWare Shell and the new NetWare Requester is provided for background information.

OPEN DATA-LINK INTERFACE (ODI)

Along with the introduction of NetWare 3.0, Novell also introduced the *Open Data-Link Interface* (ODI) architecture. It replaced the old monolithic IPX.COM driver.

Note

The ODI specification is jointly developed by Novell and Apple Computer and was published to the networking industry in 1989.

The IPX.COM driver has a number of limitations, as follows:

◆ Limited memory, I/O port, and interrupt line combination

◆ Supports only one frame type at a time

◆ Non-modular

The ODI design splits the single IPX.COM into three separate pieces: LSL.COM, NIC driver, and IPXODI.COM (see Figure 23.1).

Figure 23.1.
Open Data-Link
Interface.

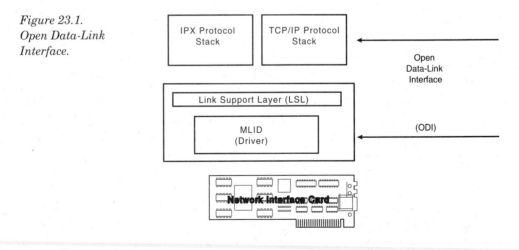

The LSL.COM file (Link Support Layer) acts as the interface between the software NIC driver and the upper layer protocol stack. IPXODI.COM provides the IPX protocol stack for the ODI architecture. The NIC driver is known as the MLID (Multiple Link Interface Driver).

ODI was designed to transparently support any network transport regardless of the underlying media. For example, ODI provides TCP/IP support, which was traditionally limited to Ethernet, over Token Ring and ARCnet.

You already may have been using ODI drivers without realizing it. All NetWare 3.x and 4.x *server* LAN drivers are ODI drivers.

It is not uncommon today to find that only ODI drivers are supported by your NIC manufacturer. As a matter of fact, the IPX.OBJ file necessary to generate the monolithic IPX.COM is no longer under development by Novell. If you encounter any incompatibilities of IPX.COM with your application, you are advised to migrate to ODI.

Note

Remember that the ODI architecture only deals with the NIC level. It does not include the NetWare Shell or Requester, which is discussed in the next section. People often consider the Shell/Requester as part of ODI, which is incorrect.

For more information about ODI technology, consult your DynaText documentation.

NETX Versus VLM

What is the difference between NETX and VLM? Traditionally, the interface driver on the workstation that decides whether a workstation request is to be handled locally or remotely is called the *NetWare Shell*. The file is NETX.EXE.

The NETX driver "sits" between the user and DOS. It intercepts user requests, and depending on the command, it routes it to the network (such as DIR F:) or passes it on to DOS (such as DIR C:). Because it comes between the user and DOS, it is very DOS-version specific. Almost every major revision of DOS results in a newer version of NETX to be released. Similar to the monolithic IPX.COM, it has many limitations and Novell has stopped development on it.

A new driver has been introduced to replace the old NETX driver. The new driver is known as the *DOS Requester* because it sits behind DOS, which means that all user commands first will be examined by DOS. Any requests that cannot be handled by DOS are routed to the network by the Requester.

The new driver is commonly called *VLM* (Virtual Loadable Module), but sometimes also is referred to as the *universal client* because it can support all versions of NetWare, including Personal NetWare (PNW), 2.2, 3.1x, and 4.x versions.

VLM has many advantages, some of which are the following:

◆ **Modular design**: The Requester is made up of a set of modules (files with .VLM extensions). This allows individual modules to be updated without having to generate the whole driver.

◆ **Better memory management**: Due to the modularity, the Requester can load into memory only what is needed at any given time. The VLM manager can also manage memory dynamically. In a way, you can compare VLMs to overlay files used by applications.

◆ **Support for NetWare Directory Services**: Only VLM has support for NDS. Therefore, to fully utilize the power of NDS, you cannot use NETX.

◆ **Better performance**: Only the VLM driver will support the Packet Burst mode. NETX does not support packet burst.

Warning

You may have been using BNETX in the past to obtain packet burst support. However, because BNETX can possibly cause data corruption, Novell no longer supports BNETX. Novell strongly advises you to switch to VLM in order to obtain packet burst support.

VLM automatically detects the type of memory you have available (expanded and extended) and will load itself accordingly, to give you the best possible memory savings. Alternatively, you can force it into a given type of memory using a command line switch—/mc, /mx, and /me for conventional, extended, and expanded memory, respectively).

Switching from NETX to VLM blindly has some drawbacks. Some applications were written to the NETX specification. Because VLM now sits behind DOS, this results in some applications not functioning correctly with VLM. In this case, you need to contact your vendor for an update.

Tip

If you are upgrading to NetWare 4.x, ensure that all NLMs currently in use will run on a 4.x platform or can obtain upgrades (as pointed out in Chapter 21).

Contact your software vendors to get assurance that their application will work with VLM.

If you are installing a new NetWare 4.*x* network, contact your software vendors *in advance* to get assurance on compatibility.

Although it is possible to use the monolithic IPX.COM driver with VLM, you will not be able to fully utilize all the performance and security features offered by VLM.

WORKSTATION CLIENT FILES

DOS and OS/2 workstation client files are supplied on the NetWare 4 CD disc. If you copied them to the server during the server software install (refer to Chapter 21 for the installation procedures), you can obtain the client files from there. Batch files are supplied with the CD so that you can create diskettes, should you need to.

You can install PC workstation clients in two ways. You can boot up the workstation and log in to the NetWare 4 server using the traditional IPX/NETX drivers under bindery emulation and then install the VLM and ODI drivers from the server. Or, you can make a set of installation diskettes from the CD and install the ODI/VLMs onto workstations, as needed.

Tip

The version of VLM shipped with NetWare 4.1 CD is VLM 1.20. It has some known bugs and problems; however, these problems have been addressed by newer VLM files, and these updates are available from the various Novell sources.

If you are installing OS/2 clients, the installation steps are similar to that of installing DOS clients. You need to keep one thing in mind, however. OS/2 Requesters are OS/2-version specific. Therefore, you cannot use the Requester shipped on the NetWare 4.1 CD for OS/2 v1.3 because it is for OS/2 version 2.1*x* and higher.

Note

If you do have OS/2 v1.3 client workstations, you can order OS/2 Requester v1.3 directly from Novell. Note, however, that it can only access your NetWare 4 servers using bindery emulation mode. NDS is not supported.

OS/2 Requester v2.11 is shipped with the NetWare 4.1 CD. Check your Novell sources for the latest updates.

DOS/WINDOWS CLIENT DISKETTES FROM CD

The DOS/Windows Client software is not shipped on diskettes with your NetWare package. It is unlikely that you will have a CD-ROM reader for each workstation or a portable CD-ROM reader that you can use for workstation driver install. It is easiest if you create the necessary diskettes from the CD and perform the install. To create DOS/Windows Client diskettes from the NetWare 4.1 CD, follow these steps:

1. Format five blank, high-density diskettes.
2. Execute the INSTALL.BAT file in the root directory of the CD.
3. From the main menu, select Create Diskettes (see Figure 23.2).

Figure 23.2.
Menu selection to create diskettes from CD.

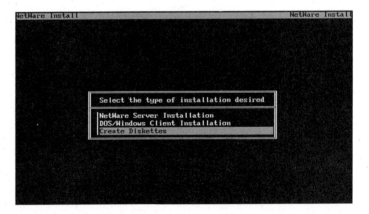

4. Select the 3.5 inch DOS & MS Windows Client (5 Diskettes) option or the 5.25 inch DOS & MS Windows Client (5 Diskettes) option, depending on your choice (see Figure 23.3).
5. Files will be copied to the diskettes and a logical label put on each diskette (see Figure 23.4). Label the diskettes accordingly.

Note

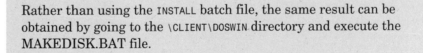

Rather than using the INSTALL batch file, the same result can be obtained by going to the \CLIENT\DOSWIN directory and execute the MAKEDISK.BAT file.

Figure 23.3.
Menu selection to create
DOS & Windows Client
diskettes.

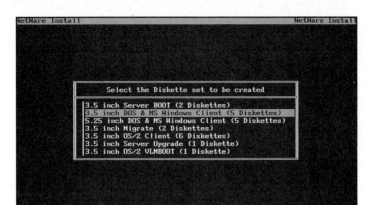

Figure 23.4.
Creating the first DOS /
Windows Client
diskette.

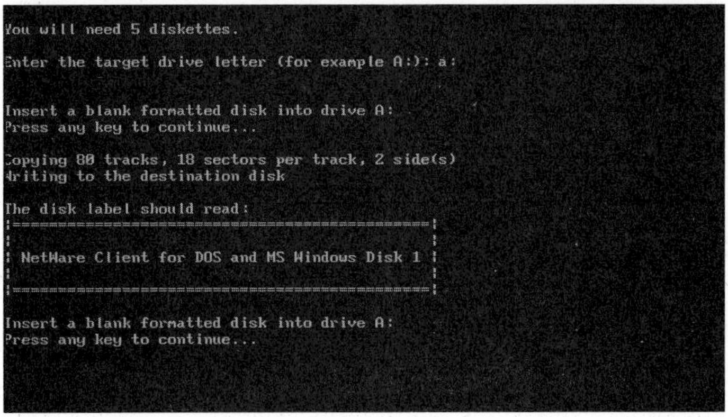

OS/2 CLIENT DISKETTES FROM CD

The OS/2 Client software is not shipped on diskettes with your NetWare package. It is unlikely that you will have a CD-ROM reader for each workstation or a portable CD-ROM reader that you can use for workstation driver install. It is easiest if you create the necessary diskettes from the CD and perform the install. To create OS/2 Client diskettes from the NetWare 4.1 CD, follow these steps:

1. Format six 3.5-inch blank, high-density diskettes.

2. Execute the INSTALL.BAT file in the root directory of the CD.

3. From the main menu, select Create Diskettes, and then select the 3.5 inch OS/2 Client (6 Diskettes) option.

4. Files will be copied to the diskettes and a logical label put on each diskette (see Figure 23.5). Label the diskettes accordingly.

23

INSTALLING NEW WORKSTATION SOFTWARE

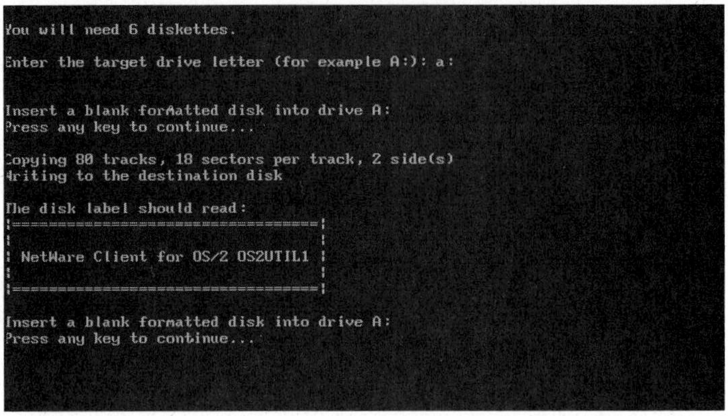

Figure 23.5.
Creating the first OS/2
Client diskette.

```
You will need 6 diskettes.
Enter the target drive letter (for example A:): a:

Insert a blank formatted disk into drive A:
Press any key to continue...

Copying 80 tracks, 18 sectors per track, 2 side(s)
Writing to the destination disk

The disk label should read:
!===================================!
!                                   !
! NetWare Client for OS/2 OS2UTIL1  !
!                                   !
!===================================!

Insert a blank formatted disk into drive A:
Press any key to continue...
```

Note

Rather than using the INSTALL batch file, the same result can be obtained by going to the \CLIENT\OS2 directory and executing the MAKEDISK.CMD file.

DOS CLIENT DISKETTES FROM SERVER

During the server software install (refer to Chapter 21 for details), you have the option of creating a directory for client installation. If you took that option, a directory called CLIENT is created under SYS:PUBLIC. Under this directory, there is a DOSWIN directory. A copy of MAKEDISK.BAT is located there, as well as the compressed DOS/Windows drivers. You create the five installation diskettes using this batch file by following the steps outlined above.

OS/2 CLIENT DISKETTES FROM SERVER

As described in the previous section, a SYS:PUBLIC\CLIENT\OS2 directory exists and contains a copy of MAKEDISK.CMD. By making this directory your default directory, you can execute the batch file as described in the previous sections to create your six installation diskettes.

INSTALLING DOS/WINDOWS CLIENTS

It is very easy and straightforward to install the DOS/Windows client files on PC workstations. The whole process is menu-driven, and ample direction is given on the different screens to help you along (see Figure 23.6).

Figure 23.6.
DOS/Windows VLM
Client installation
menu.

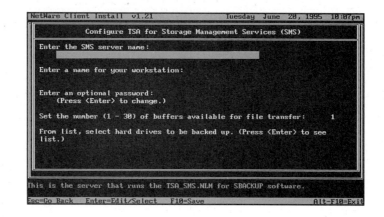

```
NetWare Client Install  v1.21                Tuesday  June  20, 1995  10:02pm
 1. Enter the destination directory:
    C:\NWCLIENT
 2. Install will modify your AUTOEXEC.BAT and CONFIG.SYS files and make
    backups.  Allow changes? (Y/N):  Yes
 3. Install support for MS Windows? (Y/N):  No


 4. Configure your workstation for back up by a NetWare server running
    software such as SBACKUP? (Y/N):  No
 5. Select the driver for your network board.
    Highlight here and press <Enter> to see list.
 6. Highlight here and press <Enter> to install.



Install will add this path to AUTOEXEC.BAT if you allow changes to the DOS
configuration files.
Esc=Go Back    Enter=Edit/Select                              Alt-F10=Exit
```

The procedure for installing the DOS/Windows Client on a PC workstation is a six-step process.

1. A directory is created on the workstation. ODI and VLM files are copied to it. Under this directory is a NLS\ENGLISH directory where message files are stored.

2. Files are copied to your Windows directory if you specified Windows support. A NetWare Tools group icon is created. A NLS\ENGLISH directory is also created under your Windows directory for message files.

3. If Windows support is installed, WIN.INI, SYSTEM.INI, and PROGMAN.INI are modified. Some NetWare-specific Windows files are copied.

4. You can specify whether the workstation will be backed up by a NetWare server running SMS-compliant software. If you indicate yes, you need to specify the SMS server and associated information (see Figure 23.7).

Figure 23.7.
Workstation SMS
configuration screen.

```
NetWare Client Install  v1.21                Tuesday  June  20, 1995  10:07pm
            Configure TSA for Storage Management Services (SMS)

   Enter the SMS server name:


   Enter a name for your workstation:


   Enter an optional password:
      (Press <Enter> to change.)

   Set the number (1 - 30) of buffers available for file transfer:      1

   From list, select hard drives to be backed up. (Press <Enter> to see
   list.)




This is the server that runs the TSA_SMS.NLM for SBACKUP software.

Esc=Go Back    Enter=Edit/Select    F10=Save                  Alt-F10=Exit
```

5. A NET.CFG file is created.

6. A STARTNET.BAT, which loads the ODI and VLM drivers, is created.

7. AUTOEXEC.BAT and CONFIG.SYS files are updated.

Note

If you are using Windows with NetWare, make sure you enabled NetWare support while installing Windows, or run SETUP to change the Windows configuration.

The installation is started by running INSTALL, located on the WSDOS_1 diskette. You must change your default working directory to that disk drive before running the batch file.

If you have an IPX driver loaded in the memory of the workstation when the install program executes, it will automatically determine the NIC settings. Otherwise, you will have to specify the settings (such as IRQ) for the given ODI driver (see Figure 23.8).

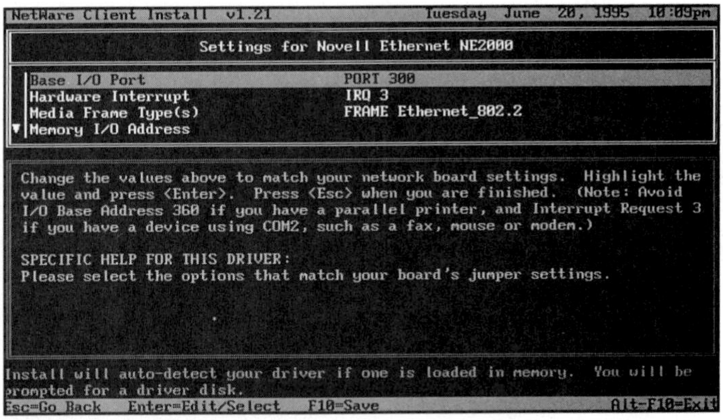

Figure 23.8.
ODI driver configuration screen.

```
NetWare Client Install  v1.21              Tuesday  June  20, 1995   10:09pm

                      Settings for Novell Ethernet NE2000

  Base I/O Port                        PORT 300
  Hardware Interrupt                   IRQ 3
  Media Frame Type(s)                  FRAME Ethernet_802.2
▼ Memory I/O Address


  Change the values above to match your network board settings.  Highlight the
  value and press <Enter>.  Press <Esc> when you are finished.  (Note: Avoid
  I/O Base Address 360 if you have a parallel printer, and Interrupt Request 3
  if you have a device using COM2, such as a fax, mouse or modem.)

  SPECIFIC HELP FOR THIS DRIVER:
  Please select the options that match your board's jumper settings.




  Install will auto-detect your driver if one is loaded in memory.  You will be
  prompted for a driver disk.
Esc=Go Back    Enter=Edit/Select    F10=Save                     Alt-F10=Exit
```

To change a setting, highlight the appropriate selection and press Enter. You will be presented with the available choices (see Figure 23.9).

Warning

The newer Ethernet drivers (circa 1993) used Ethernet_802.2 as the default frame type. Older Ethernet drivers default to Ethernet_802.3. Most NetWare 3.1x servers still use Ethernet_802.3 frame type, so if you are also connecting to NetWare 3.1x servers, check your frame

> type selection. NetWare 2.*x* does not support the Ethernet_802.2 frame type.
>
> Failure to match workstation frame type to that used by the server can render your workstation unable to communicate with the server.
>
> You can select multiple frame types by pressing F5.

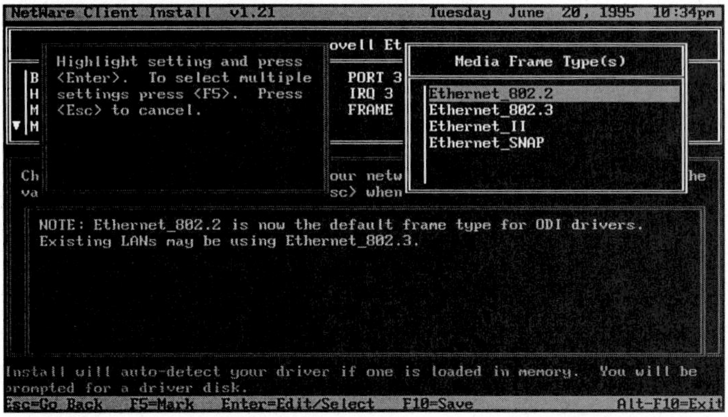

Figure 23.9.
Media Frame Type
selection menu.

In versions prior to VLM 1.10, if the driver diskettes (as created using steps given in the preceding sections or supplied with the VLM/Windows Kit you ordered from Novell) does not contain a driver for your particular network card, select Dedicated (Non-ODI) IPX driver to continue with the installation. You can edit the resulting STARTNET.BAT and NET.CFG later manually. You cannot complete the installation without selecting an NIC driver.

The INSTALL program for VLM v1.1 and higher, however, does not provide the Non-Dedicated IPX driver option. In this case, you need to select *any* driver in order to proceed with the install, and then manually edit the resulting STARTNET.BAT and NET.CFG to reflect your particular ODI driver.

In order for an ODI driver to be "installable" by the INSTALL program, it must have a companion .INS file. You can obtain this file from the NIC vendor or create one using one of the existing files as an example.

If you allowed the install process to modify your AUTOEXEC.BAT and CONFIG.SYS files, make sure you check them. Note the modification made to your AUTOEXEC.BAT (see Figure 23.10).

The install program inserts a call to the STARTNET.BAT file (for loading the ODI drivers and VLM) as the first line of AUTOEXEC.BAT. If you load any memory-

23

INSTALLING NEW WORKSTATION SOFTWARE

resident programs (TSRs), such as SHARE, in your AUTOEXEC.BAT, you will be unable to unload the ODI and VLM drivers. You should move this line to the end of the file.

Figure 23.10.
Note the location of
@CALL STARTNET.BAT.

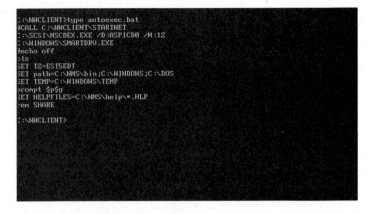

```
C:\NWCLIENT>type autoexec.bat
@CALL C:\NWCLIENT\STARTNET
C:\SCSI\MSCDEX.EXE /D:ASPICD0 /M:12
C:\WINDOWS\SMARTDRV.EXE
@echo off
:ls
SET TZ=EST5EDT
SET path=C:\NMS\bin;C:\WINDOWS;C:\DOS
SET TEMP=C:\WINDOWS\TEMP
prompt $p$g
SET HELPFILES=C:\NMS\help\*.HLP
rem SHARE

C:\NWCLIENT>
```

Warning

You need to manually add SET TZ to your AUTOEXEC.BAT file (see Figure 23.10). Without the time zone DOS variable set correctly, some of the NetWare 4 utilities will exhibit strange behavior. Check that the time zone specification is correct. For example, for Eastern Standard Time, use SET TZ=EST5EDT.

The STARTNET.BAT file is created in \NWCLIENT (default) or the directory you specified during the installation. In this file, a DOS variable called NWLANGUAGE is set. It is important that the correct language is specified so that any messages from NetWare utilities are displayed in the correct language. The batch file also loads the ODI and VLM drivers. Following is a sample STARTNET.BAT (as created by the INSTALL program for VLM v1.20):

```
SET NWLANGUAGE=ENGLISH
C:\NWCLIENT\LSL.COM

C:\NWCLIENT\NW2000.COM
C:\NWCLIENT\IPXODI.COM
C:\NWCLIENT\VLM.EXE
```

You might want to edit this file to load the various drivers into high memory, either using DOS LOADHIGH or the appropriate command for your memory manager.

WINDOWS-RELATED CHANGES

As part of the NetWare support under Windows, a NetWare Tools group is created. In it are the icons for NW Admin and User Tools programs. The NW Admin is the Windows-based administration tool for LAN administrators. User Tools is for all users. You may want to delete the NW Admin icon from the group so that users will not access it by mistake.

The following changes are made to SYSTEM.INI, WIN.INI, and PROGMAN.INI files:

SYSTEM.INI

◆ Modification of `network.drv=` to `network.drv=netware.drv` under the `[boot]` section

◆ Modification of `network.drv=` to `network.drv=NetWare (v4.0)` under the `[boot.description]` section

◆ Modification of `network=dosnet` to `network=*vnetbios,vipx.386, vnetware.386` under the `[386enh]` section

◆ Modification of `TimerCriticalSection=` to `TimerCriticalSection= 1000` under the `[386enh]` section

WIN.INI

◆ Addition of NWPOPUP.EXE to the `LOAD=` line under the `[windows]` section

PROGMAN.INI

◆ Addition of `Groupx=NWTOOLS.GRP` to the group file list

Warning

Some new Windows drivers are also copied (see Chapter 24 for details). Do not revert back to the drivers from your Windows 3.1 disks for VLM.

NET.CFG FILE FOR DOS

The NET.CFG file created by the installation is minimal (see Figure 23.11). Insert the line

```
NAME CONTEXT="name context"
```

under the `NetWare DOS Requester` section. Note that the quotation marks are required, as in the following:

```
NAME CONTEXT="OU=Consult.O=DreamLAN"
```

This line sets your default context in the NDS tree and is used in locating your user object within the NDS during the login process.

Figure 23.11.
NET.CFG as created by
the installation process.

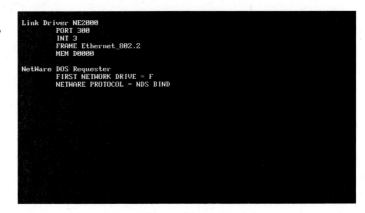

```
Link Driver NE2000
        PORT 300
        INT 3
        FRAME Ethernet_802.2
        MEM D0000

NetWare DOS Requester
        FIRST NETWORK DRIVE = F
        NETWARE PROTOCOL = NDS BIND
```

For a complete list of NET.CFG options, VLM related information, and last minute changes that are not in the (DynaText) documentation, consult the README.TXT file, which is copied to the directory you specified in the installation step. The default path for this file is C:\NWCLIENT.

INSTALLING OS/2 REQUESTER

You install the OS/2 Requester (also known as NetWare Client for OS/2) in much the same manner as the DOS Requester. The steps discussed here are for Requester v2.01; different steps for Requester v2.1x are noted where appropriate.

To start the installation, insert the WSOS2_1 disk into a floppy drive, change your default working directory to the drive, and run INSTALL. You must do this from either an OS/2 window or a full-screen box.

The following four things happen when you install the OS/2 client:

1. A directory is created on your workstation.
2. Files are copied.
3. The Novell group icon is created on the OS/2 desktop.
4. The CONFIG.SYS file is modified.

You first are prompted for the language to be used for directions and prompts, and then you are presented with the main installation menu, as shown in Figure 23.12.

Figure 23.12.
OS/2 Requester main
installation menu.

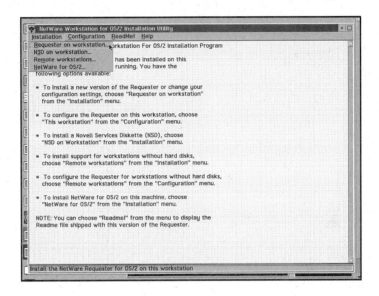

To install the requester files, select Requester on workstation... from the Installation menu. You then will be prompted for the directory into which the requester files will be installed. The default path is C:\NETWARE. You can specify any directory path you want. The example used here is C:\NETWARE2 (see Figure 23.13).

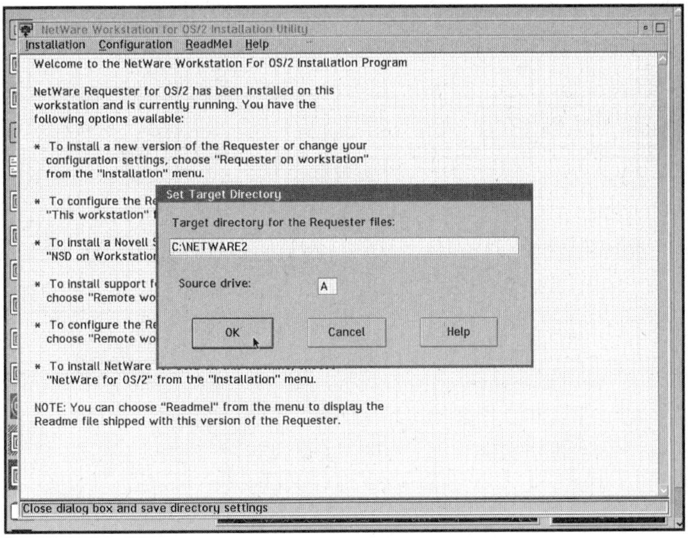

Figure 23.13.
Specify the directory
into which the client
files are to be installed.

The next screen is the Requester Installation prompt. You should choose the Edit CONFIG.SYS and Copy All Files for a first-time installation (see Figure 23.14). The other three options are for changing the initial installation.

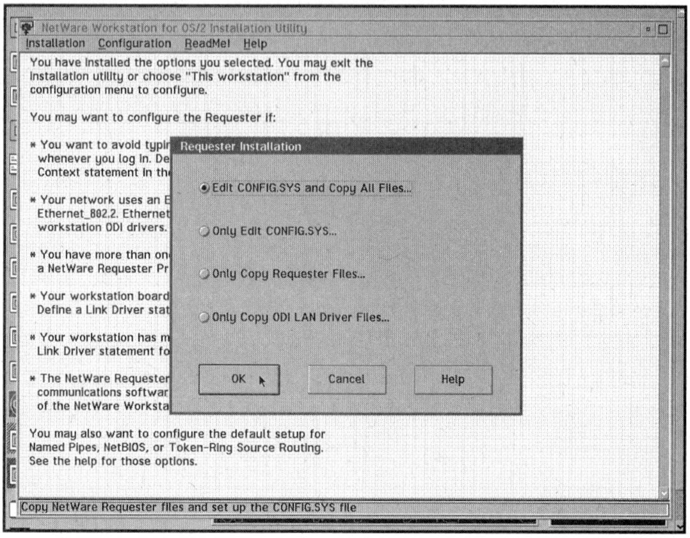

Figure 23.14. Requester Installation menu screen.

The install program appends a number of lines that are appended to the end of CONFIG.SYS. The section is clearly marked with `NetWare Requester statements BEGIN` and `NetWare Requester statements END` (see Figure 23.15). Any components you did not select (such as named pipe support) are commented out.

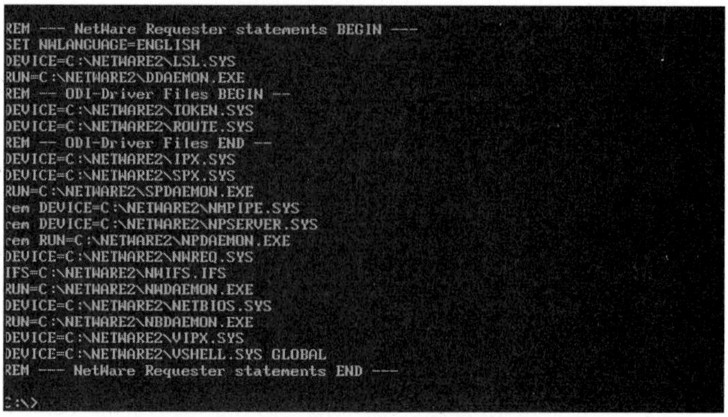

```
REM --- NetWare Requester statements BEGIN ---
SET NWLANGUAGE=ENGLISH
DEVICE=C:\NETWARE2\LSL.SYS
RUN=C:\NETWARE2\DDAEMON.EXE
REM -- ODI-Driver Files BEGIN --
DEVICE=C:\NETWARE2\TOKEN.SYS
DEVICE=C:\NETWARE2\ROUTE.SYS
REM -- ODI-Driver Files END --
DEVICE=C:\NETWARE2\IPX.SYS
DEVICE=C:\NETWARE2\SPX.SYS
RUN=C:\NETWARE2\SPDAEMON.EXE
rem DEVICE=C:\NETWARE2\NMPIPE.SYS
rem DEVICE=C:\NETWARE2\NPSERVER.SYS
rem RUN=C:\NETWARE2\NPDAEMON.EXE
DEVICE=C:\NETWARE2\NWREQ.SYS
IFS=C:\NETWARE2\NWIFS.IFS
RUN=C:\NETWARE2\NWDAEMON.EXE
DEVICE=C:\NETWARE2\NETBIOS.SYS
RUN=C:\NETWARE2\NBDAEMON.EXE
DEVICE=C:\NETWARE2\VIPX.SYS
DEVICE=C:\NETWARE2\VSHELL.SYS GLOBAL
REM --- NetWare Requester statements END ---

C:\>
```

Figure 23.15. NetWare Requester section in the OS/2 CONFIG.SYS file.

You will need to specify an ODI driver for loading. A set of drivers is shipped with the Requester on the WSDRV_1 diskette (see Figure 23.16). If it does not contain one for your particular NIC, check the driver diskette that came with your NIC or contact the manufacturer.

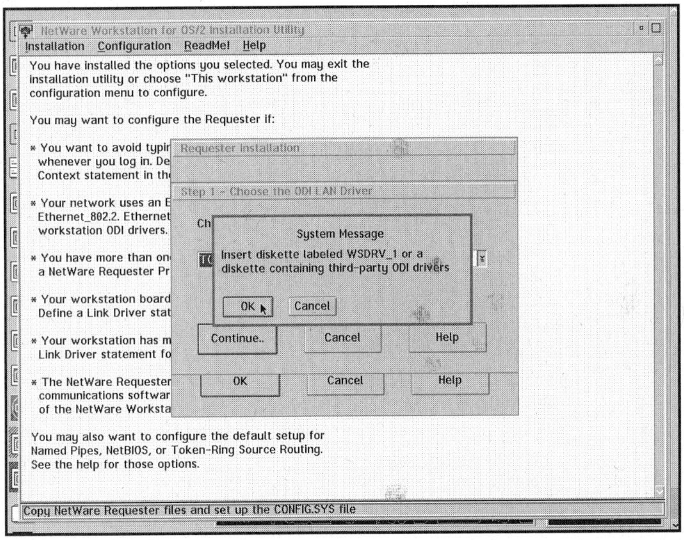

Figure 23.16.
Selecting ODI drivers.

Note

Similar to the Requester, OS/2 drivers tend to be OS/2 version specific. Make sure you have the driver for your version of OS/2.

You then are prompted to specify the type of NetWare support for DOS and Windows applications (see Figure 23.17). You have the following three choices:

◆ **Private NetWare Shell Support**: Each DOS and OS/2 session is independent from each other.

◆ **Global NetWare Shell Support**: In this mode, the DOS sessions share the same resources (such as drive mappings) as the OS/2 sessions.

◆ **No NetWare Shell Support**: No networking support

The prompts for this step are slightly different for Requester v2.1. You also will be prompted for AUTOEXEC.BAT settings. For more information about the selections, click the Help button.

You can specify additional protocol support, such as SPX and NetBIOS (see Figure 23.18). Check all applicable selection boxes. The unchecked options are commented out in the CONFIG.SYS file; therefore, if you want to use them, you can simply edit CONFIG.SYS without having to reinstall the Requester files.

23

INSTALLING NEW WORKSTATION SOFTWARE

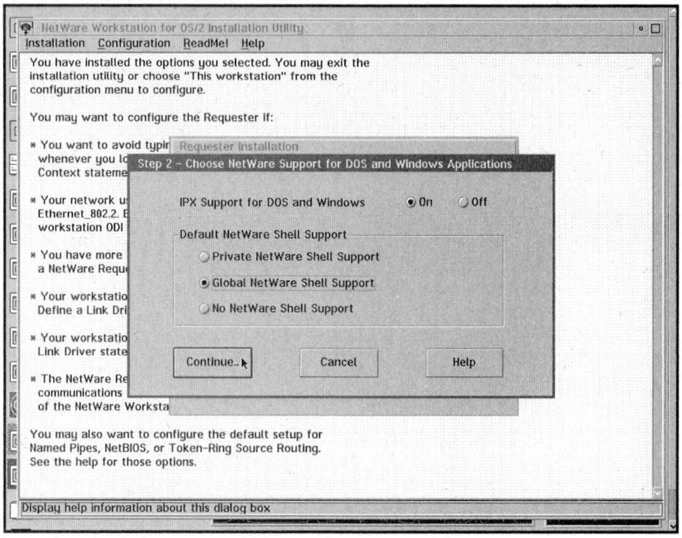

Figure 23.17.
NetWare support for
DOS and Windows
applications choices.

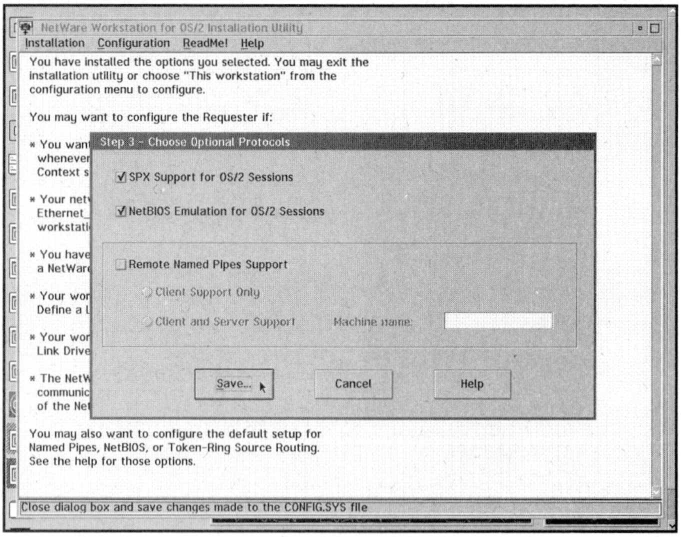

Figure 23.18.
Optional protocol
support selection menu.

A backup copy of CONFIG.SYS is made (CONFIG.BAK) before changes are saved to it.

You have the option of copying just the specified ODI driver to your workstation, or copy all the supplied drivers (see Figure 23.19). The status line at the bottom of the screen reflects the file currently being copied.

Next, you need to create a NET.CFG file to configure the workstation.

Figure 23.19.
Menu to copy ODI LAN
driver files.

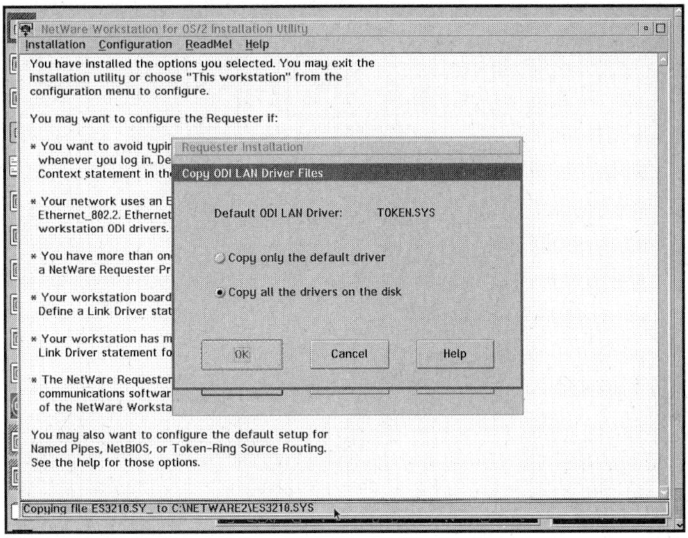

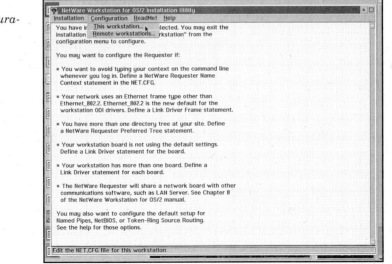

NET.CFG FILE FOR OS/2

From the main installation menu, select This Workstation from the Configuration menu (see Figure 23.20). The file should be created in the root directory of your boot drive. The exact syntax and explanation of the different NET.CFG parameters are provided by the menu (see Figure 23.21). A sample NET.CFG is shown in Figure 23.22.

Figure 23.20.
OS/2 client configura-
tion menu.

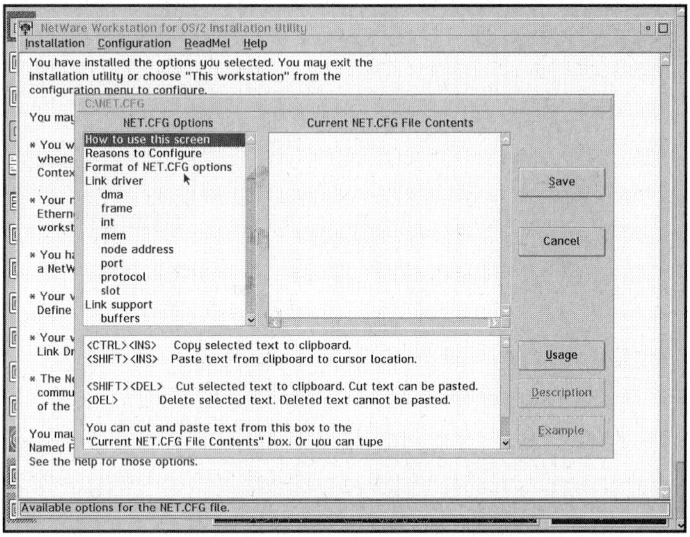

Figure 23.21.
NET.CFG parameters.

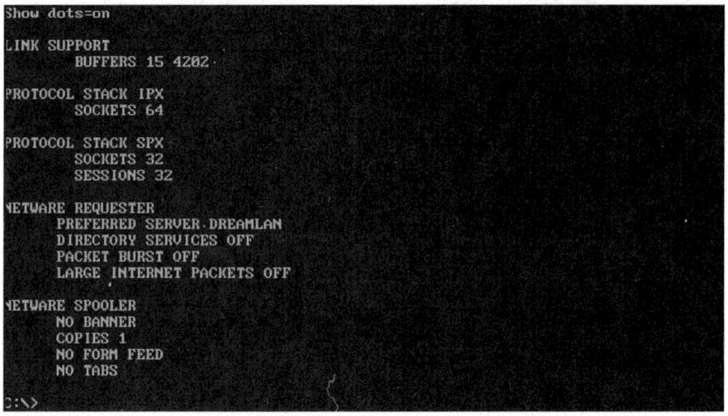

Figure 23.22.
A sample NET.CFG for
OS/2 client worksta-
tion.

Similar to the DOS NET.CFG, you should add a NAME CONTEXT statement under the
NETWARE REQUESTER section.

If you are using dual-boot (DOS and OS/2), you can combine the contents of your
DOS NET.CFG with that of OS/2's. However, make sure you leave the NET.CFG in
the root directory.

SUMMARY

This chapter discussed the ODI technology, and presented a short discussion about
NETX versus VLM. Also presented were step-by-step installation procedures for
installing DOS/Windows support for PC workstations, and OS/2 client support for
OS/2 workstations.

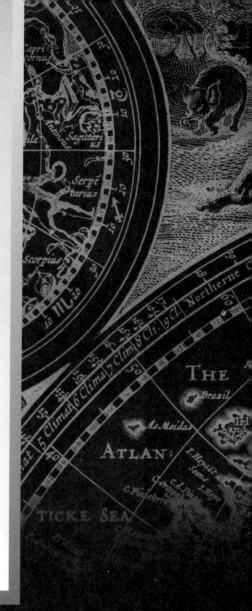

- Workstation LAN Driver

- Installing NetWare DOS Requester

- Updating NET.CFG

- Upgrading OS/2 Requester

- Updating NET.CFG

- Summary

CHAPTER 24

Upgrading Existing PC Workstations

This chapter discusses the changes required to update existing PC workstations to access NetWare 4.1 servers. The changes include reconfiguring some DOS parameters in your CONFIG.SYS file as well as some Windows configuration files, if you are using Windows.

WORKSTATION LAN DRIVER

In order to use the new NetWare DOS Requester, you must update the LAN driver for your PC workstation to use the ODI drivers. Some drivers are shipped with NetWare. If the driver you require is not included, you need to obtain it from the manufacturer of the NIC card.

Note

There is a chance that an ODI driver comes on the driver diskette shipped with your NIC card. However, you should check with the vendor for the latest version.

In the case of OS/2 workstations, make sure you have the correct driver for the OS/2 version that you are running. Check the driver diskette for your NIC or contact the vendor.

Warning

OS/2 is very specific about drivers. It has been found in the past that compatible cards may not run correctly with the original driver. For example, NE2000.SYS may not work correctly with an NE2000-compatible card. If you can, get the correct driver for the particular card.

INSTALLING NETWARE DOS REQUESTER

As described in Chapter 23, the installation of the DOS Requester is initiated by running the INSTALL program located on the WSDOS_1 diskette. You can also run the INSTALL program off the file server if you picked to copy the client files to the server during the installation using IPX/NETX (for more details, refer to Chapter 21). The DOS client files are located in the SYS:PUBLIC\DOSWIN directory (refer to Chapter 23 for the step-by-step instructions). This chapter focuses on the changes the INSTALL program makes to some of the system files.

Depending on whether you previously enabled NetWare support for Windows, some of the changes in some Windows-related files, such as WIN.INI, may have already been made.

AUTOEXEC.BAT

The installation program inserts a line `@CALL STARTNET` as the *first line* in your AUTOEXEC.BAT. You may want to move this to the end of the batch file. This line loads the ODI and VLM drivers.

A path to `C:\NWCLIENT`, assuming you used the default directory for installation, is prepended to your PATH statement, as in the following:

```
PATH C:\NWCLIENT;%PATH%
```

Note

Check to verify that the addition of this path does not exceed the DOS PATH length limit of 128 characters for your workstation.

CONFIG.SYS

Because VLM is now a DOS *requester*, it shares the same drive table as DOS. In order for VLM to access all drive letters (A-Z), the LASTDRIVE is now set to Z. This makes it incompatible with NETX.

If, for any reason, you need to run NETX, you need to edit CONFIG.SYS and remove the LASTDRIVE statement.

SYSTEM.INI

The following changes to the SYSTEM.INI file are made by the installation of VLM v1.20:

♦ Modification of `NETWORK.DRV=` to `NETWORK.DRV=NETWARE.DRV` under the `[boot]` section

♦ Modification of `NETWORK.DRV=` to `NETWORK.DRV=NetWare (v4.0)` under the `[boot.description]` section

♦ Modification of `NETWORK=DOSNET` to `NETWORK=*VNETBIOS,VIPX.386, VNETWARE.386` under the `[386enh]` section

♦ Modification of `TimerCriticalSection=` to `TimerCriticalSection= 1000` under the `[386enh]` section. For VLM 1.11 and prior, this value needs to be set to `10000`.

WIN.INI

Addition of NWPOPUP.EXE to the LOAD= line is made under the [windows] section. This allows you to receive broadcast messages from NetWare servers while in Windows.

PROGMAN.INI

A new group file list, Groupx=NWTOOLS.GRP, has been added. This group contains the NetWare Tools and NW Admin icons. The NetWare Tools icon allows you to map drives, printers, and so on from within Windows (see Figure 24.1). The NW Admin icon is a Windows-based tool for LAN administrators. You may want to remove this for end users.

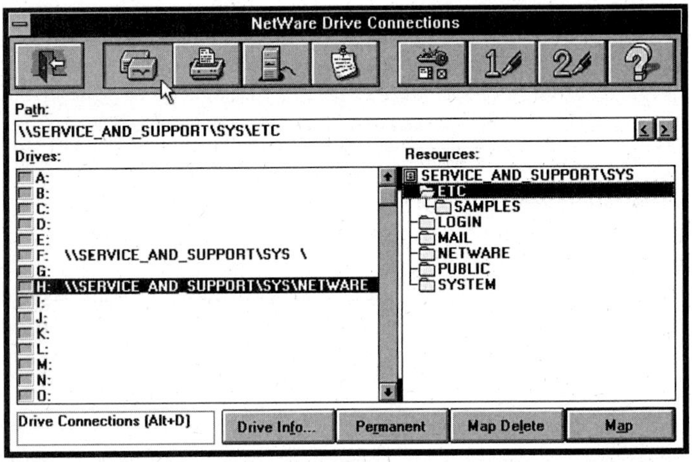

Figure 24.1.
NetWare Tools.

WINDOWS FILES

When you include Windows support for the NetWare DOS Requester, a number of DLL files are copied to the SYSTEM directory of your Windows files. The filenames and their functions are as follows:

- ◆ **NWCALLS.DLL**: APIs for NCP communication between file server and workstation
- ◆ **NWIPXSPX.DLL**: APIs for IPX/SPX communication
- ◆ **NWLOCALE.DLL**: APIs for localization and internationalization of applications

- **NWNET.DLL**: Network API support for NDS, and so on
- **NWPOPUP.EXE**: Windows utility to "pop-up" network messages in Windows
- **NWPSRV.DLL**: Contains print server services APIs
- **VIPX.386**: Virtual IPX/SPX driver for Windows enhanced mode
- **VNETWARE.386**: Virtual NetWare driver for Windows enhanced mode
- **NETWARE.DRV**: NetWare network driver
- **NETWARE.HLP**: NetWare network driver help file
- **NWGDI.DLL**: NetWare graphical device interface
- **NWUSER.EXE**: Provides an entry point into NETWARE.DRV
- **NETWARER.EXE**: NetWare English language enabled driver. (This file is copied to the NLS\ENGLISH directory of your Windows directory.)

Warning

The NETWARE.DRV driver is not compatible with the NETX driver. If you need to run the NETX shell, you need to replace NETWARE.DRV using the original copy from your Windows 3.1 disks or a copy from CompuServe.

Many times, people have problems within Windows after upgrading to VLM because of older .DLL and .386 files in the Windows directory. Check to ensure that the files in the preceding list have no duplicates elsewhere, especially along the DOS and NetWare search paths.

UPDATING NET.CFG

If you were using SHELL.CFG before, you should move the contents to NET.CFG. Although the current ODI drivers will also look for SHELL.CFG, there is no guarantee that future versions will. And you can get unpredictable results if both SHELL.CFG and NET.CFG exist. Simply merge SHELL.CFG into the beginning of NET.CFG, and make sure the lines are left-justified. Some parameters are no longer used. You can tell whether the parameters are recognized or not by seeing whether they are echoed while the ODI drivers load. If not echoed, then they are no longer supported, or the syntax has changed.

If you have any special settings used in the previous NET.CFG, combine them with the new one. Some settings now need to go under the NetWare DOS Requester section.

Tip

> You can manually create NET.CFG if you want. Make sure you have a NetWare DOS Requester section. It is a common error that the word *requester* is misspelled as *requestor*.

UPGRADING OS/2 REQUESTER

Upgrading the OS/2 Requester needs to be done from diskettes. This is because when the OS/2 workstation boots up, the requester files are loaded via CONFIG.SYS, and some files are held open by OS/2. They cannot be replaced by the upgrade process.

In preparation for the upgrade, you need to disable the loading of the requester files in CONFIG.SYS. Either delete the requester section or comment the lines out.

Tip

> It is *best* to delete the lines after a backup copy of CONFIG.SYS is made.

Boot up the OS/2 machine "clean," without the Requester, and then refer to the step-by-step instructions in Chapter 23 for the OS/2 Requester install.

UPDATING NET.CFG

If you have special parameters, such as IPX RETRY COUNTS, set in your previous NET.CFG, move them to the new one, or include them while you are creating the new copy.

Do not forget to edit NET.CFG to include a NAME CONTEXT.

Note

> For OS/2, the section name is called NetWare Requester and for DOS it is called NetWare DOS Requester. That means you can combine the two files together into one, as each has its own section heading. This is useful for dual-boot OS/2 machines, or if you want to have a "standard" NET.CFG for both OS/2 and DOS/Windows workstations.

SUMMARY

This chapter highlighted the changes necessary for the existing OS/2 and DOS/Windows workstations in order to run the new requester drivers to connect to a NetWare 4.1 server.

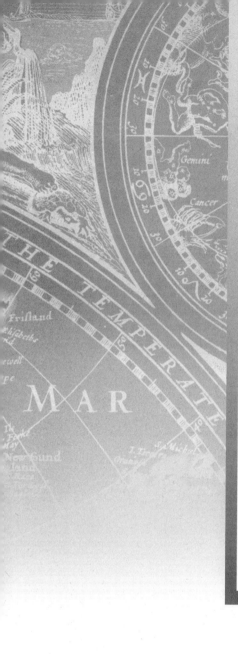

- Configuring User Accounts

- Menuing

- MHS Services

- Implementing Security

- Auditing

- Documenting Your Network

- Working with Users

- Network Printing

- Selecting Network Applications

- Remote Access

PART VI

Operation

- Creating Users

- Creating Groups

- Login Scripts

- Creating, Copying, and Modifying Your Login Scripts

- Login Script Commands and Variables

- Login Script Commands

- Login Script Identifier Variables

- Login Script Example

- Summary

CHAPTER 25

Configuring User Accounts

The success of your network is greatly dependent upon how well you can set up resources and make them available to users. This chapter deals with the specifics of setting up users, groups, and login scripts. Mastering these operations can simplify the management of a secure computing environment.

CREATING USERS

The creation of users can be accomplished by using two NetWare-provided utilities: NETADMIN, which is a text-based utility and the NetWare Administrator, which is a graphical utility. Procedures for both these utilities will be reviewed. Keep in mind that the procedures that are covered are very similar for creating other object types, such as Groups, in the NDS database.

CREATING A USER WITH NETADMIN

Before creating a user with NETADMIN, you should verify that you are running DOS 3.30 or later. You also should have sufficient rights to create objects in the intended NDS context. Following is the procedure for creating a user under NETADMIN:

1. From the DOS prompt, type

   `NETADMIN`

2. Select Manage Objects from the NetAdmin Options menu.

3. Select the container to which you want to add the users.

4. Press Insert key to create a new user.

5. Select from the Select an object class screen the object class you want to create. Remember, users can only be created under Organizations and Organizational Units. Because you are creating a user, select the User object (see Figure 25.1).

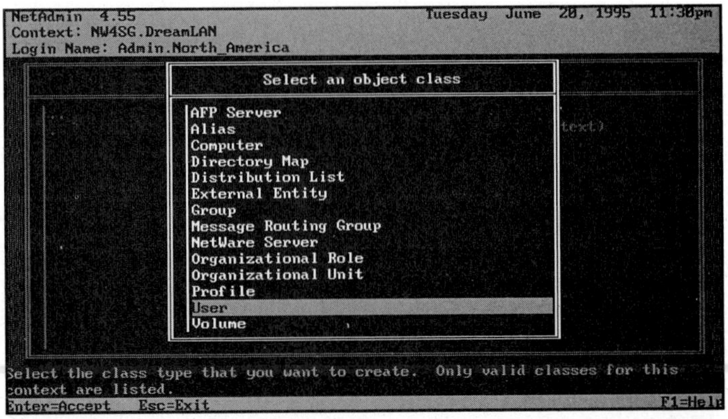

Figure 25.1.
Selecting the USER
object class.

6. Type in the prompted information (the user name and last name). If you want to continue creating other users, select Yes to the prompt to create another object. When you complete the process, press F10 to save the changes.

7. After the creation of the user, you can add additional information about the user and the configuration. To accomplish this, select the newly created user object by highlighting it, and then pressing Enter or F10.

CREATING A USER USING THE NETWARE ADMINISTRATOR

Before attempting the creation of a user using the NetWare Administrator, you should verify that you have sufficient rights to create a user in a targeted context. To run the NetWare Administrator, you should be using Windows 3.1x or OS/2 2.x. Following are the procedures for creating a user using the NetWare Administrator:

1. Click the NetWare Administrator icon from the Windows Program Manager or the OS/2 desktop.

2. Select the object that will contain the new user. This can be either an Organization or Organizational Unit.

3. Select Create from the Object menu.

4. Select the User object (see Figure 25.2).

Figure 25.2.
Selecting the USER object class in the NetWare Administrator.

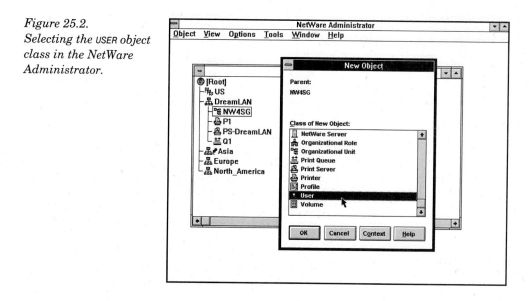

5. Enter the information into the dialog box. The user name and last name are mandatory. If you want to continue creating other users, you can select the option to continue creating other users. When completed, click on OK to create the User object.

6. Once the User object is created, you can double-click on the object and fill out other information about the user and the configuration being used.

CREATING GROUPS

Groups are useful for grouping users together for management purposes. Instead of giving each user rights to a certain application, you could give a group rights to the application and then assign users to be members of the group. The creation of groups can be accomplished by using two NetWare-provided utilities: NETADMIN, which is a text-based utility, and the NetWare Administrator, which is a graphical utility. Procedures for both of these utilities will be reviewed. Keep in mind, that the procedures that are covered are very similar for creating other object types in the NDS database.

CREATING A GROUP WITH NETADMIN

Before creating a group with NETADMIN, you should verify that you are running DOS 3.30 or later. You also should have sufficient rights to create objects in the intended NDS context. Following is the procedure for creating a group under NETADMIN:

1. From the DOS prompt, type

   `NETADMIN`

2. Select Manage Objects from the NetAdmin Options menu.

3. Select the container to which you want to add the group.

4. Press Insert to create a new group.

5. Select from the Select an Object Class screen the object class that you want to create. Remember, groups can only be created under Organizations and Organizational Units. Select the Group object type.

6. Type in the prompted information (group name). If you want to continue creating other groups, select Yes to the prompt to create another object. When you complete the information, press F10 to save the changes.

7. After the creation of the group, you can add additional information (such as which users are part of the group) about the group and its configuration. To accomplish this, select the newly created group object by first highlighting it and then pressing Enter or F10.

CREATING A GROUP USING THE NETWARE ADMINISTRATOR

Before attempting the creation of a group using the NetWare Administrator, you should verify that you have sufficient rights to create a group in a targeted context. To run the NetWare Administrator you should be using Windows 3.1*x* or OS/2 2.*x*. Following are the procedures for creating a group using the NetWare Administrator:

1. Click the NetWare Administrator icon from the Windows Program Manager or the OS/2 desktop.

2. Select the object that will contain the new group. This can be either an Organization or Organizational Unit.

3. Select Create from the Object menu.

4. Select the Group object.

5. Enter the information into the dialog box. The group name is mandatory. If you want to continue creating other groups, you can select the option to continue creating other groups. When completed, click on OK to create the Group object.

6. Once the group is created, you can double-click on the object and fill out other information (such as the members of the group) about the group and its configuration.

LOGIN SCRIPTS

Login scripts are used by both the administrator and the user to set up the network computing environment. Upon login, depending on the user's configuration, these login scripts can be executed. Like an AUTOEXEC.BAT under DOS, a login script can be used to establish path settings or drive mappings for applications, as well as providing a mechanism for executing a file (such as CAPTURE.EXE for printing). They also can be used to display information for all users, groups of users, or even a particular user.

This part of the chapter discusses different types of login scripts, how to select what to put in each, where you create and modify the scripts, the commands that can be used, and examples of login scripts.

TYPES OF LOGIN SCRIPTS

Following are the three types of login scripts you should become familiar with as an administrator:

System Login Script (or Container Login Script): This script is used to set up general network computing environments for users within a certain Organization or Organization Unit. Upon the initial login, this script would be executed first.

Profile Login Script: This script is used to set up the general network computing environment for users, much like a system login script, but at the groups level. The difference between the Profile and System Login Script is multiple Profile scripts could exist within an Organization or Organizational Unit. One of the Profile scripts could be assigned to multiple users, and another to other users. The rule is only one profile script can be assigned per user. This is ideal for groups that may want to have control over a specific general script, without letting them have control of the System Login Script. If a profile script is assigned to a user, it will be executed upon login after the System Login script.

User Login Script: This script is specific to a user. It is used to customize the environment for each user. It is executed after the Profile Login script.

Within the code of LOGIN.EXE there is a default login script that is used for users without any scripts. It contains the essential commands needed (drive mappings to NetWare) for a login from a user without any scripts (such as Admin upon initial login). The default login script cannot be modified. As an administrator, you do not need to be concerned about this script but should be aware that it exists.

LOGIN SCRIPT ESSENTIALS

As an administrator, you'll want scripts that are easy to maintain. The least amount of modifications as possible should be the ultimate goal. The following sections describe the different types of login scripts and provide brief examples of what each script type might contain.

SYSTEM LOGIN SCRIPT

The System Login Script, or Container Login Script, is executed by all the users that reside within that container. This script is used to set up the general working environment for a "department" or "division" of users and should include the following:

◆ NetWare drive mappings

◆ DOS drive mappings

◆ Generally used applications mappings

◆ E-mail drive mappings and settings

◆ Login Script greetings

◆ General displayed messages

◆ Default printer capture statements

PROFILE LOGIN SCRIPT

After establishing the general working environment for the users using the Container Login Script, you can further customize the environment for particular groups of users with the use of Profile Login Scripts. You may consider Profile Login Scripts as "group" login scripts. You should include the following in your Profile Login Scripts:

◆ Specific group application mappings

◆ Group messages

◆ Group printer capture statements

◆ Group environment settings

USER LOGIN SCRIPT

Oftentimes, the use of Container and Profile Login Scripts are sufficient to set up the proper working environment for a user. But if you need further customization, down to the individual user level, you can use User Login Scripts. In general, User Login Scripts contain the following:

◆ Personal drive mappings to local and network drives

◆ Personal messages (such as reminders)

◆ Capture statements to specific printers

Remember that NetWare login scripts are very flexible, you can do it any way you want to. If you can, keep most (global) commands and setups in the system login script and then the profile login script. This should help on minimizing administration time.

CREATING, COPYING, AND MODIFYING YOUR LOGIN SCRIPTS

NetWare 4.x provides two utilities that can be used to create, copy, and modify login scripts. You can use either the NetWare Administer graphical utility or the NETADMIN text-based utility. It is important to note that if you use the SYSCON utility that was provided with NetWare 2.x or 3.x to modify a system or user login script, those changes will not appear in Directory Services (NetWare Administer and NETADMIN).

The following is a list of the different login scripts and their association with objects found in Directory Services. When creating, copying, or modifying scripts, you will need to go to the login script property associated with the respective objects:

System Login Script   This script is a property of the Organization or Organizational Unit objects.

Profile Login Script   This script is a property of the Profile object.

User Login Script   This script is a property of the User object.

CREATING OR MODIFYING A LOGIN SCRIPT USING NETADMIN

As mentioned earlier, the NETADMIN utility is a text-based utility that will allow you to manage your login scripts. To use this utility, you should have DOS 3.3 or later loaded on your workstation. You also should log into directory services as a user with sufficient rights to make changes. Following is a list of the procedures you will need to create and modify a login script:

1. From the command line, type

   `NETADMIN`

2. Choose Manage objects from the NetAdmin options menu (see Figure 25.3).

Figure 25.3.
NetAdmin Main Menu.

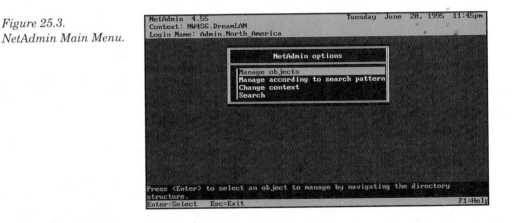

3. At this point, you have two options: you can select an object you want to modify, or you can change to a different context to find the object you want to modify.

4. Once you have selected the object you want to modify, remember that System or Container Login Script is stored in an Organization or Organizational Unit object, Profile Login Script is stored in a Profile object, and User

Login Script is associated with a User object. Select the View or edit properties of this object option (see Figure 25.4).

Figure 25.4.
Object modification
options.

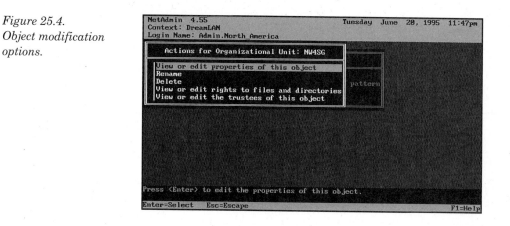

5. Select Login Script from the displayed menu.

6. If this is a new or empty script, you will be first given the option of copying a login script from another object in the directory. If you answer No to copying the login script, the cursor will move to the login script text box. If you answer Yes to copying a login script, a box will appear in which you can place the name of the object from which you want to copy. If you want, press Insert to display and a menu comes up that will allow you to "walk the tree" (navigate around the tree) and find the object you want.

7. Once you are in the login script text box, you can enter the commands and variables you will need. These commands and variable options are listed later in this chapter in the "Login Script Commands" section.

8. Upon the completion of the script change, you can press F10 to save your changes. If you have created a login script, you should read the next section to learn more about using this script.

ASSOCIATING A PROFILE SCRIPT TO A USER USING NETADMIN

If you created a profile script that must be associated with a user, you will need to assign and give the user rights to the profile login script. The following is a list of steps you will need to go through to ensure that a user will execute the profile login script.

1. From the DOS prompt, type
   `NETADMIN <Enter>`
2. Select the Manage Objects option from the NetAdmin Options.
3. Select the User object you want to modify. You may have to browse the directory tree to a different context.
4. Select the View or edit properties of this object.
5. Select Group/Security Equals/Profile.
6. Select the Profile field.
7. Enter in the name of the Profile object in the text box. If you don't remember the profile name, you can press Ins to search for the object.
8. After placing the profile object name, press F10 to save the information.
9. Now that you have associated the user with a profile, you will need to give the user rights to the profile. You can do this by first selecting the View or edit the trustees of this object.
10. Select Trustees.
11. To allow a User object to be trustee of this Profile object, press Ins.
12. Select [All Properties Rights].
13. Enter the name of the User object that needs to be the trustee of this Profile object. If you want, you can search for the object by pressing the Ins key. Once you have selected the object, press F10 to save the information.
14. To add the user as a trustee and grant the default property right, press Enter. This gives the User object Read rights to all the Profile's properties.
15. Select the User object and press Ins key.
16. Choose [Object Rights].
17. Enter the name of the User object or press Ins to search. After selecting the User object, press F10.
18. To grant the default object right, press Enter.

This completes the steps you will need to take to set up a Profile script for usage by a User object.

COPYING A LOGIN SCRIPT USING NETADMIN

Copying a login script can help save time, especially when many of the System and Profiles Login Scripts are very similar throughout the network. You should log into directory services as a user with sufficient rights to make changes. To copy login scripts, follow these steps:

1. At the DOS prompt, type
   `NETADMIN`
2. Select Manage Objects from the NetAdmin Options menu.
3. Select the object whose login script you want to copy. This can be done by finding it on the list and pressing F10 or by pressing Ins to browse for the object.
4. After selecting the object, click the View or edit properties of this object.
5. Select Login Script.
6. Within the login script text box, select the part of the script you want to copy by placing the cursor at the beginning of the text and pressing F5 to mark the text.
7. Use the arrow keys to highlight the text you want to copy.
8. Press Del to put the text into a buffer.
9. Press Ins to place the text from the buffer into the script again.
10. You now can exit the login script by pressing Esc, and selecting No when prompted to save the changes.
11. Return to the NetAdmin Options menu and select Manage Objects.
12. Select the destination object's login script. This can be done either by finding it on the displayed list and pressing F10, or by pressing Insert to walk the tree and browse for the object.
13. Select View or edit properties of this object.
14. Select Login Script.
15. Within the login script text box, place the cursor where you want to insert the copied text.
16. Press Ins to insert the text from the buffer into the login script.
17. After the text has been placed in the script, press F10 to save the changes.

CREATING OR MODIFYING A LOGIN SCRIPT USING NETWARE ADMINISTRATOR

The NetWare Administrator is a graphical-based utility that can be used to manage login scripts. You also will need to have the Write property to the objects that contain the login scripts. To create and modify login scripts, follow these steps:

1. Double-click the NetWare Administrator icon on the Windows Program Manager or the OS/2 desktop.
2. Using the Browser, select the object whose login script you want to modify or create.

3. Select Details from the Object menu.

4. Click the Login Script option button on the right hand side of the displayed menu.

5. A login script text box will appear, where you can add or delete login script commands and variables.

6. After you make the changes you want, choose OK to save the login script. If you have created a login script, you should read the next section to learn more about using this script.

ASSOCIATING A PROFILE SCRIPT TO A USER USING NETWARE ADMINISTRATOR

If you created a profile script that must be associated with a user, you will need to assign and give the user rights to the profile login script. To ensure that a user will execute the profile login script, follow these steps:

1. Using the Browser, select the User object to which you will be assigning the profile script.

2. Select Details from the Object menu.

3. Click the Login Script option button.

4. Enter the name of the Profile object you want to assign in the Default Profile field. If you want, you can search for the Profile by clicking the Browser button next to the Default Profile field.

5. After you make your changes, choose OK to save the changes.

The next few steps explain how to give the user sufficient rights to use the login script.

1. Using the Browser, select the Profile object you wish the user to have rights to.

2. Select Trustee of this Object from the Object menu.

3. Select Add Trustee.

4. Enter the name of the User object that will be using this Profile object. You can use the Browser button to search for the User object, if needed.

5. Make sure that the User has the Browse object right and the Read property right checked.

6. To save, select OK.

Copying a Login Script Using NetWare Administrator

Copying login script can help save time, especially when many of the System and Profiles Login Scripts are very similar throughout the network. You should log into directory services as a user with sufficient rights to make changes. To copy login scripts, follow these steps:

1. Double-click the NetWare Administrator icon on the Windows Program Manager or the OS/2 desktop.
2. Select the object whose login script you want to copy by using the Browser.
3. Select Details from the Object menu.
4. Select the Login Script option button.
5. Within the login script text box, highlight the text you want to copy.
6. Press Ctrl+Ins to copy the highlighted text into a buffer in memory.
7. To save and exit the login script, select OK.
8. Using the Browser, select the User object whose login script you want to paste in the text.
9. Select Detail from the Object menu.
10. Select the Login Script option button.
11. Within the login script text box, place the cursor where you want to paste the text and press Shift+Ins.
12. To save the modified login script, select OK.

Login Script Commands and Variables

The login script commands and variables are used to automate the creation of the user's environment. The environment may consist of messages, drive mappings, and DOS environment settings. With each command, an explanation, command format, and brief example will be given on how you can use a login script. The next section will provide full examples of login scripts.

Before going into details about the various commands and variables, an explanation of the command format syntax can help you determine which is mandatory or optional:

[ ]   Square brackets indicate that the enclosed item is optional.

¦   The vertical bar is used to show that either the item to the left of the bar or to the right of the bar can be used. You cannot use both items.

[option]   Options or parameters are listed with the command.

[[]]   The nested square brackets indicate that all enclosed items are optional. However, if the items within the innermost brackets are used, then you must use the items within the outermost brackets.

LOGIN SCRIPT COMMANDS

In the following sections, the various login script commands are listed, in alphabetical order. The syntax for the command and an example is given where appropriate.

#

This command (#) is used to execute an external command from within the login script. This is especially useful when you want to capture a user to a particular printer on the network through the login script. The following is the command format that you can use:

```
# [path] filename [parameter]
```

The `path` variable represents the full DOS path where the file you want to execute is located.

The `filename` variable represents the name of the file you want to have executed from the login script.

The `parameter` variable represents file parameters that may be executed with the file.

Workstations may not have enough memory to execute the LOGIN utility and the external command, the LOGIN utility, will "swap" out of conventional memory to place the LOGIN into available higher memory or onto the disk. If you want to swap LOGIN out of conventional memory every time you execute an external command, you can place the SWAP command in the login script before the # command.

If you do not want to temporarily swap to higher memory, you may use the NOSWAP command. (The NOSWAP command is discussed later in this section.)

Example: If you wanted a user to capture to PRINTQ-1 upon login, you may place this inside the login script.

```
#CAPTURE Q=PRINTQ-1 NB NFF TI=10
```

ATTACH

The ATTACH command is used to connect to bindery-based NetWare servers (NetWare 2.x and/or NetWare 3.x) or to NetWare 4.x servers using bindery emulation. The command format is

25

```
ATTACH [server[/username[;password]]]
```

The *server* variable represents the actual server name to which you are requesting a connection.

The *username* variable represents the login name you want to use when connecting to the specified server.

The *password* variable represents the password of the login name specified.

Example: If you wanted to attach to a bindery-based NetWare server called ACCOUNTING, as user DSMITH with the password of MOUNTAIN, you would add the following line to the login script:

```
ATTACH ACCOUNTING/DSMITH;MOUNTAIN
```

BREAK

The BREAK command is used to control the user's capability to use the Ctrl+C or Ctrl+Break to terminate the execution of the login script. If BREAK ON is placed in the login script, a user can terminate the execution of the login script. BREAK OFF is the default setting. The command format is

```
BREAK [ON ¦ OFF]
```

CLS

The CLS command is used to clear the display within the login process. This can be especially helpful when you want to clear the screen before displaying a message. The command format is

```
CLS
```

COMSPEC

The COMSPEC command is used to specify the location of a DOS user's command processor (COMMAND.COM). Some users on the network set their COMSPEC to a local drive. In the case where multiple DOS versions are available on your network, you will need a separate directory for each version. Later in this section, when variables are discussed, an example of setting up multiple DOS versions will be given. The command format is

```
COMSPEC = [path]COMMAND.COM
```

The *path* variable represents the full DOS path needed to find the command processor, COMMAND.COM.

If your users are running OS/2, do not include the COMSPEC variable in the login script. In the case where OS/2 users use a virtual DOS session, you will need to make sure the COMSPEC statement is in the CONFIG.SYS.

Example: If your users have a DOS directory as a second search drive (S2:, which will map to drive Y:) in the login script, you would place one of the following commands in the login script:

```
COMSPEC=S2:COMMAND.COM
COMSPEC=Y:COMMAND.COM
```

CONTEXT

The CONTEXT command is used to set the user's current context in the Directory Services tree. The command format is

```
CONTEXT [context]
```

The *context* variable represents the full context of where you want the user's context set to.

Example: If you want to switch a user's current context to the ACCOUNTING Organization Unit, within the WIDGETS Organization you would put the following line as the login script:

```
CONTEXT .ACCOUNTING.WIDGETS
```

Note

It is important to include the leading period in the preceding command. If you leave it out, LOGIN will try to change context to ACCOUNTING.WIDGETS *relative to your current context*. This may or may not be what you want.

DISPLAY

The DISPLAY command is used to display the content of a text file, much like the DOS TYPE command. This can be helpful for displaying certain messages upon login. If a file was saved in a word processor format, the codes used by the word processor may appear when being displayed. To display a file that was created and saved in a word processor format, use the FDISPLAY command, which is described later in this section. The command format is

```
DISPLAY [path]filename
```

The *path* variable represents the full DOS path of where the file you want displayed is located.

The *filename* variable represents the actual file name of the context you want displayed.

Example: To display a message upon login that is contained in the file MESSAGE.TXT in SYS:PUBLIC\MESSAGES directory, put the following in the login script:

```
DISPLAY SYS:PUBLIC\MESSAGES\MESSAGE.TXT
```

DOS BREAK

The DOS BREAK command is used to control the Ctrl+Break level of DOS. If you place the DOS BREAK ON statement within the login script, you will allow users to terminate programs (other than the login script) by using the Ctrl+Break key sequence. This command is different than the BREAK command, discussed earlier, in that the BREAK command allows users to terminate login script execution. The command format is

```
DOS BREAK [ON ¦ OFF]
```

By default, DOS BREAK is set to OFF.

Example: If you want users to use the Ctrl+Break key sequence to terminate programs, place the following statement in the login script:

```
DOS BREAK ON
```

DOS SET

The DOS SET command (much like DOS's SET command) is used to set DOS or OS/2 environment variables to specified values. For the OS/2 workstation, the DOS SET environment variable only remains valid during the execution of the login script. The command format is

```
DOS SET name = "value"
```

The *name* variable represents the actual name of the environment variable.

The *"value"* variable represents the value to which you want the environment variable set.

Example: To set a TEMP environment variable to a TEMP directory under the user's home directory, place the following in the login script:

```
DOS SET TEMP = "F:\USERS\%LOGIN_NAME\TEMP"
```

DOS VERIFY

The DOS VERIFY command is used to verify data that it copied to a local drive using the DOS COPY command. Users using the NetWare NCOPY utility to copy data will not need to use this command. The command format is

```
DOS VERIFY [ON ¦ OFF]
```

The default for DOS VERIFY is OFF.

Example: To ensure the data integrity copied to a local drive using the DOS COPY command, place the following in the login script:

```
DOS VERIFY ON
```

DRIVE

You use the DRIVE command to set your default drive. The command format is

```
DRIVE [drive: ¦ *n:]
```

The *drive* variable represents the local or network drive letter you want to make as your default.

The *n* variable represents the driver number you want as your default.

Example: To have the user exit the script to drive P:, place the following in your script:

```
DRIVE P:
```

EXIT

You use the EXIT command to terminate the execution of the LOGIN utility. This command also enables you to execute a file when exiting the script, which could be useful for putting a user in an application or menu. The command format is

```
EXIT ["filename"]
```

The "filename" represents the name of the file to which you want to exit.

Example: To have a user execute upon login a NetWare menu called SALES, place the following in the login script:

```
EXIT "NMENU SALES"
```

This command can add more functionality when used in an IF...THEN statement, which is explained in this section.

FDISPLAY

FDISPLAY (filtered display) is used to display text of a word-processed file during the login procedure. It ignores control characters placed in the file from the word processor, and only displays the text. The command format is

```
FDISPLAY [path]filename
```

The *path* variable represents the full DOS path of file that contains the text message.

The *filename* variable represents the actual file name that contains the text message.

Example: To display a message in a word-processed file named MESSAGE.TXT in the SYS:PUBLIC\MESSAGES directory, use the following in the login script:

```
FDISPLAY SYS:PUBLIC\MESSAGES\MESSAGE.TXT
```

FIRE PHASERS

You use the FIRE PHASERS command to cause a phaser sound at the workstation upon login. This can be useful for getting the user's attention when displaying a message in the login script. The command format is

```
FIRE PHASERS n [TIMES]
```

The *n* variable represents the number of times you want the phaser sound to go off.

Example: To fire phasers seven times upon login, use the following in the login script:

```
FIRE PHASERS 7 TIMES
```

GOTO

You use the GOTO command to execute a portion of the login script out of sequence. The command format is

```
GOTO label
```

The *label* variable is used to refer to the login script portion you want executed next.

Example: If you want users in a group called BYPASS to bypass all or a portion of the login script, use the GOTO statement to bypass all or portions of the script, as in the following:

```
IF MEMBER OF "BYPASS" THEN GOTO BYPASS_SCRIPT

... other script commands

BYPASS_SCRIPT:
```

In this example, if the user is a member of the group BYPASS, the GOTO statement will skip all commands between it and the label.

Warning

Do not use the GOTO command in nested IF...THEN statements because it does not work correctly.

IF...THEN

You use the IF...THEN command when you want the script to perform certain actions if the conditions are met. The command format is

```
IF conditional [AND ¦ OR [conditional] THEN commands
[ELSE commands]
[END]
```

The conditional variable can be replaced with identifier variables. The identifier variables are as follows:

The commands variable represents login script commands (such as MAP, DRIVE, DOS SET, and so on).

A conditional statement can be used to find out if a variable is equivalent to a value, such as:

```
IF MEMBER OF "USERS"
```

The preceding statement tests to see whether the user is a member of the USERS group.

Conditional statements can derive a relationship between the variable (%LOGIN_NAME) and its value (DSMITH) by using the following symbols:

Symbol	Definition
=	Equals
<>	Does not equal
>	Is greater than
>=	Is greater than or equal to
<	Is less than
<=	Is less than or equal to

Example: The following example shows how you could map users to use WordPerfect.

```
IF MEMBER OF "WORDPERFECT" THEN
MAP *3:=SYS:APPS\WP
```

END

You use the END command in conjunction with IF...THEN. If you wanted to display a meeting reminder for Wednesday with a list of list of the open action items (found in a file called ACTIONS) to be discussed, you could place the following in the script:

```
IF DAY_OF_WEEK="WEDNESDAY" THEN
CLS
WRITE "Staff meeting to be held today at 9:00 AM!!!"
WRITE "Here is a list of the open action items."
DISPLAY SYS:\PUBLIC\MESSAGES\ACTIONS
PAUSE
END
```

INCLUDE

You use the INCLUDE command to execute a file or another object's login script as subscript of the login script. This could be useful for groups or users that want to customize their own scripts, without having rights to change the main script. Only valid login script commands and variables can be used. The command format is

```
INCLUDE [path] filename
```

or

```
INCLUDE objectname
```

The path variable represents the full path needed to find the subscript file. This can either begin with a drive letter or a full directory path beginning with the NetWare volume name.

The filename variable represents the actual subscript's file name. Remember, if users are going to modify this subscript file, they must have Read and Write rights to this files. Those using the file must have Read rights.

The objectname variable represents the name of the object whose login script you are going to execute.

Example: If a group called TECHS wanted to execute a subscript they created called LOGMEIN.TXT in the PUBLIC\SCRIPTS directory on volume SYS: you would put the following in the script:

```
IF MEMBER OF "TECHS" THEN
INCLUDE SYS:PUBLIC\SCRIPTS\LOGMEIN.TXT
END
```

Or, if you wanted to have a login script execute another Organizational Unit's login script, you could place a reference in the INCLUDE command to the object's name. If the Organizational Unit is named SALES.WIDGETS, for example, you would put the following in the login script:

```
INCLUDE .OU=SALES.O=WIDGETS
```

Note

As mentioned earlier, the inclusion of the leading period may be required.

LASTLOGINTIME

You use the LASTLOGINTIME command to display the user's last login time. The command format is

```
LASTLOGINTIME
```

MACHINE

You use the MACHINE command to set the DOS machine name for the workstation; for example, IBM_PC, COMPAQ, HEWPAC, and so on. The command format is

```
MACHINE = name
```

The name variable represents the name of the actual machine. The name can be up to 15 characters.

The value set using the MACHINE command can be used by some programs (such as NETBIOS) written to run under PC DOS. The name can include such identifier variables as STATION.

Example: To set the MACHINE name to COMPAQ, place the following command in the login script:

```
MACHINE=COMPAQ
```

Note

This command is not valid under OS/2.

MAP

You use the MAP command to view and establish drives to network directories. The command format is

```
MAP [option] [drive:=path]
```

The drive variable can be replaced with the actual drive letter that you want associated with the directory path.

The *path* variable can be replaced with a drive letter, a full directory path, or a Directory Map object. When mapping drives to directories on a Directory Services file server, you should begin the path with the Volume object name. If you are mapping to a bindery-based NetWare server, you should begin the path with the server's name.

Following are some examples of uses of the *drive* and *path* variables:

◆ MAP drive:=directory—Used to map a specified drive to a certain directory. If *1 is used for the drive option, the first network drive will be mapped to the specified directory. The first network drive is set in your NET.CFG file. If *2, the next drive after *1 will be used, and so on.

```
MAP F:=SYS:USERS\DSMITH
```

or

```
MAP *1:=SYS:USERS\DSMITH
```

◆ MAP drive:=directory_map_object—With NetWare 4.*x*, you can create Directory Service Map objects that will refer to a specified file system path. The MAP command allows you to just specify the object's name to which you want to map, without specifying the full file system path. For example, if you had a Map object in Directory Services with a full name of WP.ACCOUNTING.WIDGETS with a reference to the ACCOUNTING_SYS:\APPS\WP directory, you could use the following command to map to this directory:

```
MAP S3:=.WP.ACCOUNTING.WIDGETS
```

◆ If the map object exited within your current context, you could just use the following command:

```
MAP S3:=WP
```

◆ In return, the mapping to the Map object would point your S3 drive to the ACCOUNTING_SYS:\APPS\WP directory.

◆ MAP drive:=drive:—Use this command option to map the first specified drive to the second.

```
MAP N:=M:
```

◆ MAP drive:=directory:drive:=directory...—This command option allows multiple drives and multiple directories to be mapped out, eliminating the need to initiate the MAP drive:=directory multiple times.

```
MAP F:=SYS:USERS\DSMITH; MAP L:=SYS:USERS\DSMITH\PROJECTS
```

The *option* variable can be replaced with one of the following:

◆ MAP INSERT or MAP INS *search drive:=directory*—Use this command option to insert drive mappings between existing mappings. This option is valid in login scripts and at the command line.

◆ MAP ROOT—Use this command to map a drive to a fake root directory. This is useful for applications that require reads and writes from the root directory, where most users shouldn't have rights.

◆ MAP DISPLAY ON—This command displays the current drive mappings when the user logs in. This command is only valid in a login script. MAP DISPLAY ON is the default setting.

◆ MAP DISPLAY OFF—This command option turns off the displaying of drive mappings when the user logs in. This command is only valid in a login script.

◆ MAP ERRORS ON—This command option displays any MAP error messages that may occur while the drive mappings are being assigned. MAP ERRORS ON is the default setting. This command is only valid in a login script.

◆ MAP ERRORS OFF—This command option turns off the displaying of any MAP error messages that may occur while the drive mappings are being assigned. This command is only valid in a login script.

◆ MAP CHANGE *drive:*—This command option changes a search drive mapping to a regular mapping, and a regular mapping to a search mapping. For example, if you wanted to change drive L: to a search drive, you would type the following command:

MAP CHANGE L:

◆ MAP NP (No Prompt)—This command option will not prompt the user to overwrite a conflicting mapping. Use this option with care.

◆ MAP N (Next) *directory*—This command option is used to map the next available drive without the user specifying the drive.

MAP N SYS:=USERS\DSMITH\PROJECTS

◆ MAP P (Physical)—This command option allows you to map a drive to a physical server volume, rather than a Directory Services volume. Under Director Services, it is possible to change a Volume object's name so that it is different from the original (physical) name.

If the MAP command is used without any options, it displays the current drive mapping for the workstation. You can also use the following syntax to include DOS Requester identifiers to help map directories for workstations:

MAP drive:=*directory* and *identifiers*

The most common use of this syntax is to map to the DOS directory that is on the server volume. The identifiers are set in the NET.CFG. Following is a list of the identifiers:

25

OS	The identifier for the DOS version descriptor
OS_VERSION	The identifier for the DOS version descriptor
MACHINE	The identifier for the long-machine-type descriptor
SMACHINE	The identifier for the short-machine-type descriptor

For example, you may use the MAP command to map out the DOS version in the login script. The MAP command may look like the following (where COMPAQ is the long machine name set in the NET.CFG file):

```
MAP S2:=SYS:PUBLIC\%MACHINE\%OS\%OS_VERSION
```

After the login script execution, the mapping would look something like this:

```
SEARCH2:=.Y:=[ACCOUNTING\SYS:PUBLIC\COMPAQ\MSDOS\V5.00]
```

NO_DEFAULT

The NO_DEFAULT command can be used from a system or profile script to prevent execution of the default user login script (which is built into the LOGIN.EXE program). The command format is

```
NO_DEFAULT
```

In the case where you do not want to create user login scripts, and you do not want the default user login script to be executed, you would place this command in the system or profile login script.

NOSWAP

The NOSWAP command is used to prevent the LOGIN utility from swapping out of conventional memory into available higher memory or from swapping to disk, in the case where a workstation runs out of memory while executing an external command (#). The command format is

```
NOSWAP
```

This command could save the workstation time by skipping the normal process of having LOGIN attempt a swap.

PAUSE

The PAUSE command is used to pause the executing login script, until the user presses a key. This is helpful when displaying messages to the user via login script, allowing the user to read the message before it scrolls off the screen. The command format is

```
PAUSE
```

PCCOMPATIBLE

The PCCOMPATIBLE command is used to enable the EXIT login script command to work on workstations whose names are not IBM_PC. The command format is:

```
PCCOMPATIBLE
```

If a workstation has a long name that was not set to IBM_PC (such as HEWPAC, COMPAQ, and so on) in the NET.CFG, you need to use this command in the login script to allow the exit command to work.

Example: If you had a Compaq computer with the long machine name of COMPAQ in the NET.CFG, and you wanted the workstation to exit to a menu upon login, you would place the following in the login script:

```
PCCOMPATIBLE
EXIT "NMENU SALES"
```

Note

This command does not apply to OS/2 workstations.

REMARK

You use the REMARK command to insert explanatory text into the login script. Text used with this command in front of it will not get displayed to the screen. The command format is

```
REM [ARK] [text]
```

or

```
* [ text]
```

or

```
; [ text]
```

The text variable is replaced by the explanatory text.

Example:

```
REMARK:
```

This is a remark in the login script.

SET

The SET command (much like DOS's SET command) is used to set DOS or OS/2 environment variables to specified values. For an OS/2 workstation, the SET environment variable only remains valid during the execution of the login script. The command format is

```
SET name = "value"
```

The *name* variable represents the actual name of the environment variable.

The *"value"* variable represents the value to which you want the environment variable set.

Example: To set a TEMP environment variable to a TEMP directory under the user's home directory, place the following in the login script:

```
SET TEMP = "F:\USERS\%LOGIN_NAME\TEMP"
```

SET_TIME

The SET_TIME command is used to set the workstation's time equal to the time on the NetWare server to which it first connects. The command format is

```
SET_TIME ON ¦ OFF
```

The default value is ON.

SHIFT

The SHIFT command is used to change the %n identifier variable used in the login script. This command could allow the users to enter other parameters with the LOGIN utility to change the user's environment mappings. The command format is

```
SHIFT [n]
```

The *n* represents that number of places you want to shift the command line variables. You can use positive and negative numbers to move the variable in either direction. For example, a -2 would move the % variable two positions to the left. The default is 1. When users log in, they can specify parameters with the LOGIN command. The login script then interprets these parameters as instructions to perform certain login script commands. When the server interprets the login script, it sees any percent sign (%) followed by a number in a command as corresponding to a parameter used when the LOGIN executes. The numbers can range from 0 to 10, %0 corresponding with the server name, %1 as the user name, and so on. The following LOGIN command line

```
LOGIN ACCOUNTING/DAVID 123 WP
```

would have the following corresponding variables:

```
%0 = ACCOUNTING
%1 = DAVID
%2 = 123
```

```
%3 = WP
```

To manipulate these variables in the login script, you can use an IF...THEN statement to see whether a certain condition is met, and then a command can be executed. For example, if specified at the LOGIN command line, the following script command could determine whether the user is connected to a word processor and/or a spreadsheet:

```
LOOP
IF "%2" = "123" THEN MAP S16:=ACCOUNTING/SYS:APPS\123
IF "%2" = "WP" THEN MAP S16:=ACCOUNTING/SYS:APPS\WP
SHIFT 1
IF "%2" <> " " THEN GOTO LOOP
```

As you can see, in this example, the LOGIN utility will test to see whether DAVID specified 123 and/or WP after his name. If %2 is equal to "123", a mapping is given to the respective directory. The login script then gets the command to SHIFT 1 and loop. Because of the SHIFT, the %2 now becomes WP. Upon executing the loop, the login script tests and maps a directory for WP.

With the above example, it does not matter if DAVID specified "123" first or "WP" first during his logging in. Either order will map the appropriate directories.

SWAP

The SWAP command is used to swap the LOGIN utility out of conventional memory and into higher memory (if available), or to disk when executing external commands (using the # parameter) in the login script. The command format is

```
SWAP [ path]
```

The path variable can be replaced with the NetWare volume name and path or with a drive letter and path. Make sure the user has sufficient rights to the path.

TEMP SET

The TEMP SET command (much like DOS's SET command) is used to set DOS or OS/2 environment variables to specified values, but only during the execution of the login script. For OS/2 workstations, the TEMP SET environment variable only remains valid during the execution of the login script. The command format is

```
TEMP SET name = "value"
```

The name variable represents the actual name of the environment variable.

The "value" variable represents the value to which you want the environment variable set.

Example: To set a TEMP environment variable to a TEMP directory under the user's home directory, place the following in the login script:

```
TEMP SET TEMP = "F:\USERS\%LOGIN_NAME\TEMP"
```

WRITE

You use the WRITE command to display messages to the workstation upon login. The command format is

```
WRITE "[text][%identifier]" [;][identifier]
```

The text variable can be replaced with the text you want to display on the workstation's screen upon login.

The identifier variable can be replaced with a NetWare login script variable, such as a greeting time or user's name. This command also enables you to use special characters to enhance the functionality. The following is a list of the characters, with an explanation:

Character	Meaning
\r	Invokes a carriage return
\n	Starts a new line of text
\7	Makes a beep sound
\"	Displays a quotation mark

Example: The following is an example of how you would display a message to users:

```
WRITE "Time cards are due today!!! \7"
```

Notice the \7 that will cause a beep sound.

Following is an example of how you could use the WRITE command with login script variables.

```
WRITE "Good %GREETING_TIME %LOGIN_NAME!!!"
```

LOGIN SCRIPT IDENTIFIER VARIABLES

In this section, login script variables that can be used in conjunction with the login script command discussed previously are covered. The identifier variables are broken down into eight categories, as described in the following sections.

DATE IDENTIFIER VARIABLES

There are a number of ways in which you can obtain or display date information. There are seven different date-related identifier variables, as follows:

DAY	Day number (01 through 31)
DAY_OF_WEEK	Day of week (Monday, Tuesday, Wednesday, and so on)

MONTH	Month number (01 through 12)
MONTH_NAME	Month name (January, February, March, etc.)
NDAY_OF_WEEK	Weekday number (1 through 7; 1=Sunday)
SHORT_YEAR	Last two digits of a year (91, 92, 93, and so on)
YEAR	Four digits of a year (1991, 1992, 1993, and so on)

Example: To display a date in a WRITE statement, you could use the following:

```
WRITE "Today is %DAY_OF_WEEK, %MONTH_NAME %DAY, %YEAR."
```

The login script would display the following statement upon login:

```
Today is Friday, April 23, 1993.
```

TIME IDENTIFIER VARIABLES

Using the following time identifier variables, you can obtain or display time-related information.

AM_PM	Day or night (a.m. or p.m.)
GREETING TIME	Time of day (morning, afternoon, or evening)
HOUR	Hour (12-hour scale; 1 through 12)
HOUR24	Hour (24-hour scale; 00 through 23; 00=midnight)
MINUTE	Minutes (00 through 59)
SECOND	Seconds (00 through 59)

Example: To display the time in a WRITE statement, you could use the following:

```
WRITE "Good %GREETING_TIME, the time is %HOUR:%MINUTE:%SECOND %AM_PM!!"
```

The login script would display the following upon login:

```
Good Morning, the time is 8:03:15 AM!!
```

USER IDENTIFIER VARIABLES

Often times, you would want to customize the messages so your users have a "personal touch" feeling. This can be achieved using the user identifier variables.

| FULL_NAME | User's complete Directory Services name or full bindery-based name |
| LAST_NAME | User's complete Directory Services last name or full bindery-based name |

LOGIN_NAME	User's unique login name (long names are truncated to eight)
MEMBER OF "group"	Group object to which the user is assigned
NOT MEMBER OF "group"	Group object to which the user is not assigned
PASSWORD_EXPIRES	Number of days before the password for the user expires
USER_ID	Number assigned to each user

Example: Following is one way you could use a couple of these identifier variables:

```
WRITE "Good %GREETING_TIME, %FULL_NAME"

WRITE "You have %PASSWORD_EXPIRES days before your password expires"
```

NETWORK IDENTIFIER VARIABLES

There are two network identifier variables that can help you to determine the name of the server you are logged in to, as well as the IPX network address you are on.

| FILE_SERVER | NetWare server name |
| NETWORK_ADDRESS | Network number of the cabling system (8-digit hexadecimal number) |

Example:

```
WRITE "Good %GREETING_TIME, Welcome to server %FILE_SERVER"
```

WORKSTATION IDENTIFIER VARIABLES

You can extract workstation information, such as the version of DOS using workstation identifier variables, and make use of them in the login's script.

MACHINE	Type of computer (IBM_PC, and so on) (non-OS/2); refer to your DOS manual for more information
NETWARE_REQUESTER	Version of the NetWare Requester for OS/2
OS	Type of DOS on the workstation (DR DOS, MS-DOS)
OS_VERSION	Version of DOS on the workstation (3.30, 4.00, and so on)
P_STATION	Workstation's node address (12-digit hex)
SHELL_TYPE	Version of the workstation's DOS shell (1.20, and so on); this variable is supported under 2.x and 3.x shells and the NetWare 4.x Requester for DOS

SMACHINE	Short machine name (IBM, and so on) (non-OS/2)
STATION	Workstation's connection number

Example: You can use these variables to map out the DOS directory, as in the following:

```
MAP S2:=SYS:PUBLIC\%MACHINE\%OS\%OS_VERSION
```

If you were using IBM_PC as the MACHINE type, MS-DOS as the OS type, and you had version 3.30 of DOS, you would get the following result:

```
SEARCH2:=.Y:=[ACCOUNTING\SYS:PUBLIC\IBM_PC\MSDOS\V3.30]
```

DOS ENVIRONMENT IDENTIFIER VARIABLES

You also can make use of DOS environment variables from within the login script, using the following syntax:

<variable>	Any DOS variable can be used in angle brackets (< >). If you use a DOS environment variable in a MAP command, add a percent sign (%) in front of the variable. For example, you could MAP a search drive to the path environment variable.

MISCELLANEOUS IDENTIFIER VARIABLES

Following are some miscellaneous identifier variables that you may find useful in controlling the execution of the login script.

ACCESS_SERVER	This is used to show whether the server you are logging into is an access server (TRUE=functional, FALSE=not functional)
ERROR_LEVEL	An error number (0=No errors)
%n	Replaced by parameters the user enters at the command line with the LOGIN utility

OBJECT PROPERTIES IDENTIFIER VARIABLES

Under NetWare 4, it is possible to make use of information that is stored in the NDS. In the login script, you can make use of the different attributes associated with an user object. Following is the syntax for referring to an NDS attribute:

`%property name`	Properties of the NDS objects can be used as variables. The property's name can be used like any other variable. If the property name includes a space, enclose the name in quotation marks.

Example: To map drive F: to the user's home directory, you can use the following command:

```
MAP F:=%HOME DIRECTORY
```

Note

Note that the attribute name is preceeded by a percent sign and must be in uppercase.

LOGIN SCRIPT EXAMPLE

Following is an example of a Container Login Script that made use of some of the login script commands and identifiers discussed from earlier sections of this chapter:

```
*****************************************************************
*           LOGIN SCRIPT FOR ACCOUNTING ORGANIZATION UNIT      *
*****************************************************************
*                                                              *
*       Last modified by: Jack Anderson                        *
*       Modification date: April 24, 1993                      *
*                                                              *
*       Drive mapping information:                             *
*           1. Drive G: needs to be map to E-mail director     *
*           2. Do not change the search drive 1, 2, and 3 -    *
*              for specific uses.                              *
*           3. Drive M: is reserved for database               *
*                                                              *
*****************************************************************
WRITE "Good %GREETING_TIME, %FULL_NAME!"
WRITE "Welcome to server %FILE_SERVER!!"
WRITE "Today is %DAY_OF_WEEK, %MONTH_NAME %DAY, %YEAR."
WRITE "The time is %HOUR:%MINUTE:%SECOND."
FIRE PHASERS 7

MAP DISPLAY OFF
MAP S1:=SYS:PUBLIC
MAP S2:=SYS:PUBLIC\%MACHINE\%OS\%OS_VERSION
COMSPEC=S2:COMMAND.COM
SET PROMPT = "$P $G"

IF MEMBER OF "WP51" THEN BEGIN
        MAP S3:=.WP.ACCOUNTING.WIDGETS
END
```

```
IF MEMBER OF "123" THEN
        MAP S16:=SYS:APPS\123
END

IF MEMBER OF "ACCOUNT_PAYABLE" THEN BEGIN
        DISPLAY SYS:PUBLIC\MESSAGES\MESS.TXT
        PAUSE
        SET USER = "%LOGIN_NAME"
        MAP L:=SYS:DATABASE\ACCDATA
        MAP S16:=SYS:DATABASE\ENGINE
END

IF MEMBER OF "LASER_PRINT" THEN BEGIN
        #CAPTURE Q=.CN=LASER.OU=ACCOUNTING.O=WIDGETS TI=10
END

IF MEMBER OF "LINE_PRINT" THEN BEGIN
        #CAPTURE S=SALES Q=LINE NB NFF TI=10
END

MAP DISPLAY ON
MAP
```

This login script first greets users, and then informs them of the name of the server they are logged onto, followed by date and time information. The script then sets up some drive-mapping, depending on the group the user belongs to, as well as setting up a CAPTURE command so their print jobs will be routed to the correct printers.

SUMMARY

The establishment of Users and Groups on a NetWare 4.1 server is an important part of bringing your NetWare 4.1 system online. The primary difference between Users and Groups between NetWare 4.1 and previous versions of NetWare is that Users and Groups are defined globally through NetWare Directory Services. Therefore, User and Group login scripts should reflect the global nature of NDS. NetWare 4.1 includes some new login script variables and commands that make use of NDS and its global object definitions. Finally, remember that login scripts are stored by NDS as a User object attribute. This is different from previous versions of bindery-based NetWare, which stored Login Scripts in the bindery object's SYS:MAIL directory and SYS:PUBLIC.

- Previous NetWare Menu System

- NetWare Current Menu System

- Designing a Menu

- Security Issues

- Designing, Creating, Compiling, and Executing a Menu

- Building a Turnkey System

- Converting the Old

- Summary

CHAPTER 26

Menuing

Networks undoubtedly will have a number of resources that are to be made available to the end users. The fact that these resources exist does not necessarily mean that the end user is aware of them. In order to make these resources available, they need to be presented to the user in a form that is easily understandable and that will encourage the user to utilize these resources, thereby increasing productivity.

However, users need to be shielded from the complexities of locating and invoking resources, and the best way to achieve this is through a simple user-friendly menu interface. If users have to spend time looking for applications, valuable productivity hours are lost, then training is needed which could be costly, and some degree of frustration is incurred. To solve this problem, when the user logs in to the network, a user-friendly menu could be invoked, presenting them with a list of choices of available resources that can be easily invoked by choosing an option.

Arguably, the choice of the desktop operating system will decide the need for menus. Users with workstations running MS-Windows 3.1x, OS/2 2.1x or Warp, Macintosh System 7, or any graphical environments do have less of a need for menu programs, even though they can utilize menu programs for their graphical environments.

While there might not seem to be much need for menus among the graphical environment users, there is certainly a need among users running MS-DOS. Leaving an inexperienced user at the DOS prompt after logging into the network could be intimidating for them. Taking this into account, Novell's NetWare ships with a menu program that will assist network administrators in making network resources readily available to network users.

PREVIOUS NETWARE MENU SYSTEM

With NetWare 3.11 and prior versions of the operating system, Novell shipped their product with their own proprietary menuing system. While this menu system worked decently, it had one major shortcoming. It consumed a lot of workstation memory and resulted in the inability to run a number of application programs properly at the workstation. This memory consumption initially was around 90K of RAM, but, after some time, a newer version of the menuing program was released that reduced the memory requirements roughly to around 35K of RAM. Nevertheless, this reduction was still not enough because the menuing program lacked other features as well.

NETWARE CURRENT MENU SYSTEM

With the introduction of NetWare 4.0 and 3.12, Novell introduced a new menuing technology that is far more practical in terms of memory consumption and features.

This new menu program, currently being shipped with NetWare 4.1 and 3.12, is a subset of Saber Software Corporation's Saber Menu for DOS technology. While it is not the same as the full-blown menu product that Saber Software is shipping, it offers many of the features. Shown in Table 26.1 is a comparison of the full-blown menu product and Novell's subset.

TABLE 26.1. A COMPARISON BETWEEN SABER AND NMENU.

Features	Novell	Saber
No RAM overhead during item execution	Yes	Yes
Create menus as an ASCII file	Yes	Yes
User-definable menu titles	Yes	Yes
User-definable item titles	Yes	Yes
Prompt for user input to be passed to the command line (optional or required)	Yes	Yes
Customize prompt text	Yes	Yes
Customize menu item selection (A-Z)	Yes	Yes
Date and Time displayed on top status bar	Yes	Yes
Compiled menu scripts	Yes	Yes
Function key access for menu help and system help	Yes	Yes
Define application on function keys (D/A keys)	No	Yes
Dynamically configure menu items based on User ID, Group, Station, Hardware and/or Network	No	Yes
User ID, free space, current drive/directory displayed on top status bar	No	Yes
Custom placement of menu panels on the screen	No	Yes
Custom colors of menu panel	No	Yes
Prompt for user input to be passed to the command line (specifically for file, directory, active drive, pick list)	No	Yes
Mouse support	No	Yes
Scrollable Menus	No	Yes

26

MENUING

Designing a Menu

When designing a network menu, a number of issues must be taken into consideration. Which resources are to be made available to the users via the menu is certainly the bulk of the design. Other issues include users rights within NetWare security to run the menu program and placement of temporary files.

Typically, you might want to include the following selections on a menu:

◆ Software application choices
◆ Printer choices
◆ Shell to DOS
◆ Logout of the network

These four choices cover most resources on the network, although software applications could account for most of the menu.

Security Issues

The programs that are necessary to create and execute a menu are located in the \PUBLIC directory of the SYS: volume. These two programs are *MENUMAKE.EXE*, which is a compiler to convert an ASCII source file to a compiled script file, and *NMENU.BAT*, which is a batch file that calls an executable program that runs your compiled script file producing a menu onscreen.

Because these two programs are located in the \PUBLIC directory, no explicit rights assignment are needed. To use them as NetWare 4.*x*, users inherit read and file scan rights to the SYS:PUBLIC DIRECTORY if they are created in the same container that has the server object. If the user was created in another container, then explicit rights assignments must be made to allow them to use the programs in the public directory.

A more critical issue is the rights that the user has in the directory from which they are going to run the menu program. Users need READ, FILE SCAN, WRITE, CREATE, ERASE, and MODIFY in the directory they are in while running the menu program. They also can be on their local drive while running the menu. The reason is that a number of temporary batch files are created and deleted while using the menu program. If users do not have sufficient rights, the menu program is unable to create these temporary batch files, resulting in the menu not functioning properly.

Tip

These temporary batch files are normally named MENU_0.BAT and MENU$$$.BAT. These batch files are deleted upon exiting the menu system, but they are kept in a salvageable state until the system needs more disk space.

Users, therefore, should refrain from changing directories before running their menu programs if they are not on a turnkey system. It could happen that they have insufficient rights in the directory they change over to. The menu program will not execute.

Tip

> If users reboot their station in the middle of running a menu, a number of files with a .BAT extension (the temporary batch files mentioned previously) are kept in their working directories on the network. These files could be deleted with no problem.

An excellent way of enabling users to be in any directory and still run the menu program without any difficulties is to redirect the location of the temporary batch files created while running the menu. This can be accomplished by setting a DOS environment variable. If all the users have local hard disks, you could redirect the files to their local drives by including in the container login script the following SET command:

```
SET S_FILEDIR = "C:\\"
```

When this command is executed upon logging in, the environment variable will be set and all temporary batch files created by the menu program will subsequently be redirected to the root directory of drive C.

Tip

> For best performance, direct your temporary files to a local hard drive whenever possible.

Temporary batch files should be redirected to a particular directory for performance and administrative reasons. These temporary files are deleted when exiting the menu program but never purged. The system, therefore, keeps track of them, which results in more overhead and some performance degradation. If they are located in one directory, the network supervisor could purge them on a regular basis.

You can create a directory called TEMPMENU on the network, and then the corresponding login script command could be used to direct the temporary files to the server:

```
SET S_FILEDIR="F:\\TEMPMENU\\"
```

Note

> You must use double backslashes (\\) for pathnames and trailing double backslashes at the end of the path in order for the SET S_FILEDIR command to work.

Doing this could be a problem with many users sharing the same directory or same login name. The temp files would all have similar names and overwrite each other and cause problems. To get around this second issue, you could set another DOS environment variable that will uniquely name each temporary menu batch file. To do this, include in the container login script the following command:

```
SET S_FILE="%LOGIN_NAME" or
SET S_FILE="%STATION"
```

The first SET command causes the temporary files to be named with the user's login name (such as $RANJI.BAT and #RANJI.BAT). The second SET command causes the files to be named with the connection number the user received when logging in (such as $3.BAT and #3.BAT). The first SET command will work properly if a user only logs in once. If the user logs in more than once, however, the menu program will try to create temporary batch files with the same name, and that will cause an error. The second SET command is much better to use because a user can login with the same name but will get a different connection number upon the second login. As a result, the temp files will be named with different connection id numbers and the .BAT extension.

DESIGNING, CREATING, COMPILING, AND EXECUTING A MENU

Basically, there are four steps to having a fully functioning menu system. The first involves deciding which choices are to be displayed to the end user. The second requires typing the menu script or source file using commands that are native to the menu program. The third step is the compilation of the source file from ASCII to a binary format. At this step, compilation errors, if any, are displayed. Finally, after the script is compiled successfully, it is executed, resulting in a user-friendly menu placed on-screen.

DESIGNING A MENU

Suppose that you want to design a menu that would present to the end user the following four choices:

◆ Choose MS-Windows to work with
◆ Choose some form of word-processing

♦ Search for printers in current container

♦ Exit from the menu

To create such a menu, follow the steps in the next section.

CREATING A MENU SOURCE FILE

The menu script or source file can be created with any word processor or editor; however, the file must be saved as a pure ASCII text file, with no formatting codes other than tabs and carriage returns. The file should be saved with an .SRC extension for ease of compilation; however, the file could be saved with another extension, such as .DOC, but the extension must be specified when compiling the menu script file.

Tip

You must put a filename extension on the menu script source file; if not, the file will not compile at all.

Type the following information with your text editor:

```
MENU 01, DreamLAN Admin Menu

        ITEM MS-Windows
                EXEC WIN

        ITEM Wordprocessing
                EXEC WP

        ITEM Printers in current container{PAUSE}
                EXEC NLIST PRINTER

        ITEM EXIT MENU SYSTEM
                EXEC EXIT
```

Save the information as a file named TEST.SRC and do not forget that it must be saved as an ASCII text file. Note the indentations that are in place. Indenting items is not required for the menu to function properly, but it makes the script file easier to debug and understand.

COMPILING THE SOURCE SCRIPT FILE

Now that you have a source file, the next step is to compile the file. You use the MENUMAKE.EXE file for this purpose. Type the following command at the DOS prompt:

```
MENUMAKE TEST
```

or

```
MENUMAKE TEST.SRC
```

26

MENUING

If the file has the .SRC extension, you do not have to specify the extension when using MENUMAKE.EXE; however, if the file has another extension, you must specify the extension when compiling the menu. At this point, if there are any compilation errors, they will be displayed with the line numbers where the errors occurred. If the compilation was successful, MENUMAKE.EXE produces a second file with the same name as the source file, but with a .DAT extension in the same directory as the source file.

Warning

If there are any errors in the compilation process, you must re-edit the menu source code file (.SRC extension) and then recompile it (MENUMAKE.EXE). This new compilation will create a new .DAT file, which will overwrite the old one *without warning*. Always save your source code.

You can have the MENU.DAT file in any directory when you are ready to execute it, providing that you have a search drive mapping to that directory. You cannot edit the MENU.SRC file, however, from any directory, even though you have a search drive to that directory. You must change to that directory.

You now should have two files named TEST.SRC and TEST.DAT. Figure 26.1 illustrates the compilation process.

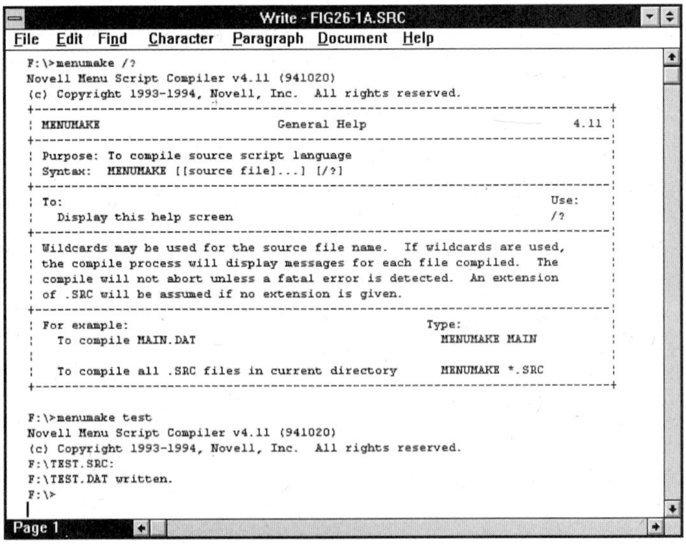

Figure 26.1.
Compiling the menu
source file.

EXECUTING THE MENU

Now that you have a compiled file named TEST.DAT, you can run the menu by simply typing:

```
NMENU TEST
```

NMENU.BAT is stored in the SYS:PUBLIC directory and can be accessed from anywhere in the network, provided that you have a search drive mapping to SYS:PUBLIC. You do not have to specify the filename extension of the compiled .DAT file when running the menu. Actually, you can rename the .DAT file to the name you want, providing that it has a filename extension; however, you must specify the entire filename including the extension when executing the menu under the new name. You cannot rename the .DAT file to a file without an extension because then the menu will not execute.

Figure 26.2 shows you what the end user will see after typing NMENU TEST.

Figure 26.2.
Executing the menu file.

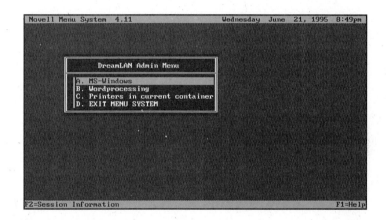

BREAKING DOWN THE SCRIPT FILE

In this section, a close look at the function of each statement of the example script file is taken. The following is the script file listing with comments for the purpose of discussion.

```
MENU 01, DreamLAN Admin Menu        Main menu title
ITEM MS-Windows                     Menu choice/option 1
EXEC WIN                            Command to be executed when option is chosen
ITEM Wordprocessing                 Menu choice/option 2
EXEC WP                             Command to be executed when option is chosen
ITEM Printers in current container {PAUSE}    Menu choice/option 3
EXEC NLIST PRINTER                  Command to be executed when option is chosen
ITEM EXIT MENU SYSTEM               Menu choice/option 4
EXEC EXIT                           Command to be executed when option is chosen
```

Looking at the first script you just created, there are a number of issues to consider when designing a menu. The first line of the script file (MENU 01, DreamLAN Admin Menu) specifies the menu title. All menu titles start with the word MENU, then a number ranging from 1 to 255. The number 1 in this case specifies that it is the first menu in the script. A menu script file can contain up to 255 menus (1 main and 254 submenus). Coming directly after the menu number, there is a comma followed by the title to be displayed on screen. A menu title cannot contain more than 40 characters. The MENU command is one of two organizational commands, while ITEM is the other command.

The second line (ITEM MS-Windows) is an option or choice on the menu. In this case, the user sees MS-Windows. Choices or options always start with the word ITEM, followed by the title that will show up as a choice. Here again, menu choices, like titles, cannot be more than 40 characters in length. There are 4 options plus a default option that you can use to customize what happens as a menu choice is being executed. These options appear after the item title. These options include {BATCH}, {CHDIR}, {PAUSE}, {SHOW}, and the default, which is invoked if no option is specified after the item title. These will be discussed in detail in a later section.

The third line (EXEC WIN) contains the file to be executed when you choose the menu option. In this case, the file is WIN, which displays MS-Windows. The file to be executed is always preceded by the word EXEC. This file can be a .BAT file, .COM file, or .EXE file. In addition to the previously mentioned types of files that EXEC can call, there are three options that are unique to the EXEC command (which are discussed in the "EXEC Options" section). The EXEC command is classified as a control command, of which there are six. The remaining five control commands, SHOW, LOAD, GETO, GETR, and GETP are discussed in the "Submenus" and "Advanced Options" sections.

The remaining lines in the sample script are repeats of menu choices and commands to be executed because there are no submenus.

Tip

The option will not execute unless you have a search drive mapping to the file that the EXEC command calls or the file is located in the directory with the menu program.

When a menu is executed, the order of the choices that appear on the menu depends on the order that the item appeared in the original source file. All items are assigned a letter from A to Z, in ascending order. You can execute a specific choice by typing the letter of that choice. In the example, the Windows choice was assigned the letter A because it appeared first in the script file, word-processing was assigned the letter B because it appeared second in the script file, and so on.

There might be times, however, when you want a specific item to be assigned a specific letter on the menu screen rather than the item appearing with a letter that was assigned, based on the order of the source file. Suppose that for the example script, you wanted MS-Windows to appear with the letter W instead of A. To do this, after the ITEM statement and before the menu choice, type a carat (^), the letter W, and then the title MS. The following example illustrates this:

```
ITEM ^WMS-Windows
          EXEC WIN
```

Tip

The order of the choice of the menu item remains the same, regardless of whether you use the carat (^) sign. The carat (^) sign forces the letter in front of the item to change. In order to actually make an item appear at the bottom of the menu, for example, you should key it in at the bottom of the source script file.

PLACEMENT OF MENUS ONSCREEN

When a menu is executed, it opens on the upper left side of your screen. Submenus open to the right of the first display. You cannot control the onscreen placement of the menu or the cascading of the submenus. Only the full-blown version of Saber's product allows you to change the position.

MENU COLOR AND SIZES

The width of a menu is determined by the widest item in the menu definition source file. Both menu titles and item titles are limited to 40 characters wide; therefore, a menu width is limited to 40 characters wide.

The height of a menu is determined automatically by the number of items in the menu. Because you can only get 12 items to display on one menu, the maximum height is that of the 12 items.

The color of a menu depends on the default Color palette that is in effect on your NetWare network. As such, your menu will probably show up in the same color as your other NetWare utilities, such as NETADMIN or FILER.

On a NetWare network, there are basically two ways to change the color of any menuing utility—either globally for everyone, or for individual users only. Color schemes are saved in a file called IBM_RUN.OVL (other files are available, depending on the type of machine being used), which is stored in the SYS:PUBLIC directory. Therefore, the file affects all utilities. You can modify this file using a program called COLORPAL.EXE.

26

MENUING

To globally change the color scheme of your menu (as well as NetWare utilities), run COLORPAL.EXE and choose the colors you want. Save your changes. This affects the IBM_RUN.OVL file stored in SYS:PUBLIC. All utilities and menus will then appear in the new color scheme.

To change an individual user's color schemes, copy IBM_RUN.OVL to the user's home directory, and then use COLORPAL.EXE to modify it. COLORPAL will modify the file in the user's home directory instead of the file contained in PUBLIC. This then will only affect the users who have their own copy of the IBM_RUN.OVL in their home directories.

Tip

When you use the COLORPAL.EXE program to change the IBM_RUN.OVL file, it gives you the appearance of changing the file. However, the file does not change and your menus appear in the previous color scheme. The reason for this is that the file is flagged Read only and does not change, even if COLORPAL prompts you to save your changes. You must first flag the file Read/Write, run COLORPAL, and then reflag it to Read only to prevent further changes.

The three commands, MENU (menu titles), ITEM (menu choices), and EXEC (files), are the building blocks of all menus. Submenus also are made up of these commands.

Note that in a simple menu that does not contain submenus, only the ITEM and EXEC commands are repeated, as in the first example. The MENU command is only used again if you have submenus.

Warning

You are only allowed up to 12 items (choices) in one menu. If you place more than 12 items in a script file, you will get a compile error. To get more than 12 items, you must use submenus.

EXEC OPTIONS

In addition to using the EXEC command to execute .BAT, .COM, and .EXE files, there are three other methods for which you can use the EXEC command.

EXEC EXIT

The EXEC EXIT option enables you to exit from the menu program and return to the DOS prompt. With the new Saber menu subset, users are not allowed to exit from the menu by pressing the Escape key. The only way out is to have the EXEC EXIT option or to reboot the system.

Note

The EXEC EXIT command *must* be UPPERCASE.

Always initially include the EXEC EXIT option when you are designing a new menu and testing it. Users designing menus can easily trap themselves in the menus if they do not include this option, resulting in the need to reboot their systems. When the menu works well, you can remove this option. This way, the user is limited to the menu, resulting in a very secure system.

EXEC DOS

The EXEC DOS option enables users to temporarily exit to the DOS prompt. Users can then execute any number of commands, provided there is sufficient memory in the workstation. To return to the menu, type EXIT. When at the DOS prompt, a portion of the menu is kept resident in RAM. The portion of RAM used varies from 4K to 48K, depending on the ITEM option used.

EXEC LOGOUT

The EXEC LOGOUT option enables users to log out of the network directly from the menu. Include this option if you want to create a turnkey system.

ITEM OPTIONS

As mentioned earlier, there are a number of options that can be used with the ITEM command. These options are placed after the title or choice that follows the ITEM command and are enclosed in braces ({ }), as in the following sample script:

```
ITEM Printers in current container {PAUSE}
```

In this example, placing the {PAUSE} command at the end of the item line causes the final screen display to pause so that you can read the results of the EXEC command before control is returned to the menu program. The display changes when a key is pressed. This option is similar to the DOS pause command.

26

MENUING

The following sections discuss in detail what each of the four options do.

{BATCH}

When a user chooses an option from the menu, such as word processing, the word processing program is loaded into memory. However, a portion of the menu program still remains resident in memory with the word processor. This portion of the menu program takes up approximately 41K of RAM. This could cause a problem with applications that need much more memory. If you include the {BATCH} parameter with the ITEM option, the menu program unloads itself from memory and loads the application, thereby making approximately 41K of RAM available to the application.

Example:

```
ITEM Wordprocessing {BATCH}
EXEC WP
```

{CHDIR}

Some application programs will change your default directory from the original directory to another directory upon exiting the application. This could cause problems with the creation of temporary files and would result in the menu program failing. The {CHDIR} option forces the menu program to return to the default directory that was in effect before the item was picked from the menu.

Example:

```
ITEM Fax Server {CHDIR}
EXEC FAX
```

{PAUSE}

The {PAUSE} parameter causes the final screen display to stop and requires pressing any key before returning to the menu screen. Pressing any key takes place after the {EXEC} command file has been executed and before control is returned to the menu screen.

Example:

```
ITEM Display Users {PAUSE}
EXEC NLIST USER
```

{SHOW}

The {SHOW} parameter causes the name of the program being executed to appear in the top left corner of the screen before the program is executed. If you don't use the {SHOW} command, the menu displays Loading *name of executable* ....

Example:

```
ITEM Word Processing {SHOW}
EXEC WP
```

In the event you need to use multiple {ITEM} options, you use one set of braces and separate the options by a space. The following example illustrates this.

Example:

```
ITEM Network Administration {SHOW BATCH}
EXEC NETADMIN
```

This concludes the parameters that can be placed with the ITEM command.

SUBMENUS

There is a distinct possibility that your LAN has more than 12 applications or choices to offer to your end users. If this is the case, you will have to develop submenus to take care of the additional features being offered, or simply for organizational purposes. The following script shows the previous menu example with a submenu:

```
MENU 01, DreamLAN Admin Menu 2
        ITEM User Utilities
                SHOW 2
        ITEM MS WINDOWS
                EXEC WIN
        ITEM WORD PROCESSING
                EXEC WP
        ITEM PRINTERS in Current Container {PAUSE}
                EXEC NLIST PRINTER
        ITEM EXIT MENU SYSTEM
                EXEC EXIT

MENU 2, User Utilities
        ITEM Filer
                EXEC FILER
        ITEM Netuser
                EXEC NETUSER
```

Of particular importance is the SHOW 2 command that comes after the line ITEM User Utilities. The SHOW command calls a submenu with a *number* following the command. This number is the number that was used in the definition of another block of menu code, which is contained within the same script source file.

When using the SHOW command, submenus are called by menu numbers and not by menu titles. The rules for creating submenus are basically the same as for creating main menus in terms of the commands, titles, indentations, and so on. You also can have submenus call other submenus, resulting in nested submenus. Bear in mind, however, that you can only display one main menu and ten nested submenus onscreen at a time. You get an error upon entering the eleventh submenu.

26

MENUING

Warning

The MENUMAKE compiler will enable you to compile menus that call more than ten nested submenus without any errors. The error only shows up when executing your nested submenus and then only after the tenth one is onscreen.

Figure 26.3 shows what the submenu display looks like.

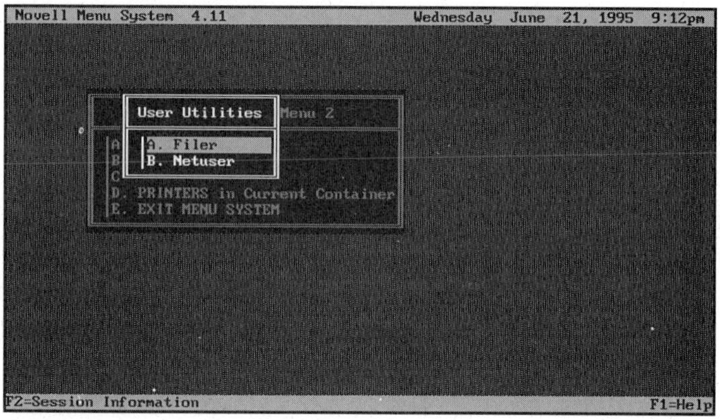

Figure 26.3.
Submenu screen.

Using the LOAD command is another way of executing a submenu that offers two advantages over the SHOW command. Following is how the sample script modified to use the LOAD command would look:

```
MENU 01, DreamLAN Admin Menu - 3

        ITEM User Utilities
                LOAD F:\PUBLIC\SUBMENU1.DAT

        ITEM MS WINDOWS
                EXEC WIN

        ITEM WORD PROCESSING
                EXEC WP

        ITEM PRINTERS in Current Container {PAUSE}
                EXEC NLIST PRINTER

        ITEM EXIT MENU SYSTEM
                EXEC EXIT
```

The LOAD statement loads a separate menu file. This file, SUBMENU1.DAT, is not in any way connected with the calling menu other than it is called from there. It is a separate file altogether. This file must have been edited (using your editor) and *compiled* (using MENUMAKE), resulting in the binary .DAT format. It is, in fact, a totally separate menu that can be executed by itself. (Don't forget that you should include an EXEC EXIT option in the submenu file if you run it by itself; if not, you will not be able to exit from the submenu.)

The two advantages of the LOAD command is that you can have many people work on a complicated menu, giving each person a section or submenu to code, and a single submenu file can be called by any other menu or submenu program or run by itself.

ADVANCED MENU OPTIONS

An excellent feature of the NMENU program is the capability to prompt the user for input during menu execution. This can be very useful to perform tasks that require user input. There are three commands that prompt the user for input. These commands are GETO, GETR, and GETP.

Tip

To continue after any user input prompt, press F10.

Following is the format for these commands:

```
GET(x) prompt to user {prepend information} length, prefill, secure {append}
```

Example:

```
GETR ENTER THE QUEUE TO PRINT TO { }8,,{ NB NFF NT TI=10}
```

GET(x) represents the GET command you are going to use.

Prompt to user is the information users will see onscreen, guiding them for some input.

Prepend is the value added to the beginning of the user response. Whatever is typed in the *prepend* field will be added to the front of whatever the user types in. This information must be placed in braces. If there is no *prepend* information (the *prepend* field is optional), empty braces are still required.

Length specifies how many characters the user can type at the prompt. You are allowed a maximum input of 80 characters.

Prefill is used to supply a default user response. The default response shows up in the input box. The user can accept it by pressing F10 or can change it.

Secure is an optional parameter that can be left out. If you use the secure parameter, when the user is asked for input, whatever the user types in shows up onscreen as asterisks (*). This is ideal for user inputs such as passwords.

append is a value that is added to the end of the user response. Whatever is typed in the *append* field will be added to the back of what the user types in at the input prompt. This information is required to be placed in braces. If there is no *append* information (the *append* field is optional), empty braces are still required.

GETO

Use GETO to prompt the user for optional input. The O in GETO stands for *optional*. When GETO is used, the information keyed in at the prompt is added to the end of the first EXEC command that comes after the GETO statement. If no information is keyed in, the command after the EXEC command is executed by itself, becoming the default command. The following sample script illustrates the use of this command:

```
MENU 01, User Input Menu
        ITEM DIRECTORY LISTING
                GETO Enter the directory to look at{ } 40, ,{/p}
                EXEC DIR
        ITEM EXIT
                EXEC EXIT
```

Figure 26.4 illustrates the results of running this menu.

Figure 26.4
The GETO prompt screen.

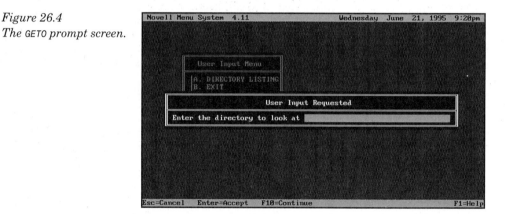

GETR

Use GETR when the user input is mandatory. The menu will not continue unless the user types in some input (the user can escape back to the main menu). Like GETO, the information that is keyed in at the prompt is added to the end of the next EXEC command that comes after the GETR statement. The following sample script illustrates this:

```
MENU 01, User Input Menu 2
        ITEM CHOOSE PRINTER QUEUE{PAUSE}
          GETR Enter the QUEUE to print to{ }8,,{ NB NFF NT TI=10}
                EXEC CAPTURE Q=
        ITEM EXIT
                EXEC EXIT
```

Figures 26.5 and 26.6 show the results of executing the menu and the corresponding CAPTURE statement.

Figure 26.5.
The GETR prompt screen.

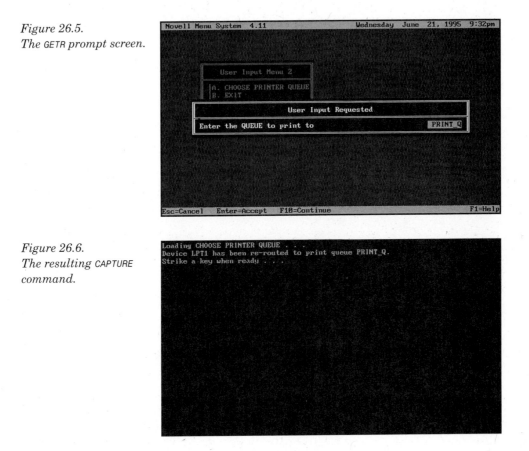

```
Novell Menu System  4.11                    Wednesday  June  21, 1995  9:32pm



                ┌─────────────────────────┐
                │    User Input Menu 2     │
                │ A. CHOOSE PRINTER QUEUE  │
                │ B. EXIT                  │
        ┌───────┴──────────────────────────┴───────────┐
        │            User Input Requested               │
        ├───────────────────────────────────────────────┤
        │ Enter the QUEUE to print to          PRINT_Q  │
        └───────────────────────────────────────────────┘




Esc=Cancel    Enter=Accept   F10=Continue                       F1=Help
```

Figure 26.6.
The resulting CAPTURE command.

```
Loading CHOOSE PRINTER QUEUE . . .
Device LPT1 has been re-routed to print queue PRINT_Q.
Strike a key when ready . . .
```

GETP

Unlike the GETO and GETR commands, which immediately apply the input typed in by the user to the end of the next EXEC statement, GETP stores the input information in the form of variables. These variables then can be used by other menu commands in other menus and submenus. The variables are referenced as %1, %2, %3, and so on.

The following script illustrates how the GETP command works:

```
MENU 01, User Input Menu 3
        ITEM Copy files from drive to drive{PAUSE}
                GETP Enter the source drive to copy from{}2,,{}
                GETP Enter the destination drive{}2,,{}
                EXEC NCOPY %1*.* %2
                EXEC DIR %2 /p
```

```
        ITEM Input Capture parameters{PAUSE}
                GETP Enter The number of copies to Print{}1,,{}
                GETP Enter The timeout for Graphics Jobs{}2,,{}
                EXEC Capture q=print_q nb nff nt copies=%1 ti=%2
        ITEM EXIT
                EXEC EXIT
```

Figures 26.7 and 26.8 show the results of the previous script being executed.

Figure 26.7.
GETP example 1.

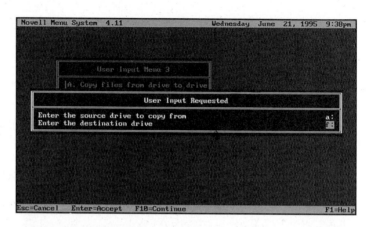

Figure 26.8.
GETP example 2.

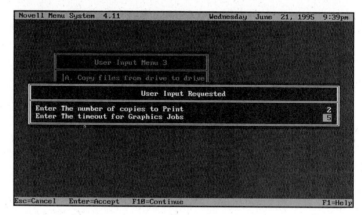

It is important to understand that in the previous sample script, the second set of the two GETP parameters in the line 'ITEM Input Capture parameters' causes the input to be stored in the %1 and %2 variables, respectively, and not in the %3 and %4 variables. It does not work if you try the %3 and %4 variables, in that order. In essence, the %1 and %2 variables are reset from the previous input commands. If you want to obtain %3 and %4 variables, you must list all GETP statements consecutively, before invoking any EXEC command.

The following script illustrates this:

```
MENU 01, User Input Menu 4
        ITEM Input Capture parameters{PAUSE}
```

```
                GETP Enter the queue to print to{}8,,{}
                GETP Enter The number of copies to Print{}1,,{}
                GETP Enter The timeout for graphics Jobs{}2,,{}
                GETP Enter banner info (no spaces allowed){}12,,{}
                EXEC Capture q=%1 nff nt copies=%2 ti=%3 b=%4
        ITEM EXIT
                EXEC EXIT
```

Figure 26.9 illustrates the outcome of this script.

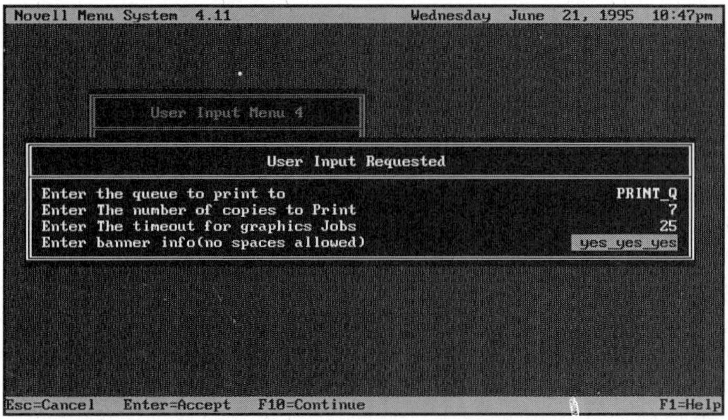

Figure 26.9.
GETP example 3.

BUILDING A TURNKEY SYSTEM

In most companies, it is better to spare the end user from all the technical details of loading up the ODI drivers, the NetWare requester, logging into the network, and executing a menu manually.

Fortunately, this entire process can be automated, so that end users only have to enter their name and passwords. Loading the ODI drivers, NetWare requester, and executing the LOGIN.EXE command can all be done from the AUTOEXEC.BAT file. Of particular importance to you is the capability to execute the menu program without the end user ever getting to a DOS prompt.

This is achieved by calling the menu program from either the system login script (this applies to the container that the user is created in), profile login script, or a personal login script.

Figure 26.10 shows how a menu is being called from a system (container) login script using the EXIT (Novell login script command) command, which is the preferred way to call a menu. You also can call the menu from any login script using the # login script command (this is a login script command; for more information on login scripts, see Chapter 25). This command causes any external .EXE or .COM file to be executed. However, the # is less used because it keeps the login script in memory, which consumes memory (approximately 10K) until the program being called has finished executing. To call the menu using the # command, the login script would say #NMENU ASIA.

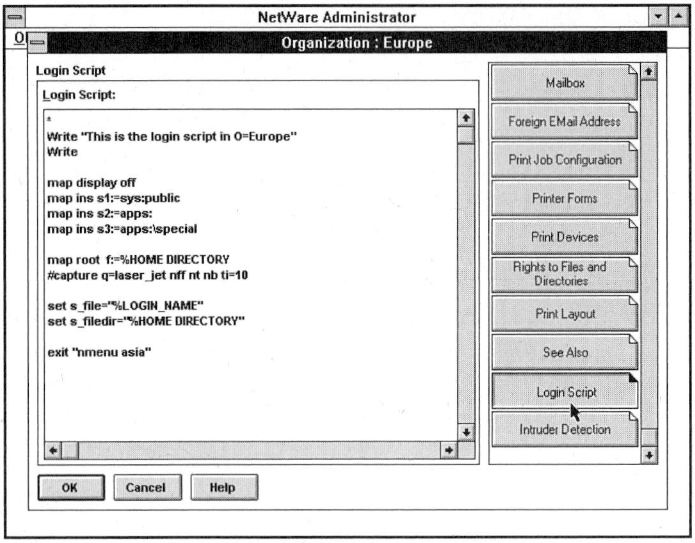

Figure 26.10.
Using user login script
to start a menu.

CONVERTING THE OLD

NetWare 4.*x* provides a program that will enable you to convert your menus that were built in NetWare versions 3.11 and 2.*x*. The menus of these older operating systems were built with Novell's proprietary menuing system. To convert a NetWare 3.11 menu called MAIN.MNU to a NetWare 3.12 or 4.*x* menu, type the following and then press Enter.

```
MENUCNVT MAIN.MNU
```

The conversion program generates a file called MAIN.SRC. If you want to change the filename as well, type the following:

```
MENUCNVT MAIN.MNU MKAMER.SRC
```

The file that is produced is an ASCII source text file that has not yet been compiled. You should edit the conversion to see whether any errors exist. After editing your file, you must compile it. Once again, use the MENUMAKE program for this purpose. Type the following:

```
MENUMAKE MKAMER
```

SUMMARY

By now, you have seen that Novell has vastly improved their menu program in NetWare 3.12 and NetWare 4.*x* over the previous versions of NetWare by incorporating a subset of Saber Software Corporation's menu technology.

You have learned in this chapter how powerful the NMENU program is for the creation of flexible, secure, and easy-to-manage menus. Designing, creating, compiling, and executing menus should become second nature. The menu program is an exceptional tool that will make your resources more easily available to your network users.

26

MENUING

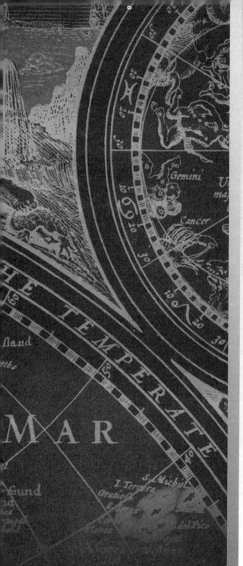

- MHS Services and NDS

- Installing MHS Services

- Configuring MHS Services

- Using FirstMail

- Summary

CHAPTER 27

MHS Services

Starting with NetWare 4.1, *Message Handling System Services* (MHS) is included with the base product. This gives you electronic mail (e-mail) capability for all your users throughout the NDS tree. MHS Services is tightly integrated with NDS. In this chapter, you will learn how to install and configure MHS Services and FirstMail, the e-mail application that comes with NetWare 4.1.

First, however, there is a brief discussion on how MHS Services is integrated with NDS.

MHS SERVICES AND NDS

When you install the MHS Services, the following NDS objects can be created:

◆ Messaging Server
◆ Message Routing Group
◆ Distribution List

The server that has MHS Services installed will have a *Messaging Server* object associated with it. There are times when you will need to install MHS Services on multiple servers; to distribute load and for different workgroups, for example. In order for these different message servers to exchange mail, they need to be placed into the same *Message Routing Group*—it is much like the group concepts for users. *Distribution lists* can be used to send messages to groups of users, depending on their location and/or functionality. For example, you can have a distribution list for Accounting, one for Engineering, and one for Finance. Therefore, rather than having to select individual user names, you can use the distribution list instead.

Other than using distribution lists, you also can address messages to the following NDS objects:

◆ **User**: If the user object has a mailbox assigned
◆ **Group**: All members of a group that have mailboxes
◆ **Container**: All users within that container that have mailboxes
◆ **Organizational Role**: All occupants of the OR that have mailboxes

Note

It is important to understand that the NDS object has a mailbox assigned before it can receive mail messages.

If you have an MHS gateway, such as Novell's Global MHS, to link you to external mail systems, such as the Internet, you can store the user's mail id for those systems as a property of the user's object in the NDS (see Figure 27.1). MHS can use this information to translate mail addresses for mail sent to and from external mail systems.

Figure 27.1.
Foreign e-mail address
for NDS user.

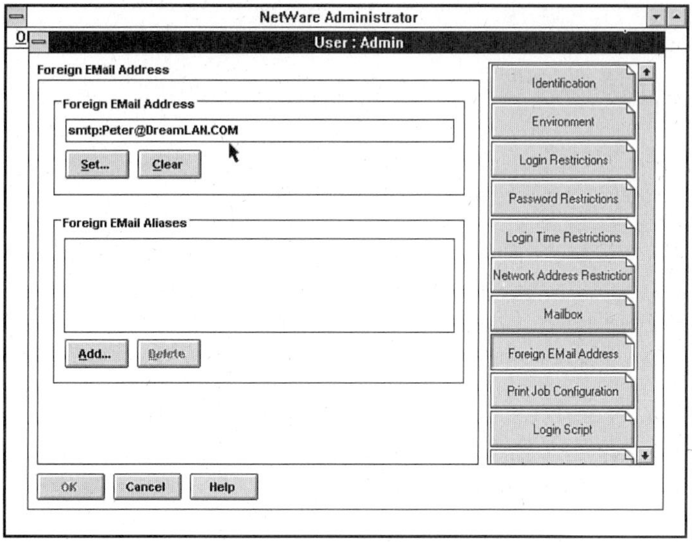

The address syntax for e-mail within MHS Services looks very similar to that of Internet e-mail—*username@container* vs. *username@domain*. For example, to address messages to user Peter that is in the OU=Toronto.O=North_America container, the address looks like the following:

PETER@TORONTO.NORTH_AMERICA

Armed with the background information, you now are ready to install and configure MHS Services, and the e-mail application FirstMail.

INSTALLING MHS SERVICES

MHS Services is included on your NetWare 4.1 Operating System CD. The INSTALL NLM is used to copy and configure the MHS Services files from the CD onto your server. From the INSTALL program, select Products option, and from it, select Install NetWare MHS Services (see Figure 27.2).

By default, INSTALL assumes the files are located on the CD-ROM. If your path for the files is different, press F3 to enter a different path. After giving the correct path, the rest of the installation is automated. You will see a status screen similar to Figure 27.3 while files (including the FirstMail application) are being copied.

You will be prompted to log into the NDS tree with a user that has the proper NDS rights to create the Messaging Server and Message Routing Group objects. This user (known as *Postmaster General*) will also become the owner of the Message Routing Group. Press F1 at the console for more information about this user. Typically you can use Admin; however, you may want to have a separate Postmaster id instead.

27

MHS SERVICES

Figure 27.2.
Installing NetWare
MHS Services.

Figure 27.3.
MHS Services file copy
status screen.

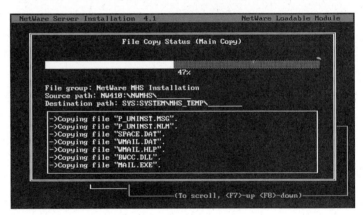

You then are prompted for the volume on which you want to install the MHS Services and user mailboxes. A directory called MHS is created off the root of the volume. You need to give some thought to the choice of volume. As a general rule, users do not like deleting mail messages: therefore, the disk usage can go up very quickly. You may want to have a dedicated e-mail volume to handle your MHS needs.

After this last step, you have successfully installed MHS Services and are ready to configure it.

To start MHS Services automatically, include the following line in your AUTOEXEC.NCF file:

```
LOAD MHS
```

Tip

After you install MHS Services, you must power down and restart the server before MHS Services will load correctly.

Note

On April 17, 1995, Novell released an update to MHS Services 1.0 (to bring it up to v1.01) that was shipped with NetWare 4.1 to address some issues. Following are the fixes and enhancements:

TimeZone: MHS Services will now correctly handle time zones east of GMT. (Ex: EST-10ESU)

Extended Addresses: Corrected parsing error due to multiple colons in an extended address

Date-Posted: Now accepts Date Posted:, header which does not contain the optional server information

MCB-Options: Fix for partial MCB-Options header

The update file is called MHSVR1.EXE and can be obtained from Novell, CompuServe, NSEPro, or the Internet.

CONFIGURING MHS SERVICES

After you have installed the MHS Services, there are a number of items to configure. For example, you need to establish mailboxes for your users and set up distribution lists to ease the task of sending mail to groups of users. They are as follows.

MHS CONSOLE

A console interface, *MHSCON*, is available as part of MHS Services to enable you to configure and manage certain MHS functions. This NLM can only be loaded after MHS is started. Figure 27.4 shows the MHSCON main screen.

Using this utility, you can configure and monitor the following eight items:

◆ **Messages**: This option shows you a list of Messaging Servers in your Message Routing Group and how many messages are waiting for delivery from your server to each of them. Also shown is the time of the last connection to each server and the current connection status (see Figure 27.5). If you highlight a Message Server and then press Enter, you will see a list of Messaging Server options, as shown in Figure 27.6. For example, from this screen, you can obtain a list of messages currently in the queue, who they are from, to whom they are sent, message size, and when the message was posted (see Figure 27.7).

27

MHS SERVICES

Figure 27.4.
MHSCON main screen.

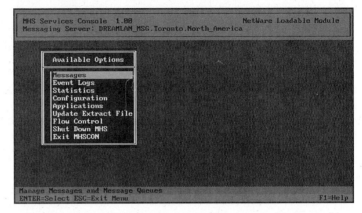

Figure 27.5.
Message statistics from
MHSCON.

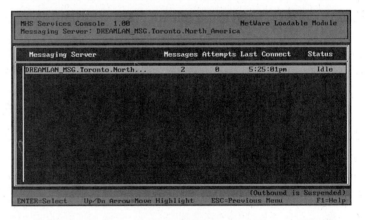

Figure 27.6.
Messaging Server
Options screen.

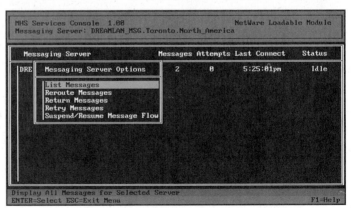

Figure 27.7.
Detailed message
information.

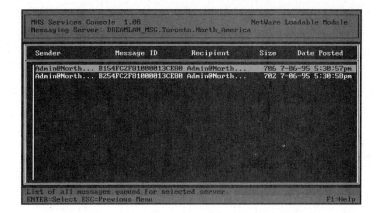

◆ **Event logs**: This option enables you to view the logs maintained by MHS Services. You also can use this option to decide which events to log, as well as to purge the event logs (see Figure 27.8).

Figure 27.8.
MHS event filters.

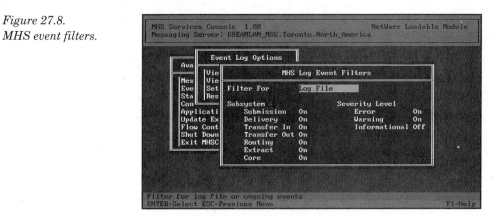

27

MHS Services

◆ **Statistics**: This screen allows you to monitor the amount of message traffic for all the Messaging Servers within the Message Routing Group or individual Messaging Servers (see Figure 27.9). You also can toggle on/off the logging of statistics by pressing F4; pressing F6 enables you to export the statistics to a file, while pressing F8 resets the statistics.

◆ **Configuration**: This option enables you to edit the MHS.CFG file that is located in SYS:SYSTEM from the server console (see Figure 27.10). Consult the DynaText for more information about each option. You need to restart MHS for the changes to take effect.

Figure 27.9.
MHSCON statistics
screen.

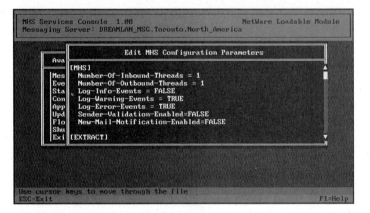

```
MHS Services Console  1.00                    NetWare Loadable Module
Messaging Server: DREAMLAN_MSG.Toronto.North_America

┌──────────────── MHS Messaging Server Statistics ────────────────┐
│ Statistics For            <All Messaging Servers>               │
│ Time of Last Reset        n/a                                   │
│                                                                 │
│ Transfer Out Messages              Transfer In Messages         │
│    Count       1                      Count       3             │
│    Total Size  0      (kb)            Total Size  1      (kb)    │
│    Maximum Size 673                   Maximum Size 706          │
│    Average Size 673                   Average Size 548          │
│    Current Rate 0     /min.           Current Rate 0    /min.   │
│    Peak Rate    4     /min.           Peak Rate    8    /min.   │
│                                                                 │
│ Total Successful Connections   0                                │
│ Total Unsuccessful Connections 0                                │
│ Last Successful Connection     n/a                              │
│ Last Unsuccessful Connection   n/a                              │
└─────────────────────────────────────────────────────────────────┘
Choose Messaging Server for which to show statistics
ENTER=Select ESC=Previous Menu  F4=Toggle Log  F6=Write  F8=Reset    F1=Help
```

Figure 27.10.
MHSCON configura-
tion screen.

```
MHS Services Console  1.00                    NetWare Loadable Module
Messaging Server: DREAMLAN_MSG.Toronto.North_America

     ┌──────────── Edit MHS Configuration Parameters ────────────┐
 ┌Ava│                                                           │
 │Mes│ [MHS]                                                     │
 │Eve│    Number-Of-Inbound-Threads = 1                          │
 │Sta│    Number-Of-Outbound-Threads = 1                         │
 │Con│    Log-Info-Events = FALSE                                │
 │App│    Log-Warning-Events = TRUE                              │
 │Upd│    Log-Error-Events = TRUE                                │
 │Flo│    Sender-Validation-Enabled=FALSE                        │
 │Shu│    New-Mail-Notification-Enabled=FALSE                    │
 │Exi│ [EXTRACT]                                                 │
     └───────────────────────────────────────────────────────────┘

Use cursor keys to move through the file
ESC=Exit                                                           F1=Help
```

◆ **Applications**: If you have more than one MHS application installed on
your server, you can use this option to register them, as well as to set each
user's preferred MHS application. That way, when an MHS message comes
in, it will be delivered to the correct application for the user.

◆ **Update Extract File**: Use this option to extract MHS user information
from the NDS and make it available to MHS applications to be used as
address books.

◆ **Flow Control**: Controls the flow of incoming and outgoing messages to and
from the server (see Figure 27.11).

◆ **Shut Down MHS**: Unloads MHS.NLM, as well as MHSCON.

In most cases, you do not need to make any changes or even use MHSCON. However,
it is available should you need it.

Figure 27.11.
Control flow of
messages.

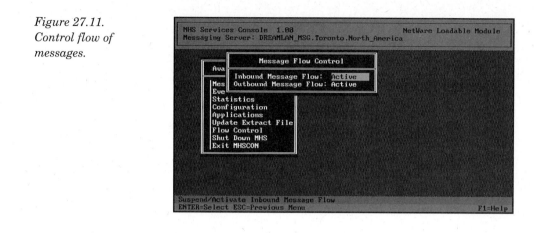

There are three other configuration tasks you may need to perform:

◆ Assign mailboxes to NDS objects

◆ Create/update Message Routing Groups

◆ Create/update Distribution lists

These configuration tasks are discussed next.

MAILBOXES

As mentioned earlier, in order for a user (or other NDS objects, such as containers and groups) to receive MHS messages, a mailbox must exist. You can create a mailbox easily by using NWAdmin or NETADMIN. NWAdmin is used to illustrate the steps necessary in assigning mailboxes to NDS objects.

Starting with NetWare 4.1, a new attribute called *Mailbox* is associated with some of the NDS objects. Shown in Figure 27.12 is the configuration for a user object. Simply enter a name of up to eight characters for the mailbox id, much like a directory name. Note that the object's name is supplied by default. Rather than specifying which server and volume that house the mailboxes, you use the Messaging Server object.

Tip

When possible, use the object's name as the mailbox id for easy identification and association.

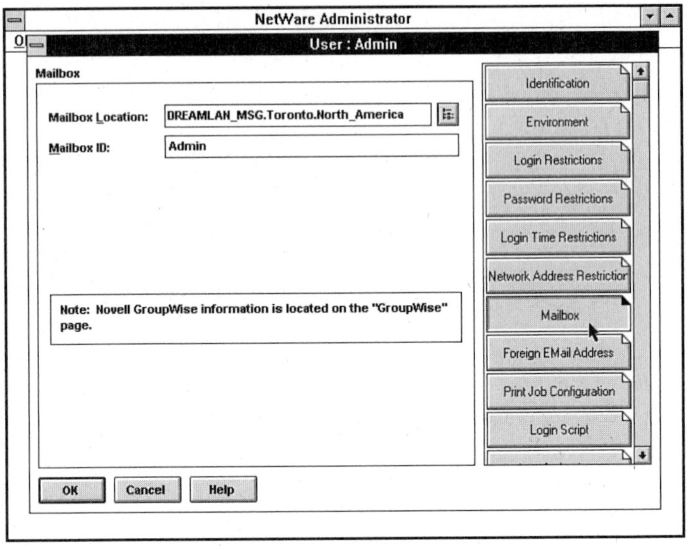

Figure 27.12.
Adding a mailbox to
user Admin.

MESSAGE ROUTING GROUPS

By default, a Message Routing Group (called MHS_ROUTING_GROUP) is created when you install MHS Services. If you have two or more Messaging Servers that will exchange mail, they must belong to the same Message Routing Group.

To add a new Messaging Server to the routing group using NWADMIN, for example, first display the Detail screen of the routing group, and then click the Messaging Server button to display a list of servers already in the group (see Figure 27.13). Then click the Add option button to include a new server into the routing group.

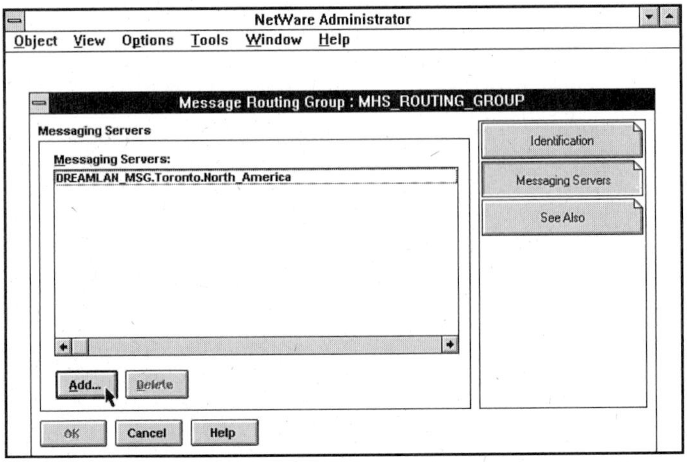

Figure 27.13.
Current Messaging
Servers in the routing
group.

To create a new routing group, simply "tree walk" to the container in which you want to create the object, press Ins and select the Message Routing Group icon. You will be asked for a name for the new routing group and the name of the Postmaster General for the routing group (see Figure 27.14).

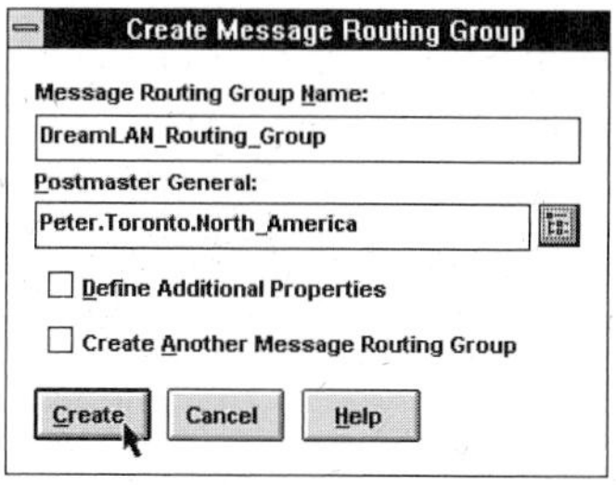

Figure 27.14.
Creating a new routing
group.

After the routing group is created, you can assign Messaging Servers as outlined earlier.

DISTRIBUTION LISTS

Distribution lists contain NDS object names, such as users, groups, containers, and Organizational Roles (see Figure 27.15).

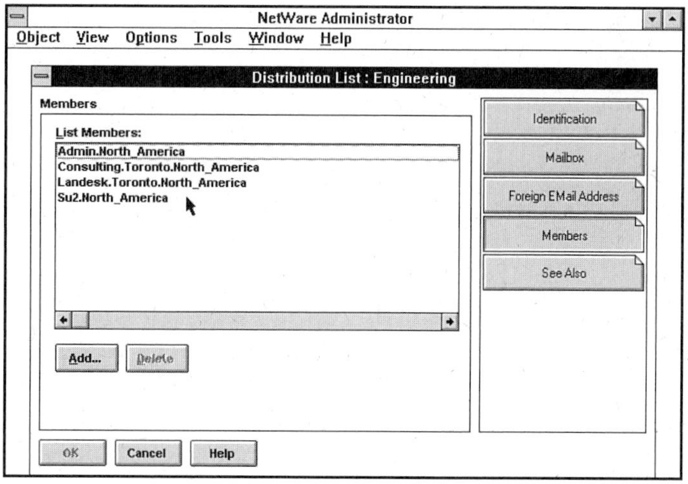

Figure 27.15.
Distribution list
contains NDS object
names.

To create a distribution list, simply "tree walk" to the container in which you want to create the object, press Ins, and click the Distribution List icon. You will be prompted for a name for the new distribution list and the location where the mailbox is (see Figure 27.16).

27

MHS SERVICES

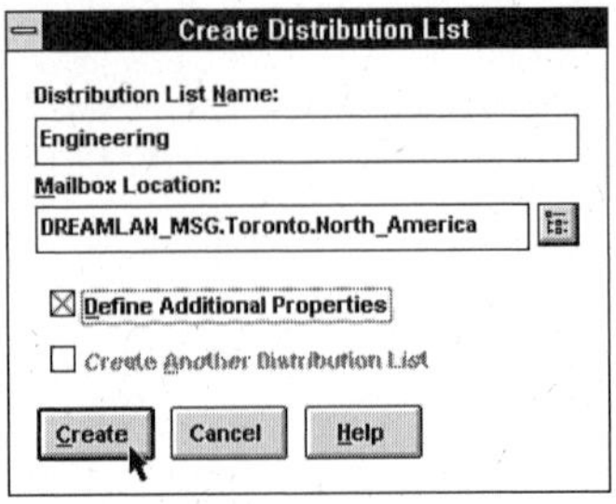

Figure 27.16.
Creating a new Distri-
bution List.

Note

Depending on where you create the Distribution List and which users need to have access to it, you may need to assign NDS object rights for the users in order for them to see and use the Distribution List.

USING FIRSTMAIL

FirstMail (FMail), based on the popular freeware e-mail package Pegasus Mail (PMail), is a simple, but powerful, MHS application that works in DOS and Windows. During the installing of MHS Services, both versions of FirstMail are also installed. FMail provides the standard e-mail feature, such as personal address books, message forwarding, file attachments, and return receipts. It is a perfect application to use if this is your first e-mail installation.

Note that any MHS application that conforms to the latest MHS messaging standards—Standard Message Format (SMF) v70 or v71, such as ExpressIT! from Infinite Technologies, will function with MHS Services, not just FirstMail. However, because FMail is available free with your NetWare 4.1 package, it is a good starter package to use until you are confortable with MHS.

Tip

Use FirstMail (for Windows or for DOS) to test your MHS Services installation by exchanging messages with users who have mailboxes. For starters, send some test messages to yourself.

There is very little configuration necessary to make FMail work the first time. The mailbox information associated with the user object is used automatically.

FIRSTMAIL FOR WINDOWS

To utilize the Windows version, you simply need to create an icon on your Windows desktop for easy access. The application file is WMAIL.EXE and is located in the SYS:PUBLIC directory of your Messaging Servers. Shown in Figure 27.17 is the opening screen of FirstMail for Windows.

Figure 27.17.
FirstMail for Windows.

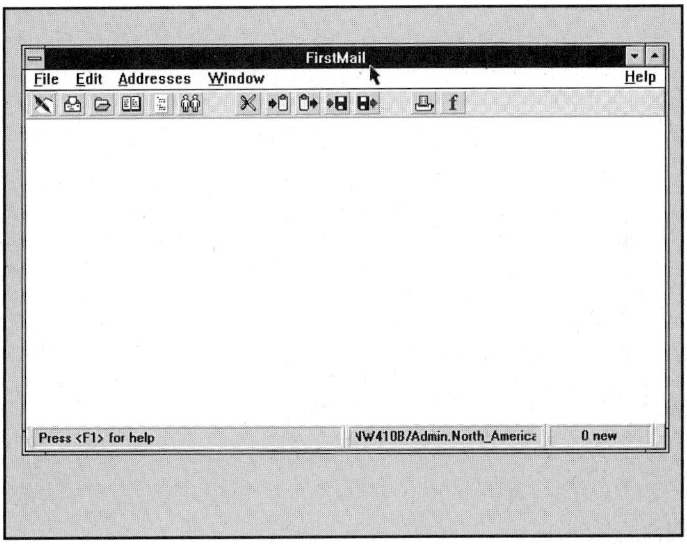

Note

On June 1, 1995 Novell released an update to FirstMail for Windows which addresses the following two problems:

◆ **Lost drive mappings**: Upon exit of WMAIL.EXE, the user reports that some of the drive mappings are lost.

◆ **Context corruption problem**: After running WMAIL.EXE, NWUSER.EXE and NWADMIN.EXE reports that NDS context is no longer valid.

The update file is called FMWIN1.EXE and can be obtained from Novell, CompuServe, NSEPro, or the Internet.

FirstMail (both DOS and Windows) is fairly intuitive to use with extensive online help available (pressing F1 will display context-sensitive help). You should know the following two things when working with addressing messages:

◆ The Address Book and Distribution List options within FMail are private to each user. To use the Distribution List you created as NDS objects, you need to use the NDS global address book option (see Figure 27.18).

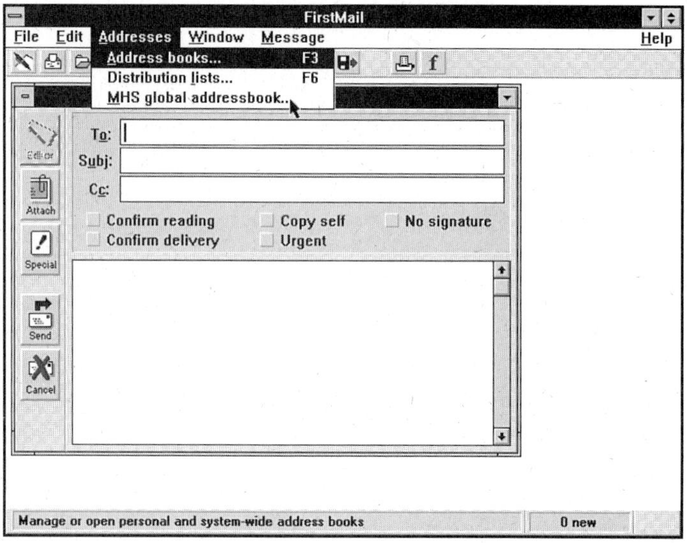

Figure 27.18.
Different addresses
within FMail.

◆ There are times new objects you created (such as a new Distribution List) in NDS are not seen from the NDS global address book option. This is because the MHS information in the NDS has not yet been made available to MHS. You need to perform an Update Extract File from within MHSCON, as outlined earlier.

FirstMail for DOS

To invoke FirstMail for DOS, make sure you have a search map to SYS:PUBLIC of a Messaging Server, and type MAIL at the DOS prompt. Shown in Figure 27.19 is the main menu for FirstMail for DOS. If you have used Pegasus Mail before, you will see that the two are striking similar.

Figure 27.19.
FirstMail for DOS.

```
07/06/95              F i r s t M a i l  ( t m )              17:43:37


               ┌──────────── Mail Options ────────────┐
               │ N: check for New mail                 │
               │ S: Send a mail message                │
               │ B: Browse mail messages               │
               │ P: Preferences                        │
               │ E: Edit a file                        │
               │ Q: Quit using FirstMail               │
               └───────────────────────────────────────┘




Press <F1> for help            Admin (1 new)            Folder <Main>
```

SUMMARY

NetWare 4.1 is shipped with Message Handling System Services (MHS) v1.0 as part of the base product. An electronic mail (e-mail) front-end, FirstMail, is also shipped with NetWare 4.1. This combination gives you e-mail capability for all your users throughout the NDS tree. MHS Services is tightly integrated with NDS. In this chapter, you learned about some of the NDS objects associated with MHS Services, such as Messaging Server and Message Routing Group. You also learned about installing and configuring MHS Services and FirstMail.

27

MHS SERVICES

- Components of
  NetWare Security

- NetWare Directory
  Services Security

- File System Security

- Administering Rights

- Administering File
  System Rights

- Administering File
  and Directory At-
  tributes

- File Server Console
  Security

- Summary

CHAPTER 28

Implementing Security

Computer networks today are crucial assets in most businesses. With this in mind, it's not surprising that network administrators need to keep the network data and resources safe.

A simple definition of security is the process of protecting a network from danger or risk of loss—making it safe from intruders, loss of data, and errors. There are many different examples of network security, including file and directory security, password protection, virus protection, and physical security of workstations and file servers. In designing NetWare, Novell recognized that customers wanted to be able to easily implement networks that were secure in all these areas, without requiring an in-depth knowledge of network security concepts.

NetWare 4.1 provides flexible, multi-level security controls embedded into the operating system. These controls allow network administrators to implement security models that range from basic, single level security to complex, secure enterprise-wide security models. NetWare 4.1's security controls are implemented through the use of administration tools that enable administrators to implement the level of security that is right for their organization.

This chapter examines the components of NetWare security to help you determine the security requirements for your network. It then takes an in-depth look at the tools provided to enable you to implement security on your network.

COMPONENTS OF NETWARE SECURITY

NetWare 4.1 includes a number of different levels of security that control who can access the network, which resources users can access, and how they can utilize those resources. These levels include the following:

◆ Login/password security
◆ NetWare Directory Services (NDS) security
◆ File system security
◆ File server console security

Login/password security controls initial access to the network. Once initial access is obtained, NDS security controls which objects (such as User objects) in the directory tree users can access. File system security controls which files and directories users can access on network volumes. And, lastly, file server console security controls who can access the file server console. Each of these levels of security are explained in greater depth in the following sections.

LOGIN/PASSWORD SECURITY

Login/password security is the first level of NetWare security. It determines who can access the network and when. To most network administrators and users, this level of security seems quite simplistic—each user has a unique login name and password and that's that. However, it's not as simple as it seems. The login process often times is considered the weakest link in network security. Because of this, it is important that network administrators understand the significance of this level of security.

There are several things that can cause security breaches during the login process. These include unauthorized user access and password breaking using techniques such as wire tapping, trojan horse attacks, and brute force attacks. These security breaches can be easily overcome by establishing and enforcing security policies and educating users on the importance of passwords and their use. NetWare 4.1 also includes features that prevent unauthorized access during the login process. These features include a sophisticated public-key cryptosystem, digital packet signatures, and other login-level security options.

RSA PUBLIC-KEY CRYPTOSYSTEM

NetWare 4.1 uses a sophisticated identification and authentication system based on a public-key cryptosystem technology developed by RSA Data Security, Inc. This system ensures that every request for login or attachment to a NetWare server passes the following test:

- ◆ The sender of the login or attachment request is a valid client
- ◆ The sender's station actually built the request
- ◆ The request originated at the workstation where the authentication data was created
- ◆ The request pertains to the current session
- ◆ The message or request has not been tampered with

When a user requests login or attachment to a NetWare 4.1 server, the VLMs transmit the user's name and encrypted password to NetWare Directory Services (NDS). NDS then generates a public and private key for that user, encrypting the private key with the user's password. The encrypted private key is then sent back to the user and is decrypted by the VLM. Neither the private key nor the password cross the network wire in an unencrypted format.

The VLM then gathers information that is unique to the user—such as the network station and the time of the login or attachment request—and combines this information to form a unique digital signature for the user's current session. The

VLM then combines this unique digital signature with the decrypted private key to form a "credential." Once the credential is formed, the VLM removes the private key from the workstation's memory.

To successfully gain login or attachment, the VLM must then transmit the credential along with "proof" back to NDS. The proof consists of encrypted contents from the original login packet. If the client's credential and proof are correct, authentication occurs and the client is logged in to NDS. This authentication process is illustrated in Figure 28.1.

Figure 28.1.
This example details
the initial authentica-
tion process used to log
a user into NDS.

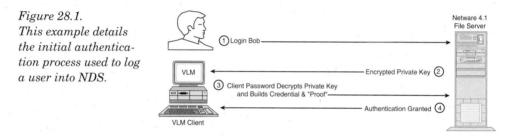

BACKGROUND AUTHENTICATION

One of the benefits of the global nature of NDS is single login. Users no longer log in to a single file server; they log in to the entire NetWare 4 network. Previous versions of NetWare and most other network operating systems require users to provide login names and passwords for each file server they need access to. In a NetWare 4 environment, users provide one login name and one password at the time of initial login. Then, through a process called *background authentication*, they are given access to additional resources on the network as long as they have the appropriate rights to access those resources.

The background authentication process in NetWare 4 uses similar algorithms as described above for initial authentication. The only difference is background authentication takes place automatically, transparent to the user. Figure 28.2 summarizes the background authentication processes.

Figure 28.2.
The background
authentication process
in NetWare 4.1.

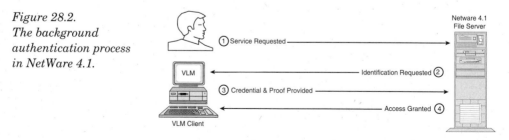

NCP PACKET SIGNATURES

NetWare 4 also includes an optional security feature, called *NCP* (NetWare Core Protocol) Packet Signature, that prevents forged packets on the network. Forged packets are another potential security breach in high-security environments. Without NCP Packet Signatures, it is possible that an NCP request packet could be injected into a privileged session to grant access to a network intruder. By enabling NCP packet signatures, a digital signature is added to each NCP packet, preventing unauthorized NCP requests from being serviced. These digital signatures are based on the RSA MD4 message digest algorithm.

NCP packet signatures are configured both at the server level and at the workstation level. There are four different NCP Packet Signature options that allow administrators to control the level of security they want to accomplish.

- ◆ Level 0—Don't do packet signatures (NCP packet signatures disabled)
- ◆ Level 1—Do packet signatures only if the workstation requires them
- ◆ Level 2—Do packet signatures if the workstation is configured to use them, but do not require them if not supported by the workstation
- ◆ Level 3—Always require packet signatures

Figure 28.3 shows the NCP Packet Signature levels at the file server. Packet Signature levels are set through the SERVMAN NLM at the server console.

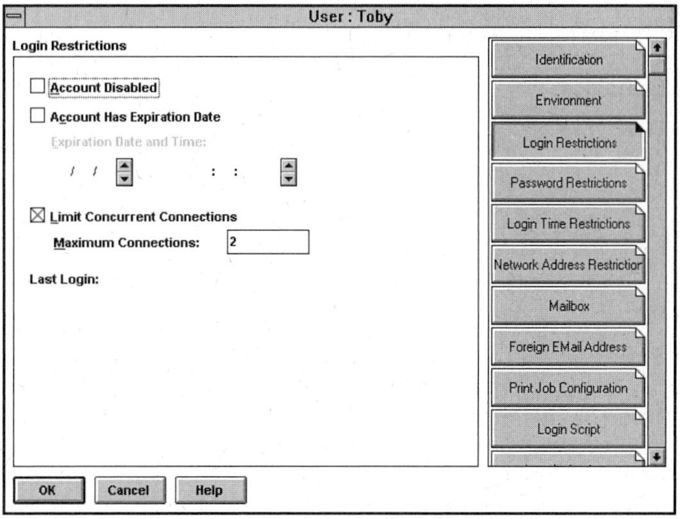

Figure 28.3.
NCP Packet signature
levels in the SERVMAN
NLM.

28

Packet signatures are set at the workstation through the NET.CFG file. The following is an example of a workstation NET.CFG file including the packet signature option (last line):

```
LINK DRIVER NE2000
        INT 3
        PORT 300
        FRAME ETHERNET_802.2

NETWARE DOS REQUESTER
        FIRST NETWORK DRIVE = F
        NETWARE PROTOCOL = NDS,BIND,PNW
        SIGNATURE LEVEL = 0
```

On the server, the signature level is established using a SET command.NCP Packet Signatures are not for every network. Generally, packet signatures are used in high-security environments when packet forging is a concern. Keep in mind that enabling packet signatures requires a lot of additional overhead and can affect the performance of your network.

OPTIONAL LOGIN SECURITY FEATURES

NetWare 4.1 includes a number of optional login security features that network administrators can choose to implement on a global or user by user level. These features include the following:

◆ Login restriction

◆ Password restrictions

◆ Login time restrictions

◆ Network address restrictions

◆ Intruder detection

LOGIN RESTRICTIONS

Login restrictions enable the network administrator to control how users can use the network. User accounts can be disabled, be given an expiration date, or limited to the number of concurrent logins.

When a user account is disabled or has expired, that user cannot log in to the network, even with a valid login name and password. Disabled or expired accounts can be released by the network administrator at any time. Disabling a user account is useful when an employee is leaving the company, voluntarily or involuntarily. Disabling the account denies the user access to the network without requiring the administrator to delete the user account. The administrator can then rename and re-enable the account when the terminated employee's replacement is hired. Similarly, account expirations are useful for temporary users that only need access to the network for a specific amount of time. When the account expires, the user can no longer access the network.

Another useful login restriction is limiting concurrent user logins. Limiting the number of concurrent logins limits the number of times a user can be logged in to the network simultaneously. A good rule of thumb is to give each user two concurrent connections. Giving them only one connection may create more administrative work than necessary. For example, if a user is forced to reboot his or her workstation without a proper logout from the network, NetWare may still be holding the user's connection open. When this occurs, if the user is configured with only one concurrent connection, access to the network will be denied until NetWare releases the original connection. Even though the original connection is generally released within a few minutes, commonly users will try to log back in immediately and when they are denied access, they call the network administrator for support.

Figure 28.4 shows the Login restrictions screen in the NetWare Administrator utility. NETADMIN provides DOS-based network administrators with similar functionality.

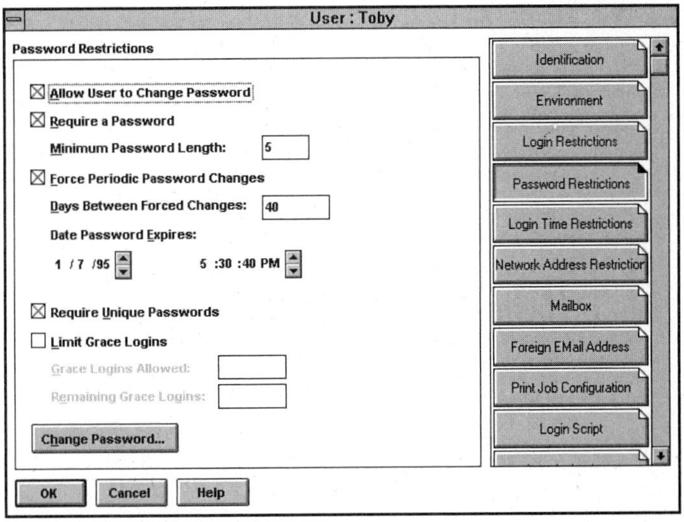

Figure 28.4.
The user login restriction screen in NetWare Administrator.

USER PASSWORD RESTRICTIONS

User password restrictions allow the network administrator to enforce certain guidelines set for user passwords. These guidelines include requiring user passwords, minimum password lengths, password expiration dates, requiring unique passwords, and allowing grace logins.

Requiring user passwords is a must in every network, regardless of the level of security you want to accomplish. Unpassworded user accounts leave the network wide open for every type of security breach possible. Unfortunately, requiring a password is not a default option in NetWare. Because of this, selecting the password required property is the first thing that should be done when each user account is created. Not only should passwords be required, a minimum password length of five or more characters should be assigned. This will prevent users from using their initials or something similar as their password. Simple precautionary measures such as these make it difficult for hackers to break into the network. Setting these parameters for the entire network can be easily done by using a global USER_TEMPLATE.

Because users frequently provide their current password to other users, it's also important to force periodic password changes. Normally, accepting the NetWare default of 40 days between password changes is sufficient. However, forcing password changes doesn't do any good unless *unique passwords* are required as well. Requiring unique password prevents users from using the same password over and over again. NetWare 4.1 keeps track of the last 20 passwords a user has used.

When a user's password expires, he or she is given the option to change the password right away or to change it later. Limiting the number of grace logins limits the number of times the user can use the old password after it expires. If a user exceeds the set number of grace logins, the account is locked and must be released by the network administrator.

Figure 28.5 shows the user password restrictions screen in NetWare Administrator. Notice that this option also allows the user password to be changed. In order for a regular user to change a password, the original password must be provided before a new password can be assigned. Network administrators can change user passwords without entering the old password first. NETADMIN provides similar functionality for DOS-based network administrators.

Figure 28.5.
The user password
restriction screen in
NetWare Administrator.

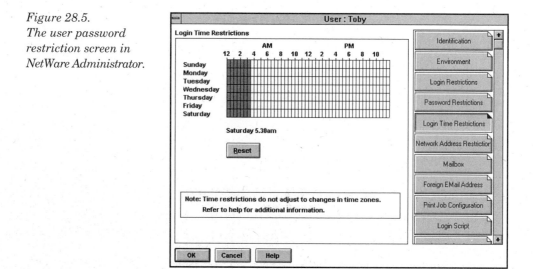

LOGIN TIME RESTRICTIONS

Login time restrictions allow the network administrator to restrict users from logging in to the network during specific times of the day. A common usage of this option is to ensure that all users are logged out before backups are performed. Many times, users will leave for the day and fail to exit their applications and log off the network. When this occurs, the open files are skipped during the backup. Setting a time restriction just prior to the backup time will not only prevent new users from logging in but will also clear the connections of any users who forgot to log out. This will ensure that all files are closed when the backup runs. Users still logged in when a time restriction approaches will be sent warning messages that a time restriction is approaching. If the warnings are ignored, the user will be automatically logged out by the system and the connection will be cleared.

Figure 28.6 shows the time restriction screen in NetWare Administrator. By default, user's login times are unrestricted. Conversely, by blocking out an area of time, a restriction is made.

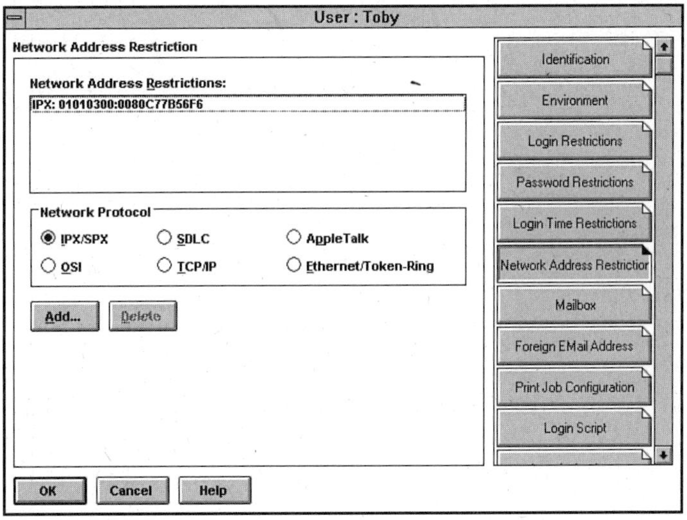

Figure 28.6.
The user time restriction screen in NetWare Administrator, showing a time restriction every day from 12:00 a.m. to 3:30 a.m.

NETWORK ADDRESS RESTRICTIONS

Network address restrictions allow administrators to define specific addresses from which users can log in. This is useful when you want to prevent users from logging in from other people's workstations. In order to make a network address restriction, the network administrator needs to know the network address and the node ID of the workstation from which the user will be logging in. The *network address* is a

28

IMPLEMENTING SECURITY

software address assigned to a network segment when the network protocol is bound to the LAN driver. The *node ID* is the unique physical hardware ID on the network interface card of each workstation. The easiest method to find this information is to use the NetWare NLIST command, as follows:

```
NLIST USER /B /A
```

This returns a display that shows the network addresses and node ID's of all currently logged in users (both Bindery and NDS).

Figure 28.7 shows the network address restriction screen in NetWare Administrator. NETADMIN provides similar functionality for DOS-based administrators.

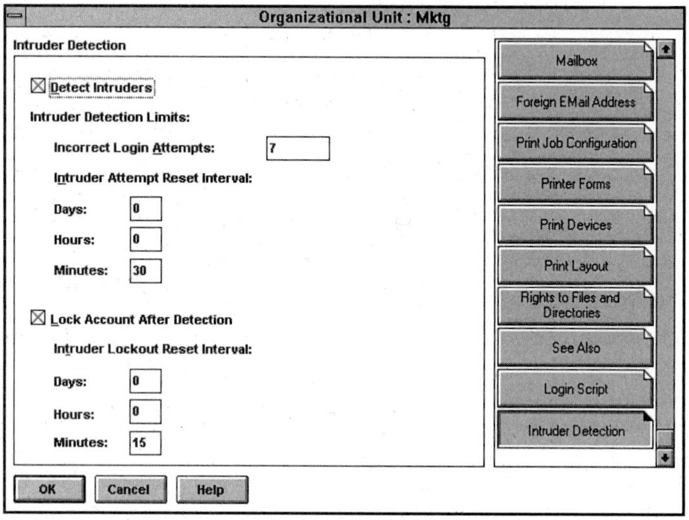

Figure 28.7.
The network address
restrictions in NetWare
Administrator.

INTRUDER DETECTION

Intruder detection is a security option that the network administrator can use to detect and lock out intruders on the network. When a user attempts to log in to the network using a valid user name but an invalid password, intruder detection is activated. Then, based on the intruder detection parameters set by the network administrator, the user account is temporarily locked if the thresholds are exceeded.

Intruder detection is set at the container level in the directory tree. When it is enabled, the network administrator configures the number of incorrect login attempts allowed in a specific period of time, and whether or not to lock the account after detection of an intruder. For example, the NetWare defaults for intruder detection shown in Figure 28.8, will lock an account if 7 incorrect login attempts are made on a single user account in 30 minutes. Once the account is locked, it will be disabled for 15 minutes and then automatically released by the system. In addition, a message will be displayed at the file server console and logged in the file server's error log, indicating the account that was locked and the network address the lockout occurred from. This allows the administrator to easily track any lockouts that occur on the network.

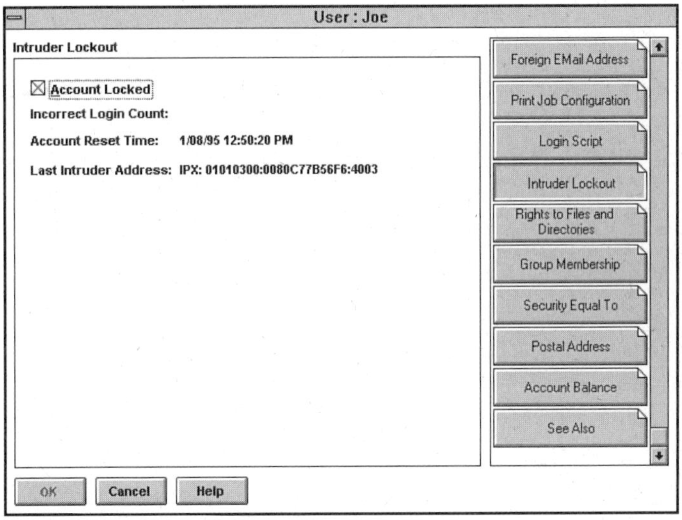

Figure 28.8.
The intruder detection screen in NetWare Administrator.

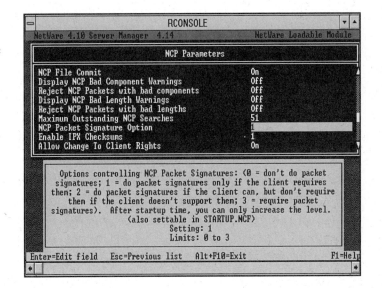

If an account is locked through intruder detection, the administrator has the option to release the account before the system releases it. This is done through the user's Intruder Lockout property, as shown in Figure 28.9.

Figure 28.9.
The administrator can release an account lock by the intruder detection feature using the Intruder Lockout user property.

28

Tip

If the Admin account is locked through the intruder detection feature, it can be immediately released by using the ENABLE LOGIN command at the file server console. This does not unlock any other user accounts, however.

NETWARE DIRECTORY SERVICES SECURITY

NetWare Directory Services (NDS) security is the second level of NetWare security. NDS security controls who can access and manage the objects in the directory tree.

When NDS is initially installed, a User object called Admin is also created. By default, Admin has all rights to the entire directory tree enabling the user to administer the tree as required. This user account is similar to the SUPERVISOR user of previous versions of NetWare, with a few exceptions. Each NetWare 2 or NetWare 3 file server had its own SUPERVISOR. Any person logged in as this user or another user made equivalent to SUPERVISOR always had complete access to the entire file server. There was never a way to block SUPERVISOR's rights.

In NetWare 4, the user Admin is not server-centric; the user is the administrator for the entire NetWare 4 network. However, unlike SUPERVISOR, it is possible to block Admin's rights. This prevents network administrators from automatically having access to sensitive information, like payroll information. In addition, it makes it possible for network administration to be delegated to multiple sub-administrators if desired. Later in this section, you learn how to create subadministrators.

OBJECT AND PROPERTY RIGHTS

NDS has two different types of rights that control how users access objects in the directory tree: *Object rights* and *Property rights*. Object rights control who can perform functions in the directory tree, such as viewing and using objects, or creating, deleting or renaming objects. Property rights are used to control who can examine or change the values of the various properties of an object in the tree. Table 28.1 shows the five NDS object rights.

TABLE 28.1. NDS OBJECT RIGHTS.

Rights	Description
Supervisor (S)	Grants all access privileges to the object. The Supervisor object right implies all other object and property rights. Can be blocked by an IRF.
Browse (B)	Grants the rights to see and use an object in the directory tree.

Rights	Description
Create (C)	Grants the right to create new objects in the directory tree. Can be only granted to container objects and volumes.
Delete (D)	Grants the right to delete an object from the directory tree.
Rename (R)	Grants the right to change the name of an object.

By default, all users are granted the Browse right to the entire directory tree. This enables them to see the entire tree structure and to use objects such as Printers. Generally, the Browse right is sufficient for a network user to accomplish day-to-day tasks, such as using printers in the tree. Network administrators, on the other hand, are given the Supervisor object right over the branch of the directory tree that they administer.

Object and property rights are separate and distinct access permissions. In other words, if a user is granted the Browse object right, it does not give him or her the capability to view an object's properties. To view the properties, he or she would need the Read property right. The only exception to this rule is in the case of the Supervisor object right. The Supervisor object right implies not only all object rights but all property rights as well. Table 28.2 shows the five NDS property rights.

TABLE 28.2. NDS PROPERTY RIGHTS.

Right	Description
Supervisor	Grants all other property rights. Can be blocked by an IRF.
Compare	Grants the right to compare the value of a property with another value to see if they are equal. Does not grant the right to see the property. Is disabled if Read is granted because Read includes Compare functionality.
Read	Grants the right to read and compare the values of a property.
Write	Grants the right to add, remove, or change the value of a property. Includes Add Self functionality.
Add (or Delete) Self	Grants a user the right to add or remove themselves from a list property such as group members. Disabled if the Write right is granted because Write includes Add Self functionality.

There are two ways in which property rights can be assigned: *all properties* or *selected properties*. All properties grants the same rights for every property of an object. Selected properties allow the network administrator to choose specific properties to give a user access to. If all property rights are granted for an object in

28

addition to selected property rights, the selected property rights will override all the property assignments for the specific property or properties.

For example, Carley has been tasked with keeping all telephone numbers and fax numbers in the Marketing department up to date. To enable her to see all of the properties of the User objects defined in her branch of the tree, she is granted the Read right to all properties. To enable her to administer the phone and fax numbers of the users, she is granted the Supervisor right to the telephone and fax number properties only.

INHERITANCE OF NDS RIGHTS

Granting rights to each individual object in the directory tree would be a huge job. So, in order to simplify this process, rights *inheritance* is used. Inheritance allows a user to receive rights to objects in the tree through a single assignment granted at a higher level in the tree. Only object rights and rights assigned with All Properties are inherited. Rights to specific properties of an object are not inherited.

To illustrate the concept of inheritance, consider the directory tree in Figure 28.10. If user Tom needs to be able to view existing objects and create new objects in the Marketing branch of the directory tree, he can be granted the Create and Browse object rights to the Marketing.SFCo container. These rights will then flow down to all of the objects below, giving him the capability to see all objects and create new objects in Marketing.SFCo and Outbound.Marketing.SFCo.

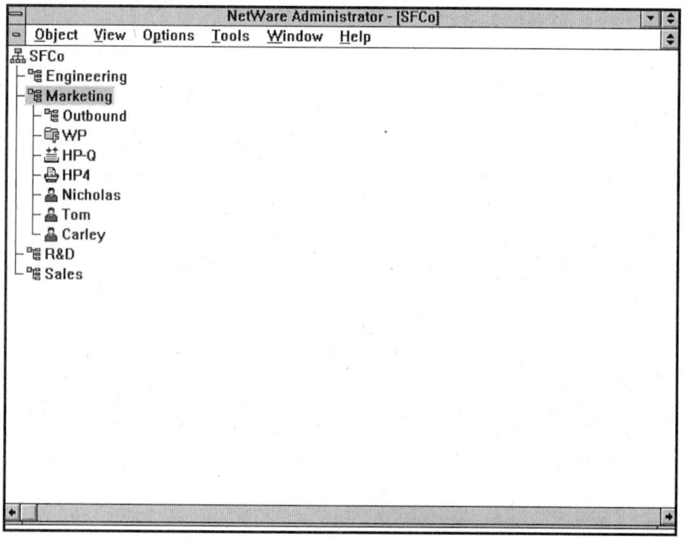

Figure 28.10.
If a user is granted rights to the Marketing container, the user will have the same rights to all objects below Marketing.

Another method of inheritance that can be used to simplify granting NDS rights is *container inheritance*. Referring again to the SFCo tree in Figure 28.10, assume, for example, that all users in the tree need to be able to use the printer HP4 in the Marketing.SFCo container. Rather than granting each user rights individually, the rights can be given to the SFCo Organization object. By doing so, all users in all containers below SFCo will inherit the rights granted to SFCo.

TRUSTEE ASSIGNMENTS

There are many different types of objects that can be granted NDS rights. Any object with rights is referred to as *a trustee* and the rights themselves are known as *trustee assignments*.

Trustee assignments can be granted to any object in the directory tree for any other object in the tree, but many times, these assignments will have no operational effect on the network. The most obvious type of trustee is an individual User object. In many cases, however, users will share common data and common network resources and require common rights. When this occurs, granting individual user rights may not be the most efficient way to administer the network so, as mentioned previously, inheritance can. Like inheritance, two other methods can be used to make granting rights to multiple users easier: *groups* and [Public].

Groups are NDS that are used to give a defined group of users rights. Each group has a Member List property. Any User object added to a group's member list will receive any rights the group is given. Users can be made members of multiple groups and the rights received from those groups are cumulative. For example, consider the directory tree in Figure 28.11.

Figure 28.11.
Rights received through multiple group memberships are cumulative.

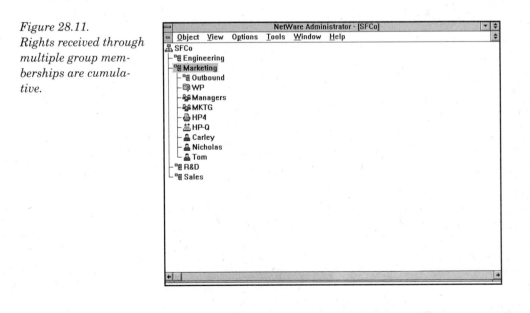

Nicholas is a member of both the MKTG group and the MANAGERS group. The MKTG group is given the Browse right to the WP Directory Map object. The MANAGERS group is given the Delete right to that same object. Nicholas' total rights to the WP Directory Map are Browse and Delete.

Group rights and explicit user rights are also cumulative. To continue the example, if Nicholas' User object is granted the Rename right to the WP Directory Map object, his total rights to that object would be Browse, Delete, and Rename.

Another method of granting rights to many users at once is through the use of the [Public] object. [Public] is a special type of NDS object that can be viewed only when granting rights.

Warning

If rights are granted to [Public], every user on the network receives those rights as well. There is no way to exclude a user from inheriting the rights of [Public] so this method of granting rights should be used with caution.

Figure 28.12 shows the [Public] object in NWAdmin.

Figure 28.12.
The [Public] object can
only be viewed when
granting rights.
Granting rights to
[Public] grants rights
to every user on the
network.

Another method that can be used to grant users rights is *security equivalence*. By making an NDS user's security equivalent to another user, you are giving that user the same rights as the other user. Security equivalences are easy to lose track of and should be used with caution. For example, assume that the network administrator makes Tom's security equivalent to Carl's. Later, Carl receives a promotion that gives him access to sensitive payroll information. The network administrator grants

Carl the new rights he needs to access the payroll records, not realizing that Tom is receiving the rights as well. Generally, security equivalences should be used only when setting up administrative accounts. For example, the network administrator, Mary, is made security equivalent to Admin giving her rights to administer the entire network.

INHERITED RIGHTS FILTER

As mentioned previously, if a user has rights to a container object, those rights will flow down the tree to all leaf and container objects below the level where the rights were granted. This inheritance of rights can be blocked using an *Inherited Rights Filter* or by granting the user another trustee assignment at a lower level. Granting another trustee assignment at a lower level revokes the rights granted above.

An *Inherited Rights Filter* (IRF) is a set of rights given to every object in the tree, both leaf and container, that determines which rights are allowed to be inherited from parent containers. By default, every object's IRF is set to all rights, indicating that all rights are allowed to be inherited from parent directories. Figure 28.13 shows the default IRF for the Outbound.Marketing.SFCo container. All rights selected indicate that any right can be inherited from a parent container.

Figure 28.13.
By default, every
object's IRF is set to all
rights, allowing any
right to be inherited
from parent containers.

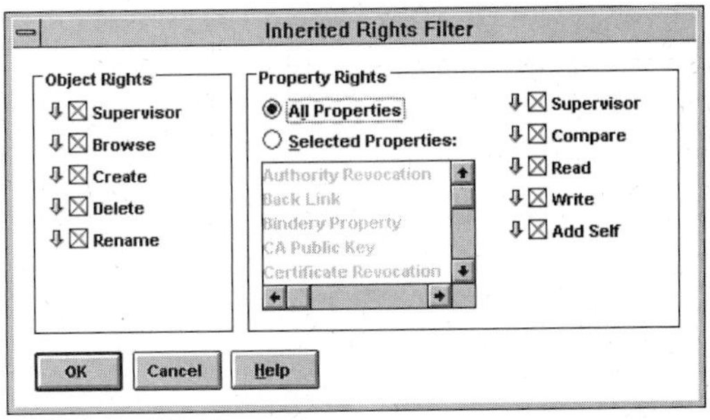

Assume that Outbound.Marketing.SFCo is only to be accessed by employees of the Outbound Marketing department. The IRF of Outbound.Marketing.SFCo can be modified, restricting rights flowing from parent containers. This is shown in Figure 28.14. By modifying the IRF, the downward flow of rights for any user with rights to Marketing.SFCo or SFCo will be blocked. This same method is used to restrict rights flowing to leaf objects as well.

Inherited Rights Filters only block rights from flowing from parent containers, not explicit trustee assignments granted at the same level as the IRF. To complete the preceding example (in order for the users in the Outbound Marketing group to have rights to the Outbound.Marketing.SFCo container) they are given an explicit assignment to that container. Because it is an explicit trustee assignment (not inherited), it is not affected by the IRF of that container.

Figure 28.14.
Modifying the IRF of
`Outbound.Marketing.SFCo`
prevents rights from
flowing from parent
containers.

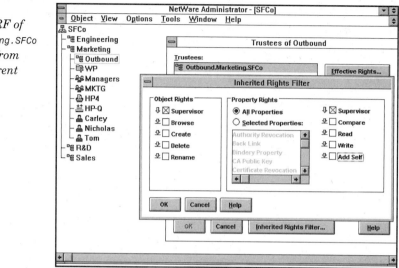

You may have noticed in the example that the `Supervisor` object and property rights were not removed from the IRF. This was done to allow any user with the `Supervisor` right in parent containers to still manage the `Outbound.Marketing.SFCo` container. If the `Supervisor` right was removed from the IRF and no other user had explicit trustee assignment to the Outbound container, administration of that branch of the tree would not be possible. The only way the `Supervisor` right can be removed from the IRF of an object is if a user has an explicit (not inherited) trustee assignment of `Supervisor` to that object. This is a safeguard built into NetWare to prevent blocking off an object from administration. However, this safeguard is not foolproof. If that user is later deleted and no other user has the `Supervisor` right to the object, administration is still blocked. Because of this, removing the `Supervisor` right from the IRF should be used with caution.

FILE SYSTEM SECURITY

In order for users to access the files and directories on network volumes, they must have the appropriate file system security access. File system security in NetWare 4.1 consists of two components: directory and file rights and file attributes. Directory and file rights determine which type of access a user has to a directory or file, such as whether the user can write to particular files or view them. Without a rights assignment, a user can do nothing, not even view files or a directory. Attribute security assigns special properties to individual directories and files that may override rights in a user's rights assignment. Directory and file rights and attribute security are described in greater depth in the following section.

DIRECTORY AND FILE RIGHTS

As mentioned previously, directory and file rights give users access to the files and directories on network volumes. NetWare 4.1 makes no assumptions when it comes to giving users file system rights. Only the user Admin has rights to files and directories by default. Rights to access files and directories must be explicitly granted to users by the network administrator.

Table 28.3 shows a list of file system rights in NetWare 4.1. These rights can be granted at the directory or subdirectory level or at the individual file level.

TABLE 28.3. FILE SYSTEM RIGHTS.

Right	Description
Supervisor (S)	Grants all rights to a file or directory. Once granted, cannot be blocked in subsequent subdirectories by an inherited rights filter.
Write (W)	Grants the right to open and write to files.
Create (C)	Grants the right to create new files in a subdirectory.
Erase (E)	Grants the right to delete files or subdirectories.
Modify (M)	Grants the right to rename or change the attributes of files and subdirectories.
File Scan (F)	Grants the right to view files and directories.
Access Control (A)	Grants the right to control who has access to a file or directory. Allows the granting of new rights (except Supervisor) as well as changing attributes.

Often times, these rights will need to be used in combinations in order to give users appropriate access to a particular file or directory. For example, if a user is required to create new files in a directory, granting the Create right alone will only allow him to create new files but not view or modify the files after creation. Table 28.4 identifies some common user tasks and the rights required for users to accomplish those tasks.

Note

Table 28.4 represents what the experts consider the minimal *functional* rights required to perform these tasks. In some cases, the task could be performed with fewer rights; however, the minimum rights may not provide the user with the functionality he or she requires. This table provides the minimum rights necessary to provide functionality without breaching security.

TABLE 28.4 MINIMAL FUNCTION RIGHTS.

Task	Rights Required
Create and view new files	[RFWCEM]
Write to existing files	[RFWCEM]
View or execute files in a directory	[RF]
Copy files from a directory	[RF]
Copy files to a directory	[RFWCE]
Give other users access to a file or directory	[RFWCEMA]
Gain full Supervisory access to a file or directory	[S]

To make it easier to determine which combinations of rights to give users, determine which of the following categories a user fits into and grant them the rights indicated:

◆ Users who need to create and write to files-[RFWCEM]

◆ Users who need to view or copy files only-[RF]

◆ Users who need to run network applications-[RF]

◆ Users who can perform administrative functions-[RFWCEMA]

TRUSTEE ASSIGNMENTS

As you saw with NDS rights, there are many different types of objects that can be granted rights. Objects with file system rights are referred to as *trustees* and the rights themselves are known as *trustee assignments*. The most obvious type of trustee is an individual user object. In most cases, however, users will share common data and common network resources and require common rights. When this occurs, granting individual user rights may not be the most efficient way to administer the network. The following objects can be used to grant users trustee assignments to files and directories:

◆ **Groups**: Group objects can be granted rights to directories and files on volumes anywhere in the directory tree. Any user who is made a member of the group will inherit the group's rights. Users can be made members of multiple groups and the rights inherited from those groups are cumulative.

◆ **Container Objects**: When a container object is granted rights to files and directories, those rights will flow down to all of the objects (both container and leaf) below that container. If rights are granted to the [Root] object, all objects in the entire tree inherit those rights.

◆ **[Public]**: [Public] is a special type of NDS object that can be viewed only when granting rights. [Public] is used to grant rights to every user on the network to a particular file or directory. There is no way to exclude a user from inheriting the rights of [Public], so this method of granting rights should be used with caution.

Another method that can be used to grant users file system rights is *security equivalences*. By making an NDS user security equivalent to another user, you are giving that user the same rights as the other user.

FILE SYSTEM RIGHTS INHERITANCE

Whether a user receives trustee rights from an explicit user trustee assignment, through a group membership or from a container object, any directory or subdirectory level right will flow down to the files and subdirectories below. For example, consider the file system directory structure in Figure 28.15.

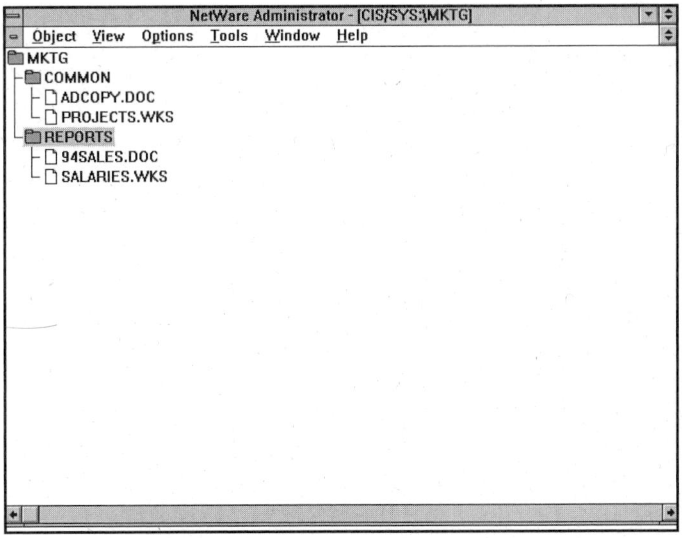

Figure 28.15.
File system rights flow down the directory structure.

If user John is granted the [RFWCEM] rights to the directory MKTG, he will have those same rights at the subdirectories COMMON and REPORTS and their files. Rights will continue to flow down the file system directory structure until another explicit assignment is given at a lower level or until an Inherited Rights Filter blocks the rights.

If John is to be given the access to view but not to change the contents of the REPORTS subdirectory, the network administrator can grant John an explicit trustee assignment of [RF] to REPORTS, overriding his previous assignment.

If rights flowing from parent directories need to be blocked for all users, an Inherited Rights Filter (IRF) can be used. An Inherited Rights Filter in the file system, similar to the IRF discussed in the NDS rights section, filters rights flowing from parent directories. When a file or directory is created, the IRF is set to all eight rights [SRFWCEDM]. To block rights flowing from parent directories, the network administrator removes rights from the IRF using NWAdmin or FILER.

To illustrate how an IRF works, consider the preceding directory structure once again.

Assume that the group MARKETING has been granted [RF] to the MKTG subdirectory, giving them the capability to view all subdirectories and files below MKTG. Because the file SALARIES.WKS contains confidential payroll information, the network administrator wants to prevent all unauthorized users from seeing the file. By setting the IRF of the file to [S   ], all users with rights other than Supervisor will be blocked from the file.

Inherited Rights Filters only block rights that are being *inherited* from parent directories; they do not block explicit trustee assignments. In other words, if the user John from our example above still needs the ability to view the contents of the SALARIES.WKS file, the network administrator can grant him [RF] explicitly at the file level. Because it is an explicit assignment and the rights are not being inherited from a parent directory, the IRF has no effect on John's rights.

ATTRIBUTE SECURITY

As you just learned, to determine a user's total rights to a file or directory, you first must check to see whether the user has an explicit trustee assignment for that file or directory. If there is not an explicit assignment, then you need to check to see whether rights are being inherited from parent directories. If they are, you then need to take into account the Inherited Rights Filter to see whether all rights are allowed to filter through. The result is the user's *effective* rights to that file or directory.

Effective rights do not always determine what a user can do in a file or directory because you have not yet considered the final level of file system security: *attribute security*.

Attributes are special properties that can be added to files or directories. Attribute security can actually override a user's effective rights. For example, if the user's effective rights give the permission to write to a file, and the file has the Read Only attribute assigned, the user will be denied write access.

Attributes can be assigned at both the file and directory level. Table 28.5 shows a list of the available attributes and a brief definition of each.

TABLE 28.5. FILE SYSTEM ATTRIBUTE.

Attribute	Description
Archive Needed (A)	Indicates file has been modified since last backup. Cleared when file is backed up. Can be assigned to files only.
Copy Inhibit (CI)	Prevents Macintosh users from copying DOS files. Can be assigned to files only.
Don't Compress (DC)	Prevents the file from being compressed even if the server-defined thresholds are reached. Can be applied to both files and directories.
Delete Inhibit (DI)	Prevents the file from being deleted, even if the trustee has been granted the Delete right. Can be assigned to both files and directories.
Don't Migrate (DM)	Prevents the file from being migrated to a secondary storage device if data migration is enabled. Can be assigned to both files and directories.
Immediate Compress (IC)	Forces immediate compression of the file without waiting for the server-defined file compression thresholds to be met. Can be applied to files only.
Execute Only (X)	Indicates that the file can be executed only. Files marked with this attribute cannot be copied or backed up and some applications cannot execute these files properly. Can only be assigned by Admin and should be used with caution. Can be applied to files only.
Hidden (H)	Prevents file from being viewed with the DOS DIR command. NetWare's NDIR command allows the viewing of Hidden files. Also prevents files from being deleted or copied. Can be applied to both files and directories.
Purge (P)	Indicates that the file should be purged immediately after deletion. Purged files cannot be salvaged with the SALVAGE utility. Can be applied to both files and directories.
Read Only (Ro)	Indicates that the file cannot be deleted, modified, or renamed. Files not flagged Read Only are automatically Read Write. Can be applied to files only.

continues

28

IMPLEMENTING SECURITY

TABLE 28.5. CONTINUED

Attribute	Description
Read Write (Rw)	Indicates that the file can be deleted, modified, or renamed. All files not flagged Read Only are automatically Read Write. Can be applied to files only.
Rename Inhibit (RI)	Prevents the file from being renamed, even if the trustee has been granted the Access Control right. Can be assigned to both files and directories.
Shareable (Sh)	Allows a file to be used by more than one user at a time. Files not flagged Shareable are automatically Non-Shareable. Can be applied to files only.
System (Sy)	Marks files used by the operating system. Files flagged system cannot be view with the DOS DIR command. NetWare's NDIR can view System files. Also prevents files from being deleted or copied. Can be applied to files and directories.
Transactional (T)	Shows that a file is protected by the Transaction Tracking System. Transactional files cannot be deleted or renamed. Can be applied to files only.

File attributes can be administered in three ways. From Windows, the NWAdmin utility can be used. Through DOS, FILER or the FLAG command can be used. Procedures for assigning file attributes are outlined later in this chapter.

ADMINISTERING RIGHTS USING NWADMIN

NetWare 4.1 provides many different methods of granting rights to objects. The method chosen will depend largely on whether you, as the network administrator, prefer to work in a Windows environment or a DOS environment. In a Windows environment, the NWAdmin utility is used. The main benefit of administering rights through NWAdmin is that the "point-and-click" and "drag-and-drop" methods commonly used in Windows applications makes administering rights fast and easy.

NDS RIGHTS

NDS rights can be granted to an object through NWAdmin by selecting the object to which you want to grant rights and by choosing Rights to Other Objects from the Object menu.

Tip

> A shortcut for granting NDS object rights is to drag and drop the object to which you want to grant rights onto the object for which you want to grant rights.

Whether the standard menu bar method is used or the short cut is used, a form is presented that enables you to select the object rights and property rights you want to grant. An example of this form is shown in Figure 28.16. Rights are granted by simply clicking on the box to the left of the permission. Also notice that the Inherited Rights Filter can be administered at this point as well.

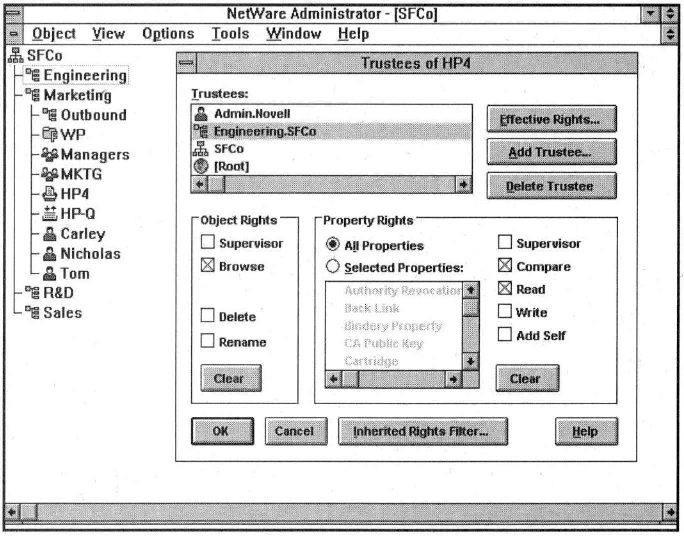

Figure 28.16.
Rights are granted in
NWAdmin by simply
clicking on the box to
the left of the permis-
sion you wish to grant.

FILE SYSTEM RIGHTS

File system rights are administered through NWAdmin by selecting the Rights to Files and Directories property in a user's Details page. The Details page is accessed by selecting the object and choosing Details from the Object menu or by double-clicking on the object.

Tip

> By selecting an object and pressing the right mouse button, a small menu appears that includes the Details option as well as other useful options.

When the `Rights to Files and Directories` property is selected, a form appears that enables you to administer file system rights. Figure 28.17 shows an example of this form. Rights are granted to a directory or file by clicking the Add button and then browsing the tree for the volume and directory or file to which you want to grant rights. Rights are then granted by clicking on the box to the left of the permission.

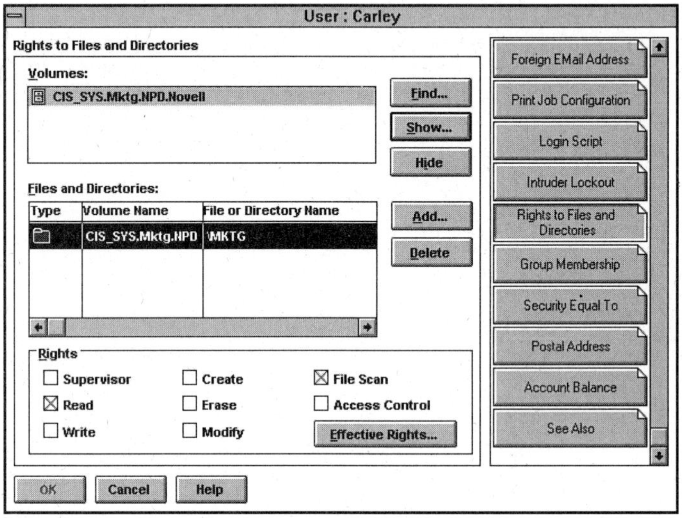

Figure 28.17.
File system rights are
granted through
NWAdmin by selecting
`Rights to Files and`
`Directories` *in a user's*
Details.

ADMINISTERING RIGHTS USING NETADMIN

For network administrators that prefer to work in a DOS-based environment, the NETADMIN utility can be used to administer rights instead of NWAdmin.

NDS RIGHTS

NDS rights are administered in NETADMIN by selecting Manage Objects from the NETADMIN and then browsing the tree until you find the object for which you want to grant rights. To grant the MANAGERS group rights to `Sales.SFCo`, for example, browse the tree and select `Sales.SFCo`.

When the object for which you want to grant rights is located, highlight it and press F10. Then select View or edit trustees of this object.

Select Trustees and then press the Insert key to browse the directory tree until you find the object to which you want to grant rights. When you locate the object, select it by pressing Enter. A list will appear that enables you to grant object rights, all property rights, or selected property rights. This list is shown in Figure 28.18.

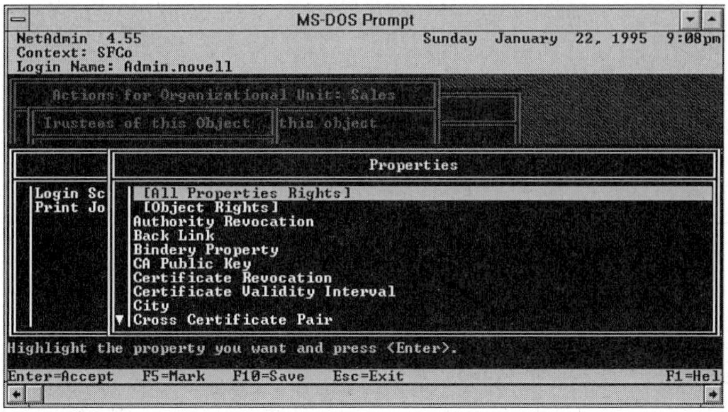

Figure 28.18.
NETADMIN allows you
to grant object rights,
all property rights, or
selected property rights
using this screen.

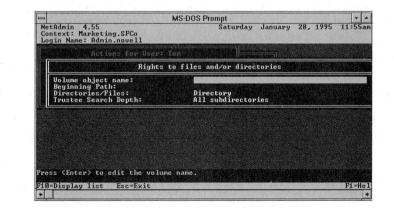

The object to which you want to grant rights can be selected by highlighting it and pressing Enter or by pressing F5 to mark multiple objects. After the object to which you want to grant rights has been selected, highlight it and press Enter. This enables you to administer the individual object or property rights. Rights can be added by pressing the Insert key and deleted by pressing the Delete key.

FILE SYSTEM RIGHTS

To administer rights to files and directories using the NETADMIN utility, select Manage Objects from the NETADMIN main menu. Then, using the arrow keys, browse the directory tree until you find the object to which you want to grant rights.

When the object to which you want to grant rights is located, highlight it and press F10 or Enter. Then, select View or edit rights to files and directories. Once selected, the form as shown in Figure 28.19 is presented.

Figure 28.19.
Viewing or editing
rights to files and
directories in
NETADMIN.

28

Using the Insert key, browse the tree to find the volume to which you wish to grant rights. When the object is located, press Enter. You then can press the Insert key again to browse the directory structure of the selected volume for the directory you want to grant rights to. If you want to grant rights to a specific file rather than a directory, select the Directory/Files option and select File. To grant a trustee assignment, press the F10 key with the Directories/Files option highlighted. As shown in Figure 28.20, rights can be granted by pressing the Insert key and deleted by using the Delete key.

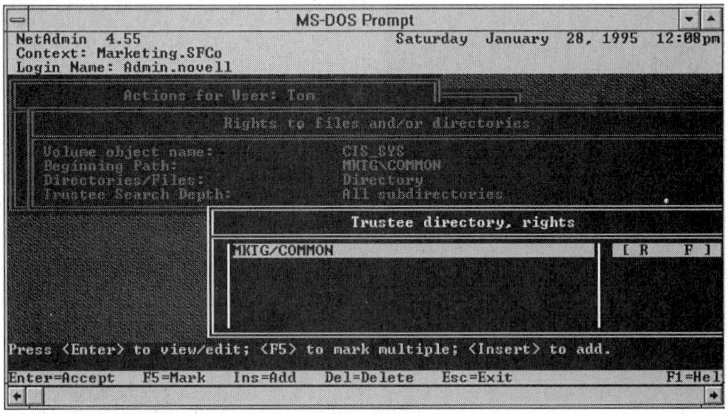

Figure 28.20.
Rights can be added or deleted using the Insert and delete keys.
Pressing F5 will allow multiple rights to be selected at once.

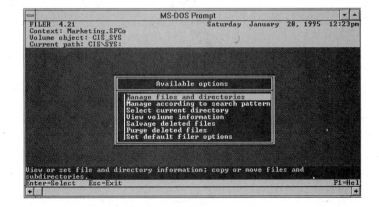

ADMINISTERING FILE SYSTEM RIGHTS USING FILER

Rights to files and directories can also be administered using the FILER utility. Like NETADMIN, the C-Worthy interface used by FILER provides a familiar interface for DOS-based network administrators. Figure 28.21 shows the FILER main menu.

Figure 28.21.
Main menu of FILER.

To grant rights, select Manage files and directories from the FILER main menu. Use the arrow keys to scroll through the directory list and press Enter to select a directory. When you locate the subdirectory or file you want, press F10 to access the Subdirectory or file options. A menu, as shown in Figure 28.22, is presented.

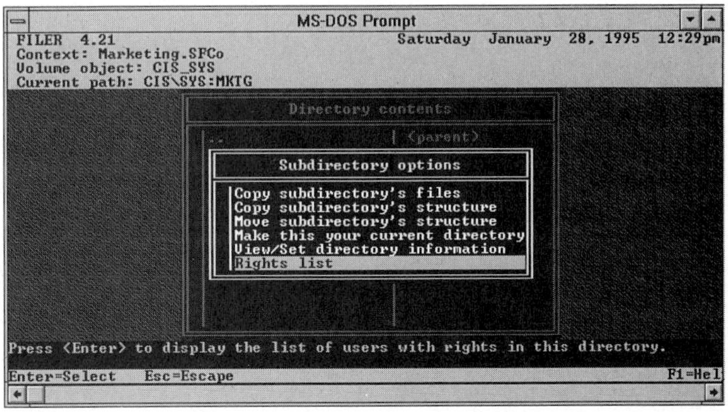

Figure 28.22.
Granting file system
rights through FILER.

Selecting the Rights list will enable you to view a list of existing trustees of this directory. Selecting View/Set directory information will allow you to view or change information, such as directory attributes, the IRF of this directory, or the Trustees (see Figure 28.23). You can add a trustee assignment by first selecting Trustees from this menu and using the Insert key to add the name of the trustee.

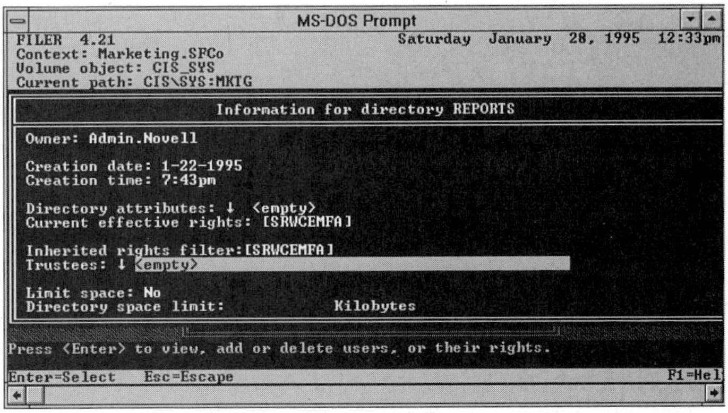

Figure 28.23.
Directory information
allows you to adminis-
ter directory attributes,
the IRF, and Trustees
of a directory.

28

ADMINISTERING FILE SYSTEM RIGHTS USING THE *RIGHTS* COMMAND

Probably the most difficult method NetWare 4.1 provides for granting rights to files and directories is the RIGHTS command. By typing RIGHTS /? from the DOS command line, a general help screen is shown for the RIGHTS command. This screen is shown in Figure 28.24.

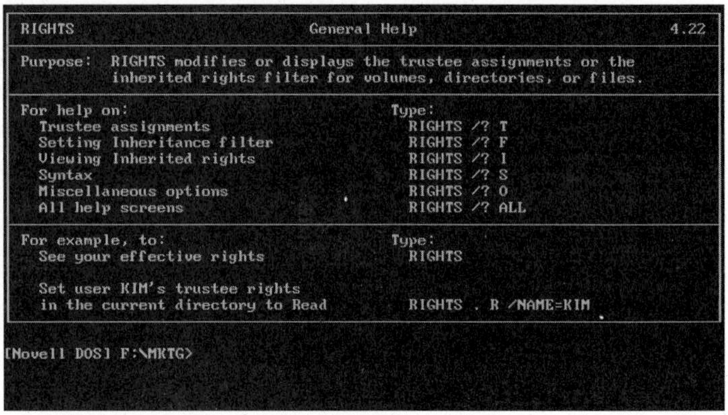

Figure 28.24.
RIGHTS general help
screen.

```
RIGHTS                        General Help                        4.22

Purpose:   RIGHTS modifies or displays the trustee assignments or the
           inherited rights filter for volumes, directories, or files.

For help on:                              Type:
   Trustee assignments                       RIGHTS /? T
   Setting Inheritance filter                RIGHTS /? F
   Viewing Inherited rights                  RIGHTS /? I
   Syntax                                    RIGHTS /? S
   Miscellaneous options                     RIGHTS /? O
   All help screens                          RIGHTS /? ALL

For example, to:                          Type:
   See your effective rights                 RIGHTS

   Set user KIM's trustee rights
   in the current directory to Read          RIGHTS . R /NAME=KIM

[Novell DOS] F:\MKTG>
```

You can get more detailed help for using the RIGHTS command. For example, typing RIGHTS /? T will give you help on setting or viewing trustee assignments and RIGHTS /? F" will provide more information for setting the IRF.

If you choose to use the DOS command line to grant rights to users, use the following syntax:

```
RIGHTS Path Rights List /NAME=object
```

For example, to grant JD the Read and File Scan rights to the SYS:MKTG\REPORTS directory, type the following:

```
RIGHTS SYS:MKTG\REPORTS RF /NAME=JD
```

If the user object JD is not in the current context, it may be necessary to provide the full NDS object name, as in the following example:

```
RIGHTS SYS:MKTG\REPORTS RF /NAME=.JD.ENGINEERING.SFCO
```

To change the inherited rights filter of a file or directory using the RIGHTS command, use the following syntax:

```
RIGHTS Path Rights List /F
```

So, if you want to restrict all rights except SUPERVISOR from being inherited from parent directories to the SALARIES.WKS file, you can use the following syntax to set the IRF:

```
RIGHTS SYS:MKTG\REPORTS\SALARIES.WKS S /F
```

Administering File and Directory Attributes

As indicated in the file system security section, you can administer file and directory attributes in three ways:

◆ Using the NWAdmin utility through Windows

◆ Using the NETADMIN utility from DOS

◆ Using the FLAG command from the DOS command line

ADMINISTERING ATTRIBUTES THROUGH NWADMIN

To administer the attributes of a file or directory using NWAdmin, browse the directory tree until you find the Volume object that the file or directory is stored on. Double-click on the volume to display the directories. Select the file or directory to which you want to assign attributes and use the Object menu or the right mouse button to select Details. From the Details page, select Attributes. A screen similar to the one displayed in Figure 28.25 will be displayed.

Figure 28.25.
Administering file
attributes through
NWAdmin.

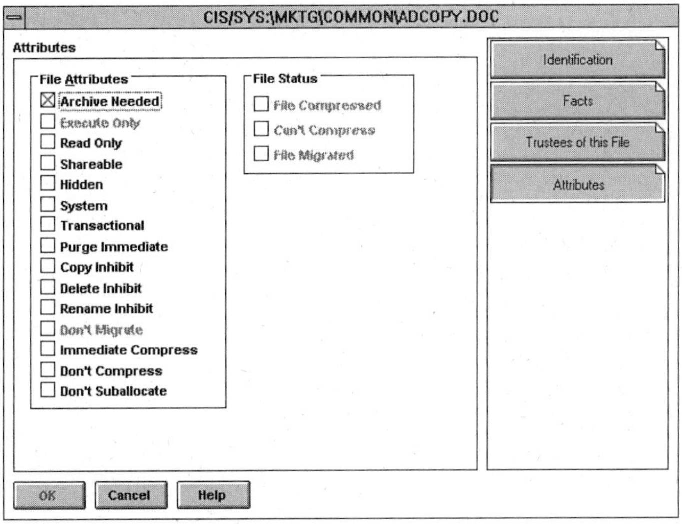

Attributes can then be applied by clicking on the box to the left of the attribute.

ADMINISTERING ATTRIBUTES THROUGH FILER

To administer file or directory attributes using the FILER utility, select Manage files and directories from the FILER main menu. Then use the arrow keys to locate the file or directory you want. When you locate the file or directory you want, highlight it and press F10 to select it. Then choose View/Set [file/directory] information. The first option enables you to change the attributes. By pressing Enter, the current file attributes are displayed (see Figure 28.26).

28

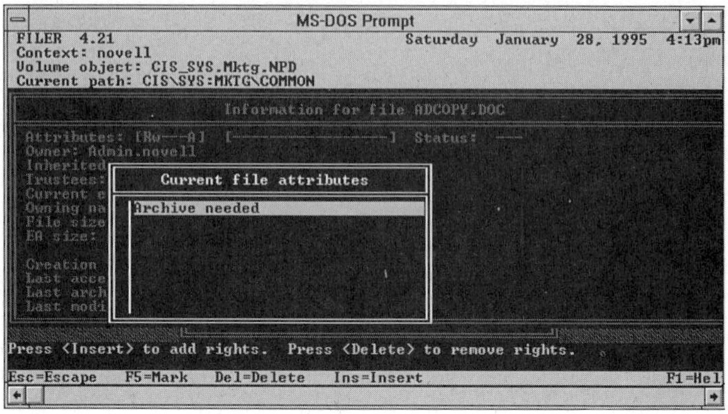

Figure 28.26.
Administering file
attributes through
FILER.

You can assign additional file attributes by pressing the Insert key. Pressing Delete enables you to delete attributes.

ADMINISTERING ATTRIBUTES USING THE *FLAG* COMMAND

For those of you who prefer the DOS command line, you can use the FLAG command to assign file or directory attributes. The FLAG syntax can be displayed by typing the following:

    FLAG /? SYNTAX

Figure 28.27 shows the FLAG syntax help screen.

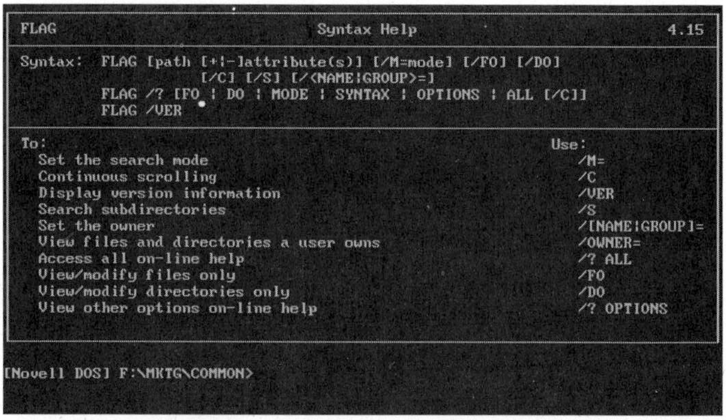

Figure 28.27.
The FLAG Syntax Help
screen.

Suppose that you want to flag the file ADCOPY.DOC in the SYS:MKTG\COMMON directory as Read Only. The syntax would be as follows:

    FLAG SYS:MKTG\COMMON\ADCOPY.DOC RO

FILE SERVER CONSOLE SECURITY

The final level of NetWare security is file server console security. File server console security protects your file server from unauthorized access. To keep your file server secure, you need to prevent unauthorized users from doing the following:

- Loading or unloading NLM
- Changing the file server's date and/or time
- Downing the file server

The easiest way to protect your file server is to lock it up. Any time your file server is stored in a location that people have general access to, you're asking for trouble. Generally, a file server is just sitting there with not a lot going on. So, the unknowing user walks up and decides he wants to use the floppy drive. When the user can't get to the A: drive, he or she decides to turn the machine off and back on again. There goes your file server.

Another issue to be aware of is the file server's date and time. In NetWare 4.1, changing the date and time at the file server console can very likely disrupt Times Synchronization on the network. Times Synchronization is important to successful synchronization of Directory Services. If Times Synchronization on the network is off, synchronization of your Directory Services replicas cannot take place. If your server console can be accessed by anyone, it is very easy to use the TIME command to change the date and time.

Also, if your server is in a common area, just about anyone can load or unload NLMs. NLMs can be loaded from the SYS:SYSTEM directory, the DOS partition, or from a floppy drive. Without proper security, it would be very easy for someone to unload a critical NLM, such as a LAN or Disk driver, or worse yet, load a rogue NLM. Rouge NLMs are NLMs that either intentionally or unintentionally cause problems on your network. Some "grow" as time goes on, using more and more memory. Others attempt to break into the system, breaching security. Some may even attempt to introduce a virus to the network.

So, the easiest way to prevent situations like these is to store your file server in a location where unauthorized users can't access it. Lock it in a closet if you have to. Remember, most of the administration in NetWare 4.1 is done from a workstation, and RCONSOLE can be used to manage the server console remotely, so don't worry about it being easily accessible for administration.

Following are some other ways to protect your server console:

- Use MONITOR.NLM to lock the console
- Use the SECURE CONSOLE command

28

From the MONITOR main menu, select the Lock file server console option to allow a software lock to be placed on the server. Once it's set, the proper password must be provided before anything can be done at the server. Figure 28.28 shows an example of a locked file server console.

Figure 28.28.
MONITOR.NLM can
be used to place a
software lock on the
server.

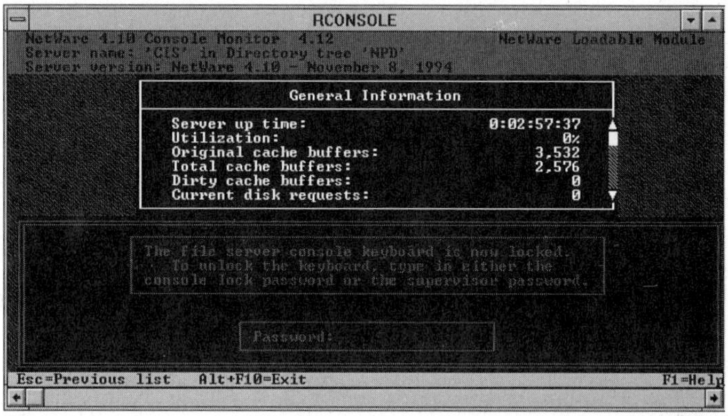

Tip

If the file console is locked through MONITOR.NLM and the password is lost or forgotten, the Admin's password can be used to release it.

The SECURE CONSOLE command can also be used to protect your file server. If you enter SECURE CONSOLE from the server console, you provide the following added security.

◆ Prevents NLMs from being loaded from any path not specified in the server's SEARCH paths

◆ Removes DOS from the server's memory, preventing NLMs from being loaded from C: or A:

◆ Prevents entry into the OS debugger. The OS Debugger is an undocumented feature of NetWare 4.1 that allows developers to directly access the server's memory from the server console. Unauthorized or uneducated access to the OS Debugger could potentially cause serious problems with your file server.

As you can see, protecting your file server console is not a difficult task. Consider using not just one but all of the techniques mentioned above to protect your server. In the long run, you'll be happy you did.

SUMMARY

Network security is an important part of network administration. NetWare 4.1 has the best security of any network operating on the market today. Administration utilities like NWAdmin and NETADMIN allow security to be administered at many different levels including Login/Password security, NDS object and property security, as well as security of files and directories. Other methods can be used to ensure that your file server console is secure, such as locking the server console with MONITOR.NLM and using the SECURE CONSOLE command to prevent other unauthorized access.

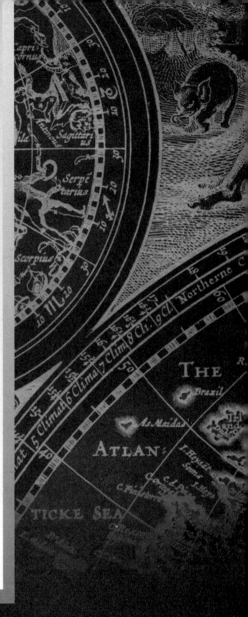

- The Need for Auditing

- Auditing Principles and Practices

- Audit Preparation

- Using AUDITCON

- Audit Files Maintenance

- Auditor Configuration

- Understanding the Audit Files

- Summary

CHAPTER 29

Auditing

In the network computing industry, there are various methods of implementing security; password protection, virus checkers, and locked server consoles are a few such security measures. Each of these levels of security are important and provide a solution for one aspect of network security; however, they do not address the most vulnerable part of a network—the user.

Any network data recovery, security, or network expert usually will agree that the biggest threat to a network's data is the user. Users are human and make mistakes; users get disgruntled and attack what they think is the company's weakest point, the network. The avenues available for users to corrupt, delete, or change network data make the user the single largest threat to the security of your network data.

Networks and their components (computers, network cards, cables, and so on) were not designed with security in mind. Thus, network security features must be properly enabled and configured to maintain system confidentiality, security, and reliability.

THE NEED FOR AUDITING

Today, nearly everyone in the business world uses some form of network computing. The use of network computing technology is not without danger. The environment in which information is being retrieved, processed, transmitted, and stored daily is not inherently secure. As mission-critical business applications find their way to the networks, the need for internal controls, security, and auditing capabilities grows, especially now that network operating systems are fulfilling an ever-increasing role in business. This increasing role of the network increases reliance on data communications systems.

Because of this reliance, computer personnel need to cooperate to establish a common goal—to make the network as reliable as possible. One method of ensuring the reliability of the data on your network is to perform auditing.

Note

Auditors should not be network administrators and should not have SUPERVISOR rights or equivalence. Otherwise, the purpose behind performing an audit is negated.

Auditors can track events and activities on the network. This form of security not only aids in creating a more secure environment, but also helps to guarantee that data has not been tampered with or altered.

NetWare 4.1's auditing features enable you to monitor and record network-wide events for any designated network resource. By auditing network resources, you can

29

verify the network is properly set up and secure. It also helps to ensure that company's security policies and procedures are adhered to.

The principle behind using NetWare 4's auditing functions are based on creating an "independent auditor" who is responsible for auditing past and present transactions on the network. This network user, the auditor, can monitor and record designated events but cannot access any resource other than the audit reports.

To access audit information, the auditor must be cleared at two password levels. Therefore, even users with supervisor equivalences do not have access to the auditing information without the appropriate passwords.

In fact, to be the most effective, an auditor should act independently of the network administrator. This creates a "check and balance" system that can help ensure that network records are accurate and confidential information is secure.

The transactions and events that can be monitored through NetWare 4's auditing console are as follows:

- Logins and logouts
- Trustee modifications
- File creations, deletions, reads, and writes
- Requests to manipulate queues
- Directory Services object creations, deletions, reads, and writes
- Events directly related to Directory Services objects
- Events directly related to users

With NetWare 4, auditors also are able to track Directory Services events, which include the creating and deleting of an object or of an object's properties. Auditing functions also are available for the file system, which include the access or use of a server's volume or files.

Note

Auditing is enabled at the volume level for file system auditing. It is enabled at the container level when auditing NetWare Directory Services events.

When an auditor designates certain network resources for auditing, the auditing information is kept in audit files, which are automatically created; that is, when a volume or container has had auditing enabled. These auditing files are similar to the records that are kept for the system error logs, except that a password can be assigned to the log file, which protects the contents from being altered.

Note

It is vital that you establish procedures for clearing the auditing files. These files will continue to accept information until the volume is full.

You should at least limit the size of the audit files, and regularly view and migrate the files to a secondary source of storage.

The *AUDITCON* audit program and files are automatically installed on the network when you install or upgrade to NetWare 4; however, auditing is not automatically initiated. For more information on initiating the auditing function in NetWare 4, see the section of this chapter entitled "Audit Preparation."

Note

By installing all the auditing files and utilities during installation, all the network auditor has to do is enable the auditing process. This separates the network administrator's roles and the auditing functions, allowing the person elected to be the auditor to perform auditing responsibilities and functions without having to perform network administrator tasks.

AUDITING PRINCIPLES AND PRACTICES

Given the flexibility of today's networks, as well as the various methods of implementing and using networks, it is virtually impossible to define auditing procedures and practices that are a "one size fits all" approach. However, there are methods you can use to help define the appropriate auditing principles and practices, regardless of network implementation or size.

The best approach for determining the auditing needs of your particular network implementation is to take a component-by-component approach. That is, look at each component of your network and determine its exact function, as well as who should have access to that particular function. The awareness of the access to the component's function, or the regularity of an audit on that given component, should directly correlate with the criticalness of that component's function to the operation of the overall network.

As you categorize each component and the component's relativeness to the overall health of the network, you should consider the auditing practice itself. Asking the simple question, "Why should I audit a particular network component?" often will help answer the question, "Who should have access to a particular component's function?"

During the process of determining your company's auditing guidelines, you should also pay close attention to the objectives of an audit, asking yourself the following questions:

◆ What is the purpose of the audit?

◆ What are the objectives?

◆ What functions should be audited, and why?

◆ Are there any company policies or standards that deserve special attention?

◆ Should management be informed of the audit process?

Note

If the audit's purpose is to determine whether managers in your company are adhering to company policies, you would most likely not inform them that an audit is being considered.

◆ Determine whether the physical security of the network has not been forgotten.

Note

After considering who should have access to specific network components and defining the objectives of the audit, you should be well on your way to implementing company audit policies and procedures. Before completely defining company policy, however, you should also consider the security of the network.

There usually is ample information about implementing the security of the network, passwords, rights, and so on; but often, the physical security of vital network components is overlooked. In other words, critical network components, such as your servers, should be placed behind lock and key. You also should ask yourself the following questions:

◆ What is the status of the system security and controls?

◆ Is sensitive data protected and well backed up?

◆ Are there company procedures in place?

◆ In case of a disaster, are techniques and procedures for continuing operation in place?

◆ Have all continuing operation plans been tested?

In the past, most communications devices were designated for a particular function; however, this is no longer true. Equipment on local area networks interoperate and act as an exchange for many applications, virtually allowing any user access to any part of the system.

To compound network security risks, networks are usually geographically dispersed, are constantly growing, and are globally accessible. The auditing process should support, not hinder, this real-time user need for flexibility.

Therefore, auditing in the network computing environment must provide one with the capability to monitor, collect, and review user activities, system-wide options, NetWare Directory Services (NDS), individual servers, and the resources that each of these network components provide.

Businesses might want to perform an audit for several reasons. For example, an internal auditor would verify that things such as regulatory requirements or processes are being followed. You may perform an audit to determine whether there are opportunities for improvement, or simply to measure compliance with company policy. It is common for external auditors, especially in the accounting profession, to perform an audit, and it is likely that this type of audit will find its way into the realm of computing. The exact approach and procedures an auditor employs depends on the objective of the audit.

Another purpose of an audit is to detect activities that may compromise the security of the system. For example, an audit would aid in determining the unauthorized access or attempted access to sensitive data or areas of the network. Audits having this type of objective could be categorized as security audits. During a security audit you should consider the following list:

♦ Creation of users

♦ Changes to a user's properties or rights

♦ Granting of Admin security equivalences

♦ Authenticating users

♦ Access system areas

♦ Changing the configuration of the system

♦ Installation and deletion of program software

♦ Modifications made to accounts

♦ Deleting or copying sensitive files

After you establish the level of security you want, you need to continually perform audits because security will tend to deteriorate over time and will weaken with the complexity and flexibility of the particular network environment.

29

Typically, the factors that contribute to the degradation of a system's security are the following types of actions:

◆ Installation of new software

◆ Employee turnover

◆ Changes in employee responsibilities

◆ Temporary employee accesses (that are not revoked)

◆ New applications updates

◆ Regular security monitoring

◆ Periodic security audits

Note

One of the biggest factors adding to the possibility of a security breach is the failure of a network administrator to perform regular security audits.

Regular monitoring of a network's security should be part of the administrator's responsibility.

Periodic security audits should be performed by someone other than the network administrator. The frequency of a security audit will depend on the size of the security risk.

The following policies enable the system administrator to control network security that can be implemented at the Directory Services, network, server, and file system levels to determine:

◆ Who can access the network

◆ Which resources (such as file system directories and files) users can access

◆ How users can utilize the resources

◆ Who can perform tasks at the server console

The auditing function of NetWare 4 helps increase the integrity of network data by tracking network events. Auditing data can be used to determine if procedures are being followed and who is performing tasks at the NetWare server level.

AUDITCON is a utility that allows auditors to specify the parts of the system to be monitored and provides functions for outputting auditing data for management review. AUDITCON also monitors the activities concerned with identification, access, and modification of network resources.

The role of the network administrator is to set up the auditor's environment or the network and enable auditing for the appropriate NDS container or volume. Once this has been completed, the network administrator gives the auditing password to the auditor, who assumes responsibility for auditing. The auditor changes the auditing password to ensure that the auditing data is secure. The auditor configures the auditing environment, sets the events to be audited, and manages the auditing data.

The auditing capability of AUDITCON provides reassurance to management and other parties interested in the security and integrity of the network. Each company should know that a user's access to and use of network resources is appropriate and authorized and that the system is operating appropriately.

AUDIT PREPARATION

Before the actual initiation of the auditing functions, the network administrator will have to perform several tasks, which will provide the auditor with the rights and accesses needed to perform an audit. The following describes these processes as well as describes the actual implementation of the auditing function.

- **Create a directory in the file system for the auditor to use**: The auditor will need space to store audit reports. Create a directory, as you did for other users (that is, if your policy is to create a directory for each user's account).

- **Create the auditor as a User object**: If the auditor will audit NetWare Directory Service events, assign him or her the Browse object right in the container objects to be audited.

- **Give the auditor trustee rights to the directory you created**: You can grant the auditor the Supervisor trustee right to the directory, or you can assign the auditor all rights but the Supervisor right.

- **Map a drive to the directory containing the audit program files**: If you have not included a search drive mapping to SYS:PUBLIC in the system login script, create a user login script for the auditor and map a drive to this directory.

Note

By default, the AUDITCON and Unicode files are located in the SYS:PUBLIC directory.

VOLUME AUDIT PREPARATION

If you have different data that will be monitored by different auditors, you can create a separate volume for each set of data. For example, you may not want someone in Human Resources to have access to the company financial information. For this type of situation, you can create separate volumes of each data set. Then each auditor could be given the appropriate rights for the data that they are suppose to audit.

To install auditing on a volume, complete the following steps:

1. Log in to the network from a DOS workstation.
2. Access the auditing utility by typing **AUDITCON** and pressing Enter. Your current server and volume are displayed at the top of the screen. To select a server or volume that is not shown, press the Insert key.
3. Select the server or volume.
4. Select Enable Volume Auditing from the Available Audit Options menu, as seen in Figure 29.1.

Figure 29.1.
Enabling volume
auditing.

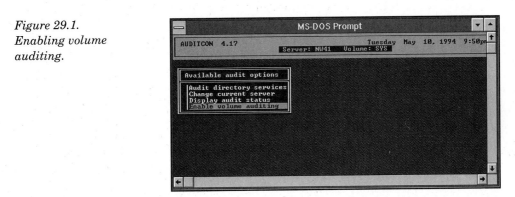

Warning

NetWare 4.0, 4.01, and 4.02 do not enable auditing. If you already have enabled auditing, you need to completely disable it. If you need auditing, you will need to upgrade your Directory Services (DS.NLM) to version 3.10 or later.

If you see a problem of high utilization on the file servers, along with extremely slow performance, you might be seeing problems associated with auditing. Disabling auditing at this point will not fix the problem; you must upgrade your NDS.

5. Enter a password for the volume, as seen in Figure 29.2.

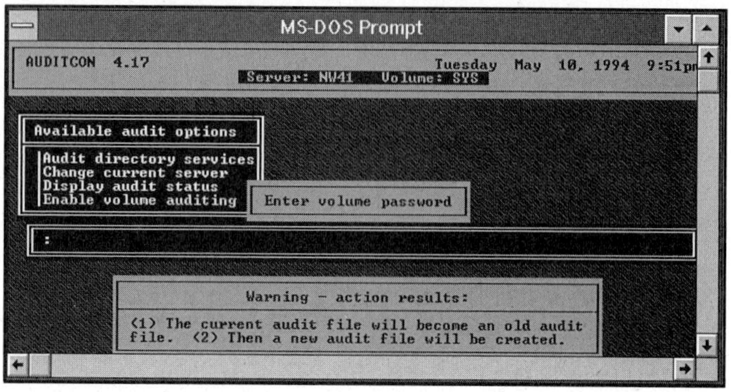

Figure 29.2.
Enter a password for
accessing volume
auditing.

6. Enter the password again when prompted.

7. Provide the password to the auditor.

After volume level auditing is enabled, the independent auditor assumes control of the program. If the auditor changes the volume password, the supervisor no longer will have access to auditing information.

ENABLING AUDITING FOR A DIRECTORY SERVICES CONTAINER

NetWare 4 also enables you to audit the use of its Directory Services. Just as with volume auditing, Directory level auditing must be enabled.

Note

> When you enable auditing for a container object (Organization or Organizational Unit), it does not enable auditing for subordinate container objects.

As an auditor, you will only "see" those containers for which you have the Browse right. If you do not see the container you want to audit, contact the network administrator.

To enable Directory auditing for a specific container, follow these steps:

1. Type AUDITCON and press Enter. Your current server name and volume are displayed at the top of the screen.

2. Select Audit Directory Services from the Available Audit Options menu. Your current context is displayed at the top of the screen.

3. Highlight the context for the container where auditing is being enabled and press Enter.

4. Press Esc to get back to the Available Audit Options menu.

5. Select Audit Directory Tree from the Audit Directory Services menu.

6. Locate the container where you are enabling auditing by pressing Enter to move around in the Directory tree.

7. Select the container you want and press F10.

8. Select Enable Container Auditing, as seen in Figure 29.3.

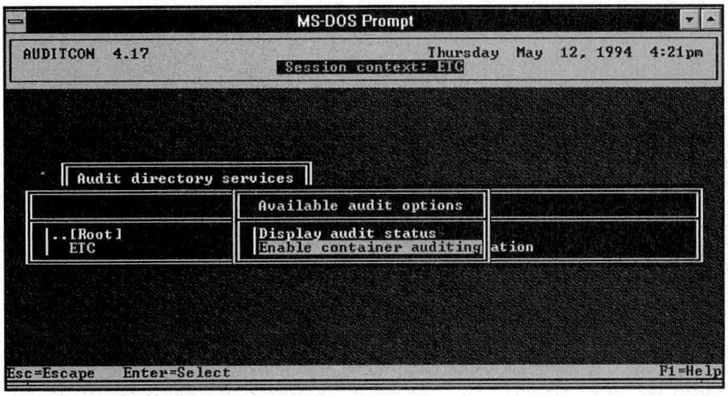

Figure 29.3.
Enabling container
auditing.

```
┌──────────────────────────────── MS-DOS Prompt ──────────────────┬──┬──┐
│                                                                  │ ▼│ ▲│
│  AUDITCON  4.17                         Thursday  May  12, 1994  4:21pm│
│                            Session context: ETC                  │
│                                                                  │
│                                                                  │
│                                                                  │
│        ┌─ Audit directory services ─┐                            │
│        │                            │  Available audit options   │
│        │ ..[Root]                   │ Display audit status       │
│        │   ETC                      │ Enable container auditing  ation│
│        │                            │                            │
│                                                                  │
│                                                                  │
│                                                                  │
│ Esc=Escape    Enter=Select                              F1=Help  │
└──────────────────────────────────────────────────────────────────┘
```

9. Enter a password for the container.

10. Verify the password when prompted.

11. Notify the auditor of the password.

USING AUDITCON

AUDITCON is the utility used by the network auditor to audit the network. To keep your audit information secure, it is suggested that as the auditor you perform the following tasks before you begin auditing:

◆ Change the auditing password given to you by the network supervisor.

◆ Log in to the volume or container using the new password.

◆ Set your preferences for the auditing environment.

From this point, you can select what you want to audit and create reports based on the audit records you collect.

With AUDITCON, you also can create reports about the activities of the items you are auditing, as well as the auditor's activities.

Tip

As an auditor, you can set an additional level of security for your audit records by enabling a second-level password.

If you set this option, a second password is required before any changes to the audit configurations or report filters can be made.

To start AUDITCON, log in to the network as a user that has been given auditing rights, and then type AUDITCON. After starting the auditor console, you will be given the following options, as shown in Figure 29.4.

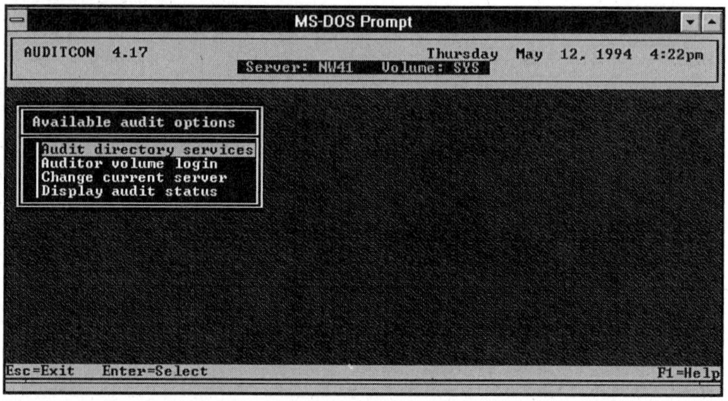

Figure 29.4.
AUDITCON's main
menu after enabling
volume auditing.

```
─                         MS-DOS Prompt                    ▼ ▲
 AUDITCON  4.17                        Thursday  May  12, 1994  4:22pm
                      Server: NW41   Volume: SYS

   ┌─Available audit options─────────┐
   │ Audit directory services        │
   │ Auditor volume login            │
   │ Change current server           │
   │ Display audit status            │
   └─────────────────────────────────┘




 Esc=Exit    Enter=Select                                    F1=Help
```

Tip

If AUDITCON does not display the menus as presented in Figure 29.4, your network administrator has not yet enabled volume auditing.

To enable auditing for a volume, see "Volume Audit Preparation," covered earlier in this section.

After enabling auditing, you will notice that the very last option will change from Enable volume auditing to Display audit status (compare Figure 29.1 with Figure 29.4).

If volume auditing has been enabled, but you do not have the password, contact the network administrator.

Once you have gained access to the auditing functions, it is recommended that you change that password to secure the auditing functions and information.

After enabling auditing, you then will need to select the option Auditor Volume Login. This option will log you into the auditing functions, where you then will have access to the volume auditing functions.

From the Available audit options menu, select Auditor container login, as seen in Figure 29.5.

Figure 29.5.
Available audit options
menu.

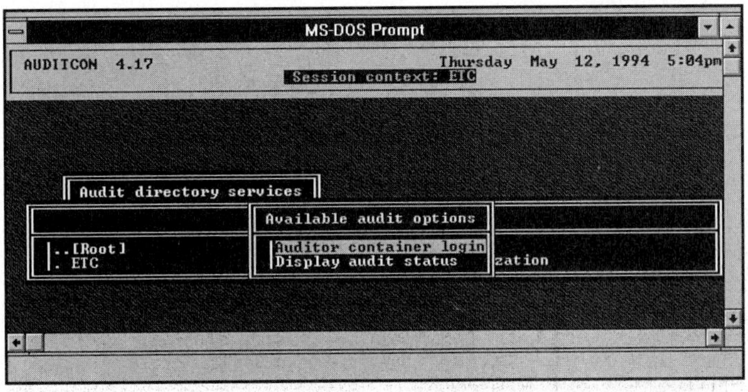

Selecting the option Audit Directory Tree will display a list of Directory Services containers that you can access. You cannot see a container unless you have access (Browse rights). You will need to have the administrator provide you with rights to all containers you want to audit.

Note

The only options that will appear will be the ones that are valid for the volume, or the container, that you are currently logged in to.

To change to a different context, highlight a container or object and press Enter. This moves you up one level in the tree.

To perform an audit on a container, highlight the container and press F10.

After selecting the Auditor login option, you will be prompted to enter the correct auditor password, as in the following:

```
Type the password and press Enter.
```

Once you have gained access, the menu as seen in Figure 29.6 will appear.

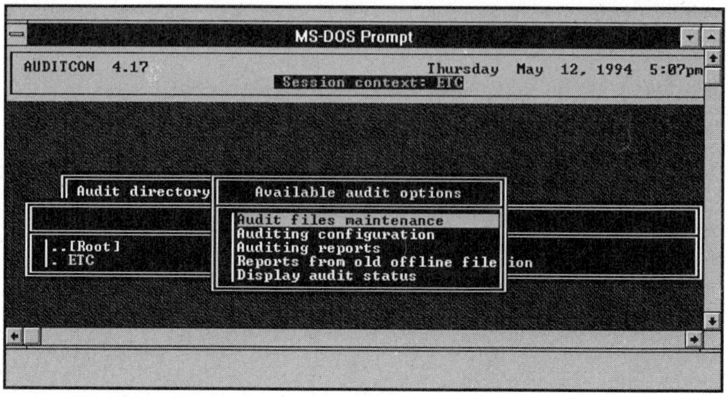

Figure 29.6.
The available
audit options,
after logging in.

The following section covers each of the options seen in the available audit options menu.

AUDIT FILES MAINTENANCE

The Audit Files Maintenance option is only available after you have logged into auditing. After logging into auditing, you can use the Audit Files Maintenance menu to select the following options:

- ◆ Close audit file
- ◆ Copy old audit file
- ◆ Delete old audit file
- ◆ Display audit status
- ◆ Reset audit data file
- ◆ Reset auditing history

Each of these respectively perform the following:

Close Old Audit File: For security and system reasons, files containing audit data remain open. Selecting Close Old Audit File will allow old audit files to be accessed outside of AUDITCON. This also means that the file may be accessible by users other than the auditor.

Copy Old Audit File: Selecting Copy Old Audit File will enable you to copy an old Audit Data file to another location. This can be useful for putting old audit files in a location where they can be compressed; this function also will enable you to leave the file as non-readable. To copy an Audit Data file in readable report format, select Report Old Audit File from the Auditing Reports menu.

29

Delete Old Audit File: This option enables you to delete old Audit Data files, without having any effect on your current Audit Data file.

Display Audit Status: This selection enables you to view information about the audit files.

Reset Audit Data File: To create a new Audit Data file, select this option. From this option you also can rename the current file.

Reset Audit History File: Select this option to delete Audit File information, without completely deleting the file. Deleting Audit File entries will clear the file, allowing you to store new information. (This is true for auditing volumes only).

AUDITOR CONFIGURATION

As an auditor, you will be required to create reports on past and present network incidents. The auditor configuration screen will allow you to select which network functions to be traced.

Selecting Audit Configuration enables you to change or select the following container auditing settings:

- ◆ Audit by DS event
- ◆ Audit by file/directory
- ◆ Audit by user
- ◆ Audit options configuration
- ◆ Change audit password
- ◆ Display volume auditing
- ◆ Display audit status

Following is a brief description of each configuration option.

AUDIT BY DS EVENTS

Selecting Audit by DS events will display a list of Directory Services events to audit.

To select a DS event you want to audit, or configure for auditing, choose the desired option and press Enter. You then will see a list of events that can be turned "on" or "off." By default, most of the events are turned off, or not audited. If you want to turn on, or audit, an event, highlight the event and press F10 to toggle that particular event. If you want to toggle all of the events, press F8.

In Figure 29.7, the Remove partition event has been toggled to on, or in other words, turned on for auditing.

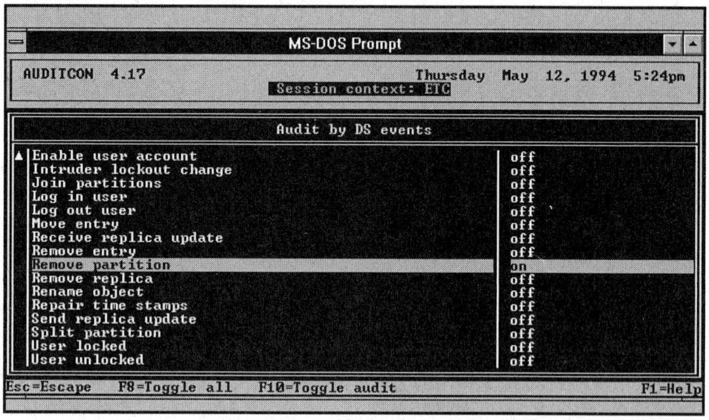

Figure 29.7.
Audit by DS event
option menu.

```
─                          MS-DOS Prompt                        ▼ ▲

  AUDITCON  4.17                          Thursday  May  12, 1994  5:24pm
                          Session context: ETC

  ┌──────────────────── Audit by DS events ────────────────────┐
  │▲ Enable user account                              │ off     │
  │   Intruder lockout change                         │ off     │
  │   Join partitions                                 │ off     │
  │   Log in user                                     │ off     │
  │   Log out user                                    │ off     │
  │   Move entry                                      │ off     │
  │   Receive replica update                          │ off     │
  │   Remove entry                                    │ off     │
  │   Remove partition                                │ on      │
  │   Remove replica                                  │ off     │
  │   Rename object                                   │ off     │
  │   Repair time stamps                              │ off     │
  │   Send replica update                             │ off     │
  │   Split partition                                 │ off     │
  │   User locked                                     │ off     │
  │   User unlocked                                   │ off     │
  └─────────────────────────────────────────────────────────────┘
  Esc=Escape   F8=Toggle all   F10=Toggle audit              F1=Help
```

Warning

The more events that are audited, the more performance degradation the server will experience. Also, the more audited events that are toggled to on, the larger the disk space required for storing the auditing file.

Audit by User

This option enables you to turn auditing on or off for user objects.

After selecting the Audit by User options, a Directory Services Browser screen will appear. This screen will list all the objects that are located in the current directory context.

Tip

Your context will be displayed at the top of the screen.

To select a user, move the highlight bar to that particular user object and press F10. An on status will appear to the right side of the screen.

Once a user is selected, all the user's transactions in this container are recorded in the Audit Data file.

29

Tip

If selecting Audit by User under Volume Auditing in AUDITCON
displays a window full of garbage characters, your Bindery Context
has not been set at the server.

To correct this problem, complete the following:

SET BINDERY CONTEXT=*valid context*

This should solve the problem, and users within that context will show
up in AUDITCON Browser.

Note

If the user object you want to audit is not listed, you will need to
change to the correct context. To change contexts, browse the directory
tree by moving the highlight bar and selecting a container by pressing
the Enter key.

Once you have marked the selected users, press the Escape key and then answer Y
to the dialog box that will appear (to save the changes).

AUDIT OPTIONS CONFIGURATION

Selecting the Audit Options Configuration option enables you to set basic audit
parameters, such as data file size, auditor login requirements, and error recovery
options. Once this option has been selected, you will be given the following options
box (see Figure 29.8).

Figure 29.8.
Audit configuration
option box.

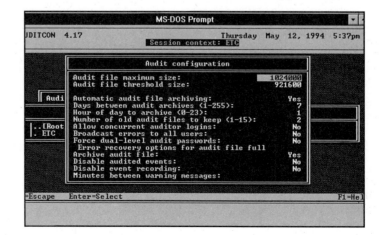

This option box is divided into three different sets of options. The first set of options allows you to specify the maximum audit file size and threshold. The middle set of options enables you to configure the automatic audit file archiving. The final set of options deals with the error recovery options when the audit file does become full. This section briefly covers the most important options; the ones that are not covered are self-explanatory.

The audit file maximum size, as its name implies, enables you to specify the maximum audit file size. This function is important, because the audit file will continue to grow until it reaches this limit.

The default audit file size is 1024000 Bytes (or 10MB), and is the same for any size disk; this default size is not based on the available disk space or the size of the disk.

Each environment will require a different size auditing file. The best way to determine the appropriate file size is to determine how much, or how long you want to audit any particular set of transactions. For example, you will want the file size set large enough to track activities for the appropriate amount of time—a day, two weeks, a month, and so on.

It is helpful to note that you can keep a total of 15 different old audit files online. These files can be migrated or kept on the disk drive. The benefit of segmenting or keeping multiple files on the drive is simply to enable you to view multiple versions for comparison.

One of the options discussed later in this section is the capability to have the volume dismount when the audit file is full. This option could be used for the ultimate in data protection. For example, you may create an audit sequence that looks at the access of certain information, or attempts to access information from a specific user. As you create this audit sequence, you could set the audit file small enough so that one incident of the action by a suspected user would cause the volume to dismount. This example may seem extreme, and probably is, but it also demonstrates the power available to an effective audit.

Note

If a volume is dismounted because the Audit Data file reached its maximum size limit and the Dismount Volume Option is set, the network supervisor must remount the volume and enable auditing again.

To remount the volume, complete the following steps:

1. At the console, mount the volume by typing

   ```
   MOUNT volume_name
   ```

2. An `Audit file full` error message appears on the server console screen and you are prompted to mount the volume with auditing disabled.

3. At the server console, enter the current auditing password for the volume.(This is the password the auditor assigned to the volume.)

4. Re-enable auditing.

Another option related to the maximum file size is the file threshold. Setting the threshold size will help ensure that this doesn't happen. The Audit file threshold size is a function that will alarm you when the file is approaching the maximum threshold size. The threshold size is by default set to 90 percent of the audit file size.

When the file reaches the maximum size, you have the option to delete it, rename it, or dismount the volume (to continue auditing, one of the options must be performed).

You also can elect to have the file automatically achieved (default setting). This provides a no hands-on backup of your audit data and audit history files. For each archived file, however, disk space is required.

From this options menu, you also can specify whether you want to provide multiple auditors concurrent access to the same container or volume, which gives them access to the same audit information.

Tip

Auditors that need access to the same volumes and containers must have knowledge of the same passwords.

If you are planning to use multiple auditors and do not want them to have access to each other's auditing information, you will want to implement your volume and directory structure accordingly. For example, if you want an auditor to have access to the company's accounting information but not to the payroll data, you will want to be sure to set these different data sets on separate volumes.

Another option in the configuration screen that you may want to take notice of is the ability to force dual-level auditing passwords. This option will require one password to be able to audit activities on the network, and a second password to configure or change the auditing parameters.

Change Audit Password

As its name implies, this option enables you to change the AUDITCON password. The process required to change the audit password is as follows:

1. Select the change audit password options.
2. Enter the current auditor password for the volume or container.
3. Enter a new auditor password for the current volume or container.
4. Confirm the change by re-entering the password when prompted.

Note

If you enter the incorrect auditing password, access to change to a new password will be denied.

Disable Container Auditing

Auditors can disable auditing, but supervisor rights are required to enable auditing.

Warning

Be careful! This is not the same as logging out of AUDITCON!

If you disable network auditing, you cannot audit the network. To re-enable auditing you will have to contact the network administrator or someone with administrative rights.

Furthermore, if auditing is disabled, the auditing file is reset, and the information contained in the original file is moved to the OLD Audit Data file.

Display Audit Status

Selecting this option will provide you with the screen similar to Figure 29.9, which enables you to view basic information about the audit files.

Note

The information presented on the Audit Status screen is for the current volume or container.

Figure 29.9.
Audit Status screen.

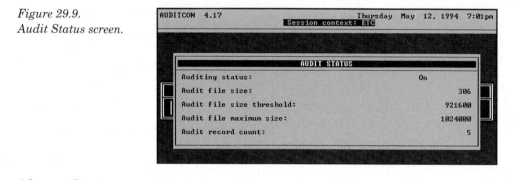

After configuring any of the audit events or configurations, press the Escape key. After pressing the Escape key, a dialog box will appear asking whether you want to save the changes.

AUDITING REPORTS

The Auditing reports option enables you to select and view data to be extracted from the audit data file that was created during the audit process. If there is information that you want, but it is not contained in the report, you will have to re-audit and make the appropriate configuration changes.

To create an audit report, complete the following steps:

1. Select Auditing Reports from the Available Audit Options menu, which will bring up a menu with the following list of options:

   Display audit status

   Edit report filters

   Report audit file

   Report audit history

   Report old audit file

   Report old audit history

   View audit file

   View audit history

   View old audit file

   View old audit history

2. From this list of options, select Report audit file, and specify where you want the file to be sent by completing one of the following steps:

Note

> If you send reports to a network directory, a user with Supervisor rights in the file system can see the file. If you want to secure your reports, you should send them to a local drive or a floppy drive on your workstation.

◆ Press Enter to copy the report to a file in your default directory. (The default filename is AUDITDAT.TXT.)

◆ Enter the directory path and filename where you want the file to be sent, and then press Enter.

Note

> AUDITCON does not create a file for you. You must specify an existing directory path and filename.

◆ Select a filter from the Select Filter list and press Enter. To create a report without a filter, select no_filter.

To create or edit a filter, complete the following steps:

1. To edit a filter in the list, press Enter.

2. To create a filter, press Insert.

Note

> The list item no_filter cannot be edited.

The following is a brief definition of the available report options.

Specify how you want the filter to be used by completing one of the following steps:

◆ To save the filter changes, select Save Filter Changes.

◆ If it is a new filter, enter a name (maximum eight characters).

◆ To use the filter once without permanently changing the filter, select Use Filter Without Saving Changes.

The report is generated with the new filter settings, and then the filter reverts to its original settings.

29

Tip

> New filters are not saved.
>
> To discard filter changes, select Discard Filter Changes.
>
> Edited filters revert to the original settings. New filters are deleted.

You will be returned to the Auditing report menu, where you can now select the View Audit file option to view the report. Or, the filtered report is sent to the directory and file you specified and can be viewed with a DOS text file format editor.

To use the View Audit File option, complete the following steps.

1. Select View Audit File from the Auditing Reports menu.
2. Select a filter from the Select Filter list and press Enter . To see a report without a filter, select no_filter from the list.

Tip

> To edit a filter in the list, press Enter.
>
> To create a filter, press Insert.
>
> The no_filter list item cannot be edited.

Specify how you want the filter to be used by completing one of the following steps:

◆ To save new changes to the filter, select Save Filter Changes.

◆ If you created a new filter, enter a name. The name should be eight characters or less.

◆ To use the filter for this report only, select Use Filter Without Saving Changes. The report is generated with the new filter settings, and then the filter reverts to its original settings.

Note

> New filters are not saved.

◆ To discard filter changes, select Discard Filter Changes.

Tip

> Edited filters revert to the original settings. New filters are deleted.

Once the report is loaded, you can use the arrow keys to scroll through the report. To exit, press Esc and answer **Yes** at the Exit View prompt. On long reports, you may want to use a DOS text editor, or a word processor.

UNDERSTANDING THE AUDIT FILES

AUDITCON automatically creates audit files when it is enabled. Each volume or container using AUDITCON will have its own audit files. The Audit Data file keeps records of all audited transactions. The auditing configuration you set determines which types of records are entered into the data file.

This file operates like a system log or error file, in that records are automatically entered into the file whenever an audited event occurs.

When you audit container objects for Directory Services events, the audit history information is combined with audit data into this file.

THE AUDIT HISTORY FILE

The Audit History file keeps a record of the auditor's activities in a volume, such as auditing configuration changes and auditor logins and logouts.

In Directory Services, the auditor's activities are recorded in the Audit Data file. There is no separate file for this information.

You can, however, use the menu options, such as View Audit History, to see auditor records, just as you would if you were auditing a volume.

RESETTING THE AUDIT DATA FILE

When the auditor resets an audit file, existing records are moved to an Old Audit Data or Old Audit History file. The original audit file continues to function as it did before.

To reset the Audit Data file, complete the following steps:

1. Select Audit Files Maintenance from the Available Audit Options menu.
2. Select Reset Audit Data File from the Audit Files Maintenance menu.

Note

A warning message appears onscreen to notify you that the current contents of the file will be moved to the Old Audit Data file. If you already have data in the old file, it will be deleted.

3. Select Yes to reset the file.

The remaining options are self-explanatory and do the following:

Audit Report Filters: Enables you to edit an existing filter or create a new filter.

Note

> You can create filters to extract specific data from the Audit Data file. Filtered information can then be copied to a separate file or viewed onscreen.

Report Audit File: Enables you to send a report from the Audit Data file to a specified file or directory.

Report Audit History: Enables you to send a report from the Audit History file to a specified file or directory.

Report Old Audit File: Enables you to send a report from the Old Audit Data file to a file or directory.

Report Old Audit History: Enables you to send a report from the Old Audit History file to a specified file or directory. This option applies to volume auditing only.

View Audit File: Enables you to see the current Audit Data file on your screen.

View Audit History: Enables you to see the current Audit History file on your screen. This option applies to volume auditing only.

View Old Audit File: Enables you to see the old Audit Data file on your screen.

View Old Audit History: Enables you to see the old Audit History file on your screen. This applies to volume auditing only.

DISPLAY AUDIT STATUS

The Display Audit Status screen shows the following information about the auditing files on the current volume or container:

Auditing Status: Indicates whether auditing has been enabled for the current volume or container.

Audit File Size: This is the current size of the Audit Data file.

Audit File Size Threshold: When the Audit Data file reaches the size shown here, a warning message is sent to the console and the system log file.

Audit File Maximum Size: This number is the maximum size allowed for the Audit Data file.

CHANGE SESSION CONTEXT

After selecting the Change Session Context, a screen similar to the one seen in Figure 29.10 will appear, enabling you to type in the context to which you would like to change.

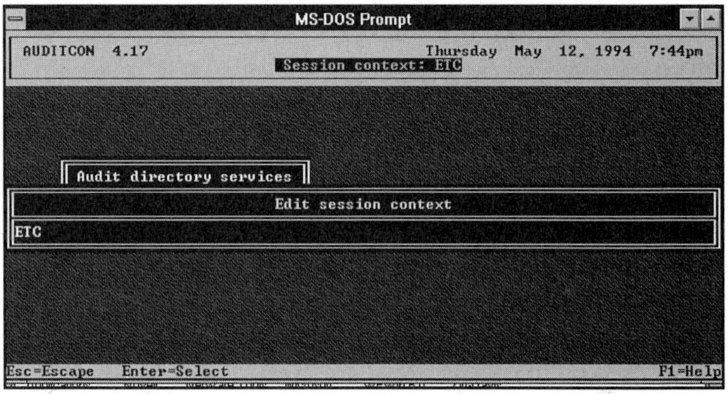

Figure 29.10.
Change Session Context
screen.

If you cannot see the container you want to audit, use Change Session Context to move to a different area of the Directory tree.

If auditing is not turned on, select the container you want to enable auditing on, and you will be given two options: Display Audit Status or Enable Container Auditing.

CHANGE CURRENT SERVER

If the volume you want to audit is not on this server, you can select a different server by choosing the Change Current Server option. After selecting this option, a dialog box will appear, from which you can select the desired server. If the server is not listed, press the Insert key. To remove a server from the list, press the Delete key.

From this location, you also can log in under a different user name by pressing the F3 or Modify key. You then will be given the option to type in the user name and appropriate password.

SUMMARY

NetWare 4.1 is one of the only network operating systems on the market that provides an enterprise network and solution, including performance, integrated messaging, fortress-like security, file services, printing services, and auditing.

With NetWare 4.1, Novell has made great progress towards helping network and security administrators, auditors, and users in creating a secure network infrastructure. This concentrated effort produces a network operating system that provides a well-balanced and expandable base for enterprise-wide secure business solutions. With these solutions, network designers, administrators, and users can implement these functions to build a trusted network computing environment at both the local and global level.

- The Ups and Downs

- The Basics

- Doing the Work

- Summary

CHAPTER 30

Documenting Your Network

Can you remember your old high school math teacher, Mr. Cal Q. Luss, ever saying, "You have to show all your work in order to get full credit!" Maybe you thought Mr. Luss was just trying to make life more difficult for you, or maybe you thought he had caught on to your deskmate's ability to produce test results amazingly similar to your own. Either way, it probably was not until later that you truly learned to appreciate the wisdom of Mr. Luss's strict policies. By learning to show your work, you discovered a practical way to improve your math skills. You could check your work and find out exactly where you went wrong.

Today, it's not summations and derivatives, it's Ethernet and twisted pair. It may have been years since you have had to deal with "The value of X in 2X - 4 = 0," but problems like "the network is slow" and "I can't print" have taken their place. Remember Mr. Luss's advice, and show your work. The job of documenting your network is no less arduous and tedious than those old math tests, but the rewards can be great.

Having invested so much time and money in your network, its operation, and its related assets, you will want to keep a close eye on it. Documenting your network is all about collecting and organizing information about your network that will give you a better understanding of how it is put together, its strengths and weaknesses, and how it is being used. In addition, documenting your network is about learning what you can do to save money and reduce costs, plan for the future, and streamline troubleshooting and maintenance.

Before you set off with your clipboard and pen in hand to count computers and map wiring, you may want to get some help and advice. This chapter explores the process of documenting your network, beginning with a brief introduction to some of the positive and negative results you can expect. This will be followed by a discussion of the different types of information you will need to collect, practical advice on what tools to use to collect it, how to get started, and, finally, how to take advantage of the results. Despite the fact that the job will never really be done, continuing the work will be up to you. The job will grow and evolve right along with your network and your organization.

THE UPS AND DOWNS

Everything has its ups and downs, its positives and its negatives. Throughout all the phases of setting up a NetWare 4 network you continue to make decisions intended to strike an ideal balance between needs and resources, solutions, and their costs. Although the cost of the decisions made during the initial Implementation phase will be considerable, those made during the remaining (and ongoing) phases of Operation, Maintenance, Troubleshooting, and finally Expansion, will be the most significant over time. Even the most subjective decision makers require data of some sort or quantitative data to make truly informed decisions.

It is important to understand that documenting your network is only part of the Operation, Maintenance, and Troubleshooting phases of installing and managing a NetWare network, but an important part, at that. Although very few network administrators have any kind of network documentation system in place, the International Standards Organization (ISO) emphasizes its importance with the following description of network management as a five-step process:

1. **Fault management**: Facilities for fault detection and isolation. Upon isolation of the apparent network problem, corrective action is taken.

2. **Accounting management**: Facilities that allow the establishment of charges for the use of managed objects. Cost identification for the use of managing objects and the method in which the charge will be administered.

3. **Configuration and name management**: Configuration of software and hardware. Initializing a network and the proper down procedures. Maintaining, adding, and updating the down part of the network configuration.

4. **Performance management**: The evaluation of network component behavior and the effectiveness of that behavior according to design, implementation, and expectation with the communication process.

5. **Security management**: The protection of managed objects or information based on an established security method design to provide the essentials in OSI network management and protection.

Among the terms just introduced, Configuration Management will be used more here to refer only to the configuration of software and hardware including the physical network. The data you collect and update while documenting your network, along with the entities they represent, are the objects of Configuration Management, managed objects, or the things to be managed.

Note

The elements of network management that deal with down procedures are better dealt with in the troubleshooting section of the book. See Chapters 35 (Network Management) and 39 (Troubleshooting NetWare 4.*x*) for more information on troubleshooting your network.

THE UPSIDE TO CONFIGURATION MANAGEMENT

The process of documenting your network itself has its own ups and downs. Even though documenting your network is vital for efficient Configuration Management, it is important to take a look at both the positive and negative results of doing so. We will start with a brief look at the more desirable results.

TRACKING NETWORK ASSETS

As a member of an organization committed to making their investment in information technology payoff, your ability to control and track the financial value of your network assets will be a high priority. By thoroughly documenting your network, you will be able to develop and maintain a plan for dealing appropriately with this challenge. Following are some things to consider:

◆ **Current investment in the network**: A snapshot of the network in its current state will allow you to estimate its monetary value to the organization and to the individual cost centers within it.

◆ **Changes to the network**: As people, resources, and organizational structures change, an accurate inventory will allow you to redistribute your network assets.

◆ **Updates or upgrades to the network**: As plans for expansion are made and executed, the network inventory will reflect the cost and value of the updates and upgrades.

PROTECTION OF NETWORK ASSETS

As network administrator, the majority of your day-to-day activities will be geared toward protecting your organization's investment in the network and information technology, making sure that everything is operating properly and efficiently. A well-documented network will make it easier for you to respond quickly when things go wrong and will allow more time for needed improvements and upgrades. Your documents should reflect the following:

◆ **Disaster recovery**: In the event of a disaster, major problems with the physical network, or a loss of data, your network documentation will help steer you to safety.

◆ **Speedy restoration of service**: Minor interruptions in service can be minimized and quickly restored when you have a clear picture of your network's makeup.

◆ **Efficient technical support**: In servicing the needs of network users, network documentation can help reduce the need for onsite support and minimize the time to problem resolution.

CONSOLIDATION OF EQUIPMENT AND FUNCTIONS

Without an accurate picture of exactly what your network contains, it can be very difficult to determine where there is a duplication of effort or where multiple standards are employed. This is often the situation with large networks that have grown quickly or over a relatively short period of time without the benefit of centralized management and control. Once your network has been documented properly, you will find it easier to control your network's growth, spot trends, and implement useful standards. Following are topics of consideration:

- ◆ **Common specifications**: By examining network documentation, you may be able to uncover areas that would benefit from the implementation of a suitable standard. Hardware, application usage, and development; security procedures, archiving and backup; and network object and resource naming conventions are usually the first problem areas that surface and should be the first areas standardized.

- ◆ **Support equipment**: You also may find that a lack of explicit standards has forced you to purchase and maintain extra support equipment.

- ◆ **Training:** When the various components of your network are too diverse, training users and support staff can grow to be very expensive and cumbersome.

- ◆ **Budgeting**: With well-established standards for hardware and software, financial planning will be more straightforward.

Controlling Expenditures

Documenting your network will also give you insight as to where you may be able to scale back some and reduce the ongoing costs of operating and maintaining your network. Just as a financial analyst needs a balance sheet to balance the budget, you will need complete documentation on your network to be able to control expenditures. Your document should provide you information on the following:

- ◆ **Unused equipment**: A complete inventory of your assets undoubtedly will turn up unused equipment. With a complete picture of your network on paper, it will be easier for you to see where you can put some of that equipment to work for you in other areas, repair it if it is broken, or sell it.

- ◆ **Lowered inventory of spare equipment**: To keep a larger network running smoothly and without significant interruptions, it will be necessary to keep on hand a certain amount of spare equipment and repair parts. Documentation that includes histories and maintenance records for those that are commonly used will help you determine exactly how much of it you will need to have standing by.

- ◆ **Site licenses and volume discounts**: If your organization seems to be using the same software, hardware, or other equipment throughout, or if you have put some usable standards in place, you may benefit from the purchase of site licenses for software, or you may qualify for volume discounts on the future purchases of hardware.

◆ **Reduced manpower requirements**: You will find that documenting your network can be an efficient way for you to stretch your manpower resources and better meet the needs and expectations of your organization.

THE DOWNSIDE TO CONFIGURATION MANAGEMENT

Documenting your network can yield some undesirable results as well. Although they will probably never be reason enough alone to prevent you from carrying on, it can be a great help to at least understand them and be prepared.

INTERRUPTION OF SERVICE

If continual, uninterrupted service is not only a goal but also a requirement within your organization, you will have to explore some pretty creative solutions to the complex problems presented by the task of documenting your network. Some sort of interruption of service is bound to occur.

The amount of time and work involved in this whole process will probably take time away from your normal duties. You may be able to get the work done outside of your organization's normal working hours, but it is more likely that you will need to bring in some sort of outside help to cover for your normal duties or help you with the grunt work of documenting your network.

Tip

> Keep in mind that there are companies for hire that specialize in inventory management. Assuming that it's within your budget, you may be able to get those companies to do a lot of the legwork for you.

It also is possible that the tools you employ will interrupt your users' normal work patterns. Many tools are activated to collect information from users' workstations when they log into the network, so you will need to look for other ways to activate these tools if your users are less than patient. Please refer to the section titled "Use the Right Tools" for more information on selecting a flexible Configuration Management tool.

RIGIDITY IN STANDARDS

Standards, although certainly beneficial in a number of ways, can be somewhat of a double-edged sword. Oftentimes, standards can get in the way. Another hardware or software product may do it faster, more efficiently, or cheaper, and any standards policy that does not make allowances for such situations may be too rigid.

It also is possible to be in a situation where development on your network or some other internal project is halted or delayed because you are forced to wait for updates from a particular vendor. Care must be taken to ensure that you minimize your reliance on out-of-date standards and technologies.

Resistance within the Organization

Configuration Management is, by its nature, something that directly involves your users. Ideally, the most any of your users would have to do would be to leave their office open late one night for you or your staff to take a physical inventory. But, your experience and common sense will probably suggest that they will be more involved than that. Some users will resist having to adhere to new or different standards, while others may simply refuse to have their service interrupted for even the shortest time.

Tip

With these things in mind, it is possible to reduce or at least be ready for the possible negative responses from your user community. Concentrate on being unobtrusive, open-minded, and team-oriented. One way to help reduce dissension would be to ensure a consensus exists before implementing any new standards. Also, be sure to involve representatives from various divisions within your organization in the planning and execution of the documentation process or any new policies that may result. People are less likely to resist something that they had a part in planning.

Different people in your organization will handle change differently. You might at first think that the "power-user" community would be the most difficult, but with an open mind, you may find their advice or complaints to be helpful. Experienced users are still users, and they view the network and the services it provides in a way that you cannot, given your differing perspectives. Making life as simple as possible on the novice or intermediate user community is still the watchword.

Warning

Don't forget to consider the effect changes will have on your own support and facility staff.

THE BASICS

No one can know everything there is to know about a network from top to bottom, but documenting your network is a great start. Perhaps you have established a powerful turnkey application menuing system for your users, but you know very little about the work your cabling contractor did for you a couple of years back. Or, perhaps, you pulled the cable yourself, but your users are on their own when it comes to running their personal productivity applications. You will soon learn, if you have not already, that your job can be very difficult without a clear view of the entire picture. By collecting, organizing, and properly using information about your network, the big picture will begin to appear.

This picture is an inventory of your network made up of many different elements. It includes an actual map of the network and buildings that contain it. It includes wiring layouts and outlet locations. It includes workstations and servers, bridges and routers, hubs and concentrators. And, more abstractly, this picture of your network includes all the data that is moved around the network. Despite the fact that data is not always something that can be accounted for directly in an inventory process, it is your network's reason for existence and cannot be left out. Your actual network was created and implemented from the physical up through the more abstract, and the documented picture of your network should be created in the same way.

This section walks you through these different levels, discussing what information is needed (in general terms) to create the big picture of your network. Having covered this, the chapter will continue with suggestions as to how you can begin to collect this information in the section called "Doing the Work."

Note

The different levels of a network discussed in the following section are very similar, in some ways, to the Open Systems Interconnect (OSI) Model, which is discussed in Chapter 5. The OSI model provides a useful framework for understanding network systems.

TOPOGRAPHY

At this level, you are concerned with everything that is physical and tangible. You can see it, touch it, and tag it. The challenge at this level is to get a good feel for the lay of the land. You are interested in only the most basic properties of the items, such as the length, gauge, and location of cables, wires, and conduits, or the location and type of servers, printers, and workstations.

Other items that should be considered to be part of your network's topography include the following:

- NetWare servers
- Mainframe and host systems
- Other servers
- Printers
- Workstations
- Cables, backbones, and general wiring
- LAN, WAN, and remote connections
- Repeaters
- Outlets
- Patch panels
- Hubs and concentrators
- Bridges and routers

Topology

Again, here the focus is still on the physical, but you are more interested in the higher functions of the individual items that make up your network. At the topological level you still want to know the length, gauge, and location of cables, wires, and conduits, but you are also interested in their configuration (bus, ring, or star), transmission protocol type, and throughput (both theoretical and effective). The location and type of servers, printers, and workstations are still important, but you will also want to know more about the make and model of the machines themselves, their connections to the network, and their primary function. It is at this level, for example, that the distinction between a print server, database server, and a fax server becomes more meaningful.

A common way to classify the various elements of a communications network at the topological level is to classify each as DTE (Data Terminal Equipment) or DCE (Data Communication Equipment). These terms can be used in a generalized manner to apply to any device found in a network. A workstation, for example, is DTE. That is to say, the data carried by the network terminates at the workstation level where it is used by an application or by the user directly. A router, on the other hand, is considered DCE, because it facilitates the propagation of data across the network.

In addition to recording the higher functions, you will want to round out your physical inventory by digging into the "guts" of all this equipment. Pay special attention to workstation and server details like those listed here:

- ◆ Make and model (Macintosh, IBM PC clone, and so on)
- ◆ Processor speed and type (Motorola 68XXX, Intel X86, and so on)
- ◆ Bus type (ISA, EISA, MCA, Local Bus, PCI, and so on)
- ◆ Installed RAM
- ◆ Fixed disk storage devices type, make, model, and configuration (capacity, drive type, cylinders, heads, and so on)
- ◆ NIC make, model, device driver version, IPX address, and configuration (IRQ, Port address, I/O address, and so on)
- ◆ Other installed adapter cards (including video adapters) make, model, device driver version, and configuration

INFORMATION AND DATA

At this level, your attention turns to the more abstract elements of your network. You cannot really see it, touch it, or tag it, but you can detect and inventory it nonetheless. Here you are primarily dealing with the substance of your business, information. As a result, you will be most interested in the contents of all of your network's mass storage devices, both online and offline, the applications, and data.

You will be particularly interested in details such as the following:

- ◆ Revision, upgrade history, location, and size of software programs installed
- ◆ Location, type, and format of data (including centralized databases)
- ◆ Network requester version (NETX, VLM, and so on)
- ◆ Operating system type and version (MS Windows, OS/2, MacOS, UNIX, and so on)
- ◆ Configuration files (NetWare .NCF, DOS, MS Windows and OS/2 AUTOEXEC.BAT and CONFIG.SYS, MS Windows and OS/2 .INI, NET.CFG, Macintosh preference files, UNIX hosts, networks, resolve, and protocol files, and so on)
- ◆ Snapshot of storage device directory structure (both server and workstation devices)
- ◆ System maintenance and repair histories
- ◆ System warranty and service agreement information. Data on the users of the network and its devices will also be important.
- ◆ User NDS tree position and context
- ◆ Name, address, mail stop, e-mail address, phone, cellular, fax, and pager number of machine user or caretaker

available today that can help you automate the process of documenting your network, and if your network is large or widely distributed, it may be difficult to do the job right without one. But, keep in mind that you may already have some good tools at your disposal.

NATIVE NETWORK OPERATING SYSTEM TOOLS

By choosing to work with NetWare 4, you have already ensured that you have access to some of the most advanced network operating system tools available today. The cornerstone of these tools is NDS. Because NDS is a multi-user, distributed, and highly extensible database, it will be an ideal complement to any additional tools you may eventually choose to implement.

With proper planning and maintenance, you can use NDS to house a great deal of documentation on your network. You will see the greatest benefit in the area of user administration. NDS can store your users' full names, office locations, addresses, telephone and fax numbers, and more. As an increasing number of software vendors begin to include support for NDS in their own network management and inventory products, you may see NDS extended to include a great deal more information about your network and its configuration.

Other features of NetWare 4, such as auditing, can also help you with the task of Configuration Management. AUDITCON, as you learned in the previous chapter, can be used as a tool for ongoing documentation and monitoring of your network and its resources. Use AUDITCON to capture some of the following information:

◆ Logins and logouts

◆ Trustee modifications

◆ File creations, deletions, reads, and writes

◆ Requests to manipulate queues

◆ Directory Services object creations, deletions, reads, and writes

◆ Events directly related to Directory Services objects

◆ Events directly related to users

Be sure to take a look at the utility included with NetWare called NVER. NVER can help you capture basic configuration information from workstations running DOS, MS Windows, or OS/2. Also, the workstation operating systems themselves often provide system inventory and diagnostic tools of their own. A particularly useful tool, called Microsoft System Diagnostics (MSD.EXE), is shipped with the more recent versions of MS-DOS and MS Windows.

Note

> Because tools like NVER and MSD are not designed to feed their output into a centralized database, it can be difficult to use these tools on a large scale basis. With a little creativity and ingenuity, however, they can still be quite useful and even indispensable.

SOFTWARE PRODUCT-SPECIFIC TOOLS

A small but growing category of high-end specialty and general purpose applications are being shipped with their own Configuration Management tools. Although most commodity and personal productivity applications do not fall into this category, more sophisticated systems, such as certain Relational Database Management Systems (RDBMS) and messaging systems, are setting high standards for those that may follow.

Among the features these applications typically provide are the capability to centrally manage and archive data distributed among multiple servers, the capability to synchronize user accounts with the NetWare bindery and NDS, and the ability to monitor application usage and performance.

Warning

> Although applications that do provide Configuration Management utilities of their own invariably provide features that general purpose tools do not, they cannot do everything. It is very likely that most networks supporting such high-end applications would still require some sort of general purpose Configuration Management tool.

THIRD-PARTY NETWORK TOOLS

It is very possible that you will not be completely at ease relying on the tools provided in the box with your network operating system and with your network applications. Fortunately, there is a large selection of tools on the market that concern themselves with Configuration Management of a network.

They vary considerably in price and features, but for the task of Configuration Management, many larger organizations find that the cost of the tool is insignificant. The Personal Computer Asset Management Institute (PCAMI), an organization based in Rochester, New York that helps companies track their personal computers and other investments in their network, estimates that the failure to track this equipment costs U.S. companies some $20 billion each year. Many larger companies can do nothing more than produce a rough estimate of the amount of money spent on this equipment. One company that the PCAMI worked with estimated the number of personal computers it owned as being somewhere between 50,000 and 90,000. A company with a problem of this scale would be eager to spend $50,000 or so on a tool if it held some promise to bring things under control.

Even though all these tools and applications really fall under the general category of network management applications, they can be divided into a couple of meaningful subcategories, as follows:

- SNMP-based general network management consoles
- General network management suites. Each of these types of products often include one or more of the following components:
    - Hardware and software inventory (may include automatic discovery and mapping of network components)
    - Application metering
    - Software distribution
    - Server and network performance monitoring and reporting
    - Virus protection
    - Remote client control
    - Network traffic analysis, monitoring and alarms.

In addition, there is a rather unique, albeit small, class of applications that are designed to assist in the task of managing wiring and cabling. In larger and more distributed networks, the costs of running cable and maintaining it afterward can be enormous. In some situations, these costs represent the majority of the total expenses related to the installation and management of the network. Fortunately, there is a fairly wide range of applications available called cable management software that can help keep costs down and simplify the management of your network's web of wires. The products themselves range in price from a few thousand dollars to more than $50,000 each, so be sure to carefully consider your individual needs before taking the plunge. The capability to import CAD architectural drawings of your organization's physical layout is one feature provided by this type of software that you may find very useful and could save you a considerable amount of duplicated effort.

SNMP-based general network management consoles are the big guns of network management. SNMP (Simple Network Management Protocol) is considered the *de facto*, universal language for exchanging management information among various objects in a network. SNMP is based on a manager-agent model. An agent is a small program which resides in a network device and responds to simple requests for information from a manager or management console. Each of these agents maintain and support a database of management data called a Management Information Base (MIB). An agent in an MS Windows workstation might include information such as .INI files, memory configuration, or installed devices, while a router's agent might include statistics and connection information.

Some well-established, SNMP-based products include those from companies such as Cabletron Systems, Computer Associates, Hewlett-Packard, IBM, NetLABs, and SunConnect, and typically run on high-end, UNIX-based workstations. Touted as mission-critical tools for managing very large networks and being popular with customers using mainframe systems along with personal computers, these expensive systems are beginning to see strong competition from less-expensive, Windows-based management platforms from the likes of Novell, Intel, Microcom, and Hewlett-Packard. These companies are drumming up interest in their low-end management systems by including more features for less money.

Some products, such as the Novell and Intel joint-venture, ManageWise, include a large selection of tools and features that span almost all of the subcategories listed above. Novell's flagship management product, NetWare Management System (NMS), has been integrated and bundled with Intel's LANDesk Manager and Virus Protect products to create a very powerful, affordable, unified, scalable, NetWare-based system that gives administrators server management, desktop management and remote control, distributed network traffic analysis, router management, hardware and software inventory, virus protection, print queue management, and an integrated SNMP-based management console. Thanks to Novell and Intel's understanding of their own systems, many feel that the ManageWise product is the best equipped to manage NetWare networks. Figure 30.1 shows off some of the advanced capabilities of ManageWise.

Figure 30.1.
ManageWise allows you
to examine the inven-
tory of any PC on the
network. By double-
clicking on a PC icon in
the network map, then
clicking on the inven-
tory summary button,
you are immediately
shown an overview of
the PC's configuration.

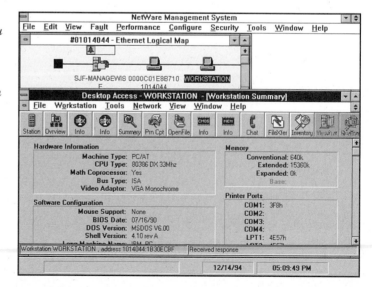

But even as the most advanced system available for managing NetWare networks, ManageWise does have some limitations. For example, its own management capabilities only reach out to manage NetWare servers, DOS and MS Windows, and Mac OS workstations, but do not extend well to other systems such as those running OS/2, UNIX, and others. For many administrators, more detailed management of these other systems can be a requirement. Fortunately, the basic architecture of ManageWise and Novell's NMS can help. Like other SNMP-based console management applications, it is open and extensible, supporting the capability to "snap-in" applications from third-parties which can significantly enhance the console's overall function set. These snap-in applications can be launched from within ManageWise and NMS and can share information with the console's management database. Administrators caught in a bind trying to manage OS/2 systems as well might look into snap-in applications from Horizons Technology Inc. (LAN Auditor) or Symantec Corp. (LANlord). In addition, those that already have a large investment in UNIX systems or a UNIX-based management console, like IBM's NetView for AIX, Hewlett-Packard's HP OpenView, Integrated System Manager (ISM) from Bull, or SunNet Manager from SunSoft, can find relief in ManageWise and NMS's ability to integrate well with those systems, providing a comprehensive enterprise management system.

Most SNMP-based products provide some form of automatic discovery and mapping of network components, and, because of this, are particularly valuable in the area of Configuration Management. After discovering the basic topography and topology of a network, some management consoles will even let you superimpose the discovered map of components onto a CAD or hand-drawn map of your organization's physical layout. Combine information and maps from several locations in a large WAN, and these management consoles provide truly global network management.

General network management suites differ from high-end systems in that they typically do not support SNMP in the same way that a management console would. Elements or portions of network management suites may implement SNMP agents of their own but will not typically interface directly with other agents on the network. Some of these suites tend to resemble a network management "toolbox" in the sense that they provide a number of different features that are only loosely integrated, while others provide a cohesive set of functions in an environment that transparently integrates the various tools that do the work. These suites tend to be more useful for the managers of small- and medium-sized networks, but some systems scale very nicely to help simplify the task of Configuration Management in large networks, too.

NETWORK INVENTORY TOOLS

For the purposes of documenting your network, hardware and software inventory should be right at the top of your list of required features for a Configuration Management tool, but be sure to consider how the other features of the product will work with other management utilities you may already have in place. Although some perform the tasks of hardware and software inventory in slightly different ways, the basic methods they use are almost always the same. The workstation inventory functions are typically initiated when a user logs into the network. In accordance with a daily or weekly schedule that you specify, each workstation will execute a program from within their login script that will handle all the dirty work, sometimes even without the user's knowledge. Because a system's hardware configuration does not change often, hardware inventory programs do not need to run as resident (TSR) programs, but the software inventory components often will.

Although hardware inventory software does not take terribly long to execute, its chore is not an easy one, especially on Intel processor-based or IBM PC clone systems. Unlike the relatively homogenous Macintosh systems from Apple Computer, IBM PC clone systems have proliferated without many strict standards for the implementation of accessories and add-on hardware components, making the job of hardware inventory much more challenging. Attempts to change this, such as IBM's recently abandoned PS/2 efforts, have met with only limited success in the past. But there is new hope for the networks of tomorrow. Hardware inventory will make a big move forward when products supporting the Plug and Play and Desktop Management Task Force (DMTF) standards begin to enter the market. These standards will help accessory manufacturers create self-configuring, self-managing system components. But, unfortunately, these standards will initially benefit only the manufacturers and will not be much help for users of older equipment. All that older equipment will have to be rolled over and replaced by equipment which adheres to the new standards before the users will see any significant benefit.

The task that software inventory packages must undertake is no less challenging. Because a user is much more likely to install new software regularly than to insert new devices or peripherals into a system, software inventory programs must keep a watchful eye on a system's software configuration. As a result, these programs are usually run resident. Inventory packages will often enable you to configure which type of software audit, if any, should be executed when the program loads, and then once the initial audit is complete, the program will stay in memory to record any changes to the system's installed software or system configuration files. The very first time you conduct a software audit on a system, that system may be tied up for quite a time. Depending on the size and number of storage devices, an initial audit may uncover hundreds of installed programs, and it is up to the inventory software to sort them out, comparing each executable to a database it maintains of popular programs. Some tools are better at this than others. Luckily, most of the tools allow you to perform incremental or differential audits where only new or different programs or configurations are detected after having completed the initial audit.

Some inventory packages will even allow you to account for systems that are not necessarily being used on the network regularly, as is the case when the system may not always be turned on and logged into the network. These inventory systems will allow you to create a diskette, or set of diskettes, that you can physically take with you when you go to gather information from these orphaned systems. By booting machines with the specially prepared diskettes, you will be able to collect and store information first to the diskettes and then later, using a data import facility, to the central inventory database. If your organization is a bit larger and you expect that you may have some strays out there, this type of feature could be a real timesaver.

Tip

> Remember that you will not be able to detect all your organization's assets over the network. Be sure to consider equipment that may be in offices used by temporary help, contractors, or interns; in the homes of telecommuters; in offices with other equipment (some users may have more than one computer); in empty offices or cubicles (where several users share equipment); and abandoned in storage after having been replaced by newer equipment.

Another feature that should top your list is the use of a centralized (and standard) database for the storing of configuration information. The tool should be able to collect and consolidate information from various locations on your network, ensuring that you have a complete view of your network even if it spans multiple sites. It can also be helpful if the database information is stored in a standard format, such as Btrieve or one of the various SQL implementations. The reporting features of most tools leave a lot to be desired; so, if your tool uses a standard database format, its reporting features can be augmented considerably by using specialized, stand-alone, database reporting tools.

Tip

> The power of using standard database formats is especially evident when you are using several tools to document your network. For example, you may use two individual tools for inventory, one that is particularly well-suited to hardware inventory and another that excels at software inventory. If both tools use some sort of standard database format, you may be able to use a single reporting tool to access and consolidate information from both systems in your reports.

Finding and purchasing the right tools is not the end, but only the beginning. Although the tools may help you discover the topography and topology of the network and may have some useful reporting mechanisms, they will not be much help when it comes to making sense of that information. How the information will affect the way your organization does business or how it purchases and maintains equipment for your network is up to you, the interpreter.

EXAMINE AND DOCUMENT THE NETWORK

Once you have established some reasonable goals and chosen appropriate tools for the job, you should be ready to jump right in with both feet and begin the real work. Well, maybe not. If you are like most network administrators, you consider this kind of work to be pure drudgery. Some companies, like Hewlett-Packard, are learning to capitalize on this hesitance network administrators seem to have for getting their hands (and feet) dirty. In the last quarter of 1994, Hewlett-Packard announced the formation of their HP Asset Management Service consulting division offering relatively simple needs analysis and inventory-control functions to complete outsourcing. With prices ranging anywhere from $3 to $8 monthly per asset, the division can also throw in consulting, physical-asset inventory capabilities, asset-database maintenance, custom reports, and tracking.

If simple math shows that your organization can simply not afford such a luxury, you are likely to be stuck doing the work on your own. The key to your success will be to "divide and conquer." In addition to the steps already discussed, consider the following remaining steps:

1. While you are still in the planning phases, be sure to get your user community involved and keep them informed to minimize surprises and unexpected interruptions in services. It would be a good idea to justify the whole process to your users as best you can.

2. Specify the exact information you are interested in collecting, and decide on what sort of database or tracking system you will use to manage it. Be sure that the system is functional, stable, and robust before you have to start keying in the information.

Warning

Even in this high-tech age, handwritten or hard copy records of your organization's assets are better than no records at all.

3. Consider investing in some sort of bar code label and reader system to assist in the tagging and tracking of physical assets. If money is tight, work up a reasonably organized system for numbering and tagging equipment on your own.

4. Begin the leg work, and start slowly. Break the project down into manageable chunks, dividing the work both geographically and chronologically. Be sure to allow plenty of time for each phase, and make sure that you are properly staffed.

5. Compile all of the information collected by keying it into your database or tracking system. Aside from the physical inventory, the most challenging step here will be deciding on the information you want to gather and how to store and retrieve that information. Use the section of this chapter called "The Basics" to help you get started with the "what." For the "how," you may choose to use a database system that you design yourself or one already offered by a tool you have chosen. If it is a system offered by a tool you already have, the type of information may already be chosen for you, but feel free to track additional information that you deem pertinent by manual means, if necessary. It will be a good idea to stick with standard database formats to simplify the tasks of integrating and reporting information.

Any physical, hands-on inventory and tagging team probably should set out after your work with software-based hardware and software inventory tools is underway. You will want to have plenty of time to familiarize yourself with the software, using it first in smaller test environments before having a go at the entire network. It is likely that you may uncover "holes" in the information these tools collect, and certain hardware or operating systems may stump your software, forcing you to collect that information by hand. Without an understanding of what your tools can and cannot provide, it will be difficult to tell your inventory team what information to uncover.

Consider the following items as part of your inventory management efforts:

◆ **Asset type:** Create a basic description of each asset. Include only the most important and distinguishing attributes. Try to establish some guidelines for consistency in these descriptions.

◆ **Brand:** Take down the make and model of each asset.

◆ **DTE/DCE:** Use these abbreviations to classify assets as Data Terminal Equipment (DTE) or Data Communication Equipment (DCE).

- **Asset ID (tag)**: Record the information shown on the physical tag marking the asset. A sample record will be a code including the year and month of purchase (YY-DD) followed by a unique identification number.
- **Serial Number**: Collect the most prominent product serial number shown on each asset. This information will be crucial to any successful security plan.
- **Department Owner and End User**: Gather information on who is responsible for each asset and who uses it on a regular basis. This information will help you determine who owns what and how much it is worth.
- **Contact Phone, Site ID, Building No., Floor No., and Room No.**: Record all information necessary to quickly locate each asset.

As you plan the leg work, everything will most likely center around some version or copy of your organization's physical plant layout. A set of blueprints in hard copy or CAD form will serve as the ideal starting point. Most architectural firms today are incorporating computer networks into their basic design with instructions for wiring closets, data outlets, and specialized wiring conduits, so you may even find a layer of the plans perfectly suited to the task of "walking" your network.

Depending on the nature of any automated inventory tools you have and use, you may be able to store away all this information in the same database. Most likely, however, you will probably find that your hardware inventory tool cannot be extended to store information like serial numbers and asset IDs. The good news is that there is a wide selection of easy-to-use, desktop, programmable databases available on the market today, and, with only a little programming knowledge, you can create a basic database that will really simplify the tracking of your organization's valuable assets. Regardless of whether you are able to implement a comprehensive system of your own to contain this information, use care to preserve it with some measure of redundancy. Keep at least two copies onsite or online, and one additional copy of the information in secure offsite or offline storage.

SUMMARY

When all is said and done, you will really begin to see your hard work pay off. Most organizations vastly underestimate the amount of time and money they have invested in their information systems, and do not take the time to check it out. Purchasing policies and procedures that have slackened over time can have a significant effect on an organization's return on investment. Your hard work will show you that you can recycle and redistribute your assets and increase the bottom line. At the same time, you will be able to lower your inventory of spare equipment, purchase site licenses, obtain volume discounts on future purchases, and reduce the size of your information services staff.

It's sometimes easy to forget why you installed a network in the first place. By taking the time to really examine and document a variety of aspects of your network, you can check to make sure that you are in line with the same goals that justified the use of a network in the first place. You will be able to analyze the higher functions of the network and how well they are implemented when you have a clear picture of what it is that is actually holding it all together. You might find that certain parts are simply not being held together well, and there might be room for new standards in system specifications, support equipment, training, budgeting, and purchasing.

Configuration Management will play an important role as you move forward with the maintenance and expansion of your organization's network. Keep the following points in mind at all times, as they will help you to better manage and troubleshoot your network:

- ◆ **Report the information**: Make the information available and accessible to all the right people: general executive staff, IS/IT executive staff, support staff, and facility staff. Use it to keep a lid on expenditures and to develop an ongoing asset security plan.

- ◆ **Troubleshoot and manage change**: The documentation you have created will prove invaluable when it comes to preventing, troubleshooting, and resolving problems with the network. You also will find that it will increase your ability to manage change within your network and your organization, as you expand or as your staff changes.

- ◆ **Maintain the information**: The information is only as good as it is current. Documenting your network is a lot like doing your homework. It's something you know you have to do, but you don't really want to do it. But, grit your teeth, buckle down and do the work, and you will be surprised at the results. And, don't forget to "show your work!"

- User Training

- Workgroup
  Administrator
  Training

- Ongoing User Support

- Summary

CHAPTER 31

Working with Users

Once you have a few workstations connected to your network, you can begin training your users and workgroup administrators. This chapter covers what users need to know and how your workgroup administrators can best help them utilize their network.

USER TRAINING

The most important people involved in your network are your users—without them, the need for a network does not exist. Therefore, it is important that your users understand the services and benefits of having a network. User training consists of determining what your users will need to know about your particular network and then instructing them in how to use the network to their advantage.

NETWORKING TERMINOLOGY

People who work with computers and computer networks tend to describe computer problems and networking components in technical terms that end users frequently will not understand. While the technical language is extremely descriptive and useful for networking professionals, the terminology can be confusing and possibly even intimidating to the average end user.

Before progressing any further, you should provide your users with a list of networking terms that you will use and their definitions. This will help facilitate easier communications between you, your users, and your workgroup administrators. Do not overwhelm your users with new terminology, but give them enough so that they can understand what you are saying when you are discussing the network with them. If you define every networking term to them and give them a massive volume of networking terms, they may get frustrated and decide that they will never understand what the network is. The trick here is to determine the most important terms your users are likely to encounter and not understand.

LOADING THE NETWARE CLIENT

If your users are working in an environment where they cannot always be connected to the NetWare 4 network, you will want to train them in how to load the NetWare client. Typically, this will consist of running the batch file called STARTNET.BAT. This file can be invoked a number of different ways, including from another batch file.

If your users will be manually loading the NetWare Client components, you will want to give them a brief education in DOS memory management. Using either the memory management that comes with the various brands of DOS or third-party memory management products, your users will be able to maximize the amount of conventional memory available for applications.

The other reason to explain how DOS memory management works is so that your users will understand why loading the NetWare Client inside of a DOS session in Windows or from a DOS shell in another application is not only a bad idea, but can lead to other problems—ranging from out of memory errors to workstation lockups.

LOGGING IN

On a workstation running DOS, your users will have four basic options for connecting to servers—logging in from DOS using the Novell LOGIN utility, connecting from within the DOS NETUSER utility or the Windows NWUSER utility, or from either DOS or Windows using a third-party product.

Logging in to a NetWare 4 system from DOS consists of running the LOGIN program, supplied by Novell and stored in the SYS:LOGIN and SYS:PUBLIC directories. The advantage to logging in from DOS is that all the scripts that you write will be executed, allowing you to map drives and capture printers automatically. However, many administrators consider logging in from DOS to be more of a hassle for your end users because of the way LOGIN handles error conditions—many of the NetWare LOGIN error messages are written in technical terms, frequently reporting an error number that needs to be looked up, and this in turn can be intimidating for an end user, especially because the error messages may only be accessible on your system only if the user is logged in. This can be frustrating for your end users, particularly if they are working outside of normal working hours and have no available means to determine what the problem is.

Note

When using VLM, you will not see the SYS:LOGIN directory show up as F:\LOGIN> prior to logging in. You will only see F:\> with its contents. This is because the VLM map roots the directory until you are authenticated into the network.

The second option for your users is to connect to the server using either NETUSER or NWUSER. Using either of these programs will only attach a user to the server, and will not cause the user's login script to run.

Under Windows, the user can make mapped drives and captured printers permanent, and can then restore those mappings once they have logged in (see Figure 31.1). This option works well if the user always logs in from the same workstation, but depending on your network environment, you may be able to get past this limitation by creatively using directory map objects in each context.

Your third option will be to look at third-party programs that allow your users to log

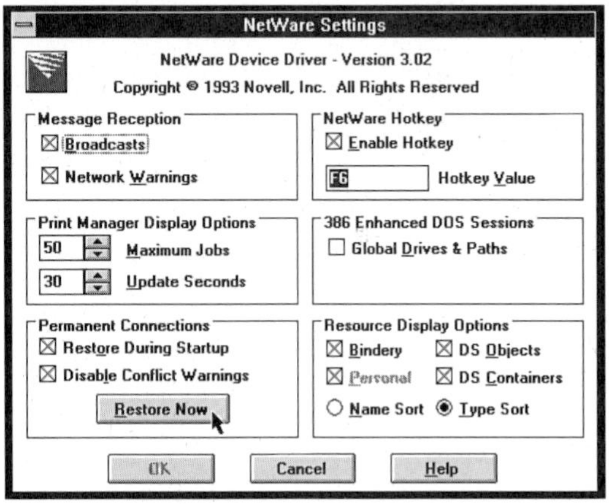

Figure 31.1.
Using the Restore Now
button to reconnect
permanent drive
mappings and captured
printers.

in from either DOS or Windows and have login scripts executed. A good source for these third-party programs is the NetWare service on CompuServe. Many third-party freeware and shareware products are posted to the NOVUSER forum library, and many of the authors of such programs frequent the various areas on NetWire.

NETWARE DIRECTORY SERVICES AND CONTEXTS

Most of your users may never need to understand the concept of their context if everything is automatically set up for them in a login script; however, there are certain types of users who may benefit from a rudimentary understanding of how NetWare Directory Services—or NDS— works. The type of user that may benefit from training in NDS and how it works can vary—mobile users, for example, may benefit greatly from an understanding of the NDS structure, as they will likely access programs and data on multiple servers. If they understand NDS enough to be able to map drives to multiple servers and redirect their output to remote printers, they will be more productive.

If your users are familiar with NetWare 3.*x*, they may have been aware that all of the objects created were part of a flat database called the bindery. However, as networks got bigger and bigger and binderies started to consist of hundreds—even thousands— of objects, response time from the network during the login process could slow considerably. Binderies also did not allow for a network-wide login process, which meant that your typical user could have several different logins for different servers, and the user would have to provide a separate login name and password every time they attached to a new server.

NetWare 4 eliminates the need for users to maintain several different logins for all of the servers on the network through the use of NDS. Through the use of a hierarchical database consisting of all objects on the network, Novell has created a structure that is not only easier for the administration team to maintain, but also makes it easier for users to navigate the network.

Even in an ideal network, where every resource that a user needs to be connected to is automatically allocated during the login process, users may still need to understand NDS in order to access resources that they normally wouldn't. For this reason, you may want to include a brief description of NDS to all of your users, and then provide one-on-one training if they need to understand more about using NDS to locate network resources.

You may find it easier to describe NDS contexts as you would describe a file directory structure. Container objects are roughly equivalent to subdirectories in a directory structure, and objects such as users, printers, print queues, and NetWare volumes would be equivalent to files.

USING CX AND NLIST

Novell has provided two DOS utilities to help facilitate locating objects and information in the NDS tree—the CX utility and the NLIST utility. Your users will benefit from a brief tutorial on the use of these utilities.

The CX utility is used to view and change the current context within the NDS structure. This utility would be used by users who have a need to use a machine that has the default name context set to a context other than where their user object is located.

As discussed in the last section, NDS is similar in many ways to a hierarchical file system structure. Just as you have the CD command to move around a DOS file system, you have the CX command to move around the NDS structure. Additionally, however, the CX utility functions as an equivalent to the DOS DIR command, because it lets users with sufficient rights browse the tree.

Just as the CX utility enables your users to browse the NDS tree for objects, the NLIST command gives your users the capability to search the tree for objects and display values for properties in the objects. Using the DOS file system metaphor, NLIST is roughly the equivalent of the DOS TYPE command.

Suppose that Mark, the MIS manager, needs to contact Bill, who works in the finance department. Assuming that Mark has sufficient rights to view Bill's telephone number property, Mark can use NLIST to look up Bill's telephone number, rather than having to go to a corporate phone directory and look it up there.

NLIST can also be used to obtain information about objects other than user objects. Suppose that Bill wanted to find the volume and pathname for a directory map object called TEST. He could issue the command

```
NLIST "DIRECTORY MAP" = "TEST" /D
```

which would display all of the property values for the directory map called TEST in the current context.

LOGIN SCRIPTS

You may want to make your users aware of the different types of login scripts that are run during the login process so that they understand the implication of using a User Login Script. These scripts are the Container Script, the Profile Script, and the User Script. Each script serves its own purpose; however, the only script that your users will be able to modify by default is the User Script. Depending on your particular network implementation, you may want to give your users the ability to modify the user script.

Warning

Because of the order in which login scripts are executed during log in, the User Login Script can potentially overwrite and change some of the settings you have established in the Container and Profile Login Scripts. If you allow users to modify their own login scripts, be sure to inform them of which settings can and cannot be changed.

As mentioned previously, on a DOS workstation, logging in under DOS is the only way that any of the three scripts will be run. If the user logs in using the NWUSER Windows utility, the login scripts assigned to the user will not be run.

You should tell your users about the functions of the different scripts. Let them know that there are certain settings that you set up in the container and profile scripts that are set up by default for everybody. Then inform your users that anything that needs to be set up on an individual basis will most likely be put in their personal login scripts. If you have given your users rights to modify their own scripts, instruct them in the basics of writing scripts, the utilities available for editing scripts, and the login script commands available to them.

Warning

If your users have no little or no experience in programming techniques, you should seriously consider not allowing them access to User Login Scripts.

When instructing users about writing login scripts, be sure to include not only information on writing scripts, but also techniques for debugging their own scripts and also ways to circumvent their login script if something they write prevents them from being able to log in. You may even want to set up the container or profile scripts with a special parameter that allows users to log in and have their personal scripts not run, even though the container and profile scripts run. This will allow users to have a search drive mapped to SYS:PUBLIC in the container script so they can run NETADMIN or NWADMIN to modify their own script without having to map the drives manually after logging in using LOGIN's /NS parameter.

USING THE FILE SYSTEM

One of the primary reasons that most organizations install a network in the first place is so users can use a shared file system. Your users will benefit from understanding how NetWare's file system rights work, as well as understanding the concepts of file system rights inheritance and the special NetWare file system attributes. Your users will also need to know about the additional features provided by the NetWare file system—features like salvaging deleted files and file compression.

If you are using home directories that are set up as fake root mappings, your users will need to understand that while all of their files are stored in a directory that looks like a root drive, it really is just a part of a larger hard drive. They will also benefit from knowing what additional features the NetWare volume will provide them with over storing files on their local drives. As the administrator, you have control over the different features enabled on each NetWare volume, and your users may benefit from knowing what some of those features are.

NetWare 4 provides all of the file system features that previous versions of NetWare provided—file sharing, security, and recovery. In addition to these standard features, there are several optional features available to you and your users. NetWare 4 introduces file compression, suballocation, and migration. If you have enabled any of these features on your NetWare volumes, you will want to describe them to your users.

File compression, when used properly, can be a valuable enhancement to your NetWare network. However, if your users misuse it, it can seriously degrade your

31

WORKING WITH USERS

server's performance. For this reason, you will want your users to know that NetWare file compression is not intended to be used in the same manner as the popular "disk doubler" products on the market for stand-alone workstations. NetWare file compression takes place on the server, running by default on files that have not been used after seven days. Compression runs on a daily basis between the hours of midnight and six o'clock in the morning. Decompression, however, runs immediately when a compressed file is written to, or the second time the file is read. Because decompression occurs on demand, your server's utilization will spike during decompression, and your users may notice a delay in accessing a compressed file while it is decompressed at the server.

Suballocation, when enabled for a volume, will save disk space. You may want to mention this feature to your users and briefly describe it; however, there are no user options for suballocation. If it is enabled for a volume, all files on the volume will be affected by it.

Migration is a method of moving files from fast hard drive storage to a slower medium, such as an optical disk jukebox. If you have migration enabled for a volume, describe it to your users, and explain the Don't Migrate file attribute to them. Users with sufficient file system rights will have control over data migration for individual files and directories.

NetWare includes a number of different file system rights, which you should list and describe to your users. The most common rights that you will give your users will be File Scan, Write, Create, Read, Erase, Access Control, and Modify. Generally speaking, the Supervisory file system right should be reserved for people on the administration team.

Once your users have an understanding of file system rights, review DOS file system attributes—Read Only, Archive, System, and Hidden. You may want to explain why, when a file is not flagged with the Read Only file system right, a user cannot modify a file when they have insufficient rights.

NetWare adds several more file attributes that your users should be aware of. Of particular interest to users will be the Purge, Execute Only, Immediate Compress, Sharable, Don't Migrate, and Don't Compress flags. These flags control how the server will manage files for the user; for example, files and directories flagged with the Purge attribute will not be salvageable.

This is usually a good time to introduce the FILER command to your users. FILER is a file management utility specifically written so that users can manage files. Of particular interest to users will be the Salvage option (see Figure 31.2). The Salvage option allows users to recover deleted files that are not flagged with the Purge flag.

Figure 31.2.
Using FILER to
salvage deleted files.

Using NetWare Print Services

Another reason that organizations install a network is so that users can share printers. Several NetWare utilities are used to manage connections to printers—CAPTURE, NETUSER, and NWUSER all are capable of connecting printers to a user's workstation. The PCONSOLE and NWADMIN utilities also allow users to view and modify jobs in NetWare print queues.

CAPTURE is the command line utility that most users will use to connect to their default printer. As the administrator, you will set up print job configurations and define the default for each user or container. Issuing the CAPTURE command with no parameters will cause the default print job for the current container or user to be used. As a general rule, the CAPTURE command will be part of your container login script.

Users can modify their printer connections using either the NETUSER or NWUSER utility. NETUSER, the DOS utility, provides a menu-driven interface that users can use to change printers for the first three printer ports allowed by NetWare (see Figure 31.3). NETUSER also provides an interface that users can use to view and modify the jobs in the print queue.

The NWUSER utility provides the functionality of modifying printer captures for all the ports available using the "drag and drop" capabilities of Windows (see Figure 31.4). All a user needs to do is browse the tree in the right hand window, and drag his or her printer selection over to the active ports window. By adding ports in the WIN.INI file's [Ports] section, you can access up to nine printer devices.

31

WORKING WITH USERS

*Figure 31.3.
Using NETUSER to
change printer assign-
ments.*

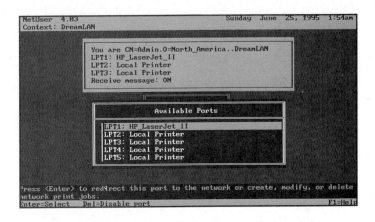

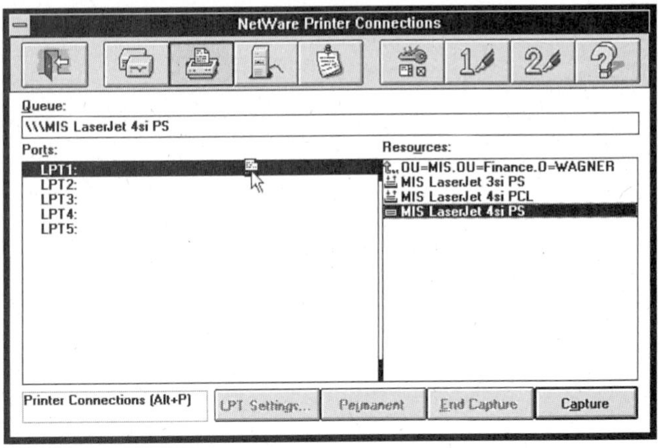

*Figure 31.4.
Using NWUSER to
change printer port
assignments.*

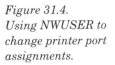

Unlike the DOS-based NETUSER utility, the Windows-based NWUSER utility does not allow a user to display and modify jobs currently in the print queue. To do this, your users can either use the PCONSOLE or NETUSER utilities in a DOS window, or they can use the NWADMIN utility. Figure 31.5 shows a sample print job detail screen. Note that in order to change any of the values displayed, your user must either be the job owner, or be listed as a queue operator.

USING E-MAIL FOR COMMUNICATING WITH YOUR USERS

Establishing an electronic mail system for communicating with your users is almost essential in any networked environment. While a telephone system may be useful for having users report immediate problems, your users can use an electronic mail system for reporting non-critical problems, and you can use it to communicate system changes, product updates, and other miscellaneous bits of information that may be of interest to your users.

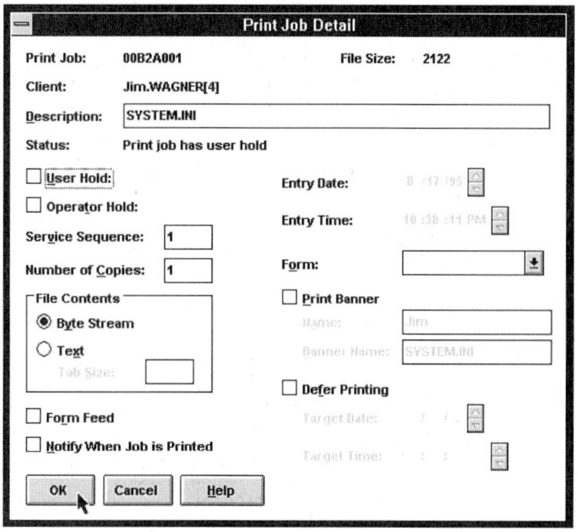

Figure 31.5.
Viewing print job
details using
NWADMIN.

Electronic mail is an effective way of passing information to groups of users. For example, you may want to establish a procedure for sending system information bulletins to your users to keep them up to date on current system developments and features. Many mail systems allow the system administrator to set up shared mail folders, which can be used as information repositories, lists of frequently asked questions, and known issues that you and your administration staff are working on.

Just as important, however, is the capability to get feedback from your users. If a user in your engineering department is working late and determines that he or she needs a file from the finance department, the user can send you mail requesting access to the file. When you log in the next morning, you will have a message in your mailbox from the user, and will be able to act on the message.

When you developed your needs assessment for your network, you should have decided on an electronic mail package to use on your network. One of the most important things to consider when looking at mail systems is ease of use—if you want users to use the system, it has to be easy to understand and use; otherwise, they will pursue other means of contacting the administration staff.

REPORTING PROBLEMS

While everyone hopes that your users will never have problems, it is likely and probable that at some point, your users will encounter some sort of problem that they will not be able to resolve by themselves. Because of this, you will want to establish methods for your users to contact the administration team when they do have problems.

If your administration team consists of several people, you may want to have those people specialize in particular types of problems. By having specialists, your administration team can be better prepared to solve complex problems.

Your procedures for reporting problems should include some sort of escalation process, which should be outlined to your users. That way, if a problem is not resolved quickly enough, the problem's priority gets moved up until the problem ends up with the highest person in the network administration group. If that person is unable to resolve the problem, you should escalate the problem to your product support people—either with the vendor, a support group, or directly with Novell. If your users perceive that you cannot get problems resolved in a reasonable amount of time, they may start to lose faith in the administration team and start using alternatives to the network that are less efficient.

If your users encounter a problem that seems to be reproducible on their computer, they should be instructed to try to determine the steps needed to recreate the problem. That way, when a member of the administration team arrives to look at the problem, they can attempt to recreate it and possibly determine what the problem is.

Many problems, however, are not reproducible on demand. For this type of problem, your users will have to remember what they were doing at the time the problem occurred. This type of problem is generally much more difficult to solve, because you can apply several possible fixes to the problem, but not get the correct combination of fixes required to actually solve the problem. When a problem like this occurs, your users should be encouraged to save their work frequently during the process of trying to solve the problem. If the user is using applications that have an automatic save feature, that feature should be enabled.

From an administration standpoint, it may be useful to have predesigned forms, either hard copy or electronic, to document the steps taken to attempt correcting a problem. This will help ensure that you do not duplicate steps.

WORKGROUP ADMINISTRATOR TRAINING

All your workgroup administrators should receive the same training your end users receive; however, they should also be included in the decision-making process for many of the policies and procedures designed to help the end users. They should also receive additional training in certain areas—for example, they should receive instruction in how to solve basic networking problems.

because that renders the protection that passwords are supposed to
less. In order to help users with password security, you and your
administrators may elect to allow your users to choose passwords of their
have the password periodically expire. This will allow users to select a
that is easy for them to remember. However, many users may chose to use
s that are not secure, such as their first or last name, a birthdate, or a social
number. Whether such passwords are secure enough for your environment
thing that you will have to determine with your workgroup administrators.

er area of security that is becoming a growing concern in large organizations
sical security of software. You and your workgroup administrators will want
cuss this issue and determine if this is an issue for your organization and what
s need to be taken to ensure the security of the software used at your site.

e possible solution would be to provide software installations from the network
d store the physical distribution media in a secure place or with a company that
ovides off-site storage. By removing the media from the site, you ensure that the
oftware will not float around the office, and that unlicensed copies of software your
rganization has purchased will be made and distributed. The manuals for the
software can be stored either in a company library where everyone can access them,
or if you purchased complete software sets for individual employees, they may want
to keep the documentation in their office. If this is the case in your environment, your
workgroup administrators should discuss the issue of security with the users and
encourage them to store any software and manuals they may have in a secure
location within their office.

Finally, if your organization requires that network administrators not be allowed
to access certain sensitive data, such as payroll or employee data, you will want to
establish an external auditor. NetWare 4 has been certified for C2 level auditing,
which allows an external auditor to monitor the activities of the administrators and
other users on the network. The primary utility used for auditing is AUDITCON. Its
main menu screen is shown in Figure 31.6.

TROUBLESHOOTING PROCEDURES

You should have a problem-reporting and escalation mechanism in place when you
start connecting users to your network. Users may have problems with the network,
and having an effective means for them to report problems and have them resolved
quickly will ease their transition to using the network.

Your reporting mechanism can be one of any number of processes. You may elect to
have your users call their workgroup administrator when they first have a problem,
and have the workgroup administrator bring problems to you they cannot solve or
that may affect users in other parts of the network. You will want to stress to your

DEFINING NETWORKING TERMINOLOGY

As discussed earlier in this chapter, your end users will need to understand basic
networking terminology. Your workgroup administrators will need to understand
the same terminology as your users, but they also will need to understand most of
the terminology in more depth and they will need to learn more than the users.

Your workgroup administrators need to realize that the majority of your end users
will not understand the terminology used to describe networks and network
problems. For example, if you are using a token ring topology for your network and
a node begins to beacon and takes down an entire ring, the only thing that will
matter to your end users is that they cannot connect to the server, and thus cannot
get work done. Always remember that when there is a problem that affects users,
they will be interested primarily in how long it will take you to get things working
again. A detailed technical description of the problem will most likely only frustrate
them, and it will also take time away from you that should be spent solving the
problem. If you can briefly explain the problem in non-technical terms and estimate
how long it will take for you to solve the problem, your users will have a better feel
for where things stand, and they won't be frustrated by terminology they do not
understand.

A good exercise for you and your workgroup administrators would be to sit down and
collectively work out what various networking terms mean, whether the individual
terms are important for your end users to know, and how to best describe common
problems in terms that your end users can understand. Not only will this help your
end users, but it will also ensure that you and your workgroup administrators are
speaking the same language to your users.

ESTABLISHING STANDARDS

In the NetWare 4 documentation, Novell describes the creation of several different
standard documents. These documents describe different standards for your network, such as object-naming conventions, default property values, and defaults to
be used when creating new users. Your workgroup administrators should sit in on
discussions about how these standards should be set, as they will likely be familiar
with their users' needs.

Other standards that should be decided upon include the brands of computers and
network cards to be used within the organization. By standardizing the hardware
used in your organization, you will reduce the number of problems you have to deal
with, and also reduce the overall number of problems. Software standards should
also be established, and a list of approved software should be distributed to your
users.

Once the standards are decided, you should establish a procedure for deviating from a standard. For example, if you decide to standardize on using your users' first names as their login name, and then realize that you have two users with the same first name in the same container, you will want to have a means of deviating from your standard so that each user has a unique login name.

HARDWARE ACQUISITIONS

Your administration team should be involved in new hardware acquisitions, as they need to be familiar with the issues related to the hardware standards that you decided on. Users should not bypass the administration group when purchasing hardware if at all possible, as new network users may not be familiar with the established hardware standards and introduce new and untested hardware into the network that could potentially cause problems.

SOFTWARE ACQUISITIONS

As described previously, you should establish a list of supported and approved software. This list of software should include commonly requested items, such as word processing and spreadsheet software. Establishing this list will not only make support easier, but will also ensure that users will be able to use each other's documents with a minimum of problems.

Your software list should include version numbers whenever possible. When a new release of a product becomes available, you will want to obtain a single copy for testing purposes and determine if the upgrade is of value to your organization. Encourage your users to work with the workgroup administrators to determine if their software needs are met by software on the list.

You will want to establish a procedure for acquiring software that falls outside of the list of approved software. Such a procedure should include a period of testing to ensure compatibility with your network. If you encounter problems with the software during the testing period, your workgroup administrators should contact you to find out if you know of any compatibility issues, and if the problems persist, you or the workgroup administrator should contact the publisher.

ADDING NEW USERS

You and your administration team should decide upon criteria for determining when a user needs to be added to the network and should establish a procedure for creating new accounts. If your network is centrally administered, you may want to have the workgroup administrator create the new account and let you know that he has created an account. However, if you have chosen to distribute your network's administration, this may not be necessary.

When creating a new account, your wor[k] standards that have been defined for nam[e] and default drive mappings. If there is any you and your administration team should [c] looked at and expanded on. For example, if you a user's first name as their login name and then because two users in the same container have the to extend your standard to have the option of addin[g] as part of the login name.

SECURITY

Any network security system can be proven to be ineffective Your workgroup administrators will need to assist you in rein[forcing] of workstation security with your users, particularly in depar[tments] tive data—such as payroll data—is handled. Your workgroup [administrators] need to help you ensure and maintain security, both at the works[tation and] server.

Workstation security can be implemented in a number of ways. [In] Windows can be set up to invoke a password-protected screen saver afte[r a period] of time to prevent unauthorized people from using a machine while t[he user has] stepped away for a few minutes.

A step up from that would be to implement a security system that w[ill prevent] unauthorized users from accessing the workstation. Novell DOS 7, for [example,] includes this type of system, which prevents unauthorized users from sta[rting a] workstation with a diskette and accessing the hard drive. Use of this type o[f security] is beneficial, however, only if the workstation is turned off while the user [is away] from the workstation—for example, at the end of the work day.

Your workgroup administrators should encourage their users to store sensitiv[e data] on the network and log out when they will be away from their workstation [for an] extended period of time. Taking this step will prevent all users—with the exce[ption] of the administrator with Supervisory rights to the volume— from accessing [the] data. As you will see later in this section, administrators with rights to the [file] system can still be audited to determine if they have been accessing critical data[, and] in many environments, using the auditing features of NetWare 4 to audit netwo[rk] administrators is not only desirable, but necessary.

Your workgroup administrators will also be responsible for enforcing password policies within their workgroups. Your workgroup administrators should ensure that their users do not store their passwords in obvious places in their office. System sign-on information should not be written on a tablet that users keep next to their

users the importance of reporting network problems to you when they occur. Impress upon your users that problems that go unreported cannot be corrected.

Figure 31.6.
The AUDITCON main
menu.

Part of having this mechanism in place should include a formal escalation process to technical support people outside your organization. By letting your users know that you have this formal escalation process in place, they will be assured that any problems they encounter that you or your workgroup administrators cannot resolve will be passed along and every attempt to resolve the problem will be made.

In order for this process to be effective, you will want to train your workgroup administrators to troubleshoot common network problems. If it is feasible for your organization to do so, you should obtain a subscription to Novell's Network Support Encyclopedia, or NSE. The NSE Professional Edition (NSEPro) includes technical information on a large number of problems and solutions logged by Novell technical support personnel.

Additionally, you should maintain clear lines of communication with all of your workgroup administrators to ensure that all of the administrators are aware of the problems that have been encountered and the solutions to those problems. This will help ensure the fastest support to the end users of your network.

VIRUS IDENTIFICATION AND ELIMINATION

One particularly difficult problem to resolve in any environment is virus infection. In many cases, a virus infection may appear to be a typical network problem. Left untreated, however, a virus has the potential to render the data on your network useless.

NetWare has some inherent protection against viruses built into it. Both the NETX and the VLM client do not recognize many of the low-level input/output functions

31

WORKING WITH USERS

that many viruses use to infect disks. For this reason, viruses like the Yale/Alameda virus will not get into your network, but they can cause odd symptoms to occur. Other things that are a part of NetWare will also help keep viruses from spreading. For example, the Yale/Alameda virus was found on a workstation running WordPerfect 5.1—the only symptom was that WordPerfect eventually would start filling up disk space on the network until NetWare told it that the disk was full because of a user disk space restriction.

Other types of viruses, such as the file infector called Jerusalem-B, use higher-level functions that are supported by the NetWare clients. This type of virus can propagate on a NetWare system without any problems.

User education about viruses and how to deal with them can be an effective way to help protect your network against a virus infection. If you can provide your users with software to protect against viruses and show them how to use it to identify and remove a virus, you greatly reduce the possibility of your network becoming infected.

Let your users know what precautions you intend to take against viruses. Whether you use server-based software, workstation-based software, or a combination of the two, if your users are aware that the software is in place, they will rest easier knowing that the threat of a virus infection is something that the administration group is concerned about.

Ongoing User Support

Above and beyond training your users, you will want to provide continuing support for them. The ways of providing ongoing support within an organization will vary greatly, depending on the way the organization is structured.

DynaText

The use of Novell's DynaText documentation will help you provide your users with ongoing support. In many cases, your users will be able to answer their own questions about NetWare by checking the online documentation. By showing your users how to use DynaText to find information quickly, you give them the advantage of getting answers to their questions without calling for support.

Earlier, this chapter discussed defining terms for your users. In addition to providing them with a printed list of terms, you may want to direct them to the DynaText version of the *NetWare Concepts* manual. Figure 31.7 shows a typical entry in this manual. By entering a search term in the "Find" part of the Window, a user will get an indication in the outline as to where the search term was found. The user can also browse the collapsible outline for the term they are looking for and select the term in the outline with the mouse. The term and its definition will then display in the text window for the user to read.

Figure 31.7.
Using DynaText to
search for information.

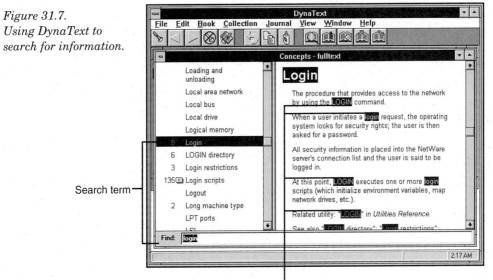

Search term

Found search term here

PHONE SUPPORT

All other means of support aside, most users are going to be the most comfortable just picking up the phone and calling someone when they have a problem. You should provide a list of phone numbers that your users can call in case they have problems. You may also want to have support available after normal hours to deal with problems that occur while the support staff is unavailable. The most popular method of providing support after hours is through the use of a pager. Some organizations provide a pager for their administration team, and then rotate the responsibilities of carrying the pager on a periodic basis.

Another advantage of having a pager is that many network servers now come with the capability of calling a pager number to inform the administrator of a network problem.

REMOTE CONTROL SOFTWARE

During the work day, users may encounter strange problems that seem to disappear when you go to look at them. In many of these instances, use of NetWare-aware remote control software will help you look at these problems more quickly. The nature of this type of software allows you to see exactly what a user is seeing without leaving your desk. In a physically large installation, this will let you look at a problem as a user sees it without having to navigate the building. Very often, while administrators run from their desks to a user's workstation to look into a problem, the user will start fiddling with the software and then not be able to reproduce the problem, or the user may actually solve the problem on their own.

Remote control software is a troubleshooting tool that can save valuable time in determining what a problem is and can help speed up resolutions for problems that are difficult to duplicate.

HELP DESK

Many large organizations use a help desk to help users with common problems. The help desk is staffed by a person who takes phone calls from users and provides solutions to common problems by looking the problems up in a database. The help desk person may also have authority to modify a user's entry in the directory services database—for example, if a user forgets their password, you may want the help desk to be able to change a user's password.

SUMMARY

This chapter discussed training users and workgroup administrators. Through the use of good tools, policies, and procedures, users can learn how to effectively use the network. When problems are encountered, users should have some options about how to deal with them and get them resolved as quickly as possible. Remember that the key to maintaining a good network is keeping the line of communications open between you, the workgroup administrators, and the end users.

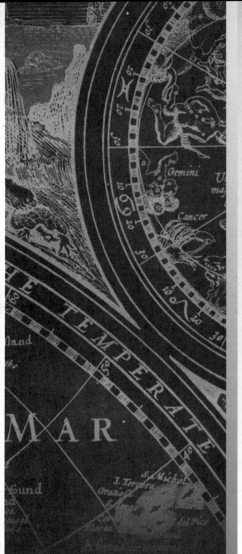

- Overview

- NetWare Print
  Services

- Workstation Setup

- Managing Print Jobs

- Managing Print
  Servers

- Setting Up and
  Customizing Printing

- Summary

CHAPTER 32

Network Printing

One of the most common uses for a local area network is the sharing of printing resources. NetWare printing services provide solid printing capabilities that are very flexible yet easy to set up. NetWare's printing environment is made up of the following five components:

- ◆ Print queues
- ◆ Printers (local or remote)
- ◆ Print servers
- ◆ Command-line utilities
- ◆ Menu utilities

This chapter gives you the necessary background information and step-by-step instructions on setting up a network printing environment in NetWare 4.

OVERVIEW

When you print from a stand-alone computer, the output goes from the workstation through the printer cable directly to the printer's buffer. Only after the entire print job has been printed or is in the printer's buffer is the computer free to perform other tasks.

When you print on a network, however, the job is sent from your workstation out through the network cable to the file server. The job then is directed into a print queue—a holding area, on the server volume. A queue assigns print jobs in the specific order in which they are printed. Queues can have English names to help you remember them, and are created through the PCONSOLE menu utility.

All print jobs are kept in the queues until the designated printer is available. The print server is in charge of polling the printers and servicing the queues to make sure that jobs are getting to the correct printers.

Generally, dedicated printers are used. However, Novell also offers the capability to share a locally attached printer. To enable the NPRINTER.EXE utility to function, you must set up a remote printer definition on a print server. The NPRINTER.EXE loads as a background task that uses approximately 5K of memory. Because of this background operation, it is not recommended to use this method for heavy printing.

NETWARE PRINT SERVICES

NetWare's printing environment consists of three primary components:

- ◆ Print queues
- ◆ Print servers
- ◆ Printers

The next three sections of this chapter discuss how to set up and configure each of these components. All the steps are accomplished using the PCONSOLE menu utility. The steps should be performed in the order given here.

Tip

If your printing needs are very simple, you can save time and effort by using the Quick Setup option in PCONSOLE (see Figure 32.1). With Quick Setup, you can easily and quickly define a print server, create a print queue, and, create and configure a printer to service that print queue.

Figure 32.1.
The Quick Setup option in PCONSOLE.

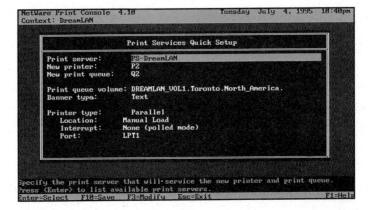

CREATE PRINT QUEUES

A print queue in NetWare is simply a directory on one of the NetWare 4 server volumes. The name of the directory is a hexadecimal number which corresponds to the print queue id. It is created as a subdirectory under \QUEUE.

Note

In NetWare 3 and prior, print queues are always created on the SYS: volume. However, starting with NetWare 4, you can place the queues on any volume of your choice.

The PCONSOLE menu utility is used to create print queues. You can use any name for the print queues, however, it is suggested that you use a combination of printer type and location to identify the queue. For example, you could use HP3_16S to indicate it is the HP III printer located on the south side of the 16th floor.

Tip

You must first create the print queues before you can set up a print server.

The following shows you the step-by-step for creating a print queue:

1. Type PCONSOLE at the DOS prompt.
2. Select the Print Queue option from the Available Options menu (see Figure 32.2).
3. Press Ins and add the new queue name, and then press Enter (see Figure 32.3).

Figure 32.2.
Main menu of
PCONSOLE.

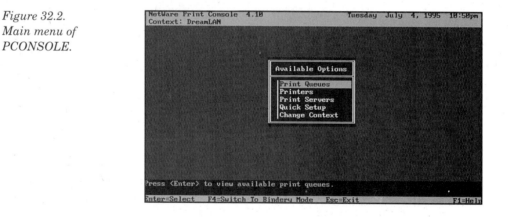

4. You then are required to specify the volume on which to place this print queue (see Figure 32.4). Use the Insert key to bring up a menu so you can "walk" the tree to locate the volume object name you want to use for the print queue.

Figure 32.3.
Creating a print queue.

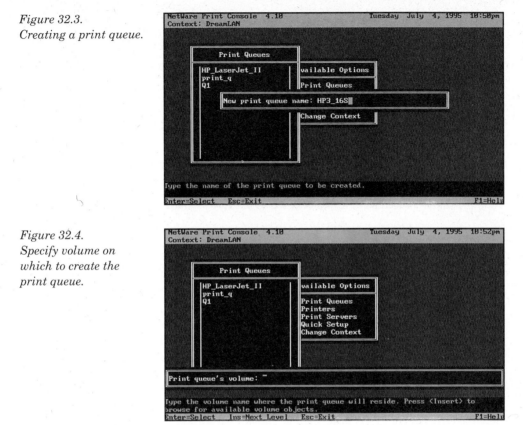

Figure 32.4.
Specify volume on
which to create the
print queue.

5. Repeat the preceding two steps for each print queue you want to create. Press Esc when you are finished. This takes you back to the main menu.

Now you are ready to create a print server.

CREATE PRINT SERVER

A print server contains information about printers, both local and remote. At the same time, it contains data that so jobs in print queues are send to the correct printer. This section shows you how to set up the print server. The next section provides the steps for creating printer definitions and associating them with print queues.

Tip

Print server names should be kept unique as they are created as NDS objects within your tree.

To create a print server, use the following steps:

1. From the PCONSOLE main menu, select the Print Servers option.
2. Press Ins and enter the new print server name (see Figure 32.5).

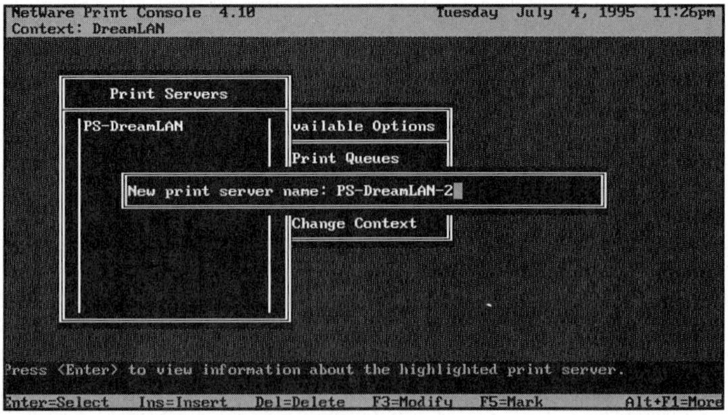

Figure 32.5.
Creating a new print
server.

You can now further configure the print server with printer information as outlined in the next section.

CREATE AND CONFIGURE NETWORK PRINTERS

In the NetWare printing environments, printers are classified either as locally attached or remotely attached. A local printer means the printer is directly attached to the machine that is running the print server software. A remote printer is one that is running the NPRINTER software on a workstation.

Note

On the market today are print server "black boxes." Some examples are HP JetDirect cards and Intel NetPort. These devices can be set up either in the dedicated print server mode or in the remote printer mode.

Use the following steps to set up your printers and associate them with the correct print queues:

1. From the Print Server list, highlight the print server you want to configure and press Enter. The Print Server Information screen will appear (see Figure 32.6).

Figure 32.6.
The Print Server
Information screen.

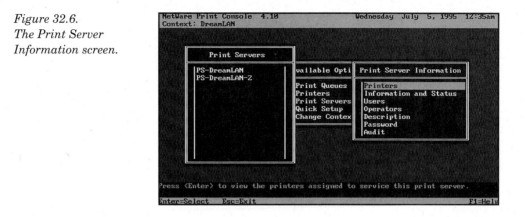

2. Select the Printers option and press Enter. If the print server is brand new, an empty Printers Serviced list will be displayed (see Figure 32.7). Otherwise, a list of defined printers are listed.

Figure 32.7.
Printers Serviced list of
the print server.

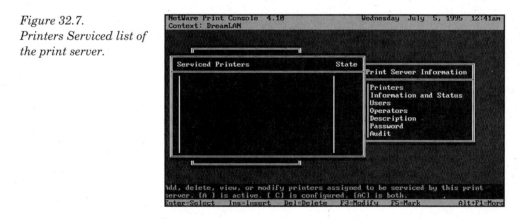

3. Press Ins to display a list of printer objects in your current NDS context. You can "tree walk" to the context in which you placed the printer. If you want to create a new printer object, press Ins again (see Figure 32.8).

Tip

The printer object name must be unique, and cannot be the same as an existing print queue name.

32

Figure 32.8.
Creating a printer NDS
object.

4. Highlight and select the printer you want to assign to the print server. The print server's printer list will be updated, as shown in Figure 32.9.

Figure 32.9.
The Printers Serviced
list is updated to
include the new printer.

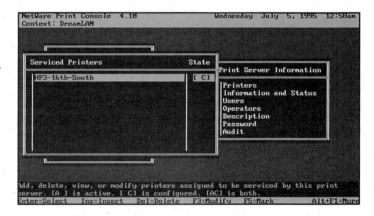

5. Highlight and select the printer from the Printers Serviced list.
6. By default, the printer is assumed to be using the parallel interface (see Figure 32.10). If your printer uses a serial interface, select Printer Type to bring up a selection.

Note

If you are using a printer that is connected directly to your network via a print server device, such as the HP JetDirect card mentioned earlier, you should set the Printer Type to Other/Unknown.

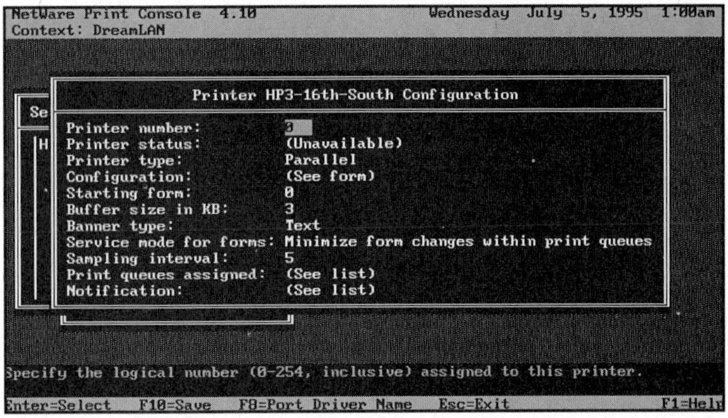

Figure 32.10.
A new printer defaults to parallel interface.

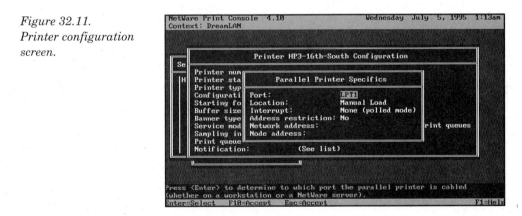

7. By default, the printer is assumed to be connected to LPT1 on a remote workstation—Manual Load (see Figure 32.11). Should the printer be locally attached to the print server machine, use the Configuration screen to change the Location setting from Manual Load to Auto Load (Local).

Figure 32.11.
Printer configuration screen.

8. Next, choose the Print Queues Assigned option to associate print queues to be serviced by this printer. Press Insert to display a list of print queue objects in your default context. Highlight and select the queue you want. This queue then is added to the list (see Figure 32.12).

Figure 32.12.
Print queue assigned to
the printer.

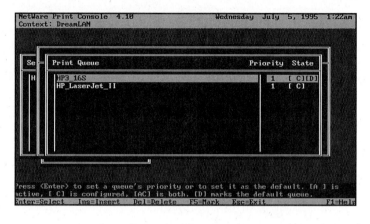

Note

You can have more than one print queue assigned to a single printer. The first print queue is designated as the "default" print queue (indicated with a [D]). It is used if a user redirects a print job using the printer reference rather than a print queue reference. The use of CAPTURE is discussed in a later section.

9. When you have finished defining all the printers you needed, press Esc to return back to the main menu.

You now are ready to load and test your print server configuration.

STARTING THE PRINT SERVER

Starting the print server is very straightforward. Because the print server software is an NLM, you need to do this at the server console (or via the use of RCONSOLE). At the server console, enter the following command:

LOAD PSERVER *print_server_name*

where the *print_server_name* should be full NDS name of the print server, if it is not located in the same context as the file server object. For example,

```
LOAD PSERVER .PS-DREAMLAN-2.DREAMLAN
```

Tip

To simplify the loading syntax, you can create an alias of the print server object and place it in the same context as the file server object. Therefore, you would not need to specify the NDS qualifiers when loading the PSERVER NLM.

You can load the PSERVER without any parameter. In this case, a menu appears and you can interactively enter the name or tree walk to the context where the print server object is located (see Figure 32.13).

Note

If you are using a printer directly attached to the print server, NPRINTER.NLM will be automatically loaded.

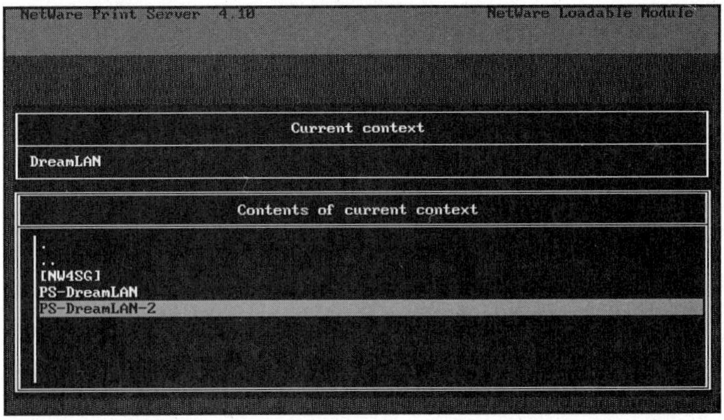

Figure 32.13.
PSERVER loading
menu.

When you have PSERVER up and running, you see a screen similar to the one shown in Figure 32.14. You have two options: Printer Status and Print Server Information.

The Printer Status option enables you to obtain detailed information about each printer you have configured for the print server (see Figure 32.15). The Print Server Information screen gives you some information about the print server software, number of printers configured, and its status (see Figure 32.16). You can use the Current Status selection to down the print server (see Figure 32.17).

32

Figure 32.14.
Print server main
menu.

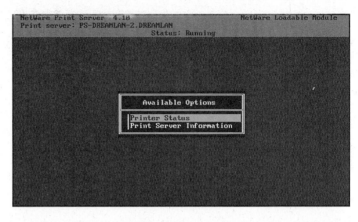

Figure 32.15.
Printer status screen on
the print server.

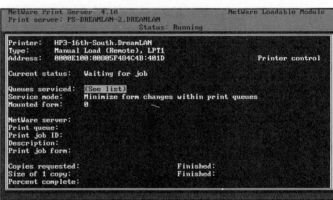

Figure 32.16.
Print Server Informa-
tion screen on the print
server.

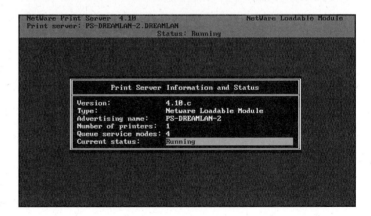

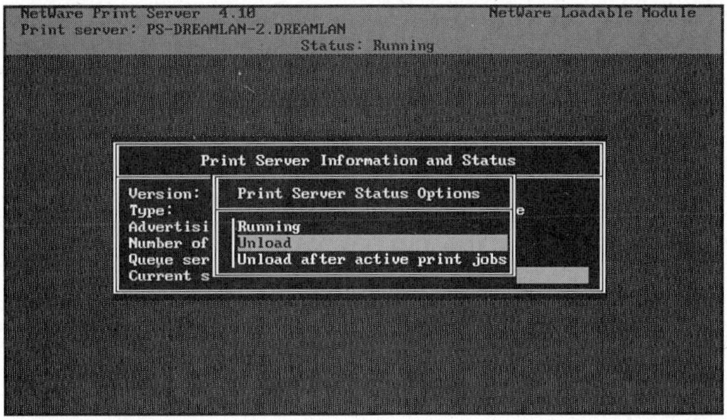

Figure 32.17.
Different options for
taking down the print
server.

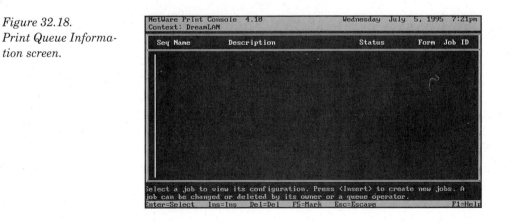

If your printer is connected locally to the print server, the Printer Status screen will show it is Connected.

TEST PRINTING

Because you have been working with PCONSOLE up to this point, you also can use PCONSOLE to submit a file to the print queue to see if the output comes out on the correct printer.

From the PCONSOLE main menu, follow these steps:

1. Select the Print Queues option.
2. Select the print queue name of interest.
3. From the Print Queue Information screen, select the Print Job option. You will see a screen similar to Figure 32.18.

Figure 32.18.
Print Queue Informa-
tion screen.

4. Press Insert to insert a print job.

5. You will be asked to specify the directory from which to print the file (see Figure 32.19). Then you will be presented with a list of files in that directory (see Figure 32.20).

Figure 32.19.
Specify directory from
which to print.

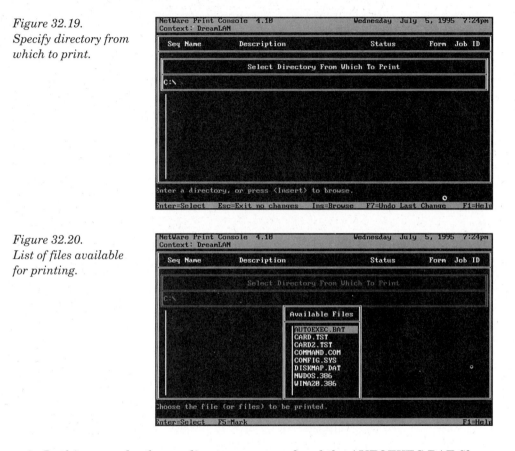

Figure 32.20.
List of files available
for printing.

6. In this example, the c:\ directory was used and the AUTOEXEC.BAT file was selected for printing. Choose the default print job configuration. If you want to print several files from the same directory, use the F5 key to mark them all before pressing Enter.

7. You have the option to modify a number of printing parameters, as shown in Figure 32.21, before you finally released the job for printing. Printing parameters are discussed in detail, later in this chapter.

8. When you are satisfied with the settings, press Esc to save the settings. Now the job is ready and awaits the print server (see Figure 32.22).

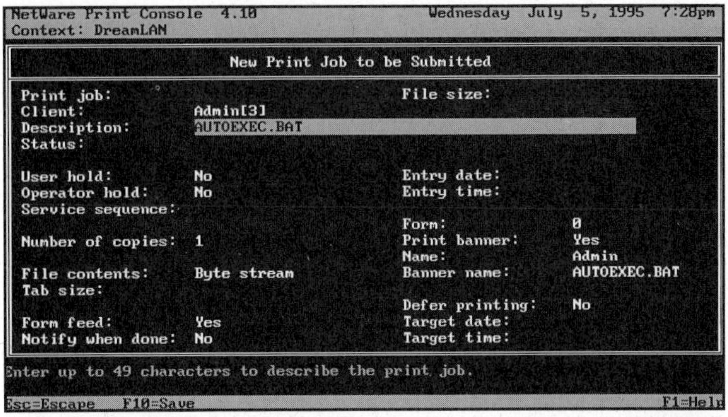

Figure 32.21.
Print job parameter
screen.

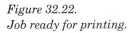

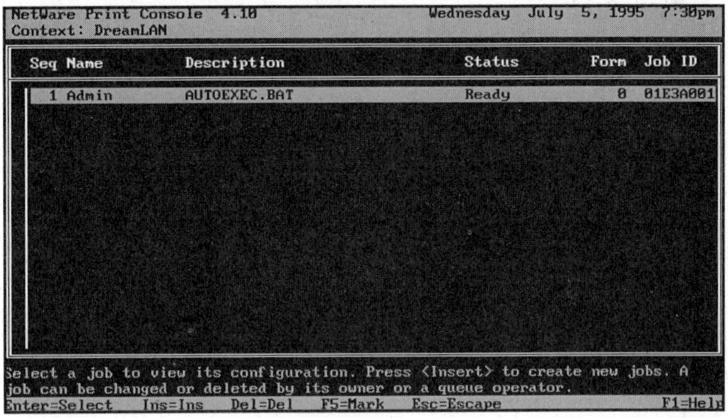

```
NetWare Print Console  4.10              Wednesday  July  5, 1995  7:28pm
Context: DreamLAN

                      New Print Job to be Submitted

Print job:                            File size:
Client:           Admin[3]
Description:      AUTOEXEC.BAT
Status:

User hold:        No                  Entry date:
Operator hold:    No                  Entry time:
Service sequence:
                                      Form:              0
Number of copies: 1                   Print banner:      Yes
                                      Name:              Admin
File contents:    Byte stream         Banner name:       AUTOEXEC.BAT
Tab size:
                                      Defer printing:    No
Form feed:        Yes                 Target date:
Notify when done: No                  Target time:

Enter up to 49 characters to describe the print job.

Esc=Escape   F10=Save                                          F1=Help
```

Figure 32.22.
Job ready for printing.

```
NetWare Print Console  4.10              Wednesday  July  5, 1995  7:30pm
Context: DreamLAN

Seq Name       Description           Status       Form  Job ID

 1 Admin       AUTOEXEC.BAT          Ready           0  01E3A001












Select a job to view its configuration. Press <Insert> to create new jobs. A
job can be changed or deleted by its owner or a queue operator.
Enter=Select  Ins=Ins  Del=Del  F5=Mark  Esc=Escape             F1=Help
```

If the print is correctly connected, the file will be printed on it shortly.

WORKSTATION SETUP

The printing setup on the workstation is comprised of the following two steps:

◆ Set up the printer so that you can print locally.

◆ Load the NPRINTER software so that the local printer becomes a shared printer.

In general, setting up a printer for local printing is no more than plugging in the power cord for the printer, and connecting the printer cable to the proper port (LPT or COM) on the workstation. If you are using serial printers, you also need to set up the correct communication rate, such as baud rate, number of data bits, and the protocol handshake (such as X-ON/X-OFF).

The loading of the NPRINTER software also is straightforward. It can be loaded with or without command-line parameters. Without command-line options, you will be presented with a menu as shown in Figure 32.23.

Note

You cannot load NPRINTER from within a DOS session in Windows. If you attempt to do so, the following message will be displayed.

```
NetWare Network Printer Driver 4.10.
(c) Copyright 1988 - 1994, Novell, Inc. All Rights Reserved.

NPRINTER-DOS-4.10-74: Windows is loaded in enhanced mode.
Load/unload NPRINTER before loading Windows.
```

Figure 32.23.
The NPRINTER menu.

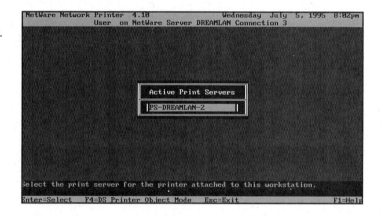

The menu will show all print servers available (active) on your network. Select the one you want to attach to. You see a list of defined printers (see Figure 32.24).

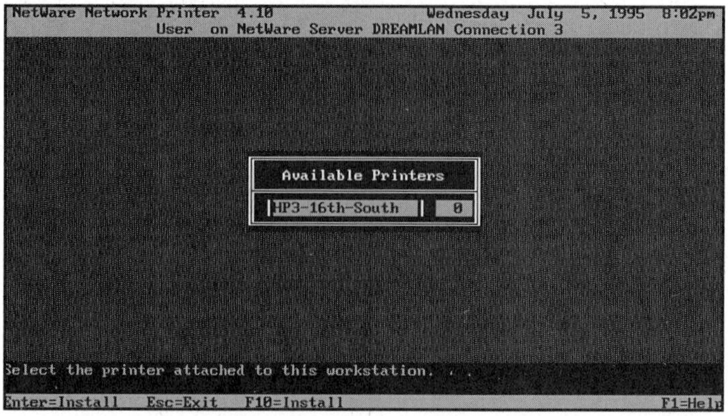

Figure 32.24.
Selecting a printer to which you want to attach.

Any jobs marked with the Held condition are not printed until the hold flag is removed. Two different hold flags can be placed on a job that has been queued to print. A User Hold can be placed on the file by pressing Enter on the job and changing the User Hold to Yes. The job owner and the queue operators can place and remove this flag. The Operator Hold flag can be placed or removed only by the queue operator. To set this flag, select the job to be held by pressing Enter, and set the Operator Hold to Yes.

The Adding condition designates a job that is in the process of being sent by a user. If the user has exited an application and the job still says ADDING, the user should type

ENDCAP

which forces the job into the Ready mode (CAPTURE and ENDCAP are discussed later).

The Waiting condition is shown when a print job has been told to wait until a specific date and time before printing. To set deferred printing, press Enter on the queued job and set Deferred Printing to Yes. You can define the Target Date and Time for that file to be printed.

Note The Ready condition is put on any job available for printing.

The sixth column, Job ID, keeps track of the print jobs that have gone through the queue.

Highlight any queued job and press Enter to display additional information about print jobs. Figure 32.26, for example, shows the information you can obtain and the parameters you can set for each queued job after pressing Enter.

Table 32.1 explains what some of the terms stand for in the Print Queue Entry

Figure 32.26.
Print job parameters.

```
NetWare Print Console  4.10                 Wednesday  July  5, 1995  9:12pm
Context: DreamLAN

                          Print Job Information

 Print job:         01E3E002              File size:       541
 Client:            Admin.North_America.[3]
 Description:       AUTOEXEC.BAT
 Status:            Print job is ready and waiting for the print server.

 User hold:         No                    Entry date:      7-5-1995
 Operator hold:     No                    Entry time:      9:03:11 pm
 Service sequence:  2
                                          Form:            0
 Number of copies:  1                     Print banner:    Yes
                                          Name:            Admin
 File contents:     Byte stream           Banner name:     AUTOEXEC.BAT
 Tab size:
                                          Defer printing:  No
 Form feed:         Yes                   Target date:
 Notify when done:  No                    Target time:

Enter up to 49 characters to describe the print job.

Esc=Exit                                                            F1=Help
```

Information screen.

TABLE 32.1. PRINT QUEUE ENTRY INFORMATION.

Item	Description
Print Job	Specifies the job number in the queue.
File Size	Specifies the size of the print job.
Client	Specifies who sent the print job.
Description	Specifies the name of the job.
Status	Denotes the condition of the job.
User Hold	Denotes the print jobs that are placed or removed by the job owner or queue operator. Held jobs are not printed.
Operator Hold	Denotes the print jobs that are placed or removed by the queue operator. Held jobs are not printed.
Service Sequence	Specifies the order in which the job is to be printed. By changing this sequence number, you can move a job ahead or behind other jobs.
Job Entry Date	Shows the date that the queue received the print job. This field cannot be altered.
Job Entry Time	Shows the time that the queue received the print job. This field cannot be altered.
Number of Copies	Specifies the number of copies of the file to be printed. This number can be set from 1 to 65,000.
File Contents	Specifies text or byte stream print jobs. Text converts indents to spaces. Byte stream enables the application to determine the printer codes.
Tab Size	Specifies the number of spaces to convert indents if File contents line is set to Text.
Suppress	Sets the form feed to On or Off.
Notify	Turns on or off notification of job upon completion.
Form	Sets the form number to use for the print job.
Print Banner	Sets the banner to On or Off.
Name	Displays the name printed on the banner. The sender's

Item	Description
	login name is the default.
Banner Name	Displays the file name by default.
Target Server	Displays the print servers that can service the current print job.
Defer Printing	Enables you to defer printing. Set to Yes or No.
Target Date	Enables you to set the time and day. The Time Default is set to the following day at 2:00 a.m.

Tip

If there are certain combinations of parameters you like to use often, you can set up a print job configuration. This is discussed later in the section entitled "Using PRINTCON."

STATUS

The Status option of the Print Queue Information menu has the following five items (see Figure 32.27):

◆ **Current number of print jobs**: Displays the number of print jobs currently in the queue.

◆ **Current number of active print servers**: Displays the number of active print servers that have this queue defined.

◆ **Allow users to submit print jobs**: Enables users to place jobs (Yes) or not place jobs (No) in this queue.

◆ **Allow service by current print server**: Enables you to have jobs printed (Yes) or not printed (No) in this queue.

◆ **Allow new print servers to attach**: Enables new print servers to service this queue (Yes) or denies new print servers access to this queue (No).

ATTACHED SERVERS

The Attached Servers option of the Print Queue Information menu shows a list of all servers servicing this queue. This option can be used to see which print servers currently are servicing jobs from the queue.

Figure 32.27.
Print queue status
screen.

```
NetWare Print Console  4.10                Wednesday  July  5, 1995  9:21pm
Context: DreamLAN

         ┌─── Print Queues ───┐
         │                    │
         │ HP_Las┌────── Print Queue Status ──────┐mation │
         │ HP3_16│                                │       │
         │ print_│ Current number of print jobs:      3   │
         │ Q1    │ Current number of active print servers: 1 │
         │       │                                │ervers │
         │       │ Operator Flags                 │       │
         │       │   Allow users to submit print jobs:    Yes │
         │       │   Allow service by current print servers: Yes │
         │       │   Allow new print servers to attach:   Yes │
         │       │                                │       │
         │       └────────────────────────────────┘       │
         │                                                 │
         │                                                 │
Choose No to prevent print jobs from entering the print queue.
Enter=Select   Esc=Exit                                   F1=Help
```

Note

All PCONSOLE screens are viewed in real time. As jobs are added
and deleted, servers attached, or print servers activated, you see the
screens change.

INFORMATION

The Information option of the Print Queue Information menu indicates the name of
the hexadecimally named subdirectory under \QUEUE with the QDR extension. Jobs
printed to this queue are held in the subdirectory until printed. It also shows the
volume and server on which the \QUEUE directory is located (see Figure 32.28).

Figure 32.28.
Information screen.

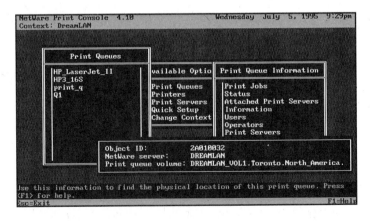

USERS

The Users option of the Print Queue Information menu lists all the users and groups that can add jobs to this queue.

Note

> The user that created the queue and the NDS container in which the print queue object is located automatically becomes queue users.

To modify this list, delete the group `container name`. You then can add users or groups to this list by pressing Insert and choosing the users or groups that can use this queue. Press Enter to accept your choices.

OPERATORS

The Operators option of the Print Queue Information menu lists all users who can manage the selected queue. Queue operators manage the queue and all jobs going through the queue. Users with NDS Supervisory rights automatically are queue operators. Queue operators can rearrange the order in which jobs print. They also can mark print jobs as Held so that they do not print. To add users or groups to this list, press Ins and select the users or groups that you want to manage this queue. Press Enter to accept your choices.

PRINT SERVERS

The Print Servers option of the Print Queue Information menu lists all the print servers that can service the selected queue. To add servers to this list, press Insert and select the desired servers. Press Enter to accept your choices. After a printer is defined and attached to the selected queue, the print server for which the printer was configured appears on this list.

MANAGING PRINT SERVERS

After you get the print server up and running using the steps described earlier, there are other setups or changes you can do to further customize your print servers.

From the Print Server Information screen (after selecting the Print Servers option from the PCONSOLE main menu), under Information and Status, a print server operator can view information about the server, similar to what you can see from the server console screen (see Figure 32.16).

In order to obtain information about a specific printer, you need to access the print server console on the file server. From the Printer Status screen, a number of status lines are available (see Figure 32.29).

The following service modes are available:

◆ **Change forms as needed**: This mode prompts the user to change forms each time a different form is encountered.

◆ **Minimize form changes across queues**: This mode specifies that the printer prints all jobs with the same form number before proceeding to the next highest form number. This procedure is done for all queues, regardless of queue priorities.

◆ **Minimize form changes within queue**: This mode specifies that the printer prints all jobs within a high-priority queue that share similar form numbers before servicing lower-priority queues.

◆ **Service only currently mounted form**: This mode prints only the jobs that have the current form number.

Figure 32.29.
Printer status screen.

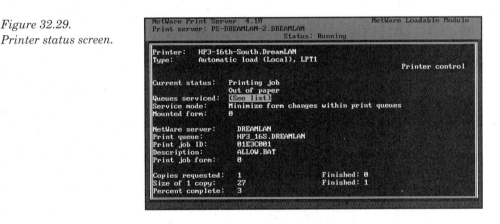

From the printer status screen, the Printer Control field can be accessed to perform certain actions on the printer. Press Enter to display the next options menu (see Figure 32.30). The following options enable you to modify the print job currently printing. These options are not available from the Print Queue options, which enable you to modify only those print jobs not currently printing.

◆ **Abort print job**: This mode enables the printer to abandon the current job. The job then is deleted from the queue. This method is the best way to stop a print job, because it clears the job from the print buffer.

◆ **Form feed**: This mode specifies that the printer advance to the top of the next page.

◆ **Mark top of form**: This mode prints a row of asterisks (*) across the top of the page to check form alignment.

◆ **Pause printer**: This mode temporarily pauses the printer. To restart the printer, select the Start Printer option.

◆ **Start printer**: This mode starts the printer if stopped or paused.

◆ **Stop printer**: This mode stops the printer and returns the print job to the queue. Printing is stopped until the printer is started again by using the Start Printer option.

Note

If you are familiar with the PSERVER software from pre-NetWare 4 versions, you will find that the Rewind Printer option is not available.

Figure 32.30.
Printer control screen.

```
NetWare Print Server  4.10                    NetWare Loadable Module
Print server: PS-DREAMLAN-2.DREAMLAN
                          Status: Running

Printer:    HP3-16th-South.DreamLAN
Type:       Automatic load (Local), LPT1
                                                    ┌──────────────────┐
                                                    │  Printer control │
Current status:    Printing job                     └──────────────────┘
                   Out of paper
Queues serviced:   (See list)                       ┌──────────────────┐
Service mode:      Minimize form changes within print qu│Abort print job│
Mounted form:      0                                │Form feed         │
                                                    │Mark top of form  │
NetWare server:    DREAMLAN                          │Pause printer     │
Print queue:       HP3_16S.DREAMLAN                  │Start printer     │
Print job ID:      01E3C001                          │Stop printer      │
Description:       ALLOW.BAT                          └──────────────────┘
Print job form:    0

Copies requested:  1                Finished: 0
Size of 1 copy:    27               Finished: 1
Percent complete:  3
```

As mentioned previously, you can down the print server from the Print Server Information screen of either the print server console screen or PCONSOLE (see Figure 32.17).

The Print Server Command (PSC), a DOS command-line utility, can be used to control and view the status of print servers. Many of the functions that you can control with PSC you can also do from within PCONSOLE. Sometimes, however, you might find that issuing a command at the DOS prompt is quicker than accessing a menu utility.

Table 32.2 lists the various flags available in the PSC command. The flags are discussed in more detail following the table.

32

TABLE 32.2. PSC FLAGS.

Flag	Description
AB	ABorts the print job
CD	Cancels a Down server
FF	Advances (Form Feeds) the printer to the top of the next page
L	Lists the print server layout
M	Marks an asterisk (*) at the printer head
MO	Specifies a different MOunt form
PAU	PAUses the printer
PRI	Specifies that the printer is PRIvate
SH	Enables the printer to be SHared
STAR	STARts the print job
STAT	Shows the STATus of the connected printers
STO	STOps the print job

The ABort flag stops the current job from printing. The job is deleted from the queue. The following command tells print server PS1 to abort the job going to printer 2:

```
PSC PS=PS1 P=2 AB
```

The Cancel Down flag enables print server operators to override the PCONSOLE command after the Going down after current jobs option in PCONSOLE is selected to down the print server. Use the following syntax when issuing this flag:

```
PSC PS=PS1 CD
```

The Form Feed flag is used to advance the printer to the top of the next page. The user must stop or pause the printer before she can issue a form feed. Use the following syntax when issuing this flag:

```
PSC PS=PS1 P=2 FF
```

The List flag allows you to list the print server information in a semi-graphical format as shown in Figure 32.31.

The Mark flag is used to position the form in the printer. The MArk flag places an asterisk (*) at the position of the printer head. The user can use any character to mark the form by placing that character after the Mark flag. When issuing this flag, use the following syntax:

```
PSC PS=PS1 P=1 M ?
```

Figure 32.31.
Print server layout.

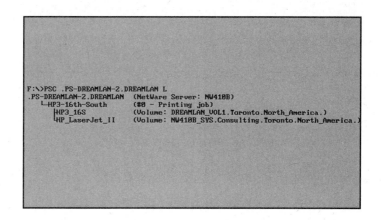

```
F:\>PSC .PS-DREAMLAN-2.DREAMLAN L
.PS-DREAMLAN-2.DREAMLAN   (NetWare Server: NW410B)
   └HP3-16th-South        (#0 - Printing job)
        ├HP3_16S          (Volume: DREAMLAN_VOL1.Toronto.North_America.)
        └HP_LaserJet_II   (Volume: NW410B_SYS.Consulting.Toronto.North_America.)
```

The MOunt form flag is used if you select a form number different from the one currently mounted. The correct syntax is MO=formnumber. Use the following syntax when issuing this flag:

PSC PS=PS1 P=0 MO=2

The PAUse flag temporarily pauses a printer. Use the following syntax when issuing the PAUse flag:

PSC PS=PS1 P=3 PAU

Use the STARt flag to resume printing.

The PRIvate flag is used when you are at a remote printer and want to prevent others from using the attached printer. This flag removes the printer from the print server list. When issuing this flag, use the following syntax:

PSC PS=PS1 P=2 PRI

The SHared flag is used after issuing the PRIvate flag. This flag enables the remote printer to be used as a network printer again. Use the following syntax when using this flag:

PSC PS=PS1 P=2 SH

The STARt flag is used to resume printing if the STOp or PAUse flags are issued. The syntax for this flag is the following:

PSC PS=PS1 P=2 STAR

Use the STATus flag to show the status of printers connected to a specific print server (see Figure 32.32).

32

STAT can display the following messages:

```
In private mode
Mark/Form feed
Mount Form n
Not Connected
Not installed
Offline
Out of paper
Paused
Printing Job
Ready to go down
Stopped
Waiting for a job
```

The STOP flag is used to stop the printer. When issuing this flag, use the following syntax:

```
PSC PS=PS1 P=3 STO
```

SETTING UP AND CUSTOMIZING PRINTING

When setting up the printing environment in NetWare, the most common command you will come across is CAPTURE. In this section, the use of CAPTURE and related commands will be discussed. Also presented are PRINTCON and PRINTDEF, two utilities that allow you to further customize your printing environment.

REDIRECTING PRINTER OUTPUT

If you are using an application written to run on a Novell NetWare network, chances are that the program knows how to "talk" to a network printer. Many newer programs enable you to define a queue name as a print device. In these instances, the user is not required to define the printing environment before entering the application.

A significant number of programs, however, still need help to print on a network. For these programs, the user must set up the printing environment before entering the program.

CAPTURE and NPRINT are two commands that enable you to print on the network. CAPTURE sets up a printing environment for the user. This command dictates the way all print jobs sent by that user are directed, and does not change unless the user reissues a CAPTURE command or logs out. NPRINT is used outside of an application to send a file to a printer. This command is intended specifically for a set of files and does not reset previous CAPTURE commands.

Note

Remember that NPRINT always requires a file name. CAPTURE does not.

THE *CAPTURE* COMMAND

CAPTURE sets up the printing environment for a user. Before using a print screen, the user must first execute a CAPTURE statement.

Figure 32.32 shows an example of a CAPTURE statement directed to the queue called HP3_16S, with no banners, no form feed, no tabs, and a timeout of 10 seconds.

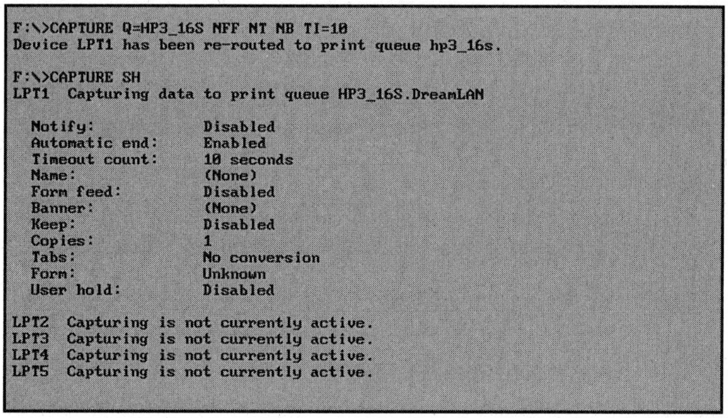

Figure 32.32.
A CAPTURE example.

```
F:\>CAPTURE Q=HP3_16S NFF NT NB TI=10
Device LPT1 has been re-routed to print queue hp3_16s.

F:\>CAPTURE SH
LPT1  Capturing data to print queue HP3_16S.DreamLAN

      Notify:              Disabled
      Automatic end:       Enabled
      Timeout count:       10 seconds
      Name:                (None)
      Form feed:           Disabled
      Banner:              (None)
      Keep:                Disabled
      Copies:              1
      Tabs:                No conversion
      Form:                Unknown
      User hold:           Disabled

LPT2  Capturing is not currently active.
LPT3  Capturing is not currently active.
LPT4  Capturing is not currently active.
LPT5  Capturing is not currently active.
```

The CAPTURE command is not used to print existing files; CAPTURE sets up the way in which a file is printed. The generic syntax when using CAPTURE is the following (the first set of options are common to both CAPTURE and NPRINT—NPRINT is discussed later):

CAPTURE *flags*

Shown in Table 32.3 are the various parameters you can use with the CAPTURE command.

TABLE 32.3. CAPTURE FLAGS.

Flag	Description
NOTI	NOTIfies when the job is done
NNOTI	Does Not NOTIfy when the job is done
S	Specifies the bindery server which holds the queue
P	Specifies the Printer (NDS object name)

continues

TABLE 32.3. CONTINUED

Flag	Description
Q	Specifies the Queue (bindery or NDS object name)
J	Specifies the Job configuration
F	Specifies the Form name
C	Specifies the number of Copies to print
T	Specifies the Tabs (TEXT)
NT	Specifies when No Tabs (BYTE STREAM) are used
B	Specifies when the Banner name is printed
NB	Specifies when No Banner is printed
NAM	Specifies the NAMe
FF	Specifies the Form Feed from the printer
NFF	Specifies No Form Feed from the printer
HOLD	Specifies the job is to be put on hold
D	Deletes the file after it is printed (NPRINT only)
EC	Specified end of capturing
TI	Specifies the TImeout period before printing
AU	Denotes AUtoendcap
NA	Denotes No Autoendcap
L	Specifies the Local port
CR	CReates a file
K	Keeps the received portion of the job in the file server and prints it
SH	SHows the current CAPTURE settings
?	Lists the available flags

When you use the NOTI flag, for example, NetWare notifies the user after the job is printed. When several jobs are buffered (temporarily stored in memory) in the printer, you might want to know when the job is ready for the user to pick up. The normal default is not to notify the user when the job has been printed. Both NOTI and NNOTI work with CAPTURE and NPRINT. Use the following syntax lines for each flag:

```
CAPTURE NOTI
```

When sending a print job to the printer as a text file, the Tabs flag is the fastest method of printing. Formatting codes are interpreted by the printer and text is printed. NetWare enables you to set the number of spaces between tabs at the command line. The default is eight.

When you use the No Tabs flag, all control characters are interpreted by the sending application. This also is called byte-stream printing. This method is slightly slower than text.

If an application is sending simple text, such as a nongraphics spreadsheet, send the job as Tabs. If the application sends more complex text, such as text created by a desktop publisher, send the job as No Tabs.

Note

If the printer adds miscellaneous characters on the page, switch printing methods. If you print the file by using the Tabs flag (text), then resend the print job and use the No Tabs flag (byte stream). The problem can occur when codes are being misinterpreted; the alternative method usually clears up any problems. No Tabs is a good default.

The T and NT flags work with both CAPTURE and NPRINT. Use the following syntax with these flags:

```
CAPTURE T=5
```

The preceding command requests a tab of five characters. The following command requests printing in byte stream:

```
CAPTURE NT
```

The network, by default, sets up a banner page before each job is printed. This page contains information about who sent the job, the name of the file, and when and where it was printed. The banner page is separated into three sections. The top section is information about the job and sender and cannot be modified. The second section is the name of the sender by default, and you can change it by using NAM=n (up to 12 characters). The third section, by default, is the name of the file; you can change it by using B=n (up to 12 characters).

If you do not have a need for a banner page, use the No Banner flag after the CAPTURE statement.

Note

Starting with NetWare 4, banner page is supported for postscript printers. However, you need to specify POSTSCRIPT for the Banner Type when setting up the printer in print server.

The Time Out option is worth some discussion here. When you print from an application, there is no way the print server will know when you have done printing and release the job. The Time Out option allows you to specify that—if there is no more print data after the "time out" period, assume the print job is complete and release it.

Warning

You need to give it some thoughts when specifying the Time Out value. If it is set too long, the user will have to wait longer in order to get their print job. If the time is too short, a single print job may end up as several ones, and may possibly be inter-mixed with other users.

TO STOP REDIRECTING PRINT JOBS

If the CAPTURE command is set up for No Autoendcap, then CAPTURE/ENDCAP must be specified at the DOS prompt before anything is printed. When used by itself, the ENDCAP option ends the CAPTURE statement to LPT1.

Note

You can also use the ENDCAP option to return the workstation ports to local use.

Table 32.4 lists the additional flags that you can use to direct the CAPTURE command when the ENDCAP (EC) option is also used.

TABLE 32.4. ADDITIONAL CAPTURE FLAGS.

Flag	Description
ALL	Ends the CAPTURE statement on all ports, such as ENDCAP ALL
L=n	Stops the CAPTURE statement to a specified port. Replaces n with the logical port number, such as ENDCAP L=1
CA	Ends the CAPTURE statement and abandons any data without printing it, such as CAPTURE EC CA

THE *NPRINT* COMMAND

The NPRINT command is used to print data files or files that have been formatted for a specific printer. The syntax for NPRINT is the following:

```
NPRINT filenames flags
```

Note

Wildcards are acceptable when indicating file names. And unlike PRINT from DOS, it is not a memory resident program.

A filename must be specified directly after the NPRINT statement and before indicating which flags to use.

The following NPRINT command prints all files with a .RPT extension to the HP3_16S print queue, without a banner page:

```
NPRINT *.RPT Q=HP3_16S NB
```

Using *PRINTCON*

You will find that there are a number of CAPTURE parameters you will use over and over again. It may become troublesome to have to type in a long string of options every time. The PRINTCON menu utility enables the system administrator or user to create print jobs with parameters similar to the CAPTURE flags. The JOB flag enables the user to call on one of the jobs that have been created. The J flag works with both CAPTURE and NPRINT. Use the following syntax with this flag:

```
CAPTURE J=LASER_LANDSCAPE
```

The print job configuration is stored either as part of an NDS user information, or if you want it be to globally available to a group of users, it can be associated with a container. Shown in Figure 32.33 is a sample print job configuration screen.

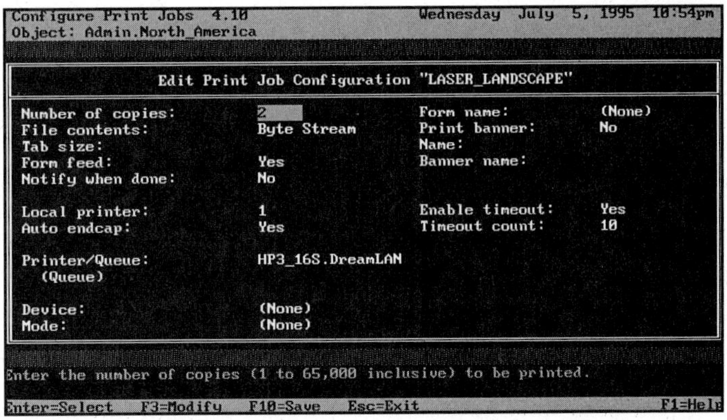

Figure 32.33.
PRINTCON screen.

```
Configure Print Jobs  4.10                    Wednesday  July  5, 1995  10:54pm
Object: Admin.North_America

            Edit Print Job Configuration "LASER_LANDSCAPE"

Number of copies:        2             Form name:        (None)
File contents:           Byte Stream   Print banner:     No
Tab size:                              Name:
Form feed:               Yes           Banner name:
Notify when done:        No

Local printer:           1             Enable timeout:   Yes
Auto endcap:             Yes           Timeout count:    10

Printer/Queue:           HP3_16S.DreamLAN
  (Queue)

Device:                  (None)
Mode:                    (None)

Enter the number of copies (1 to 65,000 inclusive) to be printed.
Enter=Select   F3=Modify   F10=Save   Esc=Exit                    F1=Help
```

Setting up Print Devices using *PRINTDEF*

If you have a printer capable of advanced features and fonts and you are using a program that does not know how to make full use of the printer's capabilities, you can solve this problem by using PRINTDEF. Perhaps you want to print a document sideways from a spreadsheet program using condensed print. This type of printing can be difficult to set up internally in the spreadsheet program. By using PRINTDEF, however, you can define a mode that has the functions necessary for the printer to print condensed and sideways.

To edit, import, or export print devices, select the Print Devices option in the PRINTDEF Options menu. The Print Device Options screen appears (see Figure 32.34).

Figure 32.34.
PRINTDEF screen.

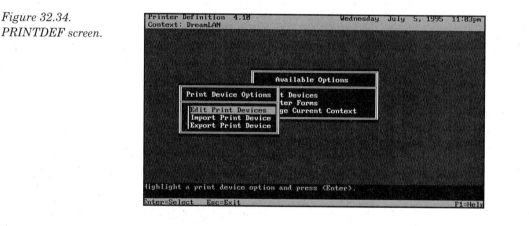

The PRINTDEF command contains a database of information about printers. Each printer has an entry in this database. If you create a print device and want it to be used on another network, you can select the Export Print Device option. This option enables you to create a file with a printer definition file (.PDF) extension that you can copy and import into another network.

Importing is done when an administrator wants to use a PDF file that someone else has created. A large list of printer definition files are included with NetWare. These files are copied into the SYS:PUBLIC directory.

Note

By default, the PDF are kept in SYS:PUBLIC.

To see a list of PDFs in the SYS:PUBLIC directory (or whatever directory contains the files), select the Import Print Device option in the Print Device Options menu. Press Enter again and NetWare displays a list of PDF files. To import a .PDF file into the list of editable items, highlight the file and press Enter.

If you activate the Edit Print Devices option, a submenu appears that enables you to edit device modes or device functions. A device mode is a list of functions that produce a desired output.

You must begin this editing process by activating the Device Functions choice. When you press Enter after highlighting the Device Functions option, NetWare displays a screen that shows all the escape sequences necessary for a specific printer (see Figure 32.35). To add new functions, press Insert and input the escape codes. You can input the codes in ASCII or hexadecimal format.

Figure 32.35.
Printer function
definition screen.

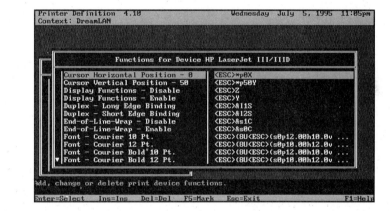

The other Edit Device option, Device Modes, enables you to combine print functions to customize the printer output. Shown in Figure 32.36 is a sample device mode for an HP III printer.

Figure 32.36.
A sample device mode
for HP III printer.

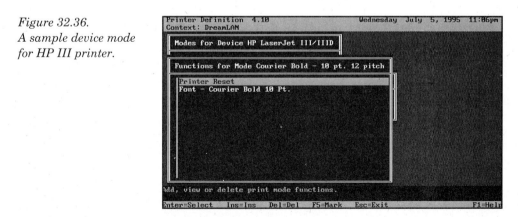

To use the modes and devices defined here, you need to set up print job configurations in PRINTCON, discussed in an earlier section.

CREATING FORMS USING *PRINTDEF*

By using the PRINTDEF menu utility, the system administrator can create forms. Forms in NetWare force a user to verify that the proper form (or special paper) is in the printer before printing begins. At the command line, the user can specify which form to use for a particular print job. The default is form 0. The Form flag works with both CAPTURE and NPRINT. Use the following syntax with this flag:

```
CAPTURE F=5
```

The second choice under the PRINTDEF Options menu is Forms. Some businesses need to share one printer for several different types of forms. By creating jobs that use different forms, you can control the printer's use. Each time the printer encounters a change of form, it waits until either a statement is typed at the file server (such as PRINTER *printer_number* MOUNT *form_number*) or the Print Server command is issued (such as PSC PS=*print_server_name* P=*printer* MO=2). You can replace *form_number* with *form_name* when mounting a form with PSC.

After you select the Forms option, NetWare displays the Forms and Form Definition screen (see Figure 32.37). Table 32.5 describes the four items that you need to fill in to define a form.

TABLE 32.5. FORM DEFINITIONS.

Item	Definition
Name	Specifies the form's name, up to 12 characters
Number	Specifies the form number, from 0 to 255
Length	Indicates the number of lines in the form, between 1 and 255
Width	Indicates the number of columns in the form, between 1 and 999

Figure 32.37. PRINTDEF's Forms screen.

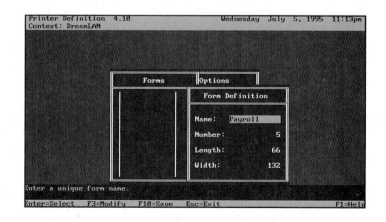

The form's length and width are there to help the Administrator keep track of the form's use. Neither the network nor the printer are affected by these numbers.

SUMMARY

NetWare's printing environment is made up of five components:

- ◆ Print queues
- ◆ Printers (local or remote)
- ◆ Print servers
- ◆ Command-line utilities
- ◆ Menu utilities

In this chapter, detailed information about creating, configuring, and managing print queues and print servers was provided. Also discussed were the use of CAPTURE, NPRINT, PRINTCON, and PRINTDEF to customize your network printing environment.

- The Value of Network Applications

- Rightsizing, Downsizing, and Upsizing

- Basic Features of a Network Application

- Taking the Plunge: From Sale to Service

- Summary

CHAPTER 33

Selecting Network Applications

Sometimes it is easy to get lost in the "how" and forget the "why." This especially is true when looking at ways that technology can help to make an organization more efficient. Product marketing is scattered all over the place and it is costing you an arm and a leg to fly people back and forth. The Art Department needs to shorten the time to publication because they are delaying product on its way to market. You are losing money because your clients' accounts are delinquent, and Accounts Receivable is tracking customer invoices on paper. It is the problem that starts you looking for a solution, and when it comes to making an organization more efficient, you recognize that better information management is part of that solution.

It is going to take planning, time, and a considerable amount of soul-searching to determine what type of changes need to be made within your organization. Some changes may be fairly straightforward, while others may require re-working or re-engineering certain business processes. People who create memos using a word processor, for example, may adjust to using an electronic mail (e-mail) package quite easily. They already know how to type, edit, spell-check, and print simple documents, and so a decent e-mail application may not be such a challenge for them. And the payback is obvious. The users can stop walking to the printer, stop waiting for the fax machine, and focus on more important matters.

If you rely too heavily on a new application itself, and ignore the need for change in other areas, your organization may end up spending a lot of money on something that never gets used. Begin by mapping out your objectives, deadlines, and your constraints. Find out how the people within your organization work. How does Product Marketing share ideas with each other and with the engineers in Manufacturing? How does the Art Department circulate copy and artwork for review? How does Accounts Receivable track delinquent accounts? Do not be immediately concerned with the lower-level details such as, "How can I connect Product Marketing's Macintoshes with the IBM PCs in Engineering?" Focus first on the objectives and then the means of encouraging the flow of information from person-to-person.

You will need to take into account which applications' tools people are already using. If your organization has not made extensive use of personal computers in the past or previous networks have been limited to a number of small workgroups, this may not be terribly important. But if people are at all familiar with, for example, a specific drafting program, word processor, or database application, and their work pattern does not necessarily need improving, you need to realize that this is experience can be an asset and not necessarily a liability. Do not force people to switch to an application simply because it is a newer version or it has more features. By easing their transition into a networked environment, you can capitalize on their experience and get more value from the network in the end. If their work pattern does not require significant change and their existing applications will work sufficiently well in the new networked environment, it may be better to wait.

Now, on the other hand, some people may not be particularly attached to a specific program, or their work pattern simply needs improving. In this case, you may have the opportunity to introduce a new network application tool that will greatly enhance their ability to function efficiently within your organization.

As your network infrastructure is just coming together or expanding into new areas, you may see the need to select some new applications for your network. A basic understanding of network applications will help you survive to realize their benefit. This chapter highlights some of the more important elements of this process.

It is best to begin by looking at the various types of network applications as the following sections will attempt to do. Although these sections will mention the names of a few specific products, they should not be construed as product endorsements. The market for network applications is too large and the solutions they provide are too numerous to make specific recommendations. Again, it will be up to you to decide what makes the most sense for your organization.

THE VALUE OF NETWORK APPLICATIONS

Now you are knee-deep in a tangle of coaxial cable and you have enough manuals lying around to open a small library. Now is the time to remember the "why." By installing and maintaining a solid, networking infrastructure you answer the "how," the answer to "why" is found in increased efficiency through network applications.

It is popular right now to think of a network as a highway for information. The cables are the roads; the routers are the road signs, junctions, and off-ramps; the servers and workstations are destinations along the way. A network provides a way for information to get from one point to another, just like a highway allows us to get to work. But the network itself does not solve any significant problems or add real perceived value. It requires some higher intelligence to make it all worthwhile. That higher intelligence is the people that the network connects and in the network applications they use.

A little more than ten years ago, networks were designed to do little more than pool and preserve physical resources. Use one instead of ten dot-matrix printers for every ten people, and sell the other nine. Swap word processing documents by copying them to and from the file server, and eliminate the use of diskettes altogether. But, today, as system software has grown more complex and hardware more powerful and less expensive, networks concentrate more on pooling and preserving ideas and information instead.

THE IDEAL APPLICATION

The essential difference between a network application and a "non-network" application is its support for multiple users. Rather than working alone, people can use the network and the applications designed for it to collaborate. Network applications can enable people to divide and conquer large projects and tasks, allowing them to work as groups.

The ideal network application understands both the network and the people that use it. It will leverage the services that the network provides, take into account all of the technical complications of a multi-user environment, and accommodate the way people work. Network software that fits this description is sometimes called *groupware*.

Although groupware is not really something that you buy once and are done with, almost all network applications these days can be considered groupware in one way or another. Groupware rather describes a way of working, and in practice, it describes applications or sets of applications that offer a variety of services which, taken together, amount to groupware. The term most likely came into widespread use in response to the growing popularity of applications such as Lotus Development Corp.'s Notes, WordPerfect Office/GroupWise from WordPerfect, and Novell, Inc.'s Applications Group. These programs are designed to facilitate conversation-like interactions and information exchange.

Warning

Products like Notes and WordPerfect Office/GroupWise are quality, popular network applications, but they are not necessarily easy to install and manage. If you are just getting a new NetWare 4 network up and running, it is recommended that you let the network grow on you and other users for a time before tackling a big project like a Lotus Notes installation.

A Marketing group might use something like Lotus Notes to encourage everyone to make comments, contributions, and observations about a new product launch plan, for example. Within a single interface, Notes users can post work that they have done in a word processor or spreadsheet application and solicit comments from others by way of free-form notes that may include the author's name, creation date and time, and other helpful information. Lotus Notes is designed to be highly customizable, and in reality, it should probably be thought of as a network application development tool itself.

Tip

Try starting with an e-mail package that will eventually work with Notes, WordPerfect Office/GroupWise, or whatever comprehensive groupware-type system you think you might adopt at a later date. Besides basic file and print services, e-mail applications are a staple on any network and one of the most popular reasons for installing a network.

These specific examples aside, following are some higher-level features you will find in only the best network applications:

◆ People who work the most with the application will get the most out of it.

◆ It will attract enough users to be successful.

◆ It will allow for flexibility in processes that are already common to the group using it.

◆ The users will be able to improvise to a certain extent.

◆ The application will not be too hard to evaluate in a test network environment.

◆ It will be easy enough for the entire group to use—from department administrator to department manager.

The situation in the real world, as you will undoubtedly find, is never quite so ideal. A little further on, some of the things previously outlined will be used to help you in your evaluation of competing network software products, but before that, it makes sense to discuss some of the basic types and categories of network applications. Two of the more important and widely used network applications are database and workflow, and so, a considerable amount of time will be spent elaborating on these topics. Perhaps, this discussion will spark some creative ideas in your mind about how to solve some of the particular problems you and your organization face.

DATABASE

The concept of a relational database management system (RDBMS) was developed by Dr. E.F. "Ted" Codd, an IBM researcher, in June 1970. But it was not until some time after that the database became a practical application on personal computers and local area networks. A database application deployed on a LAN behaves quite differently than a database on a minicomputer or mainframe, primarily because of the distributed nature of data processing on a LAN.

It used to be, and still is in a significant number of installations, that all database processing was done in one place, on the minicomputer or mainframe itself. The user worked at a dumb terminal which behaved more like a remote control device than a computer in the strict sense. The users' keystrokes were sent over a wire to the host where their program was running side-by-side with all the other users' programs, and the host responded by returning information to update the screen on the user's terminal. The host was responsible for all the hard work. It had to interface with the user and, at the same time, retrieve, update and basically manipulate data from the database.

Today's database model, the client/server database model, specifies that the user's machine and the host should share the work. Small desktop systems are now a lot more capable, available, and affordable than ever, so it makes sense to let the desktop take care of the all of the user's interface, where graphics and useability issues are a concern, and make the server handle all of the database manipulation, where massive storage and speedy information retrieval is more important.

In order to make an informed choice of your database application needs, you need to have a sound understanding of the two database models that are used today: single-user and client/server. They are discussed below.

SINGLE-USER DESKTOP MODEL

Personal computers also made possible the idea of a "personal" database, where your own computer can play terminal and host at the same time. While convenient for individuals and small organizations where only a small amount of information needs to be maintained and the need to share information is minimal, databases designed for use by a single-user on a single machine are severely limited in a LAN environment. Figure 33.1 diagrams the basic components of a single-user database application.

Figure 33.1.
A single-user database
application can assume
total ownership and
full access to its own
program code and data.

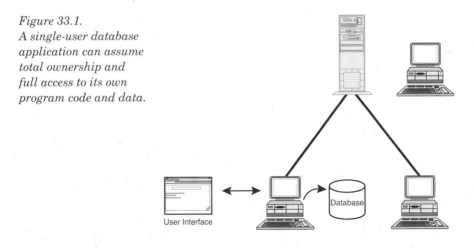

User Interface

Database

Try putting an old, single-user version of a database on a network and watch what happens when two users try to access the same database at the same time. Database applications designed for one user assume that the data is always available, and as a result, the users get really frustrated if one of the users tries to save changes to a database or a record that has already been opened by another user.

Another limitation is more obvious when the users are a considerable distance apart. One or both of the users are going to have performance problems. Single-user database applications are a little spoiled in this way. These programs are designed to run on a single machine with the program code and data stored locally where it can be read from disk quickly. Database application designers facing performance problems when creating these types of databases can save themselves a lot of hard work by keeping big chunks of data in the workstation's memory as the program works through searches, additions, and updates to the data.

It is much quicker for such an application to manipulate data that is already in memory, but in a LAN or WAN environment the cost of keeping all that data in memory can outweigh the benefit. Limitations in the performance of servers shared by a number of users or in the performance of the wide-area network connection make the single-user desktop database model impractical to retrieve large amounts of data.

CLIENT/SERVER MODEL

Dr. Codd's model for database design, although much older than the PC-inspired single-user model, fits nicely in a network environment. An Relational Database Management System (RDBMS) database application designer can separate the portion of the program responsible for controlling the user interface from the portion responsible for data manipulation, which translates into big wins for the user and database administrator. Figure 33.2 shows how a client/server database can be created using this "divide and conquer" method of application design.

When a user starts up a database program, the application running on the workstation (client) attempts to establish a connection with the appropriate database engine (server). After the user is validated with a password and the physical connection is made and operating properly, the client can request information from the server.

Note

The components of a client/server system must agree to speak the same language before any actual exchange of data can begin. The language most widely used for this type of communication is called Structured Query Language (SQL).

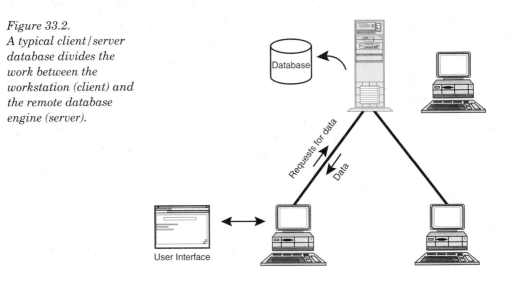

Figure 33.2.
A typical client/server
database divides the
work between the
workstation (client) and
the remote database
engine (server).

These requests can take a variety of forms, but they all have one important thing in common. Unlike requests for remote data made by a single-user database running on a LAN or WAN, client/server requests do not result in the transmission of large chunks of data. Rather, the requests sent by the client, in the form of SQL statements, are simply streams of ASCII text, usually not a whole lot more than a couple hundred characters in size. And, more importantly, the server will respond in the same way using ASCII text. The amount of information sent back to the client can be reduced to an absolute minimum because the server is capable of processing the data on its own and returning only the data the client requests. Figure 33.3 shows a basic SQL statement and the subsequent response from the server.

Besides reducing traffic on the network, a client/server database is able to deal with multiple users more effectively than a single-user database. The client portion of the database does not have to keep track of open (and, as a result, locked) files, locked records, or any changes made to the database. Instead, this is left to the server. Requests for information from the database do not actually change the information or make it any less accessible to other users. Of course, when information is changed at the client, that information will not be written back to the database until the client sends a request for the server to do so.

As the user of a client/server database application you will benefit from the following:

♦ Better performance during data retrieval, search, sort, update, and other operations

♦ Data that is assessable from anywhere on the LAN/WAN

♦ Added data security from centralized user access control

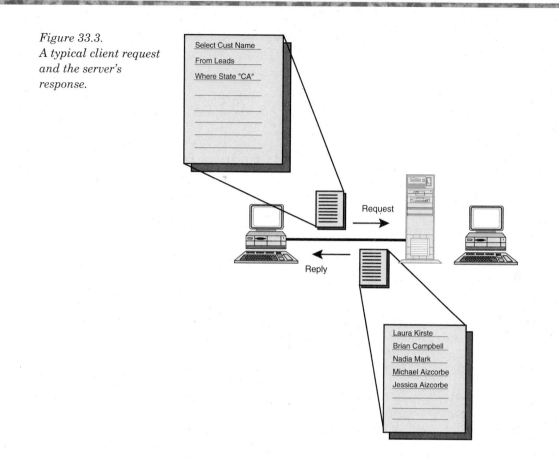

Figure 33.3.
A typical client request
and the server's
response.

Rightsizing, Downsizing, and Upsizing

In your experience in reading industry publications or researching network applications, you may come across some new buzzwords. "Rightsizing," "downsizing," or "upsizing" are terms usually used in the context of discussing the ways that businesses today are changing the way their organization handles information.

As mentioned earlier, data and database management in large organizations was handled by minicomputers and mainframes. These systems were typically terribly expensive, difficult to manage and maintain, and just plain big, often taking up entire rooms and needing specialized temperature and environmental control systems just to operate properly and efficiently.

Now, cheaper, smaller, faster rules the day. Network operating systems like NetWare 4 and the hardware they use offer organizations a better way to work. Not only have these systems grown physically smaller, but the cost of management, maintenance, and the applications they use have gone down, too. With so many types of systems to choose from, it is probably best to think of "rightsizing," "downsizing," or "upsizing" as simply ways to describe the process of finding the *right kind* of system or applications for you particular organization.

The following sections present some of the key elements to look for when choosing a particular type of application, such as the user-friendliness when selecting an electronic mail package.

WORKFLOW

Although it is a little more descriptive than some other terms, "workflow" is also one of these new buzzwords. The workflow concept pulls together elements of business process re-engineering (BPR) and client/server network systems. Workflow software essentially automates the routing of information within an organization, and it usually does so through the use of a client/server architecture.

Workflow applications are very much related to database applications in this way, and they often work with the same types of data. But the two normally differ in the way data is handled and the way it is presented. Where a basic client/server database application may simply offer a way to store and report information on customers, products, and sales, for example, a workflow application may allow users to track the progress of selling products to particular customers.

A workflow application may be the solution to the problem described in a previous example where department managers in Customer Service and Sales were butting heads over the handling of sales leads. By connecting both departments via the same client/server system, workflow software could help the Customer Service representatives route sales leads to the Sales office closest to the customer. Such a system would also help the organization's leaders better manage work by allowing them to see what customers should be pursued and what kind of income may result.

Even in this simple example, it is easy to see how workflow systems can affect both the business process and the people involved. In the process of moving to such a system, the groups must map out the way they work and the way information should flow in the handling of sales leads. In the process, they may discover inefficiencies in the previous system or duplication of effort. In a more complex example, eliminating or adding process steps may mean eliminating, shifting or changing certain jobs.

You will find that the human element plays a very important and complicated role in the search for the ideal workflow network application. You certainly do not want people to feel like they are being watched and managed by Big Brother, but at the same time, something needs to be done to keep your organization operating efficiently.

Warning

Although the capability is there and it is definitely tempting, it is not recommended that workflow systems be used to track people's performance on the job. People may reject the system to such an extent that it becomes useless.

In the discussions of messaging, multimedia, and other types of network applications to follow, you may notice that a variety of tools can be used by software developers to create and deploy workflow systems. Thomas Koulopoulos, president of Delphi Consulting Group Inc. in Boston, identified, for the sake of simplicity, the following three categories of workflow software:

- **E-mail-centric**: These products use an existing electronic mail system for routing work, and many employ utilities for creating, filling out, and tracking electronic forms.

- **Document-centric**: The focus is on the document as the basic information object in these products.

- **Process-centric**: These products are document-based in that they use an underlying database of some kind. Both process-based and document-based products can also be considered to be database-centric.

The type of workflow software that you choose for your organization depends on the type of tasks that need to be automated. If your organization is small or your workflow needs are minimal, mail-based software makes a lot of sense because it is easy for the average person to understand. For example, most people have had the experience of filling out and returning a form that they receive in the mail through the local post office. Learning to do the same thing using e-mail is a trivial matter provided that the e-mail program itself is relatively easy to use. WordPerfect InForms is a good example of an e-mail-based workflow product. It consists of a designer for creating forms and a filler for using them. Forms are routed and revised using a simple messaging system.

If your organization is larger or your workflow needs great, something more complicated and tied into a relational database makes sense. A new product from IBM, called FlowMark, is a large scale workflow application that runs in a client/server environment. According to IBM, it provides facilities for capturing and building a process model and then supporting the real-time execution of the business process.

Either way, you will learn that workflow systems basically automate two types of tasks:

◆ Structured tasks

◆ Unstructured or ad hoc tasks

Structured tasks follow a process that can be defined in advance and include a variety of information types in addition to being somewhat replicable or common. For these tasks, it is important that the tools integrate well with the existing system and provide useful management features. The basic design of a structured workflow task is portrayed in Figure 33.4.

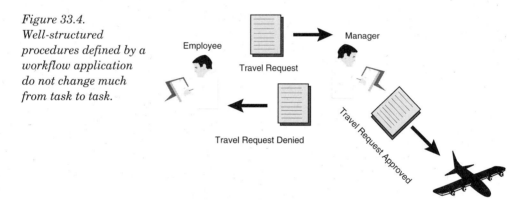

Figure 33.4.
Well-structured
procedures defined by a
workflow application
do not change much
from task to task.

Employee

Travel Request

Manager

Travel Request Approved

Travel Request Denied

Suppose that an organization requires its employees to fill out a request form before purchasing airline tickets. The process is always the same. The employee begins by filling in their name, telephone extension, desired travel dates, accommodations, and any other information that relates to their particular travel needs. The employee then signs the form and forwards it to the department manager, and, from there, the manager either approves the request by signing the form and passing it along to the general manager, or the manager returns it to the employee for modification. The process continues this way until the employee receives the tickets or until the request is denied. There is not a whole lot of room there for variation. Each request for travel is defined by a rather rigid structure. A structured workflow application designed to automate this process would add value in several ways:

◆ Expedite the process of obtaining approval for travel

◆ Prevent the employee from having to fax their travel request all over the place for approval. It might do this by sending forms over e-mail

◆ Not require that the employee know exactly who needs to approve what and how. That is, the application itself would be programmed with information such as "Forward all international travel requests directly to the general manager for approval. Domestic travel requests can be approved by the department manager alone."

◆ Allow the employee to track the progress of their request

◆ Offer management a way to immediately store and retrieve information on travel requests histories

Unstructured tasks, on the other hand, have only a limited amount of structure but tend to be adaptable to a wider variety of situations. They are not as easy to duplicate and are more closely tied to a specific project. The basic design of an unstructured workflow task is portrayed in Figure 33.5.

Figure 33.5.
Unstructured workflow
tasks need to allow
room for variation.

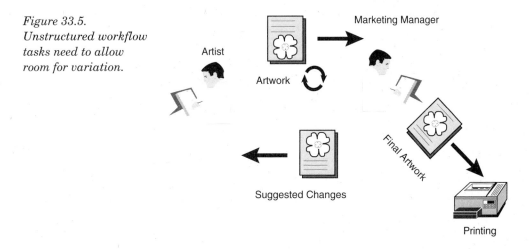

A customer service organization responsible for assisting customers in a variety of ways would need a workflow application with a rather high level of inherent flexibility. Creative services groups might be frustrated by workflow tools which discourage free and uninhibited thinking and brainstorming. Corporate executives who rely on workflow-type products to view and interpret financial data need to be able to generate reports in several different ways. Unstructured workflow applications like these would add value in several ways:

◆ Provide a basic framework or guidelines for freeform tasks. As an example, a workflow application that automatically outlines a basic business plan for a product manager to "fill in" only gives the individual a place to start. It will be up to the product manager to add the detail.

◆ Allow a number of users to collaborate on a project in a natural conversational way, while at the same time, give the project owner control over who participates and in what way.

◆ Help users record irregular or special elements of a particular project in a well-defined way so that such information does not go unnoticed by others.

You will see that workflow applications come in many forms, and that any such application designed to help with even the most mundane tasks can be considered a workflow application. The next couple of sections look briefly at a number of such network applications and discuss how they may affect the day-to-day work within your organization.

Messaging

The unintelligible, hand-scribbled meeting invitation. The not-so-sticky, yellow Post-It note. The hurried, stream-of-consciousness, voice-mail message. These are all tools for sending messages and, unfortunately, they are all too common to communication within most organizations. Networks are being installed everywhere in the hopes that people will communicate more often and more efficiently using network messaging applications.

If you are adequately prepared and provide the right follow-through, the network messaging applications you choose to use in your network will be a resounding success. But, if you are not careful or do not provide sufficient training, your users will not take to using the network for everyday communication. Concentrate on looking for ease-of-use, powerful management capabilities, and administrative features when shopping for messaging applications.

Electronic Mail

As mentioned previously, e-mail is one of the most, if not the most, popular network applications. The concept is simple, combine a basic word processing program, a directory of the individuals on the network, and an "engine" to send documents created in the word processor portion to the various individuals selected from the directory, and you have an e-mail application. Now, of course, add to that the ability to send files along with your message, the ability to send messages to multiple users by referencing a mailing list, a spell-checker, and the capability to store sent and received messages to create a "paper trail," and you now have a sophisticated messaging infrastructure.

You really need only concern yourself with the two basic elements of an e-mail system:

◆ **The user interface**: The users need to feel comfortable with the e-mail program and their ability to easily create, view, and edit messages. If the interface gets in the way and makes sending a message more difficult than some of the "old-fashioned" methods hinted at above, the application may never get very far.

◆ **The network mail delivery system**: The engine which is responsible for distributing message to other users must work right along with your network operating system and must provide useful utilities for its own management. It must also provide ways to send messages to other network environments and messaging systems like MCI Mail, CompuServe, and the Internet, to name a few.

In a NetWare 4 network, you will likely find the most value in mail engines that exploit NetWare Directory Services like Novell's own NetWare Global Message Handling System (MHS). Both the users and you, as e-mail administrator and network administrator, will then have to deal with only one directory of users on the network.

Note

The installation and configuration of MHS for NetWare 4.1 is discussed in Chapter 27.

Calendaring and Scheduling

Sometimes installed as an add-on to an existing e-mail system, calendaring and scheduling applications are designed to assist people with personal calendar and schedule keeping and group scheduling and meeting planning. They can do wonders for helping people work together and manage time efficiently, but they can also be ineffectual and, even worse, cause significant social problems if you do not consider some of these important issues surrounding their use:

◆ People may be slow to change habits in regard to how they keep their schedules and may be particularly hesitant to share their schedules with others.

◆ Many people in your organization may never use anything but their trusty, luggable, personal organizer.

◆ Without a complete commitment from the entire group to keeping the scheduling information up-to-date, such an application can be rendered worthless.

Be sure to look for a group scheduler with extensive security options so that you can preserve a certain amount of privacy for the individual users without limiting group scheduling and meeting planning functions.

The term messaging can be used to describe a number of applications in addition to e-mail, calendaring, and scheduling. Elements of imaging and multimedia are most definitely message-oriented.

IMAGING

Bearing in mind the old saying "a picture is worth a thousand words," technologists have really promoted the use of computers for creating, displaying, and sharing graphical images in recent years. Although computers of one sort or another have been able to create and display images for some time now, it has not been until only the last six to eight years that computers have been able to do so affordably, quickly, and with such an unparalleled level of quality. A personal computer costing around $2,200 today is capable of displaying color images containing more individuals hues than the human brain is even able to distinguish. To accomplish the same thing a mere ten years ago would have required hardware well beyond the reach of all but research and educational institutions.

So much of how people relate with one another is visual. A speaker gesticulates for emphasis and uses a chalkboard to get a point across. Books, magazines, and newspapers have always used pictures right along with text to educate. And young children unable to communicate effectively in any other way must watch others intently to learn more about their world. This dependence on our eyes, on seeing to believe, will persist in an increasingly technology dependent society.

Computer imaging technology provides a way for us to communicate using still pictures. It has grown out of the photographic and micrographic technologies that proceeded it, and, as it has continued to evolve, it has paved the way for multimedia technology adding moving pictures and sound to the personal computer's bag of tricks.

Keep in mind that imaging can still be rather expensive if it is to be used to a great extent within a large organization. However, many organizations, such as banks, libraries, hospitals, and government agencies that all keep extensive records of physical documents have found computer imaging technology to be indispensable and penny-wise in the long run. But you can bet that they have had to pour huge amounts of money into hardware and software to get the new processes started. Most of the dollars go into hardware upgrades. Following are some of the areas in which you should expect to spend money should you choose to dabble in imaging:

◆ Mass storage devices for network servers. Digitized images, for example, really use up a lot of storage space very quickly.

◆ Hierarchical Storage Management (HSM) systems for network servers. HSM systems allow network administrators to control the migration of infrequently used data and images offline to slower, higher-capacity storage devices like digital streaming tape.

◆ High-speed, high-color display adapters for network workstations. Look into using local-bus and Peripheral Connect Interface (PCI)-based video

33

cards at the workstations for maximum performance when viewing images at the workstation.

Tip

Remember that local-bus and PCI adapters only operate in PCs equipped to support them, so be sure to talk to your hardware or systems vendor before purchasing new video hardware.

♦ Floating-point, math coprocessors or 486/Pentium-based processors for network workstations. Most imaging functions are based on a lot of calculation-intensive mathematics.

♦ High-speed network architecture. For light imaging use and simple image manipulation, standard LAN speeds of 10 Mbps will be usually sufficient, but for heavier use, you will need a more expensive high-speed LAN based on fiber-optic, Asynchronous Transfer Mode (ATM), or packet switching technologies.

If you have decided that your organization will be able to make use of some type of imaging capabilities, consider the advantages and disadvantages carefully before committing to all of the various expenses associated with them.

SCANNING

Image scanning captures documents as they originally appear and stores them digitally for later retrieval, but the images themselves are not really machine readable. That is, text which might be part of an image is stored just like the portions containing pictures, and the user has no way of searching the images for specific text information. Even with this limitation, scanning is extremely useful for creating virtually indestructible facsimiles of important documents. Some banks use image scanning instead of microfilm because of the relative permanence of digital information.

IMAGE PROCESSING

Image processing provides a way to modify or enhance images already stored digitally. For example, it can be used to produce special effects, add or remove information from an image, and change the basic properties of an image such as color balance, brightness, sharpness, and resolution. The software and hardware required to do sophisticated image processing can be quite expensive.

OPTICAL CHARACTER RECOGNITION (OCR)

OCR is an advanced, software-only technology that is capable of reading textual information from an image, both handwritten and typed. It is usually used as means to prevent having to manually enter into a computer large amounts of text. If the original image is stored in tandem with the output of the OCR application, the original image can then be called up from a database by searching the text information for specific strings.

Tip

> Images that are visually complex, use lots of different types of text faces, or are of poor quality may present a problem for most OCR software.

STORAGE, INDEXING, RETRIEVAL, AND DOCUMENT MANAGEMENT

Storage, indexing, retrieval, and document management is the technology that makes extensive use of scanning and document archiving practical. It assists with searches for particular documents and ranks results according to relevance in order to find the documents most likely to match the search criteria. Document management goes a step farther by providing control over tracking, revisions, access and storage location. Efficiency breaks down as the size of the database grows, however, because of the significant storage and computational needs inherent to this type of technology.

DOCUMENT EXCHANGE

Document exchange allows images to be moved around easily within an organization where a number of different, not-so-compatible computer systems are in use. A UNIX system, for example, stores and displays image information differently than an IBM compatible, Microsoft Windows system. This technology allows the widest possible access to computer images.

Computer-imaging technologies overlap with a number of other technologies, and multimedia is probably considered its closest relative.

MULTIMEDIA

Psychological studies show that people's understanding and ability to learn can be greatly improved when visual presentations are combined with audio. School teachers probably welcome the excitement from children who are eager to watch an educational video and are likely pleased by the results: higher retention and greater comprehension. Automobile manufacturers can train assembly workers much quicker with a video and a little hands-on than with a procedures manual alone. And how many times have you heard from someone, "Just show me, and then I'll understand."

Audio is also already a major part of the workplace, but the telephone is really the only vehicle. In the same way, video is something most everyone is very comfortable with thanks to the television. By integrating these technologies using the network and the network workstation, you can explore multimedia and new ways to increase your organization's productivity and effectiveness.

In addition to all of the areas in which you can expect to incur expenses related to computer imaging, multimedia applications have a couple of their own, such as the following:

◆ Additional hardware and software at the workstation. The Multimedia Personal Computer (MPC) specification outlines the standard hardware requirements for a PC that will be used for multimedia applications, and it includes a requirement for audio hardware and speakers. You may need to add other components for telephone integration, like a microphone or headset.

◆ More network bandwidth control. Multimedia applications, digital audio, and digital video can really clog up the works of an average network. If you are thinking seriously about adding these things to your network, you will need to look into ways to better control network traffic. More raw bandwidth and network analysis hardware and software is a must. You may also find that you need a special program to manage multimedia data on your network, like Novell's NetWare Video product. NetWare Video controls how much and how fast multimedia data is sent across the network to prevent overloading.

Unfortunately, for most people, multimedia is not all that viable a communications tool just yet. In some ways, it is a technology looking for an application. Not only is it costly and challenging to create useful and innovative multimedia applications, but it is very expensive to put them into widespread use. Nevertheless, the following is a summary of the basic types of multimedia applications that you and your organization may be interested in investigating:

◆ Voice annotated e-mail

◆ Network based voice mail

◆ Presentations with audio or music

◆ Simultaneous voice and data transfer

- ◆ Interactive training videos
- ◆ Long-distance learning
- ◆ Video teleconferencing
- ◆ Video e-mail
- ◆ Telephone conferencing and call control via a graphical user interface

The next and final class of applications is perhaps more closely related to a network service than the other applications discussed.

General Data Communications

Improving your organization's capability to communicate directly and efficiently with other organizations can be just as important as improving your own internal communication. The telephone continues to lead as the number one tool. Now, telephones can be used to hold conference calls, control computers like your bank's automated teller, and transmit faxes and data. The worldwide telephone and telegraph network has grown into the largest network in existence, and, as a result, your own computer networks will rely heavily on telecommunications providers to provide WAN connectivity and other digital communications services within your organization.

In terms of the services they provide, general data communications applications can be considered on the same level as basic file and print services. For example, network print services allow us to pool printers, and network communications services allow us to pool modems and other communications devices. But in addition, and perhaps more importantly, a communications system can augment the usefulness of all network applications by extending your reach and access to data beyond your own organization.

The two basic services, data and fax, are really two-way services: that is, they provide a way out of the network when directly attached and a way into the network when disconnected. For this reason, they are sometimes called *dial-in* and *dial-out* services, and it is not uncommon for a single communications system to handle all four types of information transfer. Again, Novell provides a unique example with their NetWare Connect product that runs on a NetWare file server and controls a bank of up to 64 modems. Using additional software from third parties and standard modem hardware, NetWare Connect is able to handle these four types of information exchange. These software packages typically support communications systems from a range of vendors.

A product such as NetWare Connect used alone, however, is not going to do much for you. In order to leverage the power of the network, you will need to find network applications that can be used to control and manage the flow of information to and from the modems themselves. These applications can provide a variety of services including those discussed in the following sections.

DIAL-UP CONNECTIVITY TO DISPARATE NETWORKS

Some communications systems can support network-to-network connections for dial-up routing and e-mail delivery without requiring any human intervention or interaction. Especially useful in the support of an organization's remote offices, a system like this can save money by establishing a connection only when it is needed and only for as long as it is needed.

FAX AND DATA SERVICES

Fax and data services can enable a large number of users to use the same set of modems, saving the cost of purchasing, installing, and supporting all those modems throughout your organization.

With access to shared data services, your users can still pull information off public networks such as CompuServe, GEnie, and Prodigy, newswires, and Bulletin Board Systems (BBSs), as well as exchange information directly with users on other modems or with other networks. Many software packages that support and control network modems for IBM-compatible computers will usually do so via one or both of two popular standards, *Interrupt 14* (INT14) and *NetWare Asynchronous Services Interface* (NASI), which are supported by NetWare Connect. Both standards help programs use a network modem as if it were directly attached to the computer. Of course, your network applications will have to support the modems you use in the same way that a stand-alone communications application would.

Fax services give users a way to send and receive facsimiles directly from within the applications running on their workstations, eliminating the need to go to paper at all. Most network fax systems are very similar in design to a client/server type architecture. That is, part of the software runs on the user's workstation and communicates with another portion running on the communications server via the network.

Typically, a dedicated IBM-compatible workstation will serve as host to the bank of modems. Network fax products are incredibly convenient and save time and money. Because of this, they are very popular right now, but, just like anything else, no two products are the same. As it is very likely that you will want to look into this. Make sure to check for some of the following features when shopping for network fax software:

◆ Private and shared fax phone books

◆ Document exchange with popular bit-map file types like PCX, TIFF, BMP, and PIC

- Easy-to-use fax viewer
- Fax send initiates when printing from applications
- Fax send initiates when sending an e-mail message to a fax number
- At least rudimentary document management for handling incoming and outgoing fax archives
- Support for directly attached modems for when a system is mobile and disconnected from the network where network fax services are provided

REMOTE NODE ACCESS

Remote node services give mobile users a way to dial into the network and work as if attached locally which means they can, such as following :

- Access e-mail directly from the network over a telephone line
- Manipulate data stored on the network (including client/server databases)
- Use other network services that are normally available when attached locally

Remote node service may be the most important general communications service that you can add to your network, but unfortunately, you will find that it is also one of the hardest to implement. The biggest hurdles here are in the training and support of mobile IBM-compatible PC users.

The two most common types of portable computers, the IBM compatible and the Apple Macintosh, behave completely different in remote node access situations. Macintosh systems remain quite usable when run as a remote node, but IBM compatibles running DOS or Microsoft Windows require a lot of patience. This is mainly due to the fact that Apple Computer's original networking protocol for small networks of Macintosh computers, LocalTalk, ran at a rather slow speed compared to the speed of today's 10 mbps Ethernet LANs. The transition from being a directly connected node to a remote node running over a 14.4 kbps telephone line is not as drastic a change for the Macintosh as it is for IBM compatibles. As a result, you will need to use great care when implementing remote node services for your users of IBM compatibles.

One other important concern not to be ignored with regard to remote node access software is security. A network equipped with dial-in lines of any kind should be considered basically unsecured. Without such lines, a network administrator can rely to an extent on the built-in security features in NetWare such as user authentication, packet encryption, and intruder lockout, and is comforted at least to the extent that physical access to the network ports and cabling is secure. By adding dial-in lines, however, the network administrator allows for the possibility, however unlikely, of a security breach. The most popular counter measure is *dial-back support*. The remote access software on the network side is pre-programmed with a list of remote users and the phone numbers of the lines from which they will be calling. When a registered remote user dials in and is authenticated, the remote access software will drop the line and call the user back at the number stored in its dial-back phone list.

Having reviewed the various types of network applications available to choose from, the next section investigates the basic concepts behind network applications in general.

BASIC FEATURES OF A NETWORK APPLICATION

If the potential car owner kicks tires, then what does the potential network application owner kick? Just like there are certain things even the most timid auto shopper should know about cars, there are certain things you should know about network applications before you take the plunge. Is it a diesel engine or does it run on unleaded? What kind of mileage does it get? Stick-shift or automatic? Many network software and hardware vendors are notorious for committing the very same "crimes" the Big Three automakers do that infuriate us as potential car owners.

At the outset it was mentioned that the most critical difference between a network application and a "non-network" application is its support for multiple users. This remains true as these differences are explored here in more detail, but it becomes immediately obvious that the network application is a rather complex creation.

NETWORK INTEGRATION: THE OSI MODEL

The question of network interoperability and integration when applied to a network application should find its answer in whether or not the program simply tolerates a particular network environment or thrives in it. Or, quite simply, it should also answer "Will it work with what I've got?" Unfortunately, no matter how simply put, there rarely exists a simple answer.

Nevertheless, the International Standards Organization, an international standards-setting association, has gone further than any other in creating a usable and widely adopted network reference model for the integration of networking systems. The *Open Systems Interconnect* (OSI) model provides a useful framework for understanding and building integrated systems and has been a great help to vendors and users alike. Although it is considered by some to be the industry's only basic networking rulebook, universal network standards will not be available anytime soon. Proprietary networking schemes are more the rule than the exception. But, networking companies are implementing the components of the model more and more.

The OSI model answers the interoperability and integration question by defining seven functional "layers," which correspond to specific network operations. Moving through the model, layer by layer, you will see that each layer is meant to be implemented separately. Also, you will see each layer has to deliver specific signals and bits of information to the layer immediately above while, at the same time, relying on the functions provided by the layer below.

Note

The signals and bits of information passed from layer to layer are defined by a set of rules or standards called a network protocol. These protocols enable computers to communicate with one another and exchange information while minimizing the number of errors generated in the process. The OSI model places network protocols in their appropriate locations of the model to help you understand how each protocol relates to or makes use of other protocols and the network hardware.

Refer to the diagram of the model in Figure 33.6 as each of the seven layers are discussed in the following sections.

Figure 33.6.
The OSI model can help in the understanding, evaluation, and purchasing of network applications.

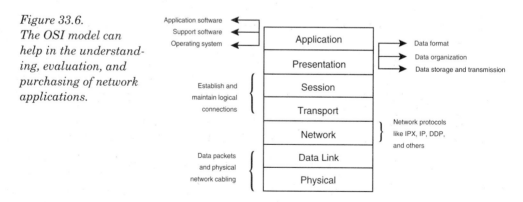

OSI Network Integration Model

APPLICATION: LAYER 7

The uppermost layer of the OSI model represents the software structure of an integrated system. Database front-end applications, word processing programs, and operating systems are all considered Application layer elements, the elements closest to the user. The Application layer can be divided into the following three sublayers:

- **Application software:** Interacts directly with user
- **Support software:** Interacts only with application software
- **Operating system:** Acts as go-between for application software, support software, and underlying hardware

PRESENTATION: LAYER 6

The OSI model's Presentation layer is concerned with the representation, organization, and storage of information. It is also divided into the following three sublayers:

- **Data format:** Includes complex representations, like word processing documents, simple ASCII text, and standards such as PostScript
- **Data organization:** Manipulates operating system file structures, such as the DOS FAT file structure
- **Data storage and transmission:** Handles ondisk representation of a data file, including proprietary and open file server protocols, such as Apple Computer's AppleTalk Filing Protocol (AFP) and TCP/IP's Networked File Server. Also makes sure that local disk activity is transparently replaced by access to a remote file server.

SESSION AND TRANSPORT: LAYERS 5 AND 4

In a network environment, these two OSI layers are in charge of establishing and maintaining a logical connection between software components operating on two different computers. They keep a complex dialog flowing in the right order and guarantee that messages sent by one party are received properly by the other. Examples are the industry-standard Transmission Control Protocol (TCP) and the Network Services Protocol found in Digital's DECnet Phase IV.

NETWORK: LAYER 3

A complicated network might connect thousands of devices over several hundred different network cables and links, each one with different transmission characteristics. The protocols found at this layer, like Novell's Internetwork Packet Exchange (IPX), the Internet Protocol (IP), and AppleTalk's Datagram Delivery Protocol (DDP), shield the higher OSI layers from this information.

Data Link and Physical: Layers 2 and 1

The protocols found at layers 2 and 1 include standardized LAN packet (Data Link) and cabling systems (Physical), such as 802.3 (Ethernet) and 802.5 (token ring). Proprietary LAN systems are also included at these levels, such as Apple's LocalTalk.

In general, the more an application sticks to its own business, interfacing directly only with the adjacent layers, the better behaved the application will be in a wider variety of environments. At the same time, however, such well-behaved applications tend to be limited by these restrictions. Application vendors know that if they cheat a little here and there, they can improve their application and make it more competitive. For example, the vendors of an application who must respond quickly to real-world events may decide that their application cannot afford to wait for its network messages to trickle down through the layers of the OSI model before making it onto the wire. As a result, they may allow their application to create network messages of its own, ignoring existing protocol standards. The application may be responsive, but at the same time it may also have difficulty running with other applications because of its disregard for the OSI model.

Determining Network Awareness

You have learned that a true multi-user application must take into account the fact that more than one user may using the program at the same time. With this understanding, it should be obvious that a true network application must take into account that it is running on a network.

NetWare, like most other Network Operating Systems (NOS), was designed from the very start to be invisible. That is to say, for NetWare to be useful, it has to support all of the same applications that users might use in a non-networked environment. So, to an application running on a network workstation, access to a NetWare file server hard disk must transparently appear as if it were access to a local hard disk.

Because of this basic design principle, all applications can be run or retrieve data from a file server hard disk without modification. Applications that have been programmed with additional knowledge of the network, however, will not just tolerate the network, but they will embrace it. The preponderance of networks today has driven vendors to make sure that most of the applications you may considering have a least some degree of explicit network support. Other vendors pursue network application markets specifically by producing applications that even require some sort of network to run.

This variation among applications in the area of network awareness cries out for classification. To satisfy our urge for order, author Michael Rockwell proposed the following three categories to describe network awareness in the December 1991 issue of *Windows-DOS Developer's Journal*.

NETWORK-BLIND

Network-blind applications are the single-user, "non-network" applications hinted at earlier. The network's fancy footwork can prevent such an application from even realizing that it is being run from a network or in a network environment. The only real value of running such an application on the network is that its management is centralized because the application is not installed on each workstation individually. Because these programs will not have any direct way to control over who runs them and how their data is used, they may even do more damage on the network than good. Those programs that open data files, read the information into memory, and then close the files are especially prone to problems. If more than one user is making changes to the same piece of data and one person saves their changes to disk before the other, their changes will be lost if the other person saves their changes afterward.

Warning

Most network-blind, single-user software is not sold with a license for use on a network. If you do install and use this kind of software on your network, make sure that you own as many single-user copies of the software as there are people will be running on the network.

NETWORK-AWARE

Network-aware applications instead take the position that at some point they may be run or share data from over a network. Though most commercial software belongs in this category, these applications are really the simplest of network applications supporting only basic file or record locking to prevent the "last to save changes wins" scenario. If a second user tries to open a document that is already opened, a network-aware application will likely warn the user that the file is in use and changes cannot be written back using the same filename. This may be sufficient for the majority of your application needs, despite the fact that a lack of special network installation and maintenance features will complicate matters for you somewhat.

NETWORK-INHERENT

Finally, network-inherent refers to applications that are closely tied to the network or a network service. Most of the products outlined in the earlier sections of this chapter fall into this category. The portions of a client/server application communicate with each other at the Transport and Session layers (layers 4 and 5 of the OSI model) using the prevailing communications protocols at those layers. E-mail applications must understand how to receive incoming messages and queue outgoing messages as they communicate with the e-mail server. Network fax software must be able to talk to the workstation or server that is host to the network modems on the network in order to send or receive faxes. You will also find that these applications come equipped with special installation and management software to help ease their integration into your network.

The following section elaborates on how applications like these use network APIs to make themselves network-aware and network-inherent.

Support for Network Application Program Interfaces (APIs)

Directly related to the ideas of network integration and network awareness is the concept of the API, or application program interface. APIs provide a way for applications to interact with other applications through the use of function calls. For example, the DOS operating system, which resides in the operating software sub-layer of the Application layer of the OSI model, makes available all sorts of functions and procedures for use by any DOS program. Some APIs handle disk I/O as well as opening and closing files, some handle printing through the parallel port, and still others may handle the display of text to the console. A DOS application developer can call certain DOS API functions within his application to make his job easier, because the code that DOS uses to accomplish these tasks is already written. Rather than having to learn all about disk access, printing, and displaying text, the developer can leverage the knowledge and capabilities of DOS. As a benefit, the developer will have more time to add valuable features to the portions that must be written from scratch.

Consider a company of several thousand employees in size. People at each level are responsible for certain job functions. The people at the higher levels orchestrate the activities of those below and then feed information back to the people above. It is vital that the high-level executives not get lost in the everyday details of running the large company, and so they must carefully decide who they should interact with directly on a daily basis for maximum gain and minimal effort. If the job descriptions of the individuals in the company are understood, and the individuals are sensitive to the "office politics" of working with others, the company is likely to be successful.

The same can be true for a network and network applications. The network applications can be thought of as the executives in this company. They are responsible for pulling together things at a lower level to successfully complete greater tasks. APIs represent individuals at the company and their respective job descriptions, defining what specific tasks an individual can and should perform. Going further, network protocols come to represent office politics, outlining exactly how elements should interact with the levels below and above. Assuming that the APIs are understood, and the network protocols are used properly, the network and the network application should likewise be successful.

The ideal network application will make extensive use of the APIs provided by the other layers in the OSI model, and at the same time, it may even make its own APIs available for use by others. You may already be familiar with some of the big standards and the APIs they support from reading other sections in this book or from your own research, but it may be helpful to take a look an example.

NetWare 4's NetWare Directory Services (NDS) API is available as part of a *System Developer Kit* (SDK), which includes documentation on how to use the API and the services it provides. A network application developer would obtain or purchase a copy of the SDK product straight from Novell. The Directory Service API, like the vast majority of SDK/API products, includes source code and sample programs written in C or C++ so the developer can see exactly how to create an NDS aware application.

The NetWare 4 Directory Services API provides access to the hierarchical NDS database architecture which stores network information on users, groups, print queues, and other objects. Among other things, the API includes functions for searching and updating database information. This API can be used as a natural complement for network applications designed to run in a NetWare 4 environment. For example, an e-mail application can synchronize its own directory of addresses with the user and group information in the Directory Services database so that the e-mail administrator need not maintain two separate directories. Table 33.1 lists some of the Directory Services API database operations and each operation's corresponding function call.

TABLE 33.1 NDS API CALLS.

Operation	Directory Function Call
Initialize the Unicode tables	NWDSInitUnicodeTables() (client applications only)
Create context	NWDSCreateContext()
Login	NWDSLogin()
Allocate buffers	NWDSAllocBuf()
Initialize buffers	NWDSInitBuf()
Define buffers	NWDSPut...()

continues

TABLE 33.1 CONTINUED

Operation	Directory Function Call
Perform the Directory Operation	`NWDSAddObject()`
	`NWDSModifyObject()`
	`...`
Retrieve buffer information	`NWDSGet...()`
Free buffers	`NWDSFreeBuf()`
Logout	`NWDSLogout()`
Free context	`NWDSFreeContext()`

It will not be easy for you to determine the exact extent to which an application is network-blind, network-aware or network-inherent, what APIs your network applications should support, and to what extent it should support those APIs, but there are some things you can do to help yourself out with this and other endeavors. The next section helps you come up with a plan of attack. It guides you through the more important decisions you will need to make when choosing a particular network application.

TAKING THE PLUNGE: FROM SALE TO SERVICE

If you are like most people, you realize that it is impossible to keep up with the technological advancements that occur almost daily in the software industry. Hundreds of vendors have flooded the market with an ever-widening selection of software, and you are getting swept away in the current, fighting your way through the flotsam and jetsam around you. But as you prepare yourself to buy network application software, hold on to your life preserver—the knowledge you have about network applications.

Your most informed decisions will come by applying what you already know and by using a little common sense. Below is a framework for common sense purchasing that will help keep you from drowning.

BEFORE YOU BUY

Remember the "why." Take the time to look closely at the way your organization operates, and how it can improve. From the basic types and categories of network applications available, determine what kind of software solution fits the bill. It may be e-mail, fax services, or client/server database, but whatever type of solution you feel you need, be sure to do your homework, and do not go it alone.

You will realize very quickly that there is probably no one perfect network application. When methodically evaluating the dozens of products in any one category, you must concentrate primarily on what will get the job done and what will meet your needs from both a technical and a business perspective. Following are some basic technical concerns:

- Ease of use
- Ease of installation, administration, and management
- Remote (or centralized) management
- Remote (or centralized) configuration
- Overall reliability

Following are some basic business concerns:

- Stability of vendor
- Support policy, training, and on-site service
- Direct, distributor, or reseller
- Initial projected costs
- Expected costs for expansion and upgrades

The amount of homework you will have to do really depends on the size and importance of your potential purchase. The following steps, however, can be adapted to your situation. For relatively minor purchase decisions, you may only briefly consider each step along the way, but for major purchases or for those that will affect a large number of people, you may want to follow along more carefully. To decide on a a network applicatoin, follow these steps:

1. Set up an evaluation team.

   Identify those groups and departments within your organization that would have some interaction with the potential application. These would definitely include those people who will use the application, but should also include the groups who will be associated with its support, installation, configuration, troubleshooting, and management and monitoring.

   Create a team with representation from each group, and charge this team with the responsibility for selecting an application that will meet the technical and business needs of the company.

2. Do a thorough needs analysis.

   As a team, analyze your business carefully and identify areas needing major change and improvement. To ensure that you adequately understand your organization's business process, carefully outline and summarize these areas in a form that you can use for executive review. This will also help you define the technical requirements your choice must eventually meet.

3. Identify and research several potential products.

Again as a team, identify several network applications that might meet the needs outlined for executive review. Then research each vendor's product by reading reviews, talking to the company's marketing and sales representatives, and asking other users' opinions. Always ask list prices and street prices. Investigate also at this point how you might purchase each product (through what channels) and how it can be licensed. Be sure you and your team consider software suite licensing issues and per-user, site, and LAN pack license arrangements (see Table 33.2).

TABLE 33.2 BASIC SOFTWARE LICENSE OPTIONS.

License Type	Description
Software suite	Highly discounted bundle of related products. Usually one license for whole suite preventing individual products from being used separately.
Per-User (single)	Full-price purchase of license for one user. No volume discounts.
Per-User (multiple)	Discount purchase of licenses for multiple users. Usually vendor-specified stratification.
LAN Pack	Discount purchase of licenses for multiple users. Usually stratified in conjunction with NOS license.
Site/Managed Licensing Agreement	Flat fee for license covering all potential users.

4. Select three finalists and create a comparison chart.

Compare your technical requirements to the information gathered during the research phase. Then select three final candidates and add to the matrix a new set of criteria for support, network management, pricing, upgrade costs and so on (see Figure 33.7).

5. Contact vendor representatives and schedule briefings.

Notify the three vendors of your intent to select an application. Indicate the number of units you may need to purchase. Schedule product briefings at their facility or at a reseller. Use a checklist to make sure you get all the information you will need to complete your matrix. This briefing should include a discussion of futures.

Figure 33.7.
A sample product
comparison chart
showing various
evaluation criteria.

	Vendor A	Vendor B	Vendor C
Basic technical concerns			
Base of use			
Base of installation, administration, and management			
Remote (or centralized) management			
Remote (or centralized) configuration			
Overall reliability			
Basic business concerns			
Stability of vendor			
Support policy, training, and on-site service			
Direct, distributor, or reseller			
Initial projected costs			
Expected costs for expansion and upgrades			

6. As a group, evaluate each vendor after the briefing.

   If possible, all team members should attend each briefing. Evaluate the vendors at the end of the day.

7. Rank each product.

   Meet later to decide, as a group, on a rating scale and assign weight to any items on the matrix that you feel need special consideration. Do this one vendor at a time for each vendor. Although this can take a lot of time, this can be the most valuable part of the process for large projects. Also, by expressing and defending their opinion each person will clarify their thinking and minimize the possibility of a misunderstanding of the facts.

8. Select a vendor and product.

   Add up the points, and then compare the spread between the first and second choices. You will most likely find that your first choice is the most expensive one, so compare the costs and benefits associated with each product carefully, and then make the final selection.

9. Notify all vendors of your decision.

   You may choose to write a letter to each vendor and give them the results. This may open the door for you to provide them with your feedback as the vendor would likely ask what they might do to improve their product to make it more competitive. By using a letter like this, the vendors will probably not pressure you to reconsider.

AFTER YOU BUY AND BEFORE YOU INSTALL

After you have taken the plunge, the real work of keeping your head above water begins. Fortunately, there are some very definite steps you can take to keep the process moving along quickly and efficiently. Do not overlook the fact that one of those steps might be to encourage the vendor to send someone out to help you on-site.

READ THE DOCUMENTATION AND THE README!

Because of the distributed nature of networks and NetWare 4 networks specifically, installing a network application requires a little more planning. A big part of that planning process is reading. Although most people do not take the time, reading the installation instructions for a network application is critical. So many different parts need to come together as a single system for the installation to run smoothly and your application operate properly.

Pay special attention to any instructions dedicated to network installations. Check the inside of the package thoroughly for special documents, and be sure to search any on-line documentation that may also be included with the product. Those products that cannot be considered network-inherent are more likely to leave you to your own devices when installing to a network. Network-inherent applications will most likely require some sort of optimization or configuration for your particular network. As an example, it is not uncommon for MS Windows–based and NetWare Loadable Module (NLM) based applications to require newer versions of certain NetWare files like the MS Windows driver, NETWARE.DRV, or the NetWare file, CLIB.NLM.

Make sure that you have the necessary supervisory rights for the target partitions of the directory or for the target servers. It can be terribly frustrating to feed a system half-a-dozen diskettes only to be told that the installation routine must be restarted with the appropriate network access rights.

PLAN THE INSTALLATION

You will need to understand, if you do not already, that consistency is very important to your users, especially the not-so-technical types. You will hear people ask questions like, "So, if I type this, then I can get my e-mail, right?" The days when these users type what they are supposed to type but nothing happens are the days you work late.

Tip

Careful planning of the installation and rollout of an application will minimize the need to make extensive and confusing changes to the network and the application later.

Break the project into manageable phases and timetables. Not all users need to begin using the application at the same time. Try working with some of the small groups that may have joined you in the original purchase planning process, and have them test things out for you. Are they able to run the application consistently? Is the application's performance acceptable? What can be done to automate the use of the application? Should the workstations be configured to use the application by making changes to the users' login scripts, or should the individual workstation configurations be altered directly?

Use the answers to these and other questions to help you determine what needs to be done before releasing the application into the wild. Always plan for half again as much time and effort in this area.

STAGE AND EXECUTE THE INSTALLATION

Before committing to an installation on the production network, you will need to stage the installation on a network which you can use as a testbed. The testbed should represent a scaled-down version of your production network by duplicating as many pertinent elements of the larger network as possible. If the application you are installing will run over a WAN connection, as an example, you may want to simulate a slower network link in your testbed to get a feel for how it affects performance and stability. A testbed is also important for the following reasons:

◆ It will minimize downtime on the production network when the application is finally rolled out.

◆ It may allow you to simply "hot-swap" some elements of the testbed over to the production network saving time and effort on the ultimate installation.

◆ You will gain a better understanding of the amount of time and effort the application takes to install and manage.

Use this time carefully. Document the application for the people that will be using it. Include information on where to find it, how to execute it, and how to get access to help and documentation. Also, work through and test any planned development projects related to the roll out of the application. For example, if you are implementing workflow software that requires customization, do as much customization work as possible during this time.

Finally, when you are comfortable with the way the testbed is operating, slip the application into the production network at an off-peak time to give you have some room to work. Be sure to lock all users out of the network beforehand. Also, double-check that everything is working properly before circulating the documentation you created to inform users of the application's availability.

AFTER YOU INSTALL AND BEFORE YOU GO CRAZY

After installation, you will naturally tend to shift from a proactive posture to a more reactive one. The key to keeping sane is to resist this temptation and continue to think in terms of preventative problem-solving.

HELP YOUR USERS

The majority of your users will be slow to adopt new applications and technologies. Unless they were involved in the purchase planning process with you, they will probably need to be "sold" on the value of the applications you install. If you have done your homework, these applications should eventually make them more productive, but holding their attention until then may still present a challenge for you. If you and your organization are going to mandate the use of a new network application, you had better make sure that you lay the groundwork and then follow through.

You need to make internal training a priority. Design and test training material right along with the application in the staging process. That way you can offer the courses concurrently with the roll out. Provide users with quick reference cards and other basic materials to help them on a day-to-day basis, and be sure to discuss basic troubleshooting strategies with the users so they feel as if they can help themselves.

Keep the channels of communication between you and the users wide open. Do what you can to make the users feel involved. Share with them the fact that you view the adoption of a new application to be more of a process than a one-time event.

Finally, some sort of attended internal help desk system might make sense if you are supporting a major application or a large number of them. It may even be a requirement of your licensing arrangement with the application vendor.

Tip

Also consider setting up an unmanned, hot-line phone number or e-mail address where users can leave anonymous comments and suggestions.

HELP YOURSELF

There is no doubt that the whole idea of selecting, purchasing, and maintaining the right network applications is to make life easier and not more complicated. You hope that the application and the new business processes related to it will make the lives of the individuals in your organization easier, but you also hope that it will not kill you and your staff in the process. So, throughout, it is vital that you focus on helping yourself, too.

In addition to what has already been discussed, you need to be on the lookout for affordable, accessible, and convenient ways to obtain helpful information and support. With the rapid growth of services like CompuServe and Prodigy along with an explosion in the use of the Internet and its e-mail, newsgroup, and World Wide Web services, more and more companies are finding that it is in their best interest to provide alternatives to traditional telephone-based technical support.

You will find that some companies will even reserve their telephone support options for resellers, distributors, and certified consultants by making them cost-prohibitive for individual users and small companies. As an example, Novell charges end-users anywhere from $50 to $200 per incident, depending on the product, for direct telephone support. Novell does this for a couple of reasons—there are simply too many NetWare users for Novell to be able to provide adequate direct support for all of them without significantly raising the price of their product, and, perhaps more importantly, Novell wants to ensure that its sales channel of resellers and distributors stay in business by supporting them directly to provide their customers with local and on-site, solution-oriented sales and support. Even if your NetWare 4 installation is quite small and relatively simplistic, you will want to make sure that you are equipped to take advantage of Novell's many alternative support options.

Spend some time during the research phase talking to vendors about these alternative support offerings. All too often, users find out what a vendor's technical support is really like at the wrong time—when they have a problem. You can avoid unpleasant surprises by considering technical support to be a product feature in and of itself. If you can afford the time and expense, place some calls into the various vendor's support departments for pre-sales technical information and assistance. Try asking the people you speak with about support alternatives and about the organization of their department itself. Do they use some sort of customer service or help desk software or is everything done in and ad hoc sort of way? Is their support department divided into groups of both experienced and front-line technicians or must you draw from one big pool when you contact them? Sometimes even knowing if the support department is physically located near product development teams will help you gauge the vendor's ability to provide quality and timely support.

Although vendors are deploying new and different ways to distribute technical information all the time, what follows are some common and well-established resources that should definitely not go overlooked.

- ◆ **Vendor publications:** Look to the individual vendors themselves for newsletters, magazines, FaxBack documents (or faxes sent on demand),

and other publications. These types of publications are very good for providing convenient access to information that is helpful to a wide range of users. The best publications will be made available free of charge and will contain only minimal advertising, sales, and promotional material, if any at all. A number of companies including Compaq Computer Corp., Hewlett-Packard Company, IBM, Microsoft Corp., and Novell Inc. have their own in-house publishers which produce comprehensive technical research publications designed to cover various aspects of designing, implementing, managing, optimizing, and troubleshooting their respective products. Talk to customer service or support to find out more about how to obtain or purchase subscriptions to vendor provided publications. As another example, Novell and others, including Microsoft, also publish on CD-ROM.

Tip

> In exploring support options for your NetWare 4 network, be sure to look into Novell's Network Support Encyclopedia Professional Volume (NSEPro). The NSEPro is a CD-ROM-based, technical information database (infobase) focused on the NetWare environment, and is refreshed and distributed about once a month. Many users find that the $1,400.00/year subscription is money well spent.

◆ **Vendor Bulletin Board Systems (BBS):** In the support of almost any software product, it is often necessary for a vendor to release and distribute updates and fixes to a product's software. A BBS can help distribute patch files in a way that is convenient and affordable for both the vendor and the user. Find out if your vendors offer such services, and check that they provide connection at a variety of transfer speeds. Most companies provide only an access number which is subject to toll charges, but this will usually be the only cost to you. Sometimes vendors will allow you to post messages and directly discuss your problems with a support representative free of charge.

◆ **CompuServe and other online services:** CompuServe is one of the more popular online services, providing extensive access to computer hardware and software vendors. Other similar services include Prodigy, GEnie, BYTE Information Exchange (BIX), and America Online (AOL). These services have access points distributed geographically to minimize the cost of your call, but they will charge for connect time. Nevertheless, these services are still relatively affordable and provide help in a way that other services cannot. That is, they allow you to interact directly with other users of a vendor's products as well as the vendor representatives themselves.

Tip

Sometimes you can learn more about a particular problem from someone in the real world. Other users tend to be more free about the problems they have had, while the vendors try may to buffer problems in order to protect sales of existing and future products.

◆ **Internet:** The Internet is an increasingly popular vehicle for the interaction of vendors and other users. Most of what goes on over the Internet today, however, does not receive too much backing and support from the vendor itself, but this is likely to change as more users begin to explore the Internet. Find out what plans your vendors have in this regard. The Internet's services can be accessed quite easily if your organization already has direct access to the Internet. If your organization is not so fortunate, you can gain access through service providers in many areas for relatively small monthly fees. You may need special software to access these services, a news reader for Usenet, a Gopher browser application for Gopher sites, and Mosaic for access to Web servers.

Tip

Because of the recent hype surrounding the Internet and its use, you will find books at your local bookstore that will explain what these services are all about as well as walk you through the entire process of gaining access to the Internet, obtaining and installing the appropriate software, and using the services available. Such references normally include directories listing summaries of the information resources accessible through the Internet.

◆ **Technical Support Alliance (TSA):** The TSA represents a partnership among the support organizations of more than 38 industry leaders designed to provide cooperative support for their mutual customers. All the problems you may encounter when using a network application will likely involve products from several different vendors, and the TSA and other similar organizations can help you by doing some of the legwork for you. For example, if you call a database front-end application vendor with a problem you both suspect is related to the access of your client/server database, and both vendors belong to a support alliance, support representatives at both companies can consult with you and with each other and hopefully arrive at a useful solution in short order. Check with your vendor to see if they belong to such an organization and to find out the names of the other members. Some of the more prominent members of the TSA include Apple Computer, Banyan Systems, Borland International, Compaq Computer, Digital Equipment, Hewlett-Packard, IBM, Intel, Microsoft, Novell, and Oracle.

◆ **Industry publications:** Because of the size of the networking market, most major industry publications today have regular networking features and special demographic editions that can go a long way toward helping you keep abreast of changes in the industry and of important support issues. Be sure to take a look at the *Network Edition* of *PC Magazine*, *NETWEEK* section in *PC WEEK*, *InfoWorld*, and any one of a number of networking industry specific publications such as *Network World*, *LAN Magazine*, and *Communications Week*.

◆ **Users groups and users groups publications:** Some vendors sponsor and directly support users groups for users of their products, and others are formed and run independently. Either way, users groups provide still another great way to interact directly with other users. Some groups, such as the Novell sanctioned NetWare Users International (NUI) groups, even have publications of their own. Your vendor's customer service department should have information on groups in your area.

◆ **Trade shows and conferences:** There are trade shows and conferences that cover just about everything in the computer industry. These events can be somewhat costly to attend, but they offer the opportunity to meet face-to-face with vendors and other users. Many conferences, like Novell's BrainShare conference, have a decidedly technical focus and offer a number of instructional seminars and technical workshops. Talk with your vendor and the representatives you deal with on a regular basis to find out more about shows and conferences your vendor may attend.

SUMMARY

If you have not already started on your quest for the perfect solution to your information management problems, do yourself a favor and make sure that you are prepared for your journey.

Understand first and foremost the exact nature of your problems. What aspects of your organization are broken? What aspects are working fine? Make sure there that a genuine problem does exist and that you are not trying to keep up with technology for technology's sake. Spend the time to talk with the people in your organization about how they work and involve them in changes you intend to make.

Then, do your homework. Focus on the "why" and not so much on the "how" in the beginning, keeping in mind some of the decision making guidelines discussed in this chapter. As you move into the "how," make sure that you explore the variety of network applications and the solutions they provide. Look closely at how these applications fit with your existing network environment by gauging their compliance with the OSI model, their level of network-awareness, and their support of network APIs. Take an organized approach to the process of choosing and purchasing a particular application from the others in its category. Finally, make sure that you have done all you can to prepare yourself and the users before actually rolling out the application.

Network applications are the end and the network is the means. Bear this in mind as you set out on your journey, and you will go far.

- When Wiring Doesn't "Reach" Far Enough

- Selecting a Modem

- Selecting a Communications Server

- Summary

CHAPTER 34

Remote Access

As companies expand, they become increasingly reliant on telecommunications technology to help run their businesses. Traveling employees, workers at branch offices, telecommuters, customers and suppliers all find it necessary to contact growing companies electronically—both for voice and data communications.

Not surprisingly, these increased demands also radically alter the complexion of their computer networking resources. These demands have forced MIS personnel to extend the reach of networking services beyond the traditional boundaries of the local-area network, or what Forrester Research has called the "LAN Internetwork" (LIN). Now, those in MIS are grappling with the thorny issues of granting remote access to networked resources to a rapidly growing profusion of computers, telecommunications devices and users.

It is out "there," in what Forrester terms the "LAN Outernetwork" or LON, that some of the networking industry's most exciting developments are occurring. Faster modems, improved data compression techniques and new high-speed digital transmission services are making remote access more and more cost-effective and transparent to end users.

But what's out "there," in the remote-access fringe, is also where many network managers fear to tread. There, they're concerned about security, management and costs—all major problems without easy answers.

It's easy, however, to understand why remote access puzzles many network administrators. The LAN Outernetwork is comprised of markedly dissimilar types of resources and users than those found in the LAN Innernetwork, where they're comfortable.

The LAN Innernetwork, for example, is made up of networking resources at an organization's primary locations—its headquarters, a campus of several buildings and large branch offices. Most network managers already understand well the dynamics of building the LAN Innernetwork.

There, they can selectively control user access to the network while also ensuring the security of the LAN-based resources. In addition, MIS personnel are accustomed to dealing with standardized hardware interfaces such as hubs, bridges and routers and their associated protocols.

LAN users, however, make strikingly different demands on a network than their local counterparts. Their connectivity needs are intermittent—a dial-up session to pick up e-mail once a day, for example. And they require different services, such as dial-up telephone lines rather than leased-lines. They also need a variety of new resources—in particular, modems, special software and perhaps even specially configured user accounts on network servers.

The key requirements of a remote-access solution thus differ considerably from those of the local LAN. Moreover, these requirements introduce a new level of complexity into today's already-complex networks.

How, for example, do organizations install, manage, maintain and equip and support users at dozens of remote sites? And with an entirely new class of users now accessing networks remotely, how do organizations handle security?

Remote users also place conflicting demands on the communications channels they use: Unlike the local network, which is up and running virtually full time, the use of LON services varies from high to low volume; at the same time, remote users require on-demand access to network-based information.

These needs translate to using some form of public dial-up services (not the leased telephone lines MIS is accustomed to dealing with) and modems, Integrated Services Digital Network (ISDN) or switched CSU/DSUs.

This chapter looks at those requirements and, where appropriate, offers suggestions, solutions and advice on incorporating remote users into a NetWare 4.x network.

WHEN WIRING DOESN'T "REACH" FAR ENOUGH

As long as users can plug their computer directly into a network, they can gain easy access to all the services, resources, and files on that network. But when they're in a location where the network cabling can't "stretch" to, such as a hotel room while traveling on business, their efforts to get at their data files and network servers becomes quite a bit more complicated.

All the reasons companies build networks—file and printer sharing, transporting electronic mail from employee to employee, and so on—don't suddenly go away just because a few employees leave company headquarters.

On the contrary. For many workers in modernized organizations, networking resources, especially e-mail, provide a vital communications link with other workers. Hence, the need for remote LAN access via the telephone network.

DIAL-IN ACCESS

Almost every worker needs to remotely access the network at one time or another. Naturally, every worker's remote-access needs will be different. They may need remote access to just e-mail. Or they may need access to data and application files.

That means the first task of any network manager planning a remote access solution is to determine "What, from home, do my users need to communicate with?" Once you've determined this, you can choose the hardware and software products that best satisfy their (and your) needs.

The primary reasons users require remote network access are to read and send electronic mail messages and access data and application files on network servers and other LAN-based computers. E-mail, in fact, is probably the most popular reason users access their network remotely.

For many—especially those at remote branch offices—e-mail is the ideal communication medium. Receiving and sending e-mail messages is as simple as logging into the network, executing the mail program, they writing or reading messages.

REMOTE NODE VERSUS REMOTE CONTROL

Whatever the end user's remote-access need, network administrators' first critical decision about providing remote LAN access has been to decide the best method for giving dial-up users entry to the network. Here, they've had two choices: Via remote-control software or as a remote node on the network.

Choosing between the two hasn't always been easy, for several reasons. First, each offers end users features and benefits the other lacks. Second, both remote-node and remote-control products are limited to 56 kbps data transmissions. Although remote-node often provides what appears to be a transparent link between the PC and remote LAN, it and remote-control are both considerably slower than the 10 Mbps or 16 Mbps rate offered by Ethernet and token ring LANs, respectively.

This means, among other things, that users' performance expectations must be clarified. It also means that companies must factor monthly long distance phone expenses into the costs of any remote LAN access solution.

A third reason they're also difficult to choose from is that both approaches generally require adding some form of communications controller, or server, to the network.

Depending on implementation, the "communications server" can be a dedicated or shared device. (The following section covers the various configurations). This, in turn, means added costs in maintenance and management requirements.

REMOTE-CONTROL

Remote-control applications allow remote users to control the screen and keyboard of another computer (called the "host"), whether the host is a stand-alone PC or a PC on a network (see Figure 34.1). In these applications, remote-control software is loaded on both the host and remote client.

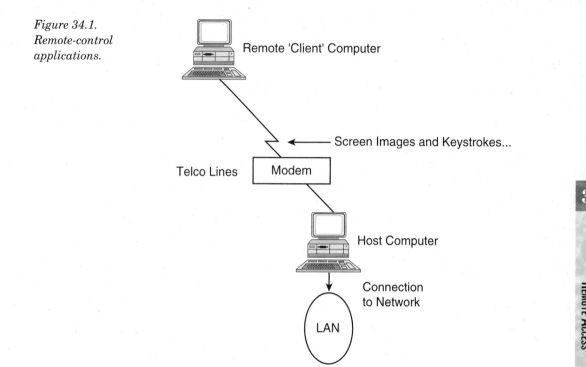

Figure 34.1.
Remote-control
applications.

The host software acts as sort of server, handling all data requests from the remote client. After receiving a request from the client, the host then transfers screen images and keystrokes over the telephone lines to the client, which displays the images on the user's monitor.

Remote-control technology minimizes the volume of data sent over telephone lines, making it useful with low-speed (300, 1200 and 2400 bits per second) modems. This explains why remote-control became popular with early laptop computer users, whose machines seldom contained the high-speed (9600 bps and 14,400 bps) modems on the market today.

Vendors have taken two tacks in developing remote-control software:

◆ Single-user solutions, which require dedicating a workstation on the LAN to serve as an application server

◆ Multiuser solutions, which use multitasking or multiple-processor systems to grant several users access to a LAN at once

Naturally, only one user can dial into and control the single-user version host at a time. Single-user solutions are cost-effective in small networks with little in the way remote-access demands because they require using dedicating only a single PC and modem on the LAN to remote communications.

Multiuser versions, obviously, grant several users access at once. Multitasking systems grant multiuser access by using multiple modems and asynchronous serial ports connected to a multitasking processor, such as an Intel 80486 operating under IBM's OS/2.

Multiprocessor systems work identically to several dedicated single-user machines. In these solutions, multiple modems grant access to multiple computing systems.

One of remote-control's key benefits is that, because all applications run on the host, server-based software licenses are not affected. This can save the costs of buying a software license for each remote user.

Poor performance is the primary disadvantage of remote-control solutions, however. Remote-control software runs significantly slower than remote-node, particularly in Windows and graphics environments.

REMOTE-NODE

Remote-node, or remote-client, products extend the LAN across standard telephone lines. First developed in the mid-1980s for NetWare 2.x LANs, the remote-node approach turns the remote computer's asynchronous communications (COM) port into a "virtual" network interface card.

Remote-node vendors have also taken two directions to developing remote-node products: LAN-to-LAN and PC-to-LAN.

In both types of remote-node implementations, remote-node users run applications on their computer, transferring only data across the telephone lines (see Figure 34.2). With all processing performed by the user's PC—a laptop or home computer in the single-node PC-to-LAN solution, an office PC in the LAN-to-LAN connection—users access the remote network as if their PC were attached directly to the LAN itself.

The growing number of powerful laptop and home-office PCs and faster modems has played a key role in increasing the popularity of remote-node solutions. Other factors in the widespread use of remote-node solutions include the prevalence of Windows and client-server applications.

One of the advantages of remote-node, in fact, is that Windows programs run as fast as the remote PC permits. Other key benefits: Data can stay on the LAN, under control of the network administrator, while remote users operate under familiar interfaces, without the need for retraining.

Remote-node solutions require powerful remote PCs and high-speed modems operating at optimum performance. Because applications run on the remote PC, remote-node solutions do not, however, support real-time database applications efficiently.

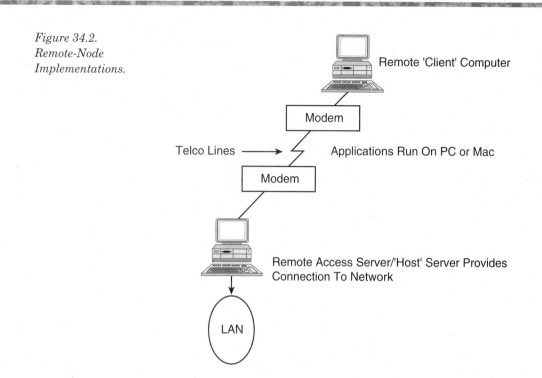

Figure 34.2.
Remote-Node
Implementations.

Remote 'Client' Computer

Modem

Telco Lines →   Applications Run On PC or Mac

Modem

Remote Access Server/'Host' Server Provides
Connection To Network

LAN

The distinguishing point between PC-to-LAN and LAN-to-LAN remote-node solutions: LAN-to-LAN remote-node solutions allow connecting two or more remotely
located LANs to one another. This permits all connected networks and their users
to share network services and data.

LAN-to-LAN remote-node, also termed dial-up LAN routing, gives the appearance
of a single LAN over dial-up telephone lines. Because it creates a single "virtual"
LAN, dial-up LAN routing is appropriate for applications that occasionally access
data on another LAN segment. These include e-mail systems, which generally use
a "store-and-forward" data-exchange scheme that requires only intermittent access
to dial-up lines, and databases.

When developing remote-node products, vendors have developed two types of
communications servers:

◆ Those built around a dedicated processor
◆ Those built around shared-processor architectures

In the shared-processor approach, the LAN-based remote-node software runs on a
PC. This can be a stand-alone PC or Macintosh dedicated to handling asynchronous
communications. It could also be a NetWare 4.X server performing multiple tasks—
file and disk sharing as well as handling asynchronous communications, for
example.

Shared-processor systems require adding asynchronous adapters to the PC/Mac or NetWare communications server. The asynchronous adapters provide the communications server with the modem connections used by remote callers when they dial into the network (see Figure 34.3).

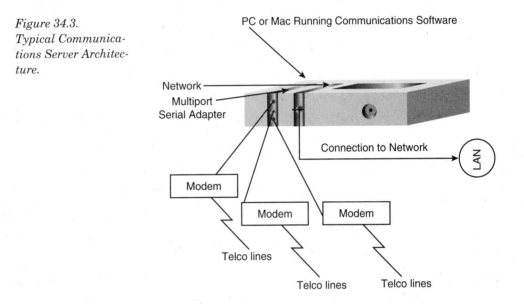

Figure 34.3. Typical Communications Server Architecture.

Novell's NetWare running a remote-node NetWare Loadable Module (NLM) application, such as Novell's own NetWare Connect, is a prime example of a server-based remote-node communications server. The advantages to this approach are its relative simplicity and the fact that—with the exception of the asynchronous adapters—it doesn't require adding computing hardware to the network.

The down side of the shared-processor system: It forces servers to work harder. The shared-processor system often slows network server response, especially when the file server/comm server combo handles multiple dial-in accesses. Poor performance is also a problem with stand-alone PC- or Mac-based communications servers.

Another issue is that shared-processor systems often support just a single networking protocol—the one running on the file server it is connected to. This means they are generally adequate only in small installations supporting one or two dial-up links but not for large, multiprotocol networks.

The dedicated-processor solution integrates a processor, network adapter and modem or multiport module (for connecting external modems) into a single package (see Figure 34.4). Dedicated-processor communications servers, such as Asante's NetConnect-RAS and Citrix Systems' A+ for NetWare, operate under specialized software that handles asynchronous communication between the remote clients and LAN-based resources, such as the file server and network operating system.

Figure 34.4.
Dedicated-processor
approach.

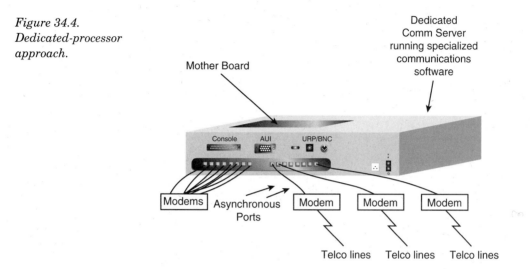

In both shared and dedicated processor systems, the client PC or Macintosh at the remote end of the communications link runs a full complement of networking software. This includes drivers for the network operating system, such as the Internetwork Packet Exchange (IPX) for Novell Inc.'s NetWare or AppleTalk for Macintoshes.

The client also runs an application that routes the input and output (I/O) of the networking software through the remote PC or Mac's serial port and modem. These applications also provide the client with a serial data-transfer protocol, such as Apple Computer's ARA. (See "Remote-Access Protocols" later in this chapter for more information on serial protocols.)

The dedicated communications server approach offers several benefits unavailable with shared-processor schemes. First, the processors in dedicated communications servers are optimized to perform only one task: handle asynchronous communications. This results in a better price-performance ratio when compared with the general-purpose CPU used in server and stand-alone PC/Mac communications servers.

Second, the dedicated communications server also centralizes remote network access into one "box," a major benefit for the LAN administrator This is important for both managing remote access—it's limited to one device—and simplifies network cabling and security issues.

Because dedicated communications servers are operating system-independent, they can also be designed to support multiple networking protocols. This is a critical requirement in large enterprise LANs, where multiple protocols are the norm.

REMOTE-ACCESS PROTOCOLS

The architecture of "remote LAN" access solutions forces them to deal with two types of protocols:

◆ The LAN-based protocol running on the network and remote clients, and

◆ A serial protocol that handles data transfer over the telephone lines between the network and remote client computer.

Each type of protocol provides its own set of "rules" that helps ensure error-free, secure and standardized ways of exchanging data between computers.

LAN-BASED PROTOCOLS

The two most prevailing LAN protocols in networks today are Apple Computer's AppleTalk, for Macintosh-based networks, and Novell's Internet Packet Exchange (IPX), for NetWare-based LANs. The AppleTalk and IPX protocols control communication between devices—PCs, printers, and servers—within the confines of a LAN.

IPX and AppleTalk are similar in many ways in that they control LAN-based communication by dictating the type and size of data packets, their address "headers," and similar issues. These ensure that data packets can pass over the network.

AppleTalk and IPX handle remote serial communication in totally dissimilar ways, however. With AppleTalk, serial communications are integral to the protocol, unlike NetWare, which requires an "add-on" protocol.

SERIAL (DIAL-IN) PROTOCOLS

The Point-to-Point Protocol (PPP) and Apple's AppleTalk Remote Access (ARA) protocols are two of the most widely implemented serial protocols for telephone-based communications. ARA and PPP control and facilitate asynchronous communication between the LAN and the remote user's PC or Mac over the telephone network.

With ARA, Apple Computer made remote communication an integral part of the AppleTalk protocol suite. This tightly integrates remote users into an AppleTalk LAN, letting them use the network resources as though they were connected locally.

ARA offers several important security features, including a call-back function, the capability to grant callers access to the LAN-based Mac but not the network it is connected to, and password protection. In addition, ARA has its own set of data-compression and filtering protocols and uses the V.42*bis* international standard for data compression, which increases data-transfer rates.

ARA also integrates the Microcom Network Protocol (NMP), which ensures the integrity of data transferred over the telephone line.

Remote users of NetWare networks, on the other hand, must rely on a non-native serial protocol, such as PPP. PPP, originally devised for the Internet, uses what is called tokenizing and compression techniques to increase data-transmission rates.

PPP doesn't perform error-handling, however. It requires using a modem that supports the V.42*bis* or MNP error-correction services for security.

Although PPP isn't an integral part of Novell's IPX, Novell permits running PPP "over" IPX. This allows remote users to access NetWare-based resources as if they were connected to the LAN locally.

Remote users requiring access to the Internet also might use still another protocol, called SLIP. SLIP is a framing scheme that puts IP packets on a serial line.

SLIP has become popular for some dial-up IP applications, with implementations available for many different types of computers.

SLIP does, however, have several deficiencies, including the fact that it contains no provisions for error detection, assuming other services will handle that. It also doesn't provide support for link-management tasks, nor for any protocol family other than IP.

DIAL-UP ROUTERS

Dial-up routers, as noted earlier, are actually communications servers that connect multiple LANs via the telephone system. These contain a LAN interface (such as an Ethernet NIC) for connection to the network cabling as well as serial asynchronous ports for connecting modems to the telco lines.

A dial-up router allows connecting two geographically separate LANs occasionally over the switched telephone network. Most dial-up routers offer only limited LAN protocol support—that is, one or two protocols. It's thus important to make sure the dial-up router you select handles the protocols running on your network.

When a dial-up router isn't handling routing chores, it can function as a shared modem, allowing local LAN users to dial out of the network. Examples of dial-up routers include Microtest's LANModem, USRobotics' LAN modem and the NetModem/E by Shiva.

NOVELL-SUPPLIED COMMUNICATIONS PRODUCTS

Novell, as noted earlier in this chapter, offers a variety of remote-access add-ons that allow remote clients to access a NetWare 4.*x* asynchronously. These include the NetWare Access Server (NAS), the NetWare Asynchronous Communication Server (NACS) and NetWare Connect, all of which provide dial-in and dial-out capabilities.

The list also includes the NetWare Remote Shell, which communicates with the Asynchronous Remote Router, and an improved version of the remote console remote-access product originally available with NetWare 3.*x*. This application allows managing a NetWare server from a remote location, either over a LAN hook-up or via the telephone network.

NetWare Remote Shell

This remote client first came with NetWare 2.12, and upgrades are available on CompuServe. The NetWare Remote Shell works with the NetWare Asynchronous Remote Router and provides access to a network over a dial-up line. With this access method, IPX/SPX must travel across the phone line. NetWare Remote Shell, similar to other dial-up solutions, is not intended for executing applications residing on the network.

Tip

To download the latest version of the NetWare Remote shell—and other NetWare updates—log into the CompuServe information service, then type GO NOVLIB at the ! prompt. You'll find the file, called PTF299.ZIP, under library nine.

NetWare Access Server

Novell's NetWare Access Server (NAS), now owned and supported by Citrix, is a software-only package that, when coupled with the necessary hardware, provides remote access to a NetWare-based LAN. It gives up to 16 users simultaneous access to all the resources on a NetWare LAN.

In addition, Macintosh users can also connect to the NAS over the LAN, then use it as a DOS application processor. This provides an easy method for letting Mac users run DOS applications across the network.

NAS supports not only asynchronous modems, but multiplexers, direct connections and X.25 Public Data Network (PDN) connections.

Users can log into the NAS with a wide range of remote-control software, such as OnLAN PC or OnLAN Mac, Symantec Corp.'s special network versions of its remote-control pcAnywhere program. OnLAN PC/Mac comes with NAS, and Novell allows users to make as many copies of OnLAN PC/Mac as they need.

After making the connection into the NAS, users can then log into a NetWare file server, gaining access to all of their usual network resources as though they were local. Security features offered by NAS include password protection, dial-back capabilities and audit file tracking, as well as NetWare's usual assortment of built-in security functions.

NAS uses Quarterdeck's DESQview multitasking environment to provide multiple concurrent sessions to remote users. A key ancillary benefit of this is the capability running multiple concurrent sessions per individual dial-up connection.

This allows a user to dial into the NAS, initiate a database query, "hot key" to a new session, then initiate another program while the database query continues to run in the background session. And if one of the sessions "locks up," the user can "hot key" to the session manager to terminate it.

NetWare Asynchronous Communications Server

Novell's NetWare Asynchronous Communications Server (NACS), an NLM-based product, also is a software-only application. When coupled with the necessary hardware, NACS gives NetWare users access to asynchronous resources. These include modems, asynchronous hosts, and X.25 network services. NACS comes in 2-, 8-, and 32-port versions.

Note

NACS since has been replaced by a new product called *NetWare Connect*. The basic operating theory, however, remains the same.

Access to the NACS allows network managers to control entry to the LAN in various ways. They can restrict users to an individual NCS server, to individual ports on a NACS server, or by authorized group. The NACS console can also be password-protected, thus banning unauthorized users from reconfiguring the NACS server.

Users want an easy-to-use communications program that recognizes the NetWare Asynchronous Services Interface (NASI). As such, dial-out communications are performed by loading the NASI TSR (terminate and stay resident) program that comes with NASI on the dial-out workstation.

This software is required because the modem isn't connected to a local serial port, as normally the case, but rather to a file server on the network. NASI thus gives LAN-based workstations the capability of dialing out of the network via a modem connected to a file server over the network.

34

REMOTE ACCESS

Note

Acquiring NASI support could be as easy as upgrading to the network version of your favorite communications program. Many popular communications applications, including those listed below, offer built-in compatibility with NACS/NASI.

- ◆ ASCOM/IV, Network
- ◆ BLAST Professional DOS
- ◆ BLAST Professional Server
- ◆ CO/Session LAN II
- ◆ CROSSTALK Mk. 4
- ◆ CROSSTALK for Windows
- ◆ DynaComm Asynchronous
- ◆ LEXUS 2000 LAN
- ◆ On/LAN PC
- ◆ pcAnywhere IV/LAN
- ◆ poly-STAR/T
- ◆ PROCOMM PLUS, Network
- ◆ Reflection/7+
- ◆ RELAY Gold/LAN
- ◆ Smartcom Exec
- ◆ SmarTerm 340
- ◆ Softerm PC
- ◆ VsComm/LAN
- ◆ WestLAW/WESTMATE
- ◆ ZSTEM 340, LAN

REMOTE SERVER CONSOLE ACCESS

Novell has incorporated an improved version of its remote console into NetWare 4.*x* for remotely managing a file server. Remote console allows managing servers from a workstation on the network or a computer linked to the LAN via a modem.

With remote console, a network manager can do the following:

- ◆ Enter the same commands remotely that are available at the server console
- ◆ Access both NetWare and DOS partitions on the server to scan directories and edit files

- Transfer files to, but not from, a NetWare 4.*x* server
- Down or reboot a NetWare 4.*x* server
- Install or upgrade NetWare on a remote server

The remote-console capability isn't difficult to master, but the network manager must remember to set the program up on the server locally before trying to access the server remotely. Typing **LOAD REMOTE** [*password*] at the server console loads the remote-console application.

The remote-console program can also be executed automatically each time the server is brought up by adding the LOAD REMOTE command to the server's AUTOEXEC.NCF start-up file. Network managers who add the REMOTE CONSOLE command to the AUTOEXEC.NCF file should refer to the next chapter in this book, Chapter 34 for instructions to encrypt their password.

There are several other things to remember when using the remote-console capabilities. To access the remote console from a workstation attached to the network, type **LOAD RSPX** at the server console. (This also must be loaded on the NetWare 4.*x* server.) To access the remote console capabilities available over a modem, the following NLMs must also be loaded on the NetWare 4.*x* server:

1. AIO.NLM, the asynchronous communications port interface (that is, type **LOAD AIO**)
2. AIOCOMX.NLM, the communications port driver (type **LOAD AIOCOMX**)
3. RS232.NLM (that is, type **RS232** [*com_port*] [*modem_speed*] [*N*] [*C*], where *com_port* is serial communications port 1 or 2, *modem_speed* is the baud rate of the attached modem, *N* refers to a null modem cable, and *C* specifies using the call-back security option).

Only after these files are loaded on the NetWare 4.*x* server can the remote PC be prepared to remotely manage the server. Set-up at the remote PC includes creating a subdirectory, such as REMAN (for REmote MANagement), then copying the following files to it:

- RCONSOLE.EXE
- RCONSOLE.HEP
- RCONSOLE.MSG
- IBM_RUN.OVL
- _RUN.OVL
- IBM_AIO.OVL
- _AIO.OVL
- TEXTUTIL.HEP

◆ TEXUTIL.IDX

◆ TEXTUTIL.MSG

Execute RCONSOLE on the PC, then choose Asynchronous from the Connection type menu. After configuring the modem, select Connect to Remote Location. Choose the server you want to manage, and you're in!

Note

When using NetWare 4.*x*'s remote-console capability to connect to a server over a modem, NetWare does not guarantee packet delivery. If, during a session, the server becomes laden with heavy disk and LAN activity, the remote console may "time out." This results in a No response from server or an Unable to send request to server message. When this occurs, simply hang up and reconnect. If this occurs frequently, you may need to wait until peak server utilization periods have passed.

NetWare Connect

NetWare Connect, a replacement for NACS, is a server-based NLM that gives NetWare LANs dial-in and dial-out capabilities for both remote-control and remote-node clients. It allows multiple remote users to access NetWare and gives LAN-based workstations access to outside resources via telephone lines.

In addition to providing basic communications capabilities, NetWare Connect offers the following:

◆ Dynamic port allocation

◆ Resource pooling

◆ Port sharing

◆ Routing of incoming calls

◆ Port and access security

◆ Support for virtually any modem type

◆ Audit trail maintenance

◆ Support for NACS 3.0

◆ Management consoles

Unlike most communications services, NetWare Connect allows dynamically allocating ports as users require them for communications. This means that ports may be used interchangeably for incoming or outgoing calls.

NetWare Connect also maximizes communications resources by sharing modems, multiport adapters, telephone lines and multiplexers. The product also provides remote clients with support for the AppleTalk Remote Access Service (ARAS), Novell's Remote Node Service and NASI Connection Service (NCS).

ARAS and RNS allow Macintosh and DOS clients, respectively, to dial into the NetWare LAN as remote nodes. NCS establishes the logical connection between a NetWare Connect port and a LAN-based workstation, essentially directing outgoing communications traffic.

SELECTING A MODEM

When developing a remote LAN access system, don't overlook the importance of the modems you'll attach to your network's communications servers. Modems, which translate a computer's digital data into audible tones that can be sent over telephone network, are a key element in the communications link between a network and its dial-in users.

Note

They're often used interchangeably, but the terms *baud rate* and *bit rate* usually refer to different data-transmission speeds. The baud rate of a modem is the actual discrete switching speed, or number of transitions (voltage or frequency changes), per second. The bit-per-second rate of a modem refers to the number of binary digits (bits) passed between two modems in a second. Modern voice-grade phone lines can handle a maximum of 2400 signal changes per second; thus, if each signal change represents a bit, then the baud rate (2400) does indeed equal the bit rate (2400). But if each baud, or signal shift, is made to represent two bits (called a "dibit"), then the 2400 baud rate yields a 4800 bps rate. With V.32*bis* modems, the modem operates at 14,400 bps and 2400 baud (5 bits per baud).

Modems determine how "fast" your remote LAN access system appears to operate to remote users. High-speed modems—this means those operating a 9600 bps and above—and modern data-compression techniques can make dial-up communications appear almost as fast as working on the LAN itself. Low-speed modems, on the other hand, can make telecommuting a drudge.

Consequently, it's important to connect the fastest modems available to your communications servers. If you're determined to stick with modems based on international standards—and you should be—that currently means selecting modems with a 14.4 kbps exchange rate.

Other choices are available, but there are tradeoffs with these options. In some situations—for example, when only modems from the same type from the same manufacturer are used at both ends of the communications link—non-standard modems can be acceptable alternatives. This is especially true when they provide a specific capability, such as a faster data rate than available with standard-based products.

V.DOT INTERNATIONAL MODEM STANDARDS

V.32 is the official designation for the current fastest accepted international modem standard for dial-up circuits, at 14.4 kbp. The V.32 label came from the CCITT (for Consultative Committee on International Telephony and Telegraph), which, until 1993, established international modem standards.

The Telecommunications Standards Bureau (TSB), an agency of the International Telecommunications Union (ITU), took over the CCITT's standard-setting role in 1993, however. The TSB and a number of modem vendors have been working to develop the next-generation modem standard, which is currently known as V.FAST but will probably be designated V.34.

V.FAST calls for data exchange at 28.8 kbps over dial-up lines. When ratified (most likely by the end of 1994), the V.FAST/V.34 specifications will include specifications for two-way simultaneous faxing at a 28.8 kbps modem transfer rate, with several auxiliary channels for management functions.

V.FAST/V.34 modems will also use the data-compression and error-correction techniques spelled out by two other CCITT standards, V.42 and v.42*bis*.

By mid-1994, V.FAST/V.34, which is unusable across transatlantic telephone circuits, was still well short of finalization. As a result, the modem market was confused, with several de facto "standards" competing for market share.

This list includes the so-called "V.terbo" modems, which operate at 16.8 kbps (data) and 19.2 kbps (fax). The proprietary work of AT&T Paradyne, V.32terbo borrows its name from the last CCITT standard (V.32) and "puns" on the word *ter*, the suffix for the third revision of a standard.

Several vendors have released V.32terbo-based products. These include Microcom. A number of other modem manufacturers have released other non-standard high-speed modems, also based on proprietary techniques.

SPEED VERSUS STANDARDS

When selecting a modem, wise network managers focus on standards and compatibility issues, not just a high data-transmission rate. This is particularly so in remote LAN access systems, which require high-speed modems to perform at optimum levels.

In LAN access environments, remote callers almost always use modems from a variety of vendors, and these are seldom the same as the modems found at the central site. Selecting standards-based modems thus ensures compatibility between the remote and central-site modems and guarantees that remote users can get onto the network.

Current international modem standards include the V.32, V.32*bis*, V.42, and V.42*bis*.

V.32

This is the CCITT standard for asynchronous and synchronous 4,800 bps and 9,600 bps full-duplex modems. It supports rate negotiation, which allows two communicating modems to transmit data at the highest rate common to them.

V.32*bis*

This is the CCITT standard for asynchronous and synchronous 4800 bps, 7200 bps, 9600 bps, 12000 bps and 14400 bps full-duplex modems. It supports rate negotiation, which allows two communicating modems to transmit data at the highest rate common to them. As noted, this is the fastest current CCITT standard.

ERROR-CORRECTION AND DATA COMPRESSION

Modern modems also incorporate a variety of schemes that compress data, thus increasing the effective data-transfer rate, and ensure that the data exchanged is error free. Again, selecting modems incorporating standards-based error-correction and data-compression schemes is vital to effective two-way communications.

These are the V.42 and V.42*bis* standards. In addition, many modems support the Microcom Networking Protocol (MNP).

MNP

MNP is a de facto error-correction standard used in many modems; in fact, the V.42 standard includes MNP as an alternative to its standards-based procedure. This means V.42-compatible modems can communicate with MNP-based modems and still ensure reliable data exchange. The MNP protocols include 10 separate classes of protocols; MNP 4 provides error control, MNP 5 data compression.

V.42

The accepted international error-correction standard is the CCITT's V.42. It prevents noisy telephone lines from causing data loss. It is a method for ensuring that the data that arrives at a receiving modem is exactly that which was sent.

Note

When both modems in a communications link support the V.42 error-correction scheme, they filter out noise on the telephone line. The modems work by sending blocks of data and exchanging an associated CRC (for cyclical redundancy check) between each other. The CRC contains a unique value that the receiving modem uses to determine whether it has received a valid data packet or a data packet corrupted by line noise. When the received CRC value fails to match that sent by the other modem, the receiving modem returns a command telling the sending modem to retransmit the associated data packet.

The V.42 standard, which uses what is known as the *Link Access Procedure Modem* (LAPM) error-correction protocol, provides an alternative protocol that is compatible with modems using the Microcom Network Protocol (MNP) levels 2 through 4 error-correction schemes.

V.42*bis*

The accepted international data-compression standard is the CCITT's V.42*bis*. V.42*bis* compresses data based on a scheme that increases modem throughput up to four times over the bit-per-second rate of the modem. This means a 2,400 bps modems implementing V.42*bis* compression transmit at 9,600 bps. The standards for V.*x*-type modems are summarized in Table 34.1.

TABLE 34.1. INTERNATIONAL MODEM STANDARDS.

CCITT Modem Standard	Description
V.22	Full-duplex 2400 bps over dial-up and two-wire leased lines with fallback to 1200 bps
V.32	Full-duplex 4,800 bps over dial-up and two-wire leased lines with fallback to 2400 bps
V.32*bis*	Full-duplex 14.4 Kbps over dial-up and two-wire leased lines, with fallback to 4800, 7200, and 9600 bps

Many high-speed modems still support MNP level 5 data compression. This scheme from Microcom, which provides a 2:1 compression ratio, preceded the V.42*bis* standard.

Note

In the BBS (electronic bulletin-board service) world, most BBS-based files are compressed, or "ZIPed," with an application called PKZIP. ZIPed files must be uncompressed (with PKUNZIP) before they're usable, but in compressed form they occupy less disk space, allowing the BBS SYSOP (system operator) to store more files in one ZIP file, while also taking less time to transmit over the telco lines. The data-compression capabilities of V.42*bis* fall well short of PKZIP, but on straight ASCII text they can still decrease the data by about 50 percent, effectively doubling the line's data-transfer rate.

Tip

Data compression between modems is effective only when the data being transferred is not already compressed.

HIGH-SPEED UARTS

When a computer receives data over a serial port from a high-speed modem, it's critical that the data flow continue without interruption. When other peripherals require "cycles" on the computer's I/O bus, however, serial data flow is often delayed, or interrupted. These delays can result in data loss, decreasing the effective throughput of the data transmission. One of the major competitors for cycles on the I/O bus is the computer's hard drive, but network interface cards (NICs) also compete heavily for bus access.

Warning

File-transfer protocols such as Ymodem/G rely on V.42 to catch data-transmission errors. If the hard drive or NIC prevents the serial port from passing information over the I/O bus, you'll lose data after the modem's V.42 capabilities have correctly received it. This data is lost in the serial port's UART (for *Universal Asynchronous Receiver / Transmitter*). This results in an aborted and/or corrupted file transfer. If your modem uses an error-correction technique such as Zmodem, the file-transfer process won't be interrupted, but the effective throughput suffers.

The solution to ending this data loss with high-speed modems is to use an intelligent, high-speed buffered UART. Most 386-class computers now come standard with the 16450 UART. An enhanced UART, the 16550AFN (AFN is the most recent and stable release of the chip), provides a 16K buffer that stores received data when the computer's I/O bus is in use by the hard drive or an NIC. The buffered data in the UART is transferred to the computer when the computer is again able to respond to the serial port's interrupt request.

Unfortunately, some communications software was not written to take advantage of the 16550 UART. In this case, the enhanced chip is functionally equivalent to the 16450 UART, and the 16550 cannot assert flow control to the modem. To overcome this weakness, some hardware vendors have produced high-speed, intelligent serial interfaces. The Hayes ESP Communications Accelerator and the Telcor T/Port are two examples of such a product. These adapters eliminate data "overrun," allow using existing software, and relieve the operating system of the overhead associated with handling high-speed serial data communications.

Tip

The performance of the new high-speed modems available now can be hindered when they're used with some serial ports. Technical advances in serial port communications seems to be lagging behind other hardware in performance upgrades. This may not be an issue when using internal modems, which connect directly to the PC's internal I/O bus and provide their own serial communications interface. It can be a problem when using external modems, which must pass data through one of the computer's serial ports. With older, slower computers, such as IBM XTs, it's often wise to consider adding an enhanced serial port.

ALTERNATIVE HIGH-SPEED COMMUNICATIONS LINKS

A variety of data-transmissions options, including Switched 56, Integrated Services Digital Network (ISDN), and SMDS (Switched Megabit Data Services) and Asynchronous Transfer Mode (ATM) are available for remote users who require faster-than-telephone access to their network. These services provide data rates in excess of the 56 kbps limitations found with standard telco circuits.

Although they offer substantially faster data-exchange rates than the telephone network, Switched 56, ISDN, ATM and SMDS all come with tradeoffs. In particular, each requires expensive terminating equipment at each end of the link, and all three are substantially more expensive than dial-up communications.

SWITCHED 56 SERVICES

Switched 56 services are often attractive when ISDN either is not available or is too expensive. Switched 56, like ISDN, is a digital service that delivers considerable bandwidth on a time-charged basis.

As its name implies it offers 56 kbps data rates, but LAN rates of up to 150 kbps to 200 kbps are possible with data compression. And, because it is often used to carry voice telephony in places where ISDN is unavailable, Switched 56 is widely available.

In addition, Switched 56 interoperates with ISDN—that is, a user on a Switched 56 circuit can place/receive calls to/from not only other Switched 56 sites, but users with ISDN basic rate services.

Long-term prospects indicate that ISDN will replace Switched 56, and ATM will eventually replace ISDN. But for the foreseeable future—the next five to seven years—Switched 56 can be a cost-effective high-speed alternative to standard telephone circuits.

INTEGRATED SERVICES DIGITAL NETWORK (ISDN)

The ISDN Basic rate service, available from a variety of services, including the Regional Bell Operating Companies (RBOCs), delivers data on up to two 64 kbps channels for services of 64 kbps or 128 kbps. ISDN is a switched service that offers pay-as-you-go applications similar to those using packet-switched technology.

The principal problem with ISDN is its varying availability and costs. It is unavailable in many large cities, while too expensive in other locations to make it cost-effective.

With compression, however, ISDN offers a considerable usefulness, with data-transfer rates of up to 400 kbps over what is called a 2B+D ISDN circuit. (ISDN services are also available in what in called a 1B-D primary rate.)

Tip

To find out about ISDN availability in your area, call 408-734-4312. This is a free online service, provided and maintained by Combinet, that provides area-code by area-code listings of ISDN service.

SMDS (SWITCHED MEGABIT DATA SERVICES)

SMDS delivers a high-bandwidth (up to 45 Mbps) packet-switched data stream. SMDS requires using high-performance communications equipment, such as

DSU/CSU and routers. CSUs (channel service units) and DSUs (data service units) act as interfaces between a local LAN and the SMDS network.

At this point, SMDS is available only within the coverage areas of a limited number of local RBOCS. With long distance carriers expected to phase SMDS in over the next two years, only short-haul local SMDS circuits are available now.

ASYNCHRONOUS TRANSFER MODE (ATM)

ATM is a provides the means to consolidate voice, data, and video into one networking scheme. It also offers an ideal private remote-access network.

As a switched technology, ATM provides "virtual" circuits that essentially guarantee that a certain level of service will be delivered to an end station. That is, both throughput and timeliness of delivery are assured. (This is a particularly important in delivering voice and video over a network.

At present, the following two types of ATM services are available:

◆ A Hewlett-Packard- and AT&T-proposed plan that transmits data at 50 mbps over twisted-pair wiring

◆ An IBM-backed measure that runs at 25 mbps

The primary downside of ATM is its costs: Adapters for ATM nodes cost in the $2,000 range, and costs for the switching hub required another $3,000 per port.

SELECTING A COMMUNICATIONS SERVER

As noted earlier, as networks expand and become more complex, the demands placed on the components in those networks increase as well. This is particularly true of communications servers.

A communications server is gateway into your network. Maintain the same level of security to this gateway as you would the doorway to a vault containing other company valuables.

Selecting the right communications server for your application can be a confusing task. There are large, expensive boxes dedicated to providing communications to those who need access. You'll also find inexpensive software-only packages that can run on a workstation to provide the same basic services.

No matter what your application, however, answering the following questions can help you pinpoint the requirements of your communications server:

◆ Who needs remote access?

◆ How many users will require access simultaneously?

- ◆ Will remote users require workstation hard disk access as well as network access?
- ◆ Will remote users require access to e-mail?
- ◆ Will users access only data files?
- ◆ Will users need to execute applications on the host?
- ◆ What other communications requirements does your organization have?

When selecting a communications server, it's critical to closely analyze the features required to ensure secure, easy-to-use, and manageable remote communications.

MULTIPROTOCOL SUPPORT

With remote LAN access products, multiprotocol support ensures dial-up flexibility for end users and enhanced management capabilities for network administrators.

By supporting multiple networking and serial protocols, remote LAN access products allow remote users to use the computing hardware and operating system they're accustomed to, not one dictated by limitations posed by communications servers.

In most LAN environments, this means a communications server should support Novell's IPX for NetWare clients and Apple's AppleTalk for Macintosh clients, two of the most widely implemented networking protocols. It may also include supporting TCP/IP, NetBIOS or any of the many other protocols found in enterprise networks.

Supporting multiple protocols in a single communications server also eases management and configuration problems for network managers. Instead of installing and managing individual "boxes" supporting each LAN protocol, they deal with just one.

STANDARDS-BASED MANAGEMENT CAPABILITIES

Remote LAN access solutions increase the number of networked devices and extend network services across large geographical areas. It is thus critical to the smooth operation of the network that the network manager be able to manage those remote links.

In particular, remote access solutions should support SNMP (*Simple Network Management Protocol*), the industry standard for network management. By supporting SNMP, including SNMP's MIB I and MIB II, remote-access solutions ensure their smooth integration into existing enterprise network management systems, such as Sun Microsystem's SunNet Manager.

34

REMOTE ACCESS

These management systems permit monitoring, configuring and controlling communications ports on communications servers. This is a key capability in ensuring secure, managed access to a LAN.

Remote access systems should also provide both in- and out-of-band management capabilities. Out-of-band management allows managing the remote access server and its associated communications via a modem from remote locations or when the network is down, and in-band services are unavailable. In-band, or over-the-network, services generally are preferred to out-of-band management, but can add traffic to an already heavily burdened network.

The management system should also provide an easy-to-use graphical interface and operate on computing hardware the network manager is familiar with. This typically means a Windows-based PC, but could also be a Sun workstation or a Macintosh.

SECURITY CAPABILITIES

Because remote access products open a gateway into the network, they must provide security capabilities that prevent unauthorized access to network services. Among the key capabilities a remote access solution should provide are user-name and password authentication schemes as well as a call-back feature, call logging and keystroke encoding.

Call-back schemes verify a user's identity by returning calls to a predetermined phone number. This certifies who the calling user is, but it also restricts access to the LAN from unauthorized phone numbers, such as a branch office employee's home number.

Keystroke encoding, which encodes passwords as they pass from the remote client to the access server, is the most secure form of protecting data in transit. Encoding makes it impossible to decode the transmitted characters without a "key" combination that allows decoding transmissions.

It's also important that remote access products be easily integrated into third-party security systems, such as Digital Pathway's Defender series of access control products.

EASY MIGRATION PATH

Remote access needs tend to increase, not diminish, as networks grow, so remote access solutions should be easily upgradable. Specifically, they should allow for modular expansion of any hardware while also permitting the upgrading of a communications server's operating software.

Modular remote access products allow starting with a basic configuration—usually, four or eight modem ports. They then allow adding modules containing additional modem ports when remote access demands have expanded.

Communications servers with "flash" EPROMs, which are electronically programmable read-only memory circuits, let the network manager download product "firmware" upgrades over the network, directly or remotely. This both avoids the tedious task of swapping EPROMs in the communications server when an upgrade is necessary, it also eliminates the time and expenses associated with traveling to remote sites to make the upgrade.

Because network cabling schemes are often upgraded, remote LAN communications servers should also offer connections to the popular networking topologies. In particular, this means Ethernet, the most widely implemented networking technology today. With Ethernet, these connections include BNC for 10Base2 (thin coaxial cable), AUI for 10Base5 (thick coax or fiber-optic cable) and RJ-45 for 10BaseT (standard telephone cable).

SUMMARY

Expanding networks place increased demands on the network's abilities to handle all types of users, especially remote users accessing the LAN via the switched telephone network. A wide variety of remote-access solutions are on the market today, but they all provide the same basic capabilities:

◆ Access to electronic mail

◆ Access to host- and other network-based data files

◆ Access to applications on the network

Various implementations of these remote access solutions include remote mail servers that grant only e-mail access, multiprocessor communications servers that allow multiple remote callers to access LAN-based data and or applications, and multitasking communications servers that also grant access to the resources on the LAN.

This chapter also looked into the problems associated with remote LAN access, discussed various ways to access the LAN from a remote location, and explained which problems are addressed by each method. It also included help in selecting the communications server and the modems attached to it.

Finally, this chapter took a brief look at some of the high-speed data-transport options available to network managers.

- Network Management

- Archiving and Backup

- Accounting

- Tuning for
  Performance

- Troubleshooting
  NetWare 4.*x*

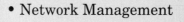

P A R T   VII

Maintenance and
Troubleshooting

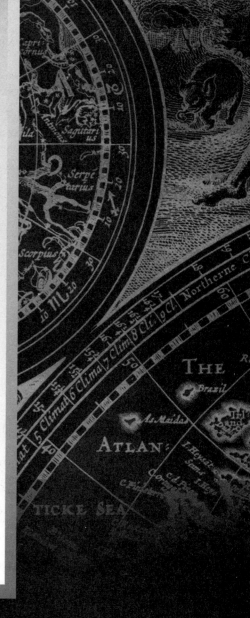

- Taking a Proactive Approach

- Tools for Managing Your Network

- NDS Partition Management

- Using NetSync

- NetWare's Remote Management Facility

- Enterprise Management Systems: Novell's NMS

- Summary

CHAPTER 35

Network Management

Networks are like children—you need to keep a constant watch on them to ensure they stay out of trouble. Without the help of network monitoring tools, it is not easy to detect and correct symptoms of a faulty LAN before it is too late. In this chapter we discuss some of the techniques you should employ as a system administrator to monitor the health of your LAN. We will specifically use Novell's NetWare Management System (NMS) as an example to illustrate to you how you can detect and rectify problems before they reduce your LAN performance or bring your LAN down.

When talking about network management, there are two general areas of interest. First, it is user management where one is looking for ways and tools to simplify the amount of work necessary to manage user information such as passwords and access rights. This is now much simplified in the case of NetWare 4 with the introduction of NetWare Directory Services (NDS). The other area of network management is the management of physical devices such as file servers and related peripherals. This chapter focuses on this later point of physical network management, however, the management of NDS is also touched upon.

Taking a Proactive Approach

There are two ways to network management—the *proactive* approach or the *reactive* approach. With any installations, you can not get away from the reactive network management approach as there are always "fires to fight." However, you can take steps to keep that to a minimum by doing more and more proactive network management.

There are many things you can do to reduce the amount of support that is needed for your network. For example, by sticking with the industry standard for hardware, use the proper cables, documenting your network and educating users will cut down on the amount of support and maintenance required. These topics are covered, respectively, in details in Chapters 6, 9, 30, and 31.

Tip

As a matter of fact, all the topics discussed in this book will in one way or another help you to operate a smooth network and quickly tackle and resolve common problems should they arise.

Deciding on a Strategy

Naturally one wants the most reliable network and the best support possible. However, this is not always possible in reality. Therefore, you must decide on a strategy. Depending on your budget, you can implement network management at either the departmental level or at the enterprise level.

Departmental network management means you put in place a set of network management tools for specific department, depending on their needs. For example, for the word processing department, it would be critical that you are notified if there is any printing problem. For planning, getting access to the central database would be more important than not being able to print; therefore, monitoring of the database server would be deemed top priority.

The advantage of implementing departmental management is that you can most likely find tools for the specific task more easily and at a lower cost. The drawback is that you don't get to see the "big picture" of your whole internet network as not all the (sub)networks have the necessary reporting and monitoring tools in place.

Enterprise network management allows you to have a "bird's eye view" of your whole network. However, it is generally a lot more expensive to implement than departmental level management. In return, you can gather a large number of statistics and information from a central location. This makes it very attractive for companies with multiple sites.

You may want to implement your network management strategy in a similar way on how you set up your Help Desk or network management structure. This way your Help staff can be notified of problems promptly. A discussion of "how to organize network administration" was given in Chapter 10.

Because NetWare 4 is designed to be an enterprise solution, we will, in this chapter, discuss Novell's enterprise network management solution, NetWare Management Services (NMS) in a later section.

AREAS OF MANAGEMENT

Before deciding on a network management software or platform, you should investigate and decide on the key areas in your network to be managed. This will help you look for the options available from the various packages.

Depending on your particular type of business or department, the areas of concern differs. For example, if your users need to access outside on-line services, such as CompuServe, it is important for you to know about the status of your modem pools and communications. If your users depends on mainframe connectivity, you need to keep close tabs on your LAN-to-mainframe gateways.

Other than establishing the areas of management, you also need to determine their priority as well as the cost of downtime. There is, unfortunately, no "hard numbers" that one can go by—it is strictly determined on a case-by-case basis.

However, no matter what your situation is, some general areas of concern are:

◆ File server availability (is the server up?)

◆ Disk space usage (how much space is left?)

◆ Router status (is the router up?)

◆ Security breaches (such as intruder detection lockouts)

Therefore, when you look for and implement a network management solution, make sure it is capable of addressing the preceding basic requirements.

ENTERPRISE MANAGEMENT PLATFORMS

Today many large sites are faced with a network management nightmare in that different devices tend to require different management tools. Therefore, an administrator has to learn about different interfaces and switch between different client platforms depending on the device in question. This reduces the effectiveness of troubleshooting and managing a distributed network.

Some of the problems inherent in using multiple tools to manage your network are

◆ Different management tools use different interfaces for the various types of information, making troubleshooting effects more difficult to perform and learn.

◆ Different reporting formats used the different tools making it difficult to obtain an overall big picture.

◆ Different applications are inconvenient to use and maintain.

One solution is to combine as much of the necessary management functions into a single environment. A good network management platform allows you to manage your entire distributed network from a centralized location. Tight integration with third-party management applications is also necessary.

There are a number of network management platforms available on the market at this time, such as the following:

◆ HP OpenView from Hewlett-Packard

◆ SunNet Manager from Sun Microsystems/SunConnect

◆ NetWare Management System (NMS) from Novell

◆ NetView/6000 from IBM

HP OpenView is available both for the DOS/Windows platform as well as UNIX machines. SunNet Manager and NetView/6000 are only available for UNIX systems. Novell's NMS is a DOS/Windows based system. All these platforms are scaleable. In other words, they can grow with your networking environment.

Depending on your requirement, NMS is suitable for a wide range of situations. Since it is designed by Novell, it has the capability to manage IPX-based devices, especially NetWare file servers. We will be discussing more about NMS in a later section in this chapter.

TOOLS FOR MANAGING YOUR NETWORK

A number of tools are available for network management purposes from a number of sources. Some simple, yet effective, tools are shipped with NetWare itself. Others are available from a range of vendors, including Novell. If you have a low network management budget, there are also good packages available as shareware as well as freeware. Check your local bulletin board systems, online information services such as CompuServe, as well as the Internet.

In this section, we will discuss some network management products shipped with NetWare as well as some available from other sources.

PRODUCTS AVAILABLE WITH NETWARE

Several tools are shipped with NetWare to assist you in managing your network:

- ◆ NW Admin (for Windows)
- ◆ NETADMIN (for DOS)
- ◆ PCONSOLE
- ◆ RCONSOLE
- ◆ Partition Manager (for Windows)
- ◆ PARTMGR (for DOS)
- ◆ NetSync

NW Admin and NETADMIN are, respectively, the Windows and DOS) version of Novell's Network Administrator that allow you to manage your NetWare Directory Services database (see Figures 35.1 and 35.2). PCONSOLE is for managing print queues/jobs and printers (see Figures 35.3 and 35.4). RCONSOLE allows you to execute server console commands (such as loading and unloading of NLMs) without being physically at the file server console (see Figure 35.5).

Figure 35.1.
Windows-based
NetWare Administrator
(NW Admin).

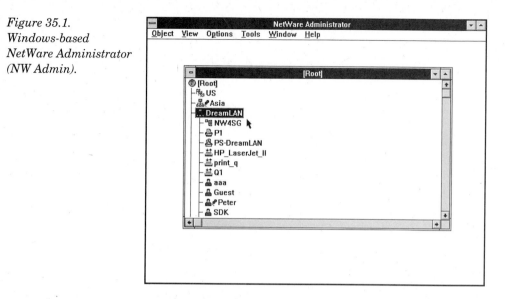

Figure 35.2.
DOS-based NetWare
Administrator
(NETADMIN).

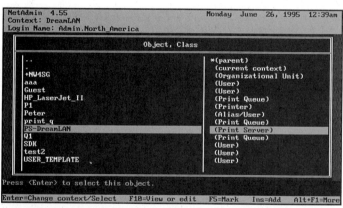

Figure 35.3.
PCONSOLE enables
you to manage print
queues and jobs.

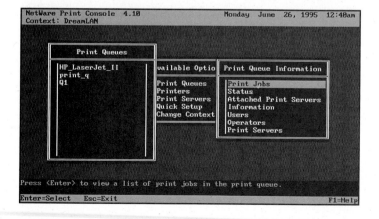

Figure 35.4.
PCONSOLE allows you
to manage printers.

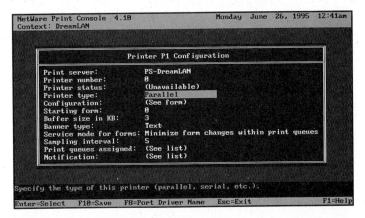

Figure 35.5.
RCONSOLE allows
you to access file server
consoles.

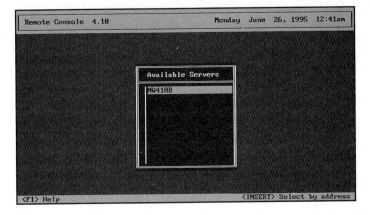

The use of NW Admin/NETADMIN has been discussed in Chapter 25 and PCONSOLE has been covered in Chapter 32. Therefore, we will only cover the use of RCONSOLE in this chapter.

The NDS partition management tools (Partition Manager and PARTMGR) are worth some detailed discussions here. Although not directly related to the health of your physical network, they do allow you to manage your NDS "network." They, along with NetSync—which allows you to manage your NetWare 3.1x servers using NetWare 4 tools—are discussed in a later section.

Note

None of the preceding programs and tools will give you information such as trend data or alerts when certain (preconfigured) thresholds are exceeded. Additional utilities are needed.

PRODUCTS FROM OTHER SOURCES

Currently on the market are a number of software tools that will help you troubleshoot, monitor, and manage the network much more easily. Some examples are:

◆ **LANDesk Manager from Intel:** Allows you to perform workstation inventory as well as accessing workstations over the LAN. Good for remote support.

◆ **NetSight from Intel**: Allows packet capture and protocol decode from the LAN cable.

◆ **Compaq Insight Manager from Compaq**: Specific to Compaq servers. Allows you to monitor performance of the server hardware remotely.

◆ **Frye Utilities for Networks from Frye Computer Systems, Inc.**: This is a suite of seven integrated network management products which includes NetWare Management, NetWare Early Warning System, NetWare Console Commander, LAN Directory, Software Update and Distribution System (SUDS), SUDS Wide Area Network Distribution Module, and Node Tracker.

◆ **NetWare Management Systems from Novell**: An enterprise network management package that allows you to manage NetWare servers, routers, and hubs from a central management console.

◆ **LANalyzer for Windows from Novell:** A DOS/Windows based packet capture and protocol analysis tool that supports both token ring and Ethernet (see Figure 35.6).

Figure 35.6.
LANalyzer for Windows
dashboard and packet
decode screens.

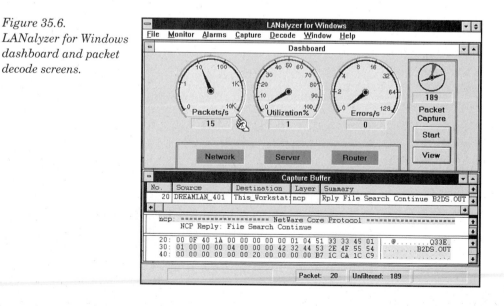

A number of free/shareware packages are available from the NOVUSER forum library on CompuServe, such as the following:

◆ NCONSOLE from Avanti Technologies allows you to record long term statistics, such as CPU utilization, cache buffers, and so on, about your NetWare 4 servers (see Figure 35.7).

◆ PacketView from Klos Technologies, Inc. allows you to capture and decode IPX, TCP/IP, Vines, and AppleTalk packets (see Figure 35.8).

◆ SmartPass for NetWare from e.g. Software, Inc. is an NLM that runs on your server and can monitor and check for commonly used passwords. You can even define a dictionary of passwords that you do not want to use (see Figure 35.9).

◆ AuditTrack, also from e.g. Software, is a management software NLM that allows you to monitor file access and other types of server access (see Figure 35.10).

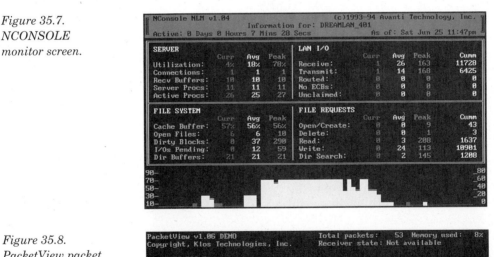

Figure 35.7.
NCONSOLE
monitor screen.

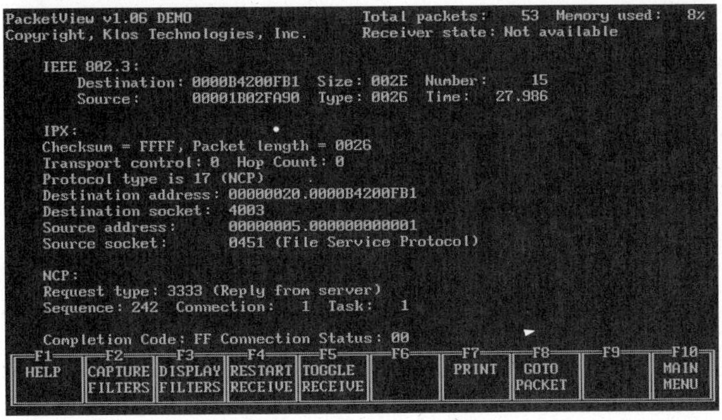

Figure 35.8.
PacketView packet
decode screen.

Figure 35.9.
SmartPass for NetWare
password scanning
screen.

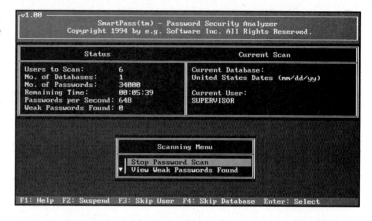

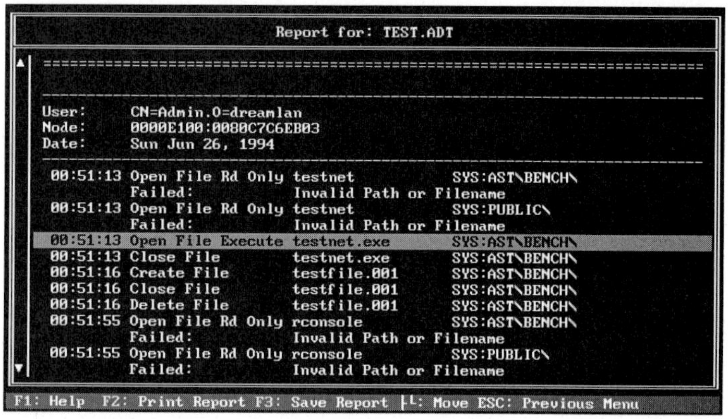

Figure 35.10.
AuditTrack access
report screen.

The software packages listed here are just a few of the available shareware and freeware network management tools.

Tip

Whether you choose a commercial or a shareware product, make sure it has the network management features that you are looking for. Most importantly, make sure it is compatible with NetWare 4.

SUPPORT FOR ENTERPRISE MANAGEMENT SYSTEMS

When choosing new network management tools, you should always keep in mind of their compatibility with your existing tools. The new tools should complement, not duplicate, your existing system.

If you already have an enterprise management system in place, such as Novell's NetWare Management System (NMS), your are should find out when purchasing additional network management tools if they can be easily integrated into your existing system.

NDS PARTITION MANAGEMENT

Partition management starts with the planning of your NDS tree and installation of servers. After you network is up and running, you should give some considerations to the sizes of partitions and placements of replicas as your network grows and environment changes. You have learned that storing your NDS database on a single server is not a very good idea. If the server is unavailable, users cannot authenticate to the network and access resources. The same issue applies on a smaller scale if you look at a partition stored on a single server. When that server goes down, your users will not have access to resources on that portion of the NDS tree.

In this section, you learn about managing partitions and replicas. NWADMIN and PARTMGR examples are used to illustrate each management function.

Note

Often it is best to use the graphical Partition Manager tool built into NWADMIN to perform partition and replica management functions as it is more visual. You can use the PARTMGR DOS utility for most of the functions except to perform container moves.

To work with NWADMIN's Partition Manager tool, select Partition Manager from NWADMIN Tools pull-down menu. A screen similar to Figure 35.11 appears. Names of partition root objects are shown in red letters and are marked with a partition icon. Servers storing replicas appear in blue letters. Double-clicking container names or the up-arrow icon walks you down or up the NDS tree. Highlighted (blacken) option buttons on the right hand side show available partition options.

Note

You need to have a tree view opened before you will have access to the Partition Manager selection in the Tools menu.

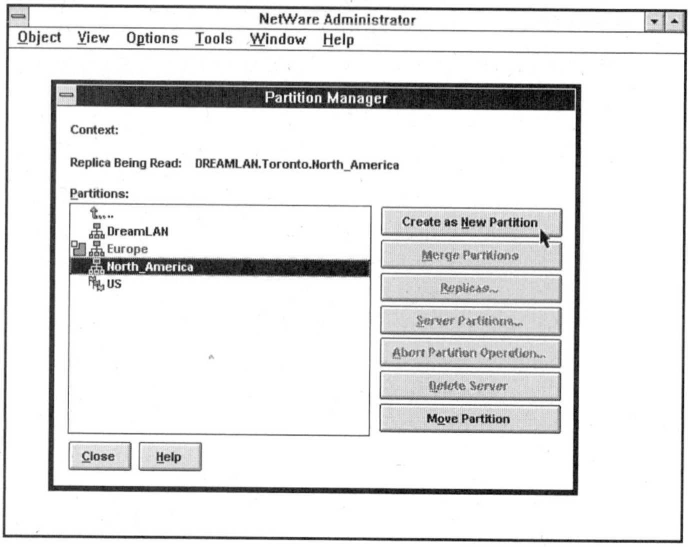

Figure 35.11.
Using Partition
Manager to view
partition information.

To use the non-graphical PARTMGR utility, type **PARTMGR** at the DOS prompt. It is located in the SYS:PUBLIC directory of each NetWare 4 server. PARTMGR's main menu has two options:

◆ Manage Partitions

◆ Change Context

Select the Manage Partitions option and a screen similar to Figure 35.12 appears. A list of container and server objects are displayed. Containers are flagged with a "plus" sign on the left hand side. On the right hand column, containers that are partition root objects show (Partition) as their class. You can walk up or down the tree by either selecting the double-dots (..) or a container name.

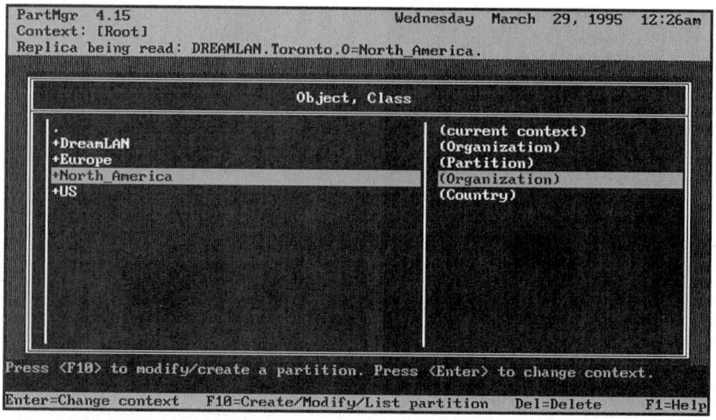

Figure 35.12.
Listing partitions
using PARTMGR.

CREATING PARTITIONS

In Partition Manager, highlight the container you want to be the partition root object, and click the Create as New Partition action button to create a new partition. A confirmation box appears, displaying the following:

```
Would you like to create a new partition? This will usually take
one to ten minutes. It may take longer depending on the
number of replicas in the partition, their size and their location.
```

Select Yes to create the partition.

With PARTMGR, the process is similar. You highlight the container you want to be the partition root object, and press F10. You are prompted to create a new partition. Select Yes to create.

MERGING PARTITIONS

There may be times that you want to combine smaller child partitions into a larger one for more efficient navigation. In such a case, from Partition Manager, you perform a Merge Partitions option after selecting the child partition you want to merge. You need to do this one child partition at a time.

In PARTMGR, if you highlight a container that is a partition root object and press F10, a Partition Management menu appears. From this menu, you have the following three choices:

- ◆ View/Edit replicas
- ◆ Abort partition operation
- ◆ Merge with the parent partition

Select the third option (Merge) to merge the partition with its parent.

MOVING CONTAINERS/PARTITIONS

NetWare 4.1 gives you the capability to move a container (and its subordinates) from one location of the NDS tree to another. Since you have to move the container and its contents, this is essentially moving a partition around.

The following two conditions must be met before you can move a container or partition:

- ◆ The container object to be move must already be a partition. If the container is not already a partition, you need to create a new partition with this container as the root object using the procedure described earlier.
- ◆ The partition can have no child partitions. If there are any child partitions, you have to merge them into the parent partition first before you can perform the move.

In Partition Manager, highlight the container you want to move, and then click the Move Partition button. The Move dialog box appears and you can browse for and select the destination (see Figure 35.13). You have the option of creating an alias container object in case any user or login scripts refer to it explicitly. This gives you the option to update the scripts at your convenience.

Figure 35.13.
Partition Manager
Move dialog box.

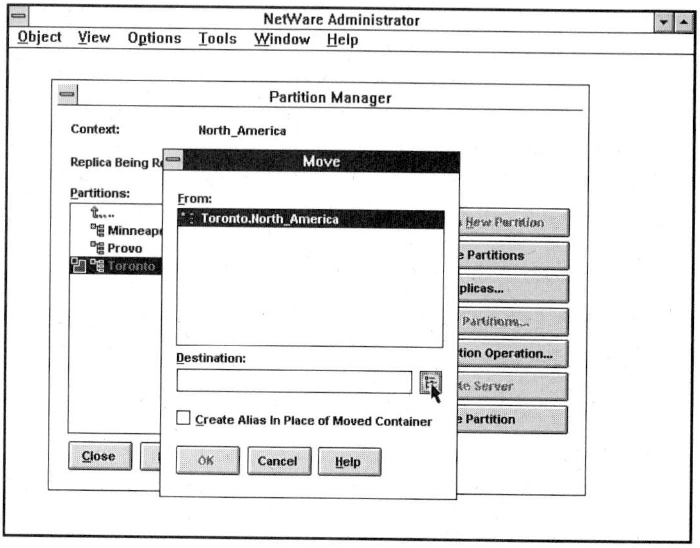

Once the container is moved, it exists as a separate partition. If you want, use the merge option to merge the moved partition into its new parent partition.

Note that you can not use PARTMGR to perform the move operation with the version that is shipped with NetWare 4.1.

Tip

Depending on the number of objects within the container and number of replicas that need updating, a move operation may take from seconds to hours. You should plan all partition management operations, such as splits and moves, for off-peak hours.

ABORTING PARTITION OPERATIONS

To protect NDS database integrity, only one partition operation can take place at any given time. If a partition operation starts, for example, and one of the servers in the replica ring becomes unavailable—downed server or downed network link—the operation becomes suspended. If you try to start another partition operation,

Partition Manager will give you a -654 error and PARTMGR will return a FD72 error (see Figure 35.14). You can either wait for the error condition to be rectified, or abort the operation.

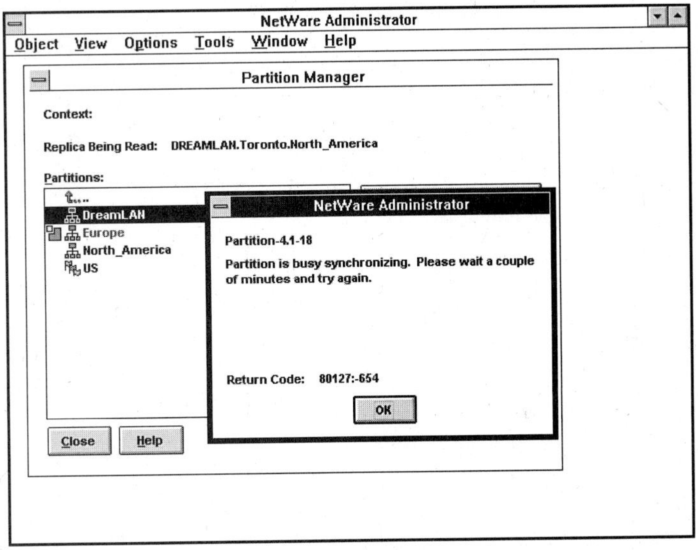

Figure 35.14.
Partition busy error code from Partition Manager.

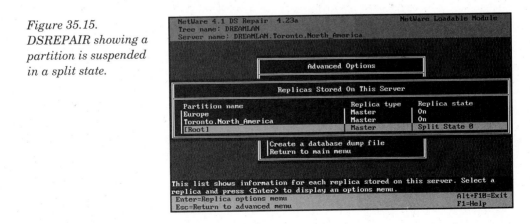

Before you can abort the operation, you have to determine which partition is busy. If you are unsure, the easiest way is to use DSREPAIR on one of the servers that holds the partitions you were working with. From its main menu, select Advanced options menu, and then select Replica and partition operations. This will display a list of all replicas and their replica state (see Figure 35.15).

Figure 35.15.
DSREPAIR showing a partition is suspended in a split state.

The F10 key will abort the partition operating in progress. Note that depending on what replica state the partition is in, it is not always possible to abort the operation.

If you do not have ready access to the server console, with a little work you can use Partition Manager or PARTMGR to determine which partition is busy and abort the operation:

◆ *Using Partition Manager.* From the displayed partition tree, walk up and down and select one partition at a time. Click Abort partition operation and examine the replica status (see Figure 35.16). The problem partition will have a none-On state. Select the Abort button to abort the operation.

◆ *Using PARTMGR.* From the displayed container and server objects list, walk up and down and select one partition at by time. Use the F10 key to bring up the Partition Management menu and select the Abort partition operation option. From the replica status table, determine whether this is the partition in question (see figure 35.17). The problem partition will have a none-On state for its replicas. Press F10 again to abort the operation.

Figure 35.16.
Replica status of a
problem partition.

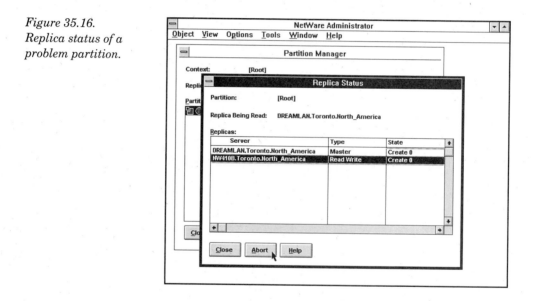

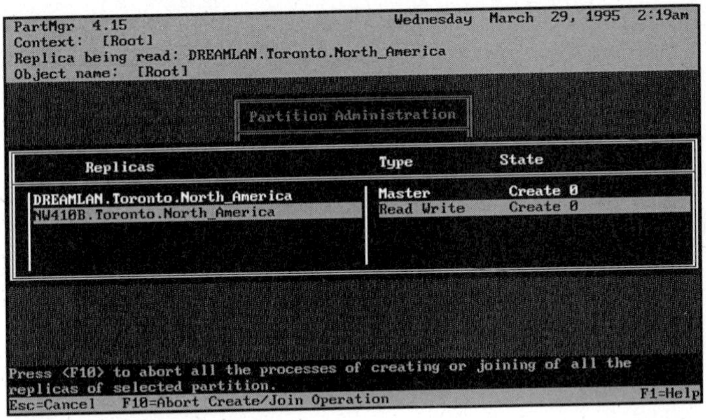

Figure 35.17.
Replica status table
from PARTMGR.

```
PartMgr  4.15                            Wednesday  March  29, 1995  2:19am
Context:  [Root]
Replica being read: DREAMLAN.Toronto.North_America
Object name:  [Root]

                        Partition Administration

        Replicas                      Type        State

   DREAMLAN.Toronto.North_America    Master      Create 0
   NW410B.Toronto.North_America      Read Write  Create 0




Press <F10> to abort all the processes of creating or joining of all the
replicas of selected partition.
Esc=Cancel    F10=Abort Create/Join Operation                    F1=Help
```

CREATING REPLICAS

To work with replicas of a given partition, select the partition in question using the utility of your choice. In Partition Manager, click on the Replicas button and a Partition Replica table appears (see Figure 35.18). To add a new replica, click the Add Replica button and a dialog box appears. Choose the replica type of the new replica by clicking on the appropriate radio button on the right; the default is Read/Write. Browse the server listing to locate the server on which you like to place the replica on. Click OK to create the replica.

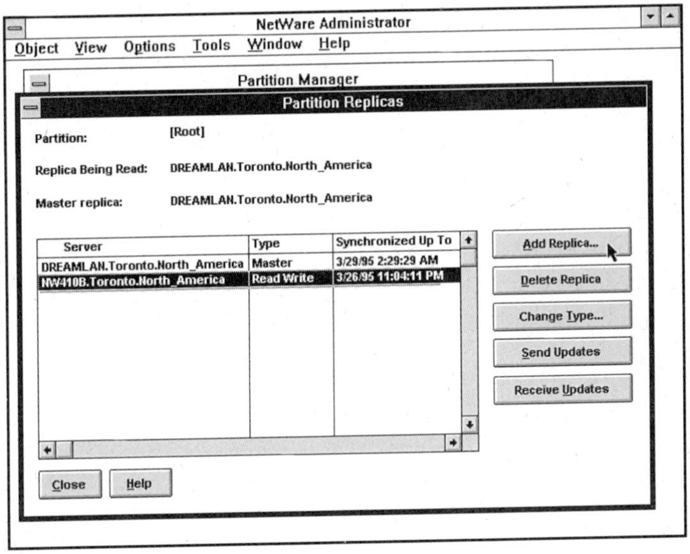

Figure 35.18.
Partition replica table
in Partition Manager.

35

NETWORK MANAGEMENT

To perform the same operation using PARTMGR, select the partition of interest, press F10 to bring up the Partition Management menu. Choose the View/Edit replicas option. You are presented with a replica table similar to that of Figure 35.18. Press Insert to add a new replica. The Add Replica box appears and prompts you to enter the replica type and the server where the replica will be stored (see Figure 35.19). Press F10 to continue and confirm you want to create a new replica.

Figure 35.19.
Add replica dialog box
in PARTMGR.

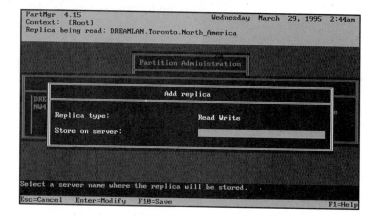

DELETING REPLICAS

The steps for deleting a replica from a server is similar to that of adding a new replica. With Partition Manager, you highlight the replica you want to remove in the Partition Replicas table and click on the Delete Replica button. In PARTMGR, instead of pressing Insert as you would when adding a new replica, highlight the replica you want to remove and press the Delete key.

CHANGING REPLICA TYPE

From Chapter 14 you learned that there are four types of replicas—Master, Read/Write (or Secondary), Read-only, and Subordinate Reference. You can readily change the replica types between Master, Read/Write, and Read-Only.

For each partition, there *must* be a Master replica. All partition operations must be performed against the Master replica. Should the server containing the Master replica is unavailable and you need to perform partition operations, you can "promote" a Read/Write to Read-only replica to become the Master.

From Partition Manager, simply select the replica you want to change the type in the Partition Replicas table and click on the Change Type button. In PARTMGR, instead of pressing Insert as you would when adding a new replica, highlight the replica you want to change type on and press the F10 key. The Replica Management menu appears and one of the three options is Change replica type (see Figure 35.20). Select it and from the resulting Modify Replica Type dialog box, press Enter to bring up a type selection list.

Figure 35.20.
Replica management
options in PARTMGR.

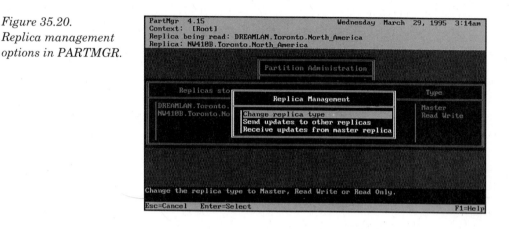

If the Master is available, and you make one of the other replicas a Master, the original Master replica will be "demoted" to a Read/Write replica automatically.

REBUILDING REPLICAS

There may be instances that a replica may become corrupted or incomplete due to one reason or another. You can try to resynchronize the information on replica using the data from the Master replica of the same partition. For example, if you restored a server's SYS: volume, you should perform a replica resynchronization using information from the Master for the restored replica is likely to contain outdated NDS information. You can wait for the normal NDS update process to update this replica, or force a replica update manually.

To resynchronize a replica to the Master replica, highlight the replica in question (the receiver), and select the Receive Update option. In Partition Manager, this is a selection button on the Partition Replicas screen. Under PARTMGR, it is one of the three Replica Management options as discussed earlier.

Warning

Do not use the rebuild replica option lightly to fix NDS problems. It may cause further problem than it is fixing. Do *not* use the rebuild replica option if you experience the following errors: -602 (FDA6), No such value; -632 (FD88), system failure and unexpected results have occurred; and -635 (FD85), remote failure.

Viewing Replicas on a Server

If you need to determine which partition replicas are stored on a given server, there are three ways to find out. From Partition Manager, select the server of interest, and then click on the Server Partitions button. A list similar to Figure 35.21 is displayed. In PARTMGR, walk the tree until you find the server you want to examine and select it. A table similar to that of the Server Partitions screen is displayed. Lastly, you can use DSREPAIR to display the list of replicas stored on a server as previously discussed.

Figure 35.21.
Server partitions
list from Partition
Manager.

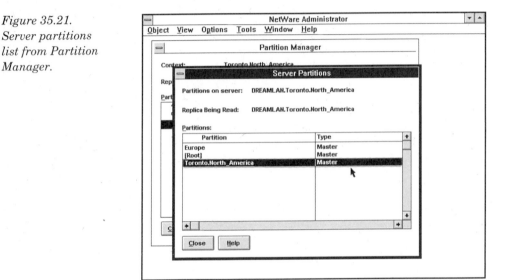

Using NetSync

A set of NLMs, collectively known as NetSync, are shipped with NetWare 4.1. They allow you to manage users and groups of NetWare 3.1*x* bindery servers through NDS tools such as NETADMIN and NW Admin. This is achieved by migrating the user and group information from the NetWare 3.1*x* bindery into the NDS. Any changes you make to these NDS objects will be reflected back to the bindery of the NetWare 3.1*x* servers. However, changes to the bindery (after the sync) are *not* sent to NDS. You will need to re-upload the bindery to reflect new changes done from the bindery side.

Tip

Once you start using NetSync to manage your bindery servers, you should *always* use the NDS tools to manage user and group changes.

The installation and configuration process of NetSync is very straightforward, therefore, only a general overview of its installation and configuration will be presented here.

INSTALLING AND CONFIGURING NETSYNC

You first need to designate a NetWare 4.1 server as the "controlling" servers for your 3.1x servers. Each NetWare 4.1 NetSync server can support up to 12 NetWare 3.1x servers. This is sometimes known as a *NetSync cluster*. For example, if you want to manage fifteen NetWare 3.1x servers, you will need two NetWare 4.1 NetSync servers, hence two clusters.

Tip

From a performance standpoint, you should have less than 12 NetWare 3.1x servers per NetWare 4.1 NetSync server.

Before starting NetSync, you need to decide which container the NetWare 3.1x bindery objects will be placed within your NDS. The NetWare 4.1 server must have its bindery context set to this container.

Warning

If you use multiple bindery contexts, make sure this container is specified *first*. Otherwise, the bindery objects will be migrated to the wrong container.

On the NetWare 4.1 server, load NETSYNC4.NLM. From its menu, you define the names of the NetWare 3.1x servers which will form this NetSync group. On the NetWare 3.1x servers, you will need to load REMAPID.NLM and NETSYNC3.NLM.

CAUTIONS ABOUT NETSYNC

The first time you start NetSync, the bindery information will be uploaded into the NDS—into the *first* bindery context of the NetWare 4.1 NetSync server. All users and group objects in the bindery context(s) of the NetWare 4.1 server will be downloaded to the bindery on each 3.1x servers within the NetSync group. As a result, the bindery of each 3.1x server will contain user and group objects from the other 3.1x servers within the NetSync group.

35

Warning

Beware that any changes (such as password, addition, or removal of users) in the NDS are propagated *immediately* to the binderies of all the 3.1x servers within the NetSync group. Therefore, if you accidentally deleted a user from the NDS, it will also be removed from the binderies of all the bindery servers.

Because all user and group objects from different 3.1x servers will be added to the same NDS container, it is important you first ensure these names are unique among the binderies before doing a NetSync. Otherwise, you will run the risk of combining user and group information from multiple 3.1x servers when you did not mean to.

REMAPID is used to translate object ids between NetWare 4.1 and NetWare 3.1x. Therefore, even if you stopped using NetSync to manage your NetWare 3.1x servers, you *must* keep on loading REMAPID.

NetWare's Remote Management Facility

Standard with NetWare 4.x is the Remote Management Facility (RMF). It is a utility that allows you to manage all your file servers from one single location by allowing a workstation to act as a file server console, or "remote console." It gives you easy access to and control of your file servers, no matter where they are located.

Note

Remote Management Facility is also shipped with NetWare 3.1x.

In many cases, file servers are locked away in secured rooms to provide physical security or are located in locations far away from you. RMF turns your workstation into a remote console and you can perform any task as though you are in front of the file server.

Access security can be set up so that only users having the correct password can perform remote management. Other than having remote access to the server's monitor and keyboard functions, you can also perform a number of other functions.

Remote Management Facility (RMF)

With the remote management facility set up, you can perform the following functions via the remote console:

◆ Load and unloading of NLMs

◆ Execute any console commands

- Perform directory scans of both the NetWare volumes and the DOS partition
- Transfer files to (but not from) a remote file server
- Transfer files to (but not from) the DOS partition of the server
- Reboot a file server

There are two types of connections that you can establish for remote console access: LAN link or via asynchronous (modem) link (see Figure 35.22). To use the modem link you need to install a modem directly on the server.

Figure 35.22.
LAN and modem
links for remote
console access.

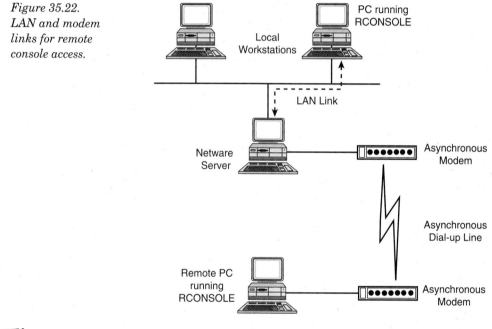

Tip

It is generally not recommended to use the modem link as the modem driver because additional overhead on the file server is due to constant polling of the communication port.

SETTING UP REMOTE MANAGEMENT FACILITY

There are two sets of software components for setting up RMF. A set of NLMs need to be loaded on the file server and the remote workstation needs to run a utility program to connect with the server NLMs.

35

Depending on the type of connection you want to set up, two NLMs need to be loaded. For the modem connection, you need to load the following:

- ◆ REMOTE.NLM
- ◆ RS232.NLM
- ◆ AIOCOMX.NLM

For a LAN connection, you need the following:

- ◆ REMOTE.NLM
- ◆ RSPX.NLM

On the workstation, whether using the LAN or modem connection, you simply need to execute the RCONSOLE utility. It is located in both SYS:SYSTEM and SYS:PUBLIC directories. However, if you want to use RCONSOLE without having to log into a file server first, you need to copy the following ten files to your workstation:

- ◆ RCONSOLE.EXE
- ◆ RCONSOLE.HEP
- ◆ RCONSOLE.MSG
- ◆ TEXTUTIL.HEP
- ◆ TEXTUTIL.IDX
- ◆ TEXTUTIL.MSG
- ◆ IBM_AIO.OVL
- ◆ IBM_RUN.OVL
- ◆ _AIO.OVL
- ◆ _RUN.OVL

SECURITY PRECAUTIONS

Because RMF gives you access to the file server console, and RCONSOLE.EXE is also located in SYS:PUBLIC where everyone has read-access to, you should establish a password to prevent unauthorized access.

By default, when you load REMOTE.NLM, you will be prompted for a password. This is the password one needs to supply when using RCONSOLE to attach to a server. The password can be different for different servers.

Tip

For maximum security you should assign different passwords for different file servers. However, this makes password management difficult, especially if you have a large number of servers on your internetwork. Perhaps it is best to have "groups" of passwords depending on the location of the server.

If the server console is locked by the MONITOR.NLM via the Lock File Server Console option RCONSOLE cannot bypass the lock (see Figures 35.23 and 35.24). You must supply the console password before you can gain access to the server console.

Figure 35.23.
Lock File Server
Console option in
MONITOR.NLM.

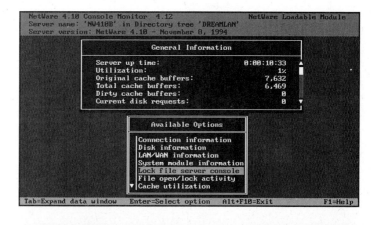

Figure 35.24.
Server console locked.

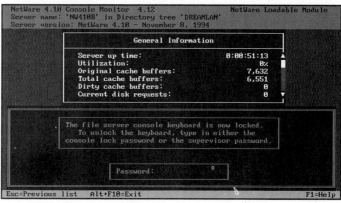

In order to have RMF available automatically every time the server is brought up, you need to put the LOAD REMOTE and LOAD RSPX (or LOAD RS232 and AIOCOMX) in the AUTOEXEC.NCF file. However, in order for REMOTE to load without prompting for a password, you need to also specify the password (in clear text) as part of the LOAD parameter, as in the following:

```
LOAD REMOTE SECRET*PASSWORD
```

This can cause a potential security risk should anyone gain access to your AUTOEXEC.NCF file.

With NetWare 4, you can encrypt this password as follows:

1. At the server console, type **LOAD REMOTE** and enter the remote console password when prompted.

2. Type **REMOTE ENCRYPT** and, when prompted, enter the password you gave for the remote console in step 1. The server displays an encryption key for the password, something similar to the following:

```
The encryption key is E1681F8D3EEAA878888888038888388
```

3. Write this encryption key down. You will use it in the AUTOEXEC.NCF file instead of the plain-text password.

4. In the AUTOEXEC.NCF file, enter the remote console startup command as follows (assuming the key given in Step 3):

```
LOAD REMOTE -E E1681F8D3EEAA878888888038888388
LOAD RSPX SIGNATURES OFF
```

Note that the encryption key is used only in the AUTOEXEC.NCF file. When you start a remote console session from a workstation, you must still enter the plain-text password as usual.

Tip

For more REMOTE options, type **REMOTE HELP** for more information after you have loaded REMOTE.NLM at the server console.

RUNNING A REMOTE CONSOLE SESSION

To start a remote console session, simply execute the RCONSOLE utility from your workstation. You will first be prompted if you want to use the asynchronous (modem) connection or LAN (SPX) connection. The default is SPX.

To use the modem link, you must define a "User Connection ID" to identify yourself as well as a "Call Back Number" (see Figure 35.25). The "Call Back Number" is used as a security precaution.

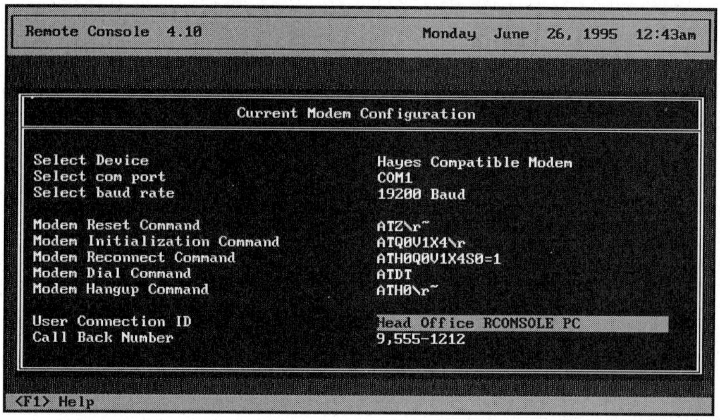

Figure 35.25.
RCONSOLE asynchro-
nous configuration
screen.

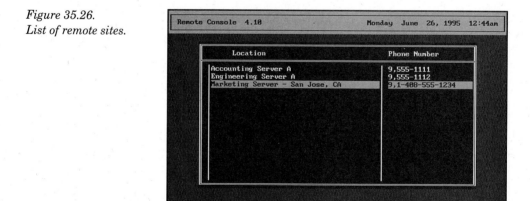

Under the Connect To Remote Location option, you define the descriptions and the phone numbers of the remote sites that you will be calling (see Figure 35.26). To add an entry, press Insert. To connect to a specific site, highlight the entry and press enter (see Figure 35.27). To modify the description or phone number of an entry, highlight and press F3.

Figure 35.26.
List of remote sites.

If you choose the SPX connection, you are presented with a list of servers that are RMF-ready (refer to Figure 35.5). Select the server you want to connect to, press Enter, then supply the password that was supplied to the REMOTE NLM (see Figure 35.28). If you give it the wrong password, you will not be able to connect to the selected server (see Figure 35.29).

Figure 35.27.
Call to remote site
in progress.

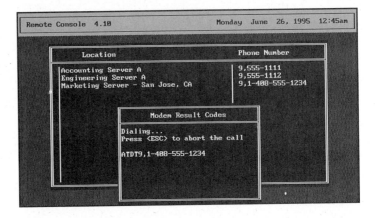

Figure 35.28.
Password prompt for
RCONSOLE.

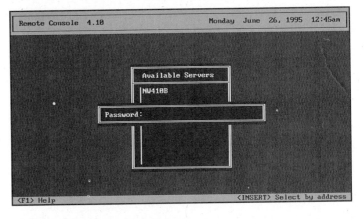

Figure 35.29.
Unable to connect if
wrong password given.

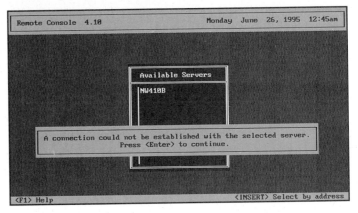

If the server console was locked using the MONITOR.NLM, you will first have to unlock it (refer to Figure 35.24). You can use either the password used to lock the keyboard *or* the SUPERVISOR password (not Admin's, but SUPERVISOR under bindery emulation mode).

Every time a RCONSOLE connection is made or cleared to a server, a console message is displayed, and an entry is made into the system error log file.

Note

As part of the connection message, the IPX network address and workstation's hardware address are also included. You can use this information to track where on the network the access is made from.

While in RCONSOLE, use the ALT+F3/F4 keys to switch between the different NLM screen instead of using Alt+Esc. To end a RCONSOLE session, press Alt+F2.

SPECIFIC ADMINISTRATIVE TASKS

Other than being able to perform all file server console functions, such as loading and unloading of NLMs, you can also do a host of other administrative tasks. Press Alt+F1 to display a menu (see Figure 35.30). You can get a directory scan of the DOS partition and copy files to the DOS partition on the file server without having to down the server (see Figures 35.31 and 35.32).

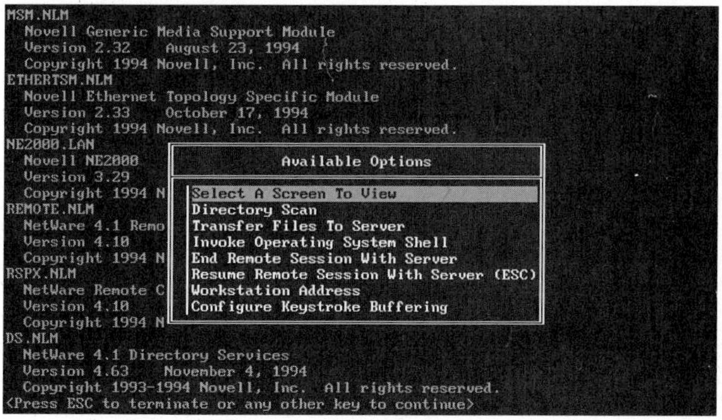

Figure 35.30.
Use ALT+F1 to bring up the Options Menu.

```
MSM.NLM
   Novell Generic Media Support Module
   Version 2.32    August 23, 1994
   Copyright 1994 Novell, Inc.  All rights reserved.
ETHERTSM.NLM
   Novell Ethernet Topology Specific Module
   Version 2.33    October 17, 1994
   Copyright 1994 Novell, Inc.  All rights reserved.
NE2000.LAN
   Novell NE2000
   Version 3.29
   Copyright 1994 N ┌──────────────────────────────────────┐
REMOTE.NLM          │          Available Options            │
   NetWare 4.1 Remo │├────────────────────────────────────┤│
   Version 4.10     ││Select A Screen To View             ││
   Copyright 1994 N ││Directory Scan                      ││
RSPX.NLM            ││Transfer Files To Server            ││
   NetWare Remote C ││Invoke Operating System Shell       ││
   Version 4.10     ││End Remote Session With Server      ││
   Copyright 1994 N ││Resume Remote Session With Server (ESC)││
DS.NLM              ││Workstation Address                 ││
   NetWare 4.1 Dire ││Configure Keystroke Buffering       ││
   Version 4.63    November 4, 1994
   Copyright 1993-1994 Novell, Inc.  All rights reserved.
<Press ESC to terminate or any other key to continue>
```

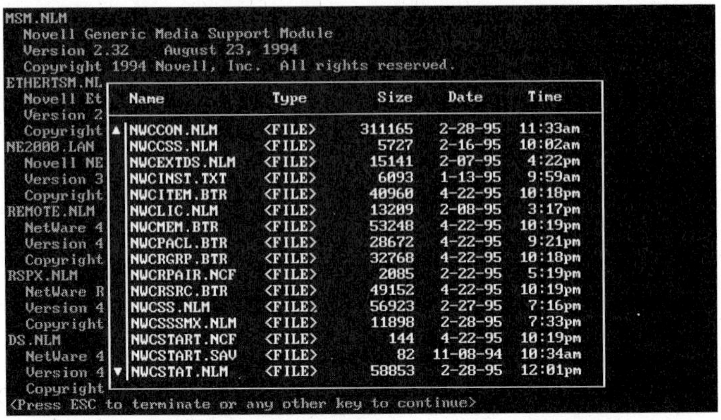

Figure 35.31.
Directory scan of
server's DOS partition.

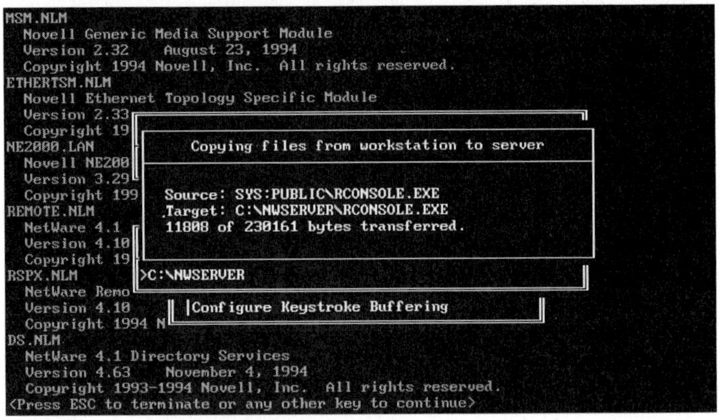

```
MSM.NLM
  Novell Generic Media Support Module
  Version 2.32    August 23, 1994
  Copyright 1994 Novell, Inc.  All rights reserved.
ETHERTSM.NL
  Novell Et  ┌───────────────────────────────────────────────────┐
  Version 2  │ Name          Type        Size    Date     Time   │
  Copyright ▲│ NWCCON.NLM    <FILE>     311165   2-28-95  11:33am │
NE2000.LAN   │ NWCCSS.NLM    <FILE>       5727   2-16-95  10:02am │
  Novell NE  │ NWCEXTDS.NLM  <FILE>      15141   2-07-95   4:22pm │
  Version 3  │ NWCINST.TXT   <FILE>       6093   1-13-95   9:59am │
  Copyright  │ NWCITEM.BTR   <FILE>      40960   4-22-95  10:18pm │
REMOTE.NLM   │ NWCLIC.NLM    <FILE>      13209   2-08-95   3:17pm │
  NetWare 4  │ NWCMEM.BTR    <FILE>      53248   4-22-95  10:19pm │
  Version 4  │ NWCPACL.BTR   <FILE>      28672   4-22-95   9:21pm │
  Copyright  │ NWCRGRP.BTR   <FILE>      32768   4-22-95  10:18pm │
RSPX.NLM     │ NWCRPAIR.NCF  <FILE>       2085   2-22-95   5:19pm │
  NetWare R  │ NWCRSRC.BTR   <FILE>      49152   4-22-95  10:19pm │
  Version 4  │ NWCSS.NLM     <FILE>      56923   2-27-95   7:16pm │
  Copyright  │ NWCSSSMX.NLM  <FILE>      11898   4-22-95   7:33pm │
DS.NLM       │ NWCSTART.NCF  <FILE>        144   4-22-95  10:19pm │
  NetWare 4  │ NWCSTART.SAV  <FILE>         82  11-08-94  10:34am │
  Version 4 ▼│ NWCSTAT.NLM   <FILE>      58853   2-28-95  12:01pm │
  Copyright  └───────────────────────────────────────────────────┘
<Press ESC to terminate or any other key to continue>
```

Figure 35.32.
Copy file to the server's
DOS partition.

```
MSM.NLM
  Novell Generic Media Support Module
  Version 2.32    August 23, 1994
  Copyright 1994 Novell, Inc.  All rights reserved.
ETHERTSM.NLM
  Novell Ethernet Topology Specific Module
  Version 2.33┌───────────────────────────────────────────────────┐
  Copyright 19│                                                   │
NE2000.LAN    │     Copying files from workstation to server      │
  Novell NE200│                                                   │
  Version 3.29│                                                   │
  Copyright 199│   Source: SYS:PUBLIC\RCONSOLE.EXE                │
REMOTE.NLM    │   Target: C:\NWSERVER\RCONSOLE.EXE                │
  NetWare 4.1 │   11808 of 230161 bytes transferred.              │
  Version 4.10│                                                   │
  Copyright 19└───────────────────────────────────────────────────┘
RSPX.NLM      >C:\NWSERVER
  NetWare Remo
  Version 4.10  ║│Configure Keystroke Buffering                  │
  Copyright 1994 N
DS.NLM
  NetWare 4.1 Directory Services
  Version 4.63    November 4, 1994
  Copyright 1993-1994 Novell, Inc.  All rights reserved.
<Press ESC to terminate or any other key to continue>
```

Note

Using the File Copy option, you can easily update all file server's SERVER.EXE (for example) from your workstation without having to visit each location.

There are times that you need to reboot the file server after changes are made to, for example, the STARTUP.NCF file. Using RCONSOLE, you can do this without having to leave your office. Just follow these steps:

1. Use a text editor (such as DOS EDIT) to create a file called REBOOT.NCF in your SYS:SYSTEM directory.

2. Add the following two lines in this file:

```
DOWN
RESTART SERVER
```

3. Connect to the server using RCONSOLE.

4. At the console prompt (:), execute the REBOOT.NCF file by typing **REBOOT** and then press Enter.

5. Exit RCONSOLE.

ENTERPRISE MANAGEMENT SYSTEMS: NOVELL'S NMS

In late 1993, Novell announced the NetWare Distributed Management Services (NDMS) strategy for managing a distributed network environment. The concept behind NDMS is different from the traditional network management philosophy. Traditionally, management services reside on the console. Network devices send information to the console via the agents that reside on a device. The console, then, has to collect, analyzer, store, and display all these data. The console and the network leading to the console can become a bottleneck. The issue becomes a bigger problem on larger networks.

On the other hand, Novell's NDMS distributes the work among the NetWare servers rather than on the console. The console is just a device to store and view the information gathered by the servers.

ARCHITECTURE

The Novell NetWare Management System (NMS) is an open network management platform based on the Simple Network Management Protocol (SNMP). Therefore, it can be used to monitor any SNMP devices that runs over IPX or IP.

NMS consists of a central management console that runs on MS Windows 3.1, and a set of NLM installed on the file servers to be monitored. A basic NMS installation consists of three separate components: a single NMS console, a single NMS NetExplorer server, and NetExplorer Plus servers (see Figure 35.33).

The *NetExplorer server* is responsible for performing network discovery. It discovers network devices, such as file servers and routers, and placed them in the NSM database. The NMS network maps are created from information stored in this database.

NetExplorer Plus NLMs provide additional information about workstations that are logged into the server. For example, usernames. It is recommended that you install NetExplorer Plus on every NetWare server on your network.

35

NETWORK MANAGEMENT

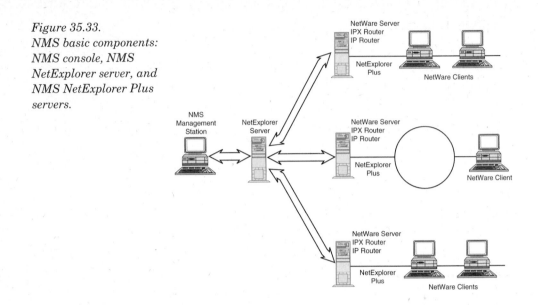

Figure 35.33.
NMS basic components:
NMS console, NMS
NetExplorer server, and
NMS NetExplorer Plus
servers.

The following are the eight categories of network devices that NetExplorer may not discover completely or correctly:

◆ ARCnet workstations. Because ARCnet stations on separate network segments are allowed to have the same address, NetExplorer is unable to keep an accurate account of ARCnet station location.

◆ Devices not equipped with the IPX diagnostic responder. For example, NetWare for UNIX servers, UnixWare servers, and Access servers are not necessarily placed correctly on the map. you may need to manually place them.

◆ NetWare SFT III servers

◆ Source route bridged token ring networks

◆ Routers that use duplicate hardware addresses (DECnet routers, for example)

◆ Non-IPX routers

◆ NetWare Multi-Protocol Routers with multiple WAN ports. This is because all WAN ports on these routers effectively have the same port address

◆ Transparent bridges

Note

Without additional assistance, NMS will only detect IP routers. No IP devices are discovered. If you want to map out IP devices, you need to have a LANtern on each Ethernet segment, or the assistance of LANalyzer Agents (this is discussed in a later section).

DATABASE

The information collected by the NetExplorer server is first stored in a data file (NETXPLOR.DAT) on the server. The data is then forwarded to the NetExplorer Manager on the NMS Console.

The database on the NMS console uses Btrieve format. Data Description File (DDF) for the NMS database is available from Novell should you want to use your own reporting tools (such as MS Access) to extract information from NMS.

MANAGEMENT PROTOCOL

The primary management protocol used by NMS is the Simple Network Management Protocol (SNMP). However, the transport used is by default IPX, and IP if loaded on the servers.

Note

It is a common misconception that SNMP only runs over IP. When SNMP was designed, it is independent of the transport protocol used. However, because it has traditionally been implemented with TCP/IP, therefore, many people mistake SNMP as being IP-based, which is not the case.

The NetExplorer server sends SNMP queries to network devices over both IPX and IP (if TCP/IP is configured on the server).

MANAGEMENT AGENTS

NetWare Management Agent (NMA) is needed if you want to manage NetWare 3.1*x* and NetWare 4.*x* servers. NMA provides you a detailed view of the server's physical and operating system characteristics. For example, you can set threshold on the file cache buffers and track your server's CPU utilization as a function of time (see Figures 35.34 and 35.35).

Figure 35.34.
Server threshold
settings.

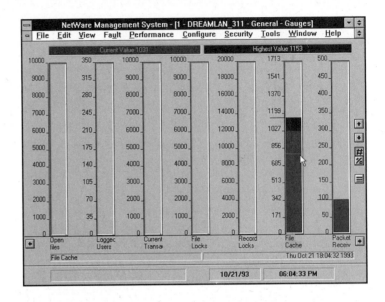

Figure 35.35.
Server CPU utilization
graph.

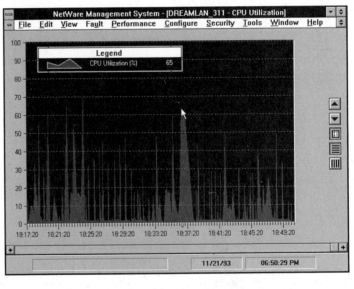

Note

You need NMA v1.6 or higher for the NetWare 4.1 servers.

The NetWare LANalyzer Agent (NLA) is a set of NLMs that provide network analysis of a given Ethernet or Token Ring segment, regardless of the protocol used by stations on the segment. It also helps NMS to discover all nodes (including IP nodes) on that segment.

The NLA is a full implementation of the Internet's RMON MIB (Remote Network Monitoring Management Information Base) standard over IPX and IP protocol. NLA comes in two versions—a single-segment version and a multi-segment version. The single-segment version will only monitor *one* segment from the server, even if there are multiple NICs installed in the server. The multi-segment version will monitor all the segments to which the server is directly attached to. Figure 35.36 shows that for a four-segment network, you only need two copies of the multi-segment version of NLA installed.

Figure 35.36.
Placement of NetWare
LANalyzer Agents on a
four-segment network.

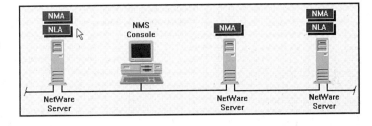

Note

The RMON MIB is made up of nine groups, as follows:

- **Statistics Group**: Features a table that tracks about 20 different traffic characteristics, such as total frames and errors.

- **History Group**. Enables you to specify frequency and intervals for traffic sampling.

- **Alarm Group**: Permits you to establish thresholds and criteria under which the agents will issue alarms.

- **Host Group**: Presents a table containing each LAN node listed by traffic statistics.

- **HostTopN Group**: Enables you to set up sorted lists and reports based on the highest statistics generated by the Host Group.

- **Matrix Group**: Keeps two tables of traffic statistics based on pairs of communicating nodes. One table is based on sending node addresses, the other is based on receiving node addresses.

- **Filter Group**: Permits you to define, by channel, particular characteristics of frames. For example, a filter may be applied to just capture IP traffic.

- **Packet Capture Group**: Works in conjunction with the Filter Group. Enables you to specify the amount of memory resources to be used for storing captured data that meet the filter criteria.

35

NETWORK MANAGEMENT

◆ **Event Group**: Enables you to specify a set of parameters or conditions to be tracked by the agent. Whenever these conditions are met, an event log will be recorded.

The advantage of using NLA over other protocol analyzers is that you have a distributed LAN monitoring and analysis system without having to invest in extra hardware. Consider this: using the distributed nature of NLA, you can monitor and capture data from different network segments at the same time. This lets you track the flow of a problem right to the source, even across routers, without even having to leave your desk.

The entry price for NLA is not as low as you also have to invest in NMS. However, it is still much lower than any available hardware options. There are no other software tools that give you this kind of flexibility.

CONSOLE INTERFACE

NMS uses an easy-to-understand graphical user interface (GUI). The main screen is divided into three sections: a pull-down menu at the top, a "work" area, and an alarm status bar at the bottom with a ticker-tape window (see Figure 35.37). A number of "background processes" are used by NMS to communicate with the NetExplorer server and to monitor and report network alarms.

Figure 35.37.
NetWare Management
System console screen.

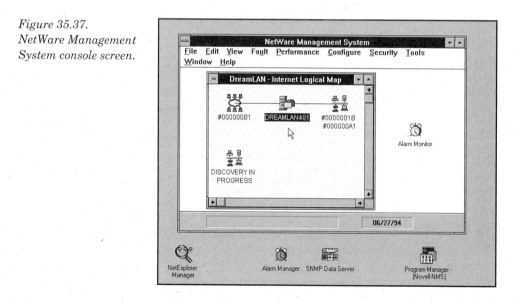

When an alarm is received by the NMS console, a ringing alarm clock is first displayed at the bottom-left corner of the desktop for 20 seconds. Optionally, a ticker-tape message is available, describing the error and the object (device) that generated the alarm (see Figure 35.38).

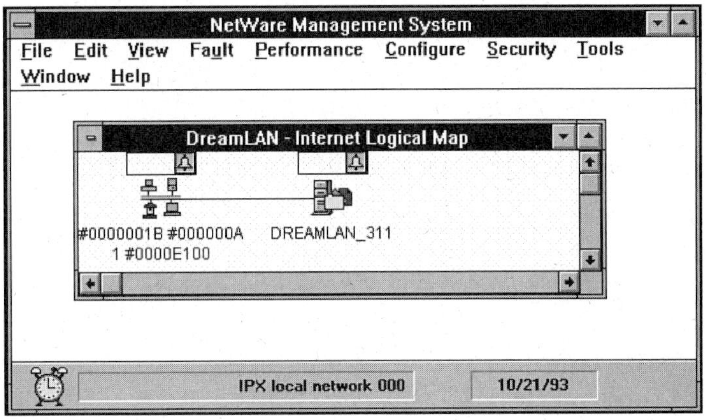

Figure 35.38.
NMS alarm
notification.

Even though the alarm bell and ticker-tape message does not last long and you may miss it, but an alarm-bell icon will be displayed over the LAN segment that originated the alarm. You can use either the Alarm Monitor or Alarm Report to find out the alarm details. Depending on the severity of the alarm, different colors is used for the alarm icon, and its position is different:

Severity	Color	Alarm bell icon location
Minor alarm	Yellow	Left
Major alarm	Magenta	Center
Critical alarm	Red	Right

THIRD-PARTY ADD-ONS

A number of third-party add-on applications are available for NMS. These tools are generally referred to as "snap-in modules" for NMS. Following are some of the more prominent snap-in modules:

- **Compaq Insight Manager from Compaq**: Allows you to monitor Compaq servers
- **LANDesk Manager from Intel**: Workstation software and hardware inventory as well as remote workstation access
- **AlertPage from Denmac**: Allows you to send NMS alarm messages to alpha-numeric pages

◆ **TrenData from Denmac**: Collects statistics and provides trend data information

◆ **Spectrum for NMS from Cabletron**: Allows you to monitor and manage Cabletron hubs over TCP/IP

◆ **Optivity for NMS from SynOptics**: Allows you to monitor and manage SynOptics hubs over IPX and IP

◆ **Cisco Router Manager from StonyBrook**: Allows you to monitor and manage Cisco routers from within NMS

◆ **Wellfleet Router Manager from StonyBrook**: Allows you to monitor and manage Wellfleet routers from within NMS

◆ **PowerNet SNMP Manager for NMS from American Power Conversion**: Allows you to monitor and manage APC's SmartUPS units

Listed here are just a small sample of available NMS snap-in modules. Shipped with NMS is a *NetWare Network Management and Internetworking Products Resource Guide* that has a comprehensive list of products that are designed to snap-in or interoperate with NMS.

SUMMARY

In this chapter, you learned how to use the following network management tools to assist you in managing your network:

◆ NW Admin (for Windows)

◆ NETADMIN (for DOS)

◆ PCONSOLE

◆ RCONSOLE

◆ Partition Manager (for Windows)

◆ PARTMGR (for DOS)

◆ NetSync

These tools are included with NetWare 4.1.

Also discussed in this chapter is how you can use Novell's NetWare Management System (NMS) to monitor and report errors from your file servers and networks.

- Importance of Archiving Network Data

- Data Archiving Requirements for NetWare 4.*x*

- Archiving Methods

- Archiving Hardware and Software

- Storage Management Services (SMS)

- Disaster Recovery

- Summary

CHAPTER 36

Archiving and Backup

Information managers and technicians who have experience working with mainframe and mini-computers never question the need for extensive data archiving. Archiving and backup solutions are part of these host computer systems at inception. It is frightening, however, that most managers and technicians who work with NetWare systems do not place as great an importance on data archiving as their host-based peers.

This chapter discusses data archiving for NetWare 4.x systems. The market for NetWare compatible data archiving hardware and software is growing fast. You are able to choose among many different types of archiving systems from basic to cutting-edge. Your job is to evaluate your data archiving requirements and to put in place an archiving system appropriate for your organization.

Importance of Archiving Network Data

Data is one of the most valuable assets of any computerized organization. In fact, much of what these organizations do today is represented by computer data: financial transactions, research and development, manufacturing, inventory, materials ordering systems, accounting, taxes, artwork, literature, music, graphics, telephone records, and so on. Computer data has become the life-blood of many modern organizations. The value of this data to an organization cannot be over emphasized.

How long should you preserve your organization's computer data? One week? One year? Most savvy organizations today archive all their data indefinitely. One software company facing a patent-infringement lawsuit presented in court archived source-code files that were almost ten years old as evidence of prior art, backing up its claim that the patent infringement suit was invalid. Ten years ago, someone at that company decided it was important to archive all data permanently. You might be surprised at how few tapes this can take if the proper scheme is used.

Depending on the types of data your organization works with, destruction of that data can cost your organization in different ways. For example, a local video store that loses its point-of-sale will be forced to work manually until the data is restored. A software development company that loses its source-code files can lose months or even years worth of engineering effort, and will have to delay shipment of its products. A factory that loses its inventory data will not be able to properly determine its materials. This may cause a shut down costing thousands or millions of dollars of heavy equipment and human resources to stand idle. A magazine that loses its articles and graphics may miss a publishing deadline, and may have to refund advertising revenue. Any organization that loses accounts receivable data is in serious jeopardy!

Many organizations never face a loss of data. Perhaps you've never experienced data loss. But this can lead to a false sense of security. Even with distributed network systems, data loss today is a relatively infrequent occurrence. However, the nature of data loss means that data loss events are impossible to predict, and impossible to prevent. If you have never had a data loss event, you are lucky, because you have simply enjoyed the odds against data loss. Past experience, however, is not a predictor of future events. Whether or not you experience a data loss is just a roll of the dice, so to speak. Because the consequence of data loss are so dire, data archiving is of paramount importance to you and everyone in your organization.

DATA ARCHIVING REQUIREMENTS FOR NETWARE 4.x

For NetWare 4.x, the basic requirements of a data archiving and retrieval system are fairly limited. The system must be able to back up and restore NetWare data including the NetWare Directory Services (NDS) and file system information. It is best if you have a system that will perform the backup without human intervention. ("Why" is discussed later.) Even these basic requirements entail some fairly sophisticated technology. Beyond the basic requirements, however, are many options which may be appropriate for your organization.

THE NETWARE FILE SYSTEM

Archiving and restoring data from a NetWare server is not as simple as it sounds. The NetWare file system, the formats and methods NetWare uses to order and update file data, is very complex. Such complexity is the result of NetWare's support for different file formats, including DOS, OS/2, Windows NT, UNIX, and OSI FTAM, and also the result of NetWare's multi-user, multi-tasking file access routines.

Any archiving system you use to back up and restore data from a NetWare server must be aware of the intricacies of the NetWare file system, and must handle these intricacies, plus errors and other conditions which may arise during normal use of the file system. NetWare-specific items, featured by archiving systems (for both backup and restoration operations), include the following:

- ◆ Support for NetWare-specific file attributes
- ◆ Support NetWare name spaces—non-DOS file formats such as UNIX, Macintosh, OS/2 HPFS, NT, and so on
- ◆ Awareness of file concurrence issues, including file and record locking
- ◆ Support for NetWare 4.x background file compression and the capability to handle compressed files

◆ Awareness of NetWare 4.*x* data migration system, and the capability to recognize migrated files

Many archiving systems on the market today handle most, if not all, of the items listed above. However, there are many archiving systems on the market today that are not designed for use with NetWare. For example, if you attempt to archive NetWare 4.*x* data using a backup program written for DOS, you will not only experience errors backing up file system data, but you will corrupt existing files when you attempt to restore archived data. The same thing can happen if you apply a backup program written for UNIX, Macintosh, or any other workstation operating system, to a NetWare 4.x file system.

NETWARE-SPECIFIC FILE ATTRIBUTES

Every file stored on a NetWare server contains 32 bits of file attributes. These file attribute bits are a superset of the 8 bits of DOS file attributes you may be familiar with. In other words, NetWare has three times the number of file attribute bits as DOS. Many of extra file attribute bits are used internally by NetWare and are not visible to users. However, some of the file attribute bits that are visible to users include the Execute Only bit, the Immediate Purge bit, and so on. A back-up system written for DOS will recognize the DOS-specific file attributes of a NetWare file, but will remain ignorant of the other NetWare file attribute bits, some of which are critical to the backup operation.

In addition, NetWare files have more information associated with them than DOS files. This extra information includes the owner of the file, users with access privileges to the file, the last access data for the file, and so on. Much of this additional information is useful to the archiving process. However, to make use of the full range of information NetWare associates with a file, the archiving system must be written specifically for NetWare.

SUPPORT FOR NAME SPACES

Name spaces are duplicate directory entries that contain non-DOS file format information. For example, UNIX name space directory entries contain the long UNIX file name, UNIX file attribute bits, and other information required by the UNIX file format. Macintosh name space entries contain the long Macintosh file name, Finder information (the Finder is the graphical desktop used by the Macintosh graphical interface), and a pointer to the Macintosh file's resource fork.

Because of the way name spaces work, a file's data is stored on the file system only once. However, that file has a separate directory entry for each file format supported. On a NetWare 4.*x* server with the UNIX and Macintosh name spaces loaded, for example, every file has three directory entries: the standard NetWare (DOS) directory entry, a UNIX directory entry, and a Macintosh directory entry.

An archiving system which does not support name spaces will be able to back up and restore all the files on a NetWare server supporting multiple name spaces. However, all the information stored in the name space directory entries will be lost. This means, for example, that DOS clients will not notice anything missing. But Macintosh and UNIX clients will not be able to gain access to any of the restored files.

Another reason to be extremely cautious of back-up systems that are not NetWare aware is binary (compiled) or executable files. Binary files with file formats other than that of your back-up system will be completely usable when restored. The backup system used will record these files in its own Binary form and restore them again in that form. The files will then be completely corrupt and unusable. Example: If the Macintosh Application file for Microsoft Word is backed up to a DOS floppy disk using the DOS BACKUP command the file would be unusable upon restoration. Although some applications are available for both MAC and DOS, the Macintosh application files are not identical in their binary form.

It is critical, then, that any archiving system you purchase support all the name spaces supported by your NetWare Server. Currently, Novell's list of supported name spaces includes the AFP (Macintosh), UNIX, OS/2, HPFS, Windows NT, and OSI FTAM name spaces.

AWARENESS OF FILE CONGRUENCY ISSUES

File congruency issues include how NetWare handles file and record locking, file sharing, file opening and closing, and file reading and writing. The NetWare file system is designed to allow many users to have open the same file concurrently. This means that NetWare must control the order in which users having a file open are allowed to read from and write to that file's data. NetWare provides extensive programming interfaces to the file system that allow an archiving system to get its job done, even when other users have files open and are reading from and writing to such files.

An archiving system which is aware of file congruency issues will be able to do the following:

◆ Archive opened files
◆ Prevent users from disrupting the archiving process by opening files that are in the process of being backed up
◆ Archive system files, including NDS information
◆ Archive online databases

Without awareness of NetWare's file congruency controls, an archiving system will not be able to perform any of the tasks listed above. In the old days, many archiving systems required that you down the NetWare server and close its bindery before performing a back up. There is no reason why you should have to put up with that kind of trouble today.

BACKGROUND FILE COMPRESSION

NetWare 4.x's new background file compression raises some interesting problems for archiving systems. When archiving a compressed file, does the backup software store the file in its compressed form or its uncompressed form? (And conversely, when restoring a file.) When scanning compressed files for archiving, how does the backup software know the size of such files when they are uncompressed? How does the backup software know when a file is compressed or uncompressed? These and other questions must be answered in order for the archiving system to work correctly with the NetWare 4.x file system.

Most archiving systems on the market today are designed to NetWare handle NetWare 4.x compressed files in the following manner:

◆ Backup software identifies compressed files by inspecting the NetWare file attribute bits.

◆ Backup software decompresses files before archiving them.

◆ When restoring files that were compressed, the backup software restores the file in an uncompressed state, and then causes NetWare to compress the file.

One issue to consider is how much space the files will take when you restore them in an uncompressed form. Most backup systems today that support NetWare 4.x are not yet aware of data compression. They simply read the file the same way any NetWare user would read it. You may find that the 1 gigabyte of data you archived now consumes 1.7 gigabytes of tape space. This can be a real problem if the total volume space you have is 1.5 gigabytes. At a minimum it will cause you to spend a great deal of time doing the restore. At the worst the program could decompress each file before it archives it and leave it in that expanded form after the copy is obtained. This action alone would fill your hard drive very quickly.

Eventually, Novell would like archiving systems to archive files in a compressed state. This would speed the backup process and raise the capacity of most backup systems. However, Novell is still developing programming interfaces that will provide archive system developers with control over the NetWare file system's compression mechanism. Until these programming interfaces are released, archiving systems will handle compressed files as discussed above. Using an archiving system that is not aware of NetWare 4.*x*'s background compression system will assuredly cause loss of data when restoring archived files.

AWARENESS OF THE NETWARE 4.*x* DATA MIGRATION SYSTEM

The NetWare 4.*x* Data Migration system is a mechanism whereby files may reside on secondary offline or near-line media, yet still remain available via the standard NetWare file system. For example, a large PCX file resides on a specially formatted optical disk, yet appears as a standard NetWare file when users issue the NDIR command. When a user attempts to open the PCX file, the Data Migration system retrieves the PCX file from the optical drive and copies the file's data to the NetWare volume. NetWare then opens the file and provides the user with access to the graphical image. When the user is finished with the file, NetWare copies the PCX file back to the optical drive, removes the file from the NetWare volume, yet retains the file's directory entry. As a result, the file remains accessible to users in the standard fashion, even though the file is stored on a specially formatted optical drive.

The Data Migration system consists of special NetWare file attributes and a low-level programming interface. Developers provide the specially formatted off-line or near-line media (such as optical, tape, CD-ROM, magneto-optical, etc.) and NLMs for controlling the movement of data between the NetWare file system and the specially formatted media. Data Migration is designed specifically for multi-media image data bases, but also has applications for leading-edge data archiving, journalized file systems, and very large data bases.

Right now there are no Data Migration applications on the market. However, several third-parties have announced development efforts designed around the data migration system.

An archiving system for NetWare 4.*x* must be aware of the following issues regarding the Data Migration system:

- ◆ How to recognize migrated files
- ◆ How to gain information about the media storing migrated files
- ◆ When archiving migrated files, how to detect and recover from migration-related errors
- ◆ When storing migrated files, how to detect and recover from migration-related errors

Novell released a Data Migration programming interface to third parties prior to the release of NetWare 4.0. However, this interface was deemed incomplete, and Novell

36

is currently in the process of providing a more functional programming interface. Hence, it is impossible for an archiving system on the market right now to be completely up-to-date with Data Migration. However, you should inquire of the archive system's vendor whether they are working with Novell to support Data Migration in the future.

Once this form of data storage is available you should keep in mind the same file considerations that where necessary for compressed files. It follows that if you must move a file to a volume, in order to back it up, you must have sufficient space available.

NETWARE CERTIFICATION

Because of the intricacies of the NetWare 4.x file system, you should only consider purchasing archiving systems that have been certified for use with NetWare 4.x. Novell Labs, based in Provo, Utah, runs a certification program. When an archiving system vendor achieves certification for its product, Novell is guaranteeing that the certified product will work correctly with NetWare. Vendors achieving certification are allowed to display a copyrighted symbol (YES! It runs with NetWare), indicating that the product has been certified for use with NetWare.

Note, however, that NetWare certification by itself does not guarantee success when using the certified product with NetWare 4.x. The product must be specifically certified for use with NetWare 4.x. Many products on the market today are certified for use with NetWare 3.11. Certification for NetWare 3.11 does not guarantee successful results when the product is applied to NetWare 4.x. The product must be certified specifically for use with NetWare 4.x—and for the particular version of NetWare 4, such as NetWare 4.1, you are using. This is especially important for archiving systems, because the NetWare 4.x file system includes the important new features of background file compression, NetWare Directory Services information, and data migration.

ARCHIVING METHODS

There are two basic types used by archiving systems to back up and restore data Image and File-by-File. From these two types of backup systems, you will find that administrators use the following several methods for backing up their data:

◆ Rotating Media

◆ Journalized Archive

◆ Perpetual Archive

Sometimes, the methods just listed are used in combination with each other.

IMAGE

An image backup is simply a copy of the NetWare server's magnetic media, sector by sector. Image backup ignores the NetWare file system completely in the sense that it does not back up files per se. Rather, it backs up the magnetic image of the server's hard drives.

Image backup has the following disadvantages:

◆ You may only archive and restore a complete hard drive.

◆ You must shut down the NetWare server for the duration of an image archive.

Image backup is used today primarily by older archiving systems, most of which are not compatible with NetWare 4.*x*.

Warning

> Image backups are an extremely precarious form of data archiving. Because of the fact that this type of backup is an image of the current hard drive at the time of the backup you may find that you are unable to restore your data to a new hard drive if yours should fail. Many image backup systems will only restore to the exact physical unit from which they originated. This makes for very bad archiving practice when what you are hoping to be able to recover from is just such a failure.

FILE-BY-FILE BACKUP AND RESTORE

Files on a NetWare server are logical structures. That is, they provide a logical order of physical data stored randomly on hard drives or other media used as a NetWare volume. Further, logical information is associated with a file, other than simply the file's data. This information includes the creation and last access date of a file, its last archiving data, its owner, and so on.

A file-by-file backup and restore orders data logically in the same manner as the NetWare file system does. This is the opposite of an image backup and restore, which ignores the logical organization of files and simply copies the magnetic image of the hard drive.

A file-by-file archiving system has the following advantages:

◆ Backup and restore operations can occur on a per-file basis.

- ◆ Because file-by-file archiving systems use the logical file structures maintained by the NetWare file system, archiving and restoration can occur while the server is up and running.

- ◆ Logical information associated with files, such as their owner and creation date, can be included in logs maintained by the archiving system.

How Much Do I Back Up?

When you use a file-by-file backup method, you must decide how much of your data you will back up. Are you going to back all of your data each time you back up, or are you only going to back up those things that have changed?

You may be wondering how your backup system will know whether a file is new or has been changed since the last backup. It is done by changing the Archive Bit (a file attribute A) attached to a file. When a file is created or modified the operating system adds the A attribute to the file to indicate the change or creation has been occurred.

You have choices. Each of the different variations on this theme have a name and a specific set of rules.

- ◆ **Full Backup:** A complete backup of all data on your File Server. All files are backed up regardless of the state of the archive bit. After this method is used the Archive bit is cleared on all files.

- ◆ **Incremental Backup:** A backup of only those files that are new or that have been changed since your last backup of any kind. After this method is used, the Archive bit is cleared on those files that are backed up.

- ◆ **Differential Backup:** A backup of all those files that have been modified since the last *full* backup. After this method is used, the Archive bit is not cleared on any files.

You can combine these methods and you must combine at least two for differential. But what ever methods you, use you have some extra items to think about. If you use Full backup every time you back up, you gain the capability to find any file on every backup set, but you use more backup media (tapes, disks, optical cartridges). If you combine a full backup with several Incremental backups, you save on backup media, but looking for files to restore can be tougher. Differential backups take up more space than incremental, but still less than continuous full backups.

Clearly, a file-by-file archiving system is superior to the old-fashioned image backup method. However, file-by-file archive sessions may take longer to complete than image backup sessions. This performance disadvantage is nullified when you consider that a file-by-file allows you to selectively back up and restore particular files and directories as well as choose the physical hard drive unit you restore to.

Archive sessions may actually complete faster under a file-by-file system, because you can eliminate archiving of redundant information, deleted files, and other data used internally by NetWare.

You clearly have many choices to make and following are some possible combinations of timing and media that may help you decide.

Rotating Media

Rotating media simply means that you have a set of media (tapes, magneto-optical cartridges, etc.), using each member of the set for archiving at regular intervals. For example, you have five tape cartridges labeled "A," "B," "C," "D," and "E." One day you use "A" for archiving data; the next day you use "B;" the third day you use "C," and so on. These schemes usually include either all Full backups, or a combination of Full and Incremental, or Full and Differential.

Rotation of media serves to protect you against media failure, but it also provides a more extensive data archive. Sophisticated media rotation schemes have been developed using anywhere from one to ten or more media cartridges. Most of these rotation schemes provide you with an extensive data archiving. You can restore data from any number of days, weeks, months, or years in the past.

One such method that allows restoration of data aged from one day to many years is the *Grandfather, Father, Son* method. This method requires a total of 20 tapes—8 tapes for the first month and one tape per month after that. In this method you mark the initial 8 tapes MONDAY, TUESDAY, WEDNESDAY, THURSDAY, FRIDAY-1, FRIDAY-2, FRIDAY-3, and FRIDAY-4. You begin the cycle on Monday by using the tape marked MONDAY and continue this process with tape TUESDAY, WEDNESDAY, THURSDAY, and FRIDAY-1 on the respective days. On the Fridays that follow, use each FRIDAY tape in order. When you have reached FRIDAY-4 you will be able to restore from tapes of 1 to 6 days old and tapes from 1 to 4 weeks old. This method can be extrapolated out by replacing you FRIDAY-1 tape each month and marking the old FRIDAY-1 tape with the month for storage. Keep the tapes from each month and before long you have quite a library of you business records and critical data.

In the early days of networks, most computer managers or technicians had to design and maintain a media rotation scheme manually. This is a lot of work and leaves room for human error. Today, most archiving systems provide software which manages media rotation, and even automates it. This is much preferable to the old manual methods.

Media rotation is usually used in combination with image backup, file-by-file backup, and journalized archiving systems.

JOURNALIZED ARCHIVE

A *journalized archive* is a special version of the file-by-file archive. Not only does a journalized archive allow you to back up and restore data on a per-file basis, it also allows you to back up and restore files as they existed on a certain day or even at a certain time on a certain day. In other words, a journalized archive system not only archives files as they presently exists, but allows you to view the entire history of files, including the manner in which files were updated over a period of time.

Journalized archive systems are especially useful in environments where documents are the main end product, such as law firms, software engineering houses, publishing houses, and so on. In environments such as these, it may be necessary to evaluate how a document has changed over time. Only a journalized archive system can maintain this information for you.

The only disadvantage of a journalized archive system is that it is media-intensive. In other words, you will may use more media cartridges over time to archive the same amount of data. However, when a journalized archive system is used in combination with a very high-capacity media, such as magneto-optical or WORM, this may not be a concern.

PERPETUAL ARCHIVE

A *perpetual archive* system is one which runs all the time, and which archives files as they are updated. In other words, whenever you close a file after writing to it, the perpetual archive system backs up that file immediately. Perpetual archiving systems eliminate the need to perform periodic backup operations. They also ensure that your data archive is completely up-to-the-minute. With a standard archiving system, you restore data that is several hours to a week old. Even though you have been able to restore your data, you've still lost between several hours and a week's worth of work. With a perpetual backup system, the most work you will ever lose is several minutes worth.

Perpetual archiving systems are fairly new to NetWare. That's because Novell never provided certain low-level programming interfaces need in order for vendors to develop the software required for perpetual archiving. However, NetWare 4.*x* includes these low-level programming interfaces. There should be a rash of perpetual archiving systems for NetWare 4.*x* on the market in the near future.

ARCHIVING HARDWARE AND SOFTWARE

The data archiving business is generally divided between hardware vendors and software vendors. Hardware vendors manufacture archiving devices, such as tape drives, magneto-optical drives, and so on. Hardware vendors usually do not tailor their products to any specific operation system or hardware architecture. Rather, they manufacture devices capable of working with various hardware architectures and operating systems, given the appropriate device controller and device driver.

Archiving hardware options for NetWare communicate with the CPU by using a disk drive controller card. Different types of drive controllers are available including mostly SCSI (Small Computer Systems Interface) or a proprietary schemes.

SCSI drive controllers are often the preferred controller type for use with backup devices. The NetWare disk driver interface has several features that take advantage of advanced SCSI commands. Another bonus is that virtually all manufacturers of archive devices produce SCSI hardware. This provides you with a wider array of hardware options. SCSI controllers are also capable of controlling up to 7 devices. This allows you to add to the number of backup devices on your CPU and not limit yourself from growth.

Archiving software vendors operate in one of two ways. Some software vendors purchase archive hardware and then tailor their software to match the hardware. This tailoring process includes writing NetWare device drivers for the archive hardware. When you purchase an archiving system from one of these vendors, you purchase an entire package—hardware, drivers, and software.

Other archiving software vendors do not tailor their software to any single hardware device. Rather, they construct their software so that it will work will most the popular archiving hardware on the market. When you purchase software from one of these vendors, you receive not only the software, but also device drivers for most of the popular archive devices on the market. You still need to purchase archive hardware separately.

ARCHIVING HARDWARE

There is a wide range of archiving hardware available today. Until a few of years ago, virtually all archiving hardware used quarter-inch magnetic tape cartridges (QIC), which had a capacity of 40MB to 300MB. These devices were reliable and inexpensive. However, hard drive manufacturers have since increased dramatically the storage capacity of the drives they produce. 4G hard drives are not uncommon on NetWare servers. This causes a problem with QIC media, because you need to use up to three tape cartridges to archive a single NetWare hard drive.

While it's possible to archive a single hard drive to multiple tape cartridges, it is problematic to do so automatically, because somebody needs to sit by the tape drive to insert the next cartridge when the previous cartridge fills up.

QIC devices are capable of archiving only around 0.5MB per minute. This is no concern if you are only archiving 20MB or so, as was the case when these devices were originally put on the market. However, if you are archiving several hundred megabtyes of data, a QIC cartridge simply doesn't have enough capacity for you.

Today, most people are using either 8mm or 4mm magnetic tape to archive their NetWare data. 8mm tape is also popular as a media for Video Camcorders; 4mm tape, also known as Digital Audio Tape (DAT), is popular among stereo enthusiasts. Both 8mm and 4mm data-grade tape cartridges are widely available today, and relatively inexpensive, given their capacity.

Most archiving devices that use either 8mm or 4mm tape cartridges can store up to 2GB of data on a single cartridge. Moreover, the electronics required for reading from and writing to 8mm and 4mm tape cartridges are more compact than the older QIC electronics. That makes it easier to build multi-cartridge devices that can archive 8 or 10G of data while running unattended.

8mm and 4mm tape devices can archive up to 5MB per minute. That means you can archive 100MB in twenty minutes. With these devices, it is possible to archive several gigabytes of data overnight.

Some archiving hardware devices use optical WORM media, or magneto-optical read/write media for archiving and restoring data. These devices share the capacity advantages of 8mm and 4mm tape, and also have the advantage of providing random access to media sectors, which gives them a performance advantage over tape. Tape remains a less expensive media to use than WORM or magneto optical, so most people today use tape as an archiving media.

ARCHIVING SOFTWARE

Archiving software has become more sophisticated over the past several years. Among today's "standard" features offered by archiving software are the following:

◆ Unattended operation

◆ Configuration and scheduling of multiple archive sessions

◆ Filters which allow you to archive selectively different types of files

◆ Storage of archive session logs in a data base format, allowing quick retrieval of specific historical information

◆ Management of multiple media cartridges, including media rotation schemes and media directories

◆ Multiple data restoration options, including restoration by file and date

◆ Multi-server archiving sessions, where data from many servers is archived to or restored from a central hardware device

◆ Archiving and restoration of workstation-based data across the network

Several years ago, some of the capabilities just listed would have seemed exotic, but now they are fairly standard fare. As NetWare sites have grown, many of which today have hundreds of servers, the degree of automation and the spectrum of operations made possible by archiving software has reflected the changes in the way organizations use NetWare.

When selecting archiving systems for your organization, you should evaluate the human resources available for performing data backup. As a rule, the more automated and featured the archiving software is, the less human-intensive the data archiving process will be. With the right software and hardware, a small Administration staff can archive an entire organization's data. Also the more automated your backup software is the less likely you are to miss a backup due to human error.

STORAGE MANAGEMENT SERVICES (SMS)

Storage Management Services (SMS) is the NetWare's data archiving platform of the future. SMS allows for network-wide data archiving, including workstations, without regard to the native file format of the data being archived or restored. SMS also provides a modular, cross-platform programming interface for developers of archiving software and archive device drivers.

The SMS architecture is built around an archive engine (called SME—Storage Management Engine), which archives data in the platform- and media-independent SMS data format. Data is sent, via the Storage Management Data Requester (SMDR), to the archive engine by SMS Target Service Agents (TSA's) residing on remote machines. The archive engine and the TSA communicate using the high-level SMS protocol, which provides for common data storage and retrieval operations.

The SMS archive engine communicates with archive hardware using the SMS driver programming interface, known as Storage Device Interface (SDI), which in turn relies on the NetWare 4.x Media Manager (a low-level media programming interface).

The basic SMS architecture is depicted in Figure 36.1.

SMS allows the archive engine to run on any machine on the network. Although Novell's SMS-complaint archive server, SBACKUP, runs on the NetWare 4.x server as an NLM, it doesn't matter to SMS whether the archive server runs on a server or a workstation.

36

ARCHIVING AND BACKUP

Figure 36.1.
The SMS architecture.

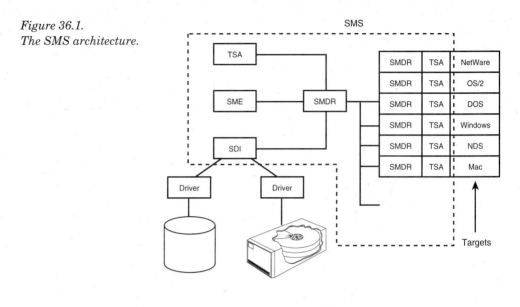

TSA = Target Service Agent

SME = Storage Management Engine

SDI = Storage Device Interface

SMDR = Storage Management Data Requester

The format SMS uses to store data is designed to be completely media- and device-independent. This means, in theory, that you can archive data in the SMS format to an 8mm tape device from vendor "A" and restore the data using an 8mm tape device from vendor "B."

Figure 36.1 shows the TSAs running on remote machines. These machines could be a NetWare server, or any other machines on the network, including workstations of different operating systems. SMS also allows the TSA to run on the same machine as the archive server, meaning you can use SMS to back up local data.

ARCHIVING SERVER DATA

NetWare 4.*x* ships with an SMS-complaint archive engine, called *SBACKUP*. NetWare 4.*x* also ships with TSAs written for NetWare 4.*x*, NetWare Directory Services (NDS), and OS/2 HPFS. Novell has indicated that it is developing TSAs for UNIX and NT workstations or servers. NetWare 4.*x* also ships with SMS-compliant device drivers for most of the popular archiving hardware on the market today.

Note

Although not shipped with NetWare 4.1, you can obtain the TSA for Macintosh from Novell directly, or download it from its FTP site or from CompuServe.

SBACKUP, the SMS-complaint archive engine shipped with NetWare 4.*x* has a good set of features but is not competitive with other archive servers on the market today. Nevertheless, you can perform most of the data archiving operations necessary for your organization with SBACKUP. Following are some operating procedures and order of NLM loading to consider:

♦ Keep at least 1MB of server hard drive space available for temporary and log files.

♦ Wait at least two hours between data compression and delayed backup.

♦ Load device driver for your specific controller—these should comes with your device hardware controller.

♦ Load TAPEDAI.DSK (optional). This a general device driver that comes with NetWare 4.*x*. You need only use this driver if you are using a SCSI backup device.

♦ Load the appropriate TSAs, such as TSANDS.

♦ Load SBACKUP.

Novell designed SMS in part to allow third-party archive software vendors to support NetWare operating systems more easily. Novell encourages these vendors to release state-of-the-art archiving software that is more complete than SBACKUP. Most large NetWare sites choose to purchase a more complete third-party archiving package, rather than use SBACKUP. (SBACKUP is perfectly acceptable for smaller organizations.)

The primary rule you should follow when purchasing a third-party archiving system for NetWare 4.*x* is that the package is compliant to SMS. SMS compliance is the only way vendors will be able to archive and restore the distributed and replicated NDS information base.

One of the most popular third-party archive systems for NetWare 3.*x* and 4.*x* today is ARCServe, by Cheyenne, Inc. Some other vendors are Legato, Palindrome, and Acadia.

ARCHIVING WORKSTATION LOCAL DATA

Choosing to archive workstation local data means a lot of extra work for the network administrator. Some NetWare sites have hundreds or thousands of workstations,

36

and most of those workstations have hard disks with a capacity of between 20 and 500MB. Local workstations represent a vast amount of data in most large organizations. Should you archive local workstation data?

The answer to the question whether or not you should archive local workstation data depends on how your organization uses its NetWare servers. Note that the answer to this question may be different from department to department.

Most Administrators follow the policy of only archiving server-based data. When this policy is communicated clearly to network users, they tend to place their important data on NetWare servers in order to ensure that their important data is archived regularly. Users tend to place utility applications and other miscellaneous files on their local hard drives, but place their important work on NetWare servers. In addition, data which needs to be available to several individuals is almost always stored on servers, because doing so provides an easy way to share data.

Some organizations, however, fall into the practice of storing critical data on workstation local hard drives. If your organization fits this description, you should either enforce a change of user's habits, which is very difficult, or archive local workstations regularly, which can be problematic.

SMS was designed to allow archiving of workstation-based data. In order for this to occur, certain conditions must be met:

◆ The local workstation must be running and have loaded an SMS TSA.

◆ The archive server must be able to communicate with the workstation over the network.

When these conditions are met, you can archive local workstation data using any SMS-compliant archive server, including Novell's SBACKUP. However, it is problematic to ensure that workstations are up and running when you have an archive session scheduled. For example, what do you do when the employee turns off his or her workstation when leaving work for the day? If you need to archive local data from 100 workstations, it is almost certain that several of those workstations will be shut down for the night.

Another factor that may come into play when archiving workstation local data is a bad attitude on the part of some users. Certain individuals are bound to resent your ability to scan their local hard drives at night while they are gone from the office. There really isn't much you can do in a situation like this. The local data will remain unarchived.

Whatever policy you decide on for your organization—to archive workstation local data or not—you must communicate this policy clearly to users. It is helpful to communicate your entire data archiving policy to users on occasion, including the frequency of backups, methods used to back up and restore data, and software used. This type of communication promotes good will and may erode some of the natural reservations some individuals may have about your ability to copy their data, whether that data be server-based or workstation-based.

DISASTER RECOVERY

Disaster recovery is a special science, related to data archiving but entailing much more. Whereas data archiving helps you to recover from data loss, disaster recovery helps you to recover from loss of computers, facilities, communications, and more. Disaster recovery is a good topic to introduce after a discussion on data archiving.

Your organization should have a disaster recovery plan in-place as soon as possible after you have your network up and running. A disaster recovery plan addresses the following non-inclusive list of topics:

◆ Procedures for recovering from total hardware system failure (machine breakdown)

◆ Offsite locations for storage of archived data

◆ Procedures for loss of power to your plant, including backup generators if appropriate

◆ Emergency evacuation plans

◆ Procedures for continuing business operations in the event your physical plant is destroyed or unavailable for a time

◆ A phone number for employees to call in the event of an emergency

◆ Insurance provisions for recovering from a disaster

Disaster recovery is a subject you and your organization should address seriously before becoming so dependent on NetWare 4.x that an interruption of computer service could cause serious damage to your organization.

SUMMARY

This chapter has discussed data archiving for NetWare 4.x. The most important thing to remember is that some archiving systems are better at backing up and restoring NetWare data than others. NetWare 4.*x* includes some new and complex file system features that must be addressed by the archiving software you select. Novell provides a certification program for NetWare 4.*x*, and you should refuse to purchase any archiving system that is not certified for use with NetWare.

SBACKUP is an archive server that ships with NetWare 4.*x*. SBACKUP provides a basic set of archiving features that are sufficient for smaller organizations. However, larger organizations may prefer to purchase a third-party archive system designed specifically for NetWare 4.*x*. The more feature-laden and automated an archiving system is, the better able you will be to perform regular backups of your organization's data.

- Purpose of Accounting

- Installation

- Configuration

- Maintenance

- Removal

- NETADMIN
  Differences

- Utilities

- Other Sources of
  Accounting
  Information

- Summary

CHAPTER 37

Accounting

"What this country needs is a good five-cent nickel."

Franklin P. Adams

If you turned to this page to find the phone number of an old friend who you heard was now doing general ledgers out in Provo, don't feel bad. That seems to be what most people think you're talking about when you say "NetWare Accounting." For the purposes of a network administrator, however, it means the function within NetWare which can be used to "account" and charge for network services. The reason for the confusion may become clear as you read on.

In the past, what has been conspicuously absent was a discussion of accounting from thorough conceptual or practical standpoints. This chapter should be seen as a supplement to the NetWare 4.*x* course manuals, the ElectroText/DynaText online documentation, and the help function available within the NWADMIN and NETADMIN utilities. The documentation included in the NetWare course manuals is somewhat sparse, NETADMIN a bit better, and NWADMIN better still.

This chapter covers the basic functions of accounting, demonstrated through the use of the Windows-based NWADMIN, NetWare Administrator, utility. Major differences in the use of NETADMIN, the DOS-based utility, for the purposes of accounting, are mentioned later in this chapter.

PURPOSE OF ACCOUNTING

The accounting feature in NetWare appears to be a carry-over from the mindset of mainframe computer management. Due to the enormous cost of mainframes, many potential users of computing services were unable to afford one of their own. This dilemma gave rise to the practice of two or more companies jointly purchasing one mainframe computer and sharing it, or one company making the purchase and charging users of the system within another company to defray the cost. In either case, it was necessary to have the capability to account and charge for use of the system. Although the costs of the first local area networks still didn't compare with those of mainframes, the capital outlay was sufficient to spawn some sharing of server resources early on. Thus, NetWare accounting.

WHAT ACCOUNTING IS

The function of accounting has remained basically unchanged since the NetWare 2.*x* series was introduced. NetWare 4.*x* accounting offers the capability to set up "charge rates" for various services provided by a file server, and record the date, time, user name, and address of users logging in and out. Information about the number of disk blocks written, read, and stored, the amount of time users are connected to the server, the number of requests that workstations sent to the server, and logins/ logouts can be stored in an accounting data file on the server for future use in charging for services. A user account balance can be assigned to control the extent of network use.

WHAT ACCOUNTING IS NOT

Accounting, in its current and previous forms, lacks even the most basic functions that a network administrator might imagine it possessing, and so poses several implementation problems. It is also often confused with an new utility for NetWare 4.*x*, auditing.

AUDITING

Accounting and auditing are completely separate functions within NetWare. Accounting is defined above. Auditing is a new feature with NetWare 4.*x*, concerned with the security of the network versus financial accountability. The two features cannot even be managed by the same person, conceptually, as the network administrator manages accounting, and one of the main functions of the "auditor" is keeping the network administrator honest. Auditing is covered in more detail in Chapter 29.

BILLING UTILITY

There is no function within accounting to assign actual money amounts to be charged. The term "charge rate" is really a misnomer as the rates are actually generic "resource units" to be charged. A more complete explanation of charge rates follows in the Configuration section of this chapter. Additionally, you might think, "Okay, I'm going to charge my network users. They're all on the network, so I'll just bill them electronically every month." Good thought, but ahead of its time. Not only can't you bill your users (or designated managerial recipients of the bad news) over the network, you can't generate a bill of any kind. There simply is no billing feature.

REPORTING UTILITY

It is reasonable to expect to be able to extract the stored accounting information in any of several formats, such as each type of charge or all charges for a given period for any user or group. Reasonable, but not possible. The only report comes from a utility called *ATOTAL*. This utility provides aggregate "unit" counts per day and week for the entire server. One additional utility, PAUDIT, was not carried over from NetWare 3.*x* to 4.*x*. This is an unfortunate omission as it had provided access to the record of user logins and logouts.

Tip

> Although not shipped with NetWare 4.x, the PAUDIT utility from NetWare 3.x will work on a 4.x server. There are two important things to note. In addition to the PAUDIT.EXE file, the NET$REC.DAT file must be copied to the 4.x server as well and although NetWare 4.0 provides a NET$REC.DAT file, PAUDIT will not work properly with it. Rename the 4.x NET$REC.DAT to NET$REC.40, for example, and then copy PAUDIT.EXE into SYS:PUBLIC and NET$REC.DAT into SYS:SYSTEM on the 4.x server. No other function in 4.x will be affected by the NET$REC.DAT swap. Try it. The information provided by PAUDIT will likely be of the most use to a network administrator, when compared with that from ATOTAL.

Any capability to extract accounting information from the auditing utility, AUDITCON, is of little use to the network administrator as the administrator is by concept not the auditor. There are third-party utilities, listed in the "Utilities" section of this chapter, which make better use of the stored accounting data.

Print Services Utility

While central funding of most network services within a company seems to make sense as these costs are more or less fixed, the expense of printing services, such as paper and toner cartridges, increase with use. If each section within a company was billed for its printing service usage, conservation would likely kick in and money might be saved. Most of the interest that I've noticed in accounting by those not yet completely familiar with it was in its conceivable capability to charge for printing services on the network. Right again! There's no function within the accounting feature to charge for printing. There is one third party utility listed later in the "Utilities" section, which counts pages printed in a network environment.

Maintenance Utility

All accounting data is stored in a file named NET$ACCT.DAT in SYS:SYSTEM. This file grows rapidly on a busy network and no maintenance utility has been provided to cull it periodically. This exclusion causes each ATOTAL report, for example, to start at the beginning of the file and include data since accounting was installed. In addition to providing old, unwanted data, the report can take awhile to percolate before appearing. The only apparent option is to delete or rename NET$ACCT.DAT.

PRACTICAL USES

Although accounting was intended to distribute the costs of operating the network, it has not been widely used for that purpose, primarily for two reasons. First, the vast majority of local area networks are each owned and operated by one entity, such as company or institution, versus being jointly owned, so the need to charge others for use of the network isn't there. Second, the accounting feature was not initially, nor is it yet, developed to an extent to be useful, so even those few who would use it for its intended purpose or those many more who would have undoubtedly found new uses for it, weren't provided the functionality to do so.

TRACKING LOGINS AND LOGOUTS

At a conference of university network managers which I recently attended, I asked for a "show of hands" on the use of accounting. Of the approximately 110 present at the time, only 10 even used accounting and all 10 were using it only to track users logging in and out, in case they ever needed to know if "Bob was logged in at 2:00 a.m. last night." No one was using accounting for its primary, financial purpose, and although there was a good amount of emerging NetWare 4.*x* users, no one was using accounting within 4.*x* yet. While researching this subject, I posed a few "Who cares about accounting" questions in the CompuServe NetWire forums and in the Novell USENET newsgroup `comp.sys.novell` on the Internet. The response from both was less, although comparable to that from the conference attendees—very few users and then only for tracking logins and logouts. Although both of these "surveys" would be scorned as inconclusive by the best in market research, the results are reasonably representative of the network administrator population.

PREPAID NETWORK USAGE

In a "pay-as-you-go" type of environment, such as student labs at some universities or other public access sites, a user could pay for a certain amount of usage, maybe as "connect time," in advance. The network administrator would set the user's account balance commensurate with the prepaid amount, and the user would be logged out by the system when his account balance was depleted, and prevented from future logins until he paid to increase his account balance. More information on setting account balances is covered later.

RESOURCE UTILIZATION

If few are using accounting, does that mean that there are no uses for it? Not quite. In addition to the need for Novell to develop Accounting to at least a minimally functional level, it seems to me that the accounting feature should be renamed to "Resource Utilization." This new name would reflect a usage of this function that would be valuable to most versus only a few. Although few network administrators need to charge their users for network services, all of them could benefit from historical, statistical data on who uses the network how much. This data could be used to project, prepare for, and help justify financially, increases in network capacity. For that reason alone, accounting could be usefully installed on all servers, even in its current state of development. Aggregate network use information can be accessed through the use of the ATOTAL utility. Although Novell doesn't provide anything else for the standard network administrator to make use of the "resource utilization" data stored in NET$ACCT.DAT, there are a few flickers of light at the end of the tunnel, which aren't the headlights of an oncoming train.

API: APPARENTLY POSITIVE INTENTIONS

Novell offers a method for programmer's to create applications that have access to the network operating system and most information that it maintains. This is the first of two "flickers of light" at the end of the accounting "tunnel." This access is in the form of an *Application Programmer Interface* or *API*. There is an API for accounting as well. Although exploration of the API is beyond the scope of this chapter, suffice it to say that custom DOS, Windows, or OS/2 applications can be written to extract accounting information and generate output in whatever format is desired. The accounting API is available from Novell only, in its NetWare Software Development Kit (SDK). This product comes on CD-ROM, costs about $190 (U.S.), has online documentation, and includes the NetWare Client SDK, NLM SDK, Novell Labs test tools, and several other development tools.

Note

The SDK product is designed for use by Microsoft C or Borland C programmers, and is not a menu-driven utility for network administrators who are non-programmers.

INSTALLATION

Activation of accounting is more akin to turning on a light switch in terms of simplicity than an "installation," per se. From the main NWADMIN window showing the NDS tree, select the server (server object) on which you want to install accounting (see Figure 37.1).

Figure 37.1.
Main NWAdmin
window.

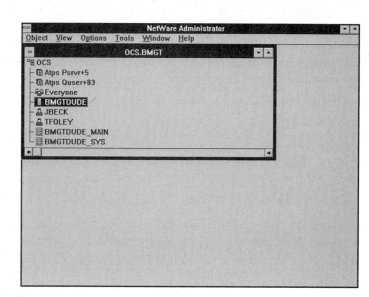

The server object information window will appear. The categories of information on
the right side of the window, such as Identification and Error Log, stop with Users.
The Accounting resource categories will appear below Users, after installation. In
the Server Object information window, click the Accounting button at the bottom of
the window. Answer Yes to Do you want to install Accounting?. Figure 37.2 shows this
window.

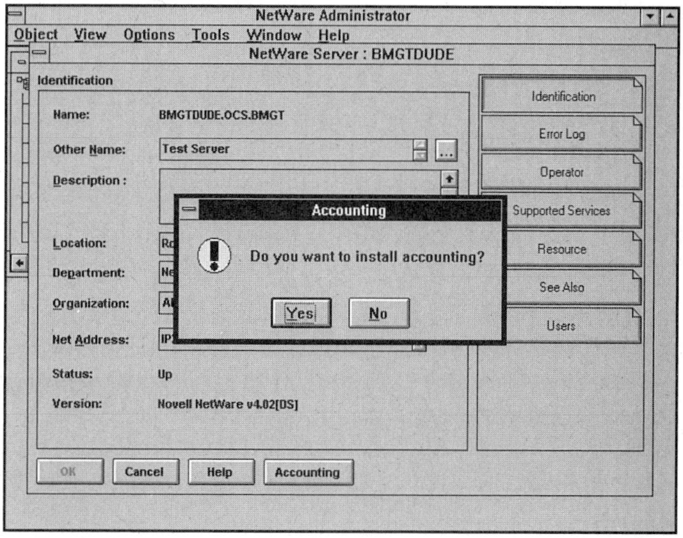

Figure 37.2.
Accounting installation
window.

Now check for the accounting resource categories on the right side of the window, such as Blocks Read and Blocks Written. There are five categories in all. If those categories now appear, you've successfully activated accounting. Now you need to configure it for charge data to accrue.

CONFIGURATION

Accounting picks up its functionality from the assignment of "charge rates" for the five different services, or "resources," and user account balance settings.

RESOURCE TYPES

The five resources are blocks read, blocks written, connect time, disk storage, and service requests. Following are explanations for all resources:

- ◆ **Blocks Read:** The charge is per disk block. Although the default block size is 4K, if you change it to 64K during installation of NetWare 4.0, for example, the user will be charged per 64K block.
- ◆ **Blocks Written:** Same as Blocks Read
- ◆ **Connect Time:** The charge is per minute of time that a user is logged in.
- ◆ **Disk Storage:** The charge is per "block day." That means that you can only charge a user once a day for file storage space used on the server. As a matter of fact, when assigning charge rates in the Disk Storage window, the assignment feature prevents rate assignment for more than one 30-minute period per day, as shown in Figure 37.3.
- ◆ **Service Requests:** Each time the workstation requests any service from the server, the user is charged. A request is not defined as simply as the use of any of the four preceding resources types. A service request is equivalent to an NCP, or Network Core Protocols, request. The simple act of logging in generates literally hundreds of service requests. This may be the most confusing resource type to charge for, and explain to users, and so can easily be left unused, that is, "No Charge" assigned.

DETERMINING CHARGE RATES

Now the amount of "resource units" (or fraction of one unit) to charge for the use of each resource needs to be determined. For illustration's sake, suppose that one resource unit equals one cent. Using Blocks Read, if a charge rate of 2/1 is assigned, two *resource units* or two cents will be charged for each block read. Conversely, 1/2 is one-half cent for each block. The first or top number is called the *multiplier* and the second or bottom number, the *divisor*. Use of the term *resource unit* is not a technicality. It was mentioned earlier that assigning actual money amounts to be charged is not possible. NetWare accounting keeps track of resources used and users' account balances in resource units. After the number of units used is known, theoretically, a value can be manually assigned to each unit and a bill prepared.

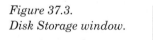

Figure 37.3.
Disk Storage window.

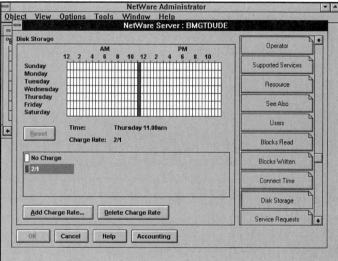

ADDING AND DELETING CHARGE RATES

To assign or *add* a charge rate, select the desired accounting resource type, such as Connect Time, from the Server Object information window. The default charge rate is No Charge, which will be reflecting throughout the Day and Time Grid and in the Charge Rates List Box. Click the Add Charge Rate button, and type in the desired multiplier and divisor, and choose OK.

Tip

Partial resource unit charge rates cannot be entered with decimals, such as 2.5/1. Whole numbers must be used. In this case,, multiply the multiplier and divisor by 10 (or enough factors of 10 to eliminate the decimal from the multiplier), and use 25/10 to achieve the same result (see Figure 37.4).

The charge rate will appear, color coded, in the Charge Rates List Box. The network administrator has no control over the colors assigned to each rate. The colors are assigned by the order of creation, not the actual charge rate, and will likely vary among resource types.

Figure 37.4.
Add Charge Rate
window.

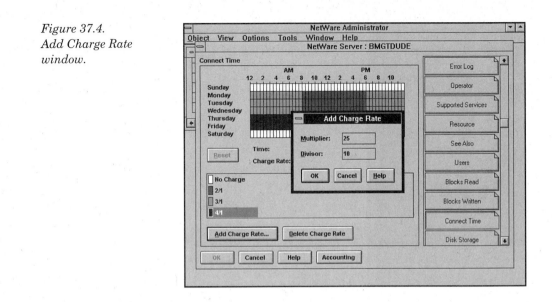

The standard recommendation is to set a charge rate for all five resources of 1/1 and give all users an unlimited account balance when you first install accounting, for a test period of time. This procedure will allow a common reference, 1/1, to monitor and analyze network usage without the management challenge associated with regularly depleting account balances. Realistic charge rates and account balances can be set later when the network administrator has determined what they should be.

Warning

Do not define more rates than are to be assigned immediately. Any charge rates defined in the Charge Rates List Box, but not assigned in the Day and Time Grid, will be deleted as soon as you choose OK and exit. Any charge rate can be added back just as it was defined originally. Because No Charge was the default charge rate and it wasn't defined by the network administrator, how can it be re-created? Use the rate of 0/1.

In order to delete a charge rate, highlight the desired charge rate in the Charge Rates List Box, and click the Delete Charge Rate button. Realistically, deleting a charge rate is really not necessary. When you stop using a given charge rate in the Day and Time Grid, it will automatically be deleted upon selecting OK and exiting from that window.

Note

You can't delete a charge rate if it's still in use anywhere in the Day and Time Grid.

MANAGING USER ACCOUNT BALANCES

The network administrator will assign each user either an unlimited account balance or a specific account balance as one of the properties of the user object. Account balance information is also a part of the new user creation template and can be set there initially. If afforded an unlimited balance, the user will be allowed to continue using network services as a negative balance accrues. If using a specific balance, the user will be given a five-minute warning to log out just after the balance has been depleted and then will be automatically logged out in five minutes, after one additional one-minute warning, if not already logged out by then (see Figure 37.5).

Figure 37.5.
Termination notice.

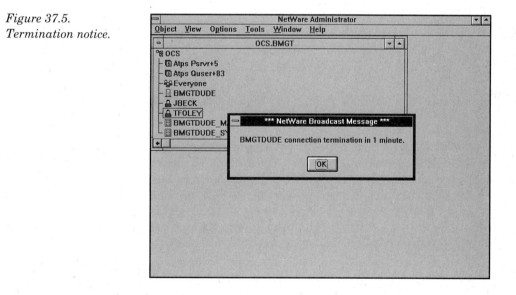

Users should be encouraged to log themselves out versus having their connections terminated as forceful termination may cause damage to any open files and will result in the loss of any unsaved data or documents.

If the user is prepaying for network usage, the administrator can reset his or her account balance when more services are paid for in advance. If the user is on "credit," the network administrator can reset the balance when each usage period is billed or as the bill is paid. For "credit" balance users, the balance should be set at least high enough to get a user through a normal billing period, such as one month or one quarter, plus a reasonable bill payment period. To assign or modify a user account balance, select the user (user object) from the main NWADMIN window. The User Identification window will appear. Scroll down the categories on the right side of the window and select Account Balance. You will see the window shown in Figure 37.6.

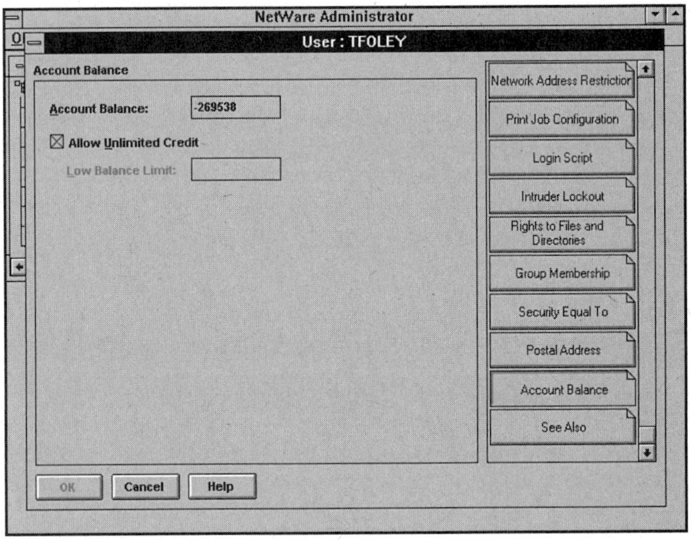

Figure 37.6.
Account Balance
window.

The current account balance, for a given user, is displayed in the top box or *field*. Replace the number in this field with the desired balance if purposely limiting the user. If the user is to be given *unlimited credit*, toggle that setting on by selecting, and thus placing an x in, the box to the left of Allow Unlimited Credit. The Low Balance Limit will only be active if a user does not have unlimited credit. Although the number in this field can be changed, the default setting of zero is best for normal use.

MAINTENANCE

The only maintenance related specifically to the accounting function concerns the accounting data collection file, NET$ACCT.DAT. This file grows rapidly and cannot be cropped. When the data in the file has outlived its usefulness or the file becomes too large, your only option is to rename or delete it. A new NET$ACCT.DAT file should be created the next time accounting information needs to be saved to disk by NetWare. Hopefully, the capability to delete portions of this file will be part of any future NetWare upgrade.

REMOVAL

Removal of accounting is as easy as, and nearly identical to, its installation. From the main NWADMIN window showing the NDS tree, select the server (server object) from which you want to remove Accounting. In the Server Object information window, click the Accounting button at the bottom of the window. Answer Yes to Do you want to remove Accounting?. Now check for the Accounting resource categories on the right side of the window, such as Blocks Read and Blocks Written. If those categories are gone, you've successfully deactivated or removed Accounting.

Warning

> The NET$ACCT.DAT file is unaffected by the removal of accounting and will remain in SYS:SYSTEM, but no additional accounting data will be stored in it. However, removal of accounting will delete all charge rate definitions and assignments, all of which have to be re-created if accounting is reinstalled.

NETADMIN DIFFERENCES

The primary difference between NWADMIN and NETADMIN is that NETADMIN is a text-based, DOS utility. Selections from menu lists give access the NDS objects and features. The Accounting Options menu, listing familiar resource types, is located about four menu choices from the main menu and can be seen in Figure 37.7.

Interestingly, NETADMIN will allow a network administrator to charge for disk space more than once per day, unlike NWADMIN. Charge rates are defined the same as in NWADMIN, but are reflected in the Day and Time Grid differently. In the grid, the rates are shown as numbers versus colors, with the first charge rate defined as Rate # 1, second rate defined is Rate # 2, and so on. The second charge rate defined may be 3/1, but will show up in the grid as a number 2, not a 3. The sample window showing charge rate assignment from NETADMIN can be seen in Figure 37.8.

Figure 37.7.
NETADMIN Account-
ing Options screen.

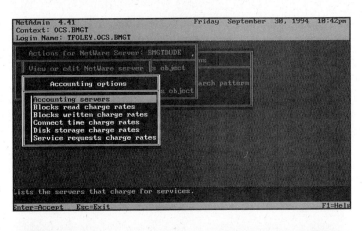

Figure 37.8.
NETADMIN Block
Read Charge Rate
screen.

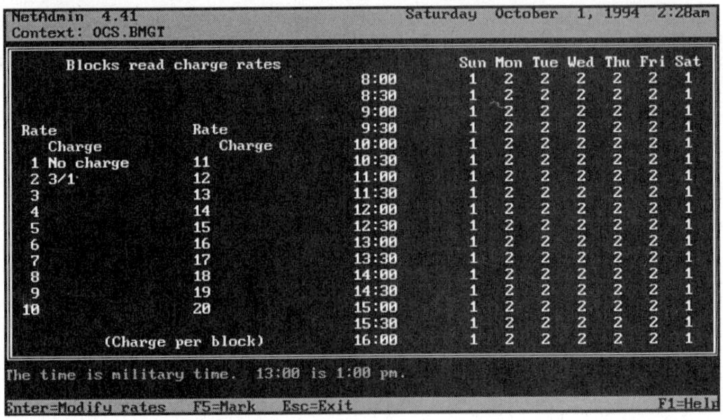

UTILITIES

Novell provides only one utility to make use of the collected accounting data. This limitation considerably detracts from the usefulness of the accounting function. A few third party companies have utilities, some within their network management software, which can extract accounting data and produce various reports.

NOVELL'S ATOTAL UTILITY

The sole utility provided with NetWare for accounting purposes is ATOTAL.EXE or the Accounting Services Total Utility. The information provided by ATOTAL lacks usefulness in that it is for the entire server, versus by user or group, and includes all information since accounting was originally installed instead of a selectable period. With this in mind, it seems realistically impossible to prepare bills for network usage without going into NWADMIN or NETADMIN to check each user's account balance manually. Following is an edited, sample ATOTAL report:

```
ACCOUNTING SERVICES TOTAL UTILITY
   Reading accounting records, please wait...
08/31/1994:
     Connect time:        597    Server requests:     54839
     Blocks read:        6254    Blocks written:       1981
     Blocks/day:          744
   (( Some days omitted for demonstration purposes ))
Totals for week:
     Connect time:        597    Server requests:     54839
     Blocks read:        6254    Blocks written:       1981
     Blocks/day:        45076
```

This report includes a daily total for each of the five resource types and a similar weekly summary. As all information since the installation of accounting is included each time the report is generated, the compilation time and the report itself can be quite long.

Note

If ATOTAL is run within a short time after installation of accounting (even up to a few hours later), it will likely abort and give the following error message

```
ATOTAL-4.04-912: The specified file cannot be found:
SYS:SYSTEM\NET$ACCT.DAT.
```

Novell's Support Encyclopedia will say that an invalid filename was specified or the file is not in the path. This is misleading. First, neither of these potential problems are accounting configuration settings. Second, checking for the existence of the file in SYS:SYSTEM will show that it doesn't exist there. Nor does it exist anywhere else for that matter. The creation of a NET$ACCT.DAT file to store accounting information does not happen immediately upon installation of accounting. It is because the accounting data initially is cached in server memory until the operating system decides to move it to disk, only then creating the NET$ACCT.DAT file. This further helps to explain why a user's account balance or the date/time of NET$ACCT.DAT doesn't always update immediately upon logout.

THIRD-PARTY TOOLS

Third-party tools constitute the second, and surely most significant, of the two "flickers of light" at the end of the accounting "tunnel."

REPORTING

Several companies that market network management software include the capability to extract information and produce reports from the information in NET$ACCT.DAT, in addition to numerous other network management functions. One of two noteworthy packages is the NetWare Management module of Frye Utilities for Networks from Frye Computer Systems, Inc. text-based reporting utility can provide accounting reports in any of several formats, such as a Connect Time Charges Report, Disk Storage Charges Report, and Login/Logout Report.

Another package is BindView NCS from the LAN Support Group, Inc. Also a text-based utility, it provides a few predefined accounting reports, such as *Accounting Activity for the Last 7 Days* and *Login Trail for the Last 7 Days*, as well as the capability to define and print reports on various accounting information fields. Both Frye and BindView NCS, as well as many others, provide some of the functionality lacking from NetWare's treatment of accounting, to include access to login and logout information, previously provided by NetWare's PAUDIT. An important point to keep in mind with both of the products mentioned above is that they currently only operate with NetWare 4.0 in bindery emulation mode.

PRINTING

Although there probably are other good products, the only shareware print counting/charge utility easily found is PCOUNTER, A Page Counting Print Server for Novell NetWare Networks. This utility is available from A.N.D. Technologies. A two-hour unregistered trial version is available on CompuServe in the Novell Users Library forum (NOVUSER). This utility is a replacement for Novell's PSERVER that counts pages on PostScript and PCL-compatible printers.

OTHER SOURCES OF ACCOUNTING INFORMATION

There are several sources to which a network administrator can turn in planning for the use of accounting or in the event of complications. The following sections give a brief overview of some of these sources, such as Novell and CompuServe. However, these sources are by no means extensive nor authoritative.

NOVELL SOURCES

There are a few sources of information available from Novell. Most of these provide basic concept information or more useful error resolution information. None approach the subject from a practical "How can a network administrator make accounting work?" angle.

NSEPro: Novell Support Encyclopedia

Overall a very good product, NSEPro provides access to an extensive database of technical support information, Novell application notes, and user experiences on all areas of NetWare through the use of a flexible Folio search interface. A search on the word accounting will provide plenty of fireside reading material. Searches on any combination of words or error message number designators are possible and will usually bear fruit. Information is provided in an Issue/Problem, then Solution format. This product is updated regularly and is available on CD-ROM via an annual subscription from Novell.

NetWare 4.x Course Texts and Manuals

These references actually provide little information about the use, configuration, and functionality of accounting beyond a basic definition and description, but are provided during Novell Authorized Education courses.

NetWare 4.x Internal "Help" Feature

This reference, built into both NWADMIN and NETADMIN, is adequate from the perspective of a "step-by-step" explanation of terms and basic concepts. Best of all, it's convenient and easy to use.

Other Books

There are not many publications specifically on accounting, and most NetWare 4.x books barely mention the subject. In general, very little good information is available in print on NetWare accounting, although that's likely related to its level of use.

CompuServe

An additional source of information on Accounting is the Novell NetWire forums on CompuServe. The "Novell NetWare 3.x" and "Novell NetWare 4.x" forums occasionally provide current discussion of accounting topics in the form of questions and answers posted as alternating messages or *threads*. Neither of these two forums has an historical library; however, some "mining" in the Novell Users Library forum may prove useful. The SysOps, or system operators, of these forums are very knowledgeable individuals who volunteer time to assist network administrators find resolutions for problems. Use of CompuServe requires a modem, an account, and an access program, the last two of which can be obtained by contacting CompuServe.

SUMMARY

Accounting is a feature of NetWare that has limited usefulness due to its immature stage of development, most prominently visible in its lack of tools to extract collected accounting information or produce reports based on the same data. The capability that existed within NetWare releases 3.*x* and earlier has been reduced with NetWare 4.*x,* with the loss of the PAUDIT utility. Although beyond the capabilities of many network administrators, an application programmer interface allows development of custom applications and reports. Several third-party companies provide menu-driven network management utilities that are capable of accessing NetWare's accounting information.

- Dynamic
  Configuration

- Determining Block
  Size

- Large Internet Packet
  (LIP)

- Assessing Server
  RAM

- Understanding and
  Tuning Packet Burst

- Summary

CHAPTER 38

Tuning for Performance

Performance optimization and benchmarking is a delicate subject because it is almost impossible to take into consideration all possible variables. And, to add disarray to confusion, it is even harder to reproduce benchmark traffic that truly represents a real-world situation. However, we all have this insatiable desire to push our operating systems to the utmost limits. Therefore, this chapter is dedicated to optimizing the performance of NetWare 4.x.

From the inception of NetWare, its engineers have been concerned with performance. The growth and success of NetWare is an indication of their successful accomplishment of this goal. A large contributing factor to this success has been Novell's philosophy of *self-optimization*. This phenomenon is often referred to as automatic optimization, automatic tuning, or dynamic configuration (this chapter will use the term *dynamic configuration*). This dynamic configuration has bolstered NetWare's success because it leaves network administrators free to oversee the network, rather than having to continually try and optimize the network for performance.

In fact, performance optimization has almost been forgotten; network parameters go unnoticed and are simply left at default settings. Forgotten is the fact, that several of these parameters, if fine-tuned, can increase network performance and make a server more efficient.

This chapter begins by introducing the concept of NetWare's dynamic configuration and explains the portions of NetWare that are dynamically tuned. It then discusses, in length, some of the dynamically adjusted parameters that can be "fine-tuned." The understanding that you will gain of NetWare's dynamic configuration will help you squeeze out every possible drop of performance.

Tip

Each time you bring your server down, NetWare's dynamic configuration mechanism will have to start over. So if nothing else, this section will inform you of the parameters that you will want to watch. After the server has been in operation for sometime, you can manually set the dynamically configurable parameters. Manually setting these parameters will mean that your server will "get back on course" the minute it starts up, rather than having to wait hours, days, or months for it to optimize itself.

DYNAMIC CONFIGURATION

NetWare's dynamic configuration is the capability to allocate a server's resources according to need and availability. When NetWare 4.x is first started, all of the server's memory is used for file caching. Other portions of the operating system require more resources, and if resources are available they will be allocated. For example, if the need for directory cache buffers increases, or, if more NLMs are loaded, memory resources will be transferred, reducing the amount of memory that was previously being used for file cache buffers. Reallocation of resources isn't done instantly, however. The operating system will wait a specified amount of time for existing resources to become available. If they do not become available in the specified amount of time, then resources will be taken from the file cache buffer area and reallocated.

Note

The "waiting period" ensures the operating system doesn't permanently allocate resources to activities that are infrequent, or for uncommon peaks in server activity.

The following section lists the parameters that are dynamically configured by NetWare 4.*x*. Although these parameters are dynamically allocated, SET commands can be used to manually determine the amount of resources available to each process (at least the minimum and maximum levels).

Using SET commands to allocate server resources can be an extremely powerful performance tool, and at the same time, provide a more efficient server. This section explains how to set these limits and provides hints and tips on some of the more adjustable dynamic configuration parameters:

◆ Directory cache buffers

◆ Disk elevator size

◆ File locks

◆ Kernel processes

◆ Kernel semaphores

◆ Maximum number of open files

◆ Memory for NLMs

◆ Router/server advertising

◆ Routing buffers

◆ Service processes

◆ TTS transactions

◆ Turbo FAT index tables

38

DIRECTORY CACHE BUFFERS

Directory cache buffers is the portion of the overall memory pool that is set aside to cache directory requests. When a NetWare server is first brought up it will eventually receive a request for a directory cache buffer. When this first request to access a directory is processed, that directory table will need to be placed in the cache buffers. So, 20 cache buffers will be immediately created (the minimum default value). A directory request will then stay in a cache buffer as long as it is being accessed frequently. (The length of time the directory table stays in cache is determined by the NonReferenced Delay time; the default value is 5.5 seconds). Once this time is elapsed, the buffer becomes available for another entry. Caching directories allows the most frequently used directories to be accessed more quickly, since they can be read from (fast) memory rather than the (slow) disk drive.

If more directory buffers are needed, NetWare waits a specified amount of time, which is called the Directory Cache Allocation Wait Time (default is 2.2 sec), before it actually allocates any more memory to caching directory requests. During this wait time other resources may become available (NonReferenced Delay time may have elapsed on some entries). If no buffers become available, a new directory cache buffer is dynamically allocated. The memory for these directory cache buffers comes from (the amount of memory itself isn't dynamic) memory previously allocated for file cache buffers (see File Cache Buffers later in this chapter). If enough directory requests are made, directory cache buffers will either reach the maximum value, or, the entire directory structure will be cached.

Following are settings related to directory cache buffers:

◆ Default minimum number of Directory Cache Buffers is 20. The range of supported minimum values are 10 to 2000.

◆ Default Maximum Directory Cache Buffers is 500. The range of supported maximum values are 20 to 4000.

◆ Default Directory Cache Allocation Wait Time is 5.5 seconds. The range of supported Allocation Wait Time = 0.5 to 2 minutes.

◆ Default Directory Cache Buffer NonReferenced Delay time is 5.5 seconds. The range of supported wait time values are 1 second to 5 minutes.

Once memory is allocated to a directory cache buffer, it is not available to cache file processes, and the only way to return the memory to the memory pool is to down the server and bring it back up. If users are being warned that the server is getting low on memory, directory cache buffers is one of the first places that you will want to manually limit memory use.

Now, with NetWare 4.x, you can use a server management utility called SERVMAN.NLM to change or monitor directory cache buffer parameters (see Figure 38.1).

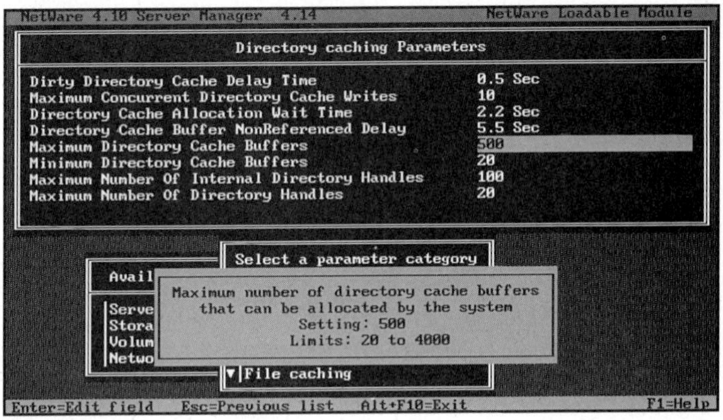

Figure 38.1.
Changing the number
of directory cache
buffers using
SERVMAN.NLM.

```
NetWare 4.10 Server Manager  4.14                NetWare Loadable Module
                          Directory caching Parameters
 Dirty Directory Cache Delay Time                    0.5 Sec
 Maximum Concurrent Directory Cache Writes            10
 Directory Cache Allocation Wait Time                 2.2 Sec
 Directory Cache Buffer NonReferenced Delay           5.5 Sec
 Maximum Directory Cache Buffers                      500
 Minimum Directory Cache Buffers                      20
 Maximum Number Of Internal Directory Handles         100
 Maximum Number Of Directory Handles                  20

                     ┌─────Select a parameter category─────┐
       Avail         │ Maximum number of directory cache buffers│
      │Serve         │   that can be allocated by the system │
      │Stora         │        Setting: 500                   │
      │Volum         │        Limits: 20 to 4000             │
      │Netwo         └──────────────────────────────────────┘
                     ▼│File caching
 Enter=Edit field    Esc=Previous list    Alt+F10=Exit          F1=Help
```

38

TUNING FOR PERFORMANCE

Tip

To change or monitor directory cache buffer parameters on a NetWare 4.1 server, do the following:

1. At the console type LOAD SERVMAN.
2. Select Server parameters from the options box.
3. Select the category Directory Caching.
4. Highlight the option you want to change.
5. Enter the new setting.

To automatically save the new parameters to the startup files, follow these steps:

1. Press Esc, to get back to Categories screen.
2. Press Esc again, and you will be presented with an Update options screen.
3. Select Update AUTOEXEC.NCF and STARTUP.NCF now option.

The next time the server is loaded, the changes will be reflected.

FILE CACHE BUFFERS

NetWare servers can provide faster file access by holding a file in its memory (it can then retrieve the file directly from memory, rather than having to retrieve it from the hard disk. The more memory you have the more files that can be stored in cache, thus the faster (on average) file accesses will be. However, memory is usually a limited commodity, meaning it needs to be used efficiently.

All free memory, after all other processes have enough, is left for file cache buffers. Therefore, the file cache buffers parameter needs to be viewed in an opposite manner from dynamically configurable options (other areas will grow in available resources). Thus, you set the minimum amount of memory to use for file cache buffers. Then when other processes ask for memory, memory designated for file cache buffers will only be allowed to get so low.

Tip

A common question is "Where should I set the minimum value for file cache buffers?"

If you set it too high, you may be saving memory for the file caching processes that are never needed; at the same time you may be handicapping other services. But, if it is set too low, file retrieval speeds will only be a smidgen of what they should be. NetWare 4.*x* has several new features that make monitoring cache utilization simpler. To determine where file cache buffers should be set, follow these steps:

1. At the server console type LOAD MONITOR.

2. Select Cache Utilization from the Options menu.

If, over time, the Long Term Cache Hits parameter remains less than 90 percent, you have too little memory to efficiently cache files (see Figure 38.2). This means that more memory needs to be added to the server, or the Minimum Cache Buffer parameter is set too low.

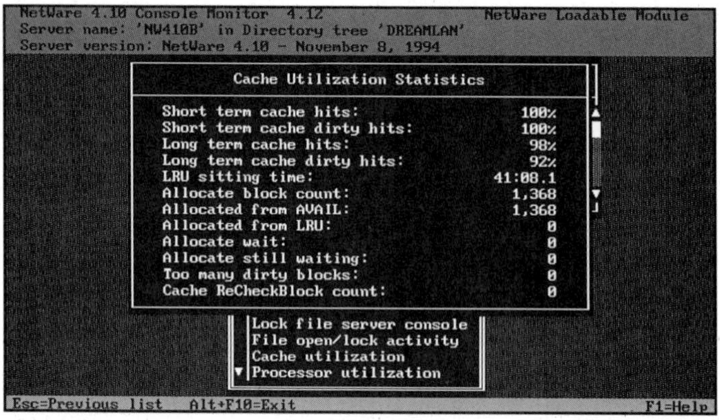

Figure 38.2.
Sample
MONITOR.NLM screen
shows cache hits.

```
NetWare 4.10 Console Monitor  4.12              NetWare Loadable Module
Server name: 'NW410B' in Directory tree 'DREAMLAN'
Server version: NetWare 4.10 - November 8, 1994

                  Cache Utilization Statistics

        Short term cache hits:                   100%  ▲
        Short term cache dirty hits:             100%  █
        Long term cache hits:                     98%  █
        Long term cache dirty hits:               92%  █
        LRU sitting time:                     41:08.1  █
        Allocate block count:                   1,368  ▼
        Allocated from AVAIL:                   1,368  ⌐
        Allocated from LRU:                         0
        Allocate wait:                              0
        Allocate still waiting:                     0
        Too many dirty blocks:                      0
        Cache ReCheckBlock count:                   0

                   Lock file server console
                   File open/lock activity
                   Cache utilization
                 ▼ Processor utilization

Esc=Previous list    Alt+F10=Exit                            F1=Help
```

DISK ELEVATOR SEEKING

Disk elevator seeking logically organizes disk operations as they arrive at the server for processing. As disk requests are queued, they are positioned in the order that the disk heads will retrieve the data (rather than simply in the order that they were requested). This allows the drive head operation to be a smooth "sweeping" fashion, rather than a completely random one.

Elevator seeking can be fine-tuned by setting the Maximum Concurrent Disk Cache Writes. This setting determines how many write requests (for data in a buffer that has been changed) can be put into the disk's elevator, before the disk begins its seek procedure. The Dirty Disk Cache Delay Time parameter, which indicates the length of time NetWare 4.x, will keep a write request (not located in a cache buffer) in the buffer before it writes it to disk.

The best way to determine whether the Maximum Concurrent Disk Cache Write parameter needs changed, is to watch the MONITOR screen. If the dirty cache buffers are more than 70 percent of the total cache buffers, you may want to increase the speed of disk writes by increasing the setting of the Maximum Concurrent Disk Cache Write parameter.

Tip

Increasing the number of Maximum Concurrent Disk Cache Writes can create more efficiency in disk write requests, while decreasing the amount creates more efficiency in disk read requests. To change the amount, use the following SET command (or SERVMAN.NLM) (supported values are 10 to 4000, default is 50) (see Figure 38.3):

Maximum Concurrent Disk Cache Writes = "X"

You can also increase the speed of disk writes by turning off Read-After-Write Verification.

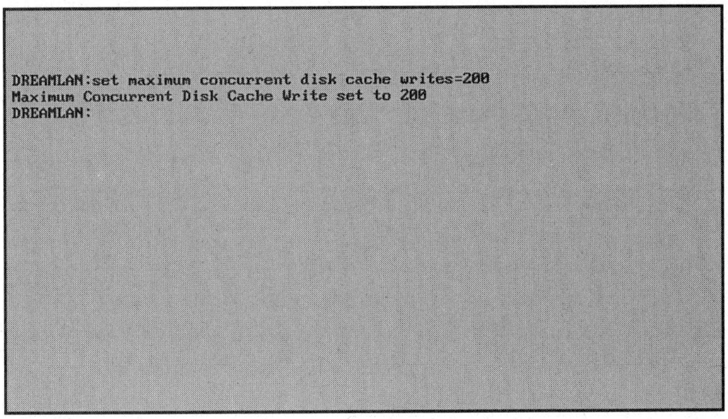

Figure 38.3.
Changing the Maximum Concurrent Disk Cache Writes from command line.

```
DREAMLAN:set maximum concurrent disk cache writes=200
Maximum Concurrent Disk Cache Write set to 200
DREAMLAN:
```

Warning

Turning off Read-After-Write Verification is not recommended for most installations because it increases the possibility of data corruption.

However, if your server does Read-After-Write Verification at the hardware level, then you can turn off NetWare's to gain some speed.

Determining the most efficient setting for the `Dirty Disk Cache Delay Time` is not quite as easy as determining what needed to be done with the `Maximum Dirty Cache` parameter. It is not as easy because the most efficient setting will be determined by the type of network traffic you have. The only tip that can honestly be given is that if your network traffic consists of lots of small writes, increasing the delay time will increase efficiency.

SETTING THE NUMBER OF PACKET RECEIVE BUFFERS

One of the most vital dynamically configurable parameters in NetWare is the number of packet receive buffers (PRBs) setting. Packets that are passed from another network, or workstation, to the server are placed in a buffer that is appropriately named a *packet receive buffer*. The packet is held until it can be processed, which creates a steady flow of work for the server.

If the packet buffer area is full, the server will wait for .01 seconds (`New Packet Receive Buffer Wait Time`) before allocating more resources to the packet buffer receive area. If the number of packet receive buffers have reached the maximum value, the server's LAN channel runs the risk of being overloaded and packets will be lost (data will not be lost because the station will simply resend the packet). This causes the network to become very sluggish, especially if the server is routing between two network segments (one slow and one fast). In extreme cases, client station response times can be impacted to the point of being unusable.

Note

Each buffer is identical in size to the `Maximum Physical Packet Receive Size` set for the operating system. The physical size of the packet is determined by the network media. Under NetWare, for example, Ethernet has a physical packet size of 1514 bytes, whereas token ring's maximum physical packet size is 4202.

Fine-tuning the number of packet receive buffers setting should only be attempted after verifying that, in fact, it needs adjustment. There are three situations that would require you to adjust the default settings: First, if you are in a multiple LAN environment (included are installations where multiple LANs reside in the same server); second, if the number of packet receive buffers are constantly reaching the maximum number; and third, if you have over 100 workstations actively using a server.

In a multiple server environment, packets are constantly being passed from one network to another, but this alone does not justify increasing the number of packet receive buffers' default setting; only increase the setting if the server is constantly reaching its maximum value. To determine if the server is reaching the maximum setting, simply look at the packet receive buffer indication on the MONITOR.NLM screen (see Figure 38.4).

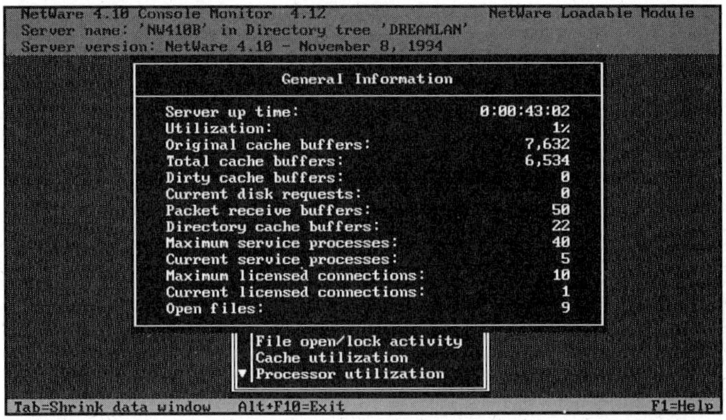

Figure 38.4.
Note the number of
packet receive buffers
used.

```
NetWare 4.10 Console Monitor  4.12                NetWare Loadable Module
Server name: 'NW410B' in Directory tree 'DREAMLAN'
Server version: NetWare 4.10 - November 8, 1994

                    ┌────────── General Information ──────────┐
                    │  Server up time:            0:00:43:02   │
                    │  Utilization:                       1%   │
                    │  Original cache buffers:         7,632   │
                    │  Total cache buffers:            6,534   │
                    │  Dirty cache buffers:                0   │
                    │  Current disk requests:              0   │
                    │  Packet receive buffers:            50   │
                    │  Directory cache buffers:           22   │
                    │  Maximum service processes:         40   │
                    │  Current service processes:          5   │
                    │  Maximum licensed connections:      10   │
                    │  Current licensed connections:       1   │
                    │  Open files:                         9   │
                    └──────────────────────────────────────────┘
                    ┌──────────────────────────────┐
                    │  File open/lock activity      │
                    │  Cache utilization            │
                    │ ▼ Processor utilization       │
                    └──────────────────────────────┘
Tab=Shrink data window    Alt+F10=Exit                            F1=Help
```

Tip

Peak periods in usage can cause the packet receive buffers to inflate, so don't jump to conclusions the first time you see the buffers coming close to reaching the maximum limit. Change is only required if the limit is continuously being reached.

The default value of 100 usually proves to be sufficient; however, in large installations it can be on the minimal side. In larger installations you should increase the packet receive buffers to include at least one buffer per workstation. Some EISA cards recommend you to increase the number of buffers. Check the documentation.

38

TUNING FOR PERFORMANCE

It is also wise to include 10 to 20 extra buffers for each bus-mastering or EISA card in the server. If you are getting the error No ECB available count, continue to increase the packet receive buffers by 10, until the errors stop. Also you can watch the LAN Driver Statistics from the MONITOR.NLM screen to determine whether the LAN board is causing the errors (see Figure 38.5).

Figure 38.5.

No ECB available counter in LAN Driver Statistics.

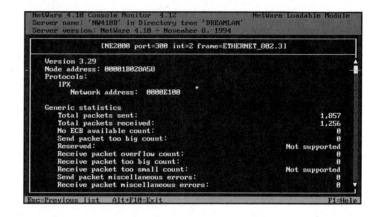

If the server continually reaches the maximum limit, it could point to a more serious problem. There are several situation where the number of packet receive buffers can climb to the maximum limit and actually hang the server, as in the following:

◆ Interrupt conflicts

◆ Faulty or poor network card drivers

◆ Bad cabling, and so on

In these situations, increasing the maximum value of the number of packet receive buffers will usually just prolong the time between server "lock up."

Watching the number of packet receive buffer limits becomes more of an issue if you are using NetWare 4.*x*'s DOS requester with packet burst loaded. A station employing packet burst (a definition of packet burst can be found later in this chapter) can use several of the available packet receive buffers because it allows stations to stream packets and send as much as 64K of packetized information in one stream. So if you have several stations using packet burst, carefully watch the packet receive buffer values.

Note

If you are upgrading from 3.1*x*, you will probably not need as many packet receive buffers. NetWare 4.*x* has increased the priority level of routing requests.

The default packet receive buffer settings are as follows:

◆ Maximum Packet Receive Buffers = 100

◆ Minimum Packet Receive Buffers = 10

◆ Maximum Physical Receive Packet Size = 4202 bytes

◆ New Packet Receive Buffer Wait Time = .01 second

It is possible to get larger packets—up to 24K—with token ring; however, at this time most NetWare token ring drivers will only support packet sizes up to 4202 bytes.

To change the number of packet receive buffer settings on NetWare 4.1:

1. Load SERVMAN.NLM at the system console.
2. Select Server parameters.
3. Select Communications.
4. Select Maximum Packet Receive Buffers (see Figure 38.6).
5. Change the value.
6. Press the Esc key twice.
7. Select Update AUTOEXEC.NCF and STARTUP.NCF

The changes will then take place after downing and restarting the server.

Figure 38.6.
Changing the maxi-
mum number of packet
receive buffers using
SERVMAN.NLM.

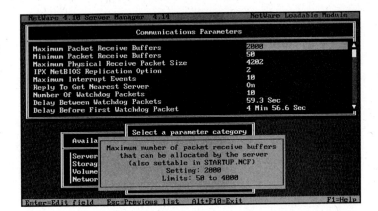

38

TUNING FOR PERFORMANCE

NUMBER OF MINIMUM PACKET RECEIVE BUFFERS

It is very uncommon to have to change any of the minimum settings of any of NetWare's dynamically configurable settings. This is because if more resources are needed they are dynamically increased. However, the number of minimum packet receive buffers is one setting that you may want to change. For example, if you have an EISA server or a server that does a lot of routing, when the server first comes up it may start spitting out the error No ECB available count. After NetWare's dynamic configuration process has had time to work, the error will generally go away. But you can increase the number of minimum packet receive buffers setting, which will allow the server to automatically increase the packet receive count to the minimum setting.

Note

Most of the dynamic parameters have a minimum setting, such as number of minimum packet receive buffers, the minimum settings are not actually a minimum, but rather, the amount that the server can automatically create without being subject to the wait times and other dynamic configuration restrictions.

FILE LOCKS

Each workstation on the network is given equal opportunity to the network resources (disregarding security). For example, there are no limitations to the amount of files that one station can have locked. However, you can use the number of File Locks parameter to restrict workstations from "hogging" the file cache area. Simply use SERVMAN.NLM to restrict the maximum amount of files that any one workstation can lock (see Figure 38.7).

To change NetWare 4.1's record locking capabilities to a minimal setting, follow these steps:

1. Load SERVMAN.NLM at the console.
2. Select Server parameters.
3. Choose Locks.
4. Change the Maximum Record Locks Per Connection=x (where x is a number 10–10000).
5. Change the File Locks Per Connection=x (where x is a number 10–1000).

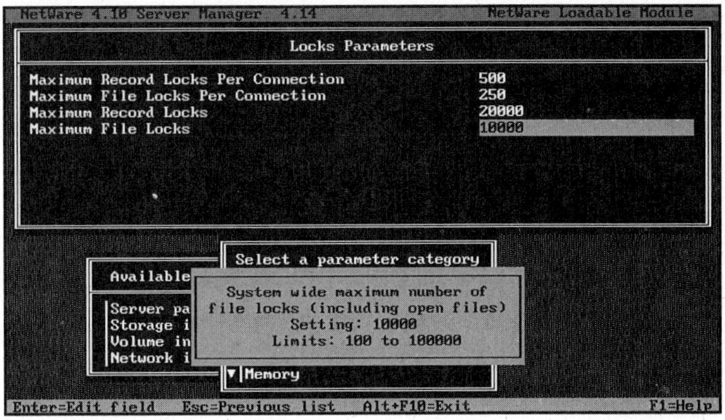

Figure 38.7.
Using
SERVMAN.NLM to
change the number of
`File Locks`.

6. Change `Maximum Record Locks` to *x* (where *x* is a number 100–200000).

7. Change `Maximum File Locks` to *x* (where *x* is a number 100–100000.)

However, by changing these parameters to a minimal amount, you may have an application fail, because it absolutely has to have *x* amount of file locks. If this is the case, use this *x* number as your minimum setting.

PRIORITIZING SERVER PROCESSES

Another important dynamically configured parameter is the execution priority of each server process. Each server contains a processor, and this processor only has a given amount of cycles. The use of these cycles are evenly divided among the load operations, unless you intervene. Intervention can help improve performance, especially if you have an application that is "cycle hungry" but used very little. For example, you may have a database that is used very little; however, it could be consuming a large percentage of your server's CPU cycles. To limit the priority of this database, or any other NLM, you can simply use the *Schedule Delay Command* in the AUTOEXEC.NCF file.

By default, each process is scheduled a delay of zero (no wait). This means that every NLM loaded is given the same amount of time, regardless of its use. To view processor statistics, follow these steps:

1. At the console, load MONITOR.NLM.

2. Select Scheduling Information.

A screen with the four columns will appear: Sch delay, Time, Count, and Load; with each column respectfully representing the value assigned to the process; the amount of CPU time spent running the application; the number of times the process ran during the sampling period; and the percent of total CPU time spent on the process (see Figure 38.8). This simple procedure enables you to pinpoint the processes that are hoarding CPU time and lets you delay the execution of a specific process; meaning that other process are given more time. To change or prioritize CPU usage, follow these steps:

1. The first process name is highlighted by default. To select a different process, use the arrow keys to scroll through the list of processes until you find the one you want.

2. You can lower or raise the scheduled delay parameter by using the plus and minus keys. For example, use the arrow key to locate and highlight MONI-TOR main, and then use the plus or minus keys to change the Sch Delay setting.

To save these settings, put the following command in the AUTOEXEC.NCF file, *after* you load MONITOR:

```
LOAD MONITOR
LOAD SCHDELAY MONITOR MAIN = 5
```

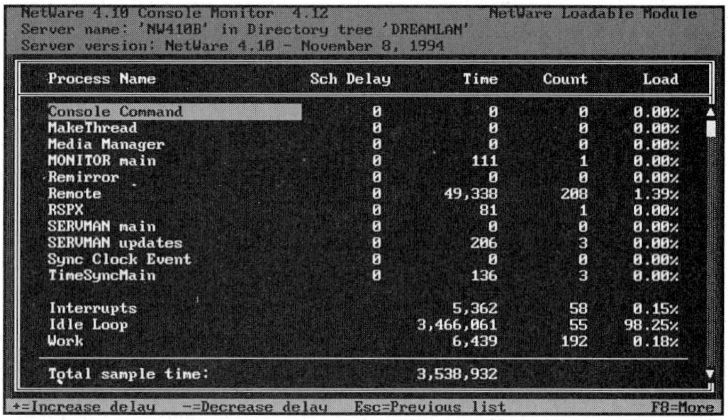

Figure 38.8.
NLM scheduling
information as
displayed by
MONITOR.NLM.

MEMORY FOR NLMS

In previous versions of NetWare, specifically NetWare 3.*x*, memory was allocated into five different memory pools, with each pool serving a different purpose. Once an application was finished using the memory (unloaded) the memory often remained unused (wasn't returned to the "available" memory pool). This lead to memory fragmentation and even meant it was possible for an application to run out of memory. NetWare 4.*x*, on the other hand, only has one memory allocation pool; when an application is finished using a section of memory, that memory is instantly returned to the available memory pool. This allows the server to operate more efficiently (the server has to perform fewer memory management operations, memory isn't fragmented, and the same segment of memory can be reused).

Note

NLMs do not use as much memory when idle, as they do when performing tasks. However, if loaded, all NLMs use some memory. Simply put, unloading unnecessary NLMs provides more memory, thereby directly increasing performance (more memory to cache files, directories, and so on).

DETERMINING BLOCK SIZE

NetWare 4.*x* has the unique capability to suballocate blocks. For an in-depth explanation of suballocation see Chapter 3. Selecting the largest possible block size will allow NetWare's Read-Ahead-Cache to read 64K instead of 4K into cache. This could be the greatest performance enhancement in 4.*x*, so be sure and take advantage of it.

Tip

If you are upgrading a server, the server's block size cannot be changed. If you have a small block size, such as 4K, you will definitely want to make sure that Read Ahead Enabled parameter is left ON (ON is default), otherwise performance will be drastically impacted.

In order to change the block size, you need to re-create the volume.

LARGE INTERNET PACKET (LIP)

Increasing the size of the packet that the server can receive is just one more way to increase the performance of your NetWare 4.*x* network. It logically makes sense, if the packet sizes are larger, more information can be sent at one time, thereby increasing performance. However, this will only help in certain situations—the most common being a network that contain routers (internal or external).

This is true because routers have no way to determine the packet size capabilities of the servers on the other side of the segment. So, in the past, these devices were forced to use the "least common denominator" 576 bytes (512 bytes of data, 30 bytes in the IPX header, and 34 bytes for the NCP/SPX header). By choosing a small packet size, the router is assured that the servers on the other side will be able to "handle" the packet.

With NetWare 4.*x* you can set the server's packet size capabilities. Because of this, when a connection is made, the packet size negotiation routine will know what packet sizes are acceptable. If the server detects a router during the packet size negotiation, the server will no longer simply default to the "lowest common denominator" of 576 bytes. Instead, when the VLM workstation driver negotiates with the server, it also tests to see the packet size that the router can handle.

Warning

Before changing this parameter, be sure that all of the cards on your network are capable of sending packets larger than 512 bytes (some older ARCnet cards cannot).

By default, LIP is enabled in NetWare 4.x. But to change the Maximum Physical Receive Packet Size, follow these instructions:

1. Load SERVMAN at the console.
2. Select Server parameters.
3. Select Communications.
4. Select Maximum Physical Receive Packet Size.
5. Change the value (see Figure 38.9).
6. Press the Esc key twice.
7. Select Update AUTOEXEC.NCF AND STARTUP .NCF

The changes will then take place after downing and restarting the server.

Figure 38.9.
Using SERVMAN to change Maximum Physical Receive Packet Size.

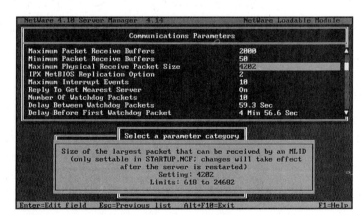

ASSESSING SERVER RAM

The most common cause for a slow network is not enough RAM. There are two ways to determine RAM requirements. The simplest way is to load MONITOR.NLM at the console, and select Cache Utilization from Available Options Menu. If the long term cache hits are less than 90 percent (over a long period of time), the server needs more RAM.

UNDERSTANDING AND TUNING PACKET BURST

The VLM drivers that ship with NetWare 4.*x* use a technology known as a *packet burst*. Packet burst takes advantage of a wire's idle time by allowing clients to submit multiple read and write requests for data blocks of up to 64K. Each block of data is considered a "packet burst" and several packet burst combined create a multi-packet burst. The client and server are continually negotiating the amount of data that should be sent. This helps optimize data delivery.

Note

This burst mode NetWare Core Protocol (NCP) technology was created to increase data transfer rates for wide area network (WAN) links. WAN links using Packet Burst experienced speed increases of up to 400 percent! These tremendous speed increases on the WAN made NetWare LAN users wonder if this technology would also increase speeds on local area networks. Now packet bursting technology is implemented with the VLM client requester.

Traditionally, IPX/NCP "ping-pongs," while burst mode packets don't have to wait for a response packet. Responses are simply "queued" until the complete burst has been received. After the burst has been received, a single response packet acknowledges the transfer (see Figure 38.10). If errors occur during a transfer, the complete burst does not have to be retransmitted. Instead of sending a transfer complete response to the client, the server sends a lost fragment list. This list informs the client of the portions of the burst that didn't make it. Thus, it is only necessary for the client to resend the fragments identified by the lost fragment response.

Figure 38.10.
Packet Burst protocol allows a group of packets to be sent for a single request packet.

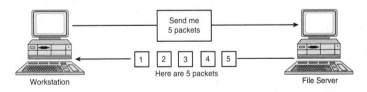

A burst mode connection is only established if both the server and the workstation support burst mode. This doesn't imply that if you won't have a connection to your file server if packet burst is loaded on one side and not the other. It simply means that packet burst technology will be ignored and that the standard request/response transfer mechanism will be used. Also, not every workstation has to be using burst mode. This interoperability lets you decide which workstations (or file servers) need Packet Burst.

Tip

To disable burst mode, set the pb buffer=0 in the NET.CFG file of the workstation. It cannot be disabled from the file server side.

Warning

A slow machine or NIC cannot transfer information fast enough to keep up with packet burst, regardless of the pb buffer setting. An example of this might be if you are using an XT workstation. In this situation, increasing your pb buffer setting will only allow the file server to completely overload the slow workstation (and possibly "traffic jamming" the entire network.) The workstation will simply digest as much of the burst as it can; obviously loosing a majority of the multi-burst packet, and then it will have to send a lost fragment list to the server. The process will start all over again, with the server bombarding the slow station.

VLM automatically and dynamically adjusts the amount of packet burst buffers "on-the-fly." No manual tuning is necessary.

Tip

If your network currently has a high speed link, multiple hops (WAN or LAN), and you transfer large files, this product could certainly help the speed of your network be more of what you want.

Increasing speeds through packet burst is simple; however, to truly optimize packet burst the speed of file servers, workstations, network cards, and the amount of network traffic need to be taken into consideration, not to mention the wire type, topology, the number of users, and so on.

UNDERSTANDING PROTOCOLS

In order to get a good handle on what goes on, you need to look at the communication process at the protocol level. Protocols are basically a set of rules that allow two or more machines communicate. This communication is a sophisticated way of packaging information and then sending that information across the network wire. There are three major elements in protocols: syntax, semantics, and timing. The syntax defines the protocol form or fields, the semantics provide meaning, and the timing works at all levels to insure a correct transfer.

Protocols are not a flat structure; they consist of different layers, giving meaning to the term `protocol stack`. When a communication channel is opened between a sending and receiving machine, the sending machine starts at the top of the stack and works down. When the receiving machine gets the packet it reads the stack in reverse order; starting at the bottom and working up (see Figure 38.11).

Figure 38.11.
Communication path of
the protocol stack.

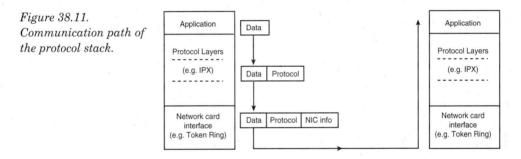

Protocols, and the way their layers operate, allow a connection to be established; information passing is possible because they make the information meaningful to the receiving station. Protocol stacks are usually divided into three sections: the lower, the middle, and the upper. Understanding the different levels of a protocol stack will assist you in your troubleshooting network and performance tuning efforts.

The lower levels of the protocol stack, or *media protocols,* deal directly with the card and media. In essence, they are responsible for getting the information through the network card and onto the wire. The two most popular types of media level protocols are CSMA/CD (used in Ethernet) and token passing (used in Token Ring and ARCnet).

The middle layers of the protocol, or *transport protocols*, are used to establish a *session*. A session consists of opening a communication channel. It is this level that specifies how information (data) should be broken into smaller segments (packets) for transmission. It also specifies how data is encapsulated (or stored) and where it will be placed within the packet structure.

The upper layers, or *service protocols*, specify how programs deal with data and how client stations request specific network services (such as printing).

Each protocol has the capability to utilize different frame types and each frame type is a variation of a specific media type that specifies a slightly different method of encapsulating data to be transported across the media. Popular Ethernet frame types are 802.3 (Raw), Ethernet_II, 802.3 with 802.2, and Ethernet_SNAP.

Note

It is important that you understand the difference between protocols and frame types. A frame type is not a protocol. It defines the various fields of the protocol, much like a template or record structure of a database.

Once a protocol is associated with a specific frame type for passage across a particular network board, the protocol must be bound to the NIC (at the file server). Binding the NIC with a protocol ensures that the card will be able to send and receive packets of that protocol and frame type.

Internet Packet eXchange (IPX) and Sequenced Packet eXchange (SPX) are two NetWare protocols that offer distinct and separate network communications. IPX, the most common, is a *connectionless* protocol. This means IPX stations don't have to undergo a handshaking process to establish a connection with another station; it takes a "best attempt" approach to deliver a packet. In other words, it merely assumes that packet delivery is going to happen; there is no guarantee.

SPX on the other hand, *guarantees* that a packet will be delivered. The SPX stations negotiate or establish a connection, which ensures that both parties are ready and available for packet delivery. The sending station will then sequence the packets and send them, in order, to the receiving station.

SPX is very useful for applications that require the packets to be in order. The most familiar example is RCONSOLE.EXE. In this environment it is necessary for the packets (think of keystrokes) to be in order, and guaranteed. The drawback of guaranteed delivery (SPX) is the acknowledgment overhead and its small packet size (512 bytes of data).

UNDERSTANDING FRAME TYPES

In defining frame types, we will use IPX as an example. Understanding the IPX protocol's frame types will provide you with an idea of how protocols work and how effective a protocol analyzer can be as a network performance tool. The following section introduces some popular Ethernet frame types and defines the fields found within these frame types.

IPX doesn't distinguish between different types of networking hardware, it merely relies on the LAN driver to transport the packet to the LAN hardware. Thus the *frame type* is responsible for the transfer.

A frame type is a standard that designates the protocol structure, or in other words, the construction of the *Ethernet packet and header* (a header is the first 22 bytes of the packet). The frame type designates where the data is encapsulated within the packet structure, where the source and destination addresses are located, and so on. A frame type is not a protocol, but is rather a designation of the media variation on which the protocol will travel (Ethernet, for example).

Tip

> Putting it simply, frame type is analogous to record structure in a database. It defines how the data is to be separated into fields.

The IPX protocol supports several frame types. The following is discussed in this section:

- ◆ Ethernet_802.3 (better known as 802.3 Raw)
- ◆ Ethernet_802.2 (also known as IEEE 802.3 or 802.3 with 802.2)
- ◆ Ethernet_SNAP
- ◆ Ethernet_II

802.3

The most common Ethernet frame type in the NetWare environment is Ethernet 802.3 (Raw). It is the most common frame type because it is the default frame type for Ethernet LAN drivers shipped with NetWare 3.11 (and below) and 2.*x* operating systems.

Novell has changed the default frame for Ethernet to 802.2. starting mid-1993. This means that if you have a mix of servers you will have to either load the 802.3 (Raw) frame type on your 4.*x* server or load the 802.2 frame type on the other servers. This will allow the entire mix of servers to "talk."

To add the 802.3 (Raw) frame type on your 4.1 server, follow these steps:

1. Load INSTALL at the console.
2. Select NCF Files Options.
3. Edit the AUTOEXEC.NCF file.
4. Locate the line that loads your Ethernet driver. Add a new line similar to it but change FRAME= to FRAME=Ethernet_802.3 (see Figure 38.12).

5. Bind IPX to the new frame type.

6. Press the Escape key to save the changes. The new lines will be activated the next time you reboot your file server.

Figure 38.12.
Multiple frame types on
the same physical NIC.

```
NetWare Server Installation  4.1                    NetWare Loadable Module

┌──────────────────────────────────────────────────────────────────────────┐
│                            File: AUTOEXEC.NCF                              │
│                                                                            │
│ search add sys:system\nwda                                               ▲ │
│ search add sys:system\commexec                                            │
│ set maximum packet receive buffers=2000                                   │
│                                                                            │
│ load c:NE2000.LAN port=300 int=2 frame=ethernet_802.3 name=IPX-NIC        │
│ bind IPX to IPX-NIC net=E100                                              │
│                                                                            │
│ load c:NE2000.LAN port=300 int=2 frame=ethernet_802.3 name=IP-NIC         │
│ bind IP to IP-NIC addr=1.1.1.1                                            │
│                                                                            │
│ mount all                                                                  │
│                                                                            │
│ ##load AIOCOMX PORT=3F8 INT=4                                            ▼ │
└──────────────────────────────────────────────────────────────────────────┘
Save file              <F10>              Previous screen      <Esc>
Mark and unmark text   <F5>               Delete marked text   <Del>
Save marked text       <F6>               Insert marked text   <Ins>
Help                   <F1>               Abort INSTALL  <Alt><F10>
```

Note

NetWare 2.*x* only supports a single frame type at a time. Under Ethernet, only Ethernet_802.3 or Ethernet_II is supported.

An Ethernet_802.3 (Raw) packet doesn't contain a field to specify what higher-level transport protocols that might be in the packet, and is therefore almost exclusively used on Novell's IPX/SPX networks (see Figure 38.13).

Figure 38.13.
An Ethernet_802.3
(Raw) frame.

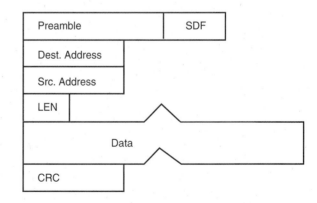

The first line of the header in an 802.3 (Raw) packet consists of the *preamble*, which is nothing more than an 7-byte field containing alternating ones and zeros. The preamble's duty is to synchronize the talking stations. Following the preamble and on the same line is a *Start Frame Delimiter* (SFD), which is a 1-byte field that also contains alternating ones and zeros, but unlike the preamble, the SFD ends with consecutive ones; the ones connote the beginning of the frame.

The second line of the header is the *packets destination address*. The destination address is a 6-byte field that houses the hardware address of the station where the packet hopes to end up. If the packet is a broadcast packet (going to every station on the network) it will contain the address of FF-FF-FF-FF-FF-FF.

The third line of the header contains the source address. The *source address*, as its name implies, contains the hardware address of the origination of the packet. However, it may not always be the actual origination of the packet; this field can contain the address of a workstation, the server, or a router. (If a packet crosses the router, the source address changes to signify the address of that router.)

The fourth line of the header is the *length field*. It indicates the length of the data portion of the frame. It is a 2-byte field and will have a decimal value of 46–1500 bytes or less. If this value is larger that 1500 bytes, the packet is too long and thus invalid (often called a *jabber* or *long* packet).

The *data field*, or fifth line of the packet, is where the header ends and the data begins. This is the actual data that is destined to another station on the network. For the packet to be valid, the data field must be at least 46 bytes long, but no more than 1500 bytes. If the data field is too short, a *padding* will be attached to the end of the data. The padding is nothing more than its name implies; something (bytes) stuck on the end of the data so that the packet meets the minimum length requirements.

The final field is the *Frame Check Sequence* (FCS) and is 4 bytes in length. The transmitting station performs a *Cyclic Redundancy Check* (CRC) check on the packet before it lets it go. When the packet arrives at the receiving station, the receiving station likewise does a CRC check. If the check value matches the value in the CRC field, then the packet is assumed to be valid.

802.2

As mentioned earlier, the 802.2 frame type is the default Ethernet frame type in NetWare 4.*x*. It contains all the fields as discussed in the 802.3 (Raw) specification, as well a few of its own (see Figure 38.14).

It additionally contains a group of fields categorized as the *Logical Link Control* (LLC) fields. The LLC area consist of three one-byte fields: The *Destination Service Access Point* (DSAP), which denotes the protocol type of the destinations network layer. The *Source Service Access Point* (SSAP), which indicates the upper or network layer of the source packet's protocol type. And the *Control Field*, which indicates the connection services that are in use.

Figure 38.14.
An Ethernet_802.2
frame.

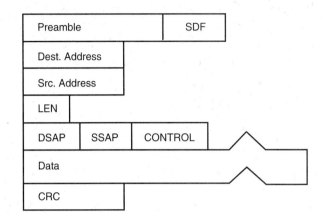

ETHERNET_SNAP

Ethernet_SNAP is a variation of the 802.2 specification. In fact, the first three fields of the Ethernet_SNAP (Sub-Network Access Protocol) frames are exactly the same as the fields found in an 802.2 packet (see Figure 38.15).

Figure 38.15.
An Ethernet_SNAP.

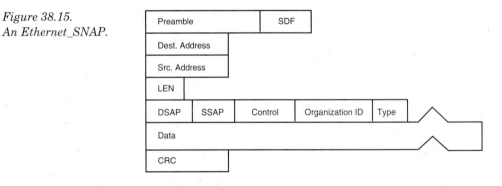

The Ethernet_SNAP protocol will contain the different values in the LLC area. The DSAP and SSAP fields will contain the value AA. The value AA indicates that the packet is of a SNAP format. Following it is the *organizational id* field. It is three bytes in size and identifies the vendor of the protocol. The next field, the type field, designates the upper layer protocol that is using the frame. For example, Novell's NetWare IPX/SPX has been assigned the value 8137 and 8138, AppleTalk 809B, IP 0800, and so on. If these protocols are encapsulated within a SNAP frame, the type field will contain the appropriate, assigned value. Encapsulating the high-level protocols within the IPX frame structure insures compatibility and allows network operating systems such as NetWare, to transport other protocols (AppleTalk Phase II, for example) over Ethernet or token ring (using token ring_SNAP frame type) media.

ETHERNET_II

Unlike all of the previously discussed frame types, Ethernet_II frame types contain a type field, rather than a length field, directly after the source address (see Figure 38.16). Ethernet_II's type field designates (even though it isn't in the same location) the upper layer protocol that is using the frame, or in other words, which type of packet is being transported within the Ethernet_II packet. The only other structural difference worth mentioning is that the preamble and SFD are combined and referred to as the Preamble.

Figure 38.16.
An Ethernet_II frame.

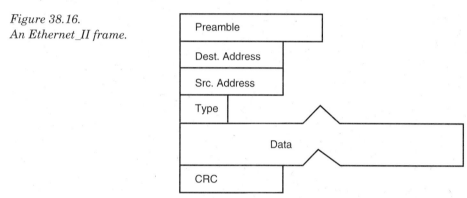

Completely understanding the differences of each protocol and all the possible frames types, is beyond the scope of this chapter; however, it is a good start. With this chapter as a reference, you will be able to at least recognize some of the packets on your network. Recognizing the packets is the first step to understanding what is actually happening on your network wire, which will help you find and alleviate network bottlenecks (which is the ultimate goal of tuning network performance).

FINDING THE BOTTLENECKS

Network errors are a miscommunication, which can cause a network to bottleneck. Errors can be caused by any one, or combination of, the following: a faulty network card, incompatible software, wiring problems, conflicting addresses, incorrectly configured drivers, transceiver jams, repeater failure, and so on. In a complex network environment, problems escalate in real-time; for example, if a network card begins clogging the line with a broadcast storm (sending out multiple long packets), collisions will reproduce like rabbits and the network will get sluggish. Uncovering such network anomalies is intimidating but vital.

TRAFFIC MONITORING

Protocol analyzers are used for monitoring traffic, a vital part of managing any network. Such monitoring allows you to determine which stations are causing the most traffic, and it aids in determining when networks are overloaded and need segmenting. Continued awareness of network traffic also provides important data on network growth, determines what percentage of time the network operates efficiently, and shows what errors are occurring and why.

However, the usefulness of a monitoring tool (analyzer) often depends on users' troubleshooting skills and their knowledge of the instrument. But, protocol analyzers can facilitate and improve any human's abilities. If, for example, while monitoring traffic, a protocol analyzer sounds an alarm declaring that a particular workstation has multiple send errors, the troubleshooter gains specific direction (it beats shutting the machines off one-by-one until the network returns to normal status). To be an effective troubleshooting tool, a product must be able to monitor traffic.

Another important reason for monitoring traffic is to obtain baseline (normal network usage) information. If baseline information is gathered and stored, you can use it to compare network usage at later times, perhaps after adding a server, workstation, or application. Being aware of what happens to the baseline after such additions is vital to understanding network performance.

TREND ANALYZERS

Each network, even if similar in configuration, will behave differently. If you have a protocol analyzer, it is simple to discover the personality of any network; this discovery will prove to be the single most important set of statistics you gather with your analyzer.

Tip

Following are several trend statistics that a good protocol analyzer can gather:

- ◆ What type of traffic is normal?
- ◆ What are my peak utilization times?
- ◆ Which stations generally impose the heaviest loads?
- ◆ Which stations normally have errors?
- ◆ Are there times we have abnormal errors?
- ◆ What percentage of total packets sent are collisions?
- ◆ Which segment hauls the heaviest load?

A baseline will be very useful performance tuning information. However, without a protocol analyzer this information is rarely, if ever, gathered. So if you have a protocol analyzer or if you plan to get one, gather the baseline information even if you are not sure what it means. This baseline will provide specialists with important direction.

A detailed discussion of baselining and review of a number of protocol analyzers, such as LANalyzer for Windows, can be found in *NetWare Unleashed* by Sams Publishing.

Summary

Fine-tuning a NetWare 4.*x* network consists of several functions:

- ◆ Understanding the dynamic configuration parameters
- ◆ Assessing server RAM
- ◆ Utilizing packet burst
- ◆ Understanding LIP

In order to keep a network error-free, you have to understand protocol, frame types, and the different types of errors.

This chapter has covered a wide variety of performance issues and has provided guidance for eliminating network errors. But the best performance advice that can be given is this: learn the particular personality of your network and then watch for any changes. If you understand your network, you will also be able to tell if minor changes (adjusting minimum and maximum parameters) actually helped or hurt performance.

38

- Change Management

- Developing a Trouble-
  shooting Methodology

- Preproduction Testing

- What Are Server
  Abends?

- The NetWare
  Debugger

- LAN Problems

- Disk Problems

- NDS Problems

- Technical Support
  Sources

- Summary

CHAPTER 39

Troubleshooting NetWare 4.*x*

Troubleshooting a distributed network system is a highly complex art form, and not a science. Unlike traditional host computer systems, which can be managed carefully, a network is a dynamic system consisting of hundreds or thousands of interrelated components. While troubleshooting is an art, it is an art that is based upon science, which we will explain shortly.

You cannot control modifications or replacements of existing network components, nor can you control the introduction of new components to the network. A user in some department can always add a new workstation to the net, add a new LAN card to an existing workstation, or even bring up an experimental server. Any user can run a new application on the network. You may even have rogue departments bringing up production servers without your sanction. You may even have unsanctioned NDS trees in your organization, distinct from your organization's NDS tree, and consisting of multiple servers.

The lack of control you have over modifications to your network is a hallmark of LAN technology, and is one of the reasons LANs are so popular with workgroups and departments. What complicates matters with NetWare 4.x is the insertion of NetWare Directory Services (NDS) into the mix. NDS demands that you have control over how servers are introduced into the network. If not, NDS will not function correctly, and you will be asking the question, "What's broken?"

Troubleshooting a network system is a complex art that is based upon the science of change management. If you can manage change on your network, you will be able to resolve problems in fairly short order. Managing change is different than controlling change. History proves that controlling changes to your NetWare 4.x system is impossible. Managing changes, however, is very possible but demanding. Troubleshooting begins with managing changes.

CHANGE MANAGEMENT

Change management is the science of documenting change and analyzing the effects of change. Change events provide a collection of data. Using the data of change events, you can develop a hypothesis regarding which change event(s) are the cause of a network breakdown. To test your hypothesis, you reverse the change event suspected as the cause of the network breakdown.

Suppose that you upgrade the Ethernet driver for a NetWare server. Later, that server begins dropping workstation connections and responding slowly to network requests, but only after it has been running for a day or so. Moreover, you see a message on the server console that the server is out or receive buffers. What happened? What do you do?

First, you answer the question, "What has changed?" Well, you installed a new Ethernet driver. The new Ethernet driver, therefore, is your best candidate for the source of the problem. You call the supplier of the Ethernet driver to report the symptoms of the problem: dropped workstation connections and loss of server receive buffers, but only after a day or so of operation. The supplier confirms a bug in the driver you received: the driver did not return receive buffers to the operating system when the Ethernet card was finished using the buffers; the server ran out of buffers and could not receive network request packets; hence, the server timed-out workstation connections.

The supplier sends you a new version of their Ethernet driver with the bug fixed. The server and the new Ethernet driver work perfectly for more than a day, which was the period you identified as necessary to prove a resolution of the problem.

In this example, you were able to solve the problem relatively quickly by identifying the source of the network breakdown. Note that you didn't diagnose the cause of the problem—only the source. You didn't, for example, identify the bug in the Ethernet driver. But you did nail the Ethernet driver as being the source of the problem. And you nailed the Ethernet driver because it was the most recent component on the server which had changed.

You never need to diagnose fully the cause of a network problem, but you always need to identify the source of the problem. You prove your diagnosis by replacing the changed component and seeing if that fixes the problem. You don't have enough time nor resources available to you to identify the root cause of every problem. But if you fix every problem, that's good enough. Change management will allow you to fix most, but no all, of your problems very quickly.

The preceding Ethernet driver example is a great troubleshooting story that actually happened in real life. Network problems usually have an element of mystery about them that you never fully understand, such as why the server would run for around a day before dropping connections. The exact amount of time the server would run before dropping connections varied by as much as an hour, which drove the Information Services (IS) technicians crazy. There seemed to be a random element involved, which is out of character for traditional computer systems.

The answer to the random element is arcane: the driver's interrupt service routine would, under certain conditions, become re-entrant (service multiple interrupts concurrently). Each time the driver's interrupt routine became re-entrant, it would fail to return one or more receive buffers to the server. Over a period of time—generally around 22 hours—the server would run out of receive buffers. The condition that caused the Ethernet driver to become re-entrant was a burst of Ethernet packets addressed to the same IPX socket number. The timing of packets over a network is always random; hence, the random character of the fault.

The lesson from this is that you don't need to fully understand the ultimate cause of network problems—only their source. Also, you shouldn't be miffed by problems that occur randomly. Networks are random systems.

IDENTIFYING CHANGE EVENTS

The most important aspect of change management is tracking, logging, and identifying change events. A change event occurs when some component on the network changes: a new workstation or server, a new LAN card, a new driver, a new application, a new user, and so on.

For a large NetWare 4.x network, logging changes is impossible to perform manually. You need software tools. NetWare provides you with the following tools:

◆ The server System Log

◆ The Auditing System

◆ The event registration application programming interface (API)

NetWare maintains a system log in every server's SYS:SYSTEM directory. This log file, SYS$LOG.ERR, contains text for every console error (including certain informational) message displayed on the NetWare server (see Figure 39.1). You can read this log using a text editor of the administration utilities shipped with NetWare 4.x. NetWare allows you to clear the system log, which deletes the actual log file and creates a new empty log file.

Figure 39.1.
Sample listing of
SYS$LOG.ERR file.

```
Established communication with server DREAMLAN.Toronto.North_America

6-30-95  11:29:08 pm:     DS-4.63-47
    Severity = 1  Locus = 17  Class = 19
    Unable to communicate with server DREAMLAN.Toronto.North_America

6-30-95  11:29:08 pm:     DS-4.63-50
    Severity = 1  Locus = 17  Class = 19
    Established communication with server DREAMLAN.Toronto.North_America

6-30-95  11:29:27 pm:     SERVER-4.10-2541
    Severity = 0  Locus = 18  Class = 19
    System time changed from file server console.
New time is  6-30-1995  11:29:15 pm

6-30-95  11:29:24 pm:     TIMESYNC-4.13-138
    Severity = 0  Locus = 17  Class = 19
    Time synchronization has been established.

6-30-95  11:37:57 pm:     DS-4.63-50
    Severity = 1  Locus = 17  Class = 19
    Established communication with server DREAMLAN.Toronto.North_America
```

Tip

It is recommended that you rename and archive the old log file rather than use NetWare's utilities to delete a large system log file.

The NetWare system log file contains important change events, such as mounting and dismounting of volumes, routing errors, and more.

The NetWare 4.*x* auditing system can record all NDS-related operations, including the creation of new NDS objects, modification of NDS objects, and deletion of NDS objects. This information can tell when new users and servers are added to the system NDS tree, which is an important indication of change.

The NetWare event registration API allows NLMs to receive notification of important system events, ranging from file system operations to loading and unloading of device drivers. If your organization has an inhouse programming staff, it may be a good idea to have them create some monitoring programs that log changes to the system. You can then use these logs for your troubleshooting efforts.

NETWORK INVENTORY PACKAGES

Chapter 30 discusses Network Inventory software products in some detail. These software products log changes to workstation configuration, including software installed on workstations, hardware installed on workstations, workstation memory, and more. Network inventory software is a critical component of a good change management system. You should purchase and use one of these packages to assist your troubleshooting efforts.

DEVELOPING A TROUBLESHOOTING METHODOLOGY

Change management will provide answers to most of your troubleshooting problems. That's because the vast majority of network faults result from changes to the existing configuration. Some network faults, however, occur because hardware components break. (Software components never break—they are either "broken" or in working order.) When a hardware component breaks down, it is possible that no changes occurred on your network. In this case, you cannot rely on change management to identify the source of the network problem. You have to rely on other indicators of the problem, such as server console messages, inability to "see" components over the network, inability to gain access to file system data, and so on.

A good troubleshooting methodology accommodates both change management and educated guessing. "Educated guessing" means that you look for immediate symptoms of the problem and make associations between the immediate symptoms and your experience with previous problems. This is where troubleshooting becomes a real art form. The remainder of this chapter provides you with information that allows you to supplement change management techniques with educated guessing.

PREPRODUCTION TESTING

An important part of your overall troubleshooting methodology should be *preproduction testing*. Simply, preproduction testing means that you run all new components through a test phase before you place them into production. Ideally, you will have a distinct test network available for this purpose.

For example, you plan on upgrading a number of servers to a new 32-bit Ethernet card. Before putting the new Ethernet cards into production, you install one of them on a test server. For at least a week, you run the test server and the new Ethernet card through a series of evaluations. These evaluations serve two purposes. First, you get a quick indication of any functional problems the new Ethernet card may have. Second, you establish a baseline performance level—a pattern of "normal" behavior for the new Ethernet card. If the Ethernet card performs acceptably during the test phase, you can use this baseline behavior as an important item of information when troubleshooting network problems.

You should run all new components through a similar test phase. This includes both software and hardware, both for workstations and for servers. The thoroughness of your testing depends on the size of your test network and the resources you have available for performing tests. Even if you belong to a small organization and don't have very many resources available for testing, you still should perform preproduction testing. Even the most cursory testing can save you time by spotting problems with new components before they go into production.

WHAT ARE SERVER ABENDS?

Most people who work with NetWare experience an abend, but don't understand exactly what is happening. *Abend* is shorthand for ABnormal END, and refers to the fate of an execution thread that encountered an error condition and was forced to stop executing.

In NetWare, an abend causes the entire operating system to stop executing. A message is displayed on the server console stating the error condition that causes the abend and the execution thread that was running when the abend occurred. The first portion of the current operating system stack memory is also displayed onscreen (see Figure 39.2).

Error conditions that cause abends on the NetWare server are grave. They include referencing nonexistent memory addresses, signaling nonexistent semaphores, relinquishing control of the CPU during interrupt processing, and more. The reason the operating system halts as the result of an abend is that the error condition is serious enough to threaten server data, were the operating system to continue execution.

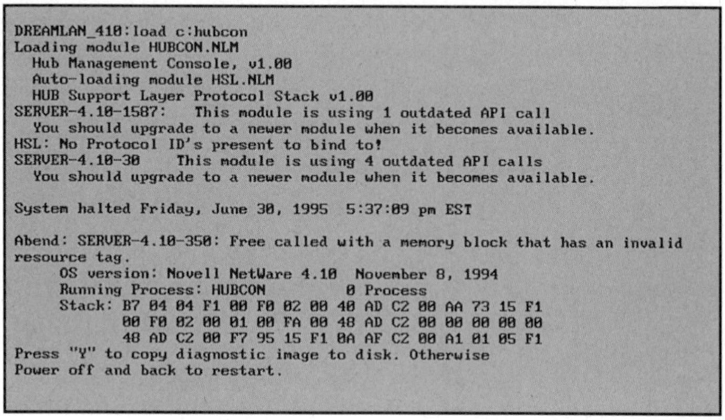

Figure 39.2.
Sample server abend
message screen.

```
DREAMLAN_410:load c:hubcon
Loading module HUBCON.NLM
   Hub Management Console, v1.00
   Auto-loading module HSL.NLM
   HUB Support Layer Protocol Stack v1.00
SERVER-4.10-1587:    This module is using 1 outdated API call
   You should upgrade to a newer module when it becomes available.
HSL: No Protocol ID's present to bind to!
SERVER-4.10-30    This module is using 4 outdated API calls
   You should upgrade to a newer module when it becomes available.

System halted Friday, June 30, 1995  5:37:09 pm EST

Abend: SERVER-4.10-350: Free called with a memory block that has an invalid
resource tag.
       OS version: Novell NetWare 4.10  November 8, 1994
       Running Process: HUBCON        0 Process
       Stack: B7 04 04 F1 00 F0 02 00 40 AD C2 00 AA 73 15 F1
              00 F0 02 00 01 00 FA 00 40 AD C2 00 00 00 00 00
              40 AD C2 00 F7 95 15 F1 0A AF C2 00 A1 01 05 F1
Press "Y" to copy diagnostic image to disk. Otherwise
Power off and back to restart.
```

In NetWare, abends are designed to shut everything down and force you to correct the condition which caused the fatal error to occur. This could mean unloading an errant NLM from the server, replacing a bad LAN card or disk controller, replacing server RAM, upgrading a device driver, or fixing some other problem.

The problem with abends is that most people can infer little information about the offending component from the abend message displayed by NetWare on the server console. However, programmers who have worked with NetWare can use the operating system's internal debugger to pinpoint the problem.

Although NetWare implemented the domain concept so that you can load NLMs into the protected memory domain, there is an important restriction you need to be aware of. In order for an NLM to fully function within the protected memory domain, it must be designed to run there in the first place. Over 90 percent of the NLMs today do not have the protected domain in mind. Therefore, it is a good idea, but developers must take advantage of it before users can benefit from that feature.

You can find out if an NLM will work in the protected memory domain by trying to load it. At worst, the NLM will not load. To set up the protected domain and load NLMs into it, follow these steps:

1. Include LOAD DOMAIN as the very *first* line of your STARTUP.NCF file. The DOMAIN.NLM is copied to your server's DOS partition during installation.

2. After you load DOMAIN.NLM, you have three additional console commands available: DOMAIN, DOMAIN HELP, and DOMAIN=<domain name>.

   DOMAIN gives you a list of NLMs that are currently loaded into the OS domain and the OS_PROTECTED domain. By default, all NLMs are loaded into the OS domain.

3. Type **DOMAIN=OS_PROTECTED** at the console to switch to the protected domain. Any LOAD command you issue from this point on will try to load the NLM into the protected domain.

4. To switch back to the OS domain, type **DOMAIN=OS** at the console.

THE NETWARE DEBUGGER

NetWare 4.x (and NetWare 3.x) has an internal debugger you can use to obtain abend-related information. The debugger is oriented toward assembly language and designed for NLM programmers to assist in software development. The debugger's interface is intimidating, even to experienced programmers. However, it does an excellent job for the purpose for which it was created—assisting NLM development.

There are a three simple things you can do with the NetWare debugger that can help you troubleshoot an abend:

◆ Retrieve the status of active threads

◆ View console screens

◆ View loaded modules, including NLMs and device drivers

ENTERING THE DEBUGGER

To enter the NetWare debugger after an abend, type **386debug**. You also use the Alt+Left Shift, Alt+Right Shift, and Esc keys concurrently.

Once you are in the debugger, you can view help screens by entering the following commands:

h	Displays main debugger help screen
.h	Displays help for debugger "dot" commands
hb	Displays debugger breakpoint help screens

The NetWare debugger has a # prompt. As long as you see a # character displayed in the first column of the server console, you'll know you are in the NetWare debugger.

RETRIEVING THE STATUS OF ACTIVE THREADS

To view the status of active threads, type **.p** at the debugger prompt. The debugger will display three groups of threads: the active thread, threads on the run queue, and threads not on the run queue. The active thread is the one you are most interested in: it is the thread that was executing when the server abended. If the active thread belongs to an NLM application, for example, this is a good indication that that NLM may have caused the problem (but not always).

Sometimes the active thread is not the cause of an abend. For example, a device driver's interrupt service routine may cause the abend. Because the interrupt service routine runs under the context of the active thread, the debugger will show that the active thread was running when the abend occurred, but will not show that the interrupt service routine was actually in control. You may be able to solve this mystery by using the ? command.

Threads on the run queue are ready to execute, but they are waiting for the active thread to relinquish control of the CPU. Threads not on the run queue are "sleeping" and can never cause an abend.

You can frequently discover whether the server was executing NLM code or a device driver interrupt service routine by using the ? command. The ? command shows the nearest label to the memory address the CPU was executing when the abend occurred. For example, if you issue the ? command and the debugger displays Memory Address in LANDRIV.LAN, you would know that the device driver named LANDRIV.LAN was executing when the abend occurred.

VIEWING CONSOLE SCREENS

Sometimes, viewing NetWare console screens can provide you with more information. This is especially true when a device driver or NLM issued a console alert just prior to the occurrence of the abend. To view console screens from within the debugger, issue the view command by typing v at the debugger prompt.

As soon as you issue the view command, the debugger will display the first screen on the server's internal screen list. This usually is the NetWare console screen. To view additional screens, press any key: the debugger will cycle to the next screen on its internal list. To continue viewing screens, simply press any key to view the next screen. When you have viewed all the screens, NetWare will return you to the debugger prompt.

The most important thing to look for when viewing screens are critical error messages, such as routing errors, volume dismounts, errors updating a volume FAT table, failure to allocate memory, and so on. When you see one of these error messages, you can look up the message in the NetWare System Error Messages manual. Error messages can be a great source of troubleshooting information. When an abend occurs, the only way to can read error messages is by using the debugger to view the server's screens.

VIEWING LOADED MODULES

Once in the NetWare debugger, you can view a list of loaded modules by typing m at the debugger prompt. NetWare will then display information about all NLMs, LAN and disk drivers, and name spaces modules loaded on the server. Information about each module includes the file name of the module, the full module name, a short description, a release date, and a version number.

OTHER DEBUGGER OPTIONS

There are many more things you can do with the NetWare internal debugger that can aid your troubleshooting efforts. However, to do more than view screens, modules, and thread status, you need to be familiar with assembly language and the general workings of NetWare's thread scheduler. Following are some useful options you can include:

◆ Disassemble loaded code

◆ Traverse the operating system's stack memory

◆ View server memory

◆ Reset the instruction pointer and step through code

If you think you may be able to perform some of these developer-related tasks with the debugger when troubleshooting, you should obtain the NetWare NLM Developer's SDK, which documents the internal workings of the NetWare operating system and the NetWare debugger.

LAN PROBLEMS

LAN problems are always easy to detect but can be difficult to diagnose. On a multi-server NetWare 4.*x* system, LAN problems may be the result of any of the following conditions:

◆ Cabling faults

◆ LAN card failures

◆ Router/Bridge failures

◆ Incorrect loading of LAN device drivers

◆ Incorrect protocol binding

◆ Not enough RAM in the NetWare server

The first three items on the preceding list—cabling faults, LAN card failures, router/bridge failures—are hardware errors that will usually shut down whole network segments. The most pressing question you need to answer when a LAN hardware failure occurs is "What station is broken?" This is not always an easy question to answer because there may be thousands of stations on your internetwork. The obvious place to start looking is on the physical LAN segment where the problem first became evident. You usually will get calls from users reporting problems, such as, "I can't see my server," or "my workstation timed-out sending a NetWare packet," or "the network is suddenly really slow."

Pinpointing cable faults can be impossible without some good tools. If you have a structured wiring system consisting of intelligent hubs (hubs that have network management software built in), the hub management console will tell you exactly where the cabling fault is. This is an excellent reason to purchase an intelligent structured wiring system.

If you don't have a structured wiring system, pinpointing a cabling fault can be difficult and time-consuming. One type of tool that is indispensable is a cable tester. Cable testers are special hardware devices that attach directly to a cable segment and perform a series of diagnostic tests. The cable segment either passes or fails the test. Some cable testers can tell you exactly what is wrong with the cable segment and even the distance (from where the tool is attached) of the cable fault.

Common cable faults include lack of grounding, lack of termination, too much cable length, shorted cable, and bad connectors. Frequently, you can breach cabling rules, such as having too much cable or too many segments, when you add a new workstation or server to the network.

Microtest makes an excellent line of cable testing products for Ethernet or token ring. Make certain the cable tester you purchase supports the types of cable at your site (twisted pair, standard (thick) Ethernet, thin Ethernet, fiber, and so on).

LAN Card failures cause different symptoms for different types of LAN systems.

Note

Ethernet card failures sometimes cause extreme numbers of collisions, which makes every station on the LAN segment slow down. This is a classic problem with Ethernet. Ethernet errors are discussed in detail, later in this chapter.

Note

Token-ring card failures usually result in the offending card being removed from the ring. The result is that the offending station is disconnected from the LAN, but other stations continue normal operation. If the offending token ring station is a NetWare server, that server "disappears" from the network, but other servers remain visible.

Router and bridge hardware errors usually cause entire network segments to "disappear" from view. Because NetWare 4.*x* servers are also internetwork routers, a routing error can be associated with some other server error condition, such as an abend. If you use dedicated routers on your internetwork, you should purchase routers that come with network management software that alerts you when an internetworking device fails.

INCORRECTLY LOADING LAN DRIVERS

Incorrectly loaded LAN drivers can cause LAN problems, just as hard failures of LAN cards, cabling, or routers can. When loading LAN drivers on either a NetWare server or a workstation, you must specify some key information, including the following:

- ◆ I/O ports
- ◆ Memory address
- ◆ Interrupt numbers
- ◆ Logical Link Control (LLC) frame types

If you load a LAN driver specifying an incorrect I/O port, interrupt number, or memory address, the driver will not be able to initialize the LAN card and will not complete its loading process. The LAN card will then be unavailable for use by the station. To load the driver correctly, you must know the interrupt, memory, and I/O settings for the card in question. Usually you can perform a visual inspection of a card's jumper settings to determine the correct hardware options with which to load the LAN card.

Note

It is possible to successfully load the TRXNET.LAN (an ARCnet driver shipped with NetWare) driver when a wrong interrupt has be given. This causes the server to be unable to communicate with other devices.

EISA and Microchannel cards can have their hardware options configured by software. This means that you must run a Microchannel SETUP program or EISA configuration program after you install the card but before you attempt to load a LAN driver for that card. When you perform software configuration, record the I/O, memory, and interrupt configuration of the card and save that information for when you load the card's LAN driver.

If you specify an incorrect LLC frame type when loading a LAN card at either a server or a workstation, things happen a little differently. First, the driver will load and will initialize the card successfully. However, the station will not be able to communicate over the network.

Tip

If you are unsure which Ethernet frame types are used on your server, type **CONFIG** at the console prompt and a report of LAN drivers and frame types used are displayed (see Figure 39.3).

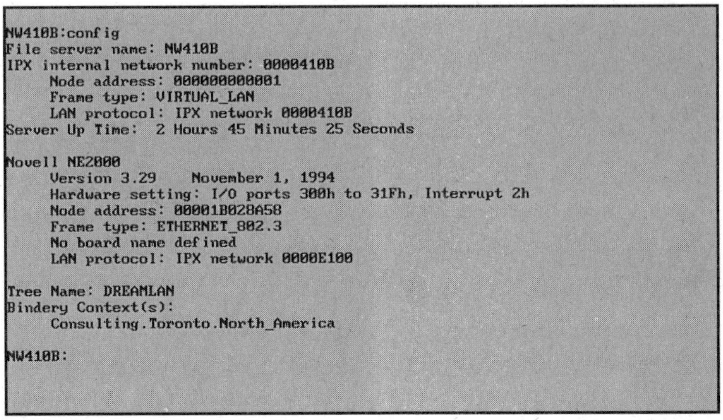

Figure 39.3.
Sample CONFIG
console command.

```
NW410B:config
File server name: NW410B
IPX internal network number: 0000410B
     Node address: 000000000001
     Frame type: VIRTUAL_LAN
     LAN protocol: IPX network 0000410B
Server Up Time: 2 Hours 45 Minutes 25 Seconds

Novell NE2000
     Version 3.29    November 1, 1994
     Hardware setting: I/O ports 300h to 31Fh, Interrupt 2h
     Node address: 00001B028A58
     Frame type: ETHERNET_802.3
     No board name defined
     LAN protocol: IPX network 0000E100

Tree Name: DREAMLAN
Bindery Context(s):
     Consulting.Toronto.North_America

NW410B:
```

For example, if all IPX communications on your network use the Ethernet 802.3 (Raw) LLC frame type, and if you bring up a new server to use the Ethernet 802.2 LLC frame type, the new server will not be able to communicate with the other stations on the network.

This turns out to be a very common problem with NetWare 4.x (the default frame type for Ethernet drivers shipped with NetWare 3.11, 2.2, and all previous releases was LLC 802.3 (Raw)). However, the default Ethernet frame type for NetWare 4.x is LLC 802.2. All current Ethernet drivers for 3.1x and 4.x defaults to LLC 802.2.

So when bringing up a NetWare 4.x server or workstation on an existing network, the default LAN driver frame type ensures that the new server or workstation will not be able to communicate over the network!

The best thing to do is load LAN drivers to use the LLC 802.3 (Raw) frame type for existing NetWare networks. If you are bringing up a NetWare 4.x network from scratch, use the LLC 802.3 (Raw) frame type when loading LAN drivers.

INCORRECT PROTOCOL BINDING

After you have a LAN driver successfully loaded (which entails successful initialization of the LAN card), you still must bind the LAN card's driver to a protocol stack. (A binding is an association of a LAN driver with a protocol stack.) This means you must assign a network address to the binding.

39

TROUBLESHOOTING NETWARE 4.x

Tip

One of the most frequent mistakes you will encounter when working with NetWare servers is the assignment of incorrect network addresses to bindings of protocol stacks with LAN card drivers. This holds true regardless of the protocol stack used in the binding: IPX, IP, AppleTalk, and so on. An incorrect network address confuses network routers.

To be correct, a network address used in a protocol binding must be consistent with all other bindings of that address on the internetwork. For example, if all NetWare servers attached to an IPX segment refer to that segment as address 00FFEE11, then you, too, must bind to that IPX segment using the address 00FFEE11.

Incorrect protocol bindings can disrupt internetwork operation in strange ways. Some servers may show up in NetWare's routing tables twice, while other servers may not show up at all. Workstations may also lose their connections to servers. For IPX networks, the best indication of an incorrect protocol binding is a series of Router Configuration Error alerts displayed on the NetWare server console (see Figure 39.4). Router Configuration Error alerts tend to show up on multiple NetWare servers, because a single incorrectly bound protocol becomes instantly visible to a large portion of the servers on the internetwork.

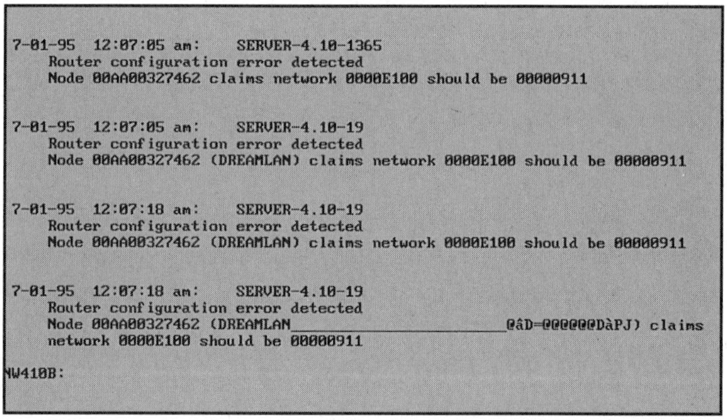

Figure 39.4.
Sample Router Configu-
ration Error message.

```
7-01-95  12:07:05 am:     SERVER-4.10-1365
         Router configuration error detected
         Node 00AA00327462 claims network 0000E100 should be 00000911


7-01-95  12:07:05 am:     SERVER-4.10-19
         Router configuration error detected
         Node 00AA00327462 (DREAMLAN) claims network 0000E100 should be 00000911


7-01-95  12:07:18 am:     SERVER-4.10-19
         Router configuration error detected
         Node 00AA00327462 (DREAMLAN) claims network 0000E100 should be 00000911


7-01-95  12:07:18 am:     SERVER-4.10-19
         Router configuration error detected
         Node 00AA00327462 (DREAMLAN                       @âD=0000000DàPJ) claims
         network 0000E100 should be 00000911

NW410B:
```

Tip

Some non-routing devices, such as HP JetDirect cards, keep track of IPX network addresses. Should you change the IPX address of a segment, make sure you reset all the HP JetDirect printers on that segment.

USING PROTOCOL ANALYZERS

Some LAN problems resist easy diagnosis or appear intermittently and unpredictably. Protocol analyzers are excellent troubleshooting tools for these types of LAN problems. Protocol analyzers, such as the Sniffer from Network General or LANalyzer for Windows from Novell, monitor all traffic that passes over a LAN segment. You can capture, filter, and trap traffic that meets certain criteria, including traffic resulting from a transmission or reception error. Network analyzers also allow you to "replay" previously capture network traffic, which may be the only way to duplicate some error conditions reliably. Protocol analyzers can also provide you with good baseline data for how your network behaves during normal conditions.

A protocol analyzer enables you to monitor the communication process that takes place between two network stations. Since networks, such as NetWare 4.*x* communicate via protocols, if problems occur, they will almost always be manifest at the protocol level.

Note

> The usefulness of a protocol analyzer depends on the user's knowledge of the instrument and troubleshooting skills. In other words, the person at the helm of the product must be able to interpret the results and decide on an appropriate action.

Protocol analyzers have several names—protocol analyzer, packet analyzer, network analyzer, packet decoder, and so on. Although these products have several names, they work under the same premise: decode traffic, monitor station connections, and provide network wire statistics.

There are two type of network analyzers: those that require special hardware and those that don't. Hardware-based analyzers are usually faster, offer more features, decode more protocols, capture more traffic, and are, unfortunately very expensive. The cost of these protocol analyzers generally directs them to the large enterprise network. The price of software analyzers starts at about $300.

ALLEVIATING ERRORS

Finding and alleviating network errors is one of the most important aspect of performance—if a network is constantly battling collisions, performance will be insufferable. Only Ethernet errors are discussed in this section. There are a number of books on the market that give a more detailed discussion on Ethernet and token ring errors, such as *NetWare Unleashed* by Sams Publishing.

Note

Collisions are errors but are a normal network occurrence in Ethernet. But how many collisions are too many? The answer is that because of factors like the amount of LAN traffic, the number of nodes, the topology of the network, and so on, all must be accounted for, it depends on the specific network. However, one error may be too many, if it is the wrong type. If you network is experiencing errors, a protocol analyzer will determine what type of errors they are, and thus, you will know "how many errors are too many."

TOO MANY COLLISIONS

Collisions are a normal network occurrence, but they are still considered an error. The best way to answer the question, "How many collisions are too many," is to compare the number of collisions as a percentage of total good packets; collisions should stay below two to five percent.

A protocol analyzer will allow you to watch the amount of collisions that occur on your network over time. This will provide you with an idea of what is normal for your network.

Note

Collisions will tend to increase in direct relation with the amount of server utilization and wire traffic. This is normal behavior for networks. If, however, collisions dramatically rise without the server utilization following, there is a good chance that the collisions are being caused by a abnormal network error. Not all errors are collisions. Errors can be caused by a faulty network card, cable, terminator, hub, repeater, and so on.

You can examine the amount of collision on your wire by using a protocol analyzer. If, however, you do not have one, you can get an idea of the amount of collision using the MONITOR.NLM. This is a statistic tracked by each Ethernet LAN driver (see Figure 39.5).

Figure 39.5.
Sample NE2000 LAN
driver statistics screen.

```
NetWare 4.10 Console Monitor  4.12            NetWare Loadable Module
Server name: 'NW410B' in Directory tree 'DREAMLAN'
Server version: NetWare 4.10 - November 8, 1994

            [NE2000 port=300 int=2 frame=ETHERNET_802.3]

    Total send OK byte count high:                          0
    Total receive OK byte count low:                  525,242
    Total receive OK byte count high:                       0
    Total group address send count:                       349
    Total group address receive count:                    424
    Adapter reset count:                                    0
    Adapter operating time stamp:                        10.6
    Adapter queue depth:                                    0
    Send OK single collision count:                         0
    Send OK multiple collision count:                       0
    Send OK but deferred:                                   0
    Send abort from late collision:                         0
    Send abort from excess collisions:                      0
    Send abort from carrier sense:                          0
    Send abort from excessive deferral:                     0
    Receive abort from bad frame alignment:                 0

Esc=Previous list    Alt+F10=Exit                        F1=Help
```

Cyclic Redundancy Check (CRC) Errors

Another error your protocol analyzer will see (other than collisions) is a *Cyclic Redundancy Check* (CRC) error. The chipset on Ethernet cards have a built-in error checking mechanism called CRC that works like this. Before a station sends a packet, it calculates a CRC value. The CRC value is then placed in a field within the packet structure called the Frame Check Sequence (FCS). When a packet arrives at its final destination, the receiving station also performs a CRC calculation. It then checks its answer against the value in the FCS field. If the destination station's value does not match the value that was placed in the FCS field by the sending station, the destination station assumes that an error occurred during the transfer. The packet containing the error goes to the "bit bucket in the sky" and the receiving station will request that the packet be resent (see Figure 39.6).

Figure 39.6.
CRC error checking.

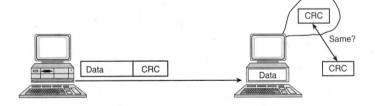

39

Troubleshooting NetWare 4.x

Tip

If a single station has continual CRC alignment errors, replace the card or update the driver.

Determining whether it is a network card causing the collisions is easy; simply watch the protocol analyzer's station monitor to determine if one station is responsible for a majority of the colliding packets (or errors). If your analyzer does not have a station monitor you can still find out if a single card is responsible. Because CSMA/CD networks allow the workstation to almost immediately retry the transmission, you can use the traffic monitor to watch for the station that seems to be transmitting directly after the collisions occur. If, by one of these methods, you think a card could be at fault, remove it and see whether the problem is eliminated.

FINDING CABLE FAULTS

Finding cabling faults is a little more tricky than the errors discussed previously; however, it can be done. First, if collisions are running wild without server utilization increasing and if you cannot point the finger at a single NIC, try to determine whether the collisions are happening locally or if the collisions are "late."

A *local collision* is a collision that happens on the same network segment. A *late collision* is a packet that meets the 64-byte minimum, but has a CRC error and the Collision Detection (CD) wire pair of the NIC is triggered.

Most network analyzers will categorize local and late collisions for you. However, if yours does not, here are some hints. Your analyzer will certainly be able to give you a list of the stations by address; a good one will also be able to read the NetWare bindery and associate the station address with a user login name. The login name (or address) will usually provide you with enough (unless the network is very large) information to know whether the collisions are local, or whether the users are on a remote segment. Now that you know what type of collision you are looking at, you can start looking for a solution.

The following are some common error conditions and possible causes and solutions:

◆ If the collisions are on a local segment, that particular segment might be too long. Collisions occur on long segments because the wire will appear to be clear for transmitting to stations on opposite ends of the wire. Check the length of the wire segment to verify whether it is within regulations (especially if you have just added a few nodes).

◆ If it is a late collision, there is a good chance the problem lies in the cabling scheme. Make sure that the cable meets specifications or that there isn't anything causing electromagnetic interference.

◆ If late collisions are happening on a remote segment, it usually means the network configuration contains a bottleneck. Check the other segments and see if each of those segments are also experiencing late collisions and if the collisions are associated with the same segment. If so, that segment is more than likely a bottleneck and causing the late collisions.

◆ If none of this applies, here are a few more things to check: If the cable doesn't have appropriate termination, a station might believe the wire is free, when in reality it is not. The station will attempt to send a packet only to be met by a collision.

◆ Some malfunctions at the workstation may talk the transmitting station into disregarding proper protocol procedures. The easiest way to check the transmitting stations (you should be able to narrow it down to two) is to "ping" each station.

◆ If a station does not answer a ping, look at the packets that contain the error to see if the packet is of proper length. Also, check to see if it passed the CRC test. If these conditions apply, the receiving station is not responding (this is sometimes called a deaf receiver). Swap out the components at the receiving end, one piece at a time.

LOST CARRIER SENSE

The *Carrier Sense Lost* error counter increases each time the interface board's transmitter loses connection with the cable. The most obvious reason for a lost carrier sense error is that the cable has "wiggled" out. So, check the connection before replacing the network board.

NETWORK JABBERS

Jabbers (also called *long packets*) are a conglomeration of packets (or something else) that disrupts the network signal; a healthy network should never experience jabbers. Jabbers fail the CRC check and generally are large packets (perhaps even larger than the 1518-byte maximum). Generally, network jabbers are caused by either a stuck card, clogged transceiver, or a bad repeater. Jabbers are extremely noticeable because network performance is always affected (they can bring the network to a crawl).

Note

The discussion on jabber errors again shows the importance of a protocol analyzer: if a protocol analyzer is not monitoring the network, you will only know that the network is slow, and not that it is slow because a station is sending out multiple long packets.

Jabbers are caused by a bad network component that disregards protocol "rules" (interrupts others that are trying to speak). This disregard for rules will cause the wire to clog. To determine which station is the culprit, simply look at the station monitor or check each station's transceiver lights (if they have one). The lights will be blinking continuously and faster than normal and the station will appear to be sending a continuous strand of transmissions.

Tip

If the lights are indicating rapid transmissions, shut the station off and watch the protocol analyzer to see whether the errors drop off. If they do, swap out that station's components.

SHORT AND LONG FRAMES

A *short frame* (some analyzers report them as *runts*) are packets that have the correct CRC, but don't meet the 64-byte minimum packet length (it's too short). Likewise, a *long frame* is too long, and will also pass the CRC.

Both long and short frames usually are attributed to the transmitting station and often are caused by bad network drivers (were they recently updated?). Again, determine which station is causing the problems and then reload the LAN drivers (an update is commonly the best fix). The invalid length packets should go away.

LATE EVENTS

Because of the rules upheld by protocols, two packets should only be able to collide if two stations transmit at almost exactly the same time. However, if a packet collides later in the transmission than should be possible, it is called a *late event*. These errors usually are caused by a disregard for topology rules and specifications (too long of a segment cable, too many repeaters, and so on). It is unlikely, but it is also possible that it could be the fault of the sending station's network card.

ALIGNMENT ERRORS

Alignment errors are packets that contain fragmented bytes (do not have 8 bits). You should rarely, if ever, see these errors. If they are present, there is a good possibility that the cabling is at fault.

Tip

If several ports on a hub report similar errors, regardless of error type, try to find a common denominator: the network card in the file server, the same punch down block, the same cable route, the same concentrator bay, and so on. If you normally have a relatively error-free network and, for no apparent reason, errors begin to flood the wires, backtrack. What was changed? Was a new station added? If these types of thought processes lead you to a dead end, start up the protocol analyzer—after all, networks communicate via protocols.

DISK PROBLEMS

Frequently, disk problems with NetWare don't lead to an immediate and total failure of the disk. Rather, a series of problems with the operation of the NetWare server occurs, growing more serious and frequent over time. Symptoms of disk problems include the following:

◆ Automatic volume dismounts

◆ Errors updating volume FAT tables

◆ Failure to mount a volume

◆ Read-after-write verification errors

Less serious disk problems frequently are masked by the fault-tolerant features of the NetWare file system. Hot-Fix redirects bad media sectors to a special reserved section of the drive media. When the media on a drive starts to go bad, you may experience no errors because Hot-Fix will correct these errors on-the-fly. The only indication you have of decaying drive media is that the reserved Hot-Fix area of the drive becomes fuller (more bad sectors are being redirected).

You can view the status of the Hot-Fix redirection area of any NetWare drive by running the MONITOR.NLM and viewing information for each NetWare drive installed on the server (see Figure 39.7). Under normal conditions, the Hot-Fix area of a NetWare drive will fill at a very slow, constant rate. If you observe that the Hot-Fix area of a NetWare drive is filling at a fast or increasing rate, this is an indication of imminent media failure.

Figure 39.7.
Use MONITOR.NLM to
check Hot-Fix area.

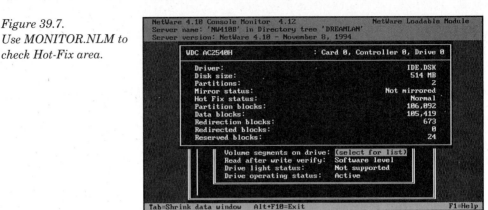

AUTOMATIC VOLUME DISMOUNTS

When NetWare detects a serious media error, it automatically dismounts the volume affected by the error. This is called an *automatic volume dismount*, and almost always indicates a failure of the hard drive or drive controller.

When a volume dismounts automatically, you might be able to repair the volume using the VREPAIR.NLM. This is appropriate if you need to recover data from the damaged volume. However, you should not put the volume back into production until you have determined the cause of the volume dismount. When you experience an automatic volume dismount, perform the following steps:

1. Repair the dismounted volume using VREPAIR.
2. Back up the volume.
3. Load INSTALL.NLM and perform a nondestructive surface test of the drive.
4. If the drive passes the surface test, reformat the drive, restore the volume, and put it back into production.
5. If the drive does not pass the surface test, replace the drive and restore the volume.

Note

It may be necessary to run VREPAIR several times. You should keep on running VREPAIR until it reports ZERO error.

Depending on the amount of disk space, it may take up to several hours per run.

ERRORS UPDATING THE FAT TABLE

Every time you create, update, or delete a file stored on a NetWare volume, the operating system must update the FAT table stored on the volume's hard drive. Errors updating the drive's FAT table cause the volume's internal data structures to become corrupt. This is a serious error condition and usually indicates imminent media failure. You should perform the preceding steps to salvage or replace the volume.

FAILURE TO MOUNT A VOLUME

After a NetWare 4.x server abends or loses its power source, you may have problems mounting volumes when you restart the server. This does not necessarily indicate media errors. The NetWare operating system has a strict protocol for dismounting volumes. This *dismount protocol* includes flushing the file cache system, updating the volume FAT and the redundant volume mirrored FAT, and more. The dismount protocol executes whenever you dismount a volume or down the server.

When a server abend occurs, however, the server shuts down without executing the dismount protocol. As a result, the mirrored copy of the volume FAT may not match the primary volume FAT, the Directory Entry Table (DET) may be internally inconsistent, or any of a series of error conditions may exist on the volume. In such a case, these error conditions are likely the result of the server's abend or power source failure and the resulting failure to execute the dismount protocol, and not the result of media failure.

When a NetWare 4.x server fails to mount a volume after a disorderly shutdown (abend of loss or power), it will run VREPAIR automatically if you have configured it (default is yes). In most cases, this will repair and mount the volume without your intervention. Sometimes, however, it may be necessary to run VREPAIR twice or more to repair and mount the volume. When a single VREPAIR session does not entirely repair the volume, you will be required to intervene manually to repair and mount the volume.

READ-AFTER-WRITE VERIFICATION ERRORS

Read-after-write verification errors almost certainly indicate an imminent media failure. When you encounter read-after-write verification errors, you should dismount the volume and perform the steps outlined in the "Automatic Volume Dismounts" section.

DRIVE MIRRORING AND DUPLEXING

When a volume has mirrored or duplexed drives, any of the error conditions discussed previously will cause the drive suffering the error condition to go offline. File service will continue using the other (undamaged) drive, but you will be running in an unmirrored (or unduplexed) state. When the replacement drive comes online, NetWare will start a background thread that synchronizes the replacement drive with the existing drive.

Warning

When a volume loses its mirrored state, the operating system generates console alerts. You should immediately replace the defective drive and restore the mirrored or duplexed state of the drive pairs using the INSTALL.NLM.

Note

Synchronization can take several hours or more for large drives. However, it occurs in the background during normal file service, so users are not affected by it.

NDS PROBLEMS

NetWare Directory Services (NDS) is a marvelous piece of technology. It has self-repairing mechanisms built into it. Most problems you will encounter with NDS will be performance-related and will require tuning of the NDS tree structure, including the creation or modification of the partition replication scheme.

Note

For in-depth information about NDS troubleshooting, consult *NDS Troubleshooting* by New Riders Publishing.

Some NDS problems, however, can disrupt normal operation of NDS. These include the following:

- ◆ Breakdown of time synchronization
- ◆ Network and routing problems
- ◆ Partitions stored on downed servers

BREAKDOWN OF TIME SYNCHRONIZATION

Time synchronization is critical to the operation of NDS because it resolves multiple updates to NDS objects. For example, two network administrators update the same NDS object using different information at around the same time. Which update gets applied to the NDS information base and ultimately becomes distributed across the network? The answer is, the update which was applied at the latest time (the most recent update). If time synchronization for your network is broken, NDS will not be able to know which of the conflicting updates is actually the most recent, and may apply the wrong update to the network-wide NDS information base.

The most telling symptom of a time synchronization breakdown is conflicting NDS object definitions residing in the NDS information base concurrently. For example, on one partition your object's phone number is listed as 123-4567, yet on a replicate partition your object's phone number is stored as 123-1234.

Another symptom of lost time synchronization is that updates to NDS objects "disappear" after they are applied. For example, you know that you changed user Joe's phone number to 123-4567, yet it remains stored in the NDS information base as 123-1234.

In general, inconsistent object definitions among NDS partitions usually are the result of a time synchronization breakdown. Other flaky types of NDS behavior, including in synchronizing NDS partitions may be the result of a time synchronization breakdown.

To verify a time synchronization breakdown, you need to find two or more NetWare 4.*x* servers that are set to different times. You can view the time setting of remote NetWare 4.*x* servers by running RCONSOLE.EXE and executing remotely the server console TIME command.

Time synchronization breakdowns are caused by the following conditions:

- ◆ A primary or reference time server with a bad clock or time source
- ◆ Failure of secondary, primary, or reference time servers to communicate over the network. This indicates a LAN or routing problem.
- ◆ Bringing test servers up as primary or reference time servers

NETWORK AND ROUTING PROBLEMS

Network routing problems can cause two major classes of NDS-related problems:

- ◆ NDS Synchronization errors
- ◆ Time Synchronization breakdown

There is a special background NDS synchronization thread that runs on every NetWare 4.x server. The job of this process is to synchronize NDS partitions with their replicated partitions. For example, to ensure a master partition, its read/write replicas and its read-only replicas are updated in a consistent fashion. When the process is working properly, every partition replica will converge to an identical state within a well-defined period of time.

When the synchronization thread is not performing normally, you may discover objects defined differently on partition replicas. This occurs because an update on one partition is not forwarded by the process to replicas of that partition. How can network or routing errors cause NDS synchronization problems? In order to "sync," the thread must be able to communicate with other NetWare 4.x servers over the network. Specifically, the synchronization thread must have a network link available to servers containing partition replicas of the machine the thread is executing on. When the thread cannot communicate across the wire with other NetWare 4.x servers, it cannot synchronize partition replicas. Hence, objects will not be synchronized across NDS partitions.

The NDS synchronization thread is designed to recover from downed networks, downed servers, and routing errors. It keeps a record of all synchronization activity and retries unsuccessful attempts to sync a remote server. This, however, causes the thread to go through a cycle of retrying synchronization operations, having those synchronization operations time-out, and retrying the operations again. The retry and time-out cycle continues for as long as the network or routing problems persist.

When the synchronization thread is in a retry and time-out cycle, server performance can be degraded dramatically. So, network and routing problems can lead to an inconsistent NDS information base, plus poor server performance. When you detect both of these symptoms together—especially when they appear on more than one server concurrently—it frequently indicates network or routing problems.

TIME SYNCHRONIZATION PROBLEMS

Network or routing errors cause NDS synchronization problems when two servers containing partition replicas cannot communicate with each other. Network or routing errors also cause a time synchronization problem when primary, reference, or secondary time servers cannot communicate with each other. In this case, the symptoms will appear as described previously in the "Breakdown of Time Synchronization" section.

PARTITIONS STORED ON DOWNED SERVERS

When a server storing an NDS partition or partition replica is down, NDS synchronization errors occur. The symptoms for this problem are exactly the same as for sync problems which occur because of network or routing errors.

The important thing to remember is that you should never allow test servers (servers that are downed frequently) to store NDS partitions or partition replicas. If they do, the synchronization process will enter the retry and time-out cycle every time the test server is down.

TECHNICAL SUPPORT SOURCES

There are a number of technical support sources available for NetWare products. Some are free and some are not. This section provides a brief discussion of the following four support sources:

- ◆ NetWire on CompuServe
- ◆ ElectroText/DynaText
- ◆ Network Support Encyclopedia (NSEPro)
- ◆ Novell Resellers, Service Centers, and User Groups
- ◆ Novell

NETWIRE

CompuServe is probably the most well known support vehicle for Novell and many other vendors. NetWire is a set of forums (special interest areas) on CompuServe sponsored by Novell.

NetWire is not Novell's official support channel, however, a number of Novell technical support staff are assigned full-time to monitor NetWire. Assisting them are a number of volunteer SysOps (Systems Operators) that are contracted by Novell. The backgrounds of these SysOps vary: some are network administrators working for large companies, some are network specialists for Fortune 100 companies, some are systems integrators, and some are consultants. They all have one thing in common: they all use NetWare products on a daily basis in their work.

A large number of experienced users use NetWire daily. The system is mostly a peer-to-peer support one. Over 90 percent of the time, you will get a response to your questions within 24 hours. Because of the non-interactive nature of a bulletin board, it is not designed for emergencies. In such situations, you should contact your local Novell Authorized Resellers or call Novell directly. A list of telephone numbers for Novell Technical Support is given in Table 39.1, later in this section.

There is no cost in using the NetWire service, except for CompuServe communication charges. You should consult CompuServe for specific charges. All you need to access NetWire and other CompuServe services is a CompuServe id.

Tip

> Often times when you purchase a modem, you will find an introductory package for CompuServe. Included in it is a $15 usage credit that can be applied to your new CompuServe account.

NetWire is one of a number of ways that Novell makes their patches and drivers update available. Therefore, it is to your advantage to monitor NetWire for the latest gossip, updates, and fixes.

A detailed discussion of NetWire can be found in *NetWare Unleashed* by Sams Publishing.

ELECTROTEXT AND DYNATEXT

Shipped with NetWare 4.*x* is a set of online documentation called ElectroText (for NetWare 4.0*x*) and DynaText for NetWare 4.1. DynaText comes with viewers for different platforms, such as Windows and UnixWare. The viewer allows you to do keyword searches to look up specific information quickly.

Although it may not contain all the error messages and solutions, it does serve as a resource for your troubleshooting needs. Its installation and usage have been described in detail in Chapter 20.

NETWORK SUPPORT ENCYCLOPEDIA (NSEPRO)

Novell has available a product called *Network Support Encyclopedia*, Professional Edition (NSEPro). It contains all known reported bugs and resolutions, FYIs (For Your Information notes), Novell Laboratory test reports, Novell Application Notes (AppNotes), and listings of patches. NSEPro, comes on a CD and contains the actual files.

NSEPro is available on a subscription basis.

NOVELL RESELLERS, SERVICE CENTERS, AND USER GROUPS

If you like a "human interface" to your problem resolution, you should contact your local Novell Resellers. There are three levels of resellers:

◆ Novell Authorized Resellers

◆ Novell Gold Authorized Resellers

◆ Novell Platinum Authorized Resellers

Each level of reseller targets a specific market. For example, Authorized Resellers usually deals with smaller companies due to their own limited resources. These resellers are not required to have a CNE (Certified NetWare Engineer) on staff. Gold Resellers deal mostly with medium-sized companies and are required to have at least one MCNE (Master Certified NetWare Engineer; formally known as ECNE or Enterprise Certified NetWare Engineer) on staff. Platinum Resellers target large corporate accounts and require at least two MCNEs on staff.

Note

In general, if you have multiple servers and multiple segments (but no wide area network connections) you want to deal with a Gold Reseller. If you have WAN connections or gateways to mini or mainframe systems, you probably want to deal with a Platinum Reseller.

In 1993, Novell introduced a new program called *Novell Authorized Service Center* (NASC). These are companies, not necessary resellers, that provide NetWare support. They have at least two CNEs and one MCNE on staff. If you call Novell for an onsite service, your call will be referred to the nearest NASC in your area. You can expect a call from the NASC within 2 hours, and someone at your site within 24 hours.

Many cities have a Novell User Group. It may be simply a group of people with the common interest (NetWare) that meets on a regular basis to swap ideas and "war stories." Sometimes, it may be part of NetWare Users International (NUI). Each year, NUI sponsors meetings around North America complete with seminars and vendor exhibits. You can call Novell to find out whether a local NUI chapter is in your area.

Tip

In many cities, there are also NPA (Network Professional Associations) chapters that hold monthly meetings. You can find out where your nearest NPA chapter is located by calling Novell.

NOVELL

Novell operates a number of support centers worldwide. There is a cost in opening a support call with these centers. Depending on the product, an incident call may cost anywhere from $50 to $250 (U.S.). Table 39.1 lists the telephone numbers of these support centers around the world.

39

TROUBLESHOOTING NETWARE 4.x

TABLE 39.1. NOVELL SUPPORT CENTERS.

North America	800-NETWARE (800-638-9273)	Provo, UT
Japan	81-3-5481-1161	Tokyo
Hong Kong	852-827-2223	Wanchai
Europe	49-211-5277-744	Dusseldorf, Germany
Australia	612-413-3077	Chatswood, NSW

Note

You can prepurchase a number of incident calls (blocks of 10) through your Novell resellers. CNEs can purchase these calls at 50 percent discount.

SUMMARY

Because NetWare 4.x is such a complex operating system, it does not make sense to perform troubleshooting in an ad-hoc manner. The most efficient approach to NetWare 4.x troubleshooting uses the science of change management to determine a starting point for the troubleshooting process. Change management, along with experience and intuition, combined with good hardware and software tools, will yield excellent results if you take these tools and methods seriously.

P A R T VIII

Internetworking and Expansion

- Examples of
  Internetworking

- Multi-Protocol
  Internetworks

- How NetWare 4.1
  Provides Multi-
  Protocol Support

- Routing NetWare's
  Native Protocols

- INETCFG

- Host Connectivity

- NetWare/IP

- Summary

CHAPTER 40

Internetworking

As a company grows and becomes more diverse, it's only natural for its network to evolve as well. A network that began with one or two file servers can very rapidly grow into a large multi-server network, supporting many different topologies and protocols. NetWare 4.1 is designed to make administration of these types of networks easy. With NetWare Directory Services (NDS), a multi-server network is viewed as a single, logical network that can be administered from a central location. Previous versions of NetWare and other network operating systems often require multi-server networks to be administered individually.

EXAMPLES OF INTERNETWORKING

Generally, when two are more file servers are installed on the same network, you are creating one of the following types of networks:

◆ Common backbone network

◆ Internetwork

A *common backbone network* is a network where multiple file servers share a single common backbone. These types of networks are common in workgroup environments and generally a single network type such as Ethernet is used. Figure 40.1 shows an example of a common backbone multi-server network.

Figure 40.1.
A common backbone
multi-server network.

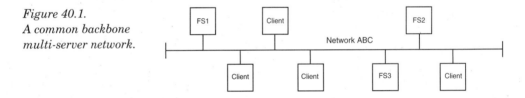

An *internetwork*, on the other hand, is a bit more complex. It is a network comprised of two or more separate physical network segments, as shown in Figure 40.2. Large networks often consist of a number of common backbone multi-server networks connected through an internetwork.

The physical network segments in an internetwork are connected by devices called *routers*. Routers have the capability to forward packets between networks independent of the underlying network media or protocol. What this means is that a router can connect networks of different types, such as Ethernet or token ring, as well as connect networks of different protocols (such as IPX and TCP/IP). This is illustrated in Figure 40.3.

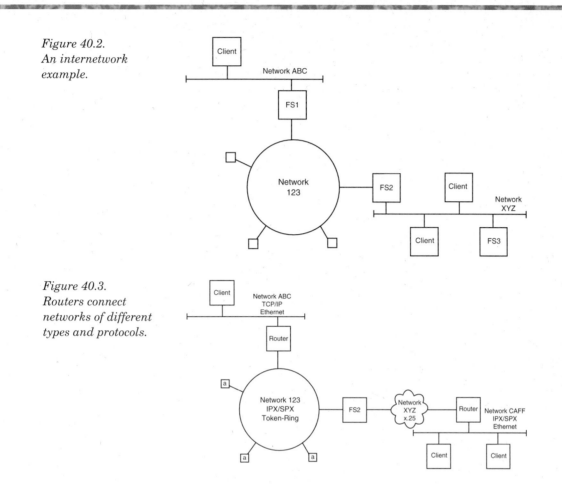

Figure 40.2.
An internetwork
example.

Figure 40.3.
Routers connect
networks of different
types and protocols.

NetWare 4.1 file servers have an internal routing mechanism built in to the operating system. By adding two or more network interface cards to a NetWare file server, you are creating what is known as an *internal router.*

In large, complex networks routers often are separate from the file server. These types of routers are known as *external routers.* External routers vary in cost and functionality. Some are only software solutions, such as Novell's Multi-Protocol Router (MPR), while others are hardware and software solutions, such as those available from router manufacturers such as Wellfleet, 3COM, and Cisco.

Software routers provide the advantage of costing less than hardware solutions but may not perform as well. When using a product like Novell's Multi-Protocol Router, routing capabilities are added by simply loading NLMs at a NetWare file server. Unlike hardware solutions that require separate hardware to be purchased and installed.

NetWare 4.1 contains all the local routing components of Novell's Multi-Protocol Router, enabling the local routing of IPX/SPX, TCP/IP and AppleTalk protocols. NetWare file servers are configured as both internal and external routers. The full Multi-Protocol Router add-on product is only required in a NetWare 4.1 environment for wide area networking capabilities such as Frame Relay or PPP connections.

Early versions of NetWare included an external router utility known as ROUTER.EXE. Due to performance issues and enhanced routing technologies, this program is no longer included with NetWare.

MULTI-PROTOCOL INTERNETWORKS

An organization's computing infrastructure is built around user and workgroup needs. A network user in the Engineering department will have different computing needs than a user in the Marketing department; a pool of secretaries will have different needs than an outside sales force. Often times, these needs dictate which desktop platforms (such as DOS, OS/2, Macintosh, UNIX, and so on) will make up an organization's network (see Figure 40.4). But even with the different desktop platforms, there is always the need for the sharing and exchange of common company information such as databases or e-mail.

Figure 40.4.
Supporting multiple
desktop environments.

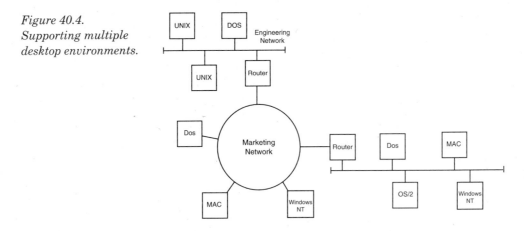

As mentioned previously, NetWare 4.1 provides routing capabilities for multiple protocols. NetWare 4.1 file servers can also store files from different desktop platforms (such as Macintosh, OS/2, or UNIX) in their native format. Together, this multi-protocol allows users of dissimilar systems to share information.

To help you better understand how multi-protocol internetworks operate, it's necessary to provide you with some background information.

What is a Protocol?

A protocol is a set of rules and procedures that enable network components to communicate. Protocols are used by software developers as basic blueprints to create products that provide network services such as file and print services. In an internetwork, each different desktop type uses a different set of protocols to communicate.

Protocols often are compared to blueprints used for building houses. These blueprints outline how many rooms the houses will contain, the size and location of those rooms, where the doors and windows should be, and so on. Similarly, network protocols outline which services will be provided on the network and how data is moved from point A to point B.

The OSI Reference Model

As mentioned previously, every different desktop supported in an internetwork uses a different set of protocols to communicate. This can make interoperability a challenge. So, in order to make supporting dissimilar systems easier, the International Standards Organization developed a set of guidelines for computer manufacturers to follow when developing protocols. These guidelines, referred to as the *Open Systems Interconnection* (OSI) reference model, provide a functional outline for network communication. Using the OSI reference model, computer manufacturers can develop protocols that will interoperate with dissimilar systems.

The OSI reference model simplifies network communication by dividing the task into seven different layers. Each layer is responsible for a different part of the network communication process but works closely with the other layers to send and receive data on the network. These seven layers are illustrated in Figure 40.5.

Figure 40.5.
Seven-Layer OSI
Reference Model.

| 7. Application |
| 6. Presentation |
| 5. Session |
| 4. Transport |
| 3. Network |
| 2. Data-Link |
| 1. Physical |

40

INTERNETWORKING

Protocols based on the seven-layer OSI model generally provide network services in the following three different areas:

◆ Physical network connection
◆ Transport of data
◆ Network Services

Physical Network Connection

Protocols at the Physical and Data-Link layers (layers 1 and 2) are responsible for the physical connection to the network. Physical layer protocols define the physical and electrical specifications of the network medium; how the raw bits of data are placed on wire. An example of a Physical layer device is a network interface card.

Data-Link layer protocols take the raw bits of network data and organize them into frames to be sent across the network. They also provide an interface between the physical hardware and the operating system (upper layers). An example of an implementation of Data-Link layer protocols is a LAN driver.

Transport of Data

In order to ensure that data is successfully sent and received on the network, the Transport and Network layers (layers 3 and 4) provide addressing and error checking services. Transport layer protocols are responsible for data integrity providing reliable, end-to-end communication. An example of a Transport layer protocol is UNIX's Transport Control Protocol (TCP). Network layer protocols are responsible for dynamically routing data on the network regardless of the underlying media. An example of a Network layer protocol is UNIX's Internet Protocol (IP).

Network Services

The Session, Presentation, and Application layers (layers 5, 6, and 7) of the OSI reference model work together to give users access to network services. Session layer protocols establish and maintain connections and control the communication dialogue. They also provide authentication services. Presentation layer protocols are responsible for translating the data to a format recognizable by the application. Application layer protocols provide the actual network services such as file and print services, e-mail, and so on. Application layer protocols are accessed by user applications to make network services available to the user. Novell's NCP and MHS (Message Handling Service) are examples of upper-layer network protocols.

Protocols written to comply to the seven-layer OSI model have the capability to interoperate in the same computing environment. Protocols used by dissimilar desktop operating systems can be supported on a network either *natively* or through the use of a *gateway*.

Supporting a desktop platform natively implies that all of the protocols that the desktop uses for communication are loaded at the file server. For example, a server that supports Macintosh clients and UNIX clients would have an AppleTalk protocol stack loaded and a TCP/IP protocol stack loaded. Files on the network are also stored in their native file-naming conventions.

Supporting multiple protocols natively is the most efficient method of multi-protocol support because no translation between protocols is necessary. NetWare 4.1 provides native protocol support.

Supporting multiple protocols through the use of a gateway should be avoided whenever possible. Gateways receive requests from a client operating system and translate the requests into a protocol supported at the file server. This process is very slow and inefficient.

HOW NETWARE 4.1 PROVIDES MULTI-PROTOCOL SUPPORT

Prior to NetWare 3.11, support for multiple protocols was an unwieldy process. Generally, additional hardware and software were required for each protocol being supported. For example, supporting Macintosh and PC users simultaneously required a network interface card in the server to support the IPX users (PCs) and one to support the AppleTalk users (Macintosh). In addition, a gateway was used to provide the translation between AppleTalk protocols and NetWare. This translation process added a lot of overhead, making this not only a costly solution but also a slow one.

With the release of NetWare 3.x, Novell introduced the *Open Data-Link Interface* (ODI) specification. This specification allows multiple protocols to share a single LAN adapter on the network. In addition, ODI allows NetWare to natively support workstations using AppleTalk (Macintosh), TCP/IP (UNIX, SUN, NeXT, and so on), IPX/SPX (DOS, OS/2, Windows, and so on) and IBM's SNA for terminal to host connectivity. ODI is now included with NetWare providing cost-effective, seamless integration of multiple protocols into the NetWare environment.

HOW ODI WORKS

When data is sent or received on the network, there are a number of ODI components involved in the communication process both at the server and at the workstation (see Figure 40.6). These components, referred to here as *layers*, allow the data to be sent through to the operating system or routed to another network regardless of the protocol.

40

INTERNETWORKING

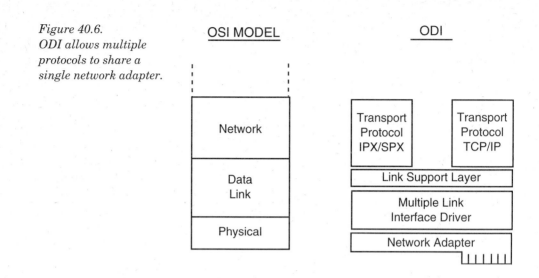

Figure 40.6.
ODI allows multiple
protocols to share a
single network adapter.

ODI AT THE SERVER

The Open Data Link interface provides multiple protocol support at both the workstation and the server. Figure 40.7 shows how ODI operates at the server level.

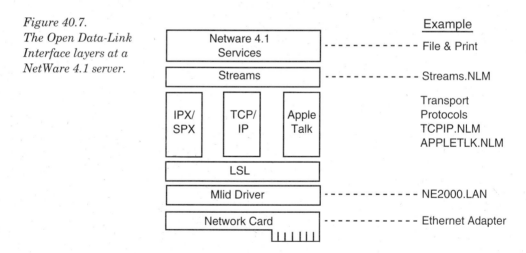

Figure 40.7.
The Open Data-Link
Interface layers at a
NetWare 4.1 server.

Table 40.1 provides a brief description of each layer.

TABLE 40.1. OPEN DATA-LINK INTERFACE LAYERS.

ODI Layer	Description
MLID	Multiple Link Interface Driver. LAN driver layer serving as an interface between the network interface card and the operating system. Supports multiple protocols simultaneously. Each 4.1 server can support up to 16 simultaneously.
LSL	Link Support Layer. Acts as a switch board to route packets between the MLID and the appropriate protocol stack.
Transport Protocol	Provides protocol stacks required to support protocols natively. Examples include IPX/SPX, AppleTalk, and TCP/IP.
STREAMS	A group of NLMs that provide a common interface between NetWare and the various transport protocols supported on the network. Allows the same set of services to be provided to users across the network, regardless of protocol.

To summarize how ODI works, data is sent and received from the network by the MLID. The MLID provides no interpretation of the data. So, data is being sent, it simply sends the data out on the network. If data is being received, its simply passed on to the Link Support Layer. MLIDs support multiple protocols by using multiple data-link layer frame types. The frame types supported with NetWare 4.1 are discussed later in this chapter.

When the Link Support Layer receives a packet from an MLID, it identifies the protocol type and passes it on to the appropriate protocol stack such as IPX, AppleTalk, and TCP/IP. When a packet is sent, the LSL determines which MLID to pass the packet to base on the protocol type again.

When a packet is passed through the various ODI layers and reaches the appropriate protocol stack, it is then either passed on to NetWare STREAMS, and ultimately on to the NetWare Operating System or it is passed back down through the layers for routing to another network.

The NetWare STREAMS interface is what allows NetWare 4.1 and the various NLMs loaded to communicate with multiple transport protocols. If an NLM is loaded that requires STREAMS support, the appropriate STREAMS support NLM will automatically be loaded.

40

INTERNETWORKING

As mentioned in Table 40.1, STREAMS is not just one NLM, but a series of NLMs. Table 40.2 summarizes the STREAMS NLMs.

TABLE 40.2. FUNCTIONS OF STREAMS AND RELATED NLMs.

NLM	Function
STREAMS	Provides routines to interface with the server applications layer. Also provides an ODI driver and the utility routines for the other STREAMS modules. Must be loaded prior to any other STREAMS module.
CLIB	A library of functions and routines that other NLMs can use. Will be automatically loaded if required. Used by STREAMS NLMs as well as by a wide variety of other NLMs. Requires STREAMS.NLM and will auto-load it if necessary.
TLI	Transport Level Interface. Provides an application programming interface that sits between STREAMS and user applications. Allows user applications to interface with the multiple transport protocols, such as IPX/SPX, TCP/IP, and AppleTalk. Required by IPXS and SPXS and will autoload if necessary. Requires STREAMS and CLIB.
IPXS/SPXS	Provides access to the IPX and SPX protocols from STREAMS. Requires and will autoloads STREAMS, CLIB and TLI.

Warning

Because the STREAMS NLMs support other NLMs, use caution when unloading them. If unloading a STREAMS NLM is necessary, you will need to unload it along with all of it's prerequisite NLMs in reverse order. For example, to unload the CLIB.NLM, you must first unload the TLI.NLM if it is loaded.

ODI AT THE WORKSTATION

In addition to allowing multiple protocols to be supported at the file server level, ODI allows network workstations to support multiple protocols. For example, a network user may concurrently access the service of a NetWare Server using IPX/SPX and a UNIX host using TCP/IP. And like ODI at the server level, this can all be done with just one network card. Figure 40.8 shows ODI at the workstation.

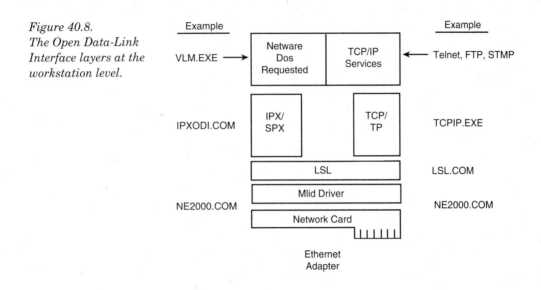

Figure 40.8.
The Open Data-Link
Interface layers at the
workstation level.

ODI at the workstation level can be best described by using the same layers previously used to describe ODI support at the server level. The main difference is that ODI is implemented through the NetWare Client software at the workstation and a series of NLMs at the file server.

ODI is enabled at the workstation by loading the following files:

◆ LSL.COM

◆ MLID files

◆ Protocol stack files

◆ NetWare DOS Requester

LSL.COM loads the link support layer. Like at the file server, the LSL at a workstation acts as a switchboard between the MLID and the transport protocol stacks (IPX, TCP/IP, and so on) loaded at the workstation. When a packet is sent, the LSL determines which MLID to route the packet to based on the protocol type. When a packet is received from an MLID, the LSL determines the appropriate protocol stack to send the packet up through.

Each ODI workstation requires a LAN driver for the network board installed. In order to support multiple protocols through a single network board, this LAN driver should be a Multiple Link Interface Driver (MLID).

In order to support multiple protocols from a workstation, the appropriate transport protocol stacks must be loaded. In the preceding example, in order for a workstation to access the NetWare server and the UNIX host simultaneously, IPXODI.COM must be loaded to access NetWare and TCPIP.EXE must be loaded to access the UNIX host.

40

INTERNETWORKING

The NetWare DOS Requester must be loaded in order to provide a workstation access to network services. This access is provided by loading a series of Virtual Loadable Modules (VLMs). VLMs and the NetWare DOS Requester were described in Chapter 23.

FRAME TYPES

An important part of supporting multiple protocols in a NetWare internetwork, is understanding the various MLID frame types and when and why you would use them.

As mentioned earlier, protocols that reside at the data-link layer of the seven-layer OSI model place network data into frames and send those frames across the network. Data-link layer frames are used to determine which station the data was indented for, who sent the data, and which network protocol used. They also provide some error checking, normally through the use of some type of cyclic redundancy check (CRC).

In a NetWare environment, the frame type that you use is configured at the time you load the MLID. NetWare supports many different MLID frame types. The network type and the protocols being used will determine the frame type needed. A NetWare 4.1 file server supports multiple frame types simultaneously however, in order for devices on the network to communicate, they must have the same frame type.

Table 40.3 provides a summary of the common frame types used in a NetWare 4.1 environment.

TABLE 40.3. SUMMARY OF FRAME TYPES.

Network Type	Frame Type	Protocol
Ethernet	Ethernet II	IPX, TCP/IP
	802.2	IPX, TCP/IP
	802.3 (Raw)	IPX
	SNAP	AppleTalk
Token ring	token ring	IPX
SNAP	AppleTalk,	TCP/IP
ARCnet	Novell_RX-NET	IPX, TCP/IP, AppleTalk

ETHERNET FRAME FORMATS

The Ethernet standard was originally introduced in the 1970s by Digital, Intel, and Xerox. At that time, the Ethernet II frame type was introduced. Later, the Institute for Electrical and Electronic Engineers (IEEE) established the "802" committee, whose purpose was to standardize local area networks. The 802 committee took the original Ethernet specification and developed it even further, adding the 802.*x* frame types and the SNAP frame type. Unfortunately, because the Ethernet specification has changed so much through out the years, the various Ethernet frame types are not compatible. In other words, a workstation using an Ethernet II frame type could not communicate with a file server that only supported Ethernet 802.3 frames.

The Ethernet II frame type is the original specification developed by Digital, Intel, and Xerox (DIX). Even though Ethernet has developed considerably since its introduction, this frame format is still very widely-used.

The Ethernet II frame contains a destination address, and a source address followed by a *type* field. The type field describes the protocol type carried in the frame. Following the type field is the IPX data and a cyclic redundancy check (CRC). The CRC performs error checking to ensure the data is received successfully. This frame is commonly used in a NetWare environment to support the TCP/IP protocol stack. It can also be used to for the IPX/SPX protocol stack.

The ODI designation for the Ethernet II frame is ETHERNET_II. The first revision of the Ethernet standard by the IEEE rendered the 802.3 *Standard* frame type. This frame format was developed to comply with the OSI standards established to provide interoperability between dissimilar systems.

The main difference between the Ethernet II and the IEEE 802.3 frame is that the IEEE frame has a length field following the source address. The Ethernet II frame uses this field to identify the protocol type. The IEEE 802.3 frame uses this field to identify the length of the data contained in the frame.

Oddly enough, the ODI designation for this frame format is Ethernet_802.2, not 802.3. The reason for this is IEEE frame uses the Logical Link Control (LLC) area to identify the protocol being carried in the frame. LLC was defined by the IEEE 802.2 committee (hence, Ethernet_802.2). This frame was designed to allow multiple protocols to share the same link layer device. Because of this, the Ethernet_802.2 frame should be used whenever possible.

The IEEE 802.3 *Raw* frame format is an implementation of the standard 802.3 frame without the LLC information. Without LLC, the 802.3 Raw frame can only carry a single network layer protocol. This frame format has traditionally been used in NetWare environments that supported IPX only. The ODI designation for this frame is Ethernet_802.3.

In the past, ETHERNET_802.3 and has been the default frame type used in NetWare. However, with the continued support of multiple protocols, NetWare 4.1 now uses ETHERNET_802.2 as the default frame format.

40

The Subnet Access Protocol(SNAP) was developed to provide a migration path from Ethernet II to IEEE 802.3 (standard format). Products that use protocols designed to work with the older Ethernet II frame formats can use the IEEE 802.3 SNAP frame types to transmit data on a multi-protocol network. Eventually, all Network Layer implementations will be updated to support the IEEE 802.3 frame format and the SNAP frame format will be phased out.

In a NetWare environment, the IEEE 802.3 SNAP frame format is used to support the AppleTalk protocol stack. Its ODI designation is ETHERNET_SNAP.

Token ring in a NetWare environment uses two basic frame formats: the standard token ring frame and a token ring SNAP frame.

The standard token ring frame was designed to use LLC, so it has the capability to simultaneously support multiple protocols (see Figure 40.9). However, as with Ethernet, some older network layer protocols do not yet support LLC, so the token ring SNAP frame is used.

Figure 40.9.
The token ring
frame format.

Start Delimiter	Access Control	Frame Check	Destination Address	Source Address	LLC (SNAP)	Data	FCS	End-Delimiter	Frame Status

In a NetWare environment, the ODI designator for the token ring frame is TOKEN-RING. This frame is used for support of the IPX protocol stack. The ODI designator for token ring SNAP is TOKEN_SNAP. TOKEN_SNAP is used to support TCP/IP and AppleTalk.

ROUTING NETWARE'S NATIVE PROTOCOLS

As indicated earlier in this chapter, an organizations internetwork will evolve around user and workgroup needs. These needs determine whether multiple protocols are used. If UNIX stations are used, TCP/IP will be required on the internetwork. If Macintoshes are used, AppleTalk protocols will be required. If the network supports just DOS and Windows workstations (which many do!), NetWare's native protocols will be used. Each of these protocols use a different mechanism to route data on the network. This section focuses on how NetWare's native protocols route data in an internetwork. In order to better understand how this process works, a discussion of the NetWare protocols involved in network communication is necessary.

Each NetWare file server uses a set of proprietary communication protocols to handle client requests and transport data across the network. These protocols ensure that data is successfully transmitted between network nodes in a fast, efficient manner. These protocols are illustrated in Figure 40.10.

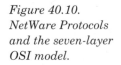

Figure 40.10.
NetWare Protocols
and the seven-layer
OSI model.

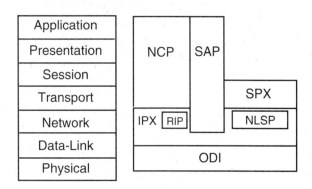

Application	NCP · SAP
Presentation	
Session	SPX
Transport	
Network	IPX · RIP · NLSP
Data-Link	ODI
Physical	

INTERNETWORK PACKET EXCHANGE (IPX)

IPX is a fast, simple protocol that provides the actual transport of data across the network. It provides an interface between the various network media type (Ethernet, token ring, and so on) and the NetWare operating system. When a request for sending data is made, IPX interacts with the MLID LAN driver to place the data into frames and then sends them over the network wire.

IPX packets include a source network and node address, as well as a destination network, node address, and a Cyclic Redundancy Check (CRC). This ensures that data is delivered to the proper destination on the network with near 100 percent accuracy.

IPX, however, is a *connectionless* protocol, which means that it will not wait for an acknowledgment from the destination device that a packet was received successfully before sending additional packets. This "best effort" delivery mechanism allows IPX to be very fast.

SEQUENCED PACKET EXCHANGE (SPX)

SPX is NetWare communication protocol that provides reliable delivery of data. SPX uses IPX to send and receive data. It is a *connection-oriented* protocol, which means that it verifies and acknowledges successful delivery of every packet sent.

This type of verification provides a more reliable delivery mechanism than IPX alone but it does so at the expense of performance. Because of this, SPX is generally used only for applications that require extra reliability. Examples of NetWare processes that use SPX for guaranteed delivery include RCONSOLE and the NetWare Print Server. Some third-party applications also use SPX to guarantee packet delivery.

NETWARE CORE PROTOCOLS (NCP)

NCP allows a NetWare server to provide distributed file and print services on the network. When a workstation requests any type of service on the network (file, print, and so on), NCP is the protocol that allows the server to accept and respond to those requests. Like other NetWare protocols, NCP is tightly integrated with IPX.

ROUTING INFORMATION PROTOCOL (RIP)

In order to get packets to the proper destination on the network, NetWare file servers have traditionally used the RIP protocol to determine the route to send packets along using IPX as a transport mechanism. In NetWare 4.1, a new protocol called *NetWare Link Services Protocol* (NLSP) was introduced as an option to RIP. NLSP is discussed later in this section.

RIP is what is known as a *distance vector* routing protocol. In a distance vector routing environment, each file server maintains a *routing information table* that allows the file server to track other file servers and routers on the network. This table contains the location of each server and the distance measured in terms of *hops* and *ticks*. A hop is the number of routers a packet must pass through in order to reach a network. A tick measures the amount of time a packet takes to reach a network. Each tick is approximately 1/18th of a second. Through this information, a NetWare file can determine the best route possible to send data.

The routing information table is built through the use of RIP broadcasts. Every NetWare server (or router) will send out its routing information to its adjacent (directly attached) routers every 60 seconds. As a router receives the RIP broadcasts, it updates its routing tables with the new information. When a new server comes up, it will automatically request information from all the other servers to build its routing table. In addition, it will also send out the routing information about itself. Conversely, if a server is taken down, it will notify the other server and routers on the network so that they can update their tables. Figure 40.11 shows an example of how RIP routing tables are built. Notice that each router builds its table based on information from adjacent routers only. In other words, each router has a very limited view of the network.

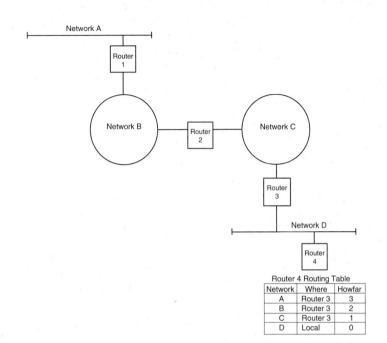

Figure 40.11.
Routers in a RIP
environment rely on
their neighbors for
routing information.

Router 4 Routing Table

Network	Where	Howfar
A	Router 3	3
B	Router 3	2
C	Router 3	1
D	Local	0

SERVICE ADVERTISING PROTOCOL (SAP)

Similar to RIP, SAP also uses a distance-vector model. In order to advertise its services on the network, a service providing device has traditionally used the SAP protocol to broadcast its availability. Examples of service providing devices include file servers, print servers, NetWare Directory Services trees, and so on. In NetWare 4.1, NLSP can be used as an alternative to SAP.

SAP broadcasts are sent out in a manner similar to RIP broadcasts. Each file server will broadcast SAP information every 60 seconds. This information includes the server's name, the type of service it provides (file, print, and so on) and its network address. As file servers receive these SAP broadcasts, the information is stored in a Server Information Table. You can view this information using the NLIST SERVER / B command from a workstation or the DISPLAY SERVERS command at the file server console. Just like RIP, as servers are brought up or down on the network, SAP is used to send out the updated information. Also, like RIP, SAP uses IPX to send and receive packets.

NETWARE LINK SERVICES PROTOCOL (NLSP)

In NetWare 4.1 NLSP is a new routing and service advertising protocol for IPX that can be used in place of RIP and SAP. NLSP uses a *link-state* routing model as opposed to the distance vector model used by RIP and SAP. Link-state routing is often preferred in internetworks because it is more reliable and requires less . overhead.

As you just saw, in a RIP and SAP environment routers/file servers, rely on their neighbors for routing information. In order to be sure that every router has accurate routing information, frequent broadcasts are required. In an NLSP environment, each router builds routing and service tables based on information received from every other router on the network, not just its adjacent routers. Using this information, a map of the network is created (see Figure 40.12). Once this map is built, updates to it are only received when there has been a change in the network or every two hours, whichever comes first.

Figure 40.12.
NLSP routers build a
map of the entire
network based on
information received
from every other router
on the network.

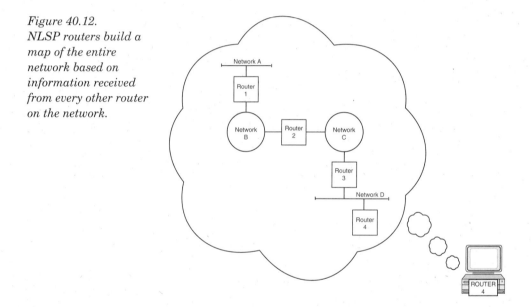

By sending out less frequent updates than RIP and SAP, NLSP has the capability to reduce routing and service advertising traffic on the network by a ratio of about 40:1. So, the bottom line is that NLSP allows more of your network bandwidth between routers to be used by user data. This can significantly increase performance on your network. In addition, NLSP provides the following features that aren't supported by RIP and SAP:

◆ Load Balancing
◆ Path Costing
◆ Hierarchical routing

Load balancing is something that is entirely new to NetWare. Using NLSP, a single file server can have two network cards attached to the same physical network segment. This provides two benefits. First, fault tolerance, if one card fails you still have a backup. Secondly, distribution of network traffic. In many instances, a single network card becomes a bottleneck in I/O intensive environments. Two network cards on the same segment relieve that bottleneck.

Path costing is another feature of NLSP not available with RIP. Each router in an NLSP environment can be assigned a *cost*. In the case of multiple routes to the same destination, routes with the lowest cost will be chosen. This allows for backup routes to be created that will only be used if the lower cost routes are not available. This is illustrated in Figure 40.13. The backup 56K link will only be used if one of the other routes is not available.

Figure 40.13.
NLSP allows path
costs to be set for
redundant routes on
an internetwork.

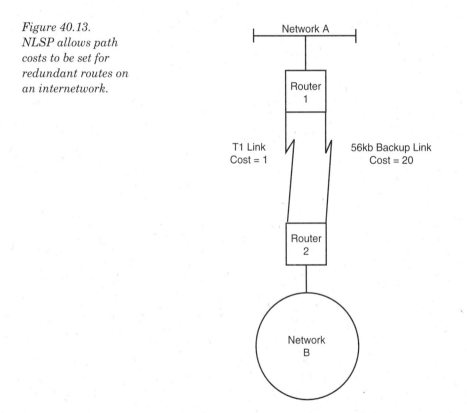

Lastly, NLSP has the capability to provide better scaleablity in large networks than RIP and SAP. Anyone who has dealt with RIP and SAP in a large environment knows that it is close to impossible to break a RIP network up into small pieces. The best solution is to set up filters, which often create administrative nightmares.

NLSP has the capability to use hierarchical addressing schemes that allow for multiple routing domains to be used. These domains are known as *routing levels*. Multiple routing levels allow large network to be broken up into smaller pieces minimizing traffic across routing domains. NLSP currently only supports a single routing level; however, future implementations will support multiple levels, as described previously.

In the past, IPX has not been considered as a goods solution for large internetworks and wide area networks. This was mostly because of the overhead (both RIP and SAP updates every 60 seconds) and other limitations. But, as you can see from the previous discussions, NLSP provides many improvements that enable IPX to be suitable for these environments. NLSP gives IPX the capability to compete in large environments where TCP/IP may have been considered the only solution.

By default, RIP and SAP are used as the default protocols for IPX. To enable NLSP, use the INETCFG utility, described later in this chapter. NLSP is fully backward-compatible with RIP and SAP and can be used simultaneously on the same internetwork.

INETCFG

NetWare 4.1 provides and internetworking configuration utility called *INETCFG*. INETCFG is an NLM that is loaded at the server console that enables you to configure your network cards, protocols, and other aspects of an internetwork. Figure 40.14 shows the INETCFG main menu.

Figure 40.14. INETCFG allows you to configure your NetWare 4.1 Internetwork.

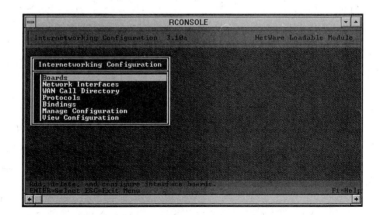

As you can see from the menu options, INETCFG allows you do much of what would normally be done through the AUTOEXEC.NCF file, such as load LAN drivers, bind protocols, and so on. In fact, when you load INETCFG for the first time, all the LOAD and BIND statements from your AUTOEXEC.NCF file are transferred to a file called NETINFO.CFG, located in the SYS:ETC directory.

Take a closer look at what is in INETCFG. The first menu option allows you to load network LAN drivers. By selecting Boards and pressing Enter, you can examine the existing LAN drivers loaded, load another by pressing Insert, or delete a loaded driver by pressing Delete(see Figure 40.15).

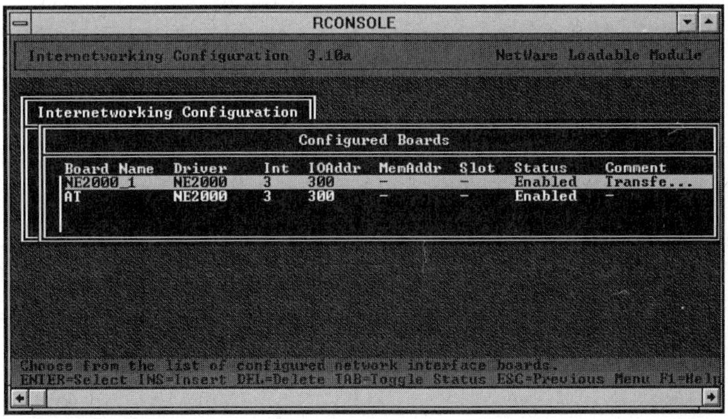

Figure 40.15.
Loading LAN drivers
through INETCFG.

The Network Interfaces option allows you to enable or disable a loaded LAN driver (see Figure 40.16).

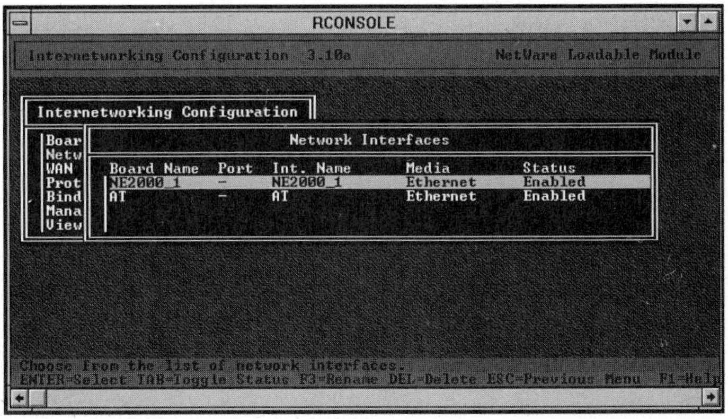

Figure 40.16.
Use this option to
enable or disable a
loaded LAN driver.

The next option is the WAN Call Directory option. This option is only available if you have installed the Novell Multi-Protocol Router add-on product. It is used to set up call locations for on-demand PPP, X.25, or Frame Relay Links.

The Protocols option enables you to configure available protocols, such as IPX, AppleTalk, and TCP/IP. This option is used to configure the IPX protocol stack to used NLSP rather than RIP and SAP.

Figure 40.17 shows the Bindings option of INETCFG. This option enables you to bind network communication protocols to your LAN cards: for example, to bind IPX to NE2000 just as you would normally in an AUTOEXEC.NCF file. The advantage to INETCFG is that you are not required to know the proper syntax; it is built into the statements for you.

Figure 40.17.
INETCFG allows you
to bind communication
protocols to your
network interfaces
without having to know
the proper syntax.

Under Manage Configuration, you will find an option that allows you to configure SNMP parameters that enable SNMP monitoring of network protocols. NetWare 4.1 provides standard Management Information Bases (MIBs) for IPX, RIP/SAP, and NLSP, allowing monitoring of those protocols through a management console called IPXCON, or any other SNMP management console. Standard SNMP monitoring also is available for AppleTalk and TCP/IP. Also under this menu option, you have the capability to configure remote access to this server through RCONSOLE. Access can either be set locally using SPX or asynchronously.

The final INETCFG option enables you to view your INETCFG configuration. This can either be done in pieces, just protocol bind commands, or in summary as shown in Figure 40.17. As mentioned previously, these commands are stored in a text file called NETINFO.CFG in the SYS:ETC directory.

CONFIGURING IPX TO USE RIP/SAP OR NLSP

From the INETCFG main menu, the Protocols option enables you to configure available protocols, such as AppleTalk, TCP/IP, or IPX.

Take a look at how to configure the IPX protocol stack to use RIP and SAP or NLSP. By selecting Protocols, and then IPX, the IPX Protocol configuration screen appears (see Figure 40.18).

When you see this screen for the first time, the Advanced IPX option is disabled. This indicates that RIP and SAP will be used for routing and that other advanced options, such as RIP and SAP filtering, will not be available.

To enable NLSP, highlight the Routing protocol option and press Enter. Your routing protocol choices will then be displayed (see Figure 40.19).

To enable NLSP on your network, select NLSP with RIP/SAP Compatibility. This enables the NLSP routing protocol with backward compatibility with RIP and SAP. None of the changes are made immediately. Once you exit the INETCFG utility and save your changes, you will need to down the server to activate the changes or use the REINITIALIZE SYSTEM command at the file server console. This activates the changes without having to bring down the server.

HOST CONNECTIVITY

Many internetworks not only connect multiple NetWare file servers, they also connect NetWare to various host systems, including IBM mainframes, AS/400 minicomputers, and UNIX systems. In order to achieve this connectivity, add-on products are available from Novell. These products include NetWare for SAA and UNIX NFS Services. For a detailed discussion about these products, refer to Chapter 4.

NETWARE/IP

From NetWare's conception, Novell has been committed to an *open-systems* platform. Many organizations have existing standards and protocols in place that they want to continue to use. One example of this is the TCP/IP protocol suite. TCP/IP has been mandated in many organizations, including government, educational institutions, and large enterprise networks. Recognizing this fact, Novell began including NetWare/IP as an optional add-on to NetWare 4.1. Unlike the other add-on products discussed, NetWare/IP is provided free of charge.

NetWare/IP allows organizations to use TCP/IP as the transport for NetWare protocols as opposed to IPX. This allows NetWare networks to be run only on TCP/IP or on a combination of TCP/IP and IPX.

When you receive NetWare 4.1, the box will contain a coupon for NetWare/IP. By returning this coupon, Novell will send you NetWare/IP free of charge.

SUMMARY

NetWare 4.1 was designed to support not only small- and medium-sized networks but large enterprise networks as well. An internetwork is a number of individual networks connected by devices known as routers. NetWare 4.1 has routing capability built in to the operating system, allowing you to connect different network types, such as Ethernet and token ring, as well as route multiple protocols like IPX/SPX, AppleTalk, and TCP/IP. The INETCFG utility is provided to help you configure your internetwork.

For connectivity to IBM mainframes, AS/400 minicomputers, and UNIX environments, Novell provides a number of add-on products to enable you to transparently connect NetWare 4.1 to those environments.

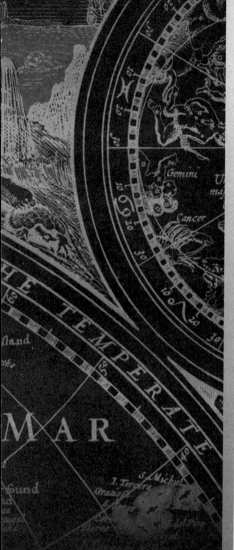

- Expanding Existing Servers

- Adding Additional Hard Drives to Your Server

- Adding Memory to Your File Server

- Adding a Network Card to Your Server

- Adding Name Space Support

- Adding Additional File Servers

- Adding a Server to the NDS Tree

- Summary

CHAPTER 41

Expand Your NetWare Installation

In the previous chapter, Chapter 40, on Internetworking, you learned how NetWare 4.1 servers connect to each other and other dissimilar systems creating internetworks. These internetworks grow as individual user and workgroup's needs grow. NetWare 4.1 was designed to grow with your organization's needs supporting networks of all sizes.

In this chapter you will take a look at how NetWare 4.1 installations can be easily expanded in the following areas:

- ◆ Expanding individual servers
- ◆ Adding a LAN segment to a server
- ◆ Adding support for additional file formats
- ◆ Adding servers to your network
- ◆ Adding servers to your NDS tree

EXPANDING EXISTING SERVERS

The NetWare 4.1 operating system is modular in design, allowing you to expand your file server at any time. The core operating system is loaded first and then other modules known as *NetWare Loadable* (NLMs) modules can be added to customize your file server.

The main benefit to this design is that your NetWare installation can be modified and expanded on-the-fly, without having to take down the server. This is done by simply loading or unloading service-providing modules.

The main component of the NetWare 4.1 operating system is SERVER.EXE. When loaded, this file loads the main core operating system into your server's memory. This is the portion of NetWare that provides basic network services, such as file services and security. NLMs provide additional services on the network, such as Directory Services, printing, backups, databases, network drivers, and network management.

NETWARE LOADABLE MODULES (NLMS)

NLMs generally fall into four categories, each adding different services to your network. Many NLMs are provided by Novell; however, a wide variety are available from third parties as well. Table 41.1 summarizes the various NLM types.

TABLE 41.1. NLM SUMMARY.

NLM Type	Extension	Description
LAN Driver	*.LAN	Provides an interface between NetWare and the network interface cards in your server.
Disk Driver	*.DSK	Provides an interface between NetWare and the disk controllers in your server.
Name Space Modules	*.NAM	Allows support for non-DOS file formats on NetWare volumes. Examples include OS/2, Macintosh, and UNIX.
NLM Utilities	*.NLM	Provides additional services on the network, such as NDS, printing, databases, and so on. Also provides management utilities, such as MONITOR and IPXCON.

Tip

If you also have Windows/NT servers on your network, you can use the OS/2 name space support on NetWare for storing Windows/NT files.

The modular design of NetWare 4.1 provides many benefits, one being the fact that any NLM can be loaded or unloaded on-the-fly. NLMs also allow you to conserve file server resources. You only load the NLMs you need, and when you're finished with an NLM, it can be unloaded, freeing the memory for other processes.

NLMs are loaded by using the LOAD command at the file server console, as in the following:

```
LOAD MONITOR
```

Similarly, NLMs are unloaded using the UNLOAD command:

```
UNLOAD MONITOR
```

ADDING ADDITIONAL HARD DRIVES TO YOUR SERVER

Another advantage of the modular design of the NetWare 4.1 operating system is the capability to easily add additional hard drives to your network. After a new hard drive is installed in your server, you can configure NetWare to recognize it by using the INSTALL NLM. When you load INSTALL, the menu shown in Figure 41.1 will appear.

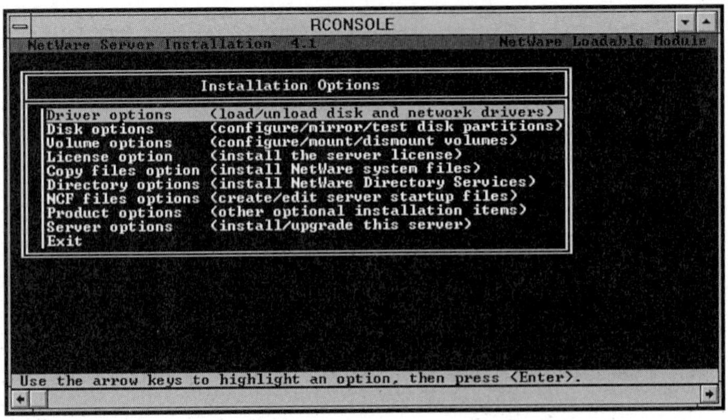

Figure 41.1.
The INSTALL
main menu.

The first step in adding a new hard drive to your file server is to load the appropriate disk driver, if necessary. If your new drive shares a disk controller with an existing drive, it won't be necessary to load another disk driver. If you have installed a new disk controller with your new drive, you will need to load a driver to allow that controller to communicate with NetWare.

Loading the driver can be done from the server command line, or can be done using the INSTALL NLM. Following is an example of loading a disk driver from the command line:

```
LOAD IDE
```

You will be prompted to enter the appropriate hardware parameters for your controller, such as the interrupt and I/O port used. To load a new driver through INSTALL, select Driver options from the main menu. The Driver options menu will appear (see Figure 41.2).

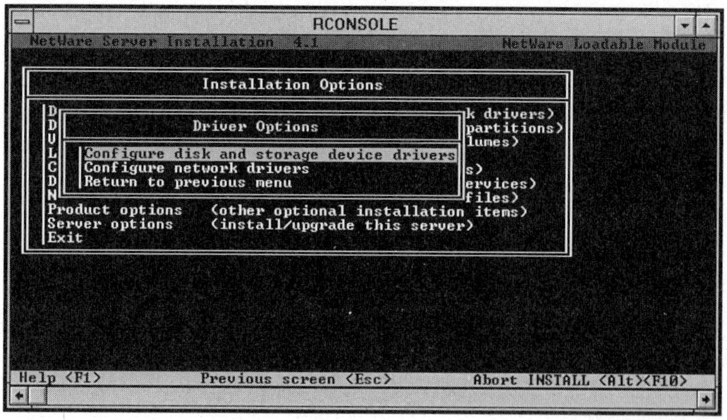

Figure 41.2.
Driver options allows
an additional disk
driver to be loaded.

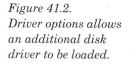

To load a disk driver, select Configure disk and storage device drivers. Using the Select additional driver option, you can load the required driver. NetWare 4.1 provides drivers for many different disk controllers; however, if the driver for the controller you are using is not shown on the list, you will need to load it from a floppy disk. This is done simply by placing the diskette that contains the driver in drive A: and pressing Insert. If you do not have the driver on floppy disk, you may need to contact the manufacturer of your drive controller.

After the disk driver is loaded, you will need to create a NetWare partition on your new drive. This is done by choosing Disk options from the INSTALL main menu. Figure 41.3 shows the Disk options menu.

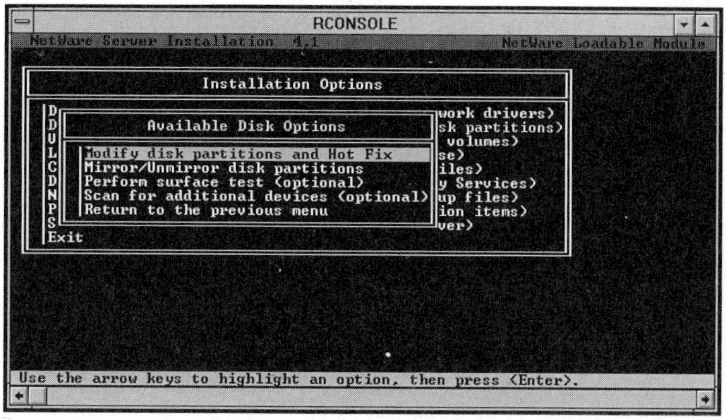

Figure 41.3.
The Disk options menu
allows you to create a
NetWare partition on a
newly installed drive.

To create a NetWare partition, select Modify disk partitions and Hot Fix. A list of your existing partitions will be displayed. You should also see "free space," as shown in Figure 41.4. By selecting Create NetWare disk partition, you can create all or a portion of the free space available as a NetWare partition. If no free space is shown, check to see that your disk driver loaded properly.

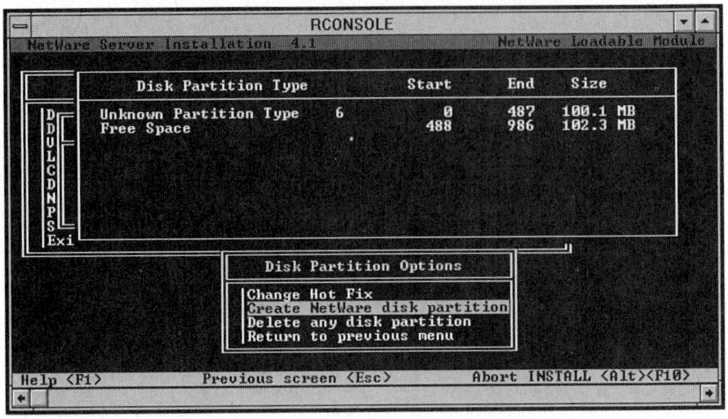

Figure 41.4.
Selecting Create
NetWare disk partition
allows the free space to
be created as a
NetWare partition.

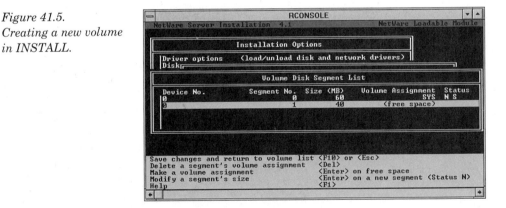

Once the NetWare partition has been created, you are ready to create a volume. NetWare 4.1 allows additional volumes to be created or existing volumes to be expanded on-the-fly. Volumes can span up to 32 physical disk drives. To add a new volume or expand an existing volume, select Volume options from the INSTALL main menu. Your existing volumes will be displayed along with free space that represents the NetWare partition you just created as in Figure 41.5.

Figure 41.5.
Creating a new volume
in INSTALL.

The menu bar at the bottom of the screen indicates that various function keys will allow you to add, view, or modify volume segments. When you press Insert, the screen shown in Figure 41.6 appears. This is where you can choose to either add this new disk drive to your existing partition or to create a new volume.

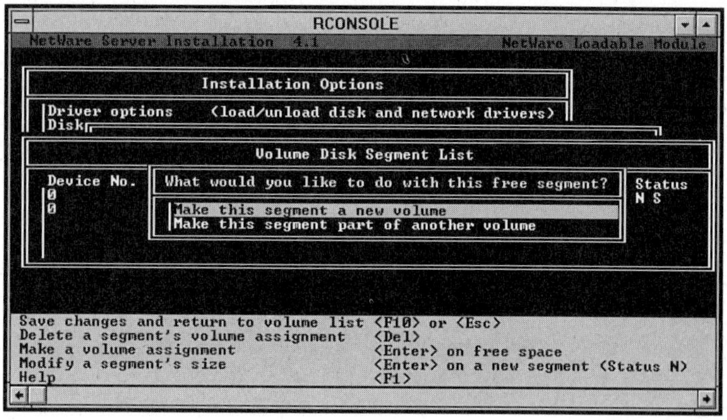

Figure 41.6.
Free disk space can
be either created as a
new volume or used
to expand an existing
volume.

When you have finished creating your volumes, you can press the Esc key to save the volume changes. You also will be given the opportunity to mount any dismounted volumes at this time. Volumes must be mounted in order to be accessed by network users. If you do not want to mount the volume at this time, you can later mount it from the console by typing the following command:

MOUNT *VOLUME_NAME*

or,

MOUNT ALL

When you finish creating your new volume, you will need to update the STARTUP.NCF file so that the new disk driver will be loaded each time you bring up the file server up. You can modify the STARTUP.NCF file by choosing .NCF files options from the INSTALL main menu. You then can choose Create STARTUP.NCF file. Two files are displayed: the original file and the new file, which should already contain the appropriate lines to load the new disk driver.

As you can see, adding additional disk space to your existing server is very easy. You can continue to add disk space as necessary. NetWare 4.1 can support up to 32 terabytes (TB) of disk space per file server. However, hardware limitations of your file server will most likely be reached before the theoretical maximum.

ADDING MEMORY TO YOUR FILE SERVER

Adding memory to your file server is just as easy as adding disk space. A NetWare 4.1 file server will support up to 4G of memory. By installing memory in your file server and bringing the server back up, NetWare will automatically recognize the new memory installed in EISA or microchannel machines. For ISA bus machines, NetWare will automatically recognize memory up to 16MB. If you have installed more than 16MB, you will need to use the REGISTER MEMORY command in order for NetWare to recognize the rest. The syntax for REGISTER MEMORY is as follows:

```
REGISTER MEMORY start_address length
```

For example,

```
REGISTER MEMORY 1000000 1250000
```

Slow performance is a good indication that your file server is low on memory. If you suspect that you need to add memory, load the MONITOR NLM and check the Cache Buffers statistic from the MONITOR main menu. If you see that the Total Cache Buffers statistic is less than 50 percent of the Original Cache Buffers, you should consider adding memory to your server. As an interim solution, be sure to unload any unnecessary NLMs.

Adding a Network Card to Your Server

By adding a network card to your server, you effectively are adding a segment to your network. Each NetWare 4.1 file server supports up to sixteen network interface cards. However, for performance and other reasons, most servers will contain no more than three or four network cards.

As you've probably already noticed, you can often accomplish a single task in NetWare in more than one way. Configuring your file server to recognize a newly installed network card is another example. Following are three ways to configure a newly installed network card:

◆ Using the INSTALL.NLM
◆ Using the INETCFG.NLM
◆ From the file server command line

Before getting into each method, there are a few background items that need to be covered.

Specifying a Frame Type

An MLID frame type must be specified at both the file server and at the workstation. The previous chapter (Chapter 40) on internetworking explains in detail the MLID frame types available with NetWare 4.1 and tells you when and why you should use each frame.

In order for a workstation and a file server to communicate on the same network segment, they must use the same frame type. In each case, the frame type is specified when you load the MLID LAN driver. If you do not specify a frame type at load time, the default frame type will be used. In NetWare 4.1, the default frame type for Ethernet is ETHERNET_802.2; for token ring the default frame type is TOKEN-RING.

At the file server, loading a LAN driver by specifying the frame type is done through the AUTOEXEC.NCF file, the NETINFO.CFG file, or from the console command line. Whichever method you choose, the command will look similar to the following:

```
LOAD NE2000 INT=3 PORT=300 FRAME=ETHERNET_802.2
```

In this example, the NE2000 network card is supporting workstations using an ETHERNET_802.2 frame only. If this network card is supporting both IPX and Macintosh clients, for example, the LAN driver can be loaded *re-entrantly* to provide support for the second frame type. Following is an example:

```
LOAD NE2000 INT=3 PORT=300 FRAME=ETHERNET_802.2 NAME=IPXNET
LOAD NE2000 INT=3 PORT=300 FRAME=ETHERNET_SNAP NAME=ATLK
```

Notice in this example that a NAME= parameter is used when the LAN drivers are loaded. This parameter makes it easier to bind multiple communication protocols to the same network card. If these commands are being loaded through an automated file such as AUTOEXEC.NCF or NETINFO.CFG, naming each board allows the bind to take place automatically. Without naming the boards, you will be prompted to specify which frame type should be bound to which protocol.

Following is an example of binding using board names:

```
BIND IPX TO IPXNET NET=12DE35F
BIND APPLETLK TO ATLK NET=10-10 ZONE={"MKTG"}
```

In order for a workstation to communicate with a particular file server, the workstation must be configured to use a frame type that the file server uses. Following is the configuration done through the NET.CFG file:

```
LINK DRIVER NE2000
  INT 3
  PORT 300
  FRAME ETHERNET_802.2
```

NETWORK ADDRESS CONSIDERATIONS

Any time you have more than one file server, you will need to properly coordinate the network addresses of those servers. Conflicting or incorrect network addresses can cause serious communication problems on your network.

NetWare 4.1 file servers are assigned two different types of software-configured network addresses:

◆ Internal IPX addresses
◆ IPX network addresses

In addition to the software addresses just listed, each node on the network (workstations and file servers) has a *hardware address* that is hard-coded on the network interface card itself. These hardware addresses are referred to as *node IDs* and must be unique across the entire network.

INTERNAL IPX ADDRESS

The internal IPX address is an address that is internal to the file server itself. It is a hexadecimal number, one to eight characters long, that is normally assigned at the time your 4.1 server is installed. If you want to view or change your server's internal IPX address, you can do this through the AUTOEXEC.NCF file. This file can be accessed by loading the INSTALL.NLM. Figure 41.7 shows an example of an internal IPX address in the AUTOEXEC.NCF.

Figure 41.7.
The Internal IPX
address in the
AUTOEXEC.NCF.

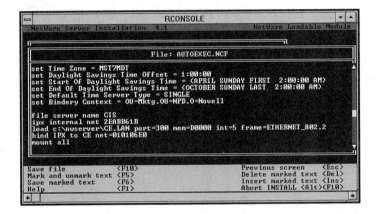

If you change your server's internal IPX address in the AUTOEXEC.NCF file, the new address will not take effect until you down the server and restart it with the new file. Also, be aware this address is used to uniquely identify each file server in your NDS tree. In large networks, a change of address may take a while to propagate throughout the entire tree.

Another method of viewing your server's internal IPX address is through the use of the CONFIG file server console command. When you type CONFIG, the information similar to what is shown in Figure 41.8 will be displayed.

Because the internal IPX address is internal to each file server, it must be unique across all file servers on the entire network. This includes common backbone multi-server networks, as well as internetworks.

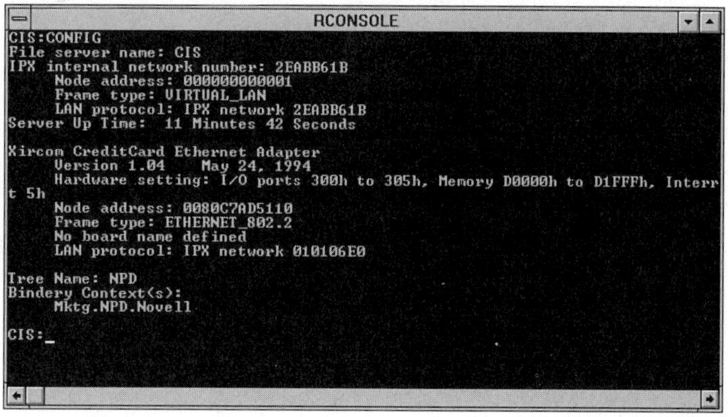

Figure 41.8.
You can use the CONFIG
console command to
view the Internal IPX
address.

```
┌──┐                          RCONSOLE                        ▼ ▲
CIS:CONFIG
File server name: CIS
IPX internal network number: 2EABB61B
    Node address: 000000000001
    Frame type: VIRTUAL_LAN
    LAN protocol: IPX network 2EABB61B
Server Up Time:  11 Minutes 42 Seconds

Xircom CreditCard Ethernet Adapter
    Version 1.04    May 24, 1994
    Hardware setting: I/O ports 300h to 305h, Memory D0000h to D1FFFh, Interr
t 5h
    Node address: 0080C7AD5110
    Frame type: ETHERNET_802.2
    No board name defined
    LAN protocol: IPX network 010106E0

Tree Name: NPD
Bindery Context(s):
    Mktg.NPD.Novell

CIS:_
←                                                                          →
```

If two servers have the same internal IPX address, sporadic and unpredictable network connection problems will occur. Often, these conflicts are very difficult to troubleshoot, especially in large internetworks. Because of this, it is a good idea to keep an accurate record of previously assigned addresses to prevent conflict when a new server comes online.

IPX NETWORK ADDRESS

The IPX network address is an address that defines a physical network segment. In a multi-server environment where all of the servers share a common backbone, each server has the same IPX network number.

In the case of an internetwork, each physical network segment that is connected through a router is considered to be a separate IPX network, and each physical network will have a different IPX network address.

Tip

To remember IPX network addressing rules, use the following expression:

Common cable, common address. Different cable, different address.

In other words, if two file servers are on the *same* physical network segment, they will have the *same* IPX network address. If they are on *different* network segments, they will have *different* addresses.

IPX network addresses are assigned when the IPX protocol is bound to a specific LAN driver. So, because NetWare file servers can have multiple network interface cards installed (creating an internal router), they also can have multiple IPX network addresses. In this case, each network interface card would create a separate network segment (different cable), so each card would be assigned a different address.

Note

The only exception to the rule of using different IPX address for a different NIC as just mentioned, is if you are using the load balancing feature of NLSP. Then, you may have more than one network interface card attached to the same physical segment, sharing the same IPX network address.

If you want to view or change an IPX network address, you can do this through the AUTOEXEC.NCF file or in the NETINFO.CFG File. Figure 41.9 shows the IPX network address in AUTOEXEC.NCF

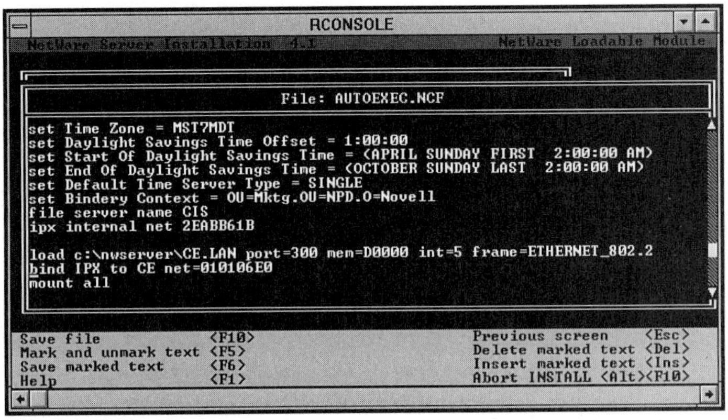

Figure 41.9.
The IPX network address in AUTOEXEC.NCF.

Another method of viewing an IPX network address is through the use of the CONFIG file server console command. When you type CONFIG, the information similar to that shown in figure 41.10 will be displayed.

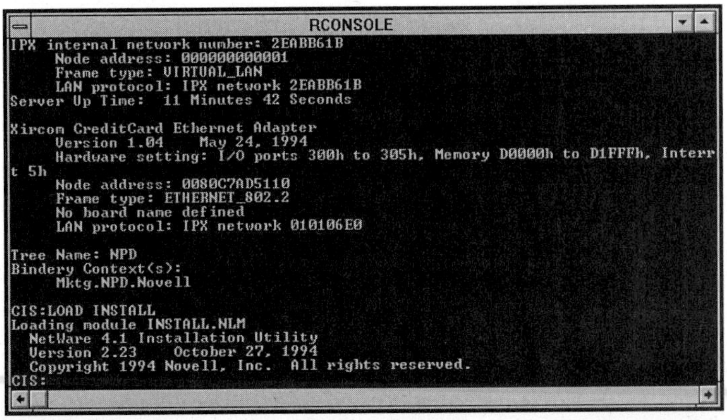

Figure 41.10.
The IPX network address can be viewed using the CONFIG command at the server console.

IPX NETWORK ADDRESS CONFLICTS

If you specify an incorrect IPX network address when you bind a LAN driver to the IPX network protocol, you will see a message similar to the following at each file server in the network segment.

```
1/11/95 6:40:48 pm: 1.1.112 Router configuration error detected
Router at node 00000C01E33A claims network 00000ADF should be 020207F1
```

This message will continue to be displayed at each file server (along with an irritating beep) until the problem is corrected. During this time, network communication will not occur on the server with the conflicting address.

To solve the problem, unbind the IPX protocol from the LAN card with the incorrect address. This is done by typing the following at the file server console:

UNBIND IPX *lan_driver name*

Then, bind IPX again using the proper network address, such as in the following:

BIND IPX *lan_driver* name **NET=ipx network number**

As with the internal IPX address, it is important to keep a record of which IPX network numbers have been assigned to various network segments. This will make it easier to add a new file server to your existing network.

ADDING A NETWORK CARD USING INSTALL.NLM

To configure the operating system to recognize a newly installed network card using the INSTALL.NLM, choose Driver Options from the main menu, as shown in Figure 41.11. Then select Configure network drivers, as shown in Figure 41.12. From the Driver Options menu, choose Configure network drivers.

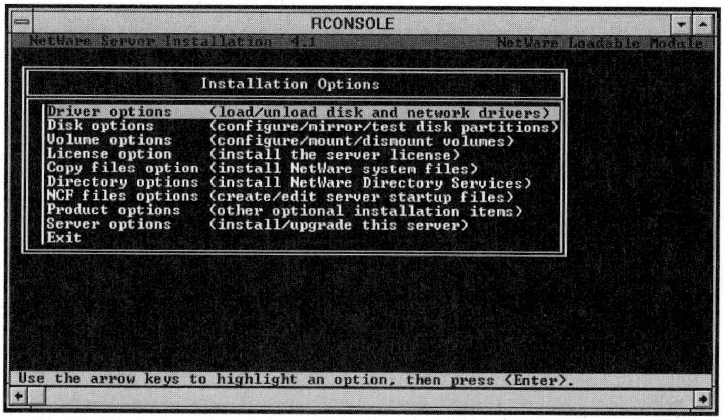

Figure 41.11.
INSTALL main menu.

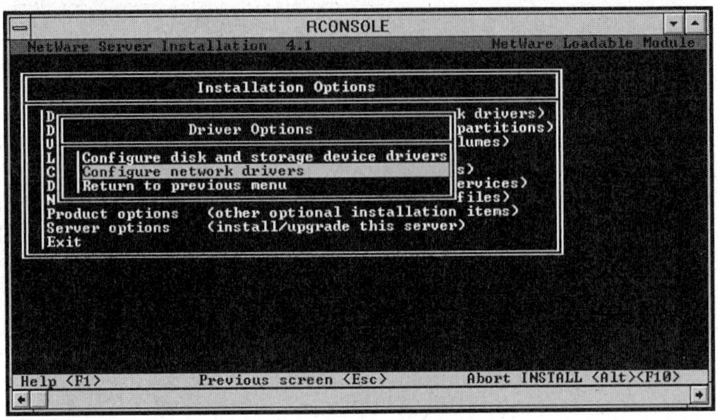

Figure 41.12.
To load an additional
LAN driver, select
Configure Network
Drivers.

You will then be presented with a list of currently loaded LAN drivers. In order for NetWare to recognize the newly installed network card, you must load the appropriate LAN driver. To load a new driver, choose Select an additional driver and choose the appropriate driver from the list. If the driver you require is not listed, you may have to load it from floppy disk or from the NetWare 4.1 Installation CD. You will also need to enter the appropriate configuration parameters this time.

After the driver has loaded successfully, you will then need to bind a communication protocol to that board. This will need to be done from the file server command line. Toggle to the server command line by press Alt+Esc. From the console, enter the BIND statement for the protocol you want to bind. For example, to bind IPX, you would type

```
BIND IPX NE2000 NET=CAFF
```

Finally, you will need to update the AUTOEXEC.NCF file so that the new driver will be loaded each time you bring up the file server. You can modify the AUTOEXEC.NCF file by choosing NCF files options from the INSTALL main menu. You can then choose Create AUTOEXEC.NCF file. Two AUTOEXEC.NCF files will appear. The original file and the new file which should already contain the appropriate lines to load the new LAN driver.

ADDING A NETWORK CARD USING INETCFG.NLM

The INETCFG utility is provided so that you can configure your NetWare 4.1 internetworking environment. Generally, you will not need to use this utility unless you will be configuring IPX to use advanced options, such as NLSP or filtering, or unless you will be configuring other protocols, such as AppleTalk or TCP/IP.

Figure 41.13 shows the INETCFG main menu.

Figure 41.13.
The INETCFG
main menu.

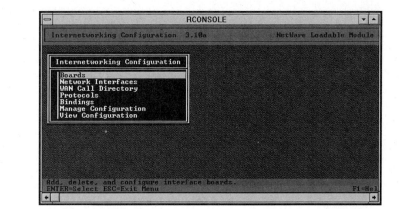

When you load the INETCFG utility for the first time, you will be prompted to transfer the LOAD and BIND commands from AUTOEXEC.NCF to this utility. When you do so, the commands will be placed in a file called NETINFO.CFG. To load a LAN driver for a newly installed network card, select Boards. A list of the currently loaded LAN drivers will appear. To load an additional driver press the Insert key. If the driver you require is not on the list, press the Insert key again and you can load the necessary driver either from the NetWare 4.1 Installation CD or from the floppy disk. You also will need to enter the board's hardware configuration at this time.

The next step is to configure your network protocols, if necessary. This is done by choosing the Protocols option from the main menu. You will only need to choose this option if you want to use a protocol other than IPX. Then you will need to enable the protocol you want. IPX is enabled by default, so for this example, you will move onto binding your protocol to the LAN driver. By selecting Bindings from the main menu, a list of your current binding will appear. To bind IPX to the new LAN card, press the Insert key, choose IPX as the protocol, and the LAN board that you configured earlier as the network interface. You will now need to specify the network number (remember the tip from the "IPX Network Address" section!) and the frame type.

When you finish, exit INETCFG. As you are exiting you, will receive a message indicating that changes made will not take effect immediately. To have the changes take effect, down the server and restart it or, type the following command at the server console:

`REINITIALIZE SYSTEM`

This command will run the NETINFO.CFG file, initializing the new network card you just configured.

ADDING NAME SPACE SUPPORT

NetWare 4.1 provides the capability for multiple desktops (DOS, OS/2, Macintosh, UNIX, and so on) to store files on a NetWare volume in their native format. This support is referred to as *name space support*. NetWare volumes by default support only the DOS file naming convention which is an 8-character filename with a 3-character extension. A Macintosh file can be up to 32 characters long, UNIX and OS/2 files can be up to 255 characters in length. In addition, each of these file formats support characters not supported by DOS, such as spaces and backslashes. To provide support for these additional naming conventions, the appropriate name space NLM must be loaded (name space NLMs have a .NAM extension) and the name space must be added to the volume. For example, to add a Macintosh name space to the volume SYS: you will need to type the following from the file server console:

```
LOAD MAC
```

This will load the Macintosh name space module. Then, add Macintosh name space support by typing

```
ADD NAME SPACE MAC TO SYS
```

Adding an OS/2 name space to a volume would be the same process, except that a different name space support module is loaded, as in the following example:

```
LOAD OS2
ADD NAME SPACE OS2 TO SYS
```

The ADD NAME SPACE command only needs to be issued once for every name space being added. However, the name space support module needs to be loaded through the STARTUP.NCF file every time the file server comes up. A volume with name space support added cannot be mounted unless the appropriate name space support module is loaded first. If you forget to include the name space support module in the STARTUP.NCF file, you can load it from the server console and then manually mount the volume. For example, to load the MAC.NAM module and mount the volume SYS manually, type the following:

```
LOAD MAC
MOUNT SYS
```

Then be sure to modify the STARTUP.NCF file to add the name space support module. You can do this using the NCF files option in the INSTALL NLM.

Adding name space support to a volume allows it to support all of the file-naming conventions of that operating system. It also creates directory entries in the directory entry table for each name space added to a volume. For example, a volume that has Macintosh and OS/2 name space added would have three directory entries for every file, as in the following:

- A DOS entry for the DOS name space (default)
- An OS/2 entry for the OS/2 name space
- A Macintosh entry for the Macintosh name space

DOS name space is the default on every volume and cannot be removed. If you are adding multiple name spaces to a volume, it is a good idea to add those name spaces at the time the volume is created. This will ensure that the all entries in the directory entry table for a particular file will be stored in the same area in the table. Adding name space to an existing volume with a number of files already created would create the possibility that the directory entries for a given file would be scattered all over the directory entry table. This would result in poor performance when retrieving that file.

Each file having a directory entry for every name space allows users to see the files stored on a volume (if they have appropriate rights), regardless of the desktop operating system that created the file. For example, a DOS user could see files created by Macintosh users and vice versa. But, because of the differences in file-naming conventions, NetWare must provide a translation of the file names (not data), depending on which type of client is viewing the file. For example, a Macintosh file saved as

```
Year End Reports
```

would be displayed to a DOS users as

```
YEARENDR
```

Notice that the characters not valid in the DOS naming convention (spaces) are removed and the file name is truncated to 8 characters to conform to the DOS 8.3 standard.

Multiple name space support on a NetWare 4.1 volume allows users of various desktop operating systems to store files on the same volume. It does not, however, provide translation of the data from one file format to another. In order for a Macintosh user and a DOS user to share the same file, for example, an application that provides file exchange between the two operating systems will have to be used. There are a number of software applications available today that provide the ability to transfer files between operating systems.

CALCULATING MEMORY REQUIREMENTS

Before adding support for additional name spaces to a volume, be sure that there is sufficient memory available to support the additional directory entries created by those name space modules. Novell provides a basic formula to help determine how much memory will be required to support volumes and their associated name spaces. The formula, as provided in the NetWare 4.1 product documentation, is as follows:

1. Calculate the memory required for each volume.

   For each DOS volume:

   ```
   M = .023 X Volume Size (in MB) / Block Size
   ```

   For each volume with name space added:

   ```
   M = .032 X Volume Size (in MB) / Block Size
   ```

2. Add the memory requirements for all volumes.

   ```
   Total Volume Memory = MSYS: + MVOL1: + MVOL2:...
   ```

3. Add 2MB for the operating system and round the figure to the next highest megabyte.

This formula provides a base memory amount to support volumes and name spaces. It does not compensate for additional memory that might be required to support NLMs and other server processes. Be sure to add those requirements to the total required memory calculated with this formula. A NetWare file server provides optimal performance when it has a large amount of memory available, so be sure to be generous when calculating memory requirements.

REMOVING NAME SPACE FROM A VOLUME

Once a name space has been added to a volume, it can only be removed by running VREPAIR NLM. If name spaced is removed using VREPAIR, all the data associated with that name space is no longer accessible.

Before VREPAIR can be run on a volume with name space added, support modules must be loaded first. V_MAC.NLM and V_OS2.NLM are examples of name space support modules for VREPAIR. These name space support modules require that VREPAIR is loaded before they can be loaded. To remove Macintosh name space from the volume SYS:, from the server console, follow these steps:

1. Load the following name space support module:

   ```
   LOAD V_OS2
   ```

2. Dismount the following volume:

   ```
   DISMOUNT SYS:
   ```

3. Load the VREPAIR NLM.

   ```
   LOAD VREPAIR
   ```

4. From the VREPAIR main menu, select the following:

   ```
   2. Set VREPAIR Options
   ```

5. From the Options menu, select the following:

   ```
   Remove Name Space Support from the volume
   ```

6. Select the name space you want to remove, as in the following:

   ```
   1. Macintosh
   ```

7. From the Options menu, select the following:

   ```
   5. Return to Main Menu
   ```

8. From the VREPAIR main menu, select the following:

   ```
   1. Repair a Volume
   ```

9. When VREPAIR pauses, press F1 and select the following:

   ```
   Do not pause after errors
   ```

ADDING ADDITIONAL FILE SERVERS

Organizations have multiple servers in their NetWare 4.1 network for many reasons. Some may have one or more servers per workgroup, some may have servers providing specialized application services, such as database or e-mail servers, and others may have a combination of both.

Determining when to have multiple servers can be a tricky process and, unfortunately, there is no single rule of thumb that can be used to determine when you need to add additional file servers. However, the following can be used as guidelines to help you determine when it might be necessary to add an additional server to your environment.

◆ User Licenses

The number of user licenses required is the most obvious reason for multiple file servers. The maximum user connections available per NetWare 4.1 file server is unlimited because you can install multiple licenses. However, the server hardware will pose a limit on how many users it can support (comfortably) concurrently.

◆ Workgroup-specific or highly sensitive data

In some cases, the types of network data stored on your network will warrant the addition of servers. For example, sensitive payroll information or other confidential information may be stored on separate servers for security purposes. Or, if various groups within an organization use department or workgroup specific applications and data, an individual server may be necessary for each group.

◆ Application servers

As mentioned previously, some servers may be dedicated to a specific application or type of application, such as database servers or e-mail servers. In environments where these types of applications are very I/O or processor-intensive, dedicating a server specifically to that application will provide better performance, not only for the specific applications, but also for the other servers as well.

◆ Server utilization

If you have continual high-server utilization, you may want to consider installing a second file server. The MONITOR NLM can be used to view server utilization. To load MONITOR, at your file server console type:

```
LOAD MONITOR
```

A screen similar to figure 41.14 will appear.

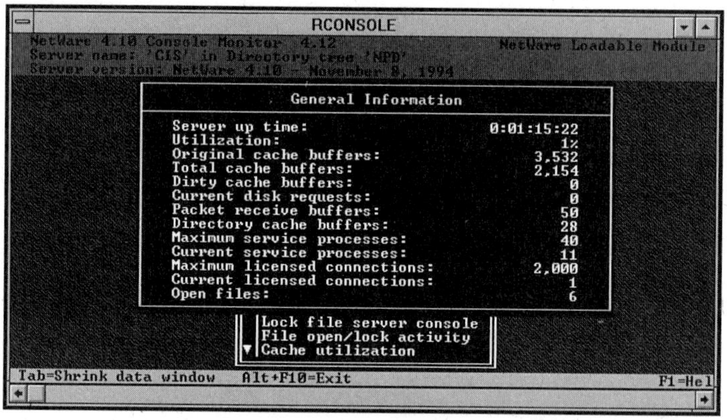

Figure 41.14.
Using MONITOR.NLM
to view server utiliza-
tion.

At the top portion of the screen, you will see statistics about this file server. Notice the Utilization statistic. If this number is greater than 80 percent on a continual basis, you should consider a second file server.

Note

High processor utilization may be caused by a malfunctioning NLM. Be sure to rule this possibility out before installing an additional server. You can do this by viewing which network resources are in use by NLMs. This is done by selecting the Resource Utilization option from the MONITOR main menu. Then, use the Processor Utilization option to determine which percentage of the total server utilization is in use by each process.

◆ Network interface card bottlenecks

Generally, if you are experiencing bottlenecks at the network interface card level, adding an additional LAN card to your existing server or replacing a 16-bit card with a 32-bit bus-mastering card will solve the problem. Under certain circumstances, however, adding an additional network card may not be possible or may not be the right solution. An example of this would be if you do not have any slots available in your existing server for an additional card. The MONITOR NLM or a network analyzer, such as Novell's LANalyzer for Windows, can be used to identify network throughput problems.

◆ Disk controller bottlenecks

Another possible bottleneck that may require an additional server is a disk channel or controller bottleneck. Disk channel bottlenecks often result in high processor utilization and slow file server response. As with network interface card bottlenecks, sometimes adding an additional or replacing the existing drive and controller with a more efficient combination will solve the problem. If it does not, an additional server may be necessary. The MONITOR NLM can be a useful tool to analyze disk channel statistics as well.

ADDING A SERVER TO THE NDS TREE

One of the main benefits of NetWare Directory Services (NDS) is global access to network resources, regardless of your physical location. One of the main network resources NDS provides access to is file servers and their associated volumes. If you are installing a new NetWare 4.1 server, in order for it to be part of this global network, it must be installed into the same NDS tree as the existing NetWare 4.1 file servers.

Installing a new server into the tree is done at the time NetWare 4.1 is installed on the new server. During the installation process, you will be prompted to install directory services. The first question asked will be if you want to install this server into an existing NDS tree. A list of existing NDS trees on your network will appear (see Figure 41.15).

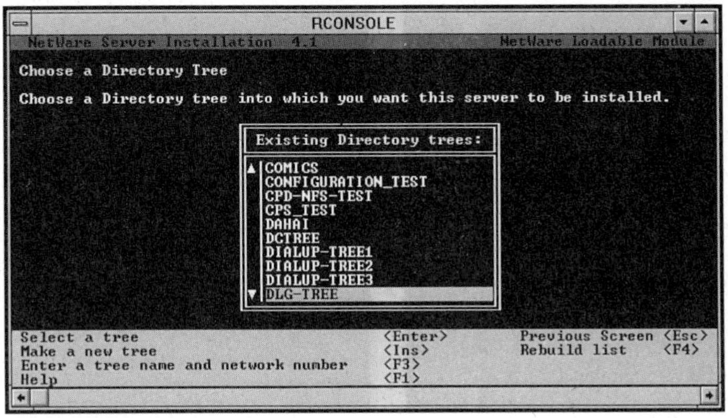

Figure 41.15.
Installing a new
NetWare 4.1 server into
an existing directory
tree.

Select the tree you want to install this server into by using the arrow keys and pressing Enter. If you choose to create a new tree at this time, users of the existing NDS tree will not be able to access resources on this file server easily because NDS users can only be logged into one NDS tree at any time.

Note

Users currently logged in to an NDS tree can access files on a file server outside of their tree through bindery services (or bindery emulation, as it is more commonly known). However, bindery emulation must be set on that file server and the user must have a valid user account to log in as.

When you select the tree to install this server into, you will be presented with a screen similar to Figure 41.16.

Figure 41.16.
Choosing the time
zone for the server.

This screen allows you to choose the time zone your file server is in. Choosing the correct time zone is important to the proper synchronization of your NDS tree. After you choose the time zone, you will see the screen shown in Figure 41.17.

This screen enables you to configure the time synchronization parameters for this file server. Notice that the default time server type is SECONDARY. This is the default because there is already a time provider (SINGLE REFERENCE, PRIMARY, or REFERENCE server) installed on this network. It is recommended that you accept the default. If you intend to make this server a time provider in the future, you can always change the time server type through the AUTOEXEC.NCF file. It is also recommended that you use the default parameters provided on this screen. Novell has made an attempt to provide the correct time information for each possible time zone. Very rarely will you have to modify the defaults. To continue, you can simply press F10.

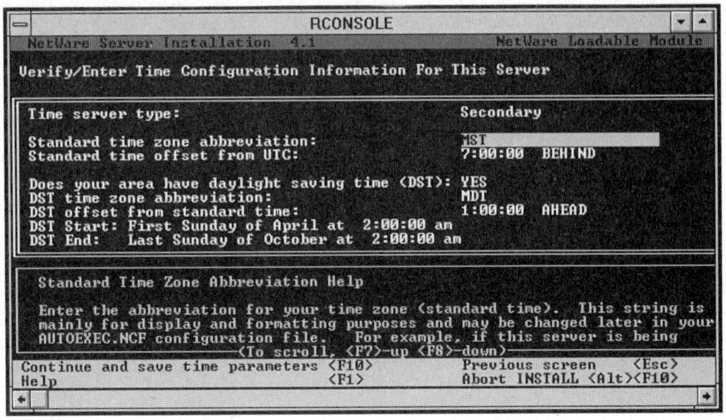

Figure 41.17.
Entering time synchro-
nization parameters.

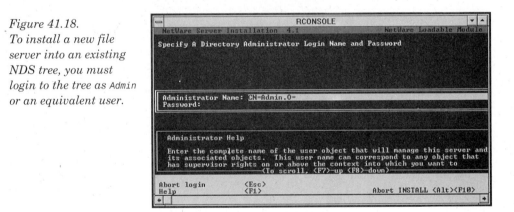

Next, you are prompted to log in to the tree you are installing this server into. This ensures that you have the appropriate rights to install the server into the tree. Figure 41.18 shows an example of this login screen.

Figure 41.18.
To install a new file
server into an existing
NDS tree, you must
login to the tree as Admin
or an equivalent user.

Notice that you are being prompted for Admin's context and password. You will need to log in as Admin or an equivalent user before you can continue. Once you have authenticated to the tree, your existing tree structure will be displayed (see Figure 41.19).

You can add this new server to an existing context in the tree by pressing Enter, or you can create a new context simply by typing the new Organization or Organizational Unit name. To save your changes, you can press F10. If you created a new context to install this server into, a screen similar to Figure 41.20 will be displayed.

Figure 41.19.
Specifying a context for
a new server in the tree.

Figure 41.20.
Creating a new context
during installation.

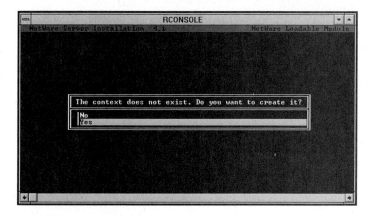

If you answer yes to the create context prompt, the new container will be created and directory services will be installed on this server. If you answer no, you will return to the previous screen.

DEFAULT PARTITIONS FOR NEWLY INSTALLED SERVERS

When a new server is installed into an NDS tree, NetWare 4.1 will provide some defaults for partitions and replicas. The first server installed into the tree will automatically receive the Master replica of the [Root] partition. Then, the next three servers installed into the tree will receive Read-Write replicas of the [Root] partition. These defaults are provided to ensure that the [Root] partition is properly replicated. Additional partitions can be created and replicated manually using the partitioning tools PARTMGR or NWAdmin.

Summary

Expanding your existing NetWare Environment is very easy. NetWare 4.1 was designed in a modular fashion to made expansion possible. Disk storage, memory, and network segments can be added to your network practically on-the-fly, just by installing the new hardware and loading the appropriate NLM drivers. NetWare 4.1 is scalable and was designed to grow as your company grows by allowing you to expand your existing servers and add new servers as required. The global nature of NetWare Directory Services allows access and management of the network transparent.

- Server Console Commands

- User Command Line Utilities

- NWADMIN and NETADMIN Utilities

- NWUSER and NETUSER Utilities

PART IX

Command Reference

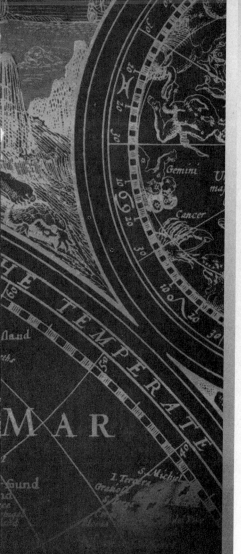

- Server Console
  Commands Summary

- New Server Console
  Commands

- NetWare Loadable
  Modules

- Summary

CHAPTER 42

Server Console Commands

This section offers an alphabetical listing of NetWare 4.1 server console commands. Each section includes a description of the command, its purpose, an example of how to use it, the command syntax, and notes and cautions concerning its use.

You can execute server console commands either at the server console itself or at a workstation via the RCONSOLE (Remote Console) workstation utility.

Enter console commands at the console prompt. You can use them for the following types of tasks:

- Monitoring server use
- Changing memory allocations
- Managing workstations' use of server resources

A second section discusses some of the major NLMs available with NetWare 4.1.

SYNTAX

Each command includes a syntax section that shows you exactly how to enter commands.

The syntax for the SEND command offers a good example of various syntax conventions:

```
SEND "message" [[TO] username ¦ connection number] [AND ¦,] username ¦ connection number]
```

Syntax explanation is as follows:

SEND	Enter words in all capitals exactly as they are spelled. (You can enter them in upper or lower case, however.)
[ ]	Items within square brackets are optional. You can enter the command with or without the bracketed item.
¦	A vertical bar stands for "either, or." Enter the value to the left of the bar or to the right, but not both.
"message"	An item within quotes indicates that you can input a value of your choice within quotes. In place of "message" you can enter "Paychecks are here", for example.
username	Items in *italics*. Replace them with the value related to your task. In the preceding example, you can replace username with the name of the user to whom you want to send the message.
[[ ]]	Nested brackets show that all enclosed items are optional. But if you enter values within the inner brackets, you must also enter values within the outer brackets.

SERVER CONSOLE COMMANDS SUMMARY

The following list summarizes the server console commands discussed in this section.

ABORT REMIRROR	Allows you to stop remirroring of a logical partition.
ADD NAME SPACE	Allows you to store non-DOS files (such as UNIX files or Macintosh files) on a NetWare volume.
BIND	Allows you to associate networking protocols (such as IPX) with drivers and with network interface cards.
BROADCAST	Allows you to send messages to a specific user, a group of users, or all users.
CLEAR STATION	Allows you to clear the connection between the file server and a workstation that has crashed.
CLS	Allows you to clear the console screen.
CONFIG	Allows you to view a variety of information related to server configuration, particularly network interface card information.
DISABLE LOGIN	Allows you to prevent users from logging in to the server.
DISABLE TTS	Allows you to disable the Transaction Tracking System (TTS).
DISKSET	Allows you to format an external hard disk through the host bus adapter.
DISMOUNT	Allows you to dismount a volume—meaning that you make the information on the disk inaccessible to network users.
DISPLAY NETWORKS	Allows you to view all networks as well as assigned network numbers recognized by the file server.
DISPLAY SERVERS	Allows you to view a list of all the servers on the network.
DOWN	Allows you to properly shut down the server.
ENABLE LOGIN	Allows users to log in to the server.
ENABLE TTS	Allows you to start the Transaction Tracking System (TTS) in the server.
EXIT	Allows you to go to the DOS command line after shutting down the server.
HELP	Allows you to get online help for using any of the server console commands.

42

LANGUAGE	Allows you to determine which language is used for NLM message files.
LIST DEVICES	Allows you to view the devices being used by the server.
LOAD	Allows you to load loadable modules.
MAGAZINE	Allows you to confirm whether magazine requests have been satisfied.
MEDIA	Allows you to confirm whether media requests have been satisfied.
MEMORY	Allows you to display how much memory the operating system can address.
MIRROR STATUS	Allows you to check the status of all mirrored logical partitions.
MODULES	Allows you to display important information about loadable modules.
MOUNT	Allows you to make the information on a volume available to users.
NAME	Allows you to view the name of the server.
OFF	Allows you to clear the console screen.
PROTOCOL	Allows you to see which protocols are registered and register new protocols and frame types.
REGISTER MEMORY	Allows the operating system to recognize installed memory above 16MB.
REMIRROR PARTITION	Allows you to begin remirroring of a logical partition.
REMOVE DOS	Allows you to remove DOS from the server's memory.
RESET ROUTER	Allows you to reset the server router table if it becomes inaccurate or corrupted.
SCAN FOR NEW DEVICES	Allows you to see if disk hardware has been installed since the server was last booted.
SEARCH	Allows you to view, add, or delete search paths.
SECURE CONSOLE	Allows you to implement several security measures by limiting what can be done at the server console. These measures include making DOS inaccessible, allowing NLMs to be loaded only from SYS:SYSTEM, and disallowing keyboard entry into OS debugger.

SEND	Allows you to send messages to a specific user, a group of users, or all users.
SERVER	Allows you to boot the server, executing the AUTOEXEC.NCF and STARTUP.NCF files and mounting the SYS volume.
SET	Allows you to check operating system parameters and configure the operating system. SET categories include communications, memory, file and directory caching, file system, locks, transaction tracking, disk, time, NetWare Core Protocol, miscellaneous, and error handling.
SET TIME	Allows you to set the date and time for the server.
SET TIME ZONE	Allows you to configure time zone information in CLIB.
SPEED	Allows you to display the speed of the central processing unit (CPU).
TIME	Allows you to view server date and time, daylight savings time status, and time synchronization data.
TRACK OFF	Allows you to configure the server so that it does not display network advertising packets received or sent on the Router Tracking Screen.
TRACK ON	Allows you to display the Router Tracking Screen and make it the active screen.
UNBIND	Allows you to unbind communication protocols from LAN drivers, change network numbers for cabling, and disable network interface cards.
UNLOAD	Allows you to unload loadable modules, drivers, or name space modules.
UPS STATUS	Allows you to check the status of the uninterruptable power supply (UPS) connected to the file server.
UPS TIME	Allows you to alter the amount of time you want to permit the network to operate on battery power.
VERSION	Allows you to check the copyright notice and version information for the server.
VOLUMES	Allows you to list all volumes mounted on the server.

42

SERVER CONSOLE COMMANDS

NEW SERVER CONSOLE COMMANDS

The following file server console commands are new with NetWare 4.1:

```
ABORT REMIRROR
HELP
LANGUAGE
LIST DEVICES
MAGAZINE
MEDIA
MIRROR STATUS
REMIRROR PARTITION
SCAN FOR NEW DEVICES
```

The following section describes each of the server console commands in detail. You can also find useful information about these commands in the following NetWare 4 manuals: *Utilities Reference*, *Supervising the Network*, and *Concepts*.

ABORT REMIRROR

PURPOSE

ABORT REMIRROR allows you to stop remirroring of a logical partition, which is a division of the directory's global database and consists of one or more containers and associated leaf objects.

SYNTAX

ABORT REMIRROR *number*

PARAMETERS

Replace *number* with the number of the appropriate logical partition.

EXAMPLE

If you want to stop remirroring for logical partition 3, enter the following at the console prompt:

ABORT REMIRROR 3

NOTES

The NetWare 4 *Concepts* manual includes a helpful section on partitions.

ADD NAME SPACE

PURPOSE

This command enables you to store non-DOS files (such as OS/2 files) on a NetWare volume.

EXAMPLE

Suppose that you want to store Macintosh files on a volume called SOCRATES. First, enter the following to see what name space support is already available:

```
ADD NAME SPACE
```

If the only loaded name space is DOS, for example, a message similar to this appears:

```
Missing name space name
Syntax:
ADD NAME SPACE <name space name>
[TO [VOLUME]] <volume name>
Loaded name spaces are:
DOS
```

Because you now know that the Macintosh name space has not yet been loaded, use the LOAD command to load the proper name space module. Next, add name space support by entering the following:

```
ADD NAME SPACE MAC TO SOCRATES
```

Macintosh name space support has now been added.

SYNTAX

```
ADD NAME SPACE name [TO [VOLUME]] volume name
```

PARAMETERS

Replace name with the variable name space for the desired module.

Replace volume name with the name of the volume where you want to store the non-DOS files.

Enter ADD NAME SPACE with no parameters to see what name spaces have already been loaded.

CAUTION

Once you add a name space to a volume, you can remove it by deleting and re-creating the volume, or by running VREPAIR.

NOTES

Use this command only once for each non-DOS file type you want to add.

NetWare supports DOS naming conventions by default.

Storing name space modules with the NetWare server boot files allows the additional name space to be added to any volume.

The following formula allows you to estimate how much memory the name space requires:

```
.032 x volume size (in MB) / block size
```

RELATED COMMANDS

The VREPAIR loadable module allows you to remove name space support from a volume. You may need to do this, for example, if you have just created a memory problem by adding name space support.

BIND

PURPOSE

This command enables you to associate networking protocols (such as IPX) with drivers and with network interface cards. This process is required for a network card to be able to process packets.

SYNTAX

```
BIND protocol [TO] lan driver ¦ board name [driver parameter ...] [protocol param-
eter ...]
```

PARAMETERS

Replace *protocol* with the name of the appropriate protocol, such as IPX.

Replace *lan driver* with the driver name loaded for the network interface card or with the name of the board that was selected when the driver was loaded.

Including *driver parameter* is optional. It is not required if you bind the protocol to a board name instead of a LAN driver. In addition, you do not need to set driver parameters if you do not install more than one network interface card of the same kind in the server.

Set driver parameters by replacing *driver parameter* with one or more of the following parameters:

DMA=*number*   DMA channel identifier. Select the same channel you selected when the driver was loaded.

FRAME=*name*   Frame type identifier. Select the same name you selected when the driver was loaded.

INT=*number*   Interrupt identifier. Select the same interrupt you selected when the driver was loaded.

MEM=*number*   Memory address identifier. Select the same address you selected when the driver was loaded.

PORT=*number*   I/O port identifier. Select the same port you selected when the driver was loaded.

SLOT=*number*   Slot identifier. This parameter applies to EISA and Micro Channel machines. Select the same slot number you selected when the driver was loaded.

Replace *protocol parameter* with the appropriate parameter. For protocols other than IPX, see the protocol documentation for parameter information.

The IPX protocol parameter is as follows:

NET=*number*   Network number identifier. This parameter is required. If applicable, use the number of the existing cabling system.

If you are using a new cabling system, choose a hexadecimal number not being used. If you selected more than one frame type for a single network card in the server, choose a number not being used.

Do not choose a number already selected for another frame type on the cabling system.

EXAMPLE

Assume that you want to install a network interface card for IPX and get it operating properly. First, install the card in the appropriate slot and connect the cable. Next, use the LOAD command to load the driver and name the card (assume you name it Kant). Further assume that the network number for the cabling system attached to the board is 10.

Now enter the following command at the console prompt:

```
BIND IPX TO KANT NET=10
```

Adding the same line to your AUTOEXEC.NCF file ensures that binding takes place whenever the filer server is booted. (In the AUTOEXEC.NCF file, the BIND line should follow load command for the driver.)

Please note, however, that the necessary BIND command may already be included in your AUTOEXEC.NCF file. The INSTALL program automatically prompts for such information after a LAN driver is loaded.

NOTES

In handling binding tasks, the INSTALL program automatically defaults to the IPX protocol.

Chapter 6 of the NetWare 4 manual, *Supervising the Network*, contains useful information on loading and binding LAN drivers.

RELATED COMMANDS

The UNBIND command allows you to remove a protocol from a driver.

The PROTOCOL command allows you to see what protocols are already registered on the server. It also allows you to register new protocols and frame types.

BROADCAST

PURPOSE

This command enables you to send messages to a specific user, a group of users, or all users.

SYNTAX

```
BROADCAST "message" [[TO] username ¦ connection number] [[AND ¦,] username ¦
connection number ...]
```

PARAMETERS

Replace *message* with the message you want to send.

Replace *username* with the name of the user or users to whom you want to send the messages.

Replace *connection number* with the number of the workstation or workstations to whic you want to send the message. (The Connection Information option in MONITOR provides information on connection numbers.)

EXAMPLE

If you want to notify user Thom that you have completed a memo, you can enter the following:

```
BROADCAST "I'VE FINISHED THE MEMO" THOM
```

Thom then sees the message on his screen.

If you want to let all users know that time cards are due, enter the following:

```
BROADCAST "TIME CARDS ARE DUE"
```

All users see the message on their screens.

NOTES

Using BROADCAST for confidential messages is not appropriate because the message automatically comes up on the workstation screen (without any request from the user) and because a message intended for one person can be accidentally sent to all users if no connection number is specified. Confidential messages are best sent via e-mail, where they are protected by passwords.

As noted previously, a message is automatically sent to all users if you do not include user or connection parameters.

When sending a message to a group of users, you can use a comma, a space, or the word AND to separate users or connection numbers.

All users logged in to the network receive BROADCAST messages, except the following:

- ◆ Those who have used the Accept None option of the SEND utility to reject messages.
- ◆ Those who are using ACS or NACS.
- ◆ Those logged in from remote workstations.
- ◆ Those using certain graphics applications.

BROADCAST messages do not alter a workstation's screen display, but the user must press Ctrl+Enter to clear the message and resume work at the station.

CAUTION

A user at a remote location using remote communications software to control one of the local LAN workstations does not see BROADCAST messages on the remote screen. However, the remote-control process is interrupted by the message, and the remote user cannot continue controlling the local station until the message is cleared with Ctrl+Enter. Therefore, remote users may want to use the SEND utility to reject all messages and avoid this problem.

RELATED COMMANDS

The SEND console command is similar to BROADCAST. The Novell documentation suggests using BROADCAST to send a message to all users and using SEND to send a message to specific users.

A workstation SEND utility is also available, and users can employ it to prevent their workstations from receiving messages.

The MONITOR loadable module provides information on connection numbers.

CLEAR STATION

PURPOSE

CLEAR STATION allows you to deal with a workstation that has crashed, such as freezing while running an application. Crashed stations leave files open on the file server, and CLEAR STATION closes those files, shuts down communications between the station and the file server, and deletes internal tables associated with the workstation.

SYNTAX

```
CLEAR STATION n
```

PARAMETERS

Replace n with the number of the workstation you want to clear.

EXAMPLE

Suppose that a given workstation crashes while calculating a spreadsheet, and you want to use CLEAR STATION. You first of all need to know the number of the workstation in question. You can obtain this information by using MONITOR at the file server console or by using NLIST USER /A /B at a workstation.

If you find that the number of the crashed station is 2, for example, type the following at the console prompt:

```
CLEAR STATION 2
```

After you enter this command, a message appears on the screen of workstation 2. If it is attached to other file servers, you see this message:

```
Current drive is no longer valid.
You can either change to another drive or log back in to the original server.
```

If workstation 2 is attached to only one file server (assume that server is named PLATO), you see this message:

```
Network error on server PLATO. Connection no longer valid.
Abort? Retry?
```

Type **A** and the station is returned to a DOS prompt.

Caution

Do not use CLEAR STATION for a workstation actively processing data. Doing so can corrupt files related to that station.

Notes

Workstations can crash for a variety of reasons. Determining the cause of a crash is not always easy. If a workstation crashes repeatedly, however, you clearly need to do some troubleshooting. If the station crashes while running an application, check the application documentation—you may need to change the FILES= line in CONFIG.SYS, for example.

If crashes seem unrelated to an application, try swapping network interface cards. Also check such items as the following: cable and board connections, network driver and requester configurations, and possible interrupt conflicts.

CLS

Purpose

CLS allows you to clear the console screen.

Syntax

CLS

Parameters

None

Example

To clear the console screen, enter the following at the console prompt:

CLS

The screen is cleared.

Notes

This is similar to the DOS CLS command, which allows you to clear DOS screens.

RELATED COMMANDS

The console command OFF accomplishes the same purpose.

CONFIG

PURPOSE

This command allows you to view a variety of information related to server configuration, particularly network interface card (NIC) information. CONFIG displays the following:

```
The name of the server
The server internal network number
Server up time
A list of loaded LAN drivers
Hardware configurations of NICs
NIC station addresses
NIC protocol information
NIC network numbers
NIC frame types
NIC names
Bindery context setting, if there is one
```

SYNTAX

```
CONFIG
```

PARAMETERS

None

EXAMPLE

To display configuration information for a given NetWare server, enter the following at the server console prompt:

```
CONFIG
```

Configuration information similar to the following is displayed:

```
File server name: HERACLITUS
IPX internal network number: 1986ABE1
    Node address: 000000000001
    Frame type: VIRTUAL_LAN
    LAN protocol: IPX network 1986ABE1
Server Up Time: 22 Hours 9 Minutes 47 Seconds

Novell NE2000
    Version 3.29     November 1, 1994
    Hardware setting: I/O Port 300h to 31Fh,
```

```
Interrupt 3h
    Node address: 00001453859A
    Frame type: ETHERNET_SNAP
    Board name: DEMOCRITUS
    LAN protocol: IPX network 00D0C200

Tree Name: DREAMLAN
Bindery Context(s):
    Consulting.Toronto.North_America
```

NOTES

Check the CONFIG information before installing new cards to avoid conflicts.

RELATED COMMANDS

DISPLAY NETWORKS allows you to view all networks as well as assigned network numbers recognized by the server.

MONITOR allows you to view a variety of network configuration information.

DISABLE LOGIN

PURPOSE

DISABLE LOGIN enables you to stop users from logging in to the server.

SYNTAX

DISABLE LOGIN

PARAMETERS

None

EXAMPLE

Suppose that you want to take care of a server maintenance task, such as running backup or installing a new application. You don't want anyone using the network while you do this. To prevent users from logging in, enter the following at the console prompt:

DISABLE LOGIN

Users are now prevented from logging in.

NOTES

This command does not stop users already logged in from continuing to use the network. Therefore, if you want to make sure no one is using the system, run DISABLE LOGIN right after booting the server.

RELATED COMMANDS

The ENABLE LOGIN command enables users to log in.

DISABLE TTS

PURPOSE

This command allows you to disable the Transaction Tracking System (TTS).

SYNTAX

```
DISABLE TTS
```

PARAMETERS

None

EXAMPLE

Suppose that you have written a database application and want to test it with TTS disabled. Enter the following:

```
DISABLE TTS
```

TTS is disabled, and the following message appears on the console screen:

```
TTS disabled by operator.
```

You can now test the application and enable TTS when you complete the test.

NOTES

TTS is a standard feature of NetWare 4. It is important even if you are not running database applications because it protects the NetWare Directory database.

TTS maintains database integrity by backing out incomplete transactions when a network failure occurs. Software bugs, power problems, server or workstation failure, or hub or repeater problems can all cause transactions to fail before they are completed. In such a case, TTS (which made a copy of the original data before the transaction began) returns the database to its pretransaction condition.

If a workstation or other network component fails, TTS rolls back the transaction immediately. If the server fails, TTS backs out the transaction when the server is rebooted.

Normally, you do not need to disable TTS. Doing so to make memory available for NLMs, for example, is dangerous and generally frees only about 40 bytes.

Warning

Do not disable TTS as it is required by the NDS database.

CAUTION

Files not made up of discrete records (such as word processing files) are not protected by TTS.

RELATED COMMANDS

ENABLE TTS causes TTS to execute. By default, TTS is enabled, so rebooting the server also enables TTS.

DISMOUNT

PURPOSE

DISMOUNT allows you to dismount a volume, meaning that you make the information on the disk inaccessible to network users.

SYNTAX

DISMOUNT *volume name*

PARAMETERS

Replace volume name with the name of the volume you want to dismount.

EXAMPLE

Suppose that you want to dismount a volume named PASCAL in order to perform various maintenance tasks while the server is still up and running.

First, use BROADCAST to inform users that they should log out of PASCAL. Then make sure all users have logged out properly.

Next, dismount the volume by entering the following:

```
DISMOUNT PASCAL
```

The volume is dismounted.

After completing maintenance, use the MOUNT command to remount the volume.

NOTES

Each mounted volume consumes memory and decreases memory available for file caching. Therefore, you may want to dismount volumes not used regularly.

RELATED COMMANDS

The INSTALL loadable module allows you to accomplish a wide variety of tasks, including dismounting volumes.

The MOUNT console command allows you to mount one or all volumes.

The VOLUMES console command allows you to list all volumes mounted on the server.

DISPLAY NETWORKS

PURPOSE

This command allows you to view all networks as well as assigned network numbers recognized by the file server.

SYNTAX

```
DISPLAY NETWORKS
```

PARAMETERS

None

EXAMPLE

If you want to see a list of networks and network numbers, enter the following at the console prompt:

```
DISPLAY NETWORKS
```

A list similar to the following comes up on the file server console screen:

```
:display networks
00000001  0/1      00000003  1/2
00000030  0/1      0000008B  2/3
There are four known networks
```

The eight-digit number is the network or cabling number; the number before the slash indicates the number of hops required to reach the network; the number after the slash shows how many ticks (1 tick is 1/18th of a second) are required for a packet to reach the network.

RELATED COMMANDS

The DISPLAY SERVERS console command lists servers on the network.

DISPLAY SERVERS

PURPOSE

This command allows you to view a list of all servers on the network.

SYNTAX

```
DISPLAY SERVERS
```

PARAMETERS

None

EXAMPLE

If you want to see a list of servers on the network, enter the following:

```
DISPLAY SERVERS
```

A list similar to the following appears on the console screen:

```
:display servers
BOND 1     GOLDFINGER     1     FLEMING    2
007  2
There are four known servers.
```

The list shows the name of each server and the number of hops required to reach that server.

NOTES

Your file server is not included in the list if the sys: volume is not mounted.

Also listed in the output are any services that advertises, such as print servers.

RELATED COMMANDS

DISPLAY NETWORKS lists networks and network numbers.

DOWN

PURPOSE

DOWN enables you to properly shut down the server.

SYNTAX

DOWN

PARAMETERS

None

EXAMPLE

Suppose that you need to shut down the server and then turn off power so that electrical maintenance can be performed. First, use BROADCAST to tell users to exit their files and logged out of the network. Then enter the following:

DOWN

If files are still open, information regarding those files—such as filename, associated user, and connection number—is displayed. A prompt then asks if you still want to down the server. If not, type n or press Enter (to accept the default of *n*).

You can then broadcast a message reminding users to exit their files or go to the workstations in question, exit the files yourself, and log out. You are then ready to enter the DOWN command again.

If you want to down the server even though files are open, answer yes to the prompt.

A message appears on the console screen informing you that the file server has been shut down. You can now type EXIT to go to the DOS command line. (If you have executed the REMOVE DOS command prior to downing the server, however, attempting to exit to DOS will reboot the server.)

Once you down the server, you can safely turn off the power.

CAUTION

To ensure data integrity, never turn off power to the server without first executing the DOWN command. Executing DOWN causes changes in cache to be written to disk, tables to be updated, and files to be closed properly.

NOTES

A downed server is still connected to the network and still accepts packets.

Executing DOWN terminates any remote console sessions.

RELATED COMMANDS

EXIT sends you to the DOS command line after you have used DOWN.

Certain commands, such as TRACK ON and TRACK OFF, are still operable after the server is shut down.

ENABLE LOGIN

PURPOSE

ENABLE LOGIN allows users to log in to the server.

SYNTAX

ENABLE LOGIN

PARAMETERS

None

EXAMPLE

If you have disabled login for any reason, such as performing routine maintenance, enter the following to allow users to log in:

ENABLE LOGIN

Users are now free to log in to the server.

NOTES

Login is enabled by default whenever the server is booted. Therefore, using ENABLE LOGIN is not normally necessary.

RELATED COMMANDS

DISABLE LOGIN prevents users from logging in to the server.

ENABLE TTS

PURPOSE

This command allows you to begin the Transaction Tracking System (TTS) in the server.

SYNTAX

ENABLE TTS

PARAMETERS

None

EXAMPLE

Assume that you have disabled TTS for some reason, such as testing a database application. To begin transaction tracking, enter the following at the server console prompt:

ENABLE TTS

TTS is now started; the following message appears on the console screen:

Transaction tracking system enabled.

Other messages can also appear on the screen. You might be informed, for example, that TTS cannot be enabled because the SYS: volume has not been mounted. If so, use MOUNT to mount the volume.

You will also be told if there is insufficient disk space for TTS backout file. If so, free up at least 1MB on the SYS: volume.

Another factor that can prevent TTS from running is insufficient memory. TTS normally requires about 40 bytes of RAM and seldom requires more than 400KB. You can make more memory available by unloading unneeded NLMs, dismounting seldom used volumes, or adding more memory to the server.

NOTES

TTS is enabled by default whenever the server is booted. NetWare automatically disables TTS, however, if the SYS: volume is full or if the server does not have enough memory to run TTS. If TTS is disabled for either of these reasons, you can use ENABLE TTS after solving the problem.

The TTS$LOG.ERR file includes information on transactions backed out by TTS. The TTS$LOG.ERR file is found in the root directory of the SYS volume and details what happened to transactions when a failure occurred.

The NetWare 4 *Concepts* manual contains a helpful section on TTS.

RELATED COMMANDS

DISABLE TTS stops transaction tracking.

The SERVMAN loadable module provides several options related to TTS.

Users can use the FLAG workstation utility to ensure that certain files are protected by TTS.

EXIT

PURPOSE

EXIT enables you to go to the DOS command line after shutting down the server with DOWN.

SYNTAX

EXIT

PARAMETERS

None

EXAMPLE

Suppose that you have downed the server and want to run DOS commands from the server console. To return to DOS, enter the following:

EXIT

The DOS command line appears; you now have access to DOS files.

If you have run REMOVE DOS before downing the server, however, EXIT reboots the server.

From the DOS command line, you can type SERVER to boot the NetWare server; pressing Ctrl+Alt+Del also causes the server to be rebooted.

RELATED COMMANDS

The DOWN command allows you to properly shut down the server.

REMOVE DOS enables the EXIT command to warm boot the server.

HELP

PURPOSE

HELP allows you to get online help for using any of the server console commands.

SYNTAX

```
HELP [console command]
```

PARAMETERS

Replace console command with the name of the command you need help with.

Enter no command name if you want to see a list of console commands.

EXAMPLE

Suppose that you want to stop remirroring of a logical partition but cannot remember the details of using ABORT REMIRROR. To get help, enter the following at the console prompt:

```
HELP ABORT REMIRROR
```

An explanation of the command, its syntax, and sample use are displayed on the server console screen.

If you simply want to view a list of console commands, enter the following:

```
HELP
```

A list of console commands appears on the screen. (Typing HELP by itself, therefore, is helpful if you cannot remember the name of a command.)

NOTES

This command is new to NetWare 4.

LANGUAGE

Purpose

This command allows you to determine which language is used for NLM message files.

Syntax

```
LANGUAGE [language_designator] [option]
```

Parameters

Replace language designator with the name or ID number of the desired language. The default ID numbers are as follows:

Canadian French	0
Chinese	1
Danish	2
Dutch	3
English	4
Finnish	5
French	6
German	7
Italian	8
Japanese	9
Korean	10
Norwegian	11
Portuguese	12
Russian	13
Spanish	14
Swedish	15

Replace option with one of the following options:

LIST	Shows available languages
REN	Renames a language (or to put it more simply, changes a language's ID number)

Therefore, to see what languages are available, enter the following:

```
LANGUAGE LIST
```

To change French's ID number from 6 to 1, enter the following:

```
LANGUAGE 6 REN 1
```

EXAMPLE

Suppose that you want to use French as the language for NLM message files. Enter the following at the console command line:

```
LANGUAGE FRENCH
```

French is now used for NLM message files. Since the ID number for French is 6, you can also enter the following the make the change:

```
LANGUAGE 6
```

NOTES

The default language for the NLM message files is English.

To see what language is currently being used, enter LANGUAGE with no parameters.

When LANGUAGE is executed, NLMs check for a directory structure containing operating system and NLM messages. The proper directory structure is as follows:

```
SYS:SYSTEM/NLS/Language ID number
```

RELATED COMMANDS

Chapter 6 of *Supervising the Network* offers instructions on using SERVER to change a server's language.

LIST DEVICES

PURPOSE

LIST DEVICES enables you to view the devices being used by the server. A device is any storage driver, such as disk drivers and tape drivers.

SYNTAX

```
LIST DEVICES
```

PARAMETERS

None

EXAMPLE

To see which device drivers are being used by your server, enter the following:

```
LIST DEVICES
```

A list of devices and their corresponding ids appears.

NOTES

The device ids are assigned by the operating system.

RELATED COMMANDS

CONFIG displays a variety of hardware information, including NIC configuration data.

LOAD

PURPOSE

This command allows you to load loadable modules, including those from Novell as well as from third parties.

SYNTAX

```
LOAD [path] loadable module [parameter...]
```

PARAMETERS

Replace *path* with the complete path to the directory containing the loadable module.

If you have mounted SYS: and do not include a path parameter, NetWare assumes the loadable module is located in SYS:SYSTEM.

Replace *loadable module* with the name of the module you want to load. The four kinds of loadable modules are as follows:

Disk drivers	Enable communications between the operating system and disk controller boards
Syntax	`LOAD [path]disk driver [driver parameter...]`
LAN drivers	Enable communications between the operating system and network interface cards
Syntax	`LOAD [path]lan driver [driver parameter...]`
NLMs	Enable communications between the operating system and network management programs.
Syntax	`LOAD [path]nlm utility [parameter...]`

Name Space Modules   Enable communications between the operating system and non-DOS naming conventions.

Syntax   `LOAD [path]name space`

Replace *parameter* with any appropriate parameters. As shown above, disk drivers, LAN driver, and NLMs can all include parameters. Check the loadable module documentation for parameter information. Name space modules do not require parameters.

EXAMPLE

To load the MONITOR program, enter the following at the console prompt:

```
LOAD MONITOR
```

To load a DCB driver from a floppy drive, enter the following:

```
LOAD A:DCB PORT=320
```

To load an ISADISK driver from a floppy disk, enter the following:

```
LOAD A:ISADISK
```

To load the TRXNET driver with parameters, enter the following:

```
LOAD TRXNET INT=3 PORT=2E0 MEM=C0000
```

To load the Macintosh name space module, enter the following:

```
LOAD MAC
```

CAUTION

Many third-party vendors have developed loadable modules to run with NetWare. Before using any of them, however, make sure they have been tested and approved by Novell. If not, arrange to test them yourself in a secure environment (by using DOMAIN, for example). Loading an unapproved or untested module can corrupt data on the server or crash the server.

Loadable modules can fail to load for a whole variety of reasons, including the following:

◆ Incorrect path

◆ Invalid parameter

◆ Another module must first be loaded

◆ Insufficient memory

◆ Incorrect drive specification

NOTES

Certain modules (LAN drivers and disk drivers, for example) must be loaded every time the server is booted. Other modules can be loaded or unloaded on the fly, without shutting down the server. When a module is unloaded, all allocated resources are returned to NetWare.

To ensure that modules are automatically loaded every time the server is booted, add the appropriate LOAD command (just as you type it on the console command line) to the AUTOEXEC.NCF file or the STARTUP.NCF file.

Loadable modules can be copied to and loaded from any of the following:

◆ A floppy disk

◆ A DOS partition

◆ NetWare directories

If SECURE CONSOLE has been executed, however, it prevents modules from being loaded from any directory except SYS:SYSTEM.

RELATED COMMANDS

The DOMAIN loadable module allows you to create operating system protected (OSP) domains for testing loadable modules before putting them into general use.

The MODULES console command lists important information about loadable modules.

MAGAZINE

PURPOSE

The MAGAZINE server console command confirms whether magazine requests (Insert Magazine and Remove Magazine) have been satisfied.

SYNTAX

MAGAZINE

PARAMETERS

Use a parameter from the following list:

Inserted	Confirms that the identified media magazine was inserted in reply to the Insert Magazine console message
Not Inserted	Confirms that the identified media magazine was not inserted in reply to the Insert Magazine console message

42

Not Removed	Confirms that the identified media magazine was not removed in reply to the `Remove Magazine` console message
Removed	Confirms that the identified media magazine was removed in reply to the `Remove Magazine` console message

EXAMPLE

To determine whether `Insert Magazine` or `Remove Magazine` requests have been met, enter the following at the console prompt:

```
MAGAZINE
```

RELATED COMMANDS

The CDROM NLM enables the server to use a CD-ROM disk as a read-only volume.

`MEDIA` confirms whether media requests were satisfied.

MEDIA

PURPOSE

This command confirms whether media requests have been satisfied.

SYNTAX

```
MEDIA
```

PARAMETERS

Use a parameter from the following list:

Inserted	Confirms that the identified media was inserted in reply to the `Insert Media` console message.
Not Inserted	Confirms that the identified media was not inserted in reply to the `Insert Media` console message.
Not Removed	Confirms that the identified media was not removed in reply to the `Remove Media` console message.
Removed	Confirms that the identified media was removed in reply to the `Remove Media` console message.

EXAMPLE

To run `MEDIA`, enter the following at the console prompt:

```
MEDIA
```

RELATED COMMANDS

The CDROM NLM enables the server to use a CD-ROM disk as a read-only volume.

MAGAZINE confirms whether magazine requests have been satisfied.

MEMORY

PURPOSE

This command lists how much memory the operating system can address.

SYNTAX

MEMORY

PARAMETERS

None

EXAMPLE

To determine how much memory the operating system can address, enter the following:

MEMORY

The total amount of addressable memory is listed on the console screen.

NOTES

On EISA and Micro Channel machines, NetWare 3.1 and above can automatically address RAM above 16MB.

On ISA machines, NetWare can automatically address RAM only up to 16MB.

RELATED COMMANDS

The REGISTER MEMORY console command allows NetWare to recognize installed memory above 16MB.

MIRROR STATUS

PURPOSE

This command allows you to check the status of all mirrored logical partitions.

SYNTAX

```
MIRROR STATUS
```

PARAMETERS

None

EXAMPLE

To check the status of mirrored logical partitions, enter the following:

```
MIRROR STATUS
```

Mirror status is displayed.

NOTES

Mirror statuses are as follows:

Not mirrored	Partition not being mirrored.
Orphaned state	Data integrity not guaranteed; use INSTALL module to unorphan partition.
Fully synchronized	Mirrored partitions contain the same data and are operating properly.
Out of sync	One server does not contain the same data and is not being remirrored.
Being remirrored	Partition being remirrored; percentage of remirroring completed is listed.

RELATED COMMANDS

The REMIRROR PARTITION console command begins remirroring of a logical partition.

MODULES

PURPOSE

MODULES lists important module information, including short names used to load modules, descriptive strings or long module names, and version numbers for LAN and disk drivers.

SYNTAX

```
MODULES
```

PARAMETERS

None

EXAMPLE

To check module information, enter the following at the server console prompt:

```
MODULES
```

A list similar to the following appears:

```
IDE.DSK
   NetWare 4.01/4.02/4.10 IDE Device Driver
   Version 5.00    September 30, 1994
   Copyright 1994 Novell, Inc.  All rights reserved.
UNICODE.NLM
   NetWare Unicode Library NLM
   Version 4.10    November 8, 1994
   Copyright 1994 Novell, Inc.  All rights reserved.
DSLOADER.NLM
   NetWare 4.1 Directory Services Loader
   Version 1.25    October 22, 1994
   Copyright 1993-1994 Novell, Inc.  All rights reserved.
```

NOTES

The "NetWare Loadable Module" section of the *Concepts* manual offers helpful information on modules.

RELATED COMMANDS

The LOAD console command allows you to load modules.

The DOMAIN module allows you to safely test loadable modules.

MOUNT

PURPOSE

MOUNT allows you to make the information on a volume available to users.

SYNTAX

```
MOUNT volume name
```

or

```
MOUNT ALL
```

42

PARAMETERS

Replace *volume name* with the name of the volume you want to mount.

The ALL parameter enables you to mount all volumes that are presently dismounted.

EXAMPLE

Suppose that you previously dismounted a seldom used volume (named HEGEL) to preserve memory and now need to access a file on that volume. To mount the volume, enter the following:

```
MOUNT HEGEL
```

The volume is now mounted and is accessible to users.

CAUTION

Although it may seem convenient to have all volumes mounted (even those not regularly used) so that they are available for use, each mounted volume consumes memory allocated for file caching. The result can be sluggish performance across the network.

It, therefore, is advisable to dismount seldom used volumes, mount them when necessary, and then dismount them, freeing up memory and improving performance.

NOTES

Volumes are normally created and mounted during the INSTALL process. Using MOUNT is therefore usually necessary only after a volume has been dismounted for some reason.

It is possible to mount and dismount volumes without shutting down the server.

You must first create a volume in INSTALL before mounting it. If you attempt to mount a mounted volume, you simply receive a message telling you it is already mounted.

Insufficient memory can prevent you from mounting a volume.

Chapter 6 of *Supervising the Network* contains valuable information on a variety of tasks related to volumes.

RELATED COMMANDS

The DISMOUNT console command allows you to dismount volumes.

The VOLUMES console command lists all mounted volumes.

The INSTALL module allows you to do all of the following:

- ◆ Create a volume
- ◆ Delete a volume
- ◆ Rename a volume
- ◆ Mount a volume
- ◆ Dismount a volume

NAME

PURPOSE

This command allows you to view the name of the server.

SYNTAX

```
NAME
```

PARAMETERS

None

EXAMPLE

To check the name of the server, enter the following:

```
NAME
```

The name of the server is displayed on the console screen in a message similar to the following (if the server were named HUME):

```
This is Server HUME
```

RELATED COMMANDS

The DISPLAY SERVERS console command lists all known servers.

The VERSION console command lists version and copyright information for the server.

OFF

PURPOSE

OFF allows you to clear the console screen.

SYNTAX

OFF

PARAMETERS

None

EXAMPLE

To clear the console screen, enter the following at the console prompt:

OFF

The screen is cleared.

RELATED COMMANDS

The console command CLS accomplishes the same purpose.

PROTOCOL

PURPOSE

PROTOCOL allows you to see which protocols are registered and register new protocols and frame types.

SYNTAX

PROTOCOL

or

PROTOCOL [REGISTER *protocol frame id#*]

PARAMETERS

Enter PROTOCOL with no parameters to see a list of registered protocols.

To register a protocol, use the REGISTER parameter.

Replace *protocol* with the name of the protocol you want to register.

Replace *frame* with the frame type name you want to bind to the protocol.

Replace *id#* with the Protocol Identification Number. This is a unique, assigned hexadecimal number that communicates with the operating system and facilitates the recognition of data transmitted via NICs with designated protocols.

The Protocol Identification Number can also be referred to as a protocol ID or PID, an Ethernet type or E-type, or a SAP.

EXAMPLE

To determine which protocols are already registered, enter the following at the console prompt:

```
PROTOCOL
```

A message similar to the following appears:

```
The following protocols are registered
Protocol: IPX Frame type: VIRTUAL_LAN Protocol ID: 0
```

CAUTION

Be sure that the LAN driver supports the specified frame type.

NOTES

The INSTALL program includes an option for loading LAN drivers, as well as an option for binding protocols to drivers. During INSTALL you are prompted for information on LAN drivers you want to load. LAN drivers register IPX by default, and other protocols register themselves. Therefore, you do not need to use PROTOCOL REGISTER under normal circumstances.

Novell Authorized Resellers can provide information on approved protocol loadable modules.

RELATED COMMANDS

The BIND console command links LAN drivers with protocols and network interface cards.

The INSTALL module allows you to load LAN drivers and bind protocols.

REGISTER MEMORY

PURPOSE

This command enables the operating system to recognize installed memory above 16MB.

SYNTAX

```
REGISTER MEMORY start_address length
```

PARAMETERS

Start_address should be replaced with the starting address where memory beyond 16MB is to begin.

Length should be replaced with a length of the memory beyond 16MB. This hexadecimal number should be divisible by 10h.

The starting address is normally 0x1000000 (equal to 16MB). The start and length values for standard PCs that begin addressing RAM above 16MB at 0x1000000 are as follows:

Total memory	Start (hex)	Length (hex)
20MB	1000000	400000
24MB	1000000	800000
28MB	1000000	C00000
32MB	1000000	1000000
36MB	1000000	1400000
40MB	1000000	1800000

EXAMPLE

Assume that you have a server with 16MB of memory. You add 4MB of memory and want to have it recognized by the operating system. Enter the following at the server console prompt:

```
REGISTER MEMORY 1000000 400000
```

If the memory addition is successful, the following message appears on the console screen:

```
Memory successfully added
```

You can now make use of the extra memory.

CAUTION

Be careful to avoid memory address conflicts if you intend to use more than 16MB of server memory. Disk adapter boards that use 16- or 24-bit Direct Memory Access (DMA) or Bus-Master DMA, for example, cause conflicts.

To resolve such problems, you can either upgrade to full 32-bit bus adapters or load modified drivers that have been certified to handle memory-addressing limitations.

NOTES

If you are not successful in adding memory, double-check the *start* and *length* values. It is also possible that the *length* value exceeds the total amount of installed memory.

The setup or reference diskette that came with the PC can help you determine how much installed memory it has.

To ensure that memory is automatically registered whenever the server is booted, add the appropriate REGISTER MEMORY line to the AUTOEXEC.NCF file. The line should be added right after the lines for the server name and the IPX internal network number.

RELATED COMMANDS

The MEMORY console command displays the total amount of memory addressable by the operating system.

The MONITOR module offers a variety of memory statistics, including total server work memory, cache buffers, and permanent memory pool.

The INSTALL module utility allows you to edit the AUTOEXEC.NCF file.

REMIRROR PARTITION

PURPOSE

This command allows you to begin remirroring of a logical partition.

SYNTAX

REMIRROR PARTITION *number*

PARAMETERS

Number should be replaced with the number of the logical partition you want to start remirroring.

EXAMPLE

Suppose that you want to begin remirroring for logical partition 3. Enter the following at the server console:

REMIRROR PARTITION 3

Remirroring now begins.

NOTES

The server remirrors partitions by default. Therefore, you should only have to use REMIRROR PARTITION if you have executed ABORT REMIRROR or the server has stopped remirroring for some other reason.

RELATED COMMANDS

The ABORT REMIRROR console command allows you to stop remirroring of a logical partition.

The MIRROR STATUS console command shows the status of all mirrored logical partitions.

REMOVE DOS

PURPOSE

The REMOVE DOS command allows you to remove DOS from the server's memory.

SYNTAX

```
REMOVE DOS
```

PARAMETERS

None

EXAMPLE

Suppose that your server is running low on memory and you want to remove DOS in order to have more RAM for file caching. Enter the following at the server console:

```
REMOVE DOS
```

DOS is removed from memory, and the following message is displayed:

```
DOS removed and its memory given to the disk cache
```

CAUTION

Once you execute this command, DOS is no longer resident on the server, and you can no longer run loadable modules located on DOS drives. This means you cannot load a disk driver from a floppy drive, for example. If you want to run such modules after removing DOS, copy them to a network drive on the file server.

Also keep in mind that the EXIT command no longer returns you to DOS but instead reboots the file server.

NOTES

There are several reasons for removing DOS from the file server's memory. As mentioned above, one is to make more memory available for file caching.

Another reason is to enhance file server security, since modules can no longer be executed from DOS partitions and floppy drives. With DOS resident on the server, an intruder can run DOS files designed for the express purpose of stealing or corrupting data.

A third reason is to allow the EXIT console command to warm boot the server. This is particularly valuable for RCONSOLE users who need to reboot the server remotely.

The SECURE CONSOLE console command also removes DOS from the server, along with implementing several other security features.

Chapter 6 of the NetWare 4 *Supervising the Network* manual includes a helpful section on disaster prevention and recovery.

RELATED COMMANDS

The EXIT console command returns you to DOS after you have downed the server (or reboots the server if you have removed DOS).

The SECURE CONSOLE console command removes DOS from the file server and also prevents several other possible security breaches.

The MONITOR module controls keyboard access to the server console.

RESET ROUTER

PURPOSE

The RESET ROUTER command allows you to reset the NetWare server router table if it becomes inaccurate or corrupted.

SYNTAX

RESET ROUTER

PARAMETERS

None

EXAMPLE

Suppose that you are running an internetwork that includes several file servers and bridges. If some of those bridges and routers go down for some reason, packets in the process of being routed can be lost. In this case, you can run RESET ROUTER in the file servers that are still up—doing so will allow accurate router tables to be constructed.

42

SERVER CONSOLE COMMANDS

To reset the router table, enter the following at the server console:

```
RESET ROUTER
```

The router table is now reset.

NOTES

Under normal circumstances, the router table is updated every two minutes. RESET ROUTER speeds up the routing process.

RESET ROUTER cannot be executed while the server is down.

SCAN FOR NEW DEVICES

PURPOSE

The SCAN FOR NEW DEVICES command allows you to see whether disk hardware has been installed since the server was last booted.

SYNTAX

```
SCAN FOR NEW DEVICES
```

PARAMETERS

None

EXAMPLE

To determine whether disk hardware has been added to the server since it was last booted, enter the following at the server console:

```
SCAN FOR NEW DEVICES
```

Any new devices are listed on the screen.

NOTES

Chapter 6 of the *NetWare Supervising the Network* manual includes valuable information on installing and managing disk hardware.

RELATED COMMANDS

The INSTALL module allows you to add an internal hard disk to the server.

SEARCH

PURPOSE

This command allows you to view, add, or delete search paths. It also gives the server information on where to find loadable module files and .NCF files.

SYNTAX

```
SEARCH [ADD [number] path]
```

or

```
SEARCH DEL number
```

PARAMETERS

Replace *number* with the number of the search drive you want to add or delete.

Path should be replaced with the complete path of the directory you want to search. The path either begins with a DOS drive letter or a NetWare volume name.

Enter SEARCH with no parameters to display a list of current search paths.

EXAMPLE

Suppose that you want to see which search paths are currently set up. Enter the following at the console prompt:

```
SEARCH
```

A message similar to the following appears on the console screen:

```
Search 1: [Server path] SYS:SYSTEM
Search 2: [DOS path   ] A:
```

To add a search path for drive B, enter the following:

```
SEARCH ADD B:
```

Drive B is added as the last search path.

To add a network directory on the file server, enter the path (beginning with the volume name). So, to add the SYS:PROGRAMS directory as a search path, enter the following:

```
SEARCH ADD SYS:PROGRAMS
```

To specify which order drives should be searched in, use 1 for first, 2 for second, and so on. So, if you want to have drive A searched first, enter the following:

```
SEARCH ADD 1 A:
```

To delete a search path, first type SEARCH by itself to display a list of search paths. Select the number of the path you want to delete (3, for example) and enter the following:

SEARCH DEL 3

The search path is deleted.

CAUTION

SEARCH is disabled once SECURE CONSOLE is executed. The SYS:SYSTEM search path is still operable, but no new search paths can be created.

If you issued the SECURE CONSOLE command, you must down the server and reboot it in order to add search paths.

NOTES

SYS:SYSTEM is the default search path. If you store loadable modules in other directories, you can add appropriate search paths—which allows you to load the modules without specifying a path.

RELATED COMMANDS

SECURE CONSOLE disables SEARCH.

SECURE CONSOLE

PURPOSE

This command allows you to enhance system security by doing the following:

◆ Making DOS inaccessible from the server.
◆ Allowing loadable modules to be loaded only from the SYS:SYSTEM directory.
◆ Allowing only the console operator to modify the server date and time.
◆ Allowing no keyboard entry into the OS debugger.

SYNTAX

SECURE CONSOLE

PARAMETERS

None

EXAMPLE

To secure the file server, enter the following at the console prompt:

SECURE CONSOLE

The security features associated with the command are now in place.

NOTES

Use SECURE CONSOLE on any file server where security is a concern.

SEARCH is disabled once SECURE CONSOLE is executed. The SYS:SYSTEM search path is still operable, but no new search paths can be created.

If you run SECURE CONSOLE, you must down the server and reboot it in order to add search paths.

It is necessary to reboot the server to disable SECURE CONSOLE.

SECURE CONSOLE protects the server against the following kinds of security breaches:

- ◆ **Trojan Horse loadable modules**: Loadable modules can be created for the express purpose of altering or removing information from the file server. Such modules are even capable of altering user account information at the server security level. SECURE CONSOLE prevents maverick modules from being loaded from diskette drives, DOS partitions, and NetWare directories.

- ◆ **Date and time alterations**: Certain security features depend on the date and time for enforcement. With SECURE CONSOLE in effect, intruders cannot bypass time-dependent features by changing the date and time.

- ◆ **Infiltration via DOS**: With DOS accessible on the server, an intruder can use a DOS file to violate security. With SECURE CONSOLE in place, an intruder has to turn off the server and power it back up again to have DOS available. (And the server will leave important clues of this breach by recording the time it was rebooted.)

In addition, if the PC you are using as a server has a power-on password feature, you can use it to prevent intruders from accessing DOS even if they turn off power to the system.

RELATED COMMANDS

REMOVE DOS removes DOS from the file server.

42

SERVER CONSOLE COMMANDS

SEND

PURPOSE

This command enables you to send messages to a specific user, a group of users, or all users.

SYNTAX

SEND "*message*" [[TO] *username* ¦ *connection number*] [[AND ¦,] *username* ¦ *connection number* ...]

PARAMETERS

Replace *message* with the message you want to send.

Replace *username* with the name of the user or users you want to send the messages to.

Replace *connection number* with the number of the workstation or workstations you want to send the message to. (The Connection Information option in MONITOR provides information on connection numbers.)

EXAMPLE

To notify user Thom that you have completed an important memo, you can enter the following:

SEND "I'VE FINISHED THE MEMO" THOM

The message within quotes then appears on Thom's screen.

To notify users at workstations 2, 3, and 4 that a meeting is beginning, enter the following:

SEND "THE MEETING IS STARTING" 2,3,4

The message appears on the screens of workstations 2, 3, and 4.

To let all users know that time cards are due the next day, enter the following at the console prompt:

SEND "TIME CARDS ARE DUE TOMORROW"

All users see the message on their screens.

NOTES

Using SEND for confidential messages is not appropriate because the message automatically comes up on the workstation screen (without any request from the user) and because a message intended for one person can be accidentally sent to all users if no connection number is specified. Confidential messages are best sent via e-mail, where they are protected by passwords.

As noted previously, a message is automatically sent to all users if you do not include user or connection parameters.

When sending a message to a group of users, you can use a comma, a space, or the word AND to separate users or connection numbers.

All users logged in to the network receive SEND messages except the following:

♦ Those who have used the Accept None option of the SEND utility to reject messages.

♦ Those who are using ACS or NACS.

♦ Those logged in from remote workstations.

♦ Those using certain graphics applications.

SEND messages do not alter a workstation's screen display, but the user must press Ctrl+Enter to clear the message and resume work at the station.

See Chapter 6 of the NetWare 4 manual, *Supervising the Network*, for more information on sending messages.

CAUTION

A user at a remote location using remote communications software to control one of the local LAN workstations does not see SEND messages on the remote screen. However, the remote-control process is interrupted by the message, and the remote user cannot continue controlling the local station until the message is cleared with Ctrl+Enter. Therefore, remote users may want to use the SEND utility to reject all messages and avoid this problem.

RELATED COMMANDS

The BROADCAST console command is similar to SEND. The Novell documentation suggests using BROADCAST to send a message to all users and using SEND to send a message to specific users.

A workstation SEND utility is also available, and users can employ it to prevent their workstations from receiving messages, to poll for messages, or to view broadcast mode.

The MONITOR loadable module provides information on connection numbers.

SET

PURPOSE

This command enables you to view and configure a wide variety of operating system parameters.

SYNTAX

```
SET [parameter]
```

PARAMETERS

Entering SET with no parameters allows you to view the 12-item list of SET categories shown previously.

Entering SET with a parameter but with no value allows you to see the current setting for that parameter.

Entering SET with a parameter followed by a value reconfigures the server. Such a command issued at the console prompt, however, stays in effect only as long as the server is up and running. As soon as the server is rebooted, SET parameters specified in the .NCF files once again take effect. Therefore, to make changes permanent, include the SET command in either AUTOEXEC.NCF or STARTUP.NCF.

Parameters for specific categories are discussed in the following sections.

EXAMPLE

To check the current SET parameters, enter the following at the console command line:

```
SET
```

A list similar to the following appears on the console screen:

```
Settable configuration parameter categories
1. Communications
2. Memory
3. File caching
4. Directory caching
5. File system
6. Locks
7. Transaction tracking
8. Disk
9. Time
10. NCP (NetWare Core Protocol)
11. Miscellaneous
12. Error handling
Which category do you want to view:
```

Select the appropriate category number.

(Each of the previously listed categories is treated separately in the following sections, as in "Setting Communications Parameters," "Setting Memory Parameters," and so on.)

CAUTION

Make sure you have a specific reason for changing any SET parameter. Improper settings can adversely affect server performance. Also, before making any change, make a note of the setting you intend to change.

NOTES

Generally, it is not necessary to change SET parameters. The default settings offer maximum performance for most installations. Depending on your situation, however, adjusting certain settings can be advantageous.

For example, the default number of maximum file locks for a single workstation is 250; the range is 10 to 1,000. An application may fail because it cannot open enough files. (OS/2 workstations in particular may require more file locks.) If an application does require more file locks, you can use the SET command to make the change.

You can run the majority of SET commands from the server console prompt and save them permanently in the AUTOEXEC.NCF file. Certain settings, however, can only be altered in the STARTUP.NCF; certain others can be altered in STARTUP.NCF, in AUTOEXEC.NCF, or at the console prompt.

If you can enter a SET command at the console prompt, you can also make the change permanent by entering the same line in AUTOEXEC.NCF. Commands included in AUTOEXEC.NCF take effect whenever the server is rebooted.

The INSTALL loadable module allows you to edit the AUTOEXEC.NCF file.

The following parameters must be set in the STARTUP.NCF. Any attempt to set them at the console prompt or in the AUTOEXEC.NCF file results in an error message.

```
Auto Register Memory Above 16 Megabytes

Auto TTS Backout Flag

Cache Buffer Size

Maximum Physical Receive Packet Size

Maximum Subdirectory Tree Depth
```

42

SERVER CONSOLE COMMANDS

```
Minimum Packet Receive Buffers

Reserved Buffers Below 16 Meg
```

The INSTALL loadable module allows you to edit the STARTUP.NCF file.

You can configure the following settings at the console prompt, in the AUTOEXEC.NCF file, or in the STARTUP.NCF file:

```
Display Spurious Interrupt Alerts

Display Lost Interrupt Alerts

Display Disk Device Alerts

Display Relinquish Control Alerts

Display Old API Names
```

Because these parameters deal with hardware and loadable module alert messages, it is advantageous to enter them at the beginning of the STARTUP.NCF file. The alerts then appear for modules you load and hardware components you install.

Certain settings manage the allocation of services. Take the case of file locks mentioned above. There is a maximum number of file locks per connection; the maximum ranges from 10 to 10,000, with a default of 250. Such limits determine how many resources the operating system can grant to a particular service, in this case file locks.

A minimum limit enables the operating system to grant a minimum number of resources as soon as a request is submitted. A low minimum limit means that a service grows slowly; a high minimum limit means that the service grows rapidly.

Take the case of directory cache buffers. With the minimum limit set to 20, the operating system grants another buffer resource as soon as a request is submitted, until 20 buffers have been allocated.

When 20 directory cache buffers have been allocated, the operating system waits for a certain length of time (the default if 2.2 seconds) when a request is submitted. If the request is still active after the waiting period, the operating system allocates another buffer.

But if the minimum limit is higher—40, for example—the operating system grants that many buffers before slowing the growth by waiting after each request.

A third category, the wait time limit, manages how quickly the operating system can grant a new resource. The TTS Unwritten Cache Wait Time, for example, determines how long cache memory holds a block of transactions before writing it to disk. The default is 1 minute, 5.9 seconds, with a range of 11 seconds to 10 minutes, 59.1 seconds.

Related Commands

The SERVMAN loadable module also allows you to configure a number of operating system parameters.

The CONFIG console command lists hardware configuration settings.

MEMORY lists the amount of memory installed on the server.

Settable Communications Parameters

Communications parameters are as follows (with the default listed first and followed by the range or options):

```
Maximum Packet Receive Buffers:
100     50-2000

Minimum Packet Receive Buffers:
10      10-1000

Maximum Physical Receive Packet Size:
4202    618-24682

Maximum Interrupt Events:
10      1-1000000

Number of Watchdog Packets:
10      5-100

Delay Between Watchdog Packets:
59.3 sec 9.9 sec-10 min, 26.2 sec

Delay Between First Watchdog Packet:
4 min, 56.6 sec     15.7 sec-20 min, 52.3 sec

New Packet Receive Buffer Wait Time:
0.1 sec   0.1-20 sec

Reply to Get Nearest Server:
ON     ON, OFF

Console Display Watchdog Logouts:
OFF    ON, OFF
```

Packet receive buffers are sections in server memory reserved to store data packets. The packets stay in the buffers while they are processed. The MONITOR module allows you to check statistics on packet receive buffers.

Watchdog packets ensure that workstations maintain their connections to the server. If the server does not receive a packet from a workstation within a given period of time (Delay Before First Watchdog Packet), the server sends a "watchdog packet" to the station.

If no response is received from the station within a given period of time (Delay Between Watchdog Packets), the server sends another watchdog packet. If a response is not

42

received after a certain number of watchdog packets are transmitted (Number of Watchdog Packets), the server concludes the workstation is no longer connected and clears the connection.

```
Maximum Packet Receive Buffers = number
Values supported: 50-2000
Default: 100
```

This parameter sets the maximum number of packet receive buffers that can be allocated by the server.

You can use MONITOR to check the server's current allocation of packet receive buffers and service processes.

If the number of packet receive buffers has reached its maximum, increase this parameter in increments of 10 until there is one packet receive buffer for each workstation.

If you are using Microchannel or EISA bus master adapters in the server, increase this parameter until there are at least five buffers for each adapter.

If you are receiving No ECB available count error messages, increase the number until there are 10 buffers for each adapter. Check the MONITOR LAN Information option to see if there are error messages.

If the number of allocated service processes is at its maximum, you can decrease the need for more packet receive buffers by increasing the Maximum Number of Service Processes.

```
Minimum Packet Receive Buffers = number
Values supported: 10-1000
Default: 10
```

You must use the STARTUP.NCF file to set this parameter.

This parameter sets the minimum number of packet receive buffers that can be allocated by the operating system.

When the server is rebooted, the minimum number of packet receive buffers is immediately allocated by the operating system.

You can use MONITOR to check on current packet receive buffer statistics.

Increase the number if the current number is above 10 and the server does not respond immediately after being booted.

If you are using Micro Channel or EISA bus master adapters in the server and are receiving No ECB available count errors (see MONITOR's "LAN Information" option) right after rebooting the server, increase this number until there are at least five packet receive buffers for each adapter.

```
Maximum Physical Receive Packet Size = number
Values supported: 618-24682
Default: 4202
```

You must use the STARTUP.NCF file to set this parameter.

This parameter sets the maximum size of packets that the server can transmit across the network.

```
Maximum Interrupt Events = number
Values supported: 1-1000000
Default: 10
```

This parameter sets the maximum number of interrupt time events allowed before a thread switch occurs.

```
Number of Watchdog Packets = number
Values supported: 5-100
Default: 10
```

This parameter sets the number of unanswered watchdog packets that the server transmits to a station before clearing the connection.

```
Delay Between Watchdog Packets = time
Values supported: 1 sec-10 min, 26.2 sec
Default: 4 min, 56.6 sec
```

This parameter sets the period of time between watchdog packets.

The server sends out the first watchdog packet; if it does not receive a response within the specified period of time, it sends out another watchdog packet.

```
Delay Before First Watchdog Packet = time
Values supported: 15.7 sec-20 min, 52.3 sec
Default: 4 min, 56.6 sec
```

This parameter sets the period of time the server waits without receiving packets from a workstation until it sends the first watchdog packet to that station.

```
New Packet Receive Buffer Wait Time = time
Values supported: 0.1 sec-20 sec
Default: 0.1 sec
```

This parameter tells the operating system how long to wait after receiving a request for a packet receive buffer before actually allocating the buffer.

This parameter ensures that the operating system does not allocate too many buffers during a sudden peak in network use.

Do not alter this parameter if you are using an EISA bus master adapter in the server.

```
Reply to Get Nearest Server = value
Values supported: ON, OFF
Default: OFF
```

This parameter determines whether the file server answers Get Nearest Server requests from workstations attempting to find a server.

```
Console Display Watchdog Logouts = value
Values supported: ON, OFF
Default: OFF
```

This parameter determines whether the console displays a message when a connection is cleared.

You probably don't need to change this setting if the server is running smoothly.

In case you are having workstation connection difficulties, setting this parameter to ON can help you determine which stations are not receiving or transmitting watchdog packets.

SETTABLE MEMORY PARAMETERS

Memory parameters are as follows (with the default listed first and followed by the range or options):

```
Auto Register Memory Above 16 Megabytes:
ON        ON, OFF

Garbage Collection Interval:
15 min    1 min-1 hour

Number of Frees for Garbage Collection:
5000      100-10,000

Minimum Free Memory for Garbage Collection:
8000      1000-1000000

Allow Invalid Pointers:
OFF       ON, OFF

Read Fault Notification:
ON        ON, OFF

Read Fault Emulation:
OFF       ON, OFF

Write Fault Notification:
ON        ON, OFF

Write Fault Emulation:
OFF       ON, OFF
```

These parameters manage the size of the dynamic memory pool and the automatic registering of memory on EISA bus machines.

```
Auto Register Memory Above 16 Megabytes = value
Values supported: ON, OFF
Default: ON
```

You must use STARTUP.NCF to set this parameter.

This parameter manages the automatic registering of memory above 16MB in EISA machines.

Select OFF if you are using a NIC or disk adapter that uses an online direct memory access (DMA) or AT bus (which can address only 16MB of RAM).

If you use one of these boards and the server addresses more than 16MB of RAM, server memory will be corrupted. Low memory is addressed by the board (instead of the assigned memory), and low memory being used by the operating system is thus corrupted.

Select ON if you want to register memory above 16MB with the operating system.

```
Garbage Collection Interval = number
Values supported: 1 min-1 hour
Default: 15 min
```

This parameter sets the maximum time between garbage collections.

```
Number of Frees for Garbage Collection = number
Values supported: 100-100000
Default: 5000
```

This parameter sets the minimum number of frees necessary for garbage collection to take place.

```
Minimum Free Memory for Garbage Collection = number
Values supported: 1000-100000
Default: 8000
```

This parameter sets the minimum number of free allocation bytes necessary to allow garbage collection.

```
Allow Invalid Pointers = value
Values supported: ON, OFF
Default: OFF
```

This parameter determines whether invalid pointers are permitted to cause a nonexistent page to be mapped in with only one notification.

```
Read Fault Notification = value
Values supported: ON, OFF,
Default: ON
```

This parameter determines whether the server console and error log receive notice of emulated read page faults.

```
Read Fault Emulation = value
Values supported: ON, OFF
Default: OFF
```

This parameter determines whether a read that results from a non-present page is emulated.

```
Write Fault Notification = value
Values supported: ON, OFF
Default: ON
```

This parameter determines whether the server console and error log receive notice of emulated write page faults.

```
Write Fault Emulation = value
Values supported: ON, OFF
Default: OFF
```

This parameter determines whether a write that results from a non-present page is emulated.

SETTABLE FILE CACHING PARAMETERS

File caching parameters are as follows (with the default listed first and followed by the range or options):

```
Read Ahead Enabled:
ON         ON, OFF

Read Ahead LRU Sitting Time Threshold:
10 sec     0 sec-1 hour

Reserved Buffers Below 16 Meg:
16         8-300

Minimum File Cache Buffers:
20         20-1000

Maximum Concurrent Disk Cache Writes:
50         10-4000

Dirty Disk Cache Delay Time:
3.3 Sec    0.1 sec-10 sec

Minimum File Cache Report Threshold:
20         0-1000
```

File caching stores frequently used files—or parts of those files—in memory and thus enables to quickly access those files.

The number of files stored in cache is dependent on the number of cache buffers permitted. This number is determined by how much memory is accessible and by the `Minimum File Cache Buffers` setting.

```
Read Ahead Enabled = value
Values supported: ON, OFF
Default: ON
```

This parameter determines whether the server carries out background reads to cache in advance of the soon-to-be-requested blocks.

Read-aheads take place only when sequential file accesses are happening.

```
Read Ahead LRU Sitting Time Threshold = number
Values supported: 0 sec-1 hour
Default: 10 sec
```

This parameter sets the minimum cache *Least Recently Used* (LRU) sitting time for read-aheads to occur.

```
Reserved Buffers Below 16 Meg = number
Values supported: 8-300
Default: 16
```

This parameter sets the number of file cache buffers that are set aside for device drivers incapable of accessing RAM above 16MB.

```
Minimum File Cache Buffers = number
Values supported: 20-1000
Default: 20
```

This parameter determines the minimum number of cache buffers that can be allocated by the operating system for file caching.

The server sends all memory not used for other purposes to the file cache. As other processes request memory, the server releases cache buffers. This parameter tells the server when to stop releasing file cache buffers to other processes.

Be careful not to set the minimum too high because other processes may not be able to run as a result. A loadable module, for instance, could fail to load because of insufficient memory.

```
Maximum Concurrent Disk Cache Writes = number
Values supported: 10-4000
Default: 50
```

This parameter sets the number of write requests for modified file data can be placed in the elevator before the disk head starts a sweep across the disk.

A high number makes for more efficient processing of write requests.

A low number makes for more efficient processing of read requests.

Use MONITOR to check dirty cache buffer statistics. If this number if higher than 70 percent of the total cache buffers, increase this parameter to optimize the write speed.

```
Dirty Disk Cache Delay Time = time
Values supported: 0.1 sec-10 sec
Default: 3.3 sec
```

This parameter determines how long the server stores a write request (that does not fill a cache buffer) in memory before sending the request to the disk.

Increasing this parameter makes disk writes more efficient if network users are making several brief write requests.

Decreasing this parameter in order to make data more secure is generally not advisable.

```
Minimum File Cache Report Threshold = number
Values supported: 0-1000
Default: 20
```

This parameter sets the minimum number of file cache buffers that can be available before the server sends out a warning that the number of buffers is getting low.

So, if the `Minimum File Cache Buffers` parameter is set at `30` and this parameter is set at `50`, the server sends out a warning when all but 80 cache buffers have been granted to other processes. The following message appears on the console screen:

```
Number of cache buffers is getting too low.
```

Whichever setting you select, the server sends out a warning when it reaches the minimum number of cache buffers. The following message appears on the console screen:

```
Cache memory allocator exceeded minimum cache buffer left limit.
```

SETTABLE DIRECTORY CACHING PARAMETERS

Directory caching parameters are as follows (with the default listed first and followed by the range or options):

```
Dirty Directory Cache Delay Time:
0.5 sec   0-10 sec

Maximum Concurrent Directory Cache Writes:
10        5-50

Directory Cache Allocation Wait Time:
2.2 sec   0.5 sec-2 min

Directory Cache Buffer NonReferenced Delay:
5.5 sec   1 sec-5 min

Maximum Directory Cache Buffers:
500       20-4000

Minimum Directory Cache Buffers:
20        10-2000
```

Directory caching enables you to quickly access frequently used directories. A directory cache buffer is a section of server memory that stores directory table entries.

A directory entry remains in a cache buffer as long as it is being regularly accessed—the default is 33 seconds.

```
Dirty Directory Cache Delay Time = time
Values supported: 0-10 sec
Default: 0.5 sec
```

This parameter determines the length of time the server holds a directory table in memory before sending it to disk.

Increasing this parameter can improve performance slightly; however, increasing the parameter also increases the chance of directory table corruption.

Decreasing this parameter decreases the chance of directory table corruption but can also reduce performance slightly.

Setting this parameter at zero decreases performance drastically.

```
Maximum Concurrent Directory Cache Writes = number
Values supported: 5-50
Default: 10
```

This parameter sets the number of write requests from directory cache buffers that can be placed in the elevator before the disk head starts a sweep across the disk.

A high number makes for more efficient processing of write requests.

A low number makes for more efficient processing of read requests.

```
Directory Cache Allocation Wait Time = number
Values supported: 0.5 sec-2 min
Default: 2.2 sec
```

This parameter sets the length of time the server has to wait after allocating a new directory cache buffer before it can allocate another.

During this period, the server ignores all requests for a new directory cache buffer.

If you set this parameter too low, high usage requests cause more resources than needed to be allocated to the directory cache.

If you set this parameter too high, the server is slow to allocate the directory cache buffers needed to service the normal number of directory requests.

In case directory searches appear slow even after the server has been up for 15 minutes, consider decreasing this parameter.

```
Directory Cache Buffer NonReferenced Delay = time
Values supported: 1 sec-5 min
Default: 5.5 sec
```

This parameter sets the length of time a directory entry has to be cached before another directory entry can overwrite it.

Increasing this number improves directory access because the server allocates more directory cache buffers.

Decreasing this number reduces directory access but also decreases the necessity for directory cache buffers.

```
Maximum Directory Cache Buffers = number
Values supported: 20-4000
Default: 500
```

This parameter sets the maximum number of cache buffers that can be allocated by the server for directory caching.

Increasing this number improves performance if the server is responding slowly to directory searches.

Decreasing this number improves performance if too much memory has been allocated for directory caching.

If the server runs low on memory, this is one of the first parameters you should reduce. For the memory to be returned to the cache buffer memory pool, however, you must reboot the server.

Once a directory cache buffer is allocated, the allocation stays in effect until the server is rebooted.

This parameter makes memory available to other processes by preventing the server from allocating too much memory to the directory cache.

```
Minimum Directory Cache Buffers = number
Values supported: 10-2000
Default: 20
```

This parameter sets the minimum number of cache buffers that can be allocated by the server for directory caching.

This number must be sufficiently high to allow directory searches to be conducted quickly. Allocating too many cache buffers, however, has an adverse effect on performance because buffers not needed by the directory cache cannot be reallocated to file caching and go unused.

Use MONITOR to check directory cache statistics. If the server is slow in responding to directory searches after it is booted, check how many directory cache buffers are normally allocated for directory caching.

If the number of buffers normally allocated is significantly higher than the Minimum Directory Cache Buffers parameter, consider increasing the number. This can remove the normal delay time the server uses for self-configuration.

SETTABLE FILE SYSTEM PARAMETERS

File system parameters are as follows (with the default listed first and followed by the range or options):

```
Minimum File Delete Wait Time:
1 min, 5.9 sec        0 sec-7 days

File Delete Wait Time:
5 min, 29.6 sec       0 sec-7 days

Allow Deletion of Active Directories:
ON                    ON, OFF
```

Maximum Percent of Volume Space Allowed for Extended Attributes:
10   5-50

Maximum Extended Attributes per File or Path:
16   4-512

Maximum Percent of Volume Used by Directory:
13   5-50

Immediate Purge of Deleted Files:
OFF   ON, OFF

Maximum Subdirectory Tree Depth:
25   10-100

Volume Low Warn All Users:
ON   ON, OFF

Volume Low Warning Reset Threshold:
256   0-100000

Volume Low Warning Threshold:
256   0-1000000

Turbo FAT Re-Use Wait Time:
5 min, 29.6 sec   0.3 sec-1 hour, 5 min, 54.6 sec

Compression Daily Check Stop Hour:
6   0-23

Compression Daily Check Starting Hour:
0   0-23

Minimum Compression Percentage Gain:
2   0-50

Enable File Compression:
ON   ON, OFF

Maximum Concurrent Compressions:
2   1-18

Convert Compressed to Uncompressed Option:
1   0-2

Decompress Percent Disk Space Free to Allow Commit:
10   0-75

Uncompress Free Space Warning Interval:
31 min, 18.5 sec   0 sec-29 days, 15 hours, 50 min, 3.8 sec

Deleted Files Compression Option:
1   0-2

Days Untouched Before Compression:
7   1-100,000

File system parameters serve a variety of purposes, including managing warnings about nearly full volumes, purging control files, controlling the reuse of turbo FATs, and managing file compression.

```
Minimum File Delete Wait Time = time
Values supported: 0 sec-7 days
Default: 1 min, 5.9 sec
```

This parameter sets the length of time a deleted file stays salvageable on the volume. The server does not automatically purge files deleted for less than this time period—even if users are unable to create new files because the volume is full.

```
File Delete Wait Time = time
Values supported: 0 sec-7 days
Default: 5 min, 29.6 sec
```

This parameter determines when the server can purge a salvageable file to create free space on the volume.

It is advisable to set this number as high as is valuable for network users. Please note, however, that doing so does not guarantee files will stay salvageable.

The server attempts to keep at least 1/32 of the available space on the volume free for new files. This setting ensures that the server does not purge files to maintain this free disk space.

If the volume is full and the server requires space for new files, it purges files that have not met this time limit.

The server identifies files deleted for longer than this number as purgeable. The oldest purgeable files are deleted first when the volume is full and requires free space.

```
Allow Deletion of Active Directories = value
Values supported: ON, OFF
Default: ON
```

This parameter determines whether a directory can be deleted with another connection having a drive mapped to it.

```
Maximum Percent of Volume Space Allowed for Extended Attributes = percentage
Values supported: 5-50
Default: 10
```

This parameter limits how much volume space the server can use for extended attribute storage.

This parameter is operable only when the volume is being mounted.

```
Maximum Extended Attributes per File or Path = number
Values supported: 4-512
Default: 16
```

This parameter limits how many extended attributes the server can assign to a file or path (subdirectory).

This setting applies to all volumes on the server.

```
Maximum Percent of Volume Used by Directory = percentage
Values supported: 5-50
Default: 13
```

This parameter limits what percentage of a volume the server can use as directory space.

```
Immediate Purge of Deleted Files = value
Values supported: ON, OFF
Default: OFF
```

This parameter determines whether deleted files can be salvaged.

If you set this parameter to OFF, you can salvage deleted files with the FILER workstation utility.

If you set this parameter to ON, the server purges deleted files immediately.

```
Maximum Subdirectory Tree Depth = number
Values supported: 10-100
Default: 25
```

You must use the STARTUP.NCF file to set this parameter.

This parameter sets the number of subdirectories to be supported by the operating system.

```
Volume Low Warn All Users = value
Values supported: ON, OFF
Default: ON
```

This parameter determines whether the server warns users when a volume is almost full.

Network managers who elect not to warn users are advised to check volume statistics at least daily via SERVMAN or MONITOR.

```
Volume Low Warning Reset Threshold = number
Values supported: 0-100000
Default: 256 blocks
```

This parameter determines how much disk space the server must free up before issuing a second warning that the volume is almost full. (The Volume Low Warn All Users parameter controls the first warning.)

```
Volume Low Warning Threshold = number
Values supported: 0-1000000
Default: 256
```

This parameter allows the server to issue a low space warning when a certain number of free blocks are remaining.

```
Turbo FAT Re-Use Wait Time = time
Values supported: 0.3 sec-1 hour, 5 min, 54.6 sec
Default: 5 min, 29.6 sec
```

This parameter sets the period of time a turbo FAT stays in memory after the operating system closes an indexed file.

The operating system is free to allocate the buffer to another indexed file as soon as the specified time period has passed.

If you elect to have the turbo FAT index stay in memory for long periods of time, increase this parameter.

If you often reopen the same file after a certain delay and know that another file opened during that delay will re-use the index, increase this parameter.

If you want to have the released memory immediately available to service the next file that requires indexing, decrease this parameter.

```
Compression Daily Check Stop Hour = number
Values supported: 0-23
Default: 6
```

This parameter determines what time during the day the compressor stops scanning each enabled volume for files requiring compression.

Use a 24-hour clock, with 0 equaling midnight, 8 equaling 8:00 a.m., 15 equaling 3:00 p.m., and so on.

```
Compression Daily Check Starting Hour = number
Values supported: 0-23
Default: 0
```

This parameter determines what time during the day the compressor begins scanning enabled volumes for files requiring compression.

Use a 24-hour clock, with 0 equaling midnight, 8 equaling 8:00 a.m., 15 equaling 3:00 p.m., and so on.

If the Compression Daily Check Stop Hour parameter is the same as the Compression Daily Starting Hour parameter, the compressor begins checking every day at that time and operates as long as is needed to compress all files meeting the compression requirements.

```
Minimum Compression Percentage Gain = number
Values supported: 0-50
Default: 2
```

This parameter determines the minimum percentage a file has to compress to stay in a compressed state.

```
Enable File Compression = value
Values supported: ON, OFF
Default: ON
```

This parameter if file compression is allowed.

With this parameter set to ON, file compression is allowed on compression-enabled volumes.

With this parameter set to OFF, no compression is allowed, and immediate compress requests are kept in a queue until the value is changed to ON.

```
Maximum Concurrent Compressions = number
Values supported: 1-8
Default: 2
```

This parameter sets the maximum number of concurrent compressions allowed by the operating system.

Concurrent compressions require multiple volumes.

```
Convert Compressed to Uncompressed Option = value
Values supported: 0-2
Default: 1
```

This parameter determines how the operating system handles uncompressed versions of files after uncompressing them.

If you want the file always left compressed, select 0.

If you want the file to stay compressed until second access if it is read only once during the period set in Days Untouched Before Compression, select 1.

If you want the file always left uncompressed, select 2.

```
Uncompress Percent Disk Space Free to Allow Commit = number
Values supported: 0-75
Default: 10
```

This parameter sets how much free disk space is required on a volume for file decompression to permanently change the compressed files to uncompressed.

This parameter stops recently uncompressed files from filling up the volume.

```
Decompress Free Space Warning Interval = number
Values supported: 0 sec-29 days, 15 hours, 50 min, 3.8 sec
Default: 31 min, 18.5 sec
```

This parameter sets the time between alerts when a lack of disk space is preventing the file system from changing compressed files to uncompressed.

```
Deleted Files Compression Option = number
Values supported: 0-2
Default: 1
```

This parameter tells the operating system if and when to compress deleted files.

Select 0 if you do not want to compress deleted files.

Select 1 if you want to compress deleted files the next day.

Select 2 if you want to compress deleted files immediately.

```
Days Untouched Before Compression = number
Values supported: 1-100000
Default: 7
```

This parameter sets how long (in days) the operating system waits after it last accessed a file before compressing that file.

SETTABLE LOCK PARAMETERS

Lock parameters are as follows (with the default listed first and followed by the range or options):

```
Maximum Record Locks Per Connection:
500       10-10000

Maximum File Locks per Connection:
250       10-1000

Maximum Record Locks:
20000     100-200000

Maximum File Locks:
10000     100-100000
```

Lock parameters manage the following:

- ◆ The number of open files each workstation can have.
- ◆ The number of open files the operating system can support.
- ◆ The number of record locks each connection can support.
- ◆ The number of record locks the operating system can support.

The different kinds of locks are as follows:

File locks: These protect an entire file and do not allow other workstations to access it.

Physical record locks: These manage data access by multiple users. They do not allow other workstations to access or change a range of bytes (or a record) within a file.

Logical record locks: These also manage data access by multiple users. The application gives a name to each part of the data that must be locked. When the application accesses the data, it locks the appropriate name.

The operating system enforces logical locks to the degree that the name is checked by the application whenever it needs to access the data.

```
Maximum Record Locks Per Connection = number
Values supported: 10-10000
Default: 500
```

This parameter determines how many record locks can be used by a workstation at one time.

If an application fails because it cannot lock enough records, increase this number.

If too many server resources are being used by workstations, decrease this number.

You can check record lock statistics with MONITOR.

```
Maximum File Locks Per Connection = number
Values supported: 10-1000
Default: 250
```

This parameter determines the number of opened and locked files that can be used by a workstation at the same time.

If an application fails because it cannot open enough files, increase this number.

OS/2 workstations might require a higher default than 250. And it may also be necessary to increase file handles in the FILES= line of the workstation's NET.CFG file.

If too many server resources are being used by workstations, decrease this number.

You can check file lock statistics with MONITOR.

```
Maximum Record Locks = number
Values supported: 100-200000
Default: 20000
```

This parameter manages the number of record locks the operating system can handle.

If users have difficulty running applications and see messages indicating insufficient record locks, increase this number.

If too many server resources are being allocated to users, decrease this number.

```
Maximum File Locks = number
Values supported: 100-100000
Default: 10000
```

This parameter manages the number of opened and locked files the operating system can support.

If the current number of open files is close to or equal to the default, increase this number.

If you want to restrict the number of available server resources, decrease this number.

You can check open file statistics with MONITOR.

SETTABLE TTS PARAMETERS

Transaction Tracking parameters are as follows (with the default listed first and followed by the range or options):

```
Auto TTS Backout Flag:
OFF                    ON, OFF
```

```
TTS Abort Dump Flag:
OFF                     ON, OFF

Maximum Transactions:
10000                   100-10000

TTS Unwritten Cache Wait Time:
1 min, 5.9 sec          11 sec-10 min, 59.1 sec

TTS Backout File Truncation Wait Time:
59 min, 19.2 sec        1 min, 5.9 sec-1 day, 2 hours, 21 min, 51.3 sec
```

These parameters manage the Transaction Tracking System (TTS). A *transaction* is a group of write operations that the operating system must complete together to maintain file and database integrity.

Write operations are made up of changes to indexes and other important components as well as data and data records. TTS ensures that a transaction will either be written to disk in its entirety or completely backed out.

Most TTS parameters should not need changing.

```
Auto TTS Backout Flag = value
Values supported: ON, OFF
Default: OFF
```

You must use the STARTUP.NCF file to set this parameter.

This parameter determines whether a crashed server running transactional files can automatically back out failed transactions when it is rebooted.

If this parameter is set to ON, the server automatically backs out failed transactions as it reboots.

If this parameter is set to OFF, the server waits for responses to prompts as it reboots.

```
TTS Abort Dump Flag = value
Values supported: ON, OFF
Default: OFF
```

This parameter determines whether the server creates a log file to store transactional backout data.

If you want to have transactional backout data written to the TTS$LOG.ERR file on the SYS: volume, set this parameter to ON.

The TTS$LOG.ERR file can either be printed or viewed with a text editor.

If you do not want to save transactional backout data, set this parameter to OFF.

```
Maximum Transactions = number
Values supported: 100-10000
Default: 10000
```

This parameter sets the number of transactions that can occur simultaneously.

```
TTS UnWritten Cache Wait Time = time
Values supported: 11 sec-10 min, 59.1 sec
Default: 1 min, 5.9 sec
```

This parameter sets the period of time the operating system can hold a block of transactional data in memory.

```
TTS Backout File Truncation Wait Time = time
Values supported: 1 min, 5.9 sec-1 day, 2 hours, 21 min, 51.3 sec
Default: 59 min, 19.2 sec
```

This parameter sets the period of time allocated blocks remain available for the TTS backout file when these blocks are unused.

SETTABLE DISK PARAMETERS

Disk parameters are as follows (with the default listed first and followed by the range or options):

```
Enable Disk Read After Write Verify:
ON                      ON, OFF

Remirror Block Size:
1                       1-8

Concurrent Remirror Requests:
4                       2-32
```

Disk parameters manage one aspect of Hot Fix redirection, which can take place during a write request, a read request, or a read-after-write verification.

Write redirection takes place when an error is reported by the disk during a write request. The operating system identifies the bad block and sends the data to a different block.

Read redirection takes place when an error is reported by the disk during a read request. If the hard disk is mirrored, the data is retrieved from the mirrored disk and the data on the primary disk is redirected. If the disk is not mirrored, the operating system identifies the bad block, but the data is lost.

Read-after-write-verify redirection takes place after the data is written to disk. The operating system then checks the data on disk and compares it to the data in memory. If the two are different, the bad block is identified and the data is sent to a different block.

```
Enable Disk Read After Write Verify = value
Values supported: ON, OFF
Default: ON
```

This parameter determines whether data written to disk is compared to data in memory.

This parameter should generally not be set to OFF.

If you are using a reliable disk mirroring system, however, you can virtually double the speed of disk writes by disabling this parameter.

```
Remirror Block Size = value
Values supported: 1-8
Default: 1
```

This parameter specifies the remirror block size in 4 K increments—so that 1 = 4K, 2 = 8K, 3 = 12K, and so on.

```
Concurrent Remirror Requests = value
Values supported: 2-32
Default: 4
```

This parameter specifies the number of remirror requests for each logical partition.

SETTABLE TIME PARAMETERS

Time parameters are as follows (with the default listed first and followed by the range or options; for some parameters a maximum length is listed):

```
TIMESYNC ADD Time Source:
Maximum length: 48

TIMESYNC Configuration File:
Maximum length: 255

TIMESYNC Configured Sources:
OFF                     ON, OFF

TIMESYNC directory Tree Mode:
ON                      ON, OFF

TIMESYNC Hardware Clock:
ON                      ON, OFF

TIMESYNC Polling Count:
3                       1-1000

TIMESYNC Polling Interval:
600                     10-2678400

TIMESYNC REMOVE Time Source:
Maximum length: 48

TIMESYNC RESET:
OFF                     ON, OFF

TIMESYNC Restart Flag:
OFF                     ON, OFF

TIMESYNC Service Advertising:
ON                      ON, OFF

TIMESYNC Synchronization Radius:
2000                    0-2147483647
```

```
TIMESYNC Time Adjustment:
Maximum length: 99

TIMESYNC Time Source:
Maximum length: 48

TIMESYNC Type:
Secondary            Reference, Primary, Secondary, Single

TIMESYNC Write Parameters:
OFF                  ON, OFF

TIMESYNC Write Value:
3                    1-3

Time Zone:
NO TIME ZONE         Maximum length: 80

Default Time Server Type:
Secondary            Reference, Primary, Secondary, Single

Start of Daylight Savings Time:
Maximum length: 79

End of Daylight Savings Time:
Maximum length: 79

Daylight Savings Time Offset:
+1:00:00             +-1:00:00

Daylight Savings Time Status:
OFF                  ON, OFF

New Time with Daylight Savings Time Status:
OFF                  ON, OFF
```

These parameters allow you to check a server's internal time and ensure that all server throughout the network use synchronized clocks.

Time parameters manage the following:

◆ Time synchronization

◆ TIMESYNC.CFG file

◆ Time zone settings

The following are time server types:

Single Reference: These servers give time to secondary servers and are the only time source on networks.

Primary: These servers synchronize the time with at least one other primary or reference server, and they also give time to secondary servers.

Reference: These servers do not alter their clocks; therefore, primary and secondary servers must synchronize their clocks with the reference server clock.

Secondary: These servers receive the time from a primary or reference server.

THE TIMESYNC CONFIGURATION FILE

The TIMESYNC.CFG file (stored by default in SYS:SYSTEM) contains time synchronization parameters. If you want to modify the time synchronization configuration, make the changes in the TIMESYNC.CFG file and then either reboot the system or use the SET console command to set the TIMESYNC Restart Flag parameter to ON.

If you store many settings in your TIMESYNC.CFG file, you may want to consider copying the file from server to server. If you do, make certain that each copied TIMESYNC.CFG file includes the correct default time server type and configured-sources list for the server it is associated with.

You can set TIMESYNC parameters at the command line (using LOAD TIMESYNC), in the TIMESYNC.CFG file, or by using the SET command or the SERVMAN module.

Keep in mind, however, that you must add the proper line to the TIMESYNC.CFG file to make changes permanent—any modifications you make in SET or SERVMAN will no longer be effective once the server is rebooted.

In addition, you should use the EDIT module rather than the following TIMESYNC parameters to accomplish certain time-related tasks (see "Managing Network Time Synchronization" in the NetWare 4 manual *Supervising the Network* for more information):

```
TIMESYNC ADD Time Source

TIMESYNC Remove Time Source

TIMESYNC RESET

TIMESYNC Time Source

TIMESYNC Type

TIMESYNC Write Parameters

TIMESYNC Write Value

TIMESYNC ADD Time Source = server name

Maximum length: 48
```

This parameter allows a server to be added to the configured time source list in TIMESYNC.CFG.

```
TIMESYNC Configuration File = path
```

```
Maximum length: 255
```

This parameter determines the path of TIMESYNC.CFG.

Example: SET TIMESYNC CONFIGURATION FILE = SYS:SYSTEM\TIMESYNC.CFG

```
TIMESYNC Configured Sources = value
Values supported: ON, OFF
Default: OFF
```

This parameter determines what time sources the server responds to.

The ON setting means that the server disregards SAP time sources and responds to time sources custom-configured with the TIMESYNC Time Source parameter.

The OFF setting means that the server responds to any advertising time source.

```
TIMESYNC Directory Tree Mode = value
Values supported: ON, OFF
Default: ON
```

This parameter manages the use of SAP packets in the NetWare Directory Services tree.

The ON setting means that time synchronization disregards SAP packets not originating from within the Directory tree the server is on.

The OFF setting means that the server can respond to SAP packets from any time source on the network.

Do not use the OFF parameter if the server has SAP set to ON. Doing so can cause time synchronization corruption for this server's Directory tree.

```
TIMESYNC Hardware Clock = value
Values supported: ON, OFF
Default: ON
```

This parameter manages hardware clock synchronization.

The ON setting means that the primary and secondary servers set the hardware clock and the single and reference servers set their time from the hardware clock at the start of each polling interval.

You should use OFF only if the server relies on an external time source (a radio clock, for example).

All servers in the same Directory tree should use the same setting.

```
TIMESYNC Polling Count = number
Values supported: 1-1000
Default: 3
```

This parameter sets the number of time packets to exchange while polling. Increasing this number unnecessarily increases network traffic.

```
TIMESYNC Polling Interval = number
Values supported: 10-2678400
Default: 600
```

This parameter sets the long polling interval. All servers in the same tree should use the same setting.

The values supported are in seconds. The maximum value translates to 31 days.

```
TIMESYNC REMOVE Time Source = server name
Maximum length: 48
```

This parameter allows a server to be deleted from the configuration list in TIMESYNC.CFG.

```
TIMESYNC RESET = value
Values supported: ON, OFF
Default: OFF
```

This parameter manages the method of resetting time synchronization. Values are reset in TIMESYNC.CFG.

The ON setting resets selected internal values and clears the configured server list.

```
TIMESYNC Restart Flag = value
Values supported: ON, OFF
Default: OFF
```

This parameter manages restarts of time synchronization.

The ON setting means that time synchronization restarts. Use ON only if you want to reload the TIMESYNC.NLM without shutting down the server and rebooting.

```
TIMESYNC Service Advertising = value
Values supported: ON, OFF
Default: ON
```

This parameter manages time source advertising.

The ON setting means that the single, reference, and primary time source advertise using SAP.

Use OFF if you are using a customized list of time sources.

```
TIMESYNC Synchronization Radius = number
Values supported: 0-2147483647
Default: 2000
```

This parameter manages the maximum time adjustment a server is given while still categorized as synchronized. Increasing this number provides a greater margin of error for time synchronization between servers.

The number value is in seconds.

Note that lowering the synchronization radius creates a greater probability that servers will lose synchronization due to randomness between clocks. Therefore, selecting a value less than the default of 2000 is not advised.

```
TIMESYNC Time Adjustment = [+ or -] hour:minute:second: at month/day/year
hour:minute:second [AM or PM]
Maximum length: 99
Default: 1 hour from the current time or 6 polling intervals (whichever is longer)
```

This parameter specifies when a time adjustment will occur. Exercise care in using this parameter because improper settings can corrupt time synchronization.

The parameter format is as follows:

```
[+][-] hour:minute:second
```

This parameter cannot be used on a secondary time server.

```
TIMESYNC Time Source = server name
Maximum length: 48
```

This parameter allows you to add a server to the configuration list in TIMESYNC.CFG.

If you do not enter a server name, the parameter lists configured servers.

```
TIMESYNC Type = type of time source
Types supported: Reference, Primary, Secondary, Single
Default: Secondary
```

This parameter determines the time source type in TIMESYNC.CFG.

```
TIMESYNC Write Parameters = value
Values supported: ON, OFF
Default: OFF
```

This parameter determines whether TIMESYNC Write Value parameters are written to the configuration file.

```
TIMESYNC Write Value = number
Values supported: 1-3
Default: 3
```

This parameter manages which parameters are written by TIMESYNC Write Parameters.

Select 1 to write internal parameters only.

Select 2 to write configured time sources only.

Select 3 to write both parameters and configured time sources.

```
Time Zone = time zone string
Maximum length: 80
Default: <<NO TIME ZONE>>
```

This parameter determines the time zone string, which indicates the following:

◆ Abbreviated time zone name

◆ Offset from Universal Time (UTC)

◆ Alternate abbreviated time zone name for use when daylight savings time is in effect.

As a result of this parameter, UTC time is recalculated from local time.

```
Default Time Server Type = type of time source
Types supported: Reference, Primary, Secondary, Single
Default: Secondary
```

This parameter sets the default time synchronization server type; other time synchronization settings can override this parameter.

```
Start of Daylight Savings Time = date and time
Maximum length: 79
```

This parameter sets the local date and time when the change to daylight savings time should take place.

Set both the start and end of daylight savings time before actually scheduling them.

```
End of Daylight Savings Time = date and time
Maximum length: 79
```

This parameter sets the local date and time when the change from daylight savings time should take place.

Set both the start and end of daylight savings time before actually scheduling them.

```
Daylight Savings Time Offset = [+][-]hour:minute:second
Default: +1:00:00
```

This parameter manages the offset associated with time calculations when daylight savings time is in effect.

Parameter format is as follows:

```
[+][-]hour:minute:second
```

As a result of this parameter, UTC time is recalculated from local time.

```
Daylight Savings Time Status = value
Values supported: ON, OFF
Default: OFF
```

This parameter specifies if daylight savings time is in effect.

If you select ON, use the Daylight Savings Time Offset parameter as well.

Changing this value does not affect the local time.

```
New Time With Daylight Savings Time Status = value
Values supported: ON, OFF
Default: OFF
```

This parameter manages the local time setting when daylight savings time is in effect.

If you use ON, this setting changes the local time by adding or subtracting the value specified in the Daylight Savings Time Offset parameter.

SETTABLE NCP PARAMETERS

NetWare Core Protocol (NCP) parameters are as follows (with the default listed first and followed by the range or options):

```
NCP File Commit:
ON                      ON, OFF

Display NCP Bad Component Warnings:
OFF                     ON, OFF

Reject NCP Packets with Bad Components:
OFF                     ON, OFF

Display NCP Bad Length Warnings:
OFF                     ON, OFF

Reject NCP Packets with Bad Lengths:
OFF                     ON, OFF

Maximum Outstanding NCP Searches:
51                      10-1000

NCP Packet Signature Option:
1                       0-3

Enable IPX Checksums:
1                       0-2

Allow Change to Client Rights:
ON                      ON, OFF

Allow LIP:
ON                      ON, OFF
```

Theses parameters allow you to do the following:

- ◆ Manage NCP packets
- ◆ Manage boundary checking
- ◆ Specify NCP Server Packet Signature levels

```
NCP File Commit = value
Values supported: ON, OFF
Default: ON
```

This parameter determines whether applications can flush pending file writes to the hard disk.

Setting this value to ON means that when a File Commit NCP is issued, the operating system sends a file from cache to disk immediately, rather than waiting for the cache manager to do so later.

```
Display NCP BAD Component Warnings = value
Values supported: ON, OFF
Default: OFF
```

This parameter determines whether the console displays NCP bad component messages.

```
Reject NCP Packets with Bad Components = value
Values supported: ON, OFF
Default: OFF
```

This parameter specifies whether the operating system rejects NCP packets that fail component checking.

```
Display NCP Bad Length Warnings = value
Values supported: ON, OFF
Default: OFF
```

This parameter specifies whether the console displays NCP bad length alert messages.

```
Reject NCP Packets with Bad Lengths = value
Values supported: ON, OFF
Default: OFF
```

This parameter specifies whether the operating system rejects NCP packets that fail boundary checking.

```
Maximum Outstanding NCP Searches = number
Values supported: 10-1000
Default: 51
```

This parameter sets the maximum number of NCP directory searches that the operating system can process simultaneously.

Usually, only one NCP directory search takes place at a time.

Increase this number only under these circumstances:

You are running applications that support multiple outstanding directory searches.

You experience difficulties with corrupted or invalid directory information.

```
NCP Packet Signature Option = number
Values supported: 0-3
Default 1
```

This parameter manages the server's NCP packet signature level.

Use one of the following values:

0	Server does not sign packets (regardless of the client level).
1	Server signs packets only if the client requests it (client level is 2 or higher).
2	Server signs packets if the client is capable of signing (client level is 1 or higher).
3	Server signs packets and requires all clients to sign packets (or logging in will fail).

NCP packet signature strengthens both server and client security by preventing forgery of packets. It does this by making it necessary for the server and client to "sign" each NCP packet.

This parameter is optional because it uses server resources and degrades performance.

```
Enable IPX Checksums = number
Values supported: 0-2
Default: 1
```

This parameter sets the enabling of IPX checksums.

Select 0 for no checksums.

Select 1 to checksum if enabled at the client.

Select 2 to require checksums.

```
Allow Change to Client Rights = value
Values supported: ON, OFF
Default: ON
```

This parameter determines whether a job server can assume the rights of a client, for NCP packet signatures.

Use the following guidelines to set this parameter:

Some job servers and third-party applications have to change to client rights in order to run. Selecting OFF can prevent some job servers from accessing the files they require.

Selecting OFF prevents packet forging via the job or print server.

```
Allow LIP = value
Values supported: ON, OFF
Default: ON
```

This parameter determines whether the operating system supports Large Internet Packet (LIP).

SETTABLE MISCELLANEOUS PARAMETERS

Miscellaneous parameters are as follows (with the default listed first and followed by the range or options):

```
Replace Console Prompt with Server Name:
ON                      ON, OFF

Alert Message Nodes:
20                      10-256

Worker Thread Execute in a Row Count:
10                      1-20
```

```
Display Disk Device Alerts:
OFF                     ON, OFF

Halt System on Invalid Parameters:
OFF                     ON, OFF

Upgrade Low Priority Threads:
OFF                     ON, OFF

Display Relinquish Control Alerts:
OFF                     ON, OFF

Display Incomplete IPX Packet Alerts:
ON                      ON, OFF

Display Old API Names:
OFF                     ON, OFF

Developer Option:
OFF                     ON, OFF

Display Spurious Interrupt Alerts:
ON                      ON, OFF

Display Lost Interrupt Alerts:
ON                      ON, OFF

Pseudo Preemption Count:
10                      1-4294967295

Global Pseudo Preemption:
OFF                     ON, OFF

Maximum Service Processes:
40                      5-100

Sound Bell for Alerts:
ON                      ON, OFF

New Service Process Wait Time:
2.2 sec                 0.3-20 sec

Automatically Repair Bad Volume:
ON                      ON, OFF

Allow Unencrypted Passwords:
OFF                     ON, OFF

Bindery Context:
Maximum length: 256
```

These parameters manage alerts, encrypted passwords, and a variety of server processes. `Allow Unencrypted Passwords` is normally the only miscellaneous parameter you should need to change.

```
Replace Console Prompt with Server Name = value
Values supported: ON, OFF
Default: ON
```

This parameter determines whether the server name replaces the console prompt.

```
Alert Message Nodes = number
Values supported: 10-256
Default: 20
```

This parameter sets the number of message nodes that have been previously allocated.

```
Worker Thread Execute in a Row Count = number
Values supported: 1-20
Default: 10
```

This parameter sets the number of times the scheduler consecutively dispatches new work before permitting other threads to run.

```
Display Disk Device Alerts = value
Values supported: ON, OFF
Default: OFF
```

This parameter manages hard disk informational messages.

The operating system generates a message whenever a hard disk is added, activated, deactivated, mounted, or dismounted.

Select ON if you want messages displayed under these circumstances:

- ◆ You load or unload a disk driver
- ◆ You either boot or shut down the server
- ◆ You are attempting to isolate a disk driver or hard disk problem

Select OFF if you are not having hard disk problems.

```
Device # 0 (20000) ISA Type 043 added.
Device # 0 (20000) ISA Type 043 activated.
Device # 0 (20000) ISA Type 043 deactivated
due to down
```

The ON setting causes the preceding types of messages to be displayed.

```
Halt System on Invalid Parameters = value
Values supported: ON, OFF
Default: OFF
```

This parameter specifies whether the system stops when it detects invalid parameters.

Select ON if you want the system to stop when it detects an invalid parameter.

Select OFF if you want the system to display a message and then continue operating when it detects an invalid parameter.

```
Upgrade Low Priority Threads = value
Values supported: ON, OFF
Default: OFF
```

This parameter specifies whether the operating system schedules low-priority threads at regular priority.

Certain NLMs can freeze up low-priority threads, which causes file compression to shut down, as well as other problems.

```
Display Relinquish Control Alerts = value
Values supported: ON, OFF
Default: OFF
```

This parameter determines whether the operating system sends CPU control messages to the server console.

Select ON if you are developing your own NLMs.

Select OFF if you are not developing your own NLMs.

```
<process name> Process did not relinquish control frequently.
Module: <module name>
Code offset in module: <memory address>
```

The preceding types of messages are displayed if NLM controls the processor for more than 0.4 seconds without giving up control to other processes.

```
Display Incomplete IPX Packet Alerts = value
Values supported: ON, OFF
Default: ON
```

This parameter specifies whether the operating system displays alert messages when IPX receives incomplete packets.

```
Display Old API Names = value
Values supported: ON, OFF
Default: OFF
```

This parameter manages messages about NetWare 3.x API calls.

Select ON if you are developing your own NLMs and are upgrading NetWare 3.0 NLMs to the new 4.x APIs.

Select OFF if you are not upgrading your NLMs to 4.x.

See the NetWare 4 manual *NetWare Utilities Reference* for more information.

```
Developer Option = value
Values supported: ON, OFF
Default: OFF
```

This parameter determines whether the operating system enables options associated with a developer environment.

```
Display Spurious Interrupt Alerts = value
Values supported: ON, OFF
Default: ON
```

This parameter manages the alert messages related to spurious interrupts.

A spurious interrupt takes place when the server hardware produces an interrupt reserved for another device.

When a spurious interrupt occurs, a message similar to the following is displayed:

```
Spurious hardware interrupt <number> detected
```

Such messages are indications of serious hardware problems.

If you receive a spurious interrupt message, remove all add-on adapters and execute SERVER. If the message no longer appears, install the adapters one at a time until you find which adapter is causing the interrupt. Then contact the party responsible for servicing that adapter.

You can set this value to OFF while you are in the process of solving the problem.

```
Display Lost Interrupt Alerts = value
Values supported: ON, OFF
Default: ON
```

This parameter manages alert messages related to lost interrupts.

A lost interrupt takes place when a driver or adapter requests a service with an interrupt call and then drops the request before the CPU can answer.

A message similar to the following is displayed when a lost interrupt occurs:

```
Interrupt controller detected a lost hardware interrupt
```

Lost interrupts can degrade performance. To isolate the problem, unload all drivers; then reload them one at a time until you find which driver is causing the problem. Then contact the responsible party. You can set this value to OFF while you are waiting for the problem to be solved.

```
Pseudo Preemption Count = number
Values supported: 1-4294967295
Default: 10
```

This parameter controls how many times threads are permitted to make file read or write system calls before a relinquish is forced.

```
Global Pseudo Preemption = value
Values supported: ON, OFF
Default: OFF
```

This parameter specifies if all threads use Pseudo Preemption.

```
Maximum Service Processes = number
Values supported: 5-100
Default: 40
```

This parameter sets the maximum number of service processes that the operating system can produce.

Lower this number temporarily if the server is running low on memory. (But if you have continual memory problems, add memory to the server.)

Raise this number if the service processes number is at the maximum. Raising this number has value only if more than 20 requests are being delayed simultaneously for a disk I/O to be completed.

MONITOR allows you to check the number of service processes that have been currently allocated.

```
Sound Bell for Alerts = value
Values supported: ON, OFF
Default: ON
```

This parameter determines whether an alert message causes a bell to sound.

```
New Service Process Wait Time = number
Values supported: 0.3 sec-20 sec
Default: 2.2 sec
```

This parameter specifies the period of time the operating system waits after receiving a request for another service process before granting the request.

```
Automatically Repair Bad Volume = value
Values supported: ON, OFF
Default: ON
```

This parameter specifies if VREPAIR executes automatically on volumes that fail to mount.

```
Allow Unencrypted Passwords = value
Values supported: ON, OFF
Default: OFF
```

This parameter manages the use of unencrypted passwords.

Select OFF if you are running NetWare v3.1x on all your servers.

Select OFF if you are running NetWare v2.12 on some servers and can copy the v3.1x utilities to these servers.

Select ON if you are running v2.12 on some servers and do not copy the utilities to those servers.

If you are running v2.12 on some servers and leave this setting at OFF, some users may have difficulty logging in.

```
Bindery Context = value
Maximum length: 256
```

This parameter determines the bindery context that NetWare Directory Services uses for bindery emulation.

Example: SET BINDERY CONTEXT = OU=SALES_LA.OU=SALES.O=NOVELL_US

SETTABLE ERROR HANDLING PARAMETERS

Error handling parameters are as follows (with the default listed first and followed by the range or options):

```
Server Log File State:
1                      0-2

Volume Log File State:
1                      0-2

Volume TTS Log File State:
1                      0-2

Server Log File Overflow Size:
4194304               65536-4294967295

Volume TTS Log File Overflow Size:
4194304               65536-4294967295

Volume Log File Overflow Size:
4194304               65536-4294967295
```

These parameters manage error log file size as well as what happens to error log files once they reach a certain size.

```
Server Log File State = number
Values supported: 0-2
Default: 1
```

This parameter determines what takes place when the SYS$LOG.ERR file is larger that the size set by the Server Log File Overflow Size parameter.

Select 0 if you want SYS$LOG.ERR to remain as it is.

Select 1 if you want to delete SYS$LOG.ERR.

Select 2 if you want to rename SYS$LOG.ERR.

```
Volume TTS Log File State = number
Values supported: 0-2
Default: 1
```

This parameter determines what takes place when the TTS$LOG.ERR file is larger than the size set by the Volume TTS Log File Overflow Size parameter.

Select 0 if you want TTS$LOG.ERR to remain as it is.

Select 1 if you want to delete TTS$LOG.ERR.

Select 2 if you want to rename TTS$LOG.ERR.

```
Volume Log File State = number
Values supported: 0-2
Default: 1
```

This parameter determines what takes place when the VOL$LOG.ERR file is larger than the size set by the Volume Log File Overflow Size parameter.

Select 0 if you want VOL$LOG.ERR to remain as it is.

Select 1 if you want to delete VOL$LOG.ERR.

Select 2 if you want to rename VOL$LOG.ERR.

```
Server Log File Overflow Size = number
Values supported: 65536-4294967295
Default: 4194304
```

This parameter sets the maximum size of the SYS$LOG.ERR file before the action set by the `Server Log File State` parameter takes place.

```
Volume TTS Log File Overflow Size = number
Values supported: 65536-4294967295
Default: 4194304
```

This parameter sets the maximum size of the TTS$LOG.ERR file before the action set by the `Volume TTS Log File State` parameter takes place.

```
Volume Log File Overflow Size = number
Values supported: 65536-4294967295
Default: 4194304
```

This parameter sets the maximum size of the VOL$LOG.ERR file before the action set by the `Volume Log File State` parameter takes place.

RELATED COMMANDS

The `EDIT` loadable module allows you to create or change text files.

The `SET TIME` console command allows you to configure the server time and date.

The `SERVMAN` loadable module allows you to check or configure time-related and other system parameters.

The `TIMESYNC` loadable module allows you to check a server's internal time to ensure that the time used by servers throughout the network is synchronized

SET TIME

PURPOSE

This command allows you to set the date and time for the server.

SYNTAX

```
SET TIME [month/day/year][hour:minute:second]
```

PARAMETERS

Enter TIME with no parameters to view the server's current date and time.

Insert the current date in place of *month/day/year*.

Insert the current time in place of *hour:minute:second*.

EXAMPLE

Suppose that you want to set the date and time on the server to June 12, 1995 at 2:00 p.m. Enter the following at the console prompt:

```
SET TIME 6/12/95 2:00:00 PM
```

or

```
SET TIME June 12, 1995 14:00:00
```

or

```
SET TIME 12 June 1995 2:00:00 PM
```

NOTES

You can enter time values in either standard or 24-hour-clock format:

> 2:00:00 PM (standard)
>
> 14:00:00 (24-hour-clock)

Use colons to separate hours, minutes, and seconds. The colon after the hour is required, but you can omit the minute and second values.

Use any of the following formats for entering the date value:

> 6/12/95
>
> June 12, 1995
>
> 12 June, 1995

Date and time can be set with the same command or they can be set separately. You can enter either value first.

If you replace only one value, the other remains unchanged.

The server always displays time in standard format (such as 2:00:00 PM).

RELATED COMMANDS

A number of SET parameters deal with such issues as synchronizing server clocks, specifying time zones, and accounting for daylight savings time changes.

SET TIME ZONE

PURPOSE

SET TIME ZONE enables you to configure time zone information in CLIB.

SYNTAX

SET TIME ZONE

or

SET TIME ZONE *zone* [[+] [*hours* [*daylight*]]]

PARAMETERS

In place of *zone*, insert an abbreviation from the following list:

Time Zone	Abbreviation
Eastern Standard Time	EST
Central Standard Time	CST
Mountain Standard Time	MST
Pacific Standard Time	PST

In place of *hours*, insert the number of hours west of Greenwich Mean Time (GMT), shown in the following list. Include a + if you are east of the GMT time zone line.

Time Zone	Hours from GMT
EST	5
CST	6
MST	7
PST	8

In place of *daylight*, insert an abbreviation from the following list (if needed):

Time Zone	Daylight Zone
EST	EDT
CST	CDT
MST	MDT
PST	PDT

EXAMPLE

To display the current time zone information, enter the following:

SET TIME ZONE

To change the time zone to California Pacific Daylight Time, enter the following:

```
SET TIME ZONE PST8PDT
```

NOTES

NLMs use time zone information to make calls to CLIB. SET TIME ZONE does not automatically change the server from standard to daylight time.

The default is EST5EDT—Eastern Standard Time, five hours west of Greenwich Mean Time, Eastern Daylight Time.

RELATED COMMANDS

SET offers parameters for changing to daylight savings time.

SPEED

PURPOSE

This command allows you to display the speed of the central processing unit (CPU).

SYNTAX

```
SPEED
```

PARAMETERS

None

EXAMPLE

To find out how fast the CPU is running, enter the following:

```
SPEED
```

NOTES

The following factors determine the processor speed rating:

◆ CPU clock speed (16 MHz, 25 MHz, and so on)

◆ CPU type (80386/SX, 80486, and so on)

◆ Number of memory wait states (0, 1, and so on)

A 16 MHz 80386/SX gets a rating of about 95, while a 16 MHz 80386 gets a rating of about 120.

Certain PCs use an AUTO or COMMON CPU speed mode that can decrease the clock speed to as little as 6 MHz.

For more information on setting the CPU speed, check the vendor documentation.

TIME

PURPOSE

This command allows you to view the server date and time, daylight savings time status, and time synchronization data.

SYNTAX

```
TIME
```

PARAMETERS

None

EXAMPLE

To check server time information, enter the following:

```
TIME
```

A list similar to the following is displayed on the server console screen:

```
ENGINEERING:time
Time zone string: "MST7MDT"
DST status: OFF
DST start: Sunday, April 4, 1993 2:00:00     am MST
DST end: Sunday, October 31, 1993 2:00:00    am MDT
Time synchronization is active.
Time is synchronization to the network.
Monday, June 12, 1995 7:06:59 pm UTC
Monday, June 12, 1995 12:06:59 pm MST
```

NOTES

See the previous section entitled "Setting Time Parameters" for information on synchronization.

RELATED COMMANDS

The SET TIME console command allows you to reset the server's date or time.

TRACK OFF

PURPOSE

The TRACK OFF command prevents the server from displaying network advertising packets that are received or sent on the Router Tracking Screen.

SYNTAX

TRACK OFF

PARAMETERS

None

EXAMPLE

To run TRACK OFF, enter the following at the server console prompt:

TRACK OFF

NOTES

This command can be executed after the server has been downed.

RELATED COMMANDS

TRACK ON allows the Router Tracking Screen to be displayed.

TRACK ON

PURPOSE

The TRACK ON command allow you to display the Router Tracking Screen and make it the active screen.

SYNTAX

TRACK ON

PARAMETERS

None

EXAMPLE

To make the Router Tracking Screen active, enter the following:

```
TRACK ON
```

NOTES

TRACK ON makes a request of the server to display all server and network advertising packets that are received or sent.

TRACK allows server, network, and connection request information to be displayed. This information is formatted according to whether the server is receiving data (IN), broadcasting data (OUT), or receiving a connection request.

TRACK ON displays incoming information in a manner similar to the following:

```
IN [00D0C200:00001B026C09] 10:53:01am PLATO 5
DEV0 3 HIKER 3 UTIL 2
IN [00D0200:00001B02609] 10:53:01am 00001EEEEEE 2/3
    5300DEEF 3/4 00001EF0 5/365 FADE2401 2/3
```

Incoming information adheres to the following format:

IN	Incoming message
00D0C200	Network number of the server transmitting the packet
0001B026C09	Node address of the server transmitting the packet.

Server information adheres to the following format:

PLATO	Server name
5	Number of hops between transmitting server and this server

Network information adheres to the following format:

00001EEE	Network number
2/	Number of hops from the transmitting server to this net work
/3	Number of ticks (1/18th of a second) required by a packet to reach this network from the transmitting server

TRACK ON displays outgoing information in a manner similar to the following:

```
OUT [1986DAD0:FFFFFFFFFFFF] 10:53:01am 00001EEE 2/3
    5300DEEF 3/4 00001EF0 5/365 FADE2401 2/3
    FEED00BB 4/5
OUT [00D0C200:FFFFFFFFFFFF] 10:53:01am
                            UTIL    2
    DEV0 3 HIKER 3 PLATO 2
```

Outgoing information adheres to the following format:

OUT	Outgoing message
1986DAD0	Network number of the server transmitting the packet
FFFFFFFFFFFF	Message is for all network nodes

The node address is followed by server or network information.

When a workstation is booted and loads the workstation drivers, it sends a GET Nearest Server request across the network.

Any server connected to the same network can answer with a Give Nearest Server message. The workstation attaches to the first server to answer.

RELATED COMMANDS

TRACK OFF allows you disable TRACK ON.

DISPLAY NETWORKS lists all the networks the server knows about.

DISPLAY SERVERS lists all the servers the server knows about.

RESET ROUTER resets the router tables to their initial state.

UNBIND

PURPOSE

This command allows you to do the following:

◆ Unbind communication protocols from LAN drivers
◆ Change network numbers for cabling
◆ Disable NICs

SYNTAX

UNBIND *protocol* [FROM] *lan driver* [*driver parameter*...]

PARAMETERS

Replace *protocol* with the name of the protocol you want to unbind.

Replace *lan driver* with the name of the appropriate driver.

If you are using more than one NIC of the same type in the server, replace *driver parameter* with one or more parameters from the following list:

[DMA=*number*]	DMA channel identifier. Select the same channel you selected when the driver was loaded.
[INT=*number*]	Interrupt identifier. Select the same interrupt you selected when the driver was loaded.
[MEM=*number*]	Memory address identifier. Select the same address you selected when the driver was loaded.
[PORT=*number*]	I/O port identifier. Select the same port you selected when the driver was loaded.
[SLOT=*number*]	Slot identifier. This parameter applies to EISA and Micro Channel machines. Select the same slot number you selected when the driver was loaded.
[*name*]	Board name. Select the same name you assigned when the driver was loaded.

EXAMPLE

Suppose that you want to unbind the NE2000 driver from the IPX protocol. Enter the following at the console prompt:

```
UNBIND IPX FROM NE2000 [INT=4]
```

NOTES

When you use UNBIND, the operating system requires information on which NIC to unbind the protocol from.

Include all information that makes the NIC different from other NICs of its type.

UNBIND changes made at the command line only stay in effect until the server is rebooted. To make such changes permanent, delete the appropriate BIND line from the AUTOEXEC.NCF file.

If you are binding multiple protocols to one NIC, it is a good idea to use the name parameter. This makes it simple to unbind one protocol from the NIC.

RELATED COMMANDS

BIND enables you to associate networking protocols (such as IPX) with drivers and with network interface cards.

The PROTOCOL command allows you to see what protocols are already registered on the server. It also allows you to register new protocols and frame types.

CAUTION

Using the UNBIND command can cause network users to lose their connections to the server. Therefore, use this command cautiously, and give proper notification to all users.

UNLOAD

PURPOSE

UNLOAD allows you unload loadable modules, drivers, or name space modules.

SYNTAX

UNLOAD *loadable module*

PARAMETERS

In place of *loadable module*, insert the name of the module you want to unload.

EXAMPLE

Suppose that you want to unload the INSTALL module. Enter the following at the console prompt:

UNLOAD INSTALL

INSTALL is unloaded and its resources are returned to the operating system.

NOTES

Before you unload name space modules, dismount any volumes using the module. You cannot remount these volumes until you reload the module.

Before you unload a disk driver, dismount any volumes stored on the disks connected to the given controller or host bus adapter.

The operating system warns you if you attempt to unload a driver without dismounting the appropriate volumes. If you override the warning, the server automatically dismounts the volumes and informs users what has happened.

Unloading a LAN driver causes it to be unbound from all protocols and NICs it was associated with.

Once you unload a LAN driver, users who have been using NICs to communicate with the server lose their connections and receive error messages similar to the following:

Network error on Server <*fileserver*>: Error receiving from network. Abort, Retry?

Users are advised to retry once to see if they can communicate with the server via an alternate bridge on another network.

If an alternate bridge is unavailable, users should try again after you reload the driver and bind the protocols.

If you intend to have the driver unloaded for longer than 15 minutes, inform users and have them log out. Otherwise, the watchdog feature will automatically terminate the connections.

RELATED COMMANDS

LOAD allows you to link loadable modules to the operating system.

UPS STATUS

PURPOSE

UPS STATUS enables you to check the status of the uninterruptable power supply (UPS) connected to the server.

SYNTAX

UPS STATUS

PARAMETERS

None

EXAMPLE

To check UPS status, enter the following at the console prompt:

UPS STATUS

An information screen similar to the following appears:

```
UPSType : DCB
Power being used     : Commercial
Discharge time requested : 20 min.    Remaining 20 min. 0 sec
Battery status : Recharged
Recharge time requested  : 160 min. Remaining 0 min 0 sec
Current network power status  : normal
Wait time requested : 15 sec. Remaining 15 sec
```

Tip

If your battery is over 6 months old, you may need to lower the discharge time. (Consult your UPS documentation for details.)

If the UPS module has not been loaded, however, the following message appears:

`"??? Unknown command???"`

If you have loaded the UPS module but have not loaded the appropriate hardware driver, the server displays a message telling you the hardware driver is not loaded.

NOTES

The following list explains the various UPS categories as reported by the UPS STATUS command:

UPS Type indicates the type of UPS hardware. The name of the NLM will be shown here if the hardware type is unrecognizable by the operating system.

Power Being Used will show either commercial or battery power is being used.

The Discharge Time Requested category estimates how long the network can operate safely on battery power.

The Remaining category shows the remaining time if the network is operating on battery power. This number is identical to Discharge Time Requested if you are using commercial power and the battery is properly charged.

Battery Status indicates if the UPS is being recharged, is low, or has recharged. Repair or replace the battery when you receive a Low status.

The Recharge Time Requested category estimates the time period the battery will require to recharge after being completely discharged.

The Remaining category estimates the time period required to recharge the battery. Of course, if the battery is fully charged and you are using commercial power, this value will be zero. If you are using battery power, this value increases.

The Current Network Power Status category supports the following values:

Normal	Operating on commercial power
Server down	Operating on battery power
Server going down in x minutes	Operating on battery power and can continue to do so for x number of minutes.

RELATED COMMANDS

The UPS loadable module allows you to connect a UPS to the server. It is the software link allowing the file server and the UPS hardware device to communicate.

You must load the UPS loadable module in order to use UPS STATUS.

The UPS TIME console command allows you to alter the amount of time you want to permit the network to operate on battery power.

UPS TIME

PURPOSE

This command enables you to alter the amount of time you want to permit the network to operate on battery power. It also enables you to alter the time you estimate the battery requires to fully recharge.

SYNTAX

```
UPS TIME [DISCHARGE=number][RECHARGE=number] [WAIT=number]
```

PARAMETERS

In place of each number parameter, insert a value based on the following information:

DISCHARGE=number	Replace number with the number of minutes you estimate the battery can safely supply power to the network. (The battery documentation should provide helpful information.)
RECHARGE=number	Replace number with the number of minutes you estimate the battery requires to recharge after the network has operated on battery power.
WAIT=number	Replace number with the number of seconds you want the UPS to wait after a power interruption before beginning operation.

```
Values supported: 1-300
Default: 15
```

EXAMPLE

Suppose that you want to change the discharge time to 15 minutes and the recharge time to 60 minutes. Enter the following at the console prompt:

```
UPS TIME DISCHARGE=15 RECHARGE=60
```

If the UPS module has not been loaded, the following message appears:

```
"??? Unknown command???"
```

If you have loaded the UPS module but have not loaded the appropriate hardware driver, the server displays a message telling you the hardware driver is not loaded.

Notes

You must load the UPS module and load the driver NLM or specify the type in order to execute UPS TIME.

The server prompts you for Discharge and Recharge parameters if you do not provide them.

As the UPS gets older, consider decreasing the discharge time and increasing the recharge time.

Any changes you make with UPS TIME are not shown on the screen until you execute UPS STATUS again.

Related Commands

The UPS module allows you to connect a UPS to the server.

The UPS STATUS command allows you to check the status of the UPS.

VERSION

Purpose

The VERSION console command allows you to check the copyright notice, version information, and the number of licensed connection for the server.

Syntax

```
VERSION
```

Parameters

None

Example

To see copyright and version information for your server, enter the following:

```
VERSION
```

The server displays a message similar to the following:

```
Novell NetWare 4.10-  November 8, 1994
(C) Copyright 1993-1994 Novell Inc.
All Rights Reserved.
Patent Pending - Novell Inc.

This server is licensed to: DreamLAN Network Consulting Ltd.
```

```
Maximum number of License Connections: 100
Current License Chain:
Serial Number    Connections    License Type    Version
12345678         50             MAIN            4.10
87654321         50             MAIN            4.10
```

RELATED COMMANDS

NAME displays the server name.

MEMORY displays the memory installed on the server.

SPEED displays the server's processor speed.

CONFIG displays server hardware settings.

VOLUMES

PURPOSE

The VOLUMES console command allows you to list all volumes mounted on the server.

SYNTAX

VOLUMES

PARAMETERS

None

EXAMPLE

To see which volumes your server has mounted, enter the following at the console prompt:

VOLUMES

The server displays information similar to the following:

```
The following volumes are mounted:
SYS
PLATO
ARISTOTLE
```

RELATED COMMANDS

MOUNT allows you to mount volumes.

DISMOUNT allows you to dismount volumes.

NETWARE LOADABLE MODULES

This section describes several important NetWare Loadable Modules (NLMs) that are new with NetWare 4.1.

The following NLMs are discussed:

- CDROM
- DOMAIN
- DSREPAIR
- KEYB
- RPL
- RTDM
- SBACKUP
- SERVMAN
- TIMESYNC

DOMAIN and SERVMAN are server management modules; DSMERGE, DSREPAIR, and TIMESYNC are NetWare Directory Services (NDS) modules; CDROM and RTDM fit in the storage management category; and SBACKUP, KEYB, and RPL are classified as backup, internationalization, and remote boot modules, respectively.

For information on other NLMs, see the NetWare 4 *Utilities Reference* manual.

NLMs link drivers, name space modules, management applications, and other functions to the operating system.

If the NLM has an interactive user interface, you can press F1 for online help.

Use the LOAD console command to run these modules. You can load most NLMs simply by entering **LOAD** followed by the module name, such as LOAD SERVMAN.

You can load modules either at the server console itself or at a workstation via the RCONSOLE (Remote Console) workstation utility.

NETWARE NLM SUMMARY

The following list summarizes some of the NetWare 4.1 NetWare loadable modules:

CDROM	Allows the server to use a CD-ROM as a read-only volume.
CLIB	Allows a loadable module to use CLIB's library of routines and functions.
DOMAIN	Allows you to create a protected OS domain to be run in ring 1, 2, or 3.

DSMERGE	Allows you to combine the roots of two separate NetWare Directory Services.
DSREPAIR	Allows you to repair and resolve errors in the NetWare Directory Services database.
EDIT	Allows you to create or change a text file.
INSTALL	Allows you to install NDS, create disk partitions, load drivers, mirror hard disks, and perform many other network management tasks.
IPXS	Allows you to load an NLM requiring STREAMS-based IPX services.
KEYB	Allows you to change keyboard type for the server console.
MATHLIB	Allows you to use MATHLIB if the server has a math coprocessor.
MATHLIBC	Allows you to use MATHLIBC if the server does not have a math coprocessor.
MONITOR	Allows you to lock the server console and view such items as server utilization, cache memory status, disk drives, loaded modules, and memory usage.
NMAGENT	Allows LAN drivers to register and pass network management information.
NUT	Allows you to load a v3.11 module requiring NUT's routine and function library.
NWSNUT	Allows you to load a 4.0 module requiring NUT's routine and function library.
PSERVER	Allows you to load the print server on the server and set up printing services for the network.
REMOTE	Allows you access the server console from a remote workstation.
ROUTE	Allows NetWare to pass packets through IBM bridges on token ring cabling systems.
RPL	Allows you to enable remote booting of IBM PC diskless workstations with network interface cards installed.
RS232	Allows you to establish a communications port for remote management.
RSPX	Allows RCONSOLE to access a NetWare server.
RTDM	Allows data migration.
SBACKUP	Allows you to back up and restore data.

SCHDELAY	Allows you to set priority for server processes and schedule processes.
SERVMAN	Allows you to view and configure many different system parameters.
SPXCONFG	Allows you to set certain SPX parameters.
SPXS	Allows you to support STREAMS-based protocol services.
STREAMS	Allows you to set up a common interface between NetWare and transport protocols.
TIMESYNC	Allows you to check the internal time on a server.
TLI	Allows you to provide TLI communications services.
UPS	Allows you to connect a UPS to the server.
VREPAIR	Allows you to repair the primary copy of the File Allocation Table.

CDROM

PURPOSE

The CDROM console command enables the server to utilize a CD-ROM disk as a read-only volume.

SYNTAX

LOAD [*path*]CDROM

PARAMETERS

Replace *path* with the complete path to the directory where CDROM.NLM is located.

EXAMPLE

Suppose that you have installed a CD-ROM drive on the network and want to use it as NetWare read-only volume. Follow these steps:

Enter the following to load the CDROM module:

LOAD CDROM

Display CD-ROM devices, device numbers, and drive numbers by entering the following:

CD DEVICE LIST

42

Enter the following to mount the CD-ROM as a volume (assuming the device number is 3 and the volume name is OPTICAL):

```
CD MOUNT 3 OPTICAL
```

Enter the following to see the contents of the CD-ROM volume's root directory:

```
CD DIR 3 OPTICAL
```

Enter the following to list data about the CD-ROM:

```
CD HELP
```

Enter the following to dismount the CD-ROM volume:

```
CD DISMOUNT 3 OPTICAL
```

NOTES

Once you have loaded CDROM, you can use CDROM commands (which are executed from the command line) to accomplish the following tasks:

- ◆ List Help information
- ◆ Display CD-ROM devices
- ◆ Display all volumes identified on CD-ROM devices
- ◆ Dismount a CD-ROM volume
- ◆ View the volume's root directory
- ◆ Mount a CD-ROM volume
- ◆ Change CD-ROM media
- ◆ Reduce time necessary to remount a volume

Each of these tasks is discussed below:

To list online help information for CDROM, enter the following:

```
CD HELP
```

To display CD-ROM devices that the server is aware of, enter the following:

```
CD DEVICE LIST
```

Device is defined as the CD-ROM drive containing the system interface and enabling the CD-ROM to read the data.

This command displays devices in groups of 10. If you give the command again, the next group of 10 devices is displayed.

For each device, the display includes the following information:

◆ Number
◆ Name
◆ Media volume name (if identified)
◆ Volume mount status

To display all volumes identified on CD-ROM devices, enter the following:

`CD VOLUME LIST`

This command displays volumes in groups of 10. If you give the command again, the next group of 10 volumes is displayed.

For each volume, the display includes the following information:

◆ Name
◆ Mount status

This command does not list information for devices that do not have media present.

To dismount a CD-ROM volume, enter the following:

`CD DISMOUNT [device number] ¦ [volume name]`

If applicable, include the *device number* or *volume name*.

After you execute CD DISMOUNT, all resources are returned to the operating system.

To view the volume's root directory, enter the following:

`CD DIR [device number] ¦ [volume name]`

If applicable, include the device number or volume name.

This command displays directory entries in DOS format, similar to the DOS DIR command.

You can use this command to check the contents of a CD-ROM volume and verify a volume root directory.

This command treats each CD-ROM as one volume for NetWare's access. You do not have to mount the volume to use the CD DIR command.

To mount a CD-ROM volume, enter the following:

`CD MOUNT [device number] ¦ [volume name]`

If applicable, include the *device number* or *volume name*.

Once CD MOUNT is executed, the CD-ROM is a NetWare read-only volume.

Unique volume names are required.

To change media in a CD-ROM, enter the following:

CD CHANGE [*device number*] ¦ [*volume name*]

If applicable, include the *device number* or *volume name*.

This command dismounts the volume and prompts you to replace the media.

CD CHANGE mounts the new media as a NetWare volume.

CD CHANGE deactivates the selected device during mounting or while a CD-ROM disk is changed.

This command enables volumes to be remounted faster because it tells the operating system to use existing data files rather than reconstructing them.

CAUTION

You must load a device driver such as CDNASPI before loading CDROM or no devices will be found when you execute a CD-ROM command.

RELATED COMMANDS

MAGAZINE confirms whether magazine requests have been satisfied.

MEDIA confirms whether media requests have been satisfied.

LOAD allows you to load modules.

MODULES lists important information about modules.

DOMAIN

PURPOSE

This loadable module allows you to produce a protected OS (OSP) domain.

SYNTAX

LOAD [*path*]DOMAIN

Replace *path* with the complete path to the directory containing the DOMAIN module.

EXAMPLE

Suppose that you have developed a loadable module called ADMIN.NLM and want to load it in a protected domain and run it in ring 1. Enter the following at the console prompt:

```
LOAD DOMAIN
DOMAIN=OS_PROTECTED
LOAD ADMIN
```

Caution

Unreliable loadable modules can cause serious network problems by corrupting data and crashing the server. Therefore, you should test modules you have written—as well as non-certified modules from third parties—in an OSP domain.

Once a module has proven itself to be reliable, you can run it in the OS domain in ring 0.

Notes

After you load DOMAIN, you can use the DOMAIN command and subcommands, as follows:

DOMAIN	Lists the current domain and its modules, followed by other domains and their modules.
DOMAIN HELP	Lists help information.
DOMAIN=domain name	Changes current domain. Replace domain name with the name of the domain you want to be the current domain (OS or OS_PROTECTED).

Related Commands

LOAD allows you to load modules.

MODULES lists important information about modules.

DSREPAIR

Purpose

The DSREPAIR loadable module allows you to repair and resolve errors in the NetWare Directory Services database.

Syntax

```
LOAD [path]DSREPAIR [=U] [-L log filename]
```

Parameters

Replace path with the complete path to the directory where the DSREPAIR module is found (not required if the DSREPAIR module is in SYS:SYSTEM).

Use the -U parameter if you want to run DSREPAIR in unattended mode (meaning that the program will execute and exit without further user input).

Use the -L parameter if you want to specify an error log file. Replace *log filename* with the filename you want to use.

EXAMPLE

Suppose that you receive a console message that the server cannot open the local database. Run DSREPAIR to solve the problem. Enter the following at the file server console prompt (assuming DSREPAIR is located in the SYS:SYSTEM directory):

```
LOAD DSREPAIR
```

DSREPAIR locks the database.

Select 1 to set options. To toggle options on and off, enter the number associated with the option. An asterisk shows that an option is selected.

Select 2 to start checking the database. If correctable problems are found, DSREPAIR saves changes in a temporary file. A prompt then asks if you want to save changes.

Select Yes if you want to save changes. The following message then appears:

```
Repair process completed
```

Select 3 to exit DSREPAIR and unlock the database. (Other users are locked out of the database until you exit.)

CAUTION

Loading DSREPAIR locks the database, and no other user can access it until you exit DSREPAIR.

NOTES

DSREPAIR finds and corrects errors related to records, schema, bindery objects, and external references.

DSREPAIR main options are as follows:

```
1.    Select Options     Shows current settings and allows you to choose
                         options.
2.    Begin Repair       Starts DSREPAIR
3.    Exit               Exits DSREPAIR
```

Selecting 1 displays the following options (with an asterisk appearing to the left of each option that is on):

1. Do not pause after each error.

   DSREPAIR pauses after each error if this option is on.

2. Do not exit automatically upon completion.

   DSREPAIR runs in unattended mode if this option is on. The =U parameter just described accomplishes the same purpose.

3. Log errors to a file: SYS:SYSTEM\DSREPAIR.LOG.

   This option specifies an error log file. Use the -L log filename parameter if you want to use a different filename. Turn this option off if you do not want to create a log file.

4. Do not check consistency of local replicas.

   If this option is on, DSREPAIR checks the consistency of replicas in the Directory tree.

5. Check for valid mail directories.

   If this option is on, DSREPAIR checks the SYS:MAIL directory for subdirectories that require the name of user IDs in the NDS database. If no object for the ID in the directory name exists, DSREPAIR deletes the mail directory for that ID.

6. Check file system for valid trustee IDs.

   DSREPAIR checks the file system for valid trustee IDs if this option is on. DSREPAIR ensures that each file system ID has a corresponding valid NDS database ID. If DSREPAIR does not find a valid trustee ID, it removes the ID from the database. Be advised that this process can require considerable time.

7. Check for valid stream files.

   DSREPAIR checks for valid stream files if this option is on. The NetWare Directory Services secure file area is checked for valid stream files that have to correspond to stream properties of objects. If a valid NDS stream file is not found, DSREPAIR removes the stream file.

8. Return to selection menu.

   Use this option to go back to the main options menu.

See Chapter 4 of the NetWare 4 manual *Supervising the Network* for more information on repairing the NetWare Directory Services Database.

See "Directory Services" in the *Concepts* manual for more information on NetWare Directory Services.

RELATED COMMANDS

VREPAIR corrects volume errors and deletes name space entries from Directory tables. (VREPAIR does not execute on mounted volumes, however.)

LOAD allows you to load modules.

MODULES lists important information about modules.

KEYB

PURPOSE

The KEYB loadable module allows you to change the server console keyboard type. Five types are available.

SYNTAX

```
LOAD [path]KEYB [parameter]
```

PARAMETERS

Replace *path* with the complete path to the directory where KEYB.NLM is located.

Replace *parameter* with the keyboard type you want to use.

To view a list of available keyboard types, enter LOAD KEYB without a parameter. The following list is displayed:

```
United States
French
German
Italian
Spanish
```

EXAMPLE

Suppose that you want to change the console keyboard type to German.

Enter the following at the server console prompt:

```
LOAD KEYB
```

A list appears. Enter the following:

```
German
```

Keyboard type is changed to German.

NOTES

The DOS code page determines keyboard types. Most keyboard types are compatible with the default code page. If changing the DOS code page setting is required, check your DOS documentation for pertinent information.

RELATED COMMANDS

Use the LANGUAGE console command to set the language that subsequently loaded NLMs will use.

RPL

PURPOSE

The RPL loadable module allows remote booting of IBM PC diskless workstations with network interface cards installed.

SYNTAX

```
LOAD [path]RPL
```

PARAMETERS

Replace *path* with the complete path to the directory where the RPL loadable module is located.

EXAMPLE

To load the RPL module, enter the following at the console prompt:

```
LOAD RPL
```

NOTES

For more information see "Remote Booting Your DOS Workstation" in the NetWare 4 manual *NetWare Workstation for DOS and Windows*.

RTDM

PURPOSE

This module allows the server to support the real-time data migration feature in NetWare 4.

SYNTAX

```
LOAD [path]RTDM
```

PARAMETERS

Replace *path* with the complete path to the directory where the RTDM loadable module is located.

EXAMPLE

To load the RTDM module, enter the following at the console prompt:

```
LOAD RTDM
```

NOTES

For more information, check the product documentation that accompanied the migration product you are using.

SBACKUP

PURPOSE

The SBACKUP loadable module allows you to back up and restore data that you identify on a NetWare server or workstation, or on a service you identify.

SYNTAX

```
LOAD [path]SBACKUP SIZE=xx BUFFER=xx
```

PARAMETERS

Replace *path* with the complete path to the directory where the SBACKUP module is located.

Select SIZE and BUFFER parameters from the following list:

Parameter	Syntax	Values
Buffer Size Default: 64	SIZE=xx	16, 32, 64, 128, 256
Number of Buffers Default: 4	Buffer=xx	2–10

EXAMPLE

To load the SBACKUP module with default values, enter the following at the server console prompt:

```
LOAD SBACKUP SIZE=64 BUFFER=4
```

The following steps show how to use SBACKUP to perform a backup:

1. From the SBACKUP main menu select the BACKUP option.
2. A list of servers appears. Select the server you want to back up.
3. Enter the username and password for the target you want to back up.
4. Select the backup device you want to use.
5. Select the directory you want to use for log and error files.
6. Select the type of backup you want to run from the Type of Backup menu (which includes such choices as Full, Differential, Incremental, Custom).
7. Enter a description of the backup session.
8. Select whether you want to append this session to others on the media (optional).
9. Save the description and continue backing up by pressing F10.
10. Indicate whether you want the backup to begin immediately or later, or if you want change the backup parameters.
11. Specify a date and time for the backup to start if you want the backup to start later.
12. Save your changes by pressing F10 and then Enter.
13. Enter a label for the media if you previously answered No to the Append to this session option (optional).

When the backup is complete, you will see a message similar to this:

```
The backup process was completed normally.
Press <Enter> to continue.
```

NOTES

You must load the appropriate TSA before loading SBACKUP.

Running SBACKUP is a complex task that requires a good deal of preparation. Chapter 8 of the NetWare 4 manual *Supervising the Network* contains valuable information on running backup.

You can find additional information in the NetWare 4 *Concepts* manual under the following headings:

◆ Backup
◆ Backup hosts and targets
◆ Data set
◆ Major resource
◆ Media manager

42

SERVER CONSOLE COMMANDS

- ◆ Minor resource
- ◆ Modify bit, Archive Needed Attribute
- ◆ Restore
- ◆ Storage Device Interface
- ◆ Storage Management Services (SMS)
- ◆ Target Service Agent (TSA)
- ◆ TSA resources

SERVMAN

PURPOSE

SERVMAN is a highly versatile loadable module that allows you to do the following:

- ◆ Check current system parameters
- ◆ Configure parameters
- ◆ Modify AUTOEXEC.NCF and STARTUP.NCF files
- ◆ Check or set up IPX/SPX parameters
- ◆ Check adapter, device, and disk partition data
- ◆ Check volume data
- ◆ Check network data

SYNTAX

```
LOAD [path]SERVMAN
```

PARAMETERS

Replace *path* with the complete path of the directory where the SERVMAN module is located.

EXAMPLE

Suppose that you want to set early warning alerts for cache buffer memory allocation. Enter the following at the console prompt:

```
LOAD SERVMAN
```

The Server Manager main screen appears.

1. Select Server parameters from the Available Options menu.
2. Select File Caching from the Categories menu.

3. Select Minimum File Cache Buffer Report Threshold from the File Caching menu.

4. Change the parameter to 100.

5. Press Esc twice to go to the Update Options menu.

6. Select Update AUTOEXEC.NCF & STARTUP.NCF now from the Update Options menu.

7. Exit SERVMAN by pressing Esc.

As the preceding procedure shows, using SERVMAN allows you to easily add changes to NCF files.

NOTES

After loading SERVMAN, press F1 for online help.

You can access additional non-documented parameters in SERVMAN by loading the NLM with the !H parameter:

```
LOAD SERVMAN !H
```

Note   These additional parameters are not discussed here.

GENERAL INFORMATION

The main screen for SERVMAN includes a General Information section that includes the following server statistics:

Processor Utilization	Percentage of time the CPU is active
Server Up Time	How long the server has been operating since it was last booted
Processor Speed	Speed at which the CPU is operating
Server Processes	How many processes the server is running
NLMs Loaded	How many NetWare Loadable Modules have been loaded
Mounted Volumes	How many volumes the server has mounted
Active Queues	How many queues are active on the server
Users Logged In	How many uses have logged in to the server
Name Spaces Loaded	How many name spaces have been loaded on the server

AVAILABLE OPTIONS

The SERVMAN main screen also includes an Available Options menu, which has the following selections:

Server parameters	Check, set operating system parameters
	Set parameters in AUTOEXEC.NCF and STARTUP.NCF
Storage Information	Check adapter, device, and partition data
Volume Information	Check volume data
Network Information	Check network data, such as packet statistics

RELATED COMMANDS

The SET console command allows you to configure a wide variety of server parameters.

The CONFIG console command allows you to view hardware configuration information.

The DISPLAY NETWORKS console command allows you to view networks and network numbers.

The DISPLAY SERVERS console command allows you to view a list of all servers on the network.

The LIST DEVICES console command allows you to view the devices being used by the server.

TIMESYNC

PURPOSE

This command allows you to check a server's internal time to ensure that the time used by servers throughout the network is synchronized.

The server automatically loads TIMESYNC.NLM every time it boots; therefore, you should seldom have to load or unload TIMESYNC. One reason you may want to load TIMESYNC is to run an alternate .CFG file.

SYNTAX

```
LOAD [path]TIMESYNC [parameter]
```

PARAMETERS

Replace *path* with the complete path to the directory where the TIMESYNC module is stored.

You can set TIMESYNC parameters at the command line (using LOAD TIMESYNC), in the TIMESYNC.CFG file, or by using the SET command or the SERVMAN module.

Keep in mind, however, that you must add the proper line to the TIMESYNC.CFG file to make changes permanent—any modifications you make in SET or SERVMAN will no longer be effective once the server is rebooted.

EXAMPLE

To load the TIMESYNC module, enter the following at the console prompt:

```
LOAD TIMESYNC
```

NOTES

The TIMESYNC.CFG file (stored by default in SYS:SYSTEM) contains time synchronization parameters. If you want to modify the time synchronization configuration, make the changes in the TIMESYNC.CFG file and then reboot the system or use the SET console command to set the TIMESYNC Restart Flag parameter to ON.

If you store many settings in your TIMESYNC.CFG file, you may want to consider copying the file from server to server. If you do, make certain that each copied TIMESYNC.CFG file includes the correct default time server type and configured-sources list for the server it is associated with.

To edit the TIMESYNC.CFG file, follow these steps:

1. Enter LOAD EDIT at the console prompt.
2. Enter SYS:SYSTEM\TIMESYNC.CFG at the Enter file to edit or press <Esc> to exit prompt. The current TIMESYNC.CFG file is displayed.
3. Move to the line you want to edit.
4. Make the desired changes to TIMESYNC parameters.
5. Save your changes by pressing Esc.
6. Answer Yes to the Do you want to save SYS:SYSTEM\TIMESYNC.CFG? prompt.
7. Exit the EDIT module by pressing Esc.

RELATED COMMANDS

The EDIT loadable module allows you to create or change text files.

42

SERVER CONSOLE COMMANDS

The SET console command allows you to configure many time-related parameters.

The SET TIME console command allows you to configure the server time and date.

The SERVMAN loadable module allows you to check or configure a variety of system parameters.

LOAD allows you to load modules.

MODULES lists important information about modules.

SUMMARY

This chapter listed and discussed all the major server console commands available in NetWare 4.1, as well as provided an in-depth discussion on some of the NLMs shipped with NetWare 4.1.

- Command Line
  Utilities

- Summary

CHAPTER 43

User Command
Line Utilities

Command line utilities are run from a workstation. They include the NetWare Administrator (Windows based), DOS text menu utilities, and DOS text workstation utilities. Almost all the utilities can be accessed by all users. The functionality of each utility is determined by the users rights.

In this chapter, the function and optional command line parameters of some of the common utilities are discussed.

ATOTAL

PURPOSE

This command line utility is used in conjunction with the accounting (not to be confused with auditing) feature of NetWare (see Figure 43.1). Assuming that the accounting feature has been enabled, it would show the total accounting charges on the network. The accounting feature is enabled through the NetWare Administrator or through NETADMIN. Charge rates can be established for blocks read, block written, usage per connection per minute, each request for service provided by the server. ATOTAL would then show all of the charges that have accrued.

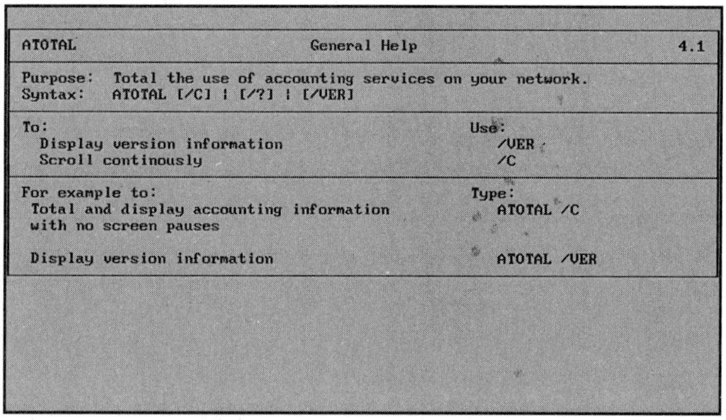

Figure 43.1.
ATOTAL help screen.

```
ATOTAL                          General Help                        4.1

Purpose:   Total the use of accounting services on your network.
Syntax:    ATOTAL [/C] ¦ [/?] ¦ [/VER]

To:                                                Use:
  Display version information                        /VER
  Scroll continuously                                /C

For example to:                                    Type:
  Total and display accounting information            ATOTAL /C
  with no screen pauses

  Display version information                         ATOTAL /VER
```

SYNTAX

ATOTAL

AUDITCON

PURPOSE

This menu utility is used in conjunction with the auditing feature of NetWare (see Figure 43.2). The main tasks that can be accomplished through AUDITCON are setting up auditing, selecting events to be audited, setting up auditing passwords, and viewing audit data. Auditing is a security feature in NetWare 4 to ensure the integrity and accuracy of the network. Once auditing has been enabled, it provides the means for a third-party auditor to track and monitor network events.

Figure 43.2.
AUDITCON main
menu.

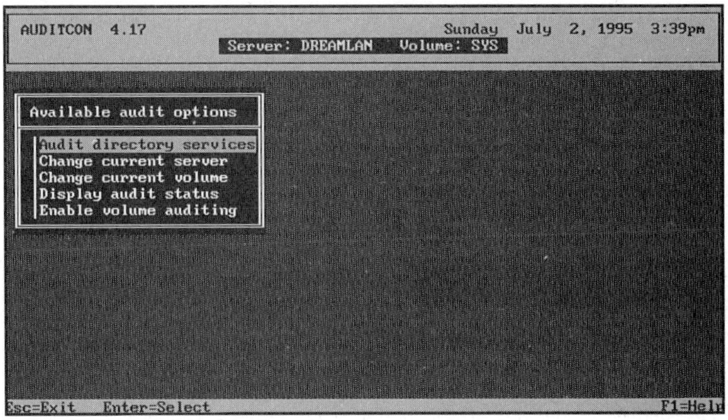

SYNTAX

AUDITCON

CAPTURE

PURPOSE

This command line utility is used to redirect print jobs from a local port on a workstation to a network queue or printer. It is used to print from within a non-network aware application or a print screen. CAPTURE can also be used to redirect data to a network file. For NetWare aware applications, such as WordPerfect, a CAPTURE statement is unnecessary.

CAPTURE *Options*	*(Abbr.)*	*Description*
AUTOEND	(AU)	Specifies that when application is exited captured data is closed and sent to the printer.
BANNER	(B)	Specifies what will be printed on the bottom half of the banner page.
COPIES	(C)	Specifies the number of copies to be printed.
CREATE	(CR)	Sends the job to a file instead of a printer or queue.

continues

CAPTURE *Options*	*(Abbr.)*	*Description*
ENDCAP	(E)	Ends the capture statement and resets the port to its original state.
FORM	(F)	If forms have been specified through the PRINTDEF utility, FORM specifies which form should be used.
FORMFEED	(FF)	Tells the printer to feed a blank piece of paper after the job is finished printing.
HELP	(?)	Displays online documentation for help.
JOB	(J)	If jobs have been specified through the PRINTCON utility, JOB specifies which job should be used.
KEEP	(K)	If the workstation hangs, KEEP specifies that data already sent to the queue is saved.
LOCAL	(L)	Specifies the local port to be captured.
NAME	(NAM)	Specifies what will be printed on the top half of the banner page.
NOAUTOEND	(NA)	Requires that a manual ENDCAP be entered before captured data will be sent to the queue.
NO BANNER	(NB)	Specifies that a banner page not be printed.
NO FORMFEED	(NFF)	Specifies that a form feed not be sent at the end of a job.
NO NOTIFY	(NNOTI)	Specifies that a user not be notified after a job is finished printing.
NO TABS	(NT)	Specifies that spaces not be included in place of tab characters.
NOTIFY	(NOTI)	Specifies that a user be notified after a print is completed.
PRINTER	(P)	Allows a user to specify which network printer a job is sent to.

QUEUE	(Q)	Allows a user to specify which queue a print job is sent to.
SERVER	(S)	In bindery emulation mode, specifies which server a print job is sent to.
SHOW	(SH)	An independently used option that shows a user how the ports are currently captured, either redirected to the network, or in local mode.
TABS	(T)	A rarely used option that specifies that when a tab character is encountered it should be replaced by the specified number of spaces.
TIMEOUT	(TI)	Specifies how long the operating system should wait before it assumes the last of the data has been received and the print job is closed out and sent to the printer.
VERBOSE	(V)	Like SHOW, it gives information on the status of CAPTURE, but provides more complete information.

SYNTAX

CAPTURE /option(s)

EXAMPLE

CAPTURE /P=LASER /C=2 /TI=5 /NT

COLORPAL

PURPOSE

This menu utility enables you to change the color of the menu windows displayed when the NMENU utility is used (see Figure 43.3).

Figure 43.3.
COLORPAL main
menu.

SYNTAX

COLORPAL

CX

PURPOSE

The CX command line utility enables you to view, change, or display your current context in the directory tree. CX is the NetWare directory services tree equivalent to the DOS CD command in the directory structure.

cx Options	(Abbr.)	Description
ALL	(A)	Shows all objects at or below the current context. use with /T or / CONT option.
CONTAINERS	(CONT)	Shows all containers at the current context or a specified context.
CONTINUOUS	(C)	Scrolls through output without pausing.
HELP	(?)	Displays online documentation for help.
ROOT	(R)	Lists the containers at the root level, or changes context from the root.
TREE	(T)	Displays all containers below the current context of the context specified.

SYNTAX

CX [*new context*] /*option(s)*

EXAMPLE

CX .MARKETING.ACME

CX /T

DOSGEN

PURPOSE

This command utility is used to create a boot image that is used with diskless workstations (see Figure 43.4). The disk image requires that the RPL.NLM be loaded at the server.

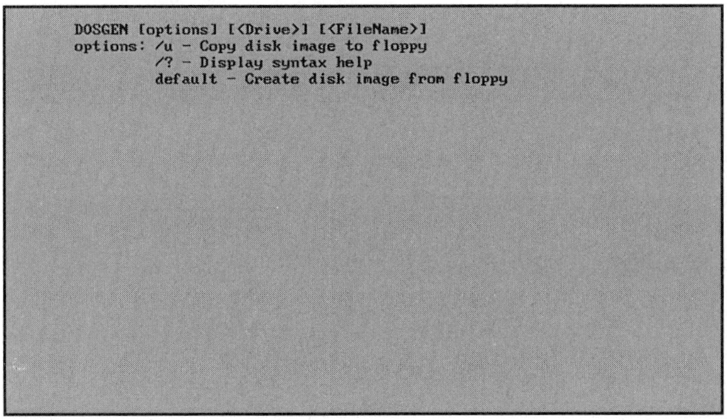

Figure 43.4.
DOSGEN help screen.

```
DOSGEN [options] [<Drive>] [<FileName>]
options: /u - Copy disk image to floppy
         /? - Display syntax help
         default - Create disk image from floppy
```

SYNTAX

DOSGEN

FILER

PURPOSE

This menu utility is used to manage the network file system (see Figure 43.5). This utility allows you to do the following:

◆ Manage files and directories

- ♦ Manage files and directories according to search patterns
- ♦ Select the current directory
- ♦ View volume information
- ♦ Salvage deleted files
- ♦ Purge deleted files
- ♦ Set default filer options

Figure 43.5.
FILER main menu.

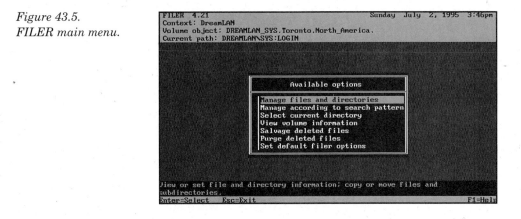

SYNTAX

FILER

FLAG

PURPOSE

This command line utility is used to view or modify file and directory attributes. It is also used to modify the owner of a directory or file. The FLAG utility is also used to view or modify the search mode of executable files.

FLAG *Options*	*(Abbr.)*	*Description*
ARCHIVE	(A)	Indicates that the file has been modified since the last backup.
COPY INHIBIT	(CI)	Only applicable to Macintosh users, keeps a file from being copied.
DELETE INHIBIT	(DI)	Keeps a file from being deleted or copied over.

DON'T COMPRESS	(DC)	Keeps a file from being compressed even if the volume default is to compress files.
DON'T MIGRATE	(DM)	Keeps a file from being migrated, even if the volume default is to migrate the file to secondary backup.
EXECUTE ONLY	(X)	Used with .COM and .EXE files. Keeps a file from being copied or copied over. Once a file is flagged X, this attribute cannot be removed.
HELP	(?)	Displays online documentation for help.
HIDDEN	(H)	Hides the file from a DOS DIR scan and keeps a file from being copied or deleted.
IMMEDIATE COMPRESS	(IC)	Compresses the file as soon as the OS is able to.
PURGE	(P)	Purges a file when it is deleted so that it cannot be recovered
READ ONLY	(RO)	Specifies that the file can be read, but not written to; setting this option automatically sets the rename inhibit and delete inhibit flags.
READ WRITE	(RW)	File can be written and read to.
RENAME INHIBIT	(RI)	Specifies that a file cannot be renamed.
SHARABLE	(SH)	Allows a file to accessed by more than one user at a time.
SYSTEM	(SY)	Hides the file from the DOS DIR scan and keeps the file from being deleted or copied.
TRANSACTIONAL	(T)	Specifies that the file is protected by Transaction Tracking System (TTS).

43

SYNTAX

```
FLAG path [ [+ ¦ -] attributes ] [option(s)]
```

LOGIN

PURPOSE

LOGIN allows you to login to the network. Using LOGIN more than once may lose any previous network connection, unless the /NS option is used.

LOGIN *Options*	*(Abbr.)*	*Description*
BINDERY	(B)	Specifies bindery emulation is being used.
HELP	(?)	Displays online documentation for help.
NO SCRIPT	(NS)	Bypasses login scripts, and keeps previous attachments
PROFILE	(pr)	Specifies profile login script to be run.
SCRIPT	(S)	Allows you to specify path and object name for objects script you want run.
SWAP	(SWAP)	Allows external commands to be run from the login script
TREE	(TR)	Specifies which tree to login to.

SYNTAX

LOGIN [server/ ¦ tree/] [user] [/option(s)]

LOGOUT

PURPOSE

This command is used to logout and terminate all network services.

LOGOUT *Options*	*(Abbr.)*	*Description*
HELP	(?)	Displays online documentation for help.
SERVER	(Name)	Server name from which you want to log out.

| TREE | (TR) | Keeps you logged in to 2.*x* and 3.*x* servers, but logs you out of the NDS tree. |
| VERSION | (VER) | Provides version information of LOGOUT.EXE |

SYNTAX

```
LOGOUT [server ¦ /option]
```

MAP

PURPOSE

The MAP command is used to view, create, or change network drive mappings and search drive mappings. It can also be used to create a fake root directory for applications that require they be installed or run at the root.

MAP *Options*	*(Abbr.)*	*Description*
CHANGE	(C)	Changes a drive mapping from a regular drive pointer to a search drive pointer.
DELETE	(DEL)	Deletes a drive pointer or search drive pointer.
HELP	(?)	Displays online documentation for help.
INSERT	(INS)	Inserts a search drive and pushes existing search drive mappings down, without overwriting them.
NEXT	(N)	Used with network drive pointers to choose the next available drive letter.
ROOT	(ROOT)	Creates a fake root directory for applications that require that they be installed at the root.

SYNTAX

```
MAP

MAP [option(s) ] [ drive:=path ]
```

43

NCOPY

Purpose

This command is used to copy network files or directories from one location to another.

NCOPY Options	(Abbr.)	Description
ARCHIVE BIT ONLY	(A)	Copies files that have the archive bit set.
ARCHIVE BIT SET	(M)	Copies files that have the archive bit set, and then sets the archive bit to off on the source file.
COPY	(C)	For file copies that will not preserve extended attributes and name space information.
FORCE SPARSE FILES	(F)	Creates sparse files.
HELP	(?)	Displays online documentation for help.
INFORM	(I)	Used for notification in the event that a file cannot be copied.
RETAIN COMPRESSION	(R)	Copies a compressed file, the source and destination file remain compressed.
RETAIN UNSUPPORTED UNCOMPRESSED	(RU)	Retains compression even if the target destination does not support compression.
SUBDIRECTORIES	(S)	Copies subdirectories.
SUBDIRECTORIES EMPTY	(E)	Copies subdirectories, even if they are empty.
VERIFY	(V)	Verifies that the files were copied correctly.

Syntax

```
NCOPY source path\filename [TO] destination path\filename [option(s)]
```

NDIR

Purpose

NDIR allows you to view information on files , directories, and volumes. NDIR also allows you to sort information based on creation date, owner, type of file, and so on. This utility can also be used to sort files based on attributes set.

NDIR Options	(Abbr.)	Description
CONTINUOUS	(C)	Scrolls through the display without pausing between screens.
DATES	(D)	Displays information on file access, creation, updates, archives, and copy information.
DETAIL	(DE)	Provides more detailed information on name space.
DIRECTORIES ONLY	(DO)	Displays only directories.
FILE COMPRESSION	(COMP)	Shows file size and compressed file size.
FILES ONLY	(FO)	Displays only files.
FIND	(FI)	Used with executable commands to find the location of a file within the search drive mappings.
HELP	(?)	Displays online documentation for help.
LONG NAMES	(LONG)	Provides information on long file names, in the event that name space other than DOS is used.
MACINTOSH	(MAC)	Shows Macintosh files.
RIGHTS	(R)	Shows the Inherited Rights Filter and effective rights for the user logged in. Also displays information on migration status, compression, and file attributes.
SUBDIRECTORIES ONLY	(SUB)	Displays and sorts subdirectories.

continues

43

NDIR Options	(Abbr.)	Description
VERSION	(VER)	Displays version information.
VOLUME	(VOL)	Displays statistics on volumes.
VOLUME SPACE	(SPA)	Displays any volume space limitations.

SYNTAX

```
NDIR [path] [option(s)]
```

NETADMIN

PURPOSE

NETADMIN is a DOS menu utility that allows you to manage objects, properties, object rights, and file system rights of network directory services (see Figure 43.6). It is the DOS equivalent of the NetWare Administrator, which is the administrators Windows utility.

Figure 43.6.
NETADMIN main
menu.

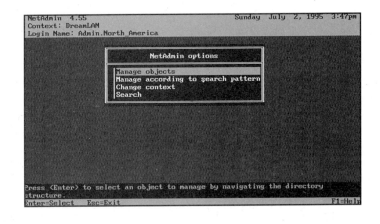

SYNTAX

```
NETADMIN
```

NETUSER

PURPOSE

NETUSER is a DOS menu utility that allows a user to manage printing, send messages, set drives, manage network attachments, and change context (see Figure 43.7). It is the DOS equivalent of User Tools, which is the users Windows utility.

Figure 43.7.
NETUSER main menu.

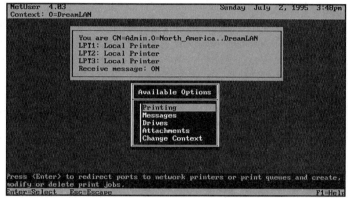

SYNTAX

NETUSER

NLIST

PURPOSE

The NLIST command allows you to view information regarding users, groups, servers, and volumes. It also allows you to search objects and object properties.

NLIST Options	(Abbr.)	Description
ACTIVE USERS	(A)	Shows who is currently logged in.
BINDERY SERVER	(B)	Lists bindery emulation information for the specified server.

continues

NLIST Options	(Abbr.)	Description
CONTEXT	(CO)	Specifies context to be searched.
CONTINUOUS	(C)	Scrolls through the information without pausing.
DETAILS	(D)	Shows details of the objects properties.
HELP	(?)	Displays online documentation for help.
NAME	(N)	Shows each objects name
PROPERTY NAME	(SHOW)	Shows specified property of object.
SEARCH ALL	(S)	From current context down, searches the NDS database.

SYNTAX

NLIST [*class type*] [*=object name*] [*/option(s)*]

NMENU

PURPOSE

NMENU is used to call a customized menu that has been created with a text editor and the MAKEMENU utility.

SYNTAX

NMENU *menuname*

NPRINT

PURPOSE

This command is used to send a DOS or ASCII text file to a queue or printer.

NPRINT Options	(Abbr.)	Description
BANNER	(B)	Specifies what will be printed on the bottom half of the banner page.
COPIES	(C)	Specifies the number of copies to be printed.

FORM	(F)	If forms have been specified through the PRINTDEF utility, FORM specifies which form should be used.
FORMFEED	(FF)	Tells the printer to feed a blank piece of paper after the job is finished printing.
HELP	(?)	Displays online documentation for help.
JOB	(J)	If jobs have been specified through the PRINTCON utility, JOB specifies which job should be used.
NAME	(NAM)	Specifies what will be printed on the top half of the banner page.
NO BANNER	(NB)	Specifies that a banner page not be printed.
NO FORMFEED	(NFF)	Specifies that a form feed not be sent at the end of a job.
NO NOTIFY	(NNOTI)	Specifies that a user not be notified after a job is finished printing.
NO TABS	(NT)	Specifies that spaces not be included in place of tab characters.
NOTIFY	(NOTI)	Specifies that a user be notified after a print is completed.
PRINTER	(P)	Allows a user to specify which network printer a job is sent to.
QUEUE	(Q)	Allows a user to specify which queue a print job is sent to.
SERVER	(S)	In bindery emulation mode, specifies which server a print job is sent to.
TABS	(T)	A rarely used option that specifies that when a tab character is encountered it should be replaced by the specified number of spaces.
VERBOSE	(V)	Like SHOW, it gives information on the status of CAPTURE but provides more complete information.

43

USER COMMAND LINE UTILITIES

SYNTAX

NPRINT *filename* [*option(s)*]

NVER

PURPOSE

NVER display information on network version information.

NVER Options	(Abbr.)	Description
CONTINUOUS	(C)	Continuous display without pause.
HELP	(?)	Displays help information.
VERSION	(VER)	Displays version information

SYNTAX

NVER [option(s)]

NWXTRACT

PURPOSE

NWXTRACT is used to extract and copy files from the distribution diskettes or CD-ROM to the network or a local drive.

SYNTAX

NWXTRACT path\filename [destination] [option(s)]

PARTMGR

PURPOSE

This DOS menu utility allows you to create or merge partitions, or to add, delete, or modify replicas (see Figure 43.8).

SYNTAX

PARTMGR

*Figure 43.8.
PARTMGR main
menu.*

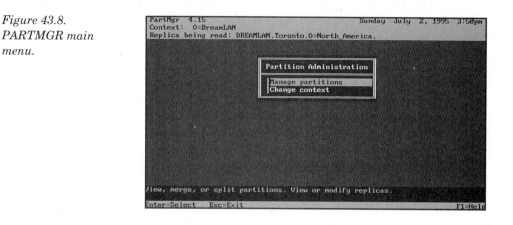

PCONSOLE

Purpose

This DOS menu utility allows you to create, modify, or delete print queues, printers, or print servers (see Figure 43.9). It also allows you to use a "quick setup" option for defining network printing.

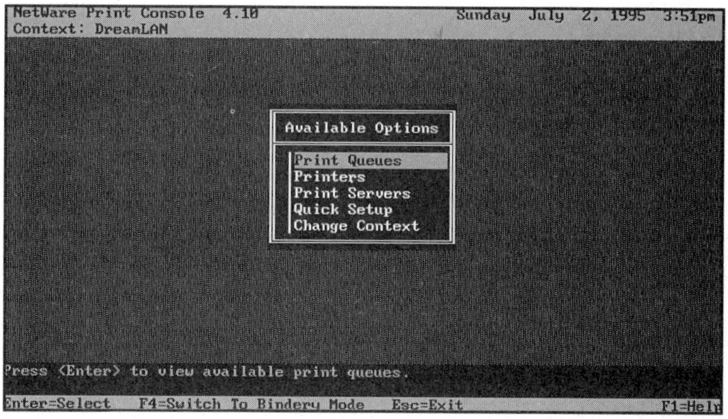

*Figure 43.9.
PCONSOLE main
menu.*

Syntax

PCONSOLE

PRINTCON

PURPOSE

PRINTCON is a DOS menu utility that allows you to edit print job configurations (see Figure 43.10). The purpose of creating print job configurations is to group options associated with CAPTURE or NPRINT for ease of use.

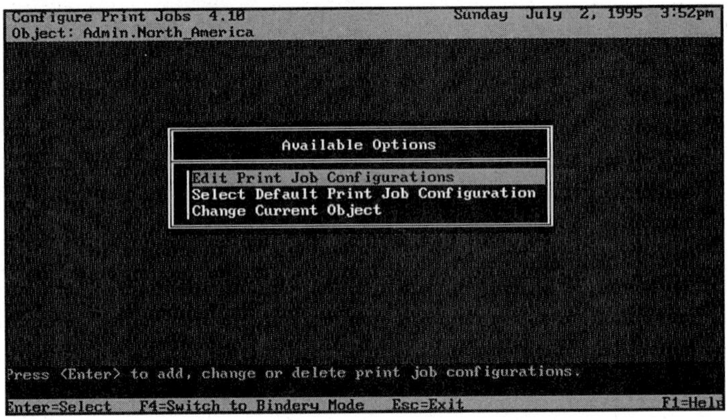

*Figure 43.10.
PRINTCON main
menu.*

SYNTAX

PRINTCON

PRINTDEF

PURPOSE

This DOS menu utility allows you to create, edit, or delete printer definitions and forms (see Figure 43.11). Defining printer definitions is usually associated with using non-NetWare aware applications.

SYNTAX

PRINTDEF

Figure 43.11.
PRINTDEF main
menu.

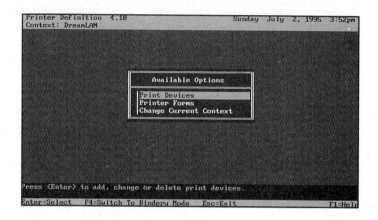

PSC

The PSC command is used in the printing environment to control network printers, network print servers, or to view network printer information.

PSC Options	(Abbr.)	Description
ABORT	(AB)	Aborts the current print job.
CANCEL DOWN	(CD)	If the print server was downed through PCONSOLE with the option Going Down After Current Jobs and the print server has not yet been downed, cancels the down command.
FORM FEED	(FF)	If the printer has been paused or stopped, causes the printer to advance to the top of the next page.
HELP	(?)	Displays online documentation for help.
MARK	(M)	Prints a row of characters in order to see which line the printer is printing on.
MOUNT FORM	(MO F)	Tells the printer which form is currently being used.

continues

43

USER COMMAND LINE UTILITIES

PSC Options	(Abbr.)	Description
PAUSE	(PAU)	Pauses the printer temporarily.
PRIVATE	(PRI)	If RPRINTER has been invoked to make a private printer a network printer, this option makes the printer private again.
SHARED	(SH)	If the PRIVATE option was invoked, the SHARED option makes the printer available to the network again.
START	(STAR)	If the printer has been stopped or paused, this option starts the printer again.
STATUS	(STAT)	Displays the status of a network printer.
STOP	(STO)	Stops the printer and deletes whatever job was being printed.

SYNTAX

    PSC PS=printserver P=printer [option(s)]

PURGE

PURPOSE

This command is used to permanently erase files that were previously deleted.

PURGE Options	(Abbr.)	Description
ALL	(A)	Purges all deleted files in current and subdirectories.
HELP	(?)	Displays help information.
VERSION	(VER)	Displays version information.

SYNTAX

    PURGE [filename ¦ path] [/option(s)]

RCONSOLE

PURPOSE

This command line utility is for network supervisors who want to run the NetWare server console as a virtual console at an attached workstation. After RCONSOLE is running, any tasks that could be done at the server console can be done at the workstation running the virtual console. Unlike the other NetWare commands, which are stored in the SYS:PUBLIC directory, RCONSOLE is stored in the SYS:SYSTEM directory.

SYNTAX

RCONSOLE

RENDIR

PURPOSE

The RENDIR command is used to rename a directory.

SYNTAX

RENDIR *path\old directory name* [TO] *new directory name*

RIGHTS

PURPOSE

The RIGHTS command is used to modify or view a users or groups rights for files, directories, or volumes.

RIGHTS *Options*	*(Abbr.)*	*Description*
CONTINUOUS	(C)	Scrolls through the information without pausing.
FILTER	(F)	Displays the inherited rights filter.

continues

RIGHTS Options	(Abbr.)	Description
GROUP	(G)	Allows you the change the rights for a group.
HELP	(?)	Displays online documentation for help.
INHERITED RIGHTS	(I)	Displays inherited rights and where the rights are inherited from.
SUBDIRECTORIES	(SUB)	Changes the rights for the subdirectories below the level you are modifying.
TRUSTEE	(T)	Displays trustee rights at the current directory.
USER	(NAME)	Changes the rights for the user specified.

SYNTAX

```
RIGHTS path [ [+ ¦ -] rights] [option(s)]
```

SEND

PURPOSE

This utility is used to send or set your machine to receive or not receive network messages.

SEND Options	(Abbr.)	Description
ACCEPT ALL	(A=A)	All messages are received.
ACCEPT FROM SERVER	(A=C)	Only messages from the server are received.
ACCEPT NONE	(A=N)	No messages are received.
BROADCAST MODE	(S)	Causes the workstation to display the current broadcast mode.
HELP	(?)	Displays online documentation for help.
POLL	(A=P)	Message will not be received until you poll for it.
POLL FOR STORED MESSAGE	(P)	Causes workstation to poll for messages at the server.

Syntax

```
SEND ["message" [TO] [user ¦ group] [option(s)] ]
```

SETPASS

Purpose

SETPASS is used to change your password. It prompt for the users old password first, the prompts two times for the new user password.

SETPASS *Options*	*(Abbr.)*	*Description*
Username	(Name)	Changes password of user if the user has rights.
Servername	(Name)	Changes password on a given server.
VERSION	(VER)	Displays version information.

Syntax

```
SETPASS [username] [/option(s)]
```

SETTTS

Purpose

This command is used to set or view the logical and physical record locks for Transaction Tracking System (TTS).

SETTTS *Options*	*(Abbr.)*	*Description*
DISABLE	(D)	Disables physical and logical settings.
HELP	(?)	Displays online documentation for help.
NORMAL	(N)	Resets the logical and physical settings to 0, the default value.

Syntax

```
SETTTS [logical level [physical level] [N ¦ D] ] [/option(s)]
```

SYSTIME

PURPOSE

SYSTIME synchronizes the workstations date and time with the servers date and time.

SYNTAX

```
SYSTIME [server]
```

UIMPORT

PURPOSE

This command takes an ASCII import file and imports user objects into the directory tree.

SYNTAX

```
UIMPORT [control file] [data file]
```

WHOAMI

PURPOSE

This command is used to view information regarding the users connection.

WHOAMI Options	(Abbr.)	Description
BINDERY	(B)	Displays bindery emulation information.
CONTINUOUS	(C)	Scrolls through output without pausing.
HELP	(?)	Displays online help.

SYNTAX

```
WHOAMI [server] [/option(s)]
```

WSUPDATE

Purpose

This supervisor command line utility is used to update local files with network files. WSUPDATE works by comparing the date on the local drives file with the date on the networks file. If the network file is newer, it updates the local file. This utility is stored in SYS:SYSTEM and should be used with caution.

WSUPDATE Options	(Abbr.)	Description
ALL	(ALL)	Searches all mapped drives for file to update.
COPY	(C)	Copies over old file without saving the old file first.
ERASE	(E)	If log file is being kept, erases existing file.
FILE	(F)	Overrides any other options, and specifies location of a file where WSUPDATE options to be used are found.
HELP	(?)	Displays online documentation for help.
LOCAL	(LOCAL)	Searches all local drives for file to update.
LOG FILE	(L)	Specifies log file to be kept of all information that is generated when WSUPDATE is executed.
PROCEED	(P)	Prompts for user input before file will be updated.
READ ONLY	(RO)	Causes a file to be updated, even if it is flagged read only.
RENAME	(R)	Copies new file when old copy is located, but saves the old copy with an .OLD extension.
SUBDIRECTORIES	(SUB)	Specifies search of subdirectories when seeking the outdated file.

43

Syntax

WSUPDATE [source path] [drive letter: ¦ volume name:] path\filename] [option(s)]

WSUPGRD

PURPOSE

This command line utility is used to upgrade the IPX.COM LAN driver on the workstation to the newer ODI driver.

WSUPGRD Options	(Abbr.)	Description
CONTINUE	(C)	Exits with error level 1 if no upgrade is performed.
NO DELETE	(N)	Does not delete the DOSIPX driver.
NO EDIT	(E0)	Does not edit AUTOEXEC.BAT.
EDIT	(E1)	Edits AUTOEXEC.BAT.
HELP	(?)	Displays help information.
EDIT and CREATE	(E2)	Creates NETSTART.BAT and edits AUTOEXEC.BAT.
NO NET.CFG	(S)	Suppresses generation of NET.CFG lines from the DOSIPX driver.

SYNTAX

WSUPGRD [path] [option(s)]

SUMMARY

This chapter presented an overview of the common command-line utilities that users have access to. The amount of information available from the utilities will depend on the individual user rights in the NDS as well as the file systems.

- NWADMIN

- Using NWADMIN

- NWADMIN's Object
  Menu

- The View Menu

- The Options Menu

- The Tools Menu

- The Window Menu

- The Help Menu

- NETADMIN

- Manage According to
  Search Pattern

- Summary

CHAPTER 44

NWADMIN and
NETADMIN Utilities

There are two types of NetWare utilities; those that are run from the server console, and those that are run from a workstation. Server console utilities are usually used for server installation, management, optimization, and server performance tuning. (Console commands and NLMs are discussed in detail in Chapter 41.)

The utilities that are run from the workstation are generally used to manage the network (not usually the server). This means adding, setting up, deleting users, assigning trustee rights and assignments, setting up security, defining the amount of network auditing that you want to implement, and so on. The workstation-based utilities can usually be used by the network administrator, but also are often used by users to perform maintenance routines on their own user accounts. This chapter covers the two main NetWare 4 utilities, NWADMIN and NETADMIN. NWADMIN is a Windows-base network administrator utility and NETADMIN is its DOS equivalent. Both of these utilities have similar functions and take the place of the NetWare 3's SYSCON utility.

NWADMIN

NWADMIN (NetWare Administrator) is Novell's new graphical tool that enables a network administrator to perform the day-to-day management procedures on a NetWare 4 network (or server). It replaces SYSCON, and can be used to perform the majority of the command-line functions. NWADMIN is also the NetWare Directory Services administration tool. NDS, of course, is the distributed network database that replaces the bindery. Users can also perform routine functions to manage their own environment.

With NetWare 4, the resources that are on the network (printers, server, volumes, and so on) can be placed in the tree, independent of their physical location. This enables network users to access any network resource, if they have rights, without having to know the exact location of the resource. Also, with NDS NetWare, networks can support multiple servers, whereas the bindery-based servers could only support a single server. This means that a user can simply be added to the network just once rather than having to add the user to each server bindery. NWADMIN is the utility that the administrator would use to perform the task of adding a user to the network.

Note

If users have the appropriate rights, they can manage, change, or configure another user's environment. Thus, you can set up workgroup managers to off-load some of the administrator's day-to-day tasks.

The network administrator can use NWADMIN to set up and administer the network environment for the user. This includes creating objects (users, servers, and printers), defining rights which rights the objects will have, setting up network auditing, creating system and user login scripts, and so on.

To start NWADMIN, double-click on its icon in Window's Program Manager, or select Run from the Window's File menu and type in the correct file location and file name (F:\SYS:\PUBLIC\NWADMIN, for example).

NWADMIN is not automatically added to a group in your windows desktop. To create a group and add NWADMIN to the group, you must perform the following steps:

You will first want to create a group in which to place the NWADMIN icon. To create a group window:

1. Start Windows, and click on the File menu in the upper left corner.
2. Then select New, and the New Program Object dialog box will appear.
3. In the New Program Object dialog box, click the Program Group button and then click on the OK button. A Program Group Properties dialog box will appear.
4. Type in a description for the group name and press Enter or click on the OK button.

    The new group icon will then be created and become active, meaning that the window will be open.

The next step is to place the icon representing NWADMIN in the new group window. To do so, complete these steps:

1. Open the group in which you which to add the NWADMIN icon. (Double-click on the group icon).
2. Click on File in Windows Program manager screen.
3. Choose New (you need to make sure the correct group icon is highlighted).
4. Select Program item and click on the OK button, or press the Enter key. The Program Item Properties dialog box will appear.
5. In the dialog box, name the icon by typing NWADMIN or some other name in the Description field.
6. Click the Browse button and use the dialog box to locate the NWADMIN executable file (by default NWADMIN.EXE is located in the Public directory on the SYS: volume).

7. When you find NWADMIN.EXE, highlight the file and click the OK button, or simply double-click on the filename. The file's location and name will then be added to the Command Line section in the Program Item Properties screen.

8. Type in the correct location for the working directory.

   If you do not specify a working directory, by default the location of the file will be used as the default working directory. Because all users will want to have access to this directory, it is best to use the PUBLIC directory or another other location in which all users have access rights.

9. Click the OK button.

   Because the NWADMIN.EXE file is in a location that may not be continuously accessible (that is, if you are not connected to the network), a Windows message box will appear, warning you that the specified location may not be available during later Windows sessions.

10. Click the Yes button, and you will be ready to run NWADMIN. An icon similar to the one shown in Figure 44.1 will appear for NWADMIN.

Figure 44.1.
Icon for NWADMIN
program.

USING NWADMIN

You now are ready to start NWADMIN. To do so, double-click on the newly created icon and the screen, similar to the one seen in Figure 44.2, will appear. NWADMIN remembers the last screen you used, therefore, the next time you start the program, the opening screen may be different.

NWADMIN has a menu across the top of the screen, as seen in Figure 44.3. Each menu selection also has several options. The following section discusses each of these options. The placement of some of the options have changed between versions of NWADMIN; therefore, the following discussion is based on NWADMIN v4.10.2, one that was originally shipped with NetWare 4.10.

Figure 44.2.
NWADMIN main
screen.

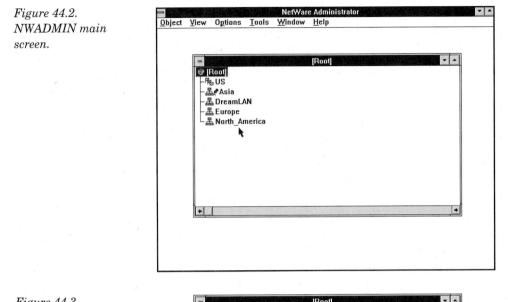

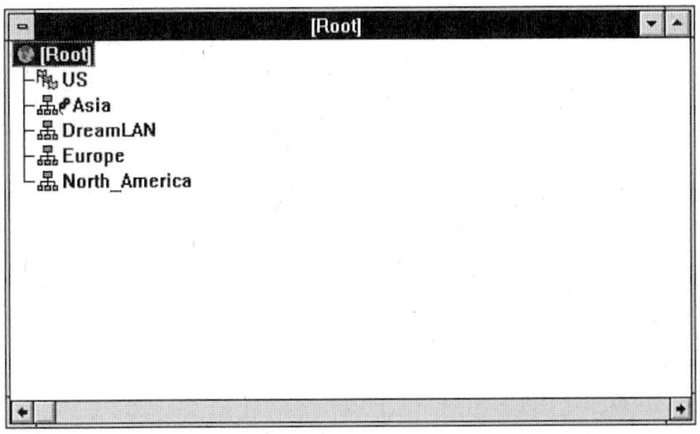

Figure 44.3.
NWADMIN main menu
selections.

NWADMIN's OBJECT MENU

NWADMIN's Object Menu is where the NetWare administrator will perform most of the management tasks. Users can also use the Object menu to manage their individual environments. The following list of options can be performed from the Object menu. This list also represents a sampling of the type of administration tasks that are performed from the Object menu.

- ◆ Create objects
- ◆ Set the details for objects

◆ Define trustee assignments and inherited rights filters.

◆ Restrict an objects rights to other parts of the tree.

◆ Salvage files and directories that have been deleted

◆ Find the details of an object

◆ Move object of files to another location within the tree

◆ Copy a file or multiple files

◆ Rename a file, directory, or object

◆ Delete a file, directory, or object

◆ Define a user template

◆ Search the directory tree for an item

◆ Print the NDS tree structure

◆ Exit NWADMIN

NWADMIN's Create Menu Option

Before you create an object, you need to make sure that you are in the container (context) in which you want the new object to be located.

Note

> If you currently have a leaf object highlighted, or if you do not have the appropriate rights to create an object in the current context, the Create option will be dimmed.

Once you are in the correct container, click on Create and a dialog box will appear, from which you can select the class of the object you want to create. Figure 44.4 shows the list of possible classes that can be selected.

Figure 44.4.
The New Object screen,
which shows the class
of objects that can be
created.

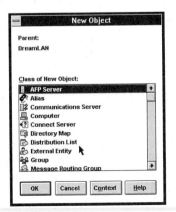

The following list briefly defines some of the available object classes that can be created.

- **AFP Server:** The AFP server (AppleTalk Filing Protocol server) object provides you with information in the Directory database about the actions and characteristics of the AFP server.

- **Alias object:** Provides a simple way to create an alternate naming path for any particular location of an object in the directory. In other words, an Alias object is used to provide an object with multiple locations in the Directory tree, which can simplify searches of the Directory tree, or can enable the network administrator to place all the objects of one type in a location, or simply allow you to place the same user in more than one directory context. When an Alias object is created, although both objects appear, only one object actually will exist.

- **Bindery object:** The representation of an object that has been upgraded from a bindery-based server. A Bindery object cannot have objects below it in the Directory tree.

- **Computer:** Designates computers that are end-user workstations. A Computer object cannot have objects below it in the Directory tree.

- **Country:** The Country object is a container object that can be used to help organize an international directory tree. A Country object can contain an Organization object, as well as an Alias object.

- **Directory Map:** A Directory Map object is a representation of a section or path of the file system directory, such as a volume. Directory Map objects cannot have objects below them in the Directory tree.

- **Group:** A Group object is a collection of users (User objects) that represents or shares a common set of needs.

- **Organization:** An Organization is a container object used in the hierarchical structuring of the directory tree. An Organization object generally is used to designate a division, department, location, or some other logical organizational arrangement. An Organization object cannot contain another Organization object; however, an Organization object can contain an Organizational Unit, any leaf object, or an Alias object.

- **Organizational Role:** An object created for the purpose of specifying a position that can be filled by people (User objects). An Organizational Role cannot have objects below it in the Directory tree.

- **Organizational Unit:** A container object that is similar to the Organization object. Like the Organization object, it is used to build and simplify the hierarchical structure of the Directory. An Organizational Unit can contain login scripts, another Organizational Unit object, an Alias object, and other leaf objects.

◆ **Profile:** A Profile object is a login script that can be accessed by users from anywhere in the Directory tree. A Profile cannot have objects below it in the Directory tree.

◆ **Root:** The Root object is the base or place holder of the Directory tree. It provides the highest point to access different Country objects as well as Organization objects. If users have rights to the Root object, they will have rights to the entire Directory tree.

◆ **User:** A User object is a person who has been given rights (of various levels) to use the network and access to the Directory tree. A user is a leaf object and cannot have objects below it in the Directory tree.

◆ **Volume:** A volume is a physical object that represents a NetWare server's volume. When creating a Volume object, it is best to not use the actual name of the volume. By not naming the Volume object the same as the volume eliminates (or reduces) the chance of having two objects with the same volume name. For example, if you had two servers in the same context, you would also have two physical volumes named SYS:. If you use the same name for the object, you will be attempting to name two objects SYS:, which is not permitted. A Volume object cannot have objects below it in the Directory tree.

To create an objects, complete the following steps:

1. Move to the container in which you want to create the object.
2. Click on the Object menu.
3. Click on Create.
4. Click on the object type you want to create.

Note

If the object type you want to create is not listed, you cannot create it in the container you selected.

5. Click the OK button.

   After clicking OK, an options box associated with that particular object type will appear. Shown in Figure 44.5 is the option box for creating a Group object.

Note

All options boxes are not necessarily the same; the object options box just mentioned is used for creating a group.

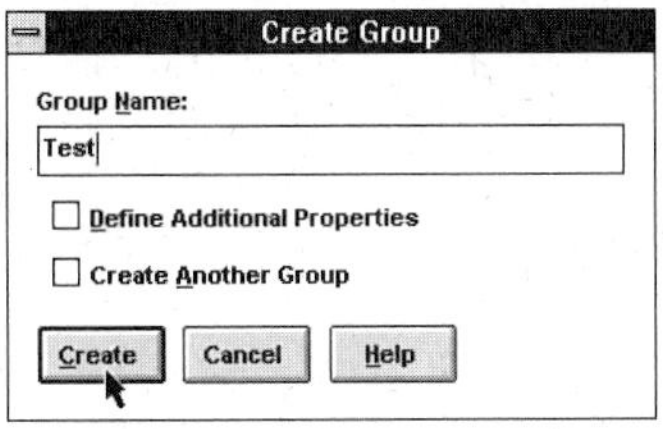

Figure 44.5.
The Create Group
object options box.

Figure 44.5.
The Create Group
object options box.

6. Fill in the appropriate information and click on the Create button.

Note

> The Create button will only become available (it will no longer be
> dimmed) after information has been put in for all the *mandatory*
> information fields.

To define additional properties for an object, if applicable, click on the Define
Additional Properties button. After an object is created you can double-click on the
object or select to the Details menu option to add or change any additional
properties.

After creating an object, it will appear in the Directory Tree Browser.

OBJECT DETAILS MENU OPTION

After using the Create menu selection to initially set up objects, such as users,
servers, volumes, and so on, you will use the Details menu option to view or change
an Organizational Unit or object. After selecting Details, the first page you will see
is the identification page for the item that is currently selected.

Note

> You can also access this page by double-clicking on a leaf object from
> the Browser. For Volume objects, however, you need to use the Details
> option and not double-click. Double-clicking a Volume object will
> display a list of files on the volume.

Each dialog box will be different, depending on the type of object you have selected,
but each dialog box will have two things in common: each will have an information
area and a page area. Each page area will be designated on the right side of the
screen with a gray button. To access the information about the object, click on the
correct page button designator. To access information about a server, for example,

44

NWADMIN AND NETADMIN UTILITIES

select the Identification button. To access the volume's statistics, select the Statistics button, and so on. Each of these pages will contain information regarding the object you have selected. Continuing the server volume example, if you select the Statistics button on a server volume, information on the volume will be displayed (see Figure 44.6).

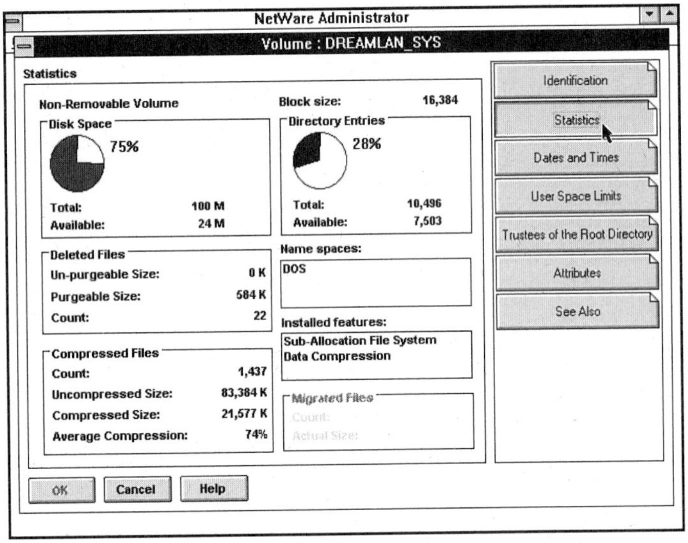

Figure 44.6.
The Volume Statistics
information screen.

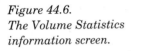

| NetWare Administrator |
| Volume : DREAMLAN_SYS |

Statistics

			Identification
Non-Removable Volume		Block size: 16,384	Statistics
Disk Space		Directory Entries	Dates and Times
75%		28%	User Space Limits
Total: 100 M		Total: 10,496	Trustees of the Root Directory
Available: 24 M		Available: 7,503	Attributes
Deleted Files		Name spaces: DOS	See Also
Un-purgeable Size: 0 K			
Purgeable Size: 584 K		Installed features:	
Count: 22		Sub-Allocation File System Data Compression	
Compressed Files			
Count: 1,437			
Uncompressed Size: 83,384 K		Migrated Files	
Compressed Size: 21,577 K		Count:	
Average Compression: 74%		Actual Size:	

OK   Cancel   Help

Warning

When you are working with an object, such as a server or a user, all the object pages (each section represented by the gray buttons) are considered the same object dialog box. Again, to open other pages of the dialog box, click on the button that represents the dialog box page in which you want to change information. Be careful, however, when you select the Cancel or OK buttons because doing this affects all the pages in the object dialog box. Suppose that you make changes in the Password Restrictions page of a user's dialog box, and then go to the Environment page and click on the cancel button. A screen will appear, prompting you want to discard all the changes. Answering "Yes, Disregard Changes" will disregard all the changes you have made for the user, not just the modification you made in the Environments page.

There are two buttons that you will see in the Details screen: the More button and the Browser button.

The More button enables you to store multiple entries for a filed and the Browser button enables you to browse and select an object's complete name. The Browser button appears next to the fields that require you to enter the complete name (distinguished name) of an object.

The Details screen is where all of the vital information about a network resource (user, server, volume) is stored. The Details section, for example, is where you can accomplish the following tasks:

- ◆ Assign user names
- ◆ Define user environment settings
- ◆ Set user password restrictions
- ◆ Create Login scripts
- ◆ Specify login restrictions
- ◆ Implement disk restriction

The preceding list obviously is not complete, but is sufficient to show you that most of the administration tasks that used to be accomplished in SYSCON now are performed from the Details section of NWADMIN.

TRUSTEES OF THIS OBJECT MENU OPTION

The next menu item of NWADMIN is the Trustees of this Object option. This menu option is used to set up NDS rights. Before getting into the specific functions of this menu option, read on to learn about security basics.

NDS security is much like the security of a file system. When implementing file system security, for example, if a user has rights to a server, volume, and file, that user can access the file and use the application that file represents.

NDS security affects the management of the NDS database, its objects, and the object's properties. NDS security allows for the creation of new objects, the deletion of existing objects, the administration of an object, or simply being able to view the information that is stored about an object.

The capability of NetWare 4 to separate the file systems rights from NDS rights strengthens the security of your network. You might, for example, have someone that needs to have rights to administer NDS, but you do not want to give that person the capability to access files. A good example of this situation is letting an IS person manage the network directory, but not allowing him or her to access the personal records or performance evaluations of other employees.

Following is a brief review of some of the file system and NDS security concepts:

A *trustee* is a user or group of users that has been given the rights to access a (file system) directory, file or even an NDS object.

A user must be defined as a trustee before they can have access rights to an object and it properties, for example. However, a trustee's rights can be implied, rather than explicitly granted. When trustee rights are said to be *explicitly granted*, it means that the network administrator has given the right to a specific user to access information on a particular item.

For example, user JSMITH has rights, or has been assigned as a trustee of the applications directory. The second method to assign trustee rights to allow the trustee rights to flow implicitly through the NDS directory or file system. In this method of assigning trustee rights, the user assumes the rights because of the location that they where placed in the directory tree.

User JSMITH, for example, has rights to the application directory because he was placed in a container that was assigned as a trustee of the application directory. In this case, the network administrator did not explicitly imply that user JSMITH is a trustee of the application directory.

In NetWare 4, these implicit and explicit methods of assigning trustee rights also applies to granting users access to information that is stored in the Directory tree. These rights are called *property rights*. The property rights that a user has affects how the user can access information about an object.

In NetWare 4, each object has properties that basically are database fields. Every property then has a value, or the actual data that is stored in that property field. When using a phone number example, the phone number is the value and the field, phone number, is the property.

Property rights can be assigned for a specific property or for all the properties. This enables the network administrator to allow users to see just a portion of the objects property values. For example, the network administrator may want to allow all users to access the values (information) stored in the phone number, e-mail address, and first name properties.

Clicking on the Trustees of this Object option will display a dialog box screen that indicates the rights of the currently selected object. If you click on the Inherited Rights Filter button found in the dialog box screen, you will be able to define, or view the current object's inherited rights. You can also click on the Effective Rights button to view the rights that another object has to this particular object. And finally, you can specify or assign trustees for the currently selected object.

With NetWare 4, you can assign rights to container, groups, organizational roles, users, and the [Public] trustee. How rights are assigned depends on the organization's needs. It often is simpler, however, to manage trustee assignments if rights are implicitly granted. This allows the network administrator to change a context's trustee rights, which in turn, will change all the user's rights that are located in the context, rather than making the network administrators change each user's individual trustee assignments.

Note

> The [Public] trustee is a new concept in NetWare 4. The [Public] trustee is a unique trustee; it is not an object, but an assignment whose assignments are received by everyone requesting authentication to the network even prior to login. Thus, you want to exercise caution when you are using the [Public] trustee (users are will be given rights before they login). Also, any actions that are performed by users that are using only public access will not be recorded by the auditing functions of NetWare 4.

In NetWare, rights are allowed to flow down the directory and file structure until the rights are reassigned (implicitly or explicitly). You can also use an Inherited Rights Filter to block the flowing of rights from one location to a lower location. Once a rights filter is put in place, it blocks all inherited rights, and by default, will affect all users. However, the filter can be overridden by explicitly granting rights.

Understanding these concepts will allow you to effectively implement NDS and the NetWare file system security. The following section walks you through some of the more important options found in the Trustees of this Object menu option.

INHERITED RIGHTS FILTER BUTTON

Selecting the Inherited Rights Filter button from the Trustees of this Object screen displays the screen seen in Figure 44.7.

Figure 44.7.
The Inherited Rights
Filter screen.

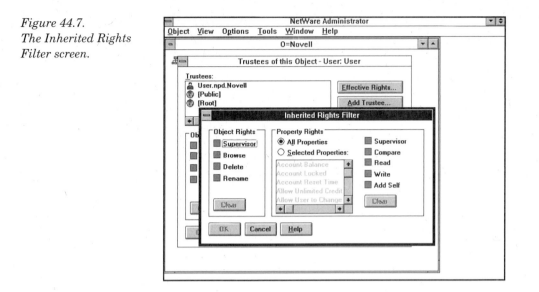

This is the Inherited Rights Filter screen where the network administrator can view or change the Inherited Rights Filter mask, for the currently selected object.

Note

To change the Inherited Rights Filter for certain properties only, select Selected Properties and then select the individual property to modify.

To change the Inherited Rights Filter for all properties of this object, select All Properties.

To remove the Inherited Rights Filter so that all rights can be inherited, choose Clear Filter.

If a box is dimmed (not available), in the Inherited Rights Filter screen, then Inherited Rights Filter exists for this particular object. If a box is white, that right cannot be inherited by a trustee with a trustee assignment above this point. If a box is marked (x), that right can be inherited.

EFFECTIVE RIGHTS TO THIS OBJECT

Clicking on the Effective Rights button in the Trustees of this object screen displays the Effective Rights screen (see Figure 44.8).

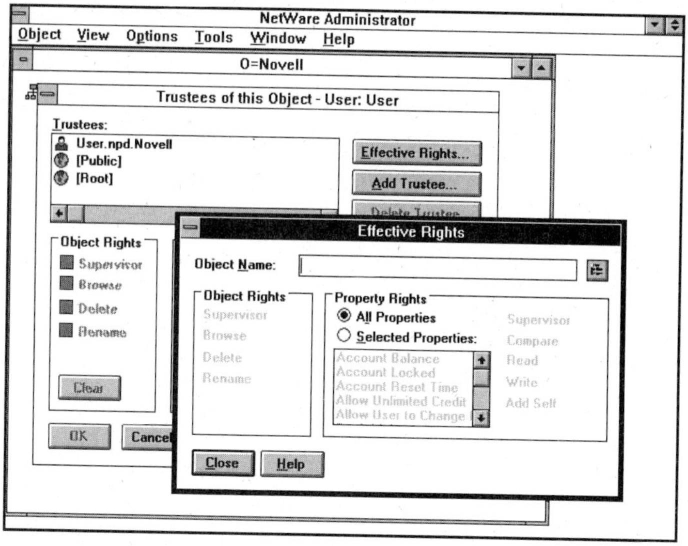

Figure 44.8.
The Effective Rights
screen.

From this location, you can see another object's effective rights to the currently selected object. Effective rights determine the type of access that a user (trustee) has to a directory, file, object, or property. A trustee's effective rights can come from several places, such as the following:

◆ Explicitly granted trustee assignments that have been made specifically to the user

◆ Trustee rights that have been inherited (or implicitly assigned) from the rights of the user's container location

◆ From security equivalencies that a user object might have been assigned

From this location in NWADMIN, you can see, change, or add, a user's or group of users capability to access property information (account balances, e-mail address, default server, and so on) for the currently selected object.

ASSIGNING A TRUSTEE TO AN OBJECT

To assign a trustee to an object, highlight the appropriate object (for example, a user). Then select Trustee of this object from the Options menu and click the Add a Trustee button, located in the upper right portion of the screen. Select the appropriate trustee object and click the OK button.

REMOVING A TRUSTEE TO THIS OBJECT

To remove a trustee of an object, highlight the appropriate object (for example, a user). Then select Trustee of this object from the options menu. Next, click on the correct Trustee icon type, and then choose the desired trustee object. Finally, click on the Delete Trustee button and answer Yes to the delete verification dialog box that will appear.

THE RIGHTS TO OTHER OBJECTS MENU OPTION

It often is important to see which rights an object has in a specific location. This task is accomplished by selecting the Rights to Other Objects option from the Object menu. After selecting this option, the first step is to specify which part of the Directory tree you want to view. This is done by choosing the Browser icon and pointing and clicking the appropriate location, or by typing the location into the dialog box that appear, and which can be seen in Figure 44.9.

Figure 44.9.
The Search Context
screen in NetWare 4.

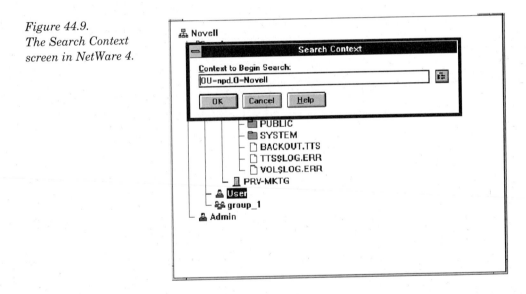

After entering the search parameters, a window showing what the selected object has rights to will appear (see Figure 44.10).

Figure 44.10.
The Rights to Other
Objects window.

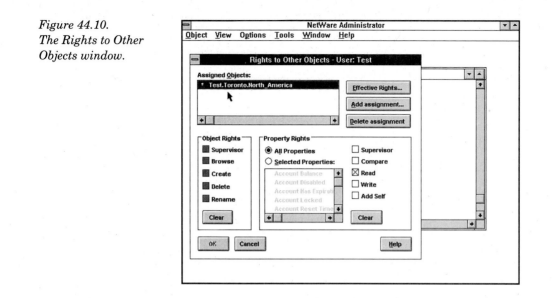

From this window, you can view both the effective rights of NetWare Directory Service objects and file system files and directories, the object, add assignments, or delete assignments. This means that you can view object and property rights, and at other times you can view file/directory rights. It also means that you can view the attributes of files or directories.

Also, from this screen, you can use the following access control and security features:

◆ Select an object and choose Trustees of this Object from the Object menu, which enables you to see the trustees of the object you selected. Along with object and property rights, it also enables you view and change the current objects Inherited Rights Filter.

◆ Select an object and choose Rights to Other Objects from the Object menu. This enables you to see where the current object is assigned as a trustee. By selecting Rights to Other objects, you also will see the current object's property and object rights to other objects. However, you cannot change or implement an Inherited Rights Filter from this location.

◆ Select an object and choose Details from the Object menu. Select the Rights to File System page in the object dialog box. You see which files and directories the object has rights to (by a trustee assignment). You see file and directory rights.

44

NWADMIN AND NETADMIN UTILITIES

◆ Select a file or directory in a volume and choose Details from the Object menu. Then select the Trustees of this file or directory page in the object dialog box. The objects that have rights granted to the file or directory through a trustee assignment are listed. You see file and directory rights. You can also view and change the file or directory's Inherited Rights Filter.

◆ Volume is a NetWare Directory Services object that allows you to work with the file system, as well. If you select a Volume and choose Trustees of this Object from the Object menu, you see a Trustees dialog box, showing who has rights to see or change the Volume object. Object and Property rights are shown. If you select a Volume and choose Details from the Object menu and then the Trustees of the Root Directory page, you see the file and directory rights that apply to the first level of directories on that volume. File and directory rights are shown.

THE MOVE AND COPY MENU OPTIONS

Selecting the Move option from the Object menu enables you to move or relocate a selected object or file to another location within the directory tree. The Copy option enables you to make a copy of a file.

To move or copy multiple leaf objects or files, press and hold down the Shift key and select the first item object or file. Then move the cursor to the last item and while holding down the Shift key and click on the last item. Multiple files, or objects, will then be highlighted. To move or copy the selected items, type in the destination location in the dialog box and click the OK button.

THE RENAME MENU OPTION

The Rename option enables you to rename any object, file, or directory. If you rename an object, you can choose to save the object's old name in the Other Names property for future reference.

THE DELETE MENU OPTION

The Delete option deletes the selected object, such as a container. However, a container can be deleted only if it is empty.

THE USER TEMPLATE MENU OPTION

Selecting the User Template option from the Object menu enables you to create a User Template that contains the default information that you want to apply to each new user object when the new object is created. This is a very effective way to assign the name default rights, property values, trustee assignments, and so on, to the each user as you are creating them. Using a User Template can be produce an extreme amount of time savings.

A User Template is a user object with the name User_Template. If NetWare "sees" that a User_Template object has been created, it will use the values stored in the template as the default setting for the new users that you create.

THE PRINT OPTION

This option enables you to print your NDS tree structure via any of the printers defined within your Windows environment. Object icons are printed along side, with the object names for easy identification. You also can send the output to a file instead of a printer.

THE SEARCH AND EXIT MENU OPTIONS

The Search option, as its name implies, enables you to search a branch of the Directory tree for objects matching a specified pattern. Selecting the Exit option from the Object menu will simply close the NetWare Administrator utility.

The remaining NWADMIN menu options do not have as much to do with the day-to-day management of the network as does the Object menu. In fact, the remaining menu options in NWADMIN focus on defining the settings for NWADMIN, rather than managing NetWare (except for the Tools menu option Partition Manager). However, because getting the most out of the NetWare utilities, such as NWADMIN is the focus of this chapter, the remaining menu options are covered in this section.

THE VIEW MENU

The selections located under the View Menu Options selection enables you to control how the Browser displays the NetWare Directory Service's objects.

THE SET CONTEXT OPTION

The context is the location of an object in the Directory Tree, which starts with the selected object in the Directory tree and goes back to the root of the Directory tree. Your context is where you are currently located in the Directory. Selecting the Set Context option displays a set context dialog box. Entering a context in the dialog box will set the context of the Browser to any location that was entered. This feature can be very helpful if you do not want to see the entire directory tree. For example, you can set the context to the object that you want to be the root of the Browser, and they you would only see from that location down the tree.

THE INCLUDE OPTION

Selecting the Include option enables you to specify which classes of objects you want to see in the Browser. After selecting this option, a screen will appear, which lists all the object class types. By default, all the object classes are represented in NWADMIN's Browser. To make it so that an object class is not represented in Browser, uncheck the Include All Objects check box. Then, hold down the Shift key and click individually on the classes you want to include.

THE SORT BY OBJECT CLASS OPTION

The Sort option enables you to select the order in which the objects are displayed onscreen. For example, you can put all your NetWare servers at the beginning of the display, and all Volume objects at the end.

THE EXPAND/COLLAPSE OPTION

The Expand and Collapse options, as their names imply, will either expand or collapse your view, as seen from NWADMIN, of the Directory Tree. More specifically, the Expand option will open the container object that you have selected. The Collapse closes the container that you have selected.

THE OPTIONS MENU

The Options menu consists of the following five selections:

- ◆ Save settings on exit
- ◆ Show Hints
- ◆ Confirm On Delete
- ◆ Get Alias Trustee
- ◆ Get Aliased Object Trustee

All the preceding selections are toggle options. In other words, clicking on the selection once will place a check mark to the left side of the menu option. If the option is selected again, the check mark will be removed.

In previous versions of NWADMIN, if you need to use settings other than the default, you have to set it up every time you start NWADMIN. In v4.10.2, you can use the Save Settings option to make your selection permanent between sessions.

NWADMIN will provide hints if the Show Hints option is a toggled on.

Selecting the Confirm option enables you to specify whether you want to see a confirmation box each time you delete an object, file, or directory. This option remains set, even after closing and re-opening NWADMIN.

The functions of the last two options are just as the description. For example, if you have selected Get Aliased Object Trustee, and if the object you selected is an Alias object, the actual object's (the "primary" object's) trustee information will be retrieved.

THE TOOLS MENU

The Tools menu consist of the Partition Manager, Browser, Salvage, and Remote Console options. Each option is a tool that will help you, in one way or another, better manage the network.

PARTITION MANAGER

Selecting the Partition Manager option starts the Partition Manager utility, which is used to manage the create, manage, and replicate NDS partitions.

NDS is a distributed, replicated database that can be divided into logical divisions (partitions). When you create a partition, it forms a distinct unit of data, which can be replicated and distributed for storage on a different server. This capability enables you to store pieces, or the entire database on multiple servers. There are several advantages of this type of distributed design: it reduces the overhead on all the servers, it ensures that the NDS database will always be accessible (even if one server goes down), and it gives the users the capability to log in to the "network" rather than each server. Also, each NDS database partition communicates with each other. So each partition, if it doesn't contain the data about a specific object, will know where it can retrieve the information. Thus, NDS is a distributed database.

Partitions form a logical part or section of the NDS database that can be duplicated, copied, and distributed to other servers. A replica is the physical portion of the NDS database that are replicated (copied) to other NetWare 4 servers.

Note

Replication makes the NDS database more fault tolerant, by eliminating a single point of failure. It also increase the availability of objects, which decreases the time it takes to access an object. Suppose that you have a server that is located in a remote location, such as Washington, and your main office is in California. If the users in Washington had to access the database across the wide area network, it would be very slow. However, if you created a partition that contained all the information about the local users and had it replicated and stored on the server in Washington, then users would not have to access object information across the slower wide area links. However, the network administrator could still manage the database from the California location.

Parition Manager is the utility that enables the network administrator to determine how the database is to be partitioned and how these partitions are to be replicate.

Note

There are three types of replicas: Master replica, Read/Write replica, and Read-only replica.

The Master replica, which as its name implies, is the first copy of the database that is used to make and copy other replicas. When a replica (copy) of the NDS database is created, a Master replica (master copy) is stored on the NetWare 4 server where the partition resides.

The Read/Write replica is the default replica type and is a copy of the original partition. The Read/Write replica is used for updating the original Master replica and provides fault tolerance. It also increases the user access and authentication speeds.

The Read-only replica is used for storing a partition in a non-changeable form.

Each replica must be synchronized. *Replica synchronization* is a background process (and is not configurable) in which replica changes, such as a user being added, are updated to every server that has a replica of the database where the new user is to reside. Replica updates are given a time stamp, which forces the changes to be applied in the proper order. These changes are collected and sent out every ten seconds.

Note

Changes made to the replica by a logged-in user are updated every five minutes.

For more information on creating and designing replicas and database partitions see Chapter 14. When using Partition Manager, remember that the location of the partitions will dramatically affect the performance of NetWare environment.

THE BROWSER MENU OPTION

When you select the Browser menu option, a new Browser window is opened. If you highlight the object for volume SYS: and then select the Browser tool, for example, a new Browser box will appear.

THE SALVAGE MENU OPTION

The Salvage option allows you to recover previously deleted, but not yet purged files. Recovering a file is possible because NetWare saves deleted files until the user or supervisor deliberately purges them, or until the NetWare server volume runs out of disk space. If the server does begin to get low on disk space, NetWare will automatically purge files on a first deleted, first purged basis. This option is also the location where you purge files. Purging files will permanently remove the files from the system.

Note

The Salvage option will be dimmed until you click on a volume or directory object. After selecting one of these objects, clicking the Salvage option will open a dialog box, as seen in Figure 44.11.

To salvage one or more files, follow these steps:

1. Select from the File List box the file(s) you want to salvage.

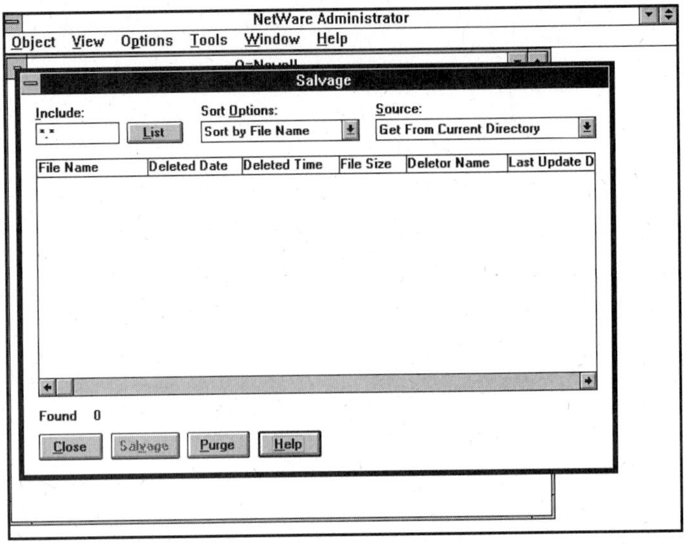

Figure 44.11.
Salvage's dialog box.

Tip

If the files you want to recover are not listed, you may not be in the correct directory location.

You must have the Create right on a file to salvage it.

If you are salvaging a file from a deleted directory, you must have Supervisor right to the root directory of the volume.

2. Choose Salvage.

After choosing Salvage, the files will disappear from the File List box and reappear in the regular file listings (DIR, NDIR, or the Browser).

Note

If you are salvaging from Deleted Directories, a DELETED.SAV directory *must* exist in the root directory of this volume; it must be flagged as Hidden (NetWare does this by default).

NetWare will then restore the recovered files in a hidden directory called DELETED.SAV. To see whether the file has been recovered, you can change into the hidden directory, even if a directory command does not see it. From the root directory type CD \DELETED.SAV and press Enter.

THE REMOTE CONSOLE MENU OPTION

Selecting the RCONSOLE menu option will launch the remote console NetWare utility in a Windows DOS session. This DOS session will look just like the server console screen. This enables the network administrator to access the server from any workstation on the network, simplifying the role of managing remote servers.

Note

> To load RCONSOLE or to use the RCONSOLE menu option, you must first load REMOTE.NLM and RSPX.NLM at the file server.

With NetWare 4, you have the choice to load RCONSOLE using an SPX connection or a asynchronous connection method. If you use SPX connection mechanism, then the workstation must have physical access to the workstation via the network wiring. The asynchronous method of communication enables the administrator to connect to the server without having to have direct physical access to the network infrastructure. However, you this method will require that you have a communication board and driver loaded at the server, as well as at the workstation.

All the actions that are performed at the remote station will happen at the server console. So if you lock the file server console, the workstation console will lock as well. With NetWare 4, the RCONSOLE commands have changed. The following list shows the new RCONSOLE commands:

◆ Alt+F1: Access the remote console available options menu

◆ Alt+F2: Exit Remote Console

◆ Alt+F3: Move backwards through the Remote Console screens

◆ Alt+F4: Move forwards through the Remote Console screens

◆ Alt+F5: Shows the current workstation address

THE WINDOW MENU

The Window menu contains options that enable you to organize or arrange windows that are used in NWADMIN. If you have several browse windows open, for example, you can select the Cascade, or Tile options to rearrange the open browse sessions. The following list briefly defines each of the options that can be selected from the Windows menu.

◆ **Cascade**: Arranges all Browser windows in overlapping style.

◆ **Tile**: Arranges all Browser windows in tile style, where none of the windows overlap, and each is smaller.

◆ **Close all**: Closes all windows.

Tip

> For every Browse window that is opened, a numbered option for the opened window is added as a line item to the Windows menu options box. So, if you are using a keyboard, or if a window is open and you cannot locate it, click on the Window menu option and then select the correct window number and that window will become active.
>
> If a window has been completely closed, to open it again, you will have to choose the Browser option from the Tools menu.

THE HELP MENU

NWADMIN's help is like any standard Windows help menu, which lists all available topics, contains a list of glossary terms, and enables you to search any topic. However, the Help menu also contains an option called *Error Messages*, which lists all error messages that can appear in the NetWare Administrator.

NETADMIN

Just as with NWADMIN, NetWare 4 is the first version of NetWare to offer the NETADMIN utility. In prior versions of NetWare, the utility known as SYSCON was used to perform the same tasks that can be accomplished using NETADMIN.

Note

> The following section assumes a certain understanding of NWADMIN, and NetWare 4's NetWare Directory Services. If you do not feel comfortable with these topics, read the first section of this chapter. Because of these assumptions, repetitious information about managing NDS will not be given. The next section will simply cover the menu options and the management functions that can be performed with NETADMIN.

NETADMIN is the text-based equivalent of NWADMIN; however, it does not include any file system management or printer management capabilities. To manage the file system from a non-Windows workstation, use FILER. To manage the printing environment from a non-windows workstation, use PRINTCON and PCONSOLE.

To start NETADMIN, login into a NetWare 4 server as a user with supervisory equivalencies and from the logged in workstation, type NETADMIN.

Note

Users without supervisory rights can also use NETADMIN to manage or change their own environments; however, without supervisory rights the functions of NETADMIN will be limited.

After typing NETADMIN, the screen as seen in Figure 44.12 will appear.

Figure 44.12.
NETADMIN main
screen.

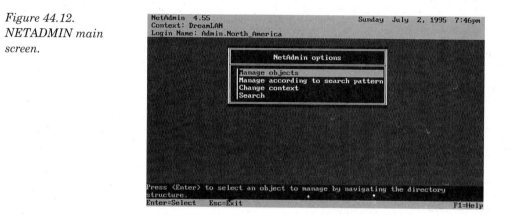

After starting NETADMIN, you will be given four main options: Manage objects, Manage according to search pattern, Change context, and Search.

Manage objects: Enables you to start working with objects.

Manage according to search pattern: Enables you to specify which objects you want to use as your working set. The capability to set filters and define a working set of objects enables network administrators to reduce the amount of objects that are visible in the Browser screen. It also can be used to find a particular object that you wan to manage, or perhaps, it could be used to find all the objects with certain properties (such as all server console operators).

Change context: Enables the network administrator move to a new location in the NDS tree, or even to a different tree.

Search: Enables you to search for a particular object or object class in the container that you specify.

Of these four options, the first, the Manage Objects option, will be used the most often. However, the later settings should be referred to first, since they will determine which objects are listed in the NETADMIN Browser screen as well as in which context you are currently working.

THE MANAGE OBJECTS MENU OPTION

Selecting Manage objects from NETADMIN's options menu displays a browse screen. The Browse screen in NETADMIN looks significantly different than its graphical cousin found in NWADMIN. However, it is used for the same purpose—to move up and down the NDS database structure.

When using NWADMIN, you can simply point and click on the object that you want to manage, with NETADMIN you must use the following conventions:

◆ To select the object that you want to view or manage, press F10.

◆ To create and object, press Insert.

◆ To delete an object, highlight the object and press Delete.

◆ To navigate down the directory tree, highlight a container object (an object with a + in front of it) and press Enter.

◆ To navigate back up the Directory tree, highlight the periods (. .) and press Enter.

When a leaf object is highlighted, pressing F10 and then Enter enables you to manage the object. For example, pressing F10 while the user object Admin is highlighted will display the Actions screen for User: Admin (see Figure 44.13).

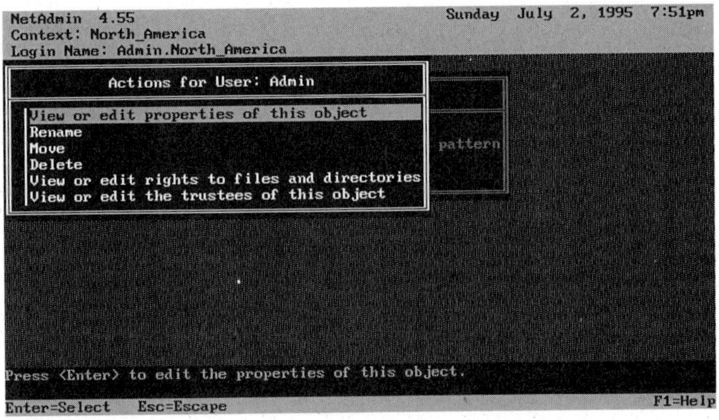

Figure 44.13.
The Actions screen for
User: Admin.

If a Container object is highlighted, however, these keys will perform different functions. If you press F10, then you will see the Actions screen for that container (see Figure 44.14).

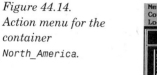

Figure 44.14.
Action menu for the container
North_America.

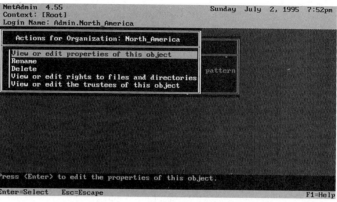

However, if the same container object is highlighted and you press Enter, then you will be moved down the NDS structure and NETADMIN's Browser screen will appear (see Figure 44.15).

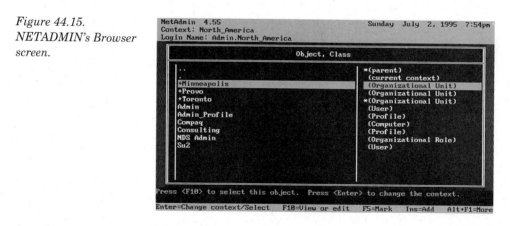

Figure 44.15.
NETADMIN's Browser
screen.

To manage an Object, use NETADMIN's Browser screen to move to the appropriate context. Select the Object by highlighting it and then pressing F10. After the object is selected, you will see an Action screen for that object. Depending on the object, the available options in the Action screens will vary. The following is a list of the actions that will be made available when you select a user object:

◆ View or edit properties of this object

◆ Rename

◆ Move

◆ Delete

◆ View or edit rights to files and directories

◆ View or edit the trustees of this object

Following is a list of actions that are provided when you select a server rather than a user:

◆ View or edit properties of this object

◆ Move

◆ Delete

◆ View or edit the trustees of this object

The list of actions that you can perform on an object will vary, depending on the type of object that is selected. However, the View or edit properties of this object option will always remain available. It is from this option that you define and manage an object, regardless of its type.

Note

Selecting an object and then choosing the option View or edit properties of this object, will provide you with the same information and management options as if you double-clicked on the object in NWADMIN.

VIEW OR EDIT PROPERTIES OF THIS OBJECT

After selecting an object, you will have the option of viewing or editing the properties of an object. Because each object type has a different set of properties, the properties screen that will appear will also be different. The list of properties offered will depend on the type of object that is selected. If a user object is selected, and the View Edit Properties of This Object is chosen, then the Actions for User screen will appear. The action options for a user object are as follows:

◆ Identification

◆ Environment

◆ Mailbox Information

◆ Account restrictions

◆ Login script

◆ Groups/Security Equals/Profile

◆ Change password

◆ Postal address

◆ See also

If a server object is selected, the View or edit NetWare server options screen will appear, offering the following list of options:

◆ Identification

◆ Accounting

◆ View Server Information

◆ View Server Error Log File

◆ Other Properties

◆ See also

Because the user and server objects are the most commonly managed objects this chapter covers both objects action items in detail. It will not, however, cover all the actions that are available for each different option. In fact, it will actually only focus on the action item View or edit properties of this object for a user object and a server object.

VIEWING AND EDITING A USER'S OBJECT PROPERTIES

After selecting a user object, select the first action option, (View or edit properties of this object) and the screen shown in Figure 44.16 will appear. A number of differnet options are available. They are as follows:

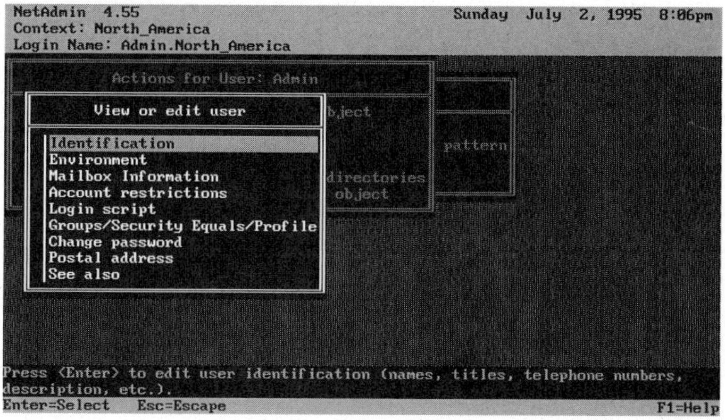

Figure 44.16.
NETADMIN's View or
edit user screen.

Identification: The identification category is where you specify the user objects identification property values. From this location, you can access all the property categories for a user object. At this point, it is important to understand that a property is simply a database field. For example, the first option in the list is Login Name. Each of these property classes are assigned a property value, which is the actual data being stored. So for the property value of Last name, the value would be Smith. All the properties assigned to a specific object help the network administrator better manage the network. The property classes and property fields that can be used to manage a user object are Login name, Last name, Other name, Title, Description, Telephone number, Fax Number, E-Mail Address, Location, and Department.

Environment: Selecting the Environment option will display the screen shown in Figure 44.17. The environment settings specified in this location are used to customize, or configure, the individual network user environments. This includes specifying the language that a particular user would like to use (dialog boxes, help screens, and so on). It includes the user's Default Server. The environment screen allows you to view the network address of the workstation that the user is currently using. It also includes the following home directory information: volume object name, Path or Volume of home directory; if you did not create a home directory for this particular user, these fields will be empty.

Figure 44.17.
NETADMIN's Environment information screen.

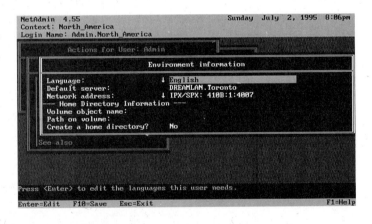

Mailbox Information: Enables you to specify where the mailbox (for MHS Services) is located for this user.

Account Restrictions: The Account Restrictions screen is used to view or edit the user's network login restrictions. Selecting Account Restrictions displays the screen containing the menu options seen in Figure 44.18.

Figure 44.18.
NETADMIN's Account
restrictions option
screen.

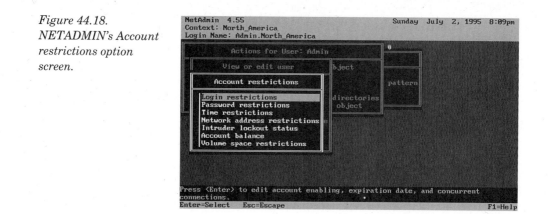

Login Scripts: Login scripts are used to specify commands that are executed when the user logs in. Each login script must be written on its own line, and all blank lines are ignored.

Groups/Security Equals/Profile: Selecting the Groups/Security Equals/ Profile option displays the dialog box shown in Figure 44.19.

Figure 44.19.
The Groups/Security
Equals/Profile screen.

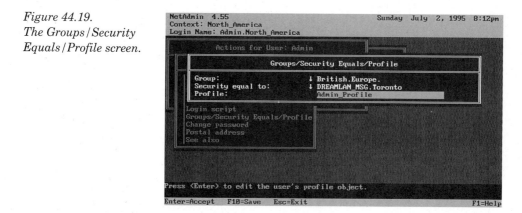

If the lists in the preceding screen are empty, highlight the "(Empty List)" designator option and press Enter. A Group Memberships (or "Security equivalences") dialog box will open. Once in the dialog box. Press the Insert key and add items to the list by pressing the Insert key again. You also can use the Browser screen to highlight and select the items to be added to the list.

If there are items listed in the field, you can position the highlight bar over the item and press Enter to change or edit the selected item.

To delete an item from the list, first select the item with the highlight bar and then press Delete. You also can delete multiple items by highlighting them while pressing F5, and then pressing the Delete key.

Note

When you make object "A" security equivalence to object "B", then object "A" has the same rights as object "B". Therefore, be sure you know what rights object "B" has before making object "A" security equal to "B" as "A" may gain rights that it should not have.

Also, every object is a security equivalent to every object in its complete name; that is, all the objects that contain it, up to the root object. These objects are not listed in this screen (you can not change these security equivalencies).

Change Password: Enables you change the password of the selected object. (You can only change the password if it is your user account, or if you have the rights to do so). After selecting this option, you will be asked to type in the old password. You then will be asked to enter the new password, and then to verify the new password.

Note

If the network administrator is changing the password of a user, you do not have to enter the old user password.

Postal Address: The Postal Address option, as it name implies, is simply a location in NDS where you can store the address of the user.

See Also: Lists any object that might have information pertaining to this user. For example, you may want to include things such as the user's immediate supervisor object, printers or server's that the user manages, and so on. If there are no items currently in the list, you can use the Insert key and Browser screen to locate and add object to this list. If you want to delete an object from the list, move the highlight bar over the entry and press the Delete key, or mark multiple entries with the F5 key and then press the Delete key.

Managing a server with NETADMIN is very similar to managing a user. The difference is the user and server objects have different properties. After highlighting a server in NETADMIN's Browser screen and pressing Enter, you will be given a list of action items that can be performed on the selected server object. These actions will be slightly different than the actions that you get when you select a user object, but the first option (View or edit properties of this object) is the same. However, after it is selected you will receive a different list of menu options, which are as follows:

- Identification
- Accounting
- View Server Information
- View Server error logs
- Other Properties
- See Also

If you select the identification option after choosing a server object, an information list with the following fields will appear; each of these field's have a descriptive name, telling you of the information that they contain.

- Server Name
- NetWare version
- Server status
- Other names
- Description
- Network address
- Operator
- User
- Location
- Department
- Organization

If you select the accounting option, you can define the following network services charge rates:

- Accounting servers
- Blocks read charge rates
- Blocks written charge rates
- Connect time charge rates
- Disk storage charge rates
- Service requests charge rates

Note

If accounting has not yet been installed and you select the accounting option, you will be asked if you want to install it. Select Y or N. If accounting has previously been installed, then selecting the accounting options will enable you to set or modify the network service charge rates.

If you select the option, View Server Information, the screen similar to Figure 44.20 will appear.

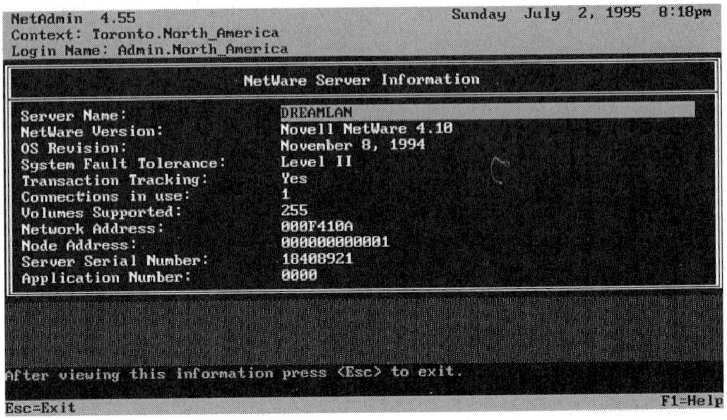

Figure 44.20.
NetWare Server
Information screen.

```
NetAdmin  4.55                                    Sunday  July  2, 1995  8:18pm
Context: Toronto.North_America
Login Name: Admin.North_America

                          NetWare Server Information

    Server Name:                  DREAMLAN
    NetWare Version:              Novell NetWare 4.10
    OS Revision:                  November 8, 1994
    System Fault Tolerance:       Level II
    Transaction Tracking:         Yes
    Connections in use:           1
    Volumes Supported:            255
    Network Address:              000F410A
    Node Address:                 000000000001
    Server Serial Number:         18408921
    Application Number:           0000



After viewing this information press <Esc> to exit.
Esc=Exit                                                              F1=Help
```

To view any errors that have been recorded by the server, select the option View Server Error Log File. A screen will appear, showing any errors that have transpired since the last deletion of the error log. If there are no errors, then no file will exist.

If the other properties option is selected, you can create, change, or view a list of other properties, such as printers, print queues, server volumes, and so on, that are managed by the server.

The See also field, as with the See also field under the user object, enables you to specify any other objects that pertain to this server object. An example of what you may want to include in this field is the printer objects (print server and printers) that are associated with this server.

MANAGE ACCORDING TO SEARCH PATTERN

The second option of NETADMIN's main menu is Manage according to search pattern. This option, as its name implies, enables you to set a search filter to select a specific object or group of objects that you want manage. After selecting the option,

Manage according to search pattern, the screen as shown in Figure 44.21 will appear.

Figure 44.21.
Selecting search
pattern.

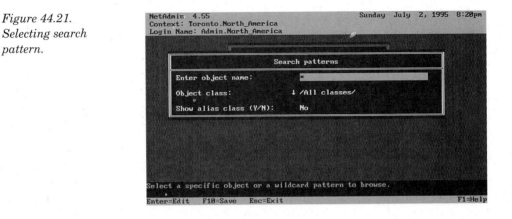

The filter screen enables you to search by object name, object class, or combination of name and object class. In the name field, you can either type in the full name of the object, or use wildcards (such as * and ?). Pressing Enter on the object class field will display a list of object "type" for you to choose from. Following is a list of some of the class types that you can choose from:

- Alias
- Computer
- NetWare server
- Organizational role
- Print server
- Printer
- Profile
- Queue
- User
- and Volume.

You can select a single object class by highlighting it and pressing Enter, or you can mark multiple object classes with the F5 key and then press Enter. Either way, your search criteria will limit the number of objects that you have to work with.

The second option in this menu is Show alias class. If this option is toggled to Yes, you can view an alias object rather than the object to which it points. If this field is set to No, then you can edit the properties of the real object (where the alias is pointing) instead of the alias object itself.

The third option in NETADMIN's main menu is Change context. Selecting Change contexts allows the network administrator to manage objects in a different portion of the tree, or in a different tree. After selecting the Change Contexts option, a single-line dialog box will appear (see Figure 44.22).

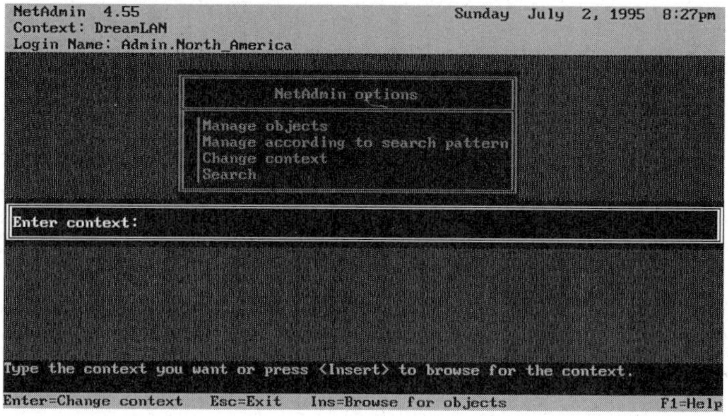

Figure 44.22.
The Change context
dialog box.

To change to a different context, type in the name of the context or the press Insert key. If you press the Insert key, the Browser screen will appear. You can then move around the NDS tree with the Browser. When you get to the context to which you want to change, press the F10 key to accept the context location.

The last option is Search. It allows you to search for a particular object by values in certain properties or search by object class (see Figure 44.23).

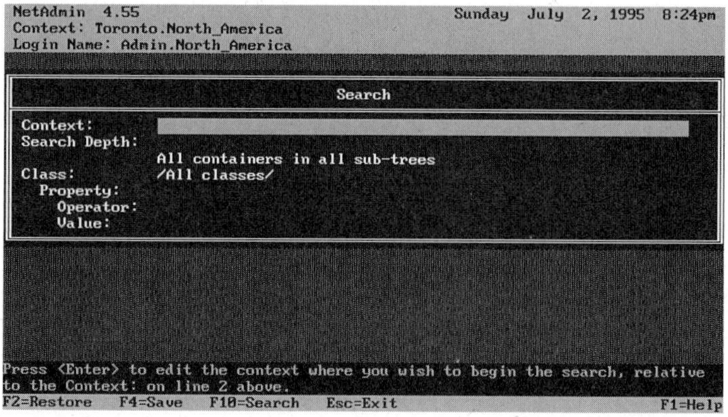

Figure 44.23.
Performing a search.

SUMMARY

NWADMIN and NETADMIN are new network management utilities for NetWare 4. NWADMIN is a Windows-based NetWare administration utility and NETADMIN is the DOS-based NetWare administration utility. These utilities perform similar functions, although NETADMIN does not offer any file management, or printer management functions. To perform these functions from a DOS workstation you must use the PCONSOLE, PRINTCON, and FILER utilities.

44

- Starting NWUSER

- Attaching to Servers

- NetWare Settings

- User-Definable Buttons

- NETUSER

- Printing

- Drives

- Attachments

- Summary

CHAPTER 45

NWUSER and NETUSER Utilities

With every version of NetWare, Novell seems to get a little bit better with NetWare's interface and utilities, making them more user-friendly. NWUSER and NETUSER are examples of this user-friendly progress. These two utilities enable the user to execute day-to-day commands from a graphical and menu-driven utility, rather than from the command line.

NWUSER is NetWare's new MS Windows user utility, and thus, has a graphical interface. It helps the user perform common functions, such as mapping drives (permanently or temporarily), attaching to a server, capturing printer ports, and so on, basically providing the user with a graphical way of accessing network resources.

NETUSER, the non-graphical DOS-based equivalent of NWUSER, enables the user to perform the same printer capturing, server attachment, message sending functions as NWUSER, but without having to have a PC that is capable of running Windows (8088, 2086, and so on). NETUSER has the familiar NetWare type (C-Worthy) interface that is easy to operate and understand. For those of you familiar with NetWare 3.*x* and 2.*x*, NETUSER is a much improved version of SESSION, a little used program in earlier versions of NetWare.

This chapter will not only help you better understand these two user utilities, it also will help the user perform day-to-day routines, such as mapping a drive, sending a message, or attaching to a server. In fact, this chapter is designed around user tasks, such as capturing a printer port. It then walks you through the step-by-step process with both utilities, with NWUSER first, followed by NETUSER.

STARTING NWUSER

As mentioned previously, NWUSER is a graphical-user utility designed for the Windows environment, which enables the users to access network resources.

To start NWUSER, double-click on its icon in Windows' Program Manager, or select Run from the Windows' File menu and type in the correct filename and path (such as F:\SYS:\PUBLIC\NWUSER.EXE). If you install the NetWare Requester client with Windows support as described in Chapter 23, you will already have a NetWare Tools group icon, with the User Tools program icon in it.

If you do not have the NetWare Tools group icon or the User Tools program icon, the following steps will help you create them.

You will first want to create a group in which to place the NWUSER icon. To create a group window, follow these steps:

1. Start Windows, and click on the File menu in the upper left corner.
2. Then select New, and the New Program Object dialog box will appear.

3. Once in this box, select the Program Group button and then click on the OK button. A Program Group Properties dialog box will appear.

4. Type in a description for the group name and press Enter or click on the OK button.

The new group icon will then be created, and it will be active, meaning that the window will be open. The next step is to place the icon representing NWUSER in the new group window. To do so, complete these steps:

1. First, open the group in which you want to add the NWUSER icon. (Double-click on the group icon).

2. Click on File in the Windows Program Manager screen.

3. Choose New (you need to make sure the correct group icon is highlighted).

4. Select the Program item and click on the OK button, or press the Enter key.

5. A Program Item Properties dialog box will appear. Name the icon by typing NWUSER or some other name in the Description field.

6. Click the Browse button and use the dialog box to locate the NWUSER executable file (by default NWUSER.EXE is located in the Public directory on the SYS: volume).

Note

When you find NWUSER.EXE, highlight the file and click the OK button, or simply double-click on the filename. The file's location and name will be added to the Command Line section in the Program Item Properties screen.

7. Type in the correct location for the working directory.

Note

If you do not specify a working directory, by default the location of the file will be used as the default working directory. Because all users will want to have access to this directory, it is best to use the PUBLIC directory, or some other location where all users have access rights.

8. Click the OK button.

Note

Because the NWUSER.EXE file is in a location that may not be continuously accessible, (if you are not connected to the network) a message box will appear, warning you that the specified location may not be available during later Windows sessions.

9. Click the Yes button, and you will be ready to run NWUSER.

Note

You also can add NWUSER to an existing group with Windows' File Manager by simply opening a file session and dragging the NWUSER.EXE file into the group window.

Figure 45.1 shows the NetWare Tools program icon.

Figure 45.1.
The NetWare Tools
program icon for
NWUSER.

To start NWUSER, double-click the NWUSER icon. A screen will appear (see Figure 45.2). Along the top of the screen is a series of buttons. The buttons (from left to right) perform the following tasks:

Exit the Utility
Map Drives
Capture printers
Attach server
Send messages
NetWare settings
Configurable buttons
Obtain help

The user interface of the NWUSER GUI utility functions in a manner similar to other Windows-based software, such as NWADMIN. To activate a specific function, click on the button; the button will appear as being "pressed."

Figure 45.2.
NWUSER menu.

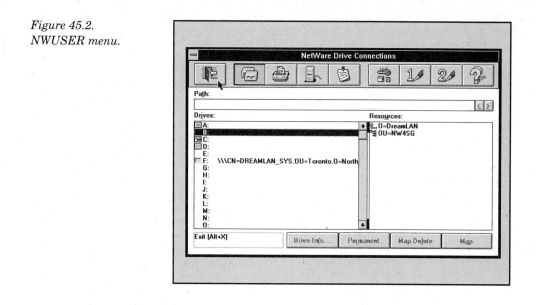

MAPPING DRIVES

Clicking the drive icon will display the screen seen in Figure 45.3. The left side of the screen, the Drives section, is a list of available drive designation letters, which include the current drive mappings. The right side of the screen, the resource section, lists the available NDS trees.

Figure 45.3.
*NWUSER's NetWare
Drive Connections
screen.*

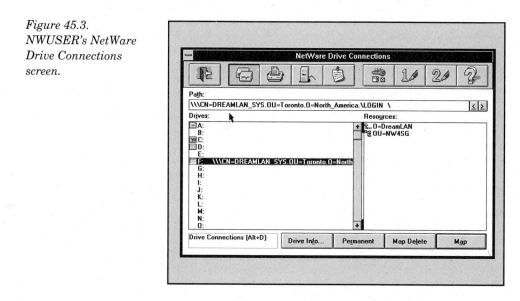

To map a drive, select the location that you would like to have mapped by clicking on the resource section of the screen.

In NetWare 4, this means you may have to begin by clicking on the Organizational unit, then the server object, and then the volume object. Once you have clicked on the volume object, you will see a list of available directory locations. The resources screen will appear. This screen looks and acts similar to Window's File Manager screen. Use the mouse to move to the directory location to which you want to map a drive. Once you have reached the destination location, drag the location designator from the resource side of the screen and drop it on top of the drive letter. Or simply highlight the resource and the drive mapping letter designator and click on the Map button located at the bottom of the NWUSER screen.

Once the resource (in this case, the directory location for which you want to create a drive mapping) is placed on the Drives side of the screen, the mapping process is complete. However, if you leave Windows and reboot the workstation, this drive mapping will be erased. To make the drive mapping "permanent" (automatically mapped each time Windows is launched), click on the Permanent button at the bottom of the screen.

Drive mappings that are permanent will have a red drive designator on the left side of the drive letter. When a drive mapping is made permanent, the drive mapping will automatically be remapped each time Windows is started—permanent drive mappings created with NWUSER, however, will not be "permanent" in DOS.

To undo or delete a permanent drive mapping, highlight the drive letter designator and click the Permanent button. Notice that the drive mapping is not deleted, but rather the permanent status indicator to the left of the drive letter disappears.

To delete a drive mapping, highlight the drive mapping and click on the Map Delete button at the bottom of the NWUSER screen.

After you map a drive, you can highlight the drive mapping and click on the Drive Info button at the bottom of the screen—or double-click the drive letter. A screen similar to the one seen in Figure 45.4 will appear. The Drive Info screen indicates the server, Path, username, and effective rights you have for the mapped directory.

To turn a mapped drive into a mapped root drive, highlight the drive mapping designator in the drive section of the screen. Notice that the Path dialog box will contain the complete path of the highlighted drive mapping. Once the path is listed, clicking on the arrows on the right end of the Path field will separate the drive path (see Figure 45.5). Clicking the arrows will leave a space between the map root and the remaining directories. The space will indicate the location of the MAP root drive mapping.

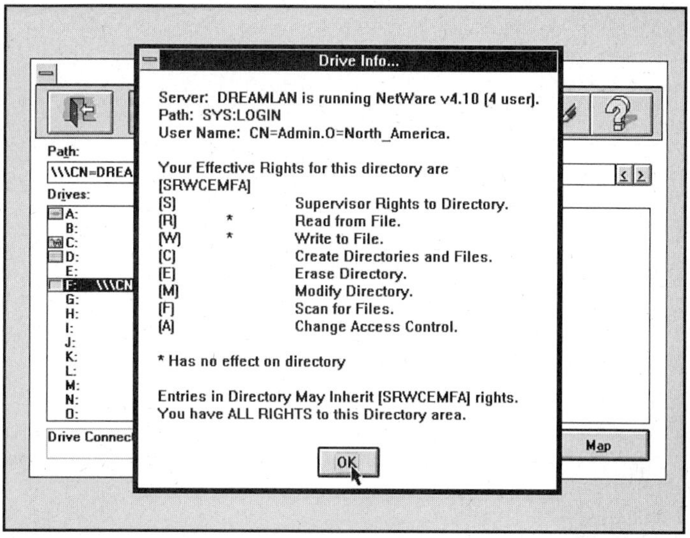

Figure 45.4.
NWUSER's Drive Info
screen.

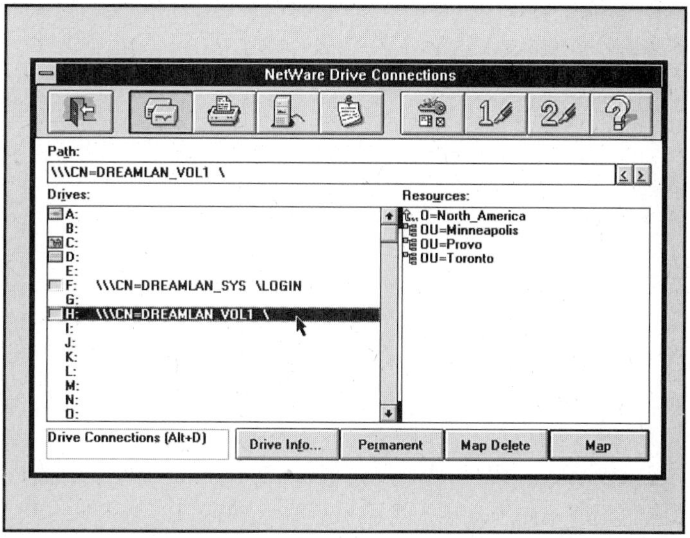

Figure 45.5.
The Path dialog box,
which contains the
Map Root arrows.

Note

When you create a map root drive mapping, the drive mapping will
still point to the same directory you originally mapped. However, with
a mapped root drive, mapping the location of the space will determine
where the root directory of the drive mapping will be (users will not be
able to move up the directory structure any further).

CAPTURING PRINTER PORTS

One of the original selling features of NetWare, and a network in general, was the capability to share printers. It was revolutionary that two computers could be hooked together and share the same peripheral device. Now, printer sharing is something users expect, even if they are not quite sure how it works. This section discusses briefly how network printing works, and how you can implement printing.

Print jobs are generated by normal applications running at the workstation. Then, when the workstation prints the print job, it sends the commands to the workstations BIOS (Basic Input Output System), which simply sends the file to be printed to the parallel or other output port. Network software, such as the NetWare command known as CAPTURE, "intercepts" the BIOS printing function, which stops a print job from printing to a local port and redirects it to a different location—a shared network printer.

Note

Actually, the print jobs are not sent directly to a network printer. They are first sent to network queues, which are defined on a file server or print server. From the queues, the print job is processed by the print server and passed to the assigned queue. After this process, print jobs are then sent to the network printer.

Some applications will allow you to print directly to the network print queue, while others are not so NetWare-aware. These "unaware" applications (which most applications are) rely on the CAPTURE command to redirect print jobs to the print queues and eventually the printer. In other words, if you do not have a printer port "captured," you will not be able to print to a network printer.

To capture a printer port with NWUSER, select the printer button. Once the printer button has been selected, the screen shown in Figure 45.6 will appear. This screen is similar to the Drive Mapping screen in that it is divided into two sections. On the left part of the screen are the ports that are available for capturing, and the right side is the Resource section. The Ports section of the screen usually contains LPT1, LPT2, and LPT3. The right side of the screen, the Resource section, lists the available network printers.

Note

When the printer button is first selected, the resources side of the screen may only show the NetWare 4 NDS tree (available contexts).

> You will have to select the context in which the print queue you want to capture resides.

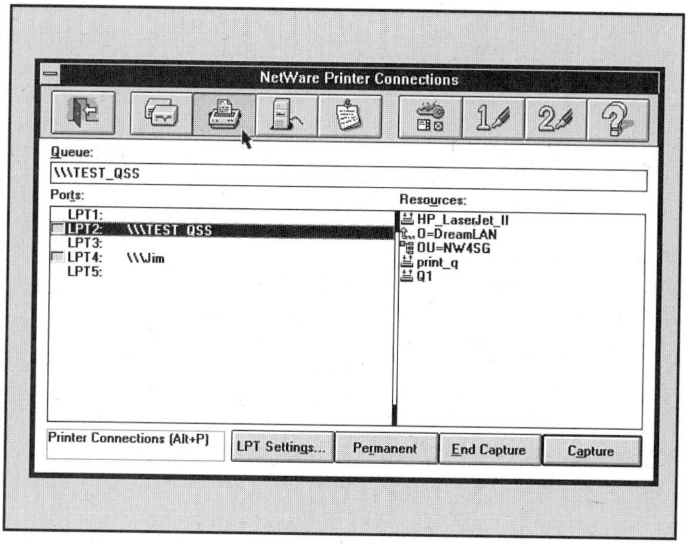

Figure 45.6.
NWUSER's print
capture screen.

Once you have located and selected the print queue or printer to which you want to send your print jobs, select the Capture button, which is in the lower left portion of the print capture screen.

As in the Drive Mapping screen, you can also drag and drop the print queue onto the port you want to capture. Once a queue or printer has been captured, it will be listed in the "Ports" section of the screen. However, if you leave Windows and reboot the workstation, the captured port will no longer be captured. To make the capture command "permanent" (to have the port automatically captured each time Windows is started), click on the Permanent button at the bottom of the screen.

Capture commands that are permanent will have a red box rather than an empty box on the left side of the port listing. When a CAPTURE command is made permanent, the port will automatically be captured each time Windows is started—similar to drive mappings, permanent capture commands created with NWUSER will not be "permanent" in DOS.

To undo or delete a permanent capture setting, highlight the port designator and click the Permanent button (this will deselect the permanent setting). Notice that the port designator is not deleted, and the permanent status indicator to the left of the port has disappeared.

To delete a capture, or rather, to release a port from its captured status, highlight the port designator (for example, LPT1) and click on the End Capture button at the bottom of the NWUSER screen.

Another important and very useful feature of NWUSER's print capture screen is the LPT Settings button, which is located on the button bar in the lower part of the NetWare Printer Connections screen. Selecting the LPT Setting button will display the NetWare settings screen, as seen in Figure 45.7.

Figure 45.7.
The NetWare Printer
Port Settings screen.

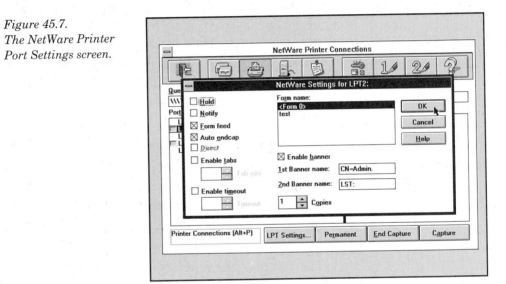

CAPTURE SETTINGS

From this location, you can customize the print capture settings by entering or changing the settings. The following is a list that describes the capture settings that can be changed:

◆ **Hold:** Sends the files to be printed to a print queue, but will "hold" the print job in the print queue until it is released by the user. This setting is often useful if you are printing a group or batch of files that require you to load special paper, such as checks, invoices, or envelopes.

◆ **Notify:** Sends the print job owner a notification that the print job is completed. This is often useful if you are not located near the printer that you print to, perhaps in a different building. It is also very useful if your printers seem to be very busy, where print jobs seem to sit in the queue for some time.

◆ **Form feed**: After each print job, the printer will send a blank page. At one time, this option was very useful (with the older dot matrix printers). It was a simple way to make sure that each print job started at the top of a new page. However, with laser printers and dot matrix printers with a rollback feature, this often wastes a page for every print job.

◆ **Auto endcap**: Sends a command to the printer at the end of a print job to indicate that the job is finished. When networks were first introduced, some applications refused to release the printer, even after the print job was finished. This meant the other print jobs sitting in the queue waiting to be printed would have to continue to wait until the printer finally timed-out. However, most applications no longer rely on the BIOS to send the end-of-job confirmation.

◆ **Direct**: Only supported if you are also running Novell's Personal NetWare as a client. If Direct to printer is enabled, print jobs will be sent directly to the printer. If you are using Personal NetWare and your application will not print, you may want to try this setting. Use it with caution, however, because it is possible that print jobs can be mixed. For example, if a print job that is coming from a queue is currently printing and you send a print job directly to the printer, you may end up with the first couple of pages of the first print job, with the direct print job in the middle.

◆ **Copies**: Specifies how many copies of a particular job you want to print. Most users use the application's capability to generate multiple copies; however, if your particular application does not support this feature, the NetWare copies feature can be a lifesaver. It also can free up your workstation because some application environments require the computer to be tied up until the application completely sends the print job to the network print queue. The default setting for copies is one, and the maximum is 255.

◆ **Enable tabs**: One of the simpler capture command parameters. It specifies the number of characters in a tab stop. Although the definition is simple, it is often difficult to know when to use the tab command. The best way to know whether your application needs to have the tab command added or changed is to look at the application documentation (check to see whether your application has an automatic formatter—most do). It often is the case, however, that the tab command can be printer-specific (as in the case of some PostScript printers). The default tab setting is 8 spaces or characters per tab stop. It can be increased up to 18 characters per tab stop.

◆ **Enable time-out**: Specifies the amount of time the printer will wait for the print job to finish. This may sound simple, but in reality is more complicated than it seems. What the time-out setting really does is this: once the printer starts receiving characters, when the first bit of data is sent to the spooling file, the file will remain open as long as data is being received. If data stops, or is interrupted (or the computer is thinking), then the spooling file will be closed and the print job will continue on its journey. Once data is no longer being received, the print mechanisms will wait the specified time—the time-out setting—and then assume the print job is finished. In certain situations, such as printing large graphic files, or when the printer is faster than the network queue, this can cause problems. Specifically, only part of the print job will print, or more than likely, only part of the graphic will print. If you find this situation happening with your print jobs, increase the time-out. Time out is not set by default; however, setting the time out will increase the speed of your network printing. The maximum time-out setting is 1000 (seconds); however, most printing environments will find a number such as 10 to 20 sufficient.

◆ **Enable banner**: The most useful or most annoying NetWare capture command feature. If banners are enabled, the printer will print a banner that indicates who sent the print job, before each print job. The banner will also contain information about the user's print capture settings, such as the port that routed the print job. Enabling banners can be very useful if you have many people using the printer and one person hand-delivering or placing the print jobs in the personal mail boxes. It is also useful to simply place ownership on print jobs. By placing ownership on each print job that is printed, many companies have found that printing resources are not as frequently wasted. The disadvantages of enabling banners are simple: it wastes paper, and it is an ASCII file, which can cause problems with some PostScript printers.

◆ **Form name**: Allows you to specify the predefined printer form. Again, this feature is very useful if you are printing on a specific piece of paper (invoice, check, application, and so on.)

ATTACHING TO SERVERS

If you select the server button located at the top of the NWUSER screen, NWUSER will display the screen similar to Figure 45.8, which enables you to do the following things:

◆ Attach network connections
◆ View individual server information
◆ Change login passwords
◆ Detach network connections

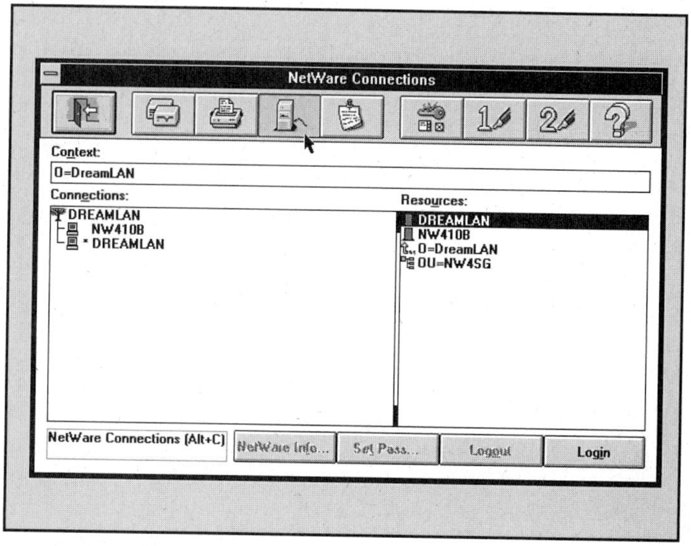

Figure 45.8.
NWUSER's NetWare
connections screen.

If you are not currently attached to any NetWare servers, the Connections side (the left side) of the screen will be empty. The right side of the screen (the Resources side) will list all the available servers.

Note

If no servers are listed, you may have to change contexts. To change contexts, click on the organization unit that contains the server to which you want to attach.

To attach to a server, highlight the server and click the Login button at the bottom right corner of the screen. After clicking the Login button, the screen seen in Figure 45.9 will appear. (You will get the same screen if you double-click the server to which you want to attach.)

After entering the correct user and user password, click the OK button. Alias username may be used.

Note

Logging in under the NDS environment, make sure that you are using the correct NDS context. The current context will be displayed in the Context dialog box, located just below the upper button bar.

You also need to be careful to not press the Enter key between typing in your user name and the user password. Instead, use the mouse or tab key to move between the User dialog box and the User password dialog box. If you pressed the Enter key after the user name, NWUSER will assume that there is no password.

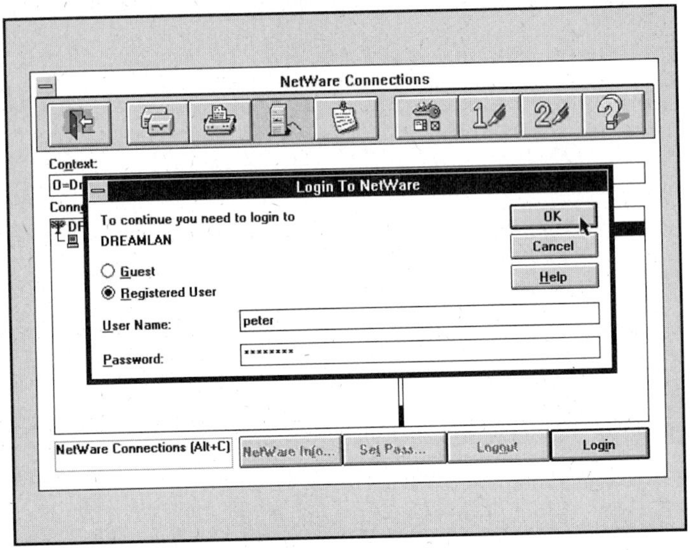

Figure 45.9.
NWUSER's login to
NetWare screen.

GETTING NETWARE CONNECTION INFORMATION

If the login procedure is successful, an icon will appear in the connections list. If you double-click on the server attachment connection in the Connections box, or highlight the attachment and click on the NetWare Info button, which is located on the lower button bar, to see the connection information, the information shown in Figure 45.10 will appear.

Tip

You also can click on a NDS tree to see authentication information.

If you are currently authenticated to NDS as a registered user, you can click on the Setpass button on the bottom of the screen to change your user password. After clicking the Setpass button, the screen shown in Figure 45.11 will appear. Type in your old password and use the Tab key or mouse to move to the next dialog box (New Password). Type in the new password and move to the next dialog box (Retype New

Password). Verify that no mistakes were made when you entered the new password by retyping it. If the passwords are identical, a screen showing that the password change was successful will appear (see Figure 45.11).

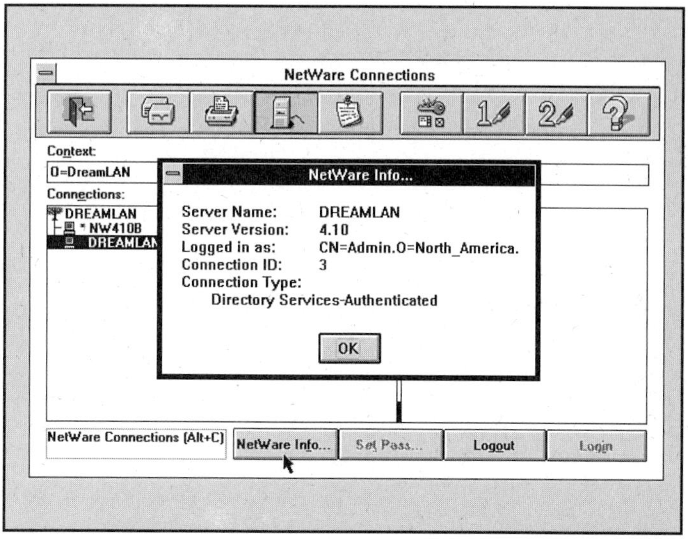

Figure 45.10.
NWUSER's NetWare
Info screen.

Note

You need to select the tree name on the left-hand side of the screen in order to access the Setpass button.

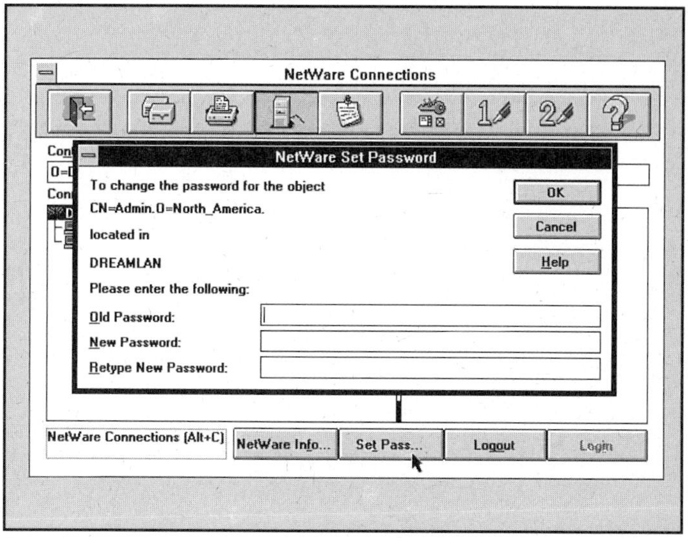

Figure 45.11.
NWUSER's NetWare
successful password
change box.

Tip

To log out, or disconnect from a resource, highlight the resource connection in the Connections side of the screen (the left side). Then select the Log out button located in the lower button bar.

SENDING MESSAGES

If you select the message button (the one with the letter tacked to the wall), the Send Message screen will appear (see Figure 45.12).

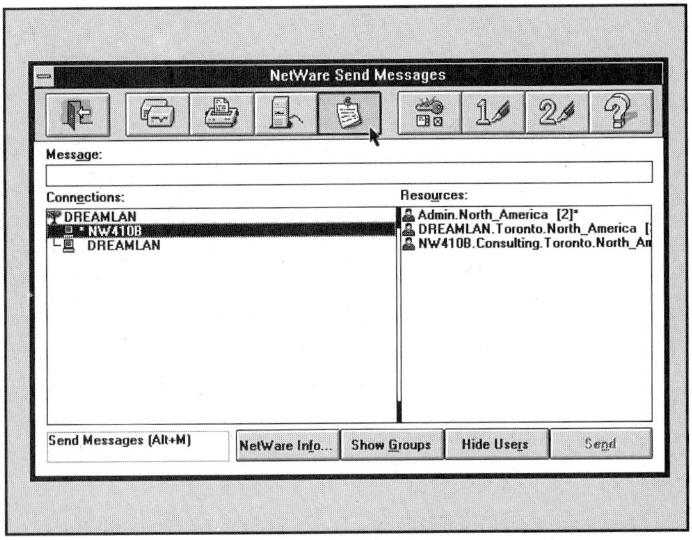

Figure 45.12.
NWUSER's Send
Message screen.

To send a message, click on the correct context on the Connections side of the screen, (the context that contains the user object to which you want to send a message). After choosing a context, the Resource screen will display the currently connected users (see Figure 45.12).

Note

You can also send a message to a group by selecting a group object. If the groups are not listed, select the Show Groups button at the bottom of the screen.

After you have the user or group selected, type the message in the dialog box.

Note

With NetWare 4, the messages you send can be up to 255 characters long (including your user name and connection ID.)

If messages annoy you, or if you are working on a project where interruptions are not allowed, NWUSER can be used to disable receive messages. To do this, click on the NetWare Settings button and then deselect the Broadcasts option under Message Reception.

NETWARE SETTINGS

Selecting the NetWare settings button, which is located in the upper button bar, will display the screen shown in Figure 45.13. From this screen, you can configure the following options:

◆ Enable the Permanent Connections button

◆ Allow or block incoming broadcast messages (under Message Reception)

◆ Enable or disable the display of Network Warnings (also under Message Reception)

◆ Set Print Manager Display Options

◆ Change Resource Display Options

◆ Define and set the Hotkey

Figure 45.13.
NWUSER's NetWare
Settings screen.

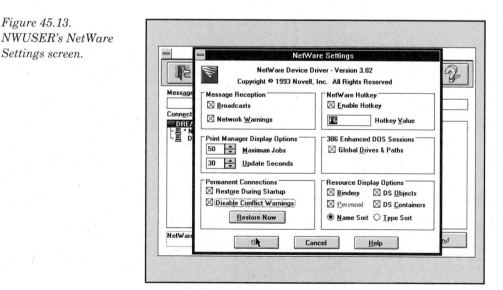

As seen in Figure 45.13, the screen configuration screen is divided into different sections. Each section represents the setting that can be set. Most of the settings, such as the Message Reception section, have check boxes beside the option. Some options, however, such as the hotkey box, require you to enter a specific value.

Because each option in the regions is fairly self explanatory, this chapter will not specifically cover every single options setting. Following, however, are explanations of the screen regions:

Permanent Connections: Restores resources connections, such as drive mappings and print capture commands, each time Windows is launched.

Message Reception: Allows the user to enable or disable the reception of messages and network warnings—replacing the SEND /A=A and SEND /A=N commands.

Print Manager Display Options: Enables you to set the number of print jobs displayed in Print Manager, as well as enables you to set the Print Manager update interval (in seconds).

Resource Display Options: Enables you to select the resources you want displayed in the resource list portion of NWUSER.

Enable Permanent Connections: Allows you to enable or disable the permanent connection button in NWUSER.

Note

If you are using a personal login script to perform drive mappings and printer connections, you should consider disabling the Restore During Startup option under the Permanent Connections setting.

Hotkey: Allows you to designate a key that will launch the NWUSER tool. This feature also can be enabled or disabled.

USER-DEFINABLE BUTTONS

Besides all the other "nifty" things NWUSER can do, it also offers two user-definable buttons. For example, you can use them to execute DOS commands or run batch files. When these buttons are first pressed, they offer a dialog box so you can define the command to be associated with each button (see Figure 45.14).

These buttons, as their names imply, allow a user to configure the buttons to perform a user definable task, such as the following:

◆ Enter a filename

◆ Enter a DOS command

◆ Enter a NetWare command-line command

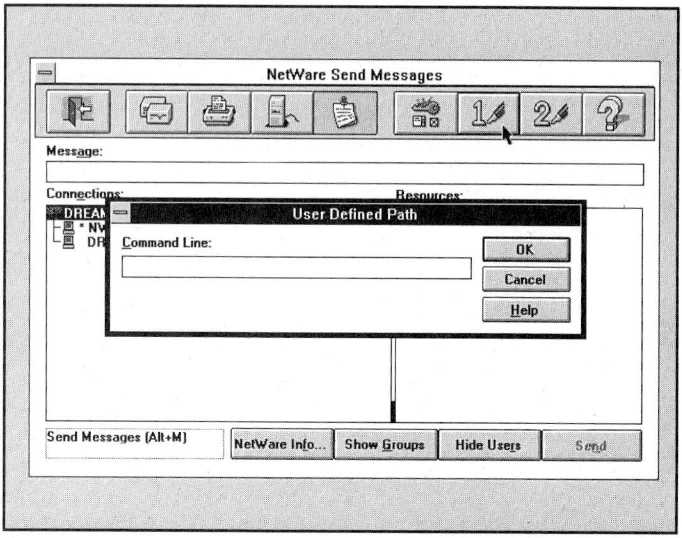

Figure 45.14.
NWUSER's User
definable buttons
dialog box.

Tip

If you have defined a user-definable button and want to change or modify what the button does, press Alt+1 or Alt+2 (depending on the button). This displays the User Defined Path dialog box, in which you can make any desired changes.

When the command has completed running its course (after a user is done using an application launched by a definable button, for example), the user will be returned to the NWUSER screen. This feature can be very useful and time saving.

Note

There is almost no limit to what can be launched with these user-definable buttons. You could use them to simplify a procedure, such as capturing a printer, or for something as complicated as running a utility (FILER) or a third-party application (WordPerfect).

Some of the settings are saved in NETWARE.INI in your Windows directory. Among them are the two user-definable keys setting. If you need to remove the definitions, you need to edit the .INI file and delete the entries. There is no option from the NWUSER menu to remove them.

NETUSER

This section covers NETUSER, the DOS text-based equivalent to NWUSER. Because these utilities perform virtually the same functions, all the options are not covered in both sections. This section only covers the basic premises and functions of the NETUSER utility.

Both utilities, NWUSER and NETUSER, are user utilities that enable the user to configure network resources, such as printers, drives, and servers. In these utilities, a user can also enable or disable message receiving, and change their context.

To start the NETUSER utility, at the DOS prompt, type NETUSER (this assumes that you have a drive mapping to the Public directory of your SYS: volume, with the appropriate rights). Figure 45.15 shows NETUSER's main menu screen.

Figure 45.15.
NETUSER main menu.

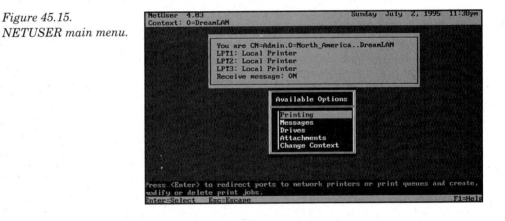

When NETUSER starts, you will see a box listing the current configuration status. The information box is just above the main menu and lists the following information:

◆ Who you are logged in as

◆ Current capture status for LPT1, LPT2, and LPT3 (even though you may have more than 3 LPTs defined)

◆ Whether the Receive messages option is on or off.

The main menu offers the following choices:

◆ Printing

◆ Messages

◆ Drives

◆ Attachments

◆ Change Context

Each of these options is covered in this section, but this section does not include as detailed information about each setting as the NWUSER section. If you are concerned or would simply like to know what a specific option setting is, review the portion in the NWUSER section that covers that specific topic.

PRINTING

Move the highlight bar to NETUSER's printing option and press Enter to see a list of printer ports that can be captured (redirected to print to a network printer). See Figure 45.16.

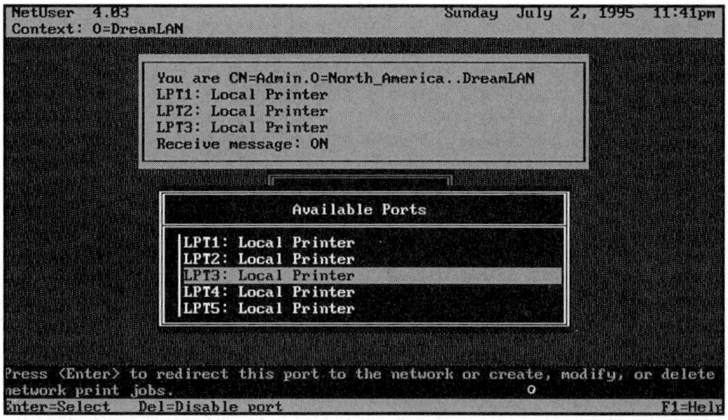

Figure 45.16.
NETUSER's Available
ports screen.

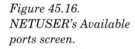

```
NetUser  4.03                            Sunday  July  2, 1995  11:41pm
Context: O=DreamLAN

            You are CN=Admin.O=North_America..DreamLAN
            LPT1: Local Printer
            LPT2: Local Printer
            LPT3: Local Printer
            Receive message: ON


                           Available Ports

            LPT1: Local Printer
            LPT2: Local Printer
            LPT3: Local Printer
            LPT4: Local Printer
            LPT5: Local Printer


Press <Enter> to redirect this port to the network or create, modify, or delete
network print jobs.                                    o
Enter=Select    Del=Disable port                                    F1=Help
```

This option enables you to select a port, change printers, and configure default print jobs. To select a port, move the highlight bar to the desired port and press Enter. An Available options screen will then appear, offering the options of Print jobs or Change printers.

If the Print Jobs option is selected, a screen will appear, listing all the current print jobs for that specific port (the print job information is updated every five seconds). From this screen a user can do the following:

◆ Press the Enter key on a selected print job to see detailed information about the job

◆ Press the Delete key to remove the selected print job (or multiple jobs) from the print queue

> ## Tip
>
> Use the F5 key to mark multiple print jobs and the F7 key to unmark all marked print jobs.

◆ Use the Insert key to add a new print job or print jobs to the print queue

◆ Exit the list by pressing the Escape key

CAPTURE PRINTERS

If you selected the Change Printers option instead of selecting the Print Jobs option, as discussed previously, NETUSER will display a list of current printers and print queues. To capture a printer or print queue, highlight the desired selection and press Enter.

MESSAGES

To send a message, select the Messages option in NETUSER's main menu. This will display the dialog box shown in Figure 45.17.

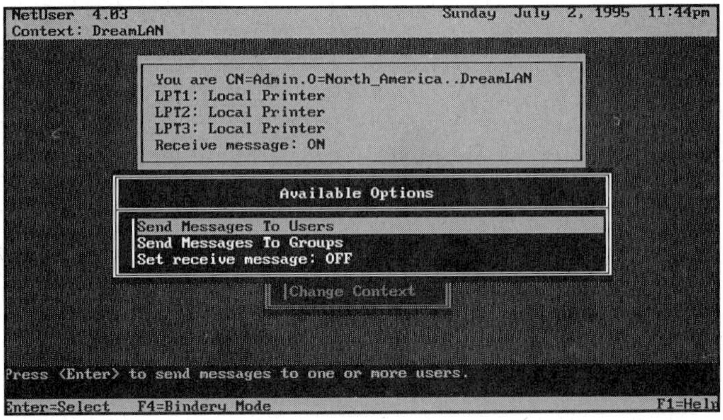

*Figure 45.17.
NETUSER's send
message Available
Options screen.*

```
NetUser  4.03                              Sunday  July  2, 1995  11:44pm
Context: DreamLAN

               You are CN=Admin.O=North_America..DreamLAN
               LPT1: Local Printer
               LPT2: Local Printer
               LPT3: Local Printer
               Receive message: ON

                       Available Options
               Send Messages To Users
               Send Messages To Groups
               Set receive message: OFF

                        Change Context

Press <Enter> to send messages to one or more users.
Enter=Select    F4=Bindery Mode                              F1=Help
```

If you select the Send Messages To Users option, a list of active users will appear. The list shows the date and time the users logged in to Directory Services, in your current context. To see which users are logged in under the bindery mode, use the F4 key to toggle you between DS and bindery mode.

Note

If you are not getting the correct time, set the time zone environment variable TZ.

To broadcast a message to a user, highlight the username, and then press Enter. You can also use the F5 key to send a message to multiple users at the same time. To unmark all marked users, press F7. From this screen, you can also send messages to groups, and set workstation to receive messages off or on.

DRIVES

Selecting the drives option will display a menu that contains the options: drive mappings and search drives.

A drive mapping allows you to access directly a particular location in the directory structure. A search mapping allows the operating system to automatically search a drive when you cannot find the requested file in the current (default) directory.

If you select the drive mapping option, a Current Drive Mappings screen will appear (see Figure 45.18). This screen will show the current local and network drives.

Figure 45.18.
NETUSER's Current
Drive Mappings screen.

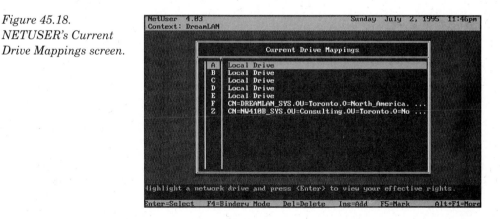

To map create a new drive mapping, press the Insert key. After pressing Insert, a small drive dialog box will appear. Type in the drive letter you want to use (one that is not currently being used) and then press Enter. The Select a Directory dialog box will appear. Type in the correct path that you want to map or continue to press the Insert key and select the path. With either method, once the path is listed in the Select a Directory box, pressing Enter will map the drive to the specified location.

To modify a drive mapping, highlight the currently mapped drive and press Enter. To delete a drive mapping, highlight the current setting and press Delete.

ATTACHMENTS

The attachment option is used to attach, detach, change login name, view file server information, and to change your user password.

After selecting the attachment option, the screen shown in Figure 45.19 will appear.

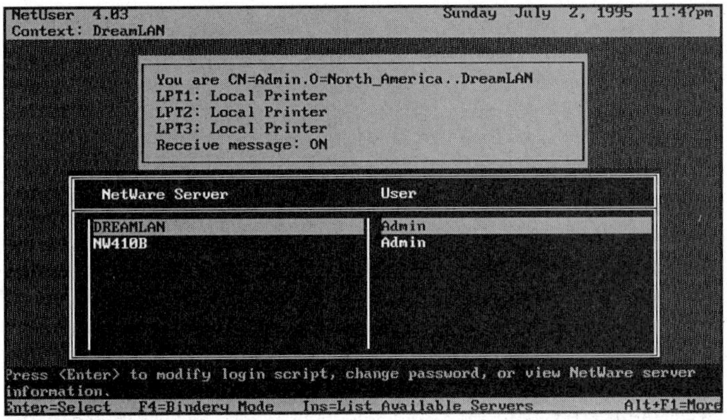

Figure 45.19.
NETUSER's current
server attachment
screen.

```
NetUser  4.03                              Sunday  July  2, 1995  11:47pm
Context: DreamLAN

        ┌──────────────────────────────────────────────────────┐
        │ You are CN=Admin.O=North_America..DreamLAN             │
        │ LPT1: Local Printer                                    │
        │ LPT2: Local Printer                                    │
        │ LPT3: Local Printer                                    │
        │ Receive message: ON                                    │
        └──────────────────────────────────────────────────────┘

      NetWare Server                  User

      ┌──────────────────┐          ┌──────────────────┐
      │ DREAMLAN         │          │ Admin            │
      │ NW410B           │          │ Admin            │
      │                  │          │                  │
      │                  │          │                  │
      │                  │          │                  │
      └──────────────────┘          └──────────────────┘

Press <Enter> to modify login script, change password, or view NetWare server
information.
Enter=Select    F4=Bindery Mode    Ins=List Available Servers        Alt+F1=More
```

The screen is split into two sections. The right side lists the servers you are currently connected to and the left side shows the user that you are attached as. While in this screen, you can use the following keys:

Key	Description
Enter	Select a file server
Ins	Attach to another server
Del	Detach from a server
F3	Login as a different user
F4	Toggle key to change NetWare mode between Directory Services and the bindery

Pressing Enter on a current attachment will display the an Available Options screen (see Figure 45.20).

Selecting the Login Script options will display the user's login script, which you then can edit. The login script specifies actions that occur when the user logs in. Each login script command must be placed on a separate line.

Figure 45.20.
NETUSER's current
attachment's Available
Options screen.

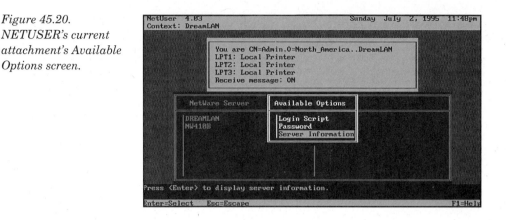

If you select the Password option, a dialog box will appear prompting you to type in the old password. After you do this, press Enter. A new dialog box will appear, prompting you to type in the new password. After entering the new password and pressing Enter, yet another dialog box will appear. This last dialog box verifies that a typing error was not made when the password was entered by asking you to retype the new password.

If you select the Server Information option, an information screen entitled Server Information will appear (see Figure 45.21).

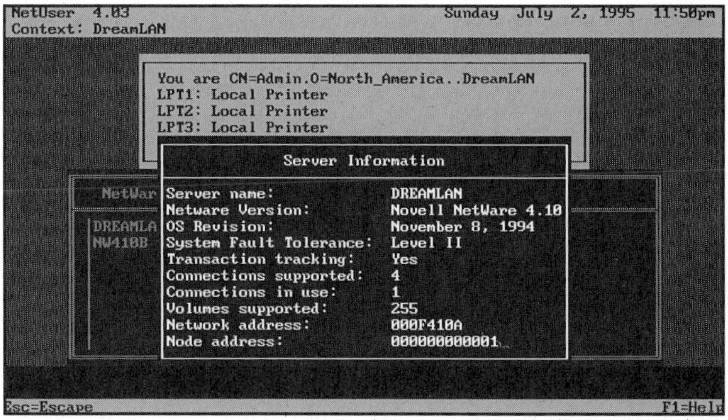

Figure 45.21.
NETUSER's Server
Information screen.

CHANGING CONTEXT

Selecting the Change Context option will display a dialog box where you can type in the path of the context to which you want to change. If you do not know the context, press the Ins key. You will then be given the NETUSER Browser screen, in which you can select the context. After you locate the context you want, press the F10 key to accept the changes and to make the selected context your current NDS location.

Note

The change context option is only available if you are currently in Directory Services mode.

SUMMARY

NWUSER is NetWare's graphical user utility. The DOS counterpart is NETUSER. NWUSER and NETUSER enable the user to navigate NetWare, creating drive mappings, printer attachments, and so on, without having to learn the intricacies of commands, such as MAP and CAPTURE.

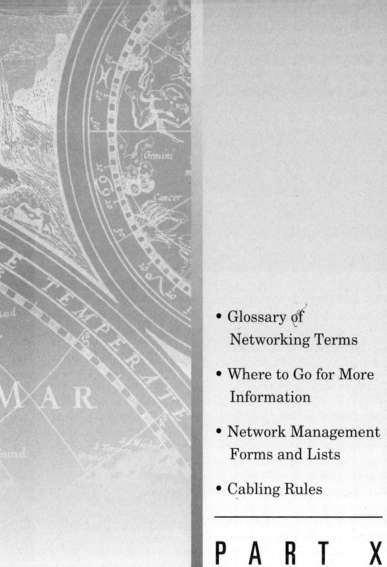

- Glossary of Networking Terms

- Where to Go for More Information

- Network Management Forms and Lists

- Cabling Rules

PART X

Appendixes

Glossary of Networking Terms

Listed in this appendix are some common networking terms used within this book. Some of them are day-to-day network related terms, while some are NetWare 4-specific.

AFP—AppleTalk Filing Protocol, a networking services protocol based upon AppleTalk. AFP is the Macintosh equivalent of NetWare's NCP.

AppleTalk—Network protocol suite from Apple Computer, Inc. AppleTalk is the native networking protocol of all Macintosh computers, and is integrated into the Macintosh operating system. NetWare 4.*x* supports AppleTalk.

ARCnet—A specification for formatting and the transmission of data over a LAN. ARCnet requires the possession of an electronic "token" before a card is allowed to transmit data. The token falls into possession of each ARCnet card on the network periodically. The use of the token avoids colliding transmissions.

Background authentication—A special background process that performs authentication automatically and transparently for each NDS connection. Authentication is required whenever a connection requests resources from a DIB partition other than the one it is currently using.

Bindery emulation—Routines and object classes within NDS that emulate the NetWare bindery. NDS servers, therefore, are backwardly compatible with bindery-based applications and utilities written for the bindery. NDS servers are also fully interoperable with bindery-based NetWare servers. Because of the bindery emulator, an NDS server appears to bindery servers as a NetWare 3.*x* server. Also called *Bindery Services*.

Bridge—A hardware and software device which connects two unlike physical network media, such as token ring and Ethernet. NetWare 4.*x* provides the ability to construct hubs using the NetWare server machine.

CLIB—C Library NLM, a special NLM developed by Novell that provides an ANSI standard C programming interface for NLM developers.

Client/Server—Client/server is the generic term applied to the basic functioning model of LANs and networked systems. Client/server implies that data processing occurs on at least two machines which are acting cooperatively. The server provides resources to the client and fulfills requests for processing tasks which are made by the client. Both the server and the client are stand-alone computers, capable of executing instructions independently of each other. However, in order to be a true client/server system, both the client and the server must be acting together. NetWare is a "server" operating system, which means it is designed to provide network resources to clients. Client/server is an overused and misused term, especially in marketing literature.

Common name—The name of an object instance. For example:

```
CN=JohnDoe
```

Communications server—A special NetWare server running NLM software which provides remote links to other types of computers and to other NetWare servers.

Containment—One DIB object is "contained" by another when the first object is further removed from the root than the second object, and when the pathway from the first object to the root passes through the second object. When both of these statements are true regarding two objects, the first object is contained by the second object.

Container—A NetWare Directory Services object that can hold other objects within. Much like a directory in a file system.

Context—The default naming information of a connection, NLM, or other entity having an NDS session. For example:

```
O=NOVELL.OU=NPD.OU=CORE OS        (context)
CN=MDAY                           (name)
O=NOVELL.OU=NPD                   (context)
OU=CORE OS.CN=MDAY                (name)
```

The context provides a "shortcut" or shorter method of naming DIB objects by providing a default location for operations.

Data bus—The mechanism by which a personal computer communicates with peripheral devices, such as modems, disk drives, network interface cards, and so on. The Data Bus contains expansion slots, into which you may install peripheral devices (cards). The peripheral devices may read data from and write data to the host computer's memory.

DIB—Directory Information Base, the actual data base maintained by NDS for use by NDS. The DIB is distributed and replicated. Replicates of a DIB partition may reside on NetWare servers. The DIB has a hierarchical tree structure.

Distinguished name—The distinguished name of an object includes the object's common name, plus all the common names of the objects that contain that specific object. The distinguished name of an object, therefore, provides the exact location of that object in the DIB tree. For example:

```
O=NOVELL.OU=NPD.OU=CORE OS.CN=MDAY
```

Distributed database—A database is distributed when portions of the database reside on different network stations yet the entire database is managed as a single logical entity. A specific portion of a distributed database is frequently referred to as a "partition."

Effective class—An effective object class allows for objects based upon it to become object instances. That is, an effective object class may be instantiated and stored as an actual object in the DIB.

EISA—Extended Industry Standard Architecture, a 32-bit extension of the original IBM PC AT data bus, Direct Memory Access, and shared memory architecture for personal computers. EISA peripherals, such as network interface cards and disk controllers, can transfer data to machine memory 32-bits at once, which is twice as fast as PC AT and clone machines. PCs conforming to the EISA specification also support peripherals, such as network interface cards, designed for the PC AT (and clones) architecture. The EISA specification was developed jointly by a group of PC manufacturers. NetWare 4.*x* takes full advantage of EISA peripherals, especially EISA network interface cards.

Ethernet—A specification for formatting and the transmission of data over a LAN. Ethernet cards transmit information whenever they sense the network media is "free." Occasionally, two Ethernet cards attempt to transmit information at the same time. When this happens, the transmissions "collide," and the transmitting Ethernet cards resend their transmission after pausing for a short random interval.

FDDI—Fiber Distributed Data Interface. A high-speed specification for formatting and transmitting data over a LAN. Like ARCnet and token ring, FDDI uses an electronic token to control transmission of data over the network. FDDI includes the capability to use redundant physical media, and operates at 100 Mbps, ten times the speed of Ethernet.

Hub—A hub is a specialized network media device that allows for the connection of several stations to the network using a single, integrated hardware device. Hubs make connection of stations to a network more modular.

Intel—Intel Corporation invented the microprocessor in the late 1970s. Today, the Intel x86 architecture is the *de facto* standard for personal computers. Most new personal computers today feature an Intel 486 microprocessor. The newest Intel Microprocessor is the Pentium (sometimes called the 586). Previous Intel microprocessors included the 8086, the 80286, and 80386. The Intel 80386 is the first 32-bit microprocessor manufactured by Intel for mass distribution. NetWare 4.*x* requires an 80386 or higher microprocessor. Although the Intel x86 architecture is the *de facto* standard for PC microprocessors, it is certainly not the only microprocessor design in wide use today. All Macintosh computers use a microprocessor manufactured by Motorola. Sun, Hewlett-Packard, Silicon Graphics, Digital Equipment, and IBM each manufacture their own proprietary designs of microprocessors for graphics workstations and other types of desktop computers.

IPX—Internetwork Packet Exchange. NetWare's native networking protocol. IPX works with all physical network media standards (Ethernet, token ring, and so on). IPX is a datagram protocol, which means that it does not guarantee delivery or sequencing of a series of network packets.

ISA—Industry Standard Architecture. The original IBM PC AT featured a 16-bit data bus and Direct Memory Access (DMA) architecture. As manufacturers began cloning the IBM PC AT, this data bus architecture became the *de facto* industry standard and, hence, became known as the Industry Standard Architecture, or ISA. Most PCs in use today conform to the ISA specification. However, most newer PCs being bought conform to either the EISA or Microchannel data bus architecture.

LAN—Local Area Network. Specifically, LAN refers to the cabling and hardware that provide network communications in a single geographic location. However, LAN also has assumed a broader meaning in recent years, taking under its umbrella not only the network hardware and cabling, but also network transport protocols, network operating systems, and network client software.

MHS—Message Handling System, an e-mail protocol supported by Novell and widely used on all types of systems (including non-NetWare systems).

Microchannel—IBM's architecture for PCs with 32-bit data buses. Microchannel is not backwardly compatible with ISA peripherals, as EISA is. Otherwise, the Microchannel architecture for PCs is very similar to the EISA. Microchannel, however, is somewhat more technically elegant and forward-looking than EISA. Because of IBM's marketing practices, Microchannel peripherals are frequently more expensive than EISA peripherals (IBM controls the design for Microchannel controller chips).

NCP—NetWare Core Protocol, NetWare's native service protocol. NetWare clients request services from NetWare servers by sending NCP request packets and receiving NCP reply packets.

NDS—NetWare Directory Services. A global naming service for NetWare, consisting of a distributed, replicated database, an object-oriented database schema, security based upon RSA public-key encryption, background authentication and synchronization, X.500 compliance, unlimited database size, and more.

Network analyzer—Network Analyzers are software or software and hardware (combined) products that capture packets "off the wire," or directly from the physical network media. Most network analyzers present a "decode," or translation of the binary data contained by network packets, and are capable of decoding most of the popular transport protocols (IPX, TCP/IP, and so on). Network analyzers are excellent network troubleshooting tools when used correctly. Using a network analyzer requires a knowledge of network transport protocols and how they work.

Network Interface Card—A hardware device that enables communication among computers over a LAN. Network Interface cards comply to different physical addressing and data formatting specifications, such as Ethernet, ARCnet, token ring, and FDDI.

Network Management—Network Management is a broad category of hardware and software products and protocols that make management, troubleshooting, and maintenance of large networks easier. Specific types of network management products include network inventory software, network analyzers, configuration management software, error reporting hardware and software, and more.

NFS—Network File System, a networking services protocol based upon TCP/IP. NFS is developed by Sun Microsystems but is licensed freely to developers of the UNIX operating system. NetWare 4.*x* supports NFS.

NLM—NetWare Loadable Module. NLMs are applications that run on the NetWare server.

Non-effective class—A non-effective class may not be instantiated and stored in the DIB. Rather, its only purpose is for effective object classes to inherit its attributes.

Object attribute—An object attribute is a specific piece of information stored in an object instance. Each object instance consists of several or many attributes. Some attributes are required for an object instance, while other attributes are optional.

Object class—The definition of a specific object type which may be stored by the DIB. An object class specifies which scalar data types may be part of the object class, which functions must be used for comparison and collation of object data items, and more. Developers may create custom object classes.

Object inheritance—Each object class may inherit object definitions from other object classes. An object class may inherit definitions from multiple classes, which is to say that the DIB supports multiple inheritance.

Object instance—A specific object stored in the DIB. Each object instance is "of a class," meaning its structure and information corresponds to an object class definition.

OSI—Open Systems Interconnection. A series of industry-standard networking protocols designed to allow unlike computer systems to work together over a network.

Partition—A portion of a distributed database.

Remote access—A class of software that, when combined with a modem and phone line, allows a user to log in to the network from a remote site.

Remote-control software—A class of software that allows one user to control the screen and keyboard of another user's computer over a network.

Replicated database—A database is replicated when one or more of its partitions are mirrored to additional network stations.

RISC—Reduced Instruction Set Computing. RISC is a generic term for newer microprocessor designs that have a minimal instruction set and which can execute one instruction per clock cycle for most instructions. RISC microprocessors are used largely in graphics and engineering workstations, and in specialized network devices, such as routers and communications controllers. Intel microprocessors contain RISC design elements, but are not RISC microprocessors.

Root, Branch, Leaf—In a hierarchical database, the top-most entry is always the "root;" each level contained by the root is a "branch;" the furthest level does not contain any other levels, and is populated by "leaves."

Router—A hardware and software device that directs network traffic across multiple LANs, ensuring that packets reach their ultimate destination. NetWare 4.*x* includes full routing capability for all protocol stacks it supports.

RSA public-key encryption—A highly secure algorithm for authenticating NDS connections. Authentication enures that an NDS connection is legitimate.

Schema—The DIB schema is, collectively, the definition of all object types that can be stored in the DIB. Objects are complex data structures. A complex data structure is a composite data type consisting of several or many scalar data types.

SFT III—System Fault Tolerance Level III, or server mirroring. SFT III NetWare is a special version of the NetWare operating system that allows for a fully redundant server machine. If any hardware component on one server fails, the redundant server continues network service without interruption.

Skulker—A special process running in the background on all NDS servers. The skulker is responsible for synchronizing DIB partitions whenever information in the DIB is updated.

SMS—Storage Management System. SMS is Novell's specification for data archival systems. SMS includes a platform-independent format for archived data.

SNA—Systems Network Architecture. IBM's blueprint for network operations. SNA includes networking, network management, and remote access protocols. NetWare 4.*x* supports the SNA blueprint.

SNMP—Simple Network Management Protocol. SNMP is an industry standard specification for hardware monitoring transmissions over a network, and for the tracking of the status of network hardware devices.

SPX—Sequenced Packet Exchange. NetWare's native session-oriented networking protocol. SPX builds upon IPX and offers sequencing and acknowledgment of network packets.

Syntax—A syntax is a scalar datatype, such as integer, character string, unsigned long, byte stream, and so on. Each object attribute consists of one or more syntaxes and a comparison and collation function.

TCNS—Thomas-Conrad Network System. A proprietary, 100 Mbps version of ARCnet developed by Thomas-Conrad.

TCP/IP—Transmission Control Protocol/Internet Protocol. A group of network protocols used widely in the UNIX market, and supported by NetWare.

Temporary connection—A special type of NDS connection used by objects when "walking the tree," or traversing the DIB in search of a specific object. Temporary connections do not count against the number of connections supported by a specific NetWare 4 server.

Token ring—A specification for the formatting and transmission of data over a LAN. Token ring networks are always arranged in a circle, or ring, of stations. Transmission of data requires the possession of an electronic token, which circles the ring in short, fixed time intervals. Token ring has robust error recovery mechanisms that go beyond those provided by Ethernet and ARCnet.

VLM—Virtual Loadable Module, a software component loadable by DOS as a TSR that provides NetWare functionality for workstations. NetWare 4.*x* client software consists of a series of VLMs, plus a programming interface which allows third-party developers to create their own VLMs.

WAN—Wide Area Network. A WAN occurs when two or more local sites are connected to each other over a long-distance network. Typically, sites on a WAN will be separated by at least 2 kilometers, and may be on other sides of the globe. WAN links are typically of a lower speed and lower capacity than LANs.

X.25—An international standard media protocol for wide area data transmission using leased phone lines.

X.400—The Open Systems Interconnection (OSI) standard for electronic mail.

X.500—The OSI Directory Services specification. NDS is compliant with the X.500 specification, except in the areas of replication and security. Replication and security are not yet fully specified by the X.500 committee.

- Novell Authorized Education

- Computer Based Training (CBTs)

- Novell CBTs

- Books

- Magazines

- Trade Shows

- User Groups

- Professional Associations

- Bulletin Board Systems

APPENDIX B

Where to Go for More Information

As NetWare 4.x continues to gain popularity, there are several sources to explore for more information. These categorically break down into:

◆ Novell Authorized Education
◆ Books
◆ Magazines
◆ Trade Shows
◆ User Groups
◆ Professional Associations
◆ Bulletin Board Systems

Novell Authorized Education

Novell is well known for having developed the industry's most well respected training program. This program includes curriculum development for instructor-led and self-study, CBT (Computer Based Training) and video development, instructor certification programs, and Novell Authorized Education Center Programs.

Novell's educational offerings are quite extensive ranging from NetWare Operating Systems classes, through Wide Area Connectivity. Following is a listing of the current Novell course offerings available as self-study or instructor-led curriculum at its worldwide Novell Authorized Education Centers (NAECs).

Instructor-Led or Self-Study Courses

Course	Course Title	Duration
105	Introduction to Networking	1/2 day
200	Networking Technologies	3 days
220	UNIX OS Fundamentals for NetWare Users	2 days
508	NetWare 3.1x Administration	4 days
518	NetWare 3.1x Advanced Administration	2 days
520	NetWare 4.x Administration	4 days
525	NetWare 4.x Advanced Administration	3 days
526	NetWare 3.x to 4.x Update	3 days
532	NetWare 4 Directory Services Design	2 days
535	Printing with NetWare	3 days
550	NetWare Navigator	2 days
601	LAN Workplace for DOS 4.1 Admin	2 days

Course	Course Title	Duration
605	NetWare TCP/IP Transport	2 days
610	NetWare NFS	2 days
611	NetWare FleX/IP	1 day
625	NetWare NFS Gateway	1 day
630	NetWare/IP	1 day
678	UnixWare Installation and Configuration	2 days
680	UnixWare System Administration	3 days
685	UnixWare Advanced System Administration	2 days
718	NetWare Connect	2 days
720	NetWare for SAA: Installation & Troubleshooting	3 days
725	NetWare for LAT	2 days
740	Novell Internetworking	5 days
750	NetWare Global MHS	2 days
801	NetWare Service and Support	5 days
802	NetWare 3.1x Installation & Configuration Workshop	2 days
804	NetWare 4.x Installation & Configuration Workshop	2 days
930	NetWare Programming: NLM development	3 days
940	NetWare Programming: Basic Services	3 days
941	NetWare Programming: Directory Services	2 days
945	NetWare Programming: Protocol Support	3 days
950	AppWare Programming: Visual AppBuilder	3 days
954	AppWare Programming: ALM Development	2 days

COURSES ONLY AVAILABLE SELF-STUDY

1100	DOS for NetWare Users	
1100	Microcomputer Concepts for NetWare Users	
1125	LANalyzer for Windows	
1540	NetWare SFT III 3.11	
1615	Administering NetWare for Macintosh 3.12	
1620	Administering NetWare for Macintosh 4.01	
1760	Administering SNADS for NetWare Global MHS	
1770	Administering SMTP for NetWare Global MHS	

Note

Due to the continuing updating and development of course material, contact Novell or your local NAECs for a list of currently available courses and related information.

NOVELL AUTHORIZED EDUCATION CENTERS (NAECs)

In the 1980s, Novell created its own channel of independently owned education centers to better meet the needs of its customers. Novell requires these companies to meet quality standards to ensure complete customer satisfaction. Among their criteria are Quality of Facilitates, Hardware and Software requirements, use of Novell Published Education Curriculum and use of only Novell Certified Instructors.

While Novell's quality standards for NAECs have kept many low quality training firms from becoming authorized, there still exists a tremendous range in the quality of NAECs. Readers are recommended to visit more than one NAEC in their area before making a selection. Aside from location and facility comfort, it is recommended to sit in on a portion of a class. It would be a good idea to speak with current students before or after their classes, or at lunch time. While no company is 100 percent perfect at all times, you will learn a lot about the company's attitude towards customer service as well. Look for companies whose entire business is network education. These firms will typically provide more courses and are better equipped than resellers or distributors who provide education just to make a few extra dollars.

Many readers might be tempted to attend non-Novell authorized classes to learn NetWare because of the reduced cost. While saving one to two thousand dollars might seem a bargain, most attendees usually end up retaking their classes at NAECs. Unfortunately, the popularity of the Novell CNE program has created a profitable situation for many scam artists and low quality training firms. For students pursuing Certified NetWare Administrator (CNA), Certified NetWare Engineer (CNE) or Enterprise Certified NetWare Engineer(ECNE) degrees—and now the Master CNE certification, it is best to avoid taking classes through non-authorized training companies. Novell develops its tests directly from Novell Authorized Courseware. The chances of both learning and passing tests are dramatically higher at NAECs.

To receive a list of Novell Authorized Education Centers in your area, you can call Novell's FaxBack Service. To call FaxBack, just dial (800) 233-3382 (North America) or (801) 429-5363 with any standard touchtone phone.

For most students, instructor-led training is the method of choice. Novell Authorized Courses are available in the evening in most parts of the country as an option for those who can not take time from work. For those with tighter time constraints or with stronger backgrounds, self-study is another option. The same Novell kits that students receive when taking classes are available for self-study at local NAECs or heavily discounted by mail order. Consult the various networking magazines for the mail order advertisements.

Certified Novell Instructors (CNIs)

All Novell classes taught at NAEC must be taught by Certified Novell Instructors or CNIs. Novell requires that CNIs be both technically competent and posses adequate presentation skills. This competency is evaluated by test scores for technical knowledge, and by requiring CNI applicants to present course material to Novell's Education department at an event known as an IPE (Instructor Performance Evaluation). Novell rates candidates in dozens of areas to ensure a satisfactory level of competency. As with NAECs, the quality of CNIs greatly ranges. When evaluating an NAEC, speaking with one or more of their CNIs will give you a good indication as to the quality of the company.

There are two categories of CNIs: NAEC-employed CNIs, and independent contract CNIs. Many of the best instructors fall into both of these categories, so this alone should not be the telltale sign of a well-run NAEC. Well run NAECs have at least three to four staff instructors and supplement their needs with contractors. Well run NAECs will utilize the same contractors on a regular basis, so they become more familiar with their facilities. Beware of centers that fly in CNIs to teach classes— many never see the instructor before the first day of class, and at that point it is a game of luck. Following are some other points to consider:

◆ Staff CNIs will be around to answer questions by phone or in person long after your class has ended.

◆ Contract CNIs are responsible for their own personal development. An easy way to tell whether a Contract CNI has chosen that career path because they are otherwise unemployable is to examine the number and level of classes they are certified to teach. The better contractors are certified to teach most of the advanced level classes such as SAA, NFS, LANalyzer, and NetWare Internetworking. Chances are that if they are not teaching these courses, they are independent for some reason.

For those of you considering a change in career path, becoming a CNI is both personally and financially rewarding. Aside from a strong technical background with NetWare, the desire to constantly learn, and the ability to organize thoughts and interact with others are important skills. For single people with a desire to travel, contractor CNI is fun way to see the country. The downsides to this status are no pay when not teaching, the costs to certify in new classes, and spending time looking for work rather than working on technical development. In the end, contractors and staff CNIs both make about the same amount of money, and the choice of status is more a lifestyle choice than financial one.

For more information on Novell's CNI program, you can retrieve the following documents from Novell's FaxBack Service:

1450   CNI Program Overview
1452   CNI Course Groups for IPEs
1453   CNI Presentation Skills for IPEs

COMPUTER BASED TRAINING (CBTs)

There are plenty of computer-based training products on the market. One of the best is from a company called *CBT Systems*. The most attractive aspect of computer-based training is its flexibility. The flexibility to train when you want for as long as you want at the speed that you can be comfortable with. This enables a vast number of extremely busy individuals to acquire training when the inflexibility of the classroom environment would deter them.

CBT system offers a wide variety of topics for self-study using multimedia effects to bring home ideas ranging from LANs and WANs, TCP/IP and OSI Standards, Systems Design, OP Systems and Programming, NetWare System Management, Integrated Computing.

CBT Systems training disks and manuals are an excellent product. They have paid a lot of attention to detail. They have broken down each topic into small easy-to-digest pieces. The text is not so dry that you lose your place. Their use of the medium is superlative. The graphics are illustrative of each point and the use of animation succeeds in enhancing them. For example, in the illustration of CSMA/CD they show the signal going out on the cable from one workstation and simultaneously from another to illustrate the collision.

Not surprisingly, the documentation is minimal. It mainly deals with installation and setup, and an overview of navigation through the curricula. There are workbooks provided with the courses that follow along with the class or may be used as review material. There is also a short Administrators Manual that explains an optional CMI (computer-managed instruction) a system for tracking user's progress through a CBT course and recording test results.

The flow of the courseware is logical and founded in sound teaching strategies. The LANs and WANs curriculum starts with basic topics such as LAN fundamentals and LAN Operations and builds to more technical matters like IEEE LAN Architecture. The latter section guides you through the OSI model and the 802.2-5 control formats.

Each section of a course builds upon the previous section. The questions are phrased in a way to lead you to conclusions. During each screen you are asked to either fill in key words pertaining to a subject or make an educated guess at an answer. In either case, if you have answered incorrectly, the program will correct you or if you are on the right track, guide you to the right answer with a hint. If you are correct, based on the difficulty of the question, the positive feedback runs from "correct" to "Excellent!" Even the highly technical material is explained in an easy to understand fashion.

For example, the IEEE LAN Architecture CBT class uses the OSI model as a reference. The learning objectives for this class are to enable the student to describe the LLC and MAC sublayers functions in detail, to describe in full detail the four IEEE protocols; 802.2-802.6, for the LLC and MAC. The class covers the material from connectionless service to resolve contention frames to Duplicate address test frames. Much to their credit CBT Systems never makes you feel as if all of this was Greek.

The Bridges, Routers, and Gateways course is approximately 12 hours long. Its aim is to enable a user to implement and manage interconnected networks built to IEEE LAN standards. This course covers topics from the need for internetworking to SMDS to the Spanning tree algorithm. The learning objectives include discussing the reasons for internetworking and how this is accomplished using various devices, identifying how LANs may differ and explaining how these differences are resolved, describing in detail the operation and function of bridges, and quite a bit more.

In addition to using clear and concise prose to illustrate and explain each point, animation was used to illuminate each of the specific ideas being explained. The illustrations were also helpful in the clarification of each point. CBT Systems can be reached at:

CBT Systems USA, Ltd.
400 Oyster Point Blvd
Suite No. 422
South San Francisco, CA 94080
800-929-9050

NOVELL CBTS

Novell also has CBTs covering many of the topics in the Certified NetWare Engineer program.

Even though the installations can be cumbersome, the programs are graphically pleasing, although the use of graphics does not enhance the material in any way or even illustrate in any detail the text that appears with them onscreen. They are designed in a hypermedia format with buttons that take you from one part of the course to another. The hypermedia is Asymetrix's Toolbook and the CBT comes with a runtime version, which is installed in its own directory during setup.

The good aspects of the Novell's computer-based training are as follows:

◆ The graphics are clear and basically illustrative of the overall topics for instance the login script section had a hand holding a pen to paper and writing in cursive.

◆ The interaction is pleasant.

◆ The course is fairly informative and organized in about the same way as the Novell written courseware.

Each section is set up with three parts: an introduction (I button), a class section (C Button), and a practice section (P button). The introduction simply states what will be covered in the following segment of the course. In the class section, the specifics of the material are gone into. And finally the practice section consists of conceptual questions when appropriate and practical applications of the NetWare commands and functions. The fact that the command line material remains within the CBT and does not affect your actual Network in any way makes working through the products much more comfortable.

The text in the CBT is clear and informative. However, it is lacking in the kind of detail that is required to pass the actual Novell certification exams.

The section on login scripts is probably the best. The writers of the program have imagined a pseudo company called Rope with a directory structure all set up, which is referred to as the scenario. You are then walked through the process of writing system script and user script. It is quite helpful to actually write login scripts with all the syntax and internal commands.

There is a test for the last section of the CBT. It covers a large portion of the curriculum that is needed to pass the CNE tests, but not all that is needed. The test never varies. It does not cover everything you need to know for the Drake exam.

This product would certainly fulfill the need of a company to get some people up to speed on NetWare in a fairly painless flexible manner. The way NetWare works is well described and explained in the material and would certainly be adequate training for someone who needed to acquire a reasonable working knowledge of NetWare.

You can obtain a complete listing of available Novell CBTs from FAXback at (801) 429-5363 or by calling Novell at 800-233-3382.

BOOKS

There are many other books besides this one that contain valuable information. The Sams *Teach Yourself CNE Administration* series is a step-by-step guide of series that includes a NetWare 4 title.

For general network information check out *Building Local Area Networks with Novell's NetWare* (Corrigan & Guy) and *Local Networks* by Stallings.

There are literally hundreds of books on a variety of subjects in your local bookstore. You should feel free to go sit and flip through them until you find the ones you like.

MAGAZINES

Computer magazines are one of the best sources for up-to-date information on a wide range of topics. Unlike books that undergo months or years between revisions, periodicals are published weekly or monthly and can help you stay up-to-date.

The following lists the major trade publications that contain information concerning NetWare and Local Area Networking. Along with the publication name, you will find a phone number for subscription information.

PC Computing	800-365-2770
PC Magazine	800-289-0429
Data Communications	800-257-9402
Computer World	800-669-1002
LAN Times	801-565-1060
Network Computing	516-562-5071
LAN Magazine	800-234-9573
Network World	508-875-6400

Another monthly publication that is invaluable is the *Novell Application Notes*, published by Novell Research. These tomes of technical details are the real goods, mostly untouched by Novell's Marketing department. They explain the inner workings of various Novell products and technologies. Recent articles have been titled "The Functions and Operations of the NetWare DOS Requester," "Managing the Branch Office," and "Implementing Naming Standards for NetWare Directory Services."

You can subscribe to *Application Notes* (AppNotes) by calling 800-377-4136 in the U.S. or 303-297-2725 internationally.

TRADE SHOWS

Industry trade shows are an excellent means to learn more about networking and NetWare. Aside from seeing live product demonstrations, attending technical seminars, and gathering product literature, trade show attendees are sure to come home with a large collection of promotional items from T-shirts to hats to gizmos.

Two of the larger national network trade shows are Networks EXPO and Networld+ Interop. To get the current schedule of these shows or to register to attend call or write to the following address:

Bruno Blenheim Inc.
Fort Lee Executive Park
One Executive Drive
Fort Lee, NJ 07024
800-829-3976

USER GROUPS

User groups are a great way to meet people facing the same kinds of problems you face and for getting support for those problems.

NetWare Users International (NUI) is open to anyone who uses NetWare. To become a member call 800-228-4NUI or 801-429-7177. Membership is fee-based, but is relatively inexpensive for the wealth of information available. Members receive a free subscription to *NetWare Connection*, which is a monthly magazine with technical tips, product reviews, and information on strategic products.

NUI also sponsors Conferences and Expositions year round. In 1994, they sponsored over 15 in the United States alone. Exhibiting vendors include 3COM, HP, Compaq, SMC and ,of course, Novell. Leading manufactures of hubs, switches, backup and storage management products regularly exhibit at these conferences. The first day usually starts with day long educational tutorials on a variety of current topics. Mini sessions are held through out the balance of the conference on topics ranging from "Intro to WANs" I to "Virus Protection" and "NetWare 4.*x* Theory."

Also available from NUI is a free magazine, called *NetWare Connection*. It is published six times a year.

The NPA, Network Professional Association, also sponsors hands-on labs at NUI conferences so that you can try products without endangering your production environment. NPA used to be called the CNEPA, Certified NetWare Engineer

Professional Association. You can become a member of NPA by calling 801-429-7227. You don't have to be a CNE to join, you can become an associate member.

NPA also holds hands-on labs at other industry shows, such as Networld+INTEROP and Networks EXPO. Both shows are held in a variety of international locations and offer comprehensive exhibitions and educational seminars.

PROFESSIONAL ASSOCIATIONS

The Network Professional Association (NPA), formerly called the Certified Network Engineer Professionals Association (CNEPA), is an extremely worthwhile avenue to explore for further education. NPA is a nonprofit organization made up of network computing professionals. It was formed as a means to disseminate technical information among peers. Today NPA has over 60 chapters worldwide, thousands of members, and is open to participation by professionals from disciplines other than Novell, although Novell professionals still represent most of the membership.

The most important benefits to NPA members are provided at a local level. Local chapters meet monthly, provide presentations by vendors of their products, and are an excellent opportunity to meet peers and discuss questions. Many chapters now have their own labs for members to use freely to gain hands on experience.

At the top level of NPA, is the executive office. This office is responsible for:

◆ Membership Accounting
◆ Production of an Excellent Publication: The NetWork News
◆ Chapter events coordination
◆ National NPA Lab presence

The National NPA labs are present at many of the industry's leading trade shows. These labs consist of hardware and software donated by NPA national sponsors and allow both NPA members and potential members the opportunity to learn hands on under the direction of instructors and lab assistants. At most trade shows, NPA members from around the world staff these labs and are a valuable resource.

While many NPA members and potential members have strong complaints about the Executive Office leadership and hidden agendas, the benefits of local membership far outweigh the negatives of joining. As with any new and rapidly growing organization, NPA is bound to improve even further as new, talented members offer their contribution. Overall, NPA is a worthwhile organization, and local chapter participation is beneficial to all.

NPA dues are currently set at $150 (U.S.) per year for members, with a six month associate membership also available. While attendees of local chapter meetings will certainly benefit the most from membership, the NPA news alone is worth the admission price. NPA members also benefit from vendor discounts on products and receive many free items from vendors. NPA members (then CNEPA members), were able to purchase a beta copy of NetWare 4.0 for only $5.00

For more information on NPA membership call 801-429-7710

BULLETIN BOARD SYSTEMS

The most cost-effective source of information is the Novell section of CompuServe called NetWire. CompuServe is a bulletin board service that charges members for connect time. You can get a free Starter Kit to CompuServe by calling 800-848-8990. The Starter Kit includes a logon id and password and some free connect time so that you do not have to pay for the privilege of figuring out how it works. All the major vendors have sections on CompuServe including IBM, Microsoft, and Banyan.

The Starter Kit includes instructions for getting online. You'll need a modem and communications software.

NetWire, the Novell part, is divided into specific sections called *forums* that address specific issues. You move around the system by typing GO and where you want to go at the system prompt (on CompuServe is the exclamation point !). To get to NetWire, log on and type **GO NETWIRE**.

A QUICK NETWIRE TOUR

If you are new to the NetWire forums, the first thing you should do is download a file called WELCOM.EXE. It contains a current map of NetWire's Forums and sections, the rules and policies you should follow while using these areas, and some examples of how to post a message. You will find WELCOM.EXE (self-extracting file) in Novell's File Library (enter **GO NOVLIB**" at the ! prompt), Library 2.

NetWire is an exceptional alternative to using Novell's telephone Hotline for technical support. Because of the large number of NetWare users, and wide range of Novell products, Novell uses more than 20 public Forums on CompuServe. A map of these forums and sections is contained within FRMORG.EXE (found in WELCOM.EXE and also on Library 2 of NOVLIB as FRMORG.EXE) therein. FRMORG.EXE is a self-extracting file.

COMMUNICATIONS SOFTWARE

If you have problems finding your way around NetWire, you may want to take a look at CompuServe's Information Manager package (CIM). There is a Novell version of CIM preconfigured for NetWire, which is called NOVCIM. You can download this package for a one-time $10 fee, which is credited back to you in connect time on CompuServe. Select Option 3 of the New User Instructions menu, or GO NOVCIM at the CompuServe prompt to download NOVCIM. This application is available for DOS or Windows. (There is also a Macintosh version which is not customized for NetWire.)

Benefits of NetWire

Novell has contracted volunteer *System Operators* (or *SysOps*) to answer your questions on NetWire. These SysOps come from various computer backgrounds and are all extremely experienced NetWare users. Together with dozens of other NetWare power-users, who also share their knowledge regularly on the service, they answer thousands of questions weekly.

When technical problems cannot be solved by the SysOps or other power-users on NetWire, SysOps escalate the issue directly to Novell Engineers in Novell's Technical Support Division—the same channels used for Hotline calls.

A major part of the NetWire service is the library of files available for downloading. These files include the most recent patches, drivers, and tips for "tweaking" your NetWare server. There also are many third-party applications and utilities available, as well as shareware.

NetWire puts you in touch with thousands of NetWare Users—most of whom are willing to share what they have learned with others. Messages are posted in public forums so that all who access NetWire can view and/or add to them. This open-forum medium leads to very accurate and complete answers to your questions. It is also an invaluable source of contacts for consulting, sales, and business opportunities within the industry.

Novell makes great efforts to see that questions posted on the NetWire service are responded to within 24 hours of posting.

NetWire has existed since 1986, during which is hase evolved NetWire into the superb support service it is today. Novell provides the NetWire service at no charge. The only costs to use the service are the connect charges to CompuServe.

Posting Messages on NetWire

For answers to technical questions, simply choose the most appropriate section for the subject of your question (refer to the map found under the Map of NetWire menu option, WELCOM.EXE or FRMORG.EXE from NOVLIB Lib 2) and post your question to SysOp or All. Your question will receive a response by the next day.

The NetWare 4 section of NetWire is broken down into topics, as follows:

◆ Printing
◆ NetWare Utilities
◆ Dsk Drvs/CDs/Cntrls
◆ LAN Cards/Drivers
◆ Install/Upgrade
◆ ElectroText/Doc's
◆ Directory Services
◆ SFT III
◆ NLM/OS/Console Util

Also of interest is the Novell Desktop forum (NOVDESKTOP) that handles the following questions about the Novell products on workstations:

◆ DRDOS/Applications
◆ DRDOS/Disk
◆ DRDOS/Memory
◆ DRDOS/Utilities
◆ Customer Service
◆ Programming Questions
◆ Dataclub
◆ NetWare Lite
◆ NetWare NT Client

There also is a forum (NOVCLIENT) dedicated to deal with workstation client software, such as VLMs:

◆ IPX/ODI Issues
◆ NETX Issues
◆ VLM Issues
◆ ODINSUP Issues
◆ NetBios Issues
◆ NetWare and Windows

You can get technical support and information about the following names from NetWire. You can find the following topics covered in the NCONNECT (Novell Connectivity) forum:

◆ NACS

- NetWare Connect
- NW for SAA
- AS/400 Connectivity
- Host Printing
- SNA Links
- LAN/LAN Links-MPR
- NetWare Macintosh
- NetWare/DEC Connectivity
- Portable NetWare
- NW/NFS, TCP/IP, NW/IP
- E-mail/MHS/FAX
- LANWrkplce/Group
- Other Connectivity Issues

For network management related issues, NOVMAN forum has the following sections:

- Network Management
- NetWare Management System
- ManageWise
- Lanalyzer for Windows
- NW for SAA Management

For information about user groups and other non-technical matters, visit the NGENERAL forum:

- Product Information
- Suggestion Box
- Application/Utils
- User Groups/Training
- CNEs
- CNEPA
- NSEPro
- AppNotes
- NASC Program
- Other Information
- The Lighter Side

Some vendors have products that run on NetWire-maintained forums on CompuServe. **GO NVENA** for the following:

- Folio
- LAN Support Group
- Computer Tyme
- Infinite Tech.
- Dell Computer
- AST Research
- Blue Lance
- Best Power
- Knowzall
- Notework
- RoseWare
- Multi-User DOS
- TriCord

In NVENB forum, you will find the following:

- Ontrack Data
- NetWorth
- Gadget
- InterConnections
- Simware
- Mountain Network

General user issues are handled in their own forum. **GO NOVUSER** for the following:

- General Q & A's
- Help Wanted
- Classifieds

If you have questions about hardware, such as Ethernet cards or cabling questions, **GO NOVHW** to find the following:

- Power Monitoring
- Token ring
- Ethernet

- ARCnet
- Backups
- Cabling/Media

The libraries (NOVLIB and NOVFILES) are full of information about various products, programs, patches, bugs, and fixes.

Tip

> Due to the ever changing nature of a BBS, in order to better serve the users, forums and libraries are reorganized from time to time. In order to use the services efficiently, you should check the forums periodically, not just when you need information.

- Documents and
  Records

APPENDIX C

Network Management
Forms and Lists

Keeping accurate and up-to-date records of your network and workstations is vital to successful troubleshooting and asset management needs. Without proper records, you may not know how many workstations you have on your network, nor where exactly where each one is located. When you are called on to troubleshoot a particular workstation, it may take you some time to even locate it. Without accurate records of workstation configurations, if a workstation loses its CMOS settings, it will take you some time to reestablish it.

In this appendix, some sample worksheets and guidelines for establishing a sound network management system are presented.

DOCUMENTS AND RECORDS

You may think that your particular network is small enough to not need any documentation. This is not true. No matter the size of your network, abundant and appropriate system documentation can save many hours in troubleshooting problems. Documentation is divided into the following three categories:

◆ The LAN system
◆ The history and use of this LAN
◆ Resources for working with this LAN

THE LAN

There are at least six important items to keep track of for the network itself, as follows:

Network Map: A detailed graphics display of the LAN that identifies the locations of all workstations, file servers, printers, bridges, routers, gateways, hubs and repeaters, and wiring closets. If possible, add wiring paths from workstations to the hubs and between wiring closets and between floors.

A blueprint of the building's floor plan is a good starting place for your network map. For example, if it is in AutoCAD or any CAD drawing format, you can easily add to it with to-the-scale accuracy. If not, a drawing package, such as Visio, would be helpful.

Novell's Network Management System (NMS) was discussed in Chapter 35. Using NMS, it can automatically discover your network topology and draw a logical network map for you. You can easily create your own floor plans using BMP files and associate them with the NMS map information.

LAN Inventory: Do you know what software and hardware you have on your network? Do you know which workstation has what software installed? Do you know how much RAM is installed in each workstation and what type of CPU is in each workstation? If you cannot answer all the preceding questions with confidence, you do not have accurate document necessary for proper asset management needs.

A number of products are available to assist you in automatically performing LAN inventory. Some of the significant products include BindView NCS from the LAN Support Group, LAN Directory from Frye Computers, PC Census from Tally Systems, and LANdesk Manager from Intel.

Cabling documentation: If this information is not already part of your network map, you should have it available separately. Especially important are the cable distances of the existing runs to ensure they are within specification.

Workstation documentation: The configuration and roles of individual workstations can be critical to a network's health and should be documented. For example, if a given workstation lost its CMOS settings, the user will not have access to its hard drive. If the user happens to be the Vice President of Sales, you would want to have the VP up and running quickly! With proper workstation documentation, this is easily done.

Change log: Use this to document changes to the network, including software and hardware upgrade and/or changes. You can use this as a "change management" record so that if something stopped working, you can look up what was changed and when, and compare to see whether the recent change is related to the network service outage.

HISTORY OF THE LAN

There are at least three things you should keep track of in terms of the historic information of your network. The three items of interest are:

◆ **User profiles**: This should include information about the users, such as their names, job function, and location. You should note their physical locations in your building so that you can easily and quickly get to their workstations in case of need. You should also note which wiring segment and wiring hub their closest workstation is attached to.

   It also is worthwhile to keep a record of the computer training users have received. Sometimes "network problems" turn out to be "pilot errors" in using new applications.

- **Baselining your network**: Keep track of the usage statistics, such as network wire traffic, CPU usage, and disk usage of your network. These items give you a feel as to what is "normal" and what is not. When you experience network problems, it's a good idea to compare the current statistics with your historic trends to see whether anything is out of order. This helps you to isolate the problem area.

- **Past problem logs**: Record past problems, especially their symptoms and resolutions. This will help you to quickly resolve the same or similar problems in the future. Also, with this record, you will be able to spot recurring issues. For example, if you continue having a problem with a particular hub, perhaps you should replace it or look into *why* it is happening to this one hub, and not others.

LAN RESOURCES

Lastly, you should have readily available to you vendor and supplier information, such as technical support phone numbers, BBS numbers, FAXback information, and any knowledge base products, such as Novell's NSEPro and Microsoft's TechNet CDs. Also, keep your service contract and warranty information up-to-date.

Listed in Appendix B of this book are additional resources, such as network-related magazines and training courses and materials to keep you up-to-date with NetWare 4 information.

- ARCnet

- Ethernet

- Token Ring

APPENDIX D

Cabling Rules

It is important when you are installing a new network or expanding an existing one that you ensure that the distance limitation and any specifications, such as cable distances, are not exceeded. This appendix gives the cabling distances and rules for ARCnet, Ethernet, and token ring.

ARCNET

ARCnet operates at 2.5 Mbps throughput and can be connected using RG-62/U coax cable or unshielded twisted pair (UTP) wiring. Although ARCnet can support up to 255 node numbers on a single network, systems of this size are not practical.

Each network interface card (NIC) on an ARCnet network is assigned a node number. This number must be unique on each network and in the range of 1 to 255.

The ARCnet topology uses coax, twisted-pair, or fiber-optic cabling to connect network devices. An ARCnet network is used primarily with either coax or twisted pair cable. Coax is an RG-62/U type cable and is terminated with 93-Ohm terminators. Twisted pair uses stranded 24- or 26-gauge wire or solid core 22-, 24-, or 26-gauge type cable and is terminated with 100-Ohm terminators. Many ARCnet networks use a mix of both coax and UTP cabling. UTP cable is simple to install and provides a reliable connection to the clients, whereas coax provides a means to span longer distances.

ARCnet can run off a linear bus topology using coax or twisted pair, as long as the cards support BUS. The most popular installations of ARCnet run off two types of hubs:

◆ **Active hubs** have active electronic signals that amplify signals and split them to multiple ports. The number of ports on an active hub varies with the manufacturer, but eight is typical. A port on an active hub can be connected to a port on another active device (such as another active hub or an NIC) or to a passive hub.

◆ **Passive hubs** cannot amplify signals. Each hub has four connectors. Because of the characteristics of passive hubs, unused ports must be equipped with a *terminator*, a connector containing a resistor that matches the ARCnet cabling characteristics. A port on a passive hub can connect only to an active device (an active hub or an NIC). Passive hubs can never be connected to passive hubs.

One of the greatest flexibilities of ARCnet is that you can integrate connections from active hubs to a linear bus connection as long as you terminate at the last connection point.

A maximum time limit of 31 microseconds is allotted for an ARCnet signal. This is also called a time-out setting. Signals on an ARCnet can travel up to 20,000 feet during the 31-microsecond default time-out period. You sometimes can extend the range of an ARCnet by increasing the time-out value. However, 20,000 feet is the distance at which ARCnet signals begin to seriously degrade. Extending the network beyond that distance can result in unreliable or failed communication. Therefore, the time-out parameter and cabling distance recommendations should be increased only with great caution.

The maximum cable distances between individual components in an ARCnet network are dependent on how the components are connected (see Table D.1).

TABLE D.1. MAXIMUM ARCNET CABLE DISTANCES

Maximum Distance	From	To
2,000 feet	Network node	Active hub
2,000 feet	Active hub	Active hub
100 feet	Active hub	Passive hub
Not supported	Passive hub	Passive hub
100 feet	Network node	Passive hub
2,000 feet	Network node	Network node
20,000 feet	Farthest node	Farthest node

In cabling ARCnet networks with coax cable, you must follow several rules:

◆ Never connect a passive hub to another passive hub directly.

◆ Passive hubs should never be used to connect two active hubs.

◆ Passive hubs are only used to connect an active hub and a node.

◆ Unused connectors on active hubs do not need to be terminated.

◆ Unused connectors on passive hubs must be terminated using a 93-Ohm terminator.

Active hubs are required to extend the network for long distances and to configure networks that have more than four nodes. Passive hubs are used as an economical means of splitting a port on an active hub to support three devices.

ETHERNET

A variety of cables can be used to implement Ethernet networks and are described in the following sections. Traditionally, Ethernet networks have been cabled with coaxial cables of several different types. Fiber-optic cables are now frequently employed to extend the geographic range of Ethernet networks.

The contemporary interest in using twisted-pair wiring has resulted in a scheme for cabling using unshielded twisted pair. The 10BaseT cabling standard, which uses UTP in a star topology, is described later.

Ethernet remains closely associated with coaxial cable, however. Two types of coaxial cable still used in small and large environments are thin net (also known as cheapernet) and thick net. The Ethernet networks have different limitations based on thin net and thick net cable specifications. The best way to remember the requirements is to use the 5-4-3 rule of thumb for each cable type.

THE 5-4-3 RULE

The 5-4-3 rule states that the following can appear between any two nodes in the Ethernet network:

◆ Up to five segments in a series

◆ Up to four concentrators or repeaters

◆ Three segments of (coax only) cable that contain nodes

10BASE2

The 10Base2 cabling topology, also referred to as thin net, generally uses the onboard transceiver of the network interface card to translate the signals to and from the rest of the network. Thin net cabling can use RG-58A/U or RG-58C/U coaxial type cable, 50-Ohm terminators, and T-connectors that directly attach to the BNC connector on the NIC. A grounded terminator must be used on one end of the network segment.

Note

Use RG-58A/U cable for Ethernet topology, not RG-58U, which is for use with cable TV setups.

You must adhere to several rules in 10Base2 Ethernet environments, including the following:

◆ The minimum cable distance between clients must be 1.5 feet, or 0.5 meters.

◆ Pig tails, also known as drop cables, from T-connectors should not be used to connect to the BNC connector on the NIC. The T-connector must be connected directly to the NIC.

◆ You may not go beyond the maximum network segment limitation of 607 feet, or 185 meters.

- ◆ The entire network cabling scheme cannot exceed 3,035 feet, or 925 meters.
- ◆ The maximum number of nodes per network segment is 30 (this includes clients and repeaters).
- ◆ A 50-Ohm terminator must be used on each end of the bus, with only one of the terminators having either a grounding strap or a grounding wire that attaches it to the screw holding an electrical outlet cover in place.
- ◆ You may not have more than five segments on a network. These segments may be connected with a maximum of four repeaters, and only three of the five segments may have network nodes. (See the 5-4-3 Rule.)

10BASE5

The 10Base5 cabling topology, also referred to as thick net, uses an external transceiver to attach to the network interface card. The NIC attaches to the external transceiver by an Attachment Universal Interface (AUI) cable to the DIX connector on the back of the card. The external transceiver clamps to the thick net cable. As with thin net, each network segment must be terminated at both ends, with one end using a grounded terminator.

Note

RG-11 is a 75-Ohm cable. 10Base5 requires 50 Ohms.

In addition to the 5-4-3 rule mentioned previously, several additional guidelines must be followed in thick Ethernet networks:

- ◆ The minimum cable distance between transceivers is 8 feet, or 2.5 meters.
- ◆ You may not go beyond the maximum network segment length of 1,640 feet, or 500 meters.
- ◆ The entire network cabling scheme cannot exceed 8,200 feet, or 2,500 meters.
- ◆ One end of the terminated network segment must be grounded.
- ◆ Drop cables can be as short as required, but cannot be longer than 50 meters from transceiver to NIC.
- ◆ Cable segments that are cut and connected using a "Vampire Tap" should come from the same cable spool to ensure that each connected piece carries the identical electrical cabling to the other.
- ◆ The maximum number of nodes per network segment is 100. (This includes all repeaters.)

10BASET

The trend in wiring Ethernet networks is to use unshielded twisted-pair (UTP) cable. UTP or 10BaseT cable is one of the three most popular implementations for Ethernet. It is based on the IEEE 802.3 standard.

10BaseT cabling is wired in a star topology. However, it functions logically like a linear bus. The cable uses RJ-45 connectors, and the network interface card can have RJ-45 jacks built into the back of the cards. External transceivers attached to a DIX connector found in combination with RJ-45 or BNC connectors on the NIC can be used to connect standard Ethernet cards into a twisted-pair topology. Figure 6.8 shows Ethernet cabling using twisted-pair cabling and a hub, also called a concentrator.

The rules for a 10BaseT network are as follows:

◆ The maximum number of network segments is 1,024.

◆ The cabling used should be 22, 24, or 26 American Wire Gauge (AWG), and be rated for an impedance of 85 to 115 Ohms at 10 MHz.

  Unshielded twisted-pair uses a terminator resistance level of 100-200 Ohms; shielded twisted-pair uses 150 Ohms.

◆ The maximum number of nodes is 512, and they may be connected on any three segments, with five being the maximum number of available line segments.

◆ The maximum unshielded cable segment length is 328 feet, or 100 meters.

Note

10BaseT requires that the UTP cable system be compliant with the Category 4 standard. Cat 4 is cable-certified to operate at 10 Mbps throughput.

TOKEN RING

Traditional token ring networks used shielded twisted pair cable. The following are standard IBM cable types for token ring:

◆ **Type 1:** A braided shield surrounds two twisted pairs of solid copper wire. Type 1 is used to connect terminals and distribution panels, or to connect between different wiring closets that are located in the same building. Type 1 uses two STPs of solid-core 22 AWG wire for long, high data-grade transmissions within the building's walls.

- **Type 2:** Type 2 uses a total of six twisted pairs: two are STPs (for networking), four are UTPs (for telephone systems). Additionally, this cable type incorporates two unshielded twisted pairs that can be used for voice circuits. This cable is used for the same purposes as Type 1, but enables both voice and data cables to be included in a single cable run.

- **Type 3:** Type 3 has unshielded twisted-pair copper with a minimum of two twists-per-inch, used as an alternative to Type 1 and Type 2 cable because of its reduced cost. It has four UTPs of 24 AWG solid-core wire for networks or telephone systems. Type 3 cannot be used for 16 mbps token ring networks. It is used primarily for long, low data-grade transmissions within walls. Signals will not travel as fast as with Type 1 cable because Type 3 does not have the shielding used by Type 1.

- **Type 5:** With Type 5, fiber-optic cable is used only on the main ring. Type 5 can use two 100-microns (micrometers) or 140-microns (micrometers) optical fibers in one fiber jacket.

- **Type 6:** A braided shield surrounds two twisted pairs of stranded copper wire. It is made up of two 26 AWG stranded-core STPs. This cable supports shorter cable runs than Type 1, but is more flexible due to the stranded conductors. Type 6 is the IBM standard for patch cables and extension cables, used also in wiring closets.

- **Type 8:** Type 8 uses a single 26 AWG stranded-core STP and is especially designed for use under carpet.

- **Type 9:** Type 9 is the same as Type 6 cable, except that it is designed to be fire-resistant for use in plenum installations. It uses two STPs of solid-core 26 AWG wire, and is used for long runs within the walls of a building.

Token ring cabling is used to connect clients to the MSAU, or to connect one MSAU to another. Cables that connect between MSAUs are called *patch cables*. Patch cables may also be made of IBM Type 6 cable.

Note

IBM defines token ring cabling in terms of two types of systems:

- Small movable
- Large nonmovable

The small movable system supports up to 96 clients and file servers and 12 MSAUs. It uses Type 6 cable to attach clients and servers to IBM Model 8228 MSAUs. Type 6 cable is a shielded twisted pair cable with stranded conductors. This cable is flexible, but has limited distance capabilities. The characteristics of this cable make it suitable for small networks and for patch cords.

D

CABLING RULES

The large nonmovable system supports up to 260 clients and file servers, with up to 33 MSAUs. This network configuration uses IBM Type 1 or Type 2 cable. These are shielded twisted pair cables with solid-wire conductors suitable for carrying signals greater distances than are possible with Type 6. The large nonmovable system also involves other wiring needs, such as punch panels or distribution panels, equipment racks for MSAUs, and wiring closets to contain the previously listed components.

IBM token ring networks use two types of connectors. NICs are equipped with a 9-pin D-connector. MSAUs, repeaters, and most other equipment use a special IBM data connector. Two types of cables are employed:

◆ **Patch cables** have IBM data connectors at both ends. These cables interconnect MSAUs, repeaters, and most other token ring components.

◆ **Token ring adapter cables** have an IBM data connector at one end and a 9-pin connector at the other. Adapter cables connect client and server NICs to other network components that use IBM data connectors.

Tip

If using more than one MSAU, connect the ring out (RO) port of each MSAU with the ring in (RI) port of the next MSAU in the loop. This must physically complete a circle or ring.

A variety of rules must be observed when configuring token rings. The following rules apply to small, movable token ring networks:

◆ The minimum patch cable distance between two MSAUs is 8 feet.

◆ The maximum patch cable distance between two MSAUs is 150 feet. Patch cables come in standard lengths of 8, 30, 75, and 150 feet for Type 6.

◆ The maximum patch cable distance connecting all MSAUs is 400 feet.

◆ The maximum adapter cable distance between an MSAU and a node is 150 feet.

A small movable IBM cable system consists of the following:

◆ Maximum 96 nodes

◆ Maximum 12 MSAUs

◆ Uses Type 6 cable

A large nonmovable IBM cable system consists of the following:

◆ Maximum 260 nodes

◆ Maximum 33 MSAUs

◆ Uses Type 1 or Type 2 cable

Note

Token ring networks also can be cabled using UTP cabling, which IBM calls Type 3 cable. The IEEE 802.5 standard describes 4 Mbps token ring using UTP cable. However, Cat 5 UTP is currently used for 16 Mbps token ring.

When using UTP cabling, the distance from workstation to the hub is 100 meters, much like that for 10BaseT Ethernet.

When using UTP wiring, a media filter must be installed between the NIC and the UTP cable. Some newer token ring NICs have built-in media filters and RJ-45 jacks ready to interface with UTP wiring.

SYMBOLS

command (login scripts), 546

^ (carat), menu source files, 577

100 Mbps Ethernet, 210-213

100BaseX/Fast Ethernet, 213

100VG-AnyLAN (Ethernet), 211-213

10Base2 (Ethernet), 206-207, 408-409, 1260-1261

10Base5 (Ethernet), 204-206, 1261

10BaseT (Ethernet), 208-209, 414-416, 1262

18 GHz Radio (wireless communications networks security), 224

386 DX processors, 120-121

386 SX processors, 120

486 processors, 121, 155-156

5-4-3 rule (Ethernet), 206, 1260

802.2 (Ethernet) frame type, 923

802.3 (Ethernet) frame type, 921-923

Index

A

A.N.D. Technologies' PCOUNTER, 898
abends (ABnormal ENDs), 934-938
ABort flag (print services), 740
ABORT REMIRROR server console command, 1018
aborting partition operations, 838-840
accessibility (Frame Relay networks), 234
accounting
 ATOTAL (Accounting Services Total) utility, 896-897
 configuration, 890-894
 information/support sources, 898-899
 installation, 888-890
 maintenance, 894-895
 management, 673
 NWADMIN versus NETADMIN, 895
 printing services, 898
 purpose and uses, 884-888
 removing, 895
 reports, 898
 total network charges, displaying, 1132
across-the-wire server upgrades, 468-476
active hubs (ARCnet), 197-199, 1258
active monitors (token ring networks), 221
active threads, viewing status, 936-937
ad hoc tasks, workflow, 765
adapter cables (token ring networks), 1264
ADD NAME SPACE server console command, 1019-1020

addressable memory, listing, 1043
addresses
 conflicts, 389-391
 hardware, 994
 server network, 993-997
Admin user object, security rights, 618
administration, *see* **network administration**
administrators, 241-242
 area administrators, 242-243
 group administrators, 242
 NETADMIN (NetWare Administrator for DOS), 1184-1194
 NWADMIN (NetWare Administrator for Windows), 1160-1184
 printing operators, 243
AFP (AppleTalk Filing Protocol), 105-106, 1228
AFP Server objects, 268, 1165
AlertPage (Denmac), 861
Alias objects, 261, 269, 1165
alignment errors, troubleshooting, 949
American Power Conversion's PowerNet SNMP Manager for NMS, 862
analog data transfer, 235
anonymous FTP mirrors (troubleshooting NetWare), 319
APIs (Application Program Interfaces)
 accounting, 888
 NDS (NetWare Directory Services), 781-782
 network applications, 780-782
AppleTalk, 82, 103, 804, 1228
AppleTalk Filing Protocol (AFP), 105-106, 1228

AppleTalk Remote Access (ARA), 804-805
Application layer (OSI model), 104-106, 777, 966-967
Application Program Interfaces, *see* **APIs**
application servers, 113-114
application sharing, 11
applications
 A.N.D. Technologies' PCOUNTER, 898
 American Power Conversion's PowerNet SNMP Manager for NMS, 862
 Avanti Technologies' NCONSOLE, 833
 Cabletron's Spectrum for NMS, 862
 Compaq Insight Manager (Compaq), 832, 861
 Denmac
  AlertPage, 861
  TrenData, 862
  AuditTrack, 833
  SmartPass for NetWare, 833
 Frye Utilities for Networks (Frye Computer Systems, Inc.), 832, 898
 Intel
  LANDesk Manager, 832, 861
  NetSight, 832
 Klos Technologies, Inc.'s PacketView, 833
 LAN Support Group, Inc.'s BindView NCS, 898
 NDS applications, 38
 network applications, 754-793
 Novell
  LANalyzer for Windows, 832

NetWare Management Systems, 832
server-based applications, 18-19, 32-33
StonyBrook
Cisco Router Manager, 862
Wellfleet Router Manager, 862
SynOptics' Optivity for NMS, 862
ARA (AppleTalk Remote Access), 804-805
archiving
file-by-file backups, 872-873
hardware, 874-876
image backups, 871
importance, 864-865
journalized archives, 874
perpetual archives, 874
requirements, 865-870
rotating media, 873
SMS (Storage Management Services), 61-63, 877-881
software, 874-877
see also backups
ARCnet, 100-101, 1228
cabling distances, 1258-1259
compatibility with ARCnet Plus, 202
data transmission, order, 199-200
Network Interface Cards (NICs), 199
node connections, 197-199
TCNS (Thomas-Conrad Network System), 1234
thin coax cable, 409
upgrading to ARCnet Plus, 202-203
ARCnet Plus architecture, 201-203
area administrators, 242-243

ARPANET (Advanced Research Projects Agency NETwork), 12
ART (automatic revision tracking), 116
assigning
charge rates for resource usage, 891-893
trustees to objects, 1173
ATM (Asynchronous Transfer Mode), 228-232, 818
ATOTAL (Accounting Services Total) command line utility, 885-886, 896-897, 1132
ATTACH command (login scripts), 546-547
Attached Servers option (managing print jobs), 735-736
attaching to servers, 1210-1214
Attachment command (NETUSER utility), 1222-1223
attenuation (cabling), 188-189
attributed security (files/directories), 628-630
attributes, 1232
directories
granting via FILER utility, 637-638
granting via FLAG command, 638
granting via NWAdmin, 637
viewing/modifying, 1138-1139
files
archiving system requirements, 866
granting via FILER utility, 637-638
granting via FLAG command, 638

granting via NWAdmin, 637
viewing/modifying, 1138-1139
audio, 771
Audit History file, 666
AUDITCON command line utility, 649-650, 653-656, 1132-1133
network documentation, 683
auditing, 47-49, 644-669, 1132-1133
Audit File Maintenance option, 656-657
audit files, 666-668
file sizes, 659-661
Audit History file, 666
audit password, changing, 662
AUDITCON utility, 649-650, 653-656, 1132-1133
configuring audits, 657-666
Directory Services events, 657-658
Directory tree containers, 652-653
disabling audits, 662
displaying status, 662-663, 667
planning audits, 646-650
preparations, 650-653
reports, 663-666
servers, changing, 668
session contexts, changing, 668
user objects, 658-659
versus accounting, 885
volume audits, 651-652
dismounting/remounting volumes, 660
AuditTrack (e.g. Software, Inc.), 833
authentication, background, 610, 1228

Authorized Resellers, 957
Authorized Service Centers (NASC), 957
Auto Detect Hard Disk option (CMOS settings), 377
AUTOEXEC.BAT file
  DOS Requester, 525
  installing NetWare, 451-452
AUTOEXEC.NCF file, installing NetWare, 463
automatic restart (servers), 116
automatic revision tracking (ART), 116
automatic volume dismounts, 950
Avanti Technologies' NCONSOLE, 833
awareness, network, 778-780

B

back-end services, 16-19
background authentication, 610, 1228
background file compression, 46-47
  archiving system requirements, 868-869
backups
  bugs, 344
  data protection, 322
  differential, 872
  directory management, 337-339
  file management, 337-339
  file-by-file backups, 872-873
  fixes, 344
  full, 872
  Grandfather-Father-Son rotation scheme, 335
  hardware, 340-341
  Hierarchical Storage Management, 343
  image backups, 871
  incremental, 872
  interfaces, 333
  maintenance, 342
  media defects, 341-342
  NDS (NetWare Directory Services), 340
  offsite storage, 342
  parallel streaming, 334
  patches, 344
  re-tensioning tapes, 334
  reliability, 333
  rotation schemes, 334-337
  SBACKUP.NLM, 339
  servers, 1124-1126
  software, 332-333
  tape devices, 334
  ten-tape rotation scheme, 335-336
  testing, 342
  Tower of Hanoi scheme, 336-337
  virus protection, 339
  viruses, 343-344
  workstation support, 339
  see also archiving
backward compatibility (NDS), 41-42, 293
bad media sectors, 22-23
balancing
  loads, 979
  server hardware, 117
banner pages (print services), 745
base memory
  address conflicts, 353-356
  CMOS settings, 375
  workstations, 379
base port addresses, 358
baselining, 927, 1256
{BATCH} option (ITEM menu command), 580
batch files, exercising disk (burn in), 366
battery power
  discharge/recharge time, setting, 1110-1111
  status, checking, 1108-1110
baud rate, 811
BBSs (bulletin board systems)
  NetWire, 1246-1251
  vendor BBSs, 790
Bearer Channels (ISDN), 235
billing, 885
BIND server console command, 1020-1022
bindery, 293-295
  compared to NDS, 37-38
  emulation, 1228
    MIGRATE, 469
  queues, 269
  server management, 844-846
Bindery objects, 269, 1165
binding protocols to LAN drivers, troubleshooting, 941-942
BindView NCS (LAN Support Group, Inc.), 898
BIOS, 372
  configuring
    for IDE drives, 362-363
    for SCSI drives, 363-364
  floppy drives, 384
  troubleshooting setup, 360
  wake-up features, 378
bit rate, 811
blocks
  sizes, optimizing, 915
  suballocation, 45
blueprints
  NDS tree structure, 284-288
  partition replication, 288-289
books (training staff), 1243
boot files, copying, 447-448
booting
  boot images, creating, 1137
  remote, 1123
bottlenecks, finding, 925-926

BREAK command (login scripts), 547, 549
BRI-2B+D (ISDN), 236
bridges, 424
  connecting networks, 225-226, 1228
  troubleshooting, 939-940
BROADCAST server console command, 1022-1024
Browser command (NWADMIN's Tools menu), 1181
budget checklist, 172-173
buffers, optimizing
  directory cache buffers, 904-905
  file cache buffers, 905-906
  PRBs (packet receive buffers), 908-912
bugs (backups), 344
bulletin board systems, *see* BBSs
burn in (server hardware), 351, 365-367
bus mastering, 125, 359
bus topology, 9, 183-184, 1229
  selecting client workstations, 157-159
  server hardware, 123-130
business processes (network documentation), 681
buttons, user-definable (NWUSER utility), 1216-1218

C

C Library NLM (CLIB), 1228
cable management software, 685
Cabletron's Spectrum for NMS, 862

cabling, 5, 187-196, 406-418
  ARCnet, 1258-1259
    node connections, 198-199
  attenuation, 188-189
  changing network numbers for, 1105-1107
  coaxial cable, 189-190, 406-411
  contractors, 427-428
  CSMA/CD (Ethernet), 209-210
  documentation, 1255
  Ethernet, 95-97, 1259-1262
    100VG-AnyLAN, 212-213
    10Base2, 206-207
    10Base5, 204-206
    10BaseT, 208-209
  external interference, 187-188
  Fast Ethernet/ 100BaseX, 213
  fiber-optic cable, 195-196, 419-420
  hiring technicians, 170-171
  MSAU (Multi-Station Access Unit) concentrators, 418-424
  multi-meters, 421
  specifications
    coax cable, 190
    EIA/TIA, 195
    IBM twisted pair cable specifications, 192-193
    Underwriters Laboratories, 193-194
  testing, 420-424
  token ring networks, 218-220, 1262-1265
  troubleshooting faults, 938-940, 946-947
  twisted pair cabling, 191-195, 412-418

caching
  CMOS settings, 378-379
  directory caching
    operating system parameters, setting, 1070-1072
    optimizing buffers, 904-905
  file caching
    operating system parameters, setting, 1068-1070
    optimizing buffers, 905-906
calendars (network applications), 767
Cancel Down flag (print services), 740
capacity (hardware backups), 341
CAPTURE command line utility, 703-704, 743-746, 1133-1135
capturing printer ports, 1206-1210, 1220
carat (^), menu source files, 577
cards (LAN), troubleshooting, 939
Carrier Sense Lost error, 947
Carrier Sense Multiple Access with Collision Detection (CSMA/CD), 209-210
Cascade command (NWADMIN's Window menu), 1183
cases (selecting client workstations), 154
CBT (computer-based training)
  CBT Systems, 1240-1241
  Novell, 1242-1243
CD-ROM
  discs as read-only volumes, 1115-1118

distribution discs, extracting/copying files from, 1148

DOS/Windows Client software diskettes, creating, 508

NetWare 3.1*x*-to-4.*x* in-place upgrades, 494-499

OS/2 Client software diskettes, creating, 509-510

CD-ROM drives
installing, 364
installing NetWare, 444-445

CDROM NLM, 1115-1118

cell-relay networks (ATMs), 229

Central Processing Units (CPUs), 155-157

centralized network administration, 246-247

certification by NetWare
archiving system requirements, 870
vendors (server hardware), 115

Certified NetWare Administrators (CNAs), 169

Certified NetWare Engineers (CNEs), 168-169

Certified Novell Instructors (CNIs), 1239-1240

Change Context command
NETADMIN utility, 1185
NETUSER utility, 1223-1224

change events, trouble-shooting, 930-933

change log (documentation), 1255

charge rates for resource usage
assigning/deleting, 891-893
determining, 890-891

{CHDIR} option (ITEM menu command), 580

checklist (planning NDS tree structure), 283-290

CIM (CompuServe Information Manager), 1246-1247

Cisco Router Manager (StonyBrook), 862

clean rooms (environmental issues), 331

cleaning floppy drives, 384

CLEAR STATION server console command, 1024-1025

clearing screen, 1025-1026, 1047-1048

CLIB (C Library NLM), 970, 1113, 1228

client diskettes, 394-396

client drivers, 396-403
DOS Requester, 397-400
NET.CFG, 400-401

client workstation identifier variables (login scripts), 563-564

client workstations, 5, 152-164
bus architecture, 157-159
cases, 154
CPUs, 155-157
dealers, 162
desktop cases, 153
disk drives, 160
documentation, 1255
installing DynaText, 433-434
keyboards, 161-162
local data, archiving, 879-881
motherboards, 154-159
mouse, 162
network operating system requirements, 163-164
ODI specification, 970-972
power supplies, 154
print services, setting up, 729-731
RAM, 159
tower cases, 153-154

UPS (Uninterruptable Power Supplies), 162
user profiles, 152
video controllers/monitors, 161
see also workstations

client/server database model, 759-760

client/server networks, 6-7, 1228

clients, 370
DOS/Windows client installation, 510-516
installing, 393-394
loading, user training, 696-697
operating system support (NetWare), 29-30
workstation client files, 507-510

clones, selecting client workstations, 162

Close All command (NWADMIN's Window menu), 1183

CLS command, 547, 1025-1026

cluster controllers, 73

clusters (NetSync), 845

CMIP (Common Management Information Protocol), 108

CMOS settings, 374-379
Auto Detect Hard Disk option, 377
base memory, 375
caching, 378-379
extended memory, 375
floppy drives, 377
hard disks, 375-377
keyboard, 378
power management, 378
primary display, 377

CNAs (Certified NetWare Administrators), 169

CNEs (Certified NetWare Engineers), 168-169

CNIs (Certified Novell Instructors), 1239-1240
coaxial cable, 189-190, 406-411
  continuity, 421
  resistance, 421
  testing, 422
  thick coax cable, 409-411
  thin coax cable, 407-409
Codd, E.F., 757
code pages, configuring (installing NetWare), 448
Collapse command (NWADMIN's View menu), 1178
collisions, troubleshooting, 944
COLORPAL command line utility, 1135-1136
colors
  menu systems, 577-578
  menu windows, changing, 1135-1136
command line (DOS), returning to, 1035-1036
commands
  #, 546
  ABORT REMIRROR, 1018
  ADD NAME SPACE, 1019-1020
  ATOTAL (Accounting Services Total), 885-886, 896-897, 1132
  ATTACH, 546-547
  Attachment (NETUSER utility), 1222-1223
  AUDITCON, 649-650, 653-656, 683, 1132-1133
  BIND, 1020-1022
  BREAK, 547, 549
  BROADCAST, 1022-1024
  CAPTURE, 703-704, 743-746, 1133-1135
  CDROM, 1115-1118
  Change Context
    NETADMIN utility, 1185
    NETUSER utility, 1223-1224

CLEAR STATION, 1024-1025
CLS, 547, 1025-1026
COLORPAL, 1135-1136
COMSPEC, 547-548
CONFIG, 1026-1027
CONTEXT, 548
CX, 1136
DISABLE LOGIN, 1027-1028
DISABLE TTS, 1028-1029
DISMOUNT, 1029-1030
DISPLAY, 548-549
DISPLAY NETWORKS, 1030-1031
DISPLAY SERVERS, 1031-1032
DOMAIN, 1118-1119
DOSGEN, 1137
DOWN, 1032-1033
DRIVE, 550
Drives (NETUSER utility), 1221-1222
DSREPAIR, 1119-1122
ENABLE LOGIN, 1033
ENABLE TTS, 1034-1035
END, 553
EXEC, 578-579
EXIT, 550, 1035-1036
FDISPLAY, 551
FILER, 1137-1138
FIRE PHASERS, 551
FLAG, 638, 1138-1139
GETO, 584
GETP, 585-587
GETR, 584-585
GOTO, 551-552
HELP, 1036
Help menu (NWADMIN utility), 1184
IF...THEN, 552
INCLUDE, 553-554
ITEM, 579-581
KEYB, 1122-1123
LANGUAGE, 1037-1038
LASTLOGINTIME, 554
LIST DEVICES, 1038-1039

LOAD, 582-583, 1039-1041
LOGIN, 1140
LOGOUT, 1140-1141
MACHINE, 554
MAGAZINE, 1041-1042
Manage according to search pattern (NETADMIN utility), 1194-1196
Manage objects (NETADMIN utility), 1186-1197
MAP, 554-557, 1141
MEDIA, 1042-1043
MEMORY, 1043
Messages (NETUSER utility), 1220-1221
MIRROR STATUS, 1043-1044
MODULES, 1044-1045
MOUNT, 1045-1047
NAME, 1047
NCOPY, 1142
NDIR, 1143-1144
NETADMIN, 895, 1144, 1184-1194
NETUSER, 1145, 1200, 1218-1224
NLIST, 1145-1146
NMENU, 1146
NO_DEFAULT, 557
NOSWAP, 557
NPRINT, 746-747, 1146-1147
NVER, 1148
NWXTRACT, 1148
Object menu (NWADMIN utility), 1163-1177
OFF, 1047-1048
PARTMGR (Partition Manager), 835-844, 1148
PAUSE, 557
PCCOMPATIBLE, 558
PCONSOLE, 1149
PRINTCON, 1150
PRINTDEF, 1150
Printing (NETUSER utility), 1219-1220

PROTOCOL, 1048-1049
PSC, 739-742, 1151-1152
PURGE, 1152
RCONSOLE,
 848-855, 1153
REGISTER MEMORY,
 1049-1051
REMARK, 558
REMIRROR PARTITION,
 1051-1052
REMOVE DOS, 1052-1053
RENDIR, 1153
RESET ROUTER,
 1053-1054
RIGHTS, 635-636,
 1153-1154
RPL, 1123
RTDM, 1123-1124
SBACKUP, 1124-1126
SCAN FOR NEW
 DEVICES, 1054
SEARCH, 1055-1056
Search (NETADMIN
 utility), 1185
SECURE CONSOLE,
 1056-1057
SEND, 1058-1059,
 1154-1155
SERVMAN, 1126-1128
SET, 549, 558-559,
 1060-1098
SET TIME, 559,
 1098-1099, 1130
SET TIME ZONE,
 1100-1101
SETPASS, 1155
SETTTS, 1155
SHIFT, 559-560
SHOW, 581-582
SPEED, 1101-1102
SWAP, 560
syntax of login script
 commands, 545-546
SYSTIME, 1156
TEMP SET, 560
TIME, 1102
TIMESYNC, 1128-1130
TRACK OFF, 1103

TRACK ON, 1103-1105
UIMPORT, 1156
UNBIND, 1105-1107
UNLOAD, 1108-1110
UPS STATUS, 1108-1110
UPS TIME, 1110-1111
VERIFY, 550
VERSION, 1111-1112
View menu (NWADMIN
 utility), 1177-1178
VOLUMES, 1112
WHOAMI, 1156
Window menu
 (NWADMIN utility),
 1183-1184
WRITE, 561
WSUPDATE, 1157
WSUPGRD, 1158
common backbone net-
works, 962
Common Management
Information Protocol
(CMIP), 108
common names (leaf
objects), 267, 1229
communications
 between hardware periph-
 erals, 352
 network applications,
 772-775
 operating system param-
 eters, setting, 1063-1066
 workstations, 370-371
communications protocols
 OSI model, 94-101
 SPX (Sequenced Packet
 Exchange), 975
communications servers,
114, 818-821, 1229
comp.sys.novell
newsgroup, 319
Compaq Insight Manager
(Compaq), 832, 861
compatibility
 ARCnet with ARCnet
 Plus, 202
 network administration
 products, 834-835

compiling menu source
 files, 573-574
complete burn in (server
 hardware), 366-367
complex data
 structures, 1233
compressing files
 background, 46-47
 *archiving system
  requirements, 868-869*
 modems, 813-815
 user training, 701-702
CompuServe
 accounting information/
 support sources, 899
 NetWire, 955-956,
 1246-1251
 *troubleshooting
  NetWare installation,
  317-319*
 network applications, 790
CompuServe Information
Manager (CIM),
1246-1247
Computer Buyer's Guide,
173-176
*Computer Database
Plus,* 174
Computer objects,
269, 1165
computer-based
 training (CBT)
 CBT Systems, 1240-1241
 Novell, 1242-1243
COMSPEC command
(login scripts), 547-548
concentrators, MSAUs
(Multi-Station Access
Units), 418-424
concurrency control, 13
conferences, network
 applications, 792
CONFIG server console
 command, 1026-1027
CONFIG.SYS file, DOS
 Requester, 525

configurations
accounting, 890-894
audits, 657-666
BIOS
for IDE drives, 362-363
for SCSI drives,
363-364
code pages, 448
country codes, 448
dynamic, *see* dynamic
configuration
hardware, troubleshoot-
ing, 348-349
information about, dis-
playing, 1026-1027
internetwork components,
980-983
keyboard mapping, 448
management, 673
advantages, 673-676
disadvantages, 676-677
software tools, 684
MHS, 595-602
mirrored servers, 27
NetSync, 845
operating system param-
eters, 1060-1098
print jobs, editing, 1150
printers, 720-724
time zone information,
1100-1101
workstations, 370-403
Confirm command
(NWADMIN's Options
menu), 1179
connecting networks,
224-228
connection-oriented
protocols, 975
connectionless
protocols, 975
connections
bridges, 424
cabling, 406-418
internetworks to hosts, 984
mainframes, 426-428
mini-computers, 426-428

NetWare for SAA, 426
packet formats, 426
physical network (OSI
layers), 966
routers, 425
temporary (servers), 1234
users, information
about, 1156
connectors
installing, 406-428
token ring networks, 1264
consistency checks (vol-
ume mounts), 24
consultants
hiring (budgeting tips),
168-170
planning NetWare instal-
lation, 305-306
troubleshooting NetWare
installation, 315
Container Login Scripts,
see **System Login Scripts**
container objects, 244-245,
260-267, 280-281
naming conventions,
273-274
templates, 285
containers, 39-40, 1229
auditing, 652-653
moving, 837-838
containment (DIB ob-
jects), 1229
CONTEXT command
(login scripts), 548
contexts, 1178, 1229
changing, 1223-1224
for auditing, 668
user training, 698-699
continuity
coaxial cable, 421
twisted pair cabling, 422
contractors (cabling),
427-428
conventional memory
(workstations), 379
converting NetWare 3.11
menu systems to
NetWare 4.x menus, 588

coordination/planning
NDS tree structure,
281-290
Copy command
(NWADMIN's Object
menu), 1176
copying
directories, 1142
files, 1142
boot files, installing
NetWare, 447-448
from distribution
diskettes /
CD-ROM, 1148
NetWare files to SYS:
volume, 457-458
login scripts
NETADMIN, 542-543
NetWare Admini-
strator, 545
copyrights (servers),
displaying information,
1111-1112
coring tools (thick coax
cable), 411
corporate rates (budget-
ing tips), 177-178
cost
budgeting tips
budget checklist,
172-173
corporate rates, 177-178
hiring consultants,
168-170
hiring technicians,
170-171
justifying costs, 178-179
Novell-approved
hardware, 167-168
researching prices,
173-177
sample shopping list,
166-167
site licensing, 177-178
staff training, 171-172
hardware backups, 340
path costing, 979
wireless communications
networks, 222

country abbreviations, 261-265

country codes, configuring, 448

Country objects, 261-265, 280-281, 1165
   naming conventions, 274

CPUs (Central Processing Units)
   selecting client workstations, 155-157
   speed, displaying, 1101-1102

crashed workstations, cleaning up, 1024-1025

CRC (Cyclic Redundancy Check) errors, troubleshooting, 945-946

Create command (NWADMIN's Object menu), 1164-1167

cross-platform printing, 60

CSMA/CD (Carrier Sense Multiple Access with Collision Detection), 209-210

customized menus, calling, 1146

CX server console command, 290, 699-700, 1136

D

DAS (Dual Attachment Stations), 215-216

data
   communications (network applications), 772-775
   compression (modems), 813-815
   fusion, 133
   migration, 29, 44-45
      real-time, 1123-1124
   network documentation, 680-681
   protecting, 322-345
   redirecting to nework files, 1133-1135

routing with NetWare's native protocols, 974-980

services, 772-774

stripping (RAID 4 level), 142-143

transmission
   ARCnet nodes, 199-200
   token ring networks, 220

unmingling, 133

data bus, 1229

Data Communication Equipment (DCE), 679

Data Link layer (OSI model), 94-101, 778, 966

Data Migration system, archiving system requirements, 869-870

Data Terminal Equipment (DTE), 679

Data Transmission Performance Level Marking (DTPLM) program, 193

data transport (OSI layers), 966

database servers, 114

databases
   bindery, 293-295
   client/server model, 759-760
   DIB (Directory Information Base), 292-295
   distributed databases, 1229
      partitions, 1232
   hierarchical databases, 1233
   network applications, 757-760
   network documentation, 689-690, 692
   replicated databases, 1233
   single-user database model, 758-759
   storing NetExplorer server data, 857

datatypes, scalar, 1234

date identifier variables (login scripts), 561-562

dates
   information about, viewing, 1102
   setting current, 1098-1099, 1130
   synchronizing, 1156

daylight savings time
   installing NetWare, 460-462
   synchronizing NDS time servers, 300

DCE (Data Communication Equipment), 679

de facto standards, 91-92

de jure standards, 91

dealers, *see* vendors

debugging
   backups, 344
   troubleshooting abends, 936-938

DEC Access, 77-78

dedicated-processor systems (remote node), 802-804

dedicated-server networks, *see* client/server networks

default partitions, 296, 1008

defining terminology
   user training, 696
   workgroup administrator training, 707

definitions (printers), creating/deleting/modifying, 1150

Delete command (NWADMIN's Object menu), 1176

deleting
   charge rates for resource usage, 891-893
   DOS from memory, 1052-1053
   name space from volumes, 1002-1003
   replicas, 842

trustees from objects, 1174
  see also removing
**Delta Channels
  (ISDN), 235**
**Demand Priority protocol
  (Ethernet), 211**
Denmac
  AlertPage, 861
  TrenData, 862
**departmental liaisons
  (network administra-
  tion), 248-249**
designing
  menu systems, 570,
    572-573
  networks, 148
**desktop cases (selecting
  client workstations), 153**
**Details command
  (NWADMIN's Object
  menu), 1167-1169**
device drivers
  binding with protocols,
    1020-1022
  client drivers, 396-403
  LAN drivers
    *binding protocols to,
    troubleshooting,
    941-942*
    *IPX.COM, updating,
    1158*
    *loading, troubleshoot-
    ing, 940-941*
  listing, 1038-1039
  loadable device-driver
    interface, 21
  mirrored servers, 27
  unbinding protocols from,
    1105-1107
  unloading, 1108-1110
**diagnostics, token ring
  networks, 221**
dial-in access
  e-mail, 797-798
  remote control, 83
  remote node, 83-85
**dial-out communications
  (LANs), 85**

**dial-up connectivity
  (network appli-
  cations), 773**
**dial-up routers (remote
  access), 805**
**DIB (Directory Informa-
  tion Base), 38, 256,
  292-295, 1229**
  archiving NDS DIB, 63
  schemas, 1233
DIB objects
  containments, 1229
  distinguished names, 1229
differential backups, 872
**direct connection, twisted
  pair cabling, 413**
**Direct Memory Access
  (DMA), 16-17**
  conflicts, 349
directories
  attributes, viewing/
    modifying, 1138-1139
  backups, 337-339
  copying, 1142
  information about,
    1143-1144
  owners, modifying,
    1138-1139
  renaming, 1153
  rights, 625-626, 1153-1154
directory caching
  operating system param-
    eters, setting, 1070-1072
  optimizing buffers,
    904-905
**Directory Information
  Base, *see* DIB**
**Directory Map objects,
  269, 1165**
**Directory Services events,
  auditing, 657-658**
directory trees, 280-290
  adding servers, 1005-1008
  auditing containers,
    652-653
  blueprint for structure,
    284-288

container objects, 260-267,
  280-281
Country objects, 280-281
current context, viewing/
  changing, 1136-1137
importing user objects
  into, 1156
leaf objects, 267-269
levels of depth, 287-288
number of trees, 281
Organization objects, 281
Organizational Unit
  objects, 281
partition replication
  blueprints, 288-289
planning/coordination,
  281-290, 311
[Root] object, 280
templates, 284-285
**DISABLE LOGIN server
  console command,
  1027-1028**
**DISABLE TTS server
  console command,
  1028-1029**
disabling audits, 662
disaster recovery, 881
**discs (CD-ROM) as read-
  only volumes, 1115-1118**
disk caching, 131-133
**disk drive mirroring,
  24-25**
disk drivers
  loading, 452-453,
    1039-1041
  troubleshooting NetWare
    installation, 465
disk drives
  disk caching, 131-133
  duplexing, 25-26
  ESDI drives, 133-134
  floppy disk drives, 160
  hard drives, 130-136, 160
    *adding to servers,
    988-991*
  IDE drives, 134
  installing, 360

mapping, 1203-1205, 1221-1222
RAID disk storage system, 136-148
SCSI drives, 135-136
selecting client workstations, 160
troubleshooting NetWare installation, 465
disk duplexing, 327-328
disk elevator seeking, optimizing, 906-908
disk hardware, checking for newly installed, 1054
disk mirroring, 327-328
disk serving systems (history of networks), 12
disk stripping (RAID 0 level), 138-139, 141-142
diskettes
client diskettes, 394-396
distribution, extracting/copying files from, 1148
DOS/Windows Client software
from CD-ROM, 508
from server, 510
OS/2 Client software
from CD-ROM, 509-510
from server, 510-514
diskless workstations, creating boot images, 1137
disks
operating system parameters, setting, 1081-1082
troubleshooting, 949-952
DISMOUNT server console command, 1029-1030
dismounting volumes
auditing, 660
automatic, 950
DISPLAY command (login scripts), 548-549
DISPLAY NETWORKS server console command, 1030-1031

DISPLAY SERVERS server console command, 1031-1032
distance vector routing protocols, 976
distinguished names (DIB objects), 1229
distributed databases, 38, 1229
DIB (Directory Information Base), 292-295
partitions, 1232
distributed network administration, 247
distributed processing, 4-6, 13
distribution diskettes/CD-ROM, extracting/copying files from, 1148
distribution lists, creating (e-mail), 601-602
DLLs (dynamic link libraries), DOS Requester, 526-527
DMA (Direct Memory Access), 16-17
channels, 359
conflicts, 349, 391-392
document exchange, 770
document management, 770
documentation, 367, 672, 1254-1256
business processes, 681
cabling documentation, 1255
client workstations, 1255
configuration management, 673-677
controlling network growth, 674-675
data/information, 680-681
ElectroText and DynaText, 956
error logs (troubleshooting network problems), 1256
goals, setting, 682

historical documentation (troubleshooting), 1255-1256
interrupted service, 676
inventory tools, 688-690
NetWare tools, 683-684
network applications, 786-787
physical inventory, 690-692
reducing maintenance expenses, 675-676
resistance from users, 677
SNMP-based tools, 685-687
software tools, 684
standards (hardware/software), 676-677
third-party network tools, 684-687
topography of network, 678-679
topology of network, 679-680
tracking financial assets, 674
troubleshooting benefits, 674
user profiles, 1255
DOMAIN NLM, 1118-1119
domains (OSP), producing, 1118-1119
DOS
command line, returning to, 1035-1036
deleting from memory, 1052-1053
FirstMail for DOS, 604
NET.CFG, 515-516
NETADMIN utility, 1184-1194
NETUSER utility, 1200, 1218-1224
network administration, 1144
partitions
creating, 364-365
installing NetWare, 443-444

PARTMGR (Partition Manager) utility, 835-844
user network management, 1145
workstation client files, 507-510
DOS environment identifier variables (login scripts), 564
DOS Requester
client drivers, 397-400
installing, 524-527
DOS/Windows Client software
diskettes from CD-ROM, 508
diskettes from server, 510
DOS/Windows clients, installing, 510-516
DOWN server console command, 323, 1032-1033
downsizing network applications, 761-775
drive bays (servers), 148
DRIVE command (login scripts), 550
drive maps, 1141
drive mirroring (RAID 1 level), 140-141
drivers, *see* device drivers
Drives command (NETUSER utility), 1221-1222
DSMERGE NLM, 1114
DSREPAIR NLM, 1119-1122
DT, *see* DynaText
DTE (Data Terminal Equipment), 679
DTPLM (Data Transmission Performance Level Marking) program, 193
Dual Attachment Stations (DAS), 215-216
DUPBIND command line utility (server upgrades), 479

duplexing disk drives, 25-26, 327-328
troubleshooting, 952
dust (environmental issues), 331
DX (overdrive) processors, 121-122
dynamic configuration, 902-903
directory cache buffers, 904-905
elevator seeking, 906-908
file cache buffers, 905-906
file/record locks, 912-913
NLM memory, 914-915
packet receive buffers (PRBs), 908-912
server process execution priority, 913-914
dynamic memory discovery, 21
dynamic volume size increasing, 22
DynaText, 432-440
installing, 433-435
NetWare, installing, 439
searching, 435-438
user training, 712-713

E

e-mail, 11, 64
configuring MHS, 595-602
dial-in access, 797-798
distribution lists, creating, 601-602
FirstMail, 602-604
installing MHS, 593-595
mailboxes, creating, 599
message routing groups, creating, 600-601
MHS (Message Handling System), 1231
MHS Console (configuring MHS), 595-599
NDS, 592-593
network applications, 766-767

Notes, 757
user training, 704-705
workflow, 763
e.g. Software, Inc.
AuditTrack, 833
SmartPass for NetWare, 833
ECC (Error Correcting Code) memory, 116
ECNEs (Enterprise Certified Network Engineers), 169
EDIT NLM, 1114
editing properties, 1188-1197
effective object classes, 1230
Effective Rights screen, 1172-1173
EIA/TIA twisted pair cable specifications, 195
EISA (Extended Industry Standard Architecture) bus, 126-127, 158, 1230
electricity
hardware protection, 323-327
power fluctuations, 326
power outages, 323-326
static electricity, 327
UPS (uninterruptable power supply), 326-327
Electro Magnetic Interference (EMI), 188
electronic mail, *see* e-mail
ElectroText, 956
elevator seeking, optimizing, 906-908
EMI (Electro Magnetic Interference), 188
ENABLE LOGIN server console command, 1033
ENABLE TTS server console command, 1034-1035
END command (login scripts), 553

Enhanced Small-Device Interface (ESDI) disk drives, 133-134
Enterprise Certified Network Engineers (ECNEs), 169
enterprise networks, 19-20
environmental issues (hardware), 330-331
Error Correcting Code (ECC) memory, 116
error correction (modems), 813-814
error handling, setting operating system parameters, 1097-1098
error logs (servers), 116
    troubleshooting network problems, 1256
Error Messages command (NWADMIN's Help menu), 1184
errors
    alignment errors, 949
    cabling faults, 946-947
    Carrier Sense Lost, 947
    causing abends (ABnormal ENDs), 934-936
    collisions, 944
    CRC (Cyclic Redundancy Check), 945-946
    jabbers (long packets), 947-948
    late events, 948
    long frames, 948
    NetWare Directory Services database, resolving, 1119-1122
    read-after-write verification, 951
    short frames (runts), 948
ESDI (Enhanced Small-Device Interface) disk drives, 133-134
Ethernet, 95-97, 203-213, 1230
    5-4-3 rule, 1260
    10Base2, 206-207, 1260-1261

    10Base5, 204-206, 1261
    10BaseT, 208-209, 1262
    100 Mbps networks, 210-213
    100VG-AnyLAN, 211-213
    802.2 frame type, 923
    802.3 (Raw) frame type, 921-923
    advantages, 203-204
    cabling distances, 1259-1262
    CSMA/CD, 209-210
    disadvantages, 204
    Fast Ethernet/100BaseX, 213
    fiber-optic cable, 420
    frame formats, 972-974
        troubleshooting NetWare installation, 465
    thin coax cable, 408-409
    twisted pair cabling, 414-416
Ethernet_II frame types, 925
Ethernet_SNAP (Sub-Network Access Protocol) frame type, 924
evaluation teams, network applications, 783
event-driven systems, 16
events, troubleshooting
    change events, 930-933
    late events, 948
EXEC command (menu systems), 578-579
EXEC DOS command (menus), 579
EXEC EXIT command (menus), 579
EXEC LOGOUT command (menus), 579
execution threads, abends (ABnormal ENDs), 934-936
exercising disk (burn in), 366

Exit command (NWADMIN's Object menu), 1177
EXIT server console command, 1035-1036
    login scripts, 550
Expand command (NWADMIN's View menu), 1178
expandability of servers, 21-22, 148-149
expanded memory (workstations), 381-382
expansion slots (servers), 149
explicitly granted trustee rights, 1170
Extended Industry Standard Architecture (EISA) bus, 126-127, 158, 1230
extended memory
    CMOS settings, 375
    workstations, 381
extensions
    menu source files, 573
    PDF (printer definition files), 748-749
external cache, 378
external interference (cabling), 187-188
external IPX addresses, 289
external routers, 963
extracting files from distribution diskettes/CD-ROM, 1148

F

Fast Ethernet media, 97
Fast Ethernet/100BaseX, 213
FAT (File Allocation Table), updating (troubleshooting), 951
fault management, 673
fault tolerance, 14, 116-117
    Frame Relay networks, 234-235

RAID, 145
system fault tolerance
level I (SFT I), 22-24
system fault tolerance
level II (SFT II), 24-26
system fault tolerance
level III (SFT III), 26-27
fax servers, 114
fax services, 772-774
**FDDI (Fiber Distributed
Data Interface), 99,
214-221, 1230**
compared to 100 Mbps
Ethernet, 210
**FDISPLAY command
(login scripts), 551**
**fiber-optic cable, 195-196,
419-420**
file caching
operating system param-
eters, setting, 1068-1070
optimizing buffers,
905-906
file servers, 4-5, 113
console security, 608,
639-640
installing DynaText, 435
naming conventions, 277
NDS tree structure
blueprint, 286-287
RAM problems, 359
see also servers
**file serving operating
systems (history of
networks), 12**
file sharing, 10
file systems
archiving system require-
ments, 865-866
capacity, 28-29
managing, 1137-1138
operating system param-
eters, setting, 1072-1078
rights
*granting via FILER
utility, 634-635*
*granting via
NETAdmin, 633-634*

*granting via NWAdmin,
631-632*
*granting via RIGHTS
command, 635-636*
security, 608, 624-630
**file-by-file backups,
872-873**
**file-service protocols,
105-106**
file-system cache, 28
filename formats, 450
**FILER command line
utility, 634-638, 1137-1138**
files
attributes
*archiving system
requirements, 866*
*viewing/modifying,
1138-1139*
audit files, 666-668
sizes, 659-661
AUTOEXEC.BAT, 451-452
AUTOEXEC.NCF, 463
background compression,
46-47
*archiving system
requirements, 868-869*
backups, 337-339
compression, user train-
ing, 701-702
concurrency control, 13
CONFIG.SYS, DOS
Requester, 525
congruency issues,
archiving system require-
ments, 867-868
copying, 1142
*from distribution
diskettes/CD-ROM,
1148*
*NetWare files to SYS:
volume, 457-458*
extensions
menu source files, 573
*PDF (printer definition
files), 748-749*
extracting from distribu-
tion diskettes/
CD-ROM, 1148

information about,
1143-1144
INSTALL.BAT, 445-446
local, updating with
network files, 1157
locks, optimizing, 912-913
migration, user
training, 702
network documentation,
680-681
network files, redirecting
data to, 1133-1135
NLM message files,
determining languages,
1037-1038
non-DOS files, storing on
NetWare volumes,
1019-1020
owners, modifying,
1138-1139
printer definition files,
748-749
purging, 1152
rights, 625-626, 1153-1154
SERVER.EXE, 986
STARTUP.NCF, 462
text files, printing,
1146-1147
TIMESYNC.CFG,
1084-1088
user training, 701-702
**filters (audit reports),
664-666**
**finding bottlenecks,
925-926**
**FIRE PHASERS command
(login scripts), 551**
FirstMail, 602-604
FirstMail for DOS, 604
**FirstMail for Windows,
603-604**
fixed disk drives, *see*
hard drives
fixes, backups, 344
**FLAG command line
utility, 638, 1138-1139**
**flexible licensing
(NetWare), 64-65**

floppy disk drives
  BIOS, 384
  cleaning, 384
  CMOS settings, 377
  installing, 383
  workstations, 382-384
   selecting, 160
FlowMark workflow, 763
fluctuations in power, 326
Form Feed flag (print services), 740
forms
  creating via PRINTDEF utility, 750-751
  printers, creating/deleting/modifying, 1150
Frame Relay networks, 232-235
frame types
  Ethernet networks, 96-97
  optimizing, 920-925
  registering, 1048-1049
frames
  formats (Ethernet), troubleshooting NetWare installation, 465
  long frames, troubleshooting, 948
  short frames (runts), troubleshooting, 948
  types, 972-974
   specifying, 992-993
freeing memory, 43
Frye Utilities for Networks (Frye Computer Systems, Inc.), 832, 898
full backups, 872
future developments (RAID disk storage system), 146

G

Get Aliased Object Trustee command (NWADMIN's Options menu), 1179

GETO command (menu systems), 584
GETP command (menu systems), 585-587
GETR command (menu systems), 584-585
goals (network documentation), 682
Gold Resellers, 957
GOTO command (login scripts), 551-552
Grandfather-Father-Son rotation scheme (backups), 335
graphics, network applications, 768-770
group administrators, 242
Group objects, 256, 269, 1165
  creating, 536-537
groups
  information about, viewing, 1145-1146
  rights, 621-622, 1153-1154
groupware, 756

H

Hamming error correction codes (RAID 2 level), 141-142
hard drives, 130-136
  adding to servers, 988-991
  CMOS settings, 375-377
  selecting client workstations, 160
hard errors, media defects, 341
hardware, 386-392
  addresses, 994
   conflicts, 389-391
  archiving hardware, 874-876
  backups, 340-341
  base memory address conflicts, 353-356
  base port addresses, 358

BIOS, 372
  troubleshooting setup, 360
bridges, 225-226
burn in, 351, 365-367
bus architecture, 1229
bus mastering devices, 359
CD-ROM drives, installing, 364
client workstations
  bus architecture, 157-159
  cases, 154
  CPUs, 155-157
  dealers, 162
  desktop cases, 153
  disk drives, 160
  keyboards, 161-162
  motherboards, 154-159
  mouse, 162
  network operating system requirements, 163-164
  power supplies, 154
  RAM, 159
  tower cases, 153-154
  UPS (Uninterruptable Power Supplies), 162
  user profiles, 152
  video controllers/ monitors, 161
CMOS settings, 374-379
communications between peripherals, 352
configuring BIOS, 362-364
disaster recovery, 881
disk drives, installing, 360
DMA (Direct Memory Access)
  channels, 359
  conflicts, 349, 391-392
documenting, 367
duplexing, 327-328
electricity, 323-327
environmental issues, 330-331
expandability, 21-22

history of networks, 12
installing, 349-351
interrupts, 386-389
inventory tools (network
  documentation), 688-690
IRQs (interrupt request
  lines), 348, 356-358
LANs, troubleshooting,
  938-940
maintenance
  contracts, 316
memory address conflicts,
  348-349
mirrored servers, 27
mirroring, 327-328
newly installed disk
  hardware, checking
  for, 1054
Novell-approved hard-
  ware, 167-168
polling, 386
port address conflicts, 348
POST test, 372-374
power conditioning
  devices, 368
power fluctuations, 326
power outages, 323-326
preproduction testing, 934
protecting, 322-345
RAM, 328-329, 359
redundancy, 327-330
repeaters, 224
replacement parts,
  367-368
routers, 226-228
servers, 112
  *386 DX processor,
    120-121*
  386 SX processor, 120
  486 processor, 121
  *application servers,
    113-114*
  balancing, 117
  *bus architectures,
    123-130*
  *communication
    servers, 114*

database servers, 114
designing networks, 148
disk caching, 131-133
drive bays, 148
*DX (overdrive) proces-
  sor, 121-122*
EISA bus, 126-127
*ESDI disk drives,
  133-134*
expandability, 148-149
expansion slots, 149
fault tolerance, 116-117
fax servers, 114
file servers, 113
*hard disk drives,
  130-136*
*Hierarchical Bus,
  129-130*
IDE disk drives, 134
ISA bus, 123-125
MCA bus, 125-126
memory, 117-119
PCI bus, 128
*Pentium processor,
  122-123*
Powerbus, 129
processors, 119-123
*RAID disk storage
  system, 136-148*
*RAM expansion,
  148-149*
*SCSI disk drives,
  135-136*
selecting, 114-117
*service contracts,
  115-116*
*TriFlex bus architec-
  ture, 129*
vendor certification, 115
VESA bus, 127-128
SFT III (system fault
  tolerance), 329
static electricity, 327
troubleshooting configurations, 348-349
UPS (uninterruptable
  power supply), 326-327

workgroup administrator
  training, hardware
  acquisitions, 708
workstations, 371-379
**HCSS (High Capacity
  Storage System), 44**
**help, accounting informa-
  tion/support sources,
  898-899**
**help desk (technical
  support), 714**
**Help menu commands
  (NWADMIN), 1184**
**HELP server console
  command, 1036**
**Hierarchical Bus architec-
  ture, 129-130**
**hierarchical
  databases, 1233**
**hierarchical network
  administration, 248**
**Hierarchical Storage
  Management,
  backups, 343**
**High Capacity Storage
  System (HCSS), 44**
**high-speed communica-
  tions links, 816**
  ATM (Asynchronous
    Transfer Mode), 818
  ISDN, 817
  SMDS (Switched Megabit
    Data Services), 817-818
  Switched 56, 817
hiring
  consultants, 168-170
  technicians, 170-171
**historical documentation
  (troubleshooting),
  1255-1256**
history of networks, 11-13
hops, 976
host computers, 798-800
  internetwork
    connectivity, 984
**host packet formats,
  connections, 426**

HostPrint, 75-77
Hot-Fix, 949
hubs, 1230
    twisted pair cabling, 412
hybrid topology, 9-10, 186

I

I/O (input/output)
    address conflicts, 389-391
    requests, disk drives,
    131-133
IBM cable types
    (token ring networks),
    1262-1263
IBM twisted pair cable
    specifications, 192-193
IDE (Integrated Drive
    Electronics) drives,
    134, 160
    configuring BIOS, 362-363
    installing multiple,
    360-361
identifier variables (login
    scripts), 561-565
    date identifier variables,
    561-562
    DOS environment identi-
    fier variables, 564
    network identifier vari-
    ables, 563
    object properties identifier
    variables, 564-565
    time identifier
    variables, 562
    user identifier variables,
    562-563
    workstation identifier
    variables, 563-564
IEEE (Institute of Electri-
    cal and Electronics
    Engineers) standards, 95
IF...THEN command
    (login scripts), 552
image backups, 871
image processing, 769
image-enabled NetWare, 66

imaging, 768-770
implementation (NetWare
    installation), 309-315
    installation/training,
    313-315
    network admini-
    stration, 250
    planning/testing, 310-312
    production, 315
    purchasing/installation,
    312-313
importing user objects
    into directory tree, 1156
in-band management, 820
in-place server upgrades,
    468, 485-499
INCLUDE command
    (login scripts), 553-554
Include command
    (NWADMIN's View
    menu), 1178
incremental backups, 872
indexing, 770
Industry Standard Archi-
    tecture (ISA) bus,
    123-125, 157, 1231
INETCFG
    (internetworking con-
    figuration) NLM, 980-983
    installing NICs, 998-999
infant mortality (server
    hardware), 365
Information option (man-
    aging print jobs), 736
infrared (wireless commu-
    nications networks), 223
inheritance
    file system rights (secu-
    rity), 627-628
    NDS rights (security),
    620-621
    object inheritance, 1232
Inherited Rights Filter
    (IRF), 623-624, 627
Inherited Rights Filter
    screen, 1171-1172
INSTALL NLM, 1114
    installing NICs, 997-998

INSTALL.BAT file, 445-446
installation time (plan-
    ning NetWare installa-
    tion), 307
installing
    accounting, 888-890
    cables, 170-171
    CD-ROM drives, 364
    clients, 393-394
    coax cable, 190
    connectors, 406-428
    disk drives, 360
    DOS Requester, 524-527
    DOS/Windows clients,
    510-516
    DynaText, 433-435
    floppy drives, 383
    hardware, 349-351
    media, 406-428
    MHS, 593-595
    multiple IDE drives,
    360-361
    multiple SCSI drives, 361
    NetSync, 845
    NetWare, 442
        AUTOEXEC.BAT file,
        451-452
        AUTOEXEC.NCF file,
        creating, 463
        CD-ROM drive setup,
        444-445
        code pages,
        configuring, 448
        copying boot files,
        447-448
        copying files to SYS:
        volume, 457-458
        country codes, configur-
        ing, 448
        disk drivers, loading,
        452-453
        DOS partitions,
        364-365, 443-444
        DynaText online
        information, 439
        filename formats, 450
        INSTALL.BAT file,
        445-446

internal IPX network numbers, 446-447
keyboard mapping, configuring, 448
LAN drivers, loading, 452-453
license disk, 456-457
NDS trees, 459-460
NetWare partitions, 454-456
planning, 304-319
registering memory, 450
registration disk, 463-464
server names, 446-447
STARTUP.NCF file, creating, 462
time zone information, 460-462
troubleshooting, 464-465
network applications, 787
NICs (network interface cards), 351-360, 384-386
OS/2 Requester, 516-522
servers, default partitions, 296
software, 504-522
instances
common names, 1229
object instances, 1232
Integrated Drive Electronics (IDE) disk drives, 134, 160
Integrated Services Digital Network (ISDN), 235-236, 817
Intel
LANDesk Manager, 832, 861
NetSight, 832
processors, 119-123
interfaces
backups, 333
NMS (NetWare Management System), 860-861
internal cache, 378

internal IPX addresses, 289, 994-995
internal IPX network numbers, 446-447
internal routers, 227-228, 963
internationalization of NetWare, 56-57
Internet, 791
Internet Packet eXchange protocol, *see* **IPX protocol**
internetworks, 12-13, 962
capabilities, 10-11
component configurations, 980-983
host connectivity, 984
multi-protocol, components, 964-974
routing data with NetWare's native protocols, 974-980
types, 962-964
interrupt request lines (IRQs), 356-358
conflicts, 348
interrupts, 386
conflicts, 387-389
intruder detection (security), 616-618
inventory (network documentation), 1255
inventory tools, 688-690
physical inventory, 690-692
inverse multiplexing, 236
IP protocols, NetWare/IP, 984
IPX (Internet Packet eXchange) protocol, 81, 804, 920, 975, 1231
configuring for RIP/SAP or NLSP use, 982-983
internal addresses, 994-995
network addresses, 289, 995-997

IPX.COM LAN drivers, updating, 1158
IPX/SPX (Internet Packet eXchange/ Sequenced Packet eXchange) protocol, 31, 101-102
IPXS NLM, 1114
IPXS/SPXS NLM, 970
IRF (Inherited Rights Filter), 623-624, 627-628
IRQs (interrupt request lines), 356-358
conflicts, 348, 387-389
ISA (Industry Standard Architecture) bus, 123-125, 157, 1231
ISDN (Integrated Services Digital Network), 235-236, 817
ISO (International Standards Organization), 775
ITEM command (menu systems), 579-581

J–K

jabbers (long packets), troubleshooting, 947-948
journalized archives, 874
justifying costs, 178-179

KEYB NLM, 1122-1123
keyboard mapping, configuring, 448
keyboards
CMOS settings, 378
selecting client workstations, 161-162
server console, changing types, 1122-1123
Klos Technologies, Inc.'s PacketView, 833

L

LAN drivers
binding protocols to,
troubleshooting, 941-942
IPX.COM, updating, 1158
loading, 452-453,
1039-1041
*troubleshooting,
940-941*
troubleshooting NetWare
installation, 465
unbinding protocols from,
1105-1107
workstation updates, 524
**LAN Innernetwork (LIN),
796-797**
**LAN Outernetwork (LON),
796-797**
**LAN Support Group, Inc.'s
BindView NCS, 898**
LAN Times Buyers' Guide,
176-177
**LAN-based protocols
(remote access), 804**
**LAN-to-LAN remote-
nodes, 801**
**LANalyzer for Windows
(Novell), 832**
**LANDesk Manager (Intel),
832, 861**
**LANGUAGE server con-
sole command, 1037-1038**
**LANs (Local Area Net-
works), 1231**
ARCnet, 196-200, 1228
*data transmission,
order, 199-200*
*Network Interface
Cards, 199*
*node connections,
197-199*
ARCnet Plus, 201-203
cabling, 406-418
clients, 370
documentation, 1254-1256

Ethernet, 203-213
10Base2, 206-207
10Base5, 204-206
10BaseT, 208-209
*100 Mbps networks,
210-213*
*100VG-AnyLAN,
211-213*
advantages, 203-204
CSMA/CD, 209-210
disadvantages, 204
*Fast Ethernet/
100BaseX, 213*
FDDI, 214-221
inventory, 1255
media, 370
messages, 370
NetWare Connect, 83-85
network maps, 1254
servers, 370
token ring, 216-221
cabling, 218-220
data transmission, 220
diagnostics, 221
MSAUs, 217-218
troubleshooting
alignment errors, 949
*binding protocols to
LAN drivers, 941-942*
cabling faults, 946-947
*Carrier Sense Lost
error, 947*
collisions, 944
*CRC (Cyclic Redun-
dancy Check) errors,
945-946*
hardware, 938-940
*jabbers (long packets),
947-948*
late events, 948
*loading LAN drivers,
940-941*
long frames, 948
short frames (runts), 948
*with protocol
analyzers, 943*

wireless communications,
221-224
workstations, 371
**Large Internet Packet
(LIP) protocol, 53-55**
optimizing, 915-916
**large non-movable sys-
tems (token ring net-
works), 1264-1265**
**LASTLOGINTIME com-
mand (login scripts), 554**
**LAT (Local Area Trans-
port) protocol, 77-78**
**late events, troubleshoot-
ing, 948**
leaf objects, 267-269
naming conventions,
275-277
NDS tree structure
blueprint, 285-286
leased lines (bridges), 424
**leaves (NDS structure),
39-40**
licensing
flexibility (NetWare),
64-65
license disk, 456-457
network applications, 784
server connections,
displaying information,
1111-1112
software (budgeting tips),
177-178
**LIN (LAN Innernetwork),
796-797**
**Link Support Layer (LSL)
ODI layer, 969, 971**
**link-state routing proto-
cols, 977-978**
**LIP (Large Internet
Packet) protocol, 53-55**
optimizing, 915-916
**LIST DEVICES server
console command,
1038-1039**
**List flag (print
services), 740**

LLC (Logical Link Control) layer, 95
load balancing, 979
LOAD server console command, 1039-1041
  menu systems, 582-583
loadable device-driver interface, 21
loadable modules
  loading, 1039-1041
  unloading, 1108-1110
loading
  disk drivers, 452-453
  LAN drivers, 452-453
    troubleshooting, 940-941
  NetWare clients (user training), 696-697
  NLMs (NetWare Loadable Modules), 987
  print servers, 724-727
local (VESA) bus, 127-128, 158
Local Area Networks, *see* LANs
Local Area Transport (LAT) protocol, 77-78
local files, updating with network files, 1157
local printers, 720
locks
  files/records, optimizing, 912-913
  operating system parameters, setting, 1078-1079
  TTS (Transaction Tracking System), setting/viewing, 1155
  workstation cases, 154
logging change events, 932-933
Logical Link Control layer (LLC), 95
logical network structure, 14

logical partitions (mirrored)
  checking status, 1043-1044
  remirroring, 1051-1052
    aborting, 1018
logical structure, NetWare Directory Services (NDS), 39-41
LOGIN command line utility, 1140
login scripts, 537-566
  command syntax, 545-546
  commands
    #, 546
    ATTACH, 546-547
    BREAK, 547
    CLS, 547
    COMSPEC, 547-548
    CONTEXT, 548
    DISPLAY, 548-549
    DOS BREAK, 549
    DOS SET, 549
    DOS VERIFY, 550
    DRIVE, 550
    END, 553
    EXIT, 550
    FDISPLAY, 551
    FIRE PHASERS, 551
    GOTO, 551-552
    IF...THEN, 552
    INCLUDE, 553-554
    LASTLOGINTIME, 554
    MACHINE, 554
    MAP, 554-557
    NO_DEFAULT, 557
    NOSWAP, 557
    PAUSE, 557
    PCCOMPATIBLE, 558
    REMARK, 558
    SET, 558-559
    SET_TIME, 559
    SHIFT, 559-560
    SWAP, 560
    TEMP SET, 560
    WRITE, 561

copying
  NETADMIN, 542-543
  NetWare Administrator, 545
creating/modifying
  NETADMIN, 540-541
  NetWare Administrator, 543-544
identifier variables, 561-565
  date, 561-562
  DOS environment, 564
  network, 563
  object properties, 564-565
  time, 562
  user, 562-563
  workstation, 563-564
menu systems, 587
Profile Login Scripts, 538-539
  associating with users (NETADMIN), 541-542
  associating with users (NetWare Administrator), 544
sample script, 565-566
System Login Scripts, 538-539
User Login Scripts, 538-539
user training, 700-701
logins
  disabling, 1027-1028
  enabling, 1033
  NetWare Directory Services (NDS), 37
  security, 608-618
  to networks, 1140
  tracking, 887
  user training, 697-698
LOGOUT command line utility, 1140-1141
logouts
  from networks, 1140-1141
  tracking, 887

LON (LAN Outernetwork), 796-797

long frames, troubleshooting, 948

long packets (jabbers), troubleshooting, 947-948

LSL (Link Support Layer) ODI layer, 969, 971

M

MAC (Media Access Control layer), 95

MACHINE command (login scripts), 554

Macintosh, selecting client workstations, 164

MAGAZINE server console command, 1041-1042

magazines
  confirming request satisfaction, 1041-1042
  training staff, 1243-1244

mailboxes, creating, 599

mainframe connections, 426-428

maintenance
  accounting files, 886, 894-895
  backups, 342
  contracts, troubleshooting NetWare installation, 316

Manage according to search pattern command (NETADMIN utility), 1194-1196

Manage objects command (NETADMIN utility), 1186-1197

Management Information Base (MIB), 106-107

ManageWise (network documentation), 686-687

MAP command line utility, 1141
  login scripts, 554-557

mapping drives, 1203-1205, 1221-1222

Mark flag (print services), 740

Master CNE program, 169

Master replicas (partitions), 288-289, 296

MATHLIB NLM, 1114

MATHLIBC NLM, 1114

MCA (Micro Channel Architecture) bus, 125-126, 157

mean time between failures (MTBF), 330

mechanical breakdowns, media defects, 342

media, 370
  bridges, 424
  cabling, 406-418
  confirming request satisfaction, 1042-1043
  defective backups, 341-342
  filters (token ring networks), 1265
  installing, 406-428
  rotating for backups, 873
  routers, 425
  sectors, fault tolerance, 22-23

Media Access Control (MAC) layer, 95

MEDIA server console command, 1042-1043

memory
  adding to servers, 991-992
  address conflicts, 348-349
  addressable, listing, 1043
  allocation speed, 44
  availability, determining, 1001-1002
  base memory address conflicts, 353-356
  BIOS setup (troubleshooting), 360
  capacity, 28
  DMA (Direct Memory Access), 16-17
    channels, 359
    conflicts, 349, 391-392

dynamic memory discovery, 21
  freeing, 43
  management, 43-44
  NetWare memory configurations, 16-17
  NLMs, optimizing, 914-915
  operating system parameters, setting, 1066-1068
  optional memory protection, 50-52
  PROM (Programmable Read Only Memory), 385
  protection, 16-17, 33
  RAM (Random Access Memory)
    expansion (servers), 148-149
    optimizing (servers), 916
    selecting client workstations, 159
    troubleshooting file servers, 359
  registering, 450, 1049-1051
  server hardware, 117-119
  shared memory, 16-17
  troubleshooting NetWare installation, 465
  virtual memory, 16-17, 120
  workstations, 379-382

MEMORY server console command, 1043

menu windows, changing colors, 1135-1136

menus, 568-589
  colors, 577-578
  comparing Saber to NetWare, 568-569
  compiling source files, 573-574
  converting from NetWare 3.11 menus, 588
  creating source files, 573, 575-577
  customized, calling, 1146

designing, 570, 572-573
executing, 575
login scripts, 587
menu system commands
   EXEC, 578-579
   GETO, 584
   GETP, 585-587
   GETR, 584-585
   GETx formats, 583-584
   ITEM, 579-581
   LOAD, 582-583
   SHOW, 581-582
placement onscreen, 577
previous NetWare menu
  systems, 568
security issues, 570-572
sizing, 577
submenus, 581-583
user input options,
  583-587
merging
partitions, 837
trees (NDS), 42
mesh topology, 8, 184
Message Handling System, *see* MHS
message routing groups, creating, 600-601
messages, 370, 766-767
receiving, 1154-1155
sending, 1022-1024,
  1058-1059, 1154-1155,
  1214-1215, 1220-1221
Messages command (NETUSER utility), 1220-1221
MHS (Message Handling System), 64, 1231
configuring, 595-602
distribution lists, creating,
  601-602
FirstMail, 602-604
installing, 593-595
mailboxes, creating, 599
message routing groups,
  creating, 600-601
NDS, 592-593

MHS Console (configuring MHS), 595-599
MIB (Management Information Base), 106-107
Micro Channel Architecture (MCA) bus, 125-126, 157
Microcom Networking Protocol (MNP), 813
Microsoft System Diagnostics, 683
MIGRATE
bindery emulation, 469
server upgrades, 468-501
migration, 29, 44-45
across-the-wire migration,
  469-476
Data Migration system,
  archiving system requirements, 869-870
in-place migration,
  485-499
real-time migration,
  1123-1124
same-server migration,
  476-484
to NetWare, 250
user training, 702
mini-computers, connections, 426-428
MIRROR STATUS server console command, 1043-1044
mirrored drives, 24-25, 327-328
logical partitions, checking
  status, 1043-1044
servers, 26
troubleshooting, 952
Mirrored Server Link (MSL), 26
MLID (Multiple Link Interface Driver) ODI layer, 969, 971
MNP (Microcom Networking Protocol), 813

modems
data compression, 813-815
error correction, 813-814
MNP (Microcom Networking Protocol), 813
selecting, 811-818
standards, 812-813
UARTs (serial port data
  transfer), 815-816
V.32 modem standard,
  812-813
V.32bis modem
  standard, 813
V.42 modem standard, 814
V.42bis modem standard,
  814-815
V.FAST modem
  standard, 812
modular design (NetWare), 17-18
modules
imformation about, listing,
  1044-1045
loadable
  loading, 1039-1041
  unloading, 1108-1110
viewing from within
  debugger, 937-938
MODULES server console command, 1044-1045
moisture (environmental issues), 331
MONITOR NLM, 1114
monitors/video controllers, selecting client workstations, 161
motherboards, 154-159
MOUNT form flag (print services), 741
MOUNT server console command, 1045-1047
mounting volumes
consistency checks, 24
troubleshooting, 951
mouse, 162
Move command (NWADMIN's Object menu), 1176

moving
 containers, 837-838
 partitions, 837-838
MPR (Multi-Protocol Router), 80-83
MS-DOS, selecting client workstations, 163
MSAUs (Multi-Station Access Units), 217-218
 concentrators, 418-424
 token ring, 417-418
MSL (Mirrored Server Link), 26
MTBF (mean time between failures), 330
Multi-Protocol Router (MPR), 80-83
multi-meters, 421
multi-protocol internetwork components, 964-974
Multi-Protocol Router, 963-964
Multi-Station Access Units, see MSAUs
multilingual support, 56-57
multimedia, 770-772
multiple IDE drives, installing, 360-361
multiple inheritance, 1232
Multiple Link Interface Driver (MLID) ODI layer, 969, 971
multiple primary time servers (NDS), 300
multiple SCSI drives, installing, 361
multiple users (network applications), 756
multiplexing, 126, 236-237
multiprotocol support (communications servers), 819
multithreading, 120

N

NACS (NetWare Asynchronous Communications Server), 807-808
NAECs (Novell Authorized Education Centers), 172, 1238-1239
NAME server console command, 1047
name space architecture, 30
name space modules
 loading, 1039-1041
 unloading, 1108-1110
name space support
 adding to servers, 1000-1003
 archiving system requirements, 866-867
names
 DIB objects, context, 1229
 directories, renaming, 1153
 naming conventions
  advantages, 272
  container objects, 273-274
  Country objects, 274
  file servers, 277
  leaf objects, 275-277
  NDS structure, 260
  object property values, 275-276
  Organization objects, 274
  Organizational Unit objects, 274
  planning, 272-273
  printer objects, 276-277
  [Root] object, 273
  user objects, 275-276
 objects (NDS structure), 40
 servers
  displaying, 1047
  installing NetWare, 446-447
NAS (NetWare Access Server), 806-807

NASCs (Novell Authorized Service Centers), 957
NCONSOLE (Avanti Technologies), 833
NCOPY command line utility, 1142
NCP (NetWare Core Protocol), 104-105, 976, 1231
 operating system parameters, setting, 1089-1091
 Packet Signatures, 611-612
NDIR command line utility, 1143-1144
NDMS (NetWare Distributed Management Services) strategy, 855
NDS (NetWare Directory Services), 13, 19-20, 36-42, 244-245, 1231
 APIs (Application Program Interfaces), 781-782
 applications, 38
 backups, 340
 backward compatibility, 41-42, 293
 compared to bindery, 37-38
 database, resolving errors/repairing, 1119-1122
 DIB (Directory Information Base), 38, 292-295
  archiving, 63
 directory trees, 280-290
  adding servers, 1005-1008
  blueprints, 284-288
  coordinating structures, 290
  current context, viewing/changing, 1136-1137
  levels of depth, 287-288
  merging/renaming, 42
  number of trees, 281
  planning/coordination, 281-290, 311
  templates, 284-285

global structure, 256-257
installing NetWare,
  459-460
IPX network
  addresses, 289
logging in, 37
logical structure, 39-41
MHS services, 592-593
network documentation
  tools, 683
objects, 259-269
organizational structure,
  257-259
partitions, 292-293,
  295-298
    administrating, 835-844
    default partitions, 296
    replicating, 295-297
    replication blueprints,
      288-289
    Skulker (updating
      partition replicas), 297
    splitting, 297
rights, granting, 630-633
security, 608, 618-624
time synchronization,
  298-300
troubleshooting, 952-955
user training, 698-699
utilities, 290
VLMs (Virtual Loadable
  Modules), 42
NEAP (Novell Education
  Alliance Partner), 172
needs analysis (network
  applications), 783
NET.CFG
  client drivers, 400-401
  DOS, 515-516
  OS/2, 521-522
  updating, 527-528
NETADMIN command
  line utility, 290, 1144,
  1184-1194
  creating group objects, 536
  creating user accounts,
    534-535

granting
  file system rights,
    633-634
  NDS rights, 632-633
login scripts
  copying, 542-543
  creating/modifying,
    540-541
profile login scripts,
  associating with user
  accounts, 541-542
versus NWADMIN utility
  (accounting), 895
NetBIOS, 103-104
NetExplorer servers,
  855-857
NetSight (Intel), 832
NetSync NLM set, 844-846
NETUSER command line
  utility, 1145, 1200
  Attachment command,
    1222-1223
  Change Context command,
    1223-1224
  Drives command,
    1221-1222
  Messages command,
    1220-1221
  Printing command,
    1219-1220
  starting, 1218-1219
  user training, 703-704
NetView, 108
NetWare
  auditing, 47-49
  back-end services, 16-19
  background file compres-
    sion, 46-47
  backwards compati-
    bility, 293
  bindery, 293-295
  bindery emulation, 1228
  block suballocation, 45
  client operating system
    support, 29-30
  data migration, 44-45
  disk caching, 131-133

dynamic memory discov-
  ery, 21
dynamic volume size
  increasing, 22
e-mail, 64
enterprise networks, 19-20
event-driven system, 16
expandability, 21-22
fault tolerance, 22-27
file system capacity, 28-29
future developments, 19
image-enabled, 66
implementation cost,
  166-179
installing, 442
  AUTOEXEC.BAT file,
    451-452
  AUTOEXEC.NCF file,
    creating, 463
  CD-ROM drive setup,
    444-445
  code pages,
    configuring, 448
  copying boot files,
    447-448
  copying files to SYS:
    volume, 457-458
  country codes, configur-
    ing, 448
  disk drivers, loading,
    452-453
  DOS partitions, 443-444
  DOS partitions, creat-
    ing, 364-365
  DynaText online
    information, 439
  filename formats, 450
  INSTALL.BAT file,
    445-446
  internal IPX network
    numbers, 446-447
  keyboard mapping,
    configuring, 448
  LAN drivers, loading,
    452-453
  license disk, 456-457
  NDS trees, 459-460

NetWare partitions,
454-456
planning the installa-
tion, 304-319
registering memory, 450
registration disk,
463-464
server names, 446-447
STARTUP.NCF file,
creating, 462
time zone information,
460-462
troubleshooting,
464-465
internal routing, 227-228
internationalization, 56-57
licensing flexibility, 64-65
loadable device-driver
interface, 21
memory capacity, 28
memory configurations,
16-17
memory management,
43-44
menu system compared to
Saber menu system,
568-569
modular design, 17-18
name space
architecture, 30
network administration
roles, 240-245
network documentation
tools, 683-684
online documentation,
67-68
optional memory protec-
tion, 33, 50-52
print services, 57-60
protocol stacks, 31
replaceable routers, 56
routing protocol support,
55-56
RSA (Rivest-Adleman-
Shamir) public-key
crypto-system, 49-50
scalability, 20
scheduler, 42-43

server-based applications,
18-19, 32-33
settings, 1215-1216
SMS (Storage Manage-
ment Services), 61-63
utilities, 66-67
WAN (wide-area net-
works) environments,
53-56
NetWare 2.x-to-3.12 in-
place upgrades, 487-493
NetWare 3.11 menu
system, 568
converting to NetWare 4.x
menus, 588
NetWare 3.1x
bindery server manage-
ment, 844-846
NetWare 3.1x-to-4.x in-
place upgrades, 493-499
NetWare 4.1. for OS/2,
65-66
NetWare 4.x, upgrad-
ing, 501
NetWare Access Server
(NAS), 806-807
NetWare Asynchronous
Communication Server
(NACS), 807-808
NetWare certification,
archiving system re-
quirements, 870
NetWare Connect, 83-85,
810-811
NetWare Core Protocol
(NCP), 104-105, 976, 1231
NetWare Directory
Services, see NDS
NetWare Distributed
Management Services
(NDMS) strategy, 855
NetWare DOS
Requester, 972
NetWare file system,
archiving system re-
quirements, 865-866
NetWare for DEC Access,
77-78

NetWare for SAA,
73-75, 426
NetWare HostPrint, 75-77
NetWare HostPrint/400,
75-77
NetWare LANalyzer Agent
(NLA), 858-860
NetWare Link Services
Protocol (NLSP), 55,
977-980
NetWare Loadable
Modules, see NLMs
NetWare Management
Agent (NMA), 857-858
NetWare Management
System, see NMS
NetWare Multi-Protocol
Router (MPR), 80-83
NetWare NFS services,
78-80
NetWare partitions
(installing NetWare),
454-456
NetWare Remote Shell, 806
NetWare servers (leaf
object), 269
NetWare Tools, 515
NetWare Users Interna-
tional (NUI), 957, 1244
NetWare/IP protocol, 984
NetWire (CompuServe
forum), 955-956, 1246
advantages, 1247
posting messages,
1247-1251
troubleshooting NetWare
installation, 317-319
network addresses
restrictions (security),
615-616
servers, 993-997
network administration,
240-251
accounting
ATOTAL (Accounting
Services Total) utility,
896-897
configuration, 890-894

*information / support
  sources, 898-899*
installation, 888-890
maintenance, 894-895
*NWADMIN versus
  NETADMIN, 895*
printing services, 898
*purpose and uses,
  884-888*
removing, 895
reports, 898
administrators, 241-242
archiving
  *file-by-file backups,
    872-873*
  hardware, 874-876
  image backups, 871
  importance, 864-865
  journalized archives, 874
  perpetual archives, 874
  requirements, 865-870
  rotating media, 873
  *SMS (Storage Manage-
    ment Services),
    877-881*
  software, 874-877
area administrators,
  242-243
bindery server manage-
  ment, 844-846
centralized network
  administration, 246-247
departmental liaisons,
  248-249
disaster recovery, 881
distributed network
  administration, 247
DOS, 1144
group administrators, 242
hierarchical network
  administration, 248
implementation/migration
  personnel, 250
management products,
  829-835
NDS (NetWare Directory
  Service), 244-245

NMS (NetWare Manage-
  ment System), 855-862
organizational structures,
  246-248
partition management,
  835-844
printing operators, 243
proactive approach,
  826-829
remote server manage-
  ment, 846-855
network analyzers, 1231
**network applications,
  754-793**
  APIs (Application Program
    Interfaces), 780-782
  audio, 771
  calendars, 767
  communications, 772-775
  CompuServe, 790
  conferences, 792
  data services, 773-774
  databases, 757-760
  dial-up connectivity, 773
  document exchange, 770
  document manage-
    ment, 770
  documentation, 786-787
  downsizing, 761-775
  e-mail, 766-767
  evaluation teams, 783
  fax services, 773-774
  groupware, 756
  imaging, 768-770
  indexing, 770
  installing, 787
  Internet, 791
  licensing, 784
  messaging, 766-767
  multimedia, 770-772
  multiple users, 756
  needs analysis, 783
  Notes, 756
  Office/GroupWise, 756
  Optical Character Recog-
    nition, 770

OSI (Open Systems
  Interconnect) model,
  775-778
planning installation,
  786-787
publications, 792
ranking products, 785
remote node access,
  774-775
research, 784
retrieval, 770
rightsizing, 761-775
scanners, 769
schedulers, 767
storage, 770
technical issues, 783
telephone support, 789
trade shows, 792
training, 788
TSA (Technical Support
  Alliance), 791
upsizing, 761-775
user issues, 788, 792
vendors, 784-785, 790
workflow, 762-766
**network awareness,
  778-780**
**network backup software,
  332-333**
**network charges, display-
  ing totals, 1132**
**Network File System
  (NFS), 105, 1232**
**network identifier vari-
  ables (login scripts), 563**
**network implementation/
  migration personnel, 250**
**Network Interface Cards,
  see NICs**
**Network layer (OSI
  model), 101-104, 777, 966**
**network management,
  672-673, 1232, 1254-1256**
  accounting
    management, 673
  cable management soft-
    ware, 685

configuration manage-
ment, 673-677
fault management, 673
performance
management, 673
remote access, 819-820
security management, 673
**network management
protocols, 106-108**
network maps, 1254
network numbers
changing for cabling,
1105-1107
listing, 1030-1031
**network operating sys-
tems (NOSs), 6, 163-164**
concurrency control, 13
fault tolerance, 14
future developments, 13
print services, 14
**Network Professional
Association (NPA), 169-
170, 1244-1246**
**network protocol stacks,
101-104**
**network services (OSI
layers), 966-967**
**Network Support Ency-
clopedia, Professional
Edition (NSEPro),
899, 956**
troubleshooting NetWare
installation, 316
**network-aware
applications, 779**
**network-blind
applications, 779**
**network-inherent
applications, 779**
**networking
workstations, 371**
networks
ARCnet, 196-200, 1228,
1258-1259
ARCnet Plus, 201-203
ATM (Asynchronous
Transfer Mode), 228-232

auditing, 644-669
audit files, 666-668
*Audit Files Mainte-
nance option, 656-657*
Audit History file, 666
*audit password, chang-
ing, 662*
*AUDITCON utility,
649-650, 653-656*
*configuring audits,
657-666*
*Directory Services
events, 657-658*
*Directory tree contain-
ers, 652-653*
disabling audits, 662
*displaying status,
662-663, 667*
file sizes, 659-661
*planning audits,
646-650*
preparations, 650-653
reports, 663-666
*resetting audit files,
666-667*
servers, changing, 668
*session contexts, chang-
ing, 668*
user objects, 658-659
volume audits, 651-652
baselining, 1256
bridges, 1228
cabling, 187-196
attenuation, 188-189
coax cable, 189-190
*external interference,
187-188*
*fiber-optic cable,
195-196*
*twisted pair cable,
191-195*
capabilities, 10-11
client/server networks,
6-7, 1228
common backbone net-
works, 962
connecting together,
224-228

cost (budgeting tips),
166-179
designing, 148
distributed processing
networks, 4-6
documenting, 367
*advantages to configu-
ration management,
673-676*
business processes, 681
*controlling network
growth, 674-675*
*data/information,
680-681*
*disadvantages to
configuration manage-
ment, 676-677*
goals, setting, 682
interrupted service, 676
inventory tools, 688-690
LANs, 1254-1256
NetWare tools, 683-684
*physical inventory,
690-692*
*reducing maintenance
expenses, 675-676*
*resistance from
users, 677*
*SNMP-based tools,
685-687*
software tools, 684
*standards (hardware/
software), 676-677*
*third-party network
tools, 684-687*
*topography of network,
678-679*
*topology of network,
679-680*
*tracking financial
assets, 674*
*troubleshooting
benefits, 674*
enterprise networks, 19-20
Ethernet, 203-213, 1230,
1259-1262
FDDI, 214-216
Frame Relay networks,
232-235

history, 11-13
hubs, 1230
ISDN (Integrated Services Digital Network), 235-236
LANs (Local Area Networks), 1231
listing, 1030-1031
logging in, 1140
logging out, 1140-1141
logical network structure, 14
menu systems, 568-589
NDS global structure, 256-257
peer-to-peer networks, 6-7
print services, 716-751
   CAPTURE command, 743-746
   forms, creating, 750-751
   NPRINT command, 746-747
   PCONSOLE utility, 717-729
   Print Queue Information menu, 731-737
   print queues, creating, 717-719
   print servers, creating, 719-720
   print servers, managing, 737-742
   print servers, starting, 724-727
   PRINTCON utility, 747
   PRINTDEF utility, 747-751
   printers, creating/configuring, 720-724
   redirecting output, 742-743
   testing, 727-729
   workstations, setting up, 729-731
remote access, 796-821
   communications servers, selecting, 818-821
   dial-in e-mail access, 797-798
   dial-up routers, 805
   LAN-based protocols, 804
   modems, selecting, 811-818
   NetWare Access Server (NAS), 806-807
   NetWare Asynchronous Communications Server (NACS), 807-808
   NetWare Connect, 810-811
   NetWare Remote Shell, 806
   network management, 819-820
   remote console, 808-810
   remote-control software, 798-800
   remote-node software, 800-804
   security, 820
   serial protocols, 804-805
   upgrading communications servers, 820-821
routers, 1233
security, 11, 608-641
   attribute security (files/directories), 628-630
   background authentication, 610
   directory/file rights, 625-626
   file server console security, 608, 639-640
   file system security, 608, 624-630
   group rights, 621-622
   intruder detection, 616-618
   IRF (Inherited Rights Filter), 623-624, 627-628
   login restrictions, 612-613
   login time restrictions, 615
   NCP Packet Signatures, 611-612
   NDS security, 608, 618-624
   network address restrictions, 615-616
   object rights, 618-624
   password restrictions, 613-614
   property rights, 618-624
   [Public] object, 622
   rights inheritance, 620-621, 627-628
   RSA public-key cryptosystem, 609-610
   security equivalence (granting rights), 622-623
   trustee assignments, 621-623, 626-627
SNA (System Network Architecture), 73-75
standards
   AFP (AppleTalk Filing Protocol), 105-106
   AppleTalk, 103
   ARCnet, 100-101
   de facto standards, 91-92
   de jure standards, 91
   Ethernet networks, 95-97
   FDDI (Fiber Distributed Data Interface), 99
   IPX/SPX, 101-102
   NCP (NetWare Core Protocol), 104-105
   NetBIOS, 103-104
   network management protocols, 106-108
   new technologies, 92
   NFS (Network File System), 105
   OSI (Open Systems Interconnections) model, 92-94

*proprietary standards,
90-91*
TCP/IP, 102
*token ring networks,
97-99*
T-carrier lines, 236-237
TCNS (Thomas-Conrad
Network System), 1234
test networks, planning
NetWare installation,
308-309, 312
token ring, 216-221, 1234
*cabling distances,
1262-1265*
*Source Route Bridge,
82-83*
topologies, 7-10, 183-186
version information,
displaying, 1148
WANs (Wide Area Net-
works), 228-237, 1234
wireless communications,
221-224
**NETX, comparing to VLM,
505-507**
**new technologies (stan-
dards), 92**
**newsgroups (trouble-
shooting NetWare), 319**
**NFS (Network File Sys-
tem), 78-80, 105, 1232**
**NICs (Network Interface
Cards), 5, 1232**
adding to servers, 992-999
ARCnet, 199
binding with protocols,
1020-1022
disabling, 1105-1107
information about, dis-
playing, 1026-1027
installing, 351-360,
384-386
**NLA (NetWare LANalyzer
Agent), 858-860**
**NLIST command line
utility, 290, 1145-1146**
user training, 699-700

**NLMs (NetWare Loadable
Modules), 32-33,
1113-1115, 1232**
CDROM, 1115-1118
development tools, 68
DOMAIN, 1118-1119
DSREPAIR, 1119-1122
INETCFG
(internetworking configu-
ration), 980-983, 998-999
INSTALL, 997-998
KEYB, 1122-1123
loading, 1039-1041
memory
freeing, 43
optimizing, 914-915
message files, determining
languages, 1037-1038
NetSync set, 844-846
RPL, 1123
RTDM, 1123-1124
SBACKUP, 1124-1126
SERVMAN, 1126-1128
STREAMS ODI layer,
969-970
TIMESYNC, 1128-1130
troubleshooting NetWare
installation, 465
types, 986-987
unloading, 987
**NLSP (NetWare Link
Services Protocol), 55,
977-980**
configuring IPX protocol
for, 982-983
**NMA (NetWare Manage-
ment Agent), 857-858**
NMAGENT NLM, 1114
**NMENU command line
utility, 1146**
**NMS (NetWare Manage-
ment System)**
architecture, 855-857
console interface, 860-861
database storage, 857
management agents,
857-860

management protocols, 857
snap-in modules (third-
party add-ons), 861-862
**NO_DEFAULT command
(login scripts), 557**
**node connections
(ARCnet), 197-199**
node IDs, 994
**noise (environmental
issue), 331**
**non-DOS files, storing on
NetWare volumes,
1019-1020**
**non-effective object
classes, 1232**
**non-preemptive schedul-
ing, 42-43**
**non-stop computing
(SFT III), 27**
**NOS (network operating
system), 6**
**NOSWAP command (login
scripts), 557**
Notes, 756-757
Novell
Authorized Education
Centers (NAECs), 172,
1238-1239
Authorized Service Center
(NASC), 957
computer-based training,
1242-1243
courses (staff training),
1236-1238
Education Alliance
Partner (NEAP), 172
LANalyzer for
Windows, 832
NetWare Management
Systems, 832
troubleshooting NetWare
installation, pay-per-
incident support, 316
**Novell-approved hard-
ware, 167-168**
**NPA (Network Profes-
sional Association),
169-170, 1244-1246**

NPRINT command line utility, 1146-1147
print services, 746-747
NSEPro (Network Support Encyclopedia, Professional Edition), 899, 956
troubleshooting NetWare installation, 316
NUI (NetWare Users International), 957, 1244
NUT NLM, 1114
NVER command line utility, 683-684, 1148
NWADMIN (NetWare Administrator) utility, 290, 515
granting
attributes (files/directories), 637
file system rights, 631-632
NDS rights, 630-631
Help menu commands, 1184
Object menu commands, 1163-1177
Options menu commands, 1178-1179
partition management, 835-844
preparing for using, 1160-1162
starting, 1162
Tools menu commands, 1179-1183
versus NETADMIN utility (accounting), 895
View menu commands, 1177-1178
Window menu commands, 1183-1184
NWSNUT NLM, 1114
NWUSER utility, 1200
Connections screen, 1210-1214
Drive Mapping screen, 1203-1205

NetWare Settings screen, 1215-1216
Print Capture screen, 1206-1210
Send Message screen, 1214-1215
starting, 1200-1202
user training, 703-704
user-definable buttons, 1216-1218
NWXTRACT command line utility, 1148

O

object classes, 1232
object instances, 1232
Object menu commands (NWADMIN), 1163-1177
object properties identifier variables (login scripts), 564-565
objects, 39-40, 256, 259-269
Admin user object, security rights, 618
AFP server objects, 268
Alias objects, 261, 269
attributes, 1232
Bindery objects, 269
Bindery queues, 269
Computer objects, 269
container objects, 260-267, 273-274, 280-281, 285
country abbreviations, 261-265
Country objects, 261-265, 274, 280-281
creating, 1166-1167
Directory maps, 269
Group objects, 536-537, 256, 269
inheritance, 1232
leaf objects, 267-269, 275-277, 285-286
modifying login scripts, 539-540
naming conventions, 272-277
NetWare servers, 269

Organization objects, 261, 265, 274, 281
Organizational Role objects, 269, 1165
Organizational Unit objects, 265-267, 274, 281
partitions, 293
Print queues, 269
Print servers, 269
Printer objects, 269, 276-277
Profile objects, 269
[Public] object, 622
rights, 618-624
[Root] object, 259-260, 273, 280
searching, 1145-1146
Unknown objects, 269
User objects, 534-536, 256, 269, 275-276
Volume objects, 269
OCR (Optical Character Recognition), 770
ODI (Open Data-Link Interface) specification, 29-30, 504-505, 967-972
OFF server console command, 1047-1048
Office/GroupWise, 756
offsite storage (backups), 342
online documentation (NetWare), 67-68
Ontrack Data Recovery for NetWare, 326
Open Data-Link Interface (ODI) specification, 29-30, 504-505, 967-972
Open Fastest Path First (OSPF), 56
Open Systems Interconnection (OSI) reference model, 92-94, 775-778, 965-967, 1232
operating systems
parameters, viewing/configuring, 1060-1098
see also network operating systems

Operators option (managing print jobs), 737
Optical Character Recognition (OCR), 770
optimizing, *see* performance optimization
optional memory protection, 33, 50-52
Options menu commands (NWADMIN), 1178-1179
Optivity for NMS (SynOptics), 862
order of data transmission
  ARCnet nodes, 199-200
  token ring networks, 220
Organization objects, 261, 265, 281, 1165
  naming conventions, 274
Organizational Role objects, 269, 1165
organizational structure (NDS), 257-259
Organizational Unit objects, 265-267, 281, 1165
  naming conventions, 274
OS/2
  NET.CFG, 521-522
  NetWare 4.1. for OS/2, 65-66
  workstation client files, 507-510
OS/2 Client software, 509-510
OS/2 Requester
  installing, 516-522
  upgrading, 528
OS/2 Warp, selecting client workstations, 163
OSGEN command line utility, 1137
OSI (Open Systems Interconnection) reference model, 92-94, 775-778, 965-967, 1232
OSP (protected OS) domains, producing, 1118-1119

OSPF (Open Fastest Path First), 56
out-of-band management, 820
outages, 323-326
owners of files/directories, modifying, 1138-1139

P

packet burst, optimizing, 917-927
Packet Burst (PBurst) protocol, 53-55
packet receive buffers (PRBs), optimizing, 908-912
packets
  formats, connections, 426
  LIP (Large Internet Packet), optimizing, 915-916
  long packets (jabbers), troubleshooting, 947-948
PacketView (Klos Technologies, Inc.), 833
parallel streaming, backups, 334
parameters (operating systems), viewing/configuring, 1060-1098
parent container objects, 260
parity information
  RAID 3 level, 142
  RAID 5 level, 143-144
Partition Manager command (NWADMIN's Tools menu), 1179-1181
partitions, 292-293, 295-298
  aborting operations, 838-840
  administrating, 835-836
  creating, 837, 1148
  defaults, 296, 1008
  distributed databases, 1229, 1232

DOS partitions, 443-444
  logical
    aborting of remirroring, 1018
    mirrored, checking status, 1043-1044
    remirroring, 1051-1052
  merging, 837, 1148
  moving, 837-838
  NDS tree structure blueprint, 286-287
  NetWare partitions, 454-456
  objects, 293
  replicas, 41, 295-297
    blueprints, 288-289
    changing types, 842-843
    creating, 841-842
    deleting, 842
    Master, 288-289, 296
    Read-Only, 288-289, 296
    Read/Write, 288-289, 296
    rebuilding, 843
    viewing on servers, 844
  Skulker (updating partition replicas), 297
  splitting, 297
  stored on downed servers, troubleshooting, 954-955
PARTMGR (Partition Manager) command line utility, 835-844, 1148
passive hubs (ARCnet), 197-199, 1258
passwords
  audit password, changing, 662
  changing, 1155
  security issues, 613-614, 709-710
  setting, 1212-1213
patch cables
  token ring networks, 1263-1264
  twisted pair cabling, 416
patches (backups), 344
path costing, 979

paths, search paths, 1055-1056

{PAUSE} option (ITEM menu command), 580

PAUSE command (login scripts), 557

PAUse flag (print services), 741

PBurst protocol, 53-55

PC-to-LAN remote nodes, 801

PCAMI (Personal Computer Asset Management Institute), 684-685

PCCOMPATIBLE command (login scripts), 558

PCI (Peripheral Component Interconnect) bus, 128, 158

PCONSOLE command line utility, 717-729, 1149

PCOUNTER (A.N.D. Technologies), 898

PCs (workstations), 371

peer-to-peer networks, 6-7

Pentium processors, 122-123, 156-157

performance
degradation (memory protection), 52
hardware redundancy, 330

performance management, 673

performance optimization
block sizes, 915
bottlenecks, finding, 925-926
dynamic configuration, 902-903
directory cache buffers, 904-905
elevator seeking, 906-908
file cache buffers, 905-906
file/record locks, 912-913

NLM memory, 914-915
packet receive buffers (PRBs), 908-912
server process execution priority, 913-914
frame types, 920-925
LIP (Large Internet Packet), 915-916
packet burst, 917-927
protocol analyzers, 926-927
protocols, 919-920
server RAM, 916
VLMs, 401-403

Peripheral Component Interconnect (PCI) bus, 128, 158

perpetual archives, 874

Personal Computer Asset Management Institute (PCAMI), 684-685

phone (twisted pair) cabling, 412-418

phone support, 713

physical inventory (network documentation), 690-692

Physical layer (OSI model), 94-101, 778, 966

planning
audits, 646-650
naming conventions, 272-273
NDS tree structure, 281-290, 311
NetWare installation, 304-319
implementation phases, 309-315
installation time, 307
project-management software, 304-305
scheduling, 304-307
technicians/consultants, scheduling, 305-306
test networks, 308-309, 312

training staff, 306-307
troubleshooting, 315-319
network application installation, 786-787

Platinum Resellers, 957

Point-to-Point Protocol (PPP), 804-805

polling, 386

port address conflicts, 348

ports (printer), capturing, 1206-1210, 1220

POST test, 372-374

posting messages (NetWire), 1247-1251

power
client workstations, selecting, 154
conditioning devices, 368
fluctuations, 326
outages, 323-326
UPS (uninterruptable power supply), 326-327
client workstations, selecting, 162
discharge/recharge time, setting, 1110-1111
status, checking, 1108-1110

power management (CMOS settings), 378

Powerbus architecture, 129

PowerNet SNMP Manager for NMS (American Power Conversion), 862

PPP (Point-to-Point Protocol), 804-805

PRBs (packet receive buffers), optimizing, 908-912

preemptive multitasking, 16-17, 120

prepaid network usage, 887

preproduction testing, 934

Presentation layer (OSI model), 777, 966-967
PRI-23B+D (ISDN), 236
primary display (CMOS settings), 377
primary time servers (NDS), 299
Print command (NWADMIN's Object menu), 1177
print jobs
  configurations,
    editing, 1150
  managing, 731-737
    Attached Servers option, 735-736
    Information option, 736
    Operators option, 737
    Print Jobs option, 732-735
    Print Servers option, 737
    Status option, 735
    Users option, 737
Print Jobs option (managing print jobs), 732-735
Print Queue Information menu (managing print jobs), 731-737
print queues, 58-59, 269
  creating, 717-719
print servers, 59, 269
  creating, 719-720
  creating/deleting/modifying, 1149
  managing, 737-742, 1151-1152
  starting, 724-727
Print Servers option (managing print jobs), 737
print services, 14, 57-60, 716-751
  accounting, 886, 898
  CAPTURE command, 743-746
  forms, creating via PRINTDEF utility, 750-751

NetWare HostPrint, 75-77
network locations, 59-60
NPRINT command, 746-747
PCONSOLE utility, 717-729
Print Queue Information menu (managing print jobs), 731-737
print queues, creating, 717-719
print servers
  creating, 719-720
  managing, 737-742
  starting, 724-727
PRINTCON command line utility, 747, 1150
PRINTDEF command line utility, 747-751, 1150
printers, adding/configuring, 720-724
protocols, 60
redirecting print jobs to network queues/printers, 742-743, 1133-1135
testing, 727-729
text files, 1146-1147
user training, 703-704
workstations, setting up, 729-731
PRINTCON command line utility, 747, 1150
PRINTDEF command line utility, 747-751, 1150
printer ports, capturing, 1206-1210, 1220
printers, 269
  adding/configuring, 720-724
  creating/deleting/modifying, 1149
  definitions/forms, 1150
  managing, 1151-1152
  naming conventions, 276-277
  redirecting output, 742-743
  referencing, 60

PRINTGRP command line utility (server upgrades), 479
printing, see print services
Printing command (NETUSER utility), 1219-1220
printing operators, 243
PRINTUSR command line utility (server upgrades), 479
PRIvate flag (print services), 741
privileges (viruses), 344
proactive approach to network administration, 826-829
processors
  RISC (Reduced Instruction Set Computing), 1233
  selecting client workstations, 155-157
  server hardware, 119-123
product research, network applications, 784
product reviews (Computer Database Plus), 174
production phase (NetWare installation), 315
professional associations (training staff), 1245-1246
Profile Login Scripts, 538-539
  NETADMIN, 541-542
  NetWare Administrator, 544
Profile objects, 269, 1166
PROGMAN.INI (DOS Requester), 526
programs, see applications; software; utilities
project-management software, planning NetWare installation, 304-305

PROM (Programmable Read Only Memory), 385

properties (objects), 256
  editing, 1188-1197
  naming conventions, 275-276
  searching, 1145-1146
  viewing, 1188-1197

property rights, 618-624, 1170

proprietary CD-ROM drives, 364

proprietary standards, 90-91

protected OS (OSP) domains, producing, 1118-1119

protecting
  data, 322-345
  hardware, 322-345
  software, 331-345

protocol analyzers, 926-927
  troubleshooting with, 943

PROTOCOL server console command, 1048-1049

protocols, 965
  AFP (AppleTalk Filing Protocol), 105-106, 1228
  AppleTalk, 82, 103, 804, 1228
  application layer protocols, 104-106
  ARA (AppleTalk Remote Access), 804-805
  binding
    to LAN drivers (troubleshooting), 941-942
    with device drivers or NICs, 1020-1022
  CMIP (Common Management Information Protocol), 108
  communications protocols (OSI model), 94-101
  connection-oriented, 975
  connectionless, 975

frame types, optimizing, 920-925
history of networks, 12
IPX (Internet Packet eXchange), 81, 804, 920, 975, 1231
  configuring for RIP / SAP or NLSP use, 982-983
  internal addresses, 994-995
  network addresses, 289, 995-997
IPX/SPX, 31, 101-102
LAT (Local Area Transport), 77-78
LIP (Large Internet Packet), 53-55
MHS (Message Handling System), 1231
MPR (Multi-Protocol Router), 80-83
multiprotocol support (communications servers), 819
NCP (NetWare Core Protocol), 104-105, 976, 1231
NetBIOS, 103-104
NetView, 108
NetWare protocol support, 31
NetWare/IP, 984
network protocol stacks, 101-104
NFS (Network File System), 105, 1232
NLSP (NetWare Link Services Protocol), 55, 977-980
NMS management, 857
ODI (Open Data Link Interface), 29-30
OSI (Open Systems Interconnection) model, 92-94, 1232
OSPF (Open Fastest Path First), 56

PBurst, 53-55
performance optimization, 919-920
PPP (Point-to-Point Protocol), 804-805
print service protocols, 60
registering, 1048-1049
RIP (Routing Information Protocol), 976
RIP/SAP (Routing Information Protocol/ *Service Advertising Protocol), 56*
SAP (Service Advertising Protocol), 977
SLIP (Serial Line Internet Protocol), 805
SNMP (Simple Network Management Protocol), 106-107, 1233
  network documentation tools, 685-687
Source Route Bridge, 82-83
SPX (Sequenced Packet eXchange), 920, 975, 1234
TCP/IP (Transmission Control Protocol/ Internet Protocol), 12, 81-82, 102, 1234
  configuring DEC servers, 78
unbinding from device drivers or NICs, 1105-1107
X.25 protocol, 1234

PSC command line utility, 739-742, 1151-1152

PSERVER NLM, 1114

[Public] object (security), 622

public-key encryption, 609-610

publications
  accounting, 898-899
  network applications, 792
  vendors, 790

punch-down block con-
nection (twisted pair
cabling), 413
purchasing/installing
(NetWare implementa-
tion phase), 312-313
PURGE command line
utility, 1152

Q–R

queues
creating/deleting/modify-
ing, 1149
redirecting print jobs to,
1133-1135

Radio Frequency Interfer-
ence (RFI), 188
RAID (Redundant Array
of Inexpensive Disks),
136-148
advantages/disadvantages,
144-146
future developments, 146
levels, 138-144
software enhance-
ments, 147
subsystem case design,
146-147
RAID 0 level, 138-139
RAID 1 level, 140-141
RAID 2 level, 141-142
RAID 3 level, 142
RAID 4 level, 142-143
RAID 5 level, 143-144
RAM (Random Access
Memory), 328-329
address conflicts, 348-349
expanding (servers),
148-149
client workstations,
selecting, 159
servers, optimizing, 916
troubleshooting
file servers, 359
NetWare instal-
lation, 465

ranking products (net-
work applications), 785
Raw (Ethernet 802.3)
frame type, 921-923
RCONSOLE command
(NWADMIN's Tools
menu), 1183
RCONSOLE command
line utility, 848-855, 1153
RDBMSs (relational
database management
systems), 757
re-tensioning backup
tapes, 334
read-after-write verification errors, 951
Read-Only replica parti-
tions, 288-289, 296
read-only volumes, CD-
ROM discs as, 1115-1118
Read/Write replica parti-
tions, 288-289, 296
real-time data migration,
1123-1124
rebuilding replicas, 843
receiving messages,
1154-1155
records (locks), optimiz-
ing, 912-913
redirecting printer out-
put, 742-743
Reduced Instruction Set
Computing (RISC), 1233
reducing maintenance
expenses (network
documentation), 675-676
redundancy
duplexing, 327-328
hardware, 327-330
mirroring, 327-328
performance, 330
RAM, 328-329
SFT III (system fault
tolerance), 329
Redundant Array of
Inexpensive Disks,
see RAID

redundant volume data
structures, 24
reference time servers
(NDS), 299
referencing printers, 60
REGISTER MEMORY
server console command,
1049-1051
registering
memory, 450, 1049-1051
protocols/frame types,
1048-1049
registration disk (installing NetWare), 463-464
relational database
management systems
(RDBMSs), 757
reliability (backups), 333
REMARK command (login
scripts), 558
REMIRROR PARTITION
server console command,
1051-1052
remirroring logical
partitions, 1051-1052
aborting, 1018
remote access, 796-821
communications servers,
selecting, 818-821
dial-in e-mail access,
797-798
dial-up routers, 805
high-speed communica-
tions links, 816-818
ATM (Asynchronous
Transfer Mode), 818
ISDN (Integrated
Services Digital
Network), 817
SMDS (Switched
Megabit Data Ser-
vices), 817-818
Switched 56, 817
LAN-based protocols, 804
modems, selecting,
811-818
data compression,
813-815

error correction,
813-814
MNP (Microcom
Networking
Protocol), 813
UARTs (serial port data
transfer), 815-816
V.32 standard, 812-813
V.32bis standard, 813
V.42 standard, 814
V.42bis standard,
814-815
V.FAST standard, 812
multiprotocol support
(communications serv-
ers), 819
NetWare Access Server
(NAS), 806-807
NetWare Asynchronous
Communications Server
(NACS), 807-808
NetWare Connect, 810-811
NetWare Remote Shell, 806
network management,
819-820
remote console, 808-810
remote-control software,
798-800
remote-node software,
800-804
security, 820
serial protocols, 804-805
upgrading communica-
tions servers, 820-821
remote access
software, 1232
remote booting, 1123
remote console, 808-810
remote control dial-in
access software, 83,
713-714, 798-800, 1233
Remote Management
Facility (RMF), 846-855
Remote Network Monitor-
ing Management Infor-
mation Base (RMON
MIB) standard, 859-860

REMOTE NLM, 1114
remote node dial-in access
software, 83-85, 774-775,
800-804
remote printers, 720
Remote Procedure Call
(RPC) technology, 52
remounting/dismounting
volumes (auditing), 660
REMOVE DOS server
console command,
1052-1053
removing
accounting, 895
see also deleting
Rename command
(NWADMIN's Object
menu), 1176
renaming
directories, 1153
trees (NDS), 42
RENDIR command line
utility, 1153
repairing NetWare Direc-
tory Services database,
1119-1122
repeaters (connecting
networks), 224
replaceable routers, 56
replacement parts (server
hardware), 367-368
replicas, 1180-1181
adding/deleting/
modifying, 1148
changing types, 842-843
creating, 841-842
defaults, 1008
deleting, 842
rebuilding, 843
stored on downed servers,
troubleshooting, 954-955
synchronizing, 1180
viewing on servers, 844
replicated databases,
38, 1233
DIB (Directory Informa-
tion Base), 292-295

replicated partitions
(NDS), 41, 295-297
Skulker (updating parti-
tion replicas), 297
reports
audit reports, 663-666
for accounting,
885-886, 898
researching
network applications, 784
prices (budgeting tips),
173-177
resellers (Novell), 956-957
RESET ROUTER server
console command,
1053-1054
resetting audit files,
666-667
resistance (coaxial
cable), 421
resources
accounting
configuration, 890
utilization, 887-888
sharing, 10
retrieval, 770
RFI (Radio Frequency
Interference), 188
rights
inheritance, 620-621,
627-628
viruses, 344
see also security
RIGHTS command line
utility, 635-636, 1153-1154
Rights to Other Objects
command (NWADMIN's
Object menu), 1174-1176
rightsizing network
applications, 761-775
ring memory protection
model, 50-52
ring topology, 9, 184
RIP (Routing Information
Protocol), 976
configuring IPX protocol
for, 982-983

RIP/SAP (Routing Infor-mation Protocol/ Service Advertising Protocol), 56
RISC (Reduced Instruc-tion Set Computing) processors, 1233
Rivest-Adleman-Shamir (RSA) public-key crypto-system, 49-50, 609-610, 1233
RMF (Remote Manage-ment Facility), 846-855
RMON MIB (Remote Network Monitoring Management Informa-tion Base) standard, 859-860
[Root] object, 39, 259-260, 280, 1166
   naming conventions, 273
root/branch/leaf (hierar-chical databases), 1233
rotating
   backups, 334-337
   media, 873
ROUTE NLM, 1114
router tables, resetting, 1053-1054
Router Tracking Screen
   displaying, 1103-1105
   turning off, 1103
ROUTER.EXE utility, 964
routers, 425
   connecting networks, 226-228, 1233
   MPR (Multi-Protocol Router), 80-83
   replaceable routers, 56
   troubleshooting, 939-940
   types, 962-964
routing data
   AppleTalk, 82
   IPX protocol, 81
   Source Route Bridge, 82-83
   TCP/IP, 81-82
   troubleshooting, 953-954
   with NetWare's native protocols, 974-980

Routing Information Protocol (RIP), 976
Routing Information Protocol/ Service Adver-tising Protocol (RIP/SAP), 56
routing information tables, 976
routing levels, 980
routing protocol support, 55-56
RPC (Remote Procedure Call) technology, 52
RPL NLM, 1123
RS232 NLM, 1114
RSA (Rivest-Adleman-Shamir) public-key crypto-system, 49-50, 609-610, 1233
RSPX NLM, 1114
RTDM NLM, 1123-1124
runts (short frames), troubleshooting, 948

S

SAA rules (NetWare for SAA), 426
Saber menu system, compared to NetWare menus, 568-569
safe rooms (environmen-tal issues), 331
Salvage command (NWADMIN's Tools menu), 1181-1182
same-server upgrades, 468, 476-484
SAP (Service Advertising Protocol) protocol, 977
   configuring IPX protocol for, 982-983
SAS (Single Attachment Stations), 215-216
Save Settings command (NWADMIN's Options menu), 1179

SBACKUP NLM, 339, 877-879, 1124-1126
scalability, 20
scalar datatypes (syn-taxes), 1234
SCAN FOR NEW DEVICES server console command, 1054
scanners (network appli-cations), 769
SCHDELAY NLM, 1115
schedulers
   NetWare, 42-43
   network applications, 767
scheduling NetWare installation, 304-307
   implementation phases, 309-315
      installation/training, 313-315
      planning/testing, 310-312
      production, 315
      purchasing/installa-tion, 312-313
   installation time, 307
   project-management software, 304-305
   technicians/consultants, 305-306
   training staff, 306-307
schemas, 1233
screens
   clearing, 1025-1026, 1047-1048
   Connections (NWUSER utility), 1210-1214
   Drive Mapping (NWUSER utility), 1203-1205
   Effective Rights, 1172-1173
   Inherited Rights Filter, 1171-1172
   NetWare Settings (NWUSER utility), 1215-1216
   Print Capture (NWUSER utility), 1206-1210

Router Tracking Screen
displaying, 1103-1105
turning off, 1103
Send Message (NWUSER
utility), 1214-1215
viewing from within
debugger, 937
**SCSI (Small Computer
System Interface)**
CD-ROM drives, 364
disk drives, 135-136, 160
*configuring BIOS,
363-364*
installing multiple, 361
**SDI (Storage Device
Interface), 61**
Search command
NETADMIN, 1185
NWADMIN's Object
menu, 1177
search paths, 1055-1056
**SEARCH server console
command, 1055-1056**
searching
DynaText online documen-
tation, 435-438
objects/properties,
1145-1146
**secondary time servers
(NDS), 299**
SECURE CONSOLE
**server console command,
1056-1057**
security, 11, 608-641
attributes (files/directo-
ries), 628-630
*granting via FILER
utility, 637-638*
*granting via FLAG
command, 638*
*granting via
NWAdmin, 637*
auditing, 47-49, 644-669,
1132-1133
*Audit Files Mainte-
nance option, 656-657*
*AUDITCON utility,
649-650, 653-656*

*configuring audits,
657-666*
*Directory tree contain-
ers, 652-653*
*planning audits,
646-650*
preparations, 650-653
volume audits, 651-652
background authentica-
tion, 610
directory/file rights,
625-626
file server console security,
608, 639-640
file system rights,
granting
FILER utility, 634-635
NETAdmin, 633-634
NWAdmin, 631-632
*RIGHTS command,
635-636*
file system security, 608,
624-630
group rights, 621-622
intruder detection,
616-618
IRF (Inherited Rights
Filter), 623-624, 627-628
login/password security,
608-618
*login restrictions,
612-613*
time restrictions, 615
menu systems, 570-572
NCP Packet Signatures,
611-612
NDS rights, granting
NETAdmin, 632-633
NWAdmin, 630-631
NDS security, 608,
618-624
network address restric-
tions, 615-616
object rights, 618-624
passwords, 613-614
changing, 1155
setting, 1212-1213
property rights, 618-624

[Public] object, 622
remote access, 820
rights, 1169-1176
*inheritance, 620-621,
627-628*
RMF (Remote Manage-
ment Facility), 848-850
RSA (Rivest-Adleman-
Shamir) public-key
crypto-system, 49-50,
609-610, 1233
securing server, 1056-1057
security equivalence
(granting rights),
622-623
trustee assignments,
621-623, 626-627
wireless communications
networks, 223-224
workgroup administrator
training, 709-710
**security equivalence
(granting rights), 622-623**
security management, 673
selecting
communications servers,
818-821
modems, 811-818
server hardware, 114-117
**SEND command line
utility, 1154-1155**
**SEND server console
command, 1058-1059**
**sending messages,
1022-1024, 1058-1059,
1154-1155, 1214-1215,
1220-1221**
**Sequenced Packet
eXchange (SPX) protocol,
920, 975, 1234**
serial ports
base port addresses, 358
data transfer, 815-816
**serial protocols (remote
access), 804-805**
server console
as virtual console, 1153
keyboard types, changing,
1122-1123

server console commands, 1015-1017
  ABORT REMIRROR, 1018
  ADD NAME SPACE, 1019-1020
  BIND, 1020-1022
  BROADCAST, 1022-1024
  CLEAR STATION, 1024-1025
  CLS, 1025-1026
  CONFIG, 1026-1027
  CX, 1136
  DISABLE LOGIN, 1027-1028
  DISABLE TTS, 1028-1029
  DISMOUNT, 1029-1030
  DISPLAY NETWORKS, 1030-1031
  DISPLAY SERVERS, 1031-1032
  DOWN, 323, 1032-1033
  ENABLE LOGIN, 1033
  ENABLE TTS, 1034-1035
  EXIT, 550, 1035-1036
  HELP, 1036
  LANGUAGE, 1037-1038
  LIST DEVICES, 1038-1039
  LOAD, 582-583, 1039-1041
  MAGAZINE, 1041-1042
  MEDIA, 1042-1043
  MEMORY, 1043
  MIRROR STATUS, 1043-1044
  MODULES, 1044-1045
  MOUNT, 1045-1047
  NAME, 1047
  new to NetWare 4.1, 1018
  OFF, 1047-1048
  PROTOCOL, 1048-1049
  REGISTER MEMORY, 1049-1051
  REMIRROR PARTITION, 1051-1052
  REMOVE DOS, 1052-1053
  RESET ROUTER, 1053-1054
  SCAN FOR NEW DEVICES, 1054
  SEARCH, 1055-1056
  SECURE CONSOLE, 1056-1057
  SEND, 1058-1059
  SET, 549, 558-559, 1060-1098
  SET TIME, 559, 1098-1099, 1130
  SET TIME ZONE, 1100-1101
  SPEED, 1101-1102
  syntax, 1014
  TIME, 1102
  TRACK OFF, 1103
  TRACK ON, 1103-1105
  UNBIND, 1105-1107
  UNLOAD, 1108-1110
  UPS STATUS, 1108-1110
  UPS TIME, 1110-1111
  VERSION, 1111-1112
  VOLUMES, 1112
Server Manager, 1126-1128
server-based applications, 18-19, 32-33
SERVER.EXE file, 986
servers, 112-150, 370
  386 DX processor, 120-121
  386 SX processor, 120
  486 processor, 121
  across-the-wire upgrades, 468-476
  adding to individual servers
    hard drives, 988-991
    memory, 991-992
    name space support, 1000-1003
    NDS (NetWare Directory Services) directory trees, 1005-1008
    NICs (Network Interface Cards), 992-999
    NLMs (NetWare Loadable Modules), 986-987
  adding to networks, 1003-1005
  application servers, 113-114
  archiving, SMS (Storage Management Services), 63
  attaching to, 1210-1214
  backups, 1124-1126
  balancing hardware, 117
  bindery, 293-295
    management, 844-846
  burn in (server hardware), 351, 365-367
  bus architectures, 123-130
  changing for auditing, 668
  communications servers, 114, 818-821, 1229
  configuration
    information about, displaying, 1026-1027
    troubleshooting, 348-349
  copyright/version/licensed connection information, displaying, 1111-1112
  data, archiving, 878-879
  database servers, 114
  designing networks, 148
  disk caching, 131-133
  documenting, 367
  DOS/Windows Client software diskettes, 510
  drive bays, 148
  DUPBIND utility (upgrades), 479
  DX (overdrive) processor, 121-122
  EISA (Extended Industry Standard Architecture) bus, 126-127
  ESDI (Enhanced System Device Interface) disk drives, 133-134
  expandability, 148-149
  expansion slots, 149
  fault tolerance, 116-117
  fax servers, 114

file servers, 4-5, 113
   console security,
    639-640
   installing DynaText, 435
   naming conventions, 277
   NDS tree structure
    blueprint, 286-287
fixed disk drives, 130-136
Hierarchical Bus, 129-130
IDE (Integrated Drive
   Electronics) disk
   drives, 134
in-place upgrades, 468,
   485-499
information about, view-
   ing, 1145-1146
installing, default partitions, 296
ISA (Industry Standard
   Architecture) bus,
   123-125
listing, 1031-1032
logging in to
   disabling, 1027-1028
   enabling, 1033
MCA (Micro Channel
   Architecture) bus,
   125-126
memory, 28, 117-119
message routing groups,
   creating, 600-601
MIGRATE utility (up-
   grades), 468
mirroring, 26, 1233
names
   displaying, 1047
   installing NetWare,
    446-447
NCP (NetWare Core
   Protocol), 104-105
NetExplorer, 855-857
ODI (Open Data-Link
   Interface) specification,
   968-970
OS/2 Client software
   diskettes, 510
partitions, 292-293

PCI (Peripheral Compo-
   nent Interconnect)
   bus, 128
Pentium processor,
   122-123
power conditioning
   devices, 368
Powerbus, 129
primary time servers
   (NDS), 299
   multiple servers, 300
print servers, 59
   creating, 719-720
   creating / deleting /
    modifying, 1149
   managing, 737-742,
    1151-1152
   starting, 724-727
PRINTGRP utility (up-
   grades), 479
PRINTUSR utility (up-
   grades), 479
process execution priority,
   optimizing, 913-914
processors, 119-123
RAID disk storage system,
   136-148
RAM (Random Access
   Memory)
   expanding, 148-149
   optimizing, 916
   troubleshooting, 359
reference time servers
   (NDS), 299
remote console, 808-810
remote management,
   846-855
replacement parts,
   367-368
same-server upgrades,
   468, 476-484
SCSI disk drives, 135-136
secondary time servers
   (NDS), 299
securing, 1056-1057
selecting hardware,
   114-117
service contracts, 115-116

shutting down, 1032-1033
single reference time
   servers (NDS), 299
temporary
   connections, 1234
TriFlex bus
   architecture, 129
upgrading, 468-501
vendor certification, 115
VESA (Video Electronics
   Standards Association)
   bus, 127-128
Service Advertising
   Protocol (SAP), 977
Service Centers
   (NASC), 957
service contracts (server
   hardware), 115-116
SERVMAN NLM,
   1126-1128
session contexts, changing
   for auditing, 668
Session layer (OSI model),
   777, 966-967
SET command (login
   scripts), 549, 558-559
Set Context command
   (NWADMIN's View
   menu), 1178
SET server console com-
   mand, 1060-1098
SET TIME server console
   command, 1098-1099
SET TIME ZONE server
   console command,
   1100-1101
SET TZ (time zones), 514
SET_TIME command
   (login scripts), 559
SETPASS command line
   utility, 1155
SETTTS command line
   utility, 1155
setup, RMF (Remote
   Management Facility),
   847-848
SFT I (system fault toler-
   ance level I), 22-24

SFT II (system fault tolerance level II), 24-26
SFT III (system fault tolerance level III), 26-27, 329, 1233
shared applications, 11
shared files, 10
SHared flag (print services), 741
shared memory, 16-17
shared processor systems (remote node), 801-802
shared resources, 10
Shielded Twisted Pair (STP) cable, 191
SHIFT command (login scripts), 559-560
shopping list, sample (budgeting tips), 166-167
short frames (runts), troubleshooting, 948
{SHOW} option (ITEM menu command), 580-581
SHOW command (menu systems), 581-582
Show Hints command (NWADMIN's Options menu), 1179
shutting down servers, 1032-1033
SIDF (Storage Independent Data Format), 61
simple burn in (server hardware), 366
Simple Network Management Protocol (SNMP), 106-107, 418, 1233
Single Attachment Stations (SAS), 215-216
single reference time servers (NDS), 299
single-user database model, 758-759
site licensing (budgeting tips), 177-178

sizes
    blocks, optimizing, 915
    dynamic volume size increasing, 22
    menu systems, 577
    packets, LIP (Large Internet Packet), 915-916
Skulker (updating partition replicas), 297, 1233
SLIP (Serial Line Internet Protocol), 805
Small Computer System Interface, see SCSI
small movable systems (token ring networks), 1263-1264
SmartPass for NetWare (e.g. Software, Inc.), 833
SMDS (Switched Megabit Data Services), 817-818
SMI (Structure and Identification of Management Information), 106
SMS (Storage Management Services), 61-63, 332-333, 877-881, 1233
SNA (System Network Architecture), 73-75, 1233
SNMP (Simple Network Management Protocol), 106-107, 418, 1233
    network documentation tools, 685-687
soft errors (media defects), 341
software
    archiving software, 874-877
    cable management software, 685
    client diskettes, 394-396
    client installation, 393-394
    configuration management tools, 684

installing, 504-522
    NetWare installation time, 307
inventory tools (network documentation), 688-690
licensing (budgeting tips), 177-178
network backups, 332-333
non-stop computing (SFT III), 27
NOS (network operating system), 6, 13-14
project-management software, planning NetWare installation, 304-305
protecting, 331-345
RAID disk storage system, 137, 147
remote access software, 1232
remote control software, 1233
SMS (Storage Management Services), 332-333
third-party network tools (network documentation), 684-687
workgroup administrator training (software acquisitions), 708
workstations, 392-396
see also applications; utilities
Sort command (NWADMIN's View menu), 1178
sound, 771
source files, menu systems
    compiling, 573-574
    creating, 573, 575-577
Source Route Bridge, 82-83
specifications (cabling)
    coax cable, 190
    EIA/TIA, 195

IBM twisted pair cable, 192-193
Underwriters Laboratories, 193-194
Spectrum for NMS (Cabletron), 862
speed
CPUs (central processing units), displaying, 1101-1102
Frame Relay networks, 235
hardware backups, 341
memory allocation, 44
wireless communications networks, 223
SPEED server console command, 1101-1102
splitting partitions, 297
spread spectrum (wireless communications network security), 223
SPX (Sequenced Packet eXchange) protocol, 920, 975, 1234
SPXCONFG NLM, 1115
SPXS NLM, 1115
SQL (Structured Query Language), 759
stacks (transport protocol), 971
staff training
books, 1243
budgeting tips, 171-172
Certified Novell Instructors (CNIs), 1239-1240
computer-based training (CBT)
CBT Systems, 1240-1241
Novell, 1242-1243
CX utility, 699-700
defining terminology, 696, 707
DynaText online documentation, 712-713
e-mail, 704-705
file system rights, 701-702

hardware acquisitions, 708
loading NetWare clients, 696-697
logging in, 697-698
login scripts, 700-701
magazines, 1243-1244
NAECs (Novell Authorized Education Centers), 1238-1239
NDS contexts, 698-699
NetWare installation, 313-315
NLIST utility, 699-700
Novell courses, 1236-1238
phone support, 713
planning NetWare installation, 306-307
print services, 703-704
professional associations, 1245-1246
security issues, 709-710
software acquisitions, 708
standards, establishing, 707-708
trade shows, 1244
troubleshooting procedures, 705-706, 710-711
user accounts, creating, 708-709
user groups, 1244-1245
user training, 696-706
viruses, 711-712
workgroup administrator training, 706-712
standards, 90-109
AFP (AppleTalk Filing Protocol), 105-106
AppleTalk, 103
ARCnet, 100-101
de facto standards, 91-92
de jure standards, 91
establishing (workgroup administrator training), 707-708
Ethernet networks, 95-97
FDDI (Fiber Distributed Data Interface), 99

Frame Relay networks, 234
IPX/SPX, 101-102
modems, 812-813
data compression, 813-815
error correction, 813-814
MNP (Microcom Networking Protocol), 813
V.32, 813
V.32bis, 813
V.42, 814
V.42bis, 814-815
NCP (NetWare Core Protocol), 104-105
NetBIOS, 103-104
network documentation, 676-677
network management protocols, 106-108
new technologies, 92
NFS (Network File System), 105
OSI (Open System Interconnections) model, 92-94
proprietary standards, 90-91
TCP/IP, 102
token ring networks, 97-99
wireless communications networks, 222
standby monitors (token ring networks), 221
star topology, 8, 185-186
STARt flag (print services), 741
starting
NETUSER utility, 1218-1219
NWADMIN (NetWare Administrator), 1162
NWUSER utility, 1200-1202
STARTUP.NCF file (installing NetWare), 462
static electricity, 327

STATus flag (print services), 741-742
Status option (managing print jobs), 735
StonyBrook
    Cisco Router Manager, 862
    Wellfleet Router Manager, 862
STOp flag (print services), 742
Storage Device Interface (SDI), 61
Storage Independent Data Format (SIDF), 61
Storage Management Services (SMS), 61-63, 332-333, 877-881, 1233
storing, 770
    files (block suballocation), 45
    non-DOS files on NetWare volumes, 1019-1020
STP (Shielded Twisted Pair) cable, 191
streaming (MCA bus), 126
STREAMS NLM, 1115
STREAMS ODI layer, 969-970
Structure and Identification of Management Information (SMI), 106
Structured Query Language (SQL), 759
structured tasks (workflow), 764
submenus, 581-583
subsystem case design (RAID), 146-147
support (network applications), 789
support centers (Novell), 957-958
SWAP command (login scripts), 560
Switched 56 services, 817
Switched Megabit Data Services (SMDS), 817-818

synchronization
    NDS (NetWare Directory Services) servers, 298-300
    troubleshooting, 952-955
SynOptics' Optivity for NMS, 862
syntax, 1234
    server console commands, 1014
SYS: volume, copying NetWare files to (installing NetWare), 457-458
system fault tolerance level I (SFT I), 22-24
system fault tolerance level II (SFT II), 24-26
system fault tolerance level III (SFT III), 26-27, 1233
System Login Scripts, 538-539
System Network Architecture (SNA), 73-75, 1233
SYSTEM.INI (DOS Requester), 525
SYSTIME command line utility, 1156

T

T-1 carrier line, 236-237
    bridges, 424
T-2 carrier line, 237
T-3 carrier line, 237
tables
    routing information, 976
    server router, resetting, 1053-1054
tagged command queuing, 133
tape devices
    backups, 334
    defective backups, 341-342
tape rotation (backups), 334-337
Target Service Agents (TSAs), 62

TCNS (Thomas-Conrad Network System), 1234
TCP/IP (Transmission Control Protocol/ Internet Protocol), 12, 81-82, 102, 1234
    configuring DEC servers, 78
technical issues (network applications), 783
Technical Support Alliance (TSA), 791
technical support sources, 955-958
    DynaText online documentation, 712-713
    help desk, 714
    network applications, 789
    phone support, 713
    remote control software, 713-714
    troubleshooting NetWare installation, 316
    user training, 705-706
    workgroup administrator training, 710-711
    see also troubleshooting
technicians
    hiring (budgeting tips), 170-171
    planning NetWare installation, 305-306
telephone (twisted pair) cabling, 412-418
telephone support (network applications), 789
TEMP SET command (login scripts), 560
temperature (environmental issues), 331
templates (NDS tree structure), 284-285
temporary batch files (menu systems), 570-572
temporary connections, 1234
ten-tape rotation scheme (backups), 335-336

terminal emulation, 72
terminators (thick coax cable), 411
test networks, planning NetWare installation, 308-309, 312
testing
 backups, 342
 burn in (server hardware), 366-367
 cabling, 420-424
 coaxial cable, 422
 preproduction testing, 934
 print services, 727-729
 twisted-pair cable, 422
text files, printing, 1146-1147
theoretical sustained transfer (bus architectures), 124
thermal cycling, 366
thick coax cable, 409-411
 coring tools, 411
 terminators, 411
 transceivers, 411
thick net, see 10Base5 (Ethernet)
thin coax cable, 407-409
 ARCnet, 409
 Ethernet, 408-409
thin net, see 10Base2 (Ethernet)
third-party network tools (network documentation), 684-687
third-party vendors (SMS compliance), 63
Thomas-Conrad Network System (TCNS), 1234
threads
 active, viewing status, 936-937
 execution, abends (ABnormal ENDs), 934-936
ticks, 976

Tile command (NWADMIN's Window menu), 1183
time
 current, setting, 1098-1099, 1130
 information about, viewing, 1102
 operating system parameters, setting, 1082-1088
 synchronizing, 1156
  checking, 1128-1130
  NDS servers, 298-300
  troubleshooting, 953
 UPS (Uninterruptable Power Supply) discharge/recharge, setting, 1110-1111
time identifier variables (login scripts), 562
TIME server console command, 1102
time servers (NDS)
 multiple, 300
 primary, 299
 reference, 299
 secondary, 299
 single reference, 299
time zones
 information, configuring, 1100-1101
 installing NetWare, 460-462
 SET TZ, 514
 synchronizing NDS time servers, 300
time-out settings (ARCnet), 1258
TIMESYNC NLM, 1128-1130
TIMESYNC.CFG file, 1084-1088
TLI (Transport Level Interface) NLM, 970, 1115
token ring network architecture, 9, 97-99, 216-221, 1234

cabling, 218-220, 1262-1265
 fiber-optic cable, 420
 twisted pair cabling, 417-418
data transmission, 220
diagnostics, 221
frame formats, 974
MSAUs, 217-218, 417-418
Source Route Bridge, 82-83
Tools menu commands (NWADMIN), 1179-1183
topography of network (network documentation), 678-679
topologies
 ARCnet node connections, 197
 ATM (Asynchronous Transfer Mode), 230-232
 FDDI architecture, 215-216
 networks, 7-10, 183-186
  bus topology, 9, 183-184, 1229
  hybrid topology, 9-10, 186
  mesh topology, 8, 184
  network documentation, 679-680
  ring topology, 9, 184
  star topology, 8, 185-186
tower cases (selecting client workstations), 153-154
Tower of Hanoi backup scheme, 336-337
TRACK OFF server console command, 1103
TRACK ON server console command, 1103-1105
tracking
 financial assets (network documentation), 674
 logins/logouts, 887

trade shows
network applications, 792
training staff, 1244
**traffic, monitoring,
926-927, 943**
training staff
books, 1243
budgeting tips, 171-172
Certified Novell Instruc-
tors (CNIs), 1239-1240
computer-based
training (CBT)
*CBT Systems,
1240-1241*
Novell, 1242-1243
CX utility, 699-700
defining terminology,
696, 707
DynaText online documen-
tation, 712-713
e-mail, 704-705
file system rights, 701-702
hardware acquisitions, 708
loading NetWare clients,
696-697
logging in, 697-698
login scripts, 700-701
magazines, 1243-1244
NAECs (Novell Authorized
Education Centers),
1238-1239
NDS (NetWare Directory
Services) contexts,
698-699
NetWare installation,
313-315
network applications, 788
NLIST utility, 699-700
Novell courses, 1236-1238
phone support, 713
planning NetWare instal-
lation, 306-307
print services, 703-704
professional associations,
1245-1246
security issues, 709-710
software acquisitions, 708
standards, establishing,
707-708

trade shows, 1244
troubleshooting proce-
dures, 705-706, 710-711
user accounts, creating,
708-709
user groups, 1244-1245
user training, 696-706
viruses, 711-712
workgroup administrator
training, 706-712
**Transaction Tracking
System (TTS), 26**
**transceivers (thick coax
cable), 411**
transfer rates
Frame Relay networks, 235
wireless communications
networks, 223
**Transmission Control
Protocol/ Internet Proto-
col, *see* TCP/IP**
transmitting data
ARCnet nodes, 199-200
token ring networks, 220
**Transport layer (OSI
model), 777, 966**
**Transport Protocol ODI
layer, 969**
**transport protocol
stacks, 971**
tree, *see* Directory tree
TrenData (Denmac), 862
**TriFlex bus architec-
ture, 129**
troubleshooting
abends (ABnormal ENDs),
934-938
base memory address
conflicts, 353-356
BIOS setup, 360
change events, 930-933
disk problems, 949-952
DynaText online documen-
tation, 432-440, 712-713
file servers (RAM prob-
lems), 359
hardware configurations,
348-349
help desk, 714

installing NICs, 351-360
IRQs (interrupt request
lines), 356-358
LANs (Local Area Net-
works)
alignment errors, 949
*binding protocols to
LAN drivers, 941-942*
cabling faults, 946-947
*Carrier Sense Lost
error, 947*
collisions, 944
*CRC (Cyclic Redun-
dancy Check) errors,
945-946*
hardware, 938-940
*jabbers (long packets),
947-948*
late events, 948
*loading LAN drivers,
940-941*
long frames, 948
short frames (runts), 948
*with protocol
analyzers, 943*
methodology,
developing, 933
NDS (NetWare Directory
Services), 952-955
NetWare installation,
315-319, 464-465
consultants, 315
*maintenance
contracts, 316*
*NetWire (CompuServe
forum), 317-319*
*Network Support
Encyclopedia, 316*
*pay-per-incident
support (Novell), 316*
network analyzers, 1231
network documentation
benefits, 674
network management,
1254-1256
phone support, 713
preproduction testing, 934
remote control software,
713-714

technical support sources, 955-958

workgroup administrator training, 710-711

see also technical support

trustees, 1170

assigning to objects, 621-623, 626-627, 1173

deleting from objects, 1174

Trustees of this Object command (NWADMIN's Object menu), 1169-1174

TSA (Technical Support Alliance), 791

TSAs (Target Service Agents), 62

TTS (Transaction Tracking System), 26

disabling, 1028-1029

enabling, 1034-1035

locks, setting/viewing, 1155

operating system parameters, setting, 1079-1081

twisted pair cabling, 191-195, 412-418

continuity, 422

direct connection, 413

Ethernet, 414-416

hubs, 412

multi-meters, 421

patch cables, 416

punch-down block connection, 413

testing, 422

token ring, 417-418

Type 5 twisted pair, 416

Type 5 twisted pair cabling, 416

U

UART (Universal Asynchronous Receiver/Transmitter), 815-816

UIMPORT command line utility, 1156

UNBIND server console command, 1105-1107

Underwriters Laboratories twisted pair cable specifications, 193-194

Uninterruptable Power Supply, *see* **UPS**

UNIX

NetWare NFS services, 78-80

selecting client workstations, 163

Unknown objects, 269

UNLOAD server console command, 1107-1108

unloading NLMs (NetWare Loadable Modules), 987

Unshielded Twisted Pair (UTP) cable, 191-192

unstructured tasks (workflow), 765

updating

FAT (File Allocation Table), troubleshooting, 951

IPX.COM LAN drivers, 1158

local files with network files, 1157

NET.CFG, 527-528

upgrading

ARCnet to ARCnet Plus, 202-203

communications servers, 820-821

NetWare 4.*x*, 501

OS/2 Requester, 528

servers, 468-501

upper memory (workstations), 380

UPS (Uninterruptable Power Supply), 326-327

client workstations, selecting, 162

discharge/recharge time, setting, 1110-1111

status, checking, 1108-1110

UPS NLM, 1115

UPS STATUS server console command, 1108-1110

UPS TIME server console command, 1110-1111

upsizing network applications, 761-775

user groups, 957

training staff, 1244-1245

user identifier variables (login scripts), 562-563

user interfaces (backups), 333

user issues (network applications), 788, 792

User Login Scripts, 538-539

user objects, 256, 269, 1166

associating Profile Login Scripts

NETADMIN, 541-542

NetWare Administrator, 544

auditing, 658-659

creating

NETADMIN, 534-535

NetWare Administrator, 535-536

workgroup administrator training, 708-709

importing into directory tree, 1156

naming conventions, 275-276

NDS structure, 256-257

user profiles

selecting client workstations, 152

troubleshooting network problems, 1255

User Template command (NWADMIN's Object menu), 1177

User Tools, 515

user utilities

NETUSER, 1200, 1218-1224

NWUSER, 1200-1218

user-definable buttons (NWUSER utility), 1216-1218
users
  account balances, managing, 893-894
  connection information, 1156
  information about, viewing, 1145-1146
  logging in
    disabling, 1027-1028
    enabling, 1033
  network management (DOS), 1145
  rights, 1153-1154
  training, 696-706
    CX utility, 699-700
    defining terminology, 696
    DynaText online documentation, 712-713
    e-mail, 704-705
    file system rights, 701-702
    loading NetWare clients, 696-697
    logging in, 697-698
    login scripts, 700-701
    NDS (NetWare Directory Services) contexts, 698-699
    NLIST utility, 699-700
    phone support, 713
    print services, 703-704
    troubleshooting procedures, 705-706
Users option (managing print jobs), 737
utilities, 66-67
  command line utilities
    ATOTAL (Accounting Services Total), 885-886, 896-897, 1132
    AUDITCON, 649-650, 653-656, 683, 1132-1133
    CAPTURE, 703-704, 743-746, 1133-1135
    COLORPAL, 1135-1136
    DOSGEN, 1137
    DUPBIND, 479
    FILER, 634-638, 1137-1138
    FLAG, 638, 1138-1139
    LOGIN, 1140
    LOGOUT, 1140-1141
    MAP, 554-557, 1141
    NCOPY, 1142
    NDIR, 1143-1144
    NETADMIN, 290, 895, 1144, 1184-1194
    NETUSER, 1145, 1200, 1218-1224
    NLIST, 290, 1145-1146
    NMENU, 1146
    NPRINT, 746-747, 1146-1147
    NVER, 683-684, 1148
    NWXTRACT, 1148
    PARTMGR (Partition Manager), 835-844, 1148
    PCONSOLE, 717-729, 1149
    PRINTCON, 747, 1150
    PRINTDEF, 747-751, 1150
    PRINTGRP, 479
    PRINTUSR, 479
    PSC, 739-742, 1151-1152
    PURGE, 1152
    RCONSOLE, 848-855, 1153
    RENDIR, 1153
    RIGHTS, 635-636, 1153-1154
    SEND, 1154-1155
    SETPASS, 1155
    SETTTS, 1155
    SYSTIME, 1156
    UIMPORT, 1156
    WHOAMI, 1156
    WSUPDATE, 1157
    WSUPGRD, 1158
  CX, 290
  INETCFG (internetworking configuration), 980-983
  NWADMIN (NetWare Administrator), 835-844, 895, 1160-1184
  NWUSER, 1200-1218
  ROUTER.EXE, 964
  see also applications; software
UTP (Unshielded Twisted Pair) cable, 191-192

V

V.32 modem standard, 812-813
V.32bis modem standard, 813
V.42 modem standard, 814
V.42bis modem standard, 814-815
V.FAST modem standard, 812
values (object properties), 256
  naming conventions, 275-276
variables, identifier variables (login scripts), 561-565
  date, 561-562
  DOS environment, 564
  network, 563
  object properties, 564-565
  time, 562
  user, 562-563
  workstation, 563-564
vendors
  BBSs, 790
  certification (server hardware), 115
  evaluating products, 310-312

network applications, 784-785
publications, 790
purchasing products, 312-313
selecting client workstations, 162
VERIFY command (login scripts), 550
VERSION server console command, 1111-1112
VESA (Video Electronics Standard Association) bus, 127-128, 158
video controllers/monitors (selecting client workstations), 161
View menu commands (NWADMIN), 1177-1178
virtual consoles, 1153
virtual memory, 16-17, 120
viruses
    backups, 339, 343-344
    workgroup administrator training, 711-712
VLM.EXE (DOS Requester), 397-400
VLMs (Virtual Loadable Modules), 42, 1234
    compared to NETX, 505-507
    optimizing, 401-403
volume data structures, 24
Volume objects, 269, 1166
volumes
    adding name space support, 1000-1003
    audits, 651-652
    automatic dismounts, 950
    dismounting, 660, 1029-1030
    dynamic volume size increasing, 22
    information about, 1143-1146
    installing NetWare, 454-456
    listing, 1112

mounting, 660, 1045-1047
    consistency checks, 24
    troubleshooting, 951
read-only, CD-ROM discs as, 1115-1118
user/group rights, 1153-1154
VOLUMES server console command, 1112
VREPAIR NLM, 324-326, 1115

W

wake-up features, 378
WANs (Wide Area Networks), 53-56, 228-237, 1234
Wellfleet Router Manager (StonyBrook), 862
WHOAMI command line utility, 1156
WIN.INI (DOS Requester), 526
window menu colors, changing, 1135-1136
Window menu commands (NWADMIN), 1183-1184
Windows
    DOS/Windows client installation, 510-516
    diskettes from CD-ROM, 508
    diskettes from server, 510
    DOS Requester, 526-527
    FirstMail for Windows, 603-604
    NetWare Tools, 515
    NW Admin, 515
    User Tools, 515
Windows 3.1, selecting client workstations, 163
Windows 95, selecting client workstations, 164
Windows for Workgroups, selecting client workstations, 163

Windows NT, selecting client workstations, 164
wireless communication networks, 221-224
    disadvantages, 222-223
    security, 223-224
workflow
    e-mail, 763
    FlowMark, 763
    network applications, 762-766
    structured tasks, 764
    unstructured tasks, 765
workgroup administrator training, 706-712
    defining terminology, 707
    hardware acquisitions, 708
    security issues, 709-710
    software acquisitions, 708
    standards, establishing, 707-708
    troubleshooting procedures, 710-711
    user accounts, creating, 708-709
    viruses, 711-712
workstation client files, 507-510
workstations, 371
    backups, 339
    base memory, 379
    BIOS, 372
    client drivers, 396-403
    CMOS settings, 374-379
    communications, 370-371
    configuring, 370-403
    conventional memory, 379
    crashed, cleaning up, 1024-1025
    diskless, creating boot images, 1137
    DOS Requester, 397-400
    expanded memory, 381-382
    extended memory, 381
    floppy drives, 382-384
    hardware, 371-379, 386-392

LAN driver updates, 524
memory, 379-382
NET.CFG, updating,
  527-528
NICs (network interface
  cards), 384-386
OS/2 Requester, upgrad-
  ing, 528
POST test, 372-374
software, 392-396, 504-522
upper memory, 380
see also client
  workstations
**WRITE command (login
  scripts), 561**
**WSUPDATE command
  line utility, 1157**
**WSUPGRD command line
  utility, 1158**

X–Y–Z

X.25 protocol, 1234
X.400 specification, 1234
X.500 standard, 260, 1234
**XNS (Xerox Network
  System), 101**

Add to Your Sams Library Today with the Best Books for Programming, Operating Systems, and New Technologies

The easiest way to order is to pick up the phone and call

1-800-428-5331

between 9:00 a.m. and 5:00 p.m. EST.
For faster service please have your credit card available.

ISBN	Quantity	Description of Item	Unit Cost	Total Cost
0-672-30481-3		Teach Yourself NetWare in 14 Days	$29.95	
0-672-30712-X		NetWare Unleashed, 2nd Edition (Book/Disk)	$45.00	
0-672-30501-1		Understanding Data Communications	$29.99	
0-672-30549-6		Teach Yourself TCP/IP in 14 Days	$29.99	
0-672-30486-4		Rightsizing Information Systems, 2nd edition (Hardcover)	$40.00	
0-672-30473-2		Client/Server Computing, 2nd edition (Hardcover)	$40.00	
0-672-30173-3		Enterprise-Wide Networking	$39.95	
0-672-30448-1		Teach Yourself C in 21 Days, Bestseller Edition	$24.95	
0-672-30620-4		Teach Yourself Visual Basic 4 in 21 Days, 3rd Edition (September release)	$35.00	
0-672-30655-7		Developing Your Own 32-Bit Operating System (Book/CD)	$49.99	
0-672-30667-0		Teach Yourself Web Publishing with HTML in a Week	$25.00	
0-672-30737-5		World Wide Web Unleashed, 2E	$39.99	
❏ 3 ½" Disk		Shipping and Handling: See information below.		
❏ 5 ¼" Disk		TOTAL		

Shipping and Handling: $4.00 for the first book, and $1.75 for each additional book. Floppy disk: add $1.75 for shipping and handling. If you need to have it NOW, we can ship product to you in 24 hours for an additional charge of approximately $18.00, and you will receive your item overnight or in two days. Overseas shipping and handling adds $2.00 per book and $8.00 for up to three disks. Prices subject to change. Call for availability and pricing information on latest editions.

201 W. 103rd Street, Indianapolis, Indiana 46290

1-800-428-5331 — Orders   1-800-835-3202 — FAX   1-800-858-7674 — Customer Service

Book ISBN 1-672-30047-8

PLUG YOURSELF INTO...

THE MACMILLAN INFORMATION SUPERLIBRARY™

Free information and vast computer resources from the world's leading computer book publisher—online!

FIND THE BOOKS THAT ARE RIGHT FOR YOU!

A complete online catalog, plus sample chapters and tables of contents give you an in-depth look at *all* of our books, including hard-to-find titles. It's the best way to find the books you need!

- **STAY INFORMED** with the latest computer industry news through our online newsletter, press releases, and customized Information SuperLibrary Reports.

- **GET FAST ANSWERS** to your questions about MCP books and software.

- **VISIT** our online bookstore for the latest information and editions!

- **COMMUNICATE** with our expert authors through e-mail and conferences.

- **DOWNLOAD SOFTWARE** from the immense MCP library:
  - Source code and files from MCP books
  - The best shareware, freeware, and demos

- **DISCOVER HOT SPOTS** on other parts of the Internet.

- **WIN BOOKS** in ongoing contests and giveaways!

TO PLUG INTO MCP: ➤   WORLD WIDE WEB: **http://www.mcp.com**

GOPHER: gopher.mcp.com

FTP: ftp.mcp.com